✍ Let's Go writers travel on your budget.

"Guides that penetrate the veneer of the holiday brochures and mine the grit of real life."

—The Economist

"The writers seem to have experienced every rooster-packed bus and lunar-surfaced mattress about which they write."

—The New York Times

"All the dirt, dirt cheap."

—People

✍ Great for independent travelers.

"The guides are aimed not only at young budget travelers but at the independent traveler; a sort of streetwise cookbook for traveling alone."

—The New York Times

"A guide should tell you what to expect from a destination. Here *Let's Go* shines."

—The Chicago Tribune

"An indispensible resource, *Let's Go*'s practical information can be used by every traveler."

—The Chattanooga Free Press

✍ Let's Go is completely revised each year.

"A publishing phenomenon...the only major guidebook series updated annually. *Let's Go* is the big kahuna."

—The Boston Globe

"Unbeatable: good sight-seeing advice; up-to-date info on restaurants, hotels, and inns; a commitment to money-saving travel; and a wry style that brightens nearly every page."

—The Washington Post

✍ All the important information you need.

"*Let's Go* authors provide a comedic element while still providing concise information and thorough coverage of the country. Anything you need to know about budget traveling is detailed in this book."

—The Chicago Sun-Times

"*Let's Go* guidebooks take night life seriously."

—The Chicago Tribune

Let's Go Publications

Let's Go: Alaska & the Pacific Northwest 2002
Let's Go: Amsterdam 2002 **New Title!**
Let's Go: Australia 2002
Let's Go: Austria & Switzerland 2002
Let's Go: Barcelona 2002 **New Title!**
Let's Go: Boston 2002
Let's Go: Britain & Ireland 2002
Let's Go: California 2002
Let's Go: Central America 2002
Let's Go: China 2002
Let's Go: Eastern Europe 2002
Let's Go: Egypt 2002 **New Title!**
Let's Go: Europe 2002
Let's Go: France 2002
Let's Go: Germany 2002
Let's Go: Greece 2002
Let's Go: India & Nepal 2002
Let's Go: Ireland 2002
Let's Go: Israel 2002
Let's Go: Italy 2002
Let's Go: London 2002
Let's Go: Mexico 2002
Let's Go: Middle East 2002
Let's Go: New York City 2002
Let's Go: New Zealand 2002
Let's Go: Paris 2002
Let's Go: Peru, Ecuador & Bolivia 2002
Let's Go: Rome 2002
Let's Go: San Francisco 2002
Let's Go: South Africa with Southern Africa 2002
Let's Go: Southeast Asia 2002
Let's Go: Southwest USA 2002 **New Title!**
Let's Go: Spain & Portugal 2002
Let's Go: Turkey 2002
Let's Go: USA 2002
Let's Go: Washington, D.C. 2002
Let's Go: Western Europe 2002

Let's Go *Map Guides*

Amsterdam	New Orleans
Berlin	New York City
Boston	Paris
Chicago	Prague
Dublin	Rome
Florence	San Francisco
Hong Kong	Seattle
London	Sydney
Los Angeles	Venice
Madrid	Washington, D.C.

Let's Go

GREECE
2002

Erzulie Coquillon editor
John Mazza associate editor

researcher-writers
Alaina Aguanno
Helen Dimos
Kate Greer
Andrew Kleimeyer
Helen Stevens
Jonathan Wood

Dan Barnes map editor
Matthew Gibson managing editor

St. Martin's Press ≈ New York

Maps by David Lindroth copyright © 2002, 2001, 2000, 1999, 1998, 1997, 1996, 1995, 1994, 1993, 1992, 1991, 1990, 1989, 1988 by St. Martin's Press.

Distributed outside the USA and Canada by Macmillan.

Let's Go: Greece Copyright © 2002 by Let's Go, Inc. All rights reserved. Printed in the United States of America. No part of this book may be used or reproduced in any manner whatsoever without written permission except in the case of brief quotations embodied in critical articles or reviews. Let's Go is available for purchase in bulk by institutions and authorized resellers. For information, address St. Martin's Press, 175 Fifth Avenue, New York, NY 10010, USA.

ISBN: 0-312-27038-0

First edition
10 9 8 7 6 5 4 3 2 1

Let's Go: Greece is written by Let's Go Publications, 67 Mount Auburn Street, Cambridge, MA 02138, USA.

Let's Go® and the thumb logo are trademarks of Let's Go, Inc.
Printed in the USA on recycled paper with biodegradable soy ink.

HOW TO USE THIS BOOK

When you set foot in Greece, you've arrived in the land of philosophers, poets, conquerors, archaeologists, apostles, saints, goddesses, and mythic beasts. We at *Let's Go* are here to rescue you from the Gorgons and vengeful Furies along the way, letting you pass unscathed to the nymphs' grottoes, sacred sites, and blessed beaches that survive in present-day Greece. Welcome, and Παμε—Let's Go!

ORGANIZATION OF THIS BOOK

INTRODUCTORY MATERIAL. The first chapter of this book, **Discover Greece,** provides you with an overview of travel in mainland Greece, the Peloponnese, and the multitude of islands that pepper the Aegean. **Suggested Itineraries** takes you to our absolute favorites: what you shouldn't miss and how long it will take to see it. The **History & Culture** chapter provides you with a general introduction to the art, history, politics, and present-day culture of Greece. The **Essentials** section outlines the practical information you will need to prepare for and execute your trip. **Cyprus** gets its own introduction at the beginning of the island's chapter.

COVERAGE. The book begins with Athens, the major city and main transportation hub; from there, the coverage radiates outward throughout the Peloponnese, the mainland, and then the islands hugging the coast. The **black tabs** in the margins will help you to navigate between chapters quickly and easily.

APPENDIX. The appendix contains useful **conversions,** a **phrasebook** of handy phrases in Greek, and a **glossary** of foreign and technical (e.g. architectural) words.

A FEW NOTES ABOUT LET'S GO FORMAT

RANKING ESTABLISHMENTS. In each section (accommodations, food, etc.), we list establishments in order from best to worst. Our absolute favorites are so denoted by the highest honor given out by Let's Go, the Let's Go thumbs-up (📖).

PHONE CODES AND TELEPHONE NUMBERS. The **phone code** for each region, city, or town appears opposite the name of that region, city, or town, and is denoted by the ☎ icon. **Phone numbers** in text are also preceded by the ☎ icon.

GRAYBOXES AND IKONBOXES. Grayboxes at times provide wonderful cultural insight, at times simply crude humor. In any case, they're usually amusing, so enjoy. **Whiteboxes,** on the other hand, provide important practical information, such as warnings (❗), helpful hints and further resources (📚), and border crossing information (🛂), etc.

BEACHES, DAYTRIPS AND THE OUTDOORS. In addition to budget-conscious coverage of Greece's archaeological and historical sites, this year's edition of *Let's Go: Greece* emphasizes the al fresco offerings of the country's varied landscape. You can follow your inner trekker on our road-tested routes through olive groves, lemon trees, springs, and dusty or verdant foothills. We've expanded outdoors coverage in the multifaceted Northeastern Aegean Islands, and continued to accentuate daytrips with descriptions of strolls to seaside towns, trips to frescoed monasteries, and an updated section of daytrips to the Turkish Aegean coast, across from the Dodecanese and Northeastern Aegean Islands.

CONTENTS

VII

MAPS

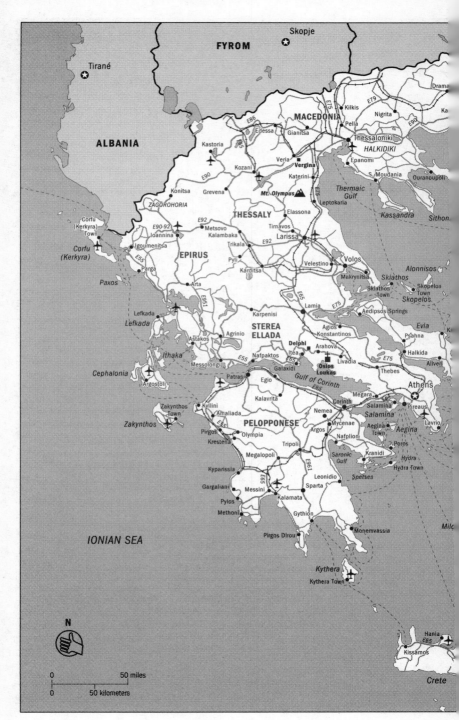

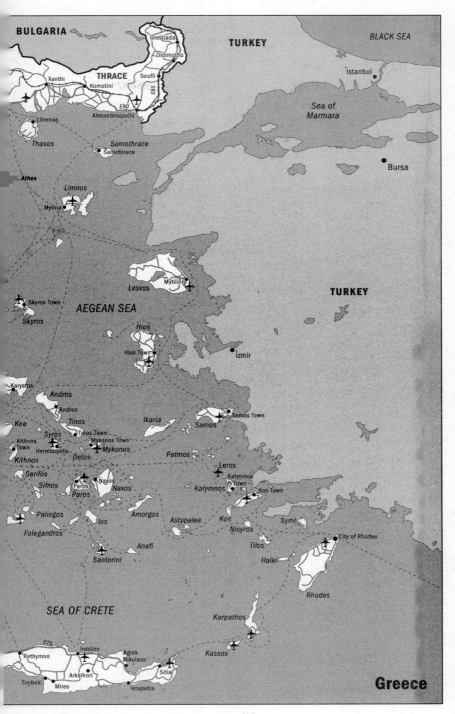

Greece

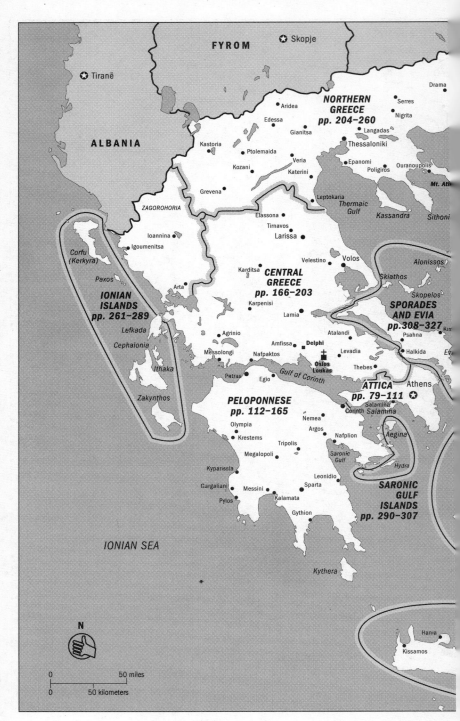

FYROM

⊗ Skopje

⊗ Tiranë

Drama
• Serres
• Nigrita

**NORTHERN
GREECE
pp. 204-260**

• Aridea
Edessa •
Gianitsa •
• Langadas
Thessaloniki

ALBANIA

Kastoria •
• Ptolemaida
Veria •
• Epanomi
Ouranoupolis
Kozani •
Katerini •
Poligiros
Mt. Ath

Grevena •
• Leptokaria
*Thermaic
Gulf*
Kassandra
Sithoni

ZAGOROHORIA
Elassona •
Tirnavos •

Ioannina •
Igoumenitsa •
Larissa •

*Corfu
(Kerkyra)*
Velestino •
Volos •
Alonissos

Paxos
Karditsa •
**CENTRAL
GREECE
pp. 166-203**
Skiathos

**IONIAN
ISLANDS
pp. 261-289**
Arta •
Karpenisi •
Skopelos

**SPORADES
AND EVIA
pp.308-327**

Lefkada
Lamia •
Atalandi •
Psahna •
Kim

Cephalonia
Agrinio •
Amfissa • ■ **Delphi**
Levadia •
Halkida •
Ev

Messolongi •
Nafpaktos
✝
**Osios
Loukas**
Thebes •

Ithaka
Patras •
Egio •
Gulf of Corinth
Levadia

**ATTICA
pp. 79-111** ⊗
Athens ⊗

Zakynthos
Salamina
Corinth Salamina

**PELOPONNESE
pp. 112-165**
Nemea •
Aegina

Olympia •
Argos •
Nafplion •

• Krestems
Tripolis •
*Saronic
Gulf*

Megalopoli •
Hydra

Kyparissia •
Leonidio •

Gargaliani •
• Messini
Sparta •
**SARONIC
GULF
ISLANDS
pp. 290-307**

Pylos •
Kalamata •

Gythion •

IONIAN SEA

Kythera

N

Hania •
Kissamos •

0 ———— 50 miles
0 ———— 50 kilometers

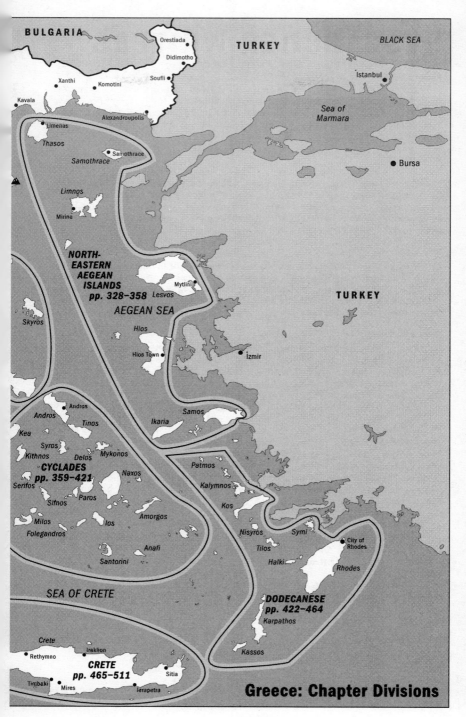

BULGARIA

TURKEY

BLACK SEA

Orestiada

Didimotho

Xanthi   Komotini   Soufli

İstanbul

Kavala

Alexandroupolis

Sea of
Marmara

Limenas

Thasos

Samothrace

Samothrace

Bursa

Limnos

Mirina

**NORTH-
EASTERN
AEGEAN
ISLANDS**
pp. 328–358

Mytlini

Lesvos

TURKEY

AEGEAN SEA

Skyros

Hios

Hios Town

İzmir

Andros

Andros

Tinos

Samos

Kea

Ikaria

Syros

Kithnos   Delos   Mykonos

CYCLADES
pp. 359–421

Naxos

Patmos

Serifos

Kalymnos

Sifnos   Paros

Kos

Milos

Amorgos

Folegandros   Ios

Nisyros   Symi

Anafi

Tilos

City of
Rhodes

Santorini

Halki

Rhodes

SEA OF CRETE

DODECANESE
pp. 422–464

Karpathos

Crete

Rethymno   Iraklion

Kassos

CRETE
pp. 465–511

Sitia

Timbaki   Mires

Ierapetra

Greece: Chapter Divisions

RESEARCHER-WRITERS

Alaina Aguanno   *Athens and the Cyclades*

Alaina stepped up to the line for Team Greece with all the poise and confidence of the track star she is. Taking the laid-back Greek lifestyle to heart, spunky, sassy Alaina paced her way through beaches and bars in the Cyclades, before a blazing sprint to the finish in The Big City, never slowed by her ever-present entourage of ▧foreign admirers.

Helen Dimos   *Cyprus and the Dodecanese*

Armed with the confidence of a native, Helen was our first to hit the high road. Upon arrival, this ▧linguist spun enough Greek lyrics to compete with Homer and to charm her countrymen. Comprehensive to the core, Helen made her in-depth researching count, constantly opening our eyes to the perks of a Greek lifestyle. Not even an infamous moped incident could steer Helen off course as she shared her homeland with the world.

Kate Greer   *Peloponnese and Ionian Islands*

Deftly bypassing a sunless summer in the Corporate World, energetic Kate lit up our lives with prompt, peppy calls and superb copy, making friends wherever she went. Using her newly-acquired outdoor orientation skills, she set our directions straight as she dashed through her itinerary, on her way to Italy and into the arms of her tow-headed ▧Latin lover.

Andrew Kleimeyer   *Central and Northern Greece*

His beloved Reds may have slumped all summer but Andrew never slowed, conquering his itinerary in enough time to spread ▧*Let's Go* cheer in Athens. Like any self-respecting budget traveler, Andrew nearly ran into a financial disaster, but his instincts and savvy kept him cruising from town to town. We set Andrew on a rocky route and this tireless worker rose to the challenge, scaling Mt. Olympus, bowing before Mt. Athos, and churning out copy smoother than butter.

Helen Stevens   *Crete and the Cyclades*

Hot-to-trot Helen of Troy stormed through the Aegean with enough style and grace to be the envy of her namesake. Equipped with the cutting wit expected of a *Lampoon* junkie, our gregarious gal painted especially thorough portraits of Greece's nude beaches, leaving no stone unturned and no clothes unshed. Although illness would eventually strike, Helen supplied us with enough entertaining accounts of her traveling ▧exploits to keep us rollin' through September.

Jonathan Wood   *Central Greece, the Sporades, Saronic Gulf, and Northeastern Aegean Islands*

Recipe for success: take one part blue Aegean water to equal parts sun, sand, and Scandinavian cohorts. Add hard work to taste. Put Jon Wood in the mix and chill for 45 days. His lyrical prose flowing like *retsina* at a Greek taverna, ▧super-star Jon rocked out across his varied route, opening our eyes to hikes and hot springs in the Northeastern Aegean Islands. Always a stellar performer, his seamless copy and first-rate research made our hearts sing.

Alexandra D. Cooley   *Bodrum, Turkey*

Kyle R. Freeney   *Çanakkale and Selçuk, Turkey*

ACKNOWLEDGMENTS

The Let's Go 2002 series is dedicated to the memory of Haley Surti

Στην υψεια σασ! **(Cheers!)** to our valiant researchers, and best of luck to the readers—we hope you have half as much fun as we did. Thanks Ben for endless entertainment and Allie for adding a dollop of sauce to the proceedings. Special thanks to: Matt for keeping us on our toes on everything from Bump Rule to baseball; James, our quirky Canadian squire, for bringing our words to the people; Jen and Caleb for supplementing our computer illiteracy with a Coke and a smile; and Dan for showing us the way. Top o' the mornin' to A&S, IRE, and SAF, and thanks for putting up with it all at all hours.

ERZ SENDS LOVE and eternal gratitude to the most amazing people I know—Mom, Naomi, GM & GP. Thanks roomies (Angie, Jean, Michelle) for a summer of laughs, and Kate & Abby for getting me into this wonderful mess in the first place. Mad love and many thanks to my *pareia* at the H—Brian, Duretti, Fitz, Ian, Iciar, Rahul, and Sean. Here's to 3 years of intoxicating good times, and many more to come. Thanks to Bertucci's, the Boss, and the Back in the Day Buffet for satisfying various summertime addictions, and to UDM for my first tantalizing taste.

MAZ OWES: this book to Erz, a true saint in the city and my legs when I couldn't walk.
SINGS: a Silent Rage to JPFlynn, Ben, Hollywood, Stan, Risherd Meh, Ed Luv, and the Smilingest Rugby Team Around; "Silver and Red" to Case, Berte, Chiz, Cannon, and Mayer.
STILL WRITES: for Vinny C. and MJDempsey.
SCOOPS: a famous sundae for Pete, Murph, Mike G., the sisters Fitz, PE, and SSICP crew.
BURNS: midnight oil with Dan and Sonja.
BUYS: the next round for Ben, Popper, P-Funk, Huyssen, Noah, the Katies, Angela, and Jean.
SENDS: thanks to Flynn, Yosh, Shearer, French, Ana, and Marc for speakin' my language; flowers to Suj (;
GIVES: bushels of love to 510 Weld, 71 Knoll, mom, dad, Angie, Dave, and Pete.

Editor
Erzulie D. Coquillon
Associate Editor
John Mazza
Managing Editor
Matthew Gibson
Map Editor
Dan Barnes

Publishing Director
Sarah P. Rotman
Editor-in-Chief
Ankur N. Ghosh
Production Manager
Jen Taylor
Cartography Manager
Dan Barnes
Design & Photo Manager
Vanessa Bertozzi
Editorial Managers
Amélie Cherlin, Naz F. Firoz, Matthew Gibson, Sharmi Surianarain, Brian R. Walsh
Financial Manager
Rebecca L. Schoff
Marketing & Publicity Managers
Brady R. Dewar, Katharine Douglas, Marly Ohlsson
New Media Manager
Kevin H. Yip
Online Manager
Alex Lloyd
Personnel Manager
Nathaniel Popper
Production Associates
Steven Aponte, Chris Clayton, Caleb S. Epps, Eduardo Montoya, Melissa Rudolph
Some Design
Melissa Rudolph
Office Coordinators
Efrat Kussell, Peter Richards

Director of Advertising Sales
Adam M. Grant
Senior Advertising Associates
Ariel Shwayder, Kennedy Thorwarth
Advertising Associate
Jennie Timoney
Advertising Artwork Editor
Peter Henderson

President
Cindy L. Rodriguez
General Manager
Robert B. Rombauer
Assistant General Manager
Anne E. Chisholm

DISCOVER GREECE

Where mythic heroes still stand silent guard among the stars and ruined antiquities poke haphazardly through modern streets, with a little imagination one may pass at will into the world of the ancients. Renaissance men long before their time, the ancient Greeks sprung to prominence with their philosophical, literary, artistic, and athletic mastery. Millennia later, schoolkids still dream of Hercules and the Medusa, Jason and the Argonauts, and outwitting the Trojans. When those kids grow up, they hanker after Greece's island beaches, free-flowing booze, and the diverse landscape, which was once the playground of a pantheon of gods. The all-encompassing Greek lifestyle is a frustrating and delicious mix of high speed and sun-inspired lounging: old men hold loud, lively debates in town plateias; young kids zoom on mopeds around the clock; unpredictable schedules force a go-with-the-flow take on life. This is a land where sacred monasteries are mountainside fixtures, three-hour sea-side siestas are standard issue, and dancing on tables till daybreak is a summer rite. Go to Greece. See the places you've read about, and do the things about which you've only dreamed.

WHEN TO GO

June through August is **high tourist season** in Greece and Cyprus. Bar-studded beaches set the scene for revelry and Dionysian indulgence, as the hundred-degree sun blazes over ancient cities and modern-day sun-worshipers alike. Hotels, domatia, clubs, and sights are, like the nightlife, in full swing. If the crowds or frantic pace of summer travel grate on you, consider visiting during May, early June, or September, when gorgeous weather smiles on thinner crowds. Avid hikers can take advantage of the mellower weather to traverse the unsullied expanses of Northern and Central Greece. In ski areas, winter brings another high season: you can hit the slopes at Mt. Parnassos (p. 170), Mt. Pelion (p. 191), or Metsovo (p. 215). The **low season,** from mid-September through May, generally has cheaper air-fares, lodging, and food prices, but many sights and accommodations have shorter hours or close altogether. At this time of year Greece hibernates, resting from summertime farming, fishing, and tourism. Ferries, buses, and trains run considerably less frequently, and life is quieter. For a temperature chart, see **Climate,** p. 556. For a list of Greek festivals, see **Festivals,** p. 34.

THINGS TO DO

Mountain chains, bougainvillea-speckled islands, silver-green olive groves, and the stark contrast of ocher land against the azure Aegean comprise the Greek landscape, the refuge of mythological beasts. This varied land of isolated villages, jasmine-scented islands, and majestic ruins satisfies even the pickiest visitor with its infinite diversions. Don't be afraid to plot out your own route: that famous Greek hospitality will make you feel welcome wherever you go. For more on regional bests, check out the **Highlights of the Region** boxes that begin each chapter.

THE ROAD TO RUIN(S)

As the birthplace of drama, democracy, and western philosophy, Greece's long history has left a wealth of sites in its impressive wake. The mother of all ruins, the **Acropolis** (p. 97), still presides over modern Athens. The gigantic, perfectly proportioned columns of the **Parthenon**, combined with the sun's beating rays and the brilliant gleam of white marble, conjures up the same awe inspired in a millennia of worshipers and pilgrims. A voyage through the **Peloponnese** will transport you back to the era of nymphs, satyrs, and gods in disguise. Take a lap around the well-preserved stadium on the way to the original Olympic fields at **Ancient Olympia** (p. 138), peer into Agamemnon's tomb at **Mycenae** (p. 120), or experience catharsis after watching the performance of an ancient tragedy in the magnificent theater at **Epidavros** (p. 128). Fast-forward (or rewind, depending on your sensibilities) to Byzantine times at the extensive city-site of **Mystras** (p. 156), the former locus of Constantine's rule in the Peloponnese. On the mainland, get to "know thyself" at the ancient **Oracle of Delphi** (p. 174). Chase after the floating island of **Delos**, birthplace of Apollo and Artemis, for a peek at the Temple of Apollo and an island-wide archaeological site (p. 374). More archaeological sites include: Heinrich Schliemann's reconstruction of the Minoan palace at **Knossos** (p. 474); Crete's *other* archaeological site, **Phaistos** (p. 479); Santorini's **Akrotiri,** a city frozen in time by a volcanic eruption (p. 410); onetime cult capital **Paleopolis** on Samothraki (p. 352); and the dual ruins of **Pella** and **Vergina** in Northern Greece, frequented by Philip II and his pride and joy Alexander the Great (p. 235). From Rhodes, you can reach the remnants of three of the seven wonders of the ancient world by daytrip. The **Colossus of Rhodes** leaves no trace today, though you can contemplate what its giant leg span must have been (p. 423). Across the water on the Turkish coast, you can venture to the city of **Halicarnassus** in modern-day Bodrum (p. 552), and Ephesus' **Temple of Artemis** (p. 555).

YOUR PLACE IN THE SUN

In Greece's summertime schedule, beach-side days melt through spectacular sunsets into starry, disco-filled nights, in a continuum of **hedonistic delight.** Roll out of bed and onto the beach around noon; nap in the late afternoon after strenuous samurai-tanning; head for a harborside dinner at 11pm; throw back after-dinner drinks, catch a movie, or hit the clubs until 5am, all under the stars; watch the sun rise over the ocean; and hit the hay before another sun-drenched day. It's nearly impossible to resist the allure of Greek sun and sea. The islands have long been a sun-worshiper's paradise (though today's crowd is more likely to love the sun than Apollo). As soon as you sail from Athens to the **Saronic Gulf Islands** (p. 290), the roasting Greek sun will bronze your (entire) body and release your inhibitions. A favorite of international vacationers, **Skiathos** in the Sporades harbors the piney Biotrope of Koukounaries beach and magical Lalaria (p. 312). In the Aegean Sea, **Santorini**'s black-sand beaches soak up the sun's hot rays and stay warm long after the stunning sunsets over the Sea of Crete (p. 404) have faded. Swim below sea caves once ransacked by pirates on the coast of **Skyros** (p. 320) or bask on the Lesvian shore, where beaches stretch out for miles from Sappho's home of **Skala Eressou** (p. 346). Stumble out of all those superfluous clothes at **Myknonos**'s wild, nude Super Paradise Beach (p. 368). If your eyes get tired of all those bare backsides, seek solace on a secluded strip of sand. The much-beloved haunt of booze-lovin' backpackers, **Corfu,** is ringed by fabulous beaches on all sides, in addition to hosting that legendary party haven, the Pink Palace (p. 261). Snorkel, waterski, or just loaf in the sun on **Ios** (p. 386) or **Naxos** (p. 397). Perfect your tan around **Paleohora** in Crete (p. 496), or at castle-crowned Haraki Beach in **Rhodes** (p. 423).

TAKE A HIKE

Greece isn't just Athens, islands, beaches, bars, and babes. If you have enough self-discipline to tear yourself away from the fun in the sun, you'll soon realize that a wilderness experience can be just as invigorating. To do so, you'll have to either bust out your walking stick or rev up your engines. Hiking or motorbiking—or a combination of the two—lets you cruise between rural villages independent of constantly changing bus schedules. On foot, you'll cross through foothills draped with olive groves, passing mountain goats and wildflowers along the way. Drowsy **Dimitsana** (p. 144) and cobblestoned **Stemnitsa** (p. 145) distinguish themselves from the tourist bustle of the rest of the Peloponnese. In the Ionian Sea, Odysseus's kingdom of **Ithaka** is an untapped hiker's paradise, where the Cave of the Nymphs—the hiding place for Odysseus's treasure and the conclusion of an enthralling hike—will seduce you (p. 276). Northern **Thassos** (p. 352) is full of secluded ruins, superior hikes, and village-to-village strolls. Rural **Alonnisos,** a largely uninhabited island in the Sporades, is crisscrossed by trails and moped-friendly roads, and hugged by beaches (p. 316) ideal for refueling after a fatiguing hike. Outlying islands are protected as part of the National Marine Park and make for a pleasant daytrip. The untouched traditional Greek villages of the **Zagorohoria** (p. 217) and their surrounding wilderness make walking an adventure. The neighboring **Vikos Gorge** (p. 218), the world's steepest canyon, challenges hikers with a six-hour-long trek. You can explore more gorgeous gorges in Crete: the **Samaria Gorge** (p. 494), Europe's longest gorge, and the quieter **Valley of Death** (p. 511) plunge you below eagles' eyries and trees clinging to the steep canyon sides.

Eighty percent of the Greek landscape is mountainous, to the delight of climbers. Clamber to the abode of the gods at **Mt. Olympus** (p. 237), ascending over 2900 steep, stunning meters to one of its eight peaks. Most trekkers start far below at little Litohoro. During the summer, Dionysus's old watering hole, **Mt. Parnassos,** makes a great hikin' and mountain-bikin' trip (p. 170); in winter, skiers storm the 2400m slopes. The trails around **Zaros** in Crete wind up to mountainside sanctuaries and to Zeus's childhood hiding place, **Kamares Cave** (p. 476).

◪ LET'S GO PICKS

BEST USE OF ANIMAL INSTINCT: Cower before the predatory **raptors** of Dadia National Reserve (p. 260). Pad quietly through the **Valley of the Butterflies** on either Paros (p. 390) or Rhodes (p. 423); just don't disturb their (mating) groove. Be amazed at animal antics at the **Pink Palace,** Corfu (p. 271).

BEST PLACE TO GET STONED: The **petrified forest** in Sigri on **Lesvos**—one of only two in the world (p. 346).

BEST BEACHES: The famous **black** and **red** sand beaches of Santorini (p. 406) satisfy those bored with golden pebbles. Get nekkid on **Paradise** beach on Mykonos (p. 368).

BEST CASTLES: Check out the famous Phaistos disc and sit in the throne room of the **Palace of Phaistos** on Crete (p. 479). Get medieval with the **Knights of St. John** in their castle on Kos (p. 436).

MOST GUT-WRENCHING RIDES: Hold on tight if you take the ride from tiny Diakofto to tinier **Kalavrita** (p. 135) on the rattling and rolling rack-railway. Imagine the fear in the eyes of those who were hauled up via rope as you take the easy way up (climbing the stairs) to the monasteries of **Meteora** (p. 201).

BEST PLACE TO USE YOUR ILLUSION: See the **Colossus of Rhodes,** one of seven wonders of the ancient world, in your mind's eye, as he stands guard over the City of Rhodes (p. 423).

BEST PLACE TO USE YOUR ILLUSION II: Mourn the absence of the **Venus de Milo** while sunning on Milos (p. 413).

WILDEST PARTIES: Visit **Pierro's,** the first gay bar in greece, on wild Mykonos (p. 368). Welcome to **The Jungle,** one of many places to **get drunk** on Ios (p. 400). Catch a ferry to the **"Bedroom of the Mediterranean,"** a.k.a. Bodrum, Turkey (p. 552), for a night you won't remember.

SUGGESTED ITINERARIES

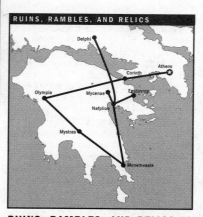

RUINS, RAMBLES, AND RELICS

POST-EURRAIL PARTY

SOUTHEASTERN AEGEAN ISLANDS

RUINS, RAMBLES, AND RELICS (1 WEEK) Put down that well-worn copy of the *Odyssey:* it's time to see the real deal. Arrive in **Athens** (p. 79) and charge straight to the gleaming **Acropolis,** which still rules over the city (p. 97). Escape the hot sun and lose yourself in the rooms and rooms of ancient treasure and statuary at the **National Archaeological Museum** (p. 104). Then head out from the capital to **Ancient Corinth,** whose fountain once quenched Pegasus's thirst (p. 116). Send up a cheer in the stadium at **Ancient Olympia,** and wonder at the life-like perfection of the Hermes of Praxiteles (p. 138). Clamber over the Byzantine wonderland of **Mystras,** a maze-like ruined city (p. 156), and to the otherworldly pedestrian and donkey-only city of **Monemvasia** (p. 162). Watch the setting sun color Venetian **Nafplion** (p. 124), then stroll the waterfront in the evening. On the way back to Athens, visit **Mycenae** and walk beneath the Lion's Gate (p. 120), then exult in the perfect acoustics of the theater at **Epidavros** (p. 128). End your journey with a pilgrimage to **Delphi,** the ancient oracle that still retains its mystic aura (p. 171).

POST-EURAIL PARTY (1 WEEK) Finish up a Eurail trip by taking the ferry from Brindisi, Italy to **Corfu** (p. 261), home to gorgeous beaches and the infamous Pink Palace. Continue on via Patras to **Athens,** where you can catch an eyeful of the Acropolis before heading out to the islands (p. 79). As soon as you get off the ferry to **Mykonos,** start shedding those inhibitions:

nude beaches abound, and nightlife sizzles (p. 368). When you've warmed up for a day, move on to **Ios,** an isle of pure bacchic hedonism (p. 400). Recuperate from the damage on the black sand beaches of **Santorini** (p. 406), then test out the tawny sand outside **Iraklion,** on Crete (p. 467).

SOUTHEAST AEGEAN ISLANDS (10 DAYS) Start your trip from **Limassol,** Cyprus, where you can wander a castle once occupied by crusading Knights Templar and visit the archaic ruins of Kourion; don't neglect the nearby beaches (p. 528). Sail on to **Rhodes,** imagining the giant Colossus that once towered over the harbor as you enter the City of Rhodes (p. 423). Sip a *frappé* as you sit between an Ottoman mosque and an Italian mansion on **Kos** (p. 436), then ferry across to the Turkish city of **Bodrum** to party until the morning ferry back (p. 552). Nurse your hangover on the deserted beaches bordering the stark cliffs of **Kalymnos** (p. 442). Find revelations on **Patmos,** where St. John wrote the last book of the Bible (p. 446), then move on to **Samos** to view its superb collection of statues (p. 332). Bust loose on wild **Mykonos** (p. 368), and return to **Athens** (p. 79) for a sight of the capital that governs them all.

loniki (p. 221) to daytrip to the ancient sites of gold-showered **Vergina** (p. 234) and nearby **Pella** (p. 235); Alexander the Great grew up in the neighborhood. For the greatest hike of them all head straight to the home of the gods on **Mt. Olympus** (p. 237). After the grueling, exultant climb, relax for a day on offshore **Thasos** before heading out (p. 355).

MAINLAND CIRUIT

Pella
Thessaloniki
Limenas
Vergina
Mt. Olympus
Zagorohoria
Monasteries of Meteroa
Ioannina
Kalambaka
Larisa
Pyli
Trikala
Volos
Mt. Pelion Peninsula
AEGEAN SEA
Karpenisi
Lamia
Proussos
Delphi
Athens

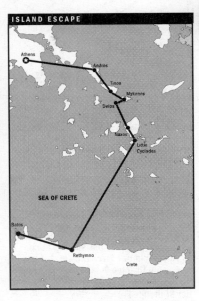

ISLAND ESCAPE

Athens
Andros
Tinos
Mykonos
Delos
Naxos
Little Cyclades
SEA OF CRETE
Balos
Rethymno
Crete

MAINLAND CIRCUIT (2 WEEKS) Set off from **Athens** (p. 79) to trek through undertouristed mainland Greece, home of cliffside Byzantine monasteries, cobble-stoned traditional villages, and the buzz of Thessaloniki. You'll probably need rented wheels of some kind. Set off for the oracle at **Delphi,** where you could receive advice about your upcoming travels in the form of a dream (p. 171). Continue on to **Lamia,** to climb the built-and-rebuilt ruins of the town Castro (p. 183). **Karpenisi,** the capital of the mountainous Evritania region, is the next stop (p. 178). From here, hike out among the tiny villages of the neighborhood; **Proussos,** with its spectacular cliffside monastery, is a highlight (p. 182). Pass through Karpenisi again on the way to Volos and the **Mt. Pelion Peninsula,** the onetime haunt of centaurs and present-day hideaway of traditional village life (p. 191). Roll out through Larisa and Trikala, as you head for the frescoed church of Porta Panagia in tiny **Pyli,** where you can dine beside a Roman footbridge (p. 196). Avoid the traditional means of ascent to the **Monasteries of Meteora**—a terrifying, free-swinging rope—and save your prayers to give thanks for the fabulous view (p. 201). Pass through Ioannina on the way to the **Zagorohoria** villages, eminently hikeable and extremely friendly (p. 217). Stay in Thessa-

ISLAND ESCAPE (2 WEEKS) For a slower, more relaxed trip, leave from Athens for **Andros,** a beach-lovers' paradise surrounded by small Neoclassical towns (p. 360). Don't miss the sunsets; you certainly won't miss the crowds that jam other beach islands. Try to tear yourself away to **Tinos,** and lie in the sand beside a ruined 4th century BC temple (p. 363). Stay the night with a local family for a truly Greek experience. Shake off your sloth at one of the crazed clubs of **Mykonos** (p. 368), and do penance for the previous night's debauchery during a daytrip to the sacred isle of **Delos,** the birthplace of Apollo and Artemis (p. 374). Next stop is **Naxos,** to snorkel among caves, sea urchins, and crystalline sand (p. 379). If the ferry schedule complies, slip away to one of the **Little Cyclades:** Koufonisia, Donousa, Iraklia, and Schinousa (p. 386). The small-town solitude will saturate your being; ease back into reality with a stopover in western Crete, around **Rethymno** (p. 484).

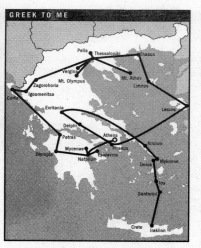

GREEK TO ME

GREEK TO ME (3 WEEKS) To see a large portion of Greece in a few weeks, start in **Athens** (p. 79), the capital for millennia; the National Archaeological Museum, the Acropolis, and the many smaller museums provide a refresher course in Greek history. Move on to **Nafplion** (p. 124), a gorgeous Venetian city and a perfect base for exploring the neighboring sights of the theater of **Epidavros** (p. 128), the alleged abode of the Atreus clan at **Mycenae** (p. 119), and the original Olympic field at sacred **Olympia** (p. 137). Head to Patras to catch the ferry to **Corfu** (p. 261), island that mixes debaucherous overdevelopment with untouched wilderness. Cross back to the mainland at Igoumenitsa on your way to the **Zagorohoria** (p. 217), a district of petite towns that stick to traditional folkways. The Byzantine sights of **Thessaloniki** beckon (p. 221), with fabulous mosaics and the awesome archaeological sites of **Vergina** (p. 234) and **Pella** (p. 235), a quick jaunt away. The industrious will set out for **Mt. Olympus** (p. 237), to grapple with the gods' abode. Men who plan ahead and collect the proper approvals and forms may visit **Mt. Athos,** the ultratraditional monastic community jutting out of Halkidiki (p. 246). Recline for a few days on the shores of **Thasos** just offshore (p. 355), then loop down to **Limnos** (p. 350) off the Turkish coast. A ferry ride carries you to the widely varied landscapes of **Lesvos** (p. 340), Sappho's home and the birthplace of Nobel laureate Odysseus Elytis, before you sail back to **Piraeus** (p. 109), Athens's modern port. From there, make a quick trip to the sacred oracle of **Delphi** (p. 171), then move on to **Evritania** (p. 178), a hilly rural district on the mainland. Hop the ferry to **Andros** (p. 360), a relaxing rural paradise that invites long hikes. Get freaky on **Mykonos** (p. 368); pay for the sins incurred with a daytrip to the sacred isle of **Delos,** birthplace of Apollo and Artemis (p. 374). Party naked on **Ios** (p. 400), then snooze on the black sand beaches of **Santorini** (p. 406); the picturesque white cliffside buildings are postcard-perfect. Finish your excursion on **Crete,** exploring the ruins of Knossos and Phaistos just outside of **Iraklion** (p. 467).

HISTORY AND CULTURE

Since antiquity, Greece has carved out its dominion of intellectual, governmental, literary, artistic, and religious majesty at the crossroads of Europe and Asia; the entire world has shared its wisdom. The relics of Crete's Minoan civilization reveal Egyptian and Babylonian influence, while in the bushy beards and long black robes of Orthodox priests, the mores of the Eastern Roman Empire have survived through the Byzantine Era to the present time. Four hundred years under the Ottoman Turks left a spice in Greek food, an Eastern twang in its *bouzouki* music, and a skyline of minarets. Greece declared independence in 1821, and now struggles to maintain the glory of Classical Athens, the splendor of Imperial Byzantium, and the religious purity of Ottoman folkways in an increasingly industrial nation governed by a reborn democracy.

HISTORY AND POLITICS

ANCIENT GREECE (THROUGH AD 324)

The romance of Ancient Greece has transfixed the world, throughout history and to the present day. The influence of the ancient Greeks pervades Western language, philosophy, and literature. Greek culture grew from agricultural and fishing communities: the coastal Aegean fostered prosperity, with its access to the ocean and its nearby olive trees, grapes, forests, and fertile land. Walled towns, constructed around a central high point, or **acropolis,** protected seaside settlements. Immigrants and traders from Anatolia, the Levant, and Egypt added a dash of global chic to the ancient Greek world.

BEGINNING OF TIME: WORLD EMERGES FROM CHAOS	The Start of the World as We Know It, and I Feel Fine. The universe's undefined mass separates into water, air, and the earth. Zeus ousts his pop Cronus to rule it; Pandora peeks into a box of evils, letting them loose on humans.

MY BRAIN HURTS Western Philosophy—"the love of wisdom"—originated in 585 BC when **Thales of Miletus** asked, "What is everything made out of?" Thales answered "water" (wrongly), and fell into a well as a lesson. **Anaximander,** Thales's pupil, guessed more safely that everything springs from the "Indefinite" and exists "according to necessity." Soon others were jostling to assert their opinions: **Heraclitus** of Ephesus, called the "Dark One" for his sour attitude, claimed that reality is usually hidden, and that "war is the father and king of all, and some he shows as gods, others as men; some he makes slaves, others free." In reply, **Parmenides** answered that appearance and reality are separate: what is *must* be, and can't *not* be, so we shouldn't even bother thinking about what doesn't exist, because we can't grasp it. His pupil **Zeno** attacked the ideas of motion and plurality as naïve—silly people, there's no motion! Anticipating a 70s rock band by several thousand years, **Empedocles** described the universe as composed of four elements—earth, air (wind), fire, and water. He believed that they constantly recombined to form all things in the world. **Pythagoras** played guru to a cult of vegetarians who tried to get in touch with their past lives; once he heard the soul of a dead friend crying out to him in a puppy's yip. In his spare time, he figured out the properties of right triangles (remember $a^2+b^2=c^2$?).

VERGINA
Ruins of the Macedonian city once home to Philip II and his son, Alexander the Great.

DODONI
The site of Zeus's oak-tree oracle.

DELPHI
One of the most important sources of wisdom in the ancient world.

OLYMPIA
The temples, training grounds and stadium of the first Olympic games.

Mycenae
Legendary home to Agamemnon and the Atreus clan of classical tragedy.

ALBANIA
FYROM
MACEDONIA
Pella
Thessaloniki
Dion
GREECE
Thermaic Gulf
TO BRINDISI, ANCONA
Vikos
Mount Olympus
Perama Cave
Ioannina
THESSALY
Meteora
EPIRUS
Acheron
Krannon
SPORADES
Nikopolis
Volos
Aktion
IONIAN
Thermon
Evia
Levadia
Eretria
Gulf of Corinth
Plataiai
ISLANDS
Athens
Isthmia
Corinth
PELOPONNESE
Nemea
Aegina
Temple of Aphaia
Olympia
Mantinia
Tiryns
Argos
Epidavros
Naos Poseidonos
Vassae
Asini
Saronic Gulf Islands
Tegea
Troizen
Saronic Gulf
Messini
Mystra
Sparta

Ionian Sea

N

MEDITERRANEAN SEA

■ Byzantine Sights
🏛 Ancient Ruins

Falasarna

0   50 miles
0   50 kilometers

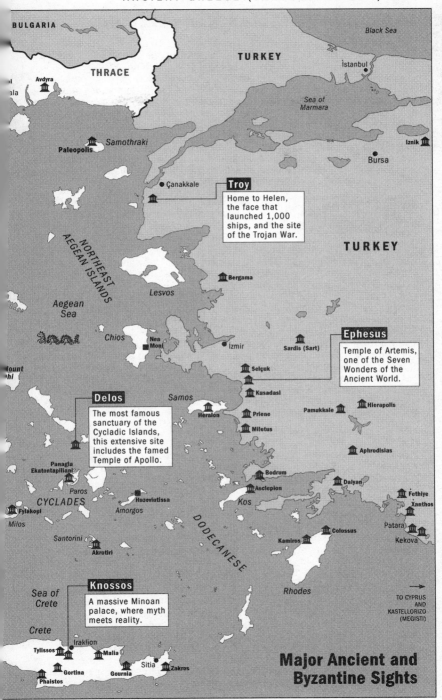

BULGARIA

THRACE

TURKEY

Black Sea

İstanbul

Sea of Marmara

Avdyra

Samothraki

Paleopolis

Iznik

Bursa

Troy

Home to Helen, the face that launched 1,000 ships, and the site of the Trojan War.

Çanakkale

TURKEY

NORTHEAST AEGEAN ISLANDS

Bergama

Lesvos

Aegean Sea

Chios

Nea Moni

İzmir

Sardis (Sart)

Ephesus

Temple of Artemis, one of the Seven Wonders of the Ancient World.

Selçuk

Mount ...hi

Samos

Kuşadası

Delos

The most famous sanctuary of the Cycladic Islands, this extensive site includes the famed Temple of Apollo.

Heraion

Priene

Miletus

Pamukkale

Hierapolis

Aphrodisias

Panagia Ekatontapiliani

Paros

Hozoviotissa

Amorgos

CYCLADES

...lakopi

Milos

Kos

Bodrum

Asclepion

Dalyan

Fethiye

Xanthos

Patara

Kekova

DODECANESE

Santorini

Akrotiri

Kamiros

Colossus

Rhodes

TO CYPRUS AND KASTELLORIZO (MEGISTI)

Sea of Crete

Knossos

A massive Minoan palace, where myth meets reality.

Crete

Tylissos

Iraklion

Malia

Sitia

Gortina

Gournia

Zakros

Phaistos

Major Ancient and Byzantine Sights

THROUGH THE TROJAN WAR (1250 BC)

THE BRONZE AGE. Though contemporary Greeks considered the **Bronze Age** (3000-1000 BC) a third-place finish after the earlier Golden and Silver Ages, the Bronze Age discovery of metalworking kicked off a high point in Greek culture. Peering over the shoulders of their eastern neighbors, Greeks learned bronze tool-making and weaponry. Three Aegean cultures built their reputations on bronze: the mainland Mycenaean, Crete's Minoan, and the islands' Cycladic. Island civiliza-tion flourished early on. The wall frescoes and marble figurines of the **Cycladic** cul-ture showed Middle Eastern influence and a strong geometric element. By about 2000 BC, the **Minoans** (named for the step-dad of the Minotaur) busily constructed palaces at Knossos (p. 474), Malia (p. 482), and Phaistos (p. 479) as centers of gov-ernment, religion, and trade; a strong fleet made Minoans the mack daddies of the Aegean. Around 1500 BC, a **Mysterious Cataclysm**—tidal waves, volcanoes, and/or alien invasions—wiped the Minoans out of existence.

1250 BC: TROJAN WAR	Worst Marital Spat of All Time Causes Ten Years of War. Helen, source of the trouble and owner of the face that launched 1000 ships, laughs, "Long live latex."

TEAM HELEN. The mainland Mycenaeans (a.k.a. Achaeans or Hellenes—named both for a tribe in Thessaly and for Helen of Troy), descended from invading warriors from Eastern Europe, overtook the Aegean after the Minoans faded. Based in Mycenae and Tyrins, they built citadels surrounded by "Cyclopean" walls—so called because later Greeks thought only a muscle-bound Cyclops could lift such massive stones. Myce-naean rule extended throughout the southern mainland, Crete, and the Cyclades and Dodecanese as far as Cyprus, where archaeologists have uncovered remnants of Mycenaean culture throughout these areas. The Mycenaeans' language, **Linear A,** has long held to be a mystery as great as the cause of the Minoans' demise. Linear B, devel-oped from the Minoan Linear A, has puzzled generations of linguists (cunning though they may have been); recently this tongue action has proven to be pre-Greek.

The Mycenaeans attacked Troy in Asia Minor around 1250 BC, igniting the most mythologized, obsessed-over, and written-about war in history. Perhaps the great-est histories of the **Trojan War,** Homer's **Iliad** and **Odyssey,** compiled the oral lore of the war into two epic poems around 850 BC (during the subsequent Dorian Era).

DORIAN BREAK-UP (1100-500 BC)

THE DORIAN INVASION. Bronze-age Aegean civilizations met an abrupt end in the 12th century BC, when invading **Dorians** burst in from the Balkan highlands just north of Greece. The invasion scattered the Mycenaeans in a **diaspora** that relo-cated Greeks to Asia Minor (where Homer may have lived) and to the Black Sea. A **Dark Age** of rule by decidedly un-dainty Dorians followed. It wasn't all bad under Dorian rule: the Greek language and alphabet settled into a single, national lan-guage, accompanied by a national identity. Tribal divisions still prevented a cen-tralized government like the Mycenaeans'. Industry, agriculture, and trade passed into the hands of hundreds of small, independent villages peopled by self-suffi-cient farmers. These villages' political independence and Dorian destruction of "high" civilization paved the path to the city-state and to Classical splendor.

THE RISE OF THE CITY-STATE. From 800-500 BC, in the aftermath of the Dorian invasion, the *polis* or **city-state** rose as the major Greek political structure. A typi-cal *polis* consisted of a city and the surrounding countryside which provided food and wood. Within the town, an **acropolis** (a fortified citadel and a religious center bedecked with **temples** to the people's patron deities) and an **agora** (the market-place and the center of commercial and social life) were major landmarks. Within the agora, thinkers waxed philosophical and traders hawked their wares amid the **stoas,** open-air paths lined with columns. Outside the city center, amphitheaters and stadia hosted political and religious gatherings and athletic games.

HALLUCINOGENIC HONEY In the 5th century BC, King Cyrus of Persia recruited a ragtag troop of jack-booted Greek thugs to pillage various villages in Asia Minor. Among the 10,000 Greeks was **Xenophon,** who recorded their misadventures in the *Anabasis.* According to Xenophon, after making a hasty retreat laden with booty, the soldiers wandered among fields of beehives brimming with honey. The tired horde sampled the combs with disastrous results: some of the soldiers ended up unconscious or plagued with violent diarrhea and vomiting. Those who consumed the nectar in moderation reported **fantastical visions** (who knows what the bees were seeing!). The morning after, the entire legion woke up with a wicked hangover and some cool but embarrassing flashbacks. After enduring a few days of detox from too many psychotropic substances, the iron-hearted Hellenes marched west to Trabzon, on the eastern end of Turkey's Black Sea coast. Travelers near the Black Sea have reported similar mind-altering effects; scientists have concluded that the bees procure their heady honey from the *Azalea pontica,* a flower that grows in the area.

By the 9th century BC, many city-states caught the imperialism bug and began to expand and colonize overseas, spreading their military influence and culture throughout the Mediterranean. Colonization had benefits, as city-states became increasingly prosperous. The isolated city-states began forming economic, religious, and military ties among themselves, further uniting Greece. Religion and sports united in the **Olympic Games** (p. 138), where the athletic fields of Olympia hosted politically-charged competitions between states. Through similar transnational events, the residents of city-states began to feel more Greek, and less Athenian or Spartan. By 700 BC, the inhabitants of Greece called themselves **Hellenes,** or Greeks. This new identity created a contrast between Greeks and foreigners, whom the Hellenes called **barbarians (barbaroi,** after the sound of foreigners' language, which Greeks thought sounded like a savage "bar bar bar").

480 BC: BATTLE OF THERMOPYLAE	Leonidas, 300 Spartan Troops Block Persian Army. New words "bottleneck," "spartan," and "self-sacrifice" were defined by the battle, which killed every Spartan soldier.

Starting in 495 BC, the Greeks were threatened by "barbarian" invasions from the eastern **Persians** under Xerxes, and from the empire of **Carthage** to the southwest. During the **Persian Wars** (490-477 BC), Athens and Sparta took the lead in defending Greece from invasion. According to Herodotus (p. 25), the Greeks defeated five million Persians (a more realistic estimate suggests 25,000-35,000) in battles at Marathon, Salamis, and Platea. In Sicily and southern Italy (called **Magna Graecia**—wider Greece—by its Italian occupants), the western Mediterranean city-states fended off Carthaginian assaults from North Africa and saved western Greece from foreign rule. The Hellenic victories ushered in a period of unprecedented prosperity and artistic, commercial, and political success.

CLASSICAL GREECE (500-400 BC)

ATHENS IN THE LEAD. At the end of the Persian Wars, Athens rose to prominence as the largest, wealthiest, and most influential *polis.* Equipped with a strong navy (built in preparation for the Persian Wars), Athens made waves in the Mediterranean and established itself as a power as head of the Delian League, an organization of Greek city-states formed to defend against Persia; which made Athens the de facto capital of Greece. Athens grew prosperous, and between 500 and 300 BC, Athens fostered the art, literature, philosophy, and government (including early democracy, a government for the ages) which still permeate Western culture. Ever a man of the people, Solon freed debt-prisoners and ended aristocratic privilege during his rule, while Pericles opened his democratic government to all male citizens, who were randomly chosen to participate in the rule of Athens. Athens was no democratic paradise, however: almost 20% of the populace were slaves.

SPARTA STRIKES BACK. Athens faced a rival city in controlling Greece: Sparta, the head of the Peloponnesian League, a collection of mainland city-states. The two powers could hardly be more different: Athens was commercial, democratic, and prided itself on its cultural achievements; Sparta was agricultural, oligarchical, and valued stoic military training above all else. Spartan men's lives from age seven to 60 were spent in military training, conquest, or defense; women trained to become fit mothers and models for their military sons. These contrasting lifestyles resulted in the Peloponnesian War (431-404 BC), sparked in part by Athenian expansion in the Peloponnese and Sicily. The war ended in a nominal defeat for Athens after a hopeless attack on Syracuse. During this period, the structure of the Greek city-state began to rot from within; the Athenian historian Thucydides, our best source on the Peloponnesian Wars, identified the problem as a *stasis*—the Greeks lost internal unity, while subject city-states chafed under Athenian rule.

MACEDONIAN RULE (400-200 BC)

PHILIP OF MACEDON. Until the Peloponnesian Wars, Athens had been the single city-state powerful enough to lead a unified Greece against common foes. After the war, Sparta and later Thebes tried to hold together a Greek alliance, but succumbed to Persian political influence. A new political force in "barbarian" **Macedonia** soon capitalized on the weakness of the rest of Greece, and seized control. **King Philip II** and his Macedonian troops conquered the Greek city-states; in 338 BC, Philip snuffed other Greek powers at the battle of Chaeronea, where he crushed an Athenian resistance led by orator and statesman **Demosthenes.** He then bound the city-states into a union subject to his monarchy.

RISE AND FALL OF EMPIRE. After Philip's assassination in 336 BC, his 20-year-old son Alexander (soon to be called Alexander the Great) took the throne. Once a student of Aristotle, Alexander ruled Greece with an iron fist—in 335 BC he mercilessly razed Thebes and seized control of his father's empire. In military control of Greece, Alexander then turned his ambitions east. Within eleven years, by the time of his sudden death at 33 years of age, he ruled Egypt and the entire Persian Empire; he had spread the Greek culture and language throughout the eastern Mediterranean. During the Hellenistic Era that followed, Athenian literary and artistic forms diffused throughout the former empire and combined with Near Eastern influences to form a distinct hybrid culture.

323 BC: ALEXANDER DIES	The Wheels Fall off the Chariot. Upon Alexander the Great's death, the united Greek and barbarian empire shatters.

The Macedonian empire quickly crumbled after Alexander's death, leaving three powers in its wake: the **Antigonids** in Macedonia, the **Seleucids** in Asia Minor, Syria, and Persia, and the **Ptolemies** in Egypt. The Ptolemies (of whom Cleopatra was the last) remained particularly tied to Greek culture. The Ptolemy capital at **Alexandria** became a legendary center of culture. Again, the collapse of an empire restored a measure of independence to the Greek city-states. Three Greek powers ruled the 3rd century BC: the Peloponnesian **Achaean Confederacy,** the Delphi-based **Aetolian Confederacy,** and the city-state of Sparta.

MAGNA GRAECIA TO MAGNA ROMA (200 BC-AD 324)

Greek self-rule was short-lived. In the 3rd century BC, **Rome** made alliances with Greek cities and began expanding its empire into Greek territory: rule of Greece was particularly satisfying for Romans, who had once been subject to Greek power, and who admired and wished to adopt Greek culture. Roman influence filled the power vacuum left by Alexander, as the Romans defeated

▥ TRUTH-SEEKING TRIUMVIRATE: WESTERN PHILOSOPHY'S BIG THREE

"The unexamined life is not worth living." Early philosophical works, surviving on fragments of papyrus and in the reports of later writers, paved the road for ▧ **Socrates** (469-399 BC), the first of the big three. Socrates was a poor, ugly convict who described himself as a gadfly nipping at the ass of the horse that was Classical Athens. He brought philosophy down from the stars and into the muddy stalls of the *agora*, where he spent his days picking over the morals and beliefs of anyone who would stop for a chat. His impersonal style of asking questions is still called the Socratic Method. All the while he insisted that he was wiser than anyone else only because he was aware of his own total ignorance. His radical lifestyle and constant questioning eventually angered influential Athenians, and he was sentenced to death for corrupting the youth. Socrates died by drinking hemlock in 399 BC.

"Until philosophers are kings...cities will never cease from ill, nor the human race." Most of what we know of Socrates comes from his disciple **Plato** (427-347 BC), one of the youths he was executed for corrupting. In his dialogues, Plato paid tribute to Socrates's questioning technique, and later referred to his mentor as the originator of his own moral and metaphysical doctrines. Plato's **Theory of Forms** described the sensory world as an illusion that was only an echo of the real truth of the pure distant world of immutable **forms,** or ideas. People could understand the forms only through intense questioning of the world and concentrated Deep Thoughts. Plato embraced reason, and used Greek mythology to support his moral arguments. His rationalism convinced him that his country's famous democracy was for stooges. Plato's *Republic* describes his vision of the ideal society, which was divided into ironclad classes by ability and birth, and ruled by an enlightened philosopher-king, who would guide society out of ignorance and into the light of wisdom.

"The whole is more than the sum of its parts." Although a student of Plato's, **Aristotle** reacted critically against his teacher's methods and teachings. Aristotle took up biology and grounded himself in concrete examples and specimens; he appreciated the palpable world and rejected abstract ideas. His empirical approach virtually founded Western science, and his work remained at the forefront of scientific thought throughout the Middle Ages. Aristotle was also a political philosopher: he disagreed with Plato and Socrates's belief (a belief shared by many even in the present) that a politically active man can't live a moral life. He saw a moral life in civic responsibility to the Greek *polis*. Indeed, his later life was spent in political service: when Athens came under pressure from Philip of Macedon (p. 12), Aristotle returned to his native Macedonia, where he took on a none-too-shabby job as tutor to Alexander the Great (p. 12).

the Seleucids of Asia Minor and conquered Macedonia in the **First and Second Macedonian Wars.** At the end of the second war in 197 BC, Greeks gained a nominal "independence;" but Rome treated Greece as its satellite, not as a free state. Greek cities began to support their former enemies against Rome, and the Achaean Confederacy openly rebelled in 146 BC. In response, Rome flexed its muscles, destroying Corinth and loading Greece with oppressive restrictions. When the cities were organized by Augustus into the Roman province of **Achaea** in 27 BC, Greece finally fell under direct Roman rule. Rome had no consistent policy toward its Greek province; while the Roman Emperor Hadrian ran public works programs and a fair government, Emperor Sulla destroyed the economy and even massacred people. Even as Roman legions took hold of Greek lands, Hellenic culture seeped into Roman society: Greek slaves often tutored Roman children, Greek sculpture was brought to Roman homes, and Roman architects imitated Greek styles. Adopting what they admired of Greek culture, the Romans created a **Greco-Roman culture** that spread Greek influence to the farthest reaches of the Roman empire.

BYZANTINE ERA (AD 324-1453)

Unlike other countries ruined by the decline and fall of the Roman Empire (Italy among them), Greece emerged from Roman rule into a **Byzantine** cultural rebirth, prosperity, and power that stretched from the Balkans through Greece to the Levant and Egypt. The Byzantines saw themselves as heirs of the classical Roman Empire; still, they were heirs to a culture more Greek than Roman, and they were Christian. Despite geographical and cultural differences between the Greeks, Syriacs, Egyptian Copts, Armenians, and Slavs in the empire, they forged a unified political state under one emperor, church, language (Greek), and tax system (even then, death and taxes were the only sure things in life). Internal pressure from religious spats and external attacks by raiders weakened the empire.

ROMAN EMPIRE: EAST SIDE (324-500)

SAILING TO BYZANTIUM. At its height, the Roman Empire became too huge to control under a single government from Rome. Thus, the eastern half of the empire split into two regions controlled by a system of four rulers. The unusual political arrangement ended in a scramble for power, finally won by **Constantine** in AD 312. Before his decisive victory, Constantine saw a vision of a cross of light in the sun, bearing the fiery inscription, "In this sign, you will conquer." The newly installed eastern emperor interpreted this as a sign from the Christian God who was winning converts throughout the former Roman Empire. Later, Constantine legalized Christianity within his empire. Founding his own *polis*, **Constantinople** (modern Istanbul), in 324, he gave the Roman Empire a new capital over the ancient city of Byzantium. Known as **New Rome** or simply the **Polis** (City), Constantinople controlled the eastern and western portions of the empire from its strategic location between the Black Sea and the Aegean. Constantinople's new strength led to the eventual administrative division between the Greek-speaking east and the Latin-speaking west after the death of Emperor Theodosius in 395.

SLOUCHING TOWARD BETHLEHEM. Constantine died in 338 after a deathbed Christian baptism; his empire didn't convert so easily. Julian the Apostate, a classically educated nephew of Constantine's, challenged the upstart religion in 361-363 and tried to return to worshipping the traditional pantheon of gods. While Constantine had given state legitimacy to Christianity, many shunned the new faith: numerous pagan monuments still dotted the ostensibly Christian city of Constantinople, yet the state grew increasingly supportive of Christian culture. Evangelical missions, Christian art, hymns, saints' biographies, theological tracts, spiritual poetry, church architecture, religious icons, and mosaics all spread the word. The church developed its doctrine through the Seven Ecumenical Councils. The Council of Nicaea in 325 (which produced the Nicene Creed still recited by Catholics daily) and the Council of Constantinople in 381 shaped the Orthodox Church into five patriarchates, or dioceses: Rome, Constantinople, Alexandria, Antioch, and Jerusalem. A patriarch or pope presided over each, as a religious and governmental official.

NETTLESOME NEIGHBORS (500-1453)

VANDALS-1, GREEKS-0. During the 6th century, **Emperor Justinian's** battles against the Sassanians of Persia and the western Vandals (who had sacked Rome) overstretched the empire's strength. Justinian attempted to simplify the empire's aging Roman laws and he undertook massive building projects such as the **Agia Sophia**, a church that still stands in Istanbul. These expensive reforms, along with military campaigns and political corruption, left the empire vulnerable to raids by Slavs, Mongols, and Avars, who attacked Greece as far as the Peloponnese around 500. In many areas of the mainland and Peloponnese, Greek culture and language were wiped out entirely, and the Greek language and script only returned after later missions from Constantinople.

SMASHING, BABY! Ensuing Arab conquests and the challenge of Islam consolidated and unified the empire, accompanied by the religious movement of **iconoclasm**—icon-smashing. Greek Christians came to believe that iconography (paintings of Christ and saints on boards or city walls for protection in battle, or any visual representation of God) violated the **second commandment** which demanded that the faithful make no graven image of God. They interpreted their defeats in battle as punishment for this violation. By the early 700s, Church doctrine demanded that all images be demolished—a policy whose enforcement depended on the Greeks' performance in war. Eventually, iconoclasm itself was smashed in 843, to the benefit of latter-day art historians.

Non-Christian conquerors created the **Byzantine Commonwealth,** which further divided Constantinople from Rome and the west. The crowning of **Charlemagne** as Holy Roman Emperor in 800 finalized the split of west and east. The bitter **Great Schism** of 1054 caused a mutual excommunication between the Greek Orthodox and Roman Catholic Churches—each church declared the other a false church.

THE CURSE OF CRUSADERS. After the separation from Rome, Greeks attempted to extend Christianity as they protected themselves from invaders. **Missionaries** reached out from the empire's contracted borders into the Slavic kingdoms and Russia, sowing the seeds of Orthodox Christianity throughout Eastern Europe. In 1071, the Byzantines lost control of eastern Anatolia to the **Selçuk Turks;** Greek monasteries in the Aegean and Black Sea areas converted to armed fortresses to ward off Turkish pirates. From 1200 to 1400, the Byzantine Empire was plagued by Norman and Venetian **Crusaders,** who conquered and looted Constantinople in 1204 and imposed western Catholic culture upon the city. Despite its strong emperors, Byzantium needed to ally with Latin, Slavic, and even Turkish rulers by marriage in order to survive. At last, the once-huge Byzantine Empire was reduced to only Constantinople and its environs, and in 1453 the **Ottoman Turks** overran the much-reduced city.

UNDER THE OTTOMAN THUMB (1453-1829)

ISTANBUL, NOT CONSTANTINOPLE

GREECE UNDER TURKEY. Old Byzantium suffered another undignified name change under the Ottoman Turks, this time renamed **Istanbul**—a Turkish adaptation of the Greek *steen Poli* (to the City)—in 1453. The city again became the seat of empire. For centuries the Ottoman Empire prospered, though eventually its diverse regions grew apart and caused it to weaken. The Muslim Turkish rulers treated their Greek subjects as a **millet**—a separate community ruled by its own religious leaders. Greeks paid the *cizye,* a head tax dictated by Islamic law, but were otherwise free to worship as they chose. The Orthodox Greek church became the moderator of culture and tradition, and the foundation of Greek autonomy. Peacefully incorporated into Ottoman society, many Greeks fared better under Muslim rule than under the Christian crusaders. Greeks formed a new merchant class in towns and served as soldiers, bureaucrats, and translators for the Turkish sultanate. Though rebellions were repressed ruthlessly, Ottoman rule brought relative peace and prosperity to Greece.

The sultans ensured army loyalty by doling out **tımars** (temporary, uninheritable land grants) as payment for military service, but as Ottoman expansion slowed (and land grants dwindled), *tımar* holders grew restless. In the 14th century, Sultan Murad I developed the **devşirme** draft system, in which male Christian children could be conscripted to serve the sultan in Istanbul, converted to Islam, and highly educated as civil servants. The position of **Janissary** (from *yeni çeri,* "new army") let Greeks rise in the military or the Ottoman bureaucracy, as *kulls* (slaves).

GRRR. Though Greeks could choose to integrate into Ottoman society, **anti-Turk nationalist sentiments** began to build, encouraged by Western Europe and Russia. Russia viewed Moscow as a Christian force and as a third Rome; Istanbul, a Muslim city that ruled Christians, the former seat of empire, naturally interested Russia immensely. Russia wanted a Greek Orthodox state at the Bosporus to control the entrance to the Black Sea, while Greeks chafed under the weakening Turkish rule. By the 19th century, Greeks were pushing for independence from the empire.

THE GREAT IDEA (1821-1900)

GREEK NATIONALIST REVOLT

WAR FOR INDEPENDENCE. On March 25, 1821, after 400 years of Ottoman rule, Bishop Germanos of Patras raised a Greek flag at the monastery of Agia Lavra and sparked an empire-wide rebellion. Middle-class rebels hoped that the Orthodox Russian czar and Greek peasants would join the revolt; when they didn't, the rebels met a crushing defeat. Disorganized but impassioned guerrillas in the Peloponnese and Aegean islands waged sporadic war on the Turkish government for 10 years. The day of the revolt, 25 Martiou, and the names Botsaris, Koundouritis, Miaoulis, Mavrokordatos, and Ypsilanti (famous rebels) now appear as street names throughout the country (and the rest of the world—Ypsilanti, Michigan, for example). The liberation movement was carefully planned for nine months before Christmas Day (see "Conceived in Liberty...?," p. 300).

In an era of European revolutions, the Greek cause attracted the attention of hundreds of **philhellenes**, Europeans seeking to restore Greece to the Classical glory they idolized. These philhellenes came to fight (and often die) for Greece's independence, drawing international attention especially after British Romantic poet George Gordon, **Lord Byron,** died there of pneumonia in 1824. The persistent Greeks and their allies finally won the nervous support of the anti-revolutionary European Great Powers and in 1827 Russia, Britain, and France pressured the Turkish sultan to ease up on Greece. After the Turkish fleet was wrecked at the **Battle of Navarino** (now called Pylos, p. 151) the hesitant Russian czar declared war. The **Treaty of Adrianople** in 1829 finally freed Greece.

A ROOM OF THEIR OWN. Russia, Britain, and France wanted a free Greece, but also wanted to restrict its power. The borders of the new Greece were narrow, including only a fraction of the six million Greeks living under Ottoman rule. For the next century, Greek politics centered around regaining the Byzantine boundaries of Greece, and unifying the Greek population scattered around the Mediterranean. The vision of unification, called the Megali Idhea—the Great Idea— eventually ended in considerable expansion, including Crete, in 1913. However, Greece never gained its great goal—making Constantinople its capital.

Post-liberation nationalism also encouraged the creation of the **Church of Greece** in 1833, although it was not recognized by the patriarch until 1850. One of a number of independent Eastern Orthodox churches, the Church of Greece has since become the official state church.

POST-REVOLUTION POLITICS

OUT OF THE FRYING PAN, INTO THE FIRE. After the War of Independence, joy soon dissolved into disappointment. Puny and poor, the new Greek state was divided by the agrarian problem that would plague it for the rest of the century: landowners clung to their traditional privileges, while peasants demanded the redistribution of lands that had motivated them to fight for independence.

The first president, **Ioannis Capodistrias,** was elected in 1827, and made an earnest (if autocratic) attempt to create a strong government. His assassination in 1831 thwarted the attempts to establish a democratic government, and prompted European intervention into Greek politics.

The European powers then declared Greece a **monarchy,** handing the crown to the young German **Prince Otho** (dubbed "Otto") in 1833. Often called an "insensitive" ruler, Otto was a rich, powerful teenager who angered Greeks by handing out high-ranking positions to his German buddies. Otto moved the capital to **Athens,** and in 1843 created a parliamentary system. Though he embraced the *Megali Idhea* (and made friends in his new country that way), his bumbling government earned him exile in 1862 for ignoring the constitution. The British stepped in and installed a Danish prince, **George I,** as king. George's rule brought stability and a new constitution (in 1864), but the land distribution problem remained unsolved.

TWENTIETH CENTURY

EXPAND AND CONTRACT. The 1864 constitution downplayed the king, and emphasized the elected prime minister. In 1920, Cretan Prime Minister Eleftherios Venizelos, immortalized in street names across Greece, wrangled new Greek territory in the aftermath of the Balkan Wars and World War I. Savvy Balkan alliances nearly doubled Greece's territory. Defying King Constantine's request for neutrality, Venizelos set up an Allied revolutionary government in Thessaloniki. After the First World War, Venizelos realized Greece wouldn't get land in Asia Minor, and so in 1919 he invaded Smyrna in Turkey. A young Atatürk rebuffed the attack, and Venizelos was soon voted out of office. The Treaty of Lausanne, signed in 1923, enacted a massive population exchange that sent a million Greeks who lived in Asia Minor to live in Greece, and sent 400,000 Turkish Muslims from Greece to Turkey. This population exchange ended the *Megali Idhea* but began a series of economic problems for Greece.

THE SECOND WORLD WAR. Political turmoil rocked the 1930s, as Greeks lived through brief intervals of democracy amid a succession of monarchies and military rule. King George II was overthrown by a series of coups that instated a democracy; Venizelos, the former Prime Minister, headed the new government for five years, though royalists eventually forced his exile. The extreme nationalist **General Metaxas** succeeded him as Prime Minister in a fixed election, as George II again took the throne in 1936. Metaxas inaugurated an oppressive military state. Most notably, Metaxas rejected Mussolini's request that Italy occupy Greece during World War II with a resounding "No!" ("Όχι!"). Greece fell to Germany in 1941 and endured four years of Axis occupation, which destroyed ancient sites, caused widespread starvation and large-scale executions, and allowed the Nazi extermination of much of Greece's Jewish community. The communist-led resistance received broad popular support, though many right-wing resistance fighters received aid from the Western powers, which were eager to prevent a communist Greece.

FORMING THE MODERN GREEK STATE

CIVIL WAR AND RECONSTRUCTION. Civil war broke out in 1944, in an early Cold War stand-off that the left-wing, Soviet-backed Democratic Army (DA) eventually lost to the US-supplied anti-communist coalition government. Through a rather disgraceful American intervention, Greece instituted the Certificate of Political Reliability, which guaranteed that the bearer had politically acceptable views. Keeping a visible hand in Greek politics, the red-scared US helped place General Papagos, Constantinos Karamanlis, and the right-wing Greek Rally Party in power. When Karamanlis resigned after the assassination of a communist official in 1963, left-wing George Papandreou came to power.

The right-wing respite was short-lived; the army staged a **coup** on April 21, 1967, which resulted in rule by a **military junta** for seven years. Making extensive use of torture, censorship, and arbitrary arrest to maintain power, the junta enjoyed official US support and investment at the height of the Cold War. It ultimately fell in 1973 after the government killed 20 protesting students and provoked a **Turkish invasion of Cyprus** by attempting to unite Cyprus and Greece (p. 514).

1975: **DEMOCRACY RETURNS**	Greece Goes Retro: Democracy Back in Style. The Prime Minister quips, "We *invented* democracy. We were into it *before* it was cool."

Former president Karamanlis returned to take power, instituting parliamentary elections and organizing a referendum on the form of government. Monarchy was defeated by a two-thirds vote, and a new constitution was drawn up in 1975, calling for parliamentary government with a ceremonial president appointed by the legislature—the system still in use today.

RECENT EVENTS

TOWARD EUROPE. Under Prime Minister and founder **Andreas Papandreou,** the leftist Panhellenic Socialist Movement (PASOK) won landslide electoral victories in 1981 and 1985. Appealing to voters with the simple campaign slogan **Allaghi** ("Change"), Papandreou promised a radical break with the past. In office, he steered Greece into the European Economic Community (EEC) and pioneered the passage of women's rights legislation, though many of his policies were anti-Western: he spoke against NATO and maintained friendships with Qaddafi and Palestinian Liberation Organization leader Yasser Arafat. When a scandal involving the chair of the Bank of Crete implicated government officials in 1989, Papandreou lost control of Parliament. After three general elections in the space of 10 months, **Constantine Mitsotakis** of the New Democracy party (Nea Demokratia, or ND) became Prime Minister by a slim parliamentary majority.

AUGMENTATION AND AUSTERITY. Attempting to solve Greece's economic and diplomatic problems and align the country with mainstream European politics, Mitsotakis imposed an **austerity program** that limited wage increases and authorized the sale of state enterprises. This policy became tremendously unpopular when it threatened thousands of public sector jobs, and in 1993, Mitsotakis was defeated by a resurgent Papandreou in an emergency election. Just two years later, poor health forced Papandreou to leave his position.

Fellow socialist **Constantine Simitis** took control of the party and has since pursued aggressive economic reforms, privatizing banks and companies despite the opposition of perpetually striking labor unions. The ruling PASOK party has also made strides in international relations by being more NATO-friendly and opening talks with Turkey. The administration has also slashed Greece's budget deficit, brought inflation down, and cut the national debt in an attempt to meet the qualifying standards for entry into the **European Monetary Union** (EMU). Simitis, who was barely reelected in the 2000 election, was instrumental in Greece's successful bid to enter the EMU in January 2001. Visitors to the **2004 Olympics in Athens** (eagerly anticipated and in elaborate preparation) will be shelling out euros instead of drachmas.

GREECE AND TURKEY: BREAKING THE ICE. One of Simitis's continuing projects is normalizing relations with nearby Turkey. The two nations have been on less-than-friendly terms in the past (see p. 16), but in January 2001 **Financial Minister George Papandreou** traveled to Turkey, the first such visit in 37 years. While there, he signed four cooperation agreements concerning tourism, the environment, the protection of investments, and terrorism. Talks have begun concerning the touchy issue of Cyprus, which remains divided into Turkish and Greek Cypriot states. Although neither country wants to relinquish hold of the island, both sides appear to be open and optimistic.

ART & ARCHITECTURE

Such is the bloom of perpetual newness upon these works which makes them ever to look like untouched by time, as though the unfaltering breath of an ageless spirit had been infused in them.
—Plutarch

Order, proportion, and symmetry have shaped the tradition of Greek art from its earliest stages. Works by masters like Praxiteles and Lysippus still fascinate art lovers and connoisseurs alike. Greek art is typically divided into three eras: Ancient, Byzantine, and Modern. Three highly influential periods of the Ancient Era still stand out: the **Archaic** (700-480 BC; see p. 10), the **Classical** (480-323 BC; see p. 11), and the **Hellenistic** (323-30 BC; see p. 12).

PERFECTION WITH A PURPOSE: ANCIENT GREECE (THROUGH AD 324)

The ancient Greeks prized aesthetics above all else, as their virtually flawless, carefully crafted works affirm. Greeks didn't produce art just to admire its beauty. Ancient works of art served religious or practical functions: decorative pottery was a hot export item, used for storing (and chugging) wine, while sculptures represented gods in temples or served as offerings or monuments to the dead. Architecture developed through the construction of temples, commercial buildings, and stadia for performance of religious plays and for governmental gatherings. The mythological scenes painted on vases and in frescoes expressed religious values, political propaganda, or even made sexual jokes.

Greek art grew out of the belief that "man is the measure of all things." The living human form became artists' favorite subject after years of dabbling with abstract and stylized geometrical shapes. Meanwhile, Greek temples incorporated light and space as integral parts of the place of worship. It is impossible to overestimate how much Western culture owes to the architectural and artistic achievements of the ancient Greeks—Augustus Caesar, Michelangelo, Jacques-Louis David, Thomas Jefferson, Constantine Brancusi, and even Salvador Dalí found inspiration in Greek works. Present-day artists still learn from 2500-year-old Greek masterpieces, though many exist only as fragments.

ROOTS

CYCLADIC AND MINOAN PERIOD (3000-1100 BC). The Bronze Age Cycladic civilizations produced a minimalist style of sculpture, mostly small marble statuettes. These miniature pieces gracefully simplified the human form; a nude goddess, arms folded straight across her body, is a typical figure. Many of these enigmatic idols dazzle visitors to the Goulandris Museum of Cycladic and Ancient Greek Art in Athens (p. 105).

The Minoans of Crete also created scores of miniature votive statuettes, like the two earthenware **snake goddesses,** decorated with opaque colored glazes, which reside in Iraklion's **Archaeological Museum** (p. 471). It was Minoan **architecture,** however, that brought them glory, as Cycladic cultures took their cue from Minoan palaces like **Knossos** (p. 389). The palaces were cities unto themselves, and their labyrinthine complexity echoed the complicated administrative and religious roles of Minoan priest-kings. The palaces' massive pillars, ceremonial stairways, and decorative stucco show Near Eastern aesthetic and structural influence, which arrived via commercial contact with Egypt and Mesopotamia.

Minoan artists used plater to sculpt bull-leaping ceremonies, gardens, and leaping dolphins in vibrantly painted and lifelike frescoes. Though a little dusty, several Minoan **frescoes** were preserved in the ash of a volcanic eruption that destroyed much of Thira (present-day Santorini) near 1500 BC, and can be seen at the **National Archaeological Museum** in Athens (p. 104). Similar fresco paintings, restored by Sir Arthur Evans, can be seen at Knossos or in Iraklion's **Archaeological Museum** (p. 471). A versatile bunch, the Minoans were also renowned throughout the Aegean for their multicolored **Kamares-style pottery,** which consisted of red and white ornamentation on a dark background. Kamares-style designs included curvy abstract patterns and stylized ocean and plant motifs.

MYCENAEAN PERIOD (1600-1100 BC). The architecture of the mainland Mycenaean culture developed in response to the Cretan Minoans. The Mycenaeans' palaces at Mycenae (p. 131), Tiryns, and Pylos (p. 160) followed a more symmetrical design than earlier architecture, and centered around the megaron, a Near East-inspired reception room. Decorative frescoes revamped the fanciful Minoan model according to Mycenaean warrior taste.

Trailblazers in their own right, the Mycenaeans were the first Europeans to produce sculpted monuments, as in the **royal tombs** and triangular **Lion's Gate** sculpture at Mycenae (p. 130). Dated to the 13th century BC, the Lion's Gate is the earliest monumental sculpture known. By 1500 BC, Mycenaean royal graves had evolved into **tholos,** beehive-shaped stone structures covered in packed earth. The relief work on these tombs shows Minoan influence, whereas the large-scale masonry is distinctly Mycenaean.

GEOMETRIC PERIOD (1100-700 BC). A new ceramics-based art evolved out of the collapse of Mycenaean civilization and the Dark Age that followed. There to pick up the pieces were the Athenians, who stood at the center of the new movement. Their pottery of the **Proto-Geometric Period** (1100-900 BC) was decorated with Mycenaean-inspired spirals, arcs, wavy lines, and concentric circles. These patterns became more intricate in the **Geometric Period,** when artists covered pottery and clay figurines with geometric motifs that resembled woven baskets. Identically posed stick-figure humans and grazing animals began to appear among the continuous, patterned bands and tight rows of thick black lines. Near Eastern contact with Greece showed up again in Syrian and Phoenician floral and animal designs. At this time, Corinth joined Athens as a major ceramic center.

Architects of the Geometric Period focused on the development of one-room temples with columned porches. These temples were essentially regarded as the houses of the gods or goddesses they honored, and each **oikos** (house) came complete with a sculpture of its inhabitant.

ARCHAIC PERIOD (700-480 BC)

During the **Archaic Period,** Greek art and architecture morphed from the stylization of the Geometric Period to the curving, human realism of the Classical Period. Sculptors and vase painters produced abstracted images of the human form, and architects fine-tuned temple-building and proportion in construction. The city-states basked in a prosperity that allowed new, expensive, and artfully conceived architecture. The acropolis, agora, amphitheater, and gymnasium were all perfected during this period. The city-states' public buildings imitated the temples that architects had pored over for hundreds of years.

COLUMNS, ON THE STRAIGHT AND NARROW. During the Archaic Period, the Doric and Ionic architectural orders—whose columns have lined many an art history student's nightmares—departed along their own paths. The Doric order gave a stone face-lift to the makeshift wood and mud-brick Geometric temple in the 7th century BC. New columns and classy marble breathed new life into the former design of a one-room *cella*, or inner sanctum, and its surrounding columns (peristyle). Around the 6th century BC, Greece's colonies along the coast of Asia Minor branched off into the more exotic Ionic order. The curlicued Ionic order differed from the more austere Doric order in gracing the tops of each column (the capitals) with twin volutes, or scrolled spiral uppers, and in the slender, fluted bodies of each column. Ionic temples, ornate and fussy, boasted forests of columns: the Temple of Hera at Samos (p. 332) sported 134.

GRIN AND BARE IT. Early Archaic sculptors began to craft large-scale figures called **kouroi.** Each *kouros* was a naked, idealized young man, symmetrically posed, with one leg forward and hands clenched at his sides, smiling goofily under stylized curls. The *kouroi* stood in temples as offerings to deities or as memorials to fallen warriors. An early example dedicated to Poseidon at Sounion (c. 590 BC) now stands in the **National Archaeological Museum** of Athens (p. 104). In the 6th century BC, technical advances and an increasing concern with the natural human form led to more lifelike *kouroi*, such as the stunning **Anavissos kouros,** also in the National Archaeological Museum. The female equivalent of the *kouros*, the **kore,** posed in the latest fashions instead of in her birthday suit; Archaic sculptors focused on the drape of the *kore*'s clothing, suggesting the female form through straight and bunched folds and zig-zag hemlines.

In the beginning of the 5th century BC, sculpture turned toward realistic depiction, which would reach its height soon afterward in the Classical Period. The relaxed posture of the free-standing **Kritios Boy** (490 BC), now in the **Acropolis Museum** in Athens (p. 101), broke the stiff, symmetrical mold of the archaic *kouroi* with an individualized personality: the Kritios Boy's weight is shifted onto one leg, and his hips and torso tilt as naturally as the Earth on its axis.

AT TEMPLE-TOP. During the Archaic Period, architectural sculpture integrated the human form into building decoration. Sculptors quit trying to fill the awkward triangular pediments above temples with mythological narratives, and looked to battle scenes to fill them. The new style placed a standing god at the central high point of the pediment, and lined falling bodies on each side. For an example, see the **Temple of Aphaia** at Aegina (p. 291). Showing the intertwined, warring figures challenged sculptors to model the human form, presaging the Classical Period's interest in the body both in architecture and in free-standing sculpture.

WALK LIKE AN EGYPTIAN. As for two-dimensional art, Athenian **vase painters** depicted humans using Corinth's **black figure technique,** drawing black silhouettes with carved features. Human figures appeared in the half-profile of ancient Egyptian art: moving figures' chests faced forward, and each person stared straight out with both eyes. The figures conveyed emotion with gestures rather than facial expression, and many figures pulled their hair in grief or flailed their limbs in joy.

CLASSICAL PERIOD (480-323 BC)

The arts flourished during the Classical Period, as Athens reached the peak of its political and economic power under Pericles and his successors (p. 11). Perfecting Doric architecture and dabbling in the Ionic style, Classical temples were more spacious and fluid than the stocky temples of the Archaic Period. The peerless Athenian **Acropolis** (p. 97), built during this period, embodied "classic" for the entire Classical world; its star attraction, the **Parthenon,** shows the fullness of the Greek obsession with perfect proportions. *Everything* on the Parthenon—from its floor space to the friezes above the columns—is in a four-to-nine ratio.

HARD BODIES. Sculptors mastered the natural representation of the human form during the Classical Period. The milestone sculptures of the **Temple of Zeus** at Olympia (p. 140) exhibit a newfound mastery of anatomical detail. Although the figures bear Archaic-style stylized hair, their unique bodies and faces expressed emotion for the first time in Greek sculpture. Indeed, the personal and mood-evoking Classical style fully broke from formulaic Archaic sculpture. Notable sculptures from the Classical Period include the bronze statues of the **Charioteer** (470 BC) at Delphi (p. 175) and the **Poseidon** from the Artemisium wreck (465 BC), now in Athens's **National Archaeological Museum** (p. 104). The charioteer's grace and Poseidon's heroism show the twin ideals toward which Classical sculpture and society strove to achieve.

By the middle of the 5th century BC, Classical sculptors had loosened the stylized stiffness of the early Archaic Period, favoring a detailed realism that still lacked much emotion in facial features. Sculptors pursued a universal perfection of the human form, suppressing the particular imperfections that make people unique. The impersonal, idealized **Severe style** embodied the idealization of Plato's forms (see "Truth-Seeking Triumvirate" p. 13) and the athletic heroism that Pindar praised in his Olympic odes (p. 25). It remained in vogue through the start of the 4th century BC. By this time, sculptors like the genius ▧**Praxiteles** had created free-standing sculptures that virtually breathed. This new generation of sculptors turned their talent away from the monumental and impersonal Severe style toward vivid representations of individual people.

OLD-SCHOOL POT. Classical potters swooned over the **red figure technique** that had been gaining steam since 540 BC; the older black figure style was *so* passé. Red figure vase painting featured a black painted background, allowing the naturally reddish clay to show through as the drawn figures. Vase-makers then painted on details with a fine brush. Inspired by the new-found realism in sculpture, anonymous early Classical masters known as the **Berlin Painter** and the **Kleophrades Painter** lent their subjects an unparalleled level of psychological depth.

Although they still showed only a limited profile of the head, vase-painters experimented with foreshortening and three-quarter views of the body, suggesting a variety of new poses, gestures, and emotions. With this newfound expressive freedom, Classical red-figure artists tackled more ordinary subjects, like boozing at parties, women lounging at home, and athletic contests. By the mid-5th century BC, vase painting fell by the wayside of the art world because of growing interest in sculpture. But vase-painters left their mark: their vigorous, sinuous lines and careful anatomical detail inspired many later European painters.

HELLENISTIC PERIOD (323-46 BC)

ALAS, POOR DORIC... After the death of Alexander the Great, a new Hellenistic Period rose out of the ashes of Classical Greece. Eastern Greeks made architecture a flamboyant affair. Scuttling the simpler Doric and Ionic styles, they whipped up ornate, flower-topped **Corinthian-style columns.** Hellenistic architects worked on a monumental scale, building complexes of temples, *stoas* (colonnaded walkways), and palaces. Astoundingly precise **acoustics** graced the enormous amphitheaters at **Argos** (p. 122) and **Epidavros** (p. 128); a coin dropped onstage is audible in the most distant seat in the theaters, even 2200 years after their construction.

Hellenistic sculpture exuded passion, displaying all the technical mastery and twice the emotion of Classical works. Artists tested the aesthetic value of ugliness, sculpting the grotesque figure of **Laocoön** as snakes writhe around him, dragging him to death; only a Roman copy of the Hellenistic original survives. The final frontier of Greek sculpture was **portraiture,** which began with the appointment of **Lysippus** as court sculptor to Alexander the Great.

DO AS THE ROMANS DO. With the arrival of the **Roman empire** in Greece, the Hellenistic style shifted to suit Roman tastes. Greek artists painted, sculpted marble, and assembled mosaics for Romans in Italy and for the old Hellenistic kingdoms of the east. Architects built mostly Christian churches; even the Parthenon was temporarily converted to a church, though it was (fortunately) left unaltered in its structure. Under the Romans, Greek art and architecture spread throughout the empire, but its innovative glory had passed.

BYZANTINE & OTTOMAN (AD 324-1829)

Ensconced in a throne and surrounded by elaborate mechanical animals and golden birds, the **Byzantine emperor** administered his holy city in the image of God ruling the cosmos. The art and architecture in Greece under Byzantine and Ottoman rule belonged more to these imperial cultures than to native Greek culture. The Byzantine empire unified religion and government, a combination that shaped the art and architecture of the empire. Byzantine artistry developed within a set of religious conventions that limited creative experimentation but still created magnificent mosaics, iconography, and church architecture.

In 529, Emperor **Justinian** restricted art to Christian subjects; afterward, Byzantine art and architecture evolved in a unified, religiously themed vein even after the fall of Constantinople in 1453.

ARCHITECTURE

GOING TO THE CHAPEL. Early Byzantine churches show their roots in Roman Christianity: based on the Roman basilica layout, the Byzantine versions were long buildings with a semicircular apse at one end and windows lining a wooden ceiling (forming a clerestory). A column-lined outer courtyard stood on a church's western side; on the eastern side, people entered the vestibule through two doors, often bronze or inlaid with silver. These doors opened onto the naos, the church proper. Inside, a central nave reached from the church's inner door to the choir rows, and was separated from two side aisles by arched colonnades.

Constantinople's **Agia Sofia**, built during Justinian's rule, stands as the prime example of Byzantine architecture. The Byzantines used two revolutionary architectural techniques: incorporating the **squinch,** an arch tucked into the corners of the square base, and the **pendentive,** a triangular section of vaulting with concave sides that transferred the dome's weight to the ground. By the reign of **Basil I** (867-886), domed basilicas like the Agia Sofia evolved into a **cross-in-square** plan, with four equal-vaulted arms holding up a central dome (see **Osios Loukas,** p. 168). On occasion, the vaulted roofs above the four arms of the cross-shaped church were replaced by four small domes, producing a five-domed church called a **quincunx.**

RETRO-CHIC ICONS. The floor and lower parts of the walls were usually covered in **marble,** while the upper parts were reserved for **mosaics** and occasionally **frescoes.** After the end of **iconoclasm** (p. 15) in the 9th century, **icon** layout in Byzantine churches was standardized along a hierarchical scheme determined by Byzantine theology. The inside of the central dome usually portrayed the **Pantocrator** (Creator of All Things); in iconoclast churches, a large cross replaced the image of Christ (smashed by Church order); the image in the central dome formed the physical and spiritual center of the rest of the church's images. Angels and evangelists lined the dome's base, and rows of saints covered the walls. The **Virgin Mary** appeared in the half-dome above the apse. The **Festival Cycle,** 12 scenes from the life of Christ that corresponded to the 12 major feast days of the Byzantine calendar, further adorned the church. The faithful assembled below these images, making the church a complete, earthly microcosm of the Christian universe.

ENLIGHTENMENT IN TWO DIMENSIONS

Byzantine artists transformed almost any flat surface they encountered into art: they illuminated manuscripts, carved ivory panels, embossed bronze doors, and covered *cloisonée* enamels with jewels. The dazzling **mosaics** and **icons** of Byzantine churches showed the greatest of Byzantine talent: artists underwent years of spiritual and technical training before gaining permission to portray sacred subjects. Byzantine icons aimed for religious authenticity, intended to transmit—not just represent—the spiritual power of the subject. Based on evocative swaths of color rather than exacting form, the Byzantine pictorial style featured flat figures with idealized facial features, wearing stylized clothes. Each figure stared out with a soul-searing gaze, adding to the power of the images; a determined frontal pose against a gold background created the illusion of the figure floating between the wall and the viewer in the church's dim light.

Byzantines used enamel, ivory, gold, wood, and mosaic to make icons. Mosaics were composed of **tesserae,** small cubes of stone or ceramic covered in glass or metallic foil. A unique shimmering effect was produced by contrasting gold and silver tesserae at sharp angles to reflect light. Sparkling examples of Byzantine mosaics can be seen in the churches of **Thessaloniki** (p. 221), at the **Monastery of Osios Loukas** (p. 169), on **Mt. Athos** (p. 246), and at **Meteora** (p. 201).

One Greek artist did separate himself from the dominant Ottoman tradition of flat, stylized, religious paintings. Domenikos Theotokopoulos (1541-1614)—**El Greco** to the world, and "god-touching" in literal Greek—was influenced by the Venetian tradition in his native Crete. El Greco moved to Spain at age 35, and there forged an international reputation.

MODERN ART (1829-PRESENT)

Nationalist sentiment after Greek independence led the government to subsidize Greek art. King Otto (p. 16) encouraged young artists to study their craft in Munich, and the **Polytechneion**, Greece's first modern art school, was established in 1838. The first wave of post-independence Greek painters—**Nicephoros Lytras** (1832-1904) and **Nicholas Gyzes** (1842-1901) among them—showed strong evidence of their German training. Sculptors, on the other hand, looked to Classical Greek works as their inspiration. **Giannoules Halepas** (1854-1938) produced graceful works which are still unparalleled among modern Greek sculpture.

FOR EUROPE. Twentieth century Greek painters have contended with European trends: painter **Konstantinos Parthenes** (1879-1965) brought Impressionism to Greece, while Expressionist **George Bouzianis** (1885-1959) used thick, vivid brush strokes to convey emotion. **Nikos Engonopoulos** (1910-85) adopted Surrealism.

FOR GREECE. Other painters rejected foreign influence, among them the much-adored Theophilos Chatzimichael (1873-1934), known simply as Theophilos. Though undistinguished in his own lifetime, this eccentric folk artist has been called the Greek Van Gogh. His oddly primitive paintings of natural and historical scenes are now admired for their harmonious composition.

In the 20th century, painter **Photis Kontoglou** (1896-1965) returned to a different set of roots, leading a movement for the revival of Byzantine art. Kontoglou also took a cue from Greek folk art, as did **Spyros Vassiliou** (1902-85)—who portrayed Greek customs and daily life in urban landscapes—and **Yiannis Tsarouhis** (1910-89), who painted his native country with emotion and sympathy. Tsarouhis, along with Yiannis Moralis (b. 1916) and Giorgos Sikeliotis (1917-84), focused his work on the relationship between artist and art. In the present day, the paintings of **Yiannis Psychopedis** (b. 1945) combine social and aesthetic criticism. Painter **Opy Zouni** (b. 1941) has won international renown for her geometric art.

LANGUAGE & LITERATURE

Wherever literature consoles sorrow or assuages pain; wherever it brings gladness to eyes which fail with wakefulness and tears, and ache for the dark house and the long sleep, there is exhibited in its noblest form the immortal influence of Greece.
—Thomas Babington Macaulay

I LAUGHED, I CRIED... Born out of the 5th century BC from a tradition of **goat songs** *(tragodoi)* dedicated to the god Dionysus, the plebeian roots of Greek drama are worlds away from our view of theater as high art. Greek drama began as a religious rite in which all attendants were both performers in the chorus and audience members. Individual acting began when, at a public competition of masked choruses in Dionysus' honor, young **Thespis** stepped out of the crowd to become Athens's first actor—hence, "thespian." By adding a second actor and other characters, **Aeschylus** (525-456 BC) composed the plays *Prometheus Bound* and the *Oresteia*, a trilogy about Agamemnon's ruinous return home from the Trojan War. **Sophocles** (496-406 BC) followed, creating the creepy, cathartic *Oedipus* trilogy, which details the ruinous tale of Oedipus, a man who becomes king by killing his father and marrying his mother. **Euripides** (485-406 BC), Sophocles' contemporary, added *Medea* and the *Bacchae* to the tradition. **Aristophanes** (450-385 BC) tossed aside the tragic medium, and wrote *The Clouds*, *Lysistrata*, and *The Frogs* in bawdy, slapstick "Old Comedy" form; Aristophanes's swipes at Socrates helped to bring about the philosopher's execution. **Menander,** creator of "New Comedy," wrote sunnier, well-mannered works; his star-crossed lovers paved the way for endless happy endings throughout Western literature.

ANCIENT GREECE

As with many things Greek, writing has a long history. Tablets scrawled with pre-Greek writing were found among Minoan palace ruins, preserved, ironically, by baking in the fires that destroyed the palaces themselves. Somewhat uninspiring in content (how many bushels of grain were received, how many cows), these palace treasury records were inscribed on tablets in scripts called Linear A and Linear B near the end of the Bronze Age (roughly 1100 BC; see p. 10). During the Dark Age under the Dorians (see p. 10), Linear B disappeared from archaeological sight.

EARLY MASTERS

SING IN ME, OH MUSE. The first written Greek did not appear until the middle of the 8th century BC, but the Greek literary tradition may have begun as much as 150 years earlier, with the epic-crooning mystery man **Homer.** The original bard may have recorded or dictated the *Iliad* and *Odyssey* in his own lifetime (if he was indeed one guy); most scholars believe that Homer simply began an oral tradition that would lead to a written epic literature in the next century. Regardless of whether or not Homer wrote the poetry, his mythic history of the Trojan War (see p. 10 and p. 28) remains a classic text, representative of such fundamental literary themes as conflict and heroism. References to his *Odyssey*, an immortal inspiration for the theme of journeys, both physical and metaphysical, appear throughout Western literature.

POEMS, POETS, POETRY. Homer's contemporary **Hesiod** composed the **Works and Days,** a farmer's-eye view of life that lamented the oppression of the aristocracy; he also composed the **Theogony,** the first Greek account of the creation of the world and the gods' wacky exploits. During the 7th century BC, anti-everything **Archilochus** of Paros inscribed the first known written poetry—anti-heroic, anti-Homeric elegies. In one particularly sour fragment, Archilochus expresses no shame at tossing his shield aside in battle to run for his life.

On the island of Lesvos, during the 6th century, lyric poet **Sappho,** the lone female poet of the ancient world, sang of love, lovin', and nature's beauty. Sappho's poems survive only in fragments, as the medieval monks who preserved much of Greek literature considered her verses filthy and evil, largely because she was a woman and bisexual. **Alcaeus,** a contemporary of Sappho's, was embroiled in Lesvos's political feuds; his angry stance colors his very personal lyric poems. **Pindar** of Thebes (518-438 BC), acclaimed by the ancients as the greatest of lyric poets, wrote Olympic odes commissioned by sports-nut nobles to commemorate athletic victories. **Theocritus,** a pastoral poet, portrayed scenes from the subdued lives of shepherds and goatherds.

Roman poet **Horace** later revived the Greek poetic model, taking its images and meters (the *sapphic* and *alcaic*), and looking to latter-day Greek poet **Callimachus** as his master. Callimachus (305-240), living in Alexandria, wrote elegies in Hellenistic Greek about the origins of rites and customs; only fragments of his work survive. Callimachus's influence shaped the Alexandrian revival in Rome, where poet **Catullus** took up his slogan **mega biblion, mega kakon**—big book, big bore.

STORY BECOMES HISTORY. Herodotus, geographer, anthropologist, and the so-called "Father of History," wrote up the epic battles and personalities of the Persian Wars in his monumental (and rather sensationalist) Histories. His incredibly detailed account of the wars must have come from interviews with elderly men with sharp memories, as the Persian Wars took place during Herodotus's childhood. Thucydides immortalized the Peloponnesian Wars, chronicling Athens's conflict with Sparta; he took the opportunity to examine the effects of war on nations and people while he was at it. Xenophon too wrote histories: see Hallucinogenic Honey for a sticky example (p. 11).

BLINDED BY SCIENCE. The philosophical-scientific writings of the ancient Greeks awed even the practically-minded Romans. Other civilizations sought religious answers to the big questions, but the scattered Greek pantheon gave no easy answers, and philosophical reasoning took over instead. The first philosopher, according to Hellenic tradition, was the 6th century BC thinker **Thales of Miletus** (see p. 7); as none of his writings survive, we'll have to take their word for it. Thales believed that the universe had an ordered structure, and that everything moved toward a predetermined end. This **teleology,** or end-oriented worldview, contributed to every major Greek philosophy. **Pythagoras,** a math whiz, came up with theorems that still make regular appearances in high school math homework (see **My Brain Hurts,** p. 7).

Plato (428-348 BC) and **Aristotle** (384-322 BC) mused about the cosmos—to them, heavenly bodies were literally divine, as their circular shapes were the most perfect in existence. The ancient Greek **universe** centered around the earth; spherical planets traveled in circular orbits. Aristotle observed spontaneous events: his science had no need for pesky experimental proof, since experiments were unnatural, fake constructions, not spontaneous and real. In the same century, **Euclid** wrote the *Elements*, the source of geometry even to the present. Euclid's geometry is one of the most widely translated works ever. **Archimedes** stole the show by creating complex mathematical formulas with circles and cylinders, and by inventing the **Archimedes screw,** a device to move water.

Greeks experimented in **medicine** as well. In the 5th century BC, before he became famous for his oath, **Hippocrates** suggested that disease might not be the result of divine punishment, but of natural causes. Combined speculation and observation yielded the idea of **four humors** flowing through the body (yellow bile, black bile, phlegm, and blood); an imbalance caused illness. Research at the museum of **Alexandria,** Egypt, in the 3rd century BC pushed medical knowledge further. Work on animal brains, hearts, and organs inspired **Galen of Pergamum** to try dissection. A pioneer in the queasy art of human dissection, Galen's work expanded knowledge about the human anatomy.

Under Roman rule, Greek natural science wilted. The Romans were impressed by the vast body of knowledge the Greeks had acquired, but confused by the concept of "knowledge for knowledge's sake." Science should be a means to a useful and practical end, thought the hard-nosed Latins. During the Middle Ages, the advancements in European medical knowledge evaporated entirely. Luckily, Greek scientists had about written their findings, and we can still read them today.

BYZANTINE LITERATURE

The pseudo-historical romance took Greece by storm in the first century AD, along with personal love poems like *Erotopaegnia (Love Games)* and erotic novels. The era of the romance novel also produced the most-read work of literature ever, the Greek-language **New Testament** of the Bible. After Emperor Constantine converted to Christianity in 338 (see p. 14), most literature was written by monastery-bound theologians or court historians.

TELL-ALL CELEBRITY BIO. Plutarch, writing around AD 100, constructed biographies of famous Greeks and Romans in *Parallel Lives.* In the 6th century, **Procopius,** one of Emperor Justinian's generals, reported on all aspects of his boss's reign. He wrote two conventional tracts for publication, *On the Wars* and *On the Buildings*, and left behind a **Secret History**—an insider's account of the **deviant debauchery** common in the court of Justinian and his wife Theodora. **Photios** (820-893), twice appointed Patriarch of Constantinople, admired the "pagan" works of Homer and encouraged their study. This avid reader was a writer as well; his massive *Biblioteca* chronicled Greek works in over 270 articles.

A LATTER-DAY HERO. Around the 10th century, folk singers began recounting a Byzantine epic about the hero **Digenis Akritas.** This epic was written down several times between the 12th and 17th centuries in both popular (Koine) and literary Greek. Akritas probably really lived, serving as an 8th-century border guard who helped defend the empire from Arabic and Turkish marauders. In the 16th century, Greek marauders composed folk ballads between raids on Ottoman posts. These bandits, called **kleftes,** would be among the first to fight for Greek independence.

MODERN LITERATURE

the language I speak has no alphabet
since even the sun and the waves are a syllabic script which you decode
only in times of grief and exile
    —Odysseas Elytis

Greece's contemporary authors, much like its modern artists, feel torn between ancient heritage and new accomplishment. Some turn to mythology, epics, the Orthodox religious legacy, and the oral tradition of folk ballads and fairy tales for inspiration; others struggle to step outside the past's long shadow. This process has forged a new national literary identity for Greece.

REVOLUTIONARY POETS. Greek independence in 1821 (see p. 16) gave rise to the **Ionian School** of modern literature, which dealt with the political and personal issues of the Greek revolution. **Andreas Kalvos's** (1796-1869) lyrical poetry pays tribute to freedom. **Dionysios Solomos** (1798-1857)—whose *Hymn to Liberty* became the Greek national anthem—is often called the "national poet of Greece." Solomos used the demotic, or spoken, Greek language, not the official *katharevousa*, a "purified" Greek that borrows obsolete words from ancient Greek; this choice proclaimed a new, modern literature for a new, free Greece.

TAKING ON HISTORY: YOUNG POETS. A flock of 20th-century poets challenged the ancient writers, and together remade Greek poetry. **Angelos Sikelianos** (1884-1951) took up the literary use of demotic Greek pioneered by Dionysios Solomos, writing lyric poetry for a modern age. **Constantine Cavafy** (1863-1933) treated Greece's ancient past with ironic nostalgia. **George Seferis** (1900-63), a **1963 Nobel Laureate**, was the first Greek Modernist. He wrote with an obsessive memory of Greek history, and spoke of the suffering of exile on personal, national, and mythic levels. **Kostas Palamas** (1859-1943) combined ancient Greek myths and history with the Byzantine Christian tradition and modern Greek folklore. **Yiannis Ritsos** (1909-90), a socialist, was arrested and exiled by the military dictatorship in 1967, and his writings were banned until the junta's fall. Winner of a **1979 Nobel Prize in Literature, ⬛Odysseas Elytis** (1911-96) looked at politics in a different light, and incorporated French Surrealism in hope of personal and national redemption. This national rebirth would combine humanity, nature, and religion.

THE WORLD'S A THEATRE, THE EARTH A STAGE...
Classical Greek theater survives as an influence on modern theater, as a body of work read and studied, and as a living, performed art. In Greece, the Athens Festival, held from June to September, features Classical drama at the ancient Theater of Herod Atticus (p. 101), as well as concerts, opera, choruses, ballet, and modern dance. At the Epidavros Festival (p. 128), from July to September, even a language barrier won't detract from the ominous chorus that, in Aeschylus's time, made "boys die of fright and women have miscarriages." Tickets and programs for the festivals are available two weeks in advance at the Athens Festival Box Office, Stadiou 4, inside the arcade; this office also sells tickets to many smaller theaters and festivals, including those at Philippi, Thassos, and Dodoni.

PROSE REVIVAL. Short-story writer **Alexandros Papadiamantis** (1851-1911)—whose last name means "father of love"—set his works on his home island of Skiathos, and used the official high-register Greek, *katharevousa*. Papadiamantis's stories describe the failings of humanity and society, but hold faith in an ultimate spiritual redemption. **George Vizyenos** (1849-96) borrowed liberally from the oral folk tradition; though he wrote in *katharevousa*, Vizyenos's work touches the mysterious and the supernatural in the realm of everyday life. **Nikos Kazantzakis** (1883-1957) may be the best known modern Greek author. His many novels include *Odyssey*, a modern sequel to the Homeric epic, *Report to Greco*, **Zorba the Greek** (1946), and **The Last Temptation of Christ** (1951); the last two have been made into successful films. *Freedom or Death*, his homage to Greek revolts against Ottoman rule on his home island of Crete, analyzes the Greek-Turkish conflict and looks into the Greek concept of masculinity.

RELIGION

ANCIENT GODS

Greek myths bubble with spicy, titillating **scandal** as they tell us how the world got to be the way it is. The colorful adventures of the often childish gods and their long-suffering mortal counterparts have inspired visual artists, writers, and even psychoanalysts.

GREEK GOD	ROMAN FAKE ID	JOB DESCRIPTION
Zeus	Jupiter	King of gods; law maker; sexual gymnast; kept order with handy thunderbolt.
Hera	Juno	Queen of Olympus; goddess of women and marriage; Zeus's sister and wife (eek!).
Ares	Mars	God of war and the spirit of battle; represented the gruesome aspects of fighting.
Hephæstus	Vulcan	Fire god; divine smith and patron of all craftsman; Aphrodite's ugly hubby.
Demeter	Ceres	Goddess of the Earth and fertility.
Aphrodite	Venus	Love goddess; patron of prostitutes; Cupid's mom and boss; noted philanderer.
Hestia	Vesta	Goddess of the family and city hearth; forever virgin (like Athena and Artemis).
Athena	Minerva	Goddess of wisdom and craft; Athens's protectress; born from Zeus's head.
Hades	Pluto	God of the Underworld; Zeus's brother; Motto: Always room for one more.
Poseidon	Neptune	God of the sea and of water; brother of Zeus; rode around in a wavetop car.
Apollo	Apollo	Sun god; patron of music, song, and poetry; python-slayer; Artemis's twin.
Artemis	Diana	Goddess of the hunt, the moon, wild animals, vegetation, chastity, and childbirth.
Hermes	Mercury	Messenger god; presided over animals, commerce, shrewdness, and persuasion; patron god of ■ travelers.

FROM HISTORY TO MYTH

Greek mythology explained natural phenomena and connected human events with a divine order, tying history to the gods. Greek literature and mythology are inextricably intertwined: from epic poems we learn of the Greek gods and their habits, and the characters of early literature become a part of mythology themselves.

Homer's semi-divine heroes project mythic shadows of Mycenaean kings and military leaders (see p. 25). **Achilles,** the hero of the *Iliad*, who spends much of the epic sulking in his tent, later rejoins battle to slay **Hector,** the Trojan prince. Though the Trojan War was long believed to be fictional, the discovery of Troy's ruins by amateur archaeologist **Heinrich Schliemann** in the 1880s proved the city really had existed, and that perhaps the Trojan War had, too. (For more on Schliemann, see p. 119.) The constant conflict between kingdoms of Greece and those on the Aegean coast of Anatolia makes a Trojan War even more likely, though in Homer's version, the gods play favorites and fight alongside the mortals.

The story of **Odysseus,** tricky hero of the *Odyssey*, reveals more than the overt plot of the story. As his story passed through generations of storytellers and across regional lines, it evolved to reflect Greek political and religious concerns. Homer's version reflects this development, as do other mythic histories that tell conflicting stories. Recent discoveries of Hellenistic-era shipwrecks in the Mediterranean lend credence to Homer's claims of ancient Greek sailing adventures on the open sea.

GODS AND MONSTERS

Greek religion evolved alongside this mythic history. Worship in the Greek pantheon centered around praying and leaving offerings to gods whose all-too-human exploits Greeks chronicled. Religious sects lacked any overarching unity or mutual exclusivity. Worship revolved around specific locations, temples, and rites. People were free to worship whomever they chose (and to develop patron gods—and enemy gods). Greek religion was thus a changeable and multifaceted creature. Though individual rites and ceremonies were preset, overall religious practices could change drastically through the centuries.

GOD, NOT THE DEVIL, MADE ME DO IT. Rituals of communion with the gods were often as scandalous as the myths that inspired them: extreme chemical **intoxication** and large-scale **orgies** were legitimate routes to a state of religious ecstasy. The Greek gods behaved very much like humans who could never die—they lacked strong morals and got into lots of silly arguments without fear of any real retribution. Appeasing the gods by rituals pleasing to humans (drunken debauchery) made sense.

The Greeks by no means thought their gods were lightweights to be trifled with: indeed, mythology is full of ugly examples of what happens to those who challenge gods. Humans were often unwilling participants in religious myths. The talented weaver **Arachne** was turned into a spider (hence the word "arachnid") because she dared to compete with Athena. **Tantalus** was condemned to stand in a pool in Hades, forever tormented by hunger and thirst with oh-so-tantalizing food and water just beyond his grasp. **King Minos,** poor fool, didn't make a sacrifice on time, so Poseidon gave Minos's wife **Pasiphaë** an insatiable lust for a bull. Pasiphaë then bore a baby, a cannibal bull-boy, the **Minotaur.**

THEY MOVE IN MYSTERIOUS WAYS. The 12 deities of the Greek pantheon were roommates on Mt. Olympus (Hades, down below, makes 13). Zeus, the team captain, liberated the higher gods from the gut of their dad, the titan Cronus, who had eaten each as he or she was born. Zeus had escaped, concealed from his father at birth. Indebted to Zeus, the rest of the gods were subject to his will. Many gods were Zeus's children, begotten from his thundering sexual exploits with Hera, various mortals, animals, and other gods. Athena, patron goddess of Athens, burst fully-formed from Zeus's head, a unique birth if ever there was one. Despite fantastic powers and immortality, gods' lives could be irritating. Hera endured her husband's endless philandering, Persephone sat bored in Hades for half the year, while her mother Demeter mourned her from above with six months of winter. Fire god Hephaestus limped around with a lame leg, and demigod Atlas quite literally had the world on his shoulders (see also chart p. 28).

Many humans and minor deities figured prominently in Greek mythology, too. The three **Fates**—Atropos, Clotho, and Lachesis—spun, measured, and snipped the threads of human lives. The **Furies,** or *Eumenides* ("Kindly Ones") punished evil-doers; their kindness was extremely one-sided. The nine **Muses** aided poets, artists, and musicians; Homer begins both the *Iliad* and the *Odyssey* with a plea for Muse-given inspiration. **Dryads** and **naiads** inhabited trees and streams; **nymphs** cavorted in the fields; **satyrs,** or goat-men with long beards and tails, frolicked with **maenads** in the holy groves.

HISTORY AND CULTURE

SEXCAPADES Although **Zeus** threw a mighty lightning bolt, **Ovid**'s lurid account in the Latin *Metamorphoses* reports that his real prowess lay in the world of romance. A bona fide nymphomaniac, Zeus would do it with almost anyone or anything, as long as his baleful and long-suffering wife **Hera** wasn't looking. Even when mortal women were unwilling or inaccessible, he always managed to get the girl: he impregnated **Danae,** safely locked away in a tower by her father, by visiting her as a golden shower of light. Oftentimes he assumed the shape of an animal in his conquests: a cuckoo when he seduced **Hera,** a swan with **Leda,** or a bull when he carried off **Europa.** His wife, powerless to injure her husband directly, lavished vengeance on the unfortunate objects of his lust. Io was turned into a cow chased by an enormous, stinging gadfly. **Leto,** pregnant with twins **Artemis** (goddess of the hunt) and **Apollo** (god of light and music), was forbidden to rest on solid ground; the itinerant island of Delos lent its shore to her to give birth. **Semele,** one of Zeus's *voluntary* cohorts, dissolved into ash. **Callisto** got off relatively easy in comparison—she was changed into a bear. What's the moral of Zeus's mythic sexcapades? *Mortals never win.*

ORTHODOX CHRISTIANITY OUSTS ZEUS

Greece, famed for its fabulous paganism, nevertheless served as a gateway for Christianity in Europe. In AD 49, **St. Paul** arrived in Philippi, Macedonia and began five years of successful preaching throughout the Greek mainland. By the 3rd century AD, the books of the **New Testament** had been written down in Greek. In the following century, **Constantine** (see p. 14) followed the flaming cross in the sky and plastered crosses across the shields of his troops. He then legalized Christianity in the empire and even converted moments before his death. Thus began the modern church, called the **Orthodox Catholic Church** in its own canonical texts, but commonly known as the "Eastern" or "Greek Orthodox" Church. Orthodoxy is defined by its adherence to the teachings of the first **seven ecumenical councils**—held in Ephesus in AD 431—and by a belief that spiritual truth is preserved not only in the Bible, but in the living **traditions** of the church. Orthodox Christianity is an apostolic religion: its members believe their church upholds the true faith as delivered to the saints by the Holy Spirit. Orthodox believers look to the lives of the saints as models for their own lives.

Orthodox practice is based on seven sacraments. Life in the church begins with **baptism,** a ritual immersion in holy water. This process of initiation is later completed by **confirmation,** an official, conscious affirmation of faith marking mature entrance into the church. The **eucharist,** or communion, recreates the Last Supper, wherein bread and wine represent the body and blood of Jesus, cleansing the faithful of sins and offering a taste of eternal life. In **confession,** supplicants ask to be forgiven for their transgressions. **Ordination** is considered the completion of apostolic succession, as the new priest is joined in spiritual lineage to St. Peter, to whom Jesus originally entrusted the church. **Marriage** is the process by which a man and a woman are united in the eyes of the church; Orthodox priests (unlike Roman Catholics) are permitted to marry before ordination. The last sacrament, **holy unction,** is the healing anointing of the sick with sanctified oil.

RELIGION TODAY

Greek Orthodoxy is the religion of 98% of the Greek population. Fortunately for the minority 2% (primarily Muslims), the constitution guarantees freedom of religion, and the Greek Orthodox Church remains separate from the Greek state.

THE CHURCH. The **Orthodox Church** is rigidly hierarchical in structure, with one archbishop of Athens, 85 bishops in 77 dioceses, and 7500 parishes. The **bishops** take responsibility for keeping the church faithful to its doctrines and for ensuring

OPA! Greeks have made music since the Bronze Age: early musical instruments from this period have been found on Crete. Although they had no system of musical notation before the 5th century BC, they devised a theory of harmonics. It was necessary for early poets to remember musical formulas, since poems were sung or chanted (partially to help poets remember endless epics). The musical choruses of religious rites naturally became part of evolving drama, and music remained essential to Classical theater. Folk music and dances flourished in the Byzantine Era. Dances from southern Greece were often tragic or funereal; northern dances celebrated war and the harvest. Cretans danced in religious and burial rites. Today, these regional distinctions have blurred. In many areas, it's common to see a wide circle of locals and tourists, hands joined, dancing to clarinets and lyres. The group leader flashes fancy footwork, twirling in circles while winding around a white handkerchief. Some dancers throw backward somersaults. The dance steps for the followers are comfortably repetitive. Don't hesitate to join in—stamp your feet, yell *Opa!* and enjoy yourself.

apostolic succession by ordaining new priests. Bishops don't have a lot of contact with their congregations on an everyday basis. **Priests,** easily recognizable by their long black robes, beards, and cylindrical hats, interact more closely with the people, but still remain fairly removed from secular life. Orthodox clergy spend most of their time praying, reflecting, and preparing the sacraments, rather than pursuing missions in the secular world at large. Greece's many isolated **monastic communities** (such as Mt. Athos, p. 246) have had considerable trouble adapting to the modern world and face dwindling numbers of recruits.

THE FAITHFUL. For the laity—the community of believers—faith and deed are intertwined; Orthodoxy is as much a worldview as an institution. The sacraments are the backbone of Orthodox doctrine, though they occur only a few times in an Orthodox Christian's life. The church plays a role in any decision made by an Orthodox Christian. Many Greeks wear crosses around their necks and hang icons in their homes. Most celebrate their name days (Greek children are always named after a saint) set aside for their patron saint, rather than their birthdays.

PEOPLE

THE MANY... Current estimates put the population at about **10.7 million** people. A Greek census took place in 2001, but the results were not yet available by the time of this book's publication in summer of 2001. The population is 98% ethnically Greek, and 98% Greek Orthodox (see p. 31), although historical and recently emerging minorities inhabit Greece, too. The extremely homogeneous ethnic and religious population is sometimes overshadowed by the large number of foreign visitors who travel in Greece.

...AND THE FEW. Both the Greek government (which does not recognize official ethnic divisions) and the Greek people generally deny any overt racism. There is a growing concern about and widespread prejudice toward a rapidly expanding refugee and migrant population. (For more information, see p. 46.)

Roughly 350,000 ethnic **Albanians** in northern Greece make up the country's largest minority population; recently, reports of violence perpetrated by the Greek border patrol against illegal Albanian immigrants have cropped up.

The **Gypsies,** or **Roma,** make up another significant minority group; they have remained on the fringes of Greek society for centuries and are now concentrated in Athens and Thessaloniki. Plagued by poor health, low literacy rates, and extensive poverty, the Gypsy population is typically viewed by Greeks as one of the country's largest social problems.

The most populous religious minority group is made up of over 130,000 Slavic and Turkish **Muslims** in Thrace who remain separated from the Greeks in both language and culture. The sizable Turkish population in Western Thrace is a result of 1923 **Population Exchange** (see p. 17). **Jewish** communities have lived in Greece since the first century AD, but the majority of the Jewish population was deported to concentration camps during the Nazi occupation of World War II. Only about 5,000 Jews live in Greece at present.

Other officially recognized minorities include the **Vlachs** and the **Sarakatsans,** both nomadic shepherds descended from Latin-speakers who settled in Greece. The Greek region of Macedonia is inhabited by some 60,000 **Slavic** people still unrecognized by the Greek government as an ethnic or cultural minority.

GOVERNMENT AND ECONOMY

ADMINISTRATION. The present Greek constitution was created on June 11, 1975, establishing a **presidential republic** and a **parliamentary democracy.** True to the oldest model of democracy, power is divided between three branches: executive, legislative, and judicial. Legislative power is vested in a single-chamber **Vouli** (parliament) composed of 300 members, who are popularly elected by secret ballot—voting is the compulsory privilege of all Greeks age 18 and older. Each member of parliament serves a 4-year term. The **President** is elected by parliament and serves a 5-year term. A constitutional amendment in 1985 significantly decreased the presidential powers, reducing the president to little more than a figurehead. The executive branch consists of the powerful **Prime Minister** (the leader of whichever party wins the national election) and the **Cabinet,** selected from the elected representatives by the Prime Minister. The full and independent judiciary has three types of courts: administrative, civil, and criminal.

PARTIES. In the Greek party system, the New Democracy (ND) and Panhellenic Socialist Movement (PASOK) dominate the political landscape, with the Communist Party of Greece (see The KKE, p. 32), and the Coalition for Left and Progress (Synaspismos) gaining a few third-party votes. The two major parties ran with similar platforms in the most recent elections, touting economic reforms aimed at gaining admission to the European Monetary Union (EMU) and the need for improved foreign relations—these reforms have succeeded, and Greece joined the EMU in 2001. The KKE, endorsing a Soviet-style communism, vocally opposed Greece's joining the EMU.

The leader of the ND, **Costas Karamanlis** (not to be confused with his uncle Constantine Karamanlis, who founded the ND) has accused **Constantine Simitis,** current Prime Minister and leader of PASOK, of neglecting rural Greek society and the workers. Simitis responded by promising to improve social welfare and reduce governmental bureaucracy during his latest term. In an April 2000 election (held five months early to avoid disruption of EMU negotiations), Simitis and his party were edged out by the surprisingly strong conservative New Democracy party, which won 157 seats to ND's 122. The KKE won 11 seats, and the remaining few went to fringe parties. In a meeting with current **President Constantine Stephanopoulous,** Simitis vowed to bring Greece up to the level of its European neighbors, economically, socially, and politically.

THE KKE The Greek Communist Party, or KKE, is the third-strongest political party in Greece, after the conservatives and socialists. Looking askance at NATO, the West, and US influence, KKE members cringe at American cultural dominance. Leave those Union Jack backpacks and Old Glory bathing suits at home, that famous Greek hospitality notwithstanding. Many KKE supporters harbor strong anti-Western sentiments, particularly the youthful, extremist set. Be prepared for a lot of angry graffiti, equating Americans with Nazis and the President with Hitler. Noisy Western patriots will probably meet with no more than angry glances or verbal harassment, but it's a good idea to lie a bit low, out of respect and common sense. (For more info, see p. 46.)

ECONOMY. With its limited natural resources and partial industrialization, the Greek economy is one of the least advanced in the European Union, with the second-to-lowest average income of all EU countries. A large **public sector** controls over 60% of the country's assets (including many banks) and is often blamed for slow economic growth. The Simitis government's Austerity policies have reduced the massive budget deficit and lowered the rate of inflation by privatizing much of the former public sector, though these reforms have led to rising unemployment and unrest among strong labor unions.

Agriculture has benefited from EU subsidies and the huge **shipping** industry remains strong. Greece **exports** fruit, olives, chromium, marble, and petroleum, and has a growing industrial sector of textiles, plastics, and chemical production.

Many fear that the economy is perilously dependent on the **tourist industry,** which caters to a yearly number of tourists greater than the country's total population. This booming business creates a need for seasonal employment, puts tremendous pressures on Greek infrastructure, and causes environmental damage.

FILM AND MEDIA

In the recent past, much of Greek media was state-owned and prone to propagandistic portrayals of government policy. More recently, private companies have bought several outlets. Many Greek-language **newspapers** are still sensationalistic (and hence exciting to read, though not overly factual). The more reputable papers include the weekly newspaper *Bima* (published Sundays), and partisan political dailies like the center-left leaning *Eleftherotipia* and *Ta Nea*, and the conservative *Kathimerini* and *Eleftheros Typos*.

The most noticeable recent change in Greek media has been in the **television** industry. Whereas ERT1 and 2 were the original stations, both state-owned and private channels like Mega Channel and ANT-1 have brought hi-tech production and those wacky, inescapable American sitcoms to the Greek viewing public. Greek **radio** plays a range of international, genre-crossing music in large cities, but in more remote locales you'll have to learn to love Greek pop.

Summertime **outdoor movies** are an essential part of the Greek experience. At twilight, cinemas set up screens in vacant lots or on high-rise rooftops. Daytime theaters may have roofs that slide away to reveal the stars. Most of the films shown in Greece are American or European imports with Greek subtitles.

REPRESSION. Greek **art house films** are a different story. During the reign of the junta, government censorship forced Greek artists to move west to comment on the political situation at home. Set in a Francophone Thessaloniki and the product of French and Greek collaboration, *Z,* directed by Costas Gavras with Yves Montand in 1969, is a thrilling, humorous, and tragic account of the regime's assassination of a rising opposition candidate and the ensuing sloppy cover-up (for a more detailed account of the political situation that inspired *Z*, see p. 17).

AND FLOWERING. After suffering under the colonels' junta, the Greek film industry rebuilt itself throughout the 1980s and has recently emerged as a distinguished and prolific presence in the international arena. This revitalization has been significantly helped along by the 1982 reestablishment of the **Greek Film Center,** a state-supported institute involved in the production of many of the most highly regarded modern Greek films. The Greek Film Center has assisted in making works by **Nikos Perakis** *(Loafing and Camouflage, Arpa-Colla),* **Pantelis Vougaris** *(The Engagement of Anna, Elefterios Venizelos)*, **Nikos Panayotopoulos** *(Varieties, O Ergenis)*, and Greece's most acclaimed filmmaker **Theo Angelopoulos** *(Voyage to Kythera, The Beekeeper, Ulysses' Gaze)*, winner of the 1998 Cannes Plame d'Or for *Eternity and a Day*. The most important event in the Greek film world (and an important event in the world film scene) is the **Thessaloniki Film Festival,** held every November (see p. 221).

BOUZOUKI PUNK ROCK Much of Greek lyric song is romantic and poetic. But a new musical style emerged from Turkey's western coast in the late 19th century, and unsettled these classical notions. Gritty, urban **rembetika** used traditional Greek instruments to sing about the ugly side of modern life, focusing on **drugs, prison, and alienation.** Convicts sang *rembetika* laments about smoking hashish and life on the run. During the population exchange with Turkey in the 1920s (see p. 17), it emerged as the cry of the underclass, as newly transplanted refugees living in urban shantytowns embraced its sorrowful expressiveness. *Rembetika* is still played on the *bouzouki* and *baglama,* although today players are few and far between. Find out more in Gail Holst-Warhaft's *Road to Rembetika* (Denise Harvey Publisher, 1994).

SPORTS

While tennis and alpine skiing have been growing in popularity recently among Greeks, **football** (soccer) and **basketball** are the national favorites. Most major Greek cities have their own municipal football teams. In addition to their home team, Greeks also favor an A-League Athenian team. Three top Athenian teams stand out in the hearts and apparel of Greek sports fans: red-jerseyed **Olympiakos** from Athens, green **Panathinaikos** from Piraeus, and the number-three team, yellow **AEK**. Almost everyone wears their favorite team's colors. **Basketball** is the country's newfound passion. The primary teams are the same as in football, but—distinctly unlike football—the Greek basketball association is among the premier European leagues. It has featured such NBA stars as Roy Tarpley, Byron Scott, Dino Radja, and Dominique Wilkins.

Figuring prominently on the horizon of Greek sporting events are the **2004 Olympic Games,** to be held in Athens in 2004. The 28th Olympiad is scheduled for August 13-29, and is expected to attract enormous crowds. Check out the official Athens 2004 Olympics website at http://www.athens2004.gr/.

HOLIDAYS & FESTIVALS

Greece celebrates a host of religious and political holidays throughout the year. Banks, shops, and most museums and sights close on holidays. Dates for 2002 include the following:

Jan. 1: Feast of St. Basil/New Year's Day. Carrying on a Byzantine tradition, Greeks cut a New Year's sweet bread called *Vassilopita,* baked with a coin inside. The person who gets the coin-hiding slice will be lucky all year.

Jan. 6: Epiphany. The Eastern Church celebrates Epiphany as the day Jesus was baptized by St. John. *Kallikantzaroi* (goblins) prowl between Christmas and Epiphany, though village bonfires try to scare them away. At Epiphany, Greeks bless the waters and throw crosses into harbors. The evil spirits leave the earth, and young men are blessed for retrieving the crosses.

February 25: Carnival. Three weeks of feasting and dancing at Carnival precede Lenten fasting. Patras (p. 129) Skyros (p. 320) and Kephalonia (p. 279) host particularly fun celebrations.

March 18: Green Monday. Start of Lent, the 4-week period of fasting preceding Easter.

March 25: Greek Independence Day. Commemorates the 1821 struggle against the Ottoman Empire. Not coincidentally, also the **Feast of the Annunciation,** celebrating when the angel Gabriel told Mary that she would bear God a son in nine months.

April 23: St. George's Day. Honors the dragon-slaying knight. Festivities at Limnos (p. 350) and Hania (p. 489) include horse races, wrestling matches, and dances.

May 1: Labor Day. A celebration of workers and a communist demonstration. Also called the **Feast of the Flowers,** because flower wreaths deck doors.

May 3: Good Friday. Commemorates Jesus's crucifixion. Greek Orthodox believers carry candles in a procession through town and around the church.

May 5: Easter. The single holiest day in the Greek calendar celebrates Jesus's resurrection from the dead. After a midnight mass and a meal, Easter celebrations commence with dancing and feasting on spit-roasted lamb and red hard-boiled Easter eggs.

June 13: Ascension. Commemorates Jesus's ascension into heaven. Celebrated 40 days after Easter, with different rituals in each region.

June 23: Pentecost. The Day of the Holy Spirit, remembering the appearance of tongues of flame (and the Holy Spirit) over Jesus's disciples. Celebrated 50 days after Easter.

Aug. 15: Feast of the Assumption of the Virgin Mary. A celebration throughout Greece, particularly on Tinos (p. 413), that honors Mary's ascent to heaven.

Sept. 8: The Virgin Mary's Birthday. To celebrate Mary's birthday, some villages hold auctions for the honor of carrying the Virgin's icon. The money pays for a village feast.

Oct. 26: Feast of St. Demetrius. Celebrated with particular enthusiasm in Thessaloniki (p. 221). The feolmast coincides with the opening of a new stock of wine.

Oct. 28: National Anniversary of Greek Independence. Called **Ohi Day** in honor of Metaxas's cry of "*Οχι!*" (No!) to Mussolini's demand to occupy Greece (see p. 17).

Nov. 17: Commemoration of an **uprising of Greek university students** against the 1974 junta. Speeches are presented at the University of Athens.

Dec. 25: Christmas. Greeks celebrate both Christmas Eve and Christmas Day. As part of the festivities, children make the rounds singing *kalanda* (Christmas carols).

FOOD & DRINK

DINNER BELL. Recent medical studies have highlighted the Greek diet as a good model for **healthy** eating; its reliance on unsaturated olive oil and vegetables has prevented high rates of heart disease despite the fairly sedentary lifestyle of the populace. Penny-pinching carnivores will thank Zeus for lamb, chicken, or beef **souvlaki** and hot-off-the-spit **gyros** stuffed into a pita. Vegetarians can also eat their fill for cheap. **Tzatziki,** a garlicky cucumber yogurt dip, with bread is a good way to start off a meal (or ripen your breath enough to ward off any overly-amorous overtures). Try the feta-piled **horiatiki** (a.k.a. Greek salad), savory pastries like **tiropita** (cheese pie, a pastry full of feta) and **spanakopita** (spinach and feta pie), and the fresh fruits and vegetables found at markets and vendor stands in most cities. Big bottles of **spring water** go for dirt cheap, so there's no excuse not to keep hydrated.

Greek-style liquid relaxation typically involves a few basic options: the strong, sweet sludge that is **Greek coffee** (drip coffee is for wimps) or the frothy, iced coffee *frappés* that take an edge off the heat in the summer. Potent **raki** and **tsipouro,** moonshine born of the remnants of wine-making, are especially popular on the mainland and Crete. **Ouzo** (a powerful, licorice-flavored Greek spirit sure to earn your respect) is often served with **mezedes,** which are snacks consisting of tidbits of octopus, cheese, and sausage.

THE PROTOCOL. Breakfast, served only in the early morning, is generally very simple: a piece of toast with *marmelada* or a pastry suffices. **Lunch,** a hearty and leisurely meal, can begin as early as noon, but is more likely eaten sometime between 2 and 5pm. After a few hours' nap, it's time to eat again. **Dinner** is a drawn-out, relaxed affair served late; 7:30pm is *very* unfashionably early for dinner. Eat with the Greeks sometime between 10pm and midnight—then party all night or head home for another nap. A Greek restaurant is known as a **taverna** or **estiatorio**; a grill is a *psistaria*. Don't be suspicious of restaurants without menus; this is common. Waiters will ask you if you want salad, appetizers, or the works, so be careful not to wind up with mountains of food, since Greek portions tend to be large. Restaurants often put bread and water on the table as a matter of course; an added charge for the bread is often listed on the menu as the couvert. You may never see ice in the glasses or butter on the table. You can ask for either, but many restaurants won't have them. Service is always included in the check, but it is customary to leave a few drachmas as an extra tip.

HISTORY AND CULTURE

MYTHOLOGY

Thomas Bulfinch. *The Age of Fable* (in *Bulfinch's Mythology*).

Robert Graves. *The Greek Myths.*

Gustav Schwab. *Gods and Heroes: Myths and Epics of Ancient Greece.*

Edward Tripp. *Dictionary of Classical Mythology.*

▣ Joseph Campbell. *The Hero with a Thousand Faces.* Part of the inspiration for George Lucas's *Star Wars*, Campbell's analysis of myth draws parallels between myth and the journey of life. He postulates that there is a single archetypical mythic hero who reflects man's search for identity.

HISTORY

Ancient: *Cambridge Illustrated History of Ancient Greece.* ed. Paul Cartledge (Cambridge University Press: NY).

The Aegean Civilization Illustrated Account of the Minoan and Mycenean Civilizations. Peter Warren (Phaidon Press: Oxford).

Byzantine: *Byzantium: the Apogee* and *Byzantium: the Decline and Fall.* John Julius Norwich (Knopf: NY).

Art: *Oxford History of Classical Art.* John Boardman (Oxford University Press: NY).

The Glory of Byzantium: Art and Culture of the Middle Byzantine Era, AD 843-1261. Ed. Helen Evans and William Wixon (Metropolitan Museum of Art: NY).

Religious: *The Orthodox Church.* Archbishop Timothy (Kallistos) Ware (Penguin: NY). Introduction to the established religion of Greece, written by the orthodox Archbishop residing at Oxford.

CONTEMPORARY ACCOUNTS

Lawrence Durell. *Prospero's Cell* and *Reflections on a Marine Venus.* Both books relate to the author's years spent on the island of Corfu (see p. 261).

Odysseus Elytis. *Oxopetra Elegies* and *Eros, Eros, Eros: Selected and Last Poems.* Collections of poetry by the Nobel Prize-winning Greek poet.

Patrick Leigh Fermer. *The Mani.* Fermer, known for rallying Cretan resistance in World War II, writes an account of his adventures in the Mani in the 1950s.

John Fowles. *The Magus.* A story of mystery and manipulation inspired by Fowles's years as a teacher on the island of Spetses (see p. 304).

Henry Miller. *The Colossus of Marousi.* Zealous account of his travels in Greece at the start of World War II.

ESSENTIALS

DOCUMENTS AND FORMALITIES

 ENTRANCE REQUIREMENTS
Passport (p. 38). Required for citizens of Australia, Canada, Ireland, New Zealand, the UK, and the US.
Visa (p. 39). Required for citizens of South Africa.
Work Permit (p. 39). Required for all foreigners planning to work in Greece.
Driving Permit (p. 70). Required for all those planning to drive.

GREEK CONSULAR SERVICES ABROAD

Australia Embassy: 9 Turrana St., Yarralumla, **Canberra,** ACT 26000 (☎(02) 6273 3011; fax 6273 2620). **Consulates:** 366 King William St., 1st Fl., **Adelaide,** SA 5000 (☎(08) 8211 8066; fax 8211 8820); Stanhill House, 34 Queens Rd., **Melbourne,** VIC 3004 (☎(03) 866 4524; fax 866 4933); 15 Castlereagh St., Level 20, **Sydney,** NSW 2000 (☎(02) 9221 2388; fax 9221 1423); 16 St. George's Terr., **Perth,** WA 6000 (☎(08) 9325 6608; fax 9325 2940).

Canada Embassy: 80 MacLaren St., **Ottawa,** ON K2P 0K6 (☎(613) 238-6271; fax 238-5676; embassy@greekembassy.ca). **Consulates:** 1170 Place du Frère André Suite 300, **Montréal,** QC H3B 3C6 (☎(514) 875-2119; fax 875-8781; info@grconsulatemtl.net); 365 Bloor St. E, Suite 1800, **Toronto,** ON M4W 3L4 (☎(416) 515-0133; fax 515-0209; toronto.consulate@greekembassy.ca); 501-1200 Burrard St. **Vancouver,** BC V6Z 2C7 (☎(604) 681-1381; fax 681-6656).

Ireland Embassy: 1 Upper Pembroke St., Dublin 2 (☎(01) 6767 2545; fax 661 88 92).

New Zealand Consulate: 5-7 Willeston St., 10th Fl., Box 24066, Wellington (☎(04) 473 7775; fax 473 7441).

South Africa Embassy: 1003 Church St. Athlone, Hatfield, 0028, **Pretoria** (☎(012) 437 35 13; fax 43 43 13). **Consulates,** 11 Wellington Rd., Parktown, 2193, **Johannesburg** (☎(011) 484 17 69; fax 484 17 69).

UK Embassy: 1a Holland Park, London W113TP (☎(0171) 229 38 50; fax 229 72 21). **Consulate:** 1a Holland Park, London W113TP (☎(0171) 221 64 67; fax 243 32 02).

US Embassy: 2221 Massachusetts Ave., NW, **Washington, D.C.** 20008 (☎(202) 939-5800; fax 939-5824; greece@greekembassy.org). **Consulates:** 2211 Massachusetts Ave. NW, **Washington, D.C.** 20008 (☎(202) 939-5818; fax 234-2803); 69 East 79th St., **New York,** NY 10021 (☎(212) 988-5500; fax 734-8492; nycons@greekembassy.org); 650 North St. Clair St., **Chicago,** IL 60611 (☎(312) 335-3915 or 6; fax 335-3958); 2441 Gough St., **San Francisco,** CA 94123 (☎(415) 775-2102 or 3; fax 776-6815); 12424 Wilshire Building, Suite 800, **Los Angeles,** CA 90025 (☎(310) 826-5555; fax 826-8670; grecon@earthlink.net); 86 Beacon St., **Boston,** MA 02108-3304 (☎(617) 523-0100 or 523-1083; fax 523-0511); Tower Place, 3340 Peachtree Rd. NE, Suite 1670, **Atlanta,** GA 30326 (☎(404) 261-3313 or 261-3391; fax 262-2798); 1360 Post Oak Blvd., Suite 2480, **Houston,** TX 77056 (☎(713) 840-7522; fax 840-0614); World Trade Center, 2 Canal St., Suite 2318, **New Orleans,** LA 70131 (☎(504) 523-1167; fax 524-5610).

CONSULAR SERVICES IN GREECE

A full listing of embassies is available at the Athens tourist office (see p. 76). Embassies are generally open only in the morning. All embassies, unless noted, are in **Athens.**

Albania: Karahristrou 1, 115 21 (☎ 723 4412; fax 723 1972). Open M-F 8:30am-noon.

Australia: D. Soutsou 37, 115 21 (☎ 644 7303 or 645 0404; telefax 21 5815). Open M-F 8:30am-12:30pm.

Brazil: Filikis Eterias 14 (☎ 721 3039). Open M-F 9am-3pm.

Canada: Ioannou Genadiou 4, 115 21 (☎ 725 9511; fax 724 7123). Open M-F 8:30am-12:30pm.

Czech Republic: Seferis 6 (☎ 671 3755). Open M-F 9am-noon.

European Community: Vasilissis Sofias 2 (☎ 724 3892). Open M-F 8:30am-1pm.

Germany: Karaoli Dimitriou 3, 106 75 (☎ 728 5111; fax 725 1205). Open M-F 9am-noon.

Hungary: Kalvou 16 (☎ 671 4889 or 672 3753). Open M-F 8:30am-12:30pm.

Ireland: Vas. Konstantinou 7, 106 74 (☎ 723 2771; telefax 21 8111). Open M-F 9am-3pm.

Romania: Em. Benaki 7 (☎ 671 8020; fax 647 9708). Open M-F 8am-1pm.

South Africa: Kifissias 60, 151 25 Maroussi (☎ 680 6645; fax 680 6640). Open M-F 8am-1pm.

Turkey: Vas. Georgiou B. 8, 106 74 (☎ 724 5915; telefax 21 4498). Open M-F 8:30am-12:30pm.

UK: Ploutarchou 1, 106 75, Athens (☎ 723 6211; fax 727 2722). Open M-F 8:30am-1pm.

US: Embassy: Vas. Sophias 91, 101 60 Athens (☎ 721 2951; fax 645 6282; www.usisathens.gr). Open M-F 8:30am-5pm, for visas 8:30-11am. **Consulate:** Tsimiski 43, 7/F, 546 23 **Thessaloniki** (☎ (031) 242 906; fax: 242 927; cons@compulink.gr). You can also contact US Information Services at USIS, Makedonon 8, 115 21 Athens (☎ (01) 643 4710 or 643 2977).

Yugoslavia: Vas. Sofias 106 (☎ 777 4355 or 777 4349; fax 779 6436). Open M-F 8:30am-1pm.

PASSPORTS

REQUIREMENTS. Citizens of Australia, Canada, Ireland, New Zealand, South Africa, the UK, and the US need valid passports to enter Greece and to re-enter their own country.

PHOTOCOPIES. Be sure to photocopy the page of your passport with your photo, passport number, and other identifying information, as well as any visas, travel insurance policies, airplane tickets, or traveler's check serial numbers. Carry one set of copies in a safe place, apart from the originals, and leave another set at home. Carry an expired passport or an official copy of your birth certificate in a part of your bag separate from other documents.

LOST PASSPORTS. If you lose your passport, immediately notify the local police and the nearest embassy or consulate of your home government. To expedite its replacement, you will need to know all information previously recorded and show identification and proof of citizenship. In some cases, a replacement may take weeks to process, and it may be valid only for a limited time. Visas stamped in your old passport will be irretrievably lost. In an emergency, ask for immediate temporary traveling papers that will permit you to re-enter your home country. Your passport is a public document belonging to your nation's government. You may have to surrender it to a foreign government official, but if you don't get it back in a reasonable amount of time, inform the nearest mission of your home country.

NEW PASSPORTS. All applications for new passports or renewals should be filed several weeks or months in advance of your planned departure date. Get a passport from your local post office, passport office (available in most major cities), or travel agency. Most passport offices offer emergency passport services for a steep fee. Citizens residing abroad who need a passport or renewal should contact the nearest consular service of their home country.

ONE EUROPE. The idea of European unity has come a long way since 1958, when the European Economic Community (EEC) was created to promote solidarity and cooperation between its six founding states. Since then, the EEC has become the **European Union (EU),** with political, legal, and economic institutions spanning 15 member states: Austria, Belgium, Denmark, Finland, France, Germany, Greece, Ireland, Italy, Luxembourg, the Netherlands, Portugal, Spain, Sweden, and the UK. What does this have to do with the average non-EU tourist? Well, in 1999 **freedom of movement** was established across 14 European countries—the entire EU minus Denmark, Ireland, and the UK, but plus Iceland and Norway. This means that border controls between participating countries have been abolished, and visa policies harmonized. While you're still required to carry a passport (or government-issued ID card for EU citizens) when crossing an internal border, once you've been admitted into one country, you're free to travel to all participating countries. For more important consequences of the EU for travelers, see **The Euro** (p. 43) and **Customs** (p. 41).

VISAS AND WORK PERMITS

VISAS. EU members, as well as citizens of the US, Canada, Australia, and New Zealand are all automatically granted leave for a three-month stay in Greece, though they are not eligible for employment during that time. South Africans need a visa. Apply for visa extensions at least 20 days prior to the three-month expiration date at the **Aliens Bureau,** Alexandras 173, Athens 11522 (☎(01) 770 5711), or check with a Greek embassy or consulate.

WORK PERMITS. For long-term employment in Greece, you must first get a **work permit** from a pre-arranged employer. Permits are available at the **Ministry of Labor,** Pireos 40, Athens 10437 (☎(01) 523 3110). Make all arrangements and negotiations before you leave. (For more information, see p. 75.)

IDENTIFICATION

When you travel, always carry two or more forms of identification on your person, including at least one photo ID. A passport combined with a driver's license or birth certificate is usually adequate. Many establishments, especially banks, require several IDs to cash traveler's checks. Never carry all of your forms of ID together; split them up in case of theft or loss. Bring extra passport-size photos to affix to the various IDs or passes you may acquire on the way.

STUDENT AND TEACHER IDENTIFICATION. The **International Student Identity Card (ISIC),** the most widely accepted form of student ID, provides discounts on sights, accommodations, food, and transport. In Greece, the card will procure you discounts at many sights and museums, a few hostels, and on the occasional ferry and Olympic Airways flight. If discounts are not listed, make sure to present the card and ask. The ISIC is preferable to an institution-specific card (such as a university ID) because it is more likely to be recognized (and honored) abroad. All cardholders have access to a 24hr. emergency helpline for medical, legal, and financial emergencies (in North America, ☎(877) 370-ISIC, elsewhere call US collect +1 (715) 342-4104; UK collect +44 20 8762 8110, or France collect +33 155 633 144), and holders of US-issued cards are also eligible for insurance benefits (see **Insurance,** p. 52). Many student travel agencies issue ISICs, including STA Travel in Australia and New Zealand; Travel CUTS in Canada; usit in the Republic of Ireland and Northern Ireland; SASTS in South Africa; Campus Travel and STA Travel in the UK; Council Travel (www.counciltravel.com/idcards/default.asp) and STA Travel in the US (see p. 61). The card is valid from September of one year to December of the following year and costs US$22. Applicants must be degree-seeking students of a secondary or post-secondary school and must be of at least 12 years of age. Because of the proliferation of fake ISICs, some services (particularly airlines) require additional proof of student identity, such as a school ID or a letter attesting to your student status, signed by your registrar and stamped with your school seal.

The **International Teacher Identity Card (ITIC)** offers the same insurance coverage as well as similar but limited discounts. The fee is AUS$13, UK£5, or US$22. For more info, contact the **International Student Travel Confederation (ISTC),** Herengracht 479, 1017 BS Amsterdam, Netherlands (☎+31 (20) 421 28 00; fax 421 28 10; istcinfo@istc.org; www.istc.org).

YOUTH IDENTIFICATION. The International Student Travel Confederation issues a discount card to travelers who are 26 years old or under but not students. Known as the **International Youth Travel Card (IYTC;** formerly the **GO 25** Card) this one-year card offers similar benefits to the ISIC, and is sold by most of the same organizations. To apply, you'll need a passport, driver's license or copy of a birth certificate, and a passport-sized photo. The fee is US$22.

ISICONNECT SERVICE. If you are an ISIC card carrier and want to avoid buying individual calling cards or wish to consolidate all your means of communication during your trip, you can activate your ISIC's ISIConnect service, a powerful new integrated communications service (powered by eKit.com). With ISIConnect, one toll-free access number (☎00 800 125 282 in Greece) gives you access to several different methods of keeping in touch via telephone and Internet, including: a reduced-rate international calling plan that treats your ISIC card as a universal calling card; a personalized voicemail box accessible from pay phones anywhere in the world or for free over the Internet; faxmail service for sending and receiving faxes via email, fax machines, or pay phones; various email capabilities, including a service that reads your email to you over the phone; an online "travel safe" for storing (and faxing) important documents and numbers; and a 24hr. emergency help line (via phone or email at ISIConnect@ekit.com) offering assistance and medical and legal referrals. To activate your ISIConnect account, visit the service's comprehensive website (www.isiconnect.ekit.com) or call the customer service number of your home country (which is also your home country's access number): in Australia 800 114 478; in Canada 877-635-3575; in Ireland 800 555 180 or 800 577 980; in New Zealand 0800 114 478; in the UK 0800 376 2366 or 0800 169 8646; in the US 800-706-1333; and in South Africa 0800 992 921 or 0800 997 285.

TOURIST BOARDS

 Tourist info in Greece is available in English 24 hours a day by dialing 171.

Start early when trying to contact tourist offices—like most things Greek, they run on their own relaxed schedule. Polite persistence and genuine excitement about visiting works wonders. Two national organizations oversee tourism: the **Greek National Tourist Organization (GNTO)** and the tourist police *(touristiki astinomia)*. The GNTO can supply general information about sights and accommodations throughout the country. (For additional info and offices abroad, see www.gnto.gr.) The main office is in Athens at Amerikis 2 (☎(01) 327 13 00; info@gnto.gr). Note that the GNTO is known as the **EOT** in Greece. The tourist police deal with more local issues: where to find a room or what the bus schedule is. The offices are open long hours and the staff is often quite willing to help, although their English may be limited. On many islands and in smaller towns, travel agencies will be more helpful (and more likely to exist) than tourist offices; feel free to stop in and ask for advice. *Let's Go* lists tourist agencies and organizations in the **Practical Information** section for most cities.

Australia and New Zealand: 3rd Fl., 51-57 Pitt St., Sydney, NSW 2000 (☎(12) 9241 1663; fax 9235 2174; hto@tpg.com.au).

Canada: 1300 Bay St., **Toronto,** ON M5R 3K8 (☎(416) 968-2220; fax 968-6533; grnto.tor@sympatico.ca; www.aei.ca/gntomtl); 1170 Place du Frére André, 3rd Fl., **Montréal,** PQ, H3B 3C6 (☎(514) 871-1535; fax 871-1498; gntomtl@aei.ca).

UK and Ireland: 4 Conduit St., London W1R ODJ (☎(4207) 734 5997; fax 287 1369; EOTgreektouristoffice@btinternet.com; www.tourist-offices.org.uk).

US: Head Office, Olympic Tower, 645 Fifth Ave., 5th Fl., New York, NY 10022 (☎(212) 421-5777; fax 826-6940;gnto@greektourism.com).

CUSTOMS

Upon entering Greece, you must declare if you've brought currency above US$1000 or if you've brought certain items from abroad. You must pay a duty on the value of those articles if it exceeds the allowance established by Greek customs. Importing biological hazards (agricultural products, raw meat, etc.) is prohibited. Selling anything while abroad is illegal; authorities expect you to return with everything except your money. Upon returning home, you must declare all articles acquired abroad and pay a duty on the value of articles in excess of your home country's allowance. Make a list of valuables brought from home and register them with customs before traveling. Keep receipts for goods acquired abroad.

DUTY-FREE ITEMS. You should also be aware that duty-free was abolished on June 30, 1999 for travel between EU member states; however, travelers between the EU and the rest of the world still get a duty-free allowance when passing through customs. Goods and gifts purchased at duty-free shops abroad are not exempt from duty or sales tax at your point of return and thus must be declared as well; "duty-free" merely means that you need not pay a tax in the country of purchase. Keeping receipts for purchases made in Greece will help establish values when you return. If you will be carrying valuables, you should make a list of their serial numbers and register it with customs. An official customs stamp will ensure that you avoid import duty charges and simplify your return. Be especially careful to document items manufactured abroad.

EUROPEAN CUSTOMS. As well as freedom of movement of people within the EU (see p. 39), travelers can also take advantage of the freedom of movement of goods. This means that there are no customs controls at internal EU borders (i.e., you can take the blue customs channel at the airport), and travelers are free to transport whatever legal substances they like as long as it is for their own personal (non-commercial) use—up to 800 cigarettes, 10L of spirits, 90L of wine (60L of sparkling wine), and 110L of beer.

VALUE ADDED TAX. The European Union imposes a value added tax (VAT) on goods and services purchased within the EU, which is included in the marked price. Non-EU citizens may obtain a refund for taxes paid on retail goods (but not services). In Greece, you must spend over 40,000dr/€117.39 to receive a refund. The percentage of your refund will vary from 11.5% to 15.3%. To file for a refund, first obtain a Tax-Free Shopping Cheque, available from shops sporting the blue, white, and silver Europe Tax-Free Shopping logo, and then save the receipts from all of the purchases for which you want to be partially refunded. Upon leaving Greece, you can present your goods, invoices, and Tax-Free Shopping Cheque to customs, which will then validate the Cheque. An immediate cash refund may be available at an ETS cash refund office, or you may have to file for a refund at home. Refunds are available for purchases made by credit card and check. Allow two hours to apply for customs endorsement at your point of departure. There are some **restrictions** on VAT refunds. Goods must be taken out of the country within three months after the end of the month of purchase, and they must be unused. For more information, visit www.globalrefund.com.

MONEY

CURRENCY AND EXCHANGE

Greek **drachmas** (abbreviated "dr") are issued in both paper notes (100, 200, 500, 1000, 5000, and 10,000dr) and coins (5, 10, 20, 50, and 100dr). If you're carrying more than US$1000 in cash when you enter Greece, you must declare it upon entry. This rule does not apply to traveler's checks. You can bring up to US$445 worth of drachmas into Greece. No more than 20,000dr can be taken out of the country when you leave. The currency chart below is based on August 2001 exchange rates. Check a large newspaper or the web (e.g. finance.yahoo.com, www.bloomberg.com, or www.letsgo.com/thumb) for the latest exchange rates.

GREEK DRACHMAS		
US$1 = 390DR	100DR = US$0.26	
CDN$1 = 255DR	100DR = CDN$0.39	
UK£1 = 555DR	100DR = UK£0.18	
IR£1 = 433DR	100DR = IR£0.23	
AUS$1 = 198DR	100DR = AUS$0.51	
NZ$1 = 160DR	100DR = NZ$0.62	
ZAR1 = 47DR	100DR = ZAR2.12	
EUR€ = 341DR	100DR = EUR€0.29	
TRL1000 =0.30DR	100DR = TRL335,443	
CYP£1 = 589DR	100DR = CYP£0.17	

It's generally cheaper to convert money in Greece and Cyprus than at home. Banks in Greece charge a commission of 2% with a minimum of 50dr and a maximum of 4500dr on cashing traveler's checks. However, you should bring enough foreign currency to last for the first 24 to 72 hours of a trip to avoid being penniless should you arrive after banking hours or on a holiday. Travelers from the US can get foreign currency from the comfort of home: **International Currency Express** (☎ (888) 278-6628) deliver foreign currency or traveler's checks overnight (US$15) or second-day (US$12) at competitive exchange rates. When changing money abroad, try to go only to banks or exchange bureaus with at most a 5% margin between their buy and sell prices. Since you lose money with every transaction, **convert large sums** (unless the currency is depreciating rapidly), **but no more than you'll need.** An **ATM card** or a **credit card** (see p. 43) will often get you the best possible conversion rates. Most towns and islands in Greece now have ATMs that are linked into major international networks.

If you use traveler's checks or bills, carry some in small denominations (the equivalent of US$50 or less) for times when you are forced to exchange money at disadvantageous rates. Bring a range of denominations, since charges may be levied per check cashed. Store your money in a variety of forms. Ideally, you will at any given time be carrying some cash, some traveler's checks, and an ATM and/or credit card. Travelers should consider carrying about US$50 or 95 German marks, which local tellers may prefer; however, avoid using non-Greek money when possible, since it marks you as a foreigner and invites price hikes and robbery.

TRAVELER'S CHECKS

Traveler's checks are one of the safest and least troublesome means of carrying funds, and are accepted in Greece (generally only at large hotels and chains; but they can be exchanged at almost any bank or exchange kiosk in urban and rural areas alike). **American Express** and **Visa** are the most recognized. Several agencies and banks sell them for a small commission. All agencies provide refunds if your checks are lost or stolen, and many provide additional services, like toll-free refund hotlines abroad, emergency message services, and stolen credit card assistance.

THE EURO. Since January 2001, the official currency of 12 members of the European Union—Austria, Belgium, Finland, France, Germany, Greece, Ireland, Italy, Luxembourg, the Netherlands, Portugal, and Spain—has been the euro. Actual euro banknotes and coins will be available beginning on January 1, 2002; but you shouldn't throw out your francs, pesetas, and Deutschmarks just yet. The old national currencies remain legal tender through July 1, 2002, after which it's all euros all the time. *Let's Go: Greece* lists prices in both denominations, euros (€) and drachmas (dr) based on actual figures or fixed conversion rates.

The currency has some important—and positive—consequences for travelers hitting more than one euro-zone country. For one thing, money-changers across the euro-zone are obliged to exchange money at the official, fixed rate (see below), and at no commission (though they may still charge a small service fee). So now you can change your guilders into escudos and your escudos into lire without losing fistfuls of money on every transaction. Second, euro-denominated travelers checks allow you to pay for goods and services across the euro-zone, again at the official rate and commission-free.

The exchange rate between euro-zone currencies was permanently fixed on January 1, 1999 at 1 EUR = 40.3399 BEF (Belgian francs) = 1.95583 DEM (German marks) = 166.386 ESP (Spanish *pesetas*) = 6.55957 FRF (French francs) = 0.787564 IER (Irish pounds) = 1936.27 ITL (Italian *lire*) = 40.3399 LUF (Luxembourg francs) = 2.20371 NLG (Dutch guilders) = 13.7603 ATS (Austrian schillings) = 200.482 PTE (Portuguese *escudos*) = 5.94573 FIM (Finnish *markka*). For more info, see www.europa.eu.int.

While traveling, keep check receipts and a record of which checks you've cashed separate from the checks themselves. Also leave a list of check numbers with someone at home. Never countersign checks until you're ready to cash them, and always bring your passport with you to cash them. If your checks are lost or stolen, immediately contact a refund center of the company that issued your checks; they may require a police report verifying the loss or theft in order to reimburse you. Less-touristed areas may not have refund centers at all, in which case you might have to wait for a refund. Ask about toll-free refund hotlines and the location of refund centers when purchasing checks, and always carry emergency cash.

American Express: Call (800) 251 902 in Australia; in New Zealand (0800) 441 068; in the UK (0800) 521 313; in the US and Canada (800) 221-7282. Elsewhere call US collect +1 (801) 964-6665; www.aexp.com. If your checks are lost, call the regional refund number, 00 800 441 27 569. Traveler's checks are available in Australian, British, Canadian, Dutch, French, German, Saudi Arabian, and US currencies at 1-4% commission at AmEx offices and banks, commission-free at AAA offices. *Cheques for Two* can be signed by either of 2 people traveling together.

Citicorp: In the US and Canada, call (800) 645-6556; in Europe, the Middle East, or Africa, call the UK +44 (020) 7508 7007; elsewhere call US collect +1 (813) 623-1709. Traveler's checks available in 7 currencies at 1-2% commission. Call 24hr.

Thomas Cook MasterCard: In the US and Canada, call (800) 223-7373; in the UK, call (0800) 62 21 01; elsewhere call UK collect +44 (1733) 31 89 50. Checks available in 13 currencies at 2% commission. Thomas Cook offices cash checks commission-free. Call toll-free in Greece at 800 441 28 455.

Visa: In the US call (800) 227-6811; in the UK call (0800) 89 50 78; elsewhere call UK collect +44 20 7937 8091. Call for the location of their nearest office.

CREDIT CARDS

Credit cards are accepted in the more touristed areas of Greece; if you're traveling off the beaten path, be prepared to use other forms of payment. Where they are accepted, credit cards often offer superior exchange rates—up to 5% better than the retail rate used by banks and other currency exchange establishments, and are sometimes required to reserve hotel rooms or rental cars. **MasterCard** (a.k.a. Euro-Card or Access in Europe) and **Visa** (a.k.a. Carte Bleue or Barclaycard) are most welcomed, with Visa being the most popular by far; **American Express** cards work at some ATMs and at AmEx offices and major airports. Credit cards often offer an array of other services, from insurance to emergency assistance. Check with your company to find out what is covered.

Credit cards are also useful for **cash advances,** which allow you to withdraw drachmas from associated banks and ATMs throughout Greece instantly. Transaction fees for credit card advances (up to US$10 per advance, plus 2-3% extra on foreign transactions after conversion) make them a costly way to withdraw cash, (more expensive than traveler's checks or cash cards), but they are very useful in emergencies. To be eligible for an advance, you'll need a **Personal Identification Number (PIN)** from your credit card company. Call in advance to arrange a PIN (see **Cash Cards (ATM Cards),** below). It's also never a bad idea to warn your credit card company that you will be traveling and will thus have an unusual spending pattern; companies have been known to freeze their customers' accounts because they thought the card had been stolen and was being used illegally.

CREDIT CARD COMPANIES. Visa (US ☎ (800) 336-8472) and **MasterCard** (US ☎ (800) 307-7309) are issued in cooperation with banks and other organizations. **American Express** (US ☎ (800) 843-2273) has an annual fee of up to US$55. AmEx cardholders may cash personal checks at AmEx offices abroad, access an emergency medical and legal assistance hotline (24hr.; in North America call (800) 554-2639, elsewhere call US collect +1 (715) 343 7977), and enjoy American Express Travel Service benefits (including plane, hotel, and car rental reservation changes; baggage loss and flight insurance; mailgram and international cable services; and held mail). The **Discover Card** (in US call (800) 347-2683, elsewhere call US +1 (801) 902-3100) offers small cashback bonuses on most purchases, but is useful only for advance arrangements: it isn't accepted in Greece.

ATM ALERT. To use a cash or credit card to withdraw money from a cash machine (ATM) in Europe, you must have a four-digit **Personal Identification Number (PIN).** If your PIN is longer than four digits, ask your bank whether you can use just the first four, or if you'll need a new one. **Credit cards** in North America don't usually come with PINs, so if you intend to hit up ATMs in Europe with a credit card to get cash advances, call your credit card company before leaving to request one. People with alphabetic, rather than numerical, PINs may also be thrown off by the lack of letters on European cash machines. The following handy chart gives the corresponding numbers to use: 1=QZ; 2=ABC; 3=DEF; 4=GHI; 5=JKL; 6=MNO; 7=PRS; 8=TUV; and 9=WXY. If you mistakenly punch the wrong code into the machine three times, it will swallow your card for good.

CASH CARDS (ATM CARDS)

Cash cards—popularly called ATM (Automated Teller Machine) cards—are widespread in larger towns, cities, and ports in Greece; only the smallest towns and remotest areas are without. You can most likely access your home checking account from abroad—savings accounts are harder to access. ATMs get the same wholesale exchange rate as credit cards, but there is often a limit on the amount of money you can withdraw per day (around US$500), and unfortunately computer networks sometimes fail. They typically charge an extra US$1-5 per withdrawal. Memorize your PIN code in numeric form, and if your PIN is longer than four digits, ask your bank for a new number.

The two major international money networks are **Cirrus** (US ☎ (800) 424-7787) and **PLUS** (US ☎ (800) 843-7587). To locate ATMs around the world, call the above numbers, or consult www.visa.com/pd/atm or www.mastercard.com/atm. All ATMs are linked to at least one of these major networks. **Visa TravelMoney** (for customer assistance in Greece, call 800 114 810 304) allows you to access money from any Visa ATM. After depositing money before you travel (plus an administration fee), you can withdraw up to that sum. These cards give you the same favorable exchange rate as a regular Visa, and are especially useful if you plan to travel through many countries. Check with your local bank to see if it issues TravelMoney cards. **Road Cash** (US ☎ (877) 762-3227; www.roadcash.com) issues cards in the US with a minimum US$300 deposit.

GETTING MONEY FROM HOME

AMERICAN EXPRESS. Cardholders can withdraw cash from their checking accounts at any of AmEx's major offices and many representative offices (up to US$1000 every 21 days; no service charge, no interest). AmEx "Express Cash" withdrawals from any AmEx ATM in Greece are automatically debited from the cardholder's checking account or line of credit. Green card holders may withdraw up to US$1000 in any seven-day period (2% transaction fee; minimum US$2.50, maximum US$20). To enroll in Express Cash, cardholders may call (800) 227-4669 in the US; elsewhere call the US collect +1 (336) 668-5041. The toll free AmEx national number in Greece is 00 800 12 3211. The Greek service center number is (01) 326 2626.

WESTERN UNION. Travelers from the US, Canada, and the UK can wire money abroad through Western Union's international money transfer services. In the US call (800) 325-6000, in Canada (800) 235-0000, in the UK (0800) 833 833, throughout Greece call (01) 927 1010. The rates for sending cash are generally US$10-11 cheaper than with a credit card, and the money is usually available at the place you're sending it to within an hour. To locate the nearest Western Union location, consult www.westernunion.com or call the national access number listed above.

US STATE DEPARTMENT (US CITIZENS ONLY). In dire emergencies, the US State Department will forward money within hours to the nearest consular office, which will then disburse it (according to instructions) for a US$15 fee. Contact the Overseas Citizens Service, American Citizens Services, Consular Affairs, Room 4811, US Department of State, Washington, D.C. 20520 (☎ (202) 647-5225; nights, Sundays, and holidays ☎ (202) 647-4000; http://travel.state.gov).

COSTS

The cost of a trip to Greece will vary considerably, depending on where you go, how you travel, and where you stay. The single biggest cost of your trip will probably be your round-trip **airfare** (see p. 61). If you choose to buy a **Eurail pass** for travel throughout Europe, it will be valid in Greece, but will cost a substantial sum. Before you go, spend some time calculating a reasonable per-day **budget** that will meet your needs. To give you a general idea, a bare-bones day in Greece, staying at hostels, campgrounds, or domatia (rooms to let), and buying food at supermarkets or at outdoor food stands, costs about US$35. Note that camping can save a substantial sum of money: about US$10-15 per day. A day with more comforts, with accommodations in a pricier domatia or budget hotel, eating one meal a day in a restaurant, and going out at night, runs US$50. For a luxurious day, the sky's the limit. Also, don't forget to factor in emergency reserve funds (at least US$200) when planning how much money you'll need.

Saving US$5 per day for a week will fund an entire additional day of travel, so learning to pinch pennies pays off. Take advantage of freebies: hit the **beach,** go **hiking,** tour churches, wander winding streets, and hunt down free open-air **concerts,** traditional **dances,** and outdoor **festivals** (especially in the summer). Do your **laundry** in the sink (where it is allowed). Split **accommodations** costs (in hotels, hostels, and domatia) with trustworthy fellow travelers, since multi-bed rooms are cheaper per person than singles. Buy food in **supermarkets** instead of eating out, split **restaurant** meals, or eat cheap, divine souvlaki from outdoor **food stands.** But don't go overboard with money management. Staying within budget is important, but don't sacrifice your sanity or your health to save a buck.

BARGAINING AND TIPPING

BARGAINING. Bargaining skills are essential in Greece, but you must know when to bargain. Paying the asked price for street wares will have the seller marveling at your naïveté, while bargaining at the shop of a master craftsman whose crafts are worth the stated tag will be seen as rude and disrespectful. The more informal the venue, the more flexible the price. If in doubt, hang back and watch someone else buy. Keep the cooperative spirit of bargaining in mind: everyone involved is looking for a fair, agreed-upon price. Merchants with any pride in their wares will refuse to sell to someone who has offended them in the negotiations.

Domatia (rooms to let, see p. 55) prices rise in summer and fall in the winter. Bargain before you get into a **taxi** (be it a boat, car, truck, or guided tour), if your trip won't be metered or ticketed. **Clothing** in general is negotiable. Obvious conveniences like pharmaceutical goods and grocery items are priced as marked, as are street food, taverna fare, and books. **Jewelry** stores usually mark up 10-50%, so shop around to get an idea of what an item is really worth. Then go back to your favorite shop and ask for a lower price. (At a good store, expect 10-20% off, more in cheaper stores; you should also be able to get deals on multiple purchases.)

TIPPING. As with bargaining, when tipping, you should offer enough to show respect, for the goods, but not so much to seem like a show-off. At all but the ritziest restaurants, service is included in the bill. A few hundred drachmas (a few euros) for a several thousand drachma meal is usually sufficient. There is no tipping for any other services (including taxis).

SAFETY AND SECURITY

EXPLORING. Solo travelers may feel quite conspicuous among Greeks, who don't usually travel alone. Westerners in particular may feel nervous around pro-KKE, anti-American, and anti-Western graffiti (see **The KKE**, p. 32). Don't worry about it; if you are heckled by anti-Westerners, just walk away. To stay safe, familiarize yourself with your surroundings before setting out, and carry yourself with confidence. If you must check a map, duck into a shop to do it. If you are traveling alone, be sure someone at home knows your itinerary. **Never admit that you're traveling alone.** When walking at night, stick to busy, well-lit streets and avoid dark alleyways. Do not attempt to cross through parks, parking lots, or other large, deserted areas. Look for children playing, women walking in the open, and other signs of an active community. Find out about unsafe areas from tourist offices, or from the manager of your hotel or hostel. You may want to carry a whistle to scare off attackers or attract attention. If you feel uncomfortable, leave as quickly and directly as you can, but don't allow fear to turn you into a hermit. Careful, persistent exploration builds confidence and will make your stay even more rewarding.

SELF DEFENSE. There is no sure-fire way to be completely prepared for every threatening situation you might encounter, but a good self-defense course will give you concrete ways to react to unwanted advances. Impact, Prepare, and Model Mugging can refer you to local self-defense courses in the US (☎(800) 345-5425) and Vancouver (☎(604) 878-3838). Workshops (2-3hr.) start at US$50; full courses run US$350-500. Visit www.impactsafety.org/chapters for a list of nearby chapters.

GETTING AROUND. Driving in Greece requires a fearless temperament and all your attention: the thousands of roadside shrines on every winding road commemorate those killed in car and moped accidents. Roads, especially on the islands and in rural areas, are narrow and poor. Some lack shoulders, barriers, and gas stations; others are plagued by roaming goats. Native Greek drivers career around the roads with astonishingly reckless confidence, but visiting drivers should take the shrines as a warning and drive slowly. Learn local driving signals and wear a seatbelt in **cars.** Children under 40lbs. should ride only

TRAVEL ADVISORIES. The following government offices provide travel information and advisories by telephone, by fax, or via the web:

Australian Department of Foreign Affairs and Trade: ☎ (2) 6261 1111; www.dfat.gov.au.

Canadian Department of Foreign Affairs and International Trade (DFAIT): In Canada call (800) 267-8376, elsewhere call +1 (613) 944-4000; www.dfait-maeci.gc.ca. Call for their free booklet, *Bon Voyage...But.*

New Zealand Ministry of Foreign Affairs: ☎ (04) 494 8500; fax 494 8506; www.mft.govt.nz/trav.html.

United Kingdom Foreign and Commonwealth Office: ☎ (020) 7270 1500; fax 7238 4545; www.fco.gov.uk.

US Department of State: ☎ (202) 647-5225, auto faxback (202) 647-4000; http://travel.state.gov. For *A Safe Trip Abroad,* call (202) 512-1800.

in a specially designed carseat, available for a small fee from most car rental agencies. Always wear a helmet on a **moped** (required by law). Driving any vehicle at night on winding roads is incredibly dangerous and even foolish; plan to take a cab instead if at all possible. Be forewarned that driving a moped is harder than it looks, and countless tourists injure themselves on the bikes. Study route maps before you hit the road, and plan ahead. You may want to bring spare parts. If your car breaks down, wait for police assistance, or locals may help you. **Sleeping in your car** is dangerous and illegal—don't do it. For info on the perils of **hitchhiking,** see p. 71.

TERRORISM. Though certainly not rampant, Greece does have some problems with terrorism, particularly with the high-profile, anti-Western, anti-NATO, anti-US **November 17** group. Claiming responsibility for the deaths of 23 people in the last 25 years, the group was also responsible for the assassination of British Defense attaché Stephen Saunders on June 8, 2000. Although the government has pledged to begin combatting terrorism more effectively, it remains on the US list of countries that have not arrested anyone for a terrorist act in over 25 years. Tourists are never targeted by these terrorist groups but should be aware of their existence.

PROTECTING YOUR VALUABLES. In Greece, you are much more likely to be **ripped off** by a cab driver, restaurant owner, or hotel owner than you are to be outright **mugged** in the street. **Pick pocketing,** however, is somewhat common, especially at major tourist sites and in Athens: be particularly careful in these locations. To avoid being swindled, do your homework. Ask around for prices for hotel rooms, food, and cab rides to find out what a fair price is: don't take a first offer. Always, always, always negotiate cab fare or accommodation price ahead of time; pay only what you agreed upon, even if they try to change the price on you later. If you think someone is trying to rip you off, contact the tourist police (listed in the **Practical Information** section for each town).

Minimize financial risks by leaving expensive watches, jewelry, cameras, and electronics (like your Discman) at home; chances are you'd break them, lose them, or get sick of lugging them around anyway. Second, carry as little cash as possible; instead carry traveler's checks, an ATM card, or credit cards (along with your passport and ID cards) in a **money belt** under your clothes. Third, keep a small cash reserve separate from your primary stash. Keep the equivalent of US$50 sewn into or stored in the depths of your pack, along with your traveler's check numbers and photocopies of your passport, plane ticket, Eurail pass, and any other valuable documents you're carrying. Leave a set of photocopies at home. Don't put a wallet with money in your back pocket. Label every piece of luggage both inside and out. Never count your money in public, and carry only as much as you'll need for the day. If you carry a purse, wear it across your body, away from the street, with the clasp against you. Always have cash stashed away, in case you are robbed.

CON ARTISTS. In larger cities and touristy towns (especially Athens), you may run into **con artists.** They often work in groups. In a classic Athenian scam, you might be invited to a club by a new friend; there you'll meet several of his friends, and everyone will have several drinks. When you get up to go, you'll be stuck with the bill for several dozen *very* expensive drinks. Be wary of such invitations, since they can cost you everything you have.

Beware of certain classic cons: sob stories that require money, rolls of bills "found" on the street, mustard spilled (or saliva spit) onto your shoulder distracting you for enough time to snatch your bag. In a suspicious situation, don't respond or make eye contact, and walk away quickly. Don't ever hand over your passport to someone whose authority you question (ask to accompany them to a police station if they insist), and **don't ever let your passport out of your sight.** Similarly, don't let your bag out of sight; never trust a "station-porter" who insists on carrying your bag or stowing it in the baggage compartment or a "new friend" who offers to guard your bag while you buy a train ticket or use the rest room. Beware of **pickpockets** in city crowds, especially on public transportation. Also, be alert in public telephone booths. If you must say your calling card number, do so very quietly; if you punch it in, make sure no one can look over your shoulder.

ACCOMMODATIONS AND TRANSPORTATION. Never leave your belongings unattended; crime occurs in even the most demure-looking hostel or hotel. Bring your own **padlock** for lockers: don't trust the original locks, and don't store valuables in lockers. If you feel unsafe, look for places with a curfew or night attendant.

Be particularly careful on **buses** and **trains;** some determined thieves wait for travelers to fall asleep. Carry your backpack in front of you where you can see it. When traveling with others, sleep in alternate shifts. When alone, use good judgement in selecting a train compartment: never stay in an empty one, and lock your pack to the luggage rack. In hostels, sleep on top bunks with your luggage above you or in bed with you. Keep important documents and valuables on your person. Don't leave valuables in a **car** while you are away from it; hide tape decks, radios, and baggage in the trunk, or take them with you.

DRUGS AND ALCOHOL. You're subject to the laws of the country in which you travel, so familiarize yourself with those laws before leaving. If you carry **prescription drugs,** it is vital to have both a copy of the prescriptions themselves and a note from a doctor, especially at border crossings. Never try to bring any illegal substances into Greece. Authorities are especially vigilant at the Turkish and Albanian borders and might carefully search your bag for anything you shouldn't have.

HEALTH

Common sense is the simplest prescription for good health while you travel. Drink lots of fluids to prevent dehydration and constipation; wear sturdy, broken-in shoes and clean socks, and use talcum powder to keep your feet dry. Bring moleskin to cover blisters.

BEFORE YOU GO

Preparation can help minimize the likelihood of contracting a disease and maximize the chances of receiving effective health care in the event of an emergency. For tips on packing a basic **first-aid kit** and other health essentials, see p. 53.

In your **passport,** write the names of people you wish to be contacted in case of a medical emergency, and add a list of your **allergies** or medical conditions. Carry up-to-date, legible prescriptions or a statement from your doctor stating the trade name, manufacturer, chemical name, and dosage of any medicine you're carrying. Matching a prescription to a foreign equivalent is not always easy, safe, or possible. While traveling, keep all medication with you in your carry-on luggage.

IMMUNIZATIONS. Travelers over two years old should have the following up-to-date immunizations: MMR (for measles, mumps, and rubella); DTaP or Td (for diptheria, tetanus, and pertussis); OPV (for polio); HbCV (for haemophilus influenza B); and HBV (for hepatitis B). Hepatitis A vaccine and/or immune globulin (IG) are recommended. For recommendations on immunizations and prophylaxis, consult the CDC (see below) in the US or the equivalent in your home country, and be sure to check with a doctor for guidance.

MEDICAL CONDITIONS. Those with diabetes, allergies to antibiotics, epilepsy, heart conditions, or other conditions can obtain a stainless steel **Medic Alert** identification tag (US$35 the first year, $20 annually thereafter), which identifies the wearer's condition and gives a 24hr. collect-call information number. Contact the Medic Alert Foundation, 2323 Colorado Ave., Turlock, CA 95382 (☎(888) 633-4298; www.medicalert.org). Diabetics can contact the **American Diabetes Association,** 1660 Duke St., Alexandria, VA 22314 (☎(800) 342-2383; www.diabetes.org), for the article "Travel and Diabetes" and a diabetic ID card, which carries messages in 18 languages explaining the carrier's diabetic status.

USEFUL ORGANIZATIONS AND PUBLICATIONS. The **US Centers for Disease Control and Prevention** (**CDC;** ☎877-FYI-TRIP; www.cdc.gov/travel) maintains an international fax information service and an international travelers hotline (☎(404)332-4559). The CDC's comprehensive booklet *Health Information for International Travel,* an annual rundown of disease, immunization, and general health advice, is free online or US$25 via the Public Health Foundation (☎(877) 252-1200). Consult the appropriate government agency of your home country for consular information sheets on health, entry requirements, and other issues for various countries (see **Consular Services,** p. 37). For quick information on health and other travel warnings, call the **Overseas Citizens Services** (☎(202) 647-5225; after hours (202) 647-4000), contact a passport agency or an embassy or consulate abroad. US citizens can send a self-addressed, stamped envelope to the Overseas Citizens Services, Bureau of Consular Affairs, #4811, US Department of State, Washington, D.C. 20520. For information on medical evacuation services and travel insurance firms, see the US government's website at http://travel.state.gov/medical.html or the **British Foreign and Commonwealth Office** (www.fco.gov.uk).

For detailed information on travel health, including a country-by-country overview of diseases, try the **International Travel Health Guide,** Stuart Rose, MD (Travel Medicine, US$24.95; www.travmed.com). For general health info, contact the **American Red Cross** (☎(800) 564-1234).

ONCE THERE

MEDICAL ASSISTANCE. In Greece, all EU travelers receive free health care with the presentation of an **E111 form.** There is a doctor on every island and in every town, and emergency treatment is available to travelers of all nationalities in public hospitals. Medical training in Greece is of high quality, but the health care system is vastly underfunded. Public hospitals are overcrowded, and hygiene may not be the best. Private hospitals generally have better care for more money; to use them, you will need good **health insurance.** If your regular policy does not cover travel abroad, you may wish to purchase additional coverage (see p. 52).

Pharmacies *(farmakia),* labeled by green or red crosses, are on every street corner. In most towns and cities, at least one pharmacy (known as *efimerevon*) is open at all hours—pharmacies post listings of 24hr. pharmacies in their windows.

If you are concerned about being able to access medical support while traveling, there are special support services you may employ. The *MedPass* from **GlobalCare, Inc.,** 2001 Westside Pkwy., #120, Alpharetta, GA 30004, USA (☎(800) 860-1111; fax (770) 475-0058; www.globalems.com), provides 24hr. international medical assistance, support, and medical evacuation resources. The **International Association for**

Medical Assistance to Travelers (IAMAT; US ☎ (716) 754-4883, Canada ☎ (416) 652-0137, New Zealand ☎ 03 352 20 53; www.sentex.net/~iamat) has free membership, lists English-speaking doctors worldwide, and offers detailed info on immunization requirements and sanitation.

ENVIRONMENTAL HAZARDS. The hot sun beats down on all of Greece all summer long: this may be why you're going to Greece. It's easy to overheat, get sunburned, and forget to drink enough water. Especially on beaches, at outdoor sights, and hiking in the sun, beware of dehydration, sunburn, and heat exhaustion. These conditions can be avoided by drinking enough water, wearing a hat and sunglasses, using sunscreen, and taking a nap during the heat of the day like Greeks do. In the **winter** or on **high-altitude** hikes, travelers should look out for hypothermia and exposure. Always dress warmly; on hikes, bring plenty of water, take it slowly to adjust to thin air, and go with a partner.

Heat exhaustion and dehydration: Heat exhaustion, characterized by dehydration and salt deficiency, can lead to fatigue, headaches, and wooziness. Avoid it by drinking plenty of clear fluids, eating salty foods (like crackers), and avoiding dehydrating beverages (e.g. alcohol, coffee, tea, and caffeinated soda). Continuous heat stress can lead to heatstroke, characterized by a rising temperature, severe headache, and cessation of sweating. Victims should be cooled off with wet towels and taken to a doctor.

Sunburn: Even if you're not prone to sunburn, bring sunscreen with you—though you can buy it in Greece, it's better to have sunscreen on hand as soon as you arrive in this sometimes fiercely hot country. Apply it liberally and often to avoid burns and risk of skin cancer. Even if you don't think you'll be in the sun much, you probably will be, and the sun is merciless, even through clouds. If you get sunburned, drink more fluids than usual and apply an aloe-based lotion.

High altitude: While skiing or hiking in the mountains, allow your body a couple of days to adjust to the reduced oxygen level before doing demanding work. At high elevations alcohol is more potent and UV rays are stronger.

FOOD- AND WATER-BORNE DISEASE. Prevention is the best cure: be sure that everything you eat is cooked properly and that the water is clean. In Greece, the tap water is fairly safe. Bottled water, however, is dirt cheap and widely available, so drink it whenever possible. Always wash your hands before eating, or bring a quick-drying anti-bacterial liquid hand cleaner. Your bowels will thank you.

Traveler's diarrhea results from drinking untreated water or eating uncooked foods. If the nasties hit you, have quick-energy, non-sugary foods with protein and carbohydrates to keep your strength up. Over-the-counter remedies (such as Pepto-Bismol or Immodium) may counteract the problems, but they can complicate serious infections. The most dangerous side effect of diarrhea is dehydration; drink 8 oz. of water with a half teaspoon of sugar or honey and a pinch of salt, try decaffeinated soft drinks, or munch on salted crackers. If you develop a fever or your symptoms don't go away after four or five days, consult a doctor. Consult a doctor for treatment of diarrhea in children.

Microbes, tapeworms, and other **parasites** hide in unsafe water and food. **Giardiasis,** for example, is acquired by drinking untreated water from streams or lakes. Symptoms include swollen glands or lymph nodes, fever, rashes or itchiness, digestive problems, eye problems, and anemia. Boil water, wear shoes, avoid bugs, and eat only cooked food.

OTHER INFECTIOUS DISEASES

Rabies: Transmitted through the saliva of infected animals; fatal if untreated. By the time symptoms appear (thirst and muscle spasms), the disease is in its terminal stage. If you are bitten, wash the wound thoroughly, seek immediate medical care, and try to have the animal located. A rabies vaccine, which consists of 3 shots given over a 21-day period, is available but is only semi-effective.

Hepatitis B: A viral infection of the liver transmitted via bodily fluids or needle-sharing. Symptoms may not surface until years after infection. Vaccinations are recommended for health-care workers, sexually active travelers, and anyone planning to seek medical treatment abroad. The 3-shot vaccination series must begin 6 mo. before traveling.

Hepatitis C: Like Hep B, but the mode of transmission differs. IV drug users, those with occupational exposure to blood, hemodialysis patients, and recipients of blood transfusions are at the highest risk, but the disease can also be spread through sexual contact or sharing items like razors and toothbrushes that may have traces of blood on them.

AIDS, HIV, AND STDS. The World Health Organization estimates that 30 million people have been infected with the **HIV** virus, the virus that causes **AIDS**. The easiest mode of HIV transmission is through direct blood-to-blood contact with an HIV-positive person, usually through shared needles; the most common way to transmit HIV is through sexual intercourse. **Latex condoms** can help prevent transmission; they are available in Greece, but it's a good idea to take a supply with you before you depart for your trip.

For detailed information on **AIDS** in Greece, call the **US Centers for Disease Control**'s 24hr. hotline at (800) 342-2437, or contact the **Joint United Nations Programme on HIV/AIDS (UNAIDS)**, Appia 20, CH-1211 Geneva 27, Switzerland (☎ +41 (22) 791 36 66; fax 791 41 87). The Council on International Educational Exchange's pamphlet, *Travel Safe: AIDS and International Travel*, is posted on their website (www.ciee.org/Isp/safety/travelsafe.htm), along with links to other online and phone resources. Greece does not require HIV tests for tourists or those with visas. Cyprus tests all foreigners applying for studying, training, or work permits for HIV.

Sexually transmitted diseases (STDs) such as gonorrhea, chlamydia, genital warts, syphilis, and herpes are easier to catch than HIV and can be just as deadly. Hepatitis B and C are also serious STDs (see Other Infectious Diseases, above). Condoms may protect you from some STDs, but oral or tactile contact transmits them, too. Warning signs include swelling, sores, bumps, or blisters on sex organs, the rectum, or the mouth; burning and pain during urination and bowel movements; itching around sex organs; swelling or redness of the throat; and flu-like symptoms. If these symptoms develop, see a doctor immediately.

WOMEN'S HEALTH. Women traveling in unsanitary conditions are vulnerable to urinary tract and bladder infections, which cause a burning sensation as well as painful and frequent urination. To try to avoid these infections, drink plenty of vitamin-C-rich juice and clean water, and urinate frequently, especially right after intercourse. Untreated, these infections can lead to kidney problems, sterility, and even death. If symptoms persist, see a doctor.

Vaginal yeast infections may flare up in hot, humid areas of Greece. Wearing loosely fitting trousers or a skirt and cotton underwear will help, as will over-the-counter remedies like Monistat or Gynelotrimin. Bring supplies from home if you are prone to infection, as they may be difficult to find on the road. In a pinch, some travelers use a natural alternative such as a plain yogurt and lemon juice douche.

Tampons and **pads** are readily available at pharmacies in cities and large towns; when heading for a remote village, bring your own supply. Although some pharmacies may be able to fill a birth control pill prescription, it is best to bring enough from home to avoid problems. Other methods of contraception, like condoms, are available everywhere.

Women considering an **abortion** should contact the **International Planned Parenthood Federation (IPPF)**, Regent's College, Inner Circle, Regent's Park, London NW1 4NS (☎ (020) 7487 7900; fax 7487 7950; www.ippf.org) for more information.

For additional women's health information, check out the *Handbook for Women Travellers* by Maggie and Gemma Moss (Piatkus Books, US$15).

INSURANCE

Travel insurance generally covers four basic areas: medical/health problems, property loss, trip cancellation/interruption, and emergency evacuation. Although your regular insurance policies may extend to travel-related accidents, consider purchasing travel insurance if the cost of potential trip cancellation or interruption is greater than you can absorb. Separately purchased travel insurance generally costs about US$50 per week for full coverage, and trip cancellation or interruption insurance may be purchased separately for about US$5.50 per US$100 of coverage.

Medical insurance (especially university policies) often covers costs incurred abroad; check with your provider. **US Medicare** does not cover foreign travel. **Canadians** are protected by their home province's health insurance plan for up to 90 days after leaving the country; check with the provincial Ministry of Health or Health Plan Headquarters for details. **Homeowners' insurance** (or your family's coverage) often covers theft during travel and loss of travel documents (passport, plane ticket, railpass, etc.) up to US$500.

ISIC and **ITIC** (see p. 39) provide basic insurance benefits, including US$100 per day of in-hospital sickness for up to 60 days, US$3000 of accident-related medical reimbursement, and US$25,000 for emergency medical transport. Cardholders have access to a toll-free 24hr. helpline (run by the insurance provider TravelGuard) for medical, legal, and financial emergencies overseas (US and Canada ☎ (877) 370-4742, elsewhere call collect +1 715-345-0505). **American Express** (US ☎ (800) 528-4800) grants some cardholders car rental insurance (collision and theft, but not liability) and ground travel accident coverage of US$100,000 on flight purchases made with the card. For information on car insurance, see p. 70.

INSURANCE PROVIDERS. Council and **STA** (see p. 61) offer a range of plans that can supplement your basic coverage. Other private insurance providers in the US and Canada include: **Access America** (☎ (800) 284-8300); **Berkely Group/Carefree Travel Insurance** (☎ (800) 323-3149; www.berkely.com); **Globalcare Travel Insurance** (☎ (800) 821-2488; www.globalcare-cocco.com); and **Travel Assistance International** (☎ (800) 821-2828; www.worldwide-assistance.com). Providers in the **UK** include **Campus Travel** (☎ 01865 25 80 00) and **Columbus Travel Insurance** (☎ 020 7375 0011). In **Australia**, try **CIC Insurance** (☎ 9202 8000).

PACKING

Pack light: lay out only what you absolutely need, then take half the clothes and twice the money. The less you have, the less you have to carry—or lose. For information on hiking, see **Camping and the Outdoors** (p. 56).

LUGGAGE. If you plan to cover most of your itinerary by foot, a sturdy **frame backpack** is unbeatable. (For the basics on buying a pack, see p. 57.) Make sure your luggage is compact and easy to transport: a **suitcase** is a very bad idea if you're going to be moving around a lot. In addition to your main piece of luggage, a **daypack** (a small backpack or courier bag) is a must.

CLOTHES. If you are in Greece at the height of summer, you'll need very little other than **comfortable shoes,** a few changes of **light clothes,** and a **fleece** or sweater. **Flip-flops** are crucial for grubby hostel showers. To visit monasteries or churches, men will need a lightweight pair of pants and women will need a long skirt; both will need covered shoulders. If you plan on taking ferries or hiking, you'll want a warm wool sweater and a windproof jacket.

CONVERTERS AND ADAPTERS. Greek electricity is 220 volts AC, enough to fry any 110V North American appliance. **Americans** and **Canadians** should buy an **adapter** (which changes the shape of the plug) and a **converter** (which changes the voltage; US$20). Don't make the mistake of using only an adapter, unless appliance instructions explicitly state otherwise. **New Zealanders** and **South Africans** (who both use 220V at home) and **Australians** (who use 240/250V) won't need a converter, but will need a set of adapters to use anything electrical.

TOILETRIES. Toothbrushes, towels, soap, talcum powder (to keep feet dry), razors, deodorant, tampons, and the all-important sunscreen and aloe vera are readily available at Greek pharmacies. Contact lenses can be expensive and difficult to obtain; bring enough extra pairs and solution for your entire trip. Also bring your **glasses** and a copy of your prescription in case you need emergency replacements. If you use heat-disinfection, you might switch temporarily to a chemical disinfection system if it's safe with your brand of lenses.

FIRST-AID KIT. For a basic first-aid kit, pack bandages, aspirin or other painkiller, antibiotic cream, a thermometer, a Swiss army knife, tweezers, sunscreen and aloe, moleskin for foot woes, decongestant, motion sickness remedy, diarrhea and upset-stomach medication, an antihistamine, insect repellent, and burn ointment.

FILM. Film and film developing in Greece can be expensive (about US$10 for a roll of 24 color exposures, though it is more reasonable in some places); try to bring enough film for your entire trip and definitely develop it at home. **Disposable cameras** may be a better option than expensive permanent ones. Airport security **X-rays** *can* fog film, so ask security to hand-inspect it or pack film in your carry-on luggage, since higher-intensity X-rays are used on checked luggage.

OTHER USEFUL ITEMS. For safety purposes, you should bring a **money belt** and a small **padlock.** Basic **outdoors equipment** (plastic water bottle, compass, waterproof matches, pocketknife, sunglasses, hat) may also prove useful. Quick repairs can be done on the road with a **needle and thread** or with **electrical tape** patches. Doing your **laundry** by hand (where it is allowed) is both cheaper and more convenient than doing it at a laundromat—bring detergent, a small rubber ball to stop up the sink, and string for a makeshift clothesline. **Other things** you're liable to forget: an umbrella; sealable **plastic bags** (for damp clothes, soap, food, shampoo, and other spillables); an **alarm clock;** safety pins; rubber bands; a flashlight; earplugs; garbage bags; and a small **calculator.**

IMPORTANT DOCUMENTS. Don't forget your passport, traveler's checks and receipts, ATM and/or credit cards, and adequate ID (see p. 39). If you need them, make sure you have a driver's license, your railpass, and travel insurance forms.

ACCOMMODATIONS

Relative to the US and elsewhere in Europe, accommodations in Greece and Cyprus remain a bargain. Budget accommodations in Greece are usually found in domatia (rooms to let), hostels, campgrounds, and budget hotels. **Prices** given in this guide are for the high season. Off-season prices (Oct.-May) are 20-40% cheaper than in high season. Prices may rise on weekends and are usually reduced for extended stays; when renting a room in a domatia, prices are completely negotiable, especially during the week and off season. This guide was researched during summer 2001, and prices may rise 10-20% in 2002. During high season (especially July and August), consider making **reservations**—you may not be able to find a room if you wait until you arrive on an island.

PLEASE CONSIDER, WHEN YOU'RE WIPING, THE POOR **TOILETS AND THEIR PIPING.** A word on Greek toilets. Some establishments have explicit signs explaining what their toilets can and cannot handle, but in general do not throw your toilet paper into the toilet. If a Greek bathroom smells a bit pungent, it is because dutiful users have been throwing their used paper into waste bins, rather than the toilet. Most Greek toilets are not designed to be able to flush toilet paper (and certainly not feminine products!) and some cannot handle more than urine, *ahem*. Check around whatever bathroom you are using to ascertain if there are indications of what that specific bathroom's guidelines are. For instance, some toilets have 4L and 10L flush options. Many have a manual flush, with which you can control the duration.

 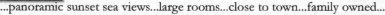

DOMATIA (ROOMS TO LET). Private homes all over Greece put up signs offering domatia (rooms to let). Domatia are perhaps the ideal budget accommodation: they are cheap and as safe as hotels, and allow you to stay in a Greek home and absorb some local culture. At more popular destinations, proprietors with rooms to let will greet your boat or bus, a practice which is theoretically illegal, but common. Always negotiate with domatia owners before settling a price. Before you accept an offer at portside, have a set destination in mind and look for people whose domatia are in the area you want. Many rooms offered at the port or bus stop are inexpensive; since the proprietors are in direct competition with the other domatia owners, good deals abound. Make owners pinpoint the location of their houses to make sure that "ten minutes away" means ten minutes on foot. Don't pay until you've seen the room.

While domatia may be run like small hotels in tourist towns, domatia in out of the way places can provide warm offers of coffee at night and friendly conversation. Prices are quite variable, but you can expect to pay about 4000-5000dr/€11.74-14.67 for a single (8000dr/€23.48 for a double) in the more remote areas of northern and central Greece, and 6000-8000dr/€17.61-23.48 for a single (8000-12,000dr/€23.48-35.22 for a double) on heavily traveled islands. Never pay more for domatia than you would for a hotel in town, and remember domatia owners can often be bargained down, *especially* when the house is not full. If in doubt, ask the tourist police: they'll usually set you up with a room and conduct the negotiations themselves. Most private rooms operate only in high season and are the best option for those arriving without reservations.

HOSTELS. Hostels—typically dorm-style accommodations, sometimes in single-sex large rooms with bunk beds—are not as prevalent in Greece as they are throughout the rest of Europe. Those that exist (usually in the most popular tourist destinations) are almost never affiliated with an international hosteling organization. Thus, a hosteling membership won't do you much good. In Greece, a bed in a hostel will average around 2000dr/€5.87. You can expect showers, sheets (free, a few euros, or several hundred drachma), and towels. Hostels are not regulated, so don't be surprised if some are less than clean or don't offer sheets and towels.

Some Greek hostels offer private rooms for families and couples. They sometimes have kitchens and utensils for your use, bike or moped rentals, storage areas, and laundry facilities. Some hostels have a maximum stay of five days. Greek **youth hostels** generally have fewer restrictions than those farther north in Europe. Many are open year-round and a few have midnight or 1am curfews (strictly enforced—you may be left in the streets if you come back too late). In summer, they usually stay open from 6-10am and 1pm-midnight (shorter hours in winter). It's advisable to book in advance in the summer at some of the more popular hostels in Athens, Santorini, Crete, or Nafplion.

HOTELS. The government oversees the construction and (seemingly random) classification of most hotels. Proprietors are permitted to charge 10% extra for stays of less than three nights, and 20% extra overall from July until September 15. Most D- and E-class hotels start at 5000dr/€14.67 for singles and 6000dr/€17.61 for doubles. A hotel with no singles may still put you in a room by yourself. More information is available from the **Hellenic Chamber of Hotels,** Stadiou 24, Athens 10564 (☎(01) 331 0022; fax 322 5449; grhotels@otenet.gr). If a hotel owner solicits you, offering to drive you, make sure you establish the location on a map: it may be miles away.

Late at night, in the off season, or in a large town, it's a buyer's market and bargaining is appropriate. As a security deposit, hotels often ask for your passport and return it when you leave. Don't give it to them—suggest that they take down your passport number or offer to pay up front. You can often leave your luggage in the reception area during the afternoon, though check-out is at 11am or noon.

To charge you more, hotel owners may offer you only their most expensive rooms, compel you to buy breakfast, squeeze three people into a hostel-size triple and charge each for a single, or quote a price for a room that includes breakfast and private shower and then charge extra for both. Don't pay until you've seen the room. If a room seems unreasonably expensive, stress that you don't want luxuries and they may give you a cheaper option. The **tourist police** are on your side. If a hotel flagrantly violates the prices shown by law at the front desk or behind each room's front door, or if you think you've been exploited, threaten to report the hotel to the tourist police. The threat alone often resolves "misunderstandings."

TRADITIONAL SETTLEMENTS. Several traditional villages and buildings have been preserved and restored by the government in an effort to maintain Greece's architectural heritage. The restoration of these Greek villages offers visitors a taste of small town Greek life and improves the regional economy. More than ten settlements host guests: **Makrynitsa** on Mt. Pelion (p. 191) and **Papingo-Zagorohoria** in Epirus (p. 217). There are 12 reconstructed towers in **Vathia, Mani** (p. 157), and an expensive hotel in the Castro in **Monemvasia** (p. 162). Doubles range 5000-10,000dr/€14.67-29.35; tourist offices make reservations and provide information.

CAMPING AND THE OUTDOORS

Camping in Greece releases you from monotonous hotel rooms and hostel regulations, and saves you a large amount of money. The Greek National Tourist Organization (GNTO, see p. 40) is primarily responsible for campgrounds; most official GNTO campgrounds have drinking water, lavatories, and electricity. Many campgrounds rent tents for a low fee (several hundred drachma or a few euros). The Hellenic Touring Club also runs a number of campgrounds, especially in northern Greece (ask at local tourist offices for more information). In addition, Greece has many private campgrounds, which may include pools, discos, mini-markets, and tavernas. **Prices** depend on the facilities; you'll usually pay roughly 1500dr/€4.40 per person, plus 1000dr/€2.93 per tent. GNTO campgrounds tend to be ritzier and more expensive (up to 1700dr/€5).

On many islands, some campers choose to bivouac on the beaches. While this is commonplace during July and August, when hotels are booked solid, it is **illegal.** Some police have been known to ignore sleeping bags in the sand, while others charge penalties from stern chastisement to stiff fines. Those who camp on beaches should always clean up after themselves. *Let's Go: Greece* doesn't recommend camping illegally. For more information on camping check out *Soft Paths*, by Bruce Hampton and David Cole (Stackpole Books, US$15); *Camping Your Way Through Europe*, by Carol Mickelsen (Affordable Press, US$15); and *Exploring Europe by RV*, by Dennis and Tina Jaffe (Globe Pequot, US$15).

CAMPING AND HIKING EQUIPMENT

WHAT TO BUY. Good camping equipment is both sturdy and light. It's also more expensive in Australia, New Zealand, and the UK than in North America.

Sleeping Bag: Good sleeping bags are rated by season. "Summer" means 30-40°F at night; "4-season" or "winter" often means below 0°F. Sleeping bags are made of **down** (warmer and lighter, but more expensive and miserable when wet) or **synthetic** (heavier, more durable, and warmer when wet). Although Greece is quite dry, a synthetic bag is a safer bet. Prices range from US$80-210 for a summer synthetic to US$250-300 for a down winter bag. Bring a **stuff sack** to keep your bag dry.

Tent: The best tents are free-standing (with their own frames and suspension systems), set up quickly, and only require staking in high winds. Low-slung dome tents are good for all-season camping, but are a bit heavy and hot in summer; good 2-person tents start at US$90, 4-person tents at US$300. Seal the seams of your tent with waterproofer and make sure it has a rain fly. For summer camping, **bivy-sacks,** one-man shelters that slide over a sleeping bag, allow sleeping under the Greek stars (US$120-200). A **battery-operated lantern,** a **plastic groundcloth,** and a **nylon tarp** might be useful.

Backpack: Internal-frame packs mold better to your back, keep a lower center of gravity, and flex adequately to allow you to hike difficult trails. **External-frame packs** are more comfortable for long hikes over even terrain, as they keep weight higher and distribute it more evenly. Make sure your pack has a strong, padded hip-belt to transfer weight to your legs. Any serious backpacking requires a pack of at least 4000 in^3 (16,000cc), plus 500 in^3 for sleeping bags in internal-frame packs. Sturdy backpacks cost anywhere from US$125-420—this is one area in which it doesn't pay to economize. Fill up any pack with something heavy and walk around the store with it to get a sense of how it distributes weight before buying it. Don't forget a **waterproof backpack cover.**

Boots: Be sure to wear hiking boots with good **ankle support.** They should fit snugly and comfortably over 1-2 pairs of wool socks and thin liner socks. Break in boots over several weeks first to spare yourself from painful and debilitating blisters.

Other Necessities: Synthetic layered clothes, like polypropylene, and a pile jacket will keep you warm when wet. A **"space blanket"** helps retain body heat and doubles as a groundcloth (US$5-15). Plastic **water bottles** are virtually shatter- and leak-proof. Bring **water-purification tablets** for when you can't boil water. Don't forget a **first-aid kit** (p. 48), **pocketknife, insect repellent, Calamine lotion, waterproof matches** or **lighter.**

WHERE TO BUY IT. Mail-order/online companies offer lower prices than many retail stores, but keep in mind that a visit to a local camping or outdoors store will give you a better sense of the look and weight of items.

WILDERNESS SAFETY

Stay warm, stay dry, and stay hydrated. Most life-threatening wilderness situations result from a breach of this rule. On any hike, however brief, pack enough equipment to keep you alive should disaster befall. This includes **raingear, hat** and **mittens,** a **first-aid kit,** a **reflector,** a **whistle, high energy food,** and extra **water.** Don't rely on **cotton** for warmth; it is useless when wet.

Check **weather forecasts** and pay attention to the skies when hiking. Weather patterns can change suddenly. Whenever possible, let someone—a friend, hostelowner, park ranger, hiking organization—know when and where you are hiking. Don't attempt a hike beyond your ability—you may be endangering your life.

ENVIRONMENTALLY RESPONSIBLE TOURISM. Leave no trace: keep your campsite at least 150 ft. (50m) from water; bury feces at least six inches (10cm) deep, above the high-water line and 150 feet or more from water supplies. Carry out your toilet paper with you; and keep your trash together and carry it with you until you reach the next trash can. For more information, contact one of the organizations listed below.

Earthwatch, 680 Mt. Auburn St., Box 403, Watertown, MA 02272 (☎(617) 776-0188; fax 926-8532; info@earthwatch.org; www.earthwatch.org).

Ecotourism Society, P.O. Box 755, North Bennington, VT 05257 (☎(802) 447-2121; ecomail@ecotourism.org; www.ecotourism.org/tesinfo.html).

EcoTravel Center: www.ecotour.com.

Tourism Concern, Stapleton House, 277-281 Holloway Rd., London N7 8HN, England (☎(0170) 753 3330; www.gn.apc.org/tourismconcern.)

KEEPING IN TOUCH
BY MAIL

Let's Go lists **post offices** in the **Practical Information** section for each city and most towns. Post offices in Greece are generally open Monday to Friday 7:30am to 2pm, although certain branches may extend their hours into the afternoon and evening, as well as into the weekend.

SENDING MAIL TO GREECE

Envelopes should be marked "air mail" or "par avion." Most countries offer both an airmail and express mail option for sending mail to Greece. For exact prices per weight, see the websites for each post office. In addition to the standard postage system whose rates are listed below, **Federal Express** (Australia ☎ 13 26 10; US and Canada ☎ (800) 247-4747; New Zealand ☎ 0800 73 33 39; UK ☎ 0800 12 38 00) handles express mail services from most home countries to Greece.

Australia: Allow 5-7 days for regular **airmail** to Greece. Postcards and letters up to 50g cost AUS$1.50; packages up to 0.5kg AUS$13, up to 2kg AUS$46. **EMS** can get a letter to Greece in 2-3 days for AUS$32. www.auspost.com.au/pac.

Canada: Allow 7-10 days for regular **airmail** to Greece. Postcards and letters up to 20g cost CDN$1.05; packages up to 0.5kg CDN$10.20, up to 2kg CDN$34. www.canada-post.ca/CPC2/common/rates/ratesgen.html#international.

Ireland: Allow 3-4 days for regular **airmail** to Greece. Postcards and letters up to 25g cost IR£0.41/€0.52. Add IR£3.30/€4.19 for **Swiftpost International.** www.anpost.ie.

New Zealand: Allow 6-10 days for regular **airmail** to Greece. Postcards NZ$1.50. Letters up to 20g cost NZ$2; small parcels up to 0.5kg NZ$16.50, up to 2kg NZ$53. www.nzpost.co.nz/nzpost/inrates.

UK: Allow 3 days for **airmail** to Greece. Letters up to 20g cost UK£0.36; packages up to 0.5kg UK£2.67, up to 2kg UK£9.42. **UK Swiftair** delivers letters a day faster for UK£2.85 more. www.royalmail.co.uk/calculator.

US: Allow 4-10 days for regular **airmail** to Greece. Postcards and aerogrammes cost US$0.70; letters under 1 oz. US$1. Packages under 1 lb. cost US$8.70; larger packages cost a variable amount (around US$15). **US Express Mail** takes 2-3 days and costs US$12.25 for 0.5 lb., US$16 for 1 lb. http://ircalc.usps.gov.

Federal Express: FedEx can get a letter from New York to Athens in 2 days for a whopping US$31; rates from non-US locations are prohibitively expensive. Australia ☎ 13 26 10; US and Canada ☎ (800) 247-4747; New Zealand ☎ (0800) 73 33 39; UK ☎ (0800) 12 38 00; Greece ☎ (01) 994 3200. www.fedex.com.

Surface mail: This is by far the cheapest and **slowest** way to send mail. It takes 1-3 months to cross the Atlantic and 2-4 to cross the Pacific—appropriate for sending large quantities of items you won't need to see for a while. When ordering books and materials from abroad, always include 1-2 **International Reply Coupons (IRCs)** as a way of providing the postage to cover delivery. IRCs (US$1.05) should be available from your local post office and those abroad.

RECEIVING MAIL IN GREECE

There are several ways to arrange pick-up of letters sent to you by friends and relatives while you are abroad. Mail can be sent to Greece through **Poste Restante** (the international phrase for General Delivery) to almost any city or town with a post office. Address Poste Restante letters to:

John Flynn
Corfu Town Post Office
Corfu, Greece 8900
POSTE RESTANTE

The mail will go to a special desk in the central post office, unless you specify another post office. As a rule, it is best to use the largest post office in the area, because mail may be sent there regardless of what is written on the envelope. When possible, it is usually safer and quicker (though much pricier) to send mail express or registered. When picking up your mail, bring a form of **photo ID**, preferably a passport. There is no surcharge for picking up Poste Restante mail in Greece. The **Practical Information** of each city and town contains information for post office listings.

American Express travel offices throughout the world will act as a mail service for cardholders if you contact them in advance. Under this free **Client Letter Service,** they will hold mail for up to 30 days and forward upon request. Address the letter in the same way shown above. Some offices will offer these services to non-cardholders (especially those who have purchased AmEx travelers cheques), but you must call ahead. *Let's Go* lists AmEx office locations in **Practical Information** when available. A complete list is available free from AmEx (US ☎ (800) 528-4800).

SENDING MAIL HOME FROM GREECE

Aerogrammes, printed sheets that fold into envelopes and travel via airmail, are available at post offices. You should mark letter both "par avion" and "air mail." Most post offices will charge exorbitant fees or simply refuse to send aerogrammes with enclosures. Airmail from Greece can take anywhere from 1-2 weeks, although times are much more unpredictable from smaller towns. Sending a postcard via airmail to an international destination costs 170dr/€0.50 within Europe and 200dr/€0.59 to the US. Domestically, postcards require 120dr/€0.35. To send a letter (up to 50g) via airmail to another European country costs 200dr/€0.59 and to anywhere else in the world, 250dr/€0.73 (up to 150g). For **express** mail service, ask for *katepeegon;* to **register** a letter, *systemeno;* for **air mail,** *aeroporikos,* and write "air mail" on the envelope.

BY TELEPHONE

CALLING HOME FROM GREECE

A **calling card** is probably your cheapest bet. **To obtain a calling card** from your national telecommunications service before leaving home, contact the appropriate company listed below (using the numbers in the first column). To **call home with a calling card,** contact the operator for your service provider in Greece by dialing the appropriate toll-free access number (listed below in the second column).

COMPANY	TO OBTAIN A CARD, DIAL:	TO CALL ABROAD, DIAL:
AT&T (US)	800-222-0300	00 800 13 11
British Telecom Direct	800 34 51 44	00 800 44 11
Canada Direct	800-668-6878	00 800 16 11
Ireland Direct	800 40 00 00	155 11 74
MCI (US)	800-444-3333	00 800 12 11
Sprint (US)	800-877-4646	00 900 14 11

All pay phones in Greece are card-operated, and you will need to purchase a card to operate the phone, even if you are going to use your own calling card to place the call (see **Calling Within Greece,** below). Although incredibly convenient, in-room hotel calls invariably include an arbitrary and sky-high surcharge (as much as US$10). For instructions on dialing direct, see **Placing International Calls.**

In an emergency, an expensive alternative to using a calling card is placing a **collect call** through an international operator. An English-speaking operator from your home nation can be reached by dialing the appropriate service provider listed above, and they will typically place a collect call even if you don't possess one of their phone cards.

CALLING WITHIN GREECE

The only way to use the phone in Greece is with a **prepaid phone card.** You can buy the cards at street-side kiosks and *peripteros* in denominations of 1000, 3000, and 5000dr. The time is measured in minutes or talk units; a 1000dr/€2.93 card will buy you 100 units, roughly equal to 30min. of local calling within Greece and 5-10min. long-distance within Greece or internationally. The Greek phone service is known as the **OTE** (Organismos Tiliepikinonion tis Elladhos); there are local offices in most towns, and cardphones are often clustered outside.

PLACING INTERNATIONAL CALLS. To call Greece from home or to place an international call from Greece, dial:

1. The **international dialing prefix.** To dial out of **Greece,** the **Republic of Ireland, New Zealand,** or the **UK,** 00; **Australia,** dial 0011; **Canada** or the **US,** 011; **South Africa,** 09.
2. The **country code** of the country you want to call. To call **Greece,** 30; **Australia,** dial 61; **Canada** or the **US,** 1; the **Republic of Ireland,** 353; **New Zealand,** 64; **South Africa,** 27; the **UK,** 44.
3. The **city or area code.** *Let's Go* lists the phone codes for cities and towns in Greece across from the city or town name, alongside the following icon: ■. If the first digit is a zero (e.g., 031 for Thessaloniki), omit it when calling from abroad (e.g., dial 011 30 31 from Canada to reach Thessaloniki).
4. The **local number.**

A few **warnings** about using card phones: type the number slowly; Greece's quirky phones get confused if you type fast. Don't remove the card until the phone tells you to do so or you will lose your remaining credit. Finally, do not make long calls from card phones, or a long line of irate people is likely to form behind you.

As of January 1, 2002, phone codes throughout Greece will change. Most will have an additional "0" at the end of the local code. At press time in summer of 2001 the specifics of these changes were not yet available; contact the Greek National Tourist Organization (GNTO, known as the EOT in Greece, see p. 40) for further information.

TIME DIFFERENCES

TIME ZONES					
Seattle San Francisco Los Angeles	Toronto New York Ottawa	London (GMT)	**Athens** Istanbul Nicosia	Hong Kong Manila Singapore	Sydney Canberra Melbourne
4am	7am	noon	2pm	8pm	10pm

BY EMAIL AND INTERNET

The availability of the Internet in Greece is rapidly expanding. In all big cities, in most small cities and large towns, and on many islands, you can find Internet access. Expect to pay between 1000-2000dr/€2.93-5.87 per hour. **Cybercafe Guide** (www.cyberiacafe.net/cyberia/guide/ccafe.htm) can help you find cybercafes in Greece. Travelers with laptops can call an Internet service provider via a **modem.** Long-distance phone cards specifically intended for such calls can defray normally high phone charges; check with your long-distance phone provider to see if it offers this option. **Internet cafes** and the occasional free Internet terminal at a public library or university are listed in the **Orientation and Practical Information** sections of major cities. Free, web-based email accounts have become popular because of their easy accessibility. Providers include Hotmail (www.hotmail.com), Operamail (www.operamail.com), and OneBox (www.onebox.com). Many free email providers are funded by advertising and some may require subscribers to fill out a questionnaire. Almost every search engine has an affiliated free email service.

GETTING THERE

BY PLANE

When it comes to airfare, a little effort can save you a bundle. If your plans are flexible enough to deal with the restrictions, courier fares are the cheapest. Tickets bought from consolidators and standby seating are also good deals, but last-minute specials, airfare wars, and charter flights often beat these fares. The key is to hunt around, to be flexible, and to persistently ask about discounts. Students, seniors, and those under 26 should never pay full price for a ticket. Read up on discount airfare in *The Worldwide Guide to Cheap Airfare*, by Michael McColl (Insider Publications, US$15) or *Discount Airfares: The Insider's Guide*, by George Hobart (Priceless Publications, US$14); and see **Other Resources** (p. 77).

Airfares to Greece peak between **June** and **September;** holidays are also expensive. Midweek (M-Th morning) round-trip flights run US$40-50 cheaper than weekend flights, but are generally more crowded and less likely to permit frequent-flier upgrades. Flights between capitals or regional hubs (particularly Athens and Thessaloniki) will offer the cheapest fares. Traveling with an **"open return" ticket** (arriving in and departing from different cities, e.g. London-Athens and Thessaloniki-London) is pricier than fixing a return date when buying the ticket.

BUDGET AND STUDENT TRAVEL AGENCIES

A knowledgeable agent specializing in flights to Greece can make your life easy and help you save, too, but agents may not spend the time to find you the lowest possible fare—they get paid on commission. Students and under-26ers holding **ISIC and IYTC cards** (see **Identification,** p. 39), respectively, qualify for big discounts from student travel agencies. Most flights from budget agencies are on major airlines, but in peak season some may sell seats on less reliable chartered aircraft.

usit World (www.usitworld.com). Over 50 usit campus branches in the UK (www.usitcampus.co.uk), including 52 Grosvenor Gardens, **London** SW1W 0AG (☎(0870) 240 1010); **Manchester** (☎(0161) 273 1721); and **Edinburgh** (☎(0131) 668 3303). Nearly 20 **usit Now** offices in Ireland, including 19-21 Aston Quay, O'Connell Bridge, **Dublin** 2 (☎(01) 602 1600; www.usitnow.ie), and **Belfast** (☎(02890) 327 111; www.usitnow.com). There is an office in **Athens** Ethinikis Antistaseos 31, 18531 Pireaus (☎+30 1 41 32 950; fax 30 1 41 32 901; etospir@usitetos.gr; www.usitetos.gr; open M-F 9 am-5pm, Sa 10 am-2pm). Offices also in Auckland, Brussels, Frankfurt, Johannesburg, Lisbon, Luxembourg, Madrid, Paris, Sofia, and Warsaw.

Council Travel (www.counciltravel.com). Countless US offices, including branches in Atlanta, Boston, Chicago, L.A., New York, San Francisco, Seattle, and Washington, D.C. Check the website or call 800-2-COUNCIL (226-8624) for the office nearest you.

CTS Travel, 44 Goodge St., **London** W1T 2AD (☎0207 636 0031; fax 0207 637 5328; ctsinfo@ctstravel.co.uk).

STA Travel, 7890 S. Hardy Dr., Ste. 110, Tempe AZ 85284 (24hr. reservations and info ☎(800) 777-0112; fax 480-592-0876; www.sta-travel.com). A student and youth travel organization with countless offices worldwide (check their website for a listing of all their offices), including US offices in Boston, Chicago, L.A., New York, San Francisco, Seattle, and Washington, D.C. Ticket booking, travel insurance, railpasses, and more. In the UK, walk-in office 11 Goodge St., **London** W1T 2PF or call (0870) 160-6070. In New Zealand, 10 High St., **Auckland** (☎09 309 0458). In Australia, 366 Lygon St., **Melbourne** Vic 3053 (☎03 9349 4344).

Student Universe, 545 Fifth Ave., Suite 640, New York, NY 10017 (toll-free customer service ☎(800) 272-9676, outside the US 212-986-8420; help@studentuniverse.com; www.studentuniverse.com), is an online student travel service offering discount ticket booking, travel insurance, railpasses, destination guides, and much more. Customer service line open M-F 9am-8pm and Sa noon-5pm EST.

Travel CUTS (Canadian Universities Travel Services Limited), 187 College St., **Toronto,** ON M5T 1P7 (☎(416) 979-2406; fax 979-8167; www.travelcuts.com). Also in the UK, 295-A Regent St., **London** W1R 7YA (☎(020) 7255 1944).

Wasteels, Skoubogade 6, 1158 **Copenhagen** K., (☎3314-4633 fax 7630-0865; www.wasteels.dk/uk). A huge chain with 165 locations across Europe. Sells Wasteels BIJ tickets discounted 30-45% off regular fare, 2nd-class international point-to-point train tickets with unlimited stopovers for those under 26 (sold only in Europe).

COMMERCIAL AIRLINES

FLIGHT PLANNING ON THE INTERNET. The web is a great place to look for travel bargain. Many airline sites offer special last-minute deals on the web. Check out **www.greeceflights.com; www.easyjet.com** lists cheap London-Athens flights; see **www.studentuniverse.com** should you happen to be a student traveler. Other sites do the legwork and compile the deals for you—www.bestfares.com, www.onetravel.com, www.lowestfare.com, and www.travelzoo.com. **STA Travel** (www.sta-travel.com) and **Council Travel** (www.counciltravel.com) provide quotes on student tickets, while **Expedia** (www.expedia.com) and **Travelocity** (www.travelocity.com) offer full travel services. **Priceline** (www.priceline.com) lets you specify a price, and obligates you to buy any ticket that meets or beats it; expect antisocial hours and odd routes. **Skyauction** (www.skyauction.com) lets you bid on both last-minute and advance-purchase tickets. One last note—to protect yourself, make sure that the site uses a secure server before handing over any credit card details.

The commercial airlines' lowest regular offer is the **APEX** (Advance Purchase Excursion) fare, which provides confirmed reservations and allows "open-jaw" tickets. Generally, reservations must be made seven to 21 days ahead of departure, with seven- to 14-day minimum-stay and up to 90-day maximum-stay restrictions. These fares carry hefty cancellation and change penalties (fees rise in summer). Book peak-season APEX fares early; by May you will have a hard time getting your desired departure date. It may be easier to purchase a ticket through a budget agency or online service (see above), in order to get the best deal on airfare. APEX fares from the commercial airlines will not be the cheapest ones to Greece, but they will give you an idea of the fares out there.

Olympic Airways (in Greece Sygrou 96, Athens 11747, ☎+30 01 926 7221, fax 926 7858, www.olympic-airways.gr), the national Greek airline, flies to and within Greece. Domestic flights in particular can be very inexpensive, saving time and money for those traveling long distances within Greece. In US 645 Fifth Ave., New York, NY 10022, ☎(800) 223-1226.

TRAVELING FROM NORTH AMERICA

Basic round-trip fares to Western Europe range from roughly US$200-750: to Frankfurt US$300-750; London US$200-600; Paris US$250-700. Standard commercial carriers like American (☎(800) 433-7300; www.aa.com) and United (☎(800) 241-6522; www.ual.com) will probably offer the most convenient flights, but they may not be the cheapest, unless you manage to grab a special promotion or airfare-war ticket. You might find flying one of the following airlines a better deal, if any of their limited departure points is convenient for you.

Icelandair: ☎(800) 223-5500; www.icelandair.com. Stopovers in Iceland for no extra cost on most transatlantic flights. Connections to Athens via Frankfurt and other European destinations. New York to Frankfurt May-Sept. US$500-730; Oct.-May US$390-$450. For last-minute offers, subscribe to their email Lucky Fares.

Finnair: ☎(800) 950-5000; www.us.finnair.com. Cheap round-trips from San Francisco, New York, and Toronto to Helsinki; connections throughout Europe.

Virgin Atlantic: ☎(800) 862-8621, www.virgin-atlantic.com. Connections to Athens via London from Boston, Chicago, New York, San Francisco, and other US cities.

TRAVELING FROM THE UK & IRELAND

Because of the myriad carriers flying from the British Isles to the continent, we only include discount airlines or those with cheap specials here. The **Air Travel Advisory Bureau** in London (☎020 7636 5000; www.atab.co.uk) provides referrals to travel agencies and consolidators that offer discounted airfares out of the UK.

easyJet: UK ☎0870 600 00 00; www.easyjet.com. London to Athens (UK£142). Online tickets.

Virgin Atlantic: ☎01293 747 74; www.virgin-atlantic.com. London to Athens M-Sa (UK£170-400).

TRAVELING FROM AUSTRALIA & NEW ZEALAND

Air New Zealand: New Zealand ☎0800 35 22 66; www.airnz.co.nz. Auckland to Athens.

Singapore Air: Australia ☎13 10 11, New Zealand ☎0800 808 909; www.singaporeair.com. Flies from Auckland, Sydney, Melbourne, and Perth to Athens.

Thai Airways: Australia ☎1300 65 19 60, New Zealand ☎09 377 38 86; www.thaiair.com. Auckland, Sydney, and Melbourne to Athens.

TRAVELING FROM SOUTH AFRICA

Air France: ☎011 880 80 40; www.airfrance.com. Johannesburg to Athens.

British Airways: ☎0860 011 747; www.british-airways.com/regional/sa. Cape Town and Johannesburg to Athens from ZAR3400.

Lufthansa: ☎011 484 47 11; www.lufthansa.co.za. From Cape Town, Durban, and Johannesburg to Athens and Thessaloniki.

Virgin Atlantic: ☎011 340 34 00; www.virgin-atlantic.co.za. Flies to Athens from both Cape Town and Johannesburg.

OTHER CHEAP ALTERNATIVES

TICKET CONSOLIDATORS. Ticket consolidators, or **"bucket shops,"** buy unsold tickets in bulk from commercial airlines and sell them at discounted rates. Look in the Sunday travel section of any major newspaper (such as the *New York Times* or the *Sydney Morning Herald*) for tiny ads from many bucket shops. Call quickly, as availability is typically extremely limited. Not all bucket shops are reliable, so insist on a receipt that gives full details of restrictions, refunds, and tickets, and pay by credit card (in spite of the 2-5% fee) so you can stop payment if you never receive your tickets. For more info, see www.travellibrary.com/air-travel/consolidators.html or pick up Kelly Monaghan's *Air Travel's Bargain Basement* (Intrepid Traveler, US$8).

CHARTER FLIGHTS. Charters are flights a tour operator contracts with an airline to fly extra loads of passengers during peak season. Charter flights fly less frequently than major airlines, make refunds particularly difficult, and are almost always fully booked. Schedules and itineraries may also change or be canceled at the last moment (as late as 48hr. before the trip, and without a full refund), and check-in, boarding, and baggage claim are often much slower. **Travelers Advantage,** Stamford, CT (☎(877) 259-2691); www.travelersadvantage.com; US$60 annual fee includes discounts, newsletters, and cheap flight directories) specializes in European travel and tour packages.

AIR COURIER FLIGHTS. Couriers help transport cargo on international flights by guaranteeing delivery of the baggage claim slips from the company to a representative overseas. Generally, couriers must travel light (carry-ons only) and deal with complex restrictions on their flight. Most flights are round-trip only with short fixed-length stays (usually one week) and a limit of a single ticket per issue. Generally, you must be over 21 (in some cases 18), have a valid passport, and procure your own visa, if necessary.

TRAVELING FROM NORTH AMERICA

Round-trip courier fares from the US to Western Europe run about US$200-500. Most flights leave from New York, Los Angeles, San Francisco, or Miami in the US; and from Montreal, Toronto, or Vancouver in Canada. Some organizations provide members with lists of opportunities and courier brokers worldwide for an annual fee (typically US$50-60). Alternatively, you can contact a courier broker directly; most charge registration fees, but a few don't. Prices quoted are round-trip.

International Association of Air Travel Couriers (IAATC), 220 South Dixie Highway #3, PO Box 1349, Lake Worth, FL 33460 (☎(561) 582-8320; fax 582-1581; www.courier.org). From 9 North American cities to Western European cities. One-year US$45-50.

Global Courier Travel, PO Box 3051, Nederland, CO 80466 (www.globalcouriertravel.com). Searchable online database. 6 departure points in the US and Canada to Athens. One-year US$40, 2 people US$55.

STANDBY FLIGHTS. Companies that specialize in standby flights don't sell tickets but the promise that you will get to your destination (or near your destination) within a certain window of time (anywhere from 1 to 5 days). One established standby company in the US is **Airhitch,** 2641 Broadway, 3rd fl., New York, NY 10025 (☎(800) 326-2009; fax 864-5489; www.airhitch.org) and Los Angeles, CA (☎(888) 247-4482), which offers one-way flights to Europe from the Northeast (US$165), West Coast and Northwest (US$233), Midwest (US$199), and Southeast (US$177). Intracontinental connecting flights within the US or Europe cost US$79-139. Airhitch has European offices in Paris (☎+33 (01) 47 00 16 30) and Amsterdam (☎+31 (20) 626 32 20). Carefully read agreements with any company offering standby flights, as tricky fine print can leave you in the lurch.

BY FERRY

Ferry travel is a popular way to get to and travel within Greece and Cyprus; their ports can be reached from a seemingly unlimited number of points, and finding a boat agency to facilitate your trip should not be difficult. Be warned that **ferries run on irregular schedules.** A few websites, like www.gptnet.com and www.ferries.fr, have tried to keep updated schedules online and are worth a try. You should try to take a look at a schedule as close to your departure as possible; you can usually find one at a tourist office or posted at the dock. That said, you should also make reservations, and check in at *least* 2hr. in advance; late boarders may find their seats gone. If you sleep on deck, bring warm clothes and a sleeping bag. Bicycles travel free, but motorcycles will have an additional charge. Don't forget motion sickness medication, toilet paper, and a hand towel. Bring food and drink to avoid high prices on board.

The major ports of departure from Italy to Greece are Ancona and Brindisi, on the southeast coast of Italy. Bari, Otranto, and Venice also have a few connections. For schedules from Greece to Italy, see Patras (p. 129), Kephalonia (p. 279), Corfu (p. 261), or Igoumenitsa (p. 206). The Brindisi-Patras route (17hr.) is heavily traveled; deck passage to Brindisi is 8000-10,000dr/€23.48-29.35, including port tax. The travel agency **Tsimaras** (☎03 061 622 602), previously Strintzis Tours, on Othonos Amalias 14 in Patras, can provide information on ferries to Italy. Ferries also run from Greece to various points on the Turkish coast. Trips from Greek islands that nearly touch the mainland are brief and fairly inexpensive. For prices, schedules, and more information, see **Turkish Daytrips** (p. 552).

BY BUS AND TRAIN

BY BUS. Although trains and railpasses are extremely popular in most of Europe, buses are a sometimes cheaper alternative. Unfortunately, there are almost no buses running directly from any European city to Greece. **Busabout,** 258 Vauxhall Bridge Rd., London SW1V 1BS, is one of the very few European bus lines that also runs to Greece (☎0171 950 1661; fax (0) 171 950 1662; info@busabout.co.uk; www.busabout.com). Only truly useful if you plan to travel elsewhere in Europe, there are five interconnecting bus circuits covering 60 cities and towns, with **"Add-ons"** that extend to Greece (via Italy) and environs. Standard/student passes are valid for times ranging from 15 days (US$249, UK£169) up to unlimited (US$1089, UK£699). "Add-ons" to **Patras** go through **Venice** (US$45, UK£29) and **Brindisi** (US$29, UK£17). The **Hellenic Railways Organization (OSE)** runs buses to **Athens** from **Sofia** (13hr.; 1 per day 8:30am; one-way 14,000dr/€41.09, round-trip 25,500dr/€74.83), and **Tirana** (17hr.; 1 per day 8am; one-way 12,000dr/€35.22, round-trip 21,500dr/€63.10). These buses are expensive and slow.

BY TRAIN. Greece is served by a number of international train routes that connect Athens, Thessaloniki, and Larisa to most European cities. **Eurail** passes are valid in Greece, and may be a useful purchase if you plan to visit one of the 17 other European countries in which they are valid. Fifteen-day youth passes (ages 25 and under) US$388; adults US$554. Eurail passes are available through travel agents, student travel agencies like STA and Council (see p. 61), and **Rail Europe,** 500 Mamaroneck Ave., Harrison, NY 10528 (US ☎(888) 382-7245, fax (800) 432-1329; Canada ☎(800) 361-7245, fax (905) 602-4198; UK ☎(0990) 84 88 48; www.raileurope.com). Unfortunately, the Greek rail system is one of Europe's most antiquated and least efficient—for example, a trip from Vienna to Athens takes at least 3 days. For information on specific routes see the **OSE** website at www.osenet.gr.

GETTING AROUND

BY FERRY AND HYDROFOIL

Widespread but unpredictable, cheap but slow, ferries will form the backbone of your travel-adventure tales. Be prepared to arrive at the dock 1-2 hours before departure for a decent seat (though a 5min.-early and a 3hr.-late departure are both real possibilities) and bring a good book, a bottle of water, food to last you the trip (snack bars are pricey), and a **windbreaker** (you'll want to wander the deck at sea). For short distances, indoor seats fill up fast; bring a hat to shield you from the sun on upper decks. For longer distances, bring **sleeping bags** or upgrade to a **cabin;** though the latter is usually expensive and disappointing, the former can be paired with insulated mats for starry sea nights on the deck.

MAKING SENSE OF FERRIES. The key to making good use of ferries is understanding ferry routes and planning your trip accordingly. Most ferries, rather than shuffling back and forth between two destinations, trace a four- or five- port route. Most ferry companies will allow you to buy your round-trip ticket **"split,"** meaning that you can ride the Piraeus-Syros-Tinos-Mykonos ferry from Piraeus to Syros, get off, get back on when the same ferry passes Syros several days later, proceed to Tinos, and so on. Besides convenience, traveling along ferry routes gives you a Greek (rather than guidebook) grouping of islands, based on commuters, local traffic, trade, and historical connections. Remember that geographic proximity is **no guarantee** that you'll be able to get to one island from another. For example, there is no ferry service from Skyros to the rest of the Sporades, nor is there service from Skyros to the NE Aegean, or from the Cyclades to the Dodecanese.

Understanding ferry routes will also help you make sense of discrepancies in ticket prices (going to Hydra from Athens via Poros and Aegina is more expensive than simply going via Poros) and travel times. **Ferry schedules,** generally available for the region from the ferry companies or posted at the port police *(limenarcheio)*, are published weekly and give the departure times, routes, and names of each departing ferry. As particular ferries, even within companies, vary widely in quality, local travelers pay close attention to the names. Ask around or check on the web (www.ferries.gr) for tips, ferry schedules, and prices.

DOLPHIN RIDES. Twice the price and twice the speed, **Flying Dolphins** provide extensive, standardized, and sanitized human transport (no cars) between islands; offices and services are listed in the **Transportation** sections of all towns. However, traveling by Dolphin is like traveling by seaborne airplane: passengers are assigned seats and required to stay in the climate-controlled cabin for the duration of the trip, which may be less than ideal for the easily seasick. If you have the money to spare and want to minimize travel time, Dolphins are convenient enough and they run like clockwork; otherwise, why sail the Aegean in a craft that won't let you get salt on your fingers and wind in your hair?

BY BUS

Spending time in Greece means traveling by bus. Service is extensive and fares are cheap. On major highways, buses tend to be more modern and efficient than in the mountainous areas of the Peloponnese or northern Greece. The **OSE** (see **By Train,** p. 66) offers limited bus service from a few cities. Unless you're sticking close to train routes, **KTEL** bus service should be sufficient.

Always check with an official source about scheduled departures; posted schedules are often outdated, and all services are curtailed significantly on Saturday and Sunday; major holidays run on Sunday schedules. The English-language weekly newspaper *Athens News* prints Athens bus schedules, and like almost everything else, they are available online (www.ktel.org). Try to arrive at least 10min. ahead of time, as Greek buses have a habit of leaving early. In major cities, KTEL bus lines may have different stations for different destinations, and schedules generally refer to **endpoints** ("the bus leaves Kalloni at three and arrives in Mytilini at four") with no mention of the numerous stops in between. In villages, a cafe or *zaccharoplasteio* (sweet-shop) often serves as the bus station, and you must ask the proprietor for a schedule.

ALL ABOARD! Ask the **conductor** before entering the bus whether it's going to your destination (the signs on the front are often misleading or wrong), and ask to be warned when you get there. If stowing bags underneath the bus, make sure they're in the compartment for your destination (conductors take great pride in packing the bus for easy unloading, and may refuse to open the "final destination" compartment at the "halfway" stop). If the bus passes your stop, stand up and yell **"Stasi!"** (STASH). On the road, stand near a Stasi sign to pick up an intercity bus. KTEL buses are generally **green** or occasionally **orange,** while intercity buses are usually **blue.** For long-distance rides, you should buy your ticket beforehand in the office (if you don't, you may have to stand throughout the journey). Prices vary by the duration of the trip; short hops cost only a few hundred drachma, while longer rides cost thousands. For shorter trips, pay the conductor after you have boarded; reasonably close change is expected. Some lines discount round-trip fares by 20%.

BY PLANE OR TRAIN

BY PLANE. In Greece, **Olympic Airways** can be found in **Athens,** Syngrou 96-100, 11741 Athens (☎(01) 926 91 11), in **Thessaloniki,** Koundouritou 3, Thessaloniki 54101 (☎(031) 26 01 21), and in many large cities and islands. In the US, contact 645 Fifth Ave., New York, NY 10022 (☎(212) 735-0200; fax (212) 735-0212). In England, contact 11 Conduit St., **London** W1R OLP (☎(870) 606 04 60; fax (207) 629 98 91). The Olympic Airways website (www.olympic-airways.com) lists information for every office around the globe. For further flight information within Greece, check regional **Practical Information** listings of airports, destinations, and prices, or get an Olympic Airways brochure at any Olympic office.

In recent years, Olympic's domestic *(esoteriko)* service has increased appreciably; from Athens, an hour's flight (US$60-90) can get you to almost any island in Greece. Even in low season, more remote destinations (Limnos, Hios) are serviced several times weekly, while more developed areas (Thessaloniki, Crete) can have several flights per day. Though somewhat frivolous for short distances, fairly cheap flights seem like more of a deal if they exempt you from overnight ferry rides and potential cost of food and beds on board (e.g., the 22hr. ferry ride from Limnos to Piraeus). Make sure to reserve your tickets one week in advance.

BY TRAIN. Although trains can be cheaper than buses, they run less frequently and take longer: as a rule, Greece has one of Europe's slowest train services. If you're lucky, you may come across a new, air-conditioned, intercity train, which is a different entity altogether: although they are slightly more expensive and rare, they are worth the price. **Eurail** passes are valid on Greek trains. **OSE** (www.osenet.gr) connects Athens to major Greek cities (like Volos and Thessaloniki). For schedules and prices in Greece, dial 145 or 147. Lines do not go to the west coast, and they are rarely useful for remote areas or archaeological sites. Bring food and a water bottle, because the on-board cafe can be pricey, and the water undrinkable. Lock your compartment and keep valuables on your person.

BY MOPED

BE CAREFUL. A word of caution about travel by moped: **most tourist-related accidents each year occur on mopeds.** Regardless of your experience driving a moped, winding, often poorly maintained mountain roads and reckless drivers make driving a moped hazardous. Always wear a helmet, and never ride with a backpack.

Motorbiking is a popular way of touring Greece's winding roads. Although renting wheels is the best and most cost efficient way to assert your independence from unreliable or inconvenient public transportation systems, you should be aware that they can be uncomfortable for long distances, dangerous in the rain, and unpredictable on rough roads. On many islands, navigable roads suddenly turn into tiny trails that can only be walked. Furthermore, moped rental shop owners often loosen the front brakes on the bikes to discourage riders from using them (relying on the front brakes makes accidents more likely), so use the back brakes. If you've never driven a moped before, a cliffside road is not the place to learn.

RENTING. Shops renting mopeds are everywhere, and most require only some sort of drivers' license (a Greek license or International Driving Permit is not necessary). Bike quality, speed of service in case of breakdown, and prices for longer periods vary drastically, but you should expect to pay at least 4000dr/€11.74 per day for a 50cc scooter, the cheapest bike with the power to tackle steep mountain roads. More powerful bikes cost 20-30% more and usually require a Greek motorcycle license. Many agencies will request your passport as a deposit, but it's wiser just to settle up in advance; if they have your passport and you have an accident or mechanical failure, they may refuse to return it until you pay for repairs. Ask before renting if the price quote includes tax, insurance, and a full tank of gas, or you may pay several hundred unexpected drachmas. Information on local moped rentals is in the **Practical Information** section for individual cities and towns.

BY CAR

Cars are a luxury in Greece, a country where public transportation is nonexistent after 7pm. Ferries will take you island-hopping if you pay a transport fee for the car. Drivers must be comfortable with a standard transmission, winding mountain roads, reckless drivers (especially in Athens), and the Greek alphabet—signs in Greek appear roughly 100m before the transliterated versions. Driving can be a cheaper alternative to trains and buses for groups of travelers, and is especially useful for exploring remote villages in northern Greece, though having a car might detract from the traveling experience.

Agencies may quote low daily rates that exclude the 20% tax and **Collision Damage Waiver (CDW)** insurance (2500dr/€7.34 per day). Without CDW, the driver is responsible for the first 15,000dr/€44.02 worth of damage if theft or accident is not the driver's fault, and the full amount otherwise. Expect to pay 16,000-18,000dr/€46.96-52.82 per day for a rental. Some places quote lower rates but hit you with hidden charges, such as exorbitant refueling bills if you come back with less than a full tank, 1.50 to 2.50dr per kilometer drop-off or special charge, or 100km per day minimum mileage. Most companies won't let you drive the car outside Greece.

Foreign drivers are required to have an **International Driving Permit** and an **International Insurance Certificate** to drive in Greece (see below). The **Automobile and Touring Club of Greece (ELPA)**, Messogion 395, Athens 11527 (☎ (01) 606 88 00), provides assistance and offers reciprocal membership to foreign auto club members. They also have 24hr. emergency road assistance (☎104) and an information line (☎174 in Athens, (01) 60 68 838 elsewhere in Greece; open M-F 7am-3pm). More information can be found at www.fia.com/tourisme/infoclub/greece.htm.

Car rental in Europe is available through the following agencies:

Auto Europe, 39 Commercial St., P.O. Box 7006, Portland, ME 04112 (US and Canada ☎ (888) 223-5555 or (207) 842-2000; fax (207) 842-2222; www.autoeurope.com).

Avis (US and Canada ☎(800) 331-1084; UK ☎(0990) 90 05 00; Australia ☎(800) 22 55 33; New Zealand ☎(0800) 65 51 11; www.avis.com).

Budget (US and Canada ☎(800) 527-0700; UK ☎(4414) 4227 6161; www.budgetrentacar.com).

Europe by Car, 1 Rockefeller Plaza, New York, NY 10020 (US ☎(800) 223-1516 or (212) 581-3040; fax 246-1458; info@europebycar.com; www.europebycar.com).

Europcar, 145 av. Malekoff, 75016 Paris (☎01 45 00 08 06); US ☎(800) 227-3876; Canada ☎(800) 227-7368; www.europcar.com).

Hertz (US ☎(800) 654-3001; Canada ☎(800) 263-0600; UK ☎(0990) 99 66 99; Australia ☎9698 2555; www.hertz.com).

Kemwel Holiday Autos (US ☎(800) 576-1590; www.kemwel.com).

INTERNATIONAL DRIVING PERMIT (IDP). If you plan to drive a car while in Greece, you are legally required to have an International Driving Permit (IDP). Although Greek proprietors may ignore the law, get one if you know you plan on driving. Your IDP, valid for one year, must be issued in your own country before you depart; AAA affiliates cannot issue IDPs valid in their own country. You must be 18 years old to receive the IDP. A valid driver's license from your home country must always accompany the IDP.

CAR INSURANCE. Most credit cards cover standard insurance. If you rent, lease, or borrow a car, you will need a **green card,** or **International Insurance Certificate,** to certify that you have liability insurance and that it applies abroad. Green cards can be obtained at car rental agencies, car dealers (for those leasing cars), some travel agents, and some border crossings. Rental agencies may require you to purchase theft insurance in areas that they consider to have a high risk of auto theft. Contact the automobile association in your country for information on obtaining an international driving permit and car insurance.

BY FOOT

Let's Go: Greece describes hikes and trails in town and city listings; local residents and fellow travelers can suggest even more. Always make sure you have comfortable shoes and a map. There's rarely any reason to trek during the hottest part of the day (1-5pm). Besides the sweltering heat and the threat of dehydration, many destinations (hilltop monasteries, campgrounds) close for the afternoon and reopen only in the evening. Good sunscreen, a hat, and water are essential.

Most islands in Greece have untamed areas through which to hike; the mainland offers an abundance of mountainous trails to trek. Some of the more famous, popular, and time-consuming hikes include **Mount Olympus** (p. 237), **Vikos Gorge** (p.

218), the villages of **Zagorohoria** (p. 217), and the monasteries of the **Meteora** (p. 201). Some hikes take more than one day to complete; be sure that you are well-informed about places to stop and sleep along your hike.

BY THUMB

 Let's Go strongly urges you to consider the risks before you choose to hitch. We do not recommend hitching as a safe means of transportation, and none of the information presented here is intended to do so.

Think before you hitch: those who hitchhike entrust their life to whoever stops beside them on the road, risking theft, assault, sexual harassment, and auto accidents. Safety-minded hitchers avoid getting in the back of a two-door car and never let go of their backpacks. If they feel threatened, they **insist on being let off,** regardless of where they are. They may also act as if they are going to open the car door or vomit on the upholstery to get a driver to stop. Experienced hitchers pick a spot outside of built-up areas, where drivers can stop, return to the road without causing an accident, and have time to inspect potential passengers as they approach; at night, experienced hitchers stand in well-lit places and expect drivers to be leery of nocturnal thumbers. Women should avoid hitching in Greece.

Greeks are not eager to pick up foreigners, and foreign cars are often filled with other travelers. Sparsely populated areas have little or no traffic—those who hitchhike risk being stuck on the road for hours. Hitchhikers write their destination on a sign in both **Greek and English.** Successful hitchers travel light and stack their belongings in a visible, compact cluster.

SPECIFIC CONCERNS

TRAVELING ALONE

There are many benefits to traveling alone, among them greater independence and challenge. Traveling alone in Greece can be a fantastic way to interact with locals and to see less-touristed areas than you might not visit with a group of sightseeing friends. On the other hand, solo travelers are more vulnerable to harassment and street theft. Lone travelers need to be well organized and look confident at all times. Follow **local customs and dress,** and be inconspicuous. **Never admit that you are traveling alone.** Maintain regular contact with someone at home who knows your itinerary. For more tips, pick up *Traveling Solo* by Eleanor Berman (Globe Pequot Press, US$17) or subscribe to **Connecting: Solo Travel Network,** 689 Park Rd., Unit 6, Gibsons, BC V0N 1V7 (☎ (604) 886-9099; www.cstn.org; membership US$28). Alternatively, several services link solo travelers with companions who have similar travel habits and interests; for a bi-monthly newsletter for single travelers seeking a travel partner (subscription US$48), contact the **Travel Companion Exchange,** P.O. Box 833, Amityville, NY 11701 (☎ (631) 454-0880 or (800) 392-1256; www.whytravelalone.com; US$48).

There are basic **common sense rules** to follow when traveling alone. Remember that no one knows where you are at all times, so be careful of going anywhere with a newfound friend. Be equally wary when hitting the nightlife, as your defenses may drop as your ouzo consumption increases. Stay alert and pay attention to your surroundings. If you feel nervous about an area or place, leave. To avoid standing out as a tourist in villages, make a *stavros* (a cross: up, down, right, left) in front of all churches as a sign of **respect** for the country's culture and customs; locals are much more likely to accept you once they realize that you respect them in return. In most Greek villages, xenophobia is directed only at rude outsiders; as soon as you show familiarity with Greek customs, people are much more friendly.

WOMEN TRAVELERS

Women exploring on their own face additional safety concerns (and **Health Concerns,** p. 48), but you can be **adventurous** without taking undue risks. If you are uneasy about traveling alone, stay in hostels with single rooms that lock from the inside or offer rooms for women only. Check the safety of communal showers in hostels before settling in. Stick to centrally located accommodations and avoid solitary nighttime treks. When traveling, carry extra money for a phone call, bus, or taxi. **Hitching** is never safe for lone women in Greece, or even for two women traveling together. Look as if you know where you're going, even when you don't.

When Greek women travel together, it tends to be to the beach, so Greeks might be curious if they see a woman or group of women traveling in what is not resort territory. The subtext of most blunt questions is: "I can't imagine anyone I know doing what you're doing. Do you really enjoy it?" Explain that you do, and insist gently on respect. **Older Greek women** in villages, towns, and cities can help you if you get in a bind; they're sharp, wise, fearless, and your best allies if you need information, advice, or a respite from persistent amorous attempts by local men.

In **cities,** you may be harassed no matter how you act or what you look like. Your best answer to verbal harassment is no answer at all: ignore catcalls and questioning by sitting motionless, and staring straight ahead, or walking away. Wearing a conspicuous **wedding band,** mentioning a "husband" back at the hotel, or carrying pictures of a "husband" or "children" may help ward off unwanted overtures. Note that Orthodox Greeks wear their wedding bands on their **right** ring fingers. (Hint: you should too.) If you do feel threatened, call attention to what is going on: yell **"AHS-se-meh"** (leave me alone), **"vo-EE-thee-ah"** (help) or **"as-te-no-MEE-ah"** (police). Alternatively, you might carry a **whistle** on your key chain to blow in an emergency. *Let's Go: Greece* lists emergency numbers in the **Practical Information** listings of most cities. Memorize the emergency numbers in the places you visit. An **IMPACT Model Mugging** self-defense course prepares people for potential attacks, and raises confidence and awareness about your surroundings (see **Self Defense,** p. 46).

BISEXUAL, GAY, & LESBIAN TRAVELERS

Though legal in Greece since 1951, homosexuality is still socially frowned upon, especially in more conservative villages. Athens and Thessaloniki offer a slew of gay bars, clubs, and hotels. The islands of **Hydra, Lesvos, Rhodes,** and **Mykonos** (arguably the most gay-friendly destination in Europe) offer gay and lesbian resorts, hotels, bars, and clubs. Gays are not legally protected from discrimination. Consult the following organizations, or pick up *Spartacus International Gay Guide,* by Bruno Gmunder Verlag (US$33); *Damron's Accommodations,* and *The Women's Traveller* (Damron Travel Guides, US$14-19); *Ferrari Guides' Gay Travel A to Z, Ferrari Guides' Men's Travel in Your Pocket,* and *Ferrari Guides' Women's Travel in Your Pocket* (Ferrari Guides, US$14-16).

Gay Greek Guide, TΘ 4228, Athens 10210 (☎(01) 381 5249; English speaker M-F 7-9pm). Call this hotline while in Greece for information on nightlife options.

International Gay and Lesbian Travel Association, 52 W Oakland Park Blvd. #237 Wilton Manors, FL 33311 (☎(954) 776-2626 or (800) 448-8550; fax 776-3303; iglta@iglta.org; www.iglta.com). AUS/NZ/Pacific Rim/ASIA: P.O. Box 1397 Rozelle NSW Australia 2039. Organization of over 1350 companies serving gay and lesbian travelers worldwide. Call for lists of travel agents, accommodations, and events.

GayGreece, at http://travel.to/gayGREECE, describes various towns and cities in Greece, listing bars and clubs in Athens, and offers a virtual tour of Mykonos.

Pridenet (www.pridenet.com/europe.html) links to other Greece-specific gay sites, and offers listings and information organized by area and island groupings.

OLDER TRAVELERS

Greeks generally have great respect for their elders, so don't expect any problems while traveling. Be aware that many sites are only reachable by strenuous hikes and the hot sun can be dangerous. Senior citizens are eligible for a wide range of discounts on transportation, museums, movies, theaters, concerts, restaurants, and accommodations. If you don't see a senior citizen price listed, ask, and you may be delightfully surprised. See *No Problem! World-wide Tips for Mature Adventurers*, by Janice Kenyon (Orca Book Pub., US$16); *A Senior's Guide to Healthy Travel*, by Donald L. Sullivan (Career Press, US$15); or *Unbelievably Good Deals and Great Adventures That You Absolutely Can't Get Unless You're Over 50*, by Joan Rattner Heilman (Contemporary Books, US$13) for information about trips for older travelers, or consult:

Elderhostel, 11 Avenue de LaFayette Boston, MA 02111, USA (☎ (877) 426-8056; fax (877) 426-2166; registration@elderhostel.org; www.elderhostel.org). Outside of the US and Canada call (978) 323-4141; fax (617) 426-0701. Organizes 1- to 4-week "educational adventures" in Greece on varied subjects for those 55+.

Walking the World, P.O. Box 1186, Fort Collins, CO 80522 (☎800-340-9255; www.walkingtheworld.com), organizes trips for 50+ travelers to Greece.

TRAVELERS WITH DISABILITIES

Greece and Cyprus are only slowly beginning to respond to the needs of travelers with disabilities; those with severe physical disabilities won't have it easy. Even the most renowned sights—even the Acropolis—are not wheelchair accessible. Some hotels, train stations, and airports have installed facilities for the disabled, as have some cruise ships that sail to Greek islands. Special air transportation is available aboard Olympic Airways to many of the larger islands.

Those with disabilities should inform airlines and hotels of their disabilities when making arrangements for travel; some time may be needed to prepare special accommodations. Call ahead to restaurants, hotels, parks, and other facilities to find out about ramps, door widths, elevator sizes, and such. **Guide dog owners** should inquire as to the specific quarantine policies ahead of time, and should carry proof of immunization against rabies. Greece's **rail** systems have very limited resources for wheelchair accessibility, but they are probably the best bet for disabled travelers. There are no handicapped-accessible **buses.** Some major **car rental** agencies (Hertz, Avis, and National) offer hand-controlled vehicles. The following organizations offer more information for disabled travelers (see **Other Resources,** p. 77, for useful publications):

Mobility International USA (MIUSA), P.O. Box 10767, Eugene, OR 97440 (☎(541) 343-1284 voice and TDD; fax 343-6812; info@miusa.org; www.miusa.org). Sells *A World of Options: A Guide to International Educational Exchange, Community Service, and Travel for Persons with Disabilities* (US$35).

Moss Rehab Hospital Travel Information Service (☎(215) 456-9600 or (800) CALL-MOSS; netstaff@mossresourcenet.org; www.mossresourcenet.org). An information resource center on travel-related concerns for those with disabilities.

The Green Book (http://members.nbci.com/thegreenbook/home.html) has a partial listing of disabled-access accommodations and sights in Greece.

MINORITY TRAVELERS (NON-GREEKS)

Greeks stare, point, whisper, and gossip as a daily pastime. The first thing to notice is that they're not just staring at *you*. Even the larger cities in Greece retain a small-village, island world view, where everyone and everything is gossip material. While Greeks tend to hold stereotypes about every group of people imaginable, they place a great value on **individualism;** you may be asked (out of curiosity, not maliciousness) all manner of questions or referred to continually as "the (insert your nationality here)," "the (insert religion here)," or simply "the foreigner" (*xenos*). If you deal with individual Greeks for any period of time, they'll treat you as you seem to be (honest, trustworthy, friendly). Still, Greek stereotypes remain global enough to be almost laughable.

Greece presents two strong and entirely different views about foreigners, and travelers should expect to encounter both. One one hand, the Greek tradition of hospitality **(philoxenia)** is unmatched in the Mediterranean. Greeks consider it almost a sacred duty to help travelers, loading them with homemade food and advice. On the other hand, it's important to remember Greece's historical position as the crossroads of empire: most European nations have at one time or another invaded, burned, betrayed, or colonized part of Greece, forging an intense "us-versus-them" Greek nationalism. If you're not obviously Greek, everyone will want to know who you are. **Minority travelers** will have more trouble blending in, and will have to deal with more stares, questions, and comments. While such curiosity may seem in-your-face and invasive by Western standards, think of its roots: 3000 years of experience have taught Greeks to beware foreigners (who could be spies, fugitives, or gods) even when they bear gifts. Once their curiosity is satisfied, they'll be happy to have you in the village, and take pleasure in showing you around.

TRAVELERS WITH CHILDREN

Greeks and Cypriots adore children. Many museums and archeological sites allow children under 18 in for free. Children under two generally fly for 10% of the adult airfare on international flights (this does not necessarily include a seat). International fares are usually discounted 25% for children from two to 11. When deciding where to stay on a family vacation, call ahead to make sure the hotels and pensions allow children; some of hotels and domatia have large rooms for families and roll-away beds for children. If you rent a car, make sure the rental company provides a car seat for younger children. Be sure that your child carries some sort of ID in case of an emergency or in case he or she gets lost.

DIETARY CONCERNS

Greek meals are traditionally organized as follows: bread and olive oil, followed by a lot of largely vegetable or seafood appetizers (fresh vegetables, vegetable pies, fried octopus), followed by a meat or fish dish, followed by fresh fruit. **Vegetarians** (but not vegans, as it is virtually impossible to avoid all animal products in Greek food) can make do if they don't mind occasionally making a meal of appetizers—green beans in oil (*fasolia*), the omnipresent Greek salad (*horiatiko*), cooked vegetables (*laderakia*), spinach-phyllo-feta pastry (*spanakopita*), greens (*horta*), flat-beans (*yigandes*), fresh bread, and wine. In smaller towns, many seemingly vegetarian entrees (like *yemista*, stuffed vegetables) can contain meat, especially in agricultural areas; **ask before you order.** Incidentally, **Lent** is an especially good time for vegetarians and vegans to visit Greece, when meat and meat stock disappear from many dishes. There are almost no Greek vegetarians though, so if questioned your best bet is to argue weather ("It's so hot I only want vegetables") or allergies ("I'm allergic to pork and beef"), as opposed to some kind of ideology: "I don't want to eat meat" will be taken with as much seriousness as "I don't want to eat my vegetables" by well-meaning local grandmothers. As far as actual **allergies** are concerned, the same rule applies: ask before you order, especially at local tavernas that simply serve you whatever is cooking in the kitchen.

Travelers who keep **kosher** should contact synagogues in larger cities for information on kosher restaurants; your own synagogue or college Hillel should have access to lists of Jewish institutions across the nation. If you are strict in your observance, you may have to prepare your own food on the road. **The Jewish Travel Guide,** which lists synagogues, kosher restaurants, and Jewish institutions in over 100 countries, is available in Europe from Vallentine Mitchell Publishers, Newbury House 890-900, Eastern Ave., Newbury Park, Ilford, Essex IG2 7HH, (☎(020) 8599 8866; fax 8599 0984) and in the US ($16.95 + $4 S&H) from ISBS, 5804 NE Hassallo St., Portland, OR 97213 (☎(800) 944-6190).

ALTERNATIVES TO TOURISM

STUDYING ABROAD

Several different types of programs are available for studying abroad in Greece: studying directly at a Greek university, studying through an international program, or going to a language school. Most of these programs are located in Greece's most highly traveled areas, especially in Athens, on Crete, and throughout the Cyclades. In addition, aspiring archeologists have a fairly unique opportunity to work on current digs while studying abroad in Greece.

Citizens of countries that can travel in Greece only on a passport need do nothing. For semester- or year-long study programs, you must first obtain admission into an academic or language program in Greece. Then, as long as you can prove financial support, you need to apply to your embassy for a student visa for however long you want to study (US$20). Programs vary tremendously in expense, academic quality, living conditions, degree of contact with local students, and exposure to local culture and languages.

Arcadia University for Education Abroad, 450 S. Easton Rd., Glenside, PA 19038, USA (☎(866) 927-2234; www.arcadia.edu/cea). Operates programs in Greece. Costs range from $8,990 (semester) to $15,990 (full-year).

The Athens Centre, Archimidous 48, Athens 11636 (☎(01) 701 2268; fax 701 8603; athenscr@compulink.gr; www.athenscentre.com). Offers a Modern Greek Language program. Semester and quarter programs on Greek civilization in affiliation with US universities. Offers 4- to 6-week summer Classics programs, a yearly summer theater program, and Modern Greek Language programs in summer on the island of Spetses.

College Year in Athens, P.O. Box 390890, Cambridge, MA 02139 (☎(617) 868-8200 from the US; fax (617) 868 8207; ☎(01) 756 0749 from Greece; cyathens@aol.com; www.cyathens.org). Runs a semester-long, full-year and summer programs for undergraduates (usually juniors), which includes travel as well as classroom instruction (in English). The program has two tracks, one in Ancient Greek civilization and one in Mediterranean area studies. Scholarships available. Students are housed in apartments in Athens' Kolonaki district. College Year in Athens also offers summer programs, including a 3-week intensive course in modern Greek on Paros, a 6-week study-travel program, and two 3-week modules that cover different subjects every year.

International Association for the Exchange of Students for Technical Experience (IAESTE), 10400 Little Patuxent Pkwy. #250, Columbia, MD 21044, USA (☎(410) 997-2200; fax (410) 992-3924; www.aipt.org or www.ntua.gr/iaeste). Facilitates 8- to 12-week paid internships in Greece for college students who have completed 2 years of technical study. US$50 application fee.

www.studyabroad.com, 1450 Edgemont Ave., Chester, PA 19013 (☎(610) 499-9200; fax (610) 499-9205; webmaster@studyabroad.com). Information and links to every type of study abroad program imaginable in Greece.

Languages Abroad, Box 502, 99 Avenue Rd., Toronto, ON M5R 2G5 (☎(800) 219-9924; www.languagesabroad.com). Runs programs from 3 to 4 weeks long in Athens. Cost varies with length, but 3-week programs start at US$2000; course only $650-750.

SUNY Brockport, Office of International Education, SUNY Brockport, 350 New Campus Dr., Brockport, NY 14420 (☎(716) 395-2119/1-800-298-SUNY; fax (716) 637-3218; www.brockport.edu/study_abroad). Offers a 2-3 week Mythological Study Tour in Greece, visiting ancient sites and relating ancient myths to Greek life. Basic program starts at $2165, with some extra costs.

WORKING AND VOLUNTEERING

WORKING. For citizens of Greece and of **EU** countries, getting a job in Greece is relatively simple. For all others, finding work in Greece can be difficult. Job opportunities are scarce and the government tries to restrict employment to citizens and visitors from the EU. If your parents were born in an EU country, you may be able to claim dual citizenship or at least the right to a work permit. Those who can teach English find a host of job openings in Greece, and in some sectors (like agricultural work) permit-less workers are rarely bothered by authorities. Students can check with their universities' foreign language departments, which may have connections to jobs abroad. Friends in Greece can expedite work permits or arrange work-for-accommodations swaps. (For info on work permits, see p. 39.) Arrive in the spring and early summer to search for **hotel jobs** (bartending, cleaning, etc.). Most night spots offer meager pay but don't require much paperwork. Check the bulletin boards of hostels in Athens and the classified ads in the *Athens News*. Check out **Other Resources** (p. 77) for more information.

International Schools Services, Educational Staffing Program, 15 Roszel Rd., Princeton, NJ 08543 (☎(609) 452-0990; fax 452-2690; edustaffing@iss.edu; www.iss.edu). Recruits teachers and administrators for American and English schools in Greece. All instruction in English. Applicants must have a bachelor's degree and 2 years of relevant experience. Nonrefundable application fee.

Office of Overseas Schools, US Department of State, Room H328, SA-1, Washington, D.C. 20522 (☎(202) 261-8200; fax 261-8224; OverseasSchools@state.gov; www.state.gov/www/about_state/schools/). Keeps a comprehensive list of schools abroad and agencies that arrange placement for Americans to teach abroad.

American Farm School runs a summer work and recreation program for high schoolers (grades 10 and up; US$500 donation). Write to: 1133 Broadway Suite 1625, New York, NY 10010 (☎(212) 463-8434; fax 463-8208; nyoffice@amerfarm.org; www.afs.edu.gr); or P.O. Box 23, GR-55102, Thessaloniki, Greece (☎(31) 49 27 00; info@afs.edu.gr).

International Jobs: Where they Are, How to Get Them, by Eric Kocher and Nina Segal (Perseus Books, US$17).

Directory of Jobs and Careers Abroad (Peterson's, US$17-18 each).

ARCHAEOLOGICAL DIGS. Archaeological Institute of America, 656 Beacon St., Boston, MA 02215-2006 (☎(617) 353-9361; www.archaeological.org), puts out the *Archaeological Fieldwork Opportunities Bulletin* (US$16 for non-members), which lists field sites in Greece. This can be purchased from Kendall/Hunt Publishing, 4050 Westmark Dr., Dubuque, Iowa 52002 (☎(800) 228-0810). **The American School of Classical Studies at Athens,** 54 Souidias, Athens 10676 (☎(01) 72 36 313; fax 72 50 584; info@ascsa.edu.gr; www.ascsa.org), is a highly competitive school offering a variety of archaeological and classical studies programs for undergraduates, graduate students, and Ph.D. candidates. Visit the website to find a list of publications and links to other archaeological programs.

VOLUNTEER. Volunteer jobs are readily available almost everywhere. You may receive room and board in exchange for your labor. You can sometimes avoid high application fees charged by organizations that arrange placement by contacting the individual work camps directly; (see **Other Resources,** p. 77).

G.S.T. (GREEK STANDARD TIME) Greeks are known the world over for their slow-paced and contemplative enjoyment of life. "Be flexible! Relax! Have fun!" This *philosophia,* unfortunately, doesn't make it particularly easy for travelers accustomed to reliable timetables. Restaurant menus and hours rotate, depending on whim. Train, bus, and ferry schedules are notoriously fickle, and owners of establishments may close up shop at any given moment to pay their respects to the sun god Helios—at the beach. Summer dance clubs return to their city locations in the winter, but will often swap beach locations from year to year. Prices for everything from food to accommodations to that garish head scarf you'll buy for Aunt Barbara are subject to change, depending on various circumstances (season, availability, whether or not you said *"yassou"* (p. 557). When a proprietor tells you your food will be here "in a minute," be warned that something might get lost in translation.

Service Civil International Voluntary Service (SCI-IVS), 814 NE 40th St., Seattle, WA 98105 (☎/fax (206) 545-6585; www.sci-ivs.org). Arranges placement in work camps in Greece for those 18+. Application fee US$125.

Volunteers for Peace, 1034 Tiffany Rd., Belmont, VT 05730, USA (☎802-259-2759; www.vfp.org). Arranges placement in work camps in Greece. Annual *International Work camp Directory* US$20. Registration fee US$200. Free newsletter.

International Directory of Voluntary Work, by Louise Whetter (Vacation Work Publications, US$16).

OTHER RESOURCES

Let's Go tries to cover all aspects of budget travel, but we can't put *everything* in our guides. Listed below are websites that can serve as jumping off points for your own research. Almost every aspect of budget travel is accessible via the **web.** Even if you don't have Internet access at home, seeking it out at a public library or at work is well worth it; within 10min. at the keyboard, you can make a reservation at a hostel in Greece, get advice on travel hotspots or experiences from other travelers who have just returned from the Cyclades, or find out exactly how much a ferry from Kephalonia to Corfu costs. Website turnover is high so use search engines (such as www.google.com) to strike out on your own.

THE ART OF BUDGET TRAVEL

How to See the World: www.artoftravel.com. A compendium of great travel tips, from cheap flights to self defense to interacting with local culture.

Rec. Travel Library: www.travel-library.com. A fantastic set of links for general information and personal travelogues.

INFORMATION ON GREECE

CIA World Factbook: www.odci.gov/cia/publications/factbook/index.html. Tons of vital statistics on Greece's geography, government, economy, and people.

Foreign Language for Travelers: www.travlang.com will help you brush up on your Greek.

MyTravelGuide: www.mytravelguide.com. Country overviews, with everything from history to transportation.

Geographia: www.geographia.com. Highlights, culture, and people of Greece.

Atevo Travel: www.atevo.com/guides/destinations. Detailed introductions, travel tips, and suggested itineraries.

World Travel Guide: www.travel-guides.com/navigate/world.asp. Helpful practical info.

TravelPage: www.travelpage.com. Links to official tourist office sites in Greece.

PlanetRider: www.planetrider.com. A subjective list of links to the "best" websites covering the culture and tourist attractions of Greece.

▨ Let's Go: www.letsgo.com. Our constantly expanding website features photos and streaming video, online ordering of all our titles, info about our books, a travel forum buzzing with stories and tips, and links that can help find all you ever wanted to know about Greece.

GENERAL TRAVEL SITES

Air Traveler's Handbook: www.cs.cmu.edu/afs/cs/user/mkant/Public/Travel/airfare.html. Help finding cheap airfare.

Rec. Travel Library: www.travel-library.com. A fantastic set of links for general information and personal travelogues.

Shoestring Travel: www.stratpub.com. An e-zine focusing on budget travel.

Eurotrip: www.eurotrip.com. This site has information and reviews on budget hostels, as well as info on traveling alone.

GREECE-SPECIFIC SITES

The Internet Guide to Greece: www.gogreece.com features maps, references, discussions, and extensive listings of Greek businesses, schools, news sources, and sports.

Phantis: www.phantis.com. A Greek-specific search engine that accommodates region-specific queries, and contains links to Greek city sites.

Hellenic Federation of Mountaineering and Climbing: www.climbing.org.gr. Learn about great hikes in Greece.

The Perseus Project: www.perseus.tufts.edu. "An evolving digital library," provides a library of classical Greek texts, translations, and an online dictionary.

United Hellas: www.united-hellas.com. A would-be database of all things Greek, from small businesses and folk art sources to places to buy a boat.

The Greek Orthodox Archdiocese of New York: www.goarch.org lists information about the religion of most Greeks.

Greek Ferries: www.ferries.gr and www.greekislands.gr claim to maintain a complete and updated list of ferry schedules over all the Greek islands.

The Ministry of Culture: www.culture.gr. Events, history, "cultural maps of Greece," and other fun stuff.

The Greek Government online: www.government.gr. In Greek with sections in English.

Cyprus homepage: http://kypros.org/Government. Links to most Cypriot government agencies and to the Cyprus virtual tour guide.

Greek poetry: www.webexpert.net/vasilios/gpoetry.htm. An extensive compilation of links to Greek poetry resources, modern and ancient.

ATHENS Αθηνα

Athens, the eye of Greece, mother of arts
And eloquence.
　—John Milton

One minute of dodging the packs of mopeds in Pl. Syndagma will prove that Athens refuses to become a museum. The city's past and present coexist in a strange yet beautiful harmony. Ancient ruins sit quietly amid the hectic modern streets as quiet testaments to its rich history, and the Acropolis looms larger than life over the city at its feet, a perpetual reminder of ancient glory. Byzantine churches recall an era of foreign invaders, when Athens was ruled from Macedonia, Rome, and Byzantium. The reborn democracy of the past two centuries has revived the city in a wave of madcap construction: the conflicted, oddly adolescent metropolis has gutted its crumbling medieval mansions to become a dense concrete jungle.

Countless vantage points from Athens's seven hills look out over this sprawling work of centuries: Lycavittos, the Acropolis, Pnyx, Strefi, Phillippapou, Hymettus, and the Hill of the Nymphs. Crowded, noisy, polluted, and totally alive, Athens will get you stuck in traffic at 2am on a Tuesday. A new subway system is up and running; it should be completed for the 2004 Olympic Summer Games. Still, civil engineers refuse to "destroy everything in the name of the underground," picking their way among subterranean antiquities, cisterns, and the springs of lost, ancient rivers that sleep beneath the city.

HIGHLIGHTS OF ATHENS

STRUT IT PAST CHIC OUTDOOR CAFES in Kolonaki (p. 90), then shake it at the hotspot seaside clubs of Glyfada (p. 97).

LOSE YOURSELF amid ancient relics at the National Archaeological Museum (p. 104).

AMBLE THROUGH THE MEDIEVAL ALLEYWAYS of Plaka (p. 85).

MAKE A PILGRIMAGE to Athena's Parthenon on the Acropolis (p. 100).

HAGGLE with wily merchants at Monastiraki's flea market (p. 85).

SCORE A WINK from the skirted, tasseled *evzones* who guard the Parliament in Pl. Syndagma (p. 85).

HISTORY

Athens's recorded history began when the Olympian gods got in a tug-of-war over who would be the Attic city's patron and namesake. They decided that whoever gave it the best gift would earn the city. Poseidon struck the Acropolis with his trident, and a sea water gushed forth from a well. But **Athena**'s wiser gift, an olive tree, won her the right to rule. Rising to political power as early as the 16th century BC, Athens was united as a *polis*, or city-state, by the hero **Theseus** (onetime slayer of the Minotaur). By the 8th century, it had become the artistic center of Greece; an initial fame for geometric pottery foreshadowed a shining future. Two centuries later, law-giver and poet **Solon** ended the servitude of native citizens, restoring rights to some slaves. After victories over the Persians at Marathon and Salamis in the 5th century BC, Athens experienced a 70-year **Golden Age** under the democracy of Pericles, the era that produced the Parthenon; the masterpiece tragedies of Aeschylus, Sophocles, and Euripides; and Aristophanes's ribald comedies.

Pericles's Athens fell apart during the bloody, drawn-out **Peloponnesian War** (431-404 BC) against Sparta. Political power shifted north under Philip of Macedon and his son **Alexander the Great,** but Athens remained a cultural center throughout the 5th and 4th centuries BC. In this period, Athens produced three of the most influential philosophers in western history—**Socrates, Plato, and Aristotle** (p. 13)—as well as the orator **Demosthenes.** By the 2nd century AD, the Roman Empire had gobbled up the city, and in AD 324 Constantine moved the capital of the Roman Empire to Byzantium, leaving the former city-state an overtaxed backwater. It remained the center of Greek education, but its status (and buildings) lapsed into ruin when the emperor Justinian banned the teaching of philosophy in 529.

Around 1000, Byzantine emperor **Basil II** visited Athens. After praying to the Virgin Mary in the Parthenon, Basil ordered craftsmen to restore Athens to its former glory. The city was reborn again and again under successive conquering crusaders—the Franks in 1205, the Catalans in 1311, the Accajioli merchant family in 1387, and the **Ottomans,** whose 400-year rule began in 1456. In 1821, Greek independence (see p. 16) brought further waves of renovation and restoration, as well as a spirit of nationalism. Modern Athens's plateias, wide boulevards, and National Garden follow the plan of architects hired by German-born monarch King Otho.

Athens's population and industry have skyrocketed in the 20th century. A 1923 **population exchange** with Turkey (see p. 17) brought an influx of ethnic Greeks from Turkish land, swelling the city, and since then rural workers have flocked to industrial jobs here. In the past 100 years, the city's population has exploded from a count of 169 families to almost half of Greece's residents. The approaching 2004 Olympic Games have sparked another urban renewal, as the transit authority fights the sinister *nephos* (smog cloud) overhead by banning cars from historic Plaka, limiting driver access downtown, and building a new mass-transit subway.

◪ INTERCITY TRANSPORTATION

Flights: El. Venizelou, Greece's new international airport, operates as 1 massive, yet easily navigable terminal (☎ 35 30 000). Arrivals are on the ground floor, departures on the 2nd floor. 4 bus lines run to and from El. Venizelou from Athens, Piraeus, and Rafina. To get from Pl. Syndagma in the Athens city center take the **E95** (40min., every 20min., 1000dr/€2.93). Pick it up on Amalias, to the right of the top right corner of Pl. Syndagma. To get from the Ethniki Amyna subway station, take either the **E94** or the **E95** (every 10min.; wait by the subway exit). Take the **E96** from *Piraeus* (every 30min.; across from Phillipis Travel in the square of busy Akti Tzelepi, across from Phillipis Travel). The bus from Rafina leaves every 30min. from the stop midway up the ramp from the waterfront. Buses deposit you at one of the 4 departure entrances; look at the screens to determine which desks are checking your flight. Buses wait outside the 5 arrivals exits; walk out of the terminal and look for your bus number, or enter the taxi queue. A **taxi** costs 2500-3000dr/€7.34-8.80 (3500-4000dr/€10.27-11.74 after midnight), with an extra 150dr/€0.44 charge for each piece of luggage over 10kg, and a 400dr/€0.88 surcharge from the airport. Watch drivers carefully; some have been known to rig the meters. Drivers may be unwilling to pick up travelers laden with luggage, and might also make you share a taxi.

Buses: Terminal A: Kifissou 100 (☎ 51 24 910 or 51 32 601). Take blue **bus #051** from the corner of Zinonos and Menandrou near Pl. Omonia (every 15min. 5am-11:30pm, 150dr/€0.44). The "information" booth at Terminal A is a privately run agency; don't buy their useless "vouchers." Buses depart for: **Corinth** (1½hr., 1 per hr. 6:30am-10:30pm, 1850dr/€5.43); **Thessaloniki** (6hr., 11 per day 7am-midnight, 9000dr/€26.41) via **Larissa; Corfu** (10hr., 3 per day 7am-8:30pm, 9100dr/€26.94); **Igoumenitsa** (8hr., 5 per day 6:30am-9pm, 9250dr/€27.15); **Patras** (3hr., 30 per day 6am-9:45pm, 4000dr/€11.74).

Terminal B: Liossion 260 (☎ 83 17 153, except Sa-Su). Take blue **bus #024** from Amalias outside the National Gardens on Panepistimiou (45min., every 20min. 5am-11pm, 120dr/€0.35). Watch the numbers on street signs—Liossion 260 is near several car mechanic shops. Buses depart for: **Delphi** (3hr., 6 per day 7:30am-8pm, 3300dr/€9.68); **Halkida** on **Evia** (1¼hr.; every 30min. 5:30am-9pm, with extra buses on Su; 1450dr/€4.26); **Katerini** (6hr., 3 per day 9:45am-10pm, 8000dr/€23.48).

Mavromateon 29: in Exarhia, between the National Archaeological Museum and Areos Park; take **trolley #18, 11, 5, 2,** or **9.** Buses to: **Marathon** (1½hr., every hr. 6am-10:30pm, 800dr/€2.35);

Rafina (1hr., every 30min. 5:40am-10:30pm, 550dr/€1.61); **Sounion** (2hr., every hr. 5:45am-5:45pm, 1350dr/€3.96; or 2¼hr., every hr. 6am-6pm, 1350dr/€3.96).

Pl. Eleftherias: from Pl. Syndagma, go west on Ermou, turn right on Athinas, and turn left on Evripidou. Buses to **Eleusis** and **Daphni**.

Ferries: Check schedules at the tourist office, in the *Athens News,* with the Port Authority of Piraeus (☎ 42 26 000), over the phone (☎ 143), or at any travel agency. Ferry schedules change daily; check as close to your departure as possible and be flexible. Most ferries dock at **Piraeus** (p. 109); some arrive at nearby **Rafina** (p. 108). Those headed for the Sporades leave from **Ag. Konstantinos** (p. 186) or **Volos** (p. 187). Those headed for the Ionian Islands leave from **Patras** (p. 129).

Piraeus: Take **Line 1** on the subway south to its end, or take green **bus #40** from Filellinon and Mitropoleos (every 10min.). To: **Iraklion, Hania,** and **Rethymno,** Crete. Also to: **Aegina, Poros, Spetses,** and **Hydra; Chios** and **Lesvos; Ios, Mykonos, Naxos,** and **Paros; Rhodes, Santorini,** and **Sifnos, Kythnos, Serifos,** and **Milos.** International ferries run to **Limassol, Cyprus** and **Haifa, Israel.** See **Piraeus** (p. 109) for prices, frequencies, and trip durations.

Rafina: Buses depart from Mavromateon 29, 2 blocks up along Areos Park, or a 15min. walk from Syndagma Square. (1hr., every 30min. 5:40am-10:30pm, 550dr/€1.61). Ferries to: **Karystos** and **Marmari** in Evia; **Andros, Tinos, Mykonos, Paros,** and **Naxos.** High-speed **catamarans** sail to: **Andros, Tinos, Amorgos,** and **Mykonos. Nel Lines** goes to: **Ag. Efstratios, Limnos, Kavala,** and **Lesvos.** See **Rafina** (p. 111) for prices, frequencies, and trip durations.

Trains: Hellenic Railways (OSE), Sina 6 (☎ 36 24 402; www.ose.gr). Call ☎ 52 97 777 for reservations; or the Greek Railway Organization information (☎ 36 24 402 or 52 97 777) for information. ☎ 145 or 147 lists timetables in Greek; schedules are subject to change. Contact the railway offices to confirm schedules before your trip.

Larissis Train Station (☎ 52 98 837 or 82 37 741) serves northern Greece and Europe. Open 24hr. Take **trolley #1** from El. Venizelou (Panepistimiou) in Pl. Syndagma (every 10min. 5am-midnight, 150dr/€0.44), or take the subway to Sepolia. Trains depart for: **Thessaloniki** (7hr., 4 per day, 4800dr/€14.21; express 5½hr., 6 per day, 9400dr/€27.83); **Bratislava, Slovakia** (30,000dr/€88.04); **Prague, Czech Republic** (35,000dr/€102.72); **Bucharest, Romania**(40,000dr/€117.39); **Budapest, Hungary** (40,000dr/€117.39). To get to Sofia, Istanbul, Bratislava, Prague, Bucharest, and Budapest, take the train from Larissis Station to **Salonica** and change there; an 8300dr/€24.36 surcharge is included in above prices.

Peloponnese Train Station (☎ 51 31 601; 52 98 739 for buses to Albania, Bulgaria, and Turkey) is in a Victorian building with a silver roof. Open 24hr. From Larissis, exit to your right and go over the footbridge; from El. Venizelou (Panepistimiou) in Syndagma, take blue **bus #057** (every 15min. 5:30am-11:30pm, 150dr/€0.44). Serves **Patras** (4¼hr., 1800dr/€5.28; express 3½hr., 3400dr/€9.98) and major towns in the Peloponnese.

Luggage Storage: There are lockers at El. Venizelou airport to the left of the Arrivals exits; from 1000dr/€2.93 per item per day. Open 24hr. Also several offices on Nikis and Filellinon, including **Pacific Ltd.,** Nikis 26 (☎ 32 41 007). 500dr/€1.47 per day, 1500dr/€4.40 per week, 3000dr/€8.80 per month. Open M-Sa 8am-8pm, Su 8am-2pm. Many **hotels** and **hostels** have free or inexpensive luggage storage.

🄴 LOCAL TRANSPORTATION

Buses: KTEL (KTEΛ) buses are punctual, so be on time. Buses around Athens and its suburbs are blue or orange and are designated by 3-digit numbers. These buses are good for travel throughout the city, and ideal for daytrips to Daphni and Kesariani. Buy blue bus/trolley **tickets** (good for both) at any street **kiosk** and validate it yourself at the orange machine on board. A standard one-way ticket for a bus or a trolley costs 150dr/€0.44. Kiosks only sell tickets for Athens and its suburbs; buy several tickets at once if you plan to use buses and trolleys frequently, or buy the "Airport 24hr." ticket (1000dr/€2.93), which grants unlimited travel on city bus, trolley, and subway within 24hr. of its validation, and need not be used to get to the airport. **Hold on to your ticket:** if you drop or don't validate your ticket—even when it seems like nobody is there to make you pay—you can be fined 6000-10,000dr/€17.61-29.35 on the spot by police. Children under 6 ride free. The tourist office's map of Athens has the most frequented **routes** labeled on it. Buses run M-Sa 5am-11:30pm, Su and public holidays 5:30am-11:30pm. **24hr. service** on the E95 from Syndagma to El. Venizelou airport,

E96 from Piraeus to El. Venizelou airport, and **040** from Piraeus to Syndagma. Check urban bus schedules (☎185) and domestic bus schedules (☎51 24 910).

Trolleys: Yellow, crowded, and sporting 1- or 2-digit numbers, trolleys are distinguished from buses by their electrical antennae. Trolleys don't accept money; buy a trolley/bus **ticket** ahead of time at a **kiosk** (150dr/€0.44). Service is frequent and convenient for short hops within town. See the detailed tourist office map for trolley **routes** and stops. Trolleys operate M-Sa 5am-midnight, Su and public holidays 5:30am-midnight.

Subway: In preparation for the 2004 Olympics, Athens is expanding and improving its **Metro.** The underground network consists of 3 lines. **M1** runs from northern Kifissia to the port of Piraeus. **M2** runs from Sepolia to Dafni. **M3** runs from Ethniki Amyna to Pl. Syndagma in central Athens. The standard ticket of 250dr/€0.73 allows for travel along any of the lines (transfer is permitted) in one direction, for up to 90min. after its validation. A ticket can be purchased at Metro stations for 200dr/€0.59, which permits travel along 1 or 2 subsequent zones of M1. Tell the cashier your destination, and they'll give you the appropriate ticket. Trains run daily 5am-midnight. Remember to **hold on to your ticket** to avoid a fine.

> **TAXI SMART** Beware! Some drivers tinker with their meters, while others may not turn on the meter at all, taking you somewhere and then charging an exorbitant fee. Ask the cost of the fare in advance, and if you don't see the meter running, yell "Meter! Meter!" In addition, if you ask for a hotel, the taxi driver may have another one in mind for you—a hotel that has paid him off. Be firm about where you're going; don't trust a driver who says your hotel is closed or there are no hostels in town.

Taxis: Meter **rates** start at 250dr/€0.73, with an additional 80dr/€0.23 per km within city limits, 150dr/€0.44 per km in the suburbs, 40dr/€0.12 per stationary min. Everything beyond the start price is 150dr/€0.44 between midnight and 5am. There's a 400dr/€1.17 surcharge for trips from the airport, and a 200dr/€0.59 surcharge for trips from port, bus, and railway terminals; add 100dr/€0.29 extra for each piece of luggage over 10kg. Pay what the meter shows rounded up to the next 50dr/€0.15 as a **tip.** Hail your taxi by shouting your destination—not the street address, but the area (e.g. "Kolonaki"). The driver will pick you up if he feels like heading that way. Get in the cab and tell the driver the exact address or site. Many drivers don't speak English, so write your destination down, in Greek if possible; include the area of the city, since streets in different parts of the city can share the same name. Empty taxis are rare; it's common to ride with other passengers going in the same direction. For an extra 400dr/€1.17, call a radio taxi: **Ikaros** (☎51 52 800); **Ermis** (☎41 15 200); **Kosmos** (☎80 11 300). You can get a full list of radio taxis in the *Athens News* or at the tourist office.

Car Rental: Try the many places on **Singrou**. All charge 10,000-15,000dr/€29.35-44 for a small car with 100km mileage (prices include tax and insurance). Some student discounts up to 50%. Prices rise in summer. International Driver's License not needed.

⁊ PRACTICAL INFORMATION

TOURIST AND FINANCIAL SERVICES

Tourist Office: The **central office** and **information booth** are at Amerikis 2 (☎33 10 561 or 33 10 562; fax 32 52 815; www.areianet.gr/infoxenios/GNTO), off Stadiou near Pl. Syndagma. Bus, train, and ferry schedules and prices; lists of museums, embassies, and banks; brochures on travel throughout Greece; and an indispensable Athens **map.**

Travel Agencies: USIT Youth Student Travel, Filellinon 3 (☎32 41 884; fax 32 38 447) sells ISIC (3000dr/€8.80) and FIYTO (3000dr/€8.80) ID cards (see p. 39). Open M-F 9am-5pm, Sa 10am-2pm. **International Student and Youth Travel Service Limited,** Nikis 11 (☎32 21 267; fax 32 23 767), sells ID cards and has student rates on transportation to the rest of Europe. Open M-F 9am-5pm, Sa 9am-1pm. **Consolas Travel,** Aiolou 100 (☎32 54 931; fax 32 10 907), next to the post office; a second office is at Filellinon 18 (☎32 32 812). Other budget travel agencies are along Nikis.

Banks: National Bank of Greece, Karageorgi Servias 2 (☎33 40 015), in Pl. Syndagma. Open M-Th 8am-2pm, F 8am-1:30pm; open for currency exchange only M-Th 3:30-6:30pm, F 3-6:30pm, Sa 9am-3pm, Su 9am-1pm. American Express, the post office, some hotels, and other banks (list available at tourist office) offer **currency exchange.** Expect commissions of about 5%. 24hr. currency exchange at the airport, but rates and commissions may be exorbitant.

American Express: Ermou 2, P.O. Box 3325 (☎32 44 975 or 32 44 979), above McDonald's in Pl. Syndagma. This A/C-endowed office cashes traveler's checks commission-free, holds mail for a month, and provides travel services for cardholders. Open M-F 8:30am-4pm, Sa 8:30am-1:30pm (only travel and mail services Sa).

LOCAL SERVICES

International Bookstores: Eleftheroudakis Book Store, Panepistimiou 17 (☎33 14 180) and Nikis 20 (☎32 29 388). A browser's delight, with Greek, English, French, and German books, classical and recent literature. Open M-F 9am-9pm, Sa 9am-3pm. **Pantelides Books,** Amerikis 11 (☎36 23 673), overflows with variety, in English. Open M and Sa 9am-4pm, Tu-F 9am-8pm. **Compendium Bookshop,** Nikis 28 (☎32 21 248), has popular new and used books, a large fiction and poetry sections with poetry readings in winter, and a **children's book room.** Open M-F 8:30am-4:30pm, Tu and Th-F 4:30pm-8:30pm, Sa 9am-3pm.

Libraries: The **American Library,** Massalias 22 (☎36 38 114), on the 4th floor of the Hellenic American Union behind the university. Open M and Th 3-7pm, Tu-W and F 11am-3pm. The 7th floor has a **Greek Library** (☎36 29 886), with English books on Greece. Open M-Th 9am-8pm, F 9am-5pm. The **British Council Library** (☎36 33 211), Pl. Filikis Eterias 17 in Kolonaki Square, is open Sept.-July M-F 9:30am-1:30pm and Tu-W 5:30-8pm.

Laundromats: Most *plinitirios* have signs reading "Laundry." At **Angelou Geront 10** in Plaka, a kind Greek grandmother will wash, dry, and fold your laundry for 2500dr/€7.27. Open M-Sa 8am-7pm, Su 9am-2pm. Syndagma has **National,** a laundromat and dry cleaners, at Apollonos 17 (☎32 32 266; wash and dry 1300dr/€3.82 per kg; open M and W 8am-4pm, T and Th-F 8am-8:30pm); or go to Zenith at **Apollonos 12 and Pentelis 1** (☎32 38 533; 1500dr/€4.40 per kg wash and dry; open M and W 8am-4pm, T and Th-F 8am-8pm). Launder one load for 2700dr/€7.92 near the train stations, at **Psaron 9** (☎52 22 856; open M-F 8am-9pm, Sa 8am-5pm, Su 8am-2pm) or get the same for 2300dr/€6.75 at **Kolokinthous 41 and Leonidou** west of Omonia Square (☎52 26 233). Open M-F 9am-9pm, Su 9am-3pm.

EMERGENCY AND COMMUNICATIONS

Telephone Number Information: (☎131).

Emergencies: Police (☎100). **Doctors** (☎105 from Athens, 101 elsewhere; line open 2pm-7am). **Ambulance** (☎166). **Poison control** (☎77 93 777). **Fire** (☎199). **AIDS Help Line** (☎72 22 222). *Athens News* lists emergency hospitals. Free emergency health care for tourists.

Tourist Police: Dimitrakopoulou 77 (☎171). Great for information, assistance, and emergencies. English spoken. Open 24hr.

Pharmacies: Identified by a **red** (signifying a doctor) or **green cross** hanging over the street. They're almost everywhere. One is always open 24hr.; check *Athens News* "Useful Information," which lists the day's emergency pharmacies, or look at the chart in pharmacy windows.

Hospitals: Emergency hospitals/clinics on duty can be reached at ☎106. **Geniko Kratiko Nosokomio** (Public State Hospital), Mesogion 154 (☎77 78 901). **Hegia,** Erithrou Stavrou 4 (☎68 27 904), is a private hospital in Maroussi. **Aeginitio** state hospital, Vas. Sofias 72 (☎72 20 811 or 72 20 812) and Vas. Sofias 80 (☎77 70 501), is closer to Athens's center. Near Kolonaki is a **public hospital,** Evangelismou 45-47 (☎72 20 101). "Hospital" is *nosokomio* in Greek; call an operator at 131.

Post Offices: Omonia, Aiolou 100 (☎32 16 023); **postal code: 10200. Syndagma** (☎32 26 253), on the corner of Mitropoleos; **postal code:** 10300. **Exarhia,** at the corner of Zaimi and K. Deligiani; **postal code:** 10691. Open M-F 7:30am-8pm, Sa 7:30am-2pm, Su 9am-1pm. An **Acropolis** branch (☎92 18 076) sells stamps and has currency exchange; **postal code:** 11742. Open M-F 7:30am-2:30pm, Sa-Su 9am-2pm.

Shipping: To send packages abroad, try parcel post, **Koumoundourou 29** (☎52 49 359; open M-F 7:30am-8pm) and **Stadiou 4** (☎32 28 940; open M-F 7:30am-2pm). **D. Alatzoglou Parcel Post and Gift Shop,** on the 1st floor of the American Express Building, provides shipping and packing services. 19,500dr/€57.23 to the US (up to 7lb.).

Internet Access:

Carousel Cybercafe, Eftixidou 32 (☎75 64 305), near Pl. Plastira in **Pangrati.** Wood-oven baked pizza after 6pm (1500dr/€4.40). Internet 1500dr/€4.40 per hr., 750dr/€2.20 minimum. Open daily 11am-midnight.

Deligrece Internet Cafe, Akadimias 87 (☎33 02 929; delice@otenet.gr), in **Exharia.** Cool enough to stand on its own, it has big-screen MTV broadcasts and cheap espresso (650dr/€1.91). Internet 1000dr/€2.93 per hr., 500dr/€1.47 minimum. Open daily 7:30am-midnight.

Internet Cafe, Stournari 49, in **Omonia.** Gaze at the city below while checking email (1000dr/€2.93 per hr.) amid crowds of Athenian students. Open M-Sa.

Ivis Internet Services, Mitropoleos 3 (☎32 43 365 or 32 43 543; fax 32 24 205). On the 2nd floor of the building across the street from the post office in **Syndagma.** Super-fast Internet connection, digital video cameras, word processing, color printing, scanning, and photoshop for only 1000dr/€2.93 per hour, 400dr/€1.17 minimum. Open daily 8:30am-midnight.

Joy Net Cafe, 67 Imittou, in **Pangrati.** Grab a fresh OJ (1000dr/€2.93) in this brand new Internet link-up. Internet 1200dr/€3.52 per hr., 500dr/€1.47 minimum. Open daily 10am-midnight.

Museum Internet Cafe, Patission 46 (☎88 33 418; museum_net_cafe@yahoo.com), in **Exharia.** After visiting the Archaeological Museum, luxuriate in oh-so-modern email. 500dr/€1.47 per 20min. Cappuccino 700dr/€2.05, beer 600-1100dr/€1.76-3.23.

Plaka Internet World, Pandrossou 29, 4th floor (☎33 16 056; plakaworld@internet.gr) in **Plaka.** 1500dr/€4.40 per hr., 500dr/€1.47 minimum.

Sofokleous.com Internet Cafe, Stadiou 5 (☎32 48 105; sofos1@ath.forthnet.gr), just up Stadiou from Pl. **Syndagma.** Owner Giorgos Kolios is friendly and PC-proficient. Complimentary coffee. 1500dr/€4.40 per hr., 500dr/€1.47 minimum.Open M-Sa 10am-10pm, Su 11am-7pm.

Telephones: OTE, Patission 85 (☎82 14 449 or 82 37 040) or Athinas 50 (☎32 16 699). Offers overseas collect calls, recent phonebooks for most European and Anglophone countries, and currency exchange (until 3pm). Open M-F 7am-9pm, Sa 8am-3pm, Su 9am-2pm. For information on **overseas calls** dial 161; for **directory assistance** in and outside Athens, dial 131. Most phone booths in the city operate by **telephone cards** (1000dr/€2.93, 7000dr/€20.54, or 11,500dr/€33.45 at OTE offices, kiosks, and tourist shops). Push the "i" button on the phones for English instructions. For rate and general info call 134; for complaints, call 135; for a domestic English-speaking operator, call 151.

 PHONE CODE. The phone code for all of Athens is **01.**

■ ORIENTATION

Athenian geography mystifies newcomers and natives alike. When you're trying to figure out the city, don't neglect the detailed **free maps** from the tourist office (p. 82): the city map includes bus, trolley, and subway routes, and the *Now in Athens* magazine has a more exacting street plan. If you lose your bearings, ask for directions back to well-lit **Syndagma** or look for a cab; if you get lost, the **Acropolis** provides a reference point, as does **Mt. Lycavittos.** Athenian streets often have **multiple spellings or names,** so check the map again before you panic about being lost.

Several English-language **publications** can help you navigate Athens. The weekly publication *Athens News* gives addresses, hours, and phone numbers for weekly happenings, as well as listings, news, and ferry information (300dr/€0.88). *Athenorama* lists entertainment information. Athens and its suburbs occupy seven hills in southwest Attica, near the coast. **Syndagma,** the central plateia containing the Parliament building, is encircled by the other major neighborhoods. Clockwise, they are: **Plaka, Monastiraki, Psiri, Omonia, Exarhia, Kolonaki,** and **Pangrati.** To get around, you can walk or take a trolley or the expanding subway line (subway maps are available at the tourist office). A half-hour car, bus, or taxi ride south takes you to the seaside suburb of **Glyfada,** where Bacchantes head to party.

SYNDAGMA. Pl. Syndagma (Συνταγμα; Constitution Square) stands at the center of Athens. The **Greek Parliament** occupies a pale yellow Neoclassical building on a large plateia uphill from the actual Syndagma square, on the edge of the **National Gardens,** once the royal gardens of Kings Otho and Amalia. The **Greek** National Tourist Office (EOT), post office, American Express office, transportation terminals, and a number of travel agencies and banks ring the lower end of the Syndagma plateia. The Syndagma subway stop is also located at the upper end of the plateia, and airport buses stop uphill from it, along the road to the right. Budget-friendly travel offices, restaurants, and hotels line **Filellinon** and **Nikis,** parallel thoroughfares that head out from Syndagma toward Plaka; **Ermou** and **Metropoleos,** which head toward Monastiraki, are similarly cheapskate-friendly. These streets are just removed enough to provide some nocturnal quiet and safety. The plateia itself buzzes around the clock: car and moped traffic mingles perilously with spaced-out pedestrians, and people-watchers can spy on lounging kids, mangy dogs, tourists and executives hailing cabs, blank-eyed drug addicts and street musicians sitting on sidewalks, and brightly clad panhandlers begging for coins.

PLAKA. Southwest of Syndagma, Plaka (Πλακα) is the center of the old city, and the temporary home of most visitors to Athens. Busy at night, Plaka undergoes a daily transformation; a vendor-vacuum by morning, it becomes the perfect place to linger over a coffee and observe the hum of Athenian life after the sun goes down. Bounded by the city's two largest ancient monuments—the **Temple of Olympian Zeus** (p. 102) and the **Acropolis** (p. 97)—the neighborhood also contains the only medieval buildings to survive the double-edged shovel of archaeologists and the frantic building of the past few decades. Many of the city's cheap hotels and tourist eateries are here, as are legions of *kamakia* ("octopus spearers," or pick-up artists) who catcall passing women. Keep walking; harassment is usually only verbal.

MONASTIRAKI. In daylight, Monastiraki's (Μοναστηρακη) frenetic flea market is home to vendors who sell rugs, furniture, leather, *bouzoukis,* and all varieties of souvenirs. Test your bargaining mettle on a stubborn merchant—haggling is the only way not to get ripped off. Because it borders the central food and flea markets, the neighborhood's three-alarm noise never pipes down. The Acropolis is nearby, as are the subway and the Agora, and the old buildings of **Psiri**—north of Ermou, bounded by Evripidou on the north and Athinas on the east—now house hot nightspots and restaurants. Go for an evening stroll—or a late night (and morning) bender—along Monastiraki's streets.

OMONIA. Northwest of Syndagma, Pl. Omonia (Ομονια) is the site of the city's **central subway station.** Trains run to Kifissia (40min.), Monastiraki (3min.), and Piraeus (20min.), among other destinations. The HQ of the **Greek Communist Party** (KKE) towers overhead. Cheap lodgings, food, clothing, and jewelry abound in Omonia, but lately the area has become increasingly unsafe. Beware of pickpockets, mind your own business, and don't travel alone at night.

Two parallel avenues, **Panepistimiou** (which becomes El. Venizelou closer to Syndagma) and **Stadiou,** connect Syndagma to Omonia. The **University** and **library** are on Panepistimiou between the two plateias. Larissis Station, serving northern Greece, and Peloponnese Station, serving the south, are on **Konstantinoupoleos,** northeast of **Pl. Karaiskaki,** accessible from Deligiani.

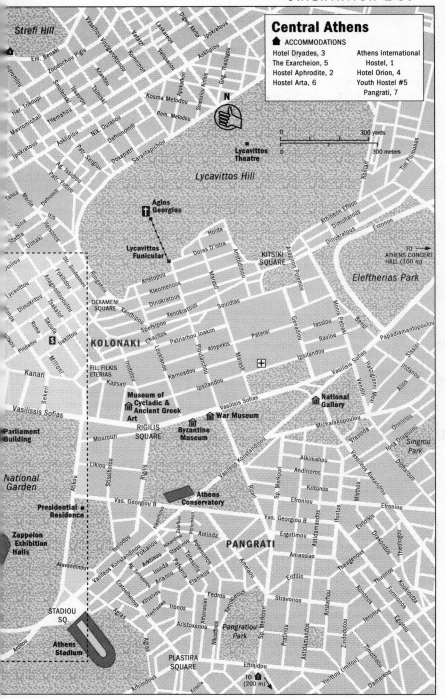

Central Athens

🏠 ACCOMMODATIONS

Hotel Dryades, 3
The Exarcheion, 5
Hostel Aphrodite, 2
Hostel Arta, 6

Athens International
Hostel, 1
Hotel Orion, 4
Youth Hostel #5
Pangrati, 7

Strefi Hill

Em. Benaki
Zoodochou Pigs
Vassiliou Vougerokinou
Isvaron
Smolenski
Tsamadou
Tilemahou
Mavromichali
Haf. Trikoupi
Ipokratous
Askilipiou
Patt. Serglou
Nik. Ourahou
Dafnonomili
Doxapatr
Sarantapichou
Kosma Melodou
Rom. Melodou
Vaatzi
Laskarou
Komminon
Tsimiski
Miaolou
Deligi Anta
Ipokratous
Terissaton
Aplahton
Sinessiou Kirinis
Grig. Theologou
Askilipiou
Ag. Issidou
Patt. Fotou

N

Lycavittos
Theatre

Lycavittos Hill

Agios
Georgios

Lycavittos
Funicular

Holda
Doras D'istra
Aristotlnou
Marasil
Anagnon Polemou

KITSIKI
SQUARE

Athineon Efvoni
Dimoharous
Dinokratous
Evzonon

Eleftherias Park

TO →
ATHENS CONCERT
HALL (100 m)

Kohari
Tim Filimonos

0   300 yards
0   300 meters

DEXAMENI
SQUARE

Rongakou
Aristopou
Kleomenous
Dinokratous
Xanthipou
Spetsipou
Xenokratous
Charitos
Patriarhou Ioakim
Loukianou
Karneadou
Ipsilandou
Souidias
Alopekis
Plotarchou
Marasil
Genadou
Iassiou
Ravine
Ipsilandou
Vasilisis Sofias
Vassili
Benzi
Papadiamantopoulou
Sissini
Iridanou
Alios
Monis Petraki

KOLONAKI

FIL. FILKIS
ETERIAS
Kapsali
Irakliiou
Inodrou
Skoura
Miltonli
Pindarou
Sekeri
Kanari
Vasilissis Sofias

National
Gallery

Vasileos
Sofias
Hazigianni Mexi
Vendiri

Michalakopoulou
Vrassida
Singrou
Park

Museum of
Cycladic &
Ancient Greek
Art

RIGILIS
SQUARE

Byzantine
Museum

War Museum

Vasilisis Sofias

Omniniou
Iona Dragoumi

Parliament
Building

Mourouzi
Likiou

Likiou
Vas. Georgiou B

Rigilis

Atikou

Stisithrou

Vasileos Konstandinou

Rizari

Alkimahou
Andinoros
Kritonos
Efroniou
Sp. Merkouri
Vassileos Alexandrou
Misthou
Diotherous
Singrou
Park

National
Garden

Presidential
Residence

Athens
Conservatory

Vas. Georgiou B

Ergotimou
Astidamandos

Vas. Georgiou B

Efroniou

Ifontos
Evridikis
Drakondos
Theodotou

Zappeion
Exhibition
Halls

Aravandinou

PANGRATI

Aminda
Amassias

Erifilis

Theagenous
Thironos
Koukatiza
Aristatiou

Vasileos Konstandinou
Tesslodou
Fotianou
Arktinou
Stassinou
Polemonos
Telesilis
Paisania
Elankou

Nikandrou
Sp. Spirsonos
Arianou
Kitssinou
Theofrasteu
Ironos

Fedrou
Xenofneous
Athenasias
Nikosthou
Stravonos
Aristathou
Kononos
Formionos

STADIOU
SQ.

Vas. Georgiou B
Agras
Agras

Aristoxenou

Pangratiou
Park

Pratinou
Astidamandos
Zindodotou
Ieronos
Eigiriou
Timotheou
Damareos

Athens
Stadium

Arhhou

PLASTIRA
SQUARE

Plaslira
Ahhindous
Kissia

Eftihidou

TO 🏛
(200 m) ↘

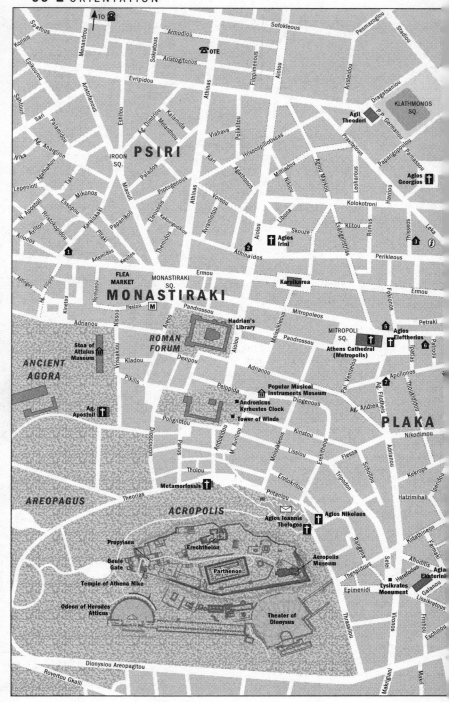

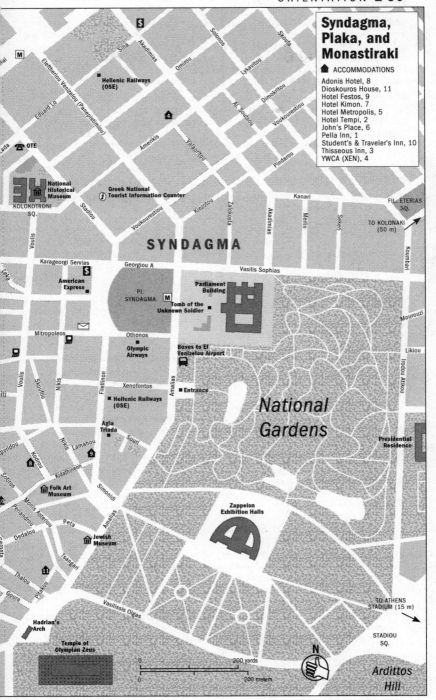

Syndagma, Plaka, and Monastiraki

ACCOMMODATIONS

Adonis Hotel, 8
Dioskouros House, 11
Hotel Festos, 9
Hotel Kimon. 7
Hotel Metropolis, 5
Hotel Tempi, 2
John's Place, 6
Pella Inn, 1
Student's & Traveler's Inn, 10
Thisseous Inn, 3
YWCA (XEN), 4

EXARHIA. Pl. Omonia's neighbor to the east, progressive Exarhia (Εξαρχια) was once the spiritual home of Greek anarchists. Over the past 10 years, international models have imported the values of capitalism, and a new population of students have arrived to match. Thanks to the crazy kids at the **University** on Panepistimiou, Exarhia sports some of Athens's most bumpin' nightlife. Cafes overflow throughout the night, as the outdoor tables open a window onto the revelry of students.

KOLONAKI. If you've got money to burn, you've found the place. Models move and shake in Exarhia, but Kolonaki's (Κολονακη) got the glitz. On this posh foothill of **Mt. Lycavittos**, swanky Greeks drop drachmas in designer boutiques, and jockey for spots for their BMWs, and for high-profile seats in the cafes, bars, and restaurants on **Plutarchou** and **Loukianou.** Kolonaki houses the British Academy, the American School of Classical Studies, and an enclave of expat students. With Plaka just down the hill and an exceptional view of the Acropolis below, Kolonaki shelters Athens's trendiest nightspots.

PANGRATI. Athenian youth chat over Fanta or coffee, jabber into cell phones, and play backgammon in Pangrati (Πανγρατι), southeast of Kolonaki. Though close to the city center, Pangrati is remarkably intimate. Not much *happens* in this peaceful area, but the safe, tree-lined streets allow for quiet strolls and exploration. Several Byzantine churches, a park, the **Olympic Stadium,** and **National Cemetery** mark the area's major monuments. Take trolley #2, 4, or 11 from Syndagma.

ACCOMMODATIONS

The **Greek Youth Hostel Association,** Dragatsaniou 4, 7th floor, lists hostels in Greece. Go up Stadiou and then left on Dragatsaniou, then take the elevators on the right as you enter the arcade. (☎ 32 34 107; fax 32 37 590. Open daily M-F 9am-3pm.) The **Hellenic Chamber of Hotels,** Karageorgi Servias 2, provides info and reservations for hotels of all classes throughout Greece. Reservations require a cash deposit, length of stay, and number of people; you must contact them at least one month in advance. (☎ 32 37 193; fax 32 25 449; www.users.otenet.gr/~grhotels/index.htm. Open May-Nov. M-Th 8:30am-2pm, F 8:30am-1:30pm, Sa 9am-12:30pm.)

SYNDAGMA

Syndagma is at the heart of Athens. Tourist services and cheap accommodations are plentiful. Though it can be a noisy area, it's a good bet for those looking for dirt-cheap hostel rates and proximity to transportation.

Hotel Festos, Filellinon 18 (☎ 32 32 455; consolas@hol.gr). This backpacker-friendly hostel charges rock-bottom prices. Located off a busy street on the border of Plaka, it's a 5min. walk to eats, shops, and transport. Breakfast 700dr/€2.05, dinner 1000-2000dr/€2.93-5.87; served in common kitchen/TV room. A/C and common bathrooms. Dorms 4000-5000dr/€11.74-14.67; singles 7000-9000dr/€20.53-26.41; doubles 8000-10,000dr/€23.48-29.35; triples 12,000-15,000dr/€35.22-44; quads 14,000- 20,000dr/€41.10-58.69. Monthly rates for students: single 80,000dr/€234.78; double 110,000dr/€322.82

YWCA (XEN), Amerikis 11 (☎ 36 24 291), up the street from the tourist office. **Women only.** Spacious building has hand-wash laundry facilities and fridges on each floor. Safe and central location compensates for strict regulations. 1000dr/€2.93 membership fee or valid YWCA membership required. Singles 6000dr/€17.61, with bath 7500dr/€22; doubles 9000-9500dr/€26.41-27.88.

Thisseos Inn, Thisseos 10 (☎ 32 45 960). Take Karageorgi Servias, which becomes Perikleous, and Thisseos is on the right. This home-turned-hostel is close to Syndagma's sights but far from its noise. Friendly staff speaks English. TV in reception area, full kitchen, fans, and common baths. Open 24hr. Towels upon request. Dorms 3500-4500dr/€10.27-13.21; singles 5000-8000dr/€14.67-23.48; doubles 7500-10,000dr/€22-29.35; triples 13,500dr/€39.62; covered roof available in summer for 2500-3000dr/€7.34-8.80 (bring your own sleeping bag).

John's Place, Patroou 5 (☎32 29 719), near Metropoleos. Well located yet off the major streets, John's has basic amenities and quiet. Dim hallways and quiet nights enhance its gothic feel. Singles 7000-9000dr/€20.53-26.41; doubles 9000-12,000dr/€26.41-35.22; triples 12,000-16,000dr/€35.22-46.96. Bargain for a better price.

PLAKA

■ **Student's and Traveler's Inn,** Kidathineon 16 (☎32 44 808 or 32 48 802; fax 32 10 065; Students-inn@ath.forthnet.gr). Unrivaled location and lively atmosphere make up for the early closing and other drawbacks. This hotel courts young backpackers with its large courtyard and balconies, travel services (open 2-10pm), and Internet access at the nearby Cyber Cafe (2500dr/€7.34 per hr., 1500dr/€4.40 minimum; open 8am-11pm). Breakfast 6-11am (limited drachmas well spent; 1000-1500dr/€2.93-4.40). Bring your own sheets, towel, and ask for toilet paper at the desk. 24hr. reception. Lockout midnight. Call for a reservation and arrive on time. Co-ed dorms 4500-5000dr/€13.21-14.67; doubles 12,000-15,000dr/€35.22-44; triples 15,000-18,000dr/€44-52.82; quads 16,000-24,000dr/€46.96-70.43. Off-season 10% discount with student ID, youth card, or hostel card. A/C and private baths extra.

■ **Hotel Metropolis,** Mitropoleos 46 (☎32 17 871 or 32 17 469), opposite Mitropoli Cathedral. Newly renovated, this hotel is a roomy step up at a good price. Its welcoming husband-and-wife owners cater to privacy-oriented travelers. Private baths in 15 of the 21 rooms; balconies have views of the Acropolis. Laundry service (2000dr/€5.87 wash and dry). Singles 10,000-14,000dr/€29.35-41.10; doubles 12,000-16,000dr/€35.22-46.96; triples 15,000-18,000dr/€44-52.82.

Dioskouros House, Pitakou 6 (☎32 48 165), on the southwest corner of the National Gardens by the Temple of Olympian Zeus. The simple wood-floored rooms are sheltered from the city center; a shaded outdoor bar serves breakfast (700dr/€2.05) and drinks until 11pm. Luggage storage (300dr/€0.88) and book exchange. Dorm 5000dr/€14.67; doubles 13,000dr/€38.15; triples 19,500dr/€57.23; quads 24,000dr/€70.43. Off-season prices around 20% less.

Adonis Hotel, Kodrou 3 (☎32 49 737 or 32 49 741; fax 32 31 602). From Filellinon on the way from Syndagma, turn right on Nikodimou and left on Kodrou, which meets Voulis. A perfect family hotel with bath and phones in each plush room, and a delightful rooftop lounge with a view of the Acropolis. Bar open daily 6:30-9:30pm. Singles 8800-12,300dr/€25.83-36.10; doubles 12,800-17,600dr/€37.56-51.65. A/C 1500dr/€4.40 extra per person. Discounts for stays of more than 2 days.

Hotel Kimon, Apollonos 27 (☎33 14 658; fax 32 14 203), 1 block from the Mitropoli Cathedral. Friendly, safe, close to the sights, and there's a quiet roof garden. Singles 8000-10,000dr/€23.48-29.35; doubles and triples 10,000-12,000dr/€29.35-35.22. Private baths 1000dr/€2.93 extra per person. A/C 1500dr/€4.40 extra.

MONASTIRAKI

Like Plaka and Syndagma, Monastiraki lies at the center of things. You'll be close to the flea market and nightlife of Psiri. It's noisy fun.

■ **Pella Inn,** Karaiskaki 1 (☎32 50 598; fax 32 50 598). Walk 10min. down Ermou from Pl. Syndagma; it's 2 blocks from the Monastiraki subway station. Near the hip hangouts of Monastiraki, Pella features a large terrace with impressive views of the Acropolis to complement the comfy rooms. Breakfast 800dr/€2.35. Free luggage storage. Common bathrooms. Dorms 3000-4000dr/€8.80-11.74; doubles 10,000-12,000dr/€29.35-35.22; triples 12,000-15,000dr/€35.22-44; quads 16,000-20,000dr/€46.96-58.69.

Hotel Tempi, Aiolou 29 (☎32 13 175 or 32 42 940; fax 32 54 179; www.travelling.gr/tempihotel). Wedged between an assortment of street vendors, Tempi rents simple rooms with ceiling fans. Rooms facing the rear are much dimmer—ask for a front-facing room. Free luggage storage. Singles 7500dr/€22; doubles 11,000dr/€32.28, with bath 12,500dr/€36.68; triples 15,000dr/€44. Off-season prices 20% less.

ATHENS

OMONIA

If you're leaving Athens on an early morning bus or train (or arriving on a late one), you can roll out of bed to your ride from Omonia. Don't travel alone at night.

Hostel Aphrodite, Einardou 12 (☎88 10 589 or 88 39 249; fax 88 16 574; hostel-aphrodite@ath.forthnet.gr). From the Victoria subway station, follow Heiden 2 blocks, then continue along Peioniou 2 more. Turn right on Michail Voda and left on Einardou. From the train station, take Filadelfias to Michail Voda. A staircase with an erotic mural leads to a swingin' 24hr. basement bar. Small, comfy rooms. Breakfast 900-1500dr/€2.64-4.40. Safety deposit box, free luggage storage, Internet access (2000dr/€5.87 per hr.), and laundry (3500dr/€10.27 per 6kg). 24hr. reception. Dorms 3500-4500dr/€10.27-13.21; doubles 11,000-13,000dr/€32.28-38.15; triples 15,000-16,500dr/€44-48.15; quads 18,000-20,000dr/€52.82-58.69. Private baths extra.

Athens International Hostel (HI), Victor Hugo 16 (☎52 34 170 and 52 31 095; fax 52 34 015; athenshostel@interland.gr). Walk down Tritis Septembriou from Pl. Omonia and take a left on Veranzerou, which becomes Victor Hugo after crossing Marni. A few minutes from the Metahourgio subway stop. A continental crowd packs this HI-affiliated youth hostel, the only one in Greece—you'll need to be an HI member or buy a membership (4200dr/€12.33) to stay here. Hot water 6-10am and 6-10pm. Laundry (2000dr/€5.87) and travel office available. Breakfast and sheets included. Call or email for reservation. Priority is given to current HI members. Dorms 2850dr/€8.36.

Hotel Arta, Nikitara 12 (☎38 27 753 or 38 22 881). Take Stadiou to Benaki from Omonia, turn left, and take the 3rd left onto Nikitara. It's in a nice part of Omonia, and very clean. Rooms vary widely so ask for another if you don't like what you see. All rooms have bath and A/C. Breakfast 1500dr/€4.40. Singles 8000-10,000dr/€23.48-29.35; doubles 12,000-14,000dr/€35.22-44; triples 15,000-17,000dr/€44-49.89.

EXARHIA

Home to Athens's student population, Exarhia has some of the city's hippest digs. Convenient to the National Archaeological Museum, the neighborhood is within walking distance of major public transportation but is quieter and brighter than nearby Pl. Omonia, making it a good choice for young budget travelers.

■ **Hotel Dryades,** Dryadon 4 (☎38 27 116 or 33 02 387). Elegant Dryades offers some of Athens's nicest budget-conscious accommodations, with large rooms and private baths. Full kitchen and TV lounge. Breakfast 1500dr/€4.40. Internet 1000dr/€2.93 per hr., 500dr/€1.47 minimum. Singles 10,000-12,000dr/€29.35-35.22; doubles 13,000-15,000dr/€38.15-44; triples 16,000-18,000dr/€46.96-52.82.

Hotel Orion, Em. Benaki 105 (☎38 27 362 or 38 20 191; fax 38 05 193). From Pl. Omonia, walk up Em. Benaki or take bus #230 from Pl. Syndagma. Filled with hip travelers intent on seeing more than Athens's tourist magnets, Orion rents small rooms with shared baths. Sunbathers relax on the rooftop with music, TV, and board games. Breakfast 1500dr/€4.40. Singles 7000-8000dr/€20.53-23.48; doubles 9000-10,000dr/€26.41-29.35; triples 11,000-12,000dr/€32.28-35.22.

The Exarcheion, Themistokleous 55 (☎38 00 731 or 38 01 256; fax 38 03 296). Enjoy the stairway's stylish mural on your way to one of the 50 rooms, each with phone, TV, and a view of Exharia. Private baths and A/C. Breakfast 1200dr/€3.52. 24hr. bar, Internet for guests (1200dr/€3.52 per hr.), and a roof garden. Make reservations. Singles 10,000dr/€29.35; doubles 12,000dr/€35.22; triples 15,000dr/€44. Off-season prices 10% less. 10% discount for *Let's Go* users.

KOLONAKI AND PANGRATI

High prices and the sizeable distance from the major sights make Kolonaki better to visit than to stay in. Though it's far from Athens's main attractions, Pangrati offers affordable accommodations.

▧**Youth Hostel #5 Pangrati,** Damareos 75 (☎75 19 530; fax 75 10 616; y-hostels@ote-net.gr). From Omonia or Pl. Syndagma take trolley #2 or 11 to Filolaou (past Imittou), or walk through the National Garden, down Eratosthenous Efthidiou, then 3 blocks to Frinis, and down Frinis until Damareos on the right. There's no sign for this cheery hostel—just the number 75 and a green door. Bulletin boards spread hosteler wit and wisdom, and the owner speaks English. TV lounge and full kitchen facilities. Hot showers 100dr/€0.29 for 5min. Sheets 250dr/€0.73, pillowcases 150dr/€0.44 each. Laundry token 1000dr/€2.93 at reception; hang your stuff to dry on the roof. Quiet hours 2-5pm and 11pm-7am. Dorms 2500dr/€7.34. Roof 2000dr/€5.87; bring a sleeping bag.

◘ FOOD

SYNDAGMA

Cheap fast food saturates Syndagma like a grease stain on paper. Chains like Goody's, Wendy's, and McDonald's dispense cheeseburgers, french fries, and sodas for 1450dr/€4.26, or traditional *tost* (a grilled sandwich) with feta and lettuce for 500dr/€1.47. **Everest** and **Delikiosk** make cheap sandwiches like ham and cheese croissants for 650dr/€1.91. For quickie eats, try the family-owned joints on Nikis: **Makrigianni,** (#54), **Mirabelle,** (#34), or **To Apollonion,** (#10).

▧**Nikis Cafe,** Nikis 3 (☎32 34 971), near Ermou. More of a cafe than an eatery, Nikis does serve fresh baguette sandwiches (900dr/€2.64) and quiche. Its bright modern art rivals its equally bright cocktails: strawberry and banana frozen margaritas 2000dr/€5.87. Open M-Sa 8am-1am.

Kentrikon, Kolokotroni 3 (☎32 32 482 or 32 35 623), near Stadiou, next to the National Historical Museum. Traditional (and lovely) Greek dishes around 2500dr/€7.34; branch out with pasta *bolognaise* (2100dr/€6.16) or veal with spinach ragout (2700dr/€7.92). Vegetarian options. Open M-F noon-6pm.

Restaurant Palea Athina, Nikis 48 (☎32 45 777). Inexpensive elegance pervades here; just go at night, when dim lighting masks the lack of scenery. Vegetable risotto 1500dr/€4.40, mussels with bacon 1900dr/€5.58. Open daily noon-12:30am.

PLAKA

For do-it-yourself meals, **minimarkets** on Nikis sell basic groceries. Most of the tavernas along Kidathineon, Plaka's main drag, are roughly equivalent; explore quieter streets like **Tripodon** and **Lysiou** for the gems. The restaurants have a traditional feel, many with live Greek music and dancing or stunning views of the Acropolis and Mt. Lycavittos. Check the menus before you sit down—the main tourist area restaurants tend to be expensive.

▧**Eden Vegetarian Restaurant,** Lissiou 12 (☎32 48 858). Take Kidathineon to Tripidon, then left on to Lysiou; it's on the first corner. Greece's first vegetarian restaurant is a mini totalitarian organic state—vegetables, beer, wine, cheese, the whole shebang. Fantastic dishes like *boureki pie* (zucchini with feta; 1600dr/€4.70), hummus (900dr/€2.64), *moussaka* with organic soy (1800dr/€5.28), and flavorful mushrooms *stifado* with onions and peppers (2900dr/€8.50). Open M and W-Su noon-midnight.

▧**Jungle Juice,** Aiolou 21, under the Acropolis (☎/fax 33 16 739; athens@junglejuice.it). Snag a turkey sandwich (500dr/€1.47) at this fresh-squeezed smoothie and sandwich stand, and wash it down with the "Leone Melone," a blended drink of cantaloupe, mango, and pineapple (900dr/€2.64). Open daily 8am-9pm.

▧**Sissofos,** Mnisikleous 31 (☎32 46 043; www.sissifos.gr). The multi-lingual manager will "rescue" you from the hilly street and set you up on the rooftop patio with dishes like "lamb with potatoes in the oven" (3100dr/€9.10). The candlelight, view, and deliciously large portions make the price tag worthwhile. Open daily 6:30pm-2am.

T. Stamatopoulos, Lissiou 26 (☎32 28 722 or 32 18 549). Family-owned since 1882, the restaurant has an outdoor terrace and—the star attraction—Greek dancing to live music (9:30-11pm). Veal in wine sauce 2200dr/€6.46. Open daily 7pm-2:30am.

MONASTIRAKI

Give up fresh breath in exchange for cheap food by eating some *tzatziki*-smothered gyros at the flea market. You can explore the chic options that stretch the boundaries of regulation Greek cooking at the markets. Stock up on groceries at **Market Sophos**, Mitropoleos 78 (☎/fax 32 26 677), near Aiolou.

■ **Savvas,** Mitropoleos 86 (☎32 45 048; fax 32 45 505), tucked in a corner off Ermou. For takeout, this grill is a budget eater's dream, with heavenly, cheap gyros (400dr/€1.17); just don't sit down—prices skyrocket. Souvlaki plate 1700dr/€5. Open 7:30am-3am.

Attalos Restaurant, Adrianou 9 (☎32 19 520), near the Thisseon area. Frequented by VIPs from the US Embassy, this traditional Greek taverna serves skewered souvlaki (1900dr/€5.58), as well as a variety of handmade *croquettes* (a vegetarian plate for 2-4 people costs 2600dr/€7.63). *Bouzouki* photos adorn the wall. Open 9am-2am.

Dia Tafta, Adrianou 37 (☎32 12 347), near the Agora. A huge bar lines one wall of the interior, but the streetside tables make it popular. Fresh Greek salad 1700dr/€5, variety platters for 4 3500-6500dr/€10.27-19.08. Open daily 9:30am-1:30am.

OMONIA

As in Syndagma, the immediate area around Pl. Omnia is filled with fast food joints—busy thoroughfares **30 Septembriou** and **28 Octovriou** (Pastission) are alive at all hours. For those with kitchen access, pick up ingredients at **Galaxias Discount Market,** Tritis Septembriou 26. To quiet late-night stomach rumblings, stop by the meat market (no, not another club) on **Athinas** between Monastiraki and Omonia, where night-owl restaurants are open 3-7am.

Healthy Food Vegetarian Restaurant, Panepistimiou 57 (☎32 10 966; fax 32 12 043). Wholesomeness to make a souvlaki stand blush—everything's made fresh. *Muesli* (1050dr/€3.08), carrot apple juice (500dr/€1.47). Open daily 8am-9:30pm.

Dafni Taverna, Iolianou 65 (☎82 13 914). From Pl. Victoria, walk down Aristotelous and turn right on Iolianou. You'll know it's a classic the second you enter the grapevine-shaded courtyard walled by barrels of *retsina*. Traditional Greek appetizers 600-1000dr/€1.76-2.93, entrees 1600dr/€4.70 or less. Open daily noon-1am.

Souvlaki Pitta Pan, Patission 8. Bite this, Captain Hook! This Greek rendition dusts the neighboring fast food behemoths—fairy-style. Souvlaki (chicken 400dr/€1.17), and full meals with fries, pita, tomato, and *tzatziki* (1500dr/€4.40). Open daily 11am-11pm.

EXARHIA

Starving twentysomethings demand inexpensive food around Exarhia. Many of the options are basic, but savory: think souvlaki, Greek classics, and a jug of wine.

■ **O Barba Giannis,** Em. Benaki 94 (☎33 00 185). From Syndagma, walk up Stadiou and make a right on Em. Benaki. Athenian students, execs, and artists all agree that "Uncle John's" is the place for cheap, delicious food and outstanding service. Lots of fish (from 1200dr/€3.52), *moussaka* (1400dr/€4.10), vegetarian dishes (1000dr/€2.93), and wine (1000dr/€2.93); ask about the day's choices. Open daily 1pm-1am; closed Su in summer. Bring a Greek phrase book, because there's no English spoken here.

Souvlaki Kavouras, Themistokleous 64 (☎38 37 981). Although its name promises souvlaki crabs, there's no seafood, just super-cheap souvlaki (300dr/€0.88) and beer (350dr/€1.03) in the rear courtyard. Open daily 10am-6am.

Yiantes, Baltetsion 44 (☎33 01 369), next to the movie theatre. Enter this blue-walled oasis of snaking vines and little tables for a traditional Greek meal (drinks and all) for 4000-5000dr/€11.74-14.67. Fresh fish 2000dr/€5.87. Open daily 1pm-1am.

Bergina, Baltetsiou 62, by Pl. Exarhia (☎33 02 136 or 38 07 992). A favorite among local Exharians, the traditional Greek food is pre-prepared at this take-out restaurant; call ahead or walk in. Entrees 1100-1500dr/€3.23-4.40. Open daily noon-1am.

KOLONAKI

The surest bargain is the Friday morning **street market** on Xenokratous, where you can grab a week's supply of peanuts, potatoes, and fresh clementines. Otherwise, this is the place to splurge with a super-swanky meal.

■ **Pluto,** Plutarchou 38 (☎72 44 713; www.thepluto.com). Owner and culinary mastermind Constandinos has created a chic restaurant with warm ambience and an international menu. Waves of Greek and international customers line up for seats at the spice-filled glass tables every night. The menu is constantly evolving, but try the grilled eggplant with feta and tomatoes (2500dr/€7.34), seafood paella (3400dr/€10), or sinful strawberry meringue (2000dr/€5.87). Open daily 11am-3am. **Pluto Sushi** is next door.

Jackson Hall, Millioni 4 (☎36 16 098), dominates the small footpath 2 blocks down the hill from Kolonaki. The spot for homesick Americans and Yankophiles, and a place to be seen. This noisy restaurant serves food (and kitsch) to please any red-blooded American. Chicken *miama* or risotto (3900dr/€11.45). Sip a beer (2000dr/€5.87) as the DJ spins 70s, 80s, and 90s pop. Open daily 10am-2am.

I Thexameni (☎72 92 578), in Pl. Thexamenis, down the sloped pathway left of Deinokratous. Eat *saganaki* (950dr/€2.79) or Greek salad (1200dr/€3.52) under the trees and street lamps of this favorite local ouzeri. Open daily 8:30am-2am.

PANGRATI

You can pick up fresh food Thursday mornings at the **street market** off Pl. Plastira. Head to Pl. Caravel for cafes and **Veropoulos,** Formionos 23, a large nearby supermarket. (Open Su-F 8am-9pm, Sa 8am-6pm.)

Evdokia, Pl. Plastira 2 (☎75 64 879), in a small storefront tucked in a corner of the square. Try the cheap veggie pizza (450dr/€1.32) or *spanakopita* (400dr/€1.17).

Dragon Palace, Andinoros 1 (☎72 42 795 or 72 35 783). From Syndagma, take Vas. Sofias, turn right onto Rizari at the War Museum, cross the lights and take a left onto Andinoros. Both the restaurant and the Peking duck (6700dr/€19.66) are large and elegant; Szechuan chicken (2100dr/€6.16) packs a spicy punch. Take-out and delivery. Open daily noon-1am; July-Aug. 7pm-1am.

Kallimarmarou, Eforiouos 13 (☎70 19 727 or 70 17 234). Rabbit with mustard sauce (3100dr/€9.10) and shrimp baked in salted biscuits (3700dr/€10.86) will wow you.

■ NIGHTLIFE

Athenian nightlife changes with the seasons. In the winter months, the neighborhoods of **Exharia, Kifissia, Psiri,** and **Syndagma** roar with action. Once summer rolls around the young and sizzling move their groove to the beach side clubs of **Glyfada, Voula, Vari,** and **Vouliagmeni.** Aside from the clubbing hotspots, much of Athens hums with that uniquely Greek hybrid, the cafe-bar, where you can start your day early with a coffee and proceed to a boozy night-time binge at the same place.

PLAKA

For a spellbinding 360° view of Athens at night, go up to **Pnyx Hill** (a.k.a. the Rock of Ares), opposite the Acropolis. Once the meeting place of the ancient Athenian assembly, the hill now brings natives and tourists together to listen to guitar-strumming by the city lights. Take care when ascending the smooth, slippery steps. Enjoy a film in the night breeze at **Cine Paris,** Kidatheneon 22. (☎32 22 071 or 32 48 057. 2nd-run English-language films at 8:50 and 11pm. Tickets 2000dr/€5.87.)

Bretto's, Kidatheneon 41 (☎32 32 110). The walls are lit up with colorful bottles of ouzo, brandy, and other liqueurs, all made by friendly Dimitris in his family's 100-year-old distilleries. Buy a bottle for later (5ml-1L), or get an immediate fix at the bar. The homemade wine in the barrels along the back wall is 1500dr/€4.40 per bottle, 500dr/€1.47 per glass. Open daily 10am-midnight.

Lava Bore, Filellinon 25 (☎32 45 335), on the corner of Simonidi by Amalias, or 200m up Kidatheneon from the Student and Traveller's Inn. This dance club tries hard to live up to its swankier, more crowded Glyfada counterparts. 1000dr/€2.93 cover includes a drink. Open Su-Th 10pm-4am, F-Sa 10pm-5am.

MONASTIRAKI

The **Psiri** district is the new place to see and be seen in Athens, and Monastiraki's nightlife has revved to up to rival Glyfada.

▨ **Vibe,** Aristophanous 1 (☎32 44 794); just beyond Plateia Iroön. The blue orbs hanging above the entrance are just a taste of the fantastic lighting effects in the bar's interior.

▨ **Bee** (☎32 12 624), at the corner of Miaoli and Themidos, off Ermou; a few blocks from the heart of Psiri. A red pillar wrapped with 1000 tiny red lights lends an amorous glow to the flirtations of all orientations below. DJs spin while the friendly staff keeps the booze flowing. Drinks 1000-2500dr/€2.93-7.34. Open daily 9pm-late.

Revekka, Miaouli 22 (☎32 11 174). Unassuming by day, this eclectic little cafe-bar blossoms at night, when tables spill out onto the sidewalk and darkness brings youth, music, and flowing drinks. Open late.

EXARHIA

Exarhia exudes its funkiness in its many bars, which showcase everything from backgammon to death metal. Check *Athens News* for showtimes of second-run movies at **Cinema Rivera,** Baltetsiou 46 (tickets 2000dr/€5.87).

Metal Cafe Dionysos, Em. Benaki 96A & Valtetsiou. Superficial conflict (backgammon vs. heavy-metal themed decor and music), leads to ultimate fun. Coffee 700dr/€2.05, beer 1000-1500dr/€2.93-4.40. Open daily 1:30pm-3am.

Rock Underground, Metaxa 21 (☎38 22 019). For a British flavor, try this cafe/bar.

Mr. Wired, Valtetsiou 61. The red parachute on the ceiling and thorn bushes painted on the walls give this rock cafe-bar an eerie Alice-in-Wonderland atmosphere. Open daily 10:30-late.

Aria, Em. Benaki 72 & Metaxa (☎38 42 077). Artsy and bright; the wine bar in the old house next door opens up when the winter months bring colder weather. Toast 1000dr/€2.93, *frappé* 900dr/€2.64. Open daily 10am-2am.

KOLONAKI

Kolonaki is brimming with cafes and bars. **Haritos** street to the right of Plutarchou is the spot for summertime action—if you're prepared to shell out major drachmas for drinks. **City, Azul, Baila,** and **Mousa** (Μουσα), all at Haritos 43, spill sophisticated patrons into the street, are open very late, and charge around 1600dr/€4.70 for a beer, 2500dr/€7.34 for a cocktail. On **Millioni** street by Jackson Hall smaller crowds chat over drinks and little outdoor tables.

Summertime performances are staged in Lycavittos Theater as part of the **Athens Festival** (p. 27), which has included acts from the Greek Orchestra to Pavarotti to the Talking Heads. The **Festival Office,** Stadiou 4, sells student tickets. An English-language schedule of events is available in mid-June. (☎32 21 459 or 32 27 944. Tickets 3000-5000dr/8.80-14.67. Open M-F 9:30am-4pm, Sa-Su 9:30am-2pm.) Open-air cinema in Dexameni square shows current movies. (Nightly shows 8:50 and 11pm. 2200dr/€6.46, students 1500dr/€4.40, children under 5 free.)

Cafe 48, Karneadou 48 (☎72 52 434), 2 blocks up the hill from Vas. Sofias. Expat classicists and student travelers exchange stories at the bar and moves on the small indoor dance floor. With a student ID, beer costs 800dr/€2.35, punch is 1000dr/€2.93, and a free shot comes with each drink on Tu and Th. Open M-Sa 9am-2am, Su 4pm-2am.

Jazz in Jazz, Dinokratous 4. From behind the well-worn wooden bar, Kostas can be persuaded to muse about jazz and teach swing lessons. Endless old jazz records draw Athens's faithful. 1500dr/€4.40 cover includes a drink. Open daily Nov.-May noon-3am.

The Daily, Xenokratous 47 (☎ 72 23 430). This small cafe-bar is where Kolonaki's chic foreign student populations converge to imbibe, take in Latin music and reggae, and watch soccer and basketball on TV. Fabulous, shaded outdoor seating and open-air bar. Pints of Heineken 1000dr/€2.93. Open daily 9am-2am.

PANGRATI

The cafes along Imittou let you people-watch in style. A walk between Imittou 128 and 67 passes people drinking coffee, playing backgammon, chatting on cell phones, and socializing. Most cafes are open daily 9am-2am. Second-run movies show twice nightly at Imittou 107 (2000dr/€5.87). **Village Cinemas,** Imittou 10 & Hremonidou, in the Millennium Center, shows the latest blockbusters in state-of-the-art theaters. (☎ 75 72 440. Shows around 1, 6, and 10pm. Call for listings.)

Sideradiko Cafe, Imittou 128 (☎ 70 18 700; fax 75 68 559; www.sideradikocafe.gr). The name ("steel"), fits the metal, stone, and mirror interior. Despite the severe decor, it offers a comfy night of Trivial Pursuit, Abalone, Scrabble, or MindTrap. Fresh fruit juices 1300dr/€3.82, beer 1200dr/€3.52. Open daily 9am-3am.

Letzos, Imittou 120 (☎ 70 19 657). The funky pop of this music cafe stretches to its tables on both sides of the street. Ice cream 1300dr/€3.82, sandwiches 500dr/€1.47, tea or coffee 600dr/€1.76. Open daily 6am-1am.

Ellas Espresso, Pl. Plastira 8 (☎ 75 62 565; www.night.gr/espresso), is a large cafe with a shaded terrace and 4 TVs suspended above its indoor bar. Greek salad 1200dr/€3.52, *frappé* 950dr/€2.79. A DJ spins in the evening. Open daily 9am-3am.

GLYFADA AND THE COAST

It's hot, you're cool…where to go? Come summertime, join the chic of the Athens club scene as they migrate to the big, swanky, seaside clubs of **Glyfada,** past the airport. Take the **A3** or the **B3 bus** from Vas. Amalias (along the street to the right of the top corner of Pl. Syndagma; 250dr/€0.73) to Glyfada, and then catch a cab from there to your club. A **taxi** to Glyfada should cost no more than 2500dr/€7.34, but the ride back into the center of Athens in the early morning—due to heavy traffic and higher nighttime rates—can cost 5000-7000dr/€14.67-20.53. Beware greedy taxi drivers. If they pack the cab with more than just your party, don't let them swindle you into a set individual price. Remember what the total should roughly be and don't agree to pay more than that.

Most of the clubs are spread out along Poseidonos Street, each a few kilometers apart. **Privilege, Venue, Prime,** and **Envy** are worth the trip out. Hoards of serious-looking bouncers with earpieces guard the doorways to swanky open-air bars beneath discoballs and strobe lights. Cover is usually 3000dr/€8.80. Drinks vary from 1200-3000dr/€3.52-8.80, but can go as high as 60,000dr/€175.08 for an individual bottle of port for your table. Also look for **+Soda, King Size,** and **Bedside.** Along Pergamon Street look for **Camel Club.** Top 40, funk, or house plays until around 2am, at which point Greek music (live or recorded) takes over. Dance, drink, and eye the beautiful crowd against the backdrop of the ocean, only a few feet away.

◉ SIGHTS

ACROPOLIS

Reach the entrance on the west side of the Acropolis either from Areopagitou to the south, by following the signs from Plaka, or by exiting the Agora to the south, following the path uphill, and turning right. Not wheelchair accessible. The marble can be slippery, so wear shoes with good traction. ☎32 10 219. Open 8am-6:30pm; winter 8am-2:30pm. Admission to site and Acropolis Museum 2000dr/€5.87, students and EU seniors 1000dr/€2.93, under 18 free. If you plan on visiting all of the sights under the Acropolis (including Hadrian's Arch, the Olympian Temple of Zeus, and the Agora) you may purchase a ticket for 4000dr/€11.74 at any of the sites, which will give you access to them all. At press time, the decision as to the number of days the ticket would be valid had not been made.

ATHENS

ATHENS

The Acropolis

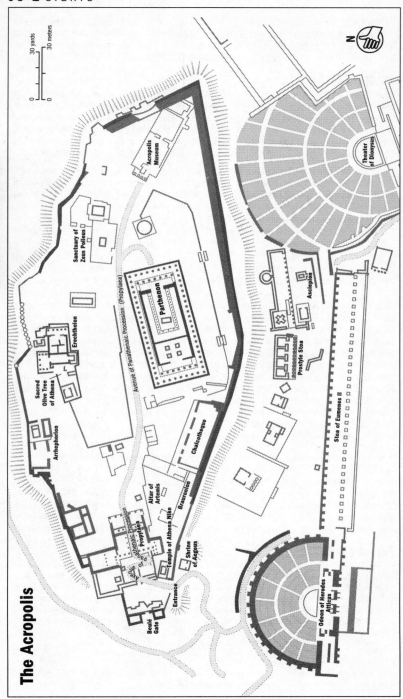

N

30 yards
30 meters

Acropolis Museum

Theater of Dionysus

Sanctuary of Zeus Polieus

Parthenon

Erechtheion

Asclepion

Sacred Olive Tree of Athena

Prostyle Stoa

Arrhephorion

Chalcotheque

Stoa of Eumenes II

Altar of Artemis

Brauronion

Temple of Athena Nike

Shrine of Aegeus

Panathenaic Procession

Propylaea

Statue of Athena

Odeon of Herodes Atticus

Entrance

Beulé Gate

Perched on a rocky plateau above the city, the Acropolis has crowned Athens since the 5th century BC. The brilliant Parthenon at its center towers over the Aegean and the plains of Attica, the greatest achievement of Athens's Classical glory and the era's most enduring architectural contribution. Although each Greek *polis* had an *acropolis* ("height of the city"), Athens's magnificent example has effectively monopolized the name. It stands timelessly, awe-inspiringly upright—though steel scaffolding and restoration work often embrace it—amid otherwise rubble-strewn grounds. Visit as early in the day as possible to avoid massive crowds and the broiling, humbling midday sun.

HISTORY

BEGINNINGS. With its view toward both land and sea, the Acropolis began as a strategically located military fortress. It was initially controlled by one ruler, who lived in a palace that doubled as a temple to a nature goddess and later to Athena. Around the 12th century BC, the original aristocrats, wealthy landowners calling themselves the **Aristoi** ("excellent ones"), ousted the monarch. They shifted government away from the Acropolis to the city's northern foothills, in an area that later became the **Agora** (see p. 101). The Acropolis became a purely religious center for worshiping Athena, whose wooden shrine celebrated both Athena Polias, goddess of crops and fertility, and Pallas Athena, loving virgin and protectress of the city (she added the name Pallas in honor of a mortal friend).

PERICLEAN PROJECT. The Acropolis's world-famous form took shape in 507 BC, when the *Aristoi* were overthown and Athens began its experiment with democracy. In 490 BC, Athenians began constructing a new temple on the Acropolis, this time in marble. Ten years later, Aegean rulers under attack from the Persians, formed the Delian League, and **Pericles** started piling up a slush fund from the taxes paid by the league to beautify Athens. He continued this practice long after the Persian threat evaporated, blowing the money on projects like the temples of the Acropolis, the **Hephaesteion** in the Agora, and the **Temple of Poseidon** at Sounion. His program was mocked as lavish and unscrupulous; Plutarch reports that Pericles was "gilding and bedizening" the city like a "wanton woman adding precious stones to her wardrobe." Nevertheless, after delays caused by the Peloponnesian War (431-404 BC), the Periclean project was completed. Four of the buildings erected thus still stand today: the **Parthenon**, the **Propylaea**, the **Temple of Athena Nike**, and the **Erechtheion**.

CAPTURE AND RESTORATION. Almost as soon as the Acropolis was completed, it fell to Sparta; ever since, its function has changed whenever it changed hands. **Byzantine Christians** added the symbolic power of the Parthenon to their faith arsenal; they turned the temple into the Church of Ag. Sophia ("Sophia," like "Athena," means wisdom). In 1205, **Frankish Crusaders** turned back the clock and again made the Acropolis into a fortress/palace/headquarters, this time for the Dukes de la Roche. Eventually, the Parthenon served as a Catholic church, Notre Dame d'Athènes. In the 15th century, **Ottomans** used the Parthenon as a mosque and the Erechtheion as the Ottoman commander's harem. In a 1687 **Venetian** siege, Ottoman gunpowder stored in the Parthenon blew its roof off; squalor ensued as Ottoman guards and their families settled on the Acropolis. In 1833, the newly independent Greeks reclaimed the hill, dismantling remnants of the Turkish occupation and resurrecting the Temple of Nike.

The subsequent preservation and restoration of the Acropolis has kicked up a swirl of impassioned controversy. The first wave of large-scale restoration began in 1898 and lasted almost forty years, transforming the site by demolishing and reconstructing the Temple of Nike. Many of the Parthenon's most important pieces have survived, since they were nicked by English ambassador Lord Elgin and spirited away to the British Museum in London. In the last 20 years, acid rain has forced works formerly displayed outside to take cover in the on-site museum.

RUINS

When you enter the Acropolis, the reconstructed **Temple of Athena Nike** lies before you. Though the Classical-era ramp that led to the Acropolis no longer exists, today's visitors still make an awe-inspiring climb. The path leads through the crumbling Roman **Beulé Gate,** named for a French archaeologist who unearthed it. It continues through the **Propylaea,** the ancient entrance famous for its ambitious multi-level design. Begun by Mnesikles between 437 and 432 BC; it was never completed. Innovative Mnesikles improved upon the Doric and Ionic styles, tying the Propylaea's Ionic columns with a massive Doric exterior.

PARTHENON. Looming over the hillside, the **Temple of Athena Parthenos** (Athena the virgin), more commonly known as the Parthenon, keeps vigil over Athens and the modern world. Iktinos designed the Parthenon to be the crowning glory of the Periclean project; he added two extra columns to the usual six in the front of the temple, thus adding a stately majesty to the traditional Doric design. More subtle refinements transformed the usual Doric boxiness: the upward bowing of the temple's *stylobate* (pedestal) and the slight swelling of its columns compensate for the optical illusion in which, from a distance, straight lines appear to bend. The Parthenon's elegance shows the Classical Athenian obsession with proportion—everything from the layout to the carved entablature shared the same four-to-nine ratio in size (a variation on the "Golden Mean"). Inside the temple, in front of a pool of water, stood Phidias's greatest sculptural masterpiece, a 40-ft. chryselephantine (ivory and gold) statue of Athena. Although the statue has been lost, the National Museum houses a 2nd-century Roman copy, which is fearsomely grand even at one-twelfth the size of the original.

Ancient Athenians saw their city as the capital of civilization, and the **metopes** (scenes in the open spaces above the columns) around the sides of the Parthenon celebrate Athens's rise. On the far right of the south side—the only side that has not been defaced—the Lapiths battle the Centaurs, while on the east side, the Olympian gods triumph over the giants. The north side faintly depicts the victory of the Greeks over the Trojans; the west side revels in their triumph over the Amazons. A well-preserved, bas relief frieze around the interior walls shows a group of Athenians hobnobbing with the gods. The **pediments** (triangular areas propped up by columns) at either end marked the zenith of Classical decorative sculpture. The **East Pediment** once depicted the birth of Athena, springing from Zeus's head, while the **West Pediment** showed Athena and Poseidon's contest for the city's eternal devotion; fragments are now housed in the Acropolis and British Museums.

TEMPLE OF ATHENA NIKE. This tiny cliff's-edge temple was raised during a respite from the Peloponnesian War called the Peace of Nikias (421-415 BC; see p. 11). The temple, known as the "jewel of Greek architecture," is ringed by eight miniature Ionic columns and once housed a statue of the winged goddess Nike. One day, in a paranoid frenzy, the Athenians were seized by a fear that Nike would flee the city and take peace with her, so they clipped the statue's wings. The remains of the 5m-thick **Cyclopean wall** lies below the temple. It predates the Classical Period, and once surrounded the entirety of the Acropolis.

ERECHTHEION. The Erechtheion, to the left of the Parthenon, was completed in 406 BC, just before Sparta defeated Athens in the Peloponnesian War. The building housed many gods in its time, grabbing its name from snake-bodied hero Erechtheus. Old Erechtheus couldn't stand up to Poseidon, who speared him with his trident in a battle over the city's patronage. When Poseidon struck a truce with Athena, he was allowed to share the temple with her—the east is devoted to the goddess of wisdom and the west to the god of the sea. The east porch, with its six Ionic columns, sheltered an olive wood statue of Athena; like the Temple of Athena Nike, it contrasts with the Parthenon's dignified

Doric columns. The Erechtheion's south side is supported by six women frozen in stone, the Caryatids. They're actually copies—the originals are safe in the Acropolis Museum (p. 101).

ACROPOLIS MUSEUM. This museum neighboring the Parthenon shelters a superb collection of sculptures, including five of the Caryatids of the Erechtheion; the sixth has been whisked off to the British Museum. The statues seem to be replicas of one another, but a close look at the folds of their drapery reveals delicately individualized detail. Compare the stylized, entranced faces and frozen poses of the Archaic Period *Moschophoros* (calf-bearer) sculpture to the more idealized, more human Classical-Period **Kritias** boy for a trip through the development of Greek sculpture. *(Open M 11am-6:30pm, Tu-Su 8am-6:30pm; off-season M 11am-2pm, Tu-Su 8am-2pm. Cameras without flash allowed; no posing next to the objects. English labels.)*

ELSEWHERE ON THE ACROPOLIS. The southwest corner of the Acropolis looks down over the reconstructed **Odeon of Herodes Atticus,** a functional theater dating from the Roman Period (AD 160). See the *Athens News* for a schedule of concerts and plays there. You'll also see nearby ruins of the Classical Theater of Dionysus, the Asclepion, and the Stoa of Eumenes II. *(Entrance on Dionissiou Areopagitou street. ☎ 32 21 459. Though the site is closed for general admission, performances are still held throughout the summer. Purchase tickets at the door or over the phone.)*

AGORA

Enter the Agora in one of three ways: off Pl. Thission, off Adrianou, or as you descend from the Acropolis. ☎ 32 10 185. Open Tu-Su 8:30am-3pm. 1200dr/€3.52, students and EU seniors 600dr/€1.76, EU students and under 18 free.

The Agora is Athens's heart, just below its soul, the Acropolis. It served as the city's marketplace, administrative center, and center of daily life from the 6th century BC through AD 500. The debates of Athenian democracy were argued in the Agora; Socrates, Aristotle, Demosthenes, Xenophon, and St. Paul all preached it here. After the 6th century AD, the Agora, like the Acropolis, passed through the hands of innumerable conquerors. The ancient Agora emerged again in the 19th century, when a residential area built above it was razed for excavations. Inhabited since 3000 BC, the Agora still stands at the center of Athens. Today, visitors have free reign over the 30-acre archaeological site it has become.

■ **HEPHAESTEION.** The Hephaesteion, on a hill in the northwest corner of the Agora, is the best-preserved classical temple in Greece. The 415 BC temple still flaunts cool **friezes,** which depict Hercules's labors and Theseus's adventures. The closer you look, the more impressed you'll be.

ODEON OF AGRIPPA. The Odeon of Agrippa, a concert hall built for Roman Emperor Augustus's son-in-law and right-hand man, now stands in ruins on the left of the Agora as you walk from the museum to the Hephaesteion. When the roof collapsed in AD 150, the Odeon was rebuilt at half its former size. From then on it served as a lecture hall. The actors' dressing room was turned into a porch supported by colossal statues, three of which still guard the site.

STOA OF ATTALOS. The elongated Stoa of Attalos was a multi-purpose building filled with shops, and home to informal philosophers' gatherings. Attalos II, King of Pergamon, built the Stoa in the 2nd century BC as a 3-D thank-you note to Athens for the education he had gotten there. Reconstructed between 1953 and 1956, it now houses the **Agora Museum,** which contains relics from the site. The stars of the collection are the excellent black figure paintings by Exekias, and a calyx-krater depicting Trojans and Greeks quarreling over Patroclus's body.

STOA BAILEIOS. Plato reports that Socrates's first trial was held at the recently excavated Stoa Basileios, the Royal Promenade of the Agora. As you cross the subway tracks at the Adrianou exit, it's on the left.

ATHENS

OTHER ANCIENT SITES

KERAMEIKOS. The Kerameikos's rigidly geometric design becomes clearly visible from above, before you enter the grounds. The site includes a large-scale cemetery and a 40m-wide boulevard that ran through the Agora and the Diplyon Gate and ended at the sanctuary of Akademos (where Plato founded his academy in the 4th century BC). **Public tombs** for state leaders, famous authors, and battle victims lined this sacred road, and worshipers began the annual Panathenaean procession along its path. The Sacred Gate arched over the Sacred Way to Eleusis, traversed in annual processions. The **Oberlaender Museum** displays finds from the burial sites; its excellent collection of highly detailed pottery and sculpture is a highlight. *(Ermou 48, northwest of the Agora. From Syndagma, walk toward Monastiraki on Ermou for 25min. ☎ 346 3552. Open Tu-Su 8:30-3pm. 500dr/€1.47, students and EU seniors 300dr/ €0.88, EU students and under 18 free.)*

TEMPLE OF OLYMPIAN ZEUS AND HADRIAN'S ARCH. In the middle of downtown Athens, you'll spot the final trace of the largest temple ever built in Greece. The 15 majestic Corinthian columns of the Temple of Olympian Zeus mark where the temple once stood. Started in the 6th century BC, it was completed 600 years later by the Roman emperor Hadrian. None too shy, Hadrian attached his name to the centuries-long effort by adding his arch, which marked the boundary between the ancient city of Theseus and Hadrian's own new city. A Roman bath (tiles and all) borders the site. *(Vas. Olgas at Amalias, next to the National Garden. ☎ 92 26 330. Open Tu-Su 8:30am-3pm. Temple admission 500dr/€1.47, EU students and under 18 free. Arch free.)*

BYZANTINE ATHENS

Viewing hours depend on each church's priest; mornings are best. Dress appropriately: long skirts for women, long pants for men, no bare shoulders.

Like their Classical counterparts, Byzantine sanctuaries have become a part of Athens's landscape. Religious Greeks often pause before churches to pay their respects before going about their business. A little time spent in a few churches gives a glimpse of the country's modern-day culture and faith.

Shoppers and pedestrians on Ermou will run right into **Kapnikaria Church,** which is stranded in the middle of the street one block beyond Aiolou. A bas relief decorates its west wall; it escaped destruction in 1834 only by the clemency of Louis I of Bavaria. Walking down Mitropoleos from Syndagma, you may notice a tiny red church on the corner of Pentelis—it's engulfed in a modern building. You'll also pass **Agios Eleftherios** and the **Mitropoli Cathedral. Agia Apostoli,** a well-preserved Byzantine church, stands at the east edge of the Agora in the heart of Athens. White-walled **Metamorphosis,** in Plaka near Pritaniou, was built in the 11th century and restored in 1956. Eleventh-century Russian Orthodox **Agia Triada,** a few blocks from Pl. Syndagma at Filellinon 21, is filled with silver angel icons.

MODERN ATHENS

OLYMPIC STADIUM. The Panathenaic Stadium is wedged between the National Gardens and Pangrati, carved into a hill. The Byzantines destroyed the Classical-era stadium, but in 1895 it was restored in Panteli marble. The site of the first modern Olympic Games in 1896, the stadium lay under a cloud of disappointment in 1996, when the centennial games were held in Atlanta. Still, in 1997, the stadium held the opening ceremonies of the World Track and Field Championships, and is now being refurbished in preparation for the **2004 Summer Olympics.** 70,000 people can pack in the stands of this preserve for athletes and sunbathing students; military parades and gymnastic displays are held here, and it's the finish line of *the* marathon. Marble *steles* near the front honor Greece's Olympic gold and silver medalists. *(On Vas. Konstandinou. From Syndagma, walk up Amalias 15min. to Vas Olgas, and follow it to the left. Or take trolley #2, 4, or 11 from Syndagma. Open daily 8am-8:30pm. Free.)*

AROUND SYNDAGMA. Be sure to catch the **changing of the guard** in front of the **Parliament** building. Every hour on the hour, two *evzones* (guards) wind up like toy soldiers, kick their tasseled heels in unison, and fall backward into symmetrical little guardhouses on either side of the **Tomb of the Unknown Warrior.** Unlike the stoic British beefeaters, *evzones* are known to give a wink and a smile. Their jovial manner matches their attire—pom-pommed clogs, *foustanelas* (short pleated skirts), and tasseled hats. Sunday at 10:45am, there's a ceremony with a band and the full guard troop. Athens's endangered species, greenery and shade, are preserved in the **National Gardens,** their natural environment. There's a duck pond and a sad little zoo. Grab a pastry (800dr/€2.35) from the *kafeneion* at the Irodou Atikou entrance to accompany you. Women shouldn't stroll here alone.

OUTDOOR MARKETS. Athens's two major markets attract bargain-hunters and browsers alike. The **Flea Market,** adjacent to Pl. Monastiraki, has a festive bazaar atmosphere: Picture a massive garage sale where old forks and teapots are sold alongside the odd family heirloom. *(Open M, W, and Sa-Su 8am-3pm; Tu and Th-F 8am-8pm; Su is the best day to go.)* If you're hankering for a **bouzouki,** seek out the master, Bill Aevorkian at Ifestou 6 (☎32 10 024). On Sunday, a sprawling **food market** takes over Athinas between Evripidou and Sofokleous. Not for the faint of heart, the **meat market** overwhelms with sights and smells of livers, kidneys, and skinned rabbits. Early risers can jostle with Athenian cooks (restauranteurs and moms alike) for choice meat, fish, fruits, vegetables, breads, and cheeses. *(Open M-Sa 8am-2pm.)*

MT. LYCAVITTOS. Of Athens's seven hills, Lycavittos is the largest and most central. Try ascending at sunset, when you can catch a last glimpse of Athens's densely packed continuous rooftops in daylight, and watch the city light up for the night. Take the **funicular** to the top (2min.; every 10-15min.; round-trip 1000dr/€2.93, children ages 3-10 500dr/€1.47)—the station is a healthy walk from the end of Ploutarchou. You can also hike up—it's a nice 15- to 20-min. walk from any approach. Bring water, watch out for slippery rocks, and don't climb alone (especially at night, when crimes, accidents, and misnavigation are most frequent). At the top you'll see the **Chapel of St. George,** where you might spy a couple tying the knot (open M-W and F-Su 8:45am-12:15am, Th 10:30am-12:15am). Light a candle (50dr/€0.15) under the ornately painted ceilings. A leisurely stroll around the church provides a view of Athens's endless panoramic expanse. Using the Acropolis as a point of reference, the neighborhoods of Monastiraki, Omonia, and Exarhia are on your right. Continuing clockwise, you will see Areos Park behind a small circular patch of green—that's Strefi, another hill. The flashy lights and music of the Lycavittos Theatre are 180° from the Acropolis. The eastern view looks out on more parks, Mt. Hymettus, and a glimpse of the Panathenaic Olympic Stadium, the National Garden, and the Temple of Olympian Zeus back near the Acropolis.

NATIONAL CEMETERY. The National Cemetery houses deceased politicians, actors, poets, and foreigners who died in Athens. There are currently two kinds of graves—family graves and rented graves that give up their bones to boxes after 3 years. Soon, space limits will allow only 3-year graves. Even VIPs will spend 3 years in the ground before moving to the Mausoleum Commons. As you enter the main gate, the Greek-speaking information bureau is on your left. The first graves are larger and more elaborate than most, as the rich and famous try to take it with them. On the left side of the first courtyard, archaeologist **Heinrich Schliemann,** excavator of Troy and Mycenae, lies in a pseudo-temple. To the left of the large statue of an angel is the tomb of **Melina Mercury,** a national film icon, who starred in *Never on Sunday* before becoming the Minister of Culture. On the main path, there is a small church where ceremonies are held for the dead. *(In Pangrati. From Pl. Syndagma walk down Amalias, turn left on Athenisiou Diakou, and then walk down Anapavseos. ☎92 21 621. Open daily 8:30am-5:30pm. Free. For guided tours call the Cultural Center, Akademias 50. ☎36 12 705 or 36 39 671. Dress respectfully.)*

NO STRINGS ATTACHED According to one story, Greek folk **shadow puppet theater** traces its origins to the 14th-century Ottoman Empire. Two men working on Sultan Orhan's new mosque, a stonemason named Karagöz and his foreman, Hacivat, were constantly distracting the rest of the crew with their fabulously witty, ribald conversations. In a rash fury, Orhan had the two jokesters executed, but soon after he found himself missing their humor. An inventive dervish attempted to entertain the bored, melancholic sultan with figures of the late twosome made from transparent camel skin, which he manipulated behind a screen lit with candles or oil lamps. Passed on from one anonymous puppet-master to the next over the following centuries, these **Karagöz** shadow shows evolved into bewitching spectacles of color, music, bawdy comedy, clever word play, slapstick, and political satire, migrating west in the early 19th century to usher in the distinctly Greek **Karaghiozis** shadow theater. Expert shadow puppet players, often an illiterate, itinerant bunch, traveled the countryside, sailed around the islands, and performed before cafe crowds sipping ouzo or coffee under the night sky. After the show, owner and puppet master split the proceeds from the food and drink. Today you can occasionally see shadow puppets on children's TV programs, or live at the one remaining permanent theater in the Athenian suburb of **Nea Smirni.** Ask at the Pl. Syndagma tourist information window for details.

🏛 MUSEUMS

NATIONAL ARCHAEOLOGICAL MUSEUM

Patission 44. A 20min. walk from Pl. Syndagma down Stadiou to Aiolou, and right onto Patission. Take trolley #2, 4, 5, 9, 11, 15, or 18 from the uphill side of Syndagma, or trolley #3 or 13 from the north side of Vas. Sofias. Or take the subway to Victoria, leave the station and walk straight to the first street, 28 Octovriou. Turn right and walk 5 blocks. ☎82 17 717. Open Apr.-Oct. M 12:30-7pm, Tu-Su 8am-7pm; Nov.-Mar. 8am-5pm; holidays 8:30am-3pm. 2000dr/€5.87, students and EU seniors 1000dr/€2.93; free Su and holidays from Nov.-Mar. No flash photography; no posing in front of the exhibits.

The jaw-dropping collection in the National Archaeological Museum deserves a spot on even the most rushed itinerary. Even a few pieces from this, the world's most extensive array of Greek artifacts, would steal the show in any other museum. Check your bags (free) and grab a **free map** of the museum. Hold on to your ticket, since the museum's arrangement redirects you to the entry several times, and you'll have to pay again if you lose it.

The museum begins with prehistoric pieces (room 4), including Heinrich Schliemann's **Mycenae** excavations (p. 120). At first glance you may think the German archaeologist discovered the Midas touch: it is a world of gold, including the ▨**Mask of Agamemnon** (the death mask of a king who lived at least 3 centuries earlier than Agamemnon himself). You'll also see samples of Bronze Age jewelry and pottery and, in the side rooms, magnificent examples of Cycladic art.

The next exhibition, made up of 29 rooms, surveys Greek **sculpture** from the 8th century BC through the 5th century AD. Buck-naked **kouroi,** or standing young men, allow the viewer to trace every last inch of Greek sculpture's development from early Archaic to late Roman. In room 12, don't miss the detailed, rippling abs of statue 13, a lifelike 540 BC work found at Megara. Compare the massive 530 BC Kouros of Sounion (item 2720), in room 8, to the 520 BC kouros named Kroisos (item 3851), in room 13; you'll notice how smoothness and fluidity seeped into sculpture over a decade. The 460 BC **bronze of Poseidon** poised to throw his trident (item 15161) seems to move—it was an inspiration to Renaissance artists in Western Europe. In room 21, the perfect bronze **Jockey of Atemision,** recovered from the sea and restored this century, is full of life.

Mentally reconstruct the scene depicted in room 30 by the 100 BC statue of Aphrodite and Eros squabbling with Pan. Move on to the fabulously sexy sculptures in room 32. The luscious neck, lips, and expression of the bust of **Antinous** (item 417), a favorite of the emperor Hadrian, will move you, while the suggestive pose of the sleeping maenad (item 261) may remind you of similar art from the pages of *Penthouse*. Sober up from such erotic exhibitions with the finds in room 48 on the second floor. Exquisite wall paintings and other finds come from **Anotiri Thira,** a 16th-century-BC civilization buried by volcanic eruption. Resembling both Egyptian and Minoan art, these images of dolphins, reeds, and a boy holding a fish highlight early fresco work. Finally, rooms 49-56 hold an overwhelming collection of 11th to 4th century-BC **pottery,** featuring pieces of every shape and style.

OTHER MUSEUMS

GOULANDRIS MUSEUM OF CYCLADIC & ANCIENT GREEK ART. This 15-year-old museum displays a stunning collection. The high-density exhibition space shows off its famous Cycladic figurines: sleek, abstract marble works, some with painted details that may represent tattoos. Many pieces were either looted from archaeological sites about 100 years ago or found in graves in the Cyclades. The figurines may represent goddesses, guides to the Underworld called *psychopompoi*, or concubines. Bronze jewelry from Skyros, a collection of vases, and Corinthian helmets share the space. Visit the extension of the Cycladic collection on the corner of Vas. Sofias and Herodotou. *(Neophytou Douka 4. A 20min. walk toward Kolonaki from Syndagma on Vas. Sofias; turn left on Neophytou Douna. It's half a block up. Accessible by trolleys #3 and 13 (120dr/€0.35). ☎72 28 321. Open M and W-F 10am-4pm, Su 10am-3pm. 1000dr/€2.93, students 500dr/€1.47, archaeologists and archaeology students free.)*

BYZANTINE MUSEUM. In an elegant Neoclassical building, the Byzantine Museum's excellent collection of Christian art spans the 4th through 19th centuries. Early Byzantine sculptures, icons from the entire period, and three reconstructed early Christian basilicas squeeze into the space. Room 4, in the back left corner of the ground floor, has a ceiling cut in the shape of the cross and mosaic-studded floor. It centers around an *omphalon* representing an eagle and a snake. Also on the ground floor, you'll find an ornately reconstructed 17th-century Kephalonian church, with the 1863 throne of the Patriarch of Constantinople. You might want to buy a guidebook (2500dr/€7.34) as exhibits are poorly marked. *(Vas. Sofias 22. ☎72 11 027 or 72 32 178. Open Tu-Su 8:30am-3pm. 500dr/€1.47; seniors 400dr/€1.17; students 300dr/€0.88; EU students, under 18, and classicists free.)*

NATIONAL GALLERY. The National Gallery (a.k.a. Alexander Soutzos Museum) exhibits the work of Greek artists, with periodic international displays. The permanent collection includes outstanding work by El Greco, as well as drawings, photographs, and sculpture gardens. Call about current exhibits. *(Vas. Konstandinou 50. Set back from Vas. Sofias, next to the Hilton. ☎72 35 857 or 72 35 937. Open M and W-Sa 9am-3pm, Su 10am-2pm. 1500dr/€4.40, students and seniors 500dr/€1.47, under 12 free.)*

WAR MUSEUM. Canons and fighter jets mark the museum, which traces Greek armaments from Neolithic times to the present. It's cool if you're into submachine guns, 5th century BC Persian invasions, or Alexander the Great. Model tanks, bombs, and booby traps amuse your inner psycho. *(Rizari 2. Next to the Byzantine Museum, off Vas. Sofias. ☎72 90 543. Open Tu-F 9am-2pm, Sa-Su 9:30am-2pm. Free.)*

FOLK ART MUSEUM. Exhibiting *laiki techni* (popular art) from all over Greece, the museum has embroidered textiles, costumes, puppets, ornamental church silverwork, and household pottery. Don't miss the temporary exhibits or **Theophilos**'s (p. 24) paintings. *(Kedatheneon 17, in Plaka. ☎32 29 031 or 32 42 066. Open Tu-Su 10am-2pm. 500dr/€1.47, EU students and children free. No flash photography.)*

POPULAR MUSICAL INSTRUMENTS MUSEUM. This interactive museum displays 18th-, 19th-, and 20th- century instruments. Grab the headphones at each exhibit to hear frenetic *kementzes* (bottle-shaped lyres) or *tsamboura* (goatskin bagpipe) music from the islands. Tapping metal coins jingle as dancers frolic. *(Diogenous 1-2, in Plaka. ☎ 32 50 198. Open Tu and Th-Su 10am-2pm, W noon-6pm. Free.)*

ILIAS LALOUNIS JEWELRY MUSEUM. An Athenian jeweller and goldsmith elected to the French Academie des Beaux-Artes, Ilias Lalounis's jewel-studded art is displayed here, in his former home. Over 3000 designs from a 50-year period gleam in cases, and other displays trace Greek jewelry from ancient to modern times. There's a workshop where visitors can watch the magic happen. *(Kallisperi 12, south of the Acropolis. ☎ 92 27 260. Open M and Th-Su 9am-4pm, W 9am-9pm. 800dr/ €2.35, students and seniors 500dr/€1.47.)*

JEWISH MUSEUM. Occupying a brand new, seven-story building, this museum charts the Jewish experience in Greece from the Hellenistic Period. The collection includes textiles, religious artifacts, and a thorough library. A reconstructed Synagogue and an exhibit on the Holocaust are also here. *(Nikis 39, in Plaka. ☎/fax 32 31 577. Open M-F 9am-2:30pm, Su 10am-2pm. Library Tu and Th 11am-1pm. 500dr/€1.47.)*

CHILDREN'S MUSEUM. This museum offers a colorful, friendly, hands-on experience in the heart of Plaka, faithfully subscribing to the motto "I hear and I forget; I see and I remember; I do and I understand." Learn about the subway system or play dress-up in a bedroom from times past. *(Kidathineon 14, in Plaka. ☎ 33 12 995 or 33 12 996. Open M and Th-F 9:30am-1:30pm, W 9:30am-6:30pm, Sa-Su 10am-2pm. Free.)*

▶ DAYTRIPS FROM ATHENS

The whites and grays of Athens's marble and smog quickly give way to the greens, browns, and blues of Greece's coast. Monasteries, ancient religious centers, and battlegrounds skirt Athens, while the ports of Piraeus and Rafina are gateways to both the frenzied and peaceful pace of the islands.

MONASTERY OF KESARIANI Μονη Καισσαριανης   ☎01

*Take **blue bus #224** from the Athens KTEL stop two blocks up Vas. Sofias from Pl. Syndagma (20min., every 15min., 120dr/€0.35). Get off at the last stop, follow the asphalt road uphill for 10min. and bear right under the overpass; stay right through 2 forks. The road splits again; stay right. After 5min., you'll see another fork. Take a stone path up to the monastery. Bring water. ☎ 72 36 619. **Open** Tu-Su 8:30am-2:30pm. **Admission** 800dr/€2.35, seniors and students 400dr/€1.17, EU students free.*

The Monastery of Kesariani is a total escape from nearby Athens. Near the peak of **Mt. Hymettus** and with a bird's-eye view of Athens, the site was originally a temple to Demeter, goddess of agriculture and nature. In the Roman Period (AD 100-300), a new temple took its place. Well-preserved 17th-century frescoes by Ioannis Ypatios adorn the tiny, cave-like chapels. The 30-40min. ends in a fabulous, peaceful view of Athens. The staircases near the monastery lead up to 3 levels of wooded picnic area. Short trails meander throughout the area; take a picnic and explore.

DAPHNI Μονη Δαφνι   ☎01

*To reach Daphni from Athens, take **blue bus #A16** (20min., every 30 min., 120dr/€0.35) from Pl. Eleftherias or from Pl. Koumoundourou. From Piraeus, take **#804** or **845** (35min., every 15min. 6am-11:30pm). Get off the bus, cross the highway and go right. ☎ 58 11 558. **Open** daily 8:30am-2:30pm. **Admission** 800dr/€2.35, students and seniors 400dr/ €1.17, EU students free. No flash photography. **Note:** The monastery was closed during summer 2001, when no definite reopening date had been determined.*

The Monastery of Daphni, surrounded by a high fortified wall, is a peaceful retreat caressed by cool breezes. It stands 10km west of Athens, along the Ancient Sacred Way at the corner of Iera and Athinon. Built on the site of the ancient Temple of Daphnios Apollo, the monastery earned its name from the sacred *daphnai*

Athens to Piraeus

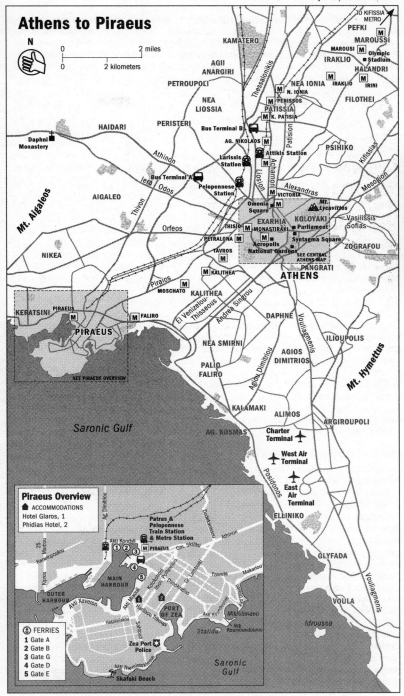

(Apollo's own laurels) that graced the ancient sanctuary. The 11th-century structure has flower-shaped windows and a smattering of birds' nests outside, while the inside holds a dozen cats and celestial mosaics of Jesus's life. Immediately to the right as you enter the octagonal room is a depiction of the *anastasis* (resurrection of Christ). The four corners of the ceiling portray (counterclockwise from near right) the angel's announcement of Mary's pregnancy, Christ's birth, His baptism in the Jordan River, and His *apotheosis* (or transfiguration). Mosaics in the narthex depict Judas's betrayal, the Last Supper, Mary's birth, and her blessing as a young girl. Christ scowls down upon visitors from the masterful mosaic dome; His displeasure with man's misdeeds was a common theme in 11th-century Christian art. This expression perhaps prophesied the later violation of the monastary's sanctity: it was used as an army camp and then as an insane asylum.

CAPE SOUNION PENINSULA Ακρωτηριο Σουνιο   ☎0232

*Two **orange-striped KTEL buses** travel to Cape Sounion from **Athens:** one leaves from the Mavromateon 14 bus stop near Areos Park and stops at all points on the Apollo Coast (2hr., every hr. 6:30am-6:30pm, 1350dr/€3.96); the other follows a less scenic inland route (2¼hr., 1 per hr. 6am-6pm, 1200dr/€5.52). Get off the bus at the last stop and head up to the right (facing the water), past the cafeteria to a ticket booth.*

The majesty of the Aegean as seen from the cliffs of Sounion so captivated Lord Byron that he included ▧**Cape Sounion** in his praise of Greek independence in the "Isles of Greece." Even his lyricism can't fully prepare you for the sight of the shimmering blue Aegean in every direction below the 60m rocky promontory.

Gracing the highest point on the Cape, the **Temple of Posiedon** has been a dazzling white landmark for sailors at sea for millennia. Originally constructed around 600 BC, the fortress of Sounion was destroyed by the Persians in 480 BC and rebuilt by Pericles in 440 BC. The 16 remaining Doric columns rise above the coast. Look closely at the graffiti for Lord Byron's name (on the square column as you face away from the cafeteria). Bits of the **Temple of Athena Sounias** litter the lower hill. (☎39 363. *Open daily 10am-sunset. 1000dr/€2.93, students 500dr/€1.47, EU students free.*)

After an hour at the temple, many people head down to the **beaches.** To reach the ocean, follow one of the paths from the inland side of the temple. Swarming with vacationing families, the beaches along the Apollo Coast between Piraeus and Cape Sounion have a carnival atmosphere on summer weekends. Towns usually have free public beaches, and some seaside stretches along the bus route remain almost empty. Drivers will let you off almost anywhere if you ask.

MARATHON Μαραθωνας   ☎0294

The bus from the Mavromateon 29 station in Athens heads to Marathon (1½hr., every hr. 5:30am-10:30pm, 800dr/€2.35), look for the bus's "Marathon" label; sit in front and remind the driver of your destination, and flag the bus down on the way back. Private transportation is the best way to see the sites, however, as they are spread out.

Gasping out two words—*Νικη ημιν,* "Victory to us"—**Phidippides** announced the Athenian victory over the Persians in the bloody 490 BC battle of Marathon; he collapsed and died immediately afterward. His 42km sprint to Athens remains legendary, and today runners trace his Marathon route twice annually, beginning at a commemorative plaque. With a car, you can explore nearby sights and beaches. At **Ramnous,** 15km northeast, lie the ruins of the **Temple of Nemesis,** goddess of divine retribution, and **Thetis,** goddess of law and justice. **Schinias** to the north and **Timvos Marathonas** to the south are popular **beaches.** Developers are building a channel at Schinias which will be the sight of the rowing events in the 2004 Olympic Games.

To reach the **Archaeological Museum of Marathonas,** ask the bus driver to drop you at the "Mouseion and Marathonas" sign, after Marathon Town and the beach. Follow the signs through 2km of farms, bearing right at the fork, to the end of the paved Plateion road at #114. The small museum's five packed rooms focus on **death rituals:** you'll find Neolithic grave pieces (4000-2500 BC), Geometric sepulchres (2500 BC), Cycladic funeral offerings, Athenian and Plateian tombs and remains from the battle of Marathon, and a first-century BC baby skeleton surrounded by two beehives. An **Athenian trophy** commemorates the battle with the Persians. Marble heads of Marathon's arts patron Herodes Atticus and his star pupil Polydenkion are on display, as are some Egyptian statues probably from a temple of Isis, and one of Atticus's poems. *(☎ 55 155. Open Tu-Su 8:30am-3pm. 500dr/ €1.47, students 300dr/€0.88, EU students, children under 18, student classicists and archaeologists free. Cemeteries from the Neolithic and Classical periods lie 2km from the museum; the oldest site dates from around 2500 BC. Ask for more information at the museum desk.)*

PIRAEUS Πειραιας ☎ 01

The natural harbor of Piraeus (also Pireas, Peiraias—literally, "port") has been Athens's port since 493 BC, when Themistocles concocted an ambitious plan to create a naval base for the growing Athenian fleet. A hilly peninsula gridded with big white apartment buildings, Piraeus has all the dirt and grime of a commercial hub, including a waterfront lined with junk shops, shipping offices, travel agencies, and banks bordered by run-down neighborhoods. However, the port stands on former glory: Plato set his *Republic* here during the height of Athenian power.

⌐ TRANSPORTATION. Piraeus is most often used as a transportation hub for travelers on their way between ferries and flights. **Bus #96** shuttles to and from the airport (every 30min., 1000dr/€2.93). Pick it up across from Philippis Tours on Akti Tzelepi. To get to Piraeus, take the **subway** west from Athens to the last stop (20min., 250dr/€0.73). The subway station is a big building adjacent to a busy square on Akti Posidonos (500m from Akti Tzelepi). To get to Northern Greece, take the subway to Omonia Square, where you transfer trains (on the same ticket) for Larissis. **Trains** bound for Patras and the Peloponnese zip around from the station just beyond the subway station.

An enormous number of ferries run from Piraeus. Unfortunately, the ferry schedule changes on a daily basis, and these listings are only approximate. **Be flexible** with your plans, since ferries are notoriously changeable. Check the *Athens News*, or stop in at a travel agency for schedules before you go. **Ferries** sail to nearly all Greek islands (except the Sporades and Ionian Islands). Among them are: **Iraklion,** Crete (8hr., 2 per day, 6900dr/€20.25); **Hania,** Crete (8hr., 2 per day, 5700dr/€16.73); and **Rethymno,** Crete (8hr., 1 per day, 6900dr/€20.25). Travel is sporadic to: **Aegina** (1hr., 1500dr/€4.40), **Hydra** (3hr., 2400dr/€7.05), **Poros** (2½hr., 2100dr/€6.16), and **Spetses** (4½hr., 3300dr/€9.68); boats leave every evening for **Chios** (9hr., 5800dr/€17.02) and **Lesvos** (12hr., 7200dr/€21.13). More regular departures are to: **Ios** (7½hr., 3 per day, 5400dr/€15.85); **Milos** (7hr., 2 per day, 5100dr/€14.97); **Mykonos** (6hr., 2 per day, 5200dr/€15.26); **Naxos** (6hr., 5 per day, 5000dr/€14.67); **Paros** (6hr., 5 per day, 5200dr/€15.26); **Rhodes** (15hr., 2 per day, 9200dr/€27); **Santorini** (9hr., 3 per day, 6000dr/€17.61); **Serifos** (4½hr., 2 per day, 3900dr/€11.45); **Sifnos** (5¼hr., 2 per day, 4400dr/€12.91). International ferries run on Thursday at 7pm to **Limassol, Cyprus** (36hr., 25,000dr/€73.37) and **Haifa, Israel** (72hr., 36,000dr/€105.65). Twice as fast and twice as expensive, **catamarans** run twice per day to Mykonos, Paros, Naxos, Syros (8800dr/€25.83), and Tinos (9400dr/€27.59); once per day to Serifos, Sifnos, Milos, and Santorini; sporadically to Aegina, Poros, Hydra, and Spetses.

▆▓ ORIENTATION AND PRACTICAL INFORMATION. Piraeus can seem chaotic and confusing at first glance, but there is a logical organization to the port. Ferries dock at five major gates, with specific gates for specific destinations. From the subway or the airport shuttle, the first group of ferries are those bound for the Cyclades, leaving from an area between **Akti Tzelepi (Gate D,** the heart of the port) and along **Akti Kondyli (Gate G)** up to the subway station **(Gate B).** Facing the water, the long street on the left side of the port is **Akti Miaouli,** where you'll find **Gate E,** the docking area for some hydrofoils, ferries to the Saronic Gulf Islands (some also at Gate G), the Dodecanese, and international destinations (at the end toward the customs house). Ferries to Crete dock at **Gate A;** those for the Northeast Aegean islands leave from **Gates A & B.** Gate A is at the end of Akti Kondyli, across from Ag. Dionysios. The large, busy street running alongside Akti Miaouli and Akti Kondyli is Akti Posidonos. The remaining hydrofoils leave from the port of **Zea** on the other side of the peninsula, a 10min. walk up and then downhill along any of the streets running inland off Akti Miaouli.

Most ticket agencies can be found on Akti Tzelepi and along Akti Posidonos. Try ▓**Philippis Tours,** in the heart of the port on Akti Tzelepi (☎41 12 767 or 41 33 182; fax 41 37 359). They sell ferry and plane tickets, help with accommodations, rent cars, exchange money, and store baggage. Most **banks** along the waterfront **exchange currency. Citibank,** Akti Miaouli 47-49, has **ATMs.** (☎41 72 153. Open M-Th 8am-2pm, F 8am-1:30pm.) There is an **American Express** office (☎42 95 120) next door. The Piraeus **port police** (☎42 26 000) are at Akti Zelopi; the Zea **port police** (☎45 93 144) are along the water and under the sidewalk. For the **tourist police,** dial 42 90 664. In an **emergency,** call the Athens police at 133, an ambulance at 166, and the fire station at 199. Stop in at **Telstar Booksellers,** just down Akti Miaouli from Citibank to grab last-minute summer reading. (☎42 93 618; fax 42 93 710; tel-star@otenet.gr. Open M-Sa 8am-8pm.) The **OTE** is at Karaoli Dimitriou 19. (Open M-F 7am-2:40pm.) Surf the Internet at **Surf In Internet Cafe,** Polytexneiou 42-44 and Platonos (1200dr/€3.52 per hr.; ☎42 27 478; www.surfin.gr; open daily 9am-9pm) or walk to **Dios Internet and...** at Sortiros Dios (a pedestrian avenue of shops) and Androutsou 170—buzz to be let in. (☎41 24 220; www.dios.gr. 1200dr/€3.52 per hr. Open daily 9:30am-11pm.) The main **post office** is off the street at the bend in the road all the way down Akti Miaouli toward the Expo Centre. (☎41 71 584. Open M-F 7:30am-2pm.) Zea's **post office** is near their port police. (☎41 83 380. Open M-F 7:30am-2pm.) **Postal code:** 18502 (Piraeus), 18504 (Zea).

▐▐█ ACCOMMODATIONS AND FOOD. Inexpensive, quality accommodations are much easier to find in Athens, but an adequate option in Piraeus is **Hotel Glaros,** Char. Trikoupi 4, off Akti Miaouli, toward the Expo Centre. (☎45 15 421; fax 45 37 889. Singles 8000dr/€23.48; doubles 10,000dr/€29.35; triples 13,000dr/€38.15.) There's also luxurious **Hotel Phidias,** Koundouriotou 189, near Zea off Bouboulinas (off Akti Miaouli), for spacious rooms, private baths, TVs and A/C. (☎42 96 160; fax 42 96 251; phidiasgr@otenet.gr. Breakfast 1700dr/€5. Singles 15,000dr/€44; doubles 18,700dr/€54.88 in high season.) Dock side fast food joints hawk average food for cheap. You can stock up on staples at **supermarkets** around town. There's a pretty restaurant and cafe area in between the buildings near Kolokatroni and Tsamadou. Dine and relax there to soft music, a welcome contrast to the jarring madness of the port. **Belle Epoque** serves an incredible fruit salad (1000dr/€2.93.) with whipped cream and blackberry sauce. (☎421 821. Open daily 8:30am-1am.) For a more substantive meal, there's also **Brazilian,** which serves Greek food; try the *bekri meze chicken.* (☎41 14 954. Open daily 6am-1:30am.)

◪ SIGHTS. The prize possession of the **Piraeus Archaeological Museum,** Char. Trikoupi 31, is the ancient **Piraeus Apollo,** a hulking hollow bronze figure with outstretched arms. Three other bronze statues of Athena and Artemis were found near the port in 1959; they had been shelved in a storeroom for safekeeping when Piraeus was besieged by Sulla in 86 BC. Notice their eyes—the strange spots of color are precious stones (☎45 21 598. Open Tu-Su 8:30am-3pm. 500dr/€1.47, students 300dr/€0.88, children ages 15 and under free.) Farther south at Zea, a stroll down the ramp to the dock at Akti Themistokleous and Botassi leads to the **Hellenic Maritime Museum,** which traces the Greek navy's history using detailed ship models. Of particular note in room B is a model of the Athenian trireme "Olympias," used in the Persian Wars (490-480 BC). The courtyard holds torpedo tubes, naval weapons, and the top part of the World War II submarine *Papanikolis.* (☎45 16 264; fax 45 16 822. Open Tu-Sa 9am-2pm. 500dr/€1.47; Sa free.)

RAFINA Ραφηνα   ☎ 0294

Rafina feels like a smaller, quieter version of Piraeus. Though there's less to do, it's easier on the eyes, ears, and lungs than its bigger, badder counterpart.

■:❼ ORIENTATION AND PRACTICAL INFORMATION. The ramp up from the waterfront leads to **Pl. Plastira. Ferries** sail to: **Karystos** in Evia (1¾hr., 2 per day, 2000dr/€5.86); **Marmari** in Evia (1¼hr., 2 per day, 1500dr/€4.40); **Andros** (2hr., 4 per day, 2500dr/€7.34); **Mykonos** (5hr., 2 per day, 4400dr/€12.91); and **Tinos** (4hr., 2 per day, 3900dr/€11.45). **Catamarans** zip, at twice ferry speed for twice ferry price, daily to **Mykonos, Paros** (2½hr., 8900dr/€26.12), **Syros,** and **Tinos** (1½hr., 7500dr/€22); 4 times per week to **Naxos** (3½hr., 9200dr/€27); 3 times per week to **Ios**; and once per week to **Amorgos** (4¼hr.; 10,100dr/€29.64). **Nel Lines** goes to **Agios Efstratios, Limnos, and Kavala** (3 per week) and **Lesvos** (1 per week); buy tickets at the office with the red door to the left of the waterfront (☎22 293). The **port authority** (☎22 300 or 28 888) has more info. Along the waterfront, English-speaking **Blue Star Ferries** (☎23 561; fax 23 350), **Rafina Tours** (☎22 700 or 24 722), or **Hellas Ferries** (☎22 292; fax 26 240), all open daily 6am-10pm, sell tickets for ferries and catamarans. Rafina is accessible by frequent **buses** from Athens's station at Mavromateon 29, two blocks up along Areos Park, a 15min. walk from Pl. Syndagma. (1hr., every 30min. 5:40am-10:30pm, 550dr/€1.61); or via airport shuttle (every 40min., 6am-9:20pm). Return buses leave Rafina from the ramp on the waterfront.

Both **Commercial Bank,** two blocks inland from the plateia (☎25 182; open M-Th 8am-2pm, F 8am-1:30pm), and the **Alpha Bank,** one block beyond the far left corner of the plateia (☎24 152; open M-Th 8am-2pm, F 8am-1:30pm), **exchange currency** and have 24hr. **ATMs. Taxis** line up in front of the plateia; call one at 23 101. Facing inland at the dock, the **post office** is two streets to the right on El. Venizelou. (☎23 777. Open M-F 7:30am-2pm.) The unmarked building that passes for an **OTE** is inland from the plateia, beside the church. (☎25 182. Open M-F 7:30am-3pm.) There's a **doctor** on El. Venizelou. (☎24 824 or 24 135. Open daily 7:30am-noon and 6-8pm.) You can find **pharmacies** on Kuprion Agoniston—look from the bottom right of the plateia, and on Eth. Antistasiou, by the Alpha Bank. **Postal code:** 19009.

❒:❒ ACCOMMODATIONS AND FOOD. Don't stay in Rafina unless you get stuck here; if you do, be prepared to pay. **Hotel Korali,** Pl. Plastira 11, rents cramped rooms with shared baths. (☎22 477. Singles 6000dr/€17.61; doubles 9000dr/€26.41; triples 14,000dr/€41.10.) Tiny inlets let you **swim** or **sunbathe** if you've got a spare hour. Head right at the top of the ramp, then right again at the end of the blue fence, then follow the coast and pick your spot. If you keep walking, you'll get to a long beach with rough sand. Cafes, pizzerias, and tavernas line the plateia and waterfront. Early ferry-catchers can try **Arktopolia,** an inexpensive bakery, on the left side of the plateia when you're facing away from the water. (☎26 083. Fresh bread 160dr/€0.47, filled croissants from 250dr/€0.73, yogurt 250dr/€0.73. Open daily 6am-11pm.) A **minimarket** sells fruits, vegetables, and toiletries off Pl. Plastira, two buildings from Arktopolia. (Open daily 8am-1:30pm and 5-9pm.)

ATHENS

PELOPONNESE
Πελοποννησος

We let the features gather, the low skies and mists, the hilltops edged with miles of old walls, fallen battlements, that particular brooding woe of the Peloponnese.
—Don DeLillo

A hand-shaped peninsula stretching its fingers into the Mediterranean, the Peloponnese is steeped in history and folklore that contribute to its otherworldly atmosphere. The remnants of ancient civilizations and their achievements mark the present-day peninsula, and its timeless natural beauty remains unchanged. The majority of Greece's best archaeological sites are here, including Olympia, Mycenae, Messene, Corinth, Mystras, and Epidavros. Uncommon landscapes, from the barren crags of the Mani to the forested peaks and flower-blanketed pastures of Arcadia, grace Pelops's former home. A world apart from the islands, the serenely beautiful and sparsely populated Peloponnese remembers 5000 years of continuous habitation, from the ancients to the traditions of village life.

HIGHLIGHTS OF THE PELOPONNESE

AN ANCIENT CITY STILL LIVES in Monemvasia, where cobbled streets and castle-like buildings line streets traversed only by donkeys and pedestrians (p. 162).

THE BYZANTINE GHOST TOWN Mystras, once the capital of the Greek part of the empire, invites you into the living architectural museum it has become (p. 156).

TAKE A BREAK FROM ANTIQUITY in the exquisite Arcadian mountain villages of mountainside Dimitsana (p. 144) and medieval Stemnitsa (p. 145).

BE A CONTENDER at ancient Olympia, where Mediterranean Greek city-states squared off in the original Olympic Games (p. 138).

DROP A COIN on the center stage of the acoustically marvelous theater of Epidavros, and a friend can hear it in the last row (p. 128).

CORINTHIA Κορινθια AND ARGOLIS Αργολιδα

Back in the day, Argos, a monster endowed with 100 unblinking eyes, stalked the north Peloponnese, subduing unruly satyrs and burly bulls. Today's Corinthia and Argolis still hold a lion's share of impressive archaeological sites, but, alas, the population of roving mythological beasts has declined sharply. Consider making Nafplion (p. 124) your base for exploring the region, as it allows access to Mycenae, Corinth, Tiryns, and Epidavros; and Nemea, Isthmia, and Argos's Heraion.

NEW CORINTH Κορινθος ☎0741

New Corinth rests on the Gulf of Corinth, just west of the canal that separates the Peloponnese from the Greek mainland. Like its ancient predecessor (7km southwest of the city), New Corinth has been rocked by several earthquakes, most recently in 1981; inhabitants wisely rebuilt their city low, secure, and shake-proof, giving it a sturdy, albeit aesthetically-challenged, appearance. Despite an attractive harbor, Corinth remains fairly dirty, busy, and hot; bypass the experience by staying at nearby campgrounds or a bus ride away in Loutraki (p. 117).

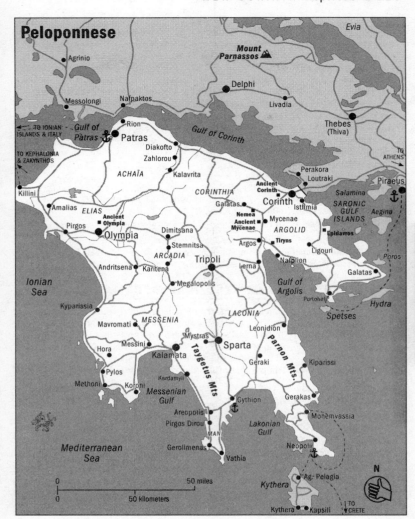

Peloponnese

Evia
Agrinio
Mount Parnassos
Delphi
Messolongi   Nafpaktos   Livadia
TO IONIAN ISLANDS & ITALY   Gulf of Patras   Rion   Patras   Gulf of Corinth   Thebes (Thiva)   TO ATHENS
TO KEPHALONIA & ZAKYNTHOS   Diakofto   Zahlorou   Perakora   Loutraki   Piraeus
ACHAÏA   Kalavrita   CORINTHIA   Ancient Corinth   Salamina   SARONIC GULF ISLANDS
Killini   Galatas   Corinth   Isthmia   Aegina
Amalias   ELIAS   Ancient Olympia   Nemea   Mycenae   Poros
Pirgos   Olympia   Dimitsana   Ancient Mycenae   ARGOLID   Epidavros
Stemnitsa   Argos   Tiryns   Galatas
ARCADIA   Tripoli   Ligouri   Poros
Ionian Sea   Andritsena   Karitena   Lerna   Nafplion   Hydra
Megalopolis   Gulf of Argolis   Portoheli
Kyparissia   LACONIA   Spetses
Mavromati   MESSENIA   Leonidion   Parnon Mts.
Hora   Messini   Mystras   Sparta   Kiparissi
Kalamata   Geraki
Pylos   Kardamyli   Gerakas
Methoni   Koroni   Messenian Gulf   Gythion   Monemvassia
Areopolis   Taygetus Mts.   Lakonian Gulf   Neopoli
Mediterranean Sea   Pirgos Dirou   MANI
Gerolimenas   Vathia   Ag. Pelagia
0   50 miles   Kythera   N
0   50 kilometers   Kythera   Kapsili   TO CRETE

PELOPONNESE

TRANSPORTATION

Buses deposit passengers and taxis line up at the city's central park, between Eth. Antistasis and Ermou. The train station is a few blocks southeast. To find the waterfront from the station, turn left out of the building onto Demokratias, then take the first right onto Damaskinou.

Buses: Terminal A: is past the train station on Demokratias. To: **Athens** (1½hr., 30 per day 5:30am-9:30pm, 1800dr/€5.28). **Terminal B:** walking inland on Eth. Anistasis, turn right on Koliatsou, halfway through the park; the terminal is outside a bakery. To: **Ancient Corinth** (20min., 20 per day, 260dr/€0.76 each way). **Terminal C:** The **Argolis Station** (☎24 403 for Nafplion or Mycenae, ☎25 645 for Isthmia, Nemea, Loutraki) is at the intersection of Eth. Antistasis and Aratou, past the park. The station is separated into counters, each serving different destinations. The 1st counter on the right as you enter off Eth. Antistasis serves **Isthmia** (10min., 5 per day, 260dr/ €0.76); **Nemea** (1hr., 7 per day, 950dr/€2.79); and **Loutraki** (20min., 2 per hr. 5:30am-10pm, 360dr/€1.06). The counter on the left serves buses to **Mycenae** (45min., 800dr/€2.35) via **Fihtia** (1.5km from the site); **Argos** (1hr., 1000dr/ €2.93); and **Nafplion** (1½hr., 1250dr/€3.67); which leave at 7am, and then every hr. 8:30am-9:30pm. To get to **Sparta** or other points south, take the Loutraki bus to the Corinth Canal and pick up the Athens bus to Sparta, Kalamata, Koroni, or Tripoli; or depart for these destinations from a new bus station south of town, but you'll need a taxi (1000dr/€2.93).

Trains: The **station** (☎ 22 523) is on Demokratias. To: **Athens** (2hr., 14 per day, 900dr/ €2.64) via **Isthmia.** Two major train lines serve the Peloponnese: one travels the northern coast from Corinth to Pirgos and south to Kyparissia; the other goes south from Corinth to Tripoli and Kalamata. To: **Argos** (1hr., 6 per day, 600dr/€1.76); **Diakofto** (1½hr., 8 per day, 700dr/€2.05); **Kalamata** (4½hr., 4 per day, 1900dr/€6.75); **Kyparissia** (5hr., 6 per day, 2300dr/€6.75); **Patras** (2½hr., 8 per day 8am-midnight, 1000dr/€2.93); **Pirgos** (4hr., 7 per day, 1600dr/€4.70); **Tripoli** (2hr., 4 per day, 900dr/€2.64). Express trains 400-1000dr/€1.17-2.93 extra. Word to the wise: bring your own toilet paper if you plan on using the facilities at the station.

Taxis: (☎ 24 844), along the park side of Eth. Antistasis.

Moped Rental: Libropoulos, Eth. Antistasis 27 (☎ 72 937). 5500dr/€16.14 per day for 50ccs of road dominance. Open daily 8am-1:30pm and 5-8:30pm.

✦❓ ORIENTATION AND PRACTICAL INFORMATION

New Corinth spreads out in a neat grid, which makes it fairly simple to navigate. The main drag, **Eth. Antistasis,** runs perpendicular to the waterfront. Both **Ermou** (to the east) and **Kolokotroni** (to the west) are parallel to Eth. Antistasis. All three intersect **Damaskinou,** which borders the harbor. Two blocks inland from the shore, between Eth. Antistasis and Ermou, is the city's central park—featuring peacocks! This is the heart of town, where most of the shops and restaurants are located.

Tourist Police: Ermou 51 (☎23 282), upstairs. Maps, brochures, and assistance. English spoken. Open daily 8am-2pm.

Banks: National Bank, Eth. Antistasis 7, 1 block up from the water, has **currency exchange** and a 24hr. **ATM.** A number of other banks with these services are also on Eth. Antistatis. Banking hours are mostly M-F 8am-2pm.

Public Toilets: Across from the park on Eth. Antistasis. Open 24hr. Toilet paper 100dr/ €0.29.

Police: Ermou 51 (☎ 100 or 81 100), facing the park. Open 24hr.

Pharmacy: Many on Eth. Anastasis and Koliatsou, most open M-F 8am-2pm and 5-8pm.

Hospital (☎25 711), on Athinaion; cross the train tracks and turn left. It's quite a walk, so take a cab or call the hospital for an **ambulance** in an emergency. Open 24hr.

Telephones: OTE, Kolokotroni 32 (☎24 499). Open M-F 7am-2:30pm.

Internet Access: Stretto, Pinarinou 17 (☎25 570), right off the first block of Eth. Antistasis. Sip coffee (500dr/€1.47) and check your email (1000dr/€2.93 per hr., 500dr/ €1.47 minimum charge). Open M-Sa 8am-noon and 5-11pm.

Post Office: Adimantou 35 (☎80 050), by the end of the street farthest from the water. Somewhat obscure, look for a vaguely official building and beware the long lines. Open M-F 7:30am-2pm. **Postal code:** 20100.

🏠 ACCOMMODATIONS AND CAMPING

Most travelers on their way to the nearby sites don't spend much time in New Corinth, so domatia, hostels, and budget hotels are rare. New Corinth's few hotels tend to be pricey, and are mostly on Eth. Antistasis and Damaskinou.

Hotel Akti, Eth. Antistasis 3 (☎23 337), is your best bet for an inexpensive stay in New Corinth. Simple, utilitarian bedrooms have private sink (toilet and showers shared), and some have balconies with great views of the water at no extra charge. Singles 4000-5000dr/€11.74-14.67; doubles 8000-10,000dr/€23.48-29.35.

Hotel Apollon, Pirinis 18 (☎22 587 or 25 920; fax 83 875). Turn left onto Demokratias after exiting the train station; Apollon is at the first intersection to your right. Clean rooms have TVs, balconies, and private baths. Singles have fans; doubles have A/C. Singles 5000dr/€22.01, 7500dr/€14.67 in high season; doubles 9000dr/€26.41, 13,000dr/€38.15.

Ephira Hotel, Eth. Antistasis 52 (☎24 021; fax 24 514), two blocks inland from the park. Posh 45-room hotel has well-furnished rooms with private bath, A/C, TV, and balconies. Enjoy breakfast (1500dr/€4.40) in a lovely, flower-laden courtyard. Singles 10,000dr/€29.35, 10,500dr/€30.81 in high season; doubles 15,000dr/€44.02, 17,000dr/€49.89 in high season; triples 18,000-20,000dr/€52.82-58.64.

Camping Korinth Beach (☎27 920) is 3km out of town. Catch a westbound bus (toward Ancient Corinth); and get off at the signs for the campground. 1100dr/€3.23 per person; 850dr/€2.49 per tent.

Blue Dolphin (☎25 766) is 1.5km beyond Camping Korinth Beach, with campsites on Lecheon beach. You can catch the Ancient Corinth-New Corinth bus back to town if the driver notices you waiting by the campground stop: make yourself visible if you want to snag the bus. 1550dr/€4.55 per person; 950dr/€2.79 per small tent, 1300dr/€3.82 per large tent; 700dr/€2.05 per car; electricity 900dr/€2.64.

🔆 FOOD

After 9pm, downtown New Corinth perks up a bit, as residents flock to the waterfront to dine outdoors in the balmy evening air. As in the daytime, speed seems to be a virtue in New Corinth; fast food is *de rigeur* and waiters deftly dodge the traffic on Damaskinou to shuttle between restaurants and their outdoor seating areas across the street on the waterfront plateia.

Axinos (Αχινος), Damaskinou 41 (☎28 889), on the waterfront plateia. The colorful chairs and tablecloths add a cheerful touch to summer evening al fresco dining. *Pastitsio* (1500dr/€4.40) and Greek salad (1300dr/€3.82) are among the many Greek specialty dishes. Open for breakfast (omelette 1200dr/€3.52). Open daily 10am-2am.

24 Oro, Ag. Nicholou 19, 1 block toward the waterfront from Damaskinou, on the right past Axinos and the museum. This taverna serves classic staples prepared with fresh ingredients, less grease, and more attention to detail. Cucumber and tomato salad 700dr/€2.05, *pastitsio* 1500dr/€4.40, *orzo* in clay bowl 1700dr/€5.

Nekkas Bakery, at the corner of Eth. Anistatis and Adimantou, by the central park. Satiate your sweet tooth with delicious pastries such as baklava and almond cookies (1000dr/€2.93 per kg) and fresh bread (150dr/€0.44). Open daily from 9am.

🎵 NIGHTLIFE

New Corinth lets down its hair at night, when motorcycle-mounted teens head west of the city to **Kalami Beach.** To reach Kalami without a motorcycle, walk four blocks past the park along Eth. Anistasis, turn right, and walk ten blocks. As the neighborhood is disconcertingly dark and empty at night, women may prefer taking a taxi from the park (500dr/€1.47); tell the driver "Kalami" or "Thalisa" (the sea). Kalami's strip has something for everyone. Mixed crowds of older couples, teens and families with small children swarm the beachfront late at night. On the waterfront street, overlooking the sparkling lights of Loutraki, an assembly of cafes and clubs strut their stuff, each with thumping bass and expansive umbrellas. **Pizza Ami** marks the middle of the strip; it's a local late-night favorite for its delicious pasta (1100-1500dr/€3.23-4.40) and pizza (1700-3000dr/€5-8.80). To the left of Pizza Ami, beyond a small amusement park (open 5pm-1am), lies a string of clubs including **Pregio** and **La Plaza.** You'll find Corinth's hip young things sipping beer (1000dr/€2.93) and mixed drinks (1700-2000dr/€5-5.87), motorcycle-watching, and listening to American dance tunes. To the right of Pizza Ami lie restaurants, such as **Cafe Mon Ami,** and more clubs and bars, such as **Club Loft** and **Freedom.** If you'd rather hang downtown, try car-free **Pinarinou** (Πιναρινοψ), right off the first block of Eth. Antistasis, as an alternative to the beach. Past the intersection with Koloktroni, the street fills with outdoor tables of cafes, pubs, and small restaurants. The typical and trendy **Saloon Giorgo** pumps bass through its doors to (relatively) quieter tables outside. As at Kalami, diverse crowds gather here.

▓ DAYTRIPS FROM CORINTH

ANCIENT CORINTH Αρχαια Κορινθος

7km southwest of New Corinth. Buses from Corinth city leave from a stop near the central park, on Koliatsou (20min.; every hr. 8am-11pm, return buses leave at half past the hour; 260dr/€0.76). ☎31 207. Open daily 8am-7pm; off-season 8am-5pm. Guidebook 2200dr/€6.46. Museum and site 1200dr/€3.52, students 600dr/€1.76.

Strategically located on the isthmus between the Corinthian and Saronic Gulfs, Ancient Corinth was once a powerful commercial center and one of the most influential cities in ancient Greece. At its height in the 5th century BC, Corinth joined forces with southern neighbor Sparta against the naval muscle of Athens—a power struggle that led to the Peloponnesian Wars (p. 12). While the war won dominance for Sparta, it weakened Corinth considerably. After Romans sacked the city in 146 BC, destroying buildings and pocketing precious objects, Corinth remained deserted until Julius Caesar rebuilt it in 44 BC.

ANCIENT SITE. The remains of the ancient city stand at the base of the **Acrocorinth** (a castle atop a large mountain). Past the exit of the museum, the archaeological site is down the stairs to your left. Its columns reconstructed from the 6th-century BC **Temple of Apollo** contrast strikingly with the vivid blue sky. Columns, engraved friezes, and pediments lie around the courtyard in majestic chaos. As you pick your way through the rubble, an unparalleled view of New Corinth and the Gulf stretches out below. Facing the entrance of the museum, the Corinthian columns on your left make up the facade of a Roman shrine. Behind the museum is the **Fountain of Glauke,** named after Jason's second wife, who was consumed by flames from an enchanted robe given to her by Jason's jilted first wife, Medea. From the Temple of Apollo and facing the mountainous Acrocorinth, the remains of the forum, the center of Roman civil life, lie in front of you. Walk down the middle of the row of central shops and you'll see the **Julian Basilica.**

To the left, near the exit at the edge of the site farthest from the museum, a broad stone stairway descends into the **Peirene Fountain,** perhaps the most impressive structure on the site. Although smoothed and patinated by the water that still flows today, the columns and fresco-covered tunnels inside the fountain have survived the centuries unharmed. The ancients believed that winged Pegasus was drinking here when Bellerophon captured him. Just past the fountain is the **Perivolos of Apollo,** an open-air court surrounded by still more columns. On the uphill edge of the site, on the side farthest from the museum, somewhat shabby sheds cover the mosaic floors of a Roman villa. Unfortunately, you'll have to peer through a rusted chain link fence, as entry is not permitted.

ARCHAEOLOGICAL MUSEUM. The Archaeological Museum houses an impressive collection of statues, well-preserved mosaics, tiny clay figurines, and pottery, tracing Corinth's history through Greek, Roman, and Byzantine rule. The Roman frescoes and mosaics date from the same period as Pompeii, and changes in pottery technique showcase Greece's evolution from Neolithic to Byzantine times. The museum's collections of sarcophagi (including one with a skeleton under glass) and headless statues in the open-air courtyard are morbidly appealing. While the exhibits are noteworthy, there isn't much explanation of their history or relationship to the site, so it's worthwhile to purchase a guidebook (2200dr/€6.46).

■ **FORTRESS AND ACROCORINTH.** Hiking to the fortress at the top of Acro-corinth is a strenuous 2hr. climb, and only for the truly dedicated. Taxis are an easy alternative. The hike down, on the other hand, is a pleasant hour of amazing views. At the summit, the Temple to Aphrodite, once served by "sacred courte-sans" who initiated diligent disciples into the "mysteries of love," remains largely intact. The relatively empty fortress contains acres of towers, mosques, gates, and walls. *(To get there from the archaeological site, call a taxi (☎31 464; 2000dr/€5.87) which will wait for an hour and drive you back down for 3000dr/€8.80.)*

ISTHMIA Ισθμια

At Terminal C, catch the bus from Corinth to Isthmia (10min., 5 per day, 260dr/€0.76). Get off at the green museum (☎0746 37 244), right of the bus stop. Open M-Sa 8:30am-3pm, Su and off-season 9:30am-2:30pm. 500dr/€1.47, students 300dr/€0.88, EU students free.

Like Olympia, Isthmia was the site of prestigious athletic contests every four years. An excellent museum compliments the remains of the ancient complex, dis-playing carefully diagrammed exhibits of finds from the Temple of Poseidon and the sites of the Isthmian games. Of particular interest are the glass *opus sectile* (mosaic panels), which survived the earthquake of AD 375 to be discovered at nearby Kenchreai. The entrance to the ruins lies to the right of the museum. All that remains of the **Temple of Poseidon** is its foundation. The **theater** is below and to the right of the temple; caves formerly home to Archaic revelry lie above it.

NEMEA Νεμυα

4km from modern Nemea; coming by bus from Corinth (1hr., 7 per day, 950dr/€2.79), ask to be let off at the ancient site. ☎0746 22 739. Site and museum open Tu-Su 8am-2:30pm, M afternoon hrs.; call to confirm. 500dr/€1.47, students 300dr/€0.88, EU students free.

The temple of **Nemean Zeus** has dwindled to three columns, but it's still worth a look. The walkway takes you past a wall built around a glass-encased grave, skele-ton and all. The site also includes a stadium (500m down the road to Corinth), well-preserved baths, and a museum with excellent explanatory notes in English, some artifacts, and reconstructions of the site.

LOUTRAKI Λουτρακι ☎0744

The pebbled beach of Loutraki, just over the isthmus of Corinth on the mainland, has attracted sun-seeking vacationers since ancient times. Visitors still come to soak in the natural springs for their reputed healing powers. This potent stuff is also the water bottled and hawked all over Greece. Though clearly a tourist haven marred by monotonous hotels, Loutraki's vacation atmosphere and beautiful sur-roundings allow for a pleasurable overnight stay on the way to neighboring sites.

▐ **TRANSPORTATION.** To get to Loutraki from Isthmia, cross the canal bridge and find the bus stop next to a railroad station sign. Stay on the bus until the last stop, a triangular road island where **El. Venizelou,** the main street, meets Periandou and Eth. Antistasis. Running parallel to the water, El. Venizelou curves away from Corinth, at the northern end of the strip and becomes Geor-giou Lekka. The change from Venizelou to G. Lekka marks the central square of Loutraki, but the beach and most of the tourist activity are along the board-walk and on Venizelou. Boat excursions are available at the dock past the park. Cruises sail to **Lake Vouliagmeni** (the Blue Lake) and down the **Corinth Canal.** Times and prices vary; see listings posted on the pier or contact the tourism office for more information. For a **taxi,** call 61 000, or stop by the stand next to the Tourist Info center on El. Venizelou. For **moped rentals,** visit **Moto-Rent** (near the bus station), one of three moped rental shops. (☎67 277. 50cc bike 6000dr/€17.61 per day.)

PRACTICAL INFORMATION. Loutraki is a tourist-information fiesta. There are two **tourist information center** kiosks: one is located on El. Venizelou one block south (Corinth-bound) from the bus station; the other is after the "curve" at the central square on G. Lekka, right at the end of the town park. The pretentiously-named **Municipal Enterprise for Touristic Development** office, in the central square, is actually a wonderful resource for any and all adventures in Loutraki: water parks, scuba-diving, hang-gliding, and other tours or cruises. (☎26 001 or 26 325; fax 21 124; loutraki@kor.forthnet.gr. Open M-F 7:30am-3pm.) To get to the **National Bank,** follow El. Venizelou to the central square. (☎22 220; fax 64 945. 24hr. **ATM** available. Open M-Th 8am-2pm, F 8am-1:30pm.) Periandrou, the first side street on the right across from the bus station's road island, is home to **Laundry Self-Service** (in the first block on your left), which provides wash and dry (3000dr/€8.80) and ironing. (☎67 367. Open M, W, Sa 8:30am-2pm; Tu, Th, F 8:30-2pm and 5:30-9pm.) The **police,** El. Venizelou 7 (☎63 000; open 24hr.), are in the same building as the **tourist police** (☎65 678; open 24hr.), 2km from downtown Loutraki, on El. Venizelou as it heads south toward Corinth. The **health center** is roughly 5km from the center of town; walk five blocks up from El. Venizelou, turn right, and continue straight. (☎26 666. Open 24hr.) One of several **pharmacies** is at El. Venizelou 21 (☎21 787). Walking north from the bus station on El. Venizelou, turn left on Hras to find **internet access** at **NetCafe@Loutraki,** on the waterfront off El. Venizelou. (1000dr/€2.93 per 30min. Open daily 9am-midnight.) The **OTE** is at El. Venizelou 10. (☎61 999. Open M-F 7:30am-3:10pm.) From the bus station, walk down El. Venizelou with the water to your left to find the **post office,** 28 Octovriou 4, a block down. (Open M-F 7:30am-2pm.) **Postal code:** 20300.

ACCOMMODATIONS. Although Loutraki draws a near-constant stream of moneyed vacationers, budget travelers do have a few options. To reach ◪**Le Petit France,** Marcou Botsari 3, from the bus station, take El. Venizelou in the direction you face upon exiting the station building; Botsari is your third right. The friendly owners of the blue-shuttered hotel extend their hospitality in every way. There is a lovely garden in back, and rooms come with balconies, ceiling fans, and bath. (☎22 401. Breakfast 1000dr/€2.93. Singles 6000dr/€17.61; doubles 8000dr/€23.48; larger, family-style rooms available. Call ahead for reservations in summer.) To find **Hotel Marko,** take the right fork (Antistasis), and the hotel will be on your right, after one block. Though it may appear a few decades outdated, the location (practically on the beach) and cleanliness improve its standing. All rooms have balcony and bath. (☎63 542. Breakfast 1000dr/€2.93. Singles 7000-9000dr/€20.53-26.41; doubles 8000-10,000dr/€23.48-29.35. A/C extra.) For domatia, call 22 456 or consult the tourist office in the central square. **Camping** is available 16km away at stunning Lake Vouliagmeni (☎0741 91 230 or 91 229) and at Isthmia Beach (☎0741 37 447 or 37 720). Transportation takes some effort. Consider a taxi or bus-walk combination; consult the tourist office.

FOOD AND NIGHTLIFE. Theoloros (Θεολορος) is on the waterfront near the park and serves generous portions of delicious food. Seafood variety plates (2000-3000dr/€5.87-8.80) and veal with spaghetti (1600dr/€4.70) are two of the best options. **Taverna Astoria** opens from the back of Hotel Achillion (on El. Venizelou near the OTE) and offers scrumptious and inexpensive dinners both à la carte (chicken *yiouvetsi* 1600dr/€4.70, *tzatziki* 700dr/€2.05) and prix-fixe (3-course meal 2000dr/€5.87). For a taste of the divine, head to **Horiatiki Taverna,** El. Venizelou 70, far down the street toward Corinth, near the Pepsi-Co. bottling company. The oldest restaurant in town, Horiatiki has been in business for 40 years, drawing crowds with its elegant, vine-bedecked garden seating area and fresh seafood (fish around 5000dr/€14.67, full meals up to 12,000dr/€35.22.) Tiny **Il Guosto Pizza,** one block behind the bus station on El. Venizelou, has an impressive variety of pizzas (1700-2300dr/€5-6.75) and Italian dishes. (☎69 200. Open daily until 1am.)

Nightlife consists of a ritual vacillation between eating and dancing. Waterfront restaurants swell in summer, staying full until midnight and beyond. From the park toward Corinth, **Cafe Coral, Jamaica** and **El Nino** pump music for steady crowds. **Bazaar** is a seasonal club in the same building as Theoloros. After midnight (when partyers let it all hang out), taxis transport the footloose to discos on the fringe of the city. **CoCoon,** at the Corinth end of the boardwalk, is a space-age venue serving food by day and parties all night long. (Beer 1500dr/€4.40, mixed drinks 1800dr/€5.28. Open daily 10am-3am.) Another option is seasonal **Baby-O,** precariously placed between a lonely-looking bottling company and a shrub-covered wasteland. Rumors have it that Baby-O's crowds can swell to over 1000.

◤ **WATER FUN.** Those seeking solace in Loutraki's healing waters can indulge in sauna treatments, whirlpool baths, and hydromassage at **Therma: Hydrotherapy Thermal Spa,** G. Lekka 26, past the central square along Venizelou/Lekka, across from the park. Four-, five-, six-, and ten-day programs are offered; call for prices and group discounts. The spa cures "rheumoatoarthritic, spondycarthritic," and "chronic gynecological diseases," or so the bilingual sign on the door promises. (☎/fax 22 215. Open daily 8am-1pm; in winter M-F.) At the carefully maintained **waterfalls,** a 12min. walk from the central square on G. Lekka, hike up and watch the water flow from fountains at the base of the cliff. (Open daily 10am-3am.) There's also a water park between Loutraki and Corinth, on beautiful Blue Lake at Perahora. With Loutraki's many beaches, don't be confined to the boardwalk area.

MYCENAE Μυκηνες   ☎ 0751

Excavations of ancient Mycenae have continued for 126 years, since Heinrich Schliemann first turned a spade here. Now one of the most visited sites in Greece, mobs stampede to the famed Lion's Gate and Tomb of Agamemnon. Most make Mycenae a daytrip from Athens, Argos, or Nafplion, but the tourist-friendly modern village can be a pleasant place to spend the night.

◾◪ **ORIENTATION AND PRACTICAL INFORMATION.** The only direct **buses** to **Mycenae** are from **Nafplion** (45min., 4 per day, 650dr/€1.91) via **Argos** (20min., 300dr/€0.88). The site is on the Corinth-Argos road; follow the sign to Mycenae from the town of Fihtia. Four buses make the return trip to **Argos** and **Nafplion,** stopping in the town of **Mycenae** (in front of the Hotel Belle Helene) and at the **site** (a 20min. walk from the town). **Trains** (5 per day) run from **Athens** to Fihtia via Corinth. Mycenae has no bank, but a mobile **post office** booth at the site offers **currency exchange.** (Open from mid-Mar. to Oct. M-Sa 9:30am-4pm.) **Postal code:** 21200.

▐◨ **ACCOMMODATIONS AND FOOD.** Mycenae is short on cheap accommodations—if campgrounds aren't your thing, browse the signs off the main road for well-priced domatia. The quiet **Hotel Belle Helene,** on the main road to the site, opened its doors in 1862; Heinrich Schliemann and crew promptly moved in for two years in the 1870s. In the lobby you can read framed photocopies of the hotel guest book, with signatures from Virginia Woolf, Claude Debussy, William Faulkner, Agatha Christie, Hans Himmler, Goebbels, and Allen Ginsberg. Grab room #3, where Schliemann stayed; it has an iron bed and period furniture. Other rooms are modern and carpeted with shared baths. (☎76 225; fax 76 179. Singles 5500-7000dr/€16.18-20.59; doubles 10,000-13,000dr/€29.41-38.23; triples 11,000-15,000dr/€32.35-44.12.) More luxurious (albeit less historic) lodgings are available next door to Belle Helen, at **Dassis Rent Rooms.** This gorgeous domatia boasts spacious rooms with balconies, baths, A/C, and even some bathtubs. (☎76 123 or (0946) 88 576. Singles 8000-10,000dr/€23.53-29.41; doubles 12,000-18,000dr/€35.29-52.94.) **Camping Mykines,** shaded by pine trees in the middle of town across from Dassis Rooms, offers laundry facilities (1000dr/€2.94), free hot showers, and a nicely-priced taverna. Breakfast 1500dr/€4.40. (☎76 121. 1500dr/€4.40 per person, 1000dr/€2.94 per child; 1100dr/€3.23 per car; 1200dr/€3.53 per small tent, 1500dr/€4.40 per large tent. Electricity 1200dr/€3.53.)

P
E
L
O
P
O
N
N
E
S
E

A few good restaurants hide among the overpriced multitude of tour-bus troughs bearing the name of gods or unfortunate members of the Atreus family. With a vast dining area that seats 500 **Achilleus Restaurant** (☎ 76 027) doesn't sacrifice quality for quantity as it serves delicious traditional Greek fare to crowds of hungry sight-seers; entrees run 500-2000dr/€1.47-5.88. Across the street, inexpensive **Spiros Restaurant and Taverna** is another source of tasty food at reasonable cost. (Omelettes 700-900dr/€2.05-2.65; grilled meats starting at 1600dr/€4.71.)

ANCIENT MYCENAE

The bus stops at the end of the asphalt road; the ruins are on the right. Open Apr.-Sept. daily 8am-7pm; Oct.-Mar. 8am-5pm. 1500dr/€4.40, students 800dr/€2.35, EU students free. Keep your ticket after the main site for Agamemnon's Tomb, or pay twice. Bring a flashlight.

Excavated ancient Mycenae rests on a rocky knoll between Mt. Ag. Elias to the north and Mt. Zara to the south. Gargantuan **Cyclopean walls,** 13m high and 10m thick, surround the site; they get their name from ancients who believed that Perseus and his descendants—the city's founders—could only have lifted such stones with the help of a superhuman Cyclops. Outside the central fortified city, several *tholoi*—most notably the so-called **Treasury of Atreus**—stand guard outside the walls. The bulk of the ruins left standing today date from 1280 BC, when the city was the center of a far-flung Mycenaean empire. Many of the unearthed relics number among the most celebrated archaeological discoveries in modern history, and are housed in the National Museum in Athens (see p. 104). A guidebook can add to the experience: try the one by S. E. Iakovidis, covering both Mycenae and Epidavros, which includes a map and is well worth the 2500dr/€7.35. Another by George E. Mylonas, director of the excavation, takes a more scholarly approach (1700dr/€5). If you want info on other ruins, try *The Peloponnese*, by E. Karpodini-Dimitriadi (3000dr/€8.80).

HISTORY

Mycenae's origins, interactions with other Near Eastern civilizations, and decline have long puzzled historians. Settled as early as 2700 BC by a colonizing tribe from the Cyclades, Mycenae (along with other nearby cities like Pylos) remained under the control of the Minoan capital Knossos for centuries. It wasn't until the cataclysmic collapse of Minoan civilization in the mid-15th century BC that Mycenae surged to the head of the Greek world, lending its name to an entire period of

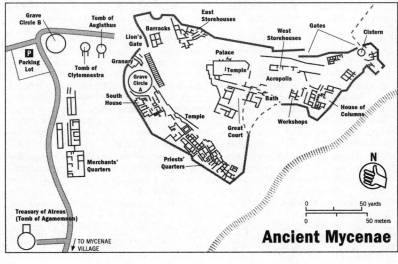

Ancient Mycenae

Grave Circle B · Tomb of Aegisthus · Lion's Gate · Barracks · East Storehouses · West Storehouses · Gates · Cistern · P Parking Lot · Tomb of Clytemnestra · Granary · Palace · Temple · Acropolis · Grave Circle A · South House · Bath · House of Columns · Temple · Great Court · Workshops · Merchants' Quarters · Priests' Quarters · Treasury of Atreus (Tomb of Agamemnon) · TO MYCENAE VILLAGE · N · 0 50 yards · 0 50 meters

Greek history (p. 10). Mycenaean culture flourished for the next centuries, until the warrior Dorians attacked from the north, burning and looting anything in their path. The Dorians conquered Greece, and Mycenae lost its hold on the Greek culture it had helped to create. Mycenae was inhabited through the Roman period, but Byzantine times saw it swallowed up by earth and forgotten.

In 1874, the German businessman, classicist and amateur archaeologist **Heinrich Schliemann** burst into Mycenae. Fresh from his successful dig at Troy and eager to further establish the historical validity of Homeric epics, he went looking for Agamemnon's city. To his delight, he found massive walls and elaborate tombs laden with dazzling artifacts, fitting Homer's description of a "well-built citadel... rich in gold." Schliemann began his dig just inside the citadel walls at the spot where several ancient authors described royal graves. Discovering 15 skeletons "literally covered with gold and jewels," Schliemann decked his new 17-year-old Greek bride with the baubles and had her pose for photographs. Believing he had unearthed the skeletons of Agamemnon and his followers, he sent a telegram to the Greek king that read, "Have gazed on face of Agamemnon." Moments after he removed its mask, the "face" underneath disintegrated. Shedding a tear at the initial reckless excavation, modern archaeologists now date the tombs to four centuries before the Trojan War.

RUINS

LION'S GATE AND GRAVE CIRCLE A. Uphill from the entrance booth, you'll spot the imposing **Lion's Gate,** the portal into the ancient city, with two lions carved in relief above the lintel. They symbolized the house of Atreus, and their heads—now missing—bore eyes of precious gems. The sculpture is one of the earliest known examples of sculpture being incorporated into a structure's support system. Schliemann found most of his artifacts in **Grave Circle A,** a large hollow area to the right, just outside the original city walls, which contains six 16th-century BC shaft graves. The barracks are up the stairs to your left just after the gate. The gate and the Cyclopean Walls of the upper citadel date from the 13th century BC.

BUILDINGS. The ruins on the hillside are the remnants of various homes, businesses, and shrines. The **palace** and the **royal apartments** are at the highest part of the citadel on the right. The open spaces here include guard rooms, private areas, and public rooms; look for the **megaron,** or royal chamber, with its round hearth framed by the bases of four pillars. To the left of the citadel sit the remaining stones of a Hellenistic **Temple of Athena.** At the far end of the city, between the palace and the **postern gate,** is the underground **cistern,** silently offering solitude and complete darkness. A flashlight is essential to explore its depths; be careful if you make the descent: the steps are worn and slippery, and drop off suddenly.

ALL IN THE FAMILY Think you have a dysfunctional family? Thank the gods that your problems pale in comparison to the epic, bloody background of Mycenae. Atreus, Mycenae's first chosen ruler, gleefully cooked his nieces and nephews for dinner to serve them to his hated brother (and the children's father), Thyestes—as revenge against Thyestes, who seduced Atreus's wife. The cannibal feast upset the gods, who pitied Thyestes and put a curse on the House of Atreus; Thyestes's son Aegisthus axed Atreus. Atreus's two sons, Agamemnon and Menelaus, fared little better. They stirred up the Trojan War when smooth-talking Paris ran off with Menelaus's gorgeous wife Helen. On the ship to the war, Agamemnon disemboweled his daughter Iphagenia for a good-luck sacrifice. Ten years later, Agamemnon returned to Mycenae as a war hero, but his wife Clytemnestra was still outraged over the fate of their daughter Iphagenia, and she and her lover Aegisthus (remember? her father-in-law's nephew and killer?) stabbed him in the bath. Agamemnon's other kids, Orestes and Electra, avenged the murder of their father by murdering their mother. The Furies then tormented Orestes until Athena finally pardoned him. Phew!

ROYAL TOMBS. Follow the asphalt road 150m back toward the town of Mycenae to the **Tomb of Agamemnon** (a.k.a. the Treasury of Athens), the largest and most impressive *tholos*, named by Schliemann for the king he desperately wanted to discover here. On your way, stop at two often-overlooked *tholoi*, the **tomb of Aegistheus** and the more interesting **tomb of Clytemnestra.** Take the paths on your left and hang on to your flashlight. Once you get to the main event, head down a 40m passage cut into the hillside that leads to Agamemnon's resting place, looking up at the 120-ton lintel stones above you. The dim, quiet interior of the *tholos* conveys a ghostly majesty befitting the grave of such a famous and tragic figure, but the tomb was found empty, having lost its valuables to grave robbers.

ARGOS Αργος   ☎ 0751

According to Homer, Argos was the kingdom of the hero Diomedes, and claimed allegiance from Mycenae's powerful king, Agamemnon. Later, Dorians invaded and captured the city in the 12th century BC, using it as their base for control of the Argolid Peninsula. Argos remained the most powerful state in the Peloponnese through the 7th century BC, defeating even Kleomenes and the Spartans, who, in the famous 494 BC battle, were unable to penetrate the city walls. Like many other ancient cities in Greece, each period of Argos's history has obliterated or buried the remains of the era preceding it. The modern city is no exception: it is built almost entirely on top of previous layers of habitation, and despite a healthy ribbon of archaeological red tape, it has managed to grow into the crowded, modern city of today. Argos may not be the most picturesque city that the Peloponnese has to offer, but the excellent museum and the ruins of the ancient theater, *agora*, and Roman baths on the southeast edge of town are worth seeing if you're in the area.

✴🛈 ORIENTATION AND PRACTICAL INFORMATION

Argos has few landmarks and can be tough to navigate, so pick up a **map** at a supermarket or local store for in-depth exploring. Most amenities, hotels, and restaurants are in or around the plateia, marked by the large **Church of St. Peter.**

Buses: The **Argolida** station (☎ 67 300), is on Kapodistriou, which runs parallel to and 1 block beyond the side of the plateia with Hotel Telesilla. Buses to: **Athens** via **Corinth** (2½hr., 15 per day, 2500dr/€7.35); **Mycenae** (30min., 5 per day, 260dr/€0.77); **Nafplion** (20min., every 30min. 6:30am-9pm, 280dr/€0.82); **Nemea** (1hr., 2 per day, 1000dr/€2.94).

Trains: (☎ 67 212), 1km from the plateia. Walk down Nikitara past the OTE and follow the signs to Nafplion from the 5-point intersection. At the next big intersection veer left; the station is at the end of the street. To: **Athens** (3hr., 6 per day, 1200dr/€3.53) via **Fihtia** (10min., 200dr/€0.59), **Nemea** (20min., 250dr/€0.74), **Corinth** (1hr., 600dr/€1.77); **Kalamata** (4hr., 4 per day, 1500dr/€4.40) via **Tripoli** (1hr., 650dr/€1.91).

Bank: National Bank (☎ 29 911), on Nikitara, off the plateia behind the small park, has **currency exchange** and an **ATM.** Open M-Th 8am-2pm, F 8am-1:30pm.

Hospital: (☎ 24 455), north on Corinth, opposite St. Nicholas Church. Open 24hr.

Police: (☎ 67 222), on the corner of Inaxou and Papaoikonomou; head out from Vas. Sofias or follow the signs from the train station. English spoken. Open 24hr.

Telephones: OTE Nikitara 8 (☎ 67 599). Facing the park from the main plateia, take the street along the left side of the park past the National Bank. Open M-F 7am-2pm.

Internet: Cafe Net (☎ 29 677), around the corner to the right from the supermarket, off the plateia. Su afternoons get free Internet access with the order of a drink. 1000dr/€2.93 per hr. Open daily 9am-1am.

Post Office: (☎ 67 366). Follow the signs from Hotel Telesilla in the plateia; it's across the plateia from the bus station. Open M-F 7:30am-2pm. **Postal code:** 21200.

🛏️🍴 ACCOMMODATIONS AND FOOD

It's a good idea to make Argos and Mycenae a daytrip from Nafplion since the sights can be seen in half a day, and Argos has few accommodations. If you stay overnight, try the **Hotel Apollon,** Papaflessa 13; take Nikitara from the plateia, then follow opposite the OTE. It's on the left; follow the signs to its spacious rooms with large shared baths, TVs, balconies, and ceiling fans. (☎ 68 065; fax 61 182. Singles 5000dr/€14.71, with bath and A/C 7000dr/€20.59; doubles 7000-10,000dr/€29.41.) The **Hotel Palladion,** Vas. Sophias 5, on the plateia, is convenient, and has private baths and TV. (☎ 67 807. Breakfast 1000dr/€2.94. Singles 8000dr/€23.53; doubles 12,000dr/€35.29; triples 15,000dr/€44; A/C 2000dr/€5.88 extra.) Argos has the Peloponnese's largest **open-air market** in the empty plateia across from the museum; vendors sell everything from olives to used clothing (W and Sa). The well-stocked **Dia Discount Supermarket,** to the right as you face the National Bank, supplements the dearth of good tavernas. (Open M-F 9am-2pm and 5:30-8:30pm, Sa 8:30am-6pm.) Next to the Hotel Mycenae, the **Retro Pub and Restaurant** is discordantly decorated with chrome and wicker. (Pizzas 1500-3500dr/€4.40-10.29.)

👁️ SIGHTS

ARCHAEOLOGICAL MUSEUM. Argos's superb archaeological museum has a large Mycenaean collection, including pottery, jewelry, and weaponry, as well as a garden courtyard with notable Roman sculptures and mosaics. In the most striking of the mosaics, 12 figures personify the months of the year in their dress, expressions, and accoutrements. On the ground floor of the museum, a detailed shard of *krater* from the 7th century BC depicts Odysseus putting out the eye of Polyphemus. In the same room, the well-preserved helmet and cuirass from the Geometric period also deserves a careful look. *(Off the plateia on Vas. Olgas. ☎ 68 819. Open Tu-Su 8:30am-3pm. 500dr/€1.47, students and seniors 300dr/€0.88, EU students and children free.)*

ANCIENT ARGOS. Archaeologists hope to uncover a large part of the ancient city of Argos, but at this point, most of it remains buried beneath the modern version. Major excavations have taken place on the city's western fringe at the site of the ancient *agora*. With a seating capacity of 20,000, the 4th-century BC **theater** was the largest of its time in the Greek world, although now it's not as well preserved as its famous counterpart in Epidavros. Across from the theater are the remains of the extensive **Roman bath complex,** whose remaining walls convey the magnitude of the structure. Many of the original wall-to-wall floor mosaics are intricate, colorful, and intact. The **Roman Odeum,** 30m from the baths, survives mostly as an outline, as the rows dissolve into the hillside. Across the street are the scattered remains of the *agora*, built in the 5th century BC and destroyed by Alaric's Visigoths in AD 395. *(Walk past the post office, turn right, and walk to the end of Theatron.)*

THE FORTRESS OF LARISA. In medieval times, Franks, Venetians, and Ottomans in turn captured and ruled Argos. As a result, the fortress is an architectural hodgepodge, combining these disparate medieval elements with Classical and Byzantine foundations. The ruins, which lie among overgrown weeds, are mainly of interest to scholars. *(Walk along Vas. Konstantinou for roughly 1hr., or climb the foot path from the ruins of the ancient theater.)*

OTHER SIGHTS. The **Argive Heraion,** 4km northeast of Argos, dedicated to Hera, goddess of the Argives, was built in the 5th century BC. It prospered well into the 2nd century AD, hosting the celebrations that followed the official ending of the Heraia Games (archery contests held at Argos in the second year after each Olympiad, see p. 138) and other annual festivals. Nearby **Prosimni,** past the Heraion, is home to a series of prehistoric graves. A few kilometers east of Agias Trias are the remains of the city of **Dendra,** where tombs yielded the preserved suit of bronze armor now in the Nafplion museum (p. 127).

NAFPLION Ναυπλιο   ☎ 0752

Beautiful old Nafplion glories in its Venetian architecture, fortresses, pebble beach, and hillside stairways. Though it's the perfect base for exploring the ancient sites of the Argolid, it may entice you to spend a few days away from the ruins. A delightful central park links the two sides over shady flower-lined paths and a large children's playground. Before the Venetians built Nafplion—named for Poseidon's son Nafplius—on a swamp in the 15th century, the city consisted entirely of the two hilltop fortresses. Passing from the Venetians to the Ottomans and back again, in 1821 it served as headquarters for the Greek revolutionary government and later as Greece's first capital (1829-1834). John Kapodistrias, former president of Greece, was assassinated here in Ag. Spyridon Church; the bullet hole is still visible in the church walls. Palamidi, the Venetian fortress where the Ottomans imprisoned Kolokotronis before the Revolutionary War of 1821, and the Bourtzi, a small island fortress that once housed retired executioners, stand as testaments to Nafplion's politically checkered past.

▐ TRANSPORTATION

The bus terminal is on **Singrou,** near the base of the Palamidi fortress. To reach **Bouboulinas,** the waterfront promenade, from the bus station, go left as you exit it and follow Singrou to the harbor—the **Old Town** is on your left. If you come by ferry, Bouboulinas is in front of you across the parking lot, parallel to the dock.

Buses: (☎28 555), on Singrou, off Pl. Kapodistrias. To: **Argos** (30min., 2 per hr. 5am-10:30pm, 280dr/€0.82); **Athens** (3hr., every hr. 5am-8pm, 2800dr/€8.23) via **Corinth** (2hr., 1500dr/€4.40); **Epidavros** (1hr., 4 per day, 650dr/€1.91); **Mycenae** (45min., 3 per day, 650dr/€1.91); **Tripoli** (2½hr., 4 per day, 1150dr/€3.38); **Tolo** (20min., every hr. 7am-9:30pm, 280dr/€0.82).

Taxis: (☎24 120 or 24 720). Congregate on Singrou across from the bus station.

Moped Rental: Motortraffic Rent-A-Moto, Sidiras 15 (☎22 702), on Sidhiras Merarchias past the post office, away from the Old Town. 50-250cc mopeds 3500-12,000dr/€10.29-35.29 per day. Open daily 8:30am-10:30pm.

◼✳▐ ORIENTATION AND PRACTICAL INFORMATION

Bouboulinas is the waterfront promenade. Three principal streets run off **Singrou,** perpendicular to Bouboulinas and the waterfont, into the Old Town. Moving inland, the first is **Amalias,** the shopping street. The second, **Vasileos Konstandinou,** ends in **Pl. Syndagma,** full of tavernas, a bookstore, bank, museum, and scores of aspiring soccer stars. The third is **Plapouta,** which becomes **Staikopoulou** in the vicinity of Pl. Syndagma; it's home to Nafplion's best restaurants. Across Singrou, Plapouta becomes **25 Martiou,** Nafplion's largest avenue. This side of Singrou, behind the statue of Kapodistrias, is the new part of town. Spreading outward from the 5-way intersection split by the roads to Argos and Tolo is the **New Town.**

Tourist Office: (☎24 444), on 25 Martiou, across from the OTE. Free pamphlets and brochures on Nafplion and surroundings. Open daily 9am-1pm and 4-8pm.

Banks: National Bank (☎23 497), in Pl. Syndagma, has an **ATM.** Other banks in Pl. Syndagma and on Amalias charge 1000dr/€2.94 commission for **currency exchange.** Open M-Th 8am-2pm, F 8am-1pm.

Bookstore: Odyssey (☎23 430), in Pl. Syndagma. Best-seller romance novels, sci-fi, and Greek plays, all in English. Open daily 8am-11pm.

Tourist Police: (☎28 131). From the Old Town, walk along 25 Martiou, 6 blocks past the turn-off for the road to Tolo and Epidavros. English spoken. Open daily 7am-10pm.

Police: (☎27 776) on Praitelous, a 15min. hike along 25 Martiou from the bus station. Follow the signs. Open 24hr.

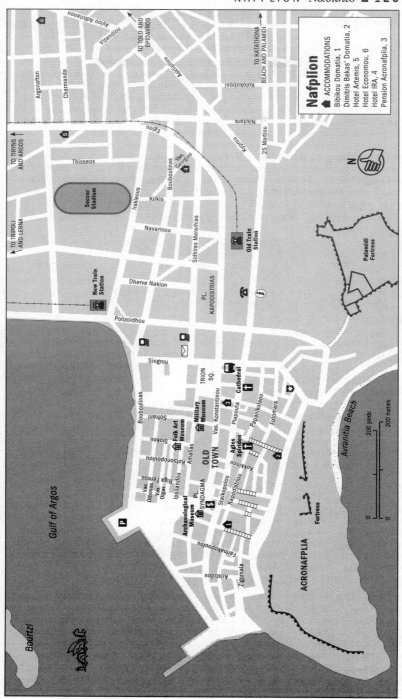

Nafplion

▲ ACCOMMODATIONS
Bibikou Domatia, 1
Dimitris Bekas' Domatia, 2
Hotel Artemis, 5
Hotel Economou, 6
Hotel IRA, 4
Pension Acronafplia, 3

PELOPONNESE

Hospital: Nafplion Hospital (☎27 309) is a 15min. walk; go down 25 Martiou and turn left onto Kolokotroni, which becomes Asklipiou. You can also call the tourist police.

Telephones: (☎22 139), on the left side of 25 Martiou as you walk toward the New Town. Open M-F 7am-10pm.

Internet Access: Filion (☎27 651), past the post office on Sidhiras Merarchias. 1500dr/€4.40 per hr; 750dr/€2.21 minimum. **Diplo Cafe,** Bouboulinas 43 (☎21 280), to the left of Singrou facing inland. 1500dr/€4.40 per hr; 500dr/€1.47 minimum. Open daily 9am-2am.

Post Office: (☎24 230), in a large yellow building on the corner of Sidhiras Merarchias and Singrou. Open M-F 7:30am-2pm. **Postal code: 21100.**

▗ ACCOMMODATIONS

Rooms in the Old Town are charming and beautifully situated, but those in the New Town have more amenities.

NEW TOWN

Hotel Artemis (☎27 862), on the road to Argos. Large rooms with balconies and baths. Singles 8000dr/€23.53; doubles 11,000dr/€32.35. Prices lower in off season.

Hotel IRA, Vas. Georgiou B9 (☎28 184), between Bouboulinas and Sidharis Merarchias. Bare lobby but airy rooms—all terrorist-free. Singles 4000-7000dr/€11.77-20.59; doubles 7500-14,000dr/€22.06-41.18. Prices vary with A/C, TV, and private baths.

Hotel Economou (☎23 955), on Argonafton off the road to Argos and a 15min. walk from the bus station. Hostel-like with shared baths (up to 4 beds in one room). Dorms 2500dr/€7.35; private doubles 9000dr/€26.47.

OLD TOWN

Dimitris Bekas' Domatia (☎24 594). Turn up the stairs onto Kokkinou, following the sign for rooms off Staikopoulou. Climb to the top, turn left, then go up another 50 steps. An evening on the roof, with its wonderful view of ocean and Palamidi, is well worth the climb. Small rooms with shared baths and fridges. Singles 4500-5200dr/€12.24-15.29; doubles 6000-6800dr/€17.65-20.

Konstadina Bibikou Domatia (☎27 708), offers rooms that are somewhat old-fashioned, but clean with common bath and kitchen just a hop, skip, and a jump away from Pl. Syndagma. Singles 6000dr/€17.65; doubles 7000dr/€20.59.

Pension Acronafplia, Vasileos Konstandinou 23 (☎24 481). If it's full, brothers George and Dimitris can show you one of their 3 other charming, conveniently-located buildings. Singles 6000-12,000dr/€17.65-35.29; doubles 7000-18,000dr/€20.59-52.94. Prices vary with A/C and private baths.

▗▗ FOOD AND NIGHTLIFE

The food in Nafplion is excellent, but pricey. The beautiful alleys of the Old Town hold an endless number of romantic tavernas, lit by soft flood lights and strewn with plants, balconies, and people. The waterfront is lined with fish restaurants that charge as much as 7000dr/€20.53 per entree. The best dining options are on Staikopoulou, the street inland from Pl. Syndagma, behind the National Bank. **Marinopoulos,** an excellent modern supermarket, is behind the post office.

■ **To Fanaria,** a street above the plateia on Staikopoulou. The trellised alleyway provides an intimate atmosphere in which to enjoy tantalizing entrees. Soups 1000dr/€2.94, spaghetti bolognese 1300dr/€4.12, and salads 550-1100dr/€1.62-3.24.

Ellas (☎27 278), in Pl. Syndagma. Refreshingly inexpensive, with a cheerful staff and seating facing the action in the plateia. Veal stew 1900dr/€5.59, fish entrees 1200-1900dr/€3.53-5.59.

The Agora Music Cafe, Vas. Konstandinou 17 (☎26 016), is perfect for an evening cocktail or ice cream. Decorated with traditional household and farm implements. American, British, and Greek pop play inside. Drinks 1300dr/€4.12, beer 750dr/€2.21, immense ice cream sundaes 1000dr/€2.94.

Although similar trendy cafes strung along the waterfront and Pl. Syndagma bustle far into the night, the search for spicier nightlife may land you in a taxi (2300dr/ €6.77) for the 15min. ride to **Tolo,** a packed beach resort where locals find themselves far outnumbered. You can also take a **minicruise** of the harbor and get a close-up view of the Bourtzi. Small *caïques* leave from the end of the dock.

SIGHTS AND BEACHES

The Old Town's architectural diversity is a historical sight in itself. Pl. Syndagma alone boasts a Venetian mansion, a Turkish mosque, and a Byzantine Church.

PALAMIDI FORTRESS. The grueling 999 steps that once provided the only access to the 18th-century fort have since been supplemented by a 3km road (taxis 1000dr/€2.94). If you opt for the steps, they begin on Plizoidhou, across the park from the bus station; bring water and avoid climbing during midday. There are spectacular views of the town, gulf, and much of the Argolid at the top of the fortress. Years ago there were eight working cisterns at the site; today you can tour the cool interiors of the two remaining underground reservoirs. (☎28 036. Open M-Su 8am-6:45pm; off-season 8:30am-5:45pm. 800dr/€2.35, students and seniors 400dr/€1.18, EU students and children free.)

ACRONAFPLIA. The fortress walls of the Acronafplia were fortified by three successive generations of conquerors—Byzantines, Franks, and Venetians. To reach the fort, take the tunnel that runs into the hill from Zigomala to the Xenia Hotel elevator. The views of the Palimidi Fortress, the Gulf, and the Old Town are fantastic. Ludwig I, King of Bavaria, had the huge Bavarian Lion carved out of a monstrous rock as a memorial to the men who died in an epidemic in 1833-34. Today the lion oversees a small park.

MUSEUMS. Nafplion's **Folklore Museum,** is exemplary and open again after years of renovation. The museum is housed in a lovely green building in the heart of the Old Town on Siokou. (☎28 379. Open W-M 9am-3pm. 1000dr/€2.93, students and children 500dr/€1.47.) The **Military Museum,** toward the New Town from Syndagma on Amalias, displays artifacts and high-quality black-and-white photos from the burning of Smyrna (İzmir), the population exchanges of the 1920s, and World War II. (☎25 591. Open Tu-Su 9am-2pm. Free.) The **Archaeological Museum,** in the Venetian mansion in Pl. Syndagma, has a small but esteemed collection of pottery and idols from Mycenaean sites, plus a Mycenaean suit of bronze armor. (☎27 502. Open Tu-Su 8:30am-3pm. 500dr/€1.47, students and seniors 300dr/€0.88, EU students and children free.)

BEACHES. Arvanitia, Nafplion's small, pebbly beach, is along the road that curves around the left-hand side of Palamidi. On hot days the shore is packed, and pop music blares over the noise of the sun-drenched crowd. For a cleaner, more serene alternative, take the footpath that runs along the water from the Arvanitia parking lot. The scenic 45min. walk will reveal three quiet, rocky **coves.** If you're desperate for a long, sandy beach, head to **Tolo,** where you can rent watersport equipment (2500-5000dr/€7.34-14.67). Buses head there from Nafplion hourly (280dr/€0.82).

DAYTRIPS FROM NAFPLION: TIRYNS Τιρυνθα

Take the Argos bus from Nafplion (10min., 2 per hr. 5am-10:30pm, 260dr/€0.76). ☎22 657. Open daily 8am-7pm. 500dr/€1.47, students 300dr/€0.88, EU students free.

About 4km northwest of Nafplion on the road to Argos lie the Mycenaean ruins of Tiryns, or **Tiryntha,** birthplace of Hercules. Heinrich Schliemann's excavation of the site began in 1875 and has been continued by the German Archaeological Institute ever since. The site is now one of the finer prehistoric sites outside Mycenae. Perched atop a 25m high hill, Tiryns was nearly impregnable during ancient times, until its capture and destruction by the Argives in the 5th century BC. Parts of the stronghold date as far back as 2600 BC, but most of what remains was built 1000 years later, in the Mycenaean era. Standing 8m high, the massive walls surrounding the site are evidence of the immensity of the original fortifications; on the eastern and southern slopes of the ancient acropolis, they reach a width of 20m. Vaulted galleries are concealed within these structures. While gems like the palace's frescoes have been taken to the National Archaeological Museum in Athens (p. 104), a huge limestone block remains to form a bathroom floor. Follow the signs left from the site to a well-preserved Mycenaean-era *tholos* tomb in a hillside.

EPIDAVROS Επιδαυρος

Buses travel to and from Nafplion (1hr., 4 per day, 650dr/€1.91). Bring lunch; there is no town near the site. Museum ☎ 22 009. Open daily 8am-7pm. Ticket office open daily 7:30am-7pm, F-Sa until 9pm during festival season. Tickets includes museum entrance and small map of the ruins; 1500dr/€4.40, students 800dr/€2.35, EU students and children free. Plan on spending at least 2hr. between the theater, ruins, and museum.

Like Olympia and Delphi, Epidavros was once both a town and a sanctuary—first to an ancient deity Maleatas, then to Apollo, who assumed the god's name and aspects of his identity, and finally to Apollo's son by Koronis, the healer Asclepius. Under the patronage of Asclepius, Epidavros became famous across the ancient world as a center of medicine, reaching its height in the early fourth century BC, when the sick would travel hundreds of kilometers for cures that mixed medical and mystical. Recent finds indicate that both surgeries and direct deity intervention took place in the sanctuary—diagnoses were made by the god in dream visitations. Over the centuries, the complex became increasingly grand with the benefactions of former patients, growing to include temples to Themis, Aphrodite, and Artemis. Operating until AD 426, the sanctuary complex was closed along with all other non-Christian sanctuaries by Byzantine emperor Theodosius II.

The theater, built in the early 2nd century BC, is the grandest structure at the site. Initially constructed to accommodate 6000 people, its capacity was expanded to 14,000 later in the same century. Despite severe earthquakes in AD 522 and 551, the theater has survived the centuries almost perfectly intact. Today, Greece's most famous ancient theater has come alive again after centuries of silence: in July and August it hosts the **Epidavros Theater Festival.**

THEATER. Built into a lovely hillside, the 55 tiers of Theater of Epidavros face half-forested, half-flaxen mountains so pretty they almost distract from the tragedies played out on the stage. The theater's acoustics are unbelievably good, as yelling, singing, coin-dropping, whispering, and even match-lighting tourists from all nations demonstrate eagerly—every sound can be heard even in the last row.

FESTIVAL. The modern sets left on stage by drama troupes may annoy those visiting the theater for its history alone, but they redeem themselves on the Friday and Saturday night shows. The festival, from late June to mid-August, trots out the National Theater of Greece and visiting companies to perform classical Greek plays translated into modern Greek. Performances begin at 9pm, and tickets can be purchased at the site. (4000dr/€11.77, students and children 2000dr/€5.88; children under six prohibited.) You can also buy tickets in advance at the Athens Festival Box Office (☎(01) 322 1459) or Nafplion's bus station. On performance nights, KTEL buses make a round-trip from Nafplion (7:30pm, 1300dr/€3.82).

MUSEUM. The museum is on the way from the theater to the ruins. Most of the museum's finest pieces have been under restoration and hidden from visitors for years. Fortunately, the three open rooms contain great pieces. The first room holds a marble pillar inscribed with a hymn to Apollo and an array of ancient medical implements. The second room is filled with elaborately decorated architectural reconstructions and randomly placed statuary. In the third room are the intricately carved **entablature** from the temple of Asclepius and the *tholos;* most of the *tholos's* beautiful decorative elements have been removed and replaced temporarily with plaster copies. Authentic and impressive, however, is the perfectly preserved Corinthian capital. It is thought to be the architect's prototype for all of the capitals of the temple of Asclepius. Archaeologists found it buried in the ground away from the site, apparently unconnected to any ruin.

SANCTUARY OF ASCLEPIUS AND THOLOS. The extensive ruins of the sanctuary can be confusing. Walking from the museum, you will pass the **Xenon** or hotel, a maze of foundations. The gymnasium containing the remains of a Roman Odeon is the first structure of the more concentrated complex of ruins. To the left is a stadium, of which only a few tiers of seats and the athletes' starting blocks survive. Two of the most important structures of the ancient sanctuary, the **Temple of Asclepius** and the famous *tholos*, are in front and to the left as you approach the ruins from the museum area. The **tholos**, thought to have been built by Polykleitos the Younger in the mid-4th century BC, is an architectural masterpiece, richly decorated with carvings. Beside the *tholos* are the remains of the **abaton**, where the sick would rest, hoping to have the correct therapy revealed in their dreams by the god. Farther from the *tholos*, along the path on the eastern edge of the site, lie the ruins of 2nd-century AD Roman baths.

ELIAS Ηλειας **AND ACHAIA** Αχαια

In rural Elias and Achaia, tomatoes and beachgoers alike redden beneath the blazing sun. Corn fields, golden beaches, and occasional ruins stud the road between their capitals, Pyrgos and Patras. First settled by Achaians from the Argolid, the region was later ruled by Romans. Afterward Franks, Ottomans, and Venetians all violently disputed this land and left their legacies behind.

PATRAS Πατρα ☎061

Patras, Greece's third-largest city, sprawls along its harbor in a mixture of urban and classical, Greek and international styles. Location, location, location—on the northwestern tip of the Peloponnese—makes Patras a busy transportation hub. Island-bound tourists often see Patras as a stopover, never looking beyond the tourist agencies and cafes. Patras's noisy exuberance makes for a lively social life; cafe-lined plateias and pedestrian-only streets overflow every night. From mid-January to Ash Wednesday, Patras breaks out with pre-Lenten Carnival madness—music, food, and an all-night festival. The port transforms into one vast dance floor, and for once, the people stand a chance against speeding vehicles. The peaceful upper city invites afternoon strolls amid elegant garden-terraced homes turned toward the turquoise gulf below.

▐▌ TRANSPORTATION

If you're coming from Athens by car, choose between the **New National Road,** which runs inland along the Gulf of Corinth, and the slower, scenic **Old National Road,** which hugs the coast. From the north, take a ferry from **Antirio** across to **Rion** on the Peloponnese (30min.; every 15min. 7am-11pm; 300dr/€0.88 per person, 1800dr/€5.28 per car), then hop on **bus #6** (30min., 270dr/€0.79) from Rion to the stop at **Kanakari** and **Aratou** streets, four blocks uphill from the main station.

> **Ferries:** From Patras, boats reach **Kephalonia, Ithaka,** and **Corfu** in Greece, and **Brindisi, Trieste, Bari, Ancona,** and **Venice** in Italy. Most ferries to Italy leave at night. Daily ferries go to **Vathy** on Ithaka (2½hr., 3500dr/€10.27) via **Sami** on Kephalonia (3hr., 3200dr/€9.41); and to **Corfu** (6-8hr., 6100dr/€17.94). Deck passage to **Brindisi** is 8000-10,000dr/€23.48-29.35 including port tax. Several ferry lines make the trip, so check the travel offices along Iroon Polytechniou and Othonas Amplias; discounts are available for those under 25. If you have a **railpass,** it will not work for domestic ferries, and it may or may not work for international ones; make sure you check with more than one line. The folks at **Tsimaras,** previously "Strintzis Tours," Othonos Amalias 14 (☎ 622 602), are very helpful. Open daily 8am-10pm.

Buses: KTEL (☎ 623 886, 887 or 888), on Othonos Amalias between Aratou and Zaïmi. Buses go to: **Athens** (3hr., 33 per day, 4000dr/€11.74); **Egio** (17 per day, 800dr/€2.35); **Ioannina** (4hr., 4 per day, 4750dr/€13.94); **Kalamata** (4hr., 2 per day, 4550dr/€13.35); **Kalavrita** (2hr., 4 per day, 1650dr/€4.84); **Pyrgos** (2hr., 10 per day, 2000dr/€5.87); **Thessaloniki** (8hr., 3 per day, 9200dr/€27); **Tripoli** (4hr., 2 per day, 3400dr/€10); **Volos** (5½hr., 2 per day, 5550dr/€16.30).

Trains: (☎ 639 110), on Othonos Amalias. To: **Athens** (8 per day; slow 5hr., 1800dr/€5.28; express 3½hr., 3400dr/€10); **Egio** (slow 400dr/€1.17, express 1300dr/€3.82); **Kalamata** (5½hr., 2 per day, 1700dr/€5); **Pyrgos,** where you can transfer to **Olympia** (1½hr.; 8 per day until 10pm; slow 1000dr/€2.93, express 2000dr/€5.87). The trains to Athens are packed, so reserve seats even if you have a railpass. **Ticket booth** open daily 6:30am-3am.

Car Rental: Many along Ag. Andreou: **Thrifty/Auto Union,** Ag. Andreou 2 (☎ 623 200), has reasonable rates. Open M-F 9am-9pm, Sa-Su 9am-2pm.

✴🛈 ORIENTATION AND PRACTICAL INFORMATION

Patras is on a grid; most hotels, restaurants, and shops are condensed in the heart of the lower city. **Iroon Polytechniou** runs parallel to the water. Walking south with the water on your right, the road curves just before the train station and becomes **Othonos Amalias.** Just beyond the train station, it runs past the palm trees, cafes, and kiosks of **Pl. Trion Simahon.** Car-free **Ag. Nikolaou,** full of hotels and cafes, runs inland from the plateia and intersects the major east-west streets of the city. From the corner of Ag. Nikolaou and **Mezanos,** walk three blocks from the water and turn right to find **Pl. Georgiou** and its sculpted fountain near the waterfront. The heart of New Patras lies between Pl. Georgiou and **Pl. Olgas,** 3 blocks to the north.

Tourist Office: On the water at the customs entrance. Multilingual staff hands out bus and ferry schedules, lodging advice, and maps. Open M-F 7am-9pm.

Banks: National Bank (☎ 278 042), in Pl. Trion Simahon on the waterfront, has a 24hr. **ATM,** as do other banks on the plateia. Open M-Th 8am-2pm, F 8am-1:30pm.

International Bookstore: Lexis Bookshop, Patreos 90 (☎ 274 831). Useful selection for travelers: language dictionaries and various books about Greek history and culture. Open M-Sa 8:30am-2pm.

Laundromat: Zaïmi 49 (☎ 620 119), past Korinthou. Wash and dry 2300dr/€6.75. Open M-F 9am-3pm and 5-8:30pm, Sa 9am-3pm.

Tourist Police: (☎ 451 833), inside the customs complex. Offers the same services as the tourist office, but goes to greater lengths. Open daily 7am-midnight.

Hospital: Red Cross First Aid (☎ 227 386), on the corner of 28 Oktovriou and Ag. Dionysiou, dispenses first aid. Open daily 8am-8pm. **Rio Hospital of Patras University** (☎ 999 111) is 5km away, accessible by taxi or bus #6.

Telephones: OTE, at Pl. Trion Simahon. Makes international collect calls. Open M-F 7am-2:30pm, Sa 7:20am-1pm.

Internet Access: Starting at Pl. Georgiou, facing the upper city, **Square** (☎ 277 828) will be on the right. 350dr/€1.03 per 30min., 750dr/€2.21 per hr. Open M-F 8am-1pm, Sa-Su 8am-9:30pm. Heading toward the upper city on Gerokostopoulou from Pl. Georgiou, **NetP@rk,** Gerokostopoulou 37 (☎ 279 699), will be on your left. 400dr/€1.17 per 30min., 800dr/€2.35 per hr. Open daily 10am-2am.

Post Office: (☎ 223 864), on Mezonos at the corner of Zaïmi. Open M-F 7:30am-8pm, Sa 7:30am-2pm. **Postal code:** 26001.

▟ ACCOMMODATIONS AND CAMPING

The tangle of buildings on **Ag. Andreou,** parallel to and one block up from the waterfront, hides hotels galore. Many of Patras's cheap hotels have closed, leaving vacant buildings with bright plastic signs. The hotels you'll see are often budget in appearance, but not in price.

Youth Hostel, Iroon Polytechniou 68 (☎ 427 278). From the port, walk away from town with the water on your left for about 1.5km. The slightly remote hostel occupies a creaky turn-of-the-century mansion that sat empty for 40 years after being used by occupying Germans. Minimalism is the key word here, but the location near the water and the relative quiet make for a pleasant atmosphere. You can leave valuables at the reception desk. Check out time 10:30am. Dorms 2000dr/€5.87.

Pension Nicos, Patreos 3 (☎ 623 757), 2 blocks off the waterfront. The best bet in Patras, cheery and conveniently located. Wood-paneled rooms have large, modern shared baths with tubs. Bar and roof terrace with perfect sunset harbor views. Singles 5000dr/€14.67; doubles 7000dr/€20.53.

Hotel El Greco, Ag. Andreou 145 (☎ 272 931; fax 272 932). Walking along Andreou with the water on your right, it's 4 blocks past Pl. Trion Simahon. Clean, cute rooms have bath, TV and A/C. Singles 10,000dr/€29.35; doubles 14,000dr/€41.10.

Rion Camping (☎ 991 585 or 991 450), 8km east in Rion, a beach-and-club suburb of Patras. Catch bus #6 at the corner of Aratou and Kamakari, get off at the port in Rion, and follow signs. 1200dr/€3.52 per person, 600dr/€1.76 per child; 1100dr/€3.23 per tent; 800dr/€2.35 per (small) car. Electricity 800dr/€2.35.

PELOPONNESE

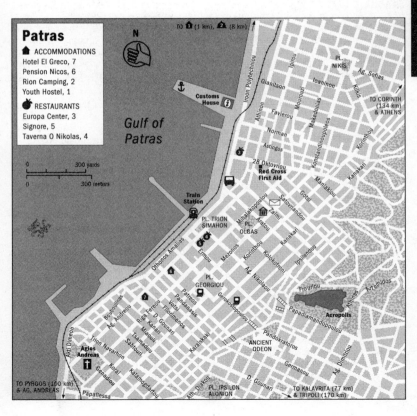

🍴 FOOD

Patras has a multitude of dining options. Cafes and bars spill onto the streets; and slightly more reserved restaurants hide around inland corners. Patras's food prices match its urban style, don't expect to find cozy tavernas serving 2500dr/ €7.34 meals. **Supermarkets** are throughout town. (Most open daily 8am-3pm.)

▨ **Taverna O Nikolas,** on Ag. Andreou just past Ag. Nikolaou, with the water on the right. A bargain meal, to be sure. Chatty Nikolas will cheerfully explain the menu to you in English. All entrees 800-2000dr/€2.35-5.87; classy bottle of wine 1000dr/€2.93 per liter. Open daily 7am-past midnight.

▨ **Europa Center** (☎437 006), on Oth. Amalias between the customs exit and bus station. This friendly cafeteria-style eatery is run by Greek-Americans ready to assist weary back-packers stumbling off ferries. In addition to tasty, low-priced dishes with large portions, (entrees 900-1800dr/€2.63-5.28, vegetarian available), they provide services such as free luggage storage, maps, and information.

Signore (☎222 212), on Ag. Andreou near Ag. Nikolaou. The quasi-Italian stand-in/take-out place serves everything from calzones (700dr/€2.05) and pizza (650dr/€1.90 per slice) to sweet and savory crepes (1000dr/€2.93). Delivery available. Open 24hr.

👁 SIGHTS

▨**ACHAIA CLAUSS WINERY.** A narrow road meanders uphill through grapevines and shaded countryside to the internationally-renowned Achaia Clauss winery, 8km southeast of Patras. Founded in 1861 by German-born Baron von Clauss, its weathered stone buildings have aged well, as has the wine. Try a complimentary sample of their famous Mavrodaphne, a superb dessert wine named for the black eyes of Clauss's ill-fated fiancée Daphne. *(Take bus #7 (30min., 270dr/€0.80) from the intersection of Kolokotroni and Kanakari; it stops at the main gate to the winery at the base of the hill. Free English tours every hour.)*

VENETIAN CASTLE. Continuously in use from the second half of the 6th century until World War II, the castle is more a tribute to the various influences that shaped it than to purely Venetian style. At the main entrance there is a map show-ing which parts of the castle are Venetian, Turkish, Palaeologean, and so on. Built atop ruins of an ancient acropolis and temple to Panachaian Athena, Patras's cas-tle has an incredible view of the entire city and waterfront. At the castle's center is a verdant courtyard with chirping birds, bright flowers, and olive and orange trees that lend the site a cheerfully medieval feel. *(Walk to the upper city from Ag. Nikolaou. If the nearest entrance through the playground is closed, walk around to the main entrance at the opposite side of the castle, along Athinas. Open Tu-Su 8am-7pm. Free.)*

ANCIENT ODEUM. West of the castle in the upper city, this ancient Roman theater was built sometime before AD 160 and used until the 3rd century. Ancient travel writer Pausanias described it as the second most impressive in Greece, after Ath-ens's Theater of Herodus Atticus (p. 101). Excavated in 1889, the theater was restored after World War II. *(Open Tu-Su 8:30am-3pm. Free.)* The theater hosts the **Patras International Festival,** where Greek and international music groups play nightly. *(Every summer June-Aug.; check for performance times and prices.)*

AGIOS ANDREAS. The largest Orthodox cathedral in Greece, Ag. Andreas is dedicated to St. Andrew, a Patras native martyred here on the X-shaped cruci-fix he requested, because he felt unworthy to die on a cross like Jesus's. A decade ago, the Catholic Church presented the Bishop of Patras with the über-relic, St. Andrew's holy head. The crown of the head is visible through its reli-quary, an ornate silver replica of the cathedral around it. The cathedral's fres-coes, gold mosaics, and delicately latticed windows enhance its otherworldly beauty. To the right of the cathedral is the equally beautiful Church of St. Andrew, with a small well allegedly built by the saint himself. Spy the well through a doorway to the right of the church. Legend holds that anyone who drinks from it will return to Patras again. *(Walk along the waterfront or Ag. Andreou with the water to your right until you reach the cathedral, roughly 1.5km from the port. Open daily 9am-dusk. Dress modestly.)*

ARCHAEOLOGICAL MUSEUM. This small museum's most striking pieces are Roman, with statuary, mosaics, glassware, oil lamps, and surprisingly intact delicate gold jewelry. *(☎ 220 829. Mezonos 42, next to Pl. Olgas at the corner of Mezonos and Aratou. Open Tu-Su 8:30am-3pm. Free.)*

CARNIVAL SEASON. From mid-January to Ash Wednesday, *karnavali* sweeps the entire town up in an indescribable energy. A seven-hour parade takes to the streets the last Sunday of Carnival. The final night climaxes in a ritual burning of King Carnival's effigy and an all-night harborside party. The festivities draw up to 300,000 people, filling every hotel room within a 100km radius, so reserve ahead.

■ NIGHTLIFE

At night, the wall of cafes and pubs swells with patrons of all tastes: younger, hardcore beer-swillers rub elbows with dainty spiked-*frappé* sippers. All gesticulate with cigarettes and jabber into cell phones. The two main plateias, Radinou (a pedestrian-only alley one block south of Pl. Olgas), and the upper part of Gerokostopolou (extending uphill from Pl. Georgiou), are especially dense with cafe umbrellas. **Blue Monday,** along Radinou, is a veritable shrine to 1950s America, playing a mix of soul and American and British rock. (Beer 700dr/€2.05; mixed drinks 1500-200dr/€4.40-5.87. Serves sandwiches during the day. Open daily 10am-3am.) **Naja,** Gerokostopoulou 57, at the base of the steps to the upper city, resembles a cave carved out of continuous rock; candles and low voices give it a mellow atmosphere. (Beer and mixed drinks 1000dr/€2.93. Open daily 10pm-3:30am.)

Though Patras itself has much to offer in the way of bars and cafes, the wildest party-goers head out of town. **Rion,** a beach satellite 8km to the northeast, accommodates Patras's club junkies with a summertime stretch of bars, clubs, restaurants, and discos. Decor is a big deal at the beach bars—the most exciting resemble theme parks. To get to Rion, take bus #6 from Kanakari and Aratou (30min., 270dr/€0.80) all the way to the port, past the beach. From the port, walk along another stretch of beach with the water on your right. The start of the strip is within 100m. Buses to Rion only run until 11pm, so count on taking a cab (1000dr/€2.93) home if you're having any fun at all. The highlights of the strip, running from the bus stop, include **Sea Through,** which really plays out the pun with white decor and expanses of glass. **KU** will take you into another world—designed to look like a pyramid from Ancient Egypt (or the bottom of one anyway) KU is covered with vines, adding a primal feel to the Rion club scene. **GAZ Club** is difficult to miss with its silver and metallic blue scaffolding, dance platforms, and lion-head fountain entrance. (Beer 700dr/€2.05; cocktails 1500dr/€4.40 along the strip.)

DIAKOFTO Διακοφτο ☎ 0691

Halfway between Corinth and Patras, at the base of precipitous mountains, Diakofto is famous for its rack-railway trains, which rumble past waterfalls and over steep cliffs through the mountains to Kalavrita. With its fruit tree-lined streets and turquoise waters, Diakofto is a town with tourist potential. Houses are planted between orange and lemon trees, with magenta bougainvillea providing shade. Accommodations are better in Kalavrita (p. 135), but if you plan to catch an early train toward Athens or Patras, Diakofto is a charming place to spend the night.

▲▼ ORIENTATION AND PRACTICAL INFORMATION. The **train station** (☎ 43 206) intersects Diakofto's main road about 10min. from the beach. As the town's social center, it is flanked by cafes and restaurants. Tiny **rack-railway trains** to **Kalavrita** make for an exhilarating ride (1hr., 4 per day, 1250dr/€3.67); halfway rides to **Zahlorou** (30min., 1100dr/€3.23) are also available. Trains to **Patras** (40min.; 9 per day, 600dr/€ 1.76, express 1500dr/€4.40) and **Corinth** (1hr.; 8 per day; 700dr/€2.05, express 1600dr/€9.70) leave from the opposite side of the tracks. Walk down the main road toward the sea to pass through a picturesque residential area and end up at the harbor and public beach. If you walk inland on the winding main road toward the mountains, you will see a **pharmacy** (☎ 41 811; open M-Sa 8am-1pm and 5-9pm), and the **National Bank**, which offers **currency exchange** and 24hr. **ATM** (open M-Th 8:45am-12:45pm, F 8:45am-12:15pm). The nearest **hospital** is a 20min. drive away in Ayion. The **post office** is on the left side of the road, as you walk inland from the train station. (☎ 41 343. Open M-F 7:30am-2pm.) **Postal code:** 25003.

▐ ACCOMMODATIONS. **Hotel Lemonies,** halfway between the train station and the beach on the main road, offers spacious rooms with bath, balcony and A/C. Downstairs is a mellow taverna, and the surrounding residential neighborhood is lovely and quiet. (☎ 41 820. Singles 7000dr/€20.53; doubles 10,000dr/€29.35; triples 12,000dr/€35.22; prices may be higher in summer.) If you're willing to squeeze your budget for comfort, try the **Chris Paul Hotel,** located a block inland from the train station, left off the main road. With the benefits of an upscale dining room, private pool, and handicapped access, Chris Paul might be worth the price. (☎ 41 715 or 41 855; fax 42 128. Singles 9000dr/€26.41; doubles 17,500dr/€51.36; triples 21,000dr/€61.63.) A ½hr. hike to the left on the beach brings you to **Camping Eleon Beach,** which sports a small playground, washing machines, kitchen, restaurant, beach bar, mini-market, and nearby disco. (☎ 41 539. 1200dr/€3.52 per person; 600dr/€1.76 per tent. Electricity 700dr/€2.05. Ask about student rates.)

◆▣ FOOD AND ENTERTAINMENT. Cafes and bars dot the shoreline and cluster around the train station, and the main street inland from the station. On the beach, **Taverna Kohuli** (Κοχυλι) sits beside a docking area for small boats and serves, among other offerings, fresh cucumber and tomato salad (600dr/€1.76), savory grilled chicken (1500dr/€4.40), and lamb (1800dr/€5.28). Next door, **El Fuego Cafe Bar** is the place for an evening drink under stars and large straw umbrellas (beer and ouzo 700dr/€2.05, mixed drinks 1300dr/€3.82). Its fashionable counterparts on the main drag are **Mess Cafe Bar,** right across from the National Bank, adorned with framed old-fashioned travel posters (ouzo and *mezedes* for 500dr/€1.47), and **Paroles**, inland from the National Bank. (Ouzo 300dr/€0.88, beer 600dr/€1.76, mixed drinks 1500dr/€4.40.)

GREAT CANYON MONASTERY Μονη Μεγαλου Σπηλαιου

Located 26km inland from Diakofto, the famous monastery is accessible only by a combination of 19th-century rack-railway and hiking. Getting there is half the fun: the 30min. railway ride winds into smoke-blackened tunnels, through spectacular canyons and gorges created by the Vouraikos River, and over old bridges, offering rollercoaster-esque excitement (1100dr/€3.23 each way). For the monastery, get off at the **Zahlorou,** the midway point on the line.

The small mountain village conjures up stock images of mining or timber towns in the old American West. A few well-shaded rustic buildings cluster around the tracks where they pass over the river. From Zahlorou you can either hike up to the monastery or drive (taxis are not abundant, so plan ahead). If you decide to hike, be prepared for a challenging walk with loose ground under foot; this is not recommended for elderly people or small children. The path that leads to the monastery is marked in English. Don't forget a water bottle, long-sleeved shirt, and sturdy shoes. After about 75min. of walking, you should reach a paved road; turn left and follow the road to the sign for Mega Spilaeou on your right. Stairs in front of the monastery lead to the main entrance. A monk will lead you to the upstairs museum with gold-encased relics and beautiful icons, such as an illustrated Bible from the 9th century. Photographs show the destruction of the centuries-old monastery by an explosion of stored gunpowder in 1934. The new monastery is built up against the cliff wall. One of the cliff's caves is accessible from the second floor of the building—peer into the darkness in search of the cave's miraculous icon, a painting of the Virgin Mary supposedly done by St. Luke.

KALAVRITA Καλαβρυτα ☎ 0692

In a small valley at the end of the rack-railway line, Kalavrita is a close-knit mountain village that caters more to winter skiers than to summer visitors. The green mountain vistas and shaded, quiet streets do make the warmer months a pleasant time to visit, however. Although it has only one sight, those who wish to make the rack-railway a two-day event may find Kalavrita an enjoyable place to stay.

🖪 **PRACTICAL INFORMATION.** Kalavrita is accesible by a tiny and fun-to-ride rack-railway line from **Diakofto** (1hr., 4 per day, 1250dr/€3.67). The two roads perpendicular to the train station that lead to the plateia are **Konstantinou** (later called **Ag. Alexiou**) to the left, and **Syngrou** (later called **25 Martiou**), initially pedestrian only, to the right. A **bus station** (☎ 22 224) has service to: **Patras** (2hr., 4 per day, 1650dr/€4.84); **Athens** (3hr, 1 per day, 3550dr/€10.42) and **Tripoli** (2hr., 1 per day, 1750dr/€5.14). To get there, take your first right off Syngrou onto Kapota, walking away from the train station. Walk several blocks until the road merges; the bus station will be on your left. **Taxis** (☎ 22 127) line up along the side of the plateia closest to the train station. The **National Bank of Greece**, 25 Martiou 4, offers **currency exchange** and a 24hr. **ATM.** (☎ 22 212. Open M-Th 8am-2pm, F 8am-1:30pm.) The **police,** Fotina 7, are to the right off of Ag. Alexiou, three blocks beyond the OTE, walking from the train station. (☎ 23 333. Open 24hr.) **Pharmacies** are sprinkled throughout the town; find one a block up Syngrou from the train station. (☎ 22 131. Open M-F 8am-2pm.) A **hospital** (☎ 22 734) is a three-block walk away from the post office, to the right. The **OTE** is at Ag. Alexiou 10 (open M-F 7:30am-3:10pm). The **post office,** on 25 Martiou, is to the right of the town hall, at the lower right corner of the plateia coming up from the train station. (☎ 22 224. Open M-F 8am-2pm.) **Postal code:** 25001.

🖪 **ACCOMMODATIONS.** Hotels in Kalavrita are pleasant but expensive, especially during ski season. Fortunately, affordable, well-appointed domatia abound; numerous signs near the train station will lead you to them. With your back to the rail station, turn right and walk three blocks. Turn right immediately after the hospital and then continue two blocks to reach **Mitsopoulos Rooms.** The spacious rooms with baths, majestic mountain views, and a common kitchen with free coffee, are all run by a friendly older woman. (☎ 22 481. Singles 6000dr/€17.61, 8000dr/€23.48 off-season; doubles 8000dr/€23.48, 15,000dr/€44.02.) **Domatia Hrysa** (Χρησα) is easy to find; just cross the tracks behind the train station and go straight down the road running perpendicular to the tracks. Comfortable ground-floor singles with TV and bath open onto a fragrant garden; more luxurious rooms are on the 3rd floor. (☎ 22 443. 6000-10,000dr/€17.61-29.35; 8000-16,000dr/€23.48-46.96 off-season. Rates are higher on weekends.) One block up Syngrou from train station, luxurious **Hotel Maria** has rooms with TVs, telephones, and slightly worn but colorful decor. (☎ 22 296. Singles 8000dr/€23.48; doubles 12,000-16,000dr/€35.22-46.96; triples 20,000dr/€58.69, 28,000dr/€82.17 in winter.)

🖪🖪 **FOOD AND NIGHTLIFE.** A collection of similar tavernas line Ag. Alexiou and Syngrou/25 Martiou. Centrally-located **Taverna Stani** offers standard fare served by a friendly staff (Greek salad 1200dr/€3.52, veal with potatoes 2000dr/€5.87). **Taverna Aistralos,** part of the Anesis Hotel, just off Ag. Alexiou facing the plateia, serves tasty dishes including spicy sausage (1500dr/€4.40) and lamb with vegetables (1900dr/€5.58) in a light and spacious dining room. (Summer prices may be lower.) Right next door is the **Tzaki Taverna,** opposite the church with good prices for Greek classics. (Tzatziki 600dr/€1.76, moussaka 1700dr/€5, stuffed tomatoes 1400dr/€4.11.) For a wild night, the **Tehni** (Τεξνι) **Music Club** offers some fun in town. Facing the plateia, turn right at the post office and walk 1 block. If you're willing to hike a bit, head 1km north on the road to Diakofto to the **Air Music Club,** housed in a real airplane.

■▲ SIGHTS AND THE OUTDOORS. One of the few sights in Kalavrita is a moving memorial to the Kalavritan men who were killed on December 13, 1943. In retaliation for the murder of one of their troopers, the occupying Nazis gathered all of the town's men and boys over age 15 on a hill outside of town, under the pretext of giving them a stern reprimand about the murder. Instead, at 2:34pm, from the trees above the hill, lurking troopers opened fire on command and then burned the town itself. Today the clock of the town's church is set permanently to 2:34, and an extensive memorial stands alongside a hanging oil lamp shrine, symbolizing the anticipated resurrection of the murdered men. To reach the memorial, follow Ag. Alexious from the train station. Signs in English point the way.

To make an afternoon of the beautiful countryside, continue walking past the memorial on the road winding up the mountain beyond. After about an hour and a half you will see signs pointing to the **Kalavrita Castle,** which appears to be an old chapel built high up on the hillside. Wear good shoes and take plenty of water. There are also several summer **hikes** around Mt. Helmos; ask around for information or a guide. In the winter months, travel to the nearby **Mt. Helmos** for fantastic **skiing.** One of the town's many ski stores and offices, the **Ski Centre,** on 25 Martiou, provides information and rentals. (☎22 175. Open Dec.-Apr. daily 8:30am-3:30pm.) Not immediately accessible in Kalavrita, but definitely worth the trip if you have transportation, is the **Cave of Lakes,** 16km away. Signs in English direct the way from up the winding mountain road behind the memorial.

KYLLINI Κυλληνη ☎0623

For a port town that handles almost all the tourist traffic to Zakynthos, Kyllini is surprisingly underdeveloped; the town has almost no bus service, few accommodations, and very little to occupy the passing traveler. If you find yourself stuck here, make the best of it by spending the afternoon at the wide sandy beach in the center of town. To bypass Kyllini entirely, take a direct bus from Zakynthos Town to any of the stops on the Patras-Athens route (p. 129).

▊ PRACTICAL INFORMATION. To leave Kyllini, take the **bus** from the kiosk near the port gate to **Pirgos** (45min., 3 per day until 4:30pm, 500dr/€1.47). Once safely in Pirgos, catch a bus to **Olympia** (40min., 16 per day, 450dr/€1.32) or a train to **Athens, Patras, Kalamata,** or **Tripoli.** For all other bus connections you will have to spend 3000dr/€8.80 on a **taxi** (☎71 764) to **Lehena,** the nearest town on the main Patras-Pirgos highway. **Ferries** sail from Kyllini to: **Argostoli** (2hr., 2 per day, 3000dr/€8.80); **Poros** on Kephalonia (1½hr., 6:30 and 10:30pm, 2000dr/€5.87); and **Zakynthos** (1hr., 1-2 per day, 1500dr/€4.40). Buy tickets from one of the two kiosks on the dock; facing inland, the kiosk on the right, near the gate, sells tickets to Zakynthos, and the one on the left sells tickets to Kephalonia. The **port police** are on the dock. (☎92 211. Open 24hr.) The path to town will take you to the **police.** (☎92 202. No English spoken.) The **post office** is a few blocks farther down, on a side street leading inland (open M-F 7:30am-2pm). **Postal code:** 27068.

▛▐ ACCOMMODATIONS AND FOOD. **Sea Garden Domatia,** above the Sea Garden Restaurant two blocks inland from the port, is nothing fancy but has pleasant rooms with ceiling fans, TVs, balconies and some private baths. (☎92 165. Singles 8000dr/€23.48; doubles 18,000dr/€52.82.) **Hotel Ionion,** across the tracks and down the beach, rents large rooms decorated in vivid shades of gray. (☎92 318. Singles 7000-9000dr/€20.53-26.41; doubles 12,000dr/€35.22; triples 14,000dr/€41.10; private baths available.) **Stivas** (☎92 045), down the street from the port gate, facing the entrance to the Sea Garden domatia, serves divine dishes cooked in a tiny, family-run kitchen; eat under a vine-laden trellis on the side patio. Dishes change daily, but a full meal with wine costs about 2500-3000dr/€7.35-8.80 per person.

OLYMPIA Ολυμπια   ☎0624

Set among meadows and shaded by cypress and olive trees, modern Olympia is a friendly and attractive town which serves as a sleeping-and-eating stopover for visitors to the ancient Olympic arena. Intense tourism has inspired vigorous recruiting tactics amongst locals who hock their wares.

◤▐ ORIENTATION AND PRACTICAL INFORMATION

Olympia consists primarily of a 1km main street called **Kondili;** buses stop in front of the tourist office on this street. Head out of town on the main road with the tourist office on your right for a 5min. walk to the Olympia ruins and archaeological museum. The road curves left just outside town; follow the signs to the site. The side road that intersects Kondili in a fork near the youth hostel has the train station, convenience store, and pricey tavernas.

Buses: Across from the tourist info shack's posted schedule. To: **Pirgos** (40min., 16 per day 6:30am-10pm, 450dr/€1.32); **Tripoli** (4hr., 3 per day, 2600dr/€7.65); **Dimitsana** (M and F 8:45am, 1300dr/€3.81); **Lala** (30min., 1:15pm, 500dr/€1.47). Service reduced Sa-Su.

Trains: At the end of the road that begins opposite the youth hostel and intersects Kondili. Despite the fact that Olympia does, indeed, have a train station, at last check in July 2001, it only had trains coming to Olympia, not leaving from. Check with the Tourist Office when you arrive in town.

Tourist Office: (☎23 100; fax 23 125), on Kondili, toward the ruins. Helpful staff, photocopier, stamps, and free **maps.** Open M-F 8am-3pm, Sa 9am-3pm.

Bank: National Bank, on Kondili between the Tourist Office and the Youth Hostel, has an **ATM** and **exchanges currency.** Open M-Th 8am-2pm, F 8am-1:30pm.

Police: Em. Kountsa 1 (☎22 100), 1 block up from Kondili directly behind the tourist office. Open daily 9am-9pm, but someone is there 24hr. There isn't much of a distinction between the police and the tourist police, but an English-speaker is usually on duty at either the police station or the tourist office.

Health Center: (☎22 222; Pirgos hospital (0621) 22 222). Olympia uses Pirgos's hospital, but has its own **health center.** Walk from the ruins down Kondili and turn left before the church on your left. Continue straight as the road winds right and then left, then take a left. Open M-F 8:30am-2pm.

Telephones: OTE (☎22 163) is on Kondili by the post office. Open M-F 7:30am-2pm.

Internet: Olympia's **Internet Cafe** (☎22 578 or 23 841) is a hip and spacious cafe/bar pumping American and British tunes late into the night. Turn off Kondili with the National Bank on your right and walk uphill two blocks; Pension Achilles and Pension Poseidon are on the same street. 500dr/€1.47 minimum; 500dr/€1.47 per 30min.; 1500dr/€4.40 per hr. Open daily 9:30am-3am.

Post Office: (☎22 578), on a nameless uphill side street just past the tourist office. Open M-F 7:30am-2pm. **Postal code:** 27065.

▐ ACCOMMODATIONS AND CAMPING

Most of Olympia's hotels offer private baths and balconies. Prices are around 5000-7000dr/14.71-20.53 per single and 8000-10,000dr/€23.48-29.35 per double.

Zounis Rooms or **Rooms for Rent.** Ask at the **Anesi Cafe-Tavern,** 13 Avgerinou and Spiliopoulou (☎22 644). Turn off Kondili facing uphill; it's 2 blocks up the road between the Youth Hostel and Pirgos (away from the Tourist Office). Pleasant rooms with balconies, nice beds, and private baths. Singles 5000dr/€14.70; doubles 7000dr/€20.53; triples 8500dr/€25.

Pension Achilleus (☎22 562), on the same street as the Internet Cafe and Pension Poseidon; turn off Kondili facing uphill with the National Bank on your right. Cheery flowers outside and serviceable rooms within for a good price. Private bathrooms. Singles 5000dr/€14.67; doubles 7000dr/€20.53; triples 9000dr/€26.41.

Youth Hostel, Kondili 18 (☎22 580). Somewhat dim, but clean and in a good location, this hostel definitely has the cheapest beds in town. Breakfast 700dr/€2.05. Free hot showers. Check-out 10:30am. Dorms 2000dr/€5.87. Separate male/female rooms. Private rooms available for an additional 1000dr/€2.93.

Camping Diana (☎22 314), uphill from the Sports Museum. With a clean pool, hot water, mini-market, helpful info (schedules and maps), and a restaurant serving ouzo with snacks (500dr/€1.47) and breakfast (1500dr/€4.40). 1700dr/€5, children 1100dr/€3.24; 1100dr/€3.24 per car; €1300dr/3.81 per small tent, 1800dr/€5.29 per large tent. Electricity 1200dr/€3.52. 10% student discounts.

▐ FOOD

Numerous **minimarkets** along Kondili sell picnic fixings. Most eateries on Kondili are overpriced, but a walk toward the railroad station or up the hill leads to enticing, inexpensive tavernas. Most restaurants are open from 8am to 1am.

Ambrosia (☎23 414), around to the right, as you face the train station. Another Ambrosia is on the road between Kondili and the train station—don't be fooled. Exceptionally delicious food in an elegant setting overlooking a quiet, cypress-lined meadow. *Mezedes* plate 2800dr/€8.22, veal with red sauce and pasta 2000dr/€5.87, lamb chops 1950dr/€5.74.

Pension Poseidon (☎22 567), 2 blocks uphill from the National Bank, on Kondili. George, the smiling owner, serves *retsina* made from the grapes that hang on the lattices overhead (800dr/€2.35 per liter), and generous, succulent portions of food made by his wife and mother. *Moussaka* 1500dr/€4.40, grilled chicken 1500dr/€4.40, omelettes 800dr/€2.35, and set menus for 2500-2900dr/€7.34-8.50.

Taverna Olympia, on the road to the train station. Away from the crowds, and low-key. Salads 700-800dr/€2.05-2.35, Greek entrees 1100-1750dr/€3.23-5.15, Italian pastas 800-1300dr/€2.35-3.82, and set menus for 2000-2600dr/€5.88-7.65.

▐ SIGHTS

At the top of the hill, on the side of town toward Pirgos, the **Museum of the Olympic Games,** a.k.a. the **Sports Museum,** on Angerinou, 2 blocks uphill from Kondili, tells the recent history of the Olympics and has paraphernalia from each of the modern games, including medals, posters, and photographs of athletes. (☎22 544. Open M-Sa 8am-3:30pm, Su 9am-4:30pm. 500dr/€1.47, children and EU students free.)

ANCIENT OLYMPIA

Site: ☎ *22 517. Open in summer daily 8am-7pm.* **Museum:** *through the parking lot opposite the ancient site.* ☎ *22 742. Open M noon-7pm, Tu-Su 8am-7pm. Cameras with flash prohibited.* **Admission** *to museum and site 2000dr/€5.87; museum or site only 1200dr/€3.53,*

NO GIRLS ALLOWED In ancient Olympia, although female athletic abilities were showcased in the prestigious Heraion footrace held every four years, most women were not allowed to attend the Olympic Games. Only young girls (more specifically, virgins) and the priestess of Demeter were allowed to watch the events. This rule was strictly enforced; as the rules specified, any women caught at the games would be thrown to her death off the summit of Mt. Typaion. While there is no record of anyone ever suffering this gruesome fate, one notable woman was caught breaking the rules. **Kallipateira,** mother of the Olympic athlete Peisirodos, entered the stadium disguised as a male trainer; her husband had died, and she wanted to watch her son compete as he could not. Peisirodos won the games, and as his victory was announced she leapt up to embrace him, disrobing herself in the process and revealing her feminine figure. Out of respect for her son, brother, and deceased husband, all of whom were Olympic champions, officials did not order her death. They *did* decree, as a preventative measure, that from then on all trainers had to wear their birthday suits.

non-EU students 600dr/€1.76; EU students and children under 18 free. A guidebook and map are vital, as the ruins are practically unmarked. Several thorough guides are available at the site—try the red Olympia *(2000dr/€5.87) and* Olympia: Complete Guide *(1500dr/€4.40) both by Spiros Photinos, or* The Blue Guide to the Museum and Sanctuary *by A. and N. Yalouris (2500dr/€7.35). Maps 500-1000dr/€1.47-2.93.*

A green tract between the rivers Kladeo and Alphios, Olympia was one of the most important cultural centers of the Greek world for a millennium. Here, participants from Sicily, Asia Minor, North Africa, Macedonia, and Greece convened to worship, compete, and get cultured among poets, musicians, and masterpieces of art and architecture. Every four years, warring city-states would call truces and travel to Olympia for the most splendid pan-Hellenic assembly of the ancient world.

Olympia was settled in the 3rd millennium BC, when it was dedicated to **Gaia,** the Earth Mother, who had an oracle at the site. Kronos disposed of Gaia and his father, who were in turn kicked out by Kronos's son Zeus and his Olympian compatriots in the Battle of the Gods and the Titans. Olympia's allegiance was quick to follow this succession, and the first athletic games commenced in Zeus's honor, only to be forgotten again until 884 BC. The first Olympic revival took place on the Oracle of Delphi's orders to Iphtos, King of Elias; prophecy held that the games would save Greece from civil war and plague. The first recorded Olympiad was in 776 BC, with **Koroibos of Elias** emerging victorious. Every four years thereafter, another champion added his name to the illustrious list, which became the first accurate chronology of Greek history. Initially, a foot-race of 192m (the stadium's length) was the only event, but longer races, wrestling, boxing, the pentathlon (long jump, discus, javelin, running, wrestling), the hoplite race (in full bronze regalia), and equestrian events eventually joined the roster. The games were celebrated through the 4th century AD, when Theodosius the Great abolished them.

👁 SIGHTS AND RUINS

The central sanctuary of the Olympic complex, which was eventually walled and dedicated to Zeus, was called the **Altis.** Over the centuries, it held temples, treasuries, and a number of monuments to the gods. The complex was surrounded by various facilities for participants and administrators, including the stadium on the far east side. Pausanias, a traveler who wrote in the 2nd century AD, mentions a whopping 69 monuments built by victors to thank the gods. Although the ruins are not especially well-preserved, few sections are corded off; you can climb up the steps of the Temple of Zeus and wander in Phidias's workshop as you please.

TRAINING GROUNDS. As you enter the site you face south, and the 2nd-century BC Gymnasium's thigh-high remains lie to your right as you follow the path, which veers slightly to the left. The Gymnasium was an open-air quadrangle surrounded by Doric columns used by runners and Pentathlon athletes for training. If you continue straight (south) through the Gymnasium, you will come to the re-erected columns of the square Palaestra, or wrestling school, built in the 3rd century BC. Always more than just an athletic facility, the Palaestra had an educational function as philosophical as it was athletic. Young men trained their minds and bodies, wrestling one moment and studying Homer the next.

PHIDIAS'S WORKSHOP. As you continue south and slightly west (out the far right corner of the Palaestra), the next group of buildings includes a walled-in building that is surprisingly intact. This is the workshop of **Phidias,** the marvelous sculptor who came to Olympia after his banishment from Athens under a cloud of scandal (it had to do with the statue of Athena he had created for the Parthenon; use your imagination). Commissioned to sculpt for the Temple of Zeus, he produced an ivory-and-gold statue of the god so magnificent that it was later called one of the **seven wonders of the ancient world.** Seven times larger than life, it stood about 12.4m high, and portrayed the god seated on his throne, his face a revelation of benevolence and glory. After viewing the sculpture, poet Philip of Salonika wrote, "Either God came down from Heaven to show you his image, Phidias, or you went to see God." When the games were abolished in the 4th century AD, the statue was moved to Constantinople; it burned in a fire there in AD 475. Adding insult to injury, the Byzantines built a **church** on top of the sculptor's workshop in the 5th century AD, constructing new walls but leaving the foundation intact. For years, the identity of the site was debated. Recent excavations of the building, however, have affirmed the traditional sources, yielding moulds, sculpting tools and, most amazing of all, shards of a plain wine jug that, when they were cleaned and mended, bore the inscription ΦΕΙΔΙΟ ΕΙΜΙ—"I belong to Phidias." These finds are in the museum (see below). The entrances to the workshop are on the south (away from the Palaestra) and east (toward the Temple of Zeus) sides. Just beyond the workshop to the south and slightly east (straight and left) is the huge **Leonidaion,** built by a wealthy man from Naxos named Leonidas and dedicated to Zeus sometime after 350 BC, and used to house game officials and other VIPs.

BOULETERION. East of the northeast corner of the Leonidaion, to the right as you face the entrance, lie the remains of the South Processional Gate to the Altis. The procession of athletes and trainers entered the sacred area on their way to the

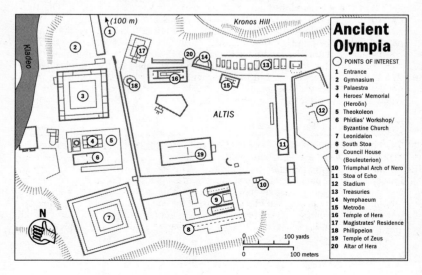

Ancient Olympia

○ POINTS OF INTEREST

1 Entrance
2 Gymnasium
3 Palaestra
4 Heroes' Memorial (Heroön)
5 Theokoleon
6 Phidias' Workshop/ Byzantine Church
7 Leonidaion
8 South Stoa
9 Council House (Bouleuterion)
10 Triumphal Arch of Nero
11 Stoa of Echo
12 Stadium
13 Treasuries
14 Nymphaeum
15 Metroön
16 Temple of Hera
17 Magistrates' Residence
18 Philippeion
19 Temple of Zeus
20 Altar of Hera

ALTIS

Kronos Hill

Kladeo

(100 m)

N

100 yards

100 meters

Bouleuterion (to the right of the Gate), where the Olympic council met. Each athlete was required to make a sacrifice to Zeus and take the sacred oath, swearing their eligibility and intent to abide by the rules of the Games.

TEMPLE OF ZEUS. To the north of the Bouleterion (toward the entrance) are the ruins of the once-gigantic Temple of Zeus, the centerpiece of the Altis after its construction in 457 BC. Home to Phidias's awe-inspiring statue of Zeus (see above), the 27m long temple was the largest completed on the Greek mainland before the Parthenon. The temple's elegant facade, impressive columns, and accurately modeled pedimental sculpture exemplified the Classical design that evolved before the Persians invaded Greece. Toppled in segments, the tremendous columns lie as they fell in a 6th-century AD earthquake.

■**STADIUM.** Continuing east past the temple (to the right as you face the entrance), you will reach the remains of the **Stoa of Echo,** which was used for the competitions between trumpeters and heralds, whose musical prowess was no doubt enhanced by the seven-fold echo the Stoa is said to have had. At the northern edge of the Stoa (toward the hill) is the **Krypte,** the official entrance to the **stadium** (farther to right and east) used by athletes and judges. This domed passageway (of which only one arch survives) and the stadium as it stands today are the products of the Hellenistic period, built over the remains of the earlier, similarly positioned stadium. Despite the efforts of powerful earthquakes, the stadium appears today much as it did 2300 years ago. The judges' stand and the start and finish lines are still in place, and the stadium's grassy banks can still seat nearly 40,000 spectators. Take a lap around, and bond with Olympians of millennia past. As you leave the passageway to the stadium, the remains of treasuries erected by distant states to house votive offerings are in a row on the north hillside to your right. Continuing west, or left as you face the hill, beyond the treasuries, you'll see the remains of the **nymphaeum** and the **metroön,** an elegant 4th-century BC temple dedicated to Rhea, the mother of gods, built in the Doric style.

HERA'S TEMPLE. Westward (to the left facing the hill), past the metroön and the nymphaeum, are the dignified remains of the Temple of Hera. Erected around 600 BC, the temple is the oldest building at Olympia, the oldest Doric temple in Greece, and the best-preserved structure at the site. Originally built for both Zeus and Hera, it was devoted solely to the goddess when Zeus moved to grander quarters in 457 BC. The *cella* of the Temple is where the magnificent Hermes of Praxiteles was unearthed during excavations; you can see the statue in the museum. This temple figured prominently in the Heraia, a women's foot-race held every four years. Today, the Olympic flame is lit at the Altar of Hera, at the northeast corner of the temple. From here, it is borne to Athens by runners who each travel 1km, then pass it from hand to hand to the site of the modern games, which can involve thousands of runners, or draw upon more modern methods of transportation like boats, planes, or even laser beam (as in the unique case of the 1976 Montreal Games). The Prytaneion is northwest (toward the entrance) of the Temple of Hera and contains a sacred hearth, the Altar of Hestia. The spirit of the Games reached its culmination here with the celebratory feasts on behalf of the victors and official guests that expressed a collective appreciation for the virtues of discipline and honor that they embodied.

MUSEUM. Many find the gleaming new ■**Archaeological Museum** a greater attraction than the ancient site itself. A team of French archaeologists began unearthing the site from 1400 years of silt in 1829; the systematic excavations that continue today commenced in 1875. Most of what has been extracted in these 124 years, from the mundane to the wildly spectacular, resides in the museum. Since military victors from across the Greek world sent spoils and pieces of their own equipment to Olympia as offerings to the gods, the new museum doubles as a museum of Greek military history, with entire rooms filled with helmets, cuirasses, greaves, swords, spear points, and other military paraphernalia. The most spectacular military offering is a common **Corinthian helmet** (490 BC), partially destroyed by oxidation. While richer, better preserved headgear can be found elsewhere in the museum, the helmet's attraction is the faint inscription on the chin guard, which reads ΜΙΛΤΙΔΕΣ ΑΝΕΘΕΚΕΝ ΤΟΙ ΔΙΙ—"Miltiades dedicated this to Zeus." The victor of one of the most famous battles in all antiquity, **Miltiades** led the outnumbered Greeks to victory over the Persians at Marathon in 479 BC; he may have worn the helmet in the battle. Beside it is another headpiece, the inscription on which reveals it to be from the Persian side of the same battle. The museum's awesome array of sculpture includes some of the greatest extant pieces in the world. Gape at the graceful perfection of the **Hermes of Praxiteles** (340-330 BC) and the **Rape of Ganymede** (470 BC), and see how the **Nike of Paionios** (421 BC) seems to float. The pedimental sculptures and metopes depicting the 12 labors of Hercules from the Temple of Zeus are in the main room. Even the lesser-known objects astound—every case holds objects that would be highlights of a lesser collection.

ARCADIA Αρκαδια

Beyond the noisy bustle of Tripoli, mountainous Arcadia is heavily forested and lightly speckled with red-roofed villages and lonely monasteries. The region's lush mountain landscapes and undisturbed serenity ushered it into mythology and literature as the pastoral archetype, home to Pan, Dionysus, and the nymphs, satyrs, and the lucky mortals who cavorted with them. While few foreign tourists make it to Arcadia's pristine outer reaches, those who do are accompanied on solitary walks by the tin bells of grazing mountain goats on atop precipitous slopes.

TRIPOLI Τριπολη   ☎071

The transportation hub of Arcadia, Tripoli is crowded and fast-paced. The narrow streets are crammed with clothing and furniture stores, and cafes and tavernas are relegated to the area bordering the park, an oasis of green amid the urban rush. Amuse yourself with a *frappé* in the park as children wreak havoc in bumper cars, or join the adolescent nightlife of techno-blaring bars along Deligianni.

■★🛈 ORIENTATION AND PRACTICAL INFORMATION

Think of Tripoli as a cross. At the center joint is **Pl. Ag. Vasiliou,** marked by the Church of Ag. Vasiliou. Four other plateias form the ends of the cross, at the ends of the four roads that branch out from Ag. Vasiliou. Most buses arrive at Arcadia station in **Pl. Kolokotronis,** to the east of the center. From the station, **Georgiou** street, to the left as you face the National Bank, takes you to Pl. Ag. Vasiliou from behind the church. Facing the church in Pl. Ag. Vasiliou, turn left and head north on **Eth. Antistasis** to reach **Pl. Petrinou,** recognizable by the large, neoclassical Maliaropouli Theater. Along with Pl. Kolokotronis, Pl. Petrinou sees most of the city's activity. Continue along Eth. Antistasis, the main shopping boulevard, past pedestrian-only **Deligianni,** which runs perpendicular to Eth. Antistasis; continue farther up Eth. Antistasis and the city park will be on your right, occupying eight city blocks. At the center of the park is **Pl. Areus,** with a 5m-high statue of War of Independence hero Kolokotronis.

Buses: Tripoli has two bus stations: one is in Pl. Kolokotronis, the other is farther southeast, outside the center of town. The **KTEL Arcadias Station** (☎222 560), in Pl. Kolokotronis, runs buses to: **Andritsena** (2hr., 2 per day, 1750dr/€5.15); **Athens** (3hr., 14 per day, 3400dr/€10); **Dimitsana** (1hr.; M-F 1:30 and 6:30pm, 8:30am M and F only, Sa-Su 1:30pm; 1400dr/€4.15); **Megalopolis** (45min., 9 per day, 700dr/€2.05); **Nafplion** and **Argos** (1hr., 4 per day, 1150dr/€3.38); and **Pirgos** (3½hr.; M-F 8:30am and 6:30pm, Sa-Su 11am; 3000dr/€8.80). **Blue buses** leave from Arcadias Station for **Tegea** and **Mantinea** (1 hr., every 15min., 300dr/€0.88). The **KTEL Messenia and Laconia** depot (☎242 086) is across from the train station. From Arcadias Station turn right onto Lagorati, which runs one block behind the eastern side of Pl.

Koloktroni; follow it past the curve near Atlantik Supermarket until it ends at the train station—the depot is on the left. Buses go to: **Kalamata** (1½hr., 12 per day, 1700dr/ €5); **Patras** (3hr., 2 per day, 3400dr/€10); **Pylos** (3hr., 2 per day, 2700dr/€7.94); and **Sparta** (1hr., 10 per day, 1100dr/€3.24).

Trains: (☎241 213), across from the Messenia and Laconia bus depot. Trains to: **Argos** (1½hr., 3 per day, 650dr/€1.91); **Athens** (4hr., 4 per day, 1500dr/€4.40); **Corinth** (2½hr., 3 per day, 1000dr/€2.94); and **Kalamata** (2½hr., 4 per day, 900dr/€2.54).

Tourist Information: There's no official tourist office, but Vrettou Vanna is a helpful woman in City Hall who might be able to give you lodging information or information about the city. She's on the 4th floor of the new city hall (☎231 844). Follow Eth. Antistasis past Pl. Petrinou. With the park on your right, take the 2nd left onto N. Dimitrakopoulou after the Greek flag-adorned old city hall on the left. The new, glass-fronted building is about 2 blocks down the street on the left. Open M-F 7am-2:30pm.

Bank: National Banks, in Pl. Kolokotroni (☎371 110) and another on Eth. Antistasis, one block from Pl. Agios Vasiliou (☎234 878). Both **exchange currency** and have a 24hr. **ATM.** Both open M-Th 8am-2pm, F 8am-1:30pm.

Police: (☎222 411), on Eth. Antistasis, in Pl. Petrinou near the theater. Open 24hr.

Hospital: (☎238 542), on Panargadon road. Walk due west from Pl. Agios Vasiliou; the road becomes E. Stavrou, which intersects with Panargadon after 500m. At the intersection, turn left. After 300m, look right.

Telephones: OTE: 28 Octovriou 29 (☎226 399). From Pl. Agios Vasiliou, take Eth. Antistasis and bear left on 28 Octovriou. Open M-Sa 7am-5pm.

Internet Access: Forth Net (☎226 407) is on Deligianni, a cafe-lined pedestrian road just off Eth. Antistasis between Pl. Petrinou and the park. 600dr/€1.76 per 30min., 1200dr/€3.53 per hr. Open late.

Post Office: (☎222 565). With your back to the church in Pl. Ag. Vasiliou, cross the plateia and pass the Galaxy Hotel on either side; the post office is one block behind it. Open M-F 7:30am-2pm. **Postal Code:** 22100.

ACCOMMODATIONS

Tripoli presents numerous bloated, mid-range hotels, better suited to business conventions than to budget travelers. Expect to pay 13,000dr/€38.24 for a double. **Hotel Alex,** Vas. Georgios 26, is between Pl. Kolokotronis and Pl. Ag. Vasiliou. The recently redone, spacious rooms are spic and span; all have A/C, TV, and private baths, and some have sitting rooms. (☎223 465; fax 223 466. Singles 10,000dr/ €29.35, doubles 13,000-15,000dr/€38.24-44.12; triples and suites available. **Hotel Menalon** is on the south side of the park. Rooms are clean and carpeted, and have immaculate private baths, phone, TV, and balcony. (☎225 450; fax 224 741. Singles 9000dr/€26.41; doubles 12,000dr/€35.22; triples 15,000dr/€44.)

FOOD

The best restaurants in Tripoli border the park. Sandwich shops on Eth. Antistasis and Georgiou pile baguettes with meat and cheese (500-700dr/€1.47-2.05). **Atlantik Supermarket,** on Lagorati, is well stocked. (Open M-F 8am-9pm, Sa 8am-6pm.)

▓ **Klimataria** (☎222 058), on Eth. Antistasis, 4 blocks past the park as you walk from Pl. Petriou. The restaurant is run by two charming brothers who inherited it from their father. Popular with regulars and visitors alike. Garden seating with fountains and overhead grape vines accent the delicious, well-priced traditional fare. Try the goat with mushrooms in egg and lemon sauce (2800dr/€8.24), or local beef with fresh tomatoes and onions (1900dr/€5.59). Salads start at 700dr/€2.05; a full meal with starter, entree, wine, and dessert will cost about 3500dr/€10.29.

H Gonia Taverna (η γωνια), (☎227 904) in Pl. Agios Vasiliou. No fancy decor, but cheap and filling. *Tzatziki* 600dr/€1.76 Greek salad 1100dr/€3.24, grilled chicken 1100dr/€3.24, and the favorite of the owner's son, pork souvlaki 250dr/€0.74.

PELOPONNESE

Alea (☎ 225 533) in Pl. Areus, facing the park. Cafe atmosphere, but serves tasty fare like their rigatoni special (1600dr/€4.70) and feta cheese (600dr/€1.76).

👁 🎵 SIGHTS AND ENTERTAINMENT

The **Archaeological Museum** is on Evangelistrias, in a yellow building surrounded by flowers. Walking from Pl. Kolokotronis to Pl. Ag. Vasiliou, take the first left and then turn left again. The museum has an especially large prehistoric collection, with room after room of pottery, jewelry, and weaponry from the Neolithic to the Mycenaean periods. Among the later pieces is a Hellenistic relief showing a figure with a scroll in hand: it's one of the few surviving artistic depictions of the predecessor to modern books. (☎ 242 148. Open Tu-Su 8:30am-2:45pm. 500dr/€1.47, seniors 300dr/€0.88, students and children free.) The large **Church of Ag. Vasiliou** is in the plateia of the same name; the shop underneath has interesting religious art.

In summer, posters advertise dance groups, choirs, and plays performed in the city's main plateias and nearby villages. Traveling companies and local performance groups stage occasional Greek-language shows in the attractive **Maliaropoulio Theater.** The theater was under restoration during summer 2001, and may not reopen by 2002; make queries at the tourist office in town hall. The **Lera Panigyris** is a 10-day **theater festival** beginning August 15. During Easter, the town's bishop roasts a lamb for all to eat in one of the plateias.

At night you can rub shoulders with Tripoli's high school students at the undisputed downtown hot spot of pedestrian-only Deligianni, off Eth Antistasis between Pl. Petrinou and the park. Especially popular is the **Cinema Classic Billiards Club,** to the right of Deligianni from Pl. Petrinou. With a big screen TV and A/C, this place fills up every night. (Beer 500dr/€1.47; cocktails 1000dr/€2.94; 1hr. of pool 1600dr/€4.70.) Numerous cafes such as **Azur,** crowd the narrow area around Deligianni and Eth. Antistasis; **The American Music Bar,** found below a "Mobile" sign near the Billiards Club, is a serious competitor on the volume scale.

DIMITSANA Δημητσανα   ☎ 0795

About 60km west of Tripoli lies the quintessential Arcadian village of Dimitsana, clinging to a steep, pine-covered mountainside with a view of the plain of Megalopolis and the Lousios River. Built on the ruins of ancient Teuthis, Dimitsana has been a center of Greek learning and revolutionary activity since the 16th century, producing several notable church fathers during the War of Independence. Today, the town is almost untouched by modern life or tourist intrusions. Wander the streets and you'll see elderly men whiling away the afternoons in cafes, and catch the scent of fresh-baked bread wafting from the open windows of stone homes.

🔁🎵 ORIENTATION AND PRACTICAL INFORMATION. Transportation can be tricky in the mountains, and locals are roughly indifferent to the passage of time. When planning connections, keep in mind that the two taxis in some towns might siesta all afternoon. There is no bus station, bus kiosk, or posted schedule. **Buses** are supposed to run to **Olympia** (1hr., at least 1 per day, 1500dr/€4.40) and **Tripoli** (2 per day, at approximately 10am and 7:30pm, 1200dr/€3.52). There is a morning bus (approximately 10am) that connects Dimitsana to the nearby mountain village of **Stemnitsa.** Schedules for all buses are erratic. Some travelers have been known to take the first bus that comes through, get off at Karkalou (or take the 20min., 1000dr/€2.93 taxi ride), then thumb down one of the more frequent buses to **Tripoli, Pirgos,** or **Olympia** from there. *Let's Go* does not recommend hitchhiking.

In Dimitsana, the bus deposits you on **Labardopoulou** (the main street), near the taxi stand, about 30m downhill from the center of town. Walking uphill into the center of town, you will pass restaurants and the **police station** (☎ 31 205; open 24hr.) to the left, followed by a small grocery store just before the turn in the road.

Opposite this road is an alley leading to rooms and a museum. Continue around the corner to the **National Bank,** with an **ATM,** on your left. (☎31 503. Open M-Th 8am-2pm, F 8am-1:30pm.) There is a nearby **health center** (☎31 401 or 31 402; open 24 hr.), and a **pharmacy** to your right as you walk uphill from the bus stop. The **post office** is past the bank. (☎31 234. Open M-F 7:30am-2pm.)

🏠🍴 ACCOMMODATIONS AND FOOD. Widespread **domatia** are really the only option, but fortunately most establishments are beautifully furnished and more like bed-and-breakfasts than the boxlike rooms to let often found elsewhere. Perhaps the best deal in town are the rooms to let above the 🏪**grocery store** in the main plateia. They include hardwood floors, great views, private baths, TV, big beds, and kitchenettes complete with breakfast fixings. (☎31 084 or 31 562. Singles 6000dr/€17.65; doubles 12,000dr/€35.29; apartment-style 24,000dr/€70.59). The home of **Basilis Tsiapa** is set back from the road with a fragrant garden, sweeping mountain views, and extremely gracious owners. Walking up the main road from the bus stop, take the last right before the road bends. Gorgeous rooms have double beds, hardwood floors, TVs, and kitchenettes. (☎31 583. Singles 10,000-13,000dr/€29.35-38.24; doubles 15,000dr/€44. Breakfast included.) In a ski-lodge style house, **Domatia Kousteni** has big, brand-new rooms with baths, TVs, kitchenettes, and access to a lounge and full kitchen. Call ahead, or head uphill in the alley next to the police station. (☎31 571. Rooms for 1-3 people 12,000dr/€35.29.)

The ouzo flows freely in the cafes lining Labardopolou, but there are fewer tavernas serving full meals. **Barougadiko** (☎31 629; ΜΠΑΡΟΥΓΑΔΙΚΟ), down the main street by the bus stop, is in a castle-like building with low arched doorways and small stone rooms. They serve skillfully prepared traditional Greek dishes like grilled pork with potatoes (1700dr/€5; salads start at 800dr/€2.35). **Barougadiko Bar** is to the right of the main street as you walk uphill from the restaurant. It's the only real bar in town, so you'll be sure to find the night owls there.

🏛 SIGHTS. Two small museums commemorate the town's ecclesiastic, scholarly, and revolutionary heritage. The **Historical Museum** shares its building with a small school. The museum displays an eclectic collection including vintage War of Independence pistols, two 15th-century illuminated psalters, and a handful of Italian edition Greek-Latin **incunabula** of various church fathers and ancient authors. To find the museum and library, walk up the alley next to the police station and look for the courtyard with the statue in it near a large church. (☎31 219. Open Tu-Sa 9am-2pm.) Walking up from the bus station, the **Icon Museum,** housed in an old mansion, is just off the main road on the last right before the bend; the same road also leads to Basilis Tsiapa Rooms. (☎31 465. Open F-Tu 10am-1:30pm and 5-7pm.)

STEMNITSA Στεμνιτσα   ☎0795

From Dimitsana, walk an easy, scenic 11km (about 2½hr.) along the winding road, or pay 1000dr/€2.93 for a taxi, to Stemnitsa, where narrow, irregular cobbled streets betray medieval roots. With its unspoiled mountain scenery and an abundance of flowers, greenery, and stucco-roofed homes, it is easy to see why this town has been called one of the most beautiful in Greece. There are **buses** that come through Stemnitsa, but as with Dimitsana, they are not necessarily regular or on time. Allegedly, there are 8am buses to **Tripoli** and 3pm buses to **Dimitsana** on weekdays. There is no post office, but the people in the **town hall** in the plateia are extremely friendly and helpful, and they speak English. (☎81 280. Open M-F 8am-3pm.) **Postal code:** 22024.

Fortunately, the only hotel in town offers outstanding quality at a reasonable price. The splendid **Hotel Triokolonion** is on the left side of the main road as you head away from Dimitsana, with an inviting terrace that offers a relaxing place to unwind after a day hiking the mountain paths. Its spacious rooms have hardwood floors, private baths, and amazing views. (☎81 297; fax 81 483. Singles 8000dr/ €23.48; doubles 11,900dr/€35; buffet breakfast included. Call ahead.) Consider tiny **Taverna Klinitsa,** just out of the plateia on the way to Dimitsana, for an inexpensive treat. Entrees run about 1000dr/€2.94; try Mama's special fried bread.

Between Dimitsana and Stemnitsa there are several monasteries, some built right into the mountain face. Many of the roads and paths leading to them are unsuitable for cars and are best attempted on foot; leave from and return to the same one. A loop from Dimitsana to a monastery and then to Stemnitsa could be up to 30km. The **Monastery of Ag. Ioannis Prodromos,** 10km from Stemnitsa and 16km from Dimitsana, is still inhabited by 12 monks, you can see icons painted on the bare stone walls and gravity-defying monastic cells that seem to hang off the mountain. Follow the road as it goes from asphalt to dirt, and finally becomes a footpath. (☎81 385. Open dawn-dusk. Modest dress required. Free.)

MESSENIA Μεσσηνια

Messenia is an oasis in the arid Peloponnese. World-renowned olives, figs, and grapes spring from the rich soil on the region's rocky coastline, which remains largely tourist-free. Most Messenians live at the head of the gulf around sprawling Kalamata, though visitors may prefer to stay in the sleepy coastal towns of Pylos, Methoni, Koroni, or Kardamyli, which luxuriate in clean, nearly empty beaches and quiet streets perfumed with the scent of fragrant blossoms.

KALAMATA Καλαματα   ☎0721

Kalamata, the second-largest Peloponnesian city, flourishes as a port and beach resort. The town played a key role in igniting the War of Independence, when, on March 23, 1821, two days before a Greek revolt was to begin, a group of impatient Kalamatans massacred local Ottomans in their sleep. A yearly reenactment of the grisly Greek victory is followed by parades and dancing. Today, fast-growing Kalamata has all the aspects of any other large city, some of which—grime, noise, and urban sprawl—may detract from its vacation appeal. For a city, however, Kalamata presents a permanent summery feel with its flowers, open air cafes, and a clean, if crowded, 4km-long beach.

▉ TRANSPORTATION

Flights: Three flights per week to **Athens** (30min., 16,200dr/€47.65). **Olympic Airways,** (☎22 376), is on the side street just to the left of Pl. Georgiou, facing the OTE. Open M-Sa 8am-3pm. Taxis to the airport—6km from town near **Messini**—cost 1500dr/€4.40.

Trains: (☎95 056), where Sideromikou Stathmou dead ends at Frantzi. As you walk away from the Old Town and toward the waterfront in Pl. Georgiou, turn right on Frantzi at the far end of the plateia and walk a few blocks. To: **Argos** (4hr., 1500dr/€4.40); **Athens** (6½hr., 4 per day, 2400dr/€7.05) via **Tripoli** (2½hr., 950dr/€2.79); **Corinth** (5¼hr., 1900dr/€5.59); **Olympia** (3hr., 1000dr/€2.94); **Patras** (5½hr., 4 per day, 1700dr/€5) via **Kyparissia** (2hr., 650dr/€1.91); **Pirgos** (3¼hr., 950dr/€2.79).

KTEL buses: Leave from the station on Artemidos (☎22 851 info line; open 7am-10pm), inland from Pl. Georgiou and across the river from Aristomenous. To get to the waterfront from the bus station, take a taxi (500-700dr/€1.47-2.05) or trudge down **Artemdios,** the bus station's street, and eventually cross to parallel Aristomenous, which leads to Pl. Georgiou. Buses go to: **Athens** (4hr., 11 per day, 4600dr/€13.53) via **Megalopolis** (1hr., 1250dr/€3.68); **Finikoundas** (2½hr., 4 per day, 1500dr/€4.40); **Koroni** (1½hr., 8 per day, 1000dr/€2.94); **Mavromati** and **Ancient Messene** (1hr., 2 per day, 500dr/€1.47); **Methoni** (1¾hr., 6 per day, 1250dr/€3.68); **Patras** (4hr., 2 per day, 4500dr/€13.24) via **Pirgos** (2hr., 2650dr/€7.80); **Pylos** (1½hr., 9 per day, 1000dr/€2.93); **Sparta** (2hr., 2 per day, 1000dr/€2.93) via **Artemisia** (30min., 500dr/€1.47); **Tripoli** (2hr., 1500dr/€4.40). To get to **Areopolis** (15min., 260dr/€0.77) and **Gythion** (1½hr., 800dr/€2.35), go to **Itilo** (2hr., 4 per day, 1500dr/€4.40) and change buses. The bus passes **Kardamyli** (800dr/€2.35) and **Stoupa** (800dr/€2.35) before it reaches Itilo.

City buses: Unfortunately for the motor-less traveler, the local city bus system (200dr/€0.59 per ride) is limited in scope. City buses depart from near Pl. 25 Martiou in the Old Town; look for the large street off Aristomenous. **Bus #1** goes down Pl. Aristomenous toward the waterfront and then runs along the water from 8am-10pm.

Taxi Service: (☎ 22 522, 23 434 or 27 366).

Moped Rental: At **Alpha Rental** (☎ 93 423 or 94 571), on Vironos near the waterfront, 1-person mopeds go for 3500dr/€10.29 per day; 2-person mopeds 5000dr/€14.70. Open daily 8:30am-8pm.

■✦❷ ORIENTATION AND PRACTICAL INFORMATION

Kalamata sprawls inland from its long beachfront, with a frustratingly spread-out plan. The city is divided into three sections. Closest to the water is a **residential section,** distinguished by the municipal park; most of the hotels and restaurants are here, clustered by the water. Heading inland, the next is **Pl. Georgiou,** home to the train station and most amenities, like stores, banks, and the post office. The **Old Town,** with the castle, market, and bus station, is farthest inland. Navigating from one end to the other can be confusing. Use a **map;** they're available at the **D.E.T.A.K. tourist office** near the bus station and the waterfront **Tourist Police.** The **bus station** and **post office** are on **Artemidos.** With your back to the bus station turn left, follow this street for about 500m, and cross the "river" on your left to **Aristomenous,** Kalamata's main street. Eventually Aristomenous meets and runs along the left side of Pl. Georgiou (coming from the bus station). Cross the river and head directly away from the bus station to get to the Old Town and castle. To get to the waterfront from the Old Town, follow Aristomenous all the way along the left side of Pl. Georgiou until it runs into the back of the Customs and Tourist Police area.

Tourist Information: Tourist police (☎ 95 555), on Maouli in the port, on the 3rd floor of a yellow building to the right of the post office. **Free maps.** Open daily 8am-2pm. More extensive tourist info and free **maps** are available near the Old Town at **D.E.T.A.K.,** Poliviou 6, just off Aristomenous near the Old Town. Open M-F 7am-2:30pm.

Bank: National Bank (☎ 28 047), on Aristomenous off the north end of Pl. Georgiou, and smaller branches in the plateia and on Akrita at the waterfront. All have 24hr. **ATMs** and **currency exchange.** Open M-Th 8am-2pm, F 8am-1:30pm.

Port police: (☎ 22 218), on the harbor near the tourist police in a blue building.

Police: (☎ 22 622), on Aristomenous, toward the water from Pl. Georgiou. Open 24hr.

Hospital: (☎ 46 000), on Athinou. Call for **medical emergencies.**

Telephones: OTE: in Pl. Georgiou, opposite a National Bank. Open M-Th 8am-1:30pm, F 8am-1pm.

Internet Access: Diktyo Internet Cafe, Nedontos 75 (☎ 97 282), just off Aristomenous and close to the OTE. 1000dr/€2.94 per hr, 500dr/€1.47 minimum. Open daily 10am-midnight. If you're farther inland, try **Winner's Cafe** (☎ 96 690), near the waterfront end of Pl. Georgiou, just up Sideromikou Stathmou from the train station. 1000dr/€2.94 per hr.; 300dr/€0.88 minimum gets you 15 minutes. Open daily 9am-1am.

Post Office: Iatropolou 4 (☎ 22 810). Follow this street from the south end of Pl. Georgiou. There's another branch on the waterfront next to the tourist police. Open M-F 7:30am-2pm. **Postal code:** 24100.

PELOPONNESE

ACCOMMODATIONS AND CAMPING

Most of Kalamata's hotels are expensive, loaded with amenities, and on the waterfront. Rooms to let and budget accommodations are uncommon here.

Hotel George (☎ 27 225), near the train station; entrance on Dagre, but visible on Frantzi as you walk from the waterfront end of Pl. Georgiou. Very convenient and charming, with TVs, balconies, and private baths. You may be paying a little more, but the immaculate rooms and baths and a great location make it well worth the extra 20%. Singles 7000dr/€20.53; doubles 8000dr/€23.48.

Hotel Nevada, Santa Rosa 9 (☎ 82 429), off Faron 1 block up from the water. Heading inland on Faron, take the 1st left, or take bus #1 from town and get off as soon as it turns left along the water. Bright rooms are large, comfortable, and wildly decorated with an assortment of kitschy posters, figurines and artificial flowers. Shared bath and kitchen. Singles 4000dr/€11.74; doubles 6000dr/€17.65; triples 9000dr/€26.41.

Camping Maria's Sea and Sun (☎ 41 060). Take bus #1 east past the other campsites. Hot showers. 1500dr/€4.40, children 1000dr/€2.93; 1000dr/€2.93 per small tent, 1200dr/€3.53 per large tent; 1000dr/€2.93 per car. Electricity 1000dr/€2.94.

FOOD

Before leaving town, sample the famous Kalamata olives and figs. The immense **New Market,** just across the bridge from the bus station, is a collection of meat, cheese, and fruit shops, as well as a daily farmer's market. Great sit-down meals can be found along the waterfront. **Tampaki Restaurant,** on the waterfront next to To Petrino serves lunch and dinner for reasonable prices. (☎ 94 152 or 23 225. Country sausage 1550dr/€4.56; entrees 800-2200dr/€2.35-6.46.) Mellow waterfront dining under a thatched straw roof and American R&B tunes make **To Petrino** stand out from the crowd. (Eggplant stuffed with meat 1300dr/€3.82; those famous Kalamata olives 500dr/€1.47.) Though rather drab and fast-food-like from the exterior, **Exociko Kentro** shines when it comes to a hearty meal, with a mean lamb and potatoes (1600dr/€4.71. ☎ 20 985.)

SIGHTS AND ENTERTAINMENT

CASTLE OF VILLEHARDOUINS. The survivor of a violent history, the Castle of the Villehardouins crowns a hill above the old city. Built by the Franks in 1208, it was blown up by the Ottomans in 1685, restored by the Venetians a decade later, and is still recovering from the damage it suffered in a 1986 earthquake. The castle encircles an open-air theater, which hosts "Cultural Summer of Kalamata" in July and August, featuring jazz, rock and classical Greek drama. *(From Pl. 25 Martiou, walk up Ipapandis past the church on the right and take the first left. Open till dusk. Free.)*

CHURCHES. At the foot of the castle you'll find the **Convent of Ag. Konstantinos and Ag. Elena,** where nuns sell bargain linen and lacework. At the far end of the site is the 14th-century **Church of the Ag. Apostoli** (Holy Apostles), site of the first Greek revolt against the Turks on March 23, 1821. A doe-eyed icon of the Virgin Mary was found here; today, the city name (good eyes) echoes the miraculous icon's appearance. *(Times are not standard but all churches should be open 7am-12pm and 5-7pm.)*

ARTS. The Old City's **Benakeion Museum** presents its small collection more artfully and professionally than most Greek museums. Highlighted by an exceptionally well-preserved mosaic floor from a ruined Roman villa nearby, the collection is enlivened by lengthy, informative placards in English. *(☎ 26 209. Open Tu-Sa 8am-2:30pm, Su 8:30am-3pm. Free.)* Just off the waterfront, Kalamata's **School of Fine Arts** exhibits work by Greek artists. *(Faron 221. Open M-Sa 9am-1pm and 6-10pm.)* Kalamata also supports two professional **theaters** and **cinemas;** ask the tourist police for info on events in the **Pantazopoulion Cultural Center** on Aristomenon *(call the municipality with any questions at 28 000).*

NIGHTLIFE. Nightlife in Kalamata revolves around the beach. The strip (1km east of the port) lacks some of the over-the-top fun you can overdose on in other towns, as there are only three clubs in town, all of which are grouped in a clump. **Palladium,** Kalamata's most bizarre night hangout, offers umbrella-topped seating, a lit-up fountain accompanied by a Disney-inspired mural of "Snow White and the Seven Dwarves" and a ball-filled play area, supposedly for "the tykes"—or for the kid in you. (Beer 700dr/€2.05; cocktails 1300dr/€3.82.) Pricier and offering a more typical club atmosphere are **Must,** ultramodern with lots of glass and steel framing, and similar **GLOK,** with lots of white framing; both are just beyond Palladium.

OUTDOORS. Shady trees arch over lovely **Train Park**'s cafes, performance space, duck pond, restaurant, and ice cream parlor, which occupies a converted old train station. Antique trains repose on the tracks. It's at the end of Aristomenous toward Pl. Georgiou. Kalamata's gravelly **beaches** empty as you go eastward, but Pylos, Methoni, and other southern beach towns are a much better bet.

▐▌ DAYTRIP FROM KALAMATA: ANCIENT MESSENE

*Take the bus to Mavromati (1hr.; leaves M-Sa 5:30am and 2pm, returns 2:30pm; 500dr/ €1.47). Taxis 5000dr/€14.67. If you rent a **moped,** you'll need 50ccs to handle the steep hills. ☎ 0724 51 046. Open all day. Free.*

Excavations on **Mt. Ithomi** over the last 15 years have yielded one of the most impressive ancient archaeological sites in Greece, which dates back 2300 years. When the battle of Leuctra in 371 BC ended Spartan domination of the Peloponnese, Theban general and statesman **Epaminodas** built Messene, naming the town for the region's first queen. While the remains of a theater, stadium, gymnasium, public baths, and nine different temples have been uncovered, it is the city's **defensive walls** that usually receive the most attention. The 3m-thick walls circle 9km, and represent the massive heft of 3rd- and 4th-century BC military architecture. Originally, huge gates reinforced with two-story towers and battlements interrupted the circuit, taking their names from the roads that they barricaded. Of the four surviving, the Arcadian gate is the best preserved, and the stone-slab road that stems from it still bears the traces of chariot wheels. A **museum** at the site houses statues and other objects. Also outside Mavromati, the 17th-century **Monastery of the Vourkan** was a starting point for rebels in the War of Independence. Its library harbors several priceless manuscripts.

KARDAMYLI ☎ 0721

The sleepy, one-road town of ▒Kardamyli is the first major bus stop south of Kalamata near Taygetus. The seaside town possesses just a few stone houses and restaurants, but its gorgeous white-pebble beach and views of the surrounding mountains captivate an increasing number of foreign visitors.

▐▐ ORIENTATION AND PRACTICAL INFORMATION. Four buses run from Kalamata every day, dropping off near the *periptera* off the main plateia. All bus times are posted inside the cafe across from the plateia. **Buses** go to **Kalamata** (1hr., 5 per day, 750dr/€2.20) and **Itilo** (30 min., 4 per day, 750dr/€2.20), where you can switch to the **Areopolis** bus (20min., 260dr/€0.77). Through the main plateia, on the road to Itilo, are the **post office** (open M-F 7:30am-2pm), a **bank** (open M and Th 9:30am-1pm) with 24hr. **ATM,** and a **pharmacy** (☎73 512) that sits across from the post office. To get to the **police station,** take a 10min. walk along the road to Kalamata and over the bridge; the station will be on a street to the left—look for signs. (☎73 209. Open 24hr.) Walking toward Itilo, turn right two blocks past the post office to use **Cafe Internet Kourearos,** across from Olympia Domatia. (☎73 148. Open 7pm-1am. 1000dr/€2.93 per 30min., 700dr/€2.05 minimum.)

▐▐ ACCOMMODATIONS AND FOOD. Domatia are everywhere, but start with the excellent, cheap rooms let by **Olympia Domatia.** To get there, turn right off the main road, across from the post office and follow the side street. Pleasant rooms are clean and spacious, most have baths, and there is a shared kitchen for all.

REALLY BIG SKYLIGHTS Throughout Greece, private homes and commercial buildings with completely finished, furnished, inhabited first floors are often topped by two or three stories of structural skeleton. Both in Greece and in Turkey, many people simply build the essentials of a house as high as they can imagine ever finishing, then fill in such niceties as walls and ceilings when they can afford them. That way, commercial ventures need not invest a load of capital before their businesses are an assured success, and families can expand their homes as they grow. Greek law once specified that a house could not be taxed until it was completed—and it wasn't completed until it had a roof. Thrifty Greeks gleefully left their top floors roofless for years of freedom from half of the supposedly inescapable Death and Taxes. A few years ago, the government revamped the tax laws and closed the loophole.

Olympia herself is delightful, fixing coffees for tenants at any time and handing out helpful information about the area. (☎73 623. Singles 6000dr/€17.61; doubles 8000dr/€23.48; triples 10,000dr/€29.35 for two rooms.) Across the way are equally comfortable and similarly priced rooms let by **Stratis Bravakos** at **Yvolvere**. (☎73 326. Singles 7000dr/€20.53; doubles 8000dr/€23.48; triples 10,000dr/€29.35; no singles in high season.) If you want beachfront (rental) property, walk toward Kalamata and turn left at the signs for **Camping Melitsana**, 1.5km down the main beach. (☎73 461. 1350dr/€3.97, 850dr/€2.50 per child; 1100dr/€3.24 per small tent; 1200dr/€3.53 per large tent; 750dr/€2.20 per car. Electricity 850dr/€2.50.)

When you get hungry, walk past the plateia toward Kalamata to find two large **supermarkets.** For delicious traditional food with a waterfront view, try the daily special menu at family-run **Taverna Kiki,** downhill from O Kypos Rooms bordering the main plateia. Menu changes daily, rotating through delicious entrees like goat and *stifado*. (☎73 148. Entrees 1400-1700dr/€4.12-5.) **Paulos,** a creative pizzeria just outside town toward Kalamata, serves eight different pizzas; each feeds two (2000-2500dr/€5.88-7.35). Try the veggie pizza with feta cheese 2400dr/€7.05.

◎◢ SIGHTS AND BEACHES. Beaches are Kardamyli's main attraction, but there are a few other things to see. A short stroll up the road to Itilo will bring you to the small but interesting ruins of the **Old Town** (across from the supermarkets). Nearby, the frescoed Monastery of Dekoulo and the 17th-century Ottoman fortress are poised on a hill. One kilometer along the waterfront toward Kalamata, you'll spot the magnificent **Ritsa beach.** On an enormous natural bay encircled by barren mountains, the white-pebble shore is ideal for swimming. From Ritsa, the winding uphill road looks out over **Limani,** the old harbor of Areopolis home to the Mavromichaeli **Castle of Potrombei.** From here, buses continue down rough roads blessed by beautiful vistas all the way to Areopolis.

▌ DAYTRIP FROM KARDAMYLI: TAYGETUS MOUNTAINS. Competing with beautiful beaches as Kardamyli's main draw is the superb **hiking** that surrounds the village. Southeast of Kalamata, the limestone mountain range of the Taygetus divides Messenia and Laconia, running from Megalopolis down through the Taenarian promontory. Sacred to Apollo and Artemis, the mountains were named after **Taygete,** daughter of Atlas, mother of Lacedaemon, and lover of Zeus. Long glorified for their size, the Taygetus Mountains were dubbed "Perimiketon," or the "long one," by Homer, while Aristophanes mentions in *Lysistrata* that "I would climb as high as the peak of Taygetus, if thus I could find peace." With its highest peak, Profitis Ilia, reaching 2407m, the mountain is home to unusual amphibians, 23 species of endemic plants, the rare *testudo marminata* turtle, and adventurous hikers, mountain bikers, climbers, and paragliders. Carry lots of water, wear good shoes, and be prepared—know your route and its approximate length. It's best to hike in the spring, as summer heat and aridity make the strenuous terrain rather exhausting to navigate for more than an hour or two. **Brochures** and **maps** with suggested routes are available in tourist shops and bookstores, and also in many of Kardamyli's accommodations. There are many possible day-hikes on any number of **color-coded trails.** One popular 1½hr. trail is marked in black and yellow, and begins from Kardamyli, heads to Old Kardamyli, Agia Sophia, then to Petrovouni.

PYLOS Πυλος   ☎ 0723

With its delightful beaches, Ottoman fortress, museum, and splendid views of
Navarino, the Peloponnese's largest natural bay, the town of Pylos is wonderfully and mystifyingly untouristed. Flower-bedecked buildings line the track of
narrow streets and steep stairways that cut from the waterfront up to the residential town.

■🔋 **ORIENTATION AND PRACTICAL INFORMATION.** Most of the town's
businesses line the plateia/bus stop and the roads leading uphill to Methoni
and Hora. The tiny **beaches,** one sand and one pebble, lie to the right of the
waterfront as you face inland, as does the 16th-century Ottoman **Neocastro** fortress on a forested hill. **Buses** (☎ 22 230) go to: **Athens** (6½hr., 2 per day, 5700dr/
€16.77); **Finikoundas** (1hr., 3 per day, 450dr/€1.32); **Kalamata** (1½hr., 9 per day,
1000dr/€2.93); and **Methoni** (15min., 6 per day, 270dr/€0.79). No buses travel
directly to **Koroni,** but you can go through Finikoundas and take a bus to
Horokorio, the stop nearest Koroni. Buses leave for **Kyparissia** (1½hr., 5 per day,
1200dr/€3.53), stopping at **Nestor's Palace** (30min., 450dr/€1.32) and **Hora**
(45min., 450dr/€1.32); service is reduced on weekends. Ask for help in catching buses, as they leave from various points around the plateia. **Rent-A-Bike,**
100m off the plateia on the road running by the police station, has a moped
monopoly. (☎ 22 707. 4000-7000dr/€11.77-20.59 per day. Open daily 9am-1pm
and 5:30-8:30pm.) The **police** are on the second floor of a building on the left
side of the waterfront, on a road going uphill. (☎ 22 316. English spoken. Open
24hr.) The **tourist police** are in the same building. (☎ 23 733. Open daily 8am-
2pm.) Continue around the curve of the waterfront road with the water on the
right to reach the **port police** (☎ 22 225). A **National Bank** with an **ATM** is in the
plateia. (Open M-Th 8am-2pm, F 8am-1:30pm.) To get to the **hospital,** take the
road right from the plateia. (☎ 22 315. Open 24hr.) For the **OTE,** pass the post
office and take your 1st left, then your 2nd right. (☎ 22 399. Open M-F 7:30am-
3:10pm.) The **post office** is on the road toward Hora and Kiparissia, uphill to the
left (facing the water) from the bus station. (☎ 22 247. Open M-F 7:30am-2pm.)
Postal code: 24001.

🏠🍴 **ACCOMMODATIONS AND FOOD.** There are several **Rooms to Let** signs as
the bus descends into town from Kalamata. In general, expect to pay 4000-6000dr/
€11.74-17.61 for singles, 6000-10,000dr/€17.61-29.35 for doubles, and 8000-
12,000dr/€23.48-35.22 for triples. Perhaps the cheapest accommodation in town is
the **Pension,** just before the OTE, which has basic high-ceilinged rooms with private baths and A/C. (☎ 22 748. Singles 5000dr/€14.67; doubles 7000dr/€20.59; triples 8000dr/€23.53.) **Hotel Nilefs,** Rene Pyot 4, has big rooms with baths and sea-
view balconies. It's on the road uphill from the waterfront on the right side of the
plateia, facing inland. (☎ 22 518. Singles 9000dr/€26.47; doubles 12,000-13,000dr/
€35.22-38.15; triples 14,000-15,000dr/€41.18-44.12.) **Navarino Beach Camping** is 6km
north at **Yialova Beach** (☎ 22 761. 1400dr/€4.12 per person, children 800dr/€2.35;
1400dr/€4.12 per large tent, 800dr/€2.35 per car. Electricity 800dr/€2.35.)
Many waterfront restaurants cook up taverna staples served alongside sunset
views over the waterfront. The best of four eating establishments with the same
name, the **Navarino** around the corner from the port police, on the waterfront, has
good, cheap meals (entrees 1100-2700dr/€3.24-7.94). At delicious **Tessera Epohes**
(Τεσσερα Εποχεζ), the last taverna on the water to the right of town (facing
inland), everything is large, cheap, and well-prepared. (☎ 22 739. *Tzatziki* 450dr/
€1.32, lamb chops 1500dr/€4.40.) Opposite the police station, **La Piazza** prepares
wonderful pasta and pizza. Try the 2000dr/€5.87 "Pizza la Piazza" made with feta,
basil, olives, green peppers and ham. (Entrees 900-1600dr/€2.64-4.70. Open daily
6pm-1am.) The classy **1930 Restaurant,** on the road into town from Kalamata, is
accented by wood paneling, antique fishing paraphernalia, and a seafood menu
with grilled octopus (2200dr/€6.47).

PELOPONNESE

◐◪ SIGHTS AND BEACHES. Fortresses guard both sides of Navarino Bay. **Neocastro,** to the south, is easily accessible from the town; walk up the road to Methoni and turn right at the sign reading Φρογριο. The well-preserved walls enclose a fast-decaying church (originally a mosque), along with a citadel and a lovely little museum. Take a look at the pictures of the Peloponnese as it was a hundred years ago. The restored hexagonal courtyard, up the hill to your right after entering the castle, shows a room of photographs detailing its restoration. (☎22 010. Open Tu-Su 8:30am-5pm. 800dr/€2.35, seniors and students 400dr/€1.17, EU students and children free.) The slight **Archaeological Museum,** on the road to Methoni, shows the contents of Mycenaean and Hellenistic tombs. A Mycenaean battle helmet made of boar's tusks catches the eye, while three richly colored glass vessels highlight the Hellenistic period. (☎22 448. Open Tu-Su 8:30am-3pm. 500dr/€1.47, seniors and students 300dr/€0.88, EU students and children free.)

To see the island of **Sfakteria** up close, you can take a **boat tour** from the port. They stop at various monuments to the allied sailors of the Battle of Navarino and show a sunken Ottoman ship. Inquire at the small booth on the waterfront, around the corner from the port police. (1½hr. 10,000dr/€29.35 for 4 people. July-Aug. only.) A few small **beaches** surround the town. Although the sand is devoured by the ocean when the tide is in, the clear, choppy water makes splashing around fun. The beautiful, long, and much wider **Yialova Beach** is 6km north of town. Only the bus to Athens goes there, so you are better off using your own transportation

▨ DAYTRIP FROM PYLOS: NESTOR'S PALACE. In the Mycenaean world, Pylos was second only to Mycenae in wealth and artistic development. The centerpiece of the archaeological site is the **palace** where Nestor met Telemachus, Odysseus's son, in Homer's *Odyssey*. The palace is thought to have been built in the 13th century BC by Nestor's father Neleus, the founder of the Neleid dynasty. It was destroyed by fire around 1200 BC. Still under excavation, the thigh-high remains of the site comprise three buildings. The main building, possibly the king's residence, originally had a second floor with official and residential quarters and storerooms. Archaeologists think an older, smaller palace stood to the southeast. To the northeast lie the ruins of a complex of isolated workshops and storerooms. Archaeologists have turned up pottery, jewelry, various bronze and ivory objects, and a cache of **Linear B tablets** explaining some of the palace's administrative operations. Most finds are displayed at the National Archaeological Museum in Athens, some pottery and surviving fragments of wall paintings are at the Hora village museum, 5km away. For 1500dr/€4.40 you can supplement your tour with the *University of Cincinnati's Guide to Nestor's Palace*. **Buses** from Pylos run through **Kyparissia** (1½hr., 5 per day, 1200dr/€3.52), and stop at **Nestor's Palace** (30min., 450dr/€1.32) on the way to Hora (45min., 450dr/€1.32); service is reduced on weekends. The last bus returns at 5:30pm. (☎31 437 or 31 358. Open daily 8:30am-3pm. 500dr/€1.47, seniors and non-EU students 300dr/€0.88, EU students and children free.) A **Mycenaean Tholos Tomb** is across the lower parking lot; look for signs.

METHONI Μεθωνη   ☎0723

With hibiscus-lined streets and a relaxed atmosphere, Methoni is a restorative reprieve from the bustle of Kalamata and Tripoli. Known as the "Camelot of Greece," Methoni was once used as bait by Agamemnon to lure the sulking Achilles back to war. The town's spectacular 15th-century castle shoots its narrow stone walkways onto rocky outcroppings in the bay. Here, Miguel de Cervantes poured out romances while imprisoned under Ottoman guard.

▰▨ ORIENTATION AND PRACTICAL INFORMATION. The town's two main streets form a Y where the Pylos-Finikoundas buses stop. Facing the fork, the lower road is on the left, and leads to the beach and the castle. There's no **bus**

station, and no posted schedule. Buses go to **Pylos** (15min., 7 per day, 260dr/€0.76) and **Finikoundas** (30min., 10 per day, 300dr/€0.88), with a reduced schedule Saturday and Sunday. There are also daily buses to **Kalamata** (2hr., 1200dr/€3.53) and infrequent buses to **Athens** (6hr., 5200dr/€15.29). Your best bet is to ask a few locals about bus schedules and frequency. The main town **beach** is a few blocks to the left end of the lower street, beside a little beachfront plateia. The campgrounds and several beach bars are on the road bordering the lengthy beach. There's also a stone walkway perfect for evening strolls by the water. The **police** are near the bus station on the upper street, just past the bank. (☎31 203. Open 24hr.) The **National Bank** with a 24hr. **ATM** is 40m down the right fork. (☎31 570. Open M-Th 8am-2pm, F 8am-1:30pm.) The **OTE** is in a poorly marked cream-colored building with blue shutters; go down the lower fork and turn left, toward the beachside plateia. (☎31 121. Open M-F 7:30am-3:10pm.) The **post office** is two blocks down the lower street on the left side. (☎31 266. Open M-F 7:30am-2pm.) **Postal code:** 24006.

⬛ ACCOMMODATIONS AND CAMPING. Since Methoni receives a fair amount of August tourism, rooms can be a bit expensive. Several **Rooms to Let** signs hang along both forks of the road. Although the rooms usually lack hotel amenities, their prices are slightly cheaper. Near the end of the lower road, make a left (heading toward the plateia) to find the unassuming **Hotel Galini,** which has rooms similar in quality to its flashier counterparts, but at cheaper prices. (☎31 467. Singles 7000-15,000dr/€20.59-44.12; doubles 8000-15,000dr/€23.53-44.12.) On the upper street, over a Tae Kwan Do center about four blocks away from the bus stop, **Ioannis Psiharis** lets spacious rooms with double beds, private baths, and balconies. (☎31 406. Singles 8000-9000dr/€23.53-26.47; doubles 9000dr/€26.47.) **Hotel Giota,** in the beachfront plateia, has modern rooms with A/C, balconies, and private baths. (☎31 290; fax 31 291. Singles 8000-12,000dr/€23.53-35.29; doubles 10,000-15,000dr/€29.41-44.12.) The same family runs nearby **Hotel Alex** (☎31 219; fax 31 291). **Seaside Camping Methoni** is a 5min. walk down the beach to the right of the plateia. (☎31 228. 1100dr/€3.23 per person; 610dr/€1.80 per car; 700dr/€2.05 per small tent; electricity 700dr/€2.05; prices lower May-June and Sept.-Oct.)

◖ FOOD. Several excellent tavernas and restaurants pepper Methoni. In the waterfront plateia, the multilingual proprietor of **Meltemi** serves excellent traditional entrees. (Feta with olive oil 600dr/€1.76, *moussaka* 1400dr/€4.11.) Humble **Oraia Methoni** accents its simple atmosphere with quality and low prices. Walking from the bus stop, turn left one block down the lower road and continue 30m. (Tomato and cucumber salad 800dr/€2.05, baked pork 3100dr/€9.12 per kg, pita souvlaki 350dr/€1.03.) **Kali Kardia,** four blocks down the upper street from the bus stop, serves a variety of dishes in a classy, spacious wooden interior. (☎31 260. Pizzas start at 1600dr/€4.71, *moussaka* 1800dr/€5.29.)

◣ SIGHTS. No visitor to the southwest Peloponnese should miss Methoni's ▧**Venetian fortress,** a 13th-century mini-city. To get to the castle, follow the upper street to its end. The castle grounds and several beach bars are on the road bordering the lengthy beach. There's also a stone walkway perfect for evening strolls by the water. Venture behind the fortified gate of the fortress to wander paths above overgrown fields strewn with wildflowers and crumbling walls. Frankish foundations, Venetian battlements, and Turkish steam baths testify to the castle's varied history. At the tip of the peninsula, a narrow bridge connects an islet and its fortified tower to the main structure with a whimsical touch of medieval defensive architecture. Early morning is the best time to visit, when the tide crashes against the steadfast stone walls and the cool earth begins to warm. (Open M-Sa 8:30am-8pm, Su 9am-8pm. Free.) The main town **beach** is a few blocks to the left of the end of the lower street, beside a little beachfront plateia.

PELOPONNESE

LACONIA Λακωνια

In the 12th century BC, the Indo-European Dorians invaded Greece from the north, driving out the Mycenaean inhabitants and ushering in the so-called Dark Age. Laconia, the territory of the ancient Spartans, has long prided itself on its minimalist aesthetic, coining its own adjective, "laconic." The starkly dramatic Taygetus Mountains has matched the traditionally stern personality of the people. Although Laconia boasts one of the Peloponnese's most popular sites, Byzantine Mystras, the region as a whole offers a peaceful break from the more touristed urban hustle of other Peloponnesian towns.

SPARTA Σπαρτη   ☎ 0731

Citizens of today's quiet Sparta make olive oil, not war. Built directly on top of the ancient warrior city, modern Sparta offers meager ruins to occupy tourists. It's by far the best base for exploring the ruins of Byzantine Mystras, 6km away. As the capital of Laconia, aggressive Sparta dominated the Peloponnese with its legendary sense of discipline and invincible armies. Spartans traced their austere daily regimens back to 8th-century law-giver **Lycurgus**, who demanded plain dress, simple food, and strict training for all citizens from a young age. Men and women were educated differently, but with equal severity. The Spartans produced little memorable literature, art, or architecture, but they were unsurpassed in arms. Finally capturing Athens in 404 BC to end the 28-year Peloponnesian War (see p. 12), Sparta won its greatest victory and effectively ruled Greece. Although its domination of Athens was brief, even a temporary hold over the Classical power is testimony to Sparta's unparalleled military prowess. In the end, the earthquake-shaken empire collapsed under the stress of slave revolts and a depleted male population.

✦ 🛈 ORIENTATION AND PRACTICAL INFORMATION

Sparta lies on a grid. The main streets, **Paleologou** and **Lykourgou** (named for law-giver Lycurgus), hold the necessary amenities, and intersect in the center of town. From this intersection, the town plateia is one block west, away from the bus station, on Lykougrou. To reach the center of town from the bus station, walk 10 blocks west, slightly uphill, on Lykourgou. The **bus station** is crowded and not particularly tourist-friendly. There are often confusing and unmentioned transfers on the bus routes, but if you stick to your guns, you'll end up where you want to be. One trick is to find a Greek traveler heading to your destination and follow him or her to ensure that you end up on the right bus, but if you ask enough people, it is likely that someone will lend a hand to point out your stop or connecting bus.

Buses: (☎ 26 441). Walk downhill on Lykourgou away from the plateia or toward the Archaeological Museum, continuing past a small forested area on your right; the station will be on your right, 10 blocks from the center of town. Buses go to: **Areopolis** (1½hr., 2 per day, 1400dr./€4.12); **Athens** (3½hr., 9 per day, 4100dr./€12.06) via **Corinth** (2½hr., 2550dr./€7.50) and **Tripoli** (1hr., 1100dr./€32.35); **Gerolimenas** (2hr., 2 per day, 2050dr./€6.03); **Gythion** (1hr., 5 per day, 850dr./€2.50); **Kalamata** (1hr., 2 per day, 850dr./€2.50); **Monemvasia** (2hr., 3 per day, 2000dr./€5.88); **Neapolis** (3hr., 4 per day, 2800dr./€8.23); **Pirgos Dirou** (1½hr., 1 per day, 1700dr./€5). Buses to **Mystras** (15min., 11 per day, 260dr./€0.77) also stop in front of the OTE on Lykourgou, and at the corner of Lykourgou and Leonidou on the left, 2 blocks past the town plateia away from the main bus station.

Tourist Office: (☎ 24 852 or 26 545), to the left of the town hall in the plateia. English spoken. Bus schedules, hotels, and information are available on specific request. Purchase their map (700dr./€2.05) at a nearby photo store. Open daily 8am-2pm.

Banks: National Bank (☎ 26 200), on Paleologou 3 blocks north (toward Ancient Sparta) from Lykourgou and the town center, has a 24hr. **ATM** and **currency exchange.** Open M-Th 8am-2pm, F 8am-1:30pm.

Police: Hilonos 8 (☎26 229), on a side street off Lykourgou, a block past the museum heading toward the bus station. Open 24hr. Earnestly helpful, English-speaking **tourist police** (☎20 492) in the same building. Open daily 8am-9pm.

Hospital: (☎28 671 or 28 675; **emergency** ☎29 106), on Nosokomeio, 1km to the north of Sparta. Open 24hr.

Pharmacies: line Lykourgou and Paleologou.

Telephone: OTE, Kleomvritou 3 (☎23 799), accessible from Lykourgou, across from the museum. Open M-F 8am-2:30pm; also Tu and Th 6-9pm.

Internet: Aerodromi (☎29 268) on Lykourgou between the bus station and the Archaeological Museum. 1200dr/€3.53 per hr., 600dr/€1.77 per 30min., 100dr/€0.29 minimum. Open M-Su 10am-midnight. **Hellas Internet Cafe,** Paleologou 34 (☎21 500), south of Lykourgou, away from Ancient Sparta. 1200dr/€3.53 per hr., 600dr/€1.77 per 30min., 300dr/€0.88 minimum. Open M-Sa 8am-11pm, Su 11am-11pm.

Post Office: (☎26 565), on Archidamou off Lykourgou. Open M-F 7:30am-2pm. **Postal code:** 23100.

ACCOMMODATIONS AND CAMPING

A bargain is hard to find among the numerous mid-range hotels on Paleologou, but TVs and private baths are a drachma a dozen.

Hotel Cecil (☎24 980), 5 blocks north of Lykourgou toward Ancient Sparta, on the corner of Paleologou and Thermopilion. Pale yellow facade and pleasant, standard rooms within, you'll spot this bright hotel from down the block. TV, A/C, phones, private baths, and wonderful light. Singles 8000dr/€23.53; doubles 12,000dr/€35.29.

Hotel Laconia (☎28 952), on Paleologou in the 1st block north (toward Ancient Sparta) from Lykourgou. Laconia caters to the vampirish—all the windows have been boarded up to allow for more rest from the sun. Rooms have TVs, dark-wood furniture, carpeting, clean private baths. Singles 7000dr/€20.59; doubles 12,000dr/€35.29.

Hotel Apollon, Thermopilion 84 (☎22 491; fax 23 936). Across Paleolougou from Hotel Cecil at a fork in the road. Flashy, mirrored lobby with a sky mural above the bar give way to colorful, patterned rooms. Each has its own personality—check out the "salmon" room on the 4th floor. TVs, private baths, phones, and A/C. Breakfast 1500dr/€4.40. Singles 8000dr/€23.53; doubles 10,000dr/€29.41.

Camping Castle View (☎83 303), near Mystras. Take the Mystras bus and get off at the signs. Pool, modern showers and toilets, and a mini-market. 1600dr/€4.70 per person, 900dr/€2.65 per child; 900dr/€2.65 per car; 900dr/€2.65 per small tent, 1200dr/€3.53 per large tent. Electricity 900dr/€2.65.

FOOD AND NIGHTLIFE

Sparta's restaurants provide uniform, standard menus at pretty reasonable prices. Superior service and a large selection spice up **Elyssé Restaurant,** on Paleologou 200m north of the main intersection, which specializes in local dishes like Greek sausage with orange peel (900dr/€2.65) and chicken *bardouniotiko* (1600dr/€4.70; ☎29 896). **Diethnes,** on Paleologou, a few meters south of Elyssé, serves tasty Greek food in a vibrant garden with orange trees, grape vines and flowers. (☎28 636. *Moussaka* 1500dr/€4.40; *taromasalata* 700dr/€2.05.) **Menelaion Hotel Restaurant,** in the Menelaion Hotel on Paleologou, two blocks north of Lykourgou toward Ancient Sparta, has an elegant pool side setting and excellent meals with surprisingly low prices. (☎22 161. Meatballs and potatoes 1300dr/€3.82, pork in wine sauce with orange peel 1800dr/€5.29.)

At night, the side of the plateia near the town hall fills with young people who while away the hours at outdoor cafes; head indoors for clubbing. **The Imago,** a hip, artsy bar, is in the alley behind the town hall. (Beer 1500dr/€4.40; cocktails 2000dr/€5.88. Open daily 9:30pm-3am.) **Caprice,** another popular club, is opposite the town hall. (Beer 1500dr/€4.40; cocktails 2000dr/€5.88. Open daily 11pm-late.)

A HARD-KNOCK LIFE A young Spartan's training for a life of war began early—before conception. Lycurgus believed two fit parents produced stronger off-spring, so he ordered all Spartan women to undergo the same rigorous training endured by men. Furthermore, newlyweds were permitted only an occasional tryst on the theory that the heightened (desperate?) desire of the parents would produce more robust children. If they weren't winnowed out as weak or deformed, seven-year-old boys began a severe regimen of training under an adult, away from their parents. They were forced to walk barefoot to toughen their feet, and wore only a single, simple garment in all seasons to expose them to drastic weather changes. The Spartan creed dictated that young men be guarded against temptations of any kind, so strict laws forbade everything from drinking to pederasty. Moreover, young Spartans were given the plainest and simplest foods for fear that rich delicacies would stunt their growth. One visitor to Sparta, upon sampling the fare, allegedly quipped, "Now I know why they do not fear death."

⊙ SIGHTS

What little remains of **ancient Sparta** lies in an olive grove 1km north of the town plateia down Paleologou. At the north end of Paleologou stands an enormous statue of **Leonidas,** the famous warrior king who fell at the Battle of Thermopylae in 480 BC. The Spartans built a large, vacant tomb for their leader, but his body was never found. The tomb is in a public park, left of the road heading up to the ruins. The ruins consist of the outline and lower rows of one of the larger theaters of antiquity, along with a few fragments of the acropolis. To get there from the bus station on Lykourgou, turn right onto Paleolourgou and walk to the end of the downtown. At the statue of Leonidas, turn left and then right at the signs for the ruins 50m from the statue; the ruins are about 400m from there.

Sparta's **Archaeological Museum,** on Lykourgou across from the OTE, hedges a beautiful, well-kept park with a fountain and assorted ancient statuary. The varied collection is worth an hour; it includes spooky votive masks used in ritual dances at the sanctuary of Artemis Orthia, a large marble statue of a warrior thought to be Leonidas, and various representations of the Dioskouri—the brothers Castor and Pollux—locally revered as symbols of brotherly love and honor. One room is devoted to prehistoric pottery, weaponry, and jewelry. Especially impressive are the "unpublished" mosaics from the Roman period. (☎28 575. Open Tu-Sa 8:30am-3pm, Su 9:30am-2:30pm. 500dr/€1.47, students and seniors 300dr/€0.88, EU students and children free.) The **National Art Gallery,** Paleologou 123, near Hotel Cecil, has a small collection of 19th-century French and Dutch paintings, mostly still-lifes and portraits, including one attributed to Gustave Courbet. Upstairs is a more contemporary exhibit by modern Greek artists, with a number of watercolor landscapes. (☎81 557. Open Tu-Sa 9am-3pm, Su 10am-2pm. Free.)

Finding the various surrounding ruins may be a challenge, but it's worth it for history buffs. Ask the tourist police for a map before heading out. Three remaining platforms of the **Shrine to Menelaus and Helen** (history's most sought-after beauty and her ditched hubby) are 5km away. The remains of a **Shrine to Apollo** are south on the road to Gythion. From the northeast corner of town, near Hotel Apollon, a short walk east along the Evrotas River leads to the **Sanctuary of Artemis Orthia,** where Spartan youths proved their courage by enduring public floggings.

⚡ DAYTRIP FROM SPARTA: MYSTRAS Μυστρας

*Buses that leave from **Sparta**'s main station and two other stops in downtown Sparta (see above; 20min., 9 per day, 260dr/€0.77) drop off **twice**: once at the main entrance to lower tier of the city and once at the Castro entrance, near the top of the city. If you get off at the lower stop, you're in for a 45min.-1hr. uphill walk to the castle. Buses pick up at the restaurant beneath the lower entrance. It gets hot—go early, bring water and wear good hiking shoes. Plan 3hr. to see the sights. Consider Guidebook Mystras by Manolis*

Chatzidakis (2000dr/€5.88) to supplement your exploration. The monasteries request modest dress, so wear long pants or a skirt; aprons are lent to forgetful visitors. ☎83 377. Open daily 8am-7pm; off-season daily 8:30am-3pm. Admission 1200dr/€3.53, students and seniors 600dr/€1.77, EU students and children free.

Mystras was once the religious center of all Byzantium, and the locus of Constantinople's rule over the Peloponnese. Its extraordinary ruins are the remains of a city of Byzantine churches, chapels, and monasteries. Mystras was founded by French crusader **Guillume de Villehardouin** in 1249 with the building of a central castle. After the final attempt to establish Frankish sovereignty over the Peloponnese failed, Mystras was ceded to the Greeks in 1262, giving them an important military base and cultural center. In the following centuries it grew from a village to a city, draining Sparta of its inhabitants as they sought protection in the city's fortress. By the early 15th century, Mystras was an intellectual center with a thriving silk industry. Unhappy under the thumb of repressive feudal lords and clergy, restless country folk surged into town, set up schools, and created an early bourgeoisie. When Turks invaded in 1460, Mystras's glory days were over. By the early 19th century, the city had crumbled to ruin. When King Otto founded modern Sparta in 1831, Mystras's fate was sealed with a table-turning exodus to its revived neighbor. Crowned by the original castle, an intricate network of paths traces through three tiers of ruins, descending from royalty to nobility to commoners. Although less well preserved than many of the religious edifices that encircle it—they're almost completely intact, if a bit faded at the frescoes—the dramatic castle delivers a breathtaking view of the site and the surrounding countryside. Most people choose to take the bus to the upper entrance, climb to the castle, then work their way down through the rest of the site. Particularly beautiful is the **Metropolis of Ag. Demetrios** on the lower tier, with its detailed frescoes, flowery courtyard, and museum of architectural fragments. Also on the lower tier are the two churches of the monastery of **Vrontochion**. The first, **Aphentiko**, glows with magnificent two-story frescoes; **Ag. Theodoros** is its neighbor. Slightly higher up is the **Pantanassa**, a convent with an elaborately ornamented facade, frescoes, and a miracle-working icon of Mary. Finally, quietly tucked away in the far corner of the lower tier, every centimeter of the awe-inspiring ⊠**Church of Peribleptos** is bathed in exquisitely detailed religious paintings. Though many were vandalized by invading Ottomans who dug the eyes out of saints and saviors alike, this remains Mystras's most stunning relic. At the top of it all is the **Castle,** which commands incredible views of the valley below and steep cliffs behind.

MANI Μανη

The name of the province of Mani comes from the Greek word *manis*, meaning wrath or fury. Sparsely settled and encircling the unforgiving Taygetus Mountains (p. 150), the region juts out into the surrounding sea unprotected. In Roman times, Mani founded the league of Laconians and broke free of Spartan domination. Ever since, Maniots have ferociously resisted foreign rule, boasting even today that nary an Ottoman set foot on their soil. While Maniots revel in their historical ferocity, they are also warm hosts to the visitors who stay in their traditional grey-stone tower houses. In more remote areas, the mountains and sea combine to create a sense of strength and independence that only the Mani could inspire.

GYTHION Γυθειο ☎0733

Gythion, "Gateway to the Mani," has a much livelier, more Mediterranean feel than the desolate landscapes to the south. Bright fishing boats bustle in and out of the port, where dockside restaurants hang strings of octopi out to dry. A short causeway connects Gythion to the tiny island of **Marathonisi,** where Paris and Helen consummated their ill-fated love, and beautiful sand and stone beaches are a short ride (but long walk) away. For those who'd like to explore the Mani on their own, Gythion is the only city in the area that rents motorbikes.

⊕ ☷ ORIENTATION AND PRACTICAL INFORMATION

Heading south from the bus station along the main harbor road with the water on your left, the causeway to Marathonisi branches off to the right before you reach Gythion's center. Continuing south, the main road leads directly to the dock, where ferries depart. As you face inland, at the left of the bay, the waterfront curves inland and forms a crescent, where most of the hotels and amenities can be found. Small **Pl. Mavromichali,** consisting mostly of cafe seating, is on the southern side of the crescent waterfront, left as you face inland. The bus stop is on the far right of the waterfront as you face inland. A number of other stores and offices crowd around the inland plateia behind the bus station.

Buses: The **station** (☎22 228) is on the north end of the waterfront, opposite a large triangle of palms. To: **Areopolis** (1hr., 4 per day, 500dr/€1.47), via the campgrounds (250dr/€0.73); **Athens** (4hr., 6 per day, 4700dr/€13.79) via **Sparta** (1hr., 850dr/€2.50); **Corinth** (3hr., 3350dr/€9.83); **Gerolimenas** (2hr., 3 per day, 1150dr/€3.37); **Kalamata** (2 per day, 2050dr/€6.02) via **Itilo** (1hr., 750dr/€2.20); **Pirgos Dirou** (1¼hr., 10:15am, 700dr/€2.05); **Tripoli** (2hr., 1850dr/€5.43).

Ferries: To **Diakofti** on Kythera (2½hr.; W 5pm; Tu, Th, Su 7:30pm; 2500dr/€7.35) and on to **Kasteli** on Crete (7hr., 1 per week W 5pm, 5300dr/€15.59).

Taxis: (☎23 423, 23 492 or 22 755). Available 24hr.

Moped Rental: Moto Makis Rent-A-Moped (☎25 111), on the waterfront, between the plateia and the causeway. 6500dr/€19.12 per day including 80km, tax, insurance, a map and a helmet. Open daily 8:30am-7pm.

Tourist Office: EOT (☎24 484). Facing the bus station, go around the left corner and walk straight along a small plateia to the right. Archaiou Theatrou will head to the right; continue straight for 200m or so, the EOT will be on your right. Open M-F 8am-2:30pm.

Travel Agency: Rozakis (☎22 650), on the waterfront near the police station, is the only place in town to buy ferry tickets. Open daily 8am-2pm and 5-9pm.

Banks: National Bank (☎22 313), just beyond the bus stop toward the water, has **currency exchange** and a 24hr. **ATM.** Open M-Th 8am-2pm, F 8am-1:30pm.

Police: (☎22 100), on the waterfront, halfway between the bus station and Pl. Mavromichali. English spoken. Open 24hr.

Port Police: (☎22 262), before the causeway, past the plateia.

Health clinic: (☎22 001, 002 or 003), on the water near the causeway.

Pharmacies: abound; try the one across from the bus station.

Telephones: OTE (☎22 799), corner of Herakles and Kapsali. As you face the bus station, take a sharp right around the left-hand side of the station onto Herakles. Open M-F 7:30am-3:10pm.

Internet: Escape Cafe (☎25 177), on Kapsali, at the corner 1 block behind the National Bank from the bus station. 1500dr/€4.40 per hr., 500dr/€1.47 minimum. Open daily 10am-1am. Behind Pl. Mavromichali, **Internet Cafe** (☎22 106) is more convenient from hotels and domatia. 1200dr/€3.53 per hr. Open daily 5pm-2am.

Post Office: (☎22 285), on Ermou. Open M-F 7:30am-2:30pm. As you face the bus station, go around the left hand corner and follow the plateia to the road that intersects it, then follow this road, Archaiou Theatrou, right two blocks. **Postal code:** 23200.

▌ ACCOMMODATIONS

While seaside accommodations are prohibitively expensive, you can find a few cheap, charming options farther inland. Gythion's campgrounds are a pleasant (and more interesting) alternative to city lodging—all are about 4km south of town toward Areopolis, and can be reached by city bus (4 per day, round-trip); taxis cost about 1000dr/€2.93. If you stay in Gythion, get some wheels for easy beach access.

Xenia Karlaftis Rooms (☎22 719), on the water 20m north of the causeway toward town. Voula and her mother, Xenia, have been letting cheap, spacious rooms for over 20 years. Their experience shows in their gracious hospitality. Kitchen with free coffee, fridges on every floor, and laundry. Clean, standard rooms with private baths. Singles 5000dr/€14.71; doubles 7000dr/€20.59; triples 10,000dr/€29.41.

Kantogiannis Domatia (☎22 518; fax 24 195), off the waterfront near the police station, above Gregori Jewelry Shop, has large white rooms with private baths, some have lovely views of the water. Singles 5000dr/€14.71; doubles 12,000-14,000dr/€35.29-41.18; triples and quads 13,000-16,000dr/€38.24-47.06.

Meltemi Camping (☎22 833), 4km south on the road toward Areopolis. Showers, washing machines, mini-market, restaurant, and pool. 1500dr/€4.40 per person, 950dr/€2.79 per child; 850dr/€2.50 per car; 1200dr/€3.53 per small tent, 1300dr/€3.82 per large tent. Electricity 900dr/€2.65.

Gythion Bay Campgrounds (☎22 522), 5km south on the road toward Areopolis. Laundry, mini-market, restaurant, and showers. 1700dr/€5 per adult, 1000dr/€2.94 per child; 1100dr/€3.24 per car; 1100dr/€3.24 per tent. Electricity 900dr/€2.65.

Mani Beach (☎23 450), 5km south on the road toward Areopolis. Washing machine, mini-market, cooking area, playground, showers, and restaurant. 1550dr/€4.56 per person, 700dr/€2.05 per child; 750dr/€2.21 per car; 1000dr/€2.94 per small tent, 1200dr/€3.53 per large tent. Electricity 1000dr/€2.94.

🍴 FOOD

Virtually identical waterfront tavernas serve up fresh seafood and views at moderate prices. A **fruit store** and **bakery** are across the street from Masouleri Kokkalis.

Taverna To Nisi (☎23 830) also called **Nisi**, is on Marathonisi, at the end of the causeway. This charming outdoor taverna is a favorite with locals and has a great view of Gythion's unique architecture. *Tzatziki* 600dr/€1.77, entrees 900-1700dr/€2.65-5.

Saga (☎23 220), on the water between the causeway and the plateia, serves delicious food served on tables pulled right up to the water. Crispy grilled and seasoned bread, cheap vegetarian salads (starting at 800dr/€2.35). Fish 10,000-14,000dr/€29.41-41.18 per kg. For a real treat, try the shrimp *saganaki* (4000dr/€11.77).

H Gonia or **The Corner** (☎22 122), is at the bend in the waterfront just past the plateia heading toward the causeway. The octopus hanging out to dry reminds you from whence your meal came. *Moussaka* 1500dr/€4.41; octopus 1800dr/€5.29.

Masouleri Kokkalis, at the center of the plateia behind all the cafe chairs. Specializes in greasy fast food and does it well. Gyros 350dr/€1.03, souvlaki 300dr/€0.88.

👁🞄 SIGHTS AND BEACHES

ANCIENT THEATER. The compact, masterfully built, 240° theater of Gythion has endured the centuries remarkably well. Even its class distinctions remain: note the differences between the seats for dignitaries in front and the simpler seats farther back. Arrive early in the evening to join the soldiers getting their nightly pep talk; any other time of day, it will most likely be deserted. Crumbling Roman walls are scattered up the hill. *(Heading away from the bus station, walk past the post office on Archaiou Theatrou until it dead ends at the theater entrance. Open daily 8am-noon and 5-8pm.)*

PALIATZOURES ANTIQUE SHOP: SIC TRANSIT GLORIA MUNDI. The last of its kind in the Peloponnese, this antique shop has furnished a number of museums in its day, as owner Costas will gladly tell you. The majority of the collection consists of 19th-century household items, artwork, furniture, coins, and assorted trinkets, but he claims to have a few medieval and even ancient items interspersed. By Greek law, foreigners may export only items made after the fall of Constantinople in 1453, but unless you plan on spending a *lot* of money, this won't be a concern. *(#25 on the waterfront, near the police. ☎22 944. Open daily 11am-2pm and 6-9pm.)*

PELOPONNESE

ON THE ROAD TO AEROPOLIS. When traveling from Gythion to Aeropolis, look for the Frankish **Castle of Pasava** on the right. The road is rough and dangerous—check to see if it has been improved or try calling the local consulate at ☎22 210 (roughly 10km down the road; taxi 1700dr/€5; tours available). Farther along, the **Castle of Kelefa** looks out to sea (taxi 2000dr/€5.88; open all day).

BEACHES. There is a disappointing **public beach** just north of the bus station, but better beaches lie outside of town. Four kilometers south, near the campgrounds, is the wide, pebble and sand beach of **Mavrovouni**, with a high surf and a number of bars (mixed drinks 900-1500dr/€2.65-4.40, beer 500-700dr/€1.47-2.05). You can get there by bus from Areopolis (4 per day), a 1000dr/€2.94 taxi, or 50min. walking. Three kilometers north is rocky **Selinitsa**, known for its incredibly clear water—look for signs. You can walk or take a 1000dr/€2.94 taxi. **Vathy** is 15km away on the road to Areopolis, and has fewer people, a lovely stretch of sand, and a quiet cove for topless sunbathing (around to the left as you face inland, after the river).

AREOPOLIS Αρεοπολη   ☎0733

Areopolis neighbors both the sea and the mountains, yet the incredible buildings of the town dominate the scenery: stone tower houses and cobbled streets just wide enough for donkey carts are framed by the dramatic purple peaks of the Taygetus. Tourists flocking to nearby coastal towns often pass right through Areopolis, leaving plenty of inexpensive, romantic accommodations available in the traditional tower houses that once defended the insular, suspicious clans of the Mani. Close by you'll find the caves at Pirgos Dirou alongside the beautiful beach at Limenas (which doubles as Areopolis's port), and lively Gythion, the harbor town on the opposite side of the peninsula

◀┃ ORIENTATION AND PRACTICAL INFORMATION

All local services can be found in the plateia, or off **Kapetan Matapan,** the main road running into the Old Town from the plateia. The **bus "station"** (☎51 229) is next to the Romeo Pub and Europa Grill, on the eastern edge of the plateia, opposite the Hotel Kouris. The road running perpendicular from the bus station is Kapetan Matapan. Follow it along the plateia, past the statue, and into the Old Town. Buses from Areopolis go to: **Athens** (6hr., 5450dr/€16.03) via **Gythion** (30min., 4 per day, 550dr/€1.62); **Itilo** (30min., 2 per day, 260dr/€0.77); and **Sparta** (2hr., 1400dr/€4.12). From Itilo, you can catch a bus to **Kalamata.** A bus running into the Mani takes you to the **Vlihada Lake Caves** (leaves 11am, returns 12:45pm; 260dr/€0.77) and **Vatheia** (1hr., 1:45pm, 850dr/€2.50) via **Gerolimenas** (40min., 600dr/€1.77). The **police** are 1km out of town toward Pirgos in the same building as the new town hall. (☎51 209. Open 24hr.) To find the **National Bank** (open M-F 9am-noon) and its 24hr. **ATM,** walk down Kapetan Matapan, turn right at the first small church, and continue up the street. The **post office** is on the same street as the National Bank, across from the Hotel Mani. (Open M-F 7:30am-2pm.) The post office **exchanges currency** and **traveler's checks** for a hefty fee. The **OTE** (☎51 299) is 50m down a street that starts in the main plateia and runs away from the ocean. Opposite the OTE is a 24hr. **health center** (☎51 242). A **pharmacy** is on Kapetan Matapan. **Postal code:** 23062.

┢┃ ACCOMMODATIONS AND FOOD

Staying at either **Tsimova's Rooms** or the **Pension** opposite may amount to taking sides in what appears to be long-standing feud. Both proprietors spend their days staring menacingly at one another's doors, but are delightful individually; choose at your own risk. To find them, turn left at the end of Kapetan Matapan. **Tsimova** rents narrow rooms with tiny doors and windows typical of tower houses—

Kolokotronis supposedly slept here—and the living room displays rifles, swords, and uniforms passed down through the owner's family from the War for Independence. The war memorabilia, religious pictures, and various knick knacks give each room its own personality. Shared baths may require a trip downstairs past the sleeping owner—try for a room with a private one. (☎51 301. Continental breakfast 1000dr/€2.94. Singles 5000-10,000dr/€14.71-29.41; doubles 10,000-15,000dr/€29.41-44.12; triples 12,000-18,000dr/€35.29-52.94; quads 20,000dr/€58.82.) Tsimova's neighbor and rival, friendly **Pierros Bozagregos Pension,** lets large, modern rooms with private baths in a classic stonework building. (☎51 354. Singles 10,000dr/€29.41; doubles 12,000-15,000dr/€35.29-44.21; triples 17,000dr/€50; quads 24,000dr/€70.59; breakfast included.) Offering spacious rooms and a newly added wing, **Hotel Mani** has huge rooms with private baths, balconies, and TVs across from the post office and near the National Bank. Walk 50m from the bus station on Kasetan Matapan, turn right at the first small church, and walk another 200m. (☎51 190; fax 51 269. Singles 8000-13,000dr/€23.53-38.24; doubles 11,000-17,000dr/€32.35-50; prices vary with A/C.)

A simple sign reading "Taverna" hangs in front of the splendid **Oinomageireio** (☎51 205), the yellow building on the left of Kapetan Matapan as you walk from the plateia. The taverna boasts intimate garden seating and first-class cooking by its internationally recognized chef and owner. Try "flower of the zucchini with mixed vegetables" (1200dr/€3.53). In the plateia, **Nicola's Place** (☎51 366), serves rotating specials, including stuffed omelettes (1500dr/€4.40), accompanied by grilled, seasoned bread (200dr/€0.59).

■ DAYTRIP FROM AREOPOLIS

PYRGOS DIROU CAVES Σπηλαιο Πυργος Διρυου

*4km from **Areopolis,** the caves are an easy bus ride but a somewhat hilly, exhaust-filled walk away; you are best off driving. (Buses leave Areopolis 11am, return 12:45pm; 260dr/€0.77.) Some tour guides speak only Greek, so you may want to purchase the guidebook* Caverns of Mani *(1500dr/€4.40) at the souvenir shop by the cave entrance. ☎(0723) 52 222. Open June-Sept. daily 8am-5:30pm; Oct.-May 8am-3pm. Ticket includes boat tour. 3700dr/€10.88; students, seniors, and children 2000dr/€5.88.*

Part of a subterranean river, the unusual **Vlihada Cave** (Spilia Dirou or Pyrgos Dirou) is cool, quiet, and strung with tiny crystalline stalactites. Vermillion stalagmites slice the 30m-deep water's surface. Discovered at the end of the 19th century, it was opened to the public in 1971 and has yet to be fully explored. Experts speculate that the cave is 70km long and may extend all the way to Sparta. The 1200m boat ride through the cave lasts about 30min.; the tiny boats rock their way through the narrow—and incredibly low—channels of the cave, forcing passengers to duck at times to avoid low-hanging stalactites. The close quarters and hollow echo of dripping water create an eerie calm. Lights floating in styrofoam rings illuminate the tour, but unlit recesses branch off on each side. Don't miss **Poseidon's Foot,** a striking hanging formation resembling (lo and behold!) a giant foot.

GEFYRA ☎0732

Byzantine enthusiasts on the way to their paradise, Monemvasia, may be puzzled when the bus drops them off in the unabashedly modern—albeit pleasant—coastal town of Gefyra. Just beyond the breaking waves off Gefyra's shore lies an impressive island, dominated by spectacular vertical cliffs. "The rock," as it is known, looks uninhabited from the mainland; only after crossing the causeway and walking along the main road for 15min. does Monemvasia appear. Before you cross, however, it's wise to take care of your needs in cheaper Gefyra.

■■ ▐ **ORIENTATION AND PRACTICAL INFORMATION.** During late July and August, an **orange bus** runs between the causeway and Monemvasia gate all day long (every 15min. 8am-midnight, 100dr/€0.29). In Gefyra, the main thoroughfares form a fork, the tail of which leads to the causeway connecting Monemvasia to the mainland. The main branch of this fork, **23 Iouliou,** runs inland from the causeway, later becoming **Spartis.** Opposite the post office on 23 Iouliou is the **bus station** located in the helpful ▓**Malvasia Travel Agency,** where superwomen Eva and Mary provide a multitude of services, including **moped rental** (5000dr/€14.67 per day), **currency exchange,** and **all tickets for Flying Dolphins and ferries.** (☎61 752; fax 61 432. Open M-Sa 8:15am-2:15pm and 6-9pm, Su 10:15am-3:15pm.) All **buses,** except for the direct express to **Athens** (6hr., 4:10am, 4500dr/€13.21), connect or stop in **Molai.** Up to three buses per day leave for: **Athens** (6hr., 6050dr/€17.79) via **Molai** (20min., 550dr/€1.62); **Corinth** (5hr., 5400dr/€15.88); **Sparta** (2½hr., 2000dr/€5.88); and **Tripoli** (4hr., 3100dr/€9.12). Twice daily **Flying Dolphins** go to **Piraeus** (9500dr/€27.94) via **Spetses** (4000dr/€11.77), **Portoheli** (4800dr/€14.12), and **Hydra** (5000dr/€14.71). Across from the bus station, the **National Bank** has a 24hr. **ATM.** (☎61 201. Open M-F 9am-1pm; off-season 1-2 days per week.) The **post office** is next door (☎61 231; open M-F 7:30am-2pm). The **police** and **tourist police** are on 23 Iouliou (☎61 210; open 24hr.). **Postal code:** 23070.

▐▐ **ACCOMMODATIONS AND FOOD.** As Gefyra's hotels tend to be expensive, the waterfront **domatia** are your best bet (doubles 5000-8000dr/€14.67-23.48). ▓**Hotel Akrogiali,** right across from Malvasia Travel on 23 Iouliou, is a diamond in the rough. Lovely white rooms with private baths and fans share a fridge. (☎61 260. Singles 6000-7000dr/€17.65-20.59; doubles 7000-10,000dr/€20.59-29.35.) **Hotel Sophos** has recently renovated rooms with balconies and baths for decent prices. (☎61 202. Singles 7000-8000dr/€20.59-23.53; doubles 8000-10,000dr/€23.53-29.35; triples 10,000-12,000dr/€29.35-35.29.) **Camping Paradise,** 3.5km along the water on the mainland, offers free hot showers, a restaurant, and mini-market. (☎61 123. 1450dr/€4.27 per person, 950d/€2.79 per child; 850dr/€2.50 per car; 950dr/€2.79 per small tent, 1300dr/€3.82 per large tent; discounts for stays longer than three days.) The many harbor front tavernas of Gefyra are the best option for dining in the area. **To Limanaki** (☎61 619), offering waterside seating on the mainland between the causeway and the harbor, serves exceptional Greek food, including the best *pastitsio* (1300dr/€3.82) and stuffed tomatoes (1150dr/€3.38) you could ever ask for. **Pipinellis Taverna,** 2km from Monemvasia on the road to Camping Paradise, has featured home-grown produce for the past 25 years, and is a favorite with locals and visitors alike. (☎61 004. Entrees 1300-1900dr/€3.82-5.58.) For cheaper dining, there is a small **supermarket** on the branch of the fork opposite 23 Iouliou in Gefyra. There is a **fruit and vegetable market** farther beyond it.

▐ **DAYTRIPS FROM GEFYRA: MONEMVASIA.** Monemvasia (Μονεμβασια) deserves the constant attention it gets; an undeniable other-worldliness pervades the old city. Entering through the single gateway (hence the town's name, which means "one way") into old Monemvasia, you feel as though you've passed into a city frozen in time. No cars or bikes are allowed through the gate, so packhorses bearing groceries and cases of beer are led back and forth to restaurants. The winding cobbled street that passes the town's tourist shops and restaurants appears immediately upon entering the gate; it continues past the strip of tourist shops to the central plateia. Facing the ocean, the church of **Christos Elkomenos** (Christ in Chains) is on the left. To get to the often-photographed 12th-century **Agia Sofia,** balanced on the edge of the rock cliffs, work your way through the maze of narrow streets—with hidden stairways, child-sized doorways, flowered courtyards, and the occasional cactus—to the edge of town farthest from the sea at the base of the mountain. There, a path climbs the cliffside to the tip of the rock;

you'll find the church on the far side of the rock. Modeled after the monastery at Daphni (p. 106), the structure of the church is still beautiful, although the faded frescoes were badly vandalized by invading Turks, who held the castle for a time. The top of the rock, scattered with crumbling castle ruins, offers splendid views of the town and sea below. In town, a small but well-labeled **Archaeological Museum** holds a single room full of masonry, pottery, and ecclesiastical sculpture attesting to Monemvasia's 13th-century prominence. (☎61 403. Open M-Su 9am-2pm. Free.)

NEAPOLI Νεαπολις   ☎0734

A necessary but uneventful stop on the path between Kythera and the southeastern Peloponnese, Neapoli is a little coastal town with lots of waterfront restaurants, a few luxury hotels, and an increasing number of Greek tourists. The pebble beaches are an uncrowded and refreshing break from the towel-to-towel sunbathers of more popular vacation spots. Unfortunately, there's not much other than Neapoli's waterfront to keep visitors occupied, so you'll probably want to stay only long enough to catch a boat or a bus to a more exciting destination.

Ferries go to **Kythera** (1hr.; W-Su 4 per day, M-Tu 3 per day; 1600dr/€4.71). **Flying Dolphins** depart five times per week (except Tu-W) to: **Monemvasia** (3hr., 10,000dr/€29.41) and **Piraeus** (4hr., 20,000dr/€58.82). The **bus station** (☎23 222), is on a street off the right side of the waterfront as you face inland, two blocks from the pier. **Buses:** go to **Ag. Nikolaos** (20min., 3 per day, 250dr/€0.74); **Athens** (6hr., 3 per day, 6850dr/€20.15); **Molai** (1hr., 3 per day, 1350dr/€3.97); and **Sparta** (2hr., 3 per day, 2800dr/€8.24).

The **port police** (☎22 228) are on the waterfront across from the sole pier. To the left of the pier as you face inland, a blue and white hut on the water's edge doles out **info** and posts ferry schedules. If it's closed, head to the **Travel Agency** to the left of the waterfront as you face inland, near the National Bank. There, Captain D. Alexandrakis gruffly dispenses **ferry** and **hydrofoil tickets**. (☎22 904. Open in summer daily 7:30am-11pm.) The **National Bank** is one block from the port police, on the other side of the street. (Open M-Th 8am-2pm, F 8am-1:30pm.) The town's main street along the water is home to many services. For **Internet** access, the **Planet Cafe** is one or two blocks inland from the small bridge near the National Bank. (☎23 779. 1500dr/€4.40 per hr., 350dr/€1.03 minimum. Open daily 9am-2pm and 5-9pm.) The **post office** is one block inland on Leoforos Democratias on the left of the waterfront as you face inland, past the bridge (open M-F 7:30am-2pm). If you decide to stay in Neapoli overnight, scour the streets for domatia, or try **Hotel Arsenakos**, run by a friendly ex-New Yorker, which is a 5min. walk from town with the water on your left. (☎22 991. A/C, TV, telephones, private baths, balconies, and fridges. Singles 5500-8500dr/€16.18-25; doubles 7500-11,000dr/€22.06-32.35.)

KYTHERA Κυθηρα

According to ancient myth, the island of Kythera rose from the waters where Zeus cast his father Kronos's severed head into the sea after castrating him. Springing from Kronos's foamy misfortune, Aphrodite washed up onto Kythera's shores and made it her homeland. In antiquity, the island supported a large temple to the goddess, where she was worshiped as Aphrodite Urania, goddess of chaste love. Though one might not associate the island's barren, mountainous landscape with the fertility for which Aphrodite is known and worshiped, its flowering shrubs, sandy beaches, and secluded villages hold a potent beauty. Like the other Ionian Islands, Kythera passed through the hands of the Venetians and the French before ending up as a British possession, yet it remains distinct in its extremely rugged scenery—desert-like in places—and its untouristed feel. Only about 3000 people live on Kythera, but improved ferry schedules (see below) have made it a more convenient destination for budget travelers. The two main island ports are northern **Agia Pelagia** and the newer, less accessible eastern port of **Diakofti**. Bus service is nearly nonexistent, making some sort of vehicle virtually essential to taking full advantage of all the island has to offer.

PELOPONNESE

AGIA PELAGIA Αγια Πελαγια ☎ 0736

If you plan a short stay on the island, and especially if you're catching a ferry, Agia Pelagia is a good place to set up camp to avoid paying for an overpriced cab or dealing with infrequent buses. The town is smaller and less picturesque than southerly Hora or Kapsali, but accommodations and moped rentals are cheaper, and its long, convenient stretch of beaches offer up both sand and pebbles.

█ ▉ ORIENTATION AND PRACTICAL INFORMATION. The island's main road runs between Agia Pelagia and **Kapsali** in the south, with small villages connected by subsidiary roads. This road also passes through **Potamos** (the island's largest town), **Livadi**, and **Kythera (Hora)**. **Ferries** leave Agia Pelagia daily for **Neapoli** (1hr., 1500dr/€4.40); and from **Diakofti** to **Gythion** (2½hr., 2400dr/€7.06); and **Kastili**, Crete (4hr., 5 per week, 4300dr/€12.65). **Flying Dolphins** leave Diakofti for **Piraeus** (5hr., 1 per day, 10,700dr/€31.47) via **Monemvasia** (1hr., 5300dr/€15.59). In Agia Pelagia, a cottage to the left of the dock as you face inland is a **Volunteer Tourist Office**, where friendly staffers provide information about accommodations and sights. (☎ 33 815. Open July-Aug. daily 8am-9pm.) A daily **bus** runs between Agia Pelagia and Kapsali in late July and August (leaves 9:30am, returns noon; 300dr/€0.88). The nearest **hospital, pharmacy, post office,** and **bank** are all in Potamos. **Easy Rider**, to the right of Agia Pelagia, rents mopeds. (☎ 33 486. Must be 21 and have a license for motorbikes. 5000dr/€14.71 per day for 50-100cc; 6000dr/€17.65 for 125cc.) Ferry tickets and schedules are also available at the two tiny shacks at the end of the pier when ferries are docking, and from the **port police** (☎ 33 280).

▉▉ ACCOMMODATIONS AND FOOD. The tourist office has a list of the few domatia owners in town, and can put you in contact with them. Otherwise, blue-and-white **Hotel Kythereia**, beside the ferry pier, has rooms with private baths, A/C, and lovely views (of either mountains or sea) for good prices. It's run by an extremely hospitable Greek-Australian family who serve a cozy continental breakfast for 1000dr/€2.94. (☎ 33 321; fax 33 825. Singles 8000dr/€23.53; doubles 10,000-20,000dr/€29.41-59.82.) Out of town, along the waterfront toward Potamos, **Maneas Domatia** lets rooms with private baths, kitchens, and phones in a large apartment-like building on the water. (☎ 33 895. Doubles 9000-11,500dr/€26.47-33.82.) The other hotels in town are more luxurious (and expensive). The **Vernados Hotel,** has a score of amenities, among them A/C, TV, free laundry, and a beautiful buffet breakfast. The hotel is just 50m inland on the road opposite the Volunteer Tourist Office cottage. (☎ 34 205 or 34 206. Singles 14,000-22,000dr/€41.17-64.71; doubles 20,000-26,000dr/€58.82-76.47; triples 24,000-30,000dr/€70.59-88.23.)

Taverna Faros, the first taverna to the right of the pier, has plenty of waterfront seating, decent prices, and good food. Try the "aubergine shoes" (stuffed eggplant) for 1500dr/€4.40. (☎ 33 348. Fish 1300-12,000dr/€3.82-35.29 per kilo, and worth every last drachma.) Farther north (right as you face inland) on the waterfront, **Restaurant Kaleris** is popular with locals and visitors alike. Children play amid diners enjoying the delicious meals. (Daily menu in Greek; try the *moussaka* 1350dr/€3.97.) Agia Pelagia has a **supermarket** opposite the beach, beside the fruit market.

▉ BEACHES. In addition to its convenience as a port town, Agia Pelagia is the only town on Kythera that boasts six beaches all within convenient walking distance of the town center. Starting from the town's main beach, continue south, toward Potamos, with the water on your left, to five more beaches. The road is initially paved as you pass the second, dark sand beach, and turns to dirt after the Aphrodite Pelagia Hotel. Each beach offers its own unique combination of coves, sand, and pebbles; the most distant beach is only a 45min. walk away. A local favorite is small and secluded **Lorenzo** beach, just past the hill with the monastery.

AROUND KYTHERA

The pint-size island has a lion's share of sights, enough to keep any visitor occupied. The peaceful beach town of **Kapsili,** east of Hora, has clear waters and a long shore. At Paleohora, in the east, are the ruins of the former fortified capital of the island, **Agios Dimitrios,** built during Byzantine rule. The town was destroyed by pirates led by the notorious Barbarossa in 1537. Even more compelling are the island's natural wonders, including the **Cave of Agia Sofia** (open Tu-Su 10am-2:30pm), near the village of Milopotamos on the western side of the island. The most impressive of the island's several caves, Agia Sofia also has beautiful **frescoes** painted on the cave walls, and is an easy walk or taxi ride away from Milopotamos. Kythera's **beaches** are gorgeous, with the ocean's variety of blues contrasting with the rocky brown landscape. The best beaches are a bit difficult to reach, accessible only by bumpy dirt roads that are perilous for mopeders (a car is safer). On the eastern coast, a steep staircase leads down to spectacular ▧**Kaladi** beach, with sparkling coves and striking rock formations. **Halkos,** near Kalamos on the southern coast, is another out-of-the-way beach; its quiet beauty makes it worth the trip.

POTAMOS Ποταμας ☎0736

Potamos is on a hill 9km south of Agia Pelagia on the main road, with narrow hilly streets bedecked with flowers and an abundance of fresh fruit markets. Accommodations are scarce here. It's worth a visit, however, to stroll through the streets and admire the traditional Kytherean architecture, as well as to take advantage of the services in the small central plateia. There's an **Olympic Airlines** office, although the airport is a taxi ride away on the eastern half of Kythera. (☎33 362. Open M-F 8am-4pm.) Olympic runs **flights** to and from Athens (1 per day, 15,400dr/€34.29). The **National Bank** and its 24hr. **ATM** are also in the plateia. (☎33 209. Open M-Th 8am-2pm, F 8am-1pm.) The **post office** is uphill from the plateia (☎33 225. Open M-F 7:30am-2pm.) The **police station** is behind the National Bank, tucked in a lemon-tree lined corner. (☎33 222. No English spoken.) The **hospital** is on the road to Hora. (☎33 325. English spoken.) **Taxis** (☎33 255 or 33 720) park in the plateia. **Selana Cafe,** in the plateia, has **Internet access.** (☎33 997. 2000dr/€5.88 per hr.) **Postal code:** 80200.

HORA Χωρα ☎0736

The whitewashed plaster houses of the island's southerly capital, Hora (also called **Kythera Town**), gleam in the bright sun. Hora hosts many of the island's visitors. This plateia holds Hora's **post office** (☎31 274; open 7:30am-2pm) and a **National Bank** with a 24hr. **ATM.** Facing the water, Hora's main street begins in the plateia's lower left-hand corner; along it you'll find the **police** (☎31 206) and **tourist police** (English spoken; open mornings only), 50m down toward the water. **Kithira Travel** has **Flying Dolphin** schedules, **currency exchange,** and is the island's main **Olympic Airways** office. (☎31 390. Open daily 9am-2pm and 7-10pm.) The **OTE** is up the stairs to the left of Kithira Travel. (☎31 299. Open 7:30am-2pm.) The nearest **hospital** is in Potamos. If you're catching a ferry in Diafkoto, a **taxi** (☎31 720 320) from Hora will cost about 6000dr/€17.65. To reach **Pension Pises,** head downhill and turn left off the main road on Ag. Elesis. It's the place for great views, shared baths, and creative decor. (☎31 070. Doubles 8000dr/€23.53.) **Camping Avlemonas,** near the town of Diakofti, offers a great location (across from the sea) and free hot showers. (☎33 742. 1000dr/€2.94 per adult, 500dr/€1.47 per child.) At the end of the main road, wildflowers have sprouted around the remains of the town's **castle,** where the wind-swept plateau offers intoxicating views of nearby Kapsali's harbor. The small, under-funded **Archaeological Museum,** on Kythera's highway just before the turn-off for Hora, has pottery, sculpture, and coins from the Classical to Byzantine periods. It also has gravestones, which are all that remain of the island's 19th-century English military base. (Open Tu-Su 8:45am-3pm. Free.) **Postal code:** 81200.

PELOPONNESE

CENTRAL GREECE

Under 19th-century Ottoman rule, Thessaly and Sterea Ellada acquired a Byzantine aura; seek it along forgotten mountain-goat paths that lead to these Byzantine treasures. Along the way, you'll encounter glorious mountain-top vistas that look out over silvery olive groves, fruit-laden trees, and patchwork farmland.

STEREA ELLADA Στερεα Ελλαδα

Small mountainside villages, monumental ruins, the country's finest honey, and superb ski slopes make up Sterea Ellada (the "Greek Continent," the only section of the mainland to join the new Greek state after the War of Independence; see p.

Central Greece

16). For thousands of years, pilgrimages from all over the Mediterranean and Asia Minor led to the Delphic Oracle, where ponderous questions met cryptic replies. The 10th-century Monastery of Osios Loukas, a modern religious center near Delphi, displays the Byzantines' architectural mastery. Be kind to strangers you meet on the road below the monastery: at the crossroads, an unknowing Oedipus met and murdered his father on the way to Thebes, where he married his mother.

THEBES (THIVA) Θηβα ☎ 0262

Buried beneath the sleepy streets and tavernas of modern Thebes lies its claim to fame—its illustrious (and notorious) past. History literally surfaces throughout as new construction projects often reveal the buried edifices of ancient Thebes. Theban history provides many street names: take a walk down the avenues of **Cadmus** (the city's legendary first king), **Oedipus** (exiled king and originator of the complex), **Antigone** (Oedipus' rebellious daughter and sister and heroine of Sophocles' play), and **Pindar** (the 5th-century BC lyric poet). Rising to prominence in the heyday of the Greek polis, from the 6th to the 4th centuries BC, Thebes capitalized on its fertile plains and strategic location between northern Greece and the Peloponnese. Alexander the Great's army cut this prosperity short around 335 BC, when its invasion from Macedonia reduced the city to rubble and spared only temples and Pindar's ancestral home. It seems that Thebes is still attempting to recover from that blow; it now warrants a brief daytrip.

▐ TRANSPORTATION. From Terminal B, platform 4 at Liossion 260 in Athens, take the **bus** to Thebes (1½hr., every hr. 6am-8pm, 1700dr/€5). Buy tickets inside the station from the desk labeled ΘHBA (Thebes). The main **bus station** is in the valley below Thebes, on Estias (☎27 512). If you ask nicely upon your arrival, the bus driver might let you off in the center of town. Otherwise, to get to town from the station, cross the parking lot with your back to the station, and turn right, following the first road uphill. You will see Eteokleous; follow it up the hill to a *plateia* where first Pindarou and then Epaminondas veer off to the right. Turn right onto Epaminonda to find hotels, tavernas, and other comforts.

From Thebes, buses depart from the station for **Athens** (1½hr., every hr. 6am-8pm, 1700dr/€5). To travel to **Halkida**, take the Athens bus to the Skimatari stop (30min., 600dr/€1.75); across the street from the Skimatari stop, catch the Athens-Halkida (10min., every 30min., 350dr/€1). A direct bus runs between Thebes and Halkida twice a day (8:40 and 11am). Regular buses run to **Livadia** (45min., every hr. 6:30am-9:30pm, 950dr/€2.90) from a stop about 2km out of town: walk all the way down Pindarou, past the Archaeological Museum, and go down the steps. First take the left fork, and then the right onto Laiou (ΛΑΙΟΨ). Take a left onto St. Athanasiou, and follow the blue signs to ΛΕΙΒΑΔΕΙΑ (Livadia) to the small metal bus shelter just before the Shell gas station, on your right. Buy your ticket on board; the conductor will come and collect your money. For **taxis** call 27 077.

▅▪▐ ORIENTATION AND PRACTICAL INFORMATION. Thebes is built on a high hill with two parallel main streets, **Epaminonda** and **Pindarou,** running from the top of the hill into the valley below. Epaminonda hosts a variety of cafes and shops; Pindarou is lined with **banks** and **pharmacies**. The **National Bank,** Pindarou 94, has a 24hr. **ATM**. (☎23 331 or 25 144. Open M-Th 8am-2pm.) The **hospital,** Pindarou 105 (☎24 444), is between the church and archaeological museum—look for Greek and Red Cross flags. An **OTE**, 14 Vourdouba, is off Epaminonda (open M-F 7:45am-1pm). The **post office,** Drakou 17, lies on a sidestreet between Pindarou and Epaminonda. (☎27 810. Open M-F 7:30am-2:30pm.) **Postal code:** 32200.

▐▐ ACCOMMODATIONS AND FOOD. If you decide to spend the night in Thebes, the English-speaking staff at **Hotel Niobh,** Epaminonda 63, offers rooms with TVs and beautifully tiled private baths at great rates. (☎29 888.

Breakfast 1000dr/€2.93. Singles 8000dr/€23.48; doubles 10,000dr/€29.35; triples 12,000dr/€35.22.) The **Hotel Meletiou,** Epaminonda 58, across the street, has comparable rooms (TVs, private baths) at slightly higher prices; try negotiating. (☎22 111. Singles 9000dr/€26.41; doubles 13,000-15,000dr/€38.15-44.02.) By evening, people of all ages fill the pedestrian-only sections of Epaminonda, as tavernas and cafes move tables into the street. A multitude of tavernas tumble across Epaminonda, and its side streets to Pindarou offer similar fare at similar prices (500-1500dr/€1.47-4.40); bakeries, fruit stands, and small gyro and souvlaki restaurants scattered among the tavernas provide cheaper eats (300-900dr/€.88-2.64).

🎦🎵 **SIGHTS AND ENTERTAINMENT.** Thebes's antiquities are its main attraction. The **Archaeological Museum** at the end of Pindarou has an extensive collection of Mycenaean artifacts, including jewelry and pottery from the era of the *Iliad* and *Odyssey,* marble statuary of well-formed women and men, pinch-faced idols, and intricate funerary boxes lamenting those trapped inside. The museum also displays Boeotian statuary from the 5th and 4th centuries BC and pottery galore. Especially notable are the Geometric style vases (larnakes), dating from 900 to 700 BC, before black-figure vase painting became commonplace (p. 21). Mosaics and funerary steles accent the courtyard, where more than half the museum's collection is simply lying about. (☎27 913. Open M noon-7pm, Tu-Su 8am-7pm. 500dr/€1.47, seniors 300dr/€.88,children and EU students free.)

Peer into the open **excavation pits**—the source of the museum's collection—sprinkled between buildings throughout the central city. Tantalizing segments of a Mycenaean palace and acropolis (dated to 1400BC) are partially visible. The largest of these, the **House of Cadmus,** shows its ancient palace walls; it is along the way to the museum on Pindarou, just between the church and the hospital. Also nearby are unimpressive ancient **Mycenaean Chamber Tombs** (take Vourdouba downhill from Pindarou, passing the remains of **Proetides Gate,** turn left on Avlidos, and right on Katsina before the high school).

🔢 **DAYTRIP FROM THEBES: LIVADIA** (Λειβαδεια). Livadia's treasures cluster around the sacred river **Herkina,** which flows below the **Oracle of Trophonius.** Tree-shaded stone bridges crisscross Herkina, which bubbles up from the dual **springs of Krya,** called *Lethe* (forgetfulness) and *Mnemosyne* (memory). Pilgrims bathed in these waters to empty their minds of everything but the oracle's instruction just before their visit. Across from the oracle, a now-graffitied 14th-century **Frankish castle** emerges from the mountain face overhead. Though the castle permits no visitors, a smooth stone path through the hills beyond the castle is open to all. Two tiny, whitewashed chapels, accessible by zig-zagging stairs carved into the mountain face, are perched high in the cliffs to the left and right of the trail. The hike up the path and the stairs takes about an hour and provides a splendid view of the countryside.

The bus stop is in front of a school on D. Papaspyrou at its intersection with G. Sefari. With the school on your right, head down Papaspyrou through the intersection where it becomes Boufidou. Follow Boufidou until it ends in a large plateia. Follow signs to Koutsopetalou which becomes El. Venizelou. With the stream on your right, follow El. Venizelou until it deadends on Katsiotou. Turn right and cross the bridge; turn left on the other side of the stream. The oracle and streams are just ahead on the left, and the castle is on the right. Along an uphill path, a modern amphitheatre is on the left; a small shrine and stone arch mark the base of the stairs to the chapels. Take a bus via Thebes (2hr., every hr. 6am-8pm, 2550dr/€7.48) or from Terminal B in Athens (p. 80). Buses run to Athens (every hr. 6am-6pm and Sa 8pm) and Arahova (30min., M-F 6:15am, 12:10, 3:40pm; Sa 12:10, 3:40pm; Su 3:40pm).

OSIOS LOUKAS Οσιος Λουκας ☎ 0267

*Bus travel between Livadia and Osios Loukas is virtually non-existent; as a result, the monastery is difficult to reach. Without a car, you'll need to hire a **taxi** (☎ 26 333 or 28 770; approx. 6000-7000dr/€17.61-20.53 each way) or **walk** along the hilly, narrow road from the town of **Distomo,** 9km west. Distomo is a 4000-5000dr/€11.74-14.67 cab ride from Livadia, the site of an annual **cultural festival** that commemorates the massacre of the town's citizenry by German soldiers during World War II. (June 6-10 annually.) Monastery ☎ 22 797. Open May 3-Sept. 15 daily 8am-2pm and 4-7pm; Sept. 16-May 2 8am-5pm. Dress modestly (long skirts for women, long pants for men, no bare shoulders). 800dr/ €2.35, seniors 400dr/€1.17, under 18 and students with ID free.*

Osios Loukas delights the eye with its mountain vistas and stunning Byzantine architecture. The exquisite monastery, built in the 10th and 11th centuries and still in use today, overlooks the fruit orchards and vineyards of Boeotia and Phokis from the green slopes of Mt. Elikon, more than 1700m above sea level. Gold-laden mosaics, vibrant frescoes, and intricate brick- and stonework adorn Osios Loukas, the most famous and perhaps the most gorgeous monastery in Greece.

HISTORY. Ironically, Christian saint Osios Loukas was born in AD 896 in Delphi (p. 171), the former religious center of the Olympian gods (see p. 28). Inclined to an ascetic life from early on, he became a monk at the age of 14. In 946, Osios Loukas settled at the lush and enchanting site of the monastery that now bears his name, building a cell, a small church, and a garden. Rumors that his relic worked miracles brought believers to his church, which led to an expansion of the grounds and the beginning of a monastery. With aid from fellow hermits and money from admirers, Osios Loukas began construction of two churches. The first, the **Church of the Panagia** (Church of the Virgin Mary), was finished soon after the saint's death in 953. The larger **Katholikon of Osios Loukas,** built in 1011, became the site of his reliquary. Osios Loukas was famed as a miracle worker during his lifetime; since his death, thousands have found cures at his tomb. Unfortunately, the monastery still bears the damage from 13th-century Frankish occupation and, more recently, from German bombing in World War II.

■ **MONASTERY.** Today, the monastery consists of the two churches, the crypt, a bell-tower, and monks' cells. Also on the grounds are an archaeology museum and several tourist shops. The handful of black-robed, bearded monks who live in the monastery and tend its gardens cheerfully accommodate tourists. The archaeology museum, on the right after the arched stone gate, sells tickets for entrance into the monastery. The museum holds a few relics from the monastery's architectural past (chunks of molding and such) and merits little more than a quick look.

The **Katholikon,** on the right after the museum, is the most impressive piece of the monastery. Built on the classic "Greek cross" basilica plan (see p. 23), the church is resplendent with brilliant frescoes and mosaics. The mosaics, crafted from minute pieces of stone, enamel, and gold, depict scenes of Christian lore: the birth, baptism, and crucifixion of Christ, and **Christ Pantokrator** (Christ in heaven, reigning in glory as savior and ruler), which gazes down from the dome.

A small passageway in the Katholikon's northwest corner links it to the smaller **Church of Panagia.** In this passageway is the monastery's most prized relic: the desiccated body of the saint himself, lying in state in a transparent glass coffin. Orthodox pilgrims come here to pray at Osios Loukas's velvet-slippered feet. Some have been even bolder: Loukas's left hand, which protrudes from his habit to hold a rosary, has lost a few fingers to relic-seekers. The Church of Panagia down the passage features extremely fine exterior brickwork and an inlaid mosaic floor.

Between the museum and the churches and accessible by an entrance in the southern exterior of the Katholikon is the **crypt**; its stunning frescoes should not be missed. Protected from the elements, the frescoes retain their original brilliance, giving us an idea of what the churches looked like originally.

PARNASSOS Παρνασσος AND ARAHOVA Αραχωβα ☎ 0267

Winter is peak season on Mt. Parnassos (2455m), as Apollo and the muses share their abode with ski buffs and bunnies flocking to the best slopes in Greece. Summer trekkers can hike the slopes undisturbed. Outdoor enthusiasts will adore Parnassos regardless of the season. From December to May, the little village of Arahova (24km away from Parnassos) becomes Greece's largest ski resort, thanks to its prime location. Drowsy and picturesque in the summer months, Arahova offers local delights like delicious unresinated red wine, Boeotian honey, that peculiar grape-seed brandy called *tsipouro* (see **Moonshine**, p. 179), and an overwhelming view of the valley 4800m below. A three-day **festival** in mid-April commemorates Arahova's role as the site of a pivotal victory over the Turks during the Ottoman War in 1821. In honor of St. George, the renowned dragon-slayer and the town's patron saint, the festival consists of athletic competitions, dances, and general merrymaking; during the festivities, residents don their best costumes.

■**⚡ ORIENTATION AND PRACTICAL INFORMATION.** From **Terminal B** in Athens (see p. 80), take the Delphi bus to **Arahova** (2½hr., 6 per day, 3300dr/€9.68). A brown and yellow "Celena Cafe" sign identifies the **bus station** (☎0265 28 226), which doubles as a restaurant. The bus station is near the center of town at the second plateia, on the left side of Delphon (the main road), approaching from Delphi. From here, **buses** make the run from Arahova to: **Delphi** (20min., 7 per day 6:15am-7:50pm, 260dr/€.76); **Livadia** (30min.; M-F 3 per day 7am-4:30pm, Sa 12:50, 4:30pm, Su 4:30, 6:30pm; 800dr/€2.35); and **Athens** (2½hr; 6 per day M-Sa 5:45am-6:15pm, Su 7:45am-9:15pm; 3300dr/€9.68). Getting from Arahova to Parnassos is slightly easier during the ski season, when a **bus** leaves in the morning and returns in the afternoon at the main plateia (8am, 3pm). During the summer months go by **car**; those without cars can hire a **taxi**. (☎31 566. Round-trip 10,000-12,000dr/€29.35-35.22.) Arahova centers on a single road, **Delphon**, which points downhill toward Delphi and has all a tourist could want. Three main plateias lie in town; directions assume you are heading into town from Delphi.

An **information office** with English-speaking staff is just to the right off the main plateia (☎29 170; fax 31 630; detpa@internet.gr; open 8am-10pm). The **police** (☎31 333) are reachable by phone. Several **pharmacies** offer balm for bruises and blisters; there's one in the second plateia, beside the big taverna, and another just past it down an alley to the right. A little past the post office, on the left, lies the **National Bank,** with a 24hr. **ATM.** (Open M-Th 8am-2pm, F 8am-1:30pm.) **Alpha Bank,** in the second plateia of cafes on the right, **exchanges money.** (Open M-Th 8am-2pm, F 8am-1:30pm.) Cafe Kivernio, next to the bus station, offers **internet access** (100dr/€.29 for 3 min.). Turning right on the cross-street in the main plateia, uphill and on the right, you'll find the **post office.** (Open M-F 7:30am-1:30pm.) **Postal code:** 32004.

⌂ ACCOMMODATIONS. Several hotels, pensions, and domatia cluster near the first plateia, and more are scattered along Delphon and at the other end town. The low-end prices listed refer to summer prices; high-end prices refer to ski season rates. ▧**Pension Petrino** (Πετρινο), down the first small alley on the right after the main plateia, offers gorgeous rooms with private baths, balconies, and high wooden ceilings. 40% discount on weekdays during ski season, and 10% off for stays longer than 3 days in summer. (☎31 384; fax 32 663. 40% discount M-F in ski season, 10% off for stays longer than 3 days in summer. Breakfast 1000dr/€2.93 in summer, included in winter. Singles 5000-16,000dr/€14.67-46.96; doubles 8000-22,000dr/€23.48-64.56.) Spend a hard day's night at **Pension Nostos,** located down the road to the right off the main plateia. Its cozy, well-appointed rooms (fridge, TV, private bath, balcony) once hosted the Beatles. (☎31 385; fax 31 765; nostospension@in.gr. Singles 6000-18,000dr/€17.61-52.82; doubles 10,000-28,800dr/

€29.35-84.52. 50% discount on weekdays in winter. Open 8 days a week.) Farther down the road past the center of town, **Hotel Apollon,** Delphi 20, has comfortable rooms with shared hall bathrooms. Some rooms have balconies with uninterrupted views of the surrounding mountains. The friendly, English-speaking owner is glad to be of service. (☎31 057. Breakfast 1500dr/€4.40 at 7:30 and 9:30am. Singles 6500-8000dr/€19.08-23.48; doubles 12,000dr/€35.22.)

◘ FOOD. The bakeries along the road to Delphi sell fresh bread and savory pastries (300-500dr/€.88-1.47). Tavernas are plentiful but indistinct and can be found along the main road. The usually moderate prices, like everything else, go up in winter. **Cafe Ekastiko** (Εικαστικο), just past the second plateia on the left, is the haunt of old Greek men downing curious liquids and greeting everyone on the street. Serves up traditional Greek fare (*moussaka* 1600dr/€4.70, *tzatziki* 600dr/€1.76). At 300dr/€.88 per glass, it has the cheapest ouzo and tsipouro prices in town. **Pizzaria** (Πιτσαρια) **Kellaria,** on the right past the second plateia, serves a variety of pizza and calzones (1600-2500dr/€4.70-7.34) from its **brick oven,** as well as savory and sweet crepes (1200-1400dr/€3.52-4.11). **Taverna Karathanassi** (Καραθαναση), up from the second plateia on, serves a variety of pastas, salads, and grilled meats (700-2000dr/€2.05-5.87) and features roof terrace dining.

◪ SKIING, HIKING, AND THE OUTDOORS. Winter activities at Parnassos are accessible at either one of its two main **ski centers, Kelaria** (☎0234 22 689 or 624) or **Terolaka** (☎0234 22 693). The ski season runs from December 17 to May 1. (Lifts: weekends 7000dr/€20.53 per day; weekdays 4000dr/€11.74 per day; full week 25,000dr/€73.37; ask about discounts for students and children, as well as family passes.) Though more goats than tourists frequent Parnassos in the summer months, it's a peaceful spot for hiking and rock climbing, with literally breathtaking views: the air becomes noticeably thinner higher up. Ski centers on the mountain provide free parking and an easy starting destination for most trips. Consult the **Greek Alpine Club** in Athens (☎01 321 2429) or the **Skiing and Mountain Climbing Association of Amfissa** (☎0265 28 577 or 29 201) about routes and refuges for climbers. In most cases, the hike will take no more than three hours. Summer hikers should note that trails are unmarked and usually deserted (goats aside). Be sure to take water and sunscreen along, and be aware of the thin air and rocky paths.

DELPHI Δελφοι ☎ 0265

The god whose oracle is at Delphi neither utters nor hides his meaning but shows it by a sign.
—Heraclitus

As any Delphinian will proudly attest, this town of 2500 marks the belly button (omphalos) of the earth. According to the ancient myth, Zeus discovered this fact by simultaneously releasing two eagles, one toward the east and one toward the west. They collided, impaling each other with their beaks, directly over Delphi. A sacred stone marks the spot. Nearby stood the most important oracle of the ancient Mediterranean. The oracle was initially devoted to Gaia (Mother Earth). Gaia was overthrown by the Olympian gods around 800 BC, when Apollo defeated the Python, Gaia's snaky, underworldly son and ruler of the site. The Apollonian oracle drew pilgrims from far and wide who sought guidance from the Pythia, the priestess of the oracle. The temples and treasury building of the ancient oracle have mostly crumbled to rubble, but Delphi remains a place of pilgrimage--for tourists. Jewelry stores, expensive restaurants, "Greek Art" trinket shops, and hotels litter the present-day town. Beyond the touristy glitter, the town's mountainside perch and its beautiful ruins make ancient Delphi a must-see daytrip.

✦ ⁊ ORIENTATION AND PRACTICAL INFORMATION

Delphi's main street, **Friderikis-Pavlou,** runs east-west through town. **Apollonas** runs uphill from and parallel to Friderikis-Pavlou. The **bus station** (☎82 317, open daily 8am-10:30pm) is at the western end of town, on Pavlou. The oracle and museum are on Pavlou at the opposite end of town, toward Athens.

Buses: From **Terminal B** in Athens (see p. 80), take a bus to **Delphi** (3½hr., 6 per day, 3100dr/€9.10). Buy your ticket at the booth labeled Δελφοι (Delphi). From Delphi, buses leave for: **Amphissa** (30min., 5 per day 6:30am-8pm, 480dr/€1.41); **Itea** (30min., 6 per day 6:30am-10pm, 400dr/€1.17); **Lamia** (2hr., 2-3 per day, 1900dr/ €5.58); **Nafpaktos** (2½hr., 3 per day, 2250dr/€6.60) via **Galaxidi** (1hr., 750dr/ €2.20); **Patras** (3hr., 1 per day, 2750dr/€8.07); **Thessaloniki** (5½hr.; M-Th, Sa 10:15am, F and Su 3:15pm; 7300dr/€21.42) via **Volos, Larisa,** and **Katerini.**

Taxi Stand (☎82 000), at the eastern end of Pavlou.

Tourist Office: Friderikis 12 or Apollonas 11 (☎82 900), housed in the town hall. From Friderikis, the office is up a flight of stairs, in a stucco courtyard to your left as you walk toward Athens, marked by an "Information" sign. Incredibly helpful, quadrilingual ▨ **Mrs. Efi** will assist you with bus schedules and accommodations. Open M-F 8am-2:30pm. If the office is closed, the bus station can provide directions and bus information. (Open 7:30am-10:30pm.)

Police (☎82 222), directly behind the church at the peak of Apollonas.

National Bank: Pavlou 32 (☎82 622), has a 24hr. **ATM.** Open M-Th 8am-2pm, F 8am-1:30pm.

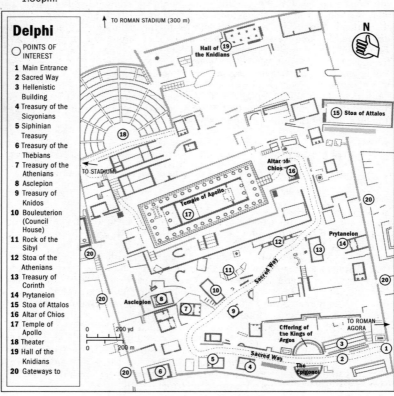

CENTRAL GREECE

Delphi

○ POINTS OF INTEREST

1 Main Entrance
2 Sacred Way
3 Hellenistic Building
4 Treasury of the Sicyonians
5 Siphinian Treasury
6 Treasury of the Thebians
7 Treasury of the Athenians
8 Asclepion
9 Treasury of Knidos
10 Bouleuterion (Council House)
11 Rock of the Sibyl
12 Stoa of the Athenians
13 Treasury of Corinth
14 Prytaneion
15 Stoa of Attalos
16 Altar of Chios
17 Temple of Apollo
18 Theater
19 Hall of the Knidians
20 Gateways to

TO ROMAN STADIUM (300 m)

N

Hall of the Knidians

Stoa of Attalos

Altar of Chios

TO STADIUM

Temple of Apollo

Prytaneion

Sacred Way

Asclepion

TO ROMAN AGORA

Offering of the Kings of Argos

Sacred Way

The Epigonoi

200 yd

200 m

Public Toilets: at the eastern end of Pavlou behind the taxi stand.

OTE: In the town hall. Open M-Th 7:30am-1pm, F 7:30am-12:30pm.

Internet Access: In a travel agency at 7 Pavlou, on the right as you walk toward Athens, next to Hotel Sybilla (1500dr/€4.40 per hr.). The agency also offers traveler's cheques and **commission-free currency exchange.** Open daily 8am-10pm.

Post Office: (☎82 376) at Pavlou 25. Open M-F 7:30am-2pm. **Postal code:** 33054.

ACCOMMODATIONS AND CAMPING

Delphi is full of hotels; most are expensive. Almost all of the many hotels can be found on Apollonas or Pavlou. Prices tend to rise during the ski season. Camping is available on the road heading west from Delphi.

Hotel Sibylla, Pavlou 9 (☎82 335), provides wonderful views (often balconies) and private baths at the best prices in town. Singles 4000dr/€11.74; doubles 6000dr/€17.61; triples 8000dr/€23.48.

Hotel Lefas, (☎82 324), on the right side of Pavlou walking toward Athens. Wood-panelled walls are the stand-out feature of this hotel, which also features TVs, private baths, and great views of the Gulf of Corinth from its balconies. Breakfast included. Check-out 10am. Singles 5000dr/€14.67; doubles 8000dr/€23.48; triples 12,000dr/€23.48.

Sunview Pension, Apollonas 84 (☎82 815/349). From the bus station, walk uphill with the gas station on your right. Make your first left onto Apollonas. Sparkling rooms with private baths and balconies overlook the Gulf. Breakfast included. Singles 8000dr/€23.48; doubles 12,000dr/€35.22; triples 15,000/€44.02.

Camping: The bus can drop you at **Delphi Camping** (☎82 745), 4km out of town (1300dr/€3.82 per person; 900dr/€2.64 per tent; 750dr/€2.20 per car); or **Chrissa Camping** (☎82 050), 10km out of town (1400dr/€4.11 per person; prices vary by season). Both sites have swimming pools.

FOOD AND ENTERTAINMENT

Several **mini-supermarkets** and a **bakery** along Pavlou and Apollonas provide for self-caterers. Delphi's tavernas are fairly indistinguishable and a bit pricey. Not one, not two, but four pizza places beckon from the western end of Pavlou. **Taverna Lefkaria,** at the peak of Apollonas, looks out over the Gulf. Its attentive waitstaff serves up tasty Greek traditional and **vegetarian** entrees, and can substitute tofu in many dishes. (Starters 700-1350dr/€2.05-3.96, entrees 1200-2000dr/€3.52-5.87.) **Taverna Elatos,** Pavlou 65, serves inexpensive starters (*tzatziki* 700dr/€2.05, *saganaki* 1000dr/€2.93), with a view. (☎82 830. Entrees 1500-2300dr/€4.40-6.75.)

Delphi's only two nightclubs are within stumbling distance of most hotels on Pavlou. Both open at 10pm and stay open until the customers leave (substantially later in the more crowded winter season). **Katoi Cub,** near Pavlou 65, boasts a large dance floor and a view of the gulf. (Cover 2000dr/€5.87, includes one drink; beer 1000dr/€2.93.) Rub elbows with tourists and the local youth at **Delphi at Night,** Pavlou 33. (Cover 1000dr/€2.93; beer 1000dr/€2.93; cocktails 1500dr/€4.40.)

Delphi Consultants (☎82 151 or 82 086), on the ground floor of the town hall, organizes traditional **Greek dances** at the Symposium Center. Call for events and dates. In July and August, the **European Cultural Center of Delphi** (☎82 731) puts on a **Festival of Greek Drama** with performances in the ancient stadium of Delphi in July and August. They also present temporary international art exhibitions. Contact their office in Athens (☎(01) 3312781-5; fax (01) 3312786; epked@culture.gr) for more information. (For more on Greek drama, see p. 27.) To find the Center, follow the Amphissa/Itea road down the hill out of town to the blue signs, turn right and head up the hill. (Open daily 9am-2pm.) Delphi is home to several other summer **festivals,** so ask around and keep a sharp eye out for posters.

KNOW THYSELF (OR ELSE) The Delphic Oracle was known for giving obscure, deceptive, metaphorical answers to pilgrims' questions. Many a suppliant went home more confused than he or she had come, having failed to draw meaning from the answer, or—worse still—having drawn the *wrong* meaning. **Croesus of Sardis,** ruler of a vast territory encompassing most of Asia Minor and the richest man in the ancient world, came to the oracle in the 6th century BC to ask about the Persian threat to his kingdom. The oracle's answer: "A great empire will be destroyed." The king returned to Sardis thinking that he would lay the smackdown to the Persians, whose empire was as large as his own. Croesus found out the hard way that the oracle had meant his own great empire would crash, as he watched his home fall to Persian invaders. Athenian leader **Themistocles** fared better when he asked the oracle how to prepare for another war with ever-pesky Persia. He was told to "build wooden walls." Most interpreted this as an order to enclose Athens in wooden walls, but Themistocles set to work building a fleet of ships. Only after Athens' decisive victory in the First Persian War at the naval battle of Salamis did the Athenians realize their leader's smarts.

👁 ORACLE OF DELPHI

Head out of town toward Athens, following the highway until you see the paved path on the left, which leads to the ruins and museum. ☎ *82 312. Museum and site 2000dr/€5.87, museum only 1200dr/€3.52, students and seniors 600dr/€1.76, EU students free; site only 1200dr/€3.52, students and seniors 600dr/€1.76, EU students free.*

A sacred site from 1500 BC or earlier, the Oracle of Delphi became the most important source of sacred wisdom in the ancient world from around the 7th century BC until the advent of Orthodox Christianity after the 4th century AD. Pilgrims ventured to the Delphic Oracle from all over Greece and the Near East (where Alexander the Great had brought Greek culture). After all, the Delphic oracle foretold **Cadmus'** founding of Thebes and prophesied the horrific fate of **Oedipus**—to kill his father and marry his mother. The oracle's authority extended beyond religious matters and personal fortune-telling; Delphic approval sanctioned many political decisions, including the reforms that led to pure democracy in Athens. The oracle's pronouncements altered nations and set off (or extinguished) military conflicts. Hoping to make powerful friends, city-states from all over the Greek world erected treasuries and donated immense sums, in respect to the oracle.

In ancient times, pilgrims approaching the oracle first cleansed themselves at the **Kastalian Spring,** then paid a tax, the *pelanon,* and sacrificed at the **Altar of Apollo.** The pilgrims' questions were submitted to the **Pythia,** an older Delphic priestess, who sat over a chasm and inhaled the vapors wafting from below. These vapors—the breath of the Python—possessed her, and she became delirious, muttering gibberish. Several priests would then interpret the mutterings, translating them into advice. The chasm, referred to in many ancient texts and whose existence no one in the ancient world doubted, was supposedly accessible from the Temple of Apollo. There is no evidence today, however, that one ever existed, although the geological instability of the area makes the original story plausible.

■**ARCHAEOLOGICAL SITE.** The inscription "Know thyself" (Γνοθι σεαυτον) has long crumbled from the portal of the ancient temple, but still governs the meditative atmosphere of peaceful, windswept ancient Delphi. Cut into the steep mountainside, the ancient oracle reigns over the brush-dotted valley below, and overlooks eagles that fly below the lofty temple. Now, as then, the thrice-destroyed **Temple of Apollo** is the centerpiece of the oracle site. A largely wooden incarnation of the temple was burned in 548 BC; it was again shattered, this time by an earthquake, in 373 BC; it still lies in ruin today. Ancient proclamations are still visible etched along the stone base. To reach the Temple of Apollo, visitors follow the **Sacred Way,** which winds up the site in the footsteps of ancient pilgrims. To the left, the treasuries of the supplicant cities line the Sacred Way, including the reconstructed **Treasury of the Athenians,** excavated in the early 20th century. Past the Temple of Apollo, the **theater,** with its geometric perfection and amazing acoustics, is no less impressive. For a taste of the oracle's life as a Roman site, slip your way up the slick steps to the **stadium** at the very top of the hill. Through the archway at the entrance, you'll see the golden brown and green dappled mountains framed before you. Take a break from the thin air to sit among Roman ghosts in the stadium's seats; then before you go, take a few laps around the stadium and imagine the turning posts and cheering crowds. *(Open 7:30am-4:45pm.)*

ARCHAEOLOGY MUSEUM. The museum contains many precious artifacts mined from the site: the frieze and two *kouroi* (see p. 20) from the Siphian Treasury, the haunting bronze ■**Charioteer of Delphi,** the altar from the temple of Athena Pronaia, enormous 7th-century bronze shields, and many ornaments and figurines in gold, silver, and ivory offered to the oracle. Nearly all of the collection was unearthed in 1939 by the **Ecole Française d'Athens.** Most labels are written in French and English as well as Greek, but a guidebook (1000-4000dr/€2.93-11.74) is still helpful. *(Open M-F 7:30am-6:45pm; Sa, Su and holidays 8:30am-2:45pm.)*

OTHER SITES. Before calling upon the oracle, pilgrims cleansed themselves both physically and spiritually in the **Kastalian Spring,** 300m past the main ruins along the road to Athens. The remains were covered by rocks until the beginning of this century, when a clever archaeologist cleared them out of the lush ravine. You can still see the niches carved into the rock for votive offerings. Drinking from the spring is said to confer the gift of eloquence. Just past the spring are the remains of an ancient **gymnasium.** About 200m farther down the road, the **Temple of Athena Pronaia** served as a lounge for pilgrims before they entered the sanctuary. The three remaining Doric columns of the **Tholos,** a round building used for an unknown purpose, are the sole evidence of its architectural mastery.

GALAXIDI Γαλαξιδι ☎ 0265

The town shares its name with a drink made of *gala* (milk) and *xithi* (vinegar), which may be an allusion to the bittersweet existence of a seaman's wife—Galaxidi used to be a prominent naval base. In its modern incarnation, seafaring has evolved into pleasure boating, as locals lead tours for vacationing Swedes and Germans. Quiet during most of the year, Galaxidi delights visitors with its peaceful waterfront, pebble beaches, and gorgeous view of the surrounding mountains.

THE WAY TO BYRON'S HEART

Seek out—less often sought than found—
A soldier's grave, for thee the best;
Then look around, and choose thy ground,
And take thy rest.
    —George Gordon, Lord Byron, "On This Day I Complete My Thirty-Sixth Year"

Though **Messolongi,** a stop on the Athens-Delphi-Astakos bus route, may not walk in beauty like the night, it does hold **Lord Byron**'s heart—literally. The city has the sad distinction of being the place Lord Byron caught fever and met his end in 1824, while leading the local troops in the War of Independence (see p. 16). A small **War of Independence Museum** in the old town hall at the center of the *plateia* includes an unexceptional collection of Byron memorabilia. A Byron pilgrim's trail points to the large statue of the poet dressed in Greek garb, in front of the Hotel Liberty, just before the entrance to the Garden of Heroes. The park consists mainly of crumbling busts and other poorly maintained monuments to national war heroes; **Byron's heart** is buried beneath his statue. The noise and dirt of modern Messolongi may be tragically unromantic, but Byron would be content that the city is indeed free.

CENTRAL GREECE

⚡ PRACTICAL INFORMATION. Galaxidi's main street, **Nik. Mama,** leads from the sole town plateia (and the **bus station**) to the cheapest hotel in town, Hotel Poseidon, and down to the harbor. **Buses** run from Galaxidi to Nafpaktos (1hr., 5 per day 6:15am-9:20pm, 1550dr/€4.55) and to Itea, where you can transfer to Delphi (1hr.; M-F 5 per day 7:15am-8pm, Sa-Su 4 per day; 400dr/€1.17). Find the **police** (☎41 222) in the main plateia across from the bus station. The **pharmacy** is one block to the right of the bus station up Nik. Mama on the left. (☎41 122. Open M-Sa 8:30am-1pm and 6-9pm.) The **National Bank** is several blocks farther down Nik. Mama, past the Hotel Poseidon on the left. (24hr. **ATM.** Open M-Th 8:30am-2pm, F 8:30am-1:30pm). **Public toilets and showers** are across the harbor from Nik. Mama before the forest on the right. Galaxidi's **post office** is next to the bank on Nik. Mama. (Open daily 7:30am-2pm.) **Postal code:** 33052.

🛏🍴 ACCOMMODATIONS AND FOOD. From the bus stop, turn right and head down Nik. Mama to find **Hotel Poseidon,** a breezy old home-turned-hotel blessed with an ultra-friendly manager, **Costas,** who just may break open a bottle of *ouzo* on the evening of your arrival. Choose rooms with old-world charm or modern convenience (A/C, TV, and private bath). (☎41 426. Breakfast included. Singles 7000-11,000dr/€20.53-32.28; doubles 10,000-13,000dr/€29.35-38.15.) On a summer weekend, expect prices to be 20% higher. Several **domatia** can also be found on sidestreets off Nik. Mama and above the restaurants along the waterfront.

To Perasma, across from the National Bank, sells old standbys for typical prices (gyros 400dr/€1.17, *souvlaki* 250dr/€.73). On Kon. Satha to the left of Nik. Mama before the Hotel Poseidon, **Taverna Albatross** is a cheap, sit-down alternative (starters 500-1000dr/€2.9-04.50, entrees 1000dr/€2.90 and up). If you're splurging, head to one of the tavernas along the harbor for a great view and tasty seafood. For the best deal, head to the bakeries on Nik. Mama (300-500dr/€.88-1.47).

📷🎭 SIGHTS AND ENTERTAINMENT. On Kon. Satha, off Nik. Mama, the **Church of Agios Nikolaos** houses many fine mosaics. The 13th-century **Monastery of the Metamorphosis,** with sublime centuries-old wood carvings and a great view of town, is 6km from Galaxidi on the uphill road outside of town. Though the unshaded, uphill trip takes an hour by foot, on a cool day the views make it a perfect hike; follow K. Papapetrou out of town past the school, beneath the highway, and follow the signs through the terraced orange orchards.

In the early spring, Galaxidi shakes off its sleepiness with the leftover Bacchanalian frenzy that is **Pre-Lenten Carnival.** Ouzo bottles are emptied by the hundreds as fantastically costumed people come from miles around for extraordinary once-a-year carousing. Revelers gyrate around a fire in traditional dances and throw brightly colored pigments at each other. If you want to keep your costume clean, stick to the dances by the town's children; they'll be in traditional garb.

Rocky shoreline stretches out past the docks on the forest side of the harbor; small, wonderful, pebbly **beaches** are scattered throughout. Walk Nik. Mama to the waterfront, then follow the harbor toward the forest to your left until you find a resting place that suits you. Several tiny islands are within easy swimming distance, ideal for solitary tanning or snoozing.

NAFPAKTOS Ναυπακτοσ ☎ 0634

From the towering battlements of the Venetian castle on the hill above the city you can look down over all of Nafpaktos, a bustling port city and a hot beach spot. Nafpaktos derives its name from its ancient role as a ship-building naval colony—its name literally means "manufacturing ships." Rarely visited by foreigners, summer weekends bring vacationing urbanites and Greek families from Patras and Athens.

🧭⚡ ORIENTATION AND PRACTICAL INFORMATION. Buses from points east drop off on **Athinon** (which becomes **Tzavella** and ultimately converges with Mesologgiou at the Old Port) at the base of the main town plateia. One block toward the water from Athinon is **Mesologgiou** which runs one way in the opposite direction to Athinon

(away from the Old Port). There are **two bus stations** in town, both near the church one street below the main plateia on Athinon. The **first station** serves **Athens** and **Antirrio.** Take a **bus** to Antirrio (15min., 2 per hr. 6am-10pm, 280dr/€0.82) to catch the **ferry** that serves the Peloponnese. Buses also leave for Athens (3½hr., 1 per hr. 10am-5pm, 4200dr/€12.33). The **second station** serves all other destinations, and is located across the street and just around the corner from the front of the church. Buses leave for: **Delphi** (2hr., 5 per day, 2250dr/€6.60); **Lamia** with a transfer at Itea (3½ hr., 8:45am and 1:30pm, 3600dr/€10.60); and **Thessaloniki** (4hr., 8:45am, 9000dr/€26.41). **Taxis** (☎27 792 or 27 678) are in the plateia, as are phones for calling them. In case of emergency, call the **police** (☎27 258). The **National Bank** and **Alpha Bank**, both on Athinon just off the main plateia, both exchange travelers checks and have 24hr. **ATMs.** (Both open M-Th 8am-2pm, F 8am-1:30pm.) There are **pharmacies** around the plateia and down Athinon, all with varying hours; if one's closed, there should be a sign indicating which others are open. You can get yourself connected (to the **Internet,** that is) at the **Golden Beach Hotel** on Psani beach, past the Old Port. (☎21 444. 1000dr/€2.93 per hr., 500dr/€1.47 minimum.) The **post office** is several blocks down Athinon from the banks, on the right side of the street. (☎27 232. Open M-F 7:30am-2pm.) **Postal code:** 30300.

⌖▣ ACCOMMODATIONS AND FOOD. ▥**Hotel Diethnes** (ΔΙΕΘΝΕΣ), on Odos Messologgiou, has hardwood floors, balconies and blindingly white private baths. Look for the purple shutters just past the Old Port plateia. (☎27 342. Singles 6000dr/€17.61; doubles 10,000dr/€29.35; triples 12,000dr/€35.22.) **Pension Aphrodite,** on Apokaykou two blocks down from the bus stop on Gribovo beach, has it all: private baths, TVs, phones, and a view, at a great price. (☎27 370. Singles 6000dr/€17.61; doubles 10,000dr/€29.35; triples 13,000dr/€38.15. Be sure to specify pension and not hotel.) **Hotel Nikh** is a convenient place to plunk down your pack. Follow Athinon two blocks from the main plateia for functional rooms with phones and private baths on a busy street. (☎28 901. Singles 5000dr/€14.67; doubles 7000dr/€20.53; triples 10,000dr/€29.35.)

Bakeries, souvlaki stands, and fast food restaurants jumble together near the central plateia and Old Port. Head to the waterfront along Gribovo beach (just a few blocks down from the main plateia) for tavernas; veer left for the best prices. The first of the bunch, **O Stavros,** offers a variety of succulent dishes and a great view. Not sure what you want? Go back to the kitchen and point at one of the many dishes being cooked and it will be on your plate in a jiffy. The Old Port is brimming with trendy cafes that become lively only after 10pm.

◨▣ SIGHTS AND ENTERTAINMENT. The ▧**Venetian castle** (Καστρο) dominates the picturesque town, with five zones of fortification from port to crest. One of the most important examples of fortress architecture in Greece, its construction was augmented in each of Nafpaktos's occupation periods, reaching its present magnificence in the 15th century under the Venetians. Besides having the best vista around, the citadel also encloses the tiny **Church of the Prophet Elias,** the remains of a **Byzantine bath** and **church,** and a large **cistern** to help the fortress weather sieges. Its walls, which reach down to the port, are now woven into the construction of modern houses on the hill. Footpaths wind around the walls, past fountains, and through century-old gates. One begins off Athinon just past the post office, on the right, as well as many other streets of Athinon-Tzavella; follow the signs "To Castle" (ΠΡΟΣ ΚΑΣΤΡΟ) and head uphill. A leisurely walk will take about 30 minutes. When you hit the road just below the main fortifications, follow it uphill about 1km to reach the **citadel.** Alternatively, drive to the citadel by following Athinon-Tzavella past the Old Port where it becomes Mesologgiou; veer right on Thermou and follow the signs for ΚΑΣΤΡΟ. The **Old Port,** enclosed by parapets and watchtowers, is the sight of the town's hottest cafes and forms a romantic backdrop for any outing. Several plaques on the parapet walls commemorate the October 7, 1571 **Battle of Lepanto** and its hero, **Miguel de Cervantes Saavedra.** Both the castle and the Old Port are lit up spectacularly at night.

Most leisure time around Nafpaktos is spent on the town's beaches; many locals take a break every afternoon to relax on the beach and swim. Nafpaktos' beaches form a large crescent with the Old Port at its center. Facing the water at the Old Port, **Gribovo beach** is to the left and **Psani beach,** the better of the two, to the right. Families dominate Psani beach; small amenities, like playgrounds and a few **public showers,** add to the experience. Cafes and *ouzeries* along Psani beach and in the Old Port are filled with customers from 8:30 until 11:30pm, when families hit the hay and everyone else hits the clubs.

Club Cinema, featuring a large dance floor and pulsing DJ mixes, is conveniently located one block off Gribovo beach on Apokaykou. (☎26 026. Open F and Sa 11pm until late.) Down Apokaykou, walking away from the Old Port by Pension Aphrodite is ultra-hip **Club Aman,** whose fluorescent blue disco lights illuminate the beachfront long into the night. **The Blue Lake** (☎51 900) claims to be open "all day, everyday" and features live, traditional Greek music on Friday, Saturday, and Sunday nights. You'll need a taxi to get there. Many other clubs open only in the summer—watch out for posters around town. On the roof of Club Cinema is the outdoor movie theatre **Cine-REX,** which features American movies and an incredible vista. (Movies at 9 and 11pm, except for long movies which show once. 2000dr/€5.87.) Nafpaktos's week-long **Pre-Lenten carnival celebration** is nothing to sniff at (although some townsfolk migrate to **Patras's** larger scale festivities), with music everywhere, dancing, free wine, and free souvlaki in the Old Port.

EVRITANIA Ευριτανια

Often called the "Switzerland of Greece," this mountainous land was once a refuge for Greeks escaping Ottoman rule. Since then it has evolved into a wildlife sanctuary where hikers and adventurers can explore clean air, green forests of fir and walnut, and trails that wander past tiny mountain villages to the highest peaks of the Louchi Mountains. Old churches and shrines dot the mountains and overlook steep gorges where water enthusiasts hop in their rafts, canoes, and kayaks and try to tame the rushing Karpenisiotis, Krikelopotamos, and Tavropos Rivers.

The best way to explore Evritania is by foot. Take a stroll up and down the sunny streets of an unhurried hillside town or hike to the peak of the closest mountain for a breathtaking change of perspective. A car, however, is the most sensible (and frequently the only) option for reaching the more remote villages. Bus service is sporadic and mostly unavailable after 1pm. There's no place to rent a car or moped in Karpenisi; the nearest rental office is **Hillco Rent-a-Car** (☎0231 37 086) in Lamia (p. 183), where cars cost 4200-6400dr/€12.33-18.78 per day (prices higher July-Sept.). They deliver cars for an extra charge of 120dr/€.35 per km.

In winter, backpackers can contact the **Hellenic Alpine Club (EOS),** which runs several mountain refuge huts throughout Evritania. (Karpenisi Office: ☎0237 23 051; Lamia Office: ☎0231 26 786.) The adventurous can outfit themselves at **Trekking Hellas,** past the Karpenisi plateia down Zinopoulou on the right (☎0237 25 940), which offers kayak, rafting, and ski packages. A map of the region is on sale at the *periptero* in the plateia in Karpenisi, and is well worth the 1000dr/€2.93 for hiking routes, a topographical key, and an invaluable guide to the area's history.

KARPENISI Καρπενησι   ☎0237

Karpenisi (pop. 10,000), at the tip of a long stretch of hairpinned roadway, is Evritania's relaxed capital and the perfect base for outdoor explorations in the surrounding countryside and villages. Founded when five agrarian settlements in the foothills of Mt. Timfristos merged early in the era of Ottoman rule, Karpenisi thrives on a healthy tourism industry, catering to Greek outdoor enthusiasts. In the broad main plateia, where old men still occasionally strum a guitar and join in a melancholy sing-along, a floor mosaic of whorled designs spells out the names of the region's old towns. South of Karpenisi, the streets give way to rolling pastures, which quickly steepen into the Karpenissiotis River gorge.

MOONSHINE Ask almost any taverna owner in Evritania for a taste of *tsipouro* and he'll give you a knowing wink, disappear into the back, and reappear with a chilled bottle of clear Greek moonshine. Regular old legal wine is distilled all over Evritania, using local grapes. When they're done with the grapes, however, the farmers don't throw them away. Instead, they boil down the leftovers for a couple of days before distilling the residue in clear river water. The result is a fiery transparent alcohol that will clear your sinuses and burn your throat with a vengeance. The Greeks aren't much for rules: despite being illegal, *tsipouro* can be found at virtually every taverna in Evritania. Beware, though: it packs a powerful punch, and tastes a bit like wine-flavored tequila mixed with lighter fluid.

TRANSPORTATION. Buses run to **Agrinio** (3½hr.; Sa-Th 1 per day 8:45am, F 3:30pm; 2150dr/€6.31); **Athens** (5hr.; 9am, noon, 3:30pm; 5250dr/€15.40); **Koryshades** (10min., M-Sa 7:20am, 260dr/€2.76); **Lamia** (1¾ hr., 4 per day 6:30am-3:30pm, 1500dr/€4.40); **Mikro Horio** and **Megalo Horio** (20min.; 7am, 1pm; 300dr/€.88); **Proussos** (M and F 5:30am, 1pm; 650dr/€2). Ask at the bus station about bus service to smaller villages. In winter, buses to the **Velouchi Ski Center** (12km) can be arranged for larger groups. **Taxis** (☎ 22 666 or 22 100) line up at the stand just downhill from the bus station.

ORIENTATION AND PRACTICAL INFORMATION. Karpenisi sits at the foot of Mt. Velouchi, which rises up about 70km west of Lamia in central Sterea Ellada. Everything of importance is within a 5min. walk from the **bus station.** From the station, Tsamboula leads downhill to the spacious plateia, where it changes its name to **Zinopoulou.** After passing the plateia, the road splits in a V, with **Karpenisioti** heading down to the right and Zinopoulou continuing on the left. Most of the town's shops are on these two streets. The other main road, **Eth. Antistaseos,** forks off to the right from Zinopoulou at the top end of the plateia. As Eth. Antistaseos passes the plateia, **Grigoriou Tsitsara** branches off to the left, running roughly parallel to Zinopoulou and Karpenisioti. The largest **church** and the **town hall** are on the north end of the plateia, near a **monument** to Greek soldiers who died in 20th-century wars. Above the bus station, the town climbs up the hillside in a tangle of steep, winding streets and narrow stairways.

Directly across the street from the taxi stand, the **tourist office** is behind an inconspicuous door, beneath a green sign. The friendly English-speaking staff offers regional maps, brochures, and ideas for excursions into the Evritanian countryside, including hiking, rafting, camping, canyoning, and parachuting. (☎/fax 21 016. Open M-Sa 10am-2pm and 5-8pm, Su 10am-2pm.) A map of Karpenisi and the surrounding villages, including extensive hiking trails, can be purchased at the *periptero* across the street (1000dr/€2.93). There are a number of 24hr. **ATMs,** including one at the **National Bank** in the plateia. (Open M-Th 8am-2pm, F 8am-1:30pm.) The **police station** (☎ 25 100; open 24hr.) and the **OTE** (open 7am-10pm) are on Eth. Antistaseos. The **hospital** (☎ 80 680) is a 10min. walk past the police station. For fast **internet access,** head down Karpenisioti and turn left at the 1st street for the Anzonopoulos computer shop (1000dr/€2.93 per hr.). The **post office** is at the bottom of Karpenisioti. (Open M-F 7:30am-2pm.) **Postal code:** 36100.

ACCOMMODATIONS. The best option is to stay in one of many **domatia:** Karpenisi brims with cheap rooms to let. The tourist office lists rooms and prices. Friendly former Boston resident **Konstandinos Kousigos** offers rooms at his house at the top of a flight of stone steps behind the taxi stand. A view, private bath, and comfy beds make it homey. (☎ 21 400. Double rooms 10,000dr/€29.35.) Rates at Karpenisi's hotels increase during ski season and summer, often by as much as 100%. In both high seasons, hotel prices also jump on weekends. **Hotel Galini,** Riga Feriou 3, is set back on a quiet side street; to reach it, walk down G. Tsitsara from Eth. Antistaseos and take the second right. True to its name ("peace"), it offers quiet, comfortable rooms with balconies, TVs, phones, and private baths at very cheap rates. (☎ 22 914; fax 25 623. Singles 6000dr/€17.61; doubles 10000dr/€29.35.) **Hotel Elvetia,** Zinopoulou 7, has pleasant rooms with TVs, radios, phones, balconies, and a lounge area. (☎ 80 111; fax 80 112. Singles 9000dr/€26.41; doubles 12,000dr/€35.22; family suite 18,000dr/€52.83. Breakfast 800/1200dr/€2.35-8.80.)

❐ **FOOD.** ▨**I Klimatria,** Kosmai Etolou 25 (☎ 22 230), 100m downhill from the top of Eth. Antistaseos, is decorated with antique local handicrafts, but offset by a 1953 Rock-Ola American jukebox, that vaults the restaurant into the 20th century. The gregarious owner, whose family has owned the restaurant for over a century, will happily translate the menu for you. Excellent seasonal dishes (1600-2400dr/€4.69-7.04), including rabbit and rooster, are all made from local ingredients. To scrounge up your own meal, visit the **bakery** and large **supermarket** on Karpenisioti. Look for a large yellow awning. Most of the restaurants in and around Karpenisi are basic *tavernas*, which serve mostly meat dishes *tis cras* (charcoal grilled). Dine outdoors on local specialties like rustic salad and fresh trout from the neighboring river at the brookside **Taverna Megampelia,** 2km south of town on the road toward Mikro Horio. If the food leaves you too weighed down to move, stay the night upstairs in their domatia. (☎ 23 171. Entrees 500-1500dr/€1.47-4.40.) Directly off the plateia, **Kitsios,** Zinopoulou 13 (☎ 25 504), soothes the sweet-tooth with fresh baked Greek pastries (300-400dr/€.88-1.17).

▨▩ **NIGHTLIFE AND ENTERTAINMENT.** The afternoon and nightlife blend seamlessly in Karpenisi as the small cafes where young Karpenisians chat over iced coffee slowly evolve into crowded bars with hopping music. Three doors down from the plateia, mild-mannered **Peros** quickly sheds its cafe image around midnight, serving beer with marvelous speed and efficiency. (☎ 22 382. Drinks 1000-1500dr/€2.93-4.40. Open daily 7am-1am.) Later, head down the street to **Byzantio,** the bar of choice for most young Karpenisian late nights; it doesn't start rocking until well after midnight. (☎ 35 606. Open daily midnight-6am.) Just past the police station (be on your best behavior) on Eth. Antiostaseos, a number of bars draw revelers out into the night. The best, **De Facto,** has an all-Greek jukebox and outdoor seating. (☎ 24 455. Drinks 1000-2000dr/€2.93-5.87. Open 6am-3am.) About 1.5km south of town on the road to Koryshades, two clubs fill up on weekends with dancers who migrate down from the slopes of the city. At Karpenisi's most popular club, **Nemesis,** tourists and Karpenisians alike groove to house and trance until 2:30am. After that, it's strictly Greek music until dawn. (Drinks 1000-2300dr/€2.93-6.75. Cover 1500dr/€4.40. Open F-Sa midnight-6am.) Down the road from Nemesis, a replica stagecoach announces the American-themed **Saloon,** where stereos blare country music, patrons slug Jack Daniel's, and dancing begins on the floor and ends up on the tables. (☎ 24 606. Drinks 1000-1500dr/€2.93-4.40. Open daily 10am-6am.) For live traditional Greek music, head to **Musikes Epafes,** Kosma Aitovou 17, a door down from the Klimataria restaurant, above the billiard parlor. (☎ 25 555. Open F-Sa.) Throughout the summer, saints' days are celebrated with religious services in the mornings and food, music, and dancing at night. In mid-July, the town hosts a 15-day *Yiortes Dhassous* ("Celebration of the Forest") replete with exhibitions and, of course, food and music.

> # HAVE ICON, WILL TRAVEL
> Local legend has it that the Virgin Mary visited Proussos in the 8th century, during the Iconoclast period (see p. 15). The Church had recently declared that traditional paintings and relief-icons of Christ and the Virgin, popular in the Byzantine Empire, violated the Second Commandment against worshiping idols. The Virgin Mary didn't bow to this anti-icon business, and personally delivered an icon to Proussos all the way from the Turkish city of Prousa. On the way, she left her footprints in the rocks near Gavros and passed through Mt. Kaliakouda, leaving a hole in her wake. Another tradition holds that two monks brought the icon when they founded the Monastery of the Virgin of Proussiotissa in the 12th century. In either case, the icon remains greatly revered throughout the area.

NEAR KARPENISI

Outside Karpenisi, small villages and traditional settlements beckon visitors to gorgeous rural views and hikes. The forested, mountainous terrain invites rambles. Old-fashioned stone houses abut lakes while sleepy herds of goats snooze on hillsides. Hotels can be expensive in the area: domatia offer much better deals. Camping is illegal and could incur a fine. The map of Evritania available at the *periptero* in Karpenisi's plateia is crucial to navigating the area.

Closed in by ominous peaks on three sides, **Koryshades** (5km southwest of Karpenisi) is a traditional, perfectly preserved Evritanian village. To get there, take the early bus from Karpenisi or hire a taxi for the short ride (1000dr/€2.93). Bright stone houses outfitted with elaborate wooden balconies, red slate roofs, and terraced gardens dot the hillsides. The National Council convened in 1944 in the schoolhouse in Koryshades; the site has been turned into a small **museum.** The only hotel and restaurant in the village, named simply **Koryschades** (☎ 25102; fax 23456) offers spectacular but expensive rooms (singles start at 15,000dr/€44.03) and a flood of information on nearby hikes and outdoor activities. West of Karpenisi lies the village of **Klafsion** (8km away), the name of which—derived from the Greek verb "to cry"—is a tribute to the hardships endured by the townspeople when they survived a 279 BC disaster caused by Galates. The church dates from the 5th century and features an ancient mosaic floor. Most of the homes in Klafsion are inhabited by vacationing Greeks for two to three months a year. Beyond lie **East** and **West Frangista** (40km from Karpenisi), home of a fresco-covered church well worth a visit. A hometown Greek feast awaits at the village tavernas where local trout, traditional sausages, *katiki* cheese, and scrumptious country bread satisfy hungry patrons. The **Monastery of Tatarnas,** west of Frangista and 70km from Karpenisi, served as a refuge for rebels against the Turks. The extensive Byzantine art collection includes an icon of "The Lord of Glory," painted in 1350. Backpackers can take the **Trans-European Footpath E4** where it passes through Evritania on a two-day hike from Karpenisi, through the village of **Krikelo,** all the way to **Mount Oxia** in the southwestern extreme of Evritania.

MIKRO HORIO

Fifteen kilometers down the road from Karpenisi and accessible by bus (15min., 300dr/€.88) are the new and old "little villages," Neo and Paleo Horio. **Paleo Mikro Horio** was largely destroyed by a landslide in 1962; only a 19th-century church and the village square, consisting of five old water fountains, survived. The cool, shaded plateia overlooks terraced farmland rising from the gorge below. After the disaster, the population relocated down the hill to **Neo Mikro Horio** (pop. 250) on the slopes of **Mt. Xelidona.** WWII bombs scarred the new village, and occupying Nazis executed the town's 13 leading dignitaries in 1944. The route to the top of the mountain (about 3hr.) starts near the bus stop; a view of the river valleys and Kremaston Lake is the reward for the uphill trek. Lodgings range from simple, cheap domatia to expensive ski lodge-style hotels. **Taverna Nyonia** has rooms to let above a restaurant. (☎41 393. Doubles 8000dr/€23.48.)

MEGALO HORIO

Megalo Horio (pop. 200) is not so much a village as a handful of stone houses tossed haphazardly down an Evritanean hillside. It is an M. C. Escher utopia precariously tilted to 45 degrees. Houses are turned at improbable angles, leaning on the mountain and each other for support. Roads turn into staircases and back to roads again. As one strolls from the top of the village down, tin-roofed weather-torn huts gradually develop into sparkling mountain vacation homes. Perched midway up the hillside, the *kafeneion* tables on the plateia overlook the breathtaking gorge of the Karpenisiotis River. An enormous gnarled plane tree shades the plateia and a semi-circle of lime trees tint the summer air with the delicate scent of their blossoms. A few meters above the plateia, the main road in Megalo Horio splits in two. From the left branch begins the trail for the 3hr. climb up

Mount Kaliakouda, marked clearly to the top with red blazes. The right branch curves quickly downhill and meanders past gorgeous homes where flowers fill every unused space. Take the same road to find the **Folk Art Museum,** whose collection houses traditional farming equipment, a shepherd's goat-wool *kapa* (coat), a Revolution-era rifle, and a still for brewing *tsipouro*. (☎41 502. Open June-Oct. daily 10am-2pm and 6-8pm; Nov.-May Th, Sa, Su only. Free.)

Reach Megalo Horio by the bus (7am and 1pm, 300dr/€0.88) that runs from Karpenisi and through Mikro Horio. Like the rest of Evritania, Megalo Horio has a number of rooms to let scattered around the village. Cheap rooms can be hard to find during high season, however, so look around before settling somewhere. The rooms at **Petrino** are beautifully furnished with local crafts, have TVs and fireplaces, and can be economical if shared with someone else. (☎41 187. Doubles 16,000-20,000dr/€46.96-58.70). Ask for **Maria Mahalioti** at the store (☎41 263) just below the plateia, and she'll display her selection of homemade sweets, jams, honey, and teas, and maybe even offer a free sample. Enjoy the clean mountain air, the shade of a twisted old tree, and the view of a river gorge at **Antigone** (☎41 395) in the plateia. Its staff serves sandwiches, omelettes, and Greek coffee all day.

PROUSSOS   ☎0237

Though small and easy to miss, Proussos is a picturesque little town, and has some of the most breathtaking views of gorges and mountainside in the Evritania region.

◪ TRANSPORTATION. Getting to **Proussos,** 15km past Megalo Horio, is an adventure in itself; enjoy the roadside scenery and admire the KTEL driver's uncanny ability to maintain control of his vehicle as it swerves alongside steep ravines past intermittent, flimsy guardrails and shrines to drivers killed on the road. From Megalo or Mikro Horio, you'll need to walk back down to the main road or to the tiny hamlet of **Gavros** to catch the Proussos-bound bus from Karpenisi (M and F 1pm; 700dr/€2.05). The village climbs upward from a central plateia, which overlooks the gasp-inducing gorge below.

◪◪ ACCOMMODATIONS AND FOOD. Proussos has no hotels, but like most of the villages in Evritania, has many homes that offer domatia for fairly inexpensive prices; most are on the road through the main village. The plateia in Proussos sports many local tavernas, most of which overlook the gorge and the river below. ▨**Proussiotissa** (☎80 768) has the best location of them all, with balcony tables hanging over the valley and looking out on the monastery and clock tower. The owner cooks up local specialties like roast goat with tomato sauce (1600dr/€4.69).

◪ SIGHTS. Just before reaching the village, a road leads down from the statue of Karaiskakis to the serene ▨**Monastery of the Virgin of Proussiotissa** that clings spectacularly to the cliffside. The monastery's innermost sanctuary is blasted out of the stone itself, and contains a miracle-working icon of the Madonna said to have been painted by St. Luke the Evangelist (see **Have Icon, Will Travel,** p. 180). Dress modestly (long skirt or pants, shoulders covered) to visit the monastery, where a monk will hospitably offer you a piece of *loukoumi*, a Greek jellied candy covered in powdered sugar. In the evenings, monks' chants mingle with the sound of rushing water from the Karpenisiotis River echoing through the ravine. Above, Proussos's clock tower belts out the hour from its precarious hilltop perch. The **Castle of Karaiskakis** is a small stone fortress near the monastery; though it's more of a crumbling tower than a castle, it emanates a mood of mystery. The dark **Black Cave,** allegedly an ancient oracle and a hideout for Greek women and children during the War of Independence, can be found along a trail that begins on the far side of Proussos, near a bridge. Bring a flashlight if you want to make like a spelunker.

LAMIA Λαμια   ☎ 0231

Bustling, rarely touristed Lamia conceals a multifaceted charm beneath a drab appearance. Lamia's four central plateias and tiny, criss-crossing pedestrian streets brim with nonstop energy. Lazy, shaded squares where old men argue for hours give way to streets crammed with slickly dressed teenagers on motorcycles. A key strategic town during the War of Independence (see p. 16), Lamia became the border gateway for the newly independent Greece before the annexation of Thessaly in 1884. A snappy archaeological museum high up within the *kastro* walls, a nighttime scene that never seems to go to bed, and the beautifully tended gardens of Agios Loukas make a brief stop in Lamia worthwhile.

▐▀ TRANSPORTATION

With five intercity bus stations and one local station, Lamia is a singularly inconvenient transportation hub. Directions to the bustling heart of the city depend on where your bus or train pulls in. The local **train station** is on **Kostantinoupoleos**; head east (left as you face the tracks) and turn left on **Satovriandou**, which runs northwest to **Pl. Parkou**, one of the city's four central plateias (the southeast corner of the quadrangle they form). From the **bus station** serving Karpenisi on **Botsari** head east (right facing away from station) half a block to Satovriandou and turn left. If arriving from Athens or Thessaloniki, on **Papakyriazi**, Satovriandou is just to your left as you face away from the station; turn right to the city center. Buses from Delphi pull in on the west side of **Thermopylon** while those from Larisa, Patras, Trikala, or Halkida stop just off Thermopylon on the east side. Walk uphill on Thermopylon, crossing the railroad tracks, until it dead-ends into **Kapodistriou**, where a left brings you to Pl. Parkou. Buses from Volos, Agia Marina, and Raches pull in on **Rozaki Angeli,** just to the east of the city center. Facing away from the station, cross the miniscule triangular park and turn right on Kapodistriou.

Buses: From the largest station (☎ 51 345 or 51 346), south of the town center and left off Satovriandou at Papakiriazi 27, buses run to **Athens** (3hr., every hr. 5am-9pm, 4700dr/€13.80) and **Thessaloniki** (4hr.; 9am, 3:15pm; 6000dr/€17.61). Take the Athens bus and ask to be let off at **Agios Kostantinos** (45min., 1000dr/€2.93) for the nearest ferry hub for the Sporades. The station for buses to **Karpenisi** (2hr., 5 per day 7am-9pm, 1450dr/€4.25) and the Evritania region is at Botsari 3 (☎ 28 955), right off of Satovriandou. At the end of Satovriandou, heading south, is the local station (☎ 51 348) at Konstantinopoulos 2, which runs buses to **Thermopylae** (15min.; 8:30, 9:30, 10am, noon, 3, 4:35pm; 380dr/€1.12), among other small locales. The station for **Delphi** (2hr., 3 per day 10:40am-7pm, 2200dr/€6.45) is at Thermopylon 58 (☎ 35 494); head along Kapodistriou from Pl. Parkou and turn right on Thermopylon. The Thessaly station (☎ 22 802) is a little farther down Thermopylon and to the left at its intersection with Nikopoleos. To: **Halkida** (2½hr.; 12:45, 7:45pm; 3250dr/€9.55); **Larisa** (2hr.; 11:15am, 12, 6:15pm; 2850dr/€8.36); **Patras** (4hr.; 12:30, 7:30pm; 3850dr/€11.30); **Trikala** (2hr., 7 per day 9:45am-7:45pm, 2050dr/€6.02). The Volos station, Rosaki Angeli 69 (☎ 22 627), down Kapodistriou, runs buses to: the beaches of **Agia Marina** (20min.; every 30min. 8am-2:30pm, every hour 3-9pm; 300dr/€0.88, 500dr/€1.47 round-trip); **Raches** (5min., 5 per day 5:45am-8pm, 700dr/€2.05, 1200dr/€3.52 round-trip); and **Volos** (2hr.; Su-F 9am, 3pm, Sa 9am; 2700dr/€7.92).

Local buses: Buses marked "Stavros (Σταυρος)" also make stops at Lionokladi, departing frequently at the corner of Drosopolou and Hatzopolou streets at Pl. Parkou.

Trains: Trains run to **Athens** (2 per day; 6am, 5:25pm) from the town station, Konstantinopoulos 1 (☎ 22 990), across from the local buses. **Lionokladi Station** (☎ 06 161) runs trains to **Thessaloniki** (3¾hr., 8 per day 9:28am-3am, 3150dr/€9.25) and **Athens** (3½hr., 7 per day 10:15am-7:20pm, 2350dr/€6.90). Take the local bus (10min., 13 per day 9:10am-7:10pm, 400dr/€1.17) from the OSE office, Averof 28. Walk down E. Venizelou from the southwest corner of Pl. Parkou to the 3rd right onto Averof.

CENTRAL GREECE

⚔🔲 ORIENTATION AND PRACTICAL INFORMATION

Just inland off the Maliakos Gulf and 160km north of Athens, Lamia's tangle of streets climbs gently into a northwesterly ridge, crowned by the **Castor** in the north. The city sprawls outward from the roughly rectangular arrangement of its four central plateias. Southeastern **Pl. Parkou** is broad, crowded, and swarming with motorcycles and banks. Maps of Lamia are posted at its northern edge. From Pl. Parkou's northeast corner, past the National Bank, **Kolokotroni** leads north to leafy and mellow **Pl. Laou,** shaded by plane trees and filled with *kafeneia* and the Greek men who idle there. West from Pl. Parkou up **Karagiannopolou** is sleepy, spacious **Pl. Diakou.** Head up Riga Feriaou in the northwest corner of Pl. Parkou to reach pulsing **Pl. Eleftherias,** home to Lamia's trendiest nightlife. Pl. Eleftherias connects with Pl. Diakou via **Diakou** on its south side and with Pl. Laou via **Kounoupi** on the east. On the north side of Pl. Eleftherias, Lamia's largest **church** and the **regional prefecture** (town hall) face each other on the corner of **Ipsilandon.** A network of small, pedestrian streets including **Rozaki Angeli** and **Karaiskaki** interlace the four squares and burst with small cafes, shops, and bakeries.

> **Tourist office:** Pl. Laou 3 (☎30 065; fax 30 066), next to the Hotel Neon Astron. The friendly, English-speaking staff can inform you about Lamia and Central Greece and provide you with an excellent map of the city. Open M-F 7am-2:30pm.
>
> **Banks:** Pl. Parkou teems with banks, including the **National Bank** on the corner of Kapodistriou with a 24hr. **ATM.** Open M-Th 8am-2pm, F 8am-1:30pm.
>
> **Police:** (☎22 331), on Patroklou, one street below Pl. Parkou off Satovriandou. Little English spoken. Open 24hr.
>
> **Hospital:** (☎56 100 or 56 200). To the north, outside of the city. Open 24hr.
>
> **OTE:** On the west side of Pl. Eleftherias. Open 24hr.
>
> **Internet Access: Internet Cafe,** Ipsilandon 6 (☎22 133), just north of Pl. Eleftherias. Sip a *frappé* (800dr/€2.35) and surf the net (1000dr/€2.93 per hr.). Open 9am-2am.
>
> **Post office:** (☎23 237; fax 33 727), on Pl. Diakou and offers Post Restante. Open M-F 7:30am-8pm. **Postal Code:** 35100.

🏠 ACCOMMODATIONS

Few tourists or budget travelers see Lamia, so hotels are scarce and expensive. Though near to noisy street traffic, **Hotel Neon Astron** (☎22 246), on Pl. Laou. offers an excellent location, airy rooms with ceiling fans, private baths, and balconies at good rates. (☎22 246. Singles 6000dr/€17.61, with TV 7000dr/€20.53; doubles 8000dr/€23.48.) **Thermopylae Hotel,** Rozaki Angeli 36 two blocks east of Pl. Laou, has 15 rooms that are small but clean and comfortable, including TV, phone, A/C, and private bath. (☎26 393 or 21 366. Singles 8500dr/€24.95; doubles 11,000dr/€32.28.) **Hotel Athena,** Rozaki Angeli 41, has cozy rooms featuring wooden floors, private baths, TV, A/C and balconies. (☎20 700 or 27 700. Singles 8500dr/€24.95; doubles 12,000dr/€35.22; triples 14,000dr/€41.10.)

🍴 FOOD

Lamia is a diner's paradise: virtually every street and side alley is crammed with pizza joints, stands hawking souvlaki and gyros, *ouzerias*, tavernas, pastry shops, and coffee bars. For fresh fruits and veggies, head to the **markets** along Rozaki Angeli and Othonos, both off Pl. Laou. Strolling south from Pl. Laou along pedestrian Karaiskaki. **Ziogas Bakery,** on Kounoupi between Pl. Laou and Pl. Eleftherias, serves a wide variety of savory and delicious pastries and breads for astonishingly low prices. Pick up a mini pizza (200dr/€0.59) and mock those who dine on pricier fare. **Taverna O Gogos,** off Pl. Laou on Aristoteli (the stairs on the north side). This romantic outdoor eatery serves tasty specialties like lamb *exohiko* (lamb, cheese, and potatoes baked in paper, 1700dr/€5; ☎23 501). **Aman Aman,** on Androutsou (the alley to the right on Kounoupi coming from Pl. Laou). Offers tasty *mezedes* (950-2050dr/€2.80-6). "Aman," which means mercy in Turkish, is the opening wail to many of the *rembetika* (see **Bouzouki Punk Rock,** p. 34) that the local intellectual crowd gathers to hear. Open 9am-12:30am.

👁 SIGHTS

KASTRO. The imposing remains of the Kastro fortifications loom eerily over the city in nighttime illumination. Built in the Classical period, it has undergone many renovations under Greece's various rulers, including the Romans, Franks, Catalans, and Ottomans. Before Greece's 1884 annexation of Thessaly and Domokos, Lamia's Kastro served as the core of the country's border defenses. The barracks building, built by King Otto in 1880, was used until World War II. It now serves as a spacious and well-organized **Archaeological Museum** displaying finds from the Neolithic to Roman periods found in tombs outside Lamia. Aside from the standard ceramic figurines and amphoras, highlights include the earliest preserved vase depicting a naval battle, a large engraving showing a pregnant mother's sacrifice to Artemis, and a fearsome collection of rusty weaponry. (*To reach the Kastro, head east out of Pl. Parkou on Kapodistriou and make the 2nd left onto Amalias. Walk up the hill and cross Eklision when Amalias dead-ends to walk up a stone stairpath. Turn right and follow the road at the top of the stairs, with the Kastro on your left.* ☎29 992. *Castle open Tu-Su 8:30am-3pm. Museum Tu-Su 8:30am-2:30pm. 500dr/€1.47, students with ID and under 18 free.*)

GARDENS OF AGIOS LOUKAS. The way to the Gardens of Agios Loukas (atop Agios Loukas hill) begins at the top of Pl. Diakou behind a gloriously posed **Statue of Athanasios Diakos,** his sword broken in battle. A War of Independence hero, he was burned to death in Lamia by the Turks in 1821. Continue up the steps behind Athanasios and you'll arrive in the beautiful shady gardens. It's a steep climb, but lovely panoramic views of the surrounding countryside, cool mountain breezes, stone paths lined with rosebushes, mulberry trees, and benches make the trek rewarding as a hot afternoon respite or a romantic evening rendezvous. On occasional summer evenings, live music fills the gardens.

🎭🎵 NIGHTLIFE AND ENTERTAINMENT

Young people from the Lamia area congregate around Pl. Eleftherias every night, zooming in on motorbikes and crowding around the bars and cheap gyro stands. For those looking to dance, there are plenty of clubs; for a more sedentary night out, check out the similar bars in northeast Pl. Eleftherias. On summer nights, most intrepid partygoers head to the seashore at **Raches** or **Agia Marina** in the countryside. These clubs are best reached by private vehicle—a taxi to the most popular clubs, **Bojo** at Raches, or the club du jour **Hakuna Matata** at Agia Marina will cost 4000-5000dr/€11.74-14.67 until midnight, when the rates double. Slightly closer to Lamia, but still requiring a taxi, are **Vorio, Caramela,** and **Paradise.** The **Municipal Theatre** (☎33 325) on Ipsilandon, past the Internet Cafe, offers a year-long program of plays, music, and movies. Visit their offices in the **movie theater** across the street.

Venezia (☎36 808), on Dikou between Pl. Diakou and Pl. Eleftherias, is *the* place to see and be seen among Lamia's would-be cosmopolitan youth. Put on your tightest garb and make your way through the clutter of motorbikes on the curb. Beer 1000dr/€2.93, drinks 1300dr/€3.82. Open 8am-4am.

Aroma Musicafe (☎36 808), next door to Venezia, vies fiercely with its neighbor for the title of Best in Show. Beer is 1300-1500dr/€3.82-4.40, but if you really want to impress that hot guy/girl at the table next to you, order the Dom Perignon (45,000dr/€132.06)...then try to get him or her to leave with you before your check bounces.

Splendid (☎52 726), on Ipsilandon, off Pl. Eleftherias. This ultra-trendy night spot serves drinks and beer to the hip and hot until 3am.

> ## 🔁 DAYTRIP FROM LAMIA

THERMOPYLAE Θερμοπυλες

*Take the bus from Lamia's local station (15min. 6 per day 8:30am-4:30pm, 380dr/€1.12)
and ask to be let off at the baths (BAN-yo), not the village of Thermopylae. To return, walk
1.5km to the village and catch the bus there.*

More a highway roadstop than a destination in itself, Thermopylae (18km south of
Lamia) is richer in history than anything else. As the gateway to southern Greece,
Thermopylae's strategic location has made it a prime target for invading armies for
thousands of years. **Leonidas** and his army of 300 Spartans fought to their heroic
deaths here in 480 BC, holding back Xerxes' vast Persian army—estimated by
Herodotus to be five million strong. More recently, both the Ottomans and the
Nazis launched fierce attacks at the straits. Sulfurous **hot springs** originate in the
mountains above and attract visitors suffering from many different ailments,
including rheumatism, arthritis, gynecological complaints, and respiratory illnesses. There is both a small swimming pool (750dr/€2.20) and numerous private
bathtubs (800dr/€2.35) that are filled with the 42-44°C waters. (Open daily 6am-
1:30pm.) Legend holds that the healing power of Thermopylae's waters once
helped Hercules regain his strength.

From the hot springs parking lot, walk down the dirt path lined with eucalyptus
and oleanders, swarming with pale yellow butterflies in summer. Continue
through a highway underpass and follow the path, turning right on a paved road
that crosses the stream of spring water. The road leads to a highway rest stop consisting of a **plaque** commemorating the battles in Greece and Crete during World
War II, the **Monument to the Thespians** and the **Statue of Leonidas.** The defiant
inscription on the statue reads "Molon Labe" ("Come and get it"). Across the highway from the statue is the **Archaeological Site,** where you can scramble around a
network of trails, see the ruins of a Classical-era wall, and catch the view from
craggy outlook points. Just beyond the Leonidas monument a dirt road runs
between an olive grove and the highway to Thermopylae village, consisting of a
deserted square with a bone-dry fountain and some crumbling benches. Flag down
one of the frequent buses to **Lamia** (380dr/€1.12) here at the rusty **bus stop.**

AGIOS KONSTANTINOS Αγιος
Κωνσταντινος   ☎0235

Agios Kostantinos is located at the meeting point of the mountainous mainland
and the Aegean. As the closest port to Athens with ferries to the Sporades, it
serves as a gateway for foreigners and Greeks alike taking to the sea. The rare visitor who resists the Sporades's siren song (or misses the ferry) and spends a night
in Agios Kostantinos has little to regret, however. From its cafe-lined plateia to the
tile-roofed Church of Agios Kostantinos, this small town's charms are open to all.

🔁 **PRACTICAL INFORMATION.** Arriving by ferry, the **bus station** (☎32 223) is
about 150m to the left along the waterfront. **Buses** go to: Athens (2½hr., every
hr. 5:45am-4:45pm and 6:15-9:30pm, 3350dr/€9.83); Lamia (45min., every hr.
8:30am-7:30pm and 8:45-11:45pm, 1000dr/€2.93); and Thessaloniki (5hr.;
7:15am, 2:15, 5:30pm; 7100dr/€20.85). The pier, immediately seaward of the
plateia, serves both **ferries** and Flying Dolphins (☎31 874). Buy your tickets at
the right side of the plateia (facing inland). One to three ferries (prices and
schedules vary depending on the season) leave daily for: Alonnisos (5½hr.,
4500-4600dr/€13.21-13.50); Skiathos (3½hr., 3400-3500dr/€10-10.30); and Skopelos (4½hr., 4200-4300dr/€12.33-12.62). One to five **Flying Dolphins** go daily to:
Alonnisos (2¾hr., 9000-9100dr/€26.41-26.70); Skiathos (1½hr., 6800-6900dr/
€20-20.25); and Skopelos (2½hr., 8500-8600dr/€24.95-25.25). Check departure

times posted outside of the ticket offices or call ahead (☎32 444 or 32 445; fax 32 234). **Taxis** line up on the opposite side of the church from the water (☎31 850). The port police (☎31 920), along the harbor, can help with ferry schedules. Facing seaward from the plateia a right-hand turn toward the bus station takes you past the National Bank, with a 24hr. **ATM.** (Open M-Th 8am-2pm, F 8am-1:30pm.) A left turn from the plateia takes you past the **OTE** (open M-F 8am-3:10pm) and a sign for the **post office,** 20m inland on a street just parallel to the park. (Open M-F 7:30am-2pm.) **Postal code:** 35006.

▮▊ ACCOMMODATIONS AND FOOD. Accommodations in Agios Kostantinos are somewhat limited. The first in the strip of hotels along the water to the right of the plateia (facing inland), **Hotel Olga** is both classy and reasonably priced. Rooms have A/C, phones, TVs, and views from private balconies. (☎32 266. Singles 5000-5500dr/€14.67-16.15; doubles 7500-8500dr/€22-24.95; triples 9000-10,000dr/€26.41-29.35.) In the center of town, **Hotel Poulia,** on Thermopylon to the right of the plateia facing inland, features small rooms with varying levels of amenities, from spartan singles to the works: TV, A/C, and private bath. (☎31 663. Singles 5000-6500dr/€14.67-19.10; doubles 7000-10,500dr/€20.53-30.80; triples 12,000dr/€35.22.) You can devour toothsome souvlaki (300-600dr/€0.88-1.76), play backgammon, and do some quality people-watching just past the main plateia. In the morning, warm bread and pastries from **Artopolia,** next door to Hotel Poulia, make painful early-morning ferries less heinous. (100-400dr/€0.29-1.17.)

THESSALY Θεσσαλια

Thessaly oscillates between the mundane and the ethereal. The region is the earthly anchor to the transcendent Meteora monasteries; at the same time, it harbors some of Greece's drabber cities. Medea supposedly dropped her witch's potions in Thessaly after returning here with Jason from Colchis and the legend won the region a reputation for sorcery and magical plants in ancient times. Thessaly's plains were once home to farmers who tended sheep and goats in summer before returning home to fish from the waters of the Pinios River. Though traditional farming has given way to modern methods, you can still buy a field guide and gather herbs off the mountain slopes or buy them in the villages. In these out-of-the-way places to the north of Karpenisi and in the green Pelion Peninsula, you'll find little English and much genuine hospitality, folk songs, and reverence for all things *hiropitios* (hand-made; literally, "poetry of the hands").

VOLOS Βολος ☎0421

Volos looms large in two of ancient Greece's best-loved myths. **Jason and the Argonauts** set sail from Volos on their quest for the Golden Fleece, a fact the city won't let its visitors forget. Two important streets and half a dozen hotels name themselves after the Argonauts' voyage. Volos was also the site of the marriage of the sea nymph Thetis to King Peleus, a wedding that would have cataclysmic repercussions (see **Who is the fairest of them all?** p. 190). A century ago, Volos was a quiet hamlet on the Pagasitic Gulf. But after the 1922 population exchange (see p. 17), ethnic Greek refugees from Turkey invigorated the port town with their love for carousing: Volos quickly became famous for the *ouzeria* that popped up all over town. Volos is a fast-growing industrial center and transportation hub, but as the visitor takes the short waterfront walk eastward from the bus station toward the beach, the cranes and oil tankers quickly become a memory. Two of the four main roads running parallel through the city are pedestrian avenues. Come nightfall, strolling couples fill the harborside, fruit vendors hawk their sweet produce, and dozens of cafes and seafood restaurants spread tables up to the water.

⌐ TRANSPORTATION

Ferries: To: **Alonnisos** (5hr., 1-2 per day, 3900dr/€11.45); **Glossa** (3hr., 2 per day, 3300dr/€9.68); **Skiathos** (3hr., 2-3 per day 2900dr/€8.51); **Skopleos** (4½hr., 2-3 per day, 3500dr/€10.27). Ferry schedules are irregular, but all destinations generally have a morning ferry between 8 and 9am and an evening ferry between 7 and 8pm. Ferries for the smaller islands of **Tinos, Paros, Santorini,** and **Iraklion** are also available, but are less frequent. Several waterfront agencies sell tickets; **Falcon Tours** (☎21 626 or 25 688), which also sells Flying Dolphin tickets, is by the docks.

Flying Dolphins: Daily to: **Alonnisos** (2¾hr., 4-7 per day, 7700dr/€22.58); **Glossa** (1¾hr., 4 per day, 6500dr/€19.08); **Skiathos** (1½hr., 4-6 per day, 5800dr/€17.02); **Skopelos** (2½hr., 5-6 per day, 7100dr/€20.82). Tickets available at any of the ticket agencies near the ferry pier.

Buses: The **bus station** (☎33 254 or 25 527), is in the Old Town, all the way at the end of Lambraki. To: **Athens** (4½hr., 10 per day 6am-10pm, 5800dr/€17.02); **Kalambaka** (3hr., 4 per day 6:30am-7pm, 3350dr/€9.83); **Larisa** (1hr., 12 per day 6am-9pm, 1200dr/€3.52); **Thessaloniki** (3hr., 6 per day 6:15am-7:30pm, 3700dr/€10.85). For service to **Trikala,** take the 1pm bus to Kalambaka. Buses to Mt. Pelion Peninsula run to: **Makrynitsa** and **Portaria** (45min., M-F 9 per day 6:15am-8:45pm, 320dr/€1.94); **Milies** (1hr., 6 per day 5:45am-6pm, 450dr/€1.32); **Tsagarada** (2hr., 3 per day 5:15am-1:30pm, 1100dr/€3.22); and other destinations. Inquire at the bus station or tourist office; most villages have daily service and can be reached in less than 3hr. Service is reduced on weekends and in winter.

Trains: The **station** (☎24 056 or 28 555) is 1 block west of the tourist office. From town, turn right at the first street past the tourist office. Walk 2-3min. down the road parallel to the track. To: **Athens** (5hr., 8 per day 5:45am-9pm, 3250dr/€9.53); **Thessaloniki** (3hr., 8 per day 5:45am-9:10pm, 2300dr/€6.75); **Larisa** (1hr., 13 per day 5:45am-9:10pm, 700dr/€2.05).

Car Rental: Avis, Argonafton 41 (☎20 849; fax 22 849), rents mopeds from 6000dr/€17.61 per day and cars from 18,000dr/€52.83 per day. **European Car Rental,** Iasonos 83 (☎36 238; fax 24 192). Rentals from 16,000dr/€46.96 per day.

◢☑ ORIENTATION AND PRACTICAL INFORMATION

Volos's **bus station** lies west of town on **Lambraki,** an easy 15min. walk from the city and the waterfront. This main road, which leads from the bus station to town, runs past the train station, **Riga Fariou Park,** and the tourist office, in that order. Lambraki splits at a fountain to become **Dimitriados** on the left and **Iasonos** on the right; both run parallel to **Argonafton** on the waterfront. The intersecting roads leading away from the harbor are lined with various hotels and other services like banks, pharmacies, and the post office. A walk along the waterfront, about 10min. from the ferry docks past a long park, brings you to the large **Church of Agios Konstantinos,** easily visible jutting out into the harbor. Here, Argonafton and Dimitriados join to become **Nik. Plastira,** which leads to the hospital, the archaeological museum, and various restaurants before ending at the **beach. Ermou,** the next street inland after Dimitriados and running parallel through the city, is a pedestrian street lined with shops selling women's clothes, shoes, and the occasional icon. Ermou leads to an open plateia containing the **Church of Agios Nikolaos.**

Tourist Office: (☎23 500 or 37 417), on Lambraki next to the town hall in Pl. Riga Fariou, in a small stone building with an orange roof. Ask for information about Volos and the Pelion Peninsula. Maps of the villages available. Open M-F 7am-2:30pm.

Banks: All major banks, including **National Bank** (☎23 382), **Agricultural Bank** (☎23 411 or 54 030), and **Bank of Greece** (☎23 442) on Iasonos. Most offer **currency**

exchange (M-Th 8am-2pm, F 8am-1:30pm) and **ATMs.** There's also a **Citibank** on the corner of Argonafton and El. Venizelou with a 24hr. **ATM.**

Police: (☎72 412). Open 24hr.

Tourist Police: 28 Octovriou 179 (☎72 421). Locals still call the street by its former name, "Alexandras." Open daily 7am-11pm.

Hospital: ☎30 126, next to the museum on the eastern waterfront. Open 24hr.

Telephone: OTE, on the corner of El. Venizelou and Sokratous, across from the fruit market. Open 24hr.

Internet Access: Diavlos Info Cafe, Topali 14 (☎25 363), off Dimitriados, offers access for 500dr/€1.47 per hour. 6 terminals and backgammon. Open daily 10am-2pm and 6-10pm. **Magic Cafe,** Argonafton 56 (☎20 992), in a loud arcade, has 9 terminals and 2 printers operated by 100dr coins. 100dr/€0.29 per 5min., 1000dr/€2.93 per hr.

Post Office: P. Melo 63, off 28 Octovriou away from the water. Open M-F 7am-8pm. Poste Restante available. **Postal code:** 38001.

ACCOMMODATIONS

Volos' hotels vary little in size, location, appeal, or amenities, and almost all are quite expensive for the financially constrained traveler. Most of the cheaper options cater to island-bound travelers and are clustered along the waterfront or on the small streets that lead away from the noisy harbor. Wave a student ID in the air and ask for a simple room *(aplo domatio)* for a small discount.

Hotel Jason, P. Melo 1 (☎26 075; fax 26 975), easy to find on the waterfront, across from the ferry dock. Most of the gleaming, scrubbed-white rooms are filled with light and have balconies overlooking the waterfront. Noisy at times. All have phones, baths, and TVs. Singles 7000dr/€20.53; doubles 10,000dr/€29.35; triples 13,000dr/€38.15.

Hotel Roussa, Iatrou Tzanou 1 (☎21 732; fax 22 987), on the corner of Plastira and Iatrou Tzanou, midway between Church of Agios Konstantinos and the beach. Look for the purple balconies. In a quieter area of town, these white rooms with neat blue trim have tiny baths, phone, A/C, and TV. Singles 7500dr/€22; doubles 9500dr/€27.88.

Hotel Santi, Topali 13, off Argonafton. These rooms, 2 blocks up from the ferry docks, are clean and bright; don't let the drab lobby fool you. Pleasant bathrooms, phones, and lots of noise from the harbor. Singles 9000dr/€26.41; doubles 18,000dr/€52.83.

FOOD

A **supermarket** on Iasonos, one block up from the ferry dock, and a **farmer's market** along Lambraki, on the way to the bus station, can provide provisions for a seaside picnic. The plentiful *ouzeria* and *tsipouradika* along Volos's waterfront are the town's saving grace. They specialize in fresh seafood and *spetsofai* (spicy sausages), and are packed with locals in the mid-afternoon.

Klasico (☎32 891), on Argonafton by the ferry docks, specializes in seafood but serves everything from fried octopus to goat soup, including a squid stuffed with cheese. Pricey but worth it. Entrees 1500-5000dr/€4.40-14.67.

Enidrio (☎27 765), on the eastern waterfront a few hundred meters west of the beach. One of the most consistently popular restaurants in the city, with tables literally 2 paces from the water, depending on your stride. Enidrio, which translates to the aquarium, specializes in seafood. Entrees 1500-2200dr/€4.40-6.46. Open until 1am.

Rotonda, Plastira 15 (☎34 973), past the Church of Agios Konstantinos on the eastern edge of town near Hotel Roussas. Specializing in fresh fish, served whole, Rotonda offers delicious calamari *psito* and swordfish souvlaki. Walk into the kitchen to pick your critter, which they'll grill up fresh. Entrees 2000-3000dr/€5.87-8.80.

ⓢ SIGHTS

The ▧**Archaeological Museum,** Athonassaki 1, a 20min. walk along the water from the ferry docks, houses tidbits from the later Paleolithic era through the Roman period in a lovely Neoclassical mansion. Check out the painted grave *steles* from ancient Demetrias in Room 4 and the rather morbid reconstructed tombs in Room 6. The panoply of miniature Neolithic objects in Room 3 includes collections of figurines, seals, spindle wheels, bits of jewelry, carbonized seeds, and small tools of bone and stone. (☎25 285. Open Tu-Su 8:30am-3pm. 600dr/€1.76, students 400dr/€1.17.) Inquire here to pick up English pamphlets with information on the nearby archaeological sites at **Dimini** and **Sesklo.** Sesklo is the oldest known settlement in Thessaly, with the oldest acropolis in Greece; the sites represent two of the oldest sites in the region: Dimini dates from 4000 BC, and Sesklo from 6500 BC. The **Art Center of Giorgio de Chirico,** Metamorphoseos 3, around the corner from Hotel Ialkos, showcases Greek landscape painting, accompanied by the racket of violins from the music school next door. The center features a collection of monotypes, lithographs, and copper prints reaching back to the Ottomans. The works of adopted Italian native and surrealist Giorgio de Chirico are upstairs, in a special collection only accessible in the morning. (☎31 701. Open Tu-Su 10am-1pm. Free.) The **Kitsos Makris Museum,** in Kitsos's own home at Afendoli 50 (a.k.a. Kitsos Makris 50), includes works by *laiki* (folk) painters **Theophilos** (see p. 24) and **Christopoulos,** as well as Byzantine icons, pottery, and wood carvings. (☎37 119. Open M-F 8:30am-2pm, Su 10am-2pm. Free.)

ⓒ ♫ NIGHTLIFE AND ENTERTAINMENT

The waterfront turns into a hive of activity at night, with cafes spilling revelers into the streets. In the quiet morning or afternoon, you'll wonder how the thousands of tables that stretch for half a kilometer down the waterfront ever get filled up. After 8pm it happens. Very quickly. The young crowd congregates at **Cafe Memory** and **Cafe Magic,** side by side on Argonafton, chatting over the loud music and pings of arcade games. A few doors down, **Lirikon** is a little more mellow; the focus here is sports on the two big screen TVs. By the museum and the beach, east-side bars thump with pounding disco beats and more tight black pants than you can shake your booty at. **Ammos** and **Yiousouri,** side by side on the beachfront across from Rotonda, alternate between pulsing house and disco's greatest misses. (Beers 800dr/€2.35, drinks 1500-2500dr/€4.40-7.34. Open nightly until 6am.) Some weekend nightspots in Volos, including **Psigeia,** are near the bus station. In late July and August, Volos hosts a **festival** in Riga Feriou Park with concerts and theater.

WHO IS THE FAIREST OF THEM ALL? Everyone has heard of the Trojan War, with its horses and subsequent odyssey. But more obscure is the knowledge that the whole 10 year conflict began on Mt. Pelion with a social *faux pas*. When King Peleus married Thetis, the sea nymph and future mother of Achilles, he invited all the gods and goddesses to the wedding—except for **Eris,** goddess of strife. Eris was infuriated by the snub, and responded by crashing the party and rolling the golden apple of discord across the floor. The apple was labeled "For the Fairest." Hera, Athena, and Aphrodite soon scared off other competitors for the title. These three babes demanded that a Trojan prince ignorant of his birth, Paris, judge the contest. Each goddess tried to bribe him: white-armed Hera offered him rule of the whole world, bright-eyed Athena promised him all-surpassing wisdom, and governess of love Aphrodite offered him the love of the most beautiful woman in the world. (Inconveniently, this woman, Helen, was already married to the Spartan king Menelaus.) Like any self-respecting red-blooded adolescent, Paris chose Aphrodite and Helen's love. The Trojan War followed, ending in Paris' death, the fall of Troy, and Helen's return to Sparta. Hormones in an uproar have never caused a bigger disaster.

MOUNT PELION PENINSULA Ορος Πηλιο

Way back before propriety, rowdy centaurs—half-men, half-horses with enormous sex drives—called the Pelion Peninsula (named for King Peleus) home. Here they had their way with whatever hot, young nymphette they could find. Chiron, a healer and tutor to Achilles, settled in Pelion despite its frat-house atmosphere; its abundant supply of over 1700 medicinal herbs lured him to the region. This plant variety stems from the peninsula's cool, moist climate, appreciated today by tourists tired of the scorching sun. Over the years, the mountains of Pelion have protected the area from invasion. While the rest of Greece groaned under Ottoman rule, the peninsula was a virtually autonomous center of Greek nationalism.

MAKRYNITSA Μακρυνιτσα   ☎0428

In Makrynitsa, one of Pelion's most beautiful villages, a wide flagstoned path bends around well preserved *archondika* (mansions) to one stunning lookout point after another. Thanks to its designation by the European Community as a protected traditional settlement, the town's roads are closed to cars. While this may bring peace and quiet within the town, the outskirts are left in traffic and tour bus gridlock. On the plateia, five immense, age-old trees form a dome of green overhead, keeping the square in perpetual shade. Nicknamed "the balcony of Pelion," the town overlooks the Pagasitic Gulf like a box seat in a giant opera house. At nightfall, the valley fills with deep indigo, broken only by the shimmer of city lights from Volos far below.

◪◪ ORIENTATION AND PRACTICAL INFORMATION. Makrynitsa is accessible by daily buses from **Volos** (45min., 9 per day 6:15am-8:45pm), which twist their way up the mountainside and through the neighboring village of **Portaria.** From the bus turn-around, take a short walk up the hill to the town parking lot, where a low road (17 Martiou) and a high road lead to the plateia. The low road passes various shops purveying both tourist kitsch and local medicinal and kitchen herbs. The high road begins with a steep flight of stone steps and runs past the village **clock tower** and the **Kimisi Theotokou church.** In Portaria one can catch buses to other Pelion destinations, including the beaches at **Agia Iannis** and **Milopotamos.** A **tourist information booth** (☎90 150), on the side of the road leading to the village just after the bus stop, offers helpful maps and advice on touring the area. A **mailbox** and **payphones** are readily available in the plateia. 24hr. **ATMs** and a **post office** can also be found in Portaria, a 20min. walk from the parking lot along the mountain road.

◪◪ ACCOMMODATIONS AND FOOD. Since Makrynitsa has been designated a traditional settlement, staying here will cost an arm and a leg. The financially constrained should stay in Volos and save by making Makrynitsa a daytrip, or stay in the neighboring town of Portaria, where loads of homes offer domatia that won't clean out your wallet. **Domatia Monousou** is in the first alley on the right a few steps past the plateia. Owned by a warm older couple, the rooms here are large and tastefully furnished with antique desks and chairs and handcrafted decorations. (Sitting room and small kitchen available. ☎99 340. Doubles 12,000dr/ €35.22.) On the north side of Portaria's plateia, two adjacent accommodations, **Hotel Pelia** (☎99 290; singles 10,000dr/€29.35; doubles 13,000dr/€38.15) and **Hotel Filoxenia** (☎99 160; singles 12,000dr/€35.22; doubles 15,000dr/€44.02), offer moderate to inexpensive rooms perched atop the immense flower-filled patio below. Both hotels have TVs, bathrooms, and include breakfast.

In Makrynitsa, a number of small restaurants offer outdoor dining and spectacular views from elevated verandas. Most notable is **Galini,** which overlooks the plateia from the north end, next to the large fountain. (☎99 256. Open 9am-5pm.) Here sentimental Greek tunes inundate the ears while patrons feast on *spetsofai* (spicy sausage) and rabbit stew. Across the way, **Pantheon** (☎99 143) monopolizes the spectacular view of the Pagasitic Gulf. Tables for two against the railing provide a romantic setting to sip a *frappé* and waste an afternoon. For dinner, the *moshari* or *kokopoulo kokkonisto* (braised veal or chicken) is delicious.

⑤ SIGHTS. Makrynitsa's **Museum of Folk Art and the History of Pelion** lies down a path that begins to the left of the church in the plateia. Follow the signs about 75m down the windy path. The curator conducts tours of the authentic clothes, scabbards, and folk art. Housed in a converted 1844 mansion with a gorgeous view down the mountainside, the museum highlights old *tsipouro* stills, a collection of 16th- and 17th-century Bibles, and paintings by **Christopoulos,** all of which depict ships, gorgons, and sundry sea-related subjects. (☎99 505. Open Tu-Su 10am-2pm and 6-10pm. 500dr/€1.47.) In the plateia, cafe **O Theophilos** contains a somewhat dim wall mural painted by folk artist Theophilos himself (see p. 24). Remarkable **churches** include the one-room **Church of Agios Yiannis the Baptist** in the main plateia and the peaceful, still-functional church of **Kimisi Theotokou,** which once housed the *krifto skolio*, a secret school that taught the forbidden Greek language during the Ottoman era. The town's churches remain open at the whim of their caretakers; early to mid-morning and evenings are your most likely opportunities for a visit. From the main parking lot, the narrow road leads steeply uphill to the **Monastery of Agios Gerasimou** (a 20min. walk). The view alone is worth the trip up. The last three churches require modest dress (long skirts for women, pants for men, no bare shoulders). Sneak a peek at the town's old houses—stained glass lanterns, false painted windows, and symbols to ward off evil spirits festoon outer walls.

LARISA Λαρισα ☎041

Seemingly uninterested in tourists, Larisa is nonetheless a pleasant place to get stranded while traveling around Central Greece. The town invites you to stroll through the elegant, tree-lined central plateias and their pedestrian sidestreets to find chic cafes and bars. Window shop at alarmingly trendy boutiques, explore the partially excavated ancient theater, or dance the transit-hub blues away at one of the packed discos outside of town. Bearing the dubious distinction of being Greece's hottest city (temperature-wise), Larisa is a ghost town on steamy summer Sundays when folks head east to the beach; on these days you can hear backgammon pieces shuffle in the *kafeneia* as you walk down the empty sidewalks.

⌐ TRANSPORTATION

Buses: (☎537 777). The main **station** is 150m north of Pl. Laou at Olympou and Georgiadou. Buses to: **Athens** (4¼hr., 6 per day 7am-midnight, 6600dr/€19.37); **Thessaloniki** (2hr.; 13 per day 6am-7:30pm, fewer Sa-Su; 3400dr/€10); **Volos** (1hr.; 12 per day M-F 6am-9pm, Sa-Su 7am-9pm; 1200dr/€3.52); **Kastoria** (4hr., 3 per day 7am-1pm, 4200dr/€12.33); **Ioannina** (4hr., 2 per day 9:30am and 3pm, 3900dr/€11.45). 2 counters at either end of the terminal sell tickets for different destinations. Buses for **Trikala** (1hr., 20 per day 5:45am-8:30pm, 1300dr/€3.82) and **Karditsa** (4hr., 11 per day 6am-8:15pm, 1350dr/€4) leave from a second station on Iroön Polytechniou (☎537 777); to get there, head south on Olympou to Plateia Laou, where Panagouli begins. Continue south on Panagouli and turn right at the 5-way intersection. Walk 600m to the gas station/bus stop on your left.

Trains: (☎236 250), at the end of Paleologou: head south on Panagouli and make a soft left (*not* sharp left) onto Paleologou at the 5-way intersection. The station is on the south side of the small park. **Intercity** express trains run to: **Athens** (4hr., 7 per day 7:45am-7:45pm, 6400dr/€18.80); **Thessaloniki** (2hr., 4 per day noon-10pm, 3500dr/€10.27); **Volos** (45min., 2 per day 8am and 3pm, 1820dr/€5.35). Regular (*aplo*) service to: **Athens** (5hr., 4 per day 10:15am-12:45am, 3000dr/€8.80); **Thessaloniki** (2½hr., 6 per day 4:45pm-11:15pm, 1700dr/€5); **Volos** (1hr., 11 per day 6:30am-10pm, 700dr/€2.05).

✦🛈 ORIENTATION AND PRACTICAL INFORMATION

Surrounded by miles of fertile corn and wheat fields, Larisa is directly southeast of the **Pinios River,** in the middle of Eastern Thessaly. The bus station in the north and the train station in the south mark the boundaries of the city's main commercial district, which is laid out in a grid. From the bus station, **Olympou** heads south to **Pl. Laou,** one of Larisa's three main plateias. **A. Panagouli** begins here and heads to the bottom of the city where it crosses **Iroön Polytechniou** at a 5-way intersection. On the way, Panagouli marks the eastern border of **Pl. Ethnarhou Makariou** (a.k.a. Pl. Tahydromiou, "post office plateia"), which is the town's *kentro,* or center. The north edge of this plateia is formed by **Papakyriazi,** which can be taken west 3 blocks to **Papanastasiou.** From here, Papanastasiou runs north to **Pl. Mikhali Sapka,** and south past the post office and tourist office.

Tourist Office, Koumoundourou 18 (☎250 919), off Papanastasiou, 2 blocks south of Papakyriazi. Friendly staff doles out city maps, pamphlets on Larisa, and advice in broken English. Open M-Sa 7am-2:30pm.

Banks: There is a 24hr. **Commercial Bank ATM** at the train station. Banks with 24hr. **ATMs** can be found all along Pl. Tahydromiou and Iroön Polytechniou.

Police: (☎683 137), on Papanastasiou, seven blocks south of Papakryiazi.

Hospital: (☎230 049), on Georgiadou, east of the main bus station. Open 24hr.

Internet Access: Planet Cafe, Skarlatou Soutsou 20 (☎252 300), founded in 1996, was Greece's first cybercafe. To find it, walk along Papakyriazi to the west (right when facing Pl. Tahydromiou) about 5 blocks until you reach A. Gazi; the cafe is in the white building on your left. Use one of its 9 high-tech terminals in the cool, quiet cafe (1000dr/€2.93 per hr.). Open M-Sa 10am-2:30am, Su 6pm-2:30am. **Arcade parlors** along pedestrian Roozvelt, running south off Pl. Tahydromiou, also offer Internet access.

Telephones: OTE (☎995 341 or 995 342), on Filellinion. Take Papanastasiou north and turn right on Kyprou. The OTE is down the 1st block on the left. Open M-F 7:30am-9pm.

Post Office (☎532 312), on the corner of Papanastasiou and Diakou, a block north of the tourist office. Open M-F 7:30am-8pm. Poste Restante service and currency exchange provided. **Postal code:** 41001.

🏠 ACCOMMODATIONS

The scarcity of hotels here highlights Larisa's indifference toward tourism. Midrange to upper-level hotels can be found among the side streets that connect the 3 main plateias. The cheapest options are near the train station and not too far from the Trikala bus, but they're a 1.5km hike south from the main bus station.

Hotel Pantheon, on Paleologou near the train station, sits atop a small taverna. Its cheap, serviceable rooms have TVs and phones—ask for one with a balcony. (☎234 810 or 236 726. Singles 6000dr/€17.61, with bath 7000dr/€20.53; doubles 9000dr/€26.41.) **Hotel Neon,** is 5 doors down from Pantheon. This hotel has only 7 small rooms, each sparsely furnished with beds and a sink. The cheery pink wallpapered rooms, however, are peaceful and spotless. (All rooms 5000dr/€14.67.)

🍴 FOOD AND CAFES

Most of Larisa's cafes, bars, and tavernas are centered around Pl. Tahydromiou and its adjacent pedestrian streets, where eating establishments blend into one never-ending series of chairs, tables, and blaring TVs. Dissatisfied *frappé* and Nescafe drinkers who yearn for the fresh-ground, hardcore stuff will find sweet fulfillment at various *kafekopteia* (coffee sellers), including one just north of Pl. Laou on the corner of Olympou, and a very good one on Skarlatou Soutsou, which runs northeast from Planet Cafe. Overpoweringly rich aromas pervade these old-fashioned stores, which also sell imported foodstuffs, candies, nuts, dried fruit, and herbs. If you prefer your groceries in neat straight aisles, head to the southern end of Panagouli, where you'll find a large **supermarket.**

Restaurants in Larisa are surprisingly rare, but tempting scents will entice you toward the *psistaria* grills on Panos, north of Kyprou one block east of the OTE, where whole chickens and bits of lamb slowly turn on spits in the window of each restaurant. On the south side of the plateia, **To Sidrivani** (☎535 933 or 531 400) offers old favorites like *pastitsio* and *moschari* for reasonable prices (entrees 1000-1800dr/€2.93-5.28). Vegetarians will enjoy the rice-stuffed tomatoes, green peppers, and palate-pleasing string beans. On the opposite side of the plateia, you can find an excellent *moussaka* and other Greek classics (and the occasional free glass of ouzo) at the quieter **Ta Dio Fengaria** ("The Two Moons"), on Asklipiou, which runs north-south from the center of Pl. Tahydromiou. The main roads of Larisa are teeming with very good *zaccharoplasteia.*

◉ SIGHTS

Larisa's **ancient theater,** fenced off in the northwest corner of town at the end of Papanastasiou, is currently being excavated and rebuilt. Just to the north are the unspectacular remains of the ancient **acropolis** (completely overgrown with weeds), the **Temple to Pallas Athena,** and the **frourio,** the city's former fortress. A slightly upscale restaurant bearing the same name now occupies the *frourio*, circling the still-standing Ottoman **Bedesten** (covered marketplace), built in the 15th-century by leader Türhanoğlu Omar Bey. Farther northeast are the **Pinios River** (a mere trickle in summer) and shady **Alcazar Park,** without a doubt the most serene spot in the city. Even the graffiti here is a bit more decorative. Modern art museum **Pinakothiki,** at Roozvelt 59, has one of the better 20th-century art collections in Greece. (☎621 205. Open W-Su 9am-1pm and 6-8pm. 100dr/€0.29.) The **Museum of Folk Art,** Mandilara 74, features rotating temporary exhibits and a permanent collection of men's and women's traditional dress, a setup of the precursor to the farmhouse kitchen, and a selection of 19th-century weapons. The exhibit captions are in both Greek and English. (☎287 516 or 287 493. Open Su-F 10am-2pm. Free.)

◉ NIGHTLIFE

For after-dinner entertainment, the lively bars of Larisa will not disappoint; hip joints like **Cafe del Mar** (☎252 464) and **Ermes** (☎621 022), on the corner of Roozvelt and Mandilara, blare until 3am. After drinks, check out some of Larisa's dynamic discos. **Club Hoya** (☎288 845), a 1000dr/€2.93 taxi ride from downtown, is an enormous open-air nightclub boasting a row of towering fountains, ten bars, and a mini club-within-a-club called **Planet Babe.** The crowd usually starts to arrive around 1am, but the top-of-the-table exhibitionism doesn't start until at least 4am. A 1500dr/€4.40 taxi ride in the other direction brings you to **Baby Boom,** Larisa's most popular club, on the outskirts of town. Packed crowds gyrate nightly to American and Greek favorites under the enormous Thessalian night sky. Nearby, about 500m toward town, is ultra-chic **Blaze,** open weekends only. All clubs have a 2000dr/€5.87 cover, which includes one drink.

TRIKALA Τρικαλα ☎0431

Greeks may snicker to hear you've vacationed in Trikala; many consider it a provincial replica of Larisa. Trikala, however, is much more pleasant than either Larisa or Volos, and is wonderful for walking. The lazy Letheos River, named for the ancient Underworld's river of forgetfulness, carves Trikala in half; acacias, chestnuts, plane trees, and pedestrian-friendly footbridges lend the town aesthetic appeal. The striking remains of a mosque designed by Ottoman-era master architect Sinan, breezy views from the *frourio* (fortress), the labyrinthine old quarter, and the Folk Art Museum will keep you from twiddling your thumbs at the bus station. At night, young people fill the streets, strolling the broad pedestrian arcades and dancing the night away in packed clubs outside town. Devotees of Asclepius, the god of healing who was born in Trikala (then known as Trikkis), can make a pilgrimage to his all-but-decimated sanctuary. According to ancient belief, a nap in the sanctuary (or maybe in a nearby hotel room?) brings a nocturnal dream-visit from Asclepius himself, who reveals the cure for whatever ails you.

▮✴▮ ORIENTATION AND PRACTICAL INFORMATION

Trikala lies 70km west of Larisa. The curvaceous Letheos River bisects the town roughly northwest to southeast: the two main plateias lie directly across the river from each other, **Pl. Riga Feriou** in the south and the rectangular **Pl. Iroön Polytechniou** in the north. The latter is home to a charming statue of a boy perpetually relieving himself into a small pond. The bus station is on **Othonos,** on the south bank of the river, to the east of Pl. Riga Feriou. **Asklipiou,** Trikala's main road, runs south from Pl. Riga Feriou, where it begins as a broad pedestrian arcade designed for glamorous strutting and coy ogling. It turns into a regular car-laden street after Kapodistriou, on its way to the train station south of town. **Vyronos** and **Garivaldi** cut diagonally across Asklipiou in succession. On the north bank, **Sarafi** leads west out of Pl. Iroön Polytechniou to **Varousi,** the old Turkish quarter, and the remains of the fortress in the northwest.

Buses: On the river's south bank, the **bus station** (☎ 73 130) is at the corner of **Othonos** and **Garivaldi** streets, about 150m east of Pl. Riga Feriou. Buses depart for: **Athens** (4½hr., 7 per day 7am-8:30pm, 5900dr/€17.30); **Ioannina** (3½hr., 2 per day 8:30am-3pm, 3050dr/€8.95); **Kalambaka** (30min., 20 per day 5:15am-9pm, 450dr/ €1.32); **Larisa** (1¼hr., 21 per day 5:45am-8:30pm, 1300dr/€3.82); **Pyli** (30min., 13 per day 5:45am-9pm, 400dr/€1.17); **Thessaloniki** (3¼hr., 6 per day 7:30am-8pm, 3950dr/€11.60); **Volos** (2½hr., 4 per day 7am-7pm, 2900dr/€8.50).

Trains: The **train station** (☎ 27 214) is located at the far southern end of Asklepiou, about 700m south of Pl. Riga Feriou. The small station was recently renovated and has a modern ticket counter and electronic departure boards. Trains leave daily for: **Athens** (7:20am, 6400dr/€18.80); **Kalambaka** (5 per day 6:30am-8:20pm, 350dr/€1.05); **Larisa** (2 per day 9:45am-9pm, 1100dr/€3.25)

Police: The **station** (☎ 27 303) is about 500m from the town center on the corner of Iannitson and Farmaki.

Banks: A National Bank with **ATM** is located right on the north side of Pl. I. Polytechniou. Open M-Th 8am-2pm, F 8am-1:30pm. There's also a 24hr. ATM on Asklepiou just south of Pl. Riga Feriou.

Internet Access: Turn left on Vyronos 1 block down Asklepiou from Pl. Riga Feriou. **Neos Kosmos** (☎ 72 591) has 9 terminals, a printer, and a full bar. Internet access 1000dr/ €2.93 per hr. Open 9am-1am.

Telephone: OTE, 25 Martiou (☎ 95 328; manager 95 315). Martiou runs parallel to Sarafi, 2 blocks away from the river; turn left after Pl. I. Polytechniou.

Post Office: The main **post office,** Sarafi 15 (☎ 27 615), provides exchange and Poste Restante. Open M-F 7am-7:30pm. Walk across the bridge from Pl. Riga Feriou and turn left on the street directly in front of you (Sarafi). A smaller post office, Asklipiou 44 (☎ 32 983), sells stamps and offers mail-related services only. Open M-F 7:30am-2pm. **Postal code:** 42100.

▮✚▮ ACCOMMODATIONS AND FOOD

The most affordable digs in town are at the **Hotel Palladion,** Vyronos 4, right along the riverbank, and one street west of Pl. Riga Feriou. All types of travelers amble across the marble floors of these spacious, comfortable, light-filled rooms. Phones, sinks, and TVs that receive more than 20 channels. (☎ 28 091 or 37 260.

Shared baths. Singles 6000dr/€17.61; doubles 9000dr/€26.41.) Other hotels are readily available, but often expensive. **Hotel Dinas,** two blocks down Asklepiou, is right above the hippest cafes in town (the sign reads *Hotel Ntina*). The brightly painted rooms have bathrooms, TVs, and A/C and are moderately priced for Trikala hotels. (☎74 777. Singles 11,000dr/€32.28; doubles 15,000dr/€44.)

Katzinetrou, one block west of Pl. Iroön Polytechniou off Martinou, has a taverna on every corner, each with outdoor seating. Three blocks north of Martinou, **Taverna Thea Atremis,** Ypsilandou 4 (☎77 533), has a large selection of Greek wines to compliment its traditional menu. The food is excellent, but bring a dictionary: neither the menu nor the owner can offer any English hints. (Entrees 1500-3000dr/ €4.40-8.80.) Pl. Riga Feriou harbors hordes of souvlaki and pizza places, including **Jimmy's,** Asklepiou 22, which offers 6 varieties of *gyros* (500-1500dr/€1.47-4.40) in addition to sandwiches, salads, fresh desserts, and crepes. (Open 8am-1am.) A **supermarket** on Vyronos, next door to Palladion Hotel, sells mini-icons of the *Panagia* (Virgin), in addition to average foodstuffs.

◖ SIGHTS

VAROUSI. Trikala's old quarter, **Varousi,** was home to the Christian community under the Ottomans. Cobblestone streets wind through the crumbling walls, past intertwined modern and historical buildings. Varousi is on the north side of town. From Pl. Riga Feriou, cross the main footbridge and turn left on Sarafi. The neighborhood is 200m on your right. One of Varousi's churches, **Agios Faneromeni,** is open to the public from 7-9am and 5:30-7:30pm. Just outside the neighborhood, the **Sanctuary of Asclepius** is under excavation, but visible through the makeshift fence.

FORT TRIKKIS. Looming above Varousi are the grand stone walls and bell tower of Fort Trikkis, first constructed in the 4th century BC and dedicated to Artemis. The fort is divided into two sections. The lovely, fountain-decked park and cafe in the lower half of the fort is an ideal setting for a cool *frappé* with a view (700dr/ €2.05). The upper half contains the bell tower and a small garden. As of summer 2001, this section was closed to the public.

◖ NIGHTLIFE

Pl. Riga Feriou and Asklipiou are packed with loud cafes blasting dance music and serving drinks a few hours shy of daybreak. If you think you look good, strut your stuff past the rows of cafes. If you *know* you look good, find a table and ration your attention sparingly. Just off Pl. Riga Feriou on Asklepiou is **Chaplin.** Always crowded, this cafe and bar has rows of comfortable lounge chairs outside and art-deco furniture inside. Anything from disco, to reggae, to Greek techno is blasted from the innumerable speakers. **Lotus,** directly across the street, has a bit more light and slightly softer music for laid-back drinking and nonchalant coolness. **Chain,** the biggest disco in the area, is about 5min. from town by taxi (1200dr/ €3.52) on the Trikala-Kalambaka road. With its exuberant beach decor and blend of Greek and American music, Chain attracts a crowd of rowdy revelers (cover 1000dr/€2.43). Just down the road is **Verykono,** which churns out Greek music in an open-air setting. The 2000dr/€5.87 cover includes one drink. Friday and Saturday nights, locals flock to **Xantres,** a dinner theater club specializing in live Greek pop (cover 2000dr/€5.87). Partying begins around 12:30am on the weekends.

PYLI Πυλη ☎ 0434

The seemingly endless plains of Thessaly finally end in tiny Pyli, portal to the forested mountains rising in the west. Notable mostly for its 12th-century Byzantine church, the Porta Panagia, Pyli is home to two spectacular monasteries and trails that climb through the trees of **Mount Kosakas.** Visit Pyli for its churches and for the cool serenity of the mountains, since it has little else to offer: the town consists of one main road and a handful of stores and tavernas.

⬛🛈 ORIENTATION AND PRACTICAL INFORMATION. Located at the foot of Mt. Kosakas, 20km southwest of Trikala, Pyli heralds the end of Thessaly's boundless flatness as it flows into mountainous terrain: *pyli* means "gateway." The highway from Trikala to Artis runs parallel to the river and directly through the center of town, where it becomes **Trikalon,** Pyli's main street and home to most of the shops and the bus station. At the bus station, the other major street, **Ermou,** breaks off from Trikalon, only to rejoin it 200m later at the small, mostly barren plateia. A few meters above the plateia, a long, narrow footbridge crosses the rocky riverbed and leads to the Porta Panagia. The bus station runs buses to **Trikala** (30min, 20 per day 6:15am-9:20pm, 400dr/€1.17) and some of the other villages in the area; inquire for service to Ellaki and Kotroni, among others. A few blocks down from the bus station is a **National Bank of Greece** offering **currency exchange** and a 24hr. **ATM.** (Open M-Th 8am-2pm, F 8am-1:30pm.) The **post office** is on Trikalon, about 400m from the bus station in the direction of Trikala. (Open M-F 7:30am-2pm.) The **OTE** is one block before the post office. (Open M-F 8am-1pm.) **Postal Code:** 42032.

🛏 ACCOMMODATIONS. Budget accommodations are very limited in Pyli. **Hotel Babanara,** housed upstairs from a cafe right across the street from the bus station, has spacious, comfortable rooms with TV, phone, and bath. The lobby doubles as a cafe, and fills up in the evening with regulars. (☎22 325. Singles 7000dr/€20.53; doubles 9000dr/€26.41.) A block down from the bus station, **Domatia To Perasma** offers fairly priced doubles and triples. All the rooms are on the 3rd floor and have TVs, phones, radios, and baths. If the door is locked, try your luck at the small market next door. (☎22 266. Doubles 14,000dr/€44.10; triples 16,000dr/€46.96.)

🍴🍷 FOOD AND ENTERTAINMENT. A few *psiterias* and cheap fast food places can be found along Trikalon and Ermou, but in general, quality restaurants are scarce. **Taverna O Theodoras,** on Ermou just below the plateia, serves good (if greasy) local specialties, including an excellent *moussaka.* (☎22 217. Entrees 700-2000dr/€2.05-5.87.) A **supermarket** can be found on Trikalon, a few doors downhill from the bus station. For a cool drink any time of the day, don't miss ■**Neromylos,** a 17th-century water mill converted to a cafe and meticulously landscaped by its owner. Water flows out of numerous fountains, cascading off of the patios, turning waterwheels, and ends up coiling through a little stream at your feet on its way to the river. To get there, take Trikalon north out of town for 500m and walk down the first road that branches right. (☎22 085. Open 10am-1am. Drinks 600-2000dr/€1.76-5.87.) After dinner Pyli is quiet at night; the streets are virtually empty. The only noise comes from **La Porta,** on the plateia, where Pyli's hip, black-clad contingent shake their groove thangs till 4am. (☎22 696. Beer 700dr/€2.05, drinks 1000-1500dr/€2.93-4.40.) **Cafe Kittara** (☎22 672), right next door, serves beer and drinks to a crowd of regulars until 2am.

◙ CHURCH OF PORTA PANAGIA. Most visitors come to Pyli to ogle the extraordinary ■**Church of Porta Panagia.** The church has rested on the banks of the Aheloös River since 1283, when it was built by Despot of Epirus **Ioannis Dukas** on the site of an ancient Greek temple. Despite a smallish, drab appearance from outside, the church's interior mosaics are jaw-dropping; light slants in from lofty windows to illuminate them. A domed *Pantokrator* ("Creator of All Things") graces the vestibule. The church's main area, the *naos,* is built in a *trikliti stavrepisteli* style: its intersecting three vertical parts and single horizontal part meet to form a cross. The church's most prized treasures are in the *naos*: a pair of 700-year-old mosaic icons, one of the *Panagia* (Virgin) and one of Christ. The positioning of Porta Panagia's icons is a bit unusual in that the icon of the *Panagia* is located to the right of Christ, not to the standard left. There's nothing unorthodox about the beautiful frescoes painted with flower-extract dyes that adorn the walls of both the vestibule and the *naos.* Some frescoes, especially in the vestibule, have been damaged by fire, earthquakes, and Nazi bullets, but most remain unscathed. *(Start in Pyli's plateia and, ignoring the signs for a moment, cross the river on the narrow footbridge. Turn left on the other side and you'll find the church on your left very shortly.* ☎22 420. *Open daily 8am-noon and 4-6pm; winter 9am-noon and 3-5pm. 400dr/€1.17.)*

KALAMBAKA Καλαμπακα   ☎ 0432

Kalambaka sits directly at the base of the Meteora rocks: all good etymologists know its name is derived from the Turkish phrase for "the rock with the cowls of monks." The lone main road channels countless package-tour buses past the town, to the rocks' summit. Though Kalambaka itself doesn't offer much beyond access to the famed monasteries, it makes a quiet, convenient base.

▐ TRANSPORTATION

Buses: Main station downhill from the local bus station on the left, past the taxi stand. To: **Athens** (5hr., 8 per day 7am-8:30pm, 5900dr/€17.30); **Ioannina** (3hr.; 8:45am and 3:20pm; 2600dr/€7.65); **Lamia** (2hr., 8 per day 7am-8:30pm, 2500dr/€7.35); **Metsovo** (2hr.; 8:45am, 3:20pm; 1450dr/€4.25); **Patras** (6hr.; Tu, Th 9am; 5950dr/€17.45); **Thessaloniki** (3hr., 6 per day 7:30am-8pm, 3950dr/€11.60); **Trikala** (30min., 25 per day 6:15am-10:30pm, 450dr/€1.32); **Volos** (3hr., 4 per day 6:15am-6:30pm, 3350dr/€9.83). Buses bound for **Meteora** (20min.; 9am, 1:20pm; 260dr/€0.76) and **Kastraki** (10min., 24 per day 6:30am-9pm, 150dr/€0.44) pick up passengers in front of the **central plateia** at the foot of the large fountain. The 9am bus to Meteora allows you time to hike around the monasteries. Most people walk back to Kalambaka (6km downhill), visiting monasteries along the way, but you can also take a bus back from **Grand Meteoron** at 2pm.

Trains: The station (☎ 22 451), on the corner of Pindou and Kondyli, is brand new and provides service to: **Athens** (4hr., 3 per day 7am-5:15pm, 6500dr/€19.08); **Thessaloniki** (3hr., 9:30am, 4200dr/€12.33); **Larisa** (2hr., 2 per day 9:30am and 8:45am, 1300dr/€3.82.) From the bus station, walk downhill 1 block and turn left on Pindou.

Taxis: (☎ 22 310 or 22 822) congregate at a small kiosk across from the central plateia. Taxi to Meteora 1500dr/€4.40. Open 6:30am-midnight.

✦ ▐ ORIENTATION AND PRACTICAL INFORMATION

Kalambaka is in the northwestern corner of Thessaly, 30km north of Trikala, near the border with Epirus. The town's central plateia is uphill from the bus station at the intersection of the town's major thoroughfares. Standing in this plateia with your back to the fountain and the Meteora cliffs, **Vlahava** is straight behind you, and **Ioanninon** runs downhill to the right toward the police station. **Patriarchou Dimitriou** goes off to your right, while **Trikalon** leads left to the sunny **Pl. Riga Fariou**, home of various banks and restaurants. A horde of cafes and bars can be found open at all hours on **Dimalou**, two blocks downhill from Pl. Riga Fariou.

Tourist Office: Vlahava 1, right on the central plateia underneath the town hall. The tourist office offers maps, bus schedules, lists of hotels and rooms to let, and information on the monasteries—most in English. Open M-F 8am-10pm. The **kiosk** by the taxi stand also provides maps of the town and of Meteora.

Banks: Both the National Bank in Pl. Riga Fariou and the Ionian Bank near the central plateia have 24hr. **ATMs.**

Police and Tourist Police: (☎ 76 100), on the road to Ioannina, about a 10min. walk from the center of town. Open 24hr.

Health Center: (☎ 24 111), 1km from town, on the road to Ioannina. Open 24hr.

Telephones: OTE (☎ 22 121), down Ioanninon. Open M-F 7:30am-2pm.

Internet Access: Cafe Hollywood, Trikalon 67 (☎ 24 964), a few blocks past Pl. Riga Fariou. 100dr/€0.29 per 6min. for use of one of its 5 coin-operated, snail-paced terminals. Open 10am-1am. **Koktel** (☎ 22 370), a block down Dimoula off of Trikalon, has 4 reliable terminals in back of the well-lit cafe.

Post Office: (☎ 22 467), between the 2 plateias on Trikalon. Poste Restante available. Open M-F 7:30am-2pm. **Postal code:** 42200.

♠ ACCOMMODATIONS AND CAMPING

Think carefully before you accept domatia offers from the dock hawks; some have been known to lure travelers with promises of good prices only to change their rates or add surcharges when it comes time to pay. Be skeptical when someone tells you that the place you're going has raised its rates or is closed, and make sure you agree on a rate before you agree to spend the night. Many moderately priced hotels are at the end of Trikalon; budget options are northeast of the city's center, closer to the base of the cliffs. A number of **campsites** line the roads around Kalambaka and Kastraki; many also rent rooms at cheap prices. **Kalambaka,** about 1km down the road to Trikala, is the closest. (☎22 309. 600dr/€1.76 per tent, 1100dr/€3.23 per car.) **Vrachos** is about as far away in the opposite direction, in nearby Kastraki. (☎22 293 or 23 134. 2000dr/€5.87 per car, 400dr/€1.17 per tent.)

■ **Koka Roka** (☎24 554). A 15min. walk from the central plateia; follow Vlachara until it ends, then bear left, following the signs to Kanari. On a quiet side street at the base of footpath to the rocks, Koka Roka offers large, airy rooms in a wholesome family setting and awe-inspiring views of Meteora. Call from the bus station for a lift. Fast internet access available. 4000dr/€11.75 per person without bath; singles with bath 6000dr/€17.61; doubles with bath 8000dr/€23.48; triples with bath 10,000dr/€29.35.

Hotel Antonadis, Trikalon 148 (☎24 387), at the edge of the commercial district, set amongst a cluster of similar, mid-level hotels. Rooms here are a bit narrow, but have TV, A/C, phones, radios, and micro-fridges. The hotel offers breakfast in the lobby and a swimming pool on the 6th floor. Singles 12,000dr/€35.22; doubles 15,000dr/€44.

Alsos Rooms (☎24 097 or mobile 097 660 929), on Kanari before Koka Roka. You'll think you're staying at the United Nations as multinational flags flap over the front gate. 14 rooms with shared baths and great views. Strain your neck to see the tops of the cliffs hanging overhead. Singles 5000dr/€14.67; doubles from 6000dr/€17.61.

♠♠ FOOD AND NIGHTLIFE

To save some cash or to slap together a picnic lunch to take to monasteries, there's a **supermarket** just off of Trikalon on Dimoula, and various **fruit stands** on Vlachara. On Fridays, Vlachara and its main intersector Kondyli turn into a full-scale **marketplace** for fresh produce and sundry household goods. Most of Kalambaka's fast food places and a few cheap tavernas are on Trikalon, south of Riga Feriou; good restaurants lean against the edge of the cliffs on the road to Karditsa.

■ **Koka Roka Taverna** (☎24 554), inside its namesake hotel. Homey, roofed outdoor tables under dried gourds make the perfect spot for chatting, backgammon, Kyria Sakkas's specialties, and chatting about backgammon while chowing on a Sakkas specialty. Entrees around 1000dr/€2.93.

Restaurant Panellinio (☎24 735). Panellinio pretty much *is* the central plateia, and very popular at night. Vegetarian eggplant *papoutsakia* (1600dr/€4.70) and *briam* (1300dr/€3.82), as well as a host of Greek lamb and veal specialties. Be sure to peek inside at the folk art and the daily specials, which are always on display and happily elaborated on by the owner. Entrees 1200-2200dr/€3.52-6.46.

Taverna Vaxchos (☎24 678), up a hill at the end of Patriarchou Dimitriou, has a large, fun-filled patio right under the Meteora rocks. Have a drink and soak up the view from the deck. *Moussaka*, lamb-and-vegetable dishes, and all kinds of country salads (1600-2700dr/€4.70-7.92) are served at intimate tables. Open noon-midnight.

The nightlife mainly centers on **Trikalon,** south of Pl. Riga Feriou, where motorcycles, cheap fast food joints, and neon signs line the streets. There's hipper atmosphere on Dimoula, home to entertaining, but indistinguishable bars, most offering beers for 700dr/€2.05 and drinks for 1200dr/€3.52. **Mateus,** 3 Dimoula, has a beach bar atmosphere with palm trees, grass umbrellas, and plenty of room for dancing.

👁 SIGHTS

In the land of monasteries, it comes as no surprise that Kalambaka's foremost attraction is the Byzantine **Church of the Assumption of the Virgin,** once the seat of the bishop of Kalambaka and Trikala. Follow the signs in the central plateia; after several blocks you'll spy the graceful bell tower of the old church. Built in the 11th century on the ruins of a 5th-century basilica, the main structure was remodeled in 1573. Unfortunately, many of the interior frescoes, painted by the Cretan monk **Neophytos** and priest **Kiriazis,** have been blackened by centuries of priestly pyromania (candles and incense). Of particular interest is the church's marble *amdo* (pulpit), located in the center of the nave. (Dress modestly: long pants or skirts and no bare shoulders. 450dr/€1.32. Open 8am-1pm and 4-8pm.) In late July, the town honors its patron saint with a **glendi** (celebration) of music, dance, and food. Nearby Kastraki holds a three-day **wine festival** with free samples in late August.

NEAR METEORA

*Buses leave for Meteora from the Kalambaka fountain M-F 9am and 1:20pm, Sa-Su 8:30am and 1:20pm. Each monastery closes for 1 day of the week, and their opening hours vary slightly. All are open Apr.-Sept. Sa-Su and W 9am-12:30pm and 3:20-6pm. **Admission:** 500dr/€1.47 per monastery. Dress modestly: long skirts for women, long pants for men, no bare shoulders, or you will not be admitted. Men with long hair may be asked to wrap it in a bun (as the monks do). Photography and filming are forbidden inside most of the monasteries; pack a picnic for the mid-day closing hours.*

No one knows how the majestic, iron-gray pinnacles of the Meteora (that's meh-TEH-o-rah to you, meaning "rocks of the air") formations were created, but they're probably the remains of large salt deposits from a primordial sea. Whatever their origin, the Meteora rear up from the plains of Thessaly and yield startling views of fields, forests, mountains, and monolithic stone; they'd be a must-see even without the 24 gravity-defying, frescoed Byzantine monasteries that cling to them. Six of these monasteries are still inhabited by religious orders and are open to the public. The largest monasteries, Grand Meteoron and Varlaam, have the most spectacular displays and cater to hordes of tourists. The other monasteries are quieter and more intimate; if you're lucky, you might even meet one of the reclusive monks. The Meteora require a full day's visit, and it's well worth the time and the walk.

HISTORY

The origins of the settlements perched atop the Meteora rocks are unknown: one likely story holds that the first recluse was a monk named **Barnabas,** who founded the *skite* of the Holy Ghost in the mid-10th century. By the 11th century, hermits and ascetics followed his example, moving to the wind-beaten pinnacles and crevices of the Meteora, worshiping in a church dedicated to the **Theotokos** (Mother of God), which can still be seen below the Agios Nikolaos monastery. As religious persecution at the hands of Serbian marauders increased in the 12th century, devout Christians scurried to the summits of these impregnable columns of rock.

In 1344, the region's first monastic community was founded when the monk **Athanasios,** his spiritual father **Gregorios,** and 14 fellow mountain-climbing monks began to build Grand Meteoron. Athanasios was a highly educated monk whose journeys brought him from his native Patras to Constantinople, Crete, and finally Mt. Athos, which he fled to avoid Turkish invasions. He preferred to occupy his time weaving baskets in a nearby cave, referring to women as "the sling" (that vaults the stones of sin into man's hearts) or as "the affliction" (addicting men to the sinful pleasures of the flesh). When the Ottomans ruled most of Greece, Meteora served as an outpost of Christianity along with Mount Athos (see p. 246), growing in the 16th century into a robust, rich community of 24 monasteries, each embellished by the age's finest artists. In the late 1700s, when donations fell off and the popularity of monastic life waned, the Greeks sold off many treasured manuscripts and books to foreign visitors for a fraction of their actual worth. A small brotherhood still exists at **Grand Meteoron, Varlaam, Agia Triada,** and **Agios Nikolaos,** while **Agios Stephanos** and **Roussanou** are now convents.

▶ WALKING THE MONASTERIES

The first ascetics scaled the sheer cliffs of the Meteora by wedging timbers into the rock crevices to construct small platforms; traces of these platforms can still be seen along the Meteora walls. After the monasteries were completed, visitors usually arrived by means of extremely long rope ladders. When these were pulled up, the summit became virtually inaccessible. Visitors who were either too weak or too timid to climb the ladders were hoisted up in free-swinging rope nets. If the pilgrims didn't fear God before the 30min. ascent, they no doubt were shakin' in their boots afterwards. Motorized winches have since replaced monk-powered rope-spool cranes, and today only provisions, not pilgrims, are yanked up by rope, though monks, obviously starved for amusement, can be seen riding miniature cable cars over the chasms. In 1922, steps were carved into the rocks and bridges built between the pillars, so even the vertigo-prone could feel secure.

It's best to begin your walking tour from **Grand Meteoron,** the uppermost monastery, and then to visit the others on your way down. From Grand Meteoron, a road leads down about 200m, where there is a turn-off for Varlaam. Another 700m beyond this point, the road splits in two. The right fork leads to **Roussanou, Agios Nikolaos,** and eventually the village of Kastraki, after a series of switchbacks down the hillside. The left fork leads to **Agia Triada** and **Agios Stephanos** and back to the village of **Kalambaka.** Large signs at every intersection make navigation easy. There is approximately a 20-30min. walk between each monastery, but the curved road between the rocks has dazzling views of the monasteries and photo opportunities.

GRAND METEORON. The **Monastery of the Transfiguration,** known as Grand Meteoron (Μεγαλου Μετεορου), is the oldest, largest, most important, and most touristed monastery in the area. Built in the late 14th century on the most imposing of the inhabited stone columns, **Platys Lithos,** the Grand Meteoron complex, looms 613m above Thessaly's plain. An engineering and architectural masterpiece, the view is accessible in nearly every direction. According to legend, Athanasios took the wings of the Holy Spirit (without ever getting a permission slip) and flew to the rocky peak to found the original church on this site, called the **Theometor.** The monastery rose to prominence when Ioannis Uresis Angelos Komninos Paleologos, many-named son of the Greco-Serbian King of Thessaly and Epirus, forsook the worldly vanities of royal power and retired to Meteora in 1388, taking on the monkish (and much more manageable) name of **Ioasaph.** Ioasaph spearheaded a period of great artistry at Grand Meteoron and is considered its second founder. Grand Meteoron reached its peak in the 16th century, when it was visited by the reigning patriarch and accorded the same privileges as the autonomous Mt. Athos. Around this time the **Church of the Transfiguration** (*Metamorphosis*) was built, to be capped by an exalted dome with a *Pantokrator* (a central image of Christ). The monastery is filled with sounds of chanting monks—unfortunately emanating from a stereo in the **folk museum,** which exhibits holy books, religious ornaments, and the traditional monastic garb. Other rooms are preserved with historical accuracy, including a dining hall, kitchen, mausoleum, and a wine cellar with the largest barrel you will ever see (15,000L). The monks here keep mostly to their private quarters on the eastern side of the monastery. *(Open W-M 9am-1pm and 3-6pm; winter Th-M 9am-1pm and 3-5pm. 500dr/€1.47.)*

VARLAAM MONASTERY. Some 800m downhill from Grand Meteoron stands Varlaam, the second-largest Meteora monastery. Varlaam was founded in the 14th century by a contemporary of Athanasios who, in a show of monkish humility, named the monastery after himself. Brothers Theophanis and Nektarios built the **Church of All Saints** in 1541. The *katholikon's* 16th-century frescoes, thought to be the babies of the Theban artist Frangos Katelanos, depict desert hermits, martyrs, an apocalyptic sea serpent swallowing doomed sinners, and St. Sisoes chatting up Alexander the Great's skeleton (symbolic of the vanity of worldly achievements). Meteora's best scribes and calligraphers worked at Varlaam in the 16th and 17th centuries; the monastery's **library** contains 290 manuscripts, including a miniature Bible from 960 that belonged to Emperor Constantine Porfitogenitou. Varlaam also has every third grade science teacher's dream—an extensive **net and pulley system**, now used for supplies, which shows how earlier visitors were hoisted. Recently the monastery has gotten a face-lift, adding new walkways, handrails (thankfully), and a clock tower. *(Open F-W 9am-1pm and 3:20-6pm; winter Sa-W 9am-1pm and 3-5pm. 500dr/€1.47)*

ROUSSANOU. Bear right at the fork in the road to reach Roussanou. Visible from most of the valley, it is spectacularly situated and frequently photographed. More than the other monasteries, Roussanou feels less like a creation of man than a natural continuation of the boulders: its steep sides—three of which overlook the sheer drop to the valley below—were built almost flush with the rock face and seem to spring out of the formation in an especially ornate flourish of stone. Founded in 1380 by the monks **Nikodemos** and **Benedict**, Roussanou was renovated and enlarged in the 16th century. Despite continuous renovation, the interior—which includes paintings of the criminal in paradise and a portrait of Constantine the Great—can't match the heavenly exterior, accessible without a ticket. Still, the *katholikon*, illuminated by stained glass, is beautiful. Roussanou celebrated its greatest moment when it housed Greek refugees fleeing the Turks in 1757 and 1897. Today, nuns maintain the monastery and are happy to offer a ticket and a smile at the door. *(Open daily 9am-6pm; in winter Th-Tu 9am-1pm and 3-5pm. 500dr/€1.47.)*

AGIOS NIKALAOS. Farther down the road lies the Monastery of Agios Nikolaos Anapafsas, only 2.5km from Kastraki. Built in 1527 by the Archbishop of Larisa and expanded in 1628, its highlight is the incomparable fresco painted by the 16th-century Cretan master **Theophanes Strelitzas-Bathas**, whose son, Neophytus, painted Kalambaka's Church of the Assumption of the Virgin (p. 198). Situated on a very narrow boulder, Agios Nikolaos grew vertically rather than horizontally; it is now the second tallest of the monasteries, next to Grand Meteoron. Excellent views open from the rooftop and the small balcony beneath it. Visitors are admitted only in small groups; wait at the top of the steps for the door to open. Allow a good 30min. for the walk past Roussanou to the next monastery, Agia Triada. *(Open Sa-Th 9am-5:30pm; closed in winter. 500dr/€1.47.)*

AGIA TRIADA. A path from Roussanou cuts off a large section of road on the way to Agia Triada and saves time. Standing on the metal bridge into Roussanou, face away from the monastery, get out your walking stick, and take the (mostly) paved path uphill on the right. When the path hits the road, bear right and keep bearing right to find Agia Triada ("Trinity"); movie buffs will recognize it from the James Bond flick *For Your Eyes Only*. Take the rock-strewn path downhill from the road and catch your breath before attempting the steep rock staircase into the monastery. Looming above Kalambaka, the peak of Agia Triada gives a soul-searing view of Kalambaka and the distant, snow-capped Pindos Mountains. Ambitious monk Dometius built the monastery in 1438, but most of the **wall paintings** weren't added for another 200 years. Sadly, most of the monastery's prized manuscripts and heirlooms were lost in WWII. Triada is now one of the least-touristed and most intimate monasteries. The caretaker, Brother John, may offer you a cup of coffee and a piece of Greek candy, called *loukoumi*, for making the trip. To get to **Kalambaka** from Agia Triada, take the (unmarked) 2km footpath leading from the bottom of the monastery's stone staircase. At the base of the cliff and with your back to the monastery, walk a few meters to your left, and then descend on the small left-hand fork in the path. The narrow, overgrown trail soon evolves into a cement-paved stone path. *(Open F-W 9am-12:30pm and 3-5pm. 500dr/€1.47.)*

AGIOS STEPHANOS. At the end of the road, past Agia Triada, is Agios Stephanos, founded as a hermitage by the Archmandrite Antonius Katakouzinos and the anti-social monk Philotheos. According to an 18th-century report, it was originally a convent; it became a monastery in the early 15th century. Today it is once again home to a large, active community of nuns. Of its two churches, only the more modern **Agios Charalambos,** built in 1798, is open to the public. The **museum** displays well-preserved icons, manuscripts, liturgical vestments, and crosses. Its wooden *iconostasis* is intricately carved into figures of birds, animals, and people. The peaceful garden out back offers spectacular views of the entire valley. *(Open Tu-Su 9am-1pm and 3:20-6pm; in winter Tu-Su 9am-1pm and 3-5pm. 500dr/€1.47.)*

CENTRAL GREECE

NORTHERN GREECE

In ancient times, snide Athenians regarded the residents of Macedonia and Thrace as primitive barbarians. Perhaps they didn't know that Orpheus, the mythical Pied Piper who tamed wild animals with his divinely inspired songs, first sang in Thrace, where cults of his devotees filled the northern hills. Having ventured to the underworld and back in a vain search for his beloved Eurydice, Orpheus recounted his tale of woe in poems resembling musical guidebooks to the underworld; commentary on one of these "Orphic" poems was found on papyrus at Derveni outside Thessaloniki. A few rural festivals still preserve pre-Christian rites that probably stem from these ancient pagan practices. Parts of Northern Greece did cling on to the ancient ways for a good long time: Romans who came to pave the Via Egnatia across the Balkans encountered uncivilized, cityless Thracian tribes. Today, the northern reaches of Greece vary greatly in their connection with modern life; Thessaloniki is a step ahead of the Next Big Thing, while the Zagorohoria region's residents barely test the waters of the 19th century.

HIGHLIGHTS OF NORTHERN GREECE

SIDESTEP SCORPIONS while trekking through Vikos Gorge (p. 218), the world's steepest of its kind.

GENUFLECT in reverence to Agios Dimitrios, Thessaloniki's oldest church, before being floored by the ancient mosaics inside (p. 230).

CATCH YOUR JAW before it hits the ground upon sight of the dazzling treasures unearthed from tombs, palaces, and mosaics at Pella (p. 235) and Vergina (p. 234).

GET LOST IN THE CLOUDS atop Mt. Olympus; the gods await your ascent (p. 237).

ABIDE by 10th century monastic doctrine at Mt. Athos' monasteries (p. 246).

FLIRT WITH FATE amid the rustling leaves of Dodoni's oracular oak (p. 214).

EPIRUS Ηπειρος

If you came in search of idyllic isolation, consider roaming Greece's northwest coast. The postcard-pretty towns and beaches of Parga see their share of visitors, but the mountains and timeless villages of Zagorohoria near the Vikos Gorge remain undisturbed. Epirus links itself to a living past—the old Latin dialect of Vlachi is still spoken in the mountain towns, and the almost perfectly preserved mosques of the dreaded Ali Pasha still grace the beautiful city of Ioannina. The region's mountains draw international hikers for some of Greece's most fulfilling outdoor rambles, with paths that link to trails through Greece and beyond.

THE PINDOS MOUNTAINS

Those who enjoy exhilaratingly fresh natural air and quality hiking will delight in the beauty of the Pindos Mountains Region. Rushing rivers and waterfalls, towering mountains, steep ravines, fertile forests, dazzling fall foliage and blossoming wildflowers constitute the breathtaking scenery that provides a refreshing change from the typical Greek tourist attractions. The **European E6** path and national **01** and **03 routes** run through the area near Ioannina (p. 209), a good base city from which to explore the

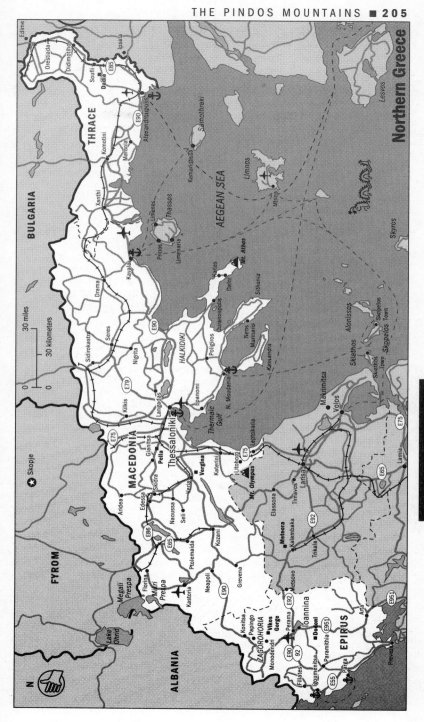

mountains. The 03 brings hikers through the Vikos Gorge, and past an array of mountaintops and villages known to offer some of the best hiking in Greece. The tourist office in Ioannina has an informative, Greek-only contour map that marks all the trails. Rock climbers can scale the faces of **Eamila, Tsouka Rossa,** and **Pirgos Astraka,** and avid spelunkers can attempt the **Provatihas Cave,** the second-deepest cave in the world, at 407m. Most of these expeditions are best undertaken with an experienced guide, or after consulting an outdoors agency in Ioannina, as maps of the region tend to be unreliable. The ⬛Hellenic Mountaineering Club (EOS), Despotatou Ipirou 2, can be reached by following the signs for the Folklore Museum down Mikhail Angelou; it's a few blocks past the museum at a multi-pronged intersection. The club supplies information and leads weekend trips throughout the region. (☎22 138. Open M-Sa 7-9pm.) **Robinson's Agency,** Merarchias 8, 2km from the city center on the airport road, arranges walking and canyoning trips. (☎29 402. Open M-F 9am-3pm.) The **Paddler Kayaking and Rafting School** (☎(0655) 23 777 or (0655) 23 101) in Konitsa gives lessons and oversees outings to local rivers. For alpine flowers, April through June is the best hiking season; colored foliage flares brilliantly in the dry autumns.

IGOUMENITSA Ηγουμενιτσα ☎0665

For many, Igoumenitsa is the first glimpse of the Greek mainland. Greece's third largest port and consummate transportation hub, the city links Central and Northern Greece, the Ionian islands, and Italy. Tourist agencies line the streets, harried backpackers scurry about in search of their ships, loitering old men keep an eye on all the comings and goings, and everyone seems in a desperate hurry. Though you may prefer to avoid staying the night in Igoumenitsa, the prevalence of early morning ferries makes this easier said than done.

⬛ TRANSPORTATION

Ferries: Igoumenitsa's endlessly long **port** has three subdivisions. **Old Port,** on the waterfront's north edge (to the right facing the water), mostly sends boats to Italy. **Corfu Port** is in the middle of the three. **New Port,** beyond the Corfu Port, sends boats to both Italy and Corfu. Tickets to **Corfu** (1½hr., every 30min. 4:30am-10pm, 1400dr/€4.11) can be purchased at the Corfu Port, in one of several white kiosks. For tickets to **Italy,** shop around at the waterfront agencies. Some budget have student rates, and some accept Eurail and Inter-Rail passes; bargain before you buy. Destinations include: **Ancona** (24hr., 4 per day, 15,000-19,000dr/€44-55.76); **Bari** (12hr., 2 per day, 11,000-13,000dr/€32.28-38.15); **Brindisi** (8hr., 2 per day, 9000-10,000dr/€26.41-29.35); and **Venice** (25hr., 2 per day, 13,000-16,000dr/€38.15-46.96). Prices do not include port dues. Most boats depart before noon or late in the evening.

Buses: Kipou 17 (☎22 309). To: **Athens** (8hr., 5 per day 8:30am-8:15pm, 9250dr/€27.15); **Ioannina** (2hr., 9 per day 6:30am-8pm, 2000dr/€5.87); **Parga** (1hr., 4 per day 5:45am-5:15pm, 1250dr/€3.67; **Preveza** (2hr., 11:45am and 3:30pm, 2200dr/€6.46); and **Thessaloniki** (7hr., 11:45am, 8600dr/€25.24). To reach the **bus station** from the ports, walk up Zalogo (past the Ionian Bank). When you reach the town plateia, turn left and walk two blocks to the **ticket office,** behind a cafe on the left marked with a blue KTEL sign.

✦🛈 ORIENTATION AND PRACTICAL INFORMATION

Igoumenitsa is on the westernmost corner of mainland Greece, about 20km from the Albanian border. **Eth. Antistaseos,** which becomes **Ag. Apostolon,** runs along the waterfront, and teems with travel agencies. To the north, after it divides, the tree-lined inland side of the street is bordered by an array of cafes and bars. Igoumenitsa's main shopping area is on **Grigariou** the first pedestrian street parallel to the waterfront. To reach the uninspiring central plateia, walk four blocks inland on **Zalogo,** which begins across from Corfu Port.

Tourist Office: (☎22 227), in the old port. Helps with transportation and accommodations. Free maps. Multilingual. Open 7am-2pm. A second **tourist office** is in the New Port, Eth. Antistaseos 68 (☎23 564). Open 7am-10pm.

Banks: National Bank (☎ 22 415), across the road from the Old Port in a string of banks with 24hr. **ATM** and automatic **currency exchange machine.**

American Express: Eth. Antistaseos 14 (☎ 22 406 or 24 333). Will **change money,** issue traveler's checks, cash all traveler's checks without commission, and give you cash from an AmEx card. Open M-F 7:30am-2pm and 4pm-11pm; Sa 4pm-11pm.

Police: Ag. Apostolon 5 (☎ 22 100), across from Corfu Port. Available 24hr.

Port Police: (☎ 25 833), in a Corfu Port booth, near customs and passport control.

Medical Center: (☎ 24 420). Basic health care. If necessary, they will help you get to the **hospital** (☎ (0664) 22 203), 15min. away. Open 24hr.

Telephones: OTE (☎ 22 399), at the end of the pedestrian street Grigariou. Open 7am-2:30pm. The new port also has an **OTE** (☎ 27 757). Open 7am-10pm.

Internet Access: Cafe Planet (☎ 29 180), on the north end of the waterfront in the cafe strip. 6 fast terminals for 800dr/€2.35 per hour. Open 11:30am-12:30am.

Post Office: Tzaveninas 2 (☎ 46 100), 1km north along the waterfront on the corner of a large playground. Poste Restante. Open 7:30am-2pm. **Postal code:** 46100.

▌ ACCOMMODATIONS

Spacious, airy rooms with private baths and comfy beds above a cafe, are found at **Stavrodromi,** Souliou 16, uphill from the InterAmerican Hotel in the main plateia. (☎ 22 343. Singles 5000dr/€14.67; doubles 10,000dr/€29.35.) **Hotel Acropolis,** on the waterfront in Old Port, has spotless, homey rooms with wooden floors, shared baths and phones along thick-carpeted hallways. The smiles radiated from the family that owns the hotel are contagious. (☎ 22 349 and 28 346. Shared fridge and water cooler. Singles 5000dr/€14.67; doubles 8000dr/€23.48.) Look for **Hotel Egnatia's** in at the central plateia's far right corner. Simple rooms have baths, TVs, phones, and A/C. (☎ 23 648. Singles 9000dr/€26.41; doubles 14,000dr/€41.10.)

◧◪ FOOD AND NIGHTLIFE

The best—and most locally popular—among the city's restaurants are on the north edge of the **waterfront,** past the ports and junk shops. Dozens of bakeries and small markets line the pedestrian street just inland from the harbor. Igoumenitsa's bland nightlife centers on a strip of bars along the waterfront. **Traffic** (☎ 23 505) and **Factory** (☎ 32 625), side by side along the water, both pump American and Greek tunes all night on the weekends. There's also a **cinema,** next to Taverna Aleko, that shows American movies at 9:30pm and 11:15pm. (1500dr/€4.40 per ticket.)

Mykonos (☎ 27 567), at the beginning of the waterfront strip, with a vine-hung patio full of loquacious Greeks. Boasts a varied menu (entrees 1400-2300dr/€4.11-6.75) that includes pizza, pasta, Greek menu mainstays and a few fish specialties. Try the feta-stuffed souvlaki (1500dr/€4.40) for a stimulating and inexpensive change of pace.

Paravda (☎ 28 169). Follow the colorful signs from the waterfront to the quiet side street behind the Ionian Bank. Imaginative takes on traditional fare and carafes of *retsina*, with live music at night under the grapevines. Entrees 1000-2000dr/€2.93-5.87.

Alekos (☎ 23 708), next door to Mykonos. Traditional Greek fare. Specializes in fish, big and small, fetched from the pristine harbor waters. Entrees 1400-2000dr/€4.11-5.87.

PARGA Πάργα ☎ 0684

Attached to the mainland by an arc of green mountains, Parga looks and feels like a Greek island town. With its luxurious beaches and bustling waterfront, Parga draws the fun- and sun-loving crowd, as well as overpriced jewelry shops, "effervescent nightlife," t-shirt vendors, and dozens of fuschia-nosed Scandinavian children wielding inflatable alligators. Parga's narrow, curling streets, its Neoclassical buildings, and its house-high bougainvillea bushes all create a pleasant and romantic mood that seems to have infected even the pastel pink supermarket.

ORIENTATION AND PRACTICAL INFORMATION. Parga is organized around its waterfront. The main waterfront road, which brims with tavernas, bars, and tourist agencies, has three different names: from west to east, they are **Lambraki, Anexartissias,** and **Athanassiou.** At **Krioneriou Beach,** which runs alongside Athanassiou, the road forks: its uphill branch is **R. Feraiou.** Running inland from the waterfront is **Al. Baga,** which leads uphill to most of Parga's municipal buildings. Al. Baga meets **Sp. Livada** at the town's main intersection.

Ferries run to **Corfu Town** (1¾hr., Su and Th 8:30am, 5500dr/€16.14). **Buses** run from Parga to: **Athens** (8½hr., 3 per day 7am-5:15pm, 8250dr/€24.21); **Igoumenitsa** (1¼hr., 4 per day 7am-6:30pm, 1250dr/€3.67); **Preveza** (1½hr., 5 per day 7am-9:15pm, 1700dr/€5) and **Thessaloniki** (8hr., 7am, 9500dr/€27.88). The bus station is a small booth next to the Chinese restaurant, at the top of Sp. Livada.

The **municipal tourist office,** across from the ferry dock, offers maps of the area and information about renting boats, cars, and mopeds. (☎32 107; fax 32 511. Open 8am-11pm.) **Tourist agencies** pack the streets around the waterfront, ready to help you find rooms, and arrange daytrips; they're generally open M-Sa 9am-2pm and 5:30-10pm. **Axis Travel,** on Riga Fereou, just up from the Balthazar Restaurant, is a good bet. (☎31 766. Open 9am-10pm.) **Internet access** is available at **Cafe Terra,** on the waterfront, halfway between the dock and the beach. (1500dr/€4.40 per hour.)

With the **OTE** building (☎31 699; open M-F 7am-2:40pm) on your left and the shore behind you, the **police station** (☎31 222; open 24hr.), and **post office** (☎31 295; open M-F 7am-2pm) are straight ahead. To the left is the **health center** and the **National Bank;** going right will bring you to a junction with the main road and the **bus stop.** Running parallel to the waterfront and having the highest density of tourist shops, **V.E. Vasila** leads up to the **Venetian castle** at the far southwest corner of town. From here, a stone path leads down the other side to **Valtos Beach.** For **emergencies** you can also call the **port police** (☎31 227). **Postal code:** 48060.

ACCOMMODATIONS AND FOOD. Parga's hotels are expensive, and prices spike in the summer months. For a cheaper bed, look around the south end of the town and the top of the hill for **rooms to let** (expect to pay 8000-10,000dr/€23.48-29.35 in high season). Across the street from the Chinese restaurant, **Domatio O Spiro,** Sp. Livada 1, lets out bright rooms with private baths five minutes from the beach and five seconds from the bus stop. (☎31 542. Singles 6000-8000dr/€17.61-23.48; doubles 9000-11000dr/€26.41-13.28.) **Thomas House,** on Tzabela, has light rooms with shared bath and a large, full kitchen. From the bus station, walk downhill and turn left at the OTE. Follow this road as it curves right and becomes V.E. Vasila. Make another right just before the Blue Bar onto Tzabela: the rooms are 20m straight ahead. (☎31 211. Doubles 7000-8000dr/€20.53-23.48.) Budget travelers can skip Parga's high-priced lodging altogether and camp on the nearby beaches. The closest is **Parga Beach Camping** (☎31 161), but **Valtos Camping,** by neighboring Valtos beach, is a bit cheaper. (☎31 287. 1200-1400dr/€3.52-4.11 per person.) **Elia Camping** (☎31 130) is 500m out on the Igoumenitsa road.

Although there are outright tourist traps among Parga's waterfront-centered restaurants, some offer memorable food at good prices. Parganites and visitors enjoy **O Psaras,** one of the first restaurants along the dock, where Christos Giakis, ever the nonconformist, cooks up innovative renditions of the standard Greek repertoire: he makes his *pastitsio* (1800dr/€5.28) with a mix of cheeses instead of pasta. (Entrees 1200-2500dr/€3.52-7.34.) A few doors down, under a blue awning, **To Souli** cooks up lamb and feta *kleftiko* (1700dr/€5), assorted salads, and fresh fish by the kilogram (6800dr/€19.96 per kilo.) By the town beach, **Restaurant Ionio** (☎31 402) has a daily *prix fixe* 3-course menu that's a steal at 2300dr/€6.75. If you're in the mood to splurge, swank Rudis serves creative Greek and Italian cuisine at the near end of the ferry dock. (Entrees 3000-6000dr/€8.80-17.61.)

◪◿ NIGHTLIFE AND ENTERTAINMENT. Scuttling waiters and rambunctious children run willy-nilly through crowds of jovially inebriated northern Europeans at Parga's many waterfront bars and cafes. **Caravel,** near the ferry dock, is one of the town's most popular cafes, with an upstairs balcony. Tourists fill the seats all day sipping either a morning orange juice, an afternoon *frappe,* or an evening cocktail. (☎31 359. Drinks 1800-2000dr/€5.28-5.87.) The more removed **Blue Bar** (☎32 067), on the road leading to the castle, is a hipper choice, with stunning views of the sea and art-deco blue-light and mirror decorations to go with the 93 cocktails mixed up by the bartenders. Try the Happy Company (6000dr/€17.61)— served in a massive ceramic jug, it packs a punch to floor you and three of your friends. Though the tourists here are of the family ilk, there are a couple of discos, which don't really start jumpin' until around 2am. The biggest scenes are ▨**Camares** (☎32 000, 1400dr/€4.11 cover) behind Caravel, and **Arena** (☎31 871), down behind the town beach. Camares packs more drunk Swedes into its cave-like interior than you'll find at a Stockholm beer festival. The reproduced Sistine ceiling frescoes which decorate the walls are rarely appreciated. Arena caters to the young, hip, beautiful set behind its mirrored facade. **Factory,** whose neon signs point up side streets from near the ferry dock, is larger but slightly less packed. All clubs stay open until 4am on weekdays and at least 6am on weekends; the cover charge is usually 1000-1500dr/€2.93-4.40, which includes one drink.

◪◿ SIGHTS AND BEACHES. Perched above Parga, the massive **fortress,** or Kastro, was built by the Normans, but controlled by the Venetians from 1401 to 1797. In its glory days, the castle held 500 homes and 5000 Pargiotes. A surprising number of walls still stand; the cannons, however, which lined their tops, have long since fallen and are now strewn about the cobblestone enclosure. Although under reconstruction, the castle remains a perfect spot for a shady picnic, stroll, or dramatic re-enactment of a Venetian-Ottoman battle. It's five minutes from the water; follow the steps from the harbor up the hill. (Open 7am-10pm.)

Krionerou Beach, Parga's little waterfront, is very family-oriented; if that's not your scene, brave the 100m swim to the islet that holds the small **Church of the Panagia. Piso Krionerou Beach** is a 5min. walk around the rocky outcropping, but is a bit more secluded. Vastly nicer is long **Valtos Beach,** on the other side of the castle: a voluptuous crescent of sole-tickling pebbles turns to sand near the middle. Endless hordes of sun-worshipers sidle up to the rim of clear turquoise water. Here you can rent anything from a beach ball to a paragliding trip, or enjoy revelry at the packed **pool club.** Boats travel to the smaller beaches, including the more secluded **Lignos Beach** (2km), accessible by car or boat (1000dr/€2.93 one-way).

Tour companies along the waterfront and on the ferry dock book a variety of prepackaged excursions to more remote beaches, most of which include cheery stops at the **River Acheron**—the River Styx, mythical gateway to the Underworld—and the **Necromonteion,** the Oracle of the Dead, excavated in 1958. It was here that Odysseus conversed with the Shades, who spoke to him only after drinking offerings of blood. (Open 8:30am-3pm. 500dr/€1.47, students 300dr/€0.80.) Both are about a 20min. drive from Parga, but trips by **boat** (2500dr/€7.34) are more frequent and significantly cheaper than by bus.

IOANNINA Ιωαννινα ☎0651

On the shores of Lake Pamvotis, 96km miles east of Igoumenitsa, lies Epirus's capital, largest city, and transportation hub. Ioannina itself might not detain you for long, but the surrounding mountains and calm lake below deliver scenic views and an uplifting breeziness to the city. Likewise, the city's post-World War II architecture is redeemed by the small, older streets near the lake and the magnificent fortress, both remnants of its Ottoman past. No visitor to Ioannina can escape the foreboding, half-legend of Ali Pasha, "Lion of Ioannina" (see p. 214). The Albanian-born Pasha of Trikala seized Ioannina in 1788 and built himself a sumptuous, well-fortified palace there. Intending to make the city the capital of his Greek-Albanian Empire, Ali ruled with an iron fist, alternately fighting with and serving the Ottoman Sultan, who was theoretically his ruler. In his quest for power, Ali flirted with Napoleon, the British, and the Venetians, until finally the Sultan swatted him for high treason in 1822. Ali left his imprint on the city: his immense fortress and private Xanadu are here, and he died on nearby Nisi Island.

ORIENTATION AND PRACTICAL INFORMATION

Ioannina is at the center of Epirus, at the edge of steely Lake Pamvotis and circled by the peaks of Pindos. Not far into the lake is a small, hilly island simply called Nisi or Nissaki ("the island" or "the islet"). Ioannina's streets change names frequently, when they are named at all. The **city center** is a major intersection near the **clock tower** in Litharitses park. **G. Averof,** lined with jewelry stores and souvlaki stands, is a broad avenue that runs from the main gate of the old city to the city center. To reach the city center from the main **bus station,** walk uphill about 20m from the station to an intersection, where you'll see an **Agricultural Bank.** Facing the bank, walk uphill along the street on the left, which begins as **Dagli** but becomes **M. Botsari** after a block—the enormous Hotel Egnatia sign makes a useful landmark. You'll pass the **post office,** (the **OTE** is behind it, but not visible from Botsari) and will emerge next to the **Ionian Bank** on Averof, facing the park. On your right, past the long building labeled "Νομαρχηιον Ιοαννινου∀" ("Prefecture of Ioannina"), the road splits. The right side (*not* the sharp right) is **Napoleonda Zerva,** to the left is **Leoforos Dodoni.** At the set of streetlights before the Prefecture building, a road leads downhill to the smaller of the two intercity bus stations. To reach the **Frourio** (fortress) and the **waterfront,** follow the signs from the city center to Averof's opposite end, and veer left at the Frourio walls. You will now be on **Karamanli,** which passes the main gate of the Frourio to the dock and waterfront.

Flights: daily to **Athens** (1hr.; 10:55am and 9:30pm; 23,700dr/€69.55) and **Thessaloniki** (45min.; W,F, Su 11:45am and Tu, Th, Sa 2pm; 17,200dr/€50.48). **Olympic Airways** (☎26 218; reservations 23 120), where G. Averoff splits into Napoleonda Zerva and Leoforos Dodoni, above the city center. Open M-F 9am-3pm.

Buses: There are two terminals in town.

   Main terminal, Zosimadon 4 (☎27 442). To: **Athens** (7hr., 9 per day 7:15am-midnight, 8100dr/ €23.77); **Igoumenitsa** (2hr., 10 per day 5am-7:45pm, 2000dr/€5.87); **Konitsa** (1hr., 6 per day 5am-6:45pm, 1250dr/€3.67); **Larisa** (4hr., 6 per day 7am-9pm, 3800dr/€11.15); **Metsovo** (1½hr., 2 per day 5am-2pm, 1200dr/€3.52); **Parga** (2½hr., 8:30am, 2000dr/€5.87); and **Thessaloniki** (7hr., 6 per day 7am-9pm, 6650dr/€19.52).

   Smaller station: Bizaniou 21 (☎25 014). To: **Agrinio** (3hr., 6 per day 5:30am-7:15pm, 3150dr/ €9.24); **Arta** (1hr., 10 per day 5:45am-7:15pm, 2150dr/€6.31); **Dodoni** (30min.: M, W, F 6:30am and 3:30pm; 450dr/€1.32); **Patras** (4hr., 4 per day 9am-5:30pm, 4750dr/€13.94); and **Preveza** (2hr., 10 per day 6am-7:45pm, 2150dr/€6.31).

Taxis: (☎46 777, 778 or 779) also in the city center and at the bus station.

Tourist Office: EOT office (☎46 662; fax 49 139), about 500m down Leoforos Dodoni on the left immediately after the playground. Has **maps** and Ioannina prefecture propaganda, with a list of Rooms to Let in the province. Worth the 10min. walk from the city center. Open M-F 7:30am-2:30pm and 5-8:30pm, Sa 9am-1pm.

Banks: There are a number of banks with 24hr. **ATMs,** including **National Bank,** on Averof, just after the archaeological museum as you walk toward the waterfront.

Police: (☎26 326). Walk along Botsari to the post office—the police and the tourist police are just around the corner on 28 Octovriou. Open 8am-10pm, but available 24hr.

Tourist Police: (☎25 673), with the police. **Free maps** and other info available. Open 8am-10pm. Another kiosk is on the waterfront on Filosoffou.

Hospital: Two hospitals, each about 5km from the center of town. One handles emergencies on even dates (☎80 111); the other on odd dates (☎99 111).

Telephones: OTE (☎22 350 or 42 777), on 28 Octovriou. Open 8am-2:30pm.

Ioannina

🏠 ACCOMMODATIONS
Hotel Ermes, 1
Hotel Metropolis, 3
Hotel Paris, 2
Hotel Bretania, 4

Internet Access: Web@r, Stoa Sarka 31-32 (☎83 215), is tucked away among shops off Nap. Zerva. Turn right down the arcade after the McDonald's. You'll see the blue-edged windows through the passageway to the left of the Casbah Cafe. Nine fast terminals, (600dr/€1.76 per hr. Open 11am-4am.) Closer to the waterfront, **Hackers** (☎77 403) has 10 terminals at the end of G. Averoff, just before the fortress wall. Open 10am-2am. 800dr/€2.35 per hr with a 400dr/€1.35 min. charge.

Post Office: (☎25 498), at the intersection of 28 Octovriou and Botsari. Open M-F 7:30am-8pm. **Postal code:** 45221.

📌 ACCOMMODATIONS

Hotel Paris, Tsirigoti 6 (☎20 541). Walk uphill from the station to the Agricultural Bank and look left for the hotel's sign. The functional rooms are close to the main bus station, with large, neatly tucked beds, and small desks. Free luggage storage. Shared baths. Singles 6000dr/€17.61; doubles 9000dr/€26.41; triples 12,000dr/€35.22.

Hotel Metropolis, Kristali 2 (☎26 207), on the corner of Averof as you walk toward the waterfront. Comfortable, spacious rooms with wooden floors and bright, spotless rugs. Conveniently located, Metropolis is a 5min. walk from anywhere in the city. Singles 6000dr/€17.61; doubles 10,000dr/€29.35. Prices lower from Oct.-Apr.

Hotel Ermes (☎75 992), across from the main bus station on Sina. Bare, cell-block rooms with sinks, shared baths, lots of street noise. But cheap and convenient for anyone just passing through. Singles 5000dr/€14.67; doubles 6000dr/€17.61.

Hotel Bretania (☎ 23 396), on G. Averoff across from the clock tower. With private baths, desks, TVs, and A/C in every room, Bretania has all the comforts of a large hotel without the expense. (Singles 10,000dr/€29.35; doubles 14,000dr/€41.10.)

🌮 🍷 FOOD AND NIGHTLIFE

Several souvlaki stands are at the end of Averof near the Frourio (and elsewhere). Seafood restaurants circle the north side of the **waterfront.**

✉ Nousias (☎ 25 075), Karamanli 1. Take the street that passes the main gate of the Frourio toward the dock and the waterfront; it's a little sweetshop, brimming with confections, pastries, chocolates, and crispy delights all baked fresh in the back. Ten different flavors of ice cream are whipped up daily (300dr/€0.88 per scoop).

Oasis (☎ 75 400), in the city center park. An enormous, open-air restaurant serving generous portions of good food at low prices. Majestic mountain views from its sprawling patio. Classic Greek entrees like *kokoretsi* (lamb liver) and awesome feta-stuffed beef are 700-3000dr/€2.05-8.80. English menu posted at the gate. Open 24hr.

Filippas (☎ 31 170), on the waterfront before Stin Ithaki. Many of the delicious specials here are given the suffix "Filippas" to help keep the patrons oriented. Large vegetarian selection. Entrees 1500-2000dr/€4.40-5.87. Open 1:30pm-midnight.

Stin Ithaki (☎ 73 012), midway down the waterfront. This local favorite serves typical Greek fare at quiet waterfront tables. Entrees 1200-2000dr/€3.52-5.87.

Propodes (☎ 81 214), along the path to the Ali Pasha Museum. Secluded tables by the lake shore. Your meal is either whisked out of the cage (quail) or the tank (frogs, eels, crayfish). Entrees 800-1800dr/€2.35-5.28.

Most of Ioannina's bars are on the waterfront in two separate clusters, both at the base of the Frourio walls: cafes to the north and late-night bars to the south. **Kura Frosuni** (☎ 73 984) is right outside the fort, on the northwest corner of the peninsula. Always crowded with young people, the cafe has the closest tables to the water and a great view of Nisi island. To the south, **Ev. Ioanninos** (☎ 21 669) takes up three sides of a small square off the road, serving drinks from its outdoor bar from 9pm to 5am; prepare to see and be seen. **Skala** (☎ 37 676) is on the fourth side, churning loud music for heavily pierced wannabe Sex Pistols. **Monopolio** is Ioannina's biggest disco; locals dance to Greek or Latin tunes nightly. It's on the end of town, past seafood restaurants. (☎ 35 985. Drinks 500dr/€1.47; cover 1000dr/€2.93.)

👁 SIGHTS

FROURIO (OLD CITY)

The town's fortress, the Frourio (a.k.a. the **Kastro** or **Old City**) presides regally over the shore, a slender minaret at each end. Its massive, overgrown stone walls enclose a placid neighborhood of narrow streets and old Turkish-style homes. The Frourio contains two separate walled areas; the larger is the **Itş Kale** (Inner Citadel). Like any self-respecting fortress, the Frourio's main entrance on Karamanli has several sharp turns, making invasion tricky. Just outside this entrance is the shrine to **St. George the Neomartyr,** Ioannina's patron saint, whose Turkish overlords tortured and hanged him in 1838 for marrying a Christian. The Frourio's old **Synagogue,** Ioustinianon 16, is inside along the wall that faces Karamanli; go left from the main gate and follow the wall until you reach the white walls with a large brick-red double door. Ioannina's Jewish population shrank from 2000 to 150 after the Second World War, but the building still has services on Friday and Saturday.

HISTORY. Most of the castle was built in the 14th century by **Thomas Preljubovic,** the Serbian ruler of Ioannina who was also known as **Albanitoktonos** ("Albanian-killer"). In order to secure the city's bloodless surrender in 1430, the Turks assured the Greeks that they could remain in their houses within the walls. After a failed 1611 Greek insurrection led by **Skilosofos,** fanatical Bishop of Trikala, however, the Turks cracked down. One Sunday, when all the Greeks were in church (offering

NORTHERN GREECE

prayers that evidently went unanswered), the sneaky Turks seized their houses and moved right in. Skilosofos, the rebellious Bishop, was flayed alive on the cliff near his namesake esplanade. When Ali Pasha came to power in 1795, he forced his Greek subjects to rebuild the pre-existing Byzantine walls on a grander scale to fortify the capital of his dreamed-of empire. The project connected the ends of a partially existing moat, insulating the walls with lake water.

ITŞ KALE. To reach the Itş Kale from the main entrance, walk forward, veering left, following the signs. The small ruined buildings to the left and right as you enter the walls were guard posts, and the cafe on the left was originally a kitchen. Over to the immediate right along the wall are the remnants of Ali Pasha's **hamam** (baths). Around what is now the Silverworks gallery, the *serai* once housed Ali, his harem, and his ornately decorated audience chambers. Ali Pasha held most of his notorious tortures and executions at the plane tree near the *serai*, running the gory gamut from skinning to impaling and suspending on hooks hung from the tree's branches. Independence War hero **Katsandonis** is said to have sung patriotic hymns while being brutally hammered to death here, a scene re-enacted frequently in Greek folk shadow puppet theater. The ruins on the right of the complex are partially preserved, and are well worth a scramble. *(Open 7am-10pm.)*

The **Byzantine Museum** in the Itş Kale has a small collection of intricately carved wooden sanctuary doors, stone carvings, calligraphied manuscripts, and post-Byzantine icons. Informative English-language wall plaques chronicle the history of Epirus and Ioannina. *(☎ 27 761 or 39 580. Open Tu-Su 8am-7pm, M 12:30-7pm. 500dr/ €1.47, students 300dr/€0.88.)* The **Fethiye Camii** (Victory Mosque) next to the museum is the third mosque in its location, a space once occupied by a 13th-century church: the first was built of wood in 1430, and the second in 1611. The current mosque was rebuilt in 1795 by Ali Pasha himself. In front of the mosque, weeds and rubble obscure the **Tomb of Ali Pasha,** a sarcophagus that contains his headless body; from the neck up, he's buried in Istanbul. The tomb was originally decorated with a gilded cage that was looted by Nazis in 1943 but it was recently replaced by a green iron approximation. Ioaninna is the silversmithing capital of Greece, and at the **Silverworks Gallery,** you'll find snuffboxes, tea services, and belt buckles to prove it. An etching beside the desk depicts the Frourio's former glory. *(☎ 25 989. Show your Byzantine Museum ticket for admission to the gallery.)*

MUNICIPAL MUSEUM. The smaller of the Frourio's walled inner areas is a little farther to the left of Itş Kale—follow signs through the crooked streets to the museum housed in the lovely **Aslan Pasha Camii.** On the left as you enter is the long, rectangular former *medrasa* (school for Quranic study). The tombstones engraved in Arabic are the remains of an **Ottoman cemetery,** and the small building behind the mosque is Aslan Pasha's mausoleum. In 1618, following Bishop Skilosofos's rebellion, the Turks destroyed the former church of St. John Prodromus and replaced it with this elegant mosque. Worshipers washed their hands and feet in the fountains outside and left their shoes in small grooves along the entranceway before going inside to pray. The Municipal Museum focuses on Ioannina's diverse ethnic past and is divided into Jewish, Greek, and Muslim exhibits. Highlights include a sword that belonged to War of Independence hero Karaiskaki and a golden dress worn by Ali Pasha's wife, Lady Vasilikis. *(☎ 26 356. Open June-Sept. 8am-8pm; Oct.-May 8am-3pm. 700dr/€2.05, students 300dr/€0.88.)*

ARCHAEOLOGICAL MUSEUM. Aside from local finds, Paleolithic to Roman, the museum's highlights are the **lead tablets** used by puzzled ancients to inscribe their questions to the oracle to Zeus in nearby **Dodoni** (p. 214). Questions range from petty suspicions ("Has Pistos stolen the wool from the mattress?") to love advice ("Am I her children's father?"), and much angst has surrounded the dilemma of which deity to honor for which cause. Check out the **copper statues** from the oracle, which would speak the words of Zeus through batons they held in their hands. *(The museum is on a small road off Averoff near the city center, across from the yellow town hall building. ☎ 33 357 or 25 490. Open Tu-Su 8:30am-3pm. 500dr/€2.05, students free.)*

NORTHERN GREECE

GOING OUT WITH(OUT) A BANG When Ali Pasha heard that the Sultan had finally tired of his rebellious, empire-dreaming antics, he decided not to go gently into that good night. Holing up on Nisi, he gave orders to Selim, his most trusted servant, to stand guard over the castle's immense casks of gunpowder with a lighted torch. If Selim heard gunshots from the island, he was to blow himself, the castle, and the city with all its inhabitants clear into Lake Pamvotis. If anyone arrived bearing Ali's rosary, all was well and he could put out the torch. The sultan's envoys, however, managed to convince Ali's Greek wife Vasilikis to betray Ali's instructions, telling her it was her duty as a Greek to save the town from destruction. Vasilikis stole Ali's rosary as he slept, and presented it to the Turks, who immediately used it to convince Selim to put out his torch. When the gun battle began on Nisi the next day, Ali waited in vain for the explosion from the mainland before discovering his rosary had vanished. Before he could order revenge against his wife, he was killed by shots fired through the floor. For her part, Vasilikis retired to the coast of Turkey, where she lived with the captain of the force sent to kill her husband.

NISI (THE ISLAND). Wandering chickens, cheap silver shops, a tiny whitewashed village, and five deteriorating monasteries cover Ioannina's peaceful island, a ten-minute ferry ride from the harbor. Ali Pasha met his death on Nisi after falling out of the sultan's favor in a big way. Discovered and trapped in the second story of the island's **St. Pantaleemon monastery**, he was killed by shots fired up through the floorboards—you can still see the bullet holes (see **Going Out With(out) a Bang**, p. 214). The victors hung Ali's severed head out for public viewing for several days before transporting it on horseback all the way to the sultan in Constantinople. The monastery now houses the **Ali Pasha Museum**, which displays Ali Pasha's enormous *nargileh*, from which he happily puffs in almost every portrait, and a large painting of the sultan ceremoniously receiving the head of his fearsome ex-governor. What goes around comes around. *(Open 8am-8pm. 200dr/€0.59.)*

Signs point the way to St. Pantaleemon and the other four monasteries. A short walk from the museum, the **frescoes** of St. Nicholas Philanthropinos, painted by Katelanou in 1542, depict saints, the life of Jesus, and seven ancient sages (including Plato, Aristotle and Plutarch, just inside the door on the left) who were said to have proclaimed the coming of Jesus. If the monastery is locked, ask politely at the house next door for a tour. At the nearby *krifto scholio* ("secret school"), the forbidden Greek language was kept alive during the Ottoman reign. The monastery of **St. John Prodromos** has a crypt leading to a secret exit and path to the lake. ☎ 25 885. *Take one of the little ferries from Ioannina's waterfront (10min.; every hr. 6:30-11:30am and every 30min. 11:30am-11pm; in winter every hr. 7am-9pm; 250dr).*

■ DAYTRIPS FROM IOANNINA

DODONI Δωδώνη

*Your best bet is the **bus** to Melig (30 min; M, Th-F 2pm; 450dr/€1.32) from **Ioannina**'s smaller station—ask to be let off at the theater. You can then catch the return bus at 5:15pm. The bus to Dodoni (30min.; M, W, F 4:30pm; 450dr/€1.32) will leave you with barely 15min. to view the site. Otherwise, hire a **taxi** (at least 5000dr/€14.67 round-trip). ☎82 287. Open 8am-7pm; in winter 8am-5pm. 500dr/€1.47, students free.*

Ancient Dodoni, the site of mainland Greece's oldest oracle, hugs the base of a mountain 22km southeast of Ioannina. The name Dodoni originates from the Linear B language, and may mean "great mother of civilization;" Dodoni was probably the deity worshipped there before being supplanted by Zeus. Excavations suggest that the oracle was used from the Bronze Age (2600-1100 BC) through Christianity's arrival in the late 4th century AD. Worship of Zeus at Dodoni was well established by Homer's time: Odysseus himself came to the oracle at "wintry Dodona" for advice on ridding his house of Penelope's suitors. At its height, Dodoni was one of the ancient world's greatest oracles and home of the **Naia festival,** a series of athletic and dramatic contests held every four years in Zeus' honor.

The large **amphitheater** near the entrance to the site was built in the third century AD. The original design seated 18,000 before the Romans expanded it and improved the drainage system to accommodate their bloodsports. The annual ancient **theater festival** may have been revived, but the theater is in dire need of restoration. Beyond the amphitheater are the ruins of the oracle itself, where Zeus would answer queries through a still-standing oak tree. A clan of priests called the **Hellopes, Helloi,** or **Selloi** interpreted the wind's effect on the oak tree leaves' rustling, the flight of doves in its branches, and the sound of wooden batons held by a bronze statue of a boy striking a row of copper cauldrons. Using their sonic data, the priests made prophecies; trying to absorb the god's messages through the soil, they walked barefoot. Wild priestesses prone to divine frenzy eventually replaced the male *Selloi*. Little remains today of the original building that housed the tree and its horde of pilgrims. Additional buildings, now almost totally vanished, once surrounded the oracle: a 5th-century BC temple and the 350 BC *bouleuterion* and *prytaneion*. Following the Aetolian sack in 219 BC, a larger Ionic temple to Zeus was built in 168-167 BC, and the great amphitheater in the early 3rd century AD.

PERAMA CAVES

Take local bus #8 from the park behind the city center (15min., every 20min., 380dr/€1.12 round-trip). At Perama, follow the signs for ΕΠΗΛΑΙΟ ("cave"). ☎81 251 or 81 440. Open 8am-8pm; in winter 8am-5pm; tours every 45min. 2000dr/€5.87, students 700dr/€2.05.

A 163-step stairway leads through the spectrally lit, glimmering yellow Perama Caves, believed to be the largest in the Balkans. Excavations have turned up bears' teeth and bones in the almost two million-year-old stalagmites and stalactites, as well as **paintings** devoted to the ancient worship of Hades and Persephone. The path leads from narrow passageways to immense **caverns** hanging with eerie rock formations. The 45min., Greek-only guided tour mainly introduces selected stalagmites which have been named after other objects they uncannily resemble: "Tower of Pisa," "Egyptian Sphinx," and so on. Always a comfortable 17°C inside, the cave makes a great excursion during the scorching Greek afternoons.

METSOVO Μετσοβο ☎0656

On a forested mountainside below the Pindos Mountains' 1690m-high Katara Pass, Metsovo is almost painfully quaint: think ski town meets intimate village. Once upon a time, Marc Antony used to pack his wife off to Metsovo when he wanted to carry on more freely with Cleopatra. Now, daytripping tour buses of all nations frequent this officially designated "traditional" settlement. There's a booming trade in postcards and handmade wooden trinkets, but despite its kitschiness, Metsovo makes an excellent base for hiking, exploring Metsovo Lake, and trekking the nearby European E6 trail. Metsovo was once an important outpost on the route from Rome to Constantinople, and its inhabitants trace their roots to the Vlachi, a tribe of Latin-speaking Romans who served as guards. Today, older villagers are among the few in the world who still speak their Latin-like tongue.

🖿🚻 ORIENTATION AND PRACTICAL INFORMATION. Metsovo is about 100km inland in eastern Epirus, halfway between Kalambaka and Ioannina. On a stone wall in the main plateia a large, nearly illegible English-language **town map** lists hotels, sights, monasteries, restaurants, discos, and a 24-hour "sanitary station" (☎41 111) for **medical emergencies.** From the main plateia, **buses** depart for Ioannina (1½hr.; M-F 3 per day 6:30am-2:45pm, Sa-Su 2 per day; 1200dr/€3.52) and to Trikala via Kalambaka (2hr.; 9:15am, 3:15pm; 1950dr/€5.72). Buses to Thessaloniki stop at the main highway above town (about 5 times per day). For **schedule info,** check any of the cafes near the bus stops. Some 6 or 7 streets are off the large, open plateia, none of which is labeled. Standing with your back to the big town map, the street on the left side of the souvenir shop leads slightly downhill to the municipal **police** (☎41 233; open 24hr.) and the **OTE** (☎42 199; open 8am-1pm). The main road is on your left, choked with souvenir stands and tavernas; it leads uphill to the path to the Tositsas Museum and the **post office**. (☎44 200. Open M-F 7:30am-2pm.) The **town hall**, on the second floor of the large yellow building where the main road meets the plateia, can provide you with a few glossy brochures of the area. (☎41 207. Open 7:30am-2pm; walk around to the building's back entrance.) On your immediate right, a road runs downhill to Hotel Athens and Agios Nikolaos monastery; another wraps around the plateia past a **National Bank** with 24-hr. **ATM,** and the art museum. **Postal code:** 44200.

⌂ ACCOMMODATIONS. Room prices peak during the two high seasons: from mid-July to early September, and from December to March for ski season. It's best to call ahead. Plentiful domatia offer the cheapest rates, most are found by veering left before the OTE, past the super market. **John Xaralabapoulos**'s rooms are large and comfortable, with TVs and phones, some with fridges and stoves. Many of the rooms have glass encased religious icons in the corners of the ceiling. An oval, handpainted sign labeled "Domatia-Rooms" marks the entrance, just past the basketball court. (☎42 086. Singles 6000dr/€17.61; doubles 8000-9000dr/€23.48-26.41; triples and suites 12,000dr/€35.22 and up; prices rise in high season.) The **Hotel Athens** is just below the main plateia, immediately to your right with your back to the town map. Family run since 1925, the hotel offers comfortable rooms with private baths, meticulously made beds, and TVs. (☎41 725. Singles 7000dr/€20.53; doubles 8000dr/€23.48.) Hikers and campers are welcome to store their gear free of charge during visits to Pindos Mountain. The owners can also suggest hiking routes, and are your best source of information in Metsovo.

◨◪ FOOD AND ENTERTAINMENT. Many of the restaurants in Metsovo are very similar and cater to large groups of tourists. The restaurant in **Hotel Athens** serves Greek specialties on their shady patio. The *fasolada* (900dr/€2.64), and other local dishes are less expensive (entrees 800-1700dr/€2.35-5) and of better quality than most restaurants in the plateia. The house wine (500dr/€1.47) is excellent and made in Athens' own wine cellar. If you'd like to eat in the plateia, try local favorite **Krifi Folia** for its grilled meats, like *kokoretsi* (1900dr/€5.58) and *kontosoufli* (1400dr/€4.11). Also on the plateia is **Kria Vrisi,** which specializes in *hilopittes fournou* (a pasta), and **Galaxias,** on the patio atop the grassy hill overlooking the plateia. Galaxias has Metsovo's largest selection of dishes, all cooked within a traditional, ivy-covered mansion. Metsovo has little nightlife, but if you need a drink or three after dinner, head to **Tositsas** street, leading uphill from the plateia. There's little difference between bars; all charge 500-1500dr/€1.47-4.40 for drinks, and quiet down by midnight.

◪ SIGHTS. Thanks to the generosity of Baron Tositsas, a Metsovo-born Swiss baron who donated his fortune to the town, and Evangelos Averoff-Tositsas, Metsovo has far more sights than you'd expect of a 3500-person town. Off the main plateia, the spacious **E. Averoff Gallery** exhibits 19th- and 20th-century Greek art labeled in English and Greek, including the private collection of Averoff-Tositsas. Highlights of the museum's 200-plus paintings include impressionistic landscapes by Pantazis (1849-84), the *Burning of the Turkish Flagship* by Lytras (1832-1904), and the postmodern *Erotic* by Gravvalos. Green clay dinosaurs gaze amiably upon visitors in the colorful **children's art room** downstairs, where dried-bean collages and delightful tempera paintings complement their oily counterparts above. (☎41 210. Open W-M 10am-7pm. 500dr/€1.47, students 300dr/€0.88.) The **Tositsas Museum,** the family abode of the town benefactors, is the stone and timber *arhontiko* (mansion) up from the main road on the left; look for the sign opposite the Shell station. In the museum's rooms you'll find the beds, sofas, rugs, jewelry, clothing, and kitchen utensils used by the Tositsas clan from 1661 until 1950. In addition, there's also a collection of local folk art and dress. (Open F-W 9:30am-1:30pm and 4-6pm. 500dr/€1.47. Visitors are admitted only in small groups; wait at the museum's door for the guide, who appears every 30min.)

A 30min. walk from the plateia, is the **Agios Nikolaos Monastery;** signs point the way. Built in the 14th century and subsequently abandoned, the crumbling chapel was a refuge for itinerant shepherds for years. The smoke from their fires completely covered the luminous frescoes painted in 1702 by noted saint biographer Efsiat Chios, perfectly preserving their colors until they were rediscovered in 1950 by Averoff-Tositsas. A Greek woman now lives in and cares for the monastery, so politely knock to be admitted and wander through the chickens and cats. For information about outdoor activities in Metsovo and **Valiakalda National Park,** contact the town hall (☎41 207) or the family that owns Hotel Athens (☎41 725).

ZAGOROHORIA Ζαγοροχωρια

The Zagorohoria is an assemblage of 46 villages north of Ioannina. According to the stipulations of Zagori custom, buildings must be crafted out of gray stone from the surrounding mountains. The villages appear, from a distance, as oddly geometric rock formations poking humbly out of the green hills. Bridging streams between villages are the famous two- and three-arched stone bridges of Epirus, best exemplified in the village of Kipi. The natural beauty hasn't prevented native Zagorians from heading to the big city, though. Some villages now function as quiet getaways for Greek and European tourists seeking clear air, simple food, and extraordinary hiking. Outside Monodendri, the Papingo villages, and Tsepelovo, however, no more than a handful of tourists visit each year, leaving the other villages as pristine as they were hundreds of years ago.

◪ **HIKING AND THE OUTDOORS.** Although the villages themselves are well worth a day or two, most tourists come to this rugged region for what lies in the hinterlands—rough-riding rivers, stark peaks, and the renowned **Vikos Gorge.** Outdoor enthusiasts of every skill level will find more than enough to satisfy them in the Zagorohoria and the surrounding **Vikos-Aoös National Park.** For more information, contact the **Hellenic Mountaineering Club (EOS)** in Ioannina (☎(0651) 22 138), Mario at **Pension Monodendri** (☎(0653) 71 300), or Nikos at **Koulis Restaurant** in Megalo Papingo (☎(0653) 41 138). Rafting and kayaking trips can be arranged in spring through **Konitsa's Paddler School** (☎(0655) 23 777 or 23 101). **Robinson Expeditions** runs guided tours, rock climbing expeditions, and rafting trips out of their office in Ioannina (☎(0651) 74 989; fax (0651) 25 071) and their activity center in Kipi (☎(0653) 71 041). The best times for hiking are late May, early June, and September. Make sure to get good maps (available through the EOS) and good directions through reliable sources before heading out. *Periptero*, in each of the Zagorohoria villages, sell excellent maps, marking all of the major trails, for 1500dr/€4.40.

MONODENDRI Μονοδενδρι ☎0653

Many an enchanted traveler has tripped dreamily through Monodendri's cobbled maze, illuminated only by celestial bodies and the summertime multitudes of fireflies. Despite a smattering of hikers, skiers, and city-escapees in summer and winter, the village remains as peaceful, unsullied, and perfect as a mountain stream. Its natural and architectural beauty makes it a pleasant base for hikers, in addition to the numerous inexpensive yet beautifully furnished hotels.

◪◪ **ORIENTATION AND PRACTICAL INFORMATION.** The single paved road in Monodendri runs through the upper end of the village; the bus stop, all of the hotels, and most of the restaurants cluster there. Buses go to **Ioannina** (45min., 7am and 5pm, 800dr/€2.35). The town plateia is accessible via a footpath descending to the right as you leave the bus stop; follow the path downhill and turn left when the road forks. The plateia is bare, save for a **phone** and **post box,** but signposts for all the trailheads begin here. The narrow cobblestone paths of Monodendri can be a disorienting maze of grey rock, but most paths meander in one way or another towards the plateia. There is **no bank,** but some hotels may be able to cash traveler's checks or change money in a pinch.

 ACCOMMODATIONS. Monodendri's plentiful accommodations are generally high in quality and low in price, making it one of the most affordable villages in the Zagorohoria. **Pension Monodendri,** just up the road from the bus stop, has extremely comfortable rooms in the traditional Zagori style: low platform beds highlight rooms strewn with cushions and colorful wool rugs, drapes, and wall hangings. There's a garden in back and a great restaurant downstairs. It's ideal lodging for hikers; the owner's English-speaking son Mario is full of info on trekking in the area. His parents, Dimitris and Katerina Daskalopoulou, can arrange to pick you up in the surrounding villages after your day hike (from Vikos village 8000dr/€23.48; from Megalo Papingo 10,000dr/€29.35) and can provide a bagged lunch (1000dr/€2.93) to take on the trail. (☎71 300 or 71 410. Singles 6000dr/€17.61; doubles 8000dr/€23.48.) The last hotel before the road curves uphill, homey **Zarkada** provides spacious rooms with wide balconies, stunning views, and sparkling modern baths. (☎71 305 or 71 308. Singles 10,000dr/€29.35; doubles 13,000dr/€38.15. Breakfast 2000dr/€5.87.) Closest to the bus station on the left is **Ladia,** a castle-like structure at the entrance to the village offering comfy, modern rooms with private baths, TVs, rugs, and the occasional fireplace. (☎71 483. Singles 7000dr/€20.54; doubles 12,000dr/€35.22. Breakfast 2000dr/€5.87.) **Kaliterimi,** to the right 40m off the main road just before Pension Monodendri, boasts spacious rooms with TVs, baths, woolly shag rugs, and the best views in Monodendri. (☎71 510 or 71 484. Singles 8000dr/€23.48; doubles 10,000dr/€29.35; triples 12,000dr/€35.22.)

 FOOD. A few tavernas are interspersed among these pensions on the main road. The friendliest is **Katerina's,** at the porch of Pension Monodendri, where Mrs. Daskalopoulou prepares an ever-changing menu for two (4500dr/€13.21), including an array of delicious traditional Zagori pies. **Oxia,** between Ladia and Zarkada, is a tour bus favorite, and has fresh local trout (1300dr/€3.82) and plenty of goat, cooked numerous ways (1200-1600dr/€3.52-4.70). Usually the most crowded, **Restaurant Vikos Gorge,** just above Pension Monodendri, has a spectacular view from its wide porch. An array of local wines complement the stuffed tomatoes (1200dr/€3.52) and *kotopita* (1300dr/€3.82).

 SIGHTS. There isn't much to see or do in Monodendri beyond admiring the architecture, breathing the mountain air, and stocking up for a foray into Vikos Gorge. Those unwilling to tackle Vikos head-on, however, can enjoy breathtaking, unparalleled views of the entire gorge at the must-see natural "balcony," about a 1½hr. walk on the main road uphill from the village. A large section of the road can be bypassed from a red-blazed trail that begins behind Pension Monodendri. The road eventually ends and gives way to a small footpath, leading to a vantage point for gazing down on the gorge's three main chasms. The sunset glow is spectacular. The abandoned Monastery of Agia Paraskevi, about 600m from the plateia, also has impressive views. From the monastery, a treacherous path (use caution on this path) skirts along the edge of the canyon and leads to a small cave not nearly as impressive as the 100m drop a few feet from the opening. Signs from the plateia point the way to Megali Spilia, another nearby cave where Zagorians used to stock food and water and hide from occasional Albanian marauders.

VIKOS GORGE Χαραδρα Βικου

According to the *Guinness Book of World Records*, the Vikos Gorge, whose walls are 900m deep but only 1100m apart, is the steepest canyon on earth. This "Greek Grand Canyon" stretches from the village of Kipi in the south to Megalo Papingo at its northernmost tip, winding its way through the center of the Zagorohoria. In spring, the river that has taken millions of years to form its eponymous gorge rushes along the 15km stretch of canyon floor. By summertime this mighty force is reduced to a feeble trickle crawling through the massive white boulders in a bone-dry riverbed. Rusted iron deposits in the gorge's sedimentary rock leave an orange-pink tint on the walls suggestive of the last gleamings of sunset. Even more colorful are the spring wildflowers, summer butterflies, autumn foliage, and views of the bright-green spring running below Vikos village. The long hike through the gorge is impressive: the nearly vertical canyon sides, to which throngs of trees stubbornly cling, tower hundreds of meters overhead.

◪ THE HIKE. The well-marked Vikos trail is part of the **Greek National O3 route.** Before you go, be sure to get a **map.** The *periptero* on the main road through Mon-odendri sells detailed maps of all the trails in Zaghoria for 1500dr/€4.40. If you get confused, just look for the red diamonds on white square backgrounds with "O3" stenciled on them, which consistently mark the path. Most enter the gorge from **Monodendri,** the highest of the villages, but it can also be accessed from **Kipi,** the **Papingo** villages, and from **Vikos village.** It takes 4½hr. to walk between Vikos village and Monodendri, and 6hr. between the Papingos and Monodendri.

To reach the gorge from Monodendri, take the marked path from the plateia. After about 40min. along the steep descending trail, you'll reach a fork in the path. Go left to enter the canyon's dry riverbed of smooth rocks and the far-off villages of Papingo and Vikos; to the right, about an hour away, lies the village of Kipi with its trademark stone bridges. Take the left fork as it climbs above the left bank of the riverbed, leaving the canyon floor. The path continues for some time, fairly level and pleasant, through a mossy, shady woodland along the riverbank. Be careful when crossing the deceptively treacherous screes (long, narrow cascades of loose rock that stretch up the canyon walls). After about two hours, there will be a sign for a **water tap** where you can fill your bottle—this is the halfway point. Continuing straight on the trail after the water tap, you'll pass some open groves mowed clean by grazing horses. Eventually you'll emerge in very bare, exposed, sunny terrain. Around this area (about 4-5hrs. from Monodendri), listen for the sound of gushing water from the previously bone-dry riverbed. These are the Void-homatis Springs, bubbling at a poorly marked **major crossroads.**

Continue on the path uphill, on the left bank, to reach **Vikos** village, about 45min. farther away. Vikos has only one accommodation: small rooms rented by **Sotiris Karpouzis** (☎ (0653) 41 176. 12,000dr/€35.22). For the **Papingo** villages, make a right and go down the slope to the inviting springs, which lie beneath a large, flat area with a campfire circle, good for tenting. Cross over the riverbed (on the right where it's still dry) and head uphill, following the red and white O3 blazes. The green, shady springs are the perfect place for a swim, if you have the time; at least wade and refill your water bottle. From here, an arduous 1½hr. ascent brings you to the twin villages of **Megalo Papingo** and **Mikro Papingo.** You'll find another small stream to drink from, but just before that a sign in Greek points the way: Megalo Papingo to the left, Mikro Papingo to the right.

MEGALO PAPINGO Μεγαλο Παπινγο ☎ 0653

The two Papingo villages are the most developed of the Zagorohoria. Their position at the end of the Vikos Gorge ensures their popularity with backpackers and independent travelers. In recent years, Megalo Papingo, the larger of the two, has also become a favorite spot for vacationing Greeks seeking a retreat from Thessaloniki and Ioannina. These villages boast 17 separate lodging choices, while most of their 44 Zagori cohorts don't have 17 full-time residents. Luckily, the influx of visitors hasn't diminished the villages' peculiar stony beauty.

◪◪ ORIENTATION AND PRACTICAL INFORMATION. The large, austere stone church and its attendant bell tower stand at the entrance to the village, at the end of the road to the outside world and next to the bus stop. From here, one cobblestone main street snakes around the town, containing most of the pensions and restaurants. The road to Mikro Papingo is clearly marked to the right of the clock tower; the trailhead for Vikos Gorge is 20m down this road on the right. Buses go to **Ioannina** (1hr.; M, W, F 7am, Su 10:30am; 1300dr/€3.82). Megalo Papingo has a phone and a mailbox, both on its main street. For information on the village and on all outdoor activities, ask for Nikos at Koulis Cafe (☎41 138). To reach it, walk uphill, to the left when facing the clock tower from the main road, and quickly take another left at the wrought-iron fence.

ACCOMMODATIONS AND FOOD. Because of its popularity with rich Greeks, lodging in Papingo is extremely expensive. Single rooms start at 10,000dr/€29.35. Food is available at most of the hotels and a number of small restaurants. **Kalliopi,** uphill to the right from the bell tower, has beautifully furnished rooms around a vine-canopied patio. (☎41 081. Singles 10,000dr/€29.35; doubles 14,000dr/€41.09.) The low-ceilinged rooms at **Pension Koulis,** with fireplaces and baths, are a good deal for groups of two or three. (☎41 138. Doubles 13,000dr/€38.15; triples 17,000dr/€49.89.) Behind its beautiful entranceway of hanging grape vines, the 120-year-old **Astraka,** on the other end of the main road, offers comfortable, pleasantly decorated rooms with baths, fireplaces, and TVs, plus a cozy living room. (☎41 693. Singles 12,000dr/€35.22; doubles 15,000dr/€44.02; triples 17,000dr/€49.89; quads 20,000dr/€58.69.) **O Nikos,** with outdoor tables just off the main plateia, has the standard menu for reasonable rates. Look for the purple "*Estiatorio*" sign uphill from the bell tower. (Entrees 1500-1850dr/€4.40-5.43.) **Restaurant Papingo** (☎41 121), to the right of the belltower in the Papingo Pension, is popular and serves delicious traditional Zagori pies.

KIPI Κηποι   ☎0653

Another option for hiking the gorge begins at its lowest point, in the tiny village of Kipi. One of the most beautiful and uncharted villages of the Zagorohoria, Kipi climbs up a hill above the one main road, its cobbled streets and stone walls rising in a gentle slope to the church and clock tower at the top. Kipi's most alluring attractions, other than the peace and quiet, are its traditional **stone bridges,** built in the 17th and 18th centuries, at the height of Zagori culture. The double- and triple-arched bridges are just outside the village; four lie within 1km on each side of the village. **Robinson Expeditions** runs an activity center in Kipi, right across the road from Hotel Artemis. The center sells hiking maps and has information on the area, as well as offering extensive guided tours of the gorge, rock climbing expeditions, rafting, and a weekly platter of events. Call ahead to find the schedule; trips are occasionally canceled if there's not enough interest. (☎71 041. Open M 2-6pm, Tu-Su 9am-3pm.) The best way to enter the gorge from Kipi is to head out on the road toward Ioannina and look for paths to the gorge floor by the bridges. The hike to Monodendri is about 2 hours along the riverbed.

The **bus** to Ioannina (45min.; M, W, F 8am; 700dr/€2.05) leaves from the road right at the bottom of the hill. To find the small plateia and the church, pick a street and follow it to the top—the town's clock tower is hard to miss. There aren't many places to stay in Kipi; your best bets are the rooms offered at **Artemis,** which are big, comfortable, and decorated in the traditional Zagori style. Follow the sign up the hill off the main road. (☎71 644. Singles 9000dr/€26.41 with breakfast; doubles 9000dr/€26.41 without breakfast.) The best dining option is **Stou Mikalis,** on the road opposite the bus stop, which serves delicious Zagori pies of chicken, vegetable, and cheese. (☎71 632. Entrees 900-2500dr/€2.64-7.34.)

TRAVEL ADVISORY. On July 26, 2001, the US State Department issued a travel warning advising American citizens against all travel to the **Former Yugoslav Republic of Macedonia.** All US citizens in the nation of Macedonia at the time were urged to depart due to rising anti-foreign sentiment and increased acts of intimidation and violence against American citizens in the country. The situation in Macedonia is unsettled and potentially dangerous as a result of armed clashes between Macedonian security forces and ethnic Albanian extremists. The unrest has resulted in periodic closures of the border between Macedonia and Kosovo. Travel restrictions on private American citizens are subject to change at short notice; see **Travel Advisories** on the US State Department website (www.state.gov) for updates.

NORTHERN GREECE

MACEDONIA Μακεδονια

Some of the most captivating Greek landscapes and sights belong to Macedonia, including the sublime Olympian hiking trails, millions of sparkling mosaic tessarae from Thessaloniki's Byzantine churches, Karala's Ottoman *imaret*, the Royal Tombs from Vergina, the austere monasteries of Mt. Athos, and the surf and sand of Halkidiki's two peninsulas. Greece's largest province tops the mainland like an ancient gold-wrought crown. You'll encounter the region's symbol, a 16-pointed star, on everything: the sidewalk at the OTE, the backs of 100-drachma coins, bumper stickers saying "Macedonia is Greece," and even Philip II's gold casket in Vergina. Though rarely touristed, it's far from a backwater: hip, lively Thessaloniki, Greece's second-largest city, keeps the whole region on its toes.

THESSALONIKI Θεσσαλονικη ☎ 031

Thessaloniki, a jumble of ancient, Byzantine, European, Turkish, Balkan, and contemporary Greek cultural and historical debris, fans out from its hilltop fortress toward the Thermaic Gulf. At its peak, the fortress oversees the Old Town's placid streets and long, congested avenues. Among glitzy and lackluster concrete facades, well-heeled Thessalonians strut their stuff, their hip-clipped cell phones swinging inches from the beggars and street children camped out on the sidewalk. Golden mosaics, frescoes, and floating domes still gleam in the industrial city's Byzantine churches. Most travelers spend a couple of days in Thessaloniki clubbing and sightseeing, and seek tranquility in countryside hikes.

Macedonia's capital and Greece's second city, Thessaloniki was founded in 316 BC. Needing a new city to name after his wife (Alexander the Great's sister), Cassander, the ruler of Macedon, picked the Thermaic Gulf shore and transplanted the citizens of 26 pre-existing towns to his new Salonica. The new burg flourished under Macedonian rule as the only port on the Via Egnatia and a vital link between trade centers. In the first century AD, the apostle Paul put Thessaloniki on the map by writing First, and possibly Second Thessalonians to pioneering Christians. A thousand years later, missionary followers of the brothers Cyril and Methodius—inventors of the Cyrillic alphabet—arrived, and set up their headquarters.

Despite frequent and bloody raids by Goths, Avars, Slavs, Bulgars, and Latin Crusaders, Salonica rose to become the Byzantine Empire's second-most important city, after Constantinople. The Turks ended these glory days, conquering the city by siege in 1421. Throughout the centuries of Ottoman rule, Thessaloniki remained a cultural and intellectual center, dominated largely by its population of Sephardic Jews, who had fled the Spanish Inquisition and arrived in 1492. In 1881, Salonica saw the birth of Mustafa Kemal, who would rise to world fame as Atatürk, founder of the Turkish Republic. Ottomans ruled Thessaloniki until the First Balkan War in 1912, 90 years after most of Greece had become independent. The Great Fire of 1917 destroyed the bulk of the city's historical downtown area, damaging many of its churches. Although the city began the 20th century with a population more European than Hellenic, the population exchange (see p. 17), the partitioning of the Ottoman Empire, and the death of almost all of the city's 50,000 Jews during the Holocaust have left Thessaloniki almost homogeneously Greek.

■ TRANSPORTATION

BY BUS

KTEL buses run out of a number of stations, each serving a region or large city. Most stations are in the no-man's-land between the port and the railway station, or just north of the railway. The **Chalkidiki Station** is east, beyond the end of Egnatia—walk down Karamanli past the hospital, turn left on Kanari, and

NORTHERN GREECE

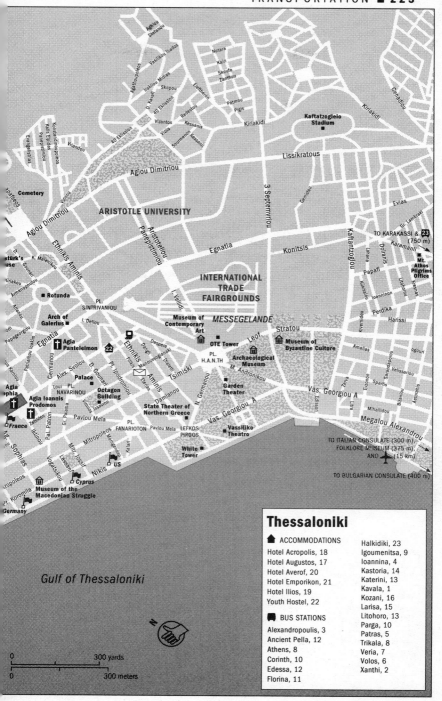

Thessaloniki

ACCOMMODATIONS
Hotel Acropolis, 18
Hotel Augustos, 17
Hotel Averof, 20
Hotel Emporikon, 21
Hotel Ilios, 19
Youth Hostel, 22

BUS STATIONS
Alexandropoulis, 3
Ancient Pella, 12
Athens, 8
Corinth, 10
Edessa, 12
Florina, 11

Halkidiki, 23
Igoumenitsa, 9
Ioannina, 4
Kastoria, 14
Katerini, 13
Kavala, 1
Kozani, 16
Larisa, 15
Litohoro, 13
Parga, 10
Patras, 5
Trikala, 8
Veria, 7
Volos, 6
Xanthi, 2

Gulf of Thessaloniki

0 ____ 300 yards
0 ____ 300 meters

right two blocks later onto Karakassi. Some stations hand out printed timetables, others post schedules on chalkboards and signs. The **EOT**, on Aristotelous (☎271 888; open M-Sa 7:30am-3pm), has info (in Greek) on schedules, fares, duration, station locations, and telephone numbers, and will call to figure out anything they don't know.

International buses (☎599 100) leave from the **main train station** (☎517 517), on Monastiriou in the city's western part; take any bus down Egnatia to get there (100dr/€0.29). Buses go to: **Istanbul, Turkey** (12hr., 2:30am, 24,300dr/€71.31); **Koritsa, Albania** (6hr., 8am and midnight, 6600dr/€19.37); **Sofia, Bulgaria** (6hr., 4 per day 7am-10pm, 5600dr/€16.43).

Domestic buses leave from different stations; check in advance.

DESTINATION	TIME	FREQUENCY	PRICE	STATION
Athens	6hr.	13 per day	9000dr/ €26.41	Monastiriou 69 (☎527 265)
Corinth	7½hr.	10:30am	10,500dr /€30.81	Monastiriou 69 (☎527 265)
Edessa	2¾hr.	14 per day 6am-8pm	1750dr/ €5.14	Anagenisseos 22 (☎525 100)
Florina	3hr.	6 per day 7:30am-7pm	3300dr/ €9.68	Anagenisseos 42 (☎522 161)
Sithonia	2hr.	8 per day 6am-7pm	2750dr/ €8.07	Karakassi 68 (☎924 444)
Igoumenitsa	8½hr.	8pm	8600dr/ €25.24	Monastiriou 51 (☎545 302)
Ioannina	7hr.	5 per day 7:30am-9:30pm	6650dr/ €19.52	Giannitsa 39 (☎512 444)
Kastoria	3½hr.	7 per day 7:30am-7:30pm	4100dr/ €12.03	Anagenisseos 4 (☎522 162)
Katerini	1hr.	every 30min. 6:30am-10:15pm	1400dr/ €4.11	Sapfous 10 (☎519 109)
Kavala	2½hr.	4 per day 9am-6pm	3150dr/ €9.24	Langadas 59 (☎525 530)
Kozani	2½hr.	every hr. 6am-8pm	2550dr/ €7.48	26 Oktovrion 20 (☎522 488)
Larisa	2hr.	14 per day 8:30am-9:45pm	3400dr/ €9.98	Enotikon 4 (☎544 133)
Litohoro	1½hr.	11 per day 6:30am-10:15pm	1900dr/ €5.58	Sapfous 10 (☎519 109)
Ouranopolis	3hr.	7 per day 6am-6:30pm	2600dr/ €7.63	Karakassi 68 (☎924 444)
Parga	8¾hr.	10am	9400dr/ €27.59	Monastiriou 69 (☎527 265)
Patras	8hr.	8:15am and 3:15pm	8250dr/ €24.21	Monastiriou 87 (☎525 253)
Ancient Pella	40min.	every 15-20min.	750dr/ €2.20	Anagenisseos 22 (☎525 100)
Trikala	3hr.	6 per day 8am-9pm	4000dr/ €11.74	Monastiriou 75 (☎510 110)
Veria	1½hr.	every hr. 8am-7pm	1450dr/ €4.26	Monastiriou 75 (☎522 160)
Volos	3½hr.	6 per day 8am-10pm	3900dr/ €11.45	Monastiriou 79 (☎512 122)
Xanthi	6½hr.	8 per day 8am-1:30am	3900dr/ €11.45	Ag. Nestoriou 22 (☎526 526)
Alexandropoulis	5hr.	6 per day 8am-10:30pm	6400dr/ €18.78	Koloniari 31 (☎514 111)

NORTHERN GREECE

BY BOAT

Ferries: Buy tickets at **Karacharisis Travel and Shipping Agency,** Koundouriotou 8 (☎524 544; fax 532 289), on the corner. Open M-F 8:30am-8pm, Sa 8:30am-2:30pm. Ferries go to: **Chios** (21hr.; Tu, F, Sa midnight; 8900dr/€26.12); **Ios** (23½hr., F 7:30pm, 9900dr/€29.05); **Iraklion** (24hr., 5 per week, 12,700dr/€37.27); **Lesvos** (9hr., W and Su 1am, 8300dr/€24.36); **Limnos** (7hr.; Tu 6pm, Su 1:30am; 5700dr/ €16.73); **Kos** (18½hr., Su 1pm, 13,000dr/€38.15); **Mykonos** (16hr.; 7 per week, 9900dr/€29.05); **Naxos** (21hr., F 7:30pm and Th 9:30pm, 9300dr/€27.29); **Paros** (18hr., 4 per week, 9900dr/€29.05); **Rhodes** (21½hr., W 4pm, 15,600dr/€45.78); **Samos** (14hr., W 1pm, 9500dr/€27.88); **Santorini** (26hr., 5 per week, 9900dr/ €29.05); **Syros** (13hr.; M 2pm, Th 9:30pm, F 7pm; 10,100dr/€29.64); **Tinos** (16hr.; Tu 3pm, F 7:30pm, Sa midnight; 9700dr/€28.47).

Flying Dolphins: Buy tickets at **Crete Air Travel,** Dragoumi 1 (☎547 407 or 534 376), with the blue awning, across from the main port. Open M-F 8:30am-9pm, Sa 8:30am-3pm, Su 9am-3pm. Flying Dolphins leave Su-F 1:45pm, Sa 8am in summer. Service to: **Alonnisos** (5hr., 8900dr/€26.12); **Skiathos** (3¾hr., 9100dr/€26.71); **Skopelos** (4½hr., 8900dr/€26.12).

BY TRAIN

To reach the **main terminal** (☎517 517), on Monastiriou in the western part of the city, take any bus down Egnatia (100dr/€0.29).

International trains to: **Istanbul, Turkey** (13hr., 7:25am 12,000dr/€35.22); **Skopje, FYR Macedonia** (5hr., 6:15pm, 4650dr/€13.65); **Sofia, Bulgaria** (10½hr., 10pm, 6150dr/€18.05). An **OSE** office (☎598 112), on the corner of Aristotelous and Ermou, sells **tickets** and has **schedules.** Open M-Sa 8am-3pm.

Domestic trains to: **Alexandroupolis** (7hr., 5 per day 7am-11:40pm, 3300dr/€9.68); **Athens** (6-8hr., 10 per day 7am-11:40pm, 4800dr/€14.09); **Edessa** (2½hr., 8 per day 6am-10pm, 1000dr/€2.93); **Florina** (4hr.; 7:30am, 9:15am, 6pm; 1450dr/€4.26); **Larisa** (2½hr., 12 per day 5:20am-11:40pm, 1600dr/€4.70); **Volos** (4hr., 4 per day 8am-10:20pm, 2300dr/€6.75); **Xanthni** (4½hr., 5 per day 5:50am-11:00pm, 2400dr/€7.04).

BY PLANE

The **airport** (☎473 720), 16km east of town, can be reached by **bus #78** (120dr/ €0.35) from the train station or Pl. Aristotelous, or by **taxi** (2500dr/€7.34). There's an **EOT** tourist office branch (☎985 215) at the airport.

Olympic Airways: office at Koundouriotou 3 (☎230 240 or 260 122; fax 229 725), is open M-Sa 7am-3:30pm. Call for reservations (☎281 880) M-Sa 7am-8pm. To: **Athens** (1hr., 10 per day, 14,000dr/€4.11); **Cyprus** (2hr., Tu and F 4pm, 30,500dr/€89.51); **Hania** (1¾hr.; Tu 8:30am, F 10:40am; 31,100dr/€91.27); **Iraklion** (1¾hr., Th and Sa 4:20pm; 28,900dr/€84.81); **Ioannina** (35min., W-M 10:30am, 13,100dr/€38.44); **Lesvos** (50min., W-F and Su 6am, 21,900dr/€64.27); **Limnos** (50min., W-M 5:45am, 15,000dr/€44.02); **Rhodes** (1¼hr.; M, F, Su 7:45am; 31,800dr/€93.32); **Istanbul,** Turkey (2hr.; Tu, Th-F, Su 3:50pm; 57,700dr/€169.33). Also to: **Chios, Corfu, Larnaka, Mykonos, Samos,** and **Santorini** (2-3 per week).

▟ LOCAL TRANSPORTATION

Thessaloniki and its suburbs are connected by an extensive public transportation network. **Local buses** cost 100dr/€0.29 and run throughout the city. An **office** across from the train station provides limited schedules. Buses #8, #10, #11, and #31 run up and down Egnatia. Buy tickets at *periptera*, or ticket booths at major stations.

NORTHERN GREECE

✦ ORIENTATION

Thessaloniki stretches out along the waterfront of the Thermaic Gulf's north shore. Its rough grid layout—established after the Great Fire of 1917—and the orienting presence of the sea make it nearly impossible to get lost, but street signs are haphazard, so a map can be helpful. **Egnatia** runs straight down the middle of town; the road was originally part of a highway from Rome to Byzantium, and now hold the city's buses, sights, and cheapest hotels congregate there. From Egnatia, running parallel to the water, the main streets are **Ermou, Tsimiski, Mitropoleos,** and **Nikis,** which go along the waterfront. Inland from Egnatia is **Ag. Dimitriou** and the **Old Town** beyond. Intersecting all these streets and leading from the water into town are **I. Dragoumi, El. Venizelou, Aristotelous, Ag. Sophias,** and **Eth. Aminis.** Tsimiski, Mitropoleos, Ag. Sophias, and all the little streets between Aristotelous and Ipodromiou are the main shopping streets. The cheaper hotels are on Egnatia, banks on Tsimiski, and waterfront bars and cafes on Nikis. Nikis leads east, past various popular bars and cafes, to the **White Tower,** Thessaloniki's favorite monument, which presides over the harbor like an oversized chess piece. The roads north of Ag. Dimitriou grow increasingly tiny and steep, toward the **Old Town**'s ancient fortress walls, marvelous walks, panoramic views, and cheap tavernas. Between Tsimiski and the Arch of Galerius, **Pl. Navarinou,** with its Roman ruins, is a meeting ground for Thessaloniki's youth. Facing inland, head left on Mitropoleos past **Pl. Elefterias** to reach **Ladadika,** a former red-light district restored into a lovely pocket of turn-of-the-century cafes, bars, and tavernas.

◪ PRACTICAL INFORMATION

Tourist Offices: EOT (☎271 888, 222 935 or 265 507; fax 265 504), Pl. Aristotelous, 1 block from the water, has **free maps,** hotel listings, transportation schedules and prices, and festival information. Exceedingly helpful; English spoken. Open M-Sa 7:30am-3pm. Another EOT office (☎985 215) is at the **airport. UTS,** Mitropoleos 28 (☎286 756; fax 283 156), is near Pl. Aristotelous; ring the bell by the door labeled "28" t and go to the 7th floor. Ask for English-speaking Liza (make sure you're carrying *Let's Go*). Open M-F 9am-5pm.

Permits for Mt. Athos: Visit the **Holy Executive of the Holy Mt. Athos Pilgrims' Bureau,** Kou. Karamanli 14, 1st fl. (☎861 611; fax 861 811). Letter of recommendation not needed, but make sure you bring your passport. Karamanli is the eastern extension of Egnatia; take **bus #12** from Mitropoleos at Pl. Aristotelous and ask to be let off at Papafio. English spoken. Open M-F 9am-2pm, Sa 10am-12pm.

Consulates: Bulgaria: N. Manou 12 (☎829 210). Open M-F 10am-noon. **Canada:** Tsimiski 17 (☎256 350). Open M-F 9am-12pm. **Cyprus:** L. Nikis 37 (☎260 611). Open M-F 9am-1pm. **Turkey:** Ag. Dimitriou 151 (☎248 452). Open M-F 9am-noon. **United Kingdom:** Venizelou 8 (☎278 006). Open M-F 8am-1pm. **United States:** Tsimiski 43 (☎242 900). Open M, W, F 9am-noon.

Banks: Banks with currency exchange and 24hr. **ATMs** line Tsimiski, including **National Bank,** Tsimiski 11 (☎538 621). Open M-F 7:45am-2pm and 6-8pm.

American Express: Memphis Travel, Aristotelous 3, 1st floor (☎282 351). Cashes **traveler's checks** (no commission) and **exchanges currency** (500dr/€1.47 flat rate). Open M-F 9:30am-3:30pm and Sa 9am-2pm.

International Bookstores: Many **kiosks** in Thessaloniki sell foreign newspapers and magazines. **Molchos Books,** Tsimiski 10 (☎275 271), across from the National Bank, has an excellent selection of English, Classical, religious, and art history books, plus international daily newspapers. Open M-Sa 8:30am-3pm. Two branches of **Prometheus International Bookstore,** Ermou 75 (☎263 786) and Vironos 4 (☎236 332), have a few shelves of novels. Open M-W and F-Sa 8am-3pm, Th 8am-2pm and 5:30-9pm.

Laundromat: Bianca, L. Antoniadou 3 (☎209 602), behind the church to the right, facing the Arch of Galerius. 1800dr/€5.28 for wash and dry. Open M-Sa 8am-3pm.

Tourist Police: Dodekanissou 4, 5th fl. (☎554 870 or 871). Free maps and brochures. English spoken. Open 24hr. For the **local police,** call 553 800 or 100. There are police and tourist police booths at the train station.

Hospital: At **Ippokration Public Hospital,** A. Papanastasiou 49 (☎837 920), some doctors speak English. **Ahepa Hospital,** Kiriakidi 1 (☎993 111), is a private alternative. **Red Cross First Aid Hospital,** Koundouriotou 6 (☎530 530), offers free minor medical care at the entrance to the port. The **EOT** can help you find an English-speaking doctor.

Telephones: OTE, Karolou Diehl 27 (☎221 899), at the corner of Ermou, 1 block east of Aristotelous. Open M-F 7:10am-2pm.

Internet Access: Pl@net, 53 Alex. Svolou (☎250 199), a block away from the hostel, is the best in town. 14 fast terminals and jazzy tunes. 600dr/€1.76 per hr. 9am-6pm; 800dr/€2.35 per hr. 6pm-3am. 300dr/€0.88 minimum. **The Web,** Gonata 4 (☎237 031), 1 block south of Svolou, near Pl. Navarino between Ipodromiou and Gounari, is often crowded but has fast terminals. 700dr/€2.05 per hr., after 5pm 900dr/€2.64 per hr. Open 24hr. The **British Council,** Eth. Aminis 9 (☎235 236 or 235 237), has **free access.** Open M-F 9am-1pm.

Post Office: On Aristotelous, just below Egnatia. Open M-F 7:30am-8pm, Sa 7:30am-2pm, Su 9am-1:30pm. A **branch** office (☎227 640), on Eth. Aminis near the White Tower, is open M-F 7am-8pm. Both offer *Poste Restante.* **Postal code:** 54101.

⚓ ACCOMMODATIONS

Welcome to the big city—don't expect to find comfort and cleanliness all at one low price. Thessaloniki's less expensive hotels are along the western end of **Egnatia,** between **Pl. Dimokratias** (500m east of the train station) and **Aristotelous.** Most are a bit gritty, ranging from ramshackle sleaze to merely cheerless, but all are easy to locate, with signs stretching from rooftop to pavement. Egnatia is loud at all hours, but rooms on the street have balconies (read: air circulation), while quieter back rooms have just a window. If you have deep pockets, more expensive hotels can be found near the waterfront, two blocks west of Aristotelous.

Hotel Augustos, Elenis Svoronou 4 (☎522 955; ☎/fax 522 500). From Egnatia, turn north at the Argo Hotel; Augustos is straight ahead. Snug rooms with wooden floors, rugs, and painted ceilings. Rooms vary; ask for a balcony. Doubles and triples with bath have A/C and TVs; all rooms have phones. Singles 6000dr/€17.61, with bath 8000dr/€23.48; doubles 7000-11,000dr/€20.54-32.28; triples 13,000dr/€38.15.

Hotel Acropolis, Tantalidou 4 (☎536 170). Tantalidou is the 2nd right off Egnatia after Dodekanissou. Coming from Pl. Dimokratias, The quiet, family-owned hotel harbors bright rooms with sinks and faux-wood floors. Storage room for bikes or motorbikes. Singles 5500dr/€16.14; doubles 7000dr/€20.54; triples 8000dr/€23.48.

Youth Hostel, Alex. Svolou 44 (☎225 946; fax 262 208). Take bus #8, 10, 11, or 31 west down Egnatia and get off at the Arch of Galerius (Kamara stop); or walk toward the water and turn left onto Svolou after 2 blocks. 10 rooms with 6 bunks each. Hot showers 7am-11pm. Reception 9-11am and 7-11pm. 2500dr/€7.34 per person.

Hotel Averof, L. Sofou 24 (☎538 840; fax 543 194), at Egnatia. Rooms are a bit bare and stuffy, but come with shiny wood furniture, friendly staff, and a communal TV room in the middle of each floor. Singles 6000dr/€17.61, with bath 10,000dr/€29.35; doubles 8000-12,000dr/€23.48-35.22.

Hotel Emporikon, Singrou 14 (☎525 560 or 514 431), at Egnatia. Simple rooms with bright balconies overlooking leafy, tranquil Singrou. Shared bathrooms and fridges, high ceilings. Quieter than most other hotels on Egnatia. Some doubles have a partitioned private shower, but all share toilets. Singles 6000dr/€17.61; doubles 9000dr/€26.41; triples 13,000dr/€38.15.

Hotel Ilios, Egnatia 27 (☎512 620). Comfortable, high-priced modern rooms with big windows, A/C, TVs, phones, and baths. Some doubles have armchairs. Ask for a room away from the noisy street. Singles 10,500dr/€30.81; doubles 15,000dr/€44.02; triples 17,000dr/€49.89.

◘ FOOD

Tucked along tiny sidestreets all over the city (and clustered along Aristotelous), Thessaloniki's *ouzeri* tables are mini altars of *mezedes*, upon which are placed offerings to the gods of good cheap food. Innovative places a block down from Egnatia between **Dragoumi** and **El. Venizelou** cater to a younger clientele and are open late. The most pleasant setting is under the trees on **Komninon** between Tsimiski and the flower market, where Thessaloniki's busiest sidewalks melt into a languid calm. Tables teem around 3:30pm and again around 11pm.

The maze of alleyways one block south of Egnatia and east of Aristotelous has an *ouzeri* on every corner. Roaming musicians squeeze their way through the tightly packed tables and strum a tune for your dinner (and for theirs). The **Aretsou** area, along the bay about 4km toward the airport, has excellent seafood. The **Old Town** brims with inexpensive family tavernas; restaurants just below the **fortress**'s tower have sweeping views over the gulf. Thessaloniki contributes its local pig's feet soup *(boutsas)* to the Greek culinary universe.

Ouzeri Melathron, in an alleyway at 23 El. Venizelou. From Egnatia, walk past the Ottoman Bedesten on El. Venizelou and make a right into the passageway between storefronts. Witty, 4ft.-long subtitled menus feature a spicy meat dish called "Lonely Nights" ("No nookie with this on your breath") and snails ("for friends of the hermaphrodite"). Entrees 1150-3600dr/€3.37-10.56.

To Adelphi (☎ 266 432), in laid-back Pl. Navarino, among a strip of similar tavernas. Carnivorous meals at good prices. Popular, delicious, and very busy. Try the special chicken: it's stuffed with cheese and wrapped in bacon. Entrees 1250-1900dr/€3.67-5.58. Open daily noon-midnight.

Mesogeios, Balanou 38 (☎ 288 460), east of Aristotelous, 1 block south of Egnatia. The largest *ouzeri* in the area—on the corner of the main intersection in the district. Delectable calamari, some English-speaking staff, and festive nighttime ambience. Try the *Bekri Meze* (1300dr/€3.82), a pork and mushroom dish cooked with wine. Mediterranean-style entrees 1300-2000dr/€3.82-5.87.

Rogoti, Venizelou 8 (☎227 766 or 227 794), on the same corner since 1928. Try the secret recipe for *soutzoukakia* (meatballs, 1650dr/€4.84) and enjoy all kinds of niceties—a black bowtie here, a tasty garnish there—at decent prices. Huge menu, almost as varied as the wide collection of beer steins. Entrees 1800-3000dr/€5.28-8.80.

Cafe Extrablatt, Alex Svolou 46 (☎256 900), next to the hostel. European-influenced cuisine, and over 50 beer options. There's an entire mushroom menu, including a mushroom gyro and the special "mushrooms Extrablatt." Sausage dishes dominate the rest of the menu. Entrees 2000-3200dr/€5.87-9.39.

◉ SIGHTS

WHITE TOWER. The White Tower is Thessaloniki's most easily recognized sight, and a natural reference point for the harbor. All that remains of a 15th-century Venetian seawall, the tower later became the Ottoman Death Row where **Janissaries**—an elite corps of Ottoman soldiers recruited from the Greek populace—carried out gruesome executions. In those days it was known as the **Bloody Tower.** In 1890, a prisoner whitewashed the whole building and inaugurated the current name. *(At the far eastern end of Nikis. ☎ 267 832. Open Tu-Su 8am-3pm. Free.)*

WALKING TOURS

Just below the surface of modern, bustling Thessaloniki lies a tangle of Roman, Byzantine, Ottoman, Sephardic, and Bulgarian legacies. Temples and baths became churches, churches were transformed into mosques, and minarets were toppled to make churches again, all in a layered pile. *Wandering Byzantine Thessaloniki,* a guide available at the White Tower for a pricey 6000dr/€17.61, will glut history buffs with Byzantine gratification.

ROMAN REMNANTS

ROTUNDA. Originally built as part of egotistical emperor Galerius's palace, the Rotunda later became a church and was renamed **Agios Georgios** by Theodosius the Great. The walls of the enormous, Pantheon-inspired, cylindrical Rotunda are plastered with some of the city's most lavish and gleaming **mosaics,** the earliest mural mosaics in the area. An estimated 36 million *tesserae* were assembled to represent gilded facades, birds, fruits, and saints; tragically, very little has survived. What mosaics can be seen are way up in the dome; bring a guidebook with pictures or a pair of binoculars. You can still see the angels' heads and hands upholding a circle of stars, and pomegranates sheaved in a rainbow band. The scaffolded **minaret** outside dates from the building's use as a mosque in the 16th century. During the day, the city's largest **open-air market** forms around the Rotunda. *(Open daily 7am-2:30pm. Free.)*

MORE OF GALERIUS'S EGO TRIP. A colonnaded processional led south from the Rotunda to the **Arch of Galerius** and the **Palace of Galerius,** once the three components of an enormous complex. Galerius built the arch to commemorate his victory over the Persians in AD 305; it's covered with **relief sculptures** detailing his triumphs. Now surrounded by a white iron fence to prevent further damage from curious hands, the arch stands at the crossroads of Egnatia and Gounari, two major thoroughfares of the ancient city. It was once paralleled by a similar structure to the east; together they formed a huge gateway commemorating the Persian defeat. The Palace of Galerius, south of the Arch on Dragoumi near Pl. Navarino, has been partially excavated to reveal a marvelous mosaic sidewalk. The centerpiece of the palace was the partially preserved **octagonal hall.**

ROMAN FORUM. Considering it's not in Rome, it's not surprising that this Roman Forum is not terribly spectacular. During the 2nd and 3rd centuries, it included a public records archive, mint, odeon, *boulaterion*, and library; today it offers a restored version of the **theater.** On the south side of the Agora's lower square was once the **colonnade** that held eight caryatid statues of mythological women. Known in Ladino, the language of the Sephardic Jews, as *las Incantadas* ("the enchanted women"), they were thought to have been magically turned to stone. When the portico was demolished in 1865, the statues were moved to the Louvre. All of the excavations at the Roman Forum are described in detail at the Archaeological Museum. *(On Egnatia, behind the Pl. Dikastiriou bus station.)*

OLD CITY

To reach the Old City, take bus #22 from Pl. Eleftherias.

North of Ag. Dimitriou you'll find the streets of the Old City. **Agios Nikolaos Orphanos,** off Apostelou Pavlou, has splendid 14th-century wall paintings, some of the illustrated biblical narratives are the most important in all of Macedonia and Serbia. From the White Tower, follow the remains of the ancient wall north along Ipodromiou, past Ag. Dimitriou, to reach the 15th-century **Trigonion Tower.** It was built as a guard post and observation point on the city's fortifications. The top of the tower is closed to the public. The **fortifications** were originally erected by the Byzantines, and later refurbished by the Ottomans to strengthen and prepare them for the new technologies of artillery warfare. Continue up through the crooked sprawl of the Old Town to reach the ruins of the **Eptapirgion Walls** ("Seven Gates"), erected during the reign of Theodosius the Great.

BYZANTINE CHURCHES

Salonica was a Big Deal in the Byzantine Empire, which graced the town with enough churches to keep devout old women crossing themselves at an aerobic rate all day. Over the centuries, earthquakes, fire, and Muslim appropriations have severely damaged most of Salonica's 90 original churches, but many—Agios Dimitrios, Agios Sofia, and the Rotunda (Agios Giorgios)—still deserve a visit. Apart from Agios Dimitrios, most churches open early (6-7am), close sometime between noon and 2pm, and reopen for a few hours in the evening (usually around 5-8pm). Come in the morning and dress modestly. Although there's no admission fee, donations are looked upon kindly. To fully appreciate the dazzling mosaics on high, get your hands on some binoculars and/or a copy of *Wandering in Byzantine Thessaloniki*, available at the Byzantine Culture Museum, the White Tower, and many bookstores (paperback 6000dr/€17.61).

■**AGIOS DIMITRIOS.** The city's oldest and most famous church is named for the city's patron saint, a Christian Roman officer who was speared to death in the Roman bath complex that once occupied the site. A small church was erected on the site of the martyr's grave in the 4th century. A 5th-century basilica soon supplanted it; pilgrims flocked to worship the saint and to collect bottles of the myrrh said to flow from the wounds of his entombed corpse. Two fires, in 620 and 1917, decimated the church, and from 1493 to 1912 it served as the Ottoman's Kasimiye Camii. The surviving fragments of the **mosaics** that once covered the inner sides of the colonnades are absolutely stunning. The **crypt,** down a flight of stairs on the east side, contains the shell of the original tiny church and the fountain where Dimitrios was killed. *(On Ag. Dimitriou, north of Aristotelous. Open daily 8am-8pm. Crypt hours reduced Su-M. Holy Liturgy held in the crypt every F 9:30-11pm.)*

PROFITIS ILIAS. The domed, 14th-century church of Profitis Ilias was once the *katholikon* (main church) of a monastery. It has since lost most of its frescoes to the passage of time, and its uniqueness lies in its architectural layout: a cross-in-square with side choruses, a style invented in 1000 by the founder of Megistis Lavras on Mt. Athos. The remaining **frescoes** detail, faintly, Herod's slaughter of the innocents. *(On Ag. Dimitriou. Open daily 6am-noon and 6-9pm.)*

OSSIOS DAVID. Originally founded in the 5th century and funded by an anonymous female donor, the dim church of Ossios David has one brilliant **mosaic** of the Epiphany in the apse. Jesus sits on a rainbow, flanked by an angel, eagle, lion, and calf (the symbols of evangelists Matthew, John, Mark, and Luke), with the prophets Ezekiel and Habakkuk in the corners and fish swimming in the river Jordan below. According to legend, the anonymous donor was **Theodora,** daughter of Galerius (who was none too fond of Christianity); she commissioned the mosaic in secret, and it was miraculously completed overnight on top of the artist's sketch. The mosaic actually dates from later years, and was more likely covered as protection from the Iconoclasts of the 8th and 9th centuries than to avoid any father's wrath. *(On Ag. Dimitrios above Profitis Ilias. Open daily 8am-noon and 6-9pm.)*

AGIA SOPHIA. Named after the cathedral in Constantinople, the magnificent, domed 7th-century Agia Sophia was erected on the site of an earlier 5th-century basilica. Gold *tesserae* gleam on the dome's 9th-century circular **mosaic** of the Ascension, where the awestruck Apostles, angels, and Virgin witness a truncated Christ ascending in a blue globe. At the southeast corner of the church, the **crypts of Agios Yiannis Prodromos** contain an underground church and winding paths with beautiful silver-plated icons. *(On Ag. Sophia. Open daily 7am-1pm and 5-7pm.)*

PANAGIA ACHIROPIITES. If you're looking for easy-to-see **mosaics,** nearby Panagia Achirpoeitos, one of the original basilica-style churches, offers examples on the undersides of its arches. Visitors to the Museum of Byzantine Culture will recall the familiar motif of heavenly delights—glittery fruits, birds, vases of water, and fish. Throughout the Ottoman occupation, Panagia Achirpoeitos was the city's official mosque, and one of the columns in the north colonnade bears the inscription of the conquering Sultan Murad II. The church's name means "created without hands" and stems from a 12th-century legend of an icon's miraculous appearance in the church. Badly damaged in the 1978 earthquake, sections of the church are still under scaffolding. *(On Ag. Sofia. Open daily 7:30am-12:30pm and 6-9pm.)*

THESSALONIKI'S JEWS
By the 16th century, Thessaloniki was nicknamed the "Mother of Israel" for its large, thriving Jewish population. The community originated when Sephardic Jews escaped the Spanish Inquisition in 1492 and emigrated to Thessaloniki; Italian, French, and Sicilian Jews joined them. In the 17th century, the *Doenmah* ("converts") sectarian group followed the self-proclaimed prophet Shabbethai Zvi to join Islam, taking a bite out of the Jewish faithful. In 1917, the community suffered a second major setback when the Great Fire destroyed 31 synagogues and countless offices and libraries (along with the rest of Thessaloniki). In April 1941, the Axis powers occupied the city, and destroyed and looted Jewish homes, businesses, and synagogues, and ripped up the gravestones of a 500-year-old Jewish cemetery (the current site of Aristotle University) to pave roads and line swimming pools. Trains for Auschwitz and Birkenau left beginning in March 1943; 18 transports carried 46,000 people to their deaths. Around 4% of the Jewish populace either escaped—fleeing to the mountains or given secret refuge by Christian friends—or numbered among the 2000 survivors of the camps.

OTTOMAN HOLDOVERS
The Ottomans ruled Thessaloniki for almost 500 years, leaving an indelible imprint on the city's landscape. Many former mosques have reverted to Orthodox churches, but the vicinity south of the forum reveals neglected but well-preserved remnants of the Ottoman legacy.

BEY HAMAMI. This 15th-century bathhouse featured a labyrinthine interior, with a cool antechamber leading to a "tepid" room and the immense domed sauna beyond. The baths once featured separate men's and women's quarters and a special apartment for the bathing *bey* himself. The bathhouse is now used to exhibit recent archaeological discoveries. (*On Egnatia, between Platonos and Venizelou. Free.*)

HAZMA BEY CAMII. Thessalonikians call this longtime mosque the **Alkazar,** for a movie theater that once screened flicks here. Built by a *bey's* daughter in 1467-68 as a *mesçid* (a hall of worship minus the minarets), the building gained a minaret and official mosque status in the late 16th century; today it is the largest mosque in Greece. (*On Egnatia, just past Venizelou.*)

BEDESTEN. A late 15th-century covered marketplace and craftsmen's workshop, the Ottoman Bedesten was said to emit delicious perfumes of musk and amber. Inscriptions carved into the domes in French, Greek, Southern Slav, and Turkish evince the variegated ethnicity of Thessaloniki in its cosmopolitan heyday. The market has lost a lot of its bustle, but the interior still houses merchants selling fabrics and sewing supplies. Southeast of the market, on the corner of Komninon and Iraklion, the 16th-century Yahudi Hamami once cleansed women and men. The name ("baths of the Jews") stems from its location in the old Jewish quarter. (*On Venizelou, one block south of Egnatia.*)

🏛 MUSEUMS

ARCHAEOLOGICAL MUSEUM. The treasures from Vergina's royal Macedonian tombs, once the highlight of Thessaloniki's collection, returned to Vergina (p. 234) in 1998, but the museum still shelters many jewels. A permanent exhibit on **Macedonian gold** has replaced the Vergina pieces in room 9. Among the **sculptures** in room 2 are Roman copies of a famously erotic Aphrodite and parts of the enormous statue of Athena that used to stand in the Roman library's central apse. Room 4 presents visual tableaux from Thessaloniki's history, from prehistoric burial figurines to the headless statue of three Muses from the Roman Forum's Odeon, accompanied by detailed wall texts on excavating the ruins. A grand **mosaic** depicting Dionysus with Ariadne, Apollo stalking Daphne, and Ganymede in Zeus's eagle talons, forms the centerpiece. There are also finds from an ancient Egyptian **temple of the Serapium**, including uncannily realistic votives of ears and feet. Surreal room 6 is full of Roman heads, while mercifully air-conditioned room 8 displays extensive finds from 121 graves at Sindos, including gold death masks and jewelry, soldiers' swords and helmets, and figurines. The museum is an ideal starting point for exploring the local Roman Forum, and the nearby sites of Vergina and Pella. (*At the western end of Tsimiski, across from the International Helexpo Fairgrounds.* ☎ *830 538 or 831 037. Open M 12:30-7pm, Tu-Su 8am-7pm; hours reduced in winter. 1500dr/€4.40, students and seniors 800dr/€2.35, EU students and under 18 free. Dual admission to the Archaeological and Byzantine museums 2000dr/€5.87.*)

MUSEUM OF BYZANTINE CULTURE. The Byzantine Museum's massive brick building, informative wall texts, and displays tracing the evolution of early Christian art and life complement its neighbor, the Archaeological Museum. The museum is divided between Early and Middle Byzantine artifacts. Room 1 showcases art salvaged from churches destroyed by the 1917 fire—check out the gold-spangled **mosaic fragments** from Ag. Demetrius. Hit the next room for a flashback to everyday Byzantine life: fish-hooks, loom weights and embroidery, belt buckles, toiletries, and dice. Well-preserved, frescoed **tombs** from the 3rd and 4th centuries fill the third room. Paintings of earthly abundance—vines, food, animals, and flowers—transformed stone tombs into Elysian fields for the benefit of their occupants, who were awaiting their resurrection at the Second Coming. The second half of the museum focuses on the pilgrimages, castles, and emperors of the Middle Byzantine era, including an exhibit of early Christian iconography recently relocated from the White Tower. (*Behind the archaeological museum, across Septemvriou 3.* ☎ *868 570 or 868 571. Open M 12:30-7pm, Tu-Su 8am-7pm; hours reduced in winter. 1000dr/€2.93, students and seniors 500dr/€1.47, EU students and under 18 free.*)

MACEDONIAN MUSEUM OF CONTEMPORARY ART. If enigmatic postmodern creations made of disco balls, papier maché, electric hot plates, and other unconventional materials are your bag, the Macedonian Museum is a must-see. Ponder **George Lazongas's** "Nike: the Idea of Nike as an Idea" (hmm) and **Takis's** ambient "Musical." Temporary spaces feature exhibits such as the luminous "Fotometaphores: Perspectives on Transportation." Outside, the whimsical rain shower **water sculpture** by Giorgos Zogoulopoulo douses a flock of rising and falling mesh umbrellas. The permanent collection is on display in an immense new addition to the museum, while smaller exhibitions rotate through the original gallery approximately eight times a year. (*At the fairgrounds. Walk through the main gates past the info center and go left from the OTE tower.* ☎ *240 002. Open Tu-Sa 10am-2pm and 6-9pm, Su 11am-3pm. 500dr/€1.47, students 300dr/€0.88, educational groups free.*)

MUSEUM OF THE MACEDONIAN STRUGGLE. Through extensive artifacts and reconstructed scenes, this museum tells the tale of Macedonia's guerrilla war for independence from both Turkey and Bulgaria, leading up to and including both **Balkan Wars.** The exhibits include personal artifacts of the rebel leader **Pavlou Melas** (including the bullet that killed him) as well as captured war booty like Turkish and Bulgarian arms and treasure. The museum is happy to provide English pamphlets on both the collection and an historical overview of the Macedonian war. (*Koromila 23, 1 block in from the water, halfway between the White Tower and Pl. Aristotelous.* ☎ *229 778. Open Tu-F 9am-2pm, Sa-Su 11am-2:30pm. Free.*)

ATATÜRK'S HOUSE. If you've just come from Turkey and miss the ubiquitous statues, streets, and museums dedicated to the creator of the modern Turkish state, here's a chance to get your fix. You'll also have a chance to walk back in time, through the pre-population exchange Ottoman household where the little tyke Atatürk (a.k.a. Mustafa Kemal) lived until age seven. Pictures of the leader adorn all the walls, and various relics (including his bathrobe) are on display upstairs. (*Apostolou Pavlou 17. Open daily 10am-5pm. Free. To visit, you must present your passport next door at the Turkish consulate, Ag. Dimitriou 151.*)

MUSEUM OF ANCIENT, BYZANTINE, AND POST-BYZANTINE MUSICAL INSTRUMENTS. Three floors display ancient music-makers that have shapes and names—tambourades, zournades, citharas—as beautiful as the sounds they made. The museum's concert hall hosts a series of **Byzantine music performances** from September to May. *(Katouni 12-14. ☎ 555 263. Open Th-Su 9am-3pm and 5-10pm. Free.)*

🎵 ENTERTAINMENT

Summer visitors looking for live *rembetika* music (see **Bouzouki Punk Rock,** p. 34) should spend a weekend night at **Iyoklima,** on tiny Axiou south of Nikis near the port, or **Palios Stathmos** (Old Station), Voutira 2 (☎ 521 892). **Alexandros,** at Eth. Aminis and Nikis by the White Tower, is an indoor movie theater, but when skies are clear, head outside to waterfront **Natali Cinema,** Vas. Olgas 3 (☎ 829 457), five minutes past the White Tower, or **Ellinis** at Pl. Chanth (☎ 292 304), across from the archaeological museum. (Films 9pm, 11pm, and 1am. 1500dr/€4.40.) You can't miss the posters plastered all over town for the theater, music, and dance performances at venues like the **Dhasous Theater** ("Forest Theater"; ☎ 218 092), **Kiprou Theater** ("Garden Theater"; ☎ 275 806), **Damari Theater,** and **Kratiko and Vassiliko Theaters** (☎ 223 785 for both). The **International Fairgrounds,** across from the Archaeological and Byzantine Museums, holds festivals throughout the year, including the **Wine Festival** (August), **International Trade Fair and Song Festival** (September), the **Dimitria Festival** (October), the internationally revered **Thessaloniki Film Festival** (November, www.filmfestival.gr), and the new **Documentary Festival** (March).

🎭 NIGHTLIFE

There are three main hubs for late-night fun in Thessaloniki: the bars and cafes of the **Ladadika** district (once the city's red-light strip), the bustling **waterfront,** and the big, open-air discos that throb in the area around the **airport** (a 2000dr/€5.87 taxi ride from the center). Most of the clubs around the airport feature live modern or traditional Greek music (3000dr/€8.80 cover includes a drink). Call ahead and dress well. Although the clubs boom until dawn, summer nightlife in the city doesn't amount to much by Thessalonikian standards—everyone who can heads out of town to the beaches of Halkidiki (p. 245).

Deka Dance (☎ 471 768), by the airport, 11km east along the main highway. One of the most popular spots in town, Deka Dance is a booming nightclub with deafening music. Features a rotating group of Greek DJs. Cover 3000dr/€8.80.

Mousis (☎ 476 106), by Deka Dance with a large red neon sign. The best club in Thessaloniki for live Greek music, Mousis has an enormous glass ceiling accented by blue neon lights shining over 5 bars, a compact stage, 100 tables, and plenty of room to bust a move. Cover 3000dr/€8.80 includes 1 drink.

Kouva, Orvilou 7 (☎ 531 944). A 2-story hotspot, with a split-level dance floor complete with catwalks and bumpin' Greek tunes. Cover 1000dr/€2.93 includes 1 drink.

Stala, L. Nikis 3 (☎ 228 237), right at the western end of the waterfront, by the port. Cool, breezy tables outside, deafening rock music and in the cavernous interior. A great place to sip a drink and people-watch before heading to the clubs of Ladadika, 2 blocks away. Cocktails 2000dr/€5.87.

Mylos, Andreou Georgiou 56 (☎ 525 968), in the far west of the city, accessible by bus #31 or by taxi. Once an old mill, now an entertainment center with art exhibits, a restaurant, and bars. Live shows include jazz and groups like Massive Attack and Patti Smith.

Podon 2000 (☎ 424 058), 11km east of the city along the main highway, across from Deka Dance. For Greek music addicts only. The most sophisticated club in Thessaloniki has an equally sophisticated cover (3000dr/€8.80 includes 1 drink). Rub elbows with Thessaloniki's hip and moneyed in the club's amphitheatric bowl, or join the crowd on stage with the live Greek pop band. The music blasts until 4:30am.

◪ DAYTRIPS FROM THESSALONIKI

With an early start from Thessaloniki, it's possible to see both Vergina and Pella in one day. The town of **Skidra** (on the junction of the Edessa-Thessaloniki and Veria roadways) can serve as a transit point, from which there are frequent buses to both Veria and Thessaloniki via Pella.

ANCIENT VERGINA Βεργινα   ☎0331

Buses run from Thessaloniki (2hr., every 30min., 1450dr/€4.26) and Edessa (1½hr., 6 per day 8am-4pm, 950dr/€2.79) to Veria. From Veria take the bus to Vergina (20min., 9 per day 6:30am-8pm, 320dr/€0.94). You'll be dropped off in the Vergina plateia; follow the signs to the archaeological sights. Buses run out of Vergina for Veria (20min., 8 per day 7:20am-8:20pm, 320dr/€0.94). Open M noon-7pm, Tu-Su 8am-7pm; winter Tu-Su 8:30am-3pm. 1200dr/€3.52, students 600dr/€1.76, EU students free.

The discovery of the ◪**ancient Vergina ruins,** 13km southeast of Veria, was an archaeological watershed. Among the enlightening finds were Greek inscriptions that proved the ancient Macedonians were a Greek tribe. In 1861, French archaeologist L. Heusey discovered portions of the palace of ancient Aigai (now called Vergina); the ruins contained ancient Macedonian remains. The extent and significance of the ruins, however, were not revealed until 1977, when Manolis Andronikos began excavating the remains of royal tombs and a large palace dating from 350 BC. The findings in the tombs display such superb artistry that scholars believe they could have belonged only to the royal Macedonian family of Philip II, father of Alexander the Great; it's likely, too, since the tombs date to 350-325 BC, during Philip's rule. Ancient sources report that one of Philip's legs was longer than the other, and the discovery of a tomb containing shin guards of different lengths had archaeologists jumping up and down: the tomb is probably Philip's. Though the Macedonian capital moved from Aigai to Pella before Philip's time, the ruins are thought to be the former capital city, since Macedonian custom required kings to be buried in the original capital.

MUSEUM. At once uncannily morbid and dazzlingly beautiful, Vergina's museum will no doubt be the highlight of your visit. Housed in Thessaloniki's Archaeological Museum (see p. 231) until 1998, most of the finds from the Vergina tombs have come home to the subterranean museum. Visitors enter the **Great Tumulus,** itself a massive burial mound more than 12m high and 110m in diameter, the largest in Greece. The Tumulus was built before the mid-3rd century BC over the foundations of an earlier, smaller mound, and housed the graves of Vergina's average citizens in addition to the massive royal tombs. The atmospherically-lit museum displays artifacts found in the Great Tumulus including Attic vases, clay and ivory figurines, gold jewelry, and the carved funerary *steles* of the commoners' graves.

Four of the majestic **royal tombs** lie in their original locations. The designs of all four are similar: each has an anterior Ionic or Doric colonnade decorated with mythological scenes. The large room behind the colonnade contains the remains of the deceased and various items to accompany him or her into the afterlife. Tombs I and IV belong to unknown royal family members. Tomb IV, looted in antiquity, stored unusually beautiful and well-preserved **frescoes,** possibly the work of master artist **Nikomachus.** The most intact depicts an anguished Persephone being abducted by a grim Hades, while Demeter watches with cold sorrow.

The **Tomb of the Prince** probably belongs to Alexander IV, son of Alexander the Great; he was murdered along with his mother at age 13 by his not-so-close relative, Cassander of Amphipolis. The silver hydra containing his bones and his spectacular leaf-mimicking gold myrtle wreath are on display, along with other artifacts. The grand **Tomb of Philip II** is accompanied by a magnificent gold chest and exquisite myrtle wreath, and by fragments of his chryselephantine couch, decorated with miniature figures made of gold, glass, and wood. A huge glass case displays the charred remains of the bountiful offerings thrown on Philip's funeral pyre; they include animal offerings, figurines, and all his treasured possessions.

The flames of the pyre acted as transformative agents, sending these items into the next world with the deceased. Philip's tomb also contained the remains of a woman, probably **Cleopatra,** one of his seven consorts. Her gold couch remains, as do shreds of the gold-embroidered purple cloth that wrapped her bones.

OTHER VERGINA RUINS. Uphill and to the south of the museum are the open ruins of the 3rd-century BC **Palace of Palatitsa,** a 20min. walk away. Although what remains of the palace is now little more than a collection of toppled columns and ancient rubble, a lovely mosaic floor on the south side still depicts vegetal motifs and half-woman, half-flower creatures. *(Open M noon-7pm, Tu-Su 8am-7pm. 1000dr/€2.93, students 500dr/€1.47, EU students free.)*

On the walk up to Palatitsa, you'll encounter the **Rhomaios Tomb,** containing a stately marble throne; its occupant remains a mystery. The tomb itself is locked, but you can climb down the stone staircase and peer through the gates at the intact inner chamber. Next to it (but still undergoing restoration) is the **tomb of Evridiki,** with a fresco of Persephone and Hades in the underworld rivaling that of Tomb IV. Farther up the road, a sign off to the left past a prickly meadow indicates the site of the **Ancient Theater.** It was here that Philip II was assassinated while celebrating the marriage of his daughter, Cleopatra.

ANCIENT PELLA Πελλα

☎ 0331

*Along the main Edessa-Thessaloniki highway, 38km west of Thessaloniki. **Buses** (40min., every 15-20min., 700dr/€2.05) to Pella depart from the station at Anagenniseos 22 (☎525 100); it's down Octovriou past the courthouse. Turn right when you see it, near the train station—make sure you're let off at "Ancient Pella," not "Nea Pella." Buses to **Thessaloniki** (2-3 per hr.) pass the site; the bus stop is across from the small cafe by the archaeological site. ☎(0382) 31 160. Open Apr.-Oct. M noon-7pm, Tu-Su 8am-7pm; Nov.-Mar. Tu-Su 8:30am-2:30pm. Both site and museum 800dr/€2.35, site or museum alone 500dr/€1.47, students 300dr/€0.88, EU students free.*

The name "Pella" derives from the ancient Macedonian word *pelli*, meaning "ashen-colored." According to legend, the city was founded by a gray ox. The ruins at Pella, discovered in 1957 by a farmer with archaeological instincts, date back to a time when the Aegean covered the surrounding fields, and Pella served as a Thermaic Gulf port and the capital of the Macedonian Empire. As the remains of 26 Neolithic settlements indicate, the area around Pella was heavily inhabited in prehistoric times. According to legend, Pella's earliest Cretan inhabitants were rapidly replaced by Macedonians barreling in from the north. Around 400 BC, King Archelaus opted to move his capital here from Aigai (Vergina), taking advantage of his new position to simultaneously foster eastern trade and cultivate a rapport with southern Greece. Pella became the largest city in Macedonia, home of such cultural luminaries as Zeuxis, one of antiquity's greatest painters, and Euripides, who lived here in his old age. Later the birthplace of Philip II, the capital prospered under his reign. As Philip united the Greek states, Pella became the first capital of a Greece ruled by Macedonian conquerors. The construction of a splendid new palace attracted great minds and talents from the entire Hellenic world to the court. Pella's halcyon days continued with the rule of Philip's son Alexander the Great and his Hellenistic successors. The gradual recession of the sea, however, made Pella a less-than-convenient port, and by the mid-4th century BC, one needed to sail upstream in a dugout boat to reach the city. Things ended abruptly when Pella was ransacked by the Roman general Aemilius Paulus in 168 BC after his victory over the Macedonians at the battle of Pydna.

MUSEUM. Pella only takes an hour to see, but the museum alone makes the trip worthwhile. It's treasures include gold-leaf jewelry, terra-cotta figurines, glazed and unglazed Macedonian pottery, and unusual molded pottery depicting some rather racy episodes. The collection's important objects are the exquisite **mosaics** of Dionysus riding a spotted panther, a lion hunt, and a gryphon devouring a deer, highlighted by grisly splashes of blood. The mosaics are composed of small sea pebbles outlined with thin lead strips; the missing eyes were likely semi-precious stones. They're the earliest-known mosaics to mimic a three-dimensional look.

NORTHERN GREECE

RUINS. Directly across the highway from the museum is Pella's vast archaeological site, still under excavation by budding young go-getters from the University of Thessaloniki. At the heart of the site are the remains of the **Agora,** the commercial center of the city in ancient times, and a few grand houses. The **House of Dionysos** and the **House of the Abduction of Helen** both have expansive, well-preserved mosaic floors. The beautifully-executed scenes in the mosaics seem to breathe, with subtle muscle gradations and shadows in the stag-hunting scene, and the swirling skirts and rearing horses in Helen's abduction. The **House of Plaster** has no mosaics, but it does have a splendid rectangular Ionic colonnade. North of the houses and the Agora are the Acropolis and palace (off-limits to visitors). The palace, built in 10 stages, is a makeshift blend of architectural styles. Expanded by Philip, it fell with the rest of Pella at the hands of Aemilius Paulus.

LITOHORO Λιτοχωρο　　　　　☎0352

For most hikers, the gateway to **Mount Olympus** is the village of Litohoro, which caters to both fearless mountain climbers and to beach-loving hedonists, who come for the sands and bars of nearby Plaka. It's also possible to make the ascent from the western side of Olympus, beginning in Kokkinopilos village, but this route can't compare to the spectacular trails that originate in Litohoro.

■■■ **ORIENTATION AND PRACTICAL INFORMATION.** Litohoro is 90km southwest of Thessaloniki, about 8km inland. **Ag. Nikolaou,** the main street in Litohoro, runs east to west, leading into the central plateia about 500m after the entrance to the town. Down Ag. Nikolaou from the bus station, you'll find the town **tourist office** in the park, providing free maps of the town and a 1000dr/€2.93 map of the mountain. (☎83 100. Open M-F 9am-12pm.) **Buses** (☎81 271) from Litohoro's KTEL station, opposite the church in the main plateia, travel to: **Athens** (6hr., 3 per day 9:30am-midnight, 8000dr/€23.48); **Larisa** (2hr., 8 per day 6am-7:45pm, 1600dr/€4.70) via **Katerini; Plaka** (10min., 12 per day 9am-8pm, 260dr/€0.76); and **Thessaloniki** (1½hr., 16 per day 6:15am-8:45pm, 1900dr/€5.58) via **Katerini** (20min., 17 per day 6:15am-8:45pm, 500dr/€1.47). **Trains** (☎22 522) stop at **Litohoro** on the **Thessaloniki-Volos** and **Thessaloniki-Athens** lines at the station, 1km from the beach **bus stop** (by the BP station, left facing the water). **Trains** from Litohoro's station run to: **Athens** (7hr., 3 per day 9:15am-7:50pm, 3800dr/€11.15); **Larisa** (1½hr., 6 per day 7:10am-8:40pm, 1100dr/€3.23); and **Thessaloniki** (1½hr., 5 per day 7:55am-8:20pm, 1000dr/€2.93). Call the Katerini station (☎0351 23 709) or the Litohoro tourist office for more information (☎83 100). A **taxi** from the train station should cost around 2000dr/€5.87. There's a **National Bank** (☎81 025) with a 24hr. **ATM** in the main plateia. The **police station** is just below the plateia, on the left as you walk downhill. (☎81 100 or 81 111. Open 24hr.) The **health center** (☎22 222) is about 5km outside of town, by the beach, and has 24hr. **emergency** facilities. **Internet access** is available at **Cafe Artio,** toward the bottom of town across from Hotel Park (☎84 038. 1000dr/€2.93 per hr.) From the plateia, cobblestoned **28 Octovriou** leads left, up to the **post office** (open M-F 7:30am-2pm). The **OTE** sits across from the tourist booth, farther down the main street. (Open 7:30am-3:10pm.) **Postal code:** 60200.

■ ■ **ACCOMMODATIONS AND FOOD.** The most affordable hotel in town is the **Hotel Park,** Ag. Nikolaou 23, down Ag. Nikolaou from the plateia and past the long park; the tight but comfortable rooms have TVs, phones, and baths. (☎81 252. Singles 6000dr/€17.61; doubles 8000dr/€23.48; triples 9000dr/€26.41.) The pleasant **Hotel Aphroditi,** next to the plateia, offers the most attractive rooms in town, while maintaining an honest price. There's a communal fridge, a social living room, and many stunning views of the mountain. (☎81 415; fax 83 646. Breakfast 1500dr/€4.40. Singles 10,000dr/€29.35; doubles 12,000dr/€35.22; triples 15,000dr/€44.02.) A cordial family owns **Hotel Enipeas,** across from Hotel Aphroditi on the plateia. The bright, very comfortable rooms have phones, TVs, and baths. There's also a lovely upstairs balcony cafe. A spacious kitchen is available in the basement. (☎84 328; fax 81 328. Singles 9000dr/€26.41; doubles 11,000dr/€32.28.) The **beach,** 5km from town, is full of **campgrounds,** of which **Olympus Zeus** (☎22 115, 22 116 or 22 117) and **Olympus Beach** (☎22 112 or 22 113) are the largest and best situated. Due to their waterfront location, expect to pay at least 3000dr/€8.80 for a site. You may get caught in crossfire should you freelance camp on the north side of the road between the town and the highway; it's a Greek army training ground.

If the munchies afflict you in Litohoro, you've got plenty of options. **To Vareladikon,** on Ag. Kinolaou past the line of bars at the end of town, has a large, varied menu of local favorites and friendly, English-speaking staff. (Entrees 1200-1600dr/€3.52-4.70.) The most consistently crowded restaurant in Litohoro is **Taverna Berekis,** with green tables 100m downhill from the plateia. (Entrees 1000-1500dr/€2.93-4.40.) On the street that forks to the right at the police station, **Zeus** roasts and grills meat dishes. (Entrees 1000-1400dr/€2.93-4.11.)

◪ **NIGHTLIFE.** If you want to party before (or instead of) hiking, the evening begins in the **bars** around the bottom of Ag. Nikolaou, and moves over to Plaka by midnight. In Litohoro, **Bolero** and **Maskes** are popular for their selective American tunes. House and techno-booming **Status** and metal-loving **Garage** see a younger and hipper crowd. At **Plaka,** techno-blasting **Kavodimo** and **White Shark,** right on the beautiful clear water, are popular, but the most jumpin' spot of them all is **On the Rocks,** where the sleekest and trendiest Litohorians get down with their black-clad selves all night long. A taxi to Plaka costs around 1500dr/€4.40.

MOUNT OLYMPUS Ολυμπος Ορος ☎0352

The charm of Olympus does not lie in its natural beauty; nor its physical magnitude;
the beauty of Olympus is spiritual, it is divine.
—Boissonade

Erupting out of the Thermaic Gulf, the 3000m height and formidable slopes of Mt. Olympus once so awed the ancients that they named it the divine dwelling place of their immortal pantheon. The sharp peaks saw no successful mortal ascent until 1913, when Christos Kakalos, a Litohorian hunter, guided two Swiss adventurers up to Mytikas's zenith. Since then, Olympus has been harnessed by a network of well-maintained hiking trails that make the summit accessible to just about anyone with sturdy legs and a taste for adventure; the climb is a fantastic must-do. Today some 20 mules make a daily trip up Olympus, carrying everything from cocoa to olive oil, walking the slopes that Iris, the ancient Olympian messenger, would leap over, going from sea level to the heavens on a dewy rainbow.

Mt. Olympus has eight peaks. **Kalogeros** (2701m), **Toumba** (2785m), **Profitis Ilias** (2803m), and **Antonius** (2817m) are dwarfed by the summits of **Skala** (2866m), **Skolio** (2911m), **Stefani** (also called "The Throne of Zeus," 2909m), and **Mytikas** (or "The Pantheon," 2919m). The entire region became Greece's first national park in 1938, and the mountain is said to contain all the climates of Europe, from the Mediterranean climate of Litohoro to the rocky tundra at the summit.

▣ **LOGISTICS OF THE CLIMB**

You'll find the most reliable resources for all aspects of hiking—updates on weather and trail conditions, advice on itineraries and routes, and reservations for any of the **Greek Alpine Club** (EOS) refuges—**EOS refuge Spilios Agapitos,** or "Refuge A." (☎81 800. See **Refuges** below for more info.) The staff has years of experience and is happy to distribute information over the phone in fluent English. In Litohoro, follow the "Alpine Club" signs from near the plateia to reach the **EOS office** just below the town parking lot. Here you'll get helpful information and some friendly banter from fellow hikers. (☎84 544. Open M-F 9am-12:30pm and 6-8:30pm, Sa-Su 9am-noon.) The **SEO office** (Association of Greek Mountain Climb-

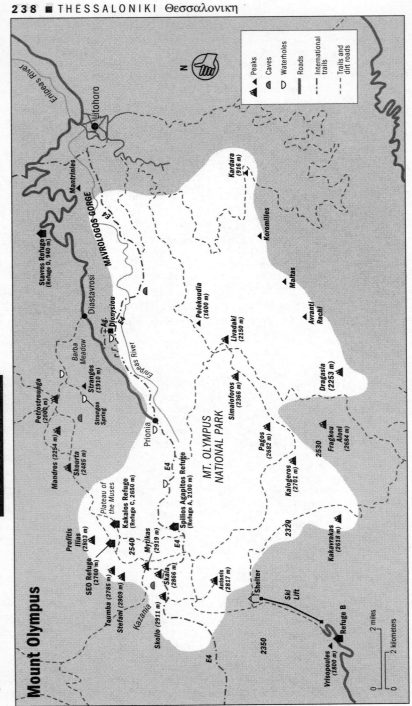

Mount Olympus

Enipéas River

Litohoro

Mantiníes

MAVROLOGOS GORGE

Stavros Refuge
(Refuge D, 940 m)

Diastavrosi

Barba Meadow

Ag.
Dionysiou

Enipéas River

Petrostrouñga
(2000 m)

Strangos
(1910 m)

Strangos
Spring

Prionia

Mandres (2254 m)

Skourta
(2485 m)

Plateau of
the Muses

Kakalos Refuge
(Refuge C, 2650 m)

Spilios Agapitos Refuge
(Refuge A, 2100 m)

E4

MT. OLYMPUS
NATIONAL PARK

Profitis
Ilias
(2803 m)

2540

Mytikas
(2919 m)

SEO Refuge
(2760 m)

2530

Fragkou
Aloni
(2684 m)

Skala
(2866 m)

Toumba (2785 m)

Stefani (2909 m)

Kazania

2320

Kakavrakas
(2618 m)

Skolio (2911 m)

Antonis
(2817 m)

Shelter

Ski
Lift

Refuge B

2350

Vrisopoules
(1800 m)

Kardara
(916 m)

Koromilies

Maltas

Avrantí
Rachi

Pelekoudia
(1600 m)

Livadaki
(2150 m)

Dragasia
(2253 m)

Simaioforos
(2366 m)

Pagos
(2682 m)

Kalogeros
(2701 m)

N

Peaks
Caves
Waterholes
Roads
**International
trails**
**Trails and
dirt roads**

0   2 miles
0   2 kilometers

ers; ☎ 83 262), behind Zeus Restaurant, acts more as a clubhouse than as an official resource, but if you happen to catch someone there they can answer questions. You can buy a colorful bilingual fold-out map with contour lines and all the major trails at the **tourist office** for 1000dr/€2.93. (☎ 83 100. Open daily 8:15am-9pm.) Produced with data from Greek Army Geographical Service, the best map is made by Anavasi and comes with a handy plastic sleeve.

PLANNING. Each winter, over 2m of snow buries Mt. Olympus, and even in late July snowfields linger in shady corners. Unless you're handy with an ice-pick and crampons, you'll want to make your ascent between May and October, when Persephone returns to Olympus from the Underworld and her mother, Demeter, warms the earth. Mytikas, the tallest peak, is not accessible without special equipment until June. **Weather** conditions can change extremely rapidly near the summits; even in the peak of summer, be prepared for chilly damp clouds, rain, and unrelenting sun above the tree line. If you make the ascent between June and September, you'll need **equipment** but nothing too special: bring sturdy shoes, sunglasses, sunscreen, head covering, some snacks, at least two liters of water, a warm wool or synthetic fleece sweater or jacket, and, ideally, an extra shirt and waterproof windbreaker. Some hikers swear by trekking poles for maintaining balance and climbing steep terrain. Take a small day-pack and leave your luggage in Litohoro, as you'll come to resent every extra pound on your shoulders.

🔥🛏 REFUGES AND FOOD

Though it's technically possible to get an early start from Prionia and climb to Mytikas and back in one day, to enjoy the mountain fully, you should try to take two or three days. This means an overnight stay in one of the social refuges or campsites on the mountain. The refuges provide blankets, beds, meals, and water, but you'll still want a full suit of warm clothes, a flashlight, and possibly earplugs. There are three refuges near the summits. The EOS-run 🏠**Spilos Agapitos refuge,** or "Refuge A," is at 2100m, about 800m below Skala and Mytikas peaks. It has 110 beds, making it the largest and cushiest, with a telephone and cold showers. The outgoing family that runs the refuge has nearly 50 years of experience and takes great pride in the refuge's cleanliness. The **kitchen** also serves meals until 9pm, with salads running around 750-1000dr/€2.20-2.93 and meat dishes around 1500dr/€4.40. (☎ 81 800. Open mid-May to late Oct.; meals served 6am-9pm; doors close and lights out at 10pm. 3000dr/€8.80 per bed; 2500dr/€7.34 for members of any mountain club; 500dr/€1.47 to tent nearby and use of facilities.) On the other side, the other EOS refuge, **Kakalos,** "Refuge C" (Γ), at 2650m, has 14 beds, no phone, and charges the same prices as Agapitos. Make reservations through Agapitos. (Open June-Sept. 15. Meals served 7am-midnight. Doors open all night.) Fifteen minutes from Kakalos, beneath Stefani and Profitis Ilias, **G. Apostolidis** (better known as **SEO Refuge;** 2760m) sleeps 90 and can accommodate extras and latecomers in its glass-walled porch or living room. The friendly proprietor will cook up a delicious meal for 1700dr/€5. (Open July-Sept. Meals served 9am-9:30pm. Doors open all night. 3000dr/€8.80 per bed; 2500dr/€7.34 with any mountain club membership.) Make reservations through the **Thessaloniki SEO,** which runs the refuge. (☎ 021 244 710. Open M-F 8-10pm; leave messages for a reservation.) Although Kakalos is smaller and more expensive than the SEO refuge, it has the best view of the rosy-fingered Dawn as she rises above the clouds.

All of the refuges, particularly the very popular Refuge A, tend to fill up on weekends in June through August. Call at least a few weeks in advance for **reservations.** Otherwise, call one to two days ahead and try your luck. Meals tend to run about 800-1000dr/€2.35-2.93 for soups and salads, 1500-1700dr/€4.40-5 for pasta and meat dishes, 1000dr/€2.93 for breakfast. Bring a flashlight to navigate your way to the bathroom after the generator is shut down in the evenings. The refuge managers are also prepared to handle emergency rescues if needed.

🏛 TRAILS: THE SLOG TO THE GODS

There are three ways to take on Olympus: all three originate at **Litohoro** (elev. 280m). Two involve heading straight to the trailheads, and one involves an alternate hike. The first trailhead is at **Prionia** (elev. 1100m), 18km from the village. The second trailhead is at **Diastavrosi** (also called **Gortsia;** elev. 1300m), 14km away. There is no bus to Prionia or Diastavrosi, so walk, drive, or take a cab (Prionia 7000dr/€20.54; Diastavrosi 2000dr/€5.87) along the asphalt road (eventually a dusty, unpaved path) that winds upward starting next to the police station in Litohoro, just below the plateia. The third route is more challenging, and involves hiking to Prionia via a trail along the **Enipeas River;** you begin in Litohoro and eventually arrive at the Pronia trailhead. After spending the night at the Agapitos refuge, you'll wind to the summit the next day and head around to the SEO and Kakalos refuges. Hikers can stay another night there and walk down the next day to Diastavrosi (about 3-4 hr., depending on how you fare going downhill), or pass the refuges and arrive at Diastavrosi in late afternoon. All of the trails are easy to follow and most are marked with red blazes.

ASCENDING MT. OLYMPUS (ENIPEAS RIVER ROUTE)

The fairly strenuous, beautiful trail from Litohoro to Prionia runs through the **Mavrologos Gorge** and along the Enipeas River, and is also an **E4 trail.** Wonderful stretches punctuate the 18km climb, but it's a difficult 4½hr. with many steep ups and downs. **Bring water.** To find the **trailhead,** walk uphill from Litohoro's main plateia past the Hotel Aphrodite, and follow signs to Mili (Μυλοι), past the town cemetery, to the Restaurant Mili. There is drinking water at the trailhead. Continue past the restaurant to the left. When you reach the concrete walkway, make a right and walk along it a short distance. Then, at a fork in the trail, follow the yellow diamond markers marked "E4" up the left side of the Mavrologos Gorge. Keep following yellow diamonds, red blazes, spray-painted numbers, and orange-and-white plastic strips tied on trees. You'll need to cross the river several times. In springtime the water may be waist-high; crossing the river when full is inadvisable. By June the water is only knee-deep, and by July, barely calf-deep. Parts of the trail have views down into the gorge. When the trail descends to the river, lovely clear green pools abound. After three hours you'll reach the tiny **chapel of Agios Spileo,** built at the source of a small spring inside a gaping cave. About 20min. farther, after a bridge crossing, follow the dirt road for 60m before turning left up the hill to see the charred shell of the **Monastery of Agios Dionysiou,** which gave refuge to Greek partisans during the World War II until the Nazis bombed it. A solitary monk lives there now, and there are a few beds he may allow you to use if you ask. You can leave a small donation here for the restoration of the large and beautifully situated monastery; you can also do yourself some good and fill your water bottle. Follow the outside wall of the monastery to a fork in the road and continue straight. You'll reach a second fork after 15min. or so. Take the left for the **falls of Perivoli** and the right to reach **Prionia** in just under an hour's walk.

ASCENDING FROM PRIONIA.

The most popular route toward the refuges begins at Prionia, where you'll find drinking **water, toilets,** and a small **restaurant.** From here, a 3hr. walk uphill takes you to the Spilios Agapitos refuge ("Refuge A," elev. 2100m). The trail is well marked, and is part of the **European E4 path** from Spain to Greece. There's one last chance for water before the refuge, about 45min. up from Prionia, but don't count on it as the spout is often dry by mid-summer. As you approach the tree line, you'll be encouraged by the brilliantly colored masses of wildflowers. Just below the refuge, the trail climbs past a steep gorge lined with dead trees uprooted by winter avalanches. This hike can take just one day up and back, if you take the 7000dr/€20.54 **taxi** ride to Prionia from Litohoro.

ASCENDING FROM DIASTAVROSI. Another approach to the peaks begins at Diastavrosi, 14km from Litohoro. This longer but more picturesque route climaxes in a stunning ridge walk with dazzling views of Poseidon's Aegean, the Macedonian plain, and Thessaloniki's smog layer. It reaches the SEO and Kakalos refuges in about six hours. Begin at the parking lot (take the right hand turn off the gravel road halfway between Litohoro and Priona) by taking the uphill path on the left, and follow the red blazes, striped plastic strips on trees, and signs of the mule caravan that uses this route. In about an hour you'll pass through the Barba meadow, and in about two hours you'll reach a cement water tank with an unhelpful painted map off to the left. Go straight here, not left, and the path leads up and up to Petrostrounga (1800m), about two and a half hours from the trailhead. Continue on; 4hr. from the trailhead you'll begin approaching the tree line, reaching Skourta Hill in another 30min. or so. The beautiful Lemos ridge (meaning "neck") leads you gently toward the peaks. About five and a half hours from the beginning of the hike you'll reach the Plateau of the Muses (Οροπεδιο Μουσον), a sweeping expanse of green under the Stefani, Toumba, and Profitis Ilias peaks. Take the clearly marked fork left for the Kakalos shelter (2650m) or right for the SEO shelter (2760m). There's also a trail up to the top of Profitis Ilias, where there's a tiny stone church. You can find water in two places along the Diastavrosi trail: at the turnoff between Barba and Spilla (1½hr. from the trailhead, marked on the trail), and at Stragos spring.

SUMMITS

ASCENDING MYTIKAS. Up at the summit area, Mytikas (2919m) has the highest elevation of the Mt. Olympus summits, and is the most climbed peak. The nearly vertical, rockslide-prone **Louki** trail, on the east face of the peak, makes for an arduous climb straight up 300m. Dotted with small plaques to honor those who fell to Hades trying to make this ascent, Louki is the more dangerous route, especially due to the risk of loose rock falling on hikers below. This trail begins 45min. south of the SEO refuge and is the best way to ascend to Mytikas from the Muses Plateau. The other trail runs along the south side of Mytikas by way of **Skala** peak (2860m), through a series of ups and downs that involves rock-climbing by handhold and foothold. This way is generally considered safer, but both trails to Mytikas are moderately dangerous, and prone to rock slides and avalanches. It's a bad idea to lug a large pack along the route or to attempt the climb in very wet weather. The Louki path should only be tackled by enthusiastic and fit hikers, and used only for the ascent. Both of the paths are marked with red dots of spraypaint. Get an early start, as clouds often hover around the peaks by mid-afternoon.

To reach Mytikas from Refuge A, walk uphill. After about 45min., you'll find a **map** at a fork in the road. The left takes you along the E4 trail to Skala and Skolio peaks; the right leads to the Louki ascent and the **Zonaria** trail, which leads to the SEO and Kakalos refuges. If you're heading toward Louki, a 40min. walk brings you to the base of the ascent. Look for the short stone wall and red blazes going straight up. From there, it's about an hour of rock climbing to the summit. A slightly more dangerous trail goes up to **Stefani** peak a little farther along, marked by a bent, rusted signpost. Past this, a 20min. walk along a stony trail leads to the SEO refuge and Plateau of the Muses. The bowl-shaped slopes are known as the **Throne of Zeus.** The god of gods rested his enormous cranium on the Stefani (crown) peak above.

Back at the fork in the road, the way to **Skala** leads left; 50m beyond the signpost, make a right at the unmarked fork (a left brings you to the top of Agios Antonios). An hour's walk brings you to Skala peak and the beginning of the **Kaki Skala** (Bad Ladder) trail to Mytikas, marked with paint blazes. The last 100m or so to the highest peak involves a fair amount of scrambling upward. The **Kazania** (Cauldron), named for the clouds of mist that usually steam up from it, drops 500m down sharply on your left. It's about a three hour hike from Refuge A to Mytikas's summit via the Skala route. Approaching the peaks from the Plateau of the Muses, it's about 90min. up to Mytikas via Louki, or four hours by the Skala route.

ASCENDING SKOLIO. If you decide not to tempt the gods by ascending Mytikas, take the 20min. hike from Skala to Skolio, the second highest peak (2911m; 6m shorter than Mytikas). The best view of Olympus's sheer western face looks out from here. It takes about 2hr. to reach the Skolio summit from the Agapitos refuge. From Skolio, a 45m-walk south along the ridge takes you to Aghios Antonis summit and a path descending to Refuge A.

EDESSA Εδεσσα   ☎0381

Atop a steep butte in the foothills of Mt. Vermion, Edessa rests on the brink of a cliff 90km west of Thessaloniki and 25km south of the border with Macedonia. Here, numerous streams channelled through stone waterways and under Edessa's arched bridges, form the country's only notable waterfalls, cascading 70m to the valley floor. One occupying Bulgarian army named this town "the waters." Historic districts, including the former Christian Varousi district and the old mills, and beautiful views over the orchard-laden plains below, make lively Edessa a refreshing and worthwhile stopover.

🔱🔃 ORIENTATION AND PRACTICAL INFORMATION

Edessa's bus station is at the corner of **Filippou** and **Pavlou Mela,** near the center of town. With your back to the station, facing the kiosk across the street, Pavlou Mela leads straight ahead to meet the town's main thoroughfares—**Egnatia** where it breaks left and **Dimokratias** where it branches to the right. A right turn on Dimokratias brings you past the cafe and playground of **Pl. Megalou Alexandrou** and leads to an intersection near the stadium, at a large, leafy park full of bars and cafes. The right fork, **25 Martiou,** leads to waterfalls, while the left, **18 Octovriou,** leads to the train station. Filippou runs parallel to Dimokratias, then merges with it near the stadium at triangular **Pl. Timendon.** Kiosks, selling city maps, are scattered around the city. One is two blocks up Pavlou Mela from the bus station.

 Buses run from the main bus station (☎23 511) to: **Athens** (7hr., 3 per day 8am-8pm, 9800dr/€28.76); **Thessaloniki** (2hr., 14 per day 6am-8pm, 1750dr/€5.14); and **Veria** (1¼hr., 6 per day 8am-4pm, 1000dr/€2.93). Buses to **Florina** (1½hr., 6 per day 8:45am-8:15pm, 1700dr/€5), **Kastoria** (2hr., 4 per day 11:15am-6:15pm, 2300dr/€6.75) and **Kozani** (2hr., 6 per day 10am-8:45pm, 2400dr/€7.04) leave from a **stop** outside a small fast food joint next to the fruit market on Filippou, one block past the main bus station; look for schedules on the *stasi* sign above the storefront. From the **train station** (☎23 510), at the end of 18 Octovriou, trains run to: **Athens** (7hr., 5000dr/€14.67); **Florina** (2hr., 700dr/€2.05); **Kozani** (2hr., 800dr/€2.35); and **Thessaloniki** (2hr., 950dr/€2.79) via **Veria** and **Naoussa**. **Taxis** (☎23 392 or 22 904) congregate on Dimokratias near the National Bank in Pl. Megalou Alexandrou.

 The **Tourist Information Office,** to the right of the waterfalls, provides maps and brochures with information in English about sights, hotels, and transportation for Edessa, the prefecture of Pella, and much of northern Greece. (☎20 300. Open daily 10am-8pm; hours reduced in winter.) The **National Bank,** Dimokratias 1, on the corner of Arch. Penteleiminos 2, has an **ATM,** as do many other banks scattered throughout town. To find the **police station,** follow Dimokratias toward the waterfalls and turn left on Iroön Polytechniou; the station is at the intersection with Arhelaou. (☎23 333. Open 24hr.) Several cafes on Edessa provide **Internet access;** the cheapest are **Monitor Cafe,** Dimokratias 38, just before the intersection at the stadium (☎26 835; open 10:30am-2am) and **Net Cafe** just around the corner at Filellinon 17, on the street that flanks the stadium (☎29 629; open 10am-1am; both charge 800dr/€2.35 per hr.). The

OTE is a blue and white building facing the Byzantine clock tower on Ag. Dimitriou (open 7am-2:40pm). Edessa also has two **post offices.** The larger (☎23 332) is at Dimokratias 26, and the smaller (☎26 030) is on Pavlou Mela one block up from the bus station; both are open 7:30am-2pm, and offer Poste Restante and **currency exchange. Postal code:** 58200.

ACCOMMODATIONS AND FOOD

There are a few good deals among Edessa's handful of hotels. Next to Hotel Pella, recently renovated **Hotel Alfa** is a bit fancy, with an astounding *two* elevators. The wide, ample rooms come with TVs, phones, balconies, and baths, and the reception has **free town maps.** (☎22 221 or 22 231; fax 24 777. Singles 9000dr/€26.41; doubles 14,000dr/€41.09; prices higher with A/C). **Hotel Pella,** Egnatia 26, is conveniently located for bus riders, a block uphill from the station. Pella has generously spacious, bright rooms with balconies, phones, TVs, baths, and a communal eating area with a fridge. (☎23 541. Singles 6000dr/€17.61; doubles 10,000dr/€29.35.) **Olympia Rented Rooms,** Octovriou 51, is near the train station with the green neon sign. Gleaming white-tiled rooms contain baths and TVs; some have balconies. (☎23 544. Doubles 8000dr/€23.48.)

Edessa has no shortage of those omnipresent cheese pies and rotisserie chicken; it also offers inexpensive restaurants. The largest, most popular, and best situated restaurant in town is the ☒**Public Waterfall Center Restaurant,** right at the top of the falls. It serves local and traditional specialties like *tseblek-kebab,* a combination of beef, eggplant, pepper, and cheese (2000dr/€26.41), and *stamnato* (1900dr/€5.58), a concoction of lamb, potatoes, vine leaves, and cheese. (☎26 810. Entrees 1500-2000dr/€4.40-5.87.) The fish taverna **Boulgouri,** under a striped awning near Octovriou 18 on the way to the train station, is a pleasant place for a fish dinner; tasty trout and a mean *tzatziki* share the menu. (Entrees 800-1500dr/€2.35-4.40.)

ENTERTAINMENT

The most picturesque and popular of Edessa's cafes is the ☒**Cafe High Rock** (Psilos Brahos), M. Alexandrou 2, in the southwest corner of town on—surprise, surprise—a high rock perched over the cliff. (☎26 793. Beer 500dr/€1.47; cocktails 1200dr/€3.52.) You'll find the complete night—dinner, drinks, and dancing—at **Kanavourgeio,** at the bottom of the glass elevator inside the old mill from which it derives its name. The disco blasts American and Greek music every Friday and Saturday night. Be careful not to mistake the giant rope-twisting machines for go-go poles. (☎20 070 or 20 102. Entrees 1100-2400dr/€3.23-7.04. Cover 1000dr/€2.93.) In the town center, the heart of nightlife is a shady park off Dimokratias right before the post office, where three similar cafe/bars draw masses of young people into tight clusters on the sidewalks. Bars popular with the young, restless, and fashionable are **Saloon** and **River,** both off Dimokratias.

SIGHTS

WATERFALLS AND ENVIRONS. Edessa's best sights revolve around the waterfall, where the town's rivers runneth over into the valley below. To reach the impressive Katarrakton (waterfall), walk down Dimokratias past the stadium, where it becomes 25 Martiou, and watch for the large waterfall signs—they'll tell you when to turn right. The descending concrete terraces let you survey the falls and the agricultural plain below while catching a little spray on your face. You'll spot a convent and the marble columns of the ancient city in the distance.

The area at the edge of the cliffs once supported a collection of water mills and textile factories. The entire area has been redesigned and reconstructed as Edessa's **Open-Air Water Museum,** featuring pre-industrial wheat and sesame mills and tanneries, built in the mid- to late-19th century, more modern textile factories, the wool mill, and the cannabis factory (**Kannavourgio**), which produced rope. Water still runs through the chutes alongside each mill, and plans are in the works to return them to working condition. The tourist office has a great free brochure showing the mill locations; get one before you go. To reach the Kannavourgio, you can follow the steps down along the waterfalls, but a more unconventional mode of transport is Edessa's **glass elevator.** Even those who haven't read Roald Dahl will enjoy the first of two glass-sided elevators sitting calmly at the top of the cliff face like a mysterious magic portal. Though the elevators are short, the view overlooking the plain is still striking. The path to the elevator begins to the right of the tourist office in the little park; the Kannavourgiou disco-cafe complex is a convenient resting place at the foot of the second elevator.

VAROUSI DISTRICT. The old church-dotted town, which remained a Christian enclave during Ottoman occupation, rests along the cliff's edge, beginning to the right of the waterfall park and continuing on behind the walls of the stadium. Examples of traditional architecture abound: upper stories miraculously protrude out on creaky old wooden beams over stone bases. The quarter's convenient location near the "safe escape" of the lowlands made it a popular spot not only for oppressed Christians, but for World War II resistance fighters—much of the area was burned by the Nazis in 1944. The new **Museum of Traditional and Folk Life** is housed in one of the old buildings on the side of the drop, a block down from the intersection of Arch. Panteleimonos and Megalou Alexandrou (ignore the big yellow "museum" sign and go left, away from Cafe High Rock). In addition to regional costumes and the run-of-the-mill bread-making, weaving, and farming tools, the museum showcases paraphernalia from Edessa's old silk mill, old geography textbooks and a Quran, colorful woven rugs, and children's toys. Ring the bell if the door is locked. (☎ 28 787. Open Tu-Su 10am-6pm. 500dr/€1.47.)

SITES. Below the town, about 3km to the southwest, the 4th-century BC ruins of the ancient city of **Loggos** are no longer terribly impressive, but a few columns along the main avenue still stand, including one from a temple devoted to **Mas,** the goddess of fertility. Try going in the evening, when the dying light makes the columns glow with celestial beauty. The fastest way to the ruins begins at the landing between the two elevators. Walk to the right on the sandy path over the little mound to find a windy path. Follow it downhill (don't go through the gates on the left) and go straight; you'll reach the city in 15min.

HOT COALS, HOLY SOULS Visitors to Northern Greece in the off season may witness some unique rural festivals. On May 21, the residents of **Langades,** north of Thessaloniki, celebrate the feast day of Saints Constantine and Helen with **fire-dancing,** which began back in the frenzied days of Dionysian worship. Orthodox Greeks imported the fire dance from Turkish Thrace during the population exchanges (p. 17). It revolves around the **Anastenarides,** a religious brotherhood of men "possessed by the saint." On the feast day, a procession carries the sacred icons of Constantine and Helen through the village, accompanied by music and drumming. The Anastenarides begin to dance around a great bonfire—slowly at first, then faster as the music accelerates, gasping and sighing all the while (*anastenazo* means "to sigh"). They enter a sort of trance, leap into the flames, and dance barefoot, calling out: "Make your vows to the Saint!" and "Restore justice lest the Saint shall destroy you!" Those who dance without damaging the feet qualify to enter the brotherhood.

The **Byzantine Clock Tower** occupies a block in the upstream direction from Dimokratias at Pl. Megalou Alexandriou. The very dilapidated, neglected remains of a 19th-century **Ottoman mosque** sink down on a side street: walk along Dimokratias a few blocks away from the city center, turn right after the Alpha Credit Bank, and veer left when the mosque's dome and de-crowned minaret come into view. To see Edessa's rivers united, follow any of the tributaries upstream until you hit the **Byzantine Bridge.** The bridge arches over the main stream that eventually splits off to form the town's countless rivulets and narrow channels.

HALKIDIKI Χαλκιδικη

The fingers of Halkidiki peninsula point south into the Aegean, sporting spectacular scenery and some of the finer beaches in Greece. Tourists with money and suntan lotion swarm to the middle and western fingers, **Sithonia** and **Kassandra,** where natural beauty tempers tourist gloss. On the eastern prong is **Mt. Athos,** a monastic community and living link to the traditions of the Byzantine Empire. Visits to Mt. Athos are strictly regulated; men must obtain permits and women are excluded entirely. Reservations for serious pilgrims should be made up to six months in advance, both for permits and for accommodations (see p. 226). Visitors to Kassandra and Sithonia have no hoops to jump through, other than the Halkidiki public transportation system. Frequent buses run between the Karakassi 68 station in Thessaloniki (☎ (031) 924 444) and the three peninsulas, but bus service does not run from finger to finger; you'll have to return to Thessaloniki. Moped rental allows for splendid cruises along Halkidiki's quiet, beautiful roads to your own private beach just around the corner.

SITHONIA PENINSULA Σιθονια ☎ 0375

Tranquility persists on the isolated beaches on the south and southwest coasts of Sithonia, though (like Kassandra), the peninsula has gradually sold its soul to BMWed visitors, plunging into the plastic world of tour buses and souvenirs. There are two back road routes through Sithonia: west via Neos Marmaras and east via Vourvourou. Not long ago, Neos Marmaras was a quiet fishing village, but recently the town has become a tourist hub. The beaches, however, remain gorgeous, and sunset views from Neos Marmaras' north end of town continue to amaze.

⛵ PRACTICAL INFORMATION. You can get to Neos Marmaras by bus or boat. **Buses** run to **Thessaloniki** (2½hr., 7 per day 6am-7:30pm, 2750dr/€8.07) and nearby small towns, including **Nea Moudania** (6 per day 6am-7:30pm, 1000dr/€2.93); timetables are posted outside of Dionysios's next door. **Taxis** (☎ 71 500) group by the beach. The nearest **ferry** service to the Sporades runs from the town of **Nea Moudania** in northernmost Kassandra. The English-speaking staff at **Marmaris Tours,** next to the bus stop, recommends rooms, **exchanges currency,** and books excursions. They also rent motorbikes and **mopeds** starting at 6000dr/€17.61 per day. (☎ 72 232 or 72 010. Open daily 9am-2pm and 6-11:30pm.) The **National Bank,** with 24hr. **ATM,** is on the main street and offers **currency exchange** on Saturdays. (☎ 72 793. Open M-Th 8am-2pm, F 8am-1:30pm, Sa 9am-1pm.) There's an **Internet cafe** (☎ 72 670) right across from the bus stop, offering 24hr. access at 600dr/€1.76 per hr. The town **post office** is in the second plateia, to the left of Plaza Cafe. (☎ 71 334. Open M-F 8am-2pm.) **Postal code:** 61381.

⛺ ACCOMMODATIONS AND CAMPING. Even with an astounding 104 proprietors in town, vacancies are scarce on midsummer weekends. A sign with a map by the beach lists every domatia; most singles run 10,000dr/€29.35, and anything below 8000dr/€23.48 will take a little haggling. **Albatross Rooms To Let,** on Themistokli, has spacious, modern rooms with kitchenettes and large balconies; ask at

Marmaris Tours, near the bus stop. They can also help you find another place if they're booked up. (☎/fax 71 738. Doubles with bath and kitchen 6000-8000dr/ €17.61-23.48; triples 10,000dr/€29.35.) **Domatia Pella** has exceptionally clean rooms with balconies, baths, and small refrigerators. Walk from the plateia between the two banks; the rooms are 20m uphill on the left. (☎71 226. Singles 7000-9000dr/€20.53-26.41; doubles 10,000dr/€29.35.) **Hotel Glaros,** next door to the Internet cafe, has small, comfortable rooms with phones and private baths. Inquire at the *ouzeri* below. (☎71 205; fax 72 340. Singles 8000dr/€23.48; doubles 9000dr/ €26.41.) **Camping Marmaras** is 2km down on the beach and clearly marked. (☎71 901. Open from May to early Oct. 1600dr/€4.70 per person; 1750dr/€5.14 per tent.)

█▐█ FOOD AND NIGHTLIFE. For Greek classics, head to a waterfront taverna, **Dionysos,** on the other side of the bus stop, which serves delicious seafood. (☎71 202. Entrees 1300-3000dr/€3.82-8.80.) Local favorite **Ta Kimata,** in the small cove 100m to the left of the bus stop, serves higher-priced, savory fish dishes (entrees 1200-3300dr/€3.52-9.68). Popular pagoda impostor **Zoe's Little China** serves a variety of Chinese dishes. (Entrees 900-3500dr/€2.64-10.27. Open daily 1pm-1:30am.) Nightlife in Neos Marmaras centers on the strip of bars and a pair of discos on the beach. The most happening bar in town is the centrally located, waveside **Pluton,** where tables float on a harbor pier. (2000dr/€5.87 cover includes one drink.) Next door at **Molos,** things are more laid back; Greeks and foreigners rub elbows, drink, and watch the surf. (1500dr/€4.40 cover includes one drink.) The big disco, **Vareladiko,** is about 2km away and plays solely Greek music.

▌▐ RURAL SITHONIA. Explore more of Sithonia by taking the **bus** around the peninsula to **Sarti** (1hr., 9 per day 9:15am-9pm, 700dr/€2.05). The bus passes by the most deserted, unblemished turf on the peninsula. Climb the road 5km south of **Porto Carras,** to a **beach** near **Agia Kiriaki,** with a small reef and an outlying island. It's a long, hard climb down, but you'll glory in the sand once you get there.

MOUNT ATHOS Αγιον Ορος ☎ 0377

The monasteries on Mt. Athos (the "Holy Mountain"), the easternmost peninsula of Halkidiki, have been the paradigm of Orthodox asceticism for more than a millennium. The community has existed since AD 883, when Basil I issued an imperial charter to Athos preventing local military officials from interfering with the monks. Today, the Holy Community of Mount Athos is an autonomous state comprised of 20 Orthodox monasteries and countless hamlets *(skites)*, with some 1600 monks who live and work there full time. The absence of technological development has helped to preserve the peninsula's luxuriant foliage. Only the jagged marble peak of Mt. Athos itself, soaring 2033m above the encircling waves of the Aegean, is exposed, and wildlife ranging from eagles to foxes roams all over the peninsula. Against the background of this lush sanctuary, the monks of Mt. Athos cloister themselves from the outside world, shunning material pleasures to pursue a wholly spiritual life. Emperor Constantine's edict of 1060 forbids women and even female domestic animals from setting foot on the peninsula.

▙✦▐ ORIENTATION AND PRACTICAL INFORMATION

Ouranoupolis, the last settlement in secular Athos, functions dually as the gateway to monastic Athos and as a hedonistic beach resort popular among Germans. With **permit** in hand, arrive here the night before your entry date into Athos, or catch the 6am bus leaving Thessaloniki for Ouranoupolis the day of your visit.

The standard approach to Athos is via Ouranoupolis, by boat to **Daphni,** then by bus to the capital city of **Karies. Buses** for Ouranoupolis leave from **Thessaloniki's** Halkidiki station (☎924 444), at Karakassi 68 (3hr., 8 per day 6am-8pm, 2600dr/ €7.63). There is one boat per day to **Daphni** from Ouranoupolis at 9:45am (3hr., 1000dr/€2.93); it returns at noon to Ouranoupolis, where one or two buses to

Thessaloniki will be waiting. From Daphni you can take Athos's one **bus line** (1 per day, 650dr/€1.91) to the capital, **Karies** (30min.), or to several of the monasteries. There is also limited (and expensive) monk-driven **taxi service** (☎23 266) between monasteries. **Boats** also travel throughout the peninsula. The main boat leaves Daphni for Agia Anna at 12:30pm; other more sporadic routes also exist. Those without a permit can view the monasteries by boat, although the boats will keep a good distance from shore. From **Ouranoupolis**, 3½hr. tours cost 4000dr/€11.74. Contact **Doucas Travel**, Venizelou 8, Thessaloniki (☎(031) 269 984), or try **Avdimiotis Theophilos** in Ouranoupolis (☎(0377) 51 207 or (0377) 51 244).

Because Athos's hikes can be long and arduous, it's a good idea to pick up a copy of the brown **Mount Athos Tourist Map** (500dr/€1.47) or buy a **guidebook** with a map (1200-3000dr/€3.52-8.80) in Ouranoupolis or Karies. Leave your pack in Ouranoupolis. **Karies,** the capital of Mt. Athos has an **OTE** next to the Athonite Holy Council Building, a **post office** (open M-F 8am-2pm), and an inexpensive hotel (4000dr/ €11.74 per person). Two restaurants in Karies also serve spartan meals, similar to those found in the monasteries (entrees 1500dr/€4.40). **Postal code:** 63086.

🛂 OBTAINING A PERMIT

Men who wish to see Mt. Athos must secure a permit in advance. To get the permit, you must call the **Mt. Athos Pilgrims' Bureau** in Thessaloniki (☎/fax (031) 861 611) six months in advance. If you can be flexible with your dates, you may call later and find a day that hasn't been fully booked up yet; only 14 non-Orthodox visitors are admitted to Mt. Athos per day. Then mail (don't fax) a copy of your passport to the office at Kon. Karamanli 14, Thessaloniki, 54638; call two weeks ahead of your visit to confirm the reservation, and visit the office with your passport to pick up the permit. (Open daily 9am-1pm; call ahead. ☎031 861 611.) In Ouranoupolis, bring your permit and passport to the Athos office, just uphill from the bus stop by the gas station, by 9am on the day your visit begins. Here you will receive your actual entrance pass called the *Diamonitirion*, complete with the blue seal of the monastic community, which you must present before boarding the ferry to Mt. Athos. The Athos office in Ouranopolis opens at 8am; come early as there will be lines of men waiting to get their passes before the ferry departs at 9:45am.

The regular permit is valid for a **four-day stay.** Passes cost 10,000dr/€29.35 for foreigners and 5000dr/€14.67 for students with ISIC under age 27. You must strictly observe the **date of arrival** on your permit: if you arrive a day late, you will be turned away. You will not be admitted without your **passport**. To extend your stay, you must ask at the peninsula's capital, Karies. Unless you have an extremely compelling reason for extending your sojourn (i.e. to become a monk), your request will almost certainly be denied. Unofficial extensions are easier to come by; especially in low season, kind monks often allow considerate, genuinely interested visitors to stay longer.

🏠🍽 ACCOMMODATIONS AND FOOD

Those staying overnight in Ouranopolis have several reasonably affordable choices. Dozens of houses offer **domatia** throughout the town, and on your arrival you will probably be greeted at the bus by offers of cheap rooms. Ask first for the location and then for the price. Any bargaining is best done before you see the room; asking for a lower price after you see the room may offend the proprietor. Most places will also store luggage while you're on Athos. **Hotel Athos**, above a supermarket one street back from the waterfront, offers elegant rooms with bath. (☎71 368. Singles 7000dr; doubles 10,000dr/€29.35.) Those looking for a last supper before their entrance into Mt. Athos—or a triumphal reward after partaking of the monks' spartan cuisine—should head to the row of similar-looking tavernas on the waterfront. **Restaurant Pyrgos** (☎71 236) and **Restaurant Karydas** (☎71 280 or 71 180) are two of the more popular establishments in the strip.

🔵 MOUNT ATHOS

Derived from the name of a Thracian giant buried by Poseidon beneath the mountain, the name "Athos" predates both Christianity and Hellenism. The Christian tradition began at Mt. Athos when the **Virgin Mary**, on a sea trip from Ephesus to visit Lazarus on Cyprus, was thrown off course and led by divine sign to the Athonite coast. The peninsula, known as **Akte,** had been a notorious center of paganism; the moment Mary's foot graced its soil, the false idols disintegrated in realization of their worthlessness. Even before Mary's time, many had tried to tame the rowdy peninsula, from Alexander the Great to Xerxes.

Although legend claims that the first monastic settlements were founded by Constantine the Great and his mother, Helen, the first record of monkish habitation does not come until the 7th century. The first monastery, **Megistis Lavras,** was built in 963 by **St. Athanasios** with the support of the Byzantine emperor, Nikephoras Phokas. Over the centuries that followed, Athos alternately flourished—at one point containing 40 settlements and 40,000 monks—and declined, as it was buffeted by natural disasters, pirate invasions, and internal squabbling. The edict banning women from the area was enacted in 1060, perhaps out of respect for the Virgin Mary, but likely because of scandalous frolicking between the monks and Vlach shepherdesses who had settled on the mountain. Unlike most of Greece, Mt. Athos retained its autonomy during the Turkish occupation by surrendering promptly to the Ottomans and accepting their rule.

During the centuries preceding the Greek liberation of 1821, Mt. Athos was supported and populated by Serbs, Bulgarians, Romanians, and Russians, who still have affiliations with particular monasteries. At the height of imperial Russia's expansionist policies, some 3000 Russian monks inhabited **Agios Panteleimon,** supplied weekly by cargo-laden ships arriving straight from Odessa.

After World War I, the Treaty of Lausanne made Mt. Athos an official port of Greece while allowing it to retain an autonomous theocratic agreement (the so-called **Agia Epistasia**—a body of monks elected from the 20 monasteries which legislate and govern the peninsula). Due to gradual attrition and the diminishing influx of young novices, Mt. Athos's eminence slowly declined through the 1950s, when it became a prime target for greedy real estate developers. In recent decades, however, Athos has been rejuvenated by hundreds of young men inspired to take vows and don the black robes and cap of Orthodox monasticism.

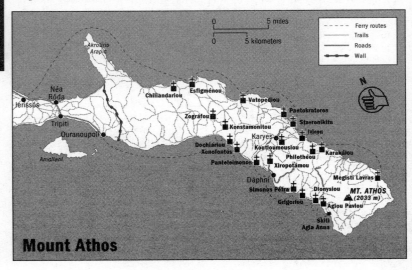

Mount Athos

2001: AN ATHOS ODYSSEY Mount Athos was once a land untouched by time. As the frenetic pace of the secular world accelerated beyond its borders, the monasteries of the Holy Mountain remained full of monks chanting the same hymns and pursuing the same austere lifestyles as their devout predecessors. But now, construction work takes place around the clock; newly paved roads are beginning to make hiking obsolete; and computers are sprouting throughout Athos. Lately, equality-minded Europeans are even attempting to force Mount Athos to let in female visitors for the first time in a millennium. Although most monks embrace the changes taking place, some remain reluctant. "The outside world is a living hell," thundered one monk at Karakallou Monastery. "Every little change we make—every little break with tradition—severs another one of our ties to God." A monk at Grigoriou had similar complaints: "When I look at the world beyond Mount Athos, I see people scurrying around blindly without any thought to where their final destination might be. Do we want the same kind of blindness to infect us too?"

LIFE ON MOUNT ATHOS

Today more than 1600 predominantly Greek monks live in the 20 communal monasteries, the smaller *skites*, or alone in hermitages on the slopes of the mountain itself. Many of the monasteries were formerly idiorrhythmic communities, where each monk was allowed to keep some personal wealth to defray the immense taxes levied on the monasteries by the sultan. Today, all the monasteries are cenobitic, with totally communal money and duties. The last idiorrhythmic monastery, Pantokratoros, converted in 1992.

Athos retains an unsurpassed wealth of Paleologian and Late Byzantine art, manuscripts, treasure, and architecture. Each monastery houses *lipsana*, remains of dead saints that only Orthodox Christian men are allowed to see and venerate. Especially impressive are the **Hand of Mary Magdalene,** who bathed Jesus, that remains (skin intact) in **Simonos Petra,** and the **belt of the Theotokos** in **Vatopediou,** the only extant relic of the Virgin Mary. Several monasteries possess fragments of the **True Cross.** The **Gifts of the Magi,** presented to Christ at his birth, are housed in St. Paul's; 5 of the 28 pieces are displayed for veneration every night.

BEING A PILGRIM

Life on Mt. Athos is dedicated to building faith and devotion to God—and, as such, is likely to induce complete culture shock. The monks operate on a schedule twice removed from our own: they use the **Julian calendar** (not Gregorian), which is 13 days behind our own, and mark the hours of the day according to the sunset as midnight. At most monasteries, the morning liturgy begins at 4am (our time) and stretches until 8am. Although only the most devout pilgrims attend the beginning of the service, the ringing of bells and tapping of wooden planks called *semanitron* keep visitors turning in their beds until they too get up and go to church. Breakfast is served directly after service in fresco-covered *trapezaries* to the sound of a **chanter,** who reads the story of a different saint's life at every meal. Only the chanter talks during meals, and everyone stops eating the moment the chanter stops. Non-Orthodox pilgrims must sit at a separate table from the monks and Orthodox visitors, and at some monasteries must eat after everyone else. Breakfast and dinner both generally consist of homegrown squash or zucchini, bread, water, and fruit, with fish and other delicacies served on feast days.

Always reach the monastery where you plan to stay before sunset, when the gates close. When you arrive, look for the *arhodariki*, or guest house. There, a monk will welcome you with a glass of ice-cold water, *tsipouro*, and a piece of "special delight" as he explains the rules of the monastery. The evening *esperino* church service usually starts at 5pm and goes until 6:30pm or so, with dinner served immediately afterward. Relics are presented for veneration either before or after dinner, depending on the monastery. Both food and lodging are free at every monastery, although it is a good idea to call ahead to make a reservation if you're planning a pilgrimage for the summer months.

While at the monasteries, be as courteous and cooperative as possible: always address monks by their title, *Patera*, and instead of hello and good-bye, say *evlog-ite* (bless us, father). Avoid talking loudly, which disturbs monks' meditation, especially during siesta and after nightfall. Be aware of each monastery's rules: some allow non-Orthodox visitors into the church, others restrict them to the narthex, and still others forbid non-Orthodox from entering the church at all.

MONASTERIES

Athos's 20 monasteries blanket the peninsula's northern and southern coasts. Despite similar architecture, each monastery has its own distinctive character. Since visitors can stay only one night in each monastery, it's a good idea to start hiking to your next destination right after breakfast. **Hikes** through Mt. Athos's winding mountain paths, speckled by fluorescent butterflies and chirping crickets, rival any in Greece. Take along a copy of the brown **Mount Athos Tourist Map** or guidebook from Ouranoupolis or Karies, and leave your pack (and any sinful thoughts) behind in Ouranoupolis. **Paths** are narrow, overgrown, and poorly marked; furthermore, the ones on the map might unexpectedly fork in four differ-ent directions or not exist at all. When possible, keep to the dirt roads for vehicles and to seaside routes, and travel in groups.

MEGISTIS LAVRAS. This monastery, on the northwestern tip of the peninsula, is the oldest, largest, and richest of the monasteries—and the only one to escape destruction by fire at some point in its history. Its monks are known to be stern and conservative. The *katholikon* architecture is in the "Athonite" style, invented here in 963. The huge complex houses multiple churches, chapels, and cells for monks and visitors, and is one of the most visited of all the monasteries. It's also the most isolated: to get here, you will need to get a ride from Karies, the capital, which costs about 20,000dr/€58.69. (☎ 23 745.)

IVIRON. Iviron is beautifully situated near a meadow overlooking the northern coast, rife with relics and icons such as the **Panagia Portaitissa**, the most renowned of Athos's miracle-working icons. According to legend, Athos will never fall as long as the Panagia Portaitissa remains within its borders. Founded by Georgian monks in 980, Iviron was the first non-Greek monastery on Mt. Athos, and rose throughout the years to a position second only to Megistis Lavras. Today, it is com-pletely Greek (the last Georgian monk died in 1955) and one of the most popular monasteries—you will need to call ahead for a reservation. (☎ 23 643.)

VATOPEDIOU. Moated and turreted like a medieval castle, Vatopediou lies on the north coast in a beautiful, secluded bay. Built in 972 and ravaged by pirates for centuries, Vatopediou is now populated largely by Greek-Cypriot monks. It houses over 3000 priceless icons, and its treasures include the **belt of the Virgin Mary** and the largest known fragment of the **True Cross**. Vatopediou is the single most visited monastery on Mt. Athos; call at least two weeks ahead for a reservation. (☎ 23 219.)

PANTOKRATOROS AND STAVRONIKITA. Pantokratoros (☎ 23 253; The Almighty) and nearby Stavronikita (☎ 23 255), lie on the north coast, close to Karies and accessible by bus. Pantokratoros was founded by officials sent to the peninsula by the Byzantine emperor Ioannis V Paleologos, who built the present monastery on the ruins of an earlier church. The 14th-century *katho-likon* houses a wooden screen carved and painted by the great Cretan artist **Kimiss Theotokou.** Stavronikita is the smallest and "youngest" monastery, com-pleted in 1536; it's also one of the friendliest and most peaceful, offering a more intimate atmosphere and direct immersion in the lives of the monks than many of the larger communities.

PHILOTHEOU. Greek for "God-loving," Philotheou is one of Mount Athos's most stunningly located monasteries, sitting on a plateau over the north coast. The abbey is surrounded by orchards, gardens, and lush chestnut forests. Founded in

1015 by two ascetic monks from Megistis Lavras, Philotheou's greatest treasure is the **arm of St. John Chrystostom,** which can be venerated every night by Orthodox visitors. Philotheou is also one of the stricter monasteries: non-Orthodox guests must eat after the faithful, and may not enter the church at all.

SIMONOS PETRA. Perched on the edge of a sheer cliff on the southern coast, Petra is spectacular. Dramatic, death-defying architecture and splendid **frescoes** could attract throngs of visitors, but there's only room for ten. Travelers can relax in the roomy guest quarters, which extend out on a balcony overlooking the cliff to the sea. Under constant renovation, the monastery is frequently booked; you'll need to call at least two weeks in advance to get a bed. (☎ 23 254.)

GRIGORIOU. In a secluded bay just east of Simonos Petra is one of the more liberal monasteries, where the meals are a little tastier, the beds a little cushier, the monks a little friendlier, and the sunset views a little more poignant. Grape vines and flowers overhang the central courtyard, and guests are treated to their own private quarters just outside the monastery walls, with breeze-blown balconies paving the way to the turquoise ocean. (☎ 23 668.)

SLAVIC MONASTERIES. In addition to these predominantly Greek monasteries, the Slavs, not to be outdone, inhabit several abbeys. At one time, there were nearly equal numbers of Greek and Slavic monks on the mountain. However, political turmoil (notably the 1917 Russian Revolution) cut off the supply of funds and novices at the source. Today, just three Slavic monasteries remain: onion-domed Russian **St. Panteleimon,** Bulgarian **Zagrafou,** and Serbian **Hilandariou.** The collapse of communism has reopened Russian wallets, and swelling church coffers now finance ongoing restoration of Panteleimon. Though 5000 Russians seek to enter the monastery, its population is barred from exceeding that of its nearest Greek neighbor, and a community of 50 fills its walls.

SKITES AND HERMITAGES. Many of Athos's monks choose to live as ascetic hermits, eschewing the material comforts of the monasteries in favor of caves and huts on the harsh slopes of Mt. Athos. Dozens of huts, cells, and tiny churches dot the southernmost end of the island, between Megistis Lavras and Ag. Pavlou, all occupied by monks who have given their lives to the reclusive study of sacred texts and contemplation of God. Many hermits will allow you to stay with them, but you must bring your own food and sleeping bag and be careful not to disturb their constant meditations. The barren southeastern slope of Athos, called **Karoulia** after the pulleys the monks use to bring food to their caves, is home to some of the most extreme ascetics. The **hike** around the base of the mountain is a difficult one, but it spans the most pristine areas of the peninsula.

Rougher than the monastic life is the hike to the top of Mt. Athos itself. The approach is by path from the skitic community of **Agia Anna** (☎ 23 320), accessible by boat daily from Daphni. A five-hour climb will take you to the **Church of the Panagia,** with beds for an overnight stay, just one hour from the summit.

KAVALA Καβαλα ☎ 051

Be forewarned: "Kavala" stems from the Greek verb meaning "to ride" (as in "cavalry"), a word connoting the same sexual innuendo as its English equivalent—that's why people may get excited when you say you're going to vacation "in Kavala." The tree-lined avenues of the bustling town stretch from the shores of the North Aegean to the slopes of Mt. Simvolo, 160km east of Thessaloniki. Modern Kavala rests upon the ruins of ancient Neapolis (later Christopolis), where the apostle Paul once preached. In the 18th century, Mehmet Ali, a future Pasha of Egypt, was born here. Most visitors use Kavala as a handy point of departure for the nearby Northeastern Aegean Islands.

NORTHERN GREECE

▐ TRANSPORTATION

Most ferries leave from the eastern end of the port in front of the string of restaurants. Thasos boats all leave from the western dock.

Buses: (☎223 593), at the corner of Eterias and Kavalas, a block north from Vas. Pavlou and the waterfront, and a block south of the post office. To: **Athens** (9½hr., 3 per day 9:15am-7:15pm, 12,200dr/€35.80); **Drama** (1hr., every 30min. 6am-9pm, 800dr/€2.35); **Iraklitsa** (20min., every 20-30min. 6am-11pm, 320dr/€0.94); **Philippi** (½hr., every 30min. 6am-9pm, 380dr/€1.12); **Thessaloniki** (3hr., 20 per day 5:30am-8:30pm, 3100dr/€9.10); **Xanthi** (1hr., 11 per day 6am-2pm, 1150dr/€3.37). To get to **Alexandroupolis** (2½hr., 6 per day 10:30am-1:30am, 3350dr/€9.83), go to the **Dore Cafe,** Erithrou Stavrou 35 (☎227 601), beyond the Oceanis Hotel; there you'll find schedules, tickets, and the bus itself.

Ferries: Nikos Milades (☎220 067 or 223 421), in a back corner of the main harbor, has ferry info for islands other than Thasos. Look behind the small park to the left of the row of tavernas. Open M-F 8:30am-1:30pm and 6-8pm, reduced hours Sa-Su. Ferries to: **Chios** (14hr., Th 9pm, 7800dr/€22.89); **Lesvos** (10hr.; Th noon, Su 10am; 6800dr/€19.96); **Limnos** (4½hr.; Th noon, Sa 5pm, Su 10am; 3900dr/€11.45); **Piraeus** (25hr., Th 9pm, 10,300dr/€30.23). **Arsinoi Travel,** K. Dimitriou 16 (☎835 671), a few doors down from Milades, sells tickets to **Samothraki** (4hr., 4-5 per week, 3300dr/€9.68); schedules change monthly. Open M-F 8:30am-8:30pm, Su 8:30am-3pm. Buy tickets to **Thasos** (2hr., 8 per day 8am-10pm, 900dr/€2.64) at the white ticket kiosk on the Thasos ferry dock, located on the busy corner one block south and one block east of the bus station.

Flying Dolphins: Hydrofoils leave from near the Thasos ferry dock for **Thasos** (45min., 5 per day 7:15am-5pm, 2400dr/€7.04) and **Samothraki;** buy your ticket on the boat.

Flights: Olympic Airways (☎223 622), a little west of the Thasos ferry dock on the corner of Eth. Andistassis and Kavalas. Open M-F 8am-3pm. Daily flights to **Athens** (1hr.; W-M 7:30am, 9pm; 18,300dr/€53.71). **Public buses** to the airport leave before scheduled airplane departures (30min.; 6am, 7:30pm; 900dr/€2.64), and from the airport to Kavala center immediately following flight arrivals.

Taxis: (☎232 001 or 227 080), in Pl. 28 Octovriou. Available 24hr.

✳ ⚡ ORIENTATION AND PRACTICAL INFORMATION

The city's main attraction, the **Panagia District,** is southeast of the port on its own peninsula, hemmed in by ancient walls under the turrets of the Byzantine fortress. The entrance is on **Poulidou** at the end of **El. Venizelou** and **Erithrou Stavrou,** two main streets that run parallel to the waterfront. On the waterfront itself is **Eth. Andistassis,** which begins at the Thasos ferry dock and runs west past the Archaeological Museum and the graffitied municipal park. A detailed **map** of Kavala can be found next to the small port police kiosk, at the Thasos ferry dock.

Tourist Office: (☎222 425, 228 762, or 231 653), on its own traffic island at the corner of El. Venizelou and Dragoumi, right on Pl. Eleftherias. Friendly English-speakers have city **maps** and a list of hotels. Open M-F 8am-8pm; off-season M-F 8am-2pm.

Police Station: Omonias 111 (☎223 167), 4 blocks north of the port. **Port police** (☎224 472) at both ports. Open 24hr.

Tourist Police: (☎222 905), on the police station ground floor. Open 7:30am-10pm.

Bank: The **National Bank** (☎222 163), on the corner of Omonias and Pavlou Mela, 1 block north of the EOT, has a 24hr. **ATM** and **currency exchange.** Smaller banks and a number of ATMs can be found closer to the harbor on El. Venizelou.

Hospital: Stavrou 113 (☎228 517). Open 24hr.

Telephones: OTE (☎222 699), on the east side of Pl. 28 Octovriou, near El. Venizelou. Open daily 7:30am-2:30pm.

Internet Access: An Internet cafe without the cafe, **Virtual Pl@net,** 55 El Venizelou (☎228 480), has 20 blazing terminals available at 700dr/€2.05 per hour, but you'll have to get your *frappé* elsewhere.

Post Office: Main branch (☎833 330), at Kavalas and Stavrou, 1 block north of the bus station. **Exchanges currency.** Open M-F 7:30am-2:30pm. **Postal code:** 65110.

ACCOMMODATIONS

Domatia are scarce, hotels aren't cheap, and many of Kavala's rooms overlook the port (the shipping industry doesn't shut down when you do).

George Alvanos Rented Rooms, Anthemiou 35 (☎221 781 or 228 412). Enter the Panagia District on Poulidou, bear left uphill on Mehmet Ali, and make a sharp left on Anathemiou. A centuries-old house in the heart of the scenic Panagia District has large rooms with fans for the lowest prices in town, far from the noise and fumes of the port. Many of the spacious, homey rooms look out over the sea; all have free use of a laundry machine and full kitchen. Singles 5000dr/€14.67; doubles 7000dr/€20.53.

Hotel Panorama (☎224 205), from the bus station walk 2 blocks away from the water and turn right on El. Venizelou. 1 block ahead on your left. Pleasant rooms with phones, and colorful drapes. Some have TV. Singles 7000dr/€20.53, with bath 8000dr/€23.48; doubles 9000dr/€26.41, with bath 11,000dr/€32.28.

Hotel Acropolis, El. Venizelou 29 (☎224 205; fax 830 752), across from Hotel Panorama. Bare, serviceable rooms have sinks, high ceilings, and sagging mattresses; some have views of the bay—or El. Venizelou. No shower is available for the rooms without baths. Singles 7000dr/€20.53, with bath 8000dr/€23.48; doubles 10,000dr/€29.35, with bath 14,000dr/€41.09.

FOOD AND NIGHTLIFE

Tavernas line the water and Poulidou in the Panagia District. Kavala's nightlife is surprisingly small. The young and hip tend to congregate at the few cafe-bars that line the waterfront. **I Kriti** (☎223 097) is a popular choice, with outdoor tables and a constant rotation of Greek and American tunes. Otherwise, take a taxi to the nearby village of **Palio** (2000-3000dr/€5.87-8.80) or the beach at **Iraklitsa.**

Cafe-Restaurant Imaret, Poulidou 32 (☎233 325 or 836 286), in the old town. Kavala's most magnificent eating experience: upstairs, tables overlook the forest of chimneys and little domes that top this former Ottoman hostel. The simple, meat-heavy menu also has a few fish options. Entrees 1300-2000dr/€3.82-5.87.

O Vangelis (☎838 885), on the east side of the harbor, at the base of the steep hill. A giant pink neon fish greets visitors. There are more fish options than you can identify, including *lithrini, sargus, plaise,* and *mourmoura.* Entrees 1000-1800dr/€2.93.

Mikros Mylos Bakery (☎228 132), on the corner of El. Venizelou and Dangli, a block south of the Municipal Museum. This first-rate bakery makes it all. Try the *pasta flora* (marzipan and fruit tart) for 400dr/€1.17.

SIGHTS

CASTRO. Follow signs from the entrance to the Panagia. Originally built in the 5th century BC, the castle and its surrounding walls were later augmented by the Byzantines and the Ottomans. The well-preserved, turreted walls survey the wide panorama of the city and the island of Thasos to the south. The small **amphitheater** hosts occasional musical and cultural performances—ask the tourist office. In the **Eleftheria Festival** in late June, students celebrate Kavala's liberation from the Ottomans by performing dances at the castle. *(Open daily 9am-1pm and 5-8pm.)*

OTTOMAN REMAINS. On the corner of Pavlidou and Mehmet Ali stands the stone and timbered **House of Muhammad Ali.** Born here in 1769, Ali later seized rule of Egypt and packed a punch in Ottoman politics during the 19th century. *(Open Tu-Su 10am-1pm and 5-7pm.)* The graceful, double-tiered 16th-century **Kamares Aqueduct,** at the north edge of the Old Town near Nikotsara, was built in 1556 by Suleyman the Magnificent to bring water into the city from mountain springs.

A TRIP DOWN MEMORY LANE If you spend enough time in Greece, you'll notice that all the street and square names are the same.

25 Martiou: March 25, 1821 is *the* Greek national holiday, celebrating Greece's declaration of independence from the Ottoman Empire.

3 Septemvriou: On September 3, 1863, Greeks rioted against monarchical rule and demanded a constitution.

11 Novembriou: Thessaloniki was liberated from the Ottomans on this day in 1912.

28 Octovriou: In 1940, President Metaxas answered Mussolini with his famous declaration of "Οχι!" (no!), refusing to submit to Italian occupation.

Athanassiou Diakou: A hero of the Greek Revolution who was roasted on a spit after being captured by the Turks.

Pavlou Melas: A guerrilla leader who freed Macedonian villages from Bulgarians.

Iroön Polytechniou: The heroes of the Polytechniou University—students who rioted against the military *junta* in 1974 and contributed to its downfall.

Riga Fereou: The great pre-Revolutionary Greek poet: "Better one day of freedom than 40 years of slavery and oppression."

Averof: The name of one of Greece's oldest, richest, and most philanthropic families. The primary beneficiary of their generosity is the village of Metsovo (p. 215).

MUNICIPAL FOLK MUSEUM. The ground floor of Kavala's small Municipal Museum houses works by famed Thassian sculptor Polygnotos Vagis (1894-1965). The marble, stone, and wooden pieces blend archaic Greek styles with modern influences like Chagall and Matisse, seen in the roughly chiseled faces of **The Moons.** Upstairs, a standard collection of traditional clothes, carpets, and farm tools stand alongside a bizarre taxidermy display featuring some ragged stuffed vultures. *(Filippou 4; take Venizelou west from the old town and turn away from the water onto Mitropelous. ☎ 222 706. Open daily 8am-2:30pm. Free.)*

BEACHES. Kavala's waterfront is home to three separate beaches. Although it's not an arduous walk from town, the best bet is an intercity bus—get off on impulse, or consult the tourist office first. Most notable is the sandy beach of **Perigali,** northwest of the city, beyond the Panagia district. The closest beach is just outside the city of **Kalamitsa,** 1500m east of the city center. There's a **GNTO campground** with a supermarket in **Batis,** 3km outside of Kavala. (☎ 243 051. 1200dr/€3.52 per person; 1500dr/€4.40 per large tent; 900dr/€2.64 per small tent; 500dr/€1.47 to swim.) Blue bus #8 treks to Batis from Kavala every 30min. The resort town of **Nea Iraklitsa,** 20km southwest of Kavala, luxuriates in long, golden beaches and some of the area's hottest nightlife.

▶ DAYTRIP FROM KAVALA: PHILIPPI

Take the bus from Kavala (every 30min., 6am-9pm, 380dr/€1.12). Make sure to tell the driver you want the archaeological site.

Roughly 15km north of Kavala, the once-proud city of **Philippi** lies in splendid ruins. Philip of Macedon founded Philippi to protect Thassian goldminers from Thracian attacks, and named it all by himself. A 42 BC Roman Civil War battle made it famous: here, Octavian (later Augustus) and Antony defeated Cassius and Brutus, the assassins of Julius Caesar. In AD 50, missionaries St. Paul and St. Silas arrived from Anatolia to preach Christianity, in the process baptizing a woman named **Lydia** the first European Christian. The **Cell of Paul** is the apostle's own budget accommodation: shut the door and peek at the Roman **latrines,** where most of the 42 marble seats are intact. For shame! All the lids have been left up. (☎ 516 470. Open daily 8am-8pm, winter 8am-2pm. 800dr/€2.35.)

THRACE Θρακη

Thrace is sliced into halves by the Evros River—Greece holds the west, Turkey the east. The region remains a political and cultural forum for both countries. Ruled by the Ottomans until 1913, the region fell under Allied control during World War I, not joining the Greek state until 1919. Continued Western interference resulted in the 1923 Treaty of Lausanne, which granted the eastern part of Thrace to Turkey. The scarring 1922 population exchange (see p. 17) relocated Greeks in Turkish territory to Greece, and Turks in Greek territory to Turkey. Although most Muslim Greeks were shipped off to Turkey, some stayed in Thrace. Seventy-five years later, they're still here. This cultural entanglement distinguishes Thrace from more homogenous Greek cities to the south.

XANTHI Ξανθη   ☎ 0541

Xanthi, Thrace's most charismatic city, may be the most pleasant place to experience the slightly edgy phenomenon of Greek multiculturalism. Strolling the sidewalks you'll see Muslims (about 10% of Xanthi's population), Christians, Gypsies, and occasional Pomaks, who descend from 16th-century Slavs. Getting lost in the cobbled streets of Xanthi's old town threads you through neighborhoods of Ottoman houses and elegant old mansions, the bounty of a tobacco industry that still buoys much of the town's economy. A winter student population from Xanthi's University of Thrace gives the modern city a smart, sophisticated feel year-round.

⌷ TRANSPORTATION. Trains go to: **Athens** (14hr., 2 per day 8:45am-4:30pm, 7200dr/ €21.13); **Komotini** (45min., 2 per day 6:30 and 9pm, 500dr/€1.47); and **Thessaloniki** (4hr., 3 per day, 2400dr/€7.04). A few faster, cooler, and pricier intercity trains run each day. Tickets are sold at the train station and the **OSE Office** in the Agora Nousi shopping area on Tsaldari, just east of the central plateia. (☎ 22 277 or 27 840. Open M-Sa 9am-1:30pm.) From the **bus station**, Dimokritou 6 (☎ 22 684), buses go to: **Athens** (11hr., 9:30am and 7pm, 13,000dr/€38.15); **Komotini** (45min., 18 per day 6:30am-8:15pm, 1150dr/€3.37); and **Thessaloniki** (3½hr., 8 per day 5:45am-7pm, 2900dr/€8.51) via **Kavala** (1hr., 1150dr/€3.37). Xanthi's **train station** (☎ 22 581) is about 2km southeast of the central plateia. To get there, head down Karaoli, go right at the rotary of Pl. Baltati, and then left onto Kapnergaton (a.k.a. Kondili). You will see signs 100m past the stadium and the tennis courts. You could also take a taxi from the central plateia for 700dr/€2.05. **Taxis** (☎ 25 900 or 22 702) wait in Pl. Dimokratias and Pl. Baltsazi.

◈⁊ ORIENTATION AND PRACTICAL INFORMATION. Xanthi is Thrace's westernmost city, about 50km northeast of Kavala. Its most important plateia is **Pl. Kentriki,** also known as **Pl. Dimokratias,** easily recognizable by the clock tower in the center. Standing in the door of the bus station, take **Dimokritou** on your left past **Pl. Balsazi,** a small traffic circle. Dimokritou becomes **Karaoli,** and leads into the central plateia. From here, streets run off like spokes of a wheel. Xanthi's main street, **28 Octovriou,** runs south to **Pl. Eleftherias,** parallel to Karaoli, and **Vas. Konstantinou** runs north into the old town, across the street from the clock tower.

Xanthi has no tourist office, but the **town hall** (☎ 24 444), on the upper end of Vas. Konstantinou, provides a **city map.** Walk 100m up Konstantinou from the plateia and take a right at the blue restaurant. The **National Bank,** which has a 24hr. **ATM** and four imposing white columns, is north of the main plateia on Konitsis. Two blocks southeast of Pl. Baltsazi is the **hospital.** (☎ 72 131. Open 24hr.) The **police** (☎ 23 333 or 28 888) are at Neston 2, north of Karaoli near the bus station. Surf the **Internet** at **Speedy Net,** Velissariou 11, north of Karaoli between the central plateia and Pl. Baltsazi, for 1000dr/€2.93 per hr. (☎ 62 950. Open 10am-2pm and 5pm-2am.) The **post office** (☎ 22 511; open M-F 7:30am-2pm) and the **OTE** (☎ 22 499; open 7am-2:30pm) are beyond the central plateia, near the clock tower. **Postal code:** 67100.

▐ ACCOMMODATIONS. Neither tourists nor budget hotels have yet discovered Xanthi, and accommodations are scarce and expensive—singles generally cost around 13,000dr/€38.15. If you have good bargaining skills, this is the time to use them. If you don't, this is the time to learn them. Your best bet is the comfortable, modern **Hotel Orfeas,** Karaoli 40, which has carpeted rooms with A/C, mini-fridges, TVs, phones, and private baths. (☎20 121 or 20 122; fax 20 998. Singles 10,000dr/ €29.35; doubles 15,000dr/€44.02.) A slightly more luxurious option is **Hotel Democritus,** 28 Octovriou 41, just below the central plateia. The black marble entrance and silver-lined elevator make for a plush journey up to your spacious carpeted room. (☎25 111; fax 25 537. Singles 13,000dr/€38.15; doubles 18,000dr/€52.82.)

◖ FOOD. Many of Xanthi's culinary specialties, including its syrupy *kariokes* or the *soutzouk-lokum*, reflect the town's strong Turkish presence. Restaurants, cafes, and bars concentrate in the central plateia and on Vas. Konstantinou. A covered **market,** off 28 Octovriou just south of the main plateia, is the perfect place to stock up on fruit, vegetables, and baked goods, as well as fish and immense slabs of meat—whole goat, anyone? (Open daily until 3pm.) Just north of the plateia on a sidestreet is **▨Midos Taverna,** Stavrou 18, serving all kinds of Greek classics in a quiet, flagstoned courtyard. Try the "Midos Special Chicken," a closely-guarded family recipe (1800dr/€5.28). **I Klimataria,** packed with locals under the shadow of the clock tower in the main plateia, has a big, tasty, inexpensive menu, specializing in local pork and goat dishes. (☎22 408. Entrees 1200-2000dr/€3.52-5.87.) **Taverna Inomagirion,** at the entrance to the old town on Konstantinou, sits in the middle of the town's most happening cafes. (☎76 681. Entrees 1500-2000dr/€4.40-5.87.)

◙ SIGHTS. On these quiet little streets you'll find stately mansions, churches, and old homes, many of them bristling with balcony satellite dishes to tune into the latest news from Turkey. Orthodox priests mingle with veiled Muslim women, and the corner stores sell a variety of Greek and Turkish newspapers. Xanthi's museums are in the Old Town, behind the Town Hall. The **Folklore Museum** houses a small, standard collection of folk clothing and farm equipment. (Open Tu-Su 8am-2:30pm. Free.) **Christos Pavlides Painting Gallery,** across the way, houses a collection of 20 brilliantly colored paintings by local luminary Christos Pavlides. (☎76 363. Open Tu-Su 8am-2pm. Free). In the hills northeast of town, vivid frescoes adorn the walls of **Panagia Archangeliotissa** convent. Ask if an English-speaking nun can show you around. (Open 7am-7pm.) Farther down, **Panagia Kalamou** is most notable for its views of the town below. (Open 8am-1pm, 4-8pm.)

◪ NIGHTLIFE. Nightlife in Xanthi is surprisingly quiet. Most of the action takes place in the central plateia, where young people gather for evenings of hanging out and people-watching. The best of the overpriced cafe-bars that line the plateia is **Retro,** where a DJ spins above-average American tunes, and the tables stretch to the middle of the square. A short walk up Konstantinou is Plateia Antika, at the entrance to the old town, where a series of lively cafes draws Xanthians of all ages out for an evening *frappé.* **Kiverno,** on nearby Vas. Sofias, provides the perfect vantage point for watching the comings and goings of Xanthi's youth. Apply hair grease liberally before you go. (Beer 800dr/€2.35, cocktails 1500dr/€4.40.)

KOMOTINI Κομοτηνη   ☎ 0531

Forty kilometers east of Xanthi, the broad Thracian plain begins to rise into the eastern Rodopi Mountains at rarely touristed Komotini. As in much of Thrace, Komotini's population is about 15% Turkish (or Greek Muslim, as the Greek authorities insist on calling them). Their influence is visible in the crooked streets of the Turkish Old Town and in the graceful minarets poking up from the forest of whitewashed apartments and church domes.

TRANSPORTATION. Komotini's **train station** (☎22 650) is at the far southwest corner of the city, a 20min. walk from the city center. Standing on Zoidi with your back to the main plateia, turn right and follow Zoidi as it curves to the left and heads southwest toward the station. Once you've passed the stadium, you're halfway there. There is an **OSE (Hellenic Railways) office** in town on Zoidou. (☎26 804. Open M-F 8am-3pm.) **Trains** go to: **Athens** (12hr., 3 per day 8:20am-midnight, 7100dr/€20.84); **Thessaloniki** (5hr., 5 per day 8:20am-11:45pm, 2650dr/€7.78); **Xanthi** (30min., 7 per day 8:20am-midnight, 500dr/€1.47); and **İstanbul, Turkey** (7hr., noon, 8600dr/€25.24). Trains at 8:20am are intercity express, where a 30% higher fare gets you there 30% faster, in icy A/C. Call ahead. The **bus station,** G. Marmeli 1 (☎22 912 or 26 111), is on the corner of **Tsounta.** To get to the city center, turn right from the bus station door, and then left at the first intersection; follow this road all the way to the central plateia. **Buses** go to: **Alexandroupolis** (1hr., 13 per day 6am-8pm, 1250dr/€3.67); **Athens** (11hr., 8:30am and 6:30pm, 14,150dr/€41.53); **Kavala** (2hr., 8 per day 5:30am-7pm, 2050dr/€6.02); **Thessaloniki** (4hr., 8 per day 5:30am-7pm, 4900dr/€14.38); and **Xanthi** (1hr., 10 per day 6:30am-8pm, 1000dr/€2.93).

▮▮ ORIENTATION AND PRACTICAL INFORMATION. Pl. Eirinis is in the very center of town. **Orfeos** runs east-west directly above it and **Zoidi** runs east-west a few blocks below it. To the north, in the Turkish part of town, is the smaller **Pl. Ifestou,** amid a maze of narrow pedestrian streets. Following Orfeos east takes you to **Pl. Vizinou,** where you'll find a large white obelisk and a wooded city park. Komotini has no tourist office, but the **police** (☎34 444), one block south of the obelisk, give out free **maps** and answer questions. The **National Bank,** Thisauis 1, north of Pl. Eirinis at the east end of Orfeos, has an **ATM.** (Open M-Th 8am-2pm, F 8am-1:30pm.) The local **hospital** (☎22 222 or 24 601) is on Sismanoglou in the southeast part of town; follow Georgiou east out of Pl. Eirinis. **Postal code:** 69100. The **post office** (☎23 195; open M-F 7:30am-2pm) and **OTE** (☎20 700; open M-F 7am-10pm, Sa-Su 7am-3pm) are neighbors on Parasiou, a side street of Pl. Eirinis.

▮ ACCOMMODATIONS. Weary but discriminating travelers take heed: Komotini's hotels are scattered, and it takes some ambling to find a decently priced room. Your best bet for affordable lodging is **Adrianopolis Hotel,** Ifestou 25, in the shadow of a mosque just north of Orfeos—the small blue hotel sign is directly across from the large yellow bell tower. The rooms above the leafy courtyard are small and worn, but quiet with shared baths and a restful feel. Listen for *muezzin* calls to prayer in the evening. (☎24 563. Singles 6000dr/€17.61; doubles and triples 8000dr/€23.48.) Another good deal is **Hotel Hellas,** Dimokritou 31, a tidy building bereft of balconies on a large intersection just north of the Archaeological Museum. Well-maintained, minimally furnished rooms with shared baths are off hallways adorned with the paintings and ceramics of the manager's artistic wife. (☎22 055. Singles 6000dr/€17.61; doubles 8000dr/€23.48; triples 10,000dr/€29.35.)

▮▮ FOOD AND NIGHTLIFE. The center for both dining and nightlife is the area around **Pl. Eirinis. To Kouti,** Orfeus 35, just south of the Pl. Eirinis, has a mouthwatering menu and mind-easing setting in a serene ivy courtyard. The reasonably priced dishes are imaginative offshoots of Greek favorites. Try the *loukarikos* (1600dr/€4.70), a baked sausage dish covered in cheese and tomatoes. (☎25 774. Entrees 1500-2000dr/€4.40-5.87.) **Taverna Aquarius,** just off Pl. Eirinis to the west, has a full menu of regional specialties, like ham and fried cheese, and chicken with mushrooms. (☎73 226. Entrees 700-1700dr/€2.05-5.) Just below the white obelisk, classy **Restaurant Dimokritos** serves shrimp dishes and classic *spetzofai* (spicy meatballs) in pink-walled splendor. (Entrees 1600-2500dr/€4.70-7.34. Open daily noon-midnight.) For comfortable *frappè*-sipping any time of the night or day, join the crowd on Pl Eirinis. **Cafe Nemesis,** Pl. Eirinis 69, is packed from morning until night. On the opposite side of the plateia is happening **Theatro** (☎30 691), where the small entryway leads to a cavernous interior packed with sharp-dressed teens.

◙ **SIGHTS.** To reach Komotini's enthralling **Archaeological Museum,** follow Zoidi westward and bear right onto the cement footpath at the park. Arranged in meticulous chronological order, the museum's artifacts are gleaned from archaeological sites from all over Thrace, including nearby Dikaia, Mesemuria, Meronia, and the banks of the Lissos River. Meronia is the modern site of Homer's ancient Ismaros, where **Odysseus** found the wine he later used to intoxicate the fearsome cyclops, **Polyphemus.** Highlights include archaic funerary statues of lions and men, a painted terra-cotta sarcophagus, a golden bust of the Roman Emperor Septimius Severus, and the 2500-year-old soles of military sandals. (☎ 22 411. Open daily 9am-6pm. Free.) The converted mansion that houses the **Museum of Folk Life and History,** Ag. Georgiou 13, has household utensils, costumes, and manuscripts depicting Greek village life. (☎ 27 344 or 25 975. Open M-Sa 10am-2pm. Free.) A 30min. taxi ride from Komotini brings you to the side-by-side beaches of **Maronia** and **Fanari,** which is popular for its strip of beach bars, while Maronia has a few seldom-visited archaeological sites, including an ancient theatre.

ALEXANDROUPOLIS ☎ 0551
Αλεξανδρουπολις

Travelers often rush through Alexandroupolis on their way to Turkey, the Northeast Aegean Islands, and the hinterlands of northern Thrace. But in the haste to get somewhere else, don't overlook the charms of Thrace's most bustling and sophisticated city. Rows of fashionable stores, cobblestone streets, and a lovely wooded waterfront make Alexandroupolis worthy of attention.

▐▀ TRANSPORTATION

Trains: The station (☎ 26 395 or 26 398) is about 400m east of the lighthouse along Alexandron, in front of Pl. Eleftherias. Open daily 6:30am-11:30pm. To: Athens (12½hr., 7:13am, 8100dr/€23.77). Four trains per day run to Thessaloniki (7½hr., 3300dr/€9.68) via Komotini (1hr., 700dr/€2.05) and Xanthi (1½hr., 1000dr/€2.93). There's also a faster intercity train with A/C to these three cities (leaves 7am), but it costs twice as much. Trains run daily to İstanbul (7hr., 1pm, 7500dr/€22).

Buses: The bus station (☎ 26 479) is at the corner of El. Venizelou and 14 Maiou, 500m from the docks. To: **Athens** (12hr., 6:15pm, 14,000dr/€41.09); **Didimotiho** (2¾hr., 18 per day 4:15am-8:45pm, 1800dr/€5.28) via **Soufli** (1½hr., 1250dr/€3.67); **Kavala** (2½hr., 7 per day 8:30am-10pm, 3350dr/€9.83); **Kipi** (30min., 6 per day 8:45am-7:30pm, 800dr/€2.35); **Komotini** (1hr., 14 per day 6:10am-8pm, 1300dr/€3.82); **Thessaloniki** (5hr., 7 per day 8:30am-10pm, 6400dr/€18.78); **Xanthi** (1½hr., 7 per day 8:30am-10pm, 2350dr/€6.90). The bus to **İstanbul** leaves from the train station (7hr., 8:30am, 6000dr/€17.61), where you can buy tickets.

Ferries: The two main ferry lines are **Saos** and **Kikon Tours.** Saos (☎ 26 721 or 23 512) is on Kyprou, a few doors up from the waterfront and sends ferries to **Samothraki** (2½hr., 1-3 per day, 2400dr/€7.04). Open 6am-4pm and 6-10pm. Kikon Tours, Venizelou 68 (☎ 25 455 or 32 378), sends one ferry per week (Tu 1pm) to: **Chios** (16hr., 7000dr/€20.53); **Kos** (24hr., 11,200dr/€32.87); **Lesvos** (11hr., 5300dr/€15.55); **Rhodes** (28hr., 12,200dr/€35.80) via **Limnos** (5hr., 3600dr/€10.56); **Samos** (21hr., 8600dr/€25.24). Open M-F 9am-9pm and 6-10pm, Sa 9am-2pm.

Flying Dolphins: Thraki (☎ 81 700), on the corner of Koundouriotou and Emporion, two blocks east of Pl. Polytechniou. Hydrofoils to: **Limnos** (1½hr., M and W 3:30pm, 7000dr/€20.53); and **Samothraki** (1hr., 2 per day, 5000dr/€14.67).

Taxis: (☎ 22 000 or 27 700). Available 24hr.

✦ 🔋 ORIENTATION AND PRACTICAL INFORMATION

Though it's a large city, everything the traveler needs or wants is within 10min. of the waterfront center, marked by a lighthouse. Standing at the lighthouse facing inland, the waterfront road, **Vas. Alexandron,** stretches left to the row of cafes, and right toward the **train station.** Halfway between the lighthouse and the train station, **Kypron** leads inland to small, leafy **Pl. Iroön Polytechniou.** The three main streets running parallel to Alexandrou—**L. Dimokratias, El. Venizelou,** and **Paleologou**—lie about three blocks inland, linked by a row of narrow cobblestone streets.

Tourist Office: On the corner of L. Dimokratias and Mitropolitou Kaviri, toward the train station. Offers maps and info on transportation and lodging. Open M-F 8am-2pm.

Banks: L. Dimokratias is one long string of banks with 24hr. **ATMs.**

Police: Karaiskaki 6 (☎37 424), 2 blocks inland from the water, just before the lighthouse. Open 24hr. **Tourist Police:** (☎37 411), with the police. Open M-F 7:30am-2pm.

Hospital: Dimitras 19 (☎25 772). Open 24hr.

Telephones: OTE, on I. Kaviri, in the block between L. Dimokratias and El. Venizelou. Open M-Sa 7am-10pm, Su 7am-6pm.

Internet Access: Arcade, Dimokratias 363 (☎36 096), just past the intersection with Trikouri. 1000dr/€2.93 per hour. Open 9am-11:30pm.

Post Office: On the water, 20m west of the lighthouse. Open M-F 7:30am-2pm. **Post code:** 68100.

🔋 ACCOMMODATIONS AND CAMPING

Alexandroupolis offers something in everyone's price range. Inexpensive choices cluster near the bus and train stations. Call ahead, especially for weekends.

Hotel Lido, Paleologou 15 (☎28 808), behind the bus station. Functional, if bare, rooms come with well-kept shared baths. Singles 5000dr/€14.67, with bath 6000dr/€17.61; doubles 6000dr-7000dr/€17.61-20.53; triples with bath 8000dr/€23.48.

Hotel Vergina, Karaoli 74 (☎23 025), directly across the street from the train station. Ten clean, well-furnished rooms around a comfortable 2nd floor lounge. Private baths, TVs, and phones. Singles 8000dr/€23.48; doubles 12,000dr/€35.22.

Camping Alexandroupolis (☎28 735), 2km west of town center on the water. 2000dr/€17.61 per person.

🔋🔋 FOOD AND NIGHTLIFE

Plenty of cheap fast food can be found on the waterfront and Dimokratias, while a number of good seafood restaurants have tables along the shore. The modest nightlife in Alexandroupolis centers almost exclusively around the waterfront, where the street closes to traffic and locals stroll past cafes.

Taverna Mylos (☎35 519), across from the post office—look for the windmill. Delicious fresh seafood served at tables overlooking the North Aegean. Plunge into the impressive *ouzo* and *tsipouro* selection. Entrees 1300-4000dr/€3.82-11.74. Open until midnight.

Neraida (☎22 827), diagonal from I. Klimataria on Pl. Polytechniou. Popular with locals. Listen for strains of the schmaltzy live music from next door as you bite into octopus pasta (1300dr/€3.82). Entrees 1000-2000dr/€2.93-5.87.

Methistaris (☎82 645), 5 minutes east of the lighthouse on the waterfront. Patrons flock here for the expansive fish selection. Try something you've never heard of, which is just about everything. Entrees 1500-5000dr/€4.40-14.67.

👁 SIGHTS

Alexandroupolis's ▨**Ecclesiastic Art Museum** is housed within the Cathedral of Ag. Nikolaos, two blocks inland from the National Bank. An 18th-century icon of Christ, portraying Jesus with his legs forming a heart, is the highlight of a collection of icons and church frescoes. If you can, get an English-speaking priest to give you a tour. You'll pick up some Thracian history and the distinctions between icon styles. (☎37 205. Open M-Sa 8am-1pm. Donation 200dr/€0.59.)

🏃 DAYTRIPS FROM ALEXANDROUPOLIS: DADIA

*Take the **bus** from Alexandroupolis to Didimotiho; it stops in **Soufli** (1½hr., 18 per day 4:30am-8:45pm, 1300dr/€3.82). From Soufli, catch the bus to Dadia (20min.; 7:30, 11:30am, 1:30pm; 300dr/€0.88). Get maps about the Reserve at the **Ecotourist Center,** across the road from the bus stop; they also rent mountain bikes for 1000dr/€2.93 per hr. ☎(90554) 32 209. Open daily June-Aug. 8:30am-8:30pm; Sept.-May 9am-7pm.*

The lush green expanse of the Dadia Forest Reserve lies 40km northeast of Alexandroupolis, covering 7300 hectares of thickly-wooded hills spread near the Turkish border. Created as a protected reserve in 1980, the forest serves as a home and breeding ground for hundreds of endangered **raptors**—rare birds of prey not unlike what you may have seen *Jurassic Park*. Of the 38 European species of these huge hunters, 36 are found only in Dadia. A well-maintained network of clearly marked **hiking trails** runs throughout the sanctuary. Blazes light the way along rugged ridges that break up the golden Thracian plain. The reserve's isolation ensures that it's one of Thrace's most beautiful and least-touristed natural attractions.

From the Ecotourist Center, a main trail leads up a hill to a **bird hide,** complete with free binoculars, where you can cringe as raptors, vultures, and other early birds catch worms in the valley opposite. Just follow the orange blazes uphill from the Center for about an hour along the clearly-marked hike. The center also runs a frequent **bus** to the bird hide (10min., every 20min., 500dr/€1.47). From the hide, trails extend in all directions, with most leading back to the center. To head straight back down to the Center, take the trail marked with yellow blazes.

IONIAN ISLANDS

Νησια Του Ιονιου

Somewhere between Calabria and Corfu the blue really begins.
—Lawrence Durrell

Just to the west of mainland Greece, the Ionian Islands create a mystique with their rugged mountains, patchwork farmland, shimmering olive groves, and pristine beaches, all surrounded by an endless expanse of varied blues. Covetous invaders have conquered and re-conquered these isles: Venetians, British, French, and Russians have all left cultural and architectural fingerprints behind. Today the islands are a favorite among vacationing Brits, Italians, Germans, and ferry-hopping backpackers heading to Italy. Multicultural for millennia, the Ionian Islands are in no danger of losing their firm grip on their unique identity.

HIGHLIGHTS OF THE IONIAN ISLANDS

SUBMIT TO THE MATING RITUALS of party animals at Corfu's Pink Palace (p. 271).

WASH ASHORE on the beaches of Ithaka, Odysseus's kingdom (p. 276).

LEAVE A TRAIL OF CANDLES to mark your path through the underground caves around a subterranean lake on Kephalonia (p. 279).

SWIM WITH SEA TURTLES in the brilliant blue waters off Zakynthos (p. 285).

CORFU Κερκυρα

Homer first sang Corfu's praise, writing of its "honied fig," "unctuous olive," and "boisterous waves"; since then, Goethe, Wilde, the Durrell brothers, Sisley, and Lear have all thrown in their two cents about Corfu's perfection. Handed down from the Franks to the Venetians to the British to today's tourist hordes, Corfu (also called Kerkyra) has captivated them all. As in most of Greece's beautiful places, those who stray from the beaten path encounter unspoiled, uncrowded beaches. Try the less frenetic resorts at Pelekas, Kalami, or Ag. Stephanos, or make Corfu Town your daytripping base. Even party-central Corfu has hidden inland villages, and beach towns remain distinctly Greek, with villagers still tending to their vineyards, olive trees, and sheep.

CORFU TOWN Κερκυρα ☎ 0661

Corfu Town flutters with activity like the two rolled *r*'s of its Greek name, Kerkyra. Laundry lines stretch from ornate iron balconies, and the Venetian loveliness of yellow-rose buildings and green-shuttered alleyways persists. A festive note pervades secluded courtyards and thronged thoroughfares, amplified at nightfall by flocks of sparrows inscribing circles on the evening sky. As dusk settles, people wander the winding streets of Old Corfu eating and chatting the night away.

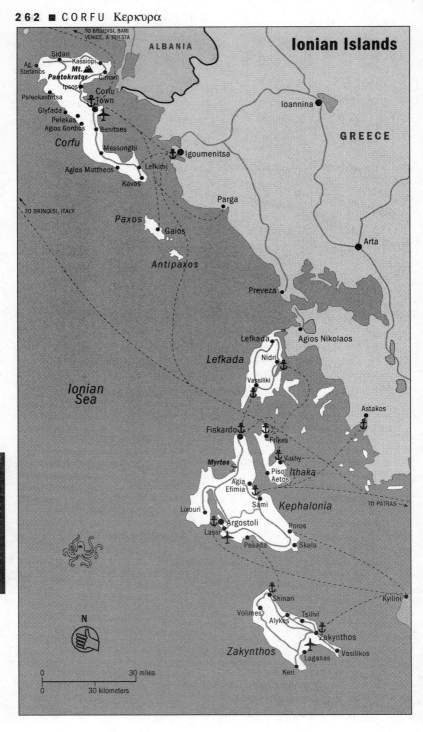

TO BRINDISI, BARI
VENICE, & TRIESTA

ALBANIA

Ionian Islands

Sidari
Ag.
Stefanos
Kassiopi
**Mt.
Pantokrator**
Gimari
Paleokastritsa
Ipsos
Corfu
Town
Glyfada
Pelekas
Agios Gordios
Benitses
Corfu
Messonghi
Agios Mattheos
Lefkimi
Kavos

Ioannina

GREECE

Igoumenitsa

TO BRINDISI, ITALY

Parga

Paxos

Gaios

Arta

Antipaxos

Preveza

*Ionian
Sea*

Lefkada

Agios Nikolaos

Lefkada

Nidri

Vassiliki

Astakos

Fiskardo

Frikes

Myrtos

Vathy

Agia
Efimia

Piso
Aetos

Ithaka

Sami

Kephalonia

Lixouri

Argostoli

Poros

Lassi

Pesada

Skala

TO PATRAS

N

Skinari

Kyllini

Volimes

Tsilivi

Alykes

Zakynthos

Zakynthos

Laganas

Vasilikos

Keri

0   30 miles

0   30 kilometers

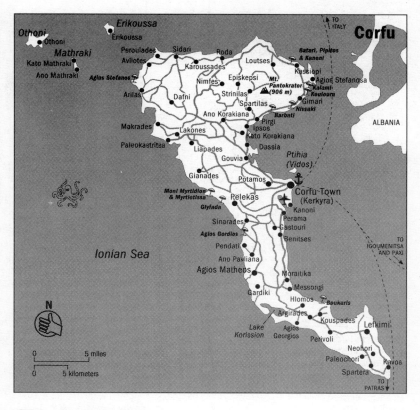

▶ TRANSPORTATION

Flights: Olympic Airways, Polila 11 (☎38 694; reservations ☎38 695). From the post office, walk 1 block on Rizopaston Voulefton toward the Old City and then turn right. Open M-F 7:30am-7:30pm. Flights to: **Athens** (1hr., 4 per day, 19,400dr/€56.93) and **Thessaloniki** (1hr.; Tu, F, Su 1 per day; 20,900dr/€61.34). In summer, almost 50 charter flights per day fly through Corfu's airport; book 2-3 days ahead. A 5min. taxi ride (agree on 2500dr/€7.34 before getting in) is the only way to the **airport** (☎33 811).

Ferries: Get your tickets at least a day in advance during high season; when traveling to **Italy,** find out if the port tax (1500-2200dr/€4.40-6.45) is included in the price of your ticket. Prices vary according to season, ferry line, and class. Try **Fragline** or **HML** for **Brindisi** and **Strindzi's Lines** for **Venice.** Check at **Blue Star Ferries** for **Eurail** and **InterRail** passes. Shipping company agents line Xen. Stratigou, opposite the new port, so shop here for the lowest fares. The jovial staff of **Corfu Mare** (☎ 32 467), at the new port beneath the Ionian Hotel, sell tickets with a friendly *"kalo taxidi!"* (good journey). Ferries to: **Ancona** (20hr., 1 per day, 19,000dr/€55.75); **Bari** (9hr., 3-4 per week, 12,400dr/€36.40); **Brindisi** (6-7hr., 3 per day, 9400-16,000dr/€27.60-46.96); **Igou-menitsa** (1½hr., 8 per day 6:30am-9pm, 1300dr/€3.82); **Patras** (6-7hr., 1-2 per day, 6100dr/€17.90); **Trieste** (24hr., 5 per week, 12,500dr/€36.68); and **Venice** (24hr., 1 per day, 14,600-20,900dr/€42.85-60.16). High-speed **catamarans** go to **Brindisi** (4hr.; 9am; check for prices, up to 30% discount for those under 26) and **Kephalonia** (3hr., W and Sa 9am, 20,000dr/€58.70 round-trip). Schedules vary by season, and some routes run only in high season, so check before planning your trip.

Buses: Two main lines serve the island: **green KTEL buses** (☎39 985), between I. Theotoki and the New Fortress (accessible from I. Theotoki or Xen. Stratigou) and **blue municipal buses,** at Pl. Sanrocco. For a detailed green bus schedule, ask at the white info kiosk at the station (open 6am-8pm); blue bus schedules are available at the ticket kiosk window in Pl. Sanrocco (open 6:30am-10pm).

Green buses head to: **Agios Gordios** (45min., 6 per day 8:15am-8pm, 350dr/€1.03); **Agios Stephanos** (1½hr., 6 per day 8:15am-8pm, 850dr/€2.50); **Barbati** (45min., 3 per day, 450dr/€1.32); **Glyfada** (45min., 6 per day 6:45am-8pm, 400dr/€1.17); **Ipsos** and **Pirgi** (30min., 8 per day 7am-8pm, 350dr/€1.03); **Kassiopi** (1hr., 4 per day 9:30am-4:30pm, 700dr/€2.05); **Kavos** (1½hr., 11 per day 5am-7:30pm, 850dr/€2.50); **Messonghi** (45min., 4 per day 9:30am-4:30pm, 500dr/€1.47); **Paleokastritsa** (45min., 7 per day 8:30am-6pm, 500dr/€1.47); **Sidari** (1hr., 9 per day 5:45am-7:30pm, 700dr/€2.05). Buy tickets on board. Reduced schedules on weekends. **KTEL** also runs buses to: **Athens** (9hr., 1 per day, 9100dr/€26.71) and **Thessaloniki** (9hr., 1 per day, 8750dr/€25.70); prices include ferry. Buy tickets at green bus station.

Blue buses: #10 to **Achilleon** (30min., 6 per day 7am-8pm, 240dr/€0.70); **#6** to **Benitses** (25min., 13 per day 6:45am-11pm, 240dr/€0.70); **#8** to **Ioannis** and **Aqualand** (30min., 7 per day 6:15am-1:15pm, 240dr/€0.70); **#2** to **Kanoni** (every 30min., 170dr/€0.50); **#11** to **Pelekas** (30min., 7 per day 7am-8:30pm, 240dr/€0.70). Buy tickets at the kiosk.

Taxis: (☎33 811), at the old port, the Spianada, Pl. Sanrocco, and G. Theotoki.

Car Rental: A small car starts at 18,000dr/€52.85 per day, but price varies by season. Ask if price includes 20% tax, third-party insurance, and mileage over 200km. **Inter-Corfu Rent a Car** (☎93 607), on the water at the new port, offers reasonable rates.

Moped Rental: Get to those untouristed areas by renting from a place on Xen. Strategiou, near customs. You shouldn't have to pay more than 6000dr/€17.61 per day. Make sure the brakes work and get a helmet. Rental fee should include third-party liability and property damage insurance.

⭐ 🗗 ORIENTATION AND PRACTICAL INFORMATION

Prepare to familiarize yourself with the Theotokos family, after whom four of Corfu Town's main streets are named: you may pass from N. to M. to G. to I. Theotoki without even realizing it. The city's peninsula juts northeast into the Ionian Sea. The endless **New Port** in the west and the smaller **Old Port** in the east span the northern coast of town. From the customs house at the New Port, it's about 1km to Corfu Town's central **Pl. Sanrocco** (also called **Pl. G. Theotoki**). Cross the intersection and walk uphill on **Avramiou,** which becomes I. Theotoki. On the way, you'll pass the driveway for the **KTEL** terminal. On the east side of Sanrocco, **G. Theotoki** leads north into the Old Town, a beautiful, befuddling tangle of old alleyways. Continuing east from Sanrocco or the Old Town, any reasonably straight walk will bring you to the **Spianada,** a large esplanade. The **Old Fortress** (Paleo Frourio) rises in the east. Arcaded buildings dotted with expensive cafes form **Liston** (Eleftherias), with narrow **Kapodistriou** running behind it. Kapodistriou curves along the waterfront, becoming **Arseniou** and **El. Venizelou,** leading back to the ports. South of town, **Dimokratias** makes a fine late-afternoon stroll along Garitsa Bay, leading to ancient Paleopolis and the Mon Repos estate. At the bay's midpoint an obelisk marks the end of tree-lined **Alexandras,** which runs back to Pl. Sanrocco.

A BRIEF *ODYSSEY* Besides enjoying notoriety for its revelry and beaches, Corfu claims the distinction of being widely regarded as the site of Homer's ancient Scheria, where Odysseus washed ashore and was taken in by the good-hearted Phaeacians. As the story goes, vengeful Poseidon, god of the sea, was looking to prevent Odysseus from returning home to his native Ithaka by attacking his ship, leaving Odysseus all washed up. Fortunately for our hero, Athena took pity on him and led Nausicaä, daughter of the King of the Phaeacians, to him as he lay on the shore. Her people nursed him back to health, and he recounted his 10-year adventure to them. Wishing to help Odysseus, the Phaeacians bestowed gifts of gold and silver on him, and offered him a ship to finish his journey. After depositing Odysseus in Ithaka, the ship returned to Scheria, where it was petrified by the furious Poseidon. Corfiot legend claims the ship can still be seen today, a large rock off the coast of Paleokastritsa—or maybe it's the small island of Pontikinossi, as a rival story claims.

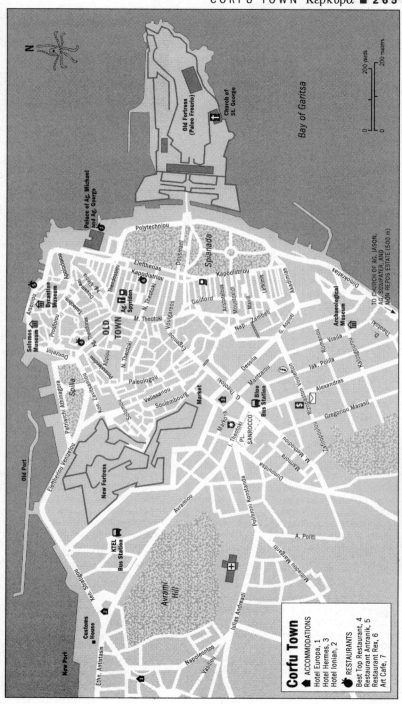

Corfu Town

▲ ACCOMMODATIONS
Hotel Europa, 1
Hotel Hermes, 3
Hotel Ionian, 2

🍴 RESTAURANTS
Best Top Restaurant, 4
Restaurant Antranik, 5
Restaurant Rex, 6
Art Cafe, 7

IONIAN ISLANDS

Old Fortress
(Paleo Frourio)

Church of
St. George

Bay of Garitsa

0   250 yards
0   200 meters

Palace of Ag. Michael
and Ag. George

Polytechniou

Eleftherias

Kapodistriou

Spianada

Kapodistriou

Byzantine
Museum

Ag.
Spiridon

Guilford

Aristotelous

N. Theotoki

M. Theotoki

Moustoxidi

Mavili

Lefkimis

Akadimias

Solomos
Museum

OLD
TOWN

Voulgareos

Evgeniou

Nap. Zambeli

G. Aspioti

Archaeological
Museum

Prosforou

Donzelot

N. Theotoki

Dessila

Mantzarou

Vraila

Paleologou

Velissariou

Market

G. Theotoki

Jak. Polila

Spilia

Patriarch Athinagora

Soulembourt

Markora

Blue
Bus Station

Alexandras

Gregoriou Marasli

Kon. Zavitsanou

Solomou

I. Theotoki

PL.
SANROCCO

M. Methodiou

New Fortress

Avramiou

Marmora

Dimouitsa

A. Politi

Eleftheriou Venizelou

KTEL
Bus Station

Avrami
Hill

Iulias Andreadi

Old Port

Xen. Stratigou

Polihroni Konstanda

Milziadou Margariti

Customs
House

Napoleontos

Vasiliou

Ethn. Antistasis

New Port

TO CHURCH OF AG. JASON,
AG. SOSSIPATER, AND
MON REPOS ESTATE (500 m)

Dimokratias

Dousmani

Spianada

Tourist Office: EOT (☎37 520 or 37 638), at the corner of Rizopaston Voulefton and Iak. Polila. The building is marked, and a sign directs you up the first flight of stairs. **Free maps** and information. Open M-F 8am-2pm.

Banks: Banks with 24hr. **ATMs** line the larger streets and the waterfront by the ports, including **Ionian Bank** in Pl. Sanrocco and **National Bank of Greece** on the corner of Alexandras and Rizopaston Voulefton across from the post office.

Luggage Storage: In the customs building at the new port (1000dr/€2.93 per day). Confirm what time you will be returning for your bags.

International Bookstores: Xenoglosso, Markora 45 (☎23 923), near the public market, has classic novels, books on Greece, and language materials. Open M, W, and Sa-Su 8:30am-2pm, Tu and Th-F 8:30am-2pm and 5-8:30pm.

Laundromat: The Peristeri, I. Theotoki 42 (☎35 304), just past Pl. Sanrocco. Wash and dry 2800dr/€8.23 per basket. Open M-Sa 8am-2pm, and Tu, Th-F 6-8pm. **New Port Laundry,** Eth. Antistaseos 12A (☎38 457), has dry cleaning; wash and dry 3200dr/€9.40 per load. Open M-F 8:30am-2:30pm and 5:30-7:30pm, Sa 8:30am-2pm.

Tourist Police: (☎30 265). Heading toward the New Port, turn right off I. Theotoki along Pl. Sanrocco onto the short street that intersects Markora; they're on the 4th floor of the police office on the left. Maps available. Open daily 7am-2:30pm. Hours may be extended in high season.

Port Police: Contact the port police (☎30 481), in the customs house at the new port, or the **port authority** (☎32 655 or 40 002) for updates on ferry schedules.

Police: (☎39 509), in the same building as the tourist police. Open 24hr.

Hospital: Corfu General Hospital (☎88 200), on Iulias Andreadi. The tourist office or tourist police can help find an English-speaking doctor. For an **ambulance,** call 166.

Telephones: OTE, Mantzarou 3, off G. Theotoki. Open M-F 7:30am-3pm. Card **phones** on the Spianada and in white mobile buildings at the Old and New ports.

Internet Access: Netoikos Cafe, Kalochairetou 14 (☎47 479), near St. Spiridon church. 500dr/€1.47 per 20min. Open daily 9am-1am. **Cafe Online** (☎46 266), after the McDonald's as you walk along Kapodistriou with the Old Fortress on your left. 1000dr/€2.93 per 30min., 2000dr/€5.87 per hr., 500dr/€1.47 minimum. Open M-Sa 9am-2am, Su 6pm-2am.

Post Office: (☎25 544), on the corner of Alexandras and Voulefton. Poste Restante and **currency exchange** available. Open M-F 7:30am-8pm. **Postal Code:** 49100.

ACCOMMODATIONS

Corfu is expensive. Budget accommodations are few, and it may require extra footwork to find them. **The Association of Owners of Private Rooms and Apartments in Corfu,** Iak. Polila 24, has a complete list of rooms in Corfu and can give you the numbers of landlords to call for rooms. (☎26 133. Open M-F 8:30am-2pm and 5:30-8pm.) Contact them several weeks prior to your trip to ensure availability. Consider staying outside the city in a base town with a nice beach and more domatia. Buses only run until 8 or 10pm, so you'll need to rent wheels to party-hop.

Hotel Europa, Giantsilio 10 (☎39 304). From the New Port customs house, cross the main street and make a right onto the street that leads back from the waterfront; Giantsilio is a tiny road on the left, just after the road becomes Napoleonta. Rooms are white and airy, at the best price in Corfu Town. Singles 5000dr/€14.67, with bath 6000dr/€17.61; doubles 7000dr/€20.53, with bath 8000dr/€23.58; triples 9000dr/€26.41.

Hotel Ionian, Xen. Stratigou 46 (☎39 915 or 30 628), at the new port, offers relatively inexpensive rooms with full bath, blessed fans and green turf-carpet suitable for mini-golf. Singles 7000-8000dr/€20.53-23.48; doubles 9000-11,000dr/€26.41-32.28; triples 12,000-16,000dr/€35.22-46.96.

Hotel Hermes, Rue G. Markora 14 (☎39 268 or 39 321; fax 31 747), by the noisy public market. A charming lobby leads to basic, high-ceilinged rooms with baths and ceiling fans. Singles 9000dr/€26.41; doubles 13,000dr/€38.15; triples 16,000dr/€46.96.

⬛ FOOD

The premier restaurant areas are near the Spianada and the Old Port. While in Corfu, try the local meat specialties: *sofrito* (veal stewed in a wine sauce with pepper and garlic), *stifado* (beef stewed with onions), and *pastitsada* (lamb or beef with noodles, flavored with tomatoes, cinnamon, onion, and pepper). Traditional pork *nuombolo* resembles prosciutto, and is available at Corfu's famous butcher shops. Corfiot treats like *chadilia* (a dense cake of almonds, pistachios, rose water, and special citrus marmalade) are served at **bakeries** throughout town. The **kumquat** plant, introduced to Corfu by the British, fills bottles of "Koum Kouat" liqueur and jars of preserves. You can taste **homemade wines** all over the island: light white *kakotrygis*, richer white *moscato*, dry *petrokorintho* red, and dark *skopelitiko*. Bottles of light yellow *tsitsibira* (ginger beer) are another imperial holdover. A daily open-air **public market** sells inexpensive produce on Dessila, off G. Theotoki below the new fortress. (Open daily 6am-2pm.) There are **supermarkets** on I. Theotoki, one in Pl. Sanrocco and another farther down the street, beyond the bus station. (Open M-F 8am-9pm, Sa 8am-6pm.)

Restaurant Antranik/Pizza Pete, Arseniou 21 (☎34 266 or 223 301), looking out over the northern waterfront. Established in 1920 by Armenian refugees, Antranik specializes in Greek dishes and seafood (entrees 1300-3200dr/€3.82-9.40). Pete's serves supreme pizzas (2000dr/€5.87). Waterfront seating gazes over Corfiot sunsets.

Restaurant Rex, Kapodistriou 66 (☎39 649), 1 block back from the Spianada. A bit pricey, but long famed as one of Corfu's best restaurants. Try the savory *sofrito* or *stifado* (both 3200dr/€9.40). Entrees 2200-4000dr/€6.45-11.74.

Best Top Restaurant, Filellinon 33 (☎24 010), on a small street perpendicular to the waterfront near Donzelot. Friendly staff serves Corfiot specialties and other dishes under spacious umbrellas in a sunny plateia by day, and by romantic candlelight by night. Entrees 1100-2700dr/€3.23-7.95.

Art Cafe, in the pretty garden behind the Palace of St. Michael and St. George. The preferred hangout of artsy local teens, it's a relaxing place to enjoy a late-afternoon ham and cheese sandwich (700dr/€2.05), and a *frappé* (650dr/€1.90).

⬛ 🏛 SIGHTS AND MUSEUMS

After invading Vandals and Goths destroyed ancient Corfu (Paleopolis) in the 5th and 6th centuries AD, Corfiots built a more defensible city between the twin peaks (called *Koryfes*, a possible root for "Corfu") of the Old Fortress. Scared of Ottoman raids, the Venetians strengthened this fortress, constructed the New Fortress, and built thick walls around the growing city. A series of **underground tunnels,** now closed, connected the Old and New Fortresses and all parts of Corfu Town. They later provided refuge for Corfiots after the first World War II air raids in 1940.

OLD FORTRESS. Finished in the late 14th century by the Venetians, the *Paleo Frourio* was considered impregnable—until the British blew it up in 1864 before leaving Corfu to the Greeks. Along with much of Corfu Town, the castle's imposing fortifications were restored to some semblance of their former glory for a 1994 EU summit. On the grounds are the **Church of St. George,** patron saint of infantry, a **Byzantine Gallery** which houses mosaics and frescoes from an early Christian basilica, a library and a nearby **museum** devoted to the role of Christianity in Byzantium, and a **bell tower** that strikes the hour for all Corfu Town. *(Just east of the Spaniada. ☎48 311. Open daily 8am-7pm. 800dr/ €2.35, students 400dr/€1.17, EU students free.)*

NEW FORTRESS. The younger, 350-year-old fort above the ferry docks opens onto panoramic views of Corfu Town ideal for sun-drenched picnics. The fort displays a small **gallery** of etchings, maps, and watercolors with nautical motifs, and an additional gallery with contemporary exhibits. Concerts and theatrical events are held here throughout the year. *(Look for signs as you walk along Velissariou from the Old Port. ☎45 000. Open daily 9am-9pm.)*

CHURCH OF AG. SPYRIDON. This site of pilgrimage for Orthodox Christians was built in 1590, and contains the embalmed body of St. Spyridon, Corfu's patron saint. Spyridon, born in AD 270, lived and died on Cyprus. When invading Saracens threatened his body, his preserved corpse was brought to Corfu in a burlap sack slung on the back of a donkey. Each year, the faithful give him a new pair of embroidered slippers—he wears out the old pair wandering the island doing good deeds. If the priests open the gold cover of the saint's casket during your visit, you can see Spyridon's blackened face. Above him, dozens of silver lamps swing beside gold votive offerings (most of ships), offering thanks and prayer. Spyridon worked his latest major miracle in 1943: when the surrounding buildings were razed in an air raid, the church and the Corfiots sheltered within went unscathed. Corfiots parade the saint's remains four times a year: on Palm Sunday, the first Sunday in November (celebrating deliverance from 17th-century plagues), on Holy Saturday (for relief from a 1550 famine), and during the two-day **festival** beginning mid-August (commemorating the end of a month-long 1716 Ottoman siege). His own feast day festival is on December 12. *(Take Ag. Spyridon off the Spianada; it's on the left, with the rose-colored onion dome. Under renovation as of June 2001. Open daily 6am-9pm.)*

BYZANTINE MUSEUM. Housed in the 15th-century Church of the Most Holy Virgin Kyra Antivouniotissa, the museum's collection of **Cretan School** icons is worth seeing, if only for the church. The beautiful courtyard is filled with flowers, and the museum has remained peacefully free of tourists, an ideal spot for a calming half hour. After the fall of Rethymno in 1646, Corfu served as a pit-stop for many artists from Venetian Crete on their way to Venice. A wall chart in the museum details their movements and activities. Striking icons include St. George with a somewhat wussy dragon, a gaudy St. Cyril of Alexandria, and St. Pantalemon granting mercy to the suffering; they're housed in the uniquely Corfiot three-sided exonarthex. *(☎ 38 313. Look for signs on Arsenion as it curls downhill from the palace. Open Tu-Su 8am-3pm. 500dr/€1.47, students and seniors 300dr/€0.88, EU students free.)*

ARCHAEOLOGICAL MUSEUM. Relics of Corfu's Mycenaean and Classical past appear in this museum's large collection. The highlight is the fantastic **Gorgon Pediment** from the Temple of Artemis in ancient Corfu, which shows the ghoulish Medusa with her children—winged Pegasus and the **Chrysoar**—born at the moment Perseus cut her head off. Statuettes of Artemis, a collection of coins depicting mythological figures from an ancient mint on Corfu, and funerary urns also deserve your attention. *(Vraila 1, on the waterfront south of Spianada. ☎ 30 680. Open Tu-Su 8:30am-3pm. 800dr/€2.35, students and seniors 400dr/€1.17, children and EU students free.)*

PALACE OF SAINT MICHAEL AND SAINT GEORGE. Presiding over the stately Spaniada is the even statelier palace, built by the Lord High Commissioner Sir Thomas Maitland to house himself, the Ionian Parliament and Senate, and various public services. It now holds the unique **Museum of Asian Art,** which displays a range of Oriental artifacts collected by diplomat Gregorios Manos. *(☎ 30 443. Open Tu-Su 8:30am-3pm. Free.)* The **Municipal Modern Art Gallery (Dimotiko Pinakothiki),** around the back of the Palace through the garden, has a small but expanding collection of Corfiot paintings and rotating special exhibits. *(☎ 48 690. Open daily 10am-9pm, but hours may vary with special exhibits. 500dr/€1.47, students 200dr/€0.60.)*

OTHER MUSEUMS. The small **Solomos Museum** honors the national poet of Greece, Dionysios Solomos (see p. 27). Born in Zante in 1798, the poet spent much of his life on Corfu. After living in Italy, Solomos dropped out of law school and began to write poetry. He was the first to use popular (Demotic) Greek in poetry, and his "Hymn to Freedom" is now the Greek National Anthem. The museum is housed in Solomos's house, reconstructed after a German bombing, and displays copies of original manuscripts, portraits, and memorabilia. *(Look for the sign in an alleyway on Arseniou just west of the Byzantine Museum, toward the New Port. ☎ 30 674. Open M-F 9:30am-2pm. 300dr/€0.88.)* Fanatical capitalists will enjoy the **Museum of Paper**

Currency, in the Ionian Bank Building down N. Theotoki from the Spianada, which holds, along with examples of all Greek currency that has ever existed, the first bank note printed in Greece. (☎41 552. Open M-F 10am-2pm. Free.)

MON REPOS ESTATE. This former summer residence of the British Commissioner was given to the Greek royal family by the British government in 1864. Since the royals' exile in 1967, the lovely Neoclassical palace has fallen into disrepair, and the large gardens of rare trees are overgrown. The forested park and its many paths are far off the beaten track. You and the cicadas will probably have the place to yourselves. (Open daily 8am-7pm. Free.) The paths lead up to the Neoclassical palace, which looks out over the sea. Past this to the left is **Kardaki beach.** It's said that anyone who drinks from its spring will remain on the island forever. To the right, a path leads to two Doric temples, the decrepit **Temple to Hera** and the more impressive **Kardaki Temple,** possibly dedicated to Poseidon, Apollo, or Asclepius. (Follow the waterfront south from the Old Fortress (away from the Palace) for about 35-40min. After a hotel and Mon Repos beach the road heads inland–the estate is about 7min. further.)

CHURCHES. One kilometer south of Corfu Town lie the remains of several churches dating back to the 12th century. Following the waterfront south from the Old Fortress (away from the Palace) after about 20min. is a sign indicating the **Church of Ag. Jason and Sosipater;** follow it to the first church in the series, the **Church of Agios Athanassios at Anemomyios.** There is a map directing you to the remaining 4 churches: the **Church of Ag. Jason and Sosipater,** an Early Christian **Basilica,** the **Monastery of Agios Theodoros,** and the **Church of Panayia Neradziha.**

FESTIVALS. The procession of the embalmed body of St. Spyridon on takes place each year during Easter celebrations, on Palm Sunday and Holy Saturday. It's a tradition for Corfiots to throw special pots full of water out of their windows at 11am on Holy Saturday—a Venetian New Year's tradition that Orthodox Greeks have appropriated to celebrate the Resurrection. The evening religious ceremonies for Holy Saturday are held in the Spaniada, and followed by music, fireworks, and a special feast including red-dyed eggs and dove-shaped breads called *colombines.* Corfu's Carnival festivities, which begin 40 days before Easter, see a mix of Greek and Venetian influence. The most striking traditions include the final Thursday's "The Gossip," a street theater performance in which women call out the latest gossip from windows across alleys in the center of the Old Town, and the last Sunday's burning of King Carnival, when the effigy "King" is tried and sentenced to death by fire for his hand in all the year's misfortunes.

NIGHTLIFE AND ENTERTAINMENT

The undisputed focus of Corfu Town's nightlife is the so-called **Disco Strip,** on Eth. Antistaseos at the waterfront, 2km west of the New Port. The many bars and clubs on the strip bustle with a multicultural crowd of locals and tourists. The typical 2000dr/€5.87 cover often includes your first drink. Beer costs 1000-1500dr/€2.93-€4.40; cocktails run 1500-2000dr/€4.40-5.87. A **taxi** from Pl. Sanrocco costs about 500-1000dr/€1.47-2.93. The more touristy and international clubs of the strip include **Coca Club,** on the hillside at the beginning of the strip, and **Apocalypsis,** an elaborate fusion of an ancient temple and a construction site, which plays only techno in its pool-equipped expanse. **Hippodrome** is next door to Apocalypsis behind the parking lot; **Sax** has a more sophisticated feel inside an old stone building. The more authentic, Greek-style clubs of the strip are **Sodoma,** which blasts mostly Greek music and flashes dizzying strobes inside, **Mobile,** next door to Hippodrome and Apocalypsis, and the bona fide hot spot of the strip: **Bouzoukia.** *The* club for Greeks who know how to party, Bouzoukia often has no cover, but you won't find a drink for under 2000dr/€5.87. If you're going to try and snag a table for the night, be prepared to shell out up to 40,000dr/€117.40. Bouzoukia's perks include live Greek music and a constant crowd of Corfu's most chic.

For a mellower night, head to **Liston** and the adjacent park under the big palm tree, where elegant little cafes stay lively until around 1am. By far the most popular among them is **Magnet,** at the top of Kapodistriou, where a babel of multilingual chatter and nearby croaking frogs echo in the shady little plateia. The **cinemas** on G. Theotoki, a few blocks from Pl. Sanrocco, and on the corner of Akadimias and G. Aspoti, screen films in English. Look for placards on G. Theotoki (tickets roughly 2000dr/€5.87). The **municipal theater** (☎33 598), between Dessila and Mantzarou one block from G. Theotoki, has occasional drama, dance, and music performances, publicized on bulletin boards all over town.

▓ DAYTRIP FROM CORFU TOWN: ACHILLION PALACE

In Gastouri. From Corfu Town, take bus #10 from 200m west of Pl. Sanrocco on Methodiou (30min., 6 per day 7am-8pm, 240dr/€0.70). ☎56 210. Open daily 9am-5pm. 1000dr/ €2.93, students 500dr/€1.47.

The 1981 James Bond flick *For Your Eyes Only* was filmed in the gardens of the eccentric and ostentatious Achillion Palace, the secluded home of Empress Elizabeth of Austria from 1892 until her 1897 assassination by an Italian anarchist in Geneva. She named her home for Achilles, an obsession of hers; she, like Achilles's mother Thetis, lost two sons. Later, German Kaiser Wilhelm II summered here until the First World War diverted his attention. Achillion Palace became a hospital and barracks in both World Wars; it was again reborn as the first Greek casino in 1962. It's now a museum, with the house as the subject.

WESTERN CORFU

Western Corfu is a beach lover's paradise, with wide expanses of golden sand and hidden crystal coves, majestic cliffs, and rock formations serving as a backdrop to the glimmering turquoise sea. While it sees its share of tour buses, it doesn't suffer from the same degree of over-development that mars the beautiful east and sad south. Instead, its towering, untouched natural beauty makes it a continual delight to explore its towns and more remote beaches.

PELEKAS Πελεκας   ☎0661

Removed from the mass tourism of the resorts, the village of ▓Pelekas sits at the top of a hill, with great views and famously beautiful sunsets. Pelekas has the best of what Corfu has to offer—beaches, beauty, great food, fun bars, architectural and cultural charm—with the added benefit of being off the beaten path. Take **bus #11** from Pl. Sanrocco in Corfu Town (30min., 7 per day 7am-8:30pm, 240dr/ €0.70). The long, sandy **beach** is a pleasant 30min. walk from town down a very steep road (plan on 45min.-1hr. back up; a shuttle bus to and from town is also available at the far left side of the beach facing inland). Rooms to let are plentiful and well priced in Pelekas, but call ahead in high season to secure a spot. ▓**Pension Tellis and Brigitte,** around the corner from the bus stop, has the friendliest hosts in town and lovely rooms in a little house covered with bougainvillea. Balconies offer superb views of the surrounding countryside. (☎94 326. Singles 5000dr/€14.67; doubles 6000-8000dr/€17.61-23.48; some with bath.) Near the **Church of Agios Nikolaos,** around the corner and above the bus stop, **Takis Kontis**'s rooms are comfortable and airy; half have fantastic balcony views. (☎94 247. All have shared baths. Singles 4000dr/€11.74; doubles 5000dr/€14.67.) On the road to the beach, next to the fork for Glyfada, the rooms at the **Pension Paradise** are a good deal, and include kitchen use. (☎94 530 or 36 217. Showers included. Singles 5000-6000dr/ €14.67-17.61; doubles 7000-10,000dr/€20.53-29.35.) The well-situated **Pelekas Cafe** purees superb milkshakes (900dr/€2.64) from a view over the island. Just outside of town on the road to Glyfada, the ▓**Pink Panther** restaurant and bar serves up terrific Greek and Italian food (pizzas start at 1800dr/€5.28). Try the Napolitana with olives, capers, and anchovies (1900dr/€5.60). If you get there early enough, the pink balcony offers great sunset views; revelry begins around midnight. **Zanzibar,** across from Pelekas Cafe, serves Foster's and Guinness on tap.

GLYFADA Γλυφαδα ☎0661

Glyfada attracts more tourists than tiny Pelekas, 5km down the coast, but its seemingly endless shore accommodates the throngs admirably. Scrubby cliffs bracket both of Glyfada's remarkably shallow **beaches,** where crashing waves make swimming extra fun. An eclectic crowd of internationals basks on the sun-speckled sand. Young sun-worshipers scope each other's tans and amuse themselves parasailing (singles 8000dr/€23.48; doubles 12,000dr/€35.22), water-skiing (5000dr/€14.67 for 10min.), or on jet skis (15min.; singles 12,000dr/€35.22, doubles 15,000dr/€44.02). Motorboats, kayaks, inner-tubes, and paddle boats are also available. Green KTEL **buses** leave from Corfu Town at the intersection above the Grand Louis Hotel (30min., 6 per day 6:45am-8pm, 400dr/€1.17), and a free bus connects Pelekas to Glyfada (10min., 4 per day 11am-8:30pm; schedules are posted throughout Glyfada and Pelekas). Budget accommodations are scarce, but it's easy to make the trip from Pelekas or Corfu Town. The nearest camping is at **Vatos Camping** (☎94 505) in Vatos Village. North of Glyfada, accessible via dirt path off the main Pelekas road, lie the isolated **beaches** of **Moni Myrtidion** and **Myrtiotissa,** extolled by Lawrence Durrell as the most beautiful in the world. A section of Myrtiotissa serves as an unofficial nude beach—unless local monks complain to the police, who reluctantly bring offending nudists to court.

PALEOKASTRITSA Παλαιοκαστριτσα ☎0663

Paleokastritsa beach rests among six small coves and sea caves that cast shadows over the blue. Although the beach is a bit narrow and can get crowded, a swim in the calm, dark-blue water encircled by cliffs, more than makes up for it. Green KTEL **buses** arrive from Corfu Town (45min., 17 per day 8:30am-6pm, 500dr/€1.47). You can hire a motorboat (2500dr/€7.35 per person; 30min. each way) or rent a pedal boat (3000dr/€8.80 per hr.) or kayak (singles 1000dr/€2.93; doubles 2000dr/€5.87 per hr.) to reach the caves where Phaecian princess Nausicaä found the shipwrecked Odysseus washed ashore (see **A Brief Odyssey,** p. 264). Jutting out on a hill over the sea, bright white **Panagia Theotokos Monastery** boasts a collection of Byzantine icons, nice views, and a so-called **sea monster's skeleton.** Come as early as possible—by mid-morning it's a mess of tour buses—and take a little bread with you to feed the monastery's tame peacocks (up the little road past the vegetable garden). The paved road up the hill leads to the monastery. The 12th-century fort of **Angelokastro** (Castle of the Holy Angels) sits above Paleokastritsa. A natural balcony with a magnificent view, **Bella Vista,** is a 1½hr. walk from Paleokastritsa. Take the road from the bus stop to the Odysseos Hotel, turn left on the path through the olive groves and continue on the trail through a village to the fort.

AGIOS GORDIOS Αγιος Γορδιος ☎0661

Ten kilometers south of Pelekas, Agios Gordios is naturally beautified by impressive rock formations and a lovely **beach.** Home of the infamous debauchery of the **Pink Palace** hotel/backpacker playground, yet it remains surprisingly quiet. The main road runs uphill, perpendicular to the beach, with a short stretch of restaurants, minimarkets, and souvenir shops. The steep rock face on the southern end of the beach was once used as a lookout for pirates. Blue **buses** run to Agios Gordios from Pl. Sanrocco in Corfu Town (45min., 6 per day 8:15am-8pm, 300dr/€0.88). The town's accommodation is the main attraction: the notorious **Pink Palace Hotel,** a favorite with American and Canadian backpackers in search of instant (and constant) gratification. Buses go to and from Athens to the Pink Palace, bypassing Patras (12,000dr/€35.25 one-way from Pink Palace; 15,000dr/€44.02 one-way from Athens). Forget mingling with the locals—there's nary a word of Greek spoken at this reincarnation of MTV Spring Break. Some Greek traditions have been appropriated to heighten the fun: toga-wrapped partiers have been known to down countless shots of ouzo as they break plates on each other's heads, in a spirit of revelry that would make Dionysus proud. The Palace's impressive list of amenities makes it a self-contained party resort: there's laundry service

IONIAN ISLANDS

(2500dr/€7.35); Internet access (1000dr/€2.93 per 30min.); a jacuzzi; basketball, volleyball, and tennis courts; an on-site nightclub; clothing-optional cliff-diving (4000dr/€11.75); boat daytrips; and various watersports. (☎53 103 or 53 104; fax 53 025. Quality-rated rooms: A-class—with A/C, telephone, private balcony and baths—9000dr/€26.41; stuffier, dorm-style B-class 7500dr/€22. Breakfast, dinner, and pick up/drop off at the Corfu Town ferry included.)

EASTERN CORFU   ☎0661

The east coast of Corfu is the most developed and least aesthetically pleasing part of the island. The first 20km north of Corfu Town are thoroughly Anglicized by throngs of rowdy expats, and the beaches are thin strips along a busy, clamorous coastal road. Despite its low points, Eastern Corfu *is* convenient and relatively inexpensive. Everything—beach, restaurants, hotels, nightlife—is consolidated in one strip, so you won't need to rent a moped, as in more remote parts of the island. It's cheaper than beautiful Corfu Town, but close enough to allow frequent trips. **Gouvia** and **Dassia,** the first two resorts north of town, thrive off package tours despite meager beaches. The visitors to notorious little **Ipsos,** a bit farther north, guzzle the day away at countless cheap bars and discos. Interchangeable souvenir stands, fast-food restaurants, and C-class hotels line the flat stretch of road across from the beach. **Pirgi,** a quieter extension of Ipsos, crawls up the base of the neighboring mountains. Hotels fill up quickly with package tour groups, so reserve ahead. There are also a few domatia and several beachside campsites in the area. Signs are posted prominently along the coastal highway for **Camping Corfu.** (☎93 579. 1350dr/€4 per person, children 800dr/€2.35. 900dr/€2.64 per small tent, 1100dr/€3.23 per large. 800dr/€2.35 per car. Electricity 900dr/€2.64.) More beachside camping is available at **Paradise** (☎93 558 or 93 552). KTEL green **buses** serve Ipsos and Pirgi (30min., 8 per day 7am-8pm, 350dr/€1.03).

NORTHERN CORFU

> ❗ **TRAVEL ADVISORY: ALBANIA.** In June 2000, the US State Department issued a warning against unnecessary travel to Albania. Violent political turmoil affects southern Albania, the location of several great archaeological sites. While improved relations between Greece and Albania have made Albania's Ionian coast accessible to tourists from Corfu, *Let's Go* discourages travel to Albania.

Past Pirgi, the road begins to wind below steep cliffs. **Mt. Pantokrator** towers 1000m above on your left, while dramatic vistas of Albania appear across the straits. Emperors Tiberius and Nero of Rome once vacationed here, though tourism has erased most traces of the ancient world on the north coast. The farther you get from overbuilt beach towns like Kassiopi and Sidari, the better off you'll be.

AGIOS STEFANOS Αγιος Ετεφανος   ☎0661

The most remote northern beach town is Agios Stefanos (not to be confused with the northeastern village of the same name). A mere 15min. drive from bustling Sidari, Agios Stefanos is mercifully underdeveloped; the wide, sandy beach is set in a long curving gulf of high sandstone cliffs. The long waves roll in toward the few determined souls who have escaped Sidari and Kassiopi. The trip there is a treat in itself: the coastal road curves inland west of Sidari, past ferny hillsides of figs, olives, and cypresses, and through a picturesque mountain village. **Buses** run from Corfu Town (1½hr., 6 per day 5:45am-7:30pm, 900dr/€2.64) and Kassiopi, via Sidari (4 per day 9:30am-4pm). The few who make it to town will find expensive hotels, but plenty of domatia, some at reasonable prices (7000-9000dr/€20.53-26.41); check the signs in front of tavernas along the main road to track them down. Be warned: there is **no bank or ATM** in town; bring enough cash for your stay.

🏖🏃 BEACHES AND THE OUTDOORS

The sheer slopes of northeastern Corfu cradle several fine **beaches** including **Barbati,** 10km north of Ipsos, nearby **Nissaki,** and the twin beaches **Kalami** and **Kouloura.** A green KTEL **bus** from Corfu Town runs to Kassiopi (1¼hr., 6 per day 5:45am-4pm, 700dr/€2.05) and stops at most beaches along the northeastern coast; ask to be let off at less popular destinations. Kouloura and Kalami beaches are a brief walk from the main road north of Gimari village. Head down from the bus stop on the main road. Soon you'll see a rusted sign on the right marking the shortcut path to Kalami. If you're heading for Kouloura, continue down the road and turn left at the fork. The right fork leads you on a long route to Kalami.

Kalami, with its wide flat-stoned beach, was home to author **Lawrence Durrell** and his family in the 1930s. His small white house is still "set like a dice on a rock" in the southern end of town; now it houses the pleasant **Taverna White Horse,** which serves typical Greek fare under wisteria vines with a sea view (entrees 1000-3000dr/€2.93-8.80). Super-secluded **Kouloura,** a 10min. walk along the road from Kalami, is a small, partially-shaded beach composed of mixed sand, eucalyptus leaves, and stones, with nary an umbrella or paddle boat in sight. **Taverna Kouloura** has a nice view of the marina (entrees 1500-9000dr/€4.40-26.41). It can be expensive to stay overnight, and there are no accommodations in Kouloura.

To hike to the high plateau of **Mt. Pantokrator** for breathtaking views of all Corfu, start at Spartillas, a village 7km north and inland from Pirgi, along the bus route. From there, follow the same path used each summer by villagers on their way to the annual festival at Pantokrator Monastery.

LEFKADA Λευκαδα

Thucydides reports that Lefkada was part of the mainland until 427 BC, when inhabitants dug a canal and made their home an island. A modern bridge now connects Lefkada to the mainland, just 50m away; it only recently replaced an archaic chain-operated ferry built by Emperor Augustus. Despite their ancestors' attempts to keep people away, modern Lefkadians are devoted to tourists. Souvenir shops and over-priced restaurants abound, especially in Nidri, which is mostly composed of tourist traps and a profusion of liquor stores. Still, miles of white-sand beaches and astonishing natural beauty remain; with a little effort, you can skirt the patches of tacky tourism and find the island's unspoiled secrets.

LEFKADA TOWN ☎0645

Lefkada Town, across from the mainland, is a little too high-end and touristed to be completely authentic, but it maintains its own brand of charm. If you stray from the waterfront and the pedestrian-only main thoroughfare, you'll find tiny alleyways full of pastel, flower-draped houses and roosters pecking in gardens—a sign that Lefkada Town retains a quiet allure beneath the busy surface.

📑🛈 ORIENTATION AND PRACTICAL INFORMATION. Archaeologist William Dörpfield claimed that Homer's Ithaka was really Lefkada; Lefkada Town thanked him by naming its main road, running down the middle of the peninsula that is the city's downtown, **Dörpfield.** It later becomes **Strategou Mela.** Dörpfield and all the little winding streets that branch off it are for pedestrians and bikes only, but cars can drive along the waterfront and inland from the peninsula.

From the **bus station** (☎22 364)—a yellow waterfront building with a gray and yellow striped awning—**buses** cross the canal to **Athens** (5½hr., 4 per day, 7000dr/€20.53) and **Aktion** (30min., 4 per day, 480dr/€1.41). **Local buses** run to: **Nidri** (30min., 13 per day, 350dr/€1.03); **Agios Nikitas** (20min., 3 per day, 300dr/€0.88); **Poros** (45min., 2 per day, 550dr/€1.62); and **Vasiliki** (1hr., 5 per day, 750dr/€2.21). Pick up a bus schedule at the station for additional routes and return times; service is reduced on Sundays. **Taxis** are available, but expensive (☎22 233 or 24 600).

Ferries leaving from **Nidri** and **Vasiliki** link Lefkada with **Ithaka** and **Kephalonia** to the south. Ferry schedules change from month to month. While the duration and price of ferries are fairly stable, departure and arrival times and locations change all the time; you are best off calling ahead. From **Nidri** (☎31 520), ferries sail to **Frikes** on Ithaka (2hr., 1500dr/€4.40) and **Fiskardo** on Kephalonia (2-3hr. depending on route, 1220dr/€3.60). From **Vasiliki**, a ferry leaves twice a day for **Fiskardo** (1hr., 1100dr/€3.23) and goes on to **Piso Aetos,** Ithaka (2hr., 1500dr/€4.40). Check travel offices for current schedules. **Excursion boats** leave Nidri each morning at 9:45am and return at 6pm cruising to **Kephalonia, Ithaka, Meganisi, Skorpios,** and **Madouri.** (7000dr/€20.53. Call ☎92 658 for more information.) For other boat excursions, inquire at waterfront kiosks or travel offices, or read the boats' hard-to-miss signs.

There is no tourist office, but the **tourist police** can be found on 8th Merarchias. Facing the bus station, walk left and follow the road as it leads away from the water; the police building will be on your left. (☎26 450. English spoken, handy brochures, and island-wide contacts for accommodations. Open 8am-10pm.) The 24hr. **police station** (☎22 346) is in the same building. For detailed info about ferries, tours, or sights, try the numerous travel agencies around the bus station. There is a **National Bank** with a 24hr. **ATM** on Dörpfield (open M-Th 8am-2pm, F 8am-1:30pm), and several **pharmacies.** Dörpfield also leads to the main plateia, with its cafes and occasional traveling music acts. For the **OTE,** turn right off St. Melas onto Skiarderesi. Turn left when it dead-ends into Ioanni Marinou. (Open Sa-M and W 7:30am-2:30pm, T and Th-F 7:30am-2:30pm and 5-8:30pm.) The **Quarta Cafe,** past the police station on 8th Merarchias on the left, offers **Internet access.** (☎21 507. 400dr/€1.17 per 30min., 800dr/€2.35 per hr. Open daily 7:30am-3am.) The **post office** is on St. Melas. (Open M-F 7:30am-2pm.) **Postal code:** 31100.

⌨ ACCOMMODATIONS AND FOOD. There are no easy-to-locate domatia in town; so if you're pinching pennies consider staying elsewhere. Lefkada Town is expensive—most rooms start at 12,000dr/€35.22. Advance booking would ease the cost. Travel agencies suggest you check in Lia, a small village 4km outside town.

One relatively affordable option is the rather deluxe **Santa Maura,** off Dörpfield about three blocks from the water. (☎21 309; fax 26 253. Singles 10,000dr/€29.35; doubles 15,000dr/€44.) In the same price range is **Hotel Nirikos,** at the end of Dörpfield on the waterfront. A shiny lobby and dining room give way to simpler, slightly worn rooms with TV, phone, and full baths. (☎24 132; fax 23 756. Breakfast included. Singles 10,000dr/€29.35; doubles 15,000dr/€44.)

By and large, dining in Lefkada town is pricey and tourist-oriented; you'll have to work a little harder to find authentic flavor. **Taverna Regentos,** off the main plateia a short walk up Verrioti, is one of the classic tavernas in Lefkada. Built into an older taverna, Regentos has been passed down from generation to generation. Peek into the pots as your palate-pleasers are prepared. (Grilled chicken with beans 1300dr/€3.82, *retsina* 700dr/€2.05 per half-liter. Open 6pm-2am.) **Taverna Riviera,** off the waterfront on the right, has low-priced traditional dishes and draws a regular crowd of locals who while away the afternoon and much of the evening. (☎21 480. Entrees 1500-2200dr/€4.40-6.46.) For a spicier night, two clubs, **X Generation** and **Capital,** are 1km to the right, facing inland, of town. The clubs are about 500m beyond the athletic center. A taxi there should cost under 1000dr/€2.93.

◧◪ SIGHTS AND BEACHES. The **Archaeological Museum,** in a modern building 1km down the waterfront road toward Ag. Nikitas, has a collection of artifacts from ancient Leukas, a prominent island city from the 7th century BC. Panels thoroughly explain the objects in English, and give interesting information about Leukas's history and culture. (☎21 635. Open 8:30am-3pm. Free.) The **folklore museum** gives a taste of Lefkada's Italian legacy. It's off the main plateia; turn right and follow the signs. It may be temporarily closed for work on the building, so call ahead to check. (☎22 473. Open M-F 11am-1pm and 6-10pm. 500dr/€1.47.) In the second half of August, Lefkada hosts the annual **Folklore Festival,** with music and dance performances in the outdoor theater just off the plateia. While Lefkada Town has

IONIAN ISLANDS

no sandy beaches, the northwest coast has miles of white pebbles and clear water. To get there, rent a **moped** (2000dr/€5.87 per day) at **Eurocar** (☎24 617) on the tip of the peninsula, or catch a bus to the best stretch of beaches, starting at ▓**Agios Nikitas** (3 per day, 300dr/€0.88) and continuing to the sweeping view at the **Faneromenis Monastery.** (☎21 105. Open 7am-10pm. Free.)

NIDRI Νιδρι

The last stop on the delightful Fiskardo-Frikes-Nidri ferry, Nidri is an anti-climactic end of the line. The waterfront, crowded with pleasure boats, has a handsome view of the dappled coves of offshore islands; the town itself is a crowded strip of tourist shops and cafes. **Ferries** go to **Frikes** on Ithaka (2hr.,1500dr/€4.40) and then to **Fiskardo** (1220dr/€3.60). **Buses** from Nidri go to **Lefkada** (30min., 13 per day, 340dr/€1) and **Vasiliki** (30min., 4 per day, 400dr/€1.17). The **buses stop** at a small KTEL bus sign on the main street; **taxis** make the trip for 3500dr/€10.27.

The crowds and glitz that make Nidri unpleasant during the daytime transform it into a party zone at night, as strobe-lit clubs on the main street throw open their doors to tourists and locals alike. Let the wind carry you to **Sail Inn,** down the main street toward Lefkada Town. The snack bar by day/club by night has a breezy atmosphere with straw umbrellas and an outdoor dance floor that opens right onto the beach. (Beer 700dr/€2.05; cocktails 1500dr/€4.40. Cafe open 10am-8pm, club open 10:30pm-early morning.) More mainstream are **Status Bar** (beer 500dr/€1.47, cocktails 1000dr/€2.93; open 9pm-2am); and **Byblos.** Be sure to hit their happy hour from 5-8pm. (Beer 1000dr/€2.93; cocktail 2000dr/€5.87. Open 5pm-late.) **Club Tropicana,** down the main street toward Vassiliki, is only for die-hards. It's doors don't even open until midnight. Just think: if you last long enough, you can catch the morning bus back to town!

VASILIKI Βαφιλικη ☎0645

Vasiliki's unique position between mountains creates distinct wind patterns that make it one of the world's premiere windsurfing towns. The town keeps a neighborly, close-knit atmosphere despite the visitors. Smaller than Lefkada Town and less touristy than Nidri, Vasiliki is the best Lefkada has to offer. With tiny pebbled coves, an attractive waterfront of excellent restaurants, and ferry connections to Kephalonia and Ithaka, Vasiliki is full of the quiet pleasures of a small beach town.

▓🛈 **ORIENTATION AND PRACTICAL INFORMATION.** Almost everything in Vasiliki lies along the waterfront or the main road running inland from the 'corner' of the harbor near Penguin Restaurant. **Buses** pick up and drop off at a T-shaped intersection, inland on the main road. Five per day run from **Lefkada** (1hr., 750dr/€2.20) and **Nidri** (30min., 450dr/€1.32). From Vasiliki, **ferries** (☎31 555 or 31 520) sail to **Fiskardo** on Kephalonia (1hr., 1100dr/€3.32) and continue on to **Piso Aetos,** Ithaka (2hr., 1500dr/€4.41); inquire at the kiosk next to the pier. Along the street between the bus stop and the waterfront, **Star Travel** (☎31 833; fax 31 834) has info about buses, accommodations, boat excursions around the islands, and **internet access.** (Internet 400dr/€1.17 per 20min., 1000dr/€2.93 per hr. Open daily 9am-11pm.) A little farther down the street, **Samba Tours** offers the same services, as well as **ferry info,** faxes, car hire, flights, photocopying, safety deposit, and book swap. (☎31 555 or 31 520; fax 31 522. Open daily 8:30am-midnight.) Both offices offer weekly trips to Lefkada's best beach, the breathtaking ▓**Porto Katsiki** (Port of the White Goat), at the base of towering white cliffs (40-50min., round trip leaves 11am and returns 5pm, 2500dr/€7.34). Renting a **moped** is a good idea. **Christo's Alex's Rental,** at the main road (i.e. the bus stop) is the cheapest place. (☎31 580; fax 31 780. Mopeds 2000dr/€5.87 per day; motorcycle 3000dr/€8.80 per day.) For **emergencies,** contact the **health center** (☎31 065); on the main road, go straight through the intersection with the road to Lefkada Town and Nidri. The 24hr. **police station** (☎31 218) is inland along the main road. The **post office** is up from Star Travel, just after the crossroads. (Open M-F 7:30am-2pm.) **Postal code:** 31082.

ℍ ACCOMMODATIONS. Rooms are plentiful along the road leading uphill from the bus stop, on the waterfront, and along the main road. With a little work, you should be able to find domatia for 5000dr/€14.67 or less in the off season, and possibly even as low as 6500dr/€19.10 in high season. The old ▓**fruit market**, which is now home of a mini-market, around the corner at the back side of the ferry dock, to the right side of the waterfront when facing inland), lets spacious rooms with private bath, balcony, and fabulous views of the water. (☎31 221. Doubles 7000dr/€20.53.) **Vasiliki Beach Camping,** popular among the windsurfing crowd, has superlative amenities including a great waterfront location, bar, mini-market, laundry and shower, not to mention a clean and flowery campsite. Head for the beach to the left of town as you face inland and make a right on the road running inland just before **Cocoon** and **Remezzo Beach Club.** (☎31 308 or 31 457; fax 31 458. 1900dr/€5.57 per person, 1400dr/€4.10 per small tent, 1300dr/€3.80 per car.) The seasonal **Hotel Lefkatas** on the main road, on the left as you walk out of town about 100m from the waterfront, is another option from summer into fall, with comfortable rooms featuring private baths and ocean-view balconies. (☎31 801 or 31 803. Call ahead. Singles 6000-10,000dr/€17.61-29.35; doubles 9000-15,000dr/€26.41-44.)

⬛⬛ FOOD AND NIGHTLIFE. Nearly all the restaurants are on a short stretch of the waterfront, where full meals can be inexpensive and well-prepared. **Miramare,** essentially on its own 'pier' at the far right of the waterfront, facing inland, has friendly service and a classy feel. It specializes in pizza (1900-2500dr/€5.59-7.35) and seafood (1500-4000dr/€4.40-11.74). Gary and Mary will offer you a warm welcome at **Penguin Restaurant,** on the waterfront at the corner of the main road running inland, which serves traditional Greek favorites (1600-2300dr/€4.70-6.75), international appetizers (400-2200dr/€1.17-6.46), great vegetarian dishes (800-1000dr/€2.35-2.93), and salads (600-2600dr/€1.76-7.63).

After dark, try **Zeus' Bar,** on the waterfront between Penguin and Dolphin restaurants, which serves up orange juice with soda water (500dr/€1.47) to soothe the salt- and sun-weary. It comes alive at night, when happy hour (7-9pm) cocktails are 1500dr/€4.40. **Remezzo Beach Bar,** all the way to the left of the waterfront (facing inland), offers the extreme of nightlife in Vasiliki for the under-25 crowd, featuring good dance music and large indoor/outdoor bars. Doors don't even open till midnight; head here if you plan to see the dawn through beer goggles. (Cover 1000dr/€2.93 includes first beer. Beer 1000dr/€2.93; cocktails 1300dr/€3.80.)

⬛ SIGHTS. A **lighthouse** built on the site of the **Temple of Lefkas Apollo** sits at the southernmost tip of the island. Worshipers exorcised evil with an annual sacrifice at the temple, in which the victim, usually a criminal or a person thought to be possessed, was launched from the cliffs into the sea. For extra fun, live birds were tied to the victim's limbs. It was from these 70m cliffs that the ancient poet **Sappho,** rejected by her lady lover Phaon, leapt to her death. The best views of **Sappho's Leap** or *Kavos tis Kiras* (Cape of the Lady) are found on various **boat excursions.**

ITHAKA Ιθάκη

The least touristed and perhaps the most beautiful of the Ionian islands, Ithaka retains a close-knit feel and is happily Greek amid heavily-touristed neighbors. Those who discover Ithaka delight in the island's pebbled, rocky hillsides and terraced olive groves. Ithaka was the kingdom that **Odysseus** left behind to fight in the Trojan War (and to wander ten years on his way home). His wife Penelope faithfully waited 20 years for his return here: crowds of suitors pressed for her hand—and Odysseus's kingdom. She bought herself time by insisting she finish the bridal cloth she was weaving (and secretly unwinding each night). However fair Penelope may have been, it is easy to see why Odysseus's kingdom attracted so many would-be successors; Ithaka is an island fit for the gods themselves.

VATHY Βαθυ   ☎0674

Ithaka's lovely capital wraps around a circular bay, where colorful fishing and
pleasure boats bob in the water and precipitous green hillsides nudge against the
water. At dusk, the dying sun deepens the tint of the red-shingled roofs and pastel-
painted houses.

■∦ ORIENTATION AND PRACTICAL INFORMATION. Facing inland, Vathy's
ferry docks are on the far right of the waterfront, about a 4min. walk to the right of
the town plateia. Depending on where you're coming from, you may need a taxi
(☎33 030) from **Piso Aetos** (10min., 3000-3500dr/€8.80-10.27) or **Frikes** (30min.,
5000-6000dr/€14.70-17.60). Be sure to call ahead for a taxi because there are not
many on the island, and Piso Aetos, for instance, is little more than a dock. **Ferries**
connect Ithaka to Sterea Ellada (at **Astakos**), the Peloponnese (at **Patras**), and
nearby **Lefkada** and **Kephalonia**. Schedules vary seasonally; check with the helpful
staff at **Delas Tours** (☎32 104; fax 33 031. Open daily 9am-2pm and 4-10pm), in the
main plateia. Or consult **Polyctor Tours,** along the far side of the plateia as you
approach from the port police. (☎33 120; fax 33 130. Open M-F 6:30-7am, 9am-
1:30pm and 3:30-9pm. Hours reduced Sa and Su.) Ferries depart from **Frikes,** on the
northern tip of Ithaka, to **Vasiliki** on Lefkada (2½hr., 1000dr/€2.93) and **Fiskardo** on
Kephalonia (1hr., 500dr/€1.47). Departures from **Piso Aetos** (near Vathy) go to:
Sami on Kephalonia (45min., 3 per day, 500dr/€1.47); **Fiskardo** on Kephalonia
(45min., 500dr/€1.47); and **Vasiliki** on Lefkada (2hr., 1400dr/€4.11). Ferries go to
mainland **Patras** in the Peloponnese (4½hr.; 7am, 4:30pm; 3900dr/€11.45). **Rent a
Scooter,** on a side street off the waterfront directly across from the Port Police, has
standard rates of 5000dr/€14.67 per day, plus gas. (☎32 840. Open 9am-2:30pm; in
summer 4:30-9:30pm.) For car rental, try **AGS Rent a Car,** on the waterfront about
two blocks to the right of the plateia. (About 14,000dr/€41.10 per day for a small
car, including insurance. ☎32 702. Open daily 8:30am-1pm and 5-9pm.) **Taxis** (☎33
030) are expensive, but can be found at the waterfront, in front of the plateia.

To reach the **hospital** (☎32 222), face inland and walk left along the waterfront
for about 1km until you see a sign. To reach the **police station** (☎32 205) coming
from the plateia, turn right on the first street after a mansion-turned-cafe and walk
inland. (Open 24hr. English spoken.) There is a **pharmacy** to the right of Delas
Tours in the plateia. For **laundry** service, **Polifimos** is behind the National Bank, in
the far right corner of the plateia. (☎32 032. 900dr/€2.65 per kg, wash and dry.)
The **National Bank** is in the far right corner of the plateia, approaching from the
Port Police, and has a 24hr. **ATM.** (Open M-Th 8am-2pm, F 8am-1:30pm.) The **OTE** is
on the waterfront, just before Hotel Mentor, coming from the plateia with the
water on your left. (Open M-F 7am-2:30pm.) **Internet access** is available at the
unmarked **Ogygia Cafe,** across from Rent a Scooter, on the side street across from
the Port Police (☎23 925. 500dr/€1.47 per 30 min., 1000dr/€2.93 per hr. Open daily
9am-2pm and 5pm-2am.) The **post office** is in the plateia. (☎32 386. Open M-F
7:30am-2pm.) **Postal code:** 28300.

∦⊡ ACCOMMODATIONS AND FOOD. Private **domatia** can cut you a very good
deal, and hotels are expensive, so they're a good way to go. Be sure to discuss
price and distance before leaving the town center. A good bet is **Andriana Domatia,**
across from the ferry dock on the far right side of the waterfront, facing inland;
immaculate rooms include bath, TV, A/C, and some have pleasant waterfront
views. (☎32 387. Singles 8000-9000dr/€23.48-26.41; doubles 13,000-14,000dr/
€38.15-41.10. Negotiate for discounts in the off season.) Many of the rooms on the
island are rented through **Delas Tours** (see above), so you might want to contact
them first to see what is available. Facing inland, **Hotel Mentor** is on the far left of
the waterfront. The swanky lobby leads to more basic rooms with linoleum floors
that include bath, A/C and TV. (☎32 433. Singles 11,000dr/€32.35, with breakfast
13,000dr/€38.15; doubles 14,000dr/€41.10, 18,000dr/€52.82 with breakfast.)

Taverna To Trexantiri, one block behind the post office off the plateia, dishes out huge portions. (Entrees under 1800dr/€5.28. ☎33 066.) **Kantouni** (☎32 910), on the right side of the waterfront facing inland, has delicious food like pork souvlaki (1900dr/€5.60), entrees between 1400-2200dr/€4.12-6.47. **O Nikos,** just down the street along the left side of the National Bank, serves traditional fare with a smile; try Nikos' famous fish soup for 2200dr/€6.46. (Entrees 1500-2500dr/€4.40-7.35. ☎33 039.) **Lo Sputino,** on the waterfront next to the Port Authority, offers pizza, pasta, and other Italian dishes for similar prices. (Entrees 1900-2400dr/€5.58-7.05.)

◙◙ SIGHTS AND THE OUTDOORS. By far the best entertainment in Vathy is to be had outdoors on the several lovely beaches, on the water, or relaxing and sipping *frappés* in open-air cafes. But museum-lovers aren't out of luck. The airy new **Folklore and Cultural Museum,** two blocks inland from the waterfront near the plateia, houses fully assembled bedrooms, a kitchen, a sitting room from Ithaka's colonial period, photographs of the 1953 earthquake devastation, and heirloom lace-trimmed clothing and linens. (☎33 398. Open M-F 9:30am-3:30pm; July-Aug. also Sa 6-10pm. 250dr/€0.74.) The tiny **Vathy Archaeological Museum** displays finds from ongoing excavations at the **Apollo sanctuary** at Aetos, a site that may be Odysseus's palace. (Open Tu-Su 8:30am-3pm. Free.)

◙◙ BEACHES AND THE OUTDOORS. Ithaka's beaches are beautiful, if a bit hard to reach. **Dexa** is the closest to Vathy, a 20min. walk from town. According to legend, this is where Odysseus landed when he returned to Ithaka. To get there from Vathy, follow the main road out of town with the water on your right, up and over the hill with the gas station on it. On the other side of Vathy, you can visit gorgeous ◙**Filiatro** and **Sarakiniko** beaches; walk with the water to your left, after Hotel Mentor turn right and keep heading toward the mountain to the left of town as you face inland. Take the steep uphill road—it's about a 40min. walk. **Ag. Ioannis,** on the island's western side, is a favorite with locals. First-rate **Gidaki** is only accessible by boat.

Homer fans and those with a poetic imagination can make the challenging hourlong, 4km **hike** up to the **Cave of the Nymphs,** where Odysseus hid the treasure the Phaeacians gave him. The cave has been under archaeological excavation in recent years, and is sometimes closed to visitors. If it is closed, you can still walk around the site and view the two separate entrances (one for the gods and one for mere mortals), and perhaps chat with a few archaeologists. To get there, walk around the harbor with the water on your right on the road out of town that leads to Piso Aetos and Stavros, then follow the signs along the road that winds up the mountain. The hike provides stunning views of Vathy; bring a flashlight for the cave. A 2hr. **hike** southeast leads to the Homeric **Arethousa Fountain,** along a steep mountain path through orchards. In summer, the fountain is dry. To find the well-marked, rocky path to the fountain, follow Evmeou St. (your first right after the Drakoulis mansion-turned-cafe when you are coming from the plateia) uphill until it becomes a dirt road. Keep an eye out for the signs.

The island's sole **bus** runs north from Vathy, passing through secluded coastal villages, including the exceptionally beautiful **Frikes** and **Kioni** on the northern coast; both have small-crystal-blue harbors. The bus doubles as a school bus, and schedules are erratic; check in town. In high season the bus usually runs 1-2 times per day (1hr., 350dr/€1.03 to Frikes). Little **Stavros** is high in the mountains on the way to Frikes and Kioni. Follow signs in town to a small museum full of excavated items from another contender for the site of Odysseus's palace. (Hours vary. A small tip is expected.) Homer described the palace site as a place from which 3 different waters could be seen; still visible from this point are the bays of Frikes, Aphales, and Polis, although several other sites on Ithaka and in Kephalonia compete for the same distinction. You can also visit the **Monastery of Panagia Katharon,** on Ithaka's highest mountain; take a taxi or moped to Anoghi and follow the signs.

PERAHORA

The small village of **Perahora** rests on the steep mountainside 4km above Vathy. It's a town devoted to the vine; it produces the island's best wine, and hosts a **wine festival** the last Sunday in July. If you make it up to Perahora, visit the ruins of **Paleohora,** the capital of the island until it was abandoned in the early 16th century. Its stone walls crumble on the hillside next to Perahora. To get there, follow the signs in Perahora to the beginning of a footpath that leads through olive groves to the ruins. The town church ruins are the first you'll encounter; although the roof is gone and the walls have nearly fallen, frescoes still cling to the inner walls. The view of Vathy from here is unbeatable. The road leading to Perahora is on the far right of the waterfront as you face inland; follow the signs.

KEPHALONIA Κεφαλονια

Massive mountains, subterranean lakes and rivers, caves, dense forests, and more than 250km of sand-and-pebble coastline make Kephalonia a nature lover's paradise. Its beauty has been fought over by the Byzantine, Frankish, Ottoman, Venetian, Napoleonic, and British Empires; during World War II, 9000 Italian soldiers occupying the island fought their alleged allies for seven days, when Germans invaded and killed all but 33 Italians. In 1953, a disastrous earthquake forced the island to rebuild, leaving only relatively undamaged Fiskardo with the Ionian pastel neoclassical look. Today, Kephalonia's beauty draws a diverse crowd, from the upscale yachting set to budget-conscious backpackers. Inconvenient bus schedules and a number of attractions make Kephalonia perfect for a longer stay.

IONIAN ISLANDS

ARGOSTOLI Αργοστολι ☎ 0671

The capital and by far the largest town in Kephalonia and Ithaka, Argostoli is a busy, noisy city with some token palm trees, but without the pleasantries or simple beauty found elsewhere on the island. The countless postcards of the island will remind you that there are nearby places more worthy of your film. There's no shortage of hotels, restaurants, or souvenir shops; and if you're looking for true Kephalonian nightlife, Argostoli's main plateia is the only place to go. Although the city may not have many picturesque charms, it does have urban convenience. Argostoli is also Kephalonia's transportation hub, so when you tire of the hubbub, just hop on the first outbound vehicle you see.

TRANSPORTATION

Flights: Olympic Airways, R. Vergoti 7 (☎ 28 808 or 28 881), has daily flights to Athens (22,300dr/€65.45). Open M-F 8am-3:30pm.

Ferries: Kephalonia has multiple ports for different destinations. Buses connect **Argostoli** to other ports, including **Sami,** where ferries leave for **Patras** and **Italy** July-Aug. (see p. 129). Prices and times are seasonal; inquire at a travel agency. From Argostoli boats go to **Kyllini** on the Peloponnese (2 per day, 3000dr/€8.80) and **Lixouri** in western Kephalonia (1 per hour until 11:30pm, 320dr/€0.94). Ferries head to the tiny port of **Skinari** on the northern end of Zakynthos from **Pesada,** a similarly small and inconvenient port on the southern coast of Kephalonia. Buses from Argostoli stop at the village of **Pesada** (30min., 2 per day, 300dr/€0.88); from the bus drop, it is a 1km walk downhill to the dock. You should arrange for transportation in Zakynthos as buses do not go regularly to Skinari.

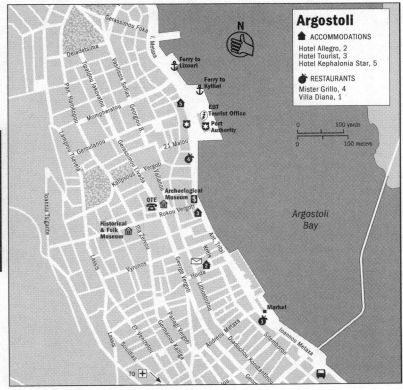

IONIAN ISLANDS

Argostoli

🏠 ACCOMMODATIONS
Hotel Allegro, 2
Hotel Tourist, 3
Hotel Kephalonia Star, 5

🍴 RESTAURANTS
Mister Grillo, 4
Villa Diana, 1

Buses: The bus station (☎ 22 281) is on the south end of the waterfront, all the way to the left as you face inland. Open 7am-8pm. Buses head to: **Skala** (2 per day, 900dr/ €2.64); **Poros** (2 per day, 1000dr/€2.94); **Fiskardo** (2hr., 2 per day, 1100dr/€3.24); **Sami** (3-4 per day, 700dr/€2.05); **Agios Gerasimos (Omala)** (3 per day, 350dr/ €1.03); **Lassi (Platis Gialos)** (7 per day, 300dr/€0.88); **Pesada** (2 per day, 350dr/ €1.03); **Kourkoumelata** (4 per day, 350dr/€1.03). For **Travliata** you can take either the Skala or Poros buses; it should cost you about 350dr/€1.03. Buses meet the ferry and continue on to **Athens** (1 per day, 8500dr/€25). Buses to Argostoli meet the ferry arriving in **Sami** (3-4 per day, 700dr/€2.05). Service is reduced Sa; none Su.

Taxis: (☎ 28 505 or 22 700). Line up in the main plateia and respond to phone calls.

Rentals: Myrtos Rent-a-Car (☎ 25 023; fax 24 230), on the waterfront. Must be over 23 to rent. 12,000-20,000dr/€35.29-58.80 per day includes the first 100km; 64dr/ €0.19 per km thereafter. Open daily 9am-1:30pm and 6-9pm. **Sunbird** (☎ 23 723), near the port authority, rents cars (15,000dr/€44) and mopeds (4000dr/€11.75). Gas not included (1500-10,000dr/€4.40-29.35). Open daily 8:30am-3pm and 5-8pm.

▰▰ ORIENTATION AND PRACTICAL INFORMATION

The town's main plateia is two blocks inland from the water on **21 Maiou,** near the Port Authority and EOT. South, or left as you face inland, from the main plateia, **Lithostrotou** is a pedestrian-only shopping area with high-rent stores like Diesel and Benetton, and dozens of leather, postcard, and jewelry shops.

Tourist Office: (☎ 22 248 or 24 466), beside the port authority near the ferry docks. Provides free maps and candid advice on accommodations, restaurants, and beaches. Open M-Sa 8am-2:30pm, also 5:30-9:30pm July-Aug.; in winter M-F 8am-2pm.

Banks: All over; try waterfront **National Bank (ATM** and 24hr. **exchange machine**).

International Bookstore: Petratos Bookstore (☎ 22 546), on Lithostrotou across from a small church, two blocks up from the water. English newspapers. Foreign newspapers and magazines. Open M-Sa 8am-8pm.

Police: (☎ 22 200), on I. Metaxa across from the tourist office. Open 24hr.

Tourist Police: In the police station. Open daily 7am-10pm.

Telephone: OTE at Rokou Vergoti and Georgiou Vergot, near the Archaeological Museum. Open M and W 7am-2:40pm, Tu and Th-F 7am-8pm, Sa 8am-3:40pm.

Post Office: (☎ 23 173), 2 blocks up from the water on Lithostrotou, at the intersection of Kerkyras. Open M-F 7:30am-2pm. **Postal code:** 28100.

▰ ACCOMMODATIONS

Private rooms are the cheapest option. Signs advertising **domatia** are all over town; for guidance, try the **Self-Catering Association of Kephalonia and Ithaka,** on the waterfront near the Port Authority. (☎ 29 109. Open M-F 9am-2pm and 6-9pm.) Bargain hard, but in high season don't expect to find a room for much less than 8000dr/ €23.48. Unless you're stuck in Argostoli awaiting a ferry, you're better off staying in the omnipresent small town domatia, where you can at least be near the beach.

Hotel Tourist (☎ 22 510 or 23 034), on the waterfront before the port authority as you approach from the bus station. A surprisingly good deal for a hotel of considerable quality. Balconies and TVs help you forgive the name. Breakfast 1500dr/€4.40. Singles 8000-12,000dr/€23.48-35.29; doubles 14,000-18,000dr/€41.10-52.82.

Hotel Kephalonia Star (☎ 23 180; fax 23 180), farther down the street on the waterfront across from the port authority, sign just says "Hotel C Star." More upscale, with extras like soundproof windows and A/C; bathrooms have tubs, and fridges are available. Singles 10,000-15,750dr/€29.35-46.22; doubles 14,000-22,500dr/€41.10-66 depending on season and the inclusion of breakfast.

Hotel Allegro (☎ 28 684), up from the waterfront on Andrea Choïda (also spelled Hoida and Xoida) halfway between the bus station and port authority. Rooms are bare but decent, with some balconies. Common baths, private baths available. Singles 6000dr/€17.61, with bath 8000dr/€23.48; doubles 8000dr/€23.48, 10,000dr/€29.35.

🍴 FOOD

Food is cheaper on the waterfront, but selection and quality are better in the plateia. A well-organized **farmers' market** takes over the waterfront near the bus station on Saturday mornings. Permanent fruit shops and bakeries line the water. **Mister Grillo**, near the port authority, has a constant crowd (go early!) and live Greek music some evenings. The great food offerings include plenty of vegetarian options like black beans in oil (900dr/€2.64) and stuffed peppers (1400dr/€4.11). Carnivores will appreciate the luscious Kephalonian meat pie (1700dr/€5), octopus (2800dr/€8.22), and *moussaka* (1500dr/€4.40). **Villa Diana,** on the waterfront next to Kalafatisis, is hosted by a friendly Canadian who will talk you through their scrumptious menu. Well-prepared traditional dishes at budget-friendly prices. (Kephalonian meat pie 1800dr/€5.28, chicken souvlaki 1950dr/€5.72.)

👁 SIGHTS

Argostoli's requisite **Archaeological Museum** is housed in a lovely brand-new building a few blocks south (left if you're facing inland) of the plateia, near the Municipal Theater on R. Vergoti. (☎ 28 300. Open Tu-Su 8:30am-3pm. 500dr/€1.47, seniors 300dr/€0.88, children and students free.) The **Historical and Folk Museum,** two blocks from the Archaeological Museum, is crammed with 19th-century objects from household items to military medals. The French coffee cups, English top hats, and antique dolls illustrate Argostoli's history of colonialism. Of particular interest are the photographs of Argostoli during the 20th century, including shots of damage from the devastating 1953 earthquake and later reconstruction. (☎ 28 835. Open M-Sa 9am-2pm. 1000dr/€2.93, students 500dr/€1.47, children free.)

📑 DAYTRIPS FROM ARGOSTOLI

Renting a moped or car gives you the freedom to roam between sights and beaches, unrestrained by inconvenient bus schedules or pricey accommodations. **Myrtos Beach,** on the west coast, is rumored to be one of Europe's best beaches.

CASTLE OF ST. GEORGE. The Venetian-built castle is 9km southeast of Argostoli, overlooking the village of T.ravliata. From its battlements, you can admire a panorama that once inspired Lord Byron. *(By moped, head toward Skala and turn when the road splits. Or take either the Poros or Skala buses (10min., about 350dr/€1.03). Open M-Sa 8am-8pm. Free.)*

LIXOURI. In the center of the western peninsula, Lixouri, former home of satirical poet Andreas Laskaratos, offers miles of essentially tourist-free coastline. You can rent **mopeds** at several places in Lixouri, and **buses** run to smaller villages in the area. *(Get there from Argostoli by boat (30min., every hr. 320dr/€0.94). Buy tickets on board.)*

SOUTH COAST BEACHES. A few beaches and interesting towns dot the area south of Argostoli. One of the best beaches is **Ormos Lourda,** in the middle of the south coast, but **Platis Gialos** is closer to Argostoli. *(Take the Lassi bus, 30min., 7 buses per day, 300dr/€0.88.)* Nearby **Metaza** (see **The Way to Byron's Heart,** p. 175) is one of the eminent Lord Byron's adopted towns; his house no longer exists. **Kourkoumelata** village was completely restored by a Greek tycoon after the 1953 earthquake. Check out the comfortable **Hotel Kourkoumi** if you decide to stay. (☎ 41 645. Doubles with bath and breakfast 6000dr/€17.61.) Outside the city in the village of **Dargoti** lies a multi-layered **Mycenaean tholos tomb,** said to belong to Odysseus himself; locals can thus claim that Kephalonia is the site of Homer's ancient Ithaka. **Poros,** on the southeast coast, is a modern beach town; rooms to let are everywhere. *(Buses run from Argostoli to Poros (1½hr., 2 per day, 1000dr/€2.93).)*

EAST OF ARGOSTOLI. The **Monastery of Ag. Gerasimos** was founded by its name-sake saint; his preserved body still rests here. On the night of August 15, nearby **Omala** hosts a festival and a vigil in the saint's church, and on the saint's name days (Oct. 20 and Aug. 16), the whole town goes wild; ask at the tourist office for info on all the fun. Omala has an excellent **Archaeological Museum** *(☎ 28 300. Open Tu-Su 8:30am-3pm. Buses run from Argostoli to Omala/Agios Gerasimos (3 per day, 350dr/€1.03).)* **Skala** is yet another Kephalonian village with an exquisite beach; in this case, it's pebble-and-sand. The remains of a 2nd-century **Roman villa** are in town; almost all its structure is gone, but the mosaic floors are remarkably well preserved. *(Look for the signs as you walk down the road from the bus drop towards the water. Open Tu-Su 9am-8pm, M 8:30am-3:30pm. Free.)* Every day two buses come to Skala from Argostoli and three return; the last runs at 5pm (1¼hr., 900dr/€2.65 each way). If you must stay, ask for rooms at **Skalini Tours** (open daily 9am-1pm and 5:30-9pm, for rooms call ☎(0972) 693 260) but be warned: they'll be expensive. Eat at the **Sun Rise Restaurant** all the way to the left of the beach, facing inland. It's on the expensive side, but the seafood is reasonably priced and rewarding; try the seafood platter for two (5000dr/ €14.67). Fish entrees start at 1800dr/€5.28, salads at 850dr/€2.50.

SAMI Σαμη   ☎ 0674

As you stroll through Sami, stunning views in all directions make it difficult to decide which is more lovely: the tempestuous blue waves crashing on the long, white-sand beach or the lush, green hills cradling the town. Despite high-season tourist traffic Sami manages to maintain its village atmosphere. It's close to the natural wonders of Melissani Lake, Drograti cave and Antisamos beach, whose beauty makes it a good place to spend the afternoon and night before catching a ferry from its small but busy port. Sami served as the set for the movie *Captain Corelli's Mandolin*, based on the best-selling novel.

▣ ↗ ORIENTATION AND PRACTICAL INFORMATION. The waterfront street is lined with restaurants and cafes, and intersects the main plateia. From Sami, **ferries** sail to: **Ithaka** (40min., 3 per day, 1500dr/€4.40); **Patras** (2½hr., 8:30am, 3400dr/ €10); and **Astakos** (high season only). In summer, international ferries go to **Brindisi** in Italy (1 per day beginning in early July; 10,000dr/€29.35). **Buses** leave the station on the left end of the waterfront for **Argostoli** (4 per day, 700dr/€2.05) and **Fiskardo** (2 per day, 900dr/€2.64). Buy tickets on board. **Taxis** (☎ 22 308) line up on the waterfront beside the plateia.

    Ferries land on either side of the town plateia. From the bus station, facing the water, turn left to reach the plateia. You may be able to glimpse the top of the blue and white **Hotel Kyma**, which sits on the (unmarked) main road of Sami; this road runs parallel to the water one block inland. The plateia lies between the road and the waterfront. If you follow it with the water on your right this main road leads to Argostoli. Heading in this direction, you'll come to the 24hr. **police station** (☎22 100), 3 blocks from the plateia on the right. There is no official tourist office, but the police may be able to answer your questions. **Sami Travel**, near the port authority on the far left end of the waterfront, is on Akti Posidonos and offers rooms, tickets to Italy, excursion tickets, and general info. (☎23 050. Open daily 7:30am-9:30pm.) The **Blue Star Ferries** office (☎22 055), on the waterfront, to the left of the ferry landing, is also helpful. There are several **banks; Emporiki Trapeza** on the waterfront, to the right of the plateia as you face inland, has an **ATM.** (Open M-Th 8am-2pm, F 8am-1pm.) The **OTE** is one block further. (Open M-F 7am-2:40pm.) **Pharmacies** are on the main road to Argostoli, one block inland from the waterfront. For **internet access,** try **Internet Break,** beneath Hotel Kastro, on the waterfront. (☎23 770. Open M-Su 10am-1:30pm and 3:30-11:30pm. 1800dr/€5.28 per hr.) The **post office** is on the road to Argostoli, two blocks out of the far right corner of the plateia. (Open M-F 7:30am-2pm.) **Postal code:** 28080.

ACCOMMODATIONS AND FOOD. Because Sami is a convenient base for travel within Kephalonia, there's a high demand for rooms, which are relatively expensive. Try the **Hotel Kyma**, in the plateia, for spectacular views, cool breezes, and decent rooms with clean baths. (☎22 064. Singles 6000-8000dr/ €17.61-23.48; doubles 10,000-15,000dr/€29.35-44.) The **Riviera Restaurant** on the waterfront lets airy rooms with double beds, private baths, and balconies. (☎22 777. Singles 7000-10,000dr/€20.53-29.35; doubles 10,000-14,000dr/€29.35-41.10.) At similar rates, **Hotel Melissana,** two blocks inland from the port authority, on the far left of the waterfront, has slightly dim rooms with many amenities: private bath, TV, telephone, balcony, and fridge. (☎22 464. Singles 7500-13,000dr/€22-38.15; doubles 10,000-17,000dr/€29.35-50.) **Karavomilos Beach Camping,** a 15min. walk down the beach from town with the water on the right, is set in a huge subdivided field with shade trees and blooming bushes. There are hot showers, electricity, laundry facilities, and a mini-market. (☎22 480. 1300dr/€3.81, 750dr/€2.20 per child; 700dr/€2.05 per car; 800dr/€2.35 per small tent, 1200dr/€3.52 per large tent. Prices higher July-Aug.) Good budget fare (gyros and salads for 500dr/€1.47) and friendly service can be found at **Taka Taka Mam** on the waterfront (open daily until 1am). More elegant meals can be found at **Mermaid Restaurant** (*moussaka* 1400dr/€4.10, *stifado* 1900dr/ €5.57), Taka's neighbor on the waterfront.

SIGHTS AND BEACHES. Play the mole in the **underground caves** of Melissani and Drogarati. **Melissani** is part of huge, underground **Lake Karavomilos.** To get there, walk along the beach with the water to your right until you come to a small ocean-fed "lake" with a waterwheel on the far side. Turn left after the restaurant by the lake, walk inland to the road about 30m, and turn right. Down this street you'll see signs to the cave (25-30min.). The boat tour of the cave lasts 15min. Lake guides will row you around the two large caverns flooded with sparkling water, studded with stalactites, and squirming with eels. Go when the sun is high. *(Open daily 9am-7pm. 1350dr/€3.97, children 700dr/ €2.05. A boatsman's tip is encouraged.)* **Drogarati** is a large cavern full of spectacular stalactites and stalagmites 5km from Sami. To get there, head inland on the road to Argostoli and follow the signs (45min.-1hr.). (☎22 950. *Open until nightfall. 1000dr/€2.93, children 500dr/€1.47.)* Agia Efimia, a pretty harbor town 10km north of Sami with few tourists and little traffic, deserves a visit. Ask the Fiskardo bus to let you off there. The often-overlooked, but very lovely ■**Antisamos beach** is a must if you are on this side of Kephalonia. Take a taxi to Antisamos (1000-1500dr/€2.93-4.40 per person), or hike (75min.) by following the waterfront left from the plateia as you face inland. Take the road between the port authority and Sami Travel. Bring plenty of water and wear good shoes.

DAYTRIPS FROM ARGOSTOLI: ■**FISKARDO.** The road north ends at must-see Fiskardo, which escaped the 1953 earthquake and is now the only remaining example of 18th- and 19th-century Kephalonian architecture. Fiskardo's crescent-shaped waterfront is tinged with the pastel hues of the modest buildings surrounding it. At night, a romantic aura pervades the town, as jazz drifts over the harbor, which twinkles with the dim lights of boats resting in the water. A playground for wealthier visitors, Fiskardo remains free of the trappings that drag other tourist towns down. A splendid walk through the woods or swim from the rocks takes you to the forested tidbit of land across the harbor, where the lighthouse and ruins of a 15th-century Venetian fortress rest. For archaeology buffs, an open excavation of a 2nd-century Roman graveyard is right next door to the harbor, along the water. Fiskardo's unbeatable beach lies 500m out of town on the hilly road back to Argostoli, in a quiet cove that offers flat rocks for sunbathing.

SUBTERRANEAN MYSTERY Melissani, a short walk from Sami, is one of Kephalonia's weirdest wonders. An underground lake and cave complex shaped like a B, it measures an astonishing 150m long, 25m wide, and 36m deep. Until 1963, the cave was accessible only to daring visitors willing to descend via a precarious rope and to swim through the lake's icy waters to reach the cave itself. Today, a tunnel eases the once-dangerous journey, and guided boat tours give the full view of the shimmering blue waters and 20,000-year-old **stalactites** (some of which twist into shapes like the "elephant's foot," "praying nun," and the ever-charming "lamb carcass"). Even more fascinating than Melissani's visual treat is its history as a place of worship of **Pan**, the musical goat-bodied god, and of the Nereids, or sea nymphs. From Mycenaean times on, worshipers descended into the cave by rope to make offerings within the eerie solemnity of an underground sanctuary. The name Melissani may be a tribute to a shepherdess who fell into the cave while looking for her lost sheep, or to the nymph Melissani, who took her life here out of unrequited love for Pan; its root word means "Honey," and remains a common English name—Melissa.

Buses for **Argostoli** leave at 6:30am and 4:30pm from the parking lot next to the church, uphill from the town. Two **buses** per day arrive from **Sami** (1hr., 900dr/ €2.64 and **Argostoli** (1½-2hr., 1100dr/€3.22). **Ferries** go to: **Piso Aetos** on Ithaka (1hr., 860dr/€2.53); **Vasiliki** (1hr., 1100dr/€3.22); and **Nidri** on Lefkada (2hr., 1500dr/ €4.40). For transportation and lodging questions or helpful info, contact **Nautilus Travel Agency,** at the right end of the waterfront. (☎41 440. Open daily 9am-9pm.)

Cliffs plunge into the sea along the coastal road north from Argostoli and Sami to Fiskardo. Just off this road lies one of the best beaches in Europe, **◪Myrtos,** which shouldn't be missed by any visitor to Kephalonia. The pure white pebbles and clear, blue water are stunning enough, but it is perhaps the beach's location, pressed against the cliffs, that has brought Myrtos its special recognition as one of Europe's premiere beaches. The **buses** from Fiskardo to Sami and Argostoli stop at the turn-off to Myrtos, 4km from the gasp-inducing beauty of the beach—hop off there and hoof it the rest of the way. Roughly 4km up the road from the Myrtos turn-off is the equally incredible Venetian castle of **Assos,** on a steep, wooded peninsula joined to the island by a narrow isthmus. Completed in the early part of the 17th century, much of the castle and its houses are well preserved. A good deal of the land inside the walls is privately owned and fenced; the owner's goats and chickens are penned in the crumbling shells of original castle buildings, adding or detracting from the medieval romance of the place, depending on your sensibilities. On August 15, the village of **Markopoulo** in the southeast celebrates the Assumption of the Virgin Mary with a strange, spooky festival involving an all-night church liturgy. According to local belief, hundreds of small snakes with black crosses on their heads slither over the icons during the service.

ZAKYNTHOS Ζακυνθος

Zakynthos's varied landscapes and seascapes comprise an exceptionally subtle palette of colors—white cliffs rise from turquoise water, sun-bleached wheat waves in the shadow of evergreens, and magenta flowers frame the twisting streets. Known as the greenest of the Ionian Islands, Zakynthos is home to thousands of flower and plant species, some of them unique to the island. Also unique to the island is the large population of **loggerhead turtles,** a source of pride to the islanders. In Zakynthos Town or its neighboring beaches, you'll see the sweaty backs of other tourists more than the beauty of your surroundings. Set out for the countryside to appreciate Zakynthos's natural sights, like its famous blue caves in the north. Those who venture there will understand why Lord Byron loved this island, which the Venetians christened *Fior di Levante*—flower of the east.

ZAKYNTHOS TOWN   ☎0695

Bustling Zakynthos Town welcomes visitors with arcaded streets and white-washed buildings. After an earthquake completely destroyed it in 1953, locals restored the city to its former state, recreating the Venetian architecture in areas such as Pl. Solomou. Head north or south of Zakynthos Town to the nearby beach communities for better nightlife, and even farther for remote beaches and the serene beauty that pervades the countryside.

⌨ TRANSPORTATION

Flights: The **airport** (☎28 322) is 6km south of town. Flights to **Athens** (45min., 2 per day, 21,700dr/€63.82). **Olympic Airways,** Alex. Roma 16 (☎28 611). Open M-F 8am-3:30pm.

Ferries: Ferries for **Kyllini** in the Peloponnese (1¼hr., 7 per day, 1500dr/€4.40) depart from Zakynthos Town at the southern dock, on the left side of the waterfront as you face inland. Tickets at the waterfront office for Kyllini ferries, between the police/tourist police and port police. Ferries from Pesada, **Kephalonia,** arrive in Skinari, north of Zakynthos Town (1½hr., 1-2 per day, 1300dr/€5.28). Be warned that both of these towns are very small and relatively inaccessible: buses in Kephalonia do not go to Pesada after noon and there are no lodgings there; buses run to Skinari only 2 days per week, and taxis to Zakynthos Town will cost 10,000dr/€29.35. Ferry tickets are available at the **boat agencies** along the waterfront. For more information, call the **port police** (☎28 117).

Buses: Filita 42 (☎22 255), on the corner of Pl. Eleftheriou; from Pl. Solomou, walk 6 blocks south (with the water on the left) and 1 block inland; from the police station, walk 3 blocks north (with the water on the right) and 1 block inland. To: **Athens** (6hr., 1 per day, 7050dr/€20.68 including ferry); **Patras** (3hr., 4-5 per day, 3100dr/€9.10 including ferry); **Thessaloniki** (10hr., 1 per day, 3250dr/€9.56). Schedules for local service are posted outside the bus station; a complete list is at the info window. Buses run to: **Alykes** (4 per day, 340dr/€1); **Argasi** (11 per day, 260dr/€0.77); **Laganas** (13 per day, 260dr/€0.77); **Kalamaki** (6 per day, 260dr/€0.77); **Keri Lake** (2 per day, 380dr/€1.12); **Tsilivi** (10 per day, 260dr/€0.77); **Vasiliko, Porto Roma,** and **Ag. Nikolaos** (3 per day, 340dr/€1).

Taxis: (☎48 400). Lining the side streets off the waterfront. Available 24hr.

Rentals: Hertz, Lomvardou 38 (☎45 706). Cars from 17,700dr/€52.06 per day in low season; prices include insurance, tax, and 100km free mileage for the first day. Must be over 21. Open daily 8am-2pm and 5:30-9:30pm. **EuroSky Rentals** (☎26 278), 1 block inland on A. Makri, charges 4000dr/€11.74 per day for mopeds, and 9000dr/€26.41 per day for motorcycles. License required, must be at least 23. Open daily 8am-midnight. **Spyros Rent a Scooter** (☎23 963 or 43 723), toward the center of Lomvardou, has the cheapest moped rates: 3500dr/€10.29 per day.

✳☷ ORIENTATION AND PRACTICAL INFORMATION

The waterfront runs between **Pl. Solomou** at the right end (facing inland) and Agios Dionysios Church at the left end. Each end has a dock: generally ferries to or from Kyllini dock at the left end by Ag. Dionysios; everything else (like daily cruise boats) docks at the right end by Pl. Solomou. The waterfront street, **Lomvardou,** runs between the two docks and is lined with restaurants, gift shops, and ferry agencies. The next street inland, parallel to Lombardou, is **Filita,** home to the bus station. Behind it are, in order, **Foskolou, Alexandrou Roma** (the main shopping street), and **Tertseti.** Three blocks inland from Pl. Solomou is **Pl. Agiou Markou,** a gathering spot with outdoor eateries.

Banks: National Bank (☎44 113), on Pl. Solomou, **exchanges currency** and has a 24hr. **ATM.** Open M-Th 8am-2pm, F 8am-1:30pm, in summer also Sa-Su 9am-1pm. Other **ATMs** on Lomvardou and around Pl. Solomou.

Police: (☎22 200), at the intersection of Lomvardou and Fra. Tzoulati, roughly equidistant on the waterfront from Pl. Solomou and Ag. Dionysios. Open 24hr.

Tourist police: (☎27 367), in the same building as the regular police. English spoken. Open daily 7:30am-10pm.

Hospital: (☎42 514 or 42 515), uphill and inland from the city center. Walk down Lomvardou to Ag. Eleftheriou. Follow this road inland to Kokkini, where the road jogs right and becomes Ag. Spiridona. The hospital is roughly 1km farther. Open 24hr.

OTE: 2 Dimokratias, (☎59 301) between the two plateias. Open M-F 7am-2:30pm.

Internet Access: Top's Cafe, Filita 38 (☎26 650), has a bar, billiards, video games, and web access (500dr/€1.47 minimum per 15 min.; 2000dr/€5.87 per hr.). Open daily 9:30am-midnight.

Post Office: (☎42 418), on Tertseti, the 4th street inland parallel to the waterfront, near Xenou, the pedestrian-only street that runs inland from the waterfront past Top's Internet Cafe. **Exchanges currency.** Open M-F 7:30am-8pm. **Postal code:** 29100.

◤ ACCOMMODATIONS

Rooms in Zakynthos Town tend to be expensive and scarce in July and August. Call ahead or look for the signs advertising domatia, and bargain.

Rooms for Rent at 40 Alex Roma (☎26 012), on the section of the street near the center of the shopping district—look for the prominent signs. Spacious rooms with private baths, some with kitchenette. Larger, apartment-style accommodations also available. Singles 4000-6000dr/€11.74-17.61; doubles 6000-8000dr/€17.61-23.48.

Athina Marouda Rooms for Rent (☎45 194), on Tzoulati and Koltoi, 2 blocks inland from the tourist police, on the left side of the street. Rooms a bit worn, but clean (as is the common bath) and Athina is friendly. Good prices, but there aren't many rooms, so they go quickly. Singles 5000dr/€14.67; doubles 10,000dr/€29.35.

Hotel Aegli, on Lomvardou, 2 blocks south from Pl. Solomou with the water on your left. Immaculate, if a bit pricey, rooms offer TV, balcony and snazzy full baths. Singles 8000dr/€23.48; doubles 10,000dr/€29.35.

◪ FOOD

Dining in Zakynthos is a pleasure. Restaurants line the waterfront and Pl. Ag. Markou; every other establishment on Alexandrou Roma is either a cafe or a candy shop. Zakynthian specialities include *melissaki* (a nougat-almond candy) and veal in tomato sauce. Fast food is everywhere (gyros 400dr/€1.17). The **Coop Supermarket,** near the police station, caters to those who cater to themselves. (Open M-F 8am-9pm, Sa 8am-6pm.)

House of Latas (Το Σπιτι του Λατα), (☎41 585), 2km above the city (follow the signs to Bohalis) near the Venetian castle. Spectacular views of Zakynthos, live local music, and inexpensive seafood (grilled swordfish 2700dr/€7.94) every evening. Salads 1000-1800dr/€2.93-5.29; entrees 1800dr/€5.29 and up. Open daily 6pm-1am.

Molos Restaurant. A popular waterfront joint with extremely affable owners and staff. The only restaurant in town with meat from its own farm—try the local favorite: spicy stuffed chicken with cheese and liver (2500dr/€7.34). Pizza 1800-2100dr/€5.29-6.16; omelettes 850-1200dr/€2.50-3.52; English breakfast 1350dr/€3.97.

The Garden, next to Ag. Dionysios, in a quiet, spacious plateia removed from the hectic waterfront. Grilled octopus 2850dr/€8.37; souvlaki 1900dr/€5.57.

Tourists to Zakynthos should note that they share the island's beaches with a resident population of **endangered sea turtles.** Careless beachgoers can destroy hundreds of the turtles' eggs just by walking. Zakynthos is gradually making efforts to protect the turtles and their nests, including encouraging waterfront properties to cover their lights, as freshly hatched baby turtles mistake the light for reflections off the ocean and follow the twinkling inland, instead of toward the sea. Ask at tour companies about which beaches are popular spots; Gerakas, Kalamaki and Laganas all have turtle populations. **Please respect their homes!**

SIGHTS AND HIKES

The **Church of Agios Dionisios** is named in honor of the island's patron saint and displays a silver chest that holds the saint's relics. (Open 7am-1pm and 5-10pm. Dress modestly.) In Pl. Solomou, the **Byzantine Museum** houses two floors of icons from the Ionian School, a distinctive local hybrid of Byzantine and Renaissance art styles, along with elaborately carved iconostases, chalices, and miscellaneous church items. Most were rescued by devout locals who risked their lives to pluck them from the steaming rubble of area churches after the 1953 earthquake; poignant photos document the effects of the disaster. (☎42 714. Open Tu-Su 9am-2pm. 800dr/€2.35, students free.) If you enjoy a good **hike,** climb 2km above town to the **Venetian Castle,** where 19th-century poet Dionysios Solomos wrote the poem that became the Greek National Anthem. Take Tertseti, later called N. Koluva, to the edge of town, or head inland from Pl. Agiou Markou, and follow the signs uphill to Bohalis, then turn left after 1km, following the signs to the Castro. You'll find panoramic views of the island and a lovely view of Zakynthos Town, particularly at night. (Open Tu-Su 8am-2:30pm.)

DAYTRIPS FROM ZAKYNTHOS TOWN

It's possible to see all of Zakynthos, including the otherwise-inaccessible **western cliffs,** by boat. Shop around for a cruise on Lomvardou. Most tours leave in the morning, usually around 9am, return around 5:30 or 6pm, and prefer a reservation the night before. Don't buy from hawkers around gift shops—they'll charge a commission (2000-3000dr/€5.87-8.80) on top of the agency's fee (usually starting around 4000dr/€11.74, although price wars sometimes cut prices). Cruises go to the **blue caves,** natural caves on the Northeast shore past Skinari, that seem to glow blue; the **"Smuggler's Wreck,"** a large boat skeleton; and **turtle beach,** a secluded beach on what is fondly known as "Turtle Island" not only for its proximity to loggerhead turtle nesting grounds, but also because the island itself resembles a turtle. Inquire at the tourist office or agencies. To explore with far less hassle, get a **moped**—there's a rental agency at each beach (3000-4500dr/€8.80-13.21). The island is developing rapidly, so many new roads don't appear on maps. Get several road maps (1000-1500dr/€2.93-4.40) and ask directions.

The closest beach to Zakynthos Town is **Tsilivi beach,** 6km up the waterfront road with the water on your right. Buses run there every day (30min., 10 per day, 260dr/€0.77). Nearby **Planos** has plenty of domatia. **Zante Camping,** 3km past Planos, is Zakynthos's only beach campsite. It has a cafeteria and minimarket. (☎(61710) 44 754. 1400dr/€4.10 per person; 810dr/€2.38 per car; 930dr/€2.73 per small tent; 1150dr/€3.37 per large tent.) Unscathed beaches carpet the peninsula that stretches out 16km from Zakynthos Town to **Vasilikos,** especially near **Porto Roma** and **Porto Zoro.** Rooms to let signs dot the road to Vasilikos, especially near **Agios Nikolaos Beach. Buses** leave Zakynthos Town for **Vasiliko** (M-F 3 per day, Sa-Su 2 per day; 340dr/€1). Romantic restaurants fill **Alykes,** 16km from Zakynthos Town. Fringed with soft, clean sand beaches, it's nicer and less crowded than its southern counterparts. Many signs along the main drag advertise domatia. **Buses** run from Zakynthos Town to Alykes (4 per day, 340dr/€1). The southern beaches near Vasilikos are pleasingly wide and sandy, with shallow, warm water full of splashing holiday-makers. Some are protected areas that must be vacated in the evenings to accommodate the sea turtles that come ashore to nest.

SKINARI Σκιναρι ☎ 0695

At the extreme northern tip of Zakynthos, a breathtaking drive away from the bustle of busier beach towns, is tiny **Skinari,** locally known as **Agios Nikolaos.** Ferries to Pesada, on Kephalonia, depart from here. Bus service is sporadic, so incoming ferry passengers often need to arrange their own transportation to Zakynthos Town. Taxis to Zakynthos Town will cost 10,000dr/€29.35 and Skinari has no rental agencies. All the same, if you can manage to get in and out of town without going bankrupt, Skinari is a lovely town and wonderful place to unwind for a day, or to use as a peaceful base for daytrips. On the waterfront, **La Grotta Restaurant** has lovely rooms with private baths and waterfront balconies. (☎ 31 224. Singles 5000dr/€14.67; doubles 10,000dr/€29.35.) Farther down the street away from the dock, **La Storia Restaurant** serves divine fare with the water at your feet; splurge for the seafood pasta (2500dr/€7.35) or settle for less extravagant dishes. (☎ 31 635. Salads start at 800dr/€2.35; seafood entrees start at 1800dr/€5.29; beer 800-900dr/€2.35-2.64.) During the day, you can buy tickets on the waterfront for a fishing boat tour of the **blue caves,** accessible only by water (1hr., 1500-2000dr/€4.40-5.87); for twice the price and time you can get a tour of the blue caves and the "Smuggler's Wreck" shipwreck. These tours are smaller and shorter than those that leave from Zakynthos Town; shop around for the best price. You can also rent canoes and boats on Skinari beach.

SARONIC GULF ISLANDS

Τα Νησια του Σαρωνικου

When 5 million Athenians flee the city each summer in search of beaches and *pareia* (Greek for something like "food, folks, and fun"), they don't flee far. Many head to the Saronic Gulf Islands. This means two things: first, you've chosen a destination approved by discriminating Greeks; second, you're not the only one. Keep in mind that, while good times are to be had *without* 50 of your closest package tourist friends, it may require a bit of creativity to shake them, and that the islands' popularity makes them a bit of a stretch on a budget traveler's wallet. Despite their geographic proximity, each of the Gulf islands retains a distinct character: Poros has a magnificent lemon grove, the Temple of Aphaia is on Aegina, Spetses's forests are pine-filled, and Hydra's streets are pollutant-free.

HIGHLIGHTS OF THE SARONIC GULF ISLANDS

BEHOLD the 360-degree view of Aegina's coastline from the 5th-century BC Temple of Aphaia (p. 296).

FOLLOW THE SCENT OF LEMONS past thousands of citrus trees on your way to a picnic in the Devil's Gorge (p. 299), near Galatas on Poros.

DON'T LOOK BOTH WAYS while crossing the street on vehicle-free Hydra (p. 301), but watch out for donkeys as you wander through the art fairs.

REFRESH YOURSELF with a slice of watermelon and a dip in the sea on Spetses's stunningly colorful Xylocheriza beach (p. 304).

AEGINA Αιγινα

Who does not know the renowned Aegina who went to bed with Zeus?
  —Bacchylides

Bright, white-washed Aegina is an easy daytrip for city-weary Athenians, and summer weekends find the island saddled with the bustle of Greece's capital. Tour groups flood the beaches and swarm the resort town of Agia Marina. The hamlet of Marathonas is ideal for a swim on a beach *sans* rented chairs. Buses pass through olive-terraced mountains and the church of Agios Nektarios. The well-preserved remains of the Temple of Aphaia still stand, securing a view of the entire island and reminding visitors of the area's more noble past.

Aegina's history is that of an island utterly different from the floating resort that exists today. Relations between Athens and the island were not particularly chummy in ancient times. The little island made up for its size with a self-determining spunk which irritated the mighty—and encroaching—Athens. The island produced the first Greek coins (silver "tortoises," which gained great finan-

Aegina

(map labels:) TO PIRAEUS · Souvala · Vaïa · Mesagros · Sanctuary of Apollo · Ag. Nektarios · Ruins of Paleohora · Temple of Aphaia · Faneromeni · Aegina · Ag. Marina · TO PIRAEUS · Marathonas · Portes · Aeginitissa · Mount Oros (532m) · Perdika · Steno Monis · TO POROS, HYDRA & SPETSES · N · 2 miles · 2 kilometers

cial leverage throughout the Greek world), and Aegina's sprinters, who practiced with jugs of water on their shoulders, zoomed past the competition at the pan-Hellenic games. With the onset of the Persian War in 491 BC, the citizens of Aegina sided at first with Xerxes's army, angering the besieged Athenians. In 480 BC they returned to the Greek side, winning the praise of the Delphic Oracle as the swiftest navy on the seas. In the peaceful inter-regnum that followed Persian defeat, island life flourished and Aegina's inhabitants built the magnificent Temple of Aphaia. With the eventual return of war, this time between Athens and Sparta, Aegina suffered the misfortune of siding with Sparta. Trounced by Athens in 459 BC, the islanders soon found themselves displaced by Athenian colonists. The island sank into geopolitical obscurity, only to emerge over two millennia later, in 1827, as the temporary capital of the partially liberated Greece.

AEGINA TOWN ☎ 0297

As soon as your ferry docks in Aegina Town, you'll know that you've entered "The Pistachio Capital of the World." Preserved, jellied, flavored, red, flaked, shelled, regular—there are as many ways to eat pistachios as there are package tour boats from the mainland. Fortunately, the tasty nuts are the stronger influence.

⌐ TRANSPORTATION

Ferries: Saronikos Lines (☎ 25 951), has service to: **Agistri** (20min., 2-3 per day, 400dr/€1.17); **Hydra** (2hr., 2 per day, 1600dr/€4.70); **Methana** (45min, 5 per day, 1000dr/€2.93); **Piraeus** (1hr., 2 per day, 1600dr/€4.70); **Poros** (1hr.; 5 per day M-F, 6-8 per day Sa-Su; 1300dr/€3.82); **Spetses** (3hr., 1 per day, 2600dr/€7.63). Buy your tickets at the kiosk at the inland end of the ferry dock.

Hydrofoils: Minoan Lines has a ticket stand on the quay (☎ 27 462). Service to **Piraeus** (35min., 12 per day, 2200dr/€6.46) and **Poros** (40min., 1 per day, 2700dr/€7.92). **Sea Falcon Lines** has a ticket stand on the quay next to Minoan. To: **Piraeus** (35min.; M-Th and Sa 4-5 per day, F and Su 7-8 per day; 1800dr/€5.28).

Buses: (☎ 22 787), in Ethnegarcias Park, at the corner of the waterfront left of the ferry quay. Buses run to **Agia Marina** and the **Temple of Aphaia** (30min., every 30min.-1hr 6:30am-8pm, 450dr/€1.32), and **Perdika** (20min., 9 per day 6:30am-8pm, 250-500dr/€0.73-1.47) via **Marathonas.** For the temple, buy a round-trip ticket.

Taxis: (☎ 22 635). Station immediately to the left of the quay along the waterfront; look for the line of grey, diesel-pumped Mercedes and Andis.

Mopeds: Moped rental places are a dime a dozen in Aegina, with prices 2000-6000dr/ €5.87-17.61 per day, varying with bells, whistles, and paint job. Try **Trust,** Leonardou Lada 1 (☎ 27 010), 1 block inland from the waterfront.

✴ ❓ ORIENTATION AND PRACTICAL INFORMATION

The central quay is expensive, but tavernas and hotels get cheaper toward either end of the waterfront street, **Republic Avenue.** Running parallel to the waterfront, **Sp. Irioti** (1 block in) is lined with supermarkets, gritty restaurants, local markets, and the occasional moped rental, while **Sp. Rodi** which becomes **Aphaias** at the intersection with **Aiakou.** Two blocks in, Aiakou runs between the National Bank and the port authority. It's home to more upscale shops, bars, and an internet cafe. **Maps** of the town are posted on the waterfront across the street from the National Bank. Ask the congenial staff at **Pipinis Travel,** one block inland on Kanari across from the ticket kiosks, for information about the island. They also rent bicycles (1500dr/€4.40 per day), mopeds (3000dr/€8.80 and up) and cars for 12,000dr/ €35.22 and up. (☎ 28 780; fax 28 779. Open all day.)

Bank: National Bank (☎ 25 697), to the right of the quay along the waterfront, just past the port police. Exchange and 24hr. **ATM.** Open M-Th 8am-2pm, F 8am-1:30pm.

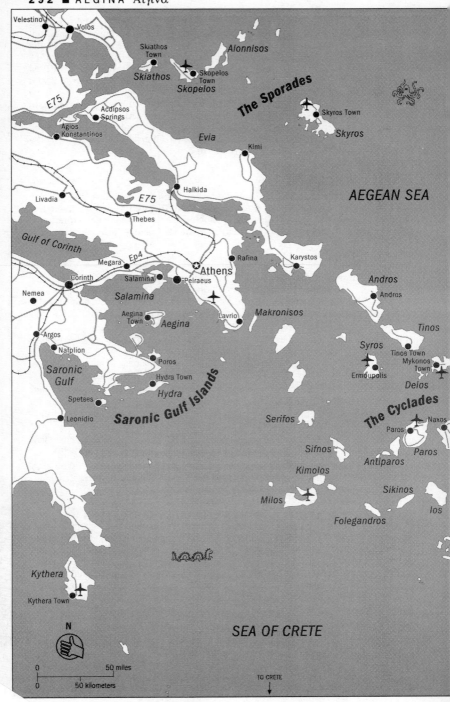

Velestino
Volos
Skiathos Town
Skiathos
Skopelos Town
Skopelos
Alonnisos
The Sporades
Skyros Town
Skyros
E75
Acdipsos Springs
Agios Konstantinos
Evia
Kimi
AEGEAN SEA
Livadia
Halkida
E75
Thebes
Gulf of Corinth
Megara
Ep4
Athens
Rafina
Karystos
Corinth
Salamina
Peiraeus
Nemea
Salamina
Andros
Andros
Argos
Aegina Town
Aegina
Lavrio
Makronisos
Tinos
Natplion
Saronic Gulf
Poros
Hydra Town
Hydra
Syros
Tinos Town
Mykonos Town
Ermoupolis
Delos
Spetses
Saronic Gulf Islands
Serifos
The Cyclades
Paros
Naxos
Leonidio
Paros
Sifnos
Antiparos
Kimolos
Sikinos
Milos
Ios
Folegandros
Kythera
Kythera Town
N
0   50 miles
0   50 kilometers
SEA OF CRETE
TO CRETE

Aegean Islands

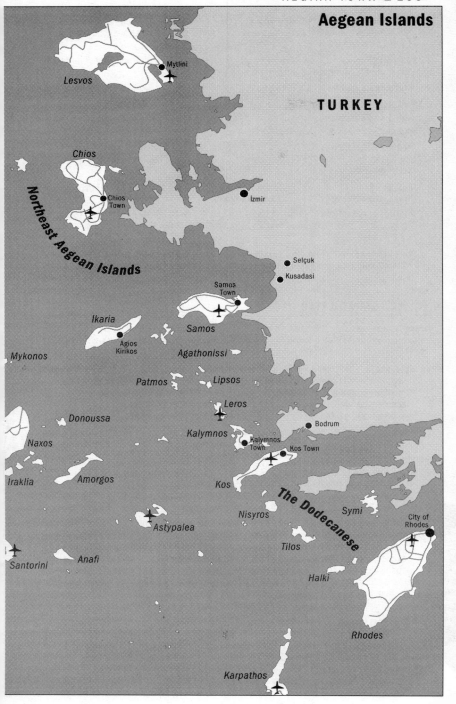

TURKEY

Lesvos

Mytlini

Chios

Northeast Aegean Islands

Chios Town

İzmir

Selçuk

Kusadasi

Samos Town

Ikaria

Samos

Agios Kirikos

Mykonos

Agathonissi

Patmos

Lipsos

Leros

Donoussa

Naxos

Kalymnos

Kalymnos Town

Bodrum

Iraklia

Amorgos

Kos Town

Kos

The Dodecanese

Symi

City of Rhodes

Astypalea

Nisyros

Santorini

Anafi

Tilos

Halki

Rhodes

Karpathos

Bookstore: Kalezis (International Press) (☎ 23 874), just past the National Bank on the waterfront. International books and magazines, phone cards, bus tickets, stamps. Open daily 8am-9:30pm.

Tourist Police: Leonardou Lada 11 (☎ 27 777). Open daily 8am-8pm. Tourist and regular police are in the same courtyard.

Police: ☎ 22 100.

Port Authority: (☎ 22 328), on the waterfront. Updated ferry schedules. English spoken. Open 24hr.

Pharmacy: Corner of Aiakou and Sp. Rodi (☎ 23 714). Open all day.

Medical Center: (☎ 22 222), 2km along the waterfront to the left of the ferry quay. Call the tourist police (☎ 27 777; **emergency** ☎ 22 100) and they will arrange transport or refer you to doctors in town.

OTE: Paleas Choras 6 (☎ 22 399; dial 161 for assistance; costs 300dr/€0.88); up Aiakou to the right. Open M-F 7:30am-3pm.

Internet access: Nesant Internet Cafe, Aphaias 13 (☎ 24 053). 1800dr/€5.28 per hr. Open daily 10am-10:30pm. **Prestige Internet Cafe,** at Sp. Rodi and Aiakou. 1800dr/ €5.28 per hr. Open late.

Post Office: Kanari 6 (☎ 22 398), Pl. Ethnegersias 1 behind the bus station. Express Mail Hellenic Post and **Poste Restante** available. Open M-F 7:30am-2pm. **Postal Code:** 18010.

ACCOMMODATIONS

Rooms here are cheaper than on any of the other Saronic Gulf Islands. In the high season, doubles go for around 8000-12,000dr/€23.48-35.22. *Domatia* owners often meet the ferries, but always bargain and discuss location before following anyone.

Hotel Plaza, Kazatzaki 4 (☎ 28 404; fax 25 600), at the far left end of the waterfront. Friendly owner Michalis Kororos runs 3 roughly equivalent pensions—Plaza, Ulrica and Christina—from the Plaza front desk. Rooms are modest and spotless, and vary in price according to amenities (A/C, TV, balcony). Singles 6000-12,000dr/€17.61-35.22; doubles 6000-16,000dr/€17.61-47. Show your *Let's Go* guide to receive a discount.

Hotel Avra, (☎ 22 303; fax 23 917) at the far left end of the waterfront. Checkered floors add a lively touch to simple rooms with phones and baths. Singles 8000-10,000dr/ €23.48-29.35; doubles 12,000-14,000dr/€35.22-41.10.

Hotel Artemis (☎ 25 195; fax 28 779), set back to the left of the post office. White rooms with A/C, private bath, and the occasional balcony. Pay the night before if you're catching a pre-10am boat. Breakfast 1500dr/€4.40. Singles 10,000dr/€29.35; doubles 14,000dr/€41.10. Discount for stays over 10 days.

Hotel Pavlou, Aeginitou 21 (☎ 22 795), behind the church on the far right of the quay. Come for the 70s decor (psychedelic curtains!) and comfortable rooms with balconies overlooking the town church. Some rooms with private bath. Payment required in advance. Owners also run the Athina, quietly tucked back 200m into the town on Telemonos, which features charmingly decorated rooms with private baths and fridges. Singles 10,000dr/€29.35; doubles 12,000dr/€35.22; triples 14,000dr/€41.10. Discounts for stays of multiple days.

FOOD AND NIGHTLIFE

No-frills tavernas line P. Irioti street, which runs parallel to the waterfront one block inland along the right side of the harbor. For make-your-own meals, try the **supermarkets** on P. Irioti.

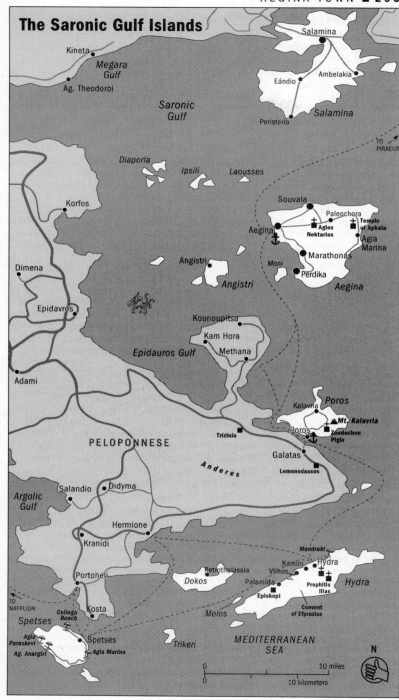

The Saronic Gulf Islands

Kineta

Megara
Gulf

Ag. Theodoroi

Saronic
Gulf

Salamina

Eándio

Ambelakia

Peristeria

Salamina

TO
PIRAEUS

Diaporia

Ipsili

Laousses

Korfos

Souvala

Paleochora

Temple
of Aphaia

Aegina

Agios
Nektarios

Agia
Marina

Dimena

Angistri

Moni

Marathonas

Perdika

Aegina

Angistri

Epidavros

Kounoupitsa

Kam Hora

Methana

Epidauros Gulf

Adami

Poros

Kalavria

Mt. Kalavria

PELOPONNESE

Trizinia

Poros

Zoodochou
Pigis

Galatas

Anderes

Lemonodassos

Salandio

Didyma

Argolic
Gulf

Hermione

Kranidi

Mandraki

Retiothalassia

Kamini

Hydra

Portoheli

Dokos

Vlihos

Palamida

Prophitis
Ilias

Hydra

TO
NAFPLION

Kosta

Episkopi

Convent
of Efpraxias

Spetses

College
Beach

Molos

MEDITERRANEAN
SEA

Agia
Paraskevi

Spetses

Ag. Anargiri

Agia Marina

Trikeri

N

0   10 miles

0   10 kilometers

To Patitiri (☎51 520), in an alley to the left off of Aikaou. Serves marvelously fresh Greek meals in a bougainvillea-filled courtyard. Entrees 1300-2400dr/€3.82-7.04.

Zachastiki Bakery, at the intersection of Aphaias and Telemonos, will lure you in with the scent of fresh bread (100-150dr/€0.29-0.44) and large croissants (250dr/€0.73). A multitude of cookies go for 1700dr/€5 per kg.

Yacht Club/Panagakis Crêperie, on the waterfront. If you can't eat another *souvlaki*, walk upstairs to the Panagakis Cafe Bar/Crêperie. Fillings range from ice cream and strawberries to tunafish and mayo. Crepes 1200-2700dr/€3.52-7.92, cocktails 2100dr/€6.16 and up.

Leo Confections, Aphaias 48, just down from the internet cafe. Local desserts and pistachio ice cream (250dr/€0.73 per scoop). Open daily 8am-11pm.

For a low-key evening, watch American movies out-of-doors at **Anesis,** to the right off Aikaou, 100m from the waterfront. (☎24 757. Shows at 9 and 11pm; 2000dr/€5.87). Get your groove on at Aegina's dance club, aptly named **The Club,** a 10min. walk along the water to the right. (☎24 570. Beer 1500dr/€4.40; cocktails 2000dr/€5.87. Cover 1500dr/€4.40, includes first drink. Open daily 10:30pm-late.) The beach bar **Inn on the Beach** is just before The Club and packs a serious crowd on summer weekends. (☎26 440. Cover 1000dr/€2.93, includes a beer.) Tempt your inner devil as you party beneath Michelangelo-esque cherubim at popular **Apokalypsis** off Aphaias. Let the painted angel be your guide.

🜊 SIGHTS

Aegina Town's archaeological fame teeters on the last half-column of the **Temple of Apollo.** The 8m-tall Doric column dates to 460 BC and stands on Kolonna hill, ancient Aegina's acropolis. The extensive archaeological site is still being excavated but it is now known to have been an important settlement since the Early Bronze Age (ca. 3000 BC). Now Byzantine-era cisterns and the foundations of prehistoric houses keep mute vigil with the monolithic column. The **archaeological museum** at the site features a magnificent early classical sphinx (460 BC), artifacts from the Temple of Aphaia, a statue of Hercules from the Temple of Apollo, and some neolithic pottery. (☎22 248. Open Tu-Su 8:30am-3:45pm. 500dr/€1.47.)

The underground church of **Faneromeni,** a 15min. walk inland just south of the town, houses a rare icon of the Virgin Mary. Locals say that the night before construction was to begin on a site above Faneromeni, the architect had a vision in which he was instructed to dig instead of build. Doing just that, he discovered the church and unearthed the icon. Contact a local travel agency to arrange a visit.

🜊 DAYTRIPS FROM AEGINA TOWN

TEMPLE OF APHAIA. The 5th-century BC remains of the Temple of Aphaia rest 2km uphill from Agia Marina. Legend holds that Aphaia, daughter of Zeus and Karme, fled to Aegina from the amorous overtures of King Minos. There she became invisible (*aphaia*). Her temple, built on the foundation of a 6th-century BC temple, boasts a spectacular set of standing double-tiered columns. At night, peacocks roam the hills by the temple. (*A small museum opens for 15min. at 9am, noon, and 1pm. The Agia Marina bus from Aegina Town stops in front. Open M-F 8:15am-7pm.*)

AGIOS NEKTARIOS. The bronze and white church of Agios Nektarios is one of the largest places of worship in the Balkans. It's part of a complex that includes Nektarios' personal residence, bed, and books. The road behind Agios Nektarios leads up to Paleohora (about 1km), the "town of 300 churches," where locals once took refuge from pirate invasions. It's worth exploring the 15 churches that remain to see their frescoes and the spectacular view from the top of the hill. (*Take the bus from Aegina Town (15min.) and ask to be let off at Agios Nektarios. Dress appropriately: long ⌐ts for men, long skirts for women, no bare shoulders.*)

■ **MARATHONAS.** Tranquil beaches reverberating with the murmuring Aegean and delicious taverns sequestered in the fading daylight make Marathonas perhaps the most agreeable location on the island. Tiny and unassuming, the town is a well-kept secret. Approaching the town on the main road, veer right onto the unpaved road after the first stand of umbrellas for the peaceful beachfront, which is lined with small tavernas and pebble beaches. **Cafe Ostria** serves specialty *melizano* (eggplant) salads and calamari. They also serve juicy slices of watermelon (400dr/ €1.17), which accompany the perfect Aegean sunsets quite nicely. (☎26 738. Entrees 1250-1850dr/€3.66-5.43.) **O Tassos** (☎24 040), family-owned for 40 years and renowned for its superb veal and fish (1800-1850dr/€5.28-5.43), is accessible from the main road just before the church. Walk the 7km road from Aegina Town (it takes an hour) to see the island's most valuable coastline.

AGIA MARINA. If you find yourself inexplicably yearning to see hordes of sun-burned tourists, overpriced beach toys and tacky towels, then by all means swing by Agia Marina. The summer resort town is at the end of a lovely 30-minute bus trip through the island's interior, and offers some quality nightlife along with the exceedingly crowded beaches. The town is built around a main avenue, called **Aph-aias,** parallel to the sea. It's lined with bars, tourist shops, and moped rentals. A multitude of hotels surround the port. Most are open only in the summer.

Hotel Myrmidon, off Aphaias, sports a courtyard with a swimming pool and a lovely footbridge. The immaculate rooms have A/C, private baths, and fridges, and *Let's Go* users enjoy a 20% discount. (☎32 691; fax 32 558. Singles 5000dr/€14.67; doubles 10,000dr/€29.35; triples 15,000dr/€44.) **Karras Travel,** next to the bus stop, offers **exchange** and sells **bus** tickets. (☎32 557. Open daily 9am-11pm.) Pricey waters-edge restaurants crammed with tourists mingle with cheaper gyro and fast food shops along Aphaias. A **supermarket** on Aphaias offers an alternative to eating out. You can rent paddle boats at the beach (2000dr/€5.87 per hr.), but consider saving your money for discos like **Zorbas.** To find Zorbas, take a right on Praxite-lous two blocks past the bus stop, then follow the signs (opens daily at 11pm). Summer clubs **Genesis** and **Manos** lie just out of town with the water on your left.

POROS Πορος

"Poros" is actually two islands separated by a shallow channel: Sphaeria hugs the Peloponnesian mainland and is covered by the sprawl of tourist-heavy Poros Town; Kalavria preserves stretches of woods and dark-watered beaches. The name Poros ("passage") refers to the 350m-wide channel separating it from the Peloponnese. In the 6th century BC, the seven-city Kalavrian League met in Poros to ward off hostile naval powers and ordered the building of the Temple of Posei-don. Three centuries later, the great orator Demosthenes, who improved his dic-tion by speaking with marbles in his mouth, killed himself beside its columns. Poros was sparsely populated until Greeks arrived from Turkey in the 1920s.

POROS TOWN ☎0298

Wrapped around Sphaeria island, Poros Town centers on the waterfront that marks its perimeter. Tourist-oriented, it brims with beach shops and tavernas that sprawl outward from the ferry dock. Quieter locations are found farther from the dock and up the hill, among the pine woods and sandy beaches of Kalavria.

▐ **TRANSPORTATION**

Ferries: Askeli Travel Agency (☎24 900, 24 767 or 24 566), across from the hydrofoil dock, sells ferry tickets and posts schedules. 5 to 8 ferries per day run to **Aegina** (1hr., 1300dr/€3.82) and **Piraeus** (2½hr., 2200dr/€6.46) via **Methana** (30min., 850dr/ €2.49). Also service to **Hydra** (1hr., 2 per day, 1100dr/€3.23) and **Spetses** (2½hr., 1 per day, 1700dr/€5).

Flying Dolphins: Askeli Travel sells tickets. Hydrofoils dock at the main landing in the center of town. To: **Aegina** (30min., 1-3 per day, 2600dr/€7.63); **Hydra** (30min., 6-7 per day, 2200dr/€6.46); **Hermione** (3 per day, 2700dr/€7.92); **Piraeus** (1¼hr., 8 per day, 4400dr/€12.91); **Portoheli** (1½hr., 1-2 per day, 3900dr/€11.45); **Spetses** (1hr., 2-3 per day, 3500dr/€10.27).

Car Ferries: Poros-Galatas (every 30min. 7am-11pm, 250-1000dr/€0.73-2.93).

Port Authority: (☎22 274). Marked entrance 1 street in from the harbor by Seven Brothers Restaurant. Up a flight of stairs and down a long dreary hallway. Open 24hr.

Moped Rental: Kosta's Bike Rental (☎23 565), left of the waterfront past Ciné Diana. Mopeds start at 2500dr/€7.34 per day (4000dr/€11.74 for 80cc). Mountain bikes 1000dr/€2.93. Open daily 9am-9pm.

Buses: Leave from the main plateia 7-8am until midnight, every 30min. The green bus goes to the **Zoodochos Pigis** (220dr/€0.65) via **Askeli Beach.** The white bus goes to **Russian Bay** (200dr/€0.59) via **Neorion.** Buses leave **Galatas** for: **Epidavros** (3 per day); **Methana** (45min., 5 per day); **Nafplion** (3 per day); **Trizina** (20min., 4 per day). Call 22 480 for schedules. The station is across from the car ferry dock, to the right of the water taxi stand.

Water Taxis: run 24hr. between Poros dock and **Galatas** (2min., 120dr/€0.35; 200dr/€0.59 after midnight).

Taxis: (☎22 00). On the waterfront to the right of the ferry landing, facing inland. Expect to pay more after midnight.

■✴🛈 ORIENTATION AND PRACTICAL INFORMATION

Ferries and hydrofoils dock in the center of the waterfront, which traces around the edge of the small island; the main plateia is to the right facing inland. **Galatas,** across the strait, has cheaper food and lodgings, and is accessible by water taxi.

Bank: The **Alpha Bank,** in the plateia to the right before the port police, has a **24hr. ATM.** Open M-Th 8am-2pm, F 8am-1:30pm.

Bookstore: International Press (☎25 205), 25m left of the ferry dock on the waterfront has international newspapers and **Internet access** (2000dr/€5.87 per hr., 500dr/€1.47 minimum). Open daily 8am-11pm. The quiet, unassuming **Skipper & Trout International Bookshop** (☎26 245), in the arcade behind Diana Cinema to the left of the main landing, is a favorite haunt of the island's expats. Buys, sells, and exchanges new and used books in many languages. Also has telephone, fax, and translation services, greeting cards, stationery, CDs, and advice. Open M-Sa 9:45am-1:45pm.

Laundromat: Suzi's Launderette Service, in an alley to the right just past international press. Wash and dry 3500dr/€10.27; ironing extra. Drop-off only. 2hr. service. Open M-Sa 9am-2pm.

Police: (☎22 256). From the post office and pharmacy turn right and head up the stairs next to Igloo Ice Cream. At the top, turn right at the church and continue past the Platanos Taverna—look for the Greek flag. **Tourist Police** (☎22 462), in the same building.

Telephone: OTE (☎22 199 or 22 399), on the waterfront left of the main landing. Telecards and telegrams. Open M-F 7:30am-3pm.

Internet Access: At **International Press,** 25m to the left of ferry dock. 2000dr/€5.87 per hr., 500dr/€1.47 minimum. Also at **Webworld Internet Cafe,** above Coconuts Bar, in the plateia to the right of the ferry dock. 2000dr/€5.87 per hr., 500dr/€1.47 minimum. Open daily 10:30am-3pm and 6:30-11pm.

Clinic: Galatas has a 24hr. clinic (☎22 222), and emergencies including minor surgery can be handled at the **Naval School;** contact the tourist police.

Post Office: (☎22 275; fax 23 451), in the 1st plateia to the right along the water. Poste Restante; specify Poros Trinzinias. Open M-F 7:30am-2pm. **Postal code:** 18020.

ACCOMMODATIONS AND CAMPING

The best deals in Poros Town are the **domatia** advertised in almost every window; expect to pay 6000-9000dr/€17.61-26.41. There's no pressing reason to stay in Poros Town, as **Galatas**, 2min. across the strait by boat (every 10-15min., 24hr., 120dr/€0.35), has similar, less expensive hotel rooms.

 Manos Pension (☎/fax 22 000 or 23 456), in Galatas. Walk left when you disembark from the small boat from Poros Town, just past the playing field. Family-run pension dedicated to your Greek experience. Friendly Manos and Beatrix can rent you motorbikes (3000-4500dr/€8.80-13.21), tell you all about the region, and invite you to their farm for traditional Greek food and dancing. Cozy rooms will make you feel right at home. Singles 6000dr/€17.61; doubles 8000dr/€23.48; triples 10,000dr/€29.35

Saronis Hotel (☎22 356; fax 25 642), across from the water taxi landing in Galatas. Simple rooms have A/C, TV, and private baths. Doubles 10,000dr/€29.35.

Hotel Seven Brothers (☎23 412; fax 23 413; 7brothrs@hol.gr), to the right of the ferry dock and inland past the Alpha Bank. One of the better deals for a decked-out port side hotel. Rooms with private bath, TV, A/C, and minibar. Singles 13,000dr/€38.15; doubles 16,000dr/€46.96; triples 19,000dr/€55.76.

Camping Kyragelo (☎24 520 or 24 521), outside Galatas. Veer left onto the road running inland across from where the water taxis land and follow it 500m out of town. 1200dr/€3.52 per person; 600dr/€1.76 per car or tent.

FOOD

Similar restaurants line the harbor, and "charming" waiters try to convince tourists to sit down; make your choice based on the view. Several grocery stores and produce markets line the waterfront to the right of the ferry dock. Cafes are open all day; more hard-core establishments start at 10:30pm.

Taverna o Bobby's (Ο ΜΠΑΜΠΗΣ) (☎23 629), in Galatas across from the car ferry dock. *The* place for fresh seafood and local atmosphere. Succulent seafood dishes start at 1500dr/€4.40; grilled dishes run 1000-2500dr/€2.93-7.34.

Taverna Poros (☎25 267), one of the more relaxed waterfront restaurants, right across from the water taxi dock. Entrees 1500dr/€4.40 and up.

Colona (☎22 366), just down the waterfront to the right of the ferry dock, meets all your fast-food-gyro needs (400dr/€1.17).

Igloo Ice Cream (☎25 515), inland around the corner to the right of the post office. Serves breakfast, pastries, ice cream (350dr/€1.03 per scoop), and build-your-own crepes from 650dr/€1.91.

SIGHTS AND ENTERTAINMENT

Poros isn't much of a party town, but there's plenty to do on weekends. Check billings by the bus station for **Diana open-air cinema,** to the left of Lela Tours, where you can see American movies (9 and 11pm; 1800dr/€5.28, children 1350dr/€3.96). Fashionable locals and tourists alike head to the waterfront bars for late-night fun; two more popular joints to soothe your dance music cravings are **Malibu** and **Typos** (drinks around 1500-2000dr/€4.40-5.87).

ARCHAEOLOGICAL MUSEUM. In Poros Town itself, the archaeological museum in the middle of the waterfront has some interesting inscriptions and photographs of the ruins at Trizina in the Peloponnese; very little of the collection is actually from Poros. (☎23 276. Open Tu-Su 8:30am-3pm. Free.) For a pretty view of the harbor, climb the **clock tower** (the stairs are next to the library, 1 block inland).

GALATAS. If you look across a thin strait to the Peloponnesian mainland from Poros, you'll spy Galatas (Γαλατας), a working village with a different feel than tourist-frequented Poros. Surrounded by beautiful farmland and cut with flat, well-paved roads, Galatas is great for bike riding and the beaches are spared the hordes of tourists that populate Poros. When you arrive, turn left (facing inland) to find the pleasant sand beaches of Plaka and Aliki. Plaka is about 2km from Galatas, marked by a wall that reads "Poros Marine," while livelier Aliki is 1km further. Caution: only the water on the ocean side is safe for swimming. About 1.5km beyond Aliki beach is Artemis, where the ruins of a temple to the goddess are visible underwater. A gravel path 1km past the turn-off for Aliki is on the right of the road and leads up through the enormous lemon grove of Lemonodassos ("lemon forest"). If you are riding a moped, leave it here before going up the dirt road. It is a pleasant, if dusty, 20min. walk up to Kardasi Taverna (☎23 100), to get a cool glass of fresh lemonade (350dr/€1.03) and a view of windmills and 38,000 lemon trees. The beaches are quieter on the opposite side of the peninsula; try Vlacheika. *(Boats run between Galatas and Poros daily (every 10min., 2min., 100dr/€0.29).)*

MONASTERY OF ZOODOCHOS PIGIS. The 18th-century Monastery of Zoodochos Pigis (Virgin of the Life-Giving Spring) is sequestered in an overgrown glade 6km from Poros Town. Monks have been drinking blessed, curative waters here since 200 BC. The monastery once served as a meeting place for Greek naval leaders Miaoulis, Jobazis, and Apostolis, who strategized the uprising of 1821. Before hopping on the bus back, stop for delicious ice cream (350dr/€1.03 per scoop) at **Samali's,** opposite the monastic complex. If you're curious, ask nicely about the tiny church next door. Between the cafe and the small church is a fountain of the **life-giving spring,** so fill up your water bottle and be invigorated. From the road below the monastery you can find the 6th-century BC **Temple of Poseidon.** The "ruins" may be best appreciated by Greek history buffs, but the view will inspire all. *(Take the green bus from the stop next to the main port (20min., every 30min. 7am-11pm, 220dr/€0.65). Open sunrise to sunset, but closed 2-4:30pm in summer. Modest dress required.)*

◼◭ BEACHES AND THE OUTDOORS

The **white bus line** runs hourly along the shore to the beach at **Russian Bay,** where Russian ships first docked to aid the Greek rebellion. Along the way are **Neorion**—featuring a long sand beach, tavernas, a watersports center; and the secluded blue-green waters and rocky sands of **Lover's Bay.** The tiny island near Lover's Bay was an undercover school during the Turkish occupation, when Greeks were forbidden an education. Ironically, it's now a popular sunning rock for kids playing hooky. The **green bus** passes sandy and crowded **Askeli beach** on the way to the monastery; the beach has a slate of tavernas, tourist shops, and watersports.

Fifteen kilometers from Galatas lies **Trizina,** mythical home to the hero **Theseus.** Take a bus (20min., 3 per day) there from Galatas and follow the signs up the hill out of town. Meager ruins have been unearthed near the town, but of far more interest is the lovely **Devil's Gorge,** so named for the cloven hoof footprint found in one of the rocks at the gorge's base. The shady, verdant area is not large, but is a perfect picnic spot, especially for those who miss trees, and the cool mountain water forms pools that will take the edge off the heat. Head uphill from the bus stop in the center of town and go right, following the paved road past olive trees and fragrant lemon groves. At the fork in the road, head left and uphill (right and downhill will take you to the ruins), passing the ancient **Tower of Diateichisma.**

CONCEIVED IN LIBERTY...? On March 25, 1821, Greek forces began the rebellion against 400 years of Ottoman occupation. The date was no accident: any Orthodox Christian will recognize March 25 as exactly nine months before Christmas Day, and thus the day of the conception of Christ. Pragmatic enough to realize that rebuilding their land would take time, yet idealistic and spiritual enough to appreciate the endless significance of March 25, the Greeks chose the date in the hopes that the new republic would be ready for birth on December 25. In actuality it took years, but freedom was won, the modern state forged, and March 25 is still celebrated annually by Greeks as the anniversary of a doubly important conception.

HYDRA Υδρα

Steep and bright, proud Hydra (EE-drah) rises out of the sea in its own bubble of smog-free, screech-free air. Even bicycles are illegal here—the steep, scaled streets only accommodate pedestrians, donkeys, and three garbage trucks. Hydra was rich long before the influx of tourist cash, first coming to prosperity as the 15th-century refuge of wealthy Greek families escaping Turkish persecution. The island then struck a deal with the Ottomans, providing the Turkish navy with the service of 30 young Hydrian men every year in return for its freedom. Hydrian youth thus learned the art of naval battle, a perk when, in 1821, Admiral Miaoulis and the Hydrian elite dedicated their fleet to the fledgling revolution. Everyone is still terribly proud of it, as the main thoroughfare is named for Miaoulis.

HYDRA TOWN   ☎ 0298

The sometimes baffling, cobbled streets of Hydra Town twist up the island's parched hills as they rise from the rich blues of the sea. Donkeys mingle with wheelbarrow-pulling fruit vendors in the quiet alleys, which wend their way toward the sky. Glowing a sleepy yellow-pink in the evenings, the port below bustles with art students and smiling tourists during the summer months. As gorgeous as summers are, the pink-blossomed spring and salt-winded fall give the town an off season like no other. Outside Hydra Town, the island's main settlement, hidden beaches are yours for the price of a sea taxi.

◼★ 🛈 ORIENTATION AND PRACTICAL INFORMATION

Hydra's famously picturesque harbor is surrounded amphitheatrically by the town, with the harbor opening facing north. Yachts and fishing boats bob in the center, accompanied by water taxis (in the southeast corner). Ferries and Flying Dolphins dock on the east edge of the harbor. Jewelry and tourist boutiques share harbor front space with pricey restaurants, bars, and cafes. **Tombazi,** in the southeast corner of the harbor, runs inland past the Internet cafe and several restaurants. **Miaouli** runs inland from the center of the harbor; **Votsi,** in the southwest corner beyond the clock tower, runs inland past the OTE, police, and medical center.

Ferries: Salanikos Ferries ticket office (☎ 54 007), upstairs in the building with the gray door across from the ferry dock. Open daily 10am-6:30pm. 2 ferries per day to: **Aegina** (2¼hr., 1700dr/€5); **Methana** (1½hr., 1600dr/€4.70); **Piraeus** (3¼hr., 2500dr/€7.34) via **Poros** (1hr., 1100dr/€3.23). Also service to **Spetses** (2hr., 1 per day, 1300dr/€3.82).

Flying Dolphins: The **ticket office** (☎ 53 813) is upstairs, on the same floor as the ferry ticket office. Open daily 6:30am-9pm. To: **Hermione** (30min., 3 per day, 1900dr/€5.58); **Piraeus** (1½hr., 8 per day, 5000dr/€14.67); **Poros** (30min., 8 per day, 2200dr/€6.46); **Portoheli** (45min., 5-6 per day, 2700dr/€7.92); **Spetses** (30min., 8 per day, 2500dr/€7.34).

Sea Taxis: (☎ 53 690). Brightly-colored motorboats parked by the mule stand in the southwest corner of the harbor. Priced per boat (not per person), reflecting length of journey. Service to: **Agios Georgios** (12,000dr/€35.22); **Agios Nikolaos** (15,000dr/€44); **Hydra Beach** (14,000dr/€41.10); **Kamina** (2000dr/€5.87); **Mandraki Beach** (3000dr/€8.80); **Metohi** (7000dr/€20.53); **Palamidas** (4000dr/€11.74); **Vlihos** (3000dr/€8.80); daytrip around the island with beach stops 30,000dr/€88.05.

Bank: National Bank (☎ 53 233), on the waterfront. 24hr. **ATM.** Open M-Th 8am-2pm, F 8am-1:30pm.

Laundry: Jasmin Laundry (☎ 53 380), in the small building behind the fruit market. 3500dr/€10.27 per load including drying. Open daily 9am-1:30pm and 5-8:30pm.

Tourist Police: (☎ 52 205). Follow the street to the right of the clock tower inland and go left at the fork. Look for the coat of arms on the right, opposite the OTE. Open 24hr.

Port Police: (☎52 279), upstairs in the big gray building flying the Greek nautical flag, in the northwest corner of the harbor. Open 24hr.

Pharmacy: Inland on Tombazi, just before the Amarillis Hotel. Open daily 9am-1:30pm and 5-8:30pm.

Hospital: (☎53 150), inland on the street to the right of the clock tower, set back on the right, just past the tourist police. Brown door with grates set in a stone wall. Open M-F 9am-1pm and by appointment; in an **emergency,** call the 24hr. nurse (☎53 150) or the tourist police.

Telephones: OTE (☎52 199 or 52 399), facing the tourist police. Open M-F 8am-2pm. **Card phones** are just past the OTE entrance on the left.

Internet Access: Flamingo Cafe (☎53 485), 20m up Tombazi on the right. 2500dr/ €7.34 per hr. Open daily 11am-11pm.

Post Office: (☎52 262), 1 block inland in the alley to the left of the Bank of Greece. Open M-F 7:30am-2pm. **Postal code:** 18040.

ACCOMMODATIONS

Hydra has the most expensive accommodations in the Saronic Gulf. Singles are practically nonexistent and doubles generally coat at least 12,000dr/€35.22 during high season. Rooms in one of Hydra's famous old mansions are usually much more expensive. Weekend accommodations are almost impossible to get due to the influx of vacationing Greeks; if you can, arrive on Thursday for the weekend or call ahead. You may also be met at the ferry dock by Hydriots offering *domatia* (probably your cheapest option), but don't expect luxurious accommodations.

Hotel Amarillis (☎53 611, 52 249 or 53 859). Walk inland on Tombazi; hang right at the fork. Rooms at this welcoming, family-run hotel have fridges, TV, and A/C. Singles 10,000dr/€29.35; doubles 15,000dr/€44; triples 18,000dr/€52.82.

Hydra Hotel (☎/fax 52 102 or 53 085; hydrahotel@aig.forthnet.gr), looms high over the waterfront on the west side, just down the street from the Koundouriotis mansion. Walk 1 block inland on Votsi, take the hard right up the stairs and around the corner, and turn right again on L. Koundouriotis (another long staircase). Wood-accented rooms have balconies with unsurpassed views and private baths. Doubles 16,400-18,400dr/ €48.13-54; triples 20,000-22,800dr/€58.69-66.91. Discounts for longer stays.

Pension Antonios (☎53 227), on Spilios J. Chasamas, across from Christina's restaurant; a 5min. walk inland on Tombazi. Bright, clean rooms off a quiet courtyard feature fridges, A/C, and private baths. Doubles 17,000dr/€49.89; triples 20,000dr/€58.69; quad or quint 30,000dr/€88.05.

FOOD

Most waterfront establishments have average food, many tourists, and prices that reflect the rent. Hidden treasures compensate for location with superb food and significantly lower prices.

Fournos Bakery, in the first alley to the left off Tombazi next to Vassilis Tours, delivers savory baked goods (100-500dr/€0.29-1.47) and has a small market, all with the best prices in town. Open daily 7am-10pm.

Taverna Xeri Elia (☎52 886), in a trellised courtyard 5min. inland on Tombazi. Classy, top-quality food and service at a range of prices. Live music to accompany your meal. Entrees 1200-3000dr/€3.52-8.80.

Christina's Taverna (☎53 615), on Spilios Charamis just to the right of Taverna Xeri Elia. Far off the beaten path, this is the place for terrific home-cooking, so don't bother with the menu—just order whatever Christina has in the kitchen. Entrees 1200-2500dr/ €3.52-7.34. Open daily 11am-11pm.

Anemoni (☎53 136). Bear left uphill from the OTE. Greek pastries (500dr/€1.47) in generous portions; stop by after dinner for fresh ice cream (600dr/€1.76 for 2 large scoops) and almond confections. Open daily 7am-11pm.

SIGHTS

HYDRA'S MERCHANT MARINERS. Despite its watery name, Hydra's land has always been too arid for prosperous agriculture. With few natural resources and a significant population of refugees from the Peloponnese, the Balkans, and Turkey, Hydra's inhabitants turned to managing the exports of others. Dodging pirates and naval blockades during the late 18th and early 19th centuries, Hydriot merchants emerged in 1821 as the financial and naval leaders in the revolt against Ottoman rule, contributing two-thirds of the revolution's 200-odd ships. The Venetian-built mansions of these merchants-turned-heroes dot the hills behind the harbor, and are definitely worth a look. George Koundouriotis was one of the many Hydriot leaders in the Greek War of Independence, and his grandson, Pavlos Koundouriotis, became the President of Greece in the 1920s.

The **Tombazis mansion,** on the east side of the harbor, now houses a famous art school—look for paint-smeared artists on the balcony. The **houses of Votsis** and **Economou,** two Hydriots who also contributed to the island's naval fame, are closer to the crest of the hill, right on Voulgari. East of the harbor, in the **Tsamados mansion,** is the first **Pilot School** of the Greek Merchant Marine.

The **Lazaros Koundouriotis Historical Mansion,** recently converted into a museum, is the yellow building high on the west side of town. Take the first hard right off Votsi and turn right again on L. Koundouriotis, then head left at the top of the long stairway. The museum exhibits an extensive array of traditional Hydriot costumes and has a brilliant view of the town. Housed in its basement is a permanent exhibition of father-and-son Hydriot painters **Periklis** and **Constantinos Byzantios.** Save your ticket for admission into the gallery. (Open Tu-Su 10am-5pm. 1000dr/€2.93, students and children 11-18 500dr/€1.47, children under 10 free.) Currently the Lazaros Koundouriotis mansion is the only one open to the general public, but you can try your luck at the others, which are privately owned.

BYZANTINE SIGHTS. Those in search of peace need only check beneath the large clock tower that dominates the port. Stepping from the busy port into the courtyard of the **Church of the Assumption of the Virgin Mary,** you are immediately struck by the stillness and angelic whiteness of the place. The small church is certainly worth a trip, if only for a peek at its gilded ceiling and a few wonderful moments of quiet contemplation. Before serving as a monastery, the structure was a convent, housing 18 nuns from 1648 to 1770. It is now dedicated to the *kemesis*, or ascension of Mary. The courtyard surrounds the tomb of Koundouriotis, his statue, and a statue of Miaoulis. Modest dress is required. Hidden away up the stairs is the lovely **Byzantine Museum,** with an extensive and impressive collection of Byzantine icons, frescoes, gospels, and liturgical vessels. Noteworthy are the holy vestments and the brightly colored, beautifully preserved scenes from the life of Christ produced in the 18th and 19th centuries. *(Open Tu-Su 10am-5pm. 500dr/€1.47.)*

HISTORICAL ARCHIVES MUSEUM. To the left of the ferry landing, the Historical Archives Museum of Hydra houses old Hydriot costumes, census records, a library, naval treasures, and relics of the revolution. Don't miss the heart of Admiral Andreas Miaoulis, which is stunningly preserved in a silver and gold urn. (☎52 355. Open Tu-Su 9am-4:30pm. 1000dr/€2.93, students 500dr/€1.47.)

MONASTERY HIKE. An arduous 90min. hike up A. Miaouli from the waterfront takes you to the **Monastery of Prophitis Ilias** and, on a lower peak overlooking the harbor, the **Convent of Efpraxia.** While the nuns at Efpraxia do beautiful embroidery work, the monastery is the prettier of the two structures, and the monks may show you around. A donkey ride up the rocks costs about 10,000dr/€29.35 and wears out the donkey—inquire at the harbor. *(Modest dress required. Both open daily 9am-5pm.)*

FESTIVALS. If you're in Hydra town during the **Miaoulia** (the 4th weekend in June), celebrate the feats of Admiral Andreas Miaoulis via an explosive mock battle held in the harbor. Greek Orthodox **Easter Weekend** (one week after Roman Catholic Easter) marks the other big festival of the year, with outdoor candlelight services on Good Friday and Holy Saturday and a ceremonial immersion of the Epitaph on Good Friday in the sea off Kamini beach.

NIGHTLIFE

If the urge to shake your groove thing overtakes you in Hydra, ascend to **Disco Heaven,** perched near to its namesake high on a cliff on the west side of town. Take the white trimmed stairs just before the Sunset Restaurant. There's an indoor, A/C dance floor as well as an outdoor bar overlooking the sea. (☎52 716. Cocktails 2300-2800dr/€6.75-8.22. Cover 1000dr/€2.93. Open daily 11pm-late, summer only.) As the large contingent of artists might suggest, the Hydrian scene is about strolling the moonlit harbor, getting invited onto yachts for drinks, and wandering through the waterfront bars. The Hydriot equivalent of a pub crawl begins around 12:30am in the lounge seats of the **Pirate Bar,** tucked into the southwest corner of the harbor. (☎52 711. Beer 1300-1500dr/€3.82-4.40; cocktails 1800-2000dr/€5.28-5.87. Open daily 10am-late.) It then meanders through the crowds to trendy **Nautilus** and **Salonicos** (cocktails 2500dr/€7.34), and ends with an early-morning swim in the deep waters off the landing past Sunset Restaurant.

BEACHES

Landings and stairs cut into the rocks around the point across the harbor from the ferry dock provide the finest swimming on Hydra. Cool, crystal and instantly deep, the waters are a popular spot for the unofficial local sport: cliff diving. A 15min. walk west along the coast takes you past the high-walled, cobbled artists' colony of **Kamini.** Just beyond it is the tiny, pebbly **beach** where the drop to the sea is less severe. Walking another 20min. brings you to slightly more populous **Vlihos Beach,** guarded by a regiment of Hawaiian-style beach umbrellas. East of town (30min. hike or 10min. water taxi) lies well-manicured **Mandraki Beach** (a.k.a. the Mira Mare Hotel, but free for all), a genuine, if gritty, sand beach. This isn't the secluded beach of your dreams, but there are plenty of fun water toys to keep you busy. (Prices per hour: paddle boats 2500dr/ €7.34, canoes 1500dr/€4.40, windsurfing 3500dr/€10.27, sailboat rental 1500-3500dr/€4.40-10.27.) If you have time and money, hire a water taxi to the far side of the island; there's room for you to find a quiet beach of your own—just be sure to agree on a pickup time before getting out.

SPETSES Σπετσες

Called *pitiousa* (pine-covered) by the ancients, Spetses derives its current name from the Venetian *spezzie* (aromatic or spiced), referring to the island's sundry vegetation. Its relaxed atmosphere belies a past that was anything but tranquil. The Turks' brutal reprisal of the 1769 Orlof Revolution left the island uninhabited until 1774, when Spetsiots returned and cultivated a profitable merchant empire that stretched throughout the Aegean. Like Hydra, the merchant-mariners devoted their sizeable fleet (armed to repel pirates) and wealth to the Greek Revolution. Today, the island commemorates the valor of one Spetsiot captain, Kosmos Barbatsis. On September 8, 1822, the intrepid sailor piloted his explosives-laden craft directly into a Turkish flagship during battle, destroying it and turning the tide of battle in favor of the Greek fleet. Every September 8th, Spetsiots honor his deed with the explosion of a mock Turkish ship in the harbor.

SPETSES TOWN   ☎ 0298

The vast majority of Spetsiots live in Spetses Town, as close to the water as possible. Cafes and bars line the 4km of water, interspersed with little pebble beaches every 50m, turning the town into a round-the-clock beach club. Jet-setters dock in Spetses's Old Harbor to the left (facing inland) of the ferry quay. Although topless sunbathing is technically illegal, Spetsiots know how to bend the rules.

⌐ TRANSPORTATION

Ferries: Depart once daily to: **Aegina** (3hr., 2600dr/€7.63); **Piraeus** (4½hr., 3500dr/ €10.27) via **Hydra** (1hr., 1300dr/€3.82); **Methana** (2¼hr., 1900dr/€5.58); **Poros** (2hr., 1700dr/€5). **Alasia Travel** (☎ 74 098), on the waterfront, sells tickets and posts schedules. Open daily 8am-9pm.

Flying Dolphins: Ticket office (☎ 73 141), inland from the dock. **Hydrofoils** and **catamarans** to: **Piraeus** (2hr., 7-9 per day, 6800dr/€19.96); **Hydra** (30min., 7 per day, 2500dr/€7.34); **Poros** (1hr., 4 per day, 3400dr/€9.98); **Monemvasia** (2½hr., 2 per day, 4500dr/€13.21.)

Water Taxis: (☎ 72 072), docked across from the Flying Dolphin ticket office, just inland of the ferry dock. Prices posted. To: **Agia Marina** (6000dr/€17.61); **Anarghiri Beach** or **Paraskevi Beach** (12,000dr/€35.22); **Costa** (3500dr/€10.27); **Emilianos** (8000dr/€23.48); **Hinitsa** (7000dr/€20.53); **Kostoula** (4500dr/€13.21); **Old Harbor** (3500dr/€10.27); **Porto Heli** (8000dr/€23.48); **Zogeria** (7500dr/€22); and trips around the island (15,000dr/€44).

Buses: Schedules and prices posted at stops. To: **Ag. Anargiri Beach** (20min., 3 per day, 450dr/€1.32), from Ag. Mamas beach, 500m down the waterfront from the dock; and to **Anargyrios College** and **Lioneri Beach** from the plateia to the right of the ferry dock by the Hotel Poseidon (15 per day 9:15am-1:30am, 300dr/€0.88).

Taxis: In front of the travel agencies to the left of the ferry dock.

Moped Rental: Several rental agencies cluster just past the Ag. Anarghiri bus stop; veer right at the kiosk. Expect to pay 4000-7000dr/€11.74-20.53 per day, according to engine-size and cool-factor. **Rent-a-Bike** (☎ 74 143), on the street running parallel to the waterfront, behind the Hotel Soleil, rents **mountain bikes.** 1500dr/€4.40 per day.

◼▨ ORIENTATION AND PRACTICAL INFORMATION

The waterfront road runs from the left of the ferry dock around the base of the town to the **Old Port**, past **Ag. Mama's** beach. To the right of the ferry dock are several restaurants and cafes, on the way to **Plateia Bouboulina**, in front of the opulent Hotel Poseidon. The first street inland parallel to the water hosts shops, pharmacies, and tavernas. The Old Port, home to waterfront bars and tavernas, is a 20min. walk or 2000dr/€5.87 carriage ride; carriages wait near the ferry dock.

Tourist Agencies: Several around the corner on the left side of the boat landing. **Alasia Travel** (☎ 74 497, 74 498, or 74 098; fax 74 053; alasia@otenet.gr), sells ferry tickets. Open daily 8am-9pm.

Banks: National Bank (☎ 72 286), next to the OTE, on the waterfront to the right of the ferry docks. Open M-Th 8am-2pm, F 8am-1:30pm. 24hr. **ATM.**

Police: (☎ 73 100). Follow signs to the Spetses Museum; 150m before the museum. Also houses the **tourist police** (☎ 73 744) in basement. Open 24hr.

Port Police: (☎ 72 245), in the rear of the OTE building; walk up the street between the National Bank and the OTE and follow the signs. Open 24hr.

First Aid Station: (☎ 72 472). Open 24hr. for **emergencies.** Call police for doctor.

Pharmacy: (☎ 72 256), in the plateia, off the street running parallel to the waterfront. Open M-Sa 8:30am-1:30pm and 5:30-9:30pm, Su 10am-1:30pm and 5:30-9:30pm.

Telephone: OTE (☎ 72 199), around to the right of the ferry dock, next to the National Bank. Open M-F 7:30am-1:30pm.

Internet Access: Delfinia Net-Cafe (☎ 75 051; delfinianet@usa.net), left of the ferry docks, next to O Roussos, just before the beach. 1500dr/€4.40 per hr., 750dr/€2.20 minimum. Open daily 9am-2am. Also at **Politis** (☎ 72 248), around to the right of the ferry dock. 1500dr/€4.40 per hr., 750dr/€2.20 minimum.

Post Office: (☎ 72 228), left of the ferry dock on the road parallel to waterfront. Open M-F 7:30am-2pm. **Postal Code:** 18050.

ACCOMMODATIONS

Accommodations are generally expensive, with prices slightly higher on weekends and rooms scarcer. A few domatia are advertised around town; you might get picked up at the ferry dock. Be sure to bargain.

Pansion Brazos (☎ 75 152), just inland of the ferry docks. Unimpressive but convenient. Rooms have baths, fridges, fans, and balconies. Singles 8000-10,000dr/€23.48-29.35; doubles and triples 12,000dr/€35.22.

Hotel Faros (☎ 72 613; fax 72 614), in the plateia off the street parallel to the water. Plain rooms with fridges, A/C, private baths, and balconies. Doubles 14,000-16,000dr/€41.10-46.96; triples 16,000-19,000dr/€46.96-55.76; quads 27,000-28,000dr/€79.24-82.17.

Hotel Klimis (☎ 73 725, 73 334, or 73 777), on the waterfront to the left of the ferry docks. Large rooms with tiled private baths, TVs, and A/C. Breakfast 2000dr/€5.87. Singles 16,000dr/€46.96; doubles 18,000dr/€52.82; triples 25,000dr/€73.37.

FOOD AND NIGHTLIFE

Tavernas abound in this tiny town, but tend to be rather pricey.

■ **Politis** (☎ 72 248), on the waterfront, just to the right of the ferry docks. Serves decadent *baklava* (450-500dr/€1.32-1.47), delicious waffle breakfasts with bottomless cups of coffee (1700dr/€5 and up), and a wide variety of cocktails. **Internet access** available upstairs (1500dr/€4.40 per hr., 750dr/€2.20 minimum).

O Roussos (☎ 72 212), on the waterfront, just before the beach. Specializes in octopus, which you'll see drying on the clothesline outside. Octopus dishes around 2000dr/€5.87. Seafood and other entrees 1000-3000dr/€2.93-8.80. Open daily 11am-late.

Il Passante (☎ 72 027), in the plateia off the road running parallel to the water. Pizzas (1700-2900dr/€5-8.50 for regular, 1950-3300dr/€5.72-9.68 for large) cooked on a wood-fire stove offer a break from the usual, as do a variety of grilled hamburgers (1600-1900dr/€4.70-5.58). Open daily 11am-midnight.

Sports fans gather for drinks at **Socrates**'s happy hour (midnight; all cocktails 1000dr/€2.93.) A younger crowd heads to **Mama's,** at Ag. Mama's beach on the way to the Old Harbor, for expensive, chic drinks. The Old Harbor itself is the site of numerous tavernas and bars: **Remezzo** and **Eazino** feature live music.

SIGHTS

The **Spetses Museum** is housed in the center of town in the crumbling, late-19th-century mansion owned by Hadjiyanni Mexi, Spetses's first governor, and has a great view of the island. The imposing building itself is worth seeing, with an old island fireplace, stained glass windows, and carved wooden doors. Its collection includes a casket of the remains of Laskarina Bouboulina (see below), coins, costumes, mastheads, folk art, and religious artifacts. (Follow the signs from between the OTE and the National Bank. ☎ 72 994. Open Tu-Su 8:30am-2:30pm. 500dr/€1.47.) The **House of Laskarina Bouboulina** sits across the park from that of Sotiros Anargyrou, the philanthropist largely responsible for the current invigoration of

Spetses's tourism. Mme. Bouboulina was a ship's captain in the Greek War of Independence, and to date the only female admiral in history. She commanded the naval blockade of Nafplion. *(Next to the park behind the National Bank and the OTE.* ☎ *72 416. Open for guided tour only; English tours run from 9:45am-9:10pm. 1000dr/€2.93, children 300dr/€0.88.)* The **Monastery of Agios Nikolaos** is opposite a square of traditional Spetsiot mosaics, above the old harbor. A memorial plaque to the left of the entrance commemorates Napoleon's nephew, Paul Marie Bonaparte, who was pickled in a barrel of rum after he died in the war for independence. The barrel was stored in a monastic cell at Agios Nikolaos from 1827 until 1832. *(Dress modestly: long pants for men, long skirts for women, no bare shoulders.)*

◢ BEACHES

Spetses's surprisingly warm beaches are invitingly shallow and a major draw to the island. Big sandy **Ag. Anargiri,** on the opposite side of the island from Spetses Town, is the leader of a pack of beaches boasting a taverna and a host of watersports. (Kayaks 2500dr/€7.34 per hr.; windsurfing 3500dr/€10.27 per hr.; parasailing 7000dr/€20.53 per person; tubing 2000dr/€5.87 per person.) In the rear of the beach's only restaurant, Manolis, are showers, changing rooms, and impeccable bathrooms. Its companion, **Ag. Paraskevi,** about 1km to the right facing seaward, has the same blanket of pine trees and a sandy-pebbly surface without the accompanying hubbub of its mentor. Midway along the Anargiri-Spetses Town bus route is the utterly peaceful **Xylocheriza.** Pure white, smooth stones contrast with the still, brightly colored waters of the bay. Refresh yourself after a swim with a hunk of watermelon big enough for two at the snack bar. Although it is most easily accessed by moped, the bus does pass by the dusty road to the beach (10-15min. on foot); check with the driver about return times before you hop off. **College Beach,** in front of Anargyrios College, is home to a popular bar and tanned tourists. **Agia Marina** beach is about a 30min. walk over the island from the far left end of the waterfront in Spetses Town, taking a right at the kiosk.

FRAPPÉ 101 You've seen them at every cafe, ubiquitous as small cellular and motor scooters—now learn to order them like a pro. *Frappés* are made-to-order blended coffee drinks. Add milk (γαλα), sugar—tell your server that you want it sweet (γλυκο)—or ice cream (παψω), and a shot of Bailey's to give it a kick. Then sit back in your skin-tight finery and watch the crowds go by.

THE SPORADES
AND EVIA

Circling into the azure depths of the Aegean, Evia and the Sporades form a family of enchanting sea maidens. Evia, the matriarch, nudges the coast of Central Greece, stretching from Karystos in the south, through bustling Halkida, to the thermal springs of Aedipsos in the north. Her children the Sporades arc across the sea to the north. Sophisticated Skopelos, the eldest, quietly welcomes the moonlight to her shores with echoing jazz melodies. Wild and independent Skiathos pays homage to the sun, flaunting her beach-ringed shores for travelers from around the world. Little Alonnisos harbors pristine wilderness crossed by hiking trails and is home to MOM (Monachus monachus), an endangered species of seal, and its wildlife preservation organization. Austere Skyros watches from afar, keeper of the old ways. They have beckoned visitors for millennia: 5th century BC Athenians, 2nd century BC Romans, 13th century AD Venetians, and 20th century tourists have all basked on their sun-lit shores and trod their shaded forests.

HIGHLIGHTS OF THE SPORADES AND EVIA

GO BANANAS on Skiathos's bare-naked Little Banana beach (p. 309).

PUNK MEETS FOLK on Skopelos, home of Giorgios Xintaris, one of Greece's last great *rembetika* performers (p. 315).

GODS AND MONSTERS fire up the Dragon House refuge of Mt. Ohi near Karystos on Evia, where Zeus and Hera fell in love (p. 326).

PONDER POETRY by Rupert Brooke among pirate spoils in Skyros Town (p. 320).

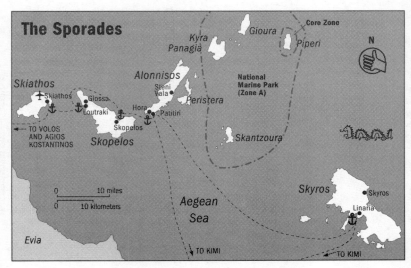

SPORADES Σποραδες

SKIATHOS Σκιαθος

Having grown up almost overnight from an innocent island daughter to a madcap dancing queen, Skiathos is the tourism (and party) hub of the Sporades. Its long waterfront, lined with travel agencies and car rental shops, gives little hint of the raw beauty of the island's beaches and rugged interior. The traveler who escapes the tourist temptations of Skiathos Town finds ethereal beaches and dignified monasteries, the childhood occupations of the Sporades's youngest daughter.

SKIATHOS TOWN   ☎ 0427

Arriving in Skiathos Town can be a bit overwhelming: dozens of Skiathans crowd the ferry landing hawking domatia, and cafes and tavernas line every street with tacky beach shops and expensive boutiques. Yet beyond the tourist gauntlet Skiathos reveals a charming and exhilarating character. From bars packed with talkative tourists, to heavenly beaches, to all-night discos, Skiathos offers something for everyone. The only thing you might find lacking is a resident Greek population.

⌷ TRANSPORTATION

Ferries: Hellas Lines (☎22 209), on the corner of Papadiamantis across from the ferry landing. Prices slightly higher in July-Aug. Ferries run to: **Agios Konstantinos** (3½hr., 1-2 per day, 3400dr/€10); **Alonnisos** (2hr., 1-2 per day, 1900dr/€5.60); **Glossa** (30min., 1-2 per day, 900dr/€2.64); **Skopelos** (1½hr., 1-3 per day, 1500dr/€4.40); **Volos** (2½hr., 1-2 per day, 2900dr/€8.50). To get to Skiathos from **Athens,** take the daily bus from the station at Liossion 260 to Ag. Konstantinos (2½hr., 16 per day, 2650dr/€7.80), and then take the ferry.

Flying Dolphins: Minoan Lines (☎22 018), at the same office. Trips to: **Agios Konstantinos** (1¼hr., 1-2 per day, 6800dr/€20); **Alonnisos** (1hr., 4-7 per day, 3800dr/€11.15); **Glossa** (15min., 3-4 per day, 1800dr/€5.30); **Skopelos** (35min., 4-6 per day, 3000dr/€8.80); **Skyros** (2½hr., 1 per day, 8400dr/€24.65); **Thessaloniki** (3¼hr., 5 per week, 8900dr/€26.15); **Volos** (1¼hr., 3-4 per day, 5800dr/€17).

Flights: Olympic Airways Office (☎22 229 or 22 220), at the airport. Call 24hr. prior to takeoff to confirm flight. Open M-F 8am-4pm. Taxis from the harbor to the airport cost about 1000dr/€2.93. One flight per day to **Athens** (50min., 19,400dr/€56.95).

Local buses: Facing inland, the **bus stop** is at the far right end of the wharf past the park. The bus to **Koukounaries beach** (every 15min. 7:15am-1am, 320dr/€0.95) makes stops at southern beaches along the main road. Heading out of Horio, sit on the driver's side for the best view. A schedule and list of stops is posted at the bus stop in Skiathos Town and at Koukounaries.

Taxis: (☎24 461). Line up along the waterfront; prices are posted on the Rooms to Let Office shack. Open 24hr.

Moped Rental: Prices run from 5000-7000dr/€14.67-20.53 per day, depending on the speed of the bike and the duration of the rental. **Euronet** (☎24 410), **Avis** (☎21 458), and **Heliotropio** (☎22 430) along the waterfront all include insurance.

Charter Boats: Boats run from the Old Port. Circuits around the island, including Lalaria and Castro beaches, cost 3000-4000dr/€8.80-11.74 per person and leave before 10am, returning in the afternoon. Boats to Tsougria, a small island just off the coast of Skiathos and a popular location for swimming and snorkeling, cost 2000dr/€5.87 per person and leave between 10am and noon, returning in the afternoon. Ask at the information kiosk next to the ferry dock for more information.

✦🛈 ORIENTATION AND PRACTICAL INFORMATION

The midpoint of Skiathos's waterfront is marked by the **Bourtzi,** a small penin-sula to the left of the ferry landing fortified by the Venetians in the 13th cen-tury. The **main waterfront** runs to the right of the Bourtzi, facing inland, and is the location of the ferry dock, vehicle rental agencies, tavernas and cafes, and tourist shops. The **Old Port** runs perpendicular to the main waterfront from the Bourtzi. **Papadiamantis,** Skiathos Town's main drag, overflows with cafes, sou-venir shops and clothing stores, and intersects the main waterfront across from the ferry dock. Farther inland, **Pandra** (left at the National Bank) and **Evangelistra** (perpendicular at the post office) intersect Papadiamantis. Paral-lel to Papadiamantis, **Polytechniou** contains a string of bars. On the far right of the waterfront facing inland, a road winds from the bus stop up to the airport and then follows the south coast of the island all the way to **Koukounaries beach. Maps** of Skiathos and the other Sporades islands are available in shops along the waterfront for about 500dr/€1.47. In the kiosk next to the ferry dock, ◣**Vasilis Korallis,** a Skiathan with a California accent, can help you with infor-mation on everything from places to stay, to beaches to visit, to how to protect Skiathos' wildlife. (Open daily 8am-1pm and 6-9pm.)

Tourist Police: (☎23 172). A small white building on the right side of Papadiamantis next to the school, just past where the road forks around an electronic info kiosk. Open most days 8am-9pm.

Banks: National Bank (☎22 400), midway up Papadiamantis on the left side. Offers **currency exchange** and an **ATM.** Open M-Th 8am-2pm, F 8am-1:30pm.

American Express: Papadiamantis 21 (☎21 463 or 21 464), on the left before Evange-listrias. Tourist services. Currency exchange. Open May-Oct.daily 9am-2pm and 5-9pm.

Bookstore: A **newsstand** on the left side of Papadiamantis past the AmEx sells interna-tional newspapers, magazines, and novels in English made for a long day on the beach.

Laundromat: Miele Laundry, about 200m up Papadiamantis on a side street across from the National Bank. The owner is in the grocery store across the street, and sells tokens and detergent. 1800dr/€5.30 per load; 2000dr/€5.87 with their soap. Open 8am-11pm. **Snow White Laundry,** on the street parallel to and behind the waterfront. 2000dr/€5.87 per load, 700dr/€2.05 per dryer, 300dr/€0.88 for soap. Drying with-out washing costs 1000dr/€2.93.

Police: (☎22 111), upstairs past the kiosk where Papadiamantis forks left. Open 24hr.

Pharmacies: Several pharmacies line Papadiamantis and its side streets.

Hospital: (☎22 040), on the "Acropolis" hill behind Skiathos Town. Open 24hr., but **emergencies** only after 1pm (go figure).

Internet Access: Internet Zone Cafe (☎22 767) on Evangelistra, to the right off Papa-diamantis. 1000dr/€2.93 per hr. Open daily 10am-midnight.

Federal Express: (☎22 006; fax 23 204), located on Simeonis, 1 block to the left of Papadiamantis before the National Bank. Open daily 9am-3pm and 5:30-8pm.

Post Office: (☎22 011), at the intersection of Papadiamantis and Evangelistra. Open M-F 7:30am-2pm. **Postal code:** 37002.

🏠 ACCOMMODATIONS AND CAMPING

Most tourists make prior reservations for July and August and tour groups often book most of the summer hotel rooms a year in advance. Dock hawks flock to meet the ferry and promote their domatia, which are generally the best deal in town. Be sure to **bargain.** Typical rooms run 6000-8000dr/€17.61-23.48 in winter, 8000-10,000dr/€23.48-29.35 in spring and fall, and 10,000-14,000dr/€29.35-41.10 in summer. Try the **Rooms to Let** office in the port's wooden kiosk, which can give you a list of rooms currently available. (☎22 990. Open daily 9am-8pm.)

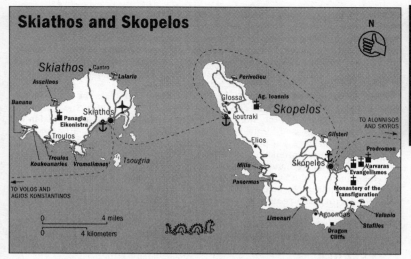

Skiathos and Skopelos

Australia Hotel (☎22 488), right on Evangelistra and in an alley to the left, is somewhat dim, but convenient. The simple rooms with baths, balconies, and fridges are cheap for 4 people. June: singles 6000dr/€17.61; doubles 9000dr/€26.41. July-Aug.: No singles; doubles 16,500dr/€48.42; triples 19,500dr/€57.23; quads 22,500dr/€66.

Pension Nikolas (May-Sept. ☎23 062; Oct.-Apr. ☎0394 32 756), just off Polytechniou to the left past Kirki bar. Centrally located, it offers private baths and fridges. Some rooms with A/C. English spoken. Doubles only. June and Sept. 9000-10,000dr/€26.41-29.35; July-Aug. 17,000dr/€49.90.

Pension Lazou (☎22 324), on the hill overlooking the Old Port. Walk along the Old Port with the water to your left, and climb the stairs at the end. A little off the beaten track, Lazou's simple, charming rooms have great views and private baths. Doubles 14,000-16,000dr/€41.10-47.

Camping Koukounaries (☎49 250), on the bus route to Koukouniares; ask the driver to let you off there. Has a restaurant, mini-market, and campground 1km from the beach. 1800dr/€5.30 per person; 1000dr/€2.93 per tent; 750dr/€2.20 per car.

🔲 FOOD

Meals in Skiathos fall conveniently into one of two categories: glamorous or functional. Foreign wads of cash pay for the ritzy food, which can be worth the splurge. Back-alley souvlaki stands and tiny tavernas off the main strip feed locals and broke backpackers. Cheap Greek food stands pack **Papadiamantis.**

Chris, Jan & Deborah's Daskalio Pub (☎0941 70 903). Follow Papadiamantis and veer right at the school. Look for a brightly painted, triangular white building on the right. Come for the tasty curries (2500-4000dr/€7.35-11.75) or "sponge of the day" (1200dr/€3.52) and stay for the English pub crowd and funky decor. Pop music quizzes Tu, Th, Sa 11pm. Bar open 7pm-3am, food until 11pm. Open May-Sept.

Primavera (☎24 086), tucked behind a church among labyrinthine streets. Turn left on Pandra before the National Bank and then left again when it intersects the end of Polytehniou. Delicious Italian food (pizza 2100-2900dr/€6.15-8.50; pasta 1700-2800dr/€5-8.25) in a romantic, Old World setting. Open daily 6:30pm-12:30am.

To Bourtzi (☎21 834), coincidentally the only cafe on the Bourtzi, offers an unparalleled view of the sea and surrounding islands from a spot quietly removed from the glitz of Papadiamantis. Sip a *frappé* and be mesmerized by the sea. Drinks only.

Crepes Kepali (☎23 840), way up Papadiamantis on the right, before the school. Serves salty and sweet crepes at decent prices (800-1200dr/€2.35-3.55). Open 24hr.

SPORADES

🜨 SIGHTS

Author Alexandros Papadiamantis's tiny 140-year-old house, set back off Papadiamantis about 1½ blocks inland, now serves as the **Papadiamantis Museum,** housing his few possessions. The museum honors the 19th-century realist who was one of Greece's best-loved prose writers. Info and short stories are available in English. (Open Tu-Su 9:30am-1pm and 5-8pm. 300dr/€0.88.)

Panagia Eikonistra or **Kounistra** ("The Blessed Icon Painter") is the most important monastery on the island. The **festival** of the Presentation of the Virgin on November 21 celebrates the monastery's miracle-working icon and the island's patron saint, the Blessed Virgin. Get off the bus at **stop #18** and follow the road signs to the monastery. The **Convent of Evangelistra,** 4km north of Skiathos Town on the slopes of Karaflitzanaka, is the site where the **first Greek national flag** (white cross on a blue background) was raised in 1807.

Ten kilometers from Skiathos Town on the north coast of the island, accessible by private vehicle or by boat, stand the ruins of a medieval walled **castle** built in the 16th century as a refuge from marauding pirates. With independence in the 19th century, the castle's occupants moved to Skiathos Town. Presently only two of Kastro's original 30 churches remain standing, notably the **Church of Christ,** which houses rare icons and frescoes and a magnificent iconostasis.

🜨 BEACHES

A single paved main road runs along the southern coast of Skiathos, between Skiathos Town and the island's most famous beach, **Koukounaries.** The bus makes many stops along the road, mostly at other beaches. A list of stops is available at the bus station in Skiathos and at Koukounaries. Many consider the 🖼**Koukounaries Beach and Biotrope** (stop #26) to be one of the most beautiful beaches in the Mediterranean. Plush sand arcs between blue waters and the verdant pines of the Biotrope, a protected forest area. Besides being the most revered beach on the island, it is also the most popular—expect throngs of crowds in July and August. Koukounaries offers a full slate of water sports (water skiing 6000dr/€17.61; parasailing 10,000dr/€29.35) and is well-equipped with showers, bathrooms, and bars.

Banana and Little Banana Beaches (stop #26) are at the end of the dusty road up the hill across from the Koukounaries bus stop. Signs lead the way. To get to curvy yellow Little Banana from Banana, walk around the rocks on the right as you face the sea. Drop your pants on the way—both are **nude beaches. Lalaria** is accessible only by charter boat (3000-4000dr/€8.80-11.75 per person) from the Old Port in Skiathos. Boats leave before 10am. Its white pebbles and magical sea caves make Lalaria one of Skiathos's best secrets. The bus also stops at other beaches, including **Megali Ammos** (stop #5), **Nostos** (stop #12), **Vromolimnos** (stop #13), **Kolios** (stop #14), **Troulos** and **Asselinos** (stop # 18) on the north coast, and **Mandraki** (stop #21).

🜨 NIGHTLIFE

Indulge yourself at the innumerable bars in **Pl. Papadiamantis,** on **Polytechniou,** or on **Evangelistra.** Beware—island novelists have a tradition of writing from real life, and you may be immortalized as a minor character by a latter-day Papadiamantis. Expect to pay 600-1000dr/€1.75-2.95 for beer, 1500dr/€4.40 for cocktails, and 1000-2000dr/€2.95-5.87 cover on very popular Saturday nights. From October to May, it's a ghost town; by July it hops.

Admiral Benbow Inn, on Polytechniou. A cozy place to begin (or end) the night, with plenty of comfy couches, a talkative crowd, decor borrowed from *The Blues Brothers,* and a 700dr/€2.05-per-pint Happy Hour (9pm-midnight) most weekends.

Kentavros (☎22 980), beyond the Papadiamantis museum. Skiathos's oldest bar serves mostly local residents who rock out to jazz and rock. Beer 1000-1300dr/€2.93-3.85; cocktails €5.87.

Kirki Bar (☎23 022), at the end of Polytechniou, features live rock music every night. Beer 800-1000dr/€2.35-2.95; cocktails 2000dr/€5.87.

Banana Bar (☎21 232), on Polytechniou, a small street parallel to Papadiamantis; take Evangelistra, then veer right. The largest TV in town entertains a rowdy tourist crowd. Beer 700-1000dr/€2.05-2.95; cocktails 1700-2000dr/€5-5.87. Open 9:30pm-4am.

Party until dawn at one (or many) of the discos that line the waterfront on the right edge of the harbor, facing inland. Clubs play everything from techno to top 40. Get your drinks beforehand, however, as beer costs about 1500dr/€4.40 a bottle during the wee hours. **Kahlua** and **Remezzo** are two of the better venues, with both interior and exterior bars and wooden dance floors.

For more sedate entertainment, the open-air **Cinema Paradiso,** just past the Papadiamantis museum on the right, screens recent Hollywood hits in English with Greek subtitles. Schedules available on signs along the waterfront or at the AmEx office across the street. (☎23 975. 2000dr/€5.87. Shows twice per night, 9 and 11:30pm.) Concerts play at the **Bourtzi,** the small peninsula jutting out next to the Flying Dolphin dock, during July and August. Ask at the information kiosk in the harbor for program schedules.

SKOPELOS Σκοπελος

Relaxed Skopelos sits between the whirlwind of Skiathos and the largely untouched wilderness of Alonnisos. Its graceful beaches and pine forests conceal a turbulent history—the islanders were brutally exterminated in 1538 by the pirate Barbaros, and the island remained uninhabited until 1600. The island has now achieved the serenity that long eluded it. By day the pious head to the hills, where monasteries and shrines hide in woods still heady with the fading sounds of *rembetika*. By night, the labyrinthine streets of Skopelos Town are filled with murmuring voices and light drips down from cafes and onto the Aegean.

SKOPELOS TOWN   ☎0424

Skopelos Town winds up the steep hills above the harbor, amphitheater to the vast stage of the Aegean. Castles and bishops peer sternly around whitewashed corners, while narrow streets twist among whitewashed buildings and beautiful churches peek from behind every bend. Lace curtains flutter behind blue shutters and cafes perch precariously among the sloping corridors. Aimless wanderings promise to be among the most interesting journeys on the island.

▐ TRANSPORTATION

Ferries and Flying Dolphins dock at the concrete landing on the left side of the harbor, facing inland. **Taxis** await near the ferry dock; the **bus station** is just down the street to the left.

Ferries: Hellas Lines (☎22 767 or 23 060; fax 23 608), directly across from the ferry dock, runs to: **Agios Konstantinos** (4hr., 1 per day Su-F, 4300dr/€12.65); **Alonnisos** (30min., 1-2 per day, 1100dr/€3.23); **Skiathos** (1hr., 2-3 per day, 1500dr/€4.40); **Volos** (4hr., 2 per day, 4300dr/€12.65). Prices slightly higher (100-200dr/€0.29-0.59) in July and August.

Flying Dolphins: Minoan Lines (☎22 767 or 23 060, fax 23 608), tickets also sold directly across from the ferry dock. To: **Agios Konstantinos** (2½hr., 1-2 per day, 8500dr/€24.95); **Alonnisos** (15min., 5-7 per day, 2200dr); **Skiathos** (45min., 4-7 per day, 2900dr/€8.50); **Thessaloniki** (4hr., 4-5 per week, 8700dr/€25.53); **Volos** (2hr., 3-4 per day, 7100dr/€20.85).

Buses: The stop is left of the ferry dock facing inland, on the left side of the road. Bus lines run a circuit between **Stafilos, Agnondas, Panormos** and **Milia** (12 per day, 7am-10:30pm), and another between **Elios, Glossa** and **Loutraki** (8 per day, 7am-10:30pm). You can also request to be let off at beaches in between stops. Check the posted schedules at the stop or call **Thalpos Travel Agency** (☎22 947).

Taxis: Available at the waterfront 7am-2am.

Moped and Car Rental: Shop around—most travel agencies arrange rentals. Mopeds 3500dr/€10.30; cars 12,000dr/€35.22. Prices vary by season, amenities, sound effects, and distance.

✦ 🔃 ORIENTATION AND PRACTICAL INFORMATION

Tourist agencies, tavernas, and cafes line the waterfront. **Galatsaniou,** a fashionable street rich with trinkets and goodies, darts upward between Cafe Cafe and Cafe Aktaion, 100m to the right of the ferry dock facing inland. **Platanos,** a small plateia brimming with souvlaki and gyros restaurants, is across from the ferry dock, with the monument on your right and the playground on your left. On the far right of the waterfront, just before the jetty, whitewashed stairs lead up the side of the town, passing many **churches** along the way.

Tourist Agencies: Most **exchange currency,** rent mopeds and cars, sell ferry tickets, and run trips to nearby islands. **Thalpos Travel Agency** (☎ 22 947; fax 23 057; thalpos@ote-net.gr), 5m to the right of Galanatsiou along the waterfront, can tip you off about everything from Dolphin tickets to catching octopi and provide you with a useful map of the town and island. English spoken. Open May-Oct. 10am-2pm and 5-10pm; Oct.-May available by fax or telephone.

Banks: National Bank (☎ 22 691), on the right side of the waterfront, has a 24hr. **ATM.** Open M-Sa 8am-2pm.

Bookstore: International Press, just out the bottom left corner of Platanos, sells international newspapers and English-language books.

Emergency: For police dial 100. For medical care, dial 22 222.

Police: (☎ 22 295), behind the National Bank.

Medical Center: (☎ 22 222). Follow the left-hand road inland from Pl. Platanos past Ag. Ioannis to the dead end, then go right at the signs. Open M-F 9am-2pm for free walk-ins; open M-F 24hr. for **emergencies.**

Telephones: OTE (☎ 22 139 or 22 121), 100m up from the water on Galatsaniou. Open M-F 7:30am-3:10pm.

Internet access: The Internet Cafe, up Galatsaniou to the right and uphill past Thalpos, behind the first row of buildings. Internet access 1500dr/€4.40 per hr, 500dr/€1.47 minimum. Printing 100dr/€0.29 per page. Faxing to Europe 800dr/€2.35 per page; US 1200dr/€3.52 per page. **Beer** (500dr/€1.47). Open 9am-11pm.

Post Office: (☎ 22 203). Head up the alley directly across from the bus station (across the playground) and between two restaurants. Look for the large yellow postbox around the corner. Open M-F 7:30am-1:30pm. **Postal code:** 37003.

🏠 🍴 ACCOMMODATIONS AND FOOD

In general, Skopelos's hotels shelter all-inclusive-resort tourists. Don't worry: the **Rooms and Apartments Association of Skopelos,** in the small stone building next to the town hall, around the waterfront to the right (facing inland), can provide a list of current **domatia.** (☎ 24 567. Open 10am-2pm and 6-10pm.) Prices vary by season, but are generally 5000-10,000dr/€14.67-29.35 for singles and 7000-12,000dr/€20.53-35.22 (and up) for doubles. Dock hawks may also offer reasonable rooms.

🏛**Pension Sotos,** on the corner of Galatsaniou on the waterfront, is a gem, both for its fantastic location (right on the waterfront in the center of town) and its diamond-in-the-rough price. A renovated Skopelian house, the pension provides baths and fans, a common kitchen, fridge, quiet courtyard, and book exchange. (☎ 22 549; fax 23 668. Singles 5500-10,000dr/€16.15-29.35; doubles 6500-10,000dr/€19.10-29.35; triples 9000-16,000dr/€26.41-46.96.)

Also Known As "Souvlaki Square," **Pl. Platanos** abounds with fast, cheap food. For slower-paced dining, **Tavera O Molos** (☎ 22 551), around the waterfront to the right facing inland, serves delicious traditional Greek food with a harbor view. Entrees run 900-2200dr/€2.64-6.45. Specialties include lamb *kleftika* (2200dr/€6.45) and chicken a la creme (1900dr/€5.60).

👁 🎵 SIGHTS AND ENTERTAINMENT

Skopelos Town has an abundance of **churches.** Thalpos Travel can provide a map that pinpoints many of them. A good place to start your tour is around the harbor to the far right, where beautiful whitewashed **Panagia ston Pirgho** perches on the rocks. Follow the stairs below the church and up along the sea-edge of the city. Along the way pass tiny, simple **Evangelismos and Athanasios**—just below the Castro—the town's oldest church, built in the 11th century. Just off to the left is **Genessis tou Christou,** a larger cruciform church with a round cupola and clock tower. Continuing up the side of the city, walk over the **Castro,** originally built by King Philip of Macedon in the 4th century BC. Today it is the site of Anatoli, a traditional tavern featuring live Greek music. On the uphill side of the Castro, wind your way into town and head for the top of the hill, where **Spiridon** rewards tired hikers. Slightly farther into the city lies **Papameletiou,** a cruciform basilica built in 1662 with a red-tile roof and small clock tower. Closer to the waterfront, **Ag. Nikolaos,** just up Galatsaniou on the left, exhibits brightly colored icons and a marble statue of the Virgin. In **Mikhail-Sinnadon,** next to the Internet cafe, a stone cruciform basilica features a remarkable iconostasis. Skopelos draws international students and recognition for its **Photographic Center of Skopelos** (☎24 121); call for more info. The **Folklore Museum,** 100m left past the OTE, has a dull collection of island artifacts, but the meticulously researched first-floor exhibit on popular religion is worth a look. (☎23 494. Open 11am-1:30pm and 7-9pm. 500dr/€1.47.)

A 10min. walk up the whitewashed stairs on the far right of the waterfront leads to **Anatoli,** the haunt of one of the world's last great *rembetika* singers, Giorgos Xintaris. Some nights (usually a little before midnight), you may be lucky enough to catch him with a group of friends singing the old songs. The sounds and setting are phenomenal. For new jazz and blues, **Platanos Jazz Club,** on the far right of the harbor facing inland, near the jetty, lets you relax with a drink by candlelight under a gargantuan tree. (☎23 661. Beer 800-1500dr/€2.35-4.40, cocktails 1700-1900dr/€5-5.60. Open 8am-3pm.) **The Blue Bar,** two blocks up Galanatsiou in an alley on the right (just past the church of Ag. Nikolaos), plays folk, rock, and blues music that accompanies the 800dr/€2.35 beers just fine. Skopelos's **dance clubs** cluster midway up a street off of Pl. Platanos. The talkative bartender at **Metro** will tell you about the island; you could meet American painting students. (☎24 446. Open May-Oct. daily, Oct.-May weekends only.) **Kavnos** (☎24 300) is Skopelos's oldest bar—8 years and counting. Top 40 and foreign hits shake the speakers.

🌊 BEACHES

Traveling Skopelos's asphalt road by bus or car to Loutraki or Glossa gives you your pick of the lovely southern beaches. Archaeologists discovered the tomb of the ancient Cretan general **Stafylos** on a nearby hillside, along with a 15th-century BC gold-plated sword that's now in the Volos museum. Stafylos beach is crowded with families; nearby **Valanio,** over the hill to the left as you face the sea, is less full. Named for the trickling spring that was a gushing fountain in Roman times, today Valanio is advertised as the only nude beach on Skopelos. Past the small town of **Agnondas,** a paved road leads about 1km to the sparkling blue beach of **Limonari;** ask the bus driver to let you off at the top of the road or take a water taxi. Farther along the asphalt road is the wide, deep bay of **Panormos,** the ancient forest. From here, a 5min. walk leads to the isolated **Adrina** beaches, named or the female pirate who terrorized the islands, leaping to her death in this cove after being cornered by angry islanders. Silvery **Milia,** the island's largest, and by many accounts most beautiful, beach is accessible by paved road, has water sports and its own little islet called **Dassia.** Closer to Loutraki, dirt paths lead to the northern beaches of **Spilia, Marraki, Keramoto,** and **Chondroyiorghi.**

❧ HIKES FROM SKOPELOS TOWN

Due to Skopelos's predominantly dirt roads, the island is best explored by moped or on foot. The island's single, 35km-long asphalt road runs from the Skopelos bus station through Stafylos (4km), Agnondas (8km), Panormos (18km), Elios (24km), Loutraki (30km), and Glossa (32km).

Dragon Cliffs. According to local lore, a fierce dragon went on a flaming bender and ate almost everyone on Skopelos, until Ag. Rigine appeared on the scene and killed it, thus becoming the island's protector. The Dragon Cliffs *(Drakondoschisma)*, where the creature was hurled to its death, are now a quiet picnicking spot with a sea view and an altar portraying the dragon's grisly demise. (To find it, take the asphalt road from Skopelos Town and turn left down a small dirt road which disappears into the woods about 1km before Agnodas beach.)

Monasteries of Mt. Palouki. Two paved roads leave the town from the bus depot on the right end of the waterfront. To reach the monasteries, follow the road out of the harbor to the left (facing inland)—signs mark the way to the monasteries ascending Mt. Palouki. **Evangelismos** was built in the 18th century as part of the Monastery of Xiropotamos of Athos, but its enormous altar screen—the genuine article from Constantinople—is 400 years older. Take the left-hand fork up the hot, winding mountain road for 45min.; start early in the morning before the heat and bugs intensify and in time to reach the monasteries before their 1-5pm daily closing. Up the right fork, another 45min. walk leads you to the **Monastery of the Transfiguration** (Metamorphosis). Its chapel, set in a flowered courtyard, dates from the 16th century. Another hour up the hill along the road takes you to two monasteries perched on precipitous ridges overlooking the sea. The first, the **Monastery of St. Barbara,** was built as a fortress in 1648. Nearby **Prodromou** contains icons dating back to the 14th and 15th centuries and wall paintings. Once a monastery, Prodromou is now a cloister dedicated to St. John the Baptist; its astounding setting surveys the entire coast. The dirt path that begins behind the building leads to the smaller monasteries of **Agia Triada** and **Agia Taxianches.**

Monasteries of Agios Ioannis. At the end of the road on the opposite side of the island from Skopelos Town, the quiet hilltop town of **Glossa** looks down on Skopelos's second port. For a four-hour round-trip hike from Glossa, walk the dirt track across the island to the **Monastery of Agios Ioannis,** clinging to a boulder above the ocean. Take the main road east from Glossa and turn left on the first dirt road to Steki Taverna; it's clear sailing after that. At the road's end, a path drops to the sea and stone steps, cut in the escarpment, lead up to the monastery. The entire road is navigable by motorbike, up to the stairs.

Monastery of Agia Anna. Another hike takes you to the eastern side of Skopelos, to the beautiful, secluded monastery of Agia Anna. Leave Skopelos Town and head toward Mt. Palouki on the road past the Monastery of St. Barbara and Ag. Triada. The road ends soon after—watch for the old sign pointing to the church.

ALONNISOS Αλοννησος

Of the twenty-odd islands within Greece's new National Marine Park, only Alonnisos is inhabited, and its fledgling tourist industry remains friendly to visitors who come to explore its sudden blues and wide open spaces. The untouched northern coast, with its cliffs awash in green pine and white sand boundary with the sea, draws hikers to its highland trails. Archaeological discoveries made on the island revealed its ancient prosperity; presently it flourishes quietly, rebuilding after a 1950 leaf blight devastated the island's famous wine industry and a 1965 earthquake forced its residents to move from Hora to Patitiri. **Gioura,** a small island to the northeast of Alonnisos, is believed to have been the home of **Polyphemus,** the cyclops whose eye was gouged out by Odysseus' sizzling lance. Though many islands claim this distinction, Gioura best fits Homer's description of Polyphemus's cavern and of the now-endangered brown goats with black crosses on their backs, which are now its sole inhabitants.

PATITIRI Πατητηρι   ☎ 0424

All boats dock at Patitiri, which is, for all intents and purposes, the only town on the island. Above, whitewashed Hora (Old Town) clings to the slopes of the hill. Sharp-angled and hastily built, it's not a postcard harbor, but it serves as an easily accessible base to explore the rest of Alonnisos and the surrounding Marine Park.

◼◪ ORIENTATION AND PRACTICAL INFORMATION

From the docks, two main parallel streets run inland: **Pelasgon** on the left, and **Ikion Dolophon** on the right. **Ferries** run to: Agios Konstantinos (5½hr., 8-9 per week, 4400dr/ €12.90); Skiathos (2hr., 1-2 per day, 1900dr/€5.58); Skopelos (30min., 1-2 per day, 1100dr/€3.23); and Volos (5¼hr., 4 per week, 3900dr/€11.45). **Flying Dolphins** go to: Agios Konstantinos (2¾hr., 1-2 per day, 9000dr/€26.41); Glossa (35min., 2-4 per day, 3800dr/€11.15); Skopelos (25min., 4-8 per day, 2200dr/€6.46); Skiathos (1¼hr., 4-8 per day, 3800dr/€11.15); Thessaloniki (4hr., 3 per week, 8700dr/€25.53); Volos (2½hr., 2-4 per day, 7700dr/€22.60). Boats to Skyros and Kimi begin running in July. Expect prices to increase by 100-200dr/€0.29-0.59 the July-Aug. high season.

The island's **bus** runs from its waterfront stop to **Hora** (every hr. 9am-3:15pm and 7-10pm, 300dr/€0.88) and to **Steni Vala** twice per day. Schedules are posted at the Patitiri, Hora, and Steni Vala stops. **Taxis,** lined up along the waterfront, run until 2am; they respond to calls any time (taxi phone numbers are posted on phone booths). **Motorbikes,** the fastest way to explore Alonnisos's charms, are available for rent at the numerous shops on Pelasgon and Ikion Dolophon. Expect to pay 3000-7000dr/€8.80-11.75 per day.

Alonnisos Travel, in the center of the waterfront, **exchanges currency,** finds rooms, books excursions, and sells ferry tickets. (☎65 188; fax 65 511. Open daily 9am-10pm.) Up Ikion Dolophon, the **Port Police** are on the corner. (☎65 595. Open 24hr.) The **National Bank** with 24hr. **ATM** lies on the left. (☎65 777. Open M-Th 8am-2pm, F 8am-1:30pm.) The **police** (☎65 205) are on the top of the hill, near the **hospital.** (☎65 208. Open daily 9am-1pm, 24hr. for emergency.) **Internet access** is available at **Il Mondo** on Ikion Dolophon, to the right just before the post office. (☎65 834. Open daily 9:30am-5:30pm. Internet 1200/€3.52 per hr, 500dr/€1.47 minimum; printing 100dr/€0.29 per page; faxes 800dr/€2.35 per page.) The **post office** is a 5min. walk up Ikion Dolophon. (☎65 560. Open M-F 7:30am-2pm.) **Postal code:** 37005.

▟ ACCOMMODATIONS

The **Rooms to Let Office** next to Ikos Travel can lend a hand to travelers looking for a place to stay. (☎66 188. Open daily 10am-2pm and 6-10pm.) **Panorama,** down the first alley on the left up Ikion Dolophon (walk up the stairs to the top of the hill and turn in at the courtyard on the right), rents bright rooms and studios with private baths, common fridges, and large, bougainvillea-covered common balconies with a port view. (☎65 240. Doubles 6000-14,000dr/€17.61-41.10; triples 7000-15,000dr/€20.53-44.) Inquire at Boutique Mary, on the right side of Pelasgon, about simple rooms with private baths at the **Dimakis Pension** next door. (☎65 294. Singles 5000-7000dr/€14.67-20.53; doubles 8000-10,000dr/€23.48-29.35.) Magdalini and Ilias Mpesinis rent immaculate **Rooms and Studios** with private baths, kitchens, and fridges, about

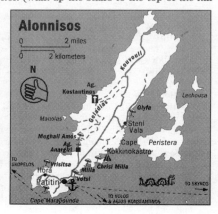

Alonnisos

0   2 miles
0   2 kilometers

N

Kouvouli
Ag. Kostantinos
Geraldias
Manolas
Glyfa
Steni Vala
Cape Peristera
Meghali Amos
Ag. Anargiri
Kokkinokastro
Lechousa
TO SKOPELOS
Vrisitsa
Milia
Chrisi Milia
Hora
Votsi
Patitiri
TO SKYROS
Cape Marapounda
TO VOLOS & AGIOS KONSTANTINOS

200m up Pelasgon on the left, across from I'M Motorbikes. A gorgeous stone stair-case and hand-painted decor adds to the atmosphere; it's worth the splurge. (☎/fax 65 451. Book exchange. Singles 6000-11,000dr/€17.61-32.28; doubles 7000-12,000dr/€20.53-35.22.)

FOOD AND NIGHTLIFE

Locals adore the little *ouzeri* **To Kamaki,** on the left side of Ikion Dolophon past the National Bank. Try the delectable warm octopus salad for 1700dr/€5. (☎ 65 245. Open daily noon-2:30pm and 7pm-late.) Stop by popular **To Steki** (☎ 65 816), on the corner of Pelasgon, for cheap but tasty souvlaki and gyros (350-450dr/€1.03-1.32.) **Artolikoudies,** just up from the harbor on the right of Pelasgon, serves delicious summer olive bread (400dr/€1.17) and traditional pastries (250-400dr/€0.73-1.17). Listen to Sting while you sip a cocktail (2000dr/€5.87) under a gnarled tree and a grape-draped terrace at water-front **Pub Dennis,** the island's oldest cafe-bar. **Club Enigma,** a bright blue building on Pelasgon, is the (only) place to boogie. (Open June-Sept. W-Sa.)

SIGHTS AND BEACHES

The **History and Folklore Museum** of Alonnisos, to the far left of the waterfront facing inland and up the stairs, features a wide variety of cultural artifacts from Alonnisos. Exhibits include weaponry from major conflicts from the Balkan Wars to World War II, historical maps of the Sporades and Greece, and, downstairs, an excellent series of **trade exhibits** on everything from winemaking to pack-saddle construction. (Open daily 11am-7pm. 1000dr/€2.93.)

Many **beaches** are accessible from the island's main road, which runs along the spine of the island from Patitiri to the port of Gherakas in the far north. A 90-minute walk on this road from Patitiri takes you to **Votsi,** the island's other major settlement. Local boys cliff-dive at Votsi beach just outside the village. Beyond Votsi, the road passes the pine-girded beaches of **Milia** and **Chrisi Milia.** The beaches are also accessible by **rented boat** from Votsi; ask at the port. Further up the coast from Chrisi Milia is the beach and archaeological site of **Kokkinocastro,** where swimmers occasionally find ancient coins. The tiny fishing village of **Steni Vala,** 12km north of Palitini, with a population fluctuating between 25 and 60, is the only other bus stop (20min., 2 per day, 400dr/€1.17)—the fantastic fish tavernas alone are worth the trip. Sandy **Glyla** beach is along the shore, north of the village.

HIKES AND THE OUTDOORS

Only the south end of the island is inhabited, leaving stretches of mountain wilderness. Though a **moped** remains the quickest way to explore—Patitiri to Gerakas takes about two hours—it's worth **hiking.** Trails are marked at regular intervals and include terrain from paved roads to steep, rocky trails. **Blue maps,** scattered throughout the island, mark trailheads and show the trail routes, which are marked by **numerical yellow signs,** but you may still want to pick up *Alonnisos on Foot* (2800dr/€8.22), a walking and swimming guide, or the Anavasi map *Nature, Culture, Footpaths and Beaches* (1000dr/€2.93), both available in Patitiri. Numbers below refer to marked trail numbers.

From Hora. Four hiking trails lead down from Hora to **beaches** and overlooks in the southern part of Alonnisos. The trail to **Mikros Mourtias (#1,** 1.5km, 45min.) begins at the bus stop. Walk through town, past the church, and up the stairs to a street lined with cafes. Turn left before the street ends and walk down the narrow side street to the trailhead. Mikros Mourtias is a small pebble beach on an inlet. **Kalovoulos (#2,** 1.5km, 45min.), is an enchanting overlook on the rocky coast east of Hora. Continue on the main road past the bus stop; the trail is on the left. A tiny beach on a secluded cove, **Vrisitsa (#3,** 1km, 30min.) is accessible by trail to the right off the main road just past the bus stop in Hora. **Patitiri (#4,** 1.5km, 45min.) trail connects the Old Town to the New, off the main road just before the bus stop.

Around Alonnisos. The **Meghalo Nero - Ag. Anarghiri - Meghali Amos - Raches - Votsi** (**#5**, 6km, 2½hr.) trail takes you along the southeastern side of Alonnisos, to the secluded **monastery** of Ag. Anarghiri and **beach** of Meghali Amos. The trailhead is just up the main road from Votsi. Head out Ikion Dolophon from Patitiri to get to the main road, then follow the signs to Votsi and Steni Vala. From Meghali Amos, two trails, **#7** (1½hr.) and **#8** (1½hr.) lead north to **Meghalo Chorafi**, east of the main road, the hub for hikes to **Ag. Laka beach** (**#14**, 45min.) and the church of **Ag. Kostantinos** (**#6**, 2hr.). From Ag. Kostantinos, hikes lead north to the church of **Ag. Georgios** (**#12**, 1hr.) and **Meleghakia** (**#13**, 1½hr.) in the more rugged part of the island. Hikes **#12** and **13** both bring you back to the main road. From **Steni Vala**, hike **#10** (1hr.) takes you south past the beach of **Ag. Petros** to **Isomata** and on to the main road. From Isomata, hike **#9** winds its way down to **Leftos** beach (45min.). Far north on the island, past Ag. George, a dirt road leads to the trailhead for trail **#11**, which leads down to the beach of **Ag. Dimitrios** (1hr.).

◆ DAYTRIPS FROM PATITIRI

HORA (OLD TOWN) Χωρα   ☎0424

The island's only bus runs from Patitiri to Hora (10min., every hr. 9am-3:15pm and 7-10pm, 300dr/€0.88). Schedules are posted at the bus stop in each town. Taxis are available (about 2000dr/€5.87 round-trip). A parching walk leads to a glorious view—start uphill on Pelasgon and continue on the main road for 1½hr. Bring water. Lots of water.

Set high on a hill to ward off pirates, Hora sprawls stony and proud, its crooked streets twisting into the dusty hills. The quiet, old alleys open suddenly onto incredible views of the island. From here, you can spy out your own private beach and head down toward it. Tiny 12th-century **Christ Church** is run by Papa Gregorias, the village priest and local legend. Many great hikes in Alonnisos begin in Hora. **Hiliadroma**, up behind the church, has wood-accented rooms with stone floors, tiled private baths, and fantastic balcony views. Some rooms have kitchenettes. (☎65 814. Doubles 12,000dr/€35.22.) Hora is host to a variety of quaint cafes and taverns, some perched on beautiful overlooks. From the bus stop, veer left up the hill past the old church, continuing up the stairs past the overlook to reach a charming paved street with several cafes; the best views are at the end of the street. **Taverna Aloni**, up the right-hand fork from the bus station at the base of an old windmill (sans blades), serves traditional Greek food with a spectacular view of the island. (Starters 700dr/€2.05; entrees 1800dr/€5.28 and up.)

NATIONAL MARINE PARK

The park islands are accessible by specially licensed boat. Most trips, advertised and sold along the Patitiri harborfront, are all-inclusive single-day trips for 10,000-12,000dr/ €29.35-35.22. MOM's HQ is open May-Oct. daily 10am-4pm and 6-10:30pm. (info@mom.gr; www.mom.gr.)

Surrounding Alonnisos are the 25 small, ecologically protected islets of Greece's National Marine Park. The largest and most important are **Peristera, Skantzoura, Piperi, Kyra Panagia, Jura,** and **Psatnoura.** They're strictly regulated and visited only by organized tour boats in summer. Psatnoura, Kyra Panagia, and Skantzoura are owned by nearby Mt. Athos (see p. 246) and are used in part for grazing goats. Visiting Jura and Piperi is forbidden in an effort to protect species once described by Homer, including the **Mediterranean monk seal.** The monk seals number only about 500 total in the Mediterranean; a growing colony of approximately 50 monk seals is now carefully monitored by MOM, an Alonnisos-based sea patrol unit named for the Latin name of the seals, *monachus monachus.* Unless you're a MOM official, forget about seeing the monk seals. Enthusiasts *are* free to draw a **"Save the Seals"** poster for the gallery in MOM's Alonnisos ferry dock headquarters. They provide crayons, paper, and info in English about ecology and conservation efforts.

SKYROS
Σκυρος

From the sea, Skyros's cliffs and rippled hills spread out in greens and yellows under an infinitely blue sky. The hilly terrain once fortified the island against marauding pirates, but now the island is now trying to fight off modern culture. Skyros Town, its capital, and the island's northern and southern wilds remain traditional and separate, the last stand of ghosts, poets, and pirate kings.

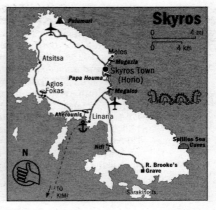

SKYROS TOWN (HORIO)   ☎ 0222

Splashed against the mountains like a breaker foaming against rocky shores, stark-white Skyros Town hangs frozen in time, suspended between a growing modern tourist economy and traditional folkways. Here old men sew sandals by porchlight late into the evening, women embroider patterns learned from pirates, and a crazed goat-man spooks the streets at Carnival. Maze-like and haunted, cobbled and china-plated, the town is a swiftly closing window to a strange dream.

▐ TRANSPORTATION

The best way to get to Skyros is to take the **bus** from **Athens** to **Kimi** on Evia (3½hr., 2 per day, 2600dr/€7.63), then the **ferry** to Skyros from Kimi (2 per day, 2500dr/€7.34). Note: buses to **Kimi** stop in the town, 5km from the ferry port; less frequent buses to **Skyros** go directly to and from the ferry dock. If you land in Kimi proper, either take a **taxi** from the bus station or walk down the long winding road. No ferries run to the other Sporades.

Flying Dolphins travel twice per day along two routes to: **Thessaloniki** (13,400dr/€39.33) via **Alonnisos** (1¼hr., 8000dr/€23.48), **Skopelos** (1¾hr., 8000dr/€23.48), **Skiathos** (2¼hr., 8400dr/€24.65) and **Moudania**; and **Volos** (4½hr., 14,100dr/€41.38) via **Alonnisos** (1¼hr., 8000dr/€23.48), **Skopelos** (1¾hr., 8000dr/€23.48) and **Skiathos** (2¼hr., 8400dr/€24.65). Boats to Skyros arrive in **Linaria,** the tiny western port; a **local bus** to Skyros Town picks up when ferries and hydrofoils arrive (20min., 3 per day, 260dr/€0.76) and leaves Skyros Town about one hour prior to ferry departures; another bus runs from Skyros Town to **Molos** (10min., 1 per day, 280dr/€0.82). Skyros Travel posts schedules. Buses stop in Skyros Town (Horio—"the village"—to locals) at the base of **Agoras**, the town's backbone road, which heads straight uphill from the stop. Veering left and downhill from the stop, the road winds around the base of hill, passing Magazia on its way to Molos. The **military airport** (☎91 607), 20km from Skyros Town on the island's northern tip, flies to Athens (35min., 2 per week, 16,000dr/€46.96); you'll have to take a cab there (2500dr/€7.34). **Taxis** (☎91 666) wait by the central plateia or the bus stop; they aren't available late at night or during siesta hours.

✦ ⁊ ORIENTATION AND PRACTICAL INFORMATION

Shops, pharmacies, bars, and restaurants ascend the hill in Skyros Town along **Agoras.** Mazelike residential streets scatter out in every direction along the hillsides. Buildings are numbered counter-intuitively, and few streets are named; when venturing off Agoras, pick out landmarks on your way. At the far end of

HAVING HIS DAY Poet **Rupert Brooke**, known, among other things, for coining the expression "every dog has his day," was a British national hero long before his death. Golden-haired Brooke was the empire's articulate darling, lettered and muscled, bright and impetuous. He signed up with the Hood Battalion of the Royal Naval Division in September 1914: "Well, if Armageddon's *on*, I suppose one should be there." After the disastrous Antwerp expedition, he became more patriotic and more serious, continuing to fight for his country despite presentiments of death. Brooke sailed with the British Mediterranean Expeditionary Force in February 1915, during the ill-fated Dardanelles campaign. He made it to Limnos and Egypt before dying of blood poisoning aboard a French hospital ship at Skyros on April 23, Ag. George's Day. At night, by torchlight, he was buried about a mile inland. His grave, a simple wooden cross bearing his name and dates of birth and death, is accessible from Linaria on the southwestern part of the island by car or foot. In a prophetic poem, Brooke left instructions for those who might visit his final resting place: "If I should die, think only this of me: / There is some corner of a foreign field / That is forever England."

town, **Pl. Rupert Brooke,** looking out across Molos and the sea, is dedicated to British poet Brooke and to "immortal poetry" (Αθανατη την ποιησι). To reach Pl. Brooke, walk up Agoras through town until it forks left at Calypso Bar. Head left along the wall and walk up until you reach a sign pointing to "Brooke & Museums" (right) and Γιαλος (beach, left). Veer right and follow the narrow street to the plateia. At the top of the hill, before descending to the plateia, a sign points the way up marble-edged steps to the **Monastery of Ag. George** and the **castle.** At Pl. Rupert Brooke, the stairs to the right pass the **archaeological museum** on a 15min. descent to the beach; stairs straight ahead lead to the **Faltaits Museum.**

Skyros Travel, past the central plateia on Agoras, sells **Olympic Airways** tickets; it's also a de facto tourist office, organizing bus and boat excursions and helping visitors find lodging. The **port office** in Linaria opens according to ferry and hydrofoil arrivals. (☎91 123 or 91 600; fax 92 123. Open daily 9am-2:30pm and 6:30-11pm.) The **National Bank,** just past the central plateia, has a 24hr. **ATM.** (Open M-Th 8am-2pm and F 8am-1:30pm.) The **hospital** (☎92 222) is just out of town behind the Hotel Nefeli. Ask at the **police** station for **doctors** in town; turn right just past Skyros Travel, walk to the end of the road, and take another right. It's the white building with light blue gates. (☎91 274. Open 24hr., but small staff may be away on another call.) There are **pharmacies** on the right near the central plateia (☎91 617; open 8:30am-1pm and 6:30-10pm) and on the right past Skyros Travel. (☎91 111. Open daily 9am-2pm and 6pm-1am.) **Internet access** is available at **Mepoh Cafe** on Agoras. (☎91 016. 1500dr/€4.40 per hr., 500dr/€1.47 minimum; printing 150dr/€ 0.44 per page.) The **OTE** is opposite the police. (☎91 399. Open M-F 7:30am-1pm.) The **post office** is across the central plateia from Agoras. (☎91 208. Open M-F 7:30am-2pm.) **Postal code:** 34007.

ACCOMMODATIONS AND CAMPING

Coming to Skyros and staying in a hotel is like coming to Greece to paddle in a pool—you've got to stay in a Skyrian house. You'll be met at the bus stop by old women offering domatia; you can also wander the narrow stairs with any sort of luggage, and you'll be asked the simple question, *"Domatia?"* The thick-walled houses are treasure troves, brimming with Delft ceramics, Italian linens, icons, embroidery, metalwork, and fine china bought from long-dead pirates who looted throughout the Mediterranean. Expect to pay 5000-12,000dr/€14.67-35.22 for a room, depending on size and season. If you decide to stay in a Skyrian house, always **bargain** over the price and look carefully for landmarks and house numbers, as the streets may be extremely confusing, and it's easy to lose your way. The aid of a travel agency will cost you an arm, a leg, and the essence of the whole experience. If you arrive during siesta, the town is dead as a doornail, and your calls for a domatia may be answered only with snores from within.

If you don't feel like searching for a room, try **Hotel Elena,** just up the road from the bus station on Agoras. The spartan but comfortable rooms have private baths, balconies, and common fridges. (☎91 738 or 91 070. Singles 5000dr/€14.67; doubles 10,000dr/€29.35; triples 12,000dr/€35.22.) On the road leading from Pl. Rupert Brooke down to the beach, **Camping Skyros** offers the amenities of a restaurant and a mini-market. (☎92 458. 1500dr/€4.40 per person; tents 1000dr/€2.93.)

🚶🍴 FOOD AND NIGHTLIFE

After a long afternoon swim, you can't go wrong with Skyrian food. The incredible 🍽O **Pappou Kai Ego** ("Grandpa and Me"), toward the top of Agoras on the right—look for the light green chairs—concocts a brilliant chicken *o pappous* floating in a light cream sauce over rice, as well as many Skyrian specialties, including nannygoat au lemon. (☎93 200. Entrees 1600-2500dr/€4.70-7.34. Open daily 8am-2pm and 8pm-late. Get there early to avoid a long wait.) **Kristina's at Pegasus,** down the alley to the left just past Skyros Travel, cooks up some vegetarian entrees in a quiet courtyard. Try the fresh hot herb bread (700dr/€2.05) or other delicious dishes (1600-1800dr/€4.70-5.28). Just before O Pappas, **Obelistirio** serves up a slow-cooked, just-shy-of-healthy, but incredibly delicious 450dr/€1.32 gyro. (☎92 205. Open daily 6pm-2am.) **Kalypso Bar,** at the top of Agoras past O Pappous, is a mellow place to sip a nightcap after a tasty Skyrian meal. Jazz music keeps the mood in concert with the dusky night. (Cocktails 1800dr/€5.28.)

📷🎵 SIGHTS AND ENTERTAINMENT

The 🏛**Faltaits Museum,** just past Pl. Rupert Brooke, is the private collection of a Skyrian ethnologist, and shouldn't be missed. Tours available in English guide you through the frozen-in-time ancestral home of the Faltaits family. The extensive holdings include beautiful examples of embroidery, carved furniture, pottery, costumes, copperware, rare books, and relics from the island's annual carnival—it's an excellent introduction to the island's traditional culture. The wise, friendly staff speak perfect English, affectionately calling the museum "a place where the nine muses meet." Conferences and cultural activities are held here throughout the year, including a **theater and dance festival** in late July and August; ask the staff for dates and times. (☎91 232 or 91 150; faltaits@otenet.gr. Open daily 10am-1pm and 6-9pm. 500dr/€1.47.) Down the stairs to the right of Pl. Rupert Brooke, the **Archaeological Museum** holds significant island artifacts culled from on-going excavations around the island, including Bronze-Age and Mycenaean relics. (☎91 327. Open Tu-Su 8:30am-3pm. 500dr/€1.47.) Both museums have rooms decorated as traditional Skyrian homes. Most Skyrians are very proud of their abodes—don't be afraid to knock on a door in the evening and ask to peek inside.

High above Skyros Town, the thousand-year-old **Monastery of Ag. George** and the **Castle of Licomidus** command magnificent views of Skyrian sunsets. Follow Agoras uphill, veering left before Kalypso bar; at the top of the hill, a small sign points the way right up marble-edged steps, which lead you to the monastery and castle. What looks like a ruin from below is actually a beautiful, rose-gardened monastic complex. Wear good shoes, as the worn stones are slippery, and dress modestly: the official sign demands that you not be "half-naked" if you want to peek at the monastery's 11th-century fresco of Ag. George. Then climb to the *castro,* generally believed to be a stellar Venetian repair of an earlier Byzantine castle. If you need a miracle, light a candle in the church of Ag. George—the saints' active presence often aids grateful locals, who have dedicated two-thirds of the island to him. (Open daily Mar.-Aug. 7am-10pm, Sept.-Feb. 7:30am-6pm.)

Skyros is best known among Hellenes for its **Skyrian Carnival,** which runs every weekend in February, culminating on the first day of Lent, 40 days before Easter. On this *Kathari Deftera,* an old man dressed in a goat mask and a costume covered with clanging sheep bells leads two young men, one dressed as a Skyrian bride and the other as a 17th-century European (with a large bell hanging from his

waist), on a wild dance through town to the monastery. The festival commemorates a land dispute between shepherds and farmers and draws upon many myths
and religious customs. One hypothesis holds that the transvestism alludes to
Achilles, who dodged the Trojan War draft on Skyros by dressing as a girl.

BEACHES

The pleasant beach below town stretches along the coast through the villages of
Magazia and **Molos,** and continues around the point. Crowded and crawling with
children in July and August, it's undeniably convenient. The local nude beach,
ironically named *Tou papa to homa* (The Sands of the Priest), remains clean and
uncrowded, just south of the local beach. To get there, follow the seaside road
south past Club Skyropoula and some low-ceilinged concrete structures (10-
12min.); a narrow, spiky-plant-lined, slippery dirt path leads downhill along a wire
fence. Be especially careful on the last 10ft. of the trail. From here, you'll have a
beautiful view of the **Southern Mountain,** famous in local literature and poetry for
its hourly color changes in the sloping island light. Once home to nymphs, the
now-deserted **natural spring** at **Nifi Beach,** south of Linaria, allows you to frolic solo.
Scenically barren beaches and **Rupert Brooke's grave** on the southern portion of the
island are accessible only by dusty paths or by boat. If you ask, buses from Linaria
to Skyros Town may stop at the beaches of **Aherounis,** on the west coast, and **Mia-
los** on the east. Boats can explore the one-time pirate grottoes at **Spillies,** on the
southeastern coast, and **Sarakino Island,** formerly Despot's Island and one of the
largest pirate centers in the Aegean. During Ottoman rule, it was an important hid-
ing-place for ships. Keep an eye out for the endangered **Skyrian horses.**

EVIA Ευβοια

The second-largest island in Greece (and one of the most convenient for Athenians), Evia is a microcosmic vacation continent of warm waters, forested highlands, therapeutic baths, and archaeological treasures. Its capital, Halkida,
reaches out to the mainland via a new suspension bridge. Ferries from ports near
Athens connect the mainland at other locations along the western coast of the
island: Aedipsos, Marmari, and Karystos. Kimi, on the island's east coast, is a convenient ferry hub for the Sporades. Though flooded by Greek vacationers in the
summer season, Evia remains a beautiful, diverse destination for all travelers.

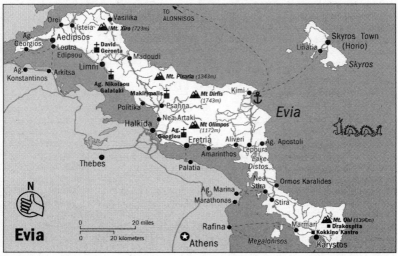

HALKIDA Χαλκιδα ☎ 0221

Sprawling, modern Halkida (also known as Chalkyda or Chalkis)—the third largest city in Greece—is the capital of Evia as well as its major transportation hub, connecting the island to the mainland. Its sparkling waterfront promenade and archaeological artifacts, nearby beaches and fresh seafood make Halkida a prime starting point for exploration of the island.

TRANSPORTATION

Halkida's main thoroughfare is tree-lined **El. Venizelou,** which runs inland perpendicular to **Voudouri** (the waterfront) for about 12 blocks before bending left into **Eikost Oktovriou.** The **Erippon Bridge,** or **Old Bridge,** connects Halkida to the mainland at the end of the waterfront to the left off El. Venizelou, and points due west, with Halkida at your back. Halkida also joins the mainland via the new **suspension bridge** on the city's south edge, now the connection point for most ground transportation. Halkida's hangar-like **bus terminal** is just off **Papanastasiou,** which intersects with El. Venizelou. **Buses** travel to: **Aedipsos Springs** (2½hr., 3 per day 10:15am-5:15pm, 2250dr/€6.61); **Athens** (2 per hr., 1450dr/€4.25); **Karystos** (3½hr., 3 per day 6am-5:30pm, 2500dr/€7.35); **Kimi** (1½hr., 9 per day, 1800dr/€5.28); **Limni** (2hr., 4 per day 8:30am-5:15pm, 1700dr/€5). **Trains** go to **Athens** (17 per day, 900dr/€2.64). From the train station, cross the Old Bridge and take a left along the waterfront; Venizelou intersects it five blocks down. **Taxis** (☎ 25 220) are available 24hr.

ORIENTATION AND PRACTICAL INFORMATION

The **port authority,** across the Old Bridge in the huge building, can help you with information about the city. (☎ 28 888. Open daily 8am-3pm.) The **National Bank** is on El. Venizelou 2 blocks from the water, with a 24hr. **ATM** and **currency exchange.** (Open M-Th 8am-2pm, F 8am-1:30pm.) The English-speaking **tourist police** are only available in the mornings and are entirely inconvenient; their office is a 25min. walk up Venizelou and onto Oktovriou, in the same building as the regular **police.** Call instead. (☎ 77 777. Open 24hr. except when out on call.) To get to the **hospital** (☎ 21 901), head up Venizelou away from the water and turn left onto Arethoussas, the next left after Papanastasiou. Follow the street as it curves and turn left on Chatzopoulou. The hospital is two blocks down on the right. **Dollars** (☎ 79 446), located half a block up from the waterfront around the corner from Hotel Kentrikon, has fast **internet access.** (1200dr/€3.52 per hr. Open daily noon-3am.) On the way you'll pass **Pl. Agios Nikolas,** spilling back from the waterfront, where the **public library** and the **Church of Agios Nikolas** rest. Dress modestly to enter the church. The **OTE** (☎ 22 599), is at the intersection of El. Venizelou and Papanastasiou. The **post office** is on Karamourtzouni between El. Venizelou and Pl. Agios Nikolas, the 2nd left from the waterfront. (Open M-F 7:30am-2pm.) **Postal code:** 34100.

ACCOMMODATIONS AND FOOD

Most hotels here are of the 25,000dr/€73.37-per-night variety, catering to business travelers or Athenian families, so Halkida is not an ideal place to spend the night. That said, there are two good options. **Hotel Kentrikon,** the peach-colored building at Ageli Gobiou 5—the last left off El. Venizelou heading toward the water—has a Greek-Canadian proprietor, George Giotas, who is happy to help you make sense of the city. The spartan, functional rooms have TVs, phones, and sinks; most have shared baths. (☎ 22 375 or 27 260; hotel_Kentrikon@hotmail.com; www.geocities.com/hotel_kentrikon. 24hr. reception. Singles 7000dr/€20.53; doubles 9000-13,000dr/€26.41-38.15; triples 9000-10,000dr/€26.41-29.35.) On the mainland across the Old Bridge, **Hotel Hara** is a sharp right turn on Karoni, which runs uphill behind the Port Authority. The bright white rooms (TV, private bath, balconies) are a bargain for larger groups—look for the flags about a block down. (☎ 76 305; fax 76 309. Singles 10,000dr/€29.35; doubles 16,000dr/€46.96; triples 18,000dr/€52.83.)

Like hotels, restaurants in Halkida are budget-busting, though the fresh seafood available along the waterfront may justify the cost. Several bakeries hide on streets around Ag. Nikolas; fast food joints are bunched at the base of El. Venizelou and near the Old Bridge on the waterfront. For a traditional meal head to **Folia** (Φωλια), across from the park on the Evia side of the Old Bridge. Entrees (600-1500dr/€1.76-4.40) rotate daily; try the *dolmades* (900dr/€2.64) on Monday or the *soupies stifado* (squid with onions, 1400dr/€4.10) on Wednesday.

👁 SIGHTS

Halkida's kilometer-long waterfront promenade, **Venidou,** which stretches from the Old Bridge to the Red House, is a worthy sight in and of itself. Breezy and palm-lined, Venidou makes for a splendid evening stroll. The fresh seafood available at many restaurants along its length, though pricey, may be worth the splurge. Or save a few drachmas sipping a *frappé*, and do some quality people watching.

The **Archaeological Museum,** on El. Venizelou across from the National Bank, is full of findings from the Neolithic, Classical and Roman eras. It's worth a look for its impressive collection of marble statuary and busts, pottery, and shimmering gold laurels. (☎76 131. Open Tu-Su 8:30am-3pm. 500dr/€1.47, under 18 free.) The white **Church of Ag. Nikolas,** just off of Venidou to the right of El. Venizelou, displays beautiful paintings and vaulted arches. Proper attire required. (Usually open 9am-1pm.) You can trace the Halkidian life of **Nikos Skalkotas,** artist and composer, at his childhood and adult homes; he grew up at Kotsouparlou 35 in the maze behind Oktovriou street, and later moved out to the pale yellow dock's-end cube past the internet cafe. Call the tourist police (☎77 777) for an appointment.

🔁 DAYTRIPS FROM HALKIDA

AEDIPSOS SPRINGS Λουτρα Αιδηψου

*Buses run from **Halkida** (3hr.; 10:15am, 12:30, 5:15pm; 2150dr/€6.31). Ferries run to and from **Arkitsa** (45min., 9 per day, 550dr/€1.62; buy tickets on the dock) on the mainland (30min. by bus from Ag. Konstantinos, 350dr/€1.03). The **bus station** (☎22 250) is on Thermopotamou, which runs inland from 28 Oktovriou, the waterfront strip. The hot springs are in a large complex on a road heading inland from the left end of the waterfront facing the water, 100m past the post office. ☎23 502. Open daily 7am-1pm and 5-7pm. 1100dr/€3.22 buys you 30min. in the swimming pool.*

The village of Aedipsos, northwest of Halkida on the coast of Evia, earned praise from Herodotus, Aristotle, and Aristophanes for its healing sulphurous waters. Aedipsos is worth a daytrip for anyone who wishes to enjoy the hot springs' relaxing vibes, but be aware that the spring's main patrons are those with "rheumatism, arthritis, and gynecological complaints." Don't swim longer than 30 minutes, as too much of the good bathing thing will leave you in a none-too-therapeutic stupor. Check out the various specialized pools and equipment. Crossing the street from the springs complex, walk past the leafy park to the shore, where the springs plunge into the ocean. Several small, natural pools of running spring water collect at the outlet, perfect for free bathing. To cool off, you can jump right into the sea.

ERETRIA   ☎0229

*Eretria is accessible by **bus** from Halkida. Buses going to Karystos, Kimi, and Amarinthos all swing through. (1-2 per hour 5am-8pm, 450dr/€1.32.) Buses stop 3 blocks inland and parallel to the waterfront. Facing the street from the bus station, turn left and walk to a large tree-lined avenue, Archaiou Theatrou. The waterfront is to the right, the museum and House of Mosaics to the left. At the water, Archaiou Theatrou intersects in a traffic circle with Amar. Artemidos, which runs along one edge of the L-shaped harbor while Archaiou Theatrou continues along the other.*

Now a popular destination for beach-bound Athenians, Eretria's former status as one of ancient Evia's most important cities has waned. Its past, however, is magnificently preserved in the archaeological excavations which today provide the best reason for a stop in Eretria. The **Archaeological Museum** is at the inland end of

Archaiou Theatrou, in a courtyard brimming with marble statues, friezes, and pillars. The collection displays some quality pieces, including 3 large *pithoi* south of the House of the Mosaics—the remaining 6 are in the museum at Athens—and the mysterious six-fingered **Centaur of Lefkandi,** (whose body and head were inexplicably found in separate tombs) which dates from 750-900 BC. Exhibits are in Greek and French, but you can buy an English guidebook for 2000dr/€5.87.

Museum admission lets you into the **House of the Mosaics,** a 10min. walk from the museum; just trade your passport for the keys at the front desk of the museum. Coming out of the museum, walk to the right along the main road for three blocks, turning left at the marked road. The three 4th-century BC mosaics are incredibly well preserved, and are among the oldest in existence. The Swiss School of Archaeology in Greece publishes a brochure on the house's history, available from the museum for 1000dr/€2.93. (☎62 206. Open Tu-Su 8:30am-3pm. 500dr/€1.47, students and under 18 free.) Beyond the museum is a large excavated portion of **Ancient Eretria;** highlights include the ancient theatre and the ruins of the ancient city's dense residential section. Should you choose to spend the night in Eretria, inexpensive options are few and far between. Try **Pension Diamado,** on Archaiou Theatrou, past the traffic circle. The rooms are wood-panelled, and feature TV, A/C, and private baths. (☎62 214. Singles 8000-8800dr/€23.48-25.83; doubles 10,000-12,000dr/€29.35-35.22; triples 11,000-14,000dr/€32.28-41.10.)

KARYSTOS Καρυστος   ☎0224

Cut off from the rest of Evia by a mountain chain, Karystos blooms in summer: there are lush trees, pink flowers, sand that squishes between toes, and glimmering bars. The city's streets are laid out with geometric regularity; the modern city was laid out by the German architect Bierbach in a grid at the behest of Greece's first king, Otho. The long bus ride from Halkida passes some unexciting strip towns, but the view of Marmari's bay more than compensates; wind-generators stand guard over the sea, while sunlight flashes from wave to wave.

■☐ ORIENTATION AND PRACTICAL INFORMATION. Though lacking the adventurous street mazes of other Greek towns, Karystos' grid layout makes the city easily navigable. The central plateia along the waterfront is connected by **I. Kotsika** running straight uphill to the **city hall;** the long waterfront, **Kriezotou,** is lined with tavernas and melts into beaches in both directions along the shore. Facing the water, **Kremala beach** is to the right. **Psili beach** curves around the bay on the left, past the **Bourtzi,** the unmistakable stone building on the waterfront. The city hall sits on a plateia circled by **El. Amerikis,** which heads out of town to the west.

The **bus** stops one block above the central plateia on I. Kotsika; look for the KTEL sign above a restaurant on the right side of the street. Buses from Karystos travel to: **Halkida** (4hr., 2 per day, 2500dr/€7.35); **Marmari** (30min., 4 per day, 400dr/€1.17); and **Stira** (45min., 2 per day, 600dr/€1.76). No buses run from Karystos on Sundays. **Ferries** travel to and from **Rafina** (1½hr., 1-2 per day, 1950dr/€5.72). **Flying Dolphins** leave once per day for **Mykonos** (2hr., 7000dr/€20.53); **Paros** (2½hr., 8000dr/€23.48); **Naxos** and **Santorini** (4½hr., 8000dr/€23.48); and **Tinos** (1½hr., 5500dr/€16.14). Buy your tickets at **South Evia Tours,** on the left side of the central plateia (through Kozmos), where ◾**Popi** and friends can help you with everything from **car rental** (10,000-12,000dr/€29.35-35.22 per day) to local excursions. (☎26 200 or 29 010; fax 29 011; root@set.hlk.forthnet.gr; http://setours.tripod.com. Open daily 9am-2:30pm and 6-11pm.) **Taxis** (☎26 500) are in the central plateia.

The **National Bank,** just uphill from the bus stop at the intersection of I. Kotsika and Karystou, has 24hr **ATM.** (Open M-Th 8am-2pm, F 8am-1:30pm.) To find the **police** (☎22 262), turn into the small alley just past the bank and climb the stairs. Find a **pharmacy** (☎23 505) on the corner on the left past the bus stop. The **OTE** is on Amerikis, to the right off I. Kotsika at the plateia. (☎22 399. Open daily 7:45am-1pm.) **Internet access** is available for 1200dr/€3.52 per hour at **Cafe Kalypso,** on the left side of Kriezotou 150m past the Bourtzi. The **post office** is on **Th. Kotsika,** one street over from I. Kotsika, to the left facing inland, just above El. Amerikis. (Open M-F 7:30am-2pm.) **Postal code:** 34001.

ℱ ACCOMMODATIONS. Hotel Ais, on the corner of Th. Kotsika and the waterfront, offers plain rooms with TV, A/C, private baths, and balconies. (☎22 202 or 203; fax 25 002. Singles 7000-9000dr/€20.53-26.41; doubles 11,000-13,000dr/€32.28-38.15; triples 13,000-15,000dr/€38.15-44.) On the far right of the waterfront, facing the water, **Hotel Galaxy,** run by a hospitable English-speaking couple, has similar rooms with TV, A/C, and private baths. (☎22 600; fax 22 463. Breakfast included. Singles 8500-10,000dr/€24.95-29.35; doubles 14,000-15,500dr/€41.10-45.50.)

◨◧ FOOD AND NIGHTLIFE. Fresh seafood abounds in the many waterfront restaurants; all have similar entrees at similar prices. Following the waterfront along Kremala beach (to the right as you face the water), you'll come to the all-Greek crowd at **Kalamia,** which serves hearty Greek fare. (☎22 223. Entrees 1250-2500dr/€3.67-7.35.) Miss McDonalds? Revive your inner teen at ▧**Tastyland** (☎25 000) on the waterfront—don your disco gear and get a burger to go (450dr/€1.32).

Lazy during the day, Karystos hosts an active nightlife on weekends. Start your night at either pseudo-tropical **Archipelagos** or mellow **Ostria Bar,** on Kremala beach at the right edge of the waterfront, with a drink and a moonlit bay view. (Beer 700-1200dr/€2.05-3.52; cocktails 1300-1500dr/€3.81-4.40.) Around midnight, make your way to the other end of the waterfront (100m past the Bourtzi) to popular Psili beach club **Kohyli,** which keeps the dance music—and an occasional golden oldie—thumping till late. Around 3am the party staggers uphill to **Barbados** disco, about 1.5km out of town to the west on Amerikis. You can catch a cab at the central plateia, though the walk might be more amusing. (Beer 1000dr/€2.93; cocktails 1200dr/€3.52 and up.) For a quieter evening, **Ciné Aura,** one block in from the waterfront on **Sachtouri,** shows American movies. (9 and 11pm; 1800dr/€5.28.)

◉ SIGHTS. Peek into one of the holes at the back of the **Fort of Bourtzi,** the impossible-to-miss structure on the waterfront. In the 11th century, your peephole was used to pour boiling oil on attackers. Today, the fort is regularly invaded by theater-goers swarming in to watch student productions in August; ask at South Evia Tours (☎25 700 or 26 200) about schedules. The **Archaeological Museum,** on Kriezotou just past the Bourtzi, houses a small collection of marble statues and inscripted tablets, as well as artifacts from the *drakospita* of Stira and Mt. Ohi. (☎25 661. Open Tu-Su 8:30am-3pm. 500dr/€1.47. Free Su.)

▨ DAYTRIPS FROM KARYSTOS. The widely varied terrain of the Karystos region features many spectacular daytrips. Some are most easily accessed by private vehicle. Among the most haunting ruins in the region, the *drakospita*, or **Dragon House,** rests high on **Mt. Ohi** (1398m), above Karystos where Zeus and Hera are rumored to have fallen in love. The most convenient point of departure is the nearby village of **Mili.** Take a cab. You can also walk the 3km by following Aiolou, one block east of the plateia, out of town. From Mili, a 2½hr. hike up the path brings you to the *drakospita* on the top of Mt. Ohi, passing the **refuge** on the way. It is believed to have been a temple dedicated to Zeus and Hera; local legend holds that it was inhabited by a dragon who terrorized the region.

Running from the heights of Mt. Ohi to the sea below, the **Dimosari Gorge** is a natural wonder that those with an extra day should not miss. Clear, cold water cascades down its length in pools shaded by verdant forest. The gorge is accessible by car at **Kallianou** (41km north of Karystos), or hike over the summit of Mt. Ohi and follow the gorge down the north slope of the mountain. On the slopes above Karystos is the majestic **Castello Rosso** (Kokkino Castro or Red Castle) named for the blood spilled there in the many battles for its control. From Mili, it's a 20min. hike up the hill on the left and across the stone bridge. Other interesting sites in the region include the mysterious and massive **columns** near Mili, the **Roman aqueduct** past the Red Castle, and **stone church** and **cave** at **Agia Triada,** accessible by hike from **Nikasi,** where the bus can drop you off (400dr/€1.17). **Hiking maps** (1000dr/€2.93) are available at South Evia Tours.

NORTHEAST AEGEAN ISLANDS

For centuries, the northeast Aegean islands have had to protect themselves, and recent Turkish occupations have left the islanders somewhat embittered. Many islands continue to isolate themselves from the influx of tourism, hoping to preserve their authenticity. Intricate, rocky coastlines and unassuming port towns enclose thickly wooded mountains, which give way to unspoiled villages and beaches. Despite proximity to the Turkish coast and a noticeable military presence, the northeast Aegean islands dispense a taste of undiluted Greek culture.

HIGHLIGHTS OF THE NORTHEAST AEGEAN

SEEK YOUR MUSE on Lesvos (p. 340), Greece's premier lesbian destination, and inspiration to poetic minds—from the ancient sensual lyricist Sappho to the Modernist Nobel Laureate Odysseus Elytis.

LOUNGE under rare palms on Samos (p. 332), birthplace of Pythagoras and Epicurus.

BOW before the Sanctuary of Great Gods of Anatolia on Samothraki (p. 352), where Alexander the Great's parents met, loved, wooed, and worshiped.

IKARIA Ικαρια ☎ 0275

Ikaria takes its name from reckless young Icarus, who plunged to his death off the island's coast when his wax wings—made by his father Daedalus so they could escape the Cretan labyrinth—melted as he gleefully flew too close to the sun. Today, Ikaria's villages adhere to a daily schedule in which stores and restaurants are closed by day and open much of the night, keeping up the bad-boy lifestyle of their namesake. The island pays little attention to tourism, which is a mixed blessing. Today's mostly Greek visitors generally arrive hoping to be healed by Ikaria's medicinal springs. Split by a rocky mountain chain, the odd landscape harbors around 2500 species of plant, mostly herbs, which subtly color and scent the island. Despite being devastated by fires in 1993 and 1997, much of the landscape is surprisingly verdant.

AGIOS KIRYKOS Αγιος Κηρυκος

As Ikaria's main port, Agios Kirykos is the most convenient base for a visiting the thermal springs, but summer rooms are sparse due to the springs' popularity.

🏧🛈 ORIENTATION AND PRACTICAL INFORMATION. The town's pier is marked by a large sculpture of Icarus plummeting to the ground. Coming off the ferry, walk up the pier onto the main waterfront road, then turn right to reach the town plateia, which shelters all the tourist services.

Ikaria's new **airport** serves **Athens** (1 per day, 20,700dr/€60.88) through the **Olympic Airways** office (☎ 22 214; open M-Sa 8:15am-2pm, Su 3-4pm). It's on the island's northeast tip, near Fanari Beach. **Ferry tickets** are available at the plateia's **G.A. office** (☎ 22 426). Ferries run to: **Fourni** (1hr., 3 per week, 1700dr/€5); **Paros** (4hr., 3 per week, 3300dr/€9.71); **Piraeus** (10hr., 2 per day, 5700dr/€16.76); and **Samos Town** (3hr., 1 per day, 2800dr/€8.24). Boats alternate stops at **Evdilos** in the north and **Agios Kirykos,** where taxis await to shuttle passengers to the other port (7000-10,000dr/€20.59-29.41). **Flying Dolphins** leave for: **Fourni** (30min., 5 per week,

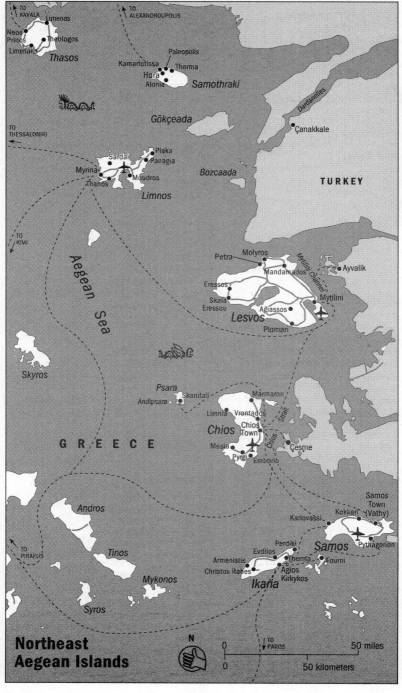

TO
KAVALA
Limenas
Neos
Prinos
Limenaria
Theologos
Thasos

TO
ALEXANDROUPOLIS
Paleopolis
Kamariotissa
Therma
Hora
Alonia
Samothraki

Gökçeada

TO
THESSALONIKI

Çanakkale

Dardanelles

Plaka
Sardai
Panagia
Myrina
Moudros
Thanos
Limnos

Bozcaada

TURKEY

TO
KIMI

*Aegean
Sea*

Petra
Molyros
Mandamados
Ayvalik
Eressos
Mytilini Channel
Skala
Eressou
Agiassos
Mytilini
Lesvos
Plomari

Skyros

Psara
Skandali
Marmaron
Andipsara
Limnia
Vrontados
Chios
Chios
Town
Mesta
Çesme
Pyrgi
Emborio
Chios Strait

G R E E C E

Samos
Town
(Vathy)
Karlovassi
Kokkari
Andros
Perdiki
Pythagorion
Evdilos
Samos
Tinos
Armenistis
Therma
Fourni
Christos Rahes
Agios
Kirkykos
Mykonos
Ikaria

TO
PIRAEUS

Syros

**Northeast
Aegean Islands**

N

0   50 miles
TO
PAROS
0   50 kilometers

2800dr/€8.24); **Patmos** (1hr., 5 per week, 3700dr/€10.86); and **Samos** (1½hr., 5 per week, 4600dr/€13.53). Daily **caïques** depart for Fourni at 10am and return at 6pm (4000dr/€11.76). **Bus** schedules can be erratic, but, in theory, run once daily between **Agios Kirykos** and **Armenistis** via **Evdilos** (1400dr/€4.12.), and every 20min. to **Therma** (400dr/€1.18). The owner of Akti Pension runs a **bus** that leaves from Ag. Kyrinos and Therma 2hr. before daily flights to Athens. On the way to the town plateia from the ferry dock you will pass **Ikariada Travel,** which offers friendly English-speaking service. They can arrange rooms, vehicle rentals, excursion trips, or Flying Dolphin services. (☎23 322; fax 23 708. Open daily 8am-10pm.)

The **port police** (☎22 207), **police** (☎22 222), and **tourist police** (☎22 207) share a building. Climb the steps left of Dolihi Tours and continue up the road (all open 24hr.). The **pharmacy** is next to the G.A. Ferry ticket office. (☎22 989 or 22 220. Open daily 8:30am-2pm.) For emergency after-hours care, try the pharmacist (☎(0932) 199 089). The local **hospital** (☎22 330 or 22 336) is two streets up from the pier. The island's banks, including the **National Bank,** are in Agios Kirykos, in the plateia near the ferry offices. (☎22 553. Open M-Th 8am-2pm, F 8am-1:30pm.) A 24hr. **ATM** is next door to Dolihi Travel. After hours, tourist offices and big hotels offer **currency exchange. Internet access** is available at the **Internet Club** to the left of Dolihi Travel. (☎22 864. 500dr/€1.47 per 20min. Open daily 10am-3pm and 6-11pm.) About 100m up the street are the **post office** (☎22 413; open M-F 7:30am-2pm), and the **OTE** (☎22 599; open M-F 7:30am-2pm). **Postal code:** 83300.

▐▛▟ ACCOMMODATIONS AND FOOD. Finding lodging can be rough on your first night, so check your port of arrival beforehand and call ahead for reservations. To reach **Akti Pension,** climb the stairs on the right-hand side of Dolihi Travel and take your first right. A pleasant courtyard enhances basic rooms built around a lovely seaside patio. Owner Marsha knows a lot about the island and is very accommodating. (☎22 694 or 23 905. Singles 5000-8000dr/€14.71-44.12; doubles 8000-12,000dr/€23.53-35.29; triples 10,000-15,000dr/€29.41-44.12.) The modern rooms of the **Hotel Castro,** on the road leading left from the police station, have TVs, baths, balconies, phones, and fridges. (☎23 480; fax 23 700. Singles 12,000-15,000dr/€35.29; doubles 14,000-17,000dr/€41.18-50.) Next to Akti Pension is the **Hotel O'Karras,** offering simple sky-blue rooms and spacious baths. (☎22 494. Singles 6000dr/€17.65; doubles 8000-10,000dr/€23.53-29.41.) Taverna **A Klimataria** is a block inland from the plateia. (*Briam*, an eggplant dish, 1200dr/€3.53; entrees up to 1600dr/€4.71. ☎22 686. Open daily noon-4pm and 7pm-midnight.) **Dedalos,** on the right of the plateia, stirs up a wonderful omelette breakfast (up to 1300dr/€3.82) and traditional Greek cuisine with ocean-side seating. (Entrees from 1200-1700dr/€3.53-5. ☎22 473. Open daily 9am-late.)

▐▛◢ NIGHTLIFE AND BEACHES. At **Flik-Flak,** 1km out of town, get down to popular radio tunes on Ag. Kirykos's only dance floor. (☎41 587. Cocktails 2000dr/€5.88. Open daily 11pm-4am.) *Barakia* (little curb-side bars) line the stoned pathways leading inland from the plateia, where nightlife is just as easily overpowered by families. **Therino Cinema/Bar,** on the road to Therma, provides outdoor film screenings and refreshing *lemonita* (600dr/€11.76). Shows are nightly at 9:30pm; look for the posters next to Ikariada Travel. There are some rocky **beaches** west of the ferry dock. To the east of town, you can clamber down to the sandy beaches of the coves past the tourist police office. **Agios Georgios,** between Fanari and the airport, is this part of the island's best beach.

EVDILOS Ευδηλος

Heading north from Agios Kirykos, the tiny road to red-roofed Evdilos snakes along sheer cliffs through florid hill country, opening wide coastal vistas—and a safety risk to moped drivers. From the island's eastern heights you can see Samos, Patmos, and the Fourni Archipelago. On the way to Evdilos, the road passes a few tiny villages and beaches, many of which have limited tourist accommodations.

YOU'VE GOT MAIL Two things you need to know about Greek post offices: when to go and what to wear. Anyone who has ever tried to send mail from Greece during the first week of the month may find that hundreds of Greeks seem to have had the same idea. This is because Greek post offices are not just for sending or receiving mail, but also for paying electric, gas, and light bills. It is thus fundamentally impossible to do any of the above in less than two hours. If you can't wait a week, at least go prepared. Women, this means tight (preferably short) clothing, and enough makeup to form a comfortable cushion between you and the person ahead of you in line. Men, break out the swim trunks and flip-flops, and please remember that shirts may inhibit your arm gestures when explaining how someone cut you off in line. Introverts, grumble quietly and constantly to yourselves; extroverts, push hard. At no time should you doubt the Greek gift for creating challenge where there was none before—after all, this is the country that gave us democracy.

PRACTICAL INFORMATION. Buses are supposed to run daily between **Agios Kirykos** and **Armenistis** via **Evdilos,** but service is unreliable at best (1400dr/€4.12 one-way). **Taxis** may be your best bet; sharing a cab will cut costs. (☎31 275. Agios Kirykos to Evdilos 8000dr/€23.53; Agios Kirykos to Armenistis 9000dr/€26.47; Armenistis to Evdilos 3000dr/€8.82.)

The **post office** sits at the top of a set of white stairs that lead to the right of the plateia. (☎31 225. Open M-F 7:30am-2pm.) The **OTE** (☎31 559) is past the post office, across from the church. The **pharmacy** (☎31 394) is between the town and ferries arrival dock. In case of emergency call for **first aid** (☎31 228). The **port police** (☎31 007) are directly inland from the plateia, next to the pharmacy. **Blue Nice Holidays** handles ferries, Flying Dolphins, excursions, flights, and car rentals, **exchanges currency,** and posts a weekly schedule for ferries serving both Evdilos and Agios Kirykos, as well as Flying Dolphins serving Agios Kirykos. (☎31 990 or 31 428; fax 31 572. Open daily 9am-2:30pm and 7-10pm.) An **Alpha Bank** is at the port across from Blue Nice Holidays. (Open M-Th 8am-2pm, F 8am-1:30pm.)

ACCOMMODATIONS AND FOOD. For the best view of crashing waves and a gorgeous sunset, try ■**Apostolos Stenos' Rooms to Rent.** From the port, take the winding uphill road to the top; continue straight at the small square and then take a right. Ask for directions on the way. (☎31 365. Singles 7000-9000dr/€20.59-26.47; doubles 8000-10,500dr/€23.53-30.88; prices are flexible.) **Hambas' Rooms** are very gentle on the budget. They're directly inland from the kiosk in the main square. (☎31 523. Singles 3000dr/€8.82; doubles 5000dr/€14.71.) **Ioannis Spanos** offers basic rooms with shared bath near the plateia at the base of the hill along the Agios Kirykos-Armenistis road. (☎31 220. Doubles 8000dr/€23.53.)

Restaurants and *kafeneions* fill the plateia, each one offering surprisingly distinct flavor. **Cuckoo's Nest,** with tables strategically surrounding the square's central monument, serves up intriguing dishes highlighted by *ouzeri.* Try the chicken in wine sauce for 1300dr/€3.82. (☎31 540. Open M-Sa 7pm-late.) Catering to the late-night ferry arrivals with an array of sweets, coffees, and baked goods, **Ta Kimata** (☎31 952), next to Blue Nice Travel, is open 24hr.

DAYTRIPS FROM EVDILOS. Stone idle fountains hidden under the canopy of shady green leaves mark the entrance to the small town of **Christos Rahes** (Χριστος τος της Ραχης), the apotheosis of a traditional Ikarian village. The best time to visit is after 11pm, when the locals have finished their daily livestock care and produce gathering, and are ready to run their daily errands, shopping until 3 or 4am. Visit the local baker on the main road below the plateia, where the brick-oven-baked loaves (100dr/€0.29) are left out for patrons to grab. Deposit the money in a little basket on the honor system. Ikaria's best-organized hiking trails originate from here and are marked by little orange footprints. Pick up the very handy *Guide Map and Information* or the *Round of Rahes on Foot* (1200dr/€3.53) at any bookstore or tourist shop. Highlights include the Monastery of Evangelistria.

A short distance from Agios Kyrikos on the way to the airport, **Therma** (Θερμα) makes for an ideal daytrip. It's very accessible; **buses** run every 20min., and the **walk** is only 2km on the path beside the police station. The village is built in a little valley with houses on the steep cliffs surrounding it. Elderly people crowd the main plateia while children clamber around the beach, people with ailments ranging from rheumatism to gynecological difficulties venture to the three springs of Therma. Each of the springs is naturally radioactive and used for different treatments. 20min. in a warm bath costs a mere 450dr/€1.32, so take your time.

West of Armenistis, the asphalt runs out, leaving a dirt road running to **Nas,** one of the Aegean's undiscovered gems. The inspiring beach, flanked by huge rock walls, separates an aggressive sea from a serene river. Bordered by the beach, a freshwater pool forms the river's final destination. A 25min. hike south takes you to the small waterfall that forms its beginning. To reach the falls, head inland toward the wood past the pool. With no set path, the hike is best accomplished by hugging the river, which may mean getting your feet wet. Approaching the final leg of the hike, notice the cavernous rock enclosure perched atop the eastern ledge. Think twice about trying to claim it for a nap as this is a favorite haunt for local goats. The smallish waterfall lies a few minutes beyond this point.

FOURNI ☎ 0275

Although few visitors stay overnight, Fourni island presents rewards for both daytrippers and those willing to stay longer. Most come for the fresh seafood served at waterfront restaurants, but pleasant beaches and easy hiking are also easily accessible. The island consists of three little villages: Kampos, Chrysomilia, and Thymeria, on the neighboring island of the same name.

The main port has more tourist facilities than one would imagine. Almost everything is either located on the waterfront or the main street that runs perpendicular to it. Weather permitting, Fourni is easily accessible by daily **caïque** from **Ikaria** (4000dr/€11.76 round-trip). There is also limited **ferry** service three times per week from **Ikaria** (1700dr/€5) and **Patmos** (3500dr/€10.27). The **port police** (☎51 207) and **police** (☎51 222) share a white building at the end of the dock. The friendly, English-speaking staff answer questions about the island. Walking away from the water heading inland, there is daily 7am-1pm). To the right (facing inland) **Hotel Nectaria** provides spacious rooms with baths, fridges, and fans. (☎/fax 51 365. Doubles 10,000-12,000dr/€29.41-35.29; triples 12,000-15,000dr/€35.29-44.12.) Next door, **Toula Rooms** has immaculate studios with baths, kitchens, and fans (☎/fax 51 332. Doubles 10,000-12,000dr/€29.41-35.29; triples 12,000-14,000dr/€35.29-41.18.) The island's two best beaches, **Kambe** and **Psili Ammos,** are accessible from here.

SAMOS Σαμος

Lush and lovely Samos accommodates a more scholarly crowd than some of its wilder siblings in the Cyclades and Dodecanese. While short-sighted tourists see the island as little more than a necessary stepping-stone on the way to Kuşadası and the ruins of Ephesus on the Turkish coast (p. 555), this green island has been a destination in its own right for centuries. A procession of architects, sculptors, poets, philosophers, and scientists (among them Pythagoras, Epicurus, Aesop, and Aristarchus, who called the sun the center of the universe 1800 years before Copernicus) have all spent thoughtful hours on Samos's shores.

VATHY Βαθυ ☎ 0273

Palm trees shade quiet inland streets, an engaging archaeological museum stands across from a garden, and red roofs speckle the neighboring hillside of Vathy (also called **Samos Town**), one of the northeast Aegean's most appealing port cities.

⌐ TRANSPORTATION

Flights: Olympic Airways (☎27 237). Pass the municipal gardens and make a right after the church; the office is 20m up the street on your left. To: **Athens** (1hr., 5 per day, 21,500dr/€63.10) and **Thessaloniki** (3 per week, 30,000dr/€88.04). Open M-F 8:30am-3:30pm. Samos's **airport** (☎61 219), past Pythagorion, is only reachable by taxi (20min., 3500dr/€10.27).

Ferries: To: **Chios** (5hr., 4 per week, 3000dr/€8.80); **Kos** (4hr., 2 per week, 5600dr/ €16.43); **Mykonos** (6hr., 6 per week, 5400dr/€15.85); **Naxos** (6hr., 3 per week, 5300dr/€15.55) via **Paros** (4500dr/€13.21); **Piraeus** (12hr., 1 per day, 7100dr/ €20.84); **Rhodes** (2 per week, 7800dr/€22.89). Catamarans to **Kuşadası, Turkey,** leave from Samos Town (1¼hr.; 5 per week; 10,000dr/€29.35 one-way, 14,000dr/ €41.09 open-return ticket; 3000dr/€8.80 Greek port tax). Turkish entrance **visas** must be purchased at the Turkish border by Americans ($45), British (UK£10), Canadians (CAN$45), and Irish (IRE£5) planning to stay for more than 1 day.

Flying Dolphins: Zip from Samos Town to **Chios, Fourni, Ikaria, Kalymnos, Kos, Lesvos,** and **Patmos,** in half the time and at twice the price.

Buses: Follow the waterfront past Pl. Pythagoras, turn left onto Lekati, and continue 1 block to the **station.** To: **Avlakia** via **Agios Konstantinos** (7 per day); **Chrissi Ammos** (3 per week); **Heraion** (3 per day); **Marathokambs** (1-2 per day); **Pythagorion** (12 per day); **Tsainadon** via **Kokkari** and **Lemonakia** (9 per day); **Vourliotes** (3 per week).

Taxis: (☎28 404). Available 24hr. in Pl. Pythagoras.

⊟⚡ ORIENTATION AND PRACTICAL INFORMATION

Samos Town unfurls around a crescent-shaped waterfront. **Pl. Pythagoras,** identifiable by its four large palm trees, consists of cafes, taxis, and a giant lion statue. Turn onto the side streets between the port and Pl. Pythagoras to hit the most densely packed pension neighborhood on the island. Heading along the waterfront away from the port, past Pl. Pythagoras, will take you to the **Municipal Gardens,** circled by the town's public amenities and the archaeological museum.

Tourist Office: (☎28 530 or 28 582), on a side street 1 block before Pl. Pythagoras. Open July-Aug. M-Sa 8:30am-2pm.

Tourist Agencies: Samos Tours (☎27 715), on the waterfront at the dock, helps with accommodations and general information. Open daily 8am-late and when boats arrive.

Banks: National Bank, on the waterfront just beyond Pl. Pythagoras, has a 24hr. **ATM.** Open M-Th 8am-2pm, F 8am-1:30pm.

Police: (☎22 100), after Pl. Pythagoras on the far right of the waterfront (facing inland). Doubles as the **tourist police.** Some English spoken.

Hospital: (☎27 426), a 10min. walk to the left as you leave the ferry dock. Open 24hr.

Telephones: OTE, across from Olympic Airways, behind the church. Open 7am-10pm.

Internet Access: Net Cafe (☎22 535) is on the waterfront past Pl. Pythagoras. 1000dr/ €2.93 per hr., 400dr/€1.17 minimum. Open daily 10am-11pm.

Post Office: (☎28 503). Walk past the municipal gardens, turn right after the church and left after the Olympic Airways office. Open M-F 7:30am-2pm. **Postal code:** 83100.

⌂ ACCOMMODATIONS

Samos has just few enough rooms to make it advisable to call head during the high season. If you arrive and all the beds listed below are filled, try the pensions around the Ionia or get help from a travel agent.

Pension Trova, Kalomiris 26 (☎27 759). Turn right at the end of the ferry dock and walk 100m along the waterfront, to take a left onto E. Stamatiadou before the Hotel Aiolis. Take the 2nd left onto Manoli Kalomiri which wraps uphill around the bend to Kalomiris. Cool, traditionally furnished rooms, some with bath and balcony, all with full hospitality. Singles 6000dr/€17.61; doubles 7000dr/€20.53.

Pension Avli, Areos 2 (☎22 939). Turn right at the end of the ferry dock and walk 100m along the waterfront to take a left onto E. Stamatiadou before the Hotel Aiolis. Take the 2nd right onto Manoli Kalomiri and then your 2nd left onto Areos. Simple 70s-ish rooms around an elegant courtyard. Open summer only. Doubles 8000dr/€23.48.

Pension Dreams, Areos 9 (☎24 350), just up from Pension Avli. Compulsively neat rooms with fridge, bath, TV, and—the owners' pride and joy—coffee makers. Singles 6000dr/€17.61; doubles 7000dr/€20.53; triples 8000dr/€23.48.

⬛ FOOD

Gourmands will find their time well-spent in savoring sweet Samian wine, served at all of the island's nearly indistinguishable restaurants, which otherwise offer a standard spate of traditional meals. **Gregory's,** just past the post office heading inland, is a worthy local favorite. The menu is the same as everywhere else in town, but it just tastes better here. Similarly priced and more conveniently located is **Christos,** in Pl. Nicolaos behind Pl. Pythagoras, with outdoor seating for optimal people-watching in the main square.

⬛ SIGHTS

The phenomenal ⬛**Archaeological Museum** sits behind the municipal gardens. Its broad collection looks at Samos's past glory as a commercial and religious center for worshiping Hera. Finds from ancient Heraion, the temple of Hera, and other local digs are enshrined in two recently renovated buildings full of informative notes; you'll find more proof of Heraion's bygone splendor here than at the crumbled remains at the site. The first building houses intricate Laconian ivory carvings of mythological notables, and awesome statues like a colossal 5m **Kouros** from 56 BC. Pieces of this magnificent *kouros* were found at different times, some of them built into existing walls and cisterns. There's also the stunning Geneleas group. A nearly life-size votive offering depicting a family, which is named after its sculptor and once graced ancient Heraion's Sacred Way. In the second building, an exhibit on Hera-worship parades offerings made to the goddess, remarkable for their workmanship and expense. Objects from Ancient Egypt, Cyprus, and the Near East testify to the island's early trade. In the last room, a case of gorgeously nightmarish **protomes** (cauldron handles) is not to be missed. (☎27 469. Open Tu-Su 8:30am-3pm. 800dr/€2.35, seniors and students 400dr/€1.17, EU students free.)

During the months of July and August, Samos hosts a number of fine classical and jazz concerts featuring Greek artists as part of the **Manolis Kalomiris Festival.** Contact the tourist office for a schedule of events.

⬛ DAYTRIPS FROM VATHY

ANCIENT PYTHAGORION Πυθαγορειο

A bus from Samos Town arrives at Pythagorion (20min., 300dr/€0.88). The beach town of Pythagorion, 14km south of Samos Town, sits atop the ancient city of the same name.

The ancient city of Pythagorion, once the island's capital, thrived during the second half of the 6th century BC under the reign of **Polykrates the Tyrant.** Herodotus reports that Polykrates undertook the three most daring engineering projects in the Hellenic world, among them the **Tunnel of Eupalinos,** 1500m up the hill to the north of town. The "tunnel" was in fact an underground aqueduct that diverted water from a natural spring to the city below. It may owe its misnomer to its size, which is just big enough to fit a person. An impressive 1.3km long, it's in remarkably good condition, although only about 200m of damp cavern are open to visitors. To reach the tunnel, walk back inland from the bus stop in town and follow the signs. The 20min. walk to the tunnel's entrance leads past minor ancient ruins, including a Hellenistic villa and some wells; rolling hills and grazing goats fill the intervals. (☎61 400. Open Tu-Su 8:45am-2:45pm, last entrance 2:15pm. 500dr/€1.47, students 300dr/€0.88, EU students free.) You can also check out Polykrates's second feat, the 40m deep **harbor mole** (rock pier), which supports the modern pier.

SEXY SAINT On July 22nd, every sinner on the island of Chios gathers by the beach at Volissos to celebrate the feast of Chios's own Saint Markella, one of the Orthodox faith's most beloved martyrs and the victim of a gruesome death. Her mother died when she was a child, and upon reaching adolescence, her blossoming beauty drew the lecherous gaze of her father. To resist his increasingly bold advances, she ran away to find refuge in the mountains. He pursued and found her; then began Markella's final escape. She ran as her father followed, shooting arrows at her. She prayed that the ground would swallow her, and it did—but only up to her waist. Markella's father attacked the trapped girl with his sword: he cut off her breasts and then her head, which he cast into the ocean. To this day, the girl's blood is believed to bless the waters around Volissos with its sacred healing powers.

Blocks, columns, wall fragments, and entablatures are strewn throughout Pythagorion. The presentation in the small **Archaeological Museum** is no different. A little over half of the collection fits into the building; many of the ruins are haphazardly scattered on the sidewalk in front. (☎61 400. Open Tu-Su 9am-2:30pm. Free.) On the south side of town are the ruins of the **Castle of Lycurgus,** built during the beginning of the 19th century by Lycurgus, a native of Samos and a leader in the Greek War of Independence. The **Church of the Transfiguration** is a pale blue variation on classic Orthodox architecture.

HERAION Ηπαιον

The bus from Pythagorion (10min., 300dr/€0.88) leaves you in Heraion Town. ☎95 277. Open T-Su 8:30am-3pm. 800dr/€2.35, students 400dr/€1.17.

Polykrates' magnum opus is in Heraion (EAR-ion). Seven centuries worth of pilgrims had worshiped Hera on Samos when Polykrates began enlarging her temple. Eventually, 134 columns supported the 118m-long, 58m-wide 530 BC version of the **Temple of Hera.** Since a fire damaged it in 525 BC, it has been only minimally reconstructed. On the site, you'll see the lone standing column of the once-majestic colonnade, and casts of the Geneleas group (now in the Samos Museum). A walk along the beach brings you back to the temple at your own pace. If you can't enter through the beachside back gate, a path brings you inland to the main road and the entrance, farther along the beach past two houses. Follow custom and wrap yourself up in your best toga and carry along a jug of libations on this path, which runs close to the ancient **Iera Odos** (Sacred Way) from Pythagorion to the temple.

NORTHERN AND WESTERN SAMOS

◪ **BEACHES.** The northern coast of Samos has many crowded, sandy beaches and a few sparsely visited pebble beaches tucked into little coves. Most of the coast is easily accessible from the road to **Karlovassi.** On a peninsula 10km west of Samos Town, you'll find the village of **Kokkari,** skirted by white pebble shores and clear waters. **Lemonakia Beach,** 1km west of Kokkari next to Tsamadou, and the wide white beach west of **Avlakia** are both alluring. Kokkari, Lemonakia, and Avlakia are accessible from Samos Town via the irregular KTEL **bus** service (7-9 buses per day). Infrequent buses (1-2 per day) shouldn't keep you from the splendid beaches of southwest Samos. A few kilometers west of the peaceful red-roofed hamlet of **Marathokampos** is the spacious beach at **Votsalakia.** A bit farther is an even better beach at **Psili Ammos.**

◪ **HIKES.** From the village of **Agios Konstantinos,** on the northern coast of Samos, you can trek into the mountains through the Valley of the Nightingales, where songbirds regale the green-treed valley just after midnight. The village of **Vourliotes,** 5km south of Avlakia, got hyped up by actress Melina Mercury, who exalted the village for years after her visit there. Several kilometers above the town, the 16th-century monastery **Moni Vrontianis** polices the behavior of the populace below. (Modest dress required. Open daily 8am-noon and 4-6pm.) Two kilometers west of **Paleo,** a path (through a pond and up a series of ropes) leads to three successive waterfalls in the island's northwest corner.

CHIOS Χιος

Chios (KHEE-ohs) is where the wild things *were:* Orion hunted every last beast down, leaving the island's mountainsides to pine and cypress trees, and to native son Homer. Ever since, human occupants have cultivated and exported the trees' *masticha*—a bittersweet, gummy resin used in a number of things from chewing gum to color TVs. Medieval Genovese and Venetian Crusaders, among them Christopher Columbus, made themselves at home here for a while, and in 1822 Chios hosted a failed Greek nationalist rebellion. A military base and shipping center for years, it only recently opened the gates to tourist infiltrators. As its striking volcanic beaches and medieval villages become more accessible, Chios flashes back to the pre-Orion days, as tourists on the way Çeşme do the Wild Thing all night long.

CHIOS TOWN   ☎ 0271

Merchant ships and the occasional tourist ferry dock at Chios Town. Shipping provides the lion's share of this affluent island's wealth, and tourists are the exception instead of the rule at the waterfront tavernas and trendy cafes. Inland, a crumbling medieval fortress keeps several centuries worth of island history intact within its decayed bulk. Today, visitors infiltrate the fallen fortifications daily, partaking of the markets and tavernas that are the fortress's contemporary occupants.

⬛ TRANSPORTATION

Ferries go to: **Alexandroupolis** (1 per week, 9000dr/€26.41); **Kos** (1 per week 6am, 6000dr/€17.61); **Lesvos** (3hr., 1 per week, 3500dr/€10.27); **Limnos** (2 per week, 5500dr/€16.14); **Piraeus** (8 hr., 1-2 per day, 6300dr/ €18.49); **Rhodes** (1 per week, 7100dr); **Samos** (4hr., 1 per week, 3300dr/€9.68); and **Çeşme,** Turkey (45min., 1 per day, 17,000dr/€49.89). Non-Greek citizens will have to purchase a **visa** if staying more than one day (by date) in Turkey: Americans ($45), Australians (AUS$20), British (UK£10), Canadians (CAN$45), and Irish (IR£5). **Tickets** are available at Hatzelenis Tourist Agency (see below). **Olympic Airways,** on the waterfront on Psychari (☎ 23 998; open M-F 8am-4pm) sends 5 **flights** per day to Athens (23,000dr/€67.50). **KTEL buses** (☎ 27 507 or 24 257) leave from both sides of Pl. Vounakio, right off the municipal gardens coming from the waterfront. **Blue buses** (☎ 23 086), in the plateia on Dimokratias, are for travel within the vicinity of Chios Town (9km), making 5-6 daily trips to Daskalopetra, Kontari, Karfas, Karies, and Vrondados. **Green buses,** on the left side of the municipal gardens, make trips to Emborios Beach, Pyrgi, and Volissos.

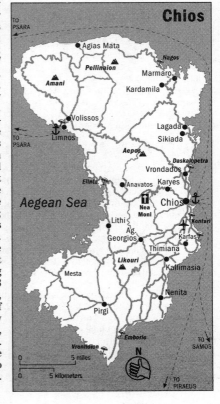

Chios

TO PSARA

Agias Mata

Nagos

Pellinaion

Marmaro

▲ Amani

Kardamila

Volissos

Lagada

TO PSARA

Limnos

Sikiada

Aepos

Daskalopetra

Vrondados

Elinta

Anavatos

Karyes

Aegean Sea

Nea Moni

Chios

Lithi

Ag. Georgios

Kontari

Karfas

Thimiana

Likouri ▲

Kallimasia

Mesta

Nenita

Pirgi

Emborio

TO SAMOS

Vronidion

N

0   5 miles

0   5 kilometers

TO PIRAEUS

ORIENTATION AND PRACTICAL INFORMATION

Walking left from the ferry dock along the waterfront, you'll pass a bevy of cafes and restaurants. A right on **Kanari** takes you inland to **Pl. Vounakio**, the social center of town, where most services, buses, and taxis plant themselves on one side or another of the **Municipal Gardens.** Left of Vounakio lies the **market street,** where groceries and bakeries are open for business. Between the ferry dock and the Municipal Gardens, fortress walls hug the Old Town, a residential area with a few small shops and tavernas.

To reach the **tourist office,** Kanari 18, turn off the waterfront onto Kanari, walk toward the plateia and look for the "i" sign. They provide maps and help with transportation and accommodations. (☎44 344 or 44 389. Open May-Oct. daily 7am-10pm.) **Hatzelenis Tourist Agency** lies at the end of the ferry dock and the start of town. The extremely friendly staff sells **ferry tickets** for all lines except NEL. (☎26 743 or 20 002; mano2@otenet.gr. Open daily 4am-2pm and 5-10pm.) NEL has its own exclusive agency in the center of the waterfront. (☎25 848. Open M-Sa 7am-1:30pm and 6-9pm, Su 10am-1pm and 6-9pm.) The **Ionian Bank,** Kanari 16, is next to the tourist office and offers a 24hr. **ATM** and **currency exchange.** (☎23 522 or 23 434. Open M-Th 8am-2pm, F 8am-1:30pm.) A 24hr. **hospital** (☎44 303) is 2km north of Chios. The **OTE,** Kanari 1, is across from the Ionian bank, and phones are on the waterfront. **Enter Internet Cafe,** Aigeou 98, is on the second floor of a waterfront building. (600dr/€1.76 per 30min. ☎41 058. Open daily 9:30am-late.) To find the **post office,** follow Omirou one block inland. (☎443 50. Open M-F 7:30am-2pm.) **Postal code:** 82100.

Chios Town

ACCOMMODATIONS
Giannis Rooms to Let, 1
Chios Rooms, 2

ACCOMMODATIONS AND FOOD

Most of Chios Town's accommodations are on the far end of the waterfront from the ferry dock, in high-ceilinged, turn-of-the-century mansions. In high season, seek help from a tourist agency to get a room. In a yellow building at the far right end of the waterfront, the hospitable owners at **Chios Rooms,** Leofores 114, offer bright and breezy rooms with polished hard-wood floors, most with a sea view and some with bath. (☎20 198. Doubles 8000dr/€23.48; triples 10,000dr/€29.35, 12,000dr/€35.22 with bath. Monthly rental available in winter.) One block behind Aigeou on the waterfront, **Giannis Rooms to Let,** M. Livanou 48, has rooms with baths, a common kitchen, and a lovely backyard garden shaded by grapevines heavy with fruit. (☎27 433. Open May-Oct. Doubles 8000-12,000dr/€23.48-35.22.)

Myriad vendors set up shop near Pl. Vounakio. For lunch on the cheap, bite into the fresh *spanakopita* or *tyropita* available in **bakeries.** Love is in the ruins at elegant **Ouzeri Ikobou Plita,** Ag. Giorgios 20, where open-air tables nestle into the tumbledown walls of the Byzantine fortress. To get there, walk past Hatzelenis on Aigeou and make the fourth right. There's no menu; just eyeball the options and pick whatever looks good. Turning off the waterfront on the way to the Archaeology Museum brings you shortly to the **Two Brothers** (☎21 313) on Livanou, who serve good Greek grub in their garden restaurant.

SIGHTS

The **Archaeology Museum,** Michalon 10, inland toward the left end of the waterfront, dissects Chios's role in the ancient Aegean world, with an extensive collection of artifacts and detailed explanatory placards. Don't miss the 3rd-century AD statue of Leda and the Swan, with just enough limbs left on both parties to suggest how the dirty deed was done. (☎82 100. Open Tu-Su 8:30am-3pm. 500dr/€1.47, students 300dr/€0.88, EU students free.) Relics of the town's past encircle Pl. Vounakio. To the right of the plateia, the walls of the **Byzantine Castro,** reconstructed by the Genovese, enclose the narrow streets of the **Old Town.** The castle houses a handful of well-restored 14th-century Byzantine wall paintings in the **Justinian Palace.** (☎26 866. Open Tu-Su 9am-3pm. 500dr/€1.47, students 300dr/€0.88.) The minaret of the nearby **Ottoman Mosque** is visible from far away, though almost every surface has a storefront built in front of it. The main room contains a Byzantine collection, including a short hallway of paintings and a small courtyard of Venetian, Genovese, and Ottoman sculptural pieces. (Open Tu-Sa 10am-1pm, Su 10am-3pm. 500dr/€1.47, students 300dr/€0.88.) The **Folklore Museum,** on the first floor of the **Korais Library,** is next to the **Mitropolis** cathedral. The collection of textiles and tools is more extensive than most, but there are no explanatory placards, just pretty designs. (Open M-Th 8am-2pm, F 8am-2pm and 5-7:30pm, Sa 8am-12:30pm.)

DAYTRIPS FROM CHIOS TOWN

NEA MONI Νεα Μονι AND ANAVATOS Αναβατος

Check with the tourist office or the green bus terminal in Chios for information on excursions to both sites. Taxi drivers may agree to drive you to the site, wait 30min., and bring you back; a taxi-tour of Nea Moni and Anavatos costs around 8000dr/€23.48.

A FORK AND A DREAM Although it's built in the twisting alleyways of a medieval castle, little Pyrgi in southern Chios is most recognizable for its *ksista,* the unique geometric patterns that cover the walls of every house in the village. Instead of whitewashing their homes, as is common in the Cyclades, Pyrgian craftsmen first coat each house with a paint made from the gray stone at Emborio. The houses are then whitewashed, and, while the paint is still wet, the craftsmen press in geometric patterns with a fork, creating the village's trademark design. After both coats have dried, artists add splendidly colorful designs to the black-and-white geometry.

On the eastern half of the island, several sites, among them Nea Moni and Anavatos, silently recall the invasion of the island by the Ottoman Turks in 1822. Pine-covered mountains 16km west of Chios Town cradle Nea Moni (New Monastery). Built in the 11th century, the **monastery** was inspired by the miraculous appearance of an icon of the Virgin Mary to three hermits. Over the centuries, the monastery complex, always one of the world's most important Byzantine monuments, has been rebuilt and enlarged. An 1881 earthquake destroyed much of the complex itself, but most of its structures have been carefully restored. Before entering the main chapel, you'll pass through the inner narthex, where 11th-century gold **mosaics** are stunning despite their age. These artists were also responsible for the mosaics of Hagia Sophia in Istanbul. An adjoining chapel beside the entrance to the complex houses a **memorial**—gut-wrenchingly real, with its skulls and bones—to monks and villagers massacred by the Turks in 1822, when the island's population was reduced from 118,000 to 18,000. The skeletons were once 600 priests and 3500 women and children who sought refuge in the chapel. Elsewhere on the island, 23,000 residents were killed and 47,000 sold into slavery. (Open daily 9am-1pm and 4-8pm. Free. Modest dress required.) An on-site **museum** displays church garments and religious items. Open daily 8:30am-1pm. 500dr/€1.47. Free Su.)

Anavatos, 15km west of Nea Moni, is a beautiful, abandoned village built into the hillside. The village's women and children threw themselves from these cliffs in resistance to the 1822 invasion. A walk among the ruins of these fortifications provides amazing views of the hills. Stop into the church near the right of the site's entrance to see a spectacular folk-art rendition of the massacre of 1822.

PYRGI Πυργι

You can get to Pyrgi via bus from Chios.

The villages in the southern half of the island, called *Mastichochoria*, are home to Chios's famous resin, produced by squat mastic or lentisk trees. Pyrgi, high in the hills 25km from Chios, is one of Greece's most uniquely beautiful villages, thanks to the black and white geometric designs tattooing its buildings. Pyrgi is also home to the 12th-century **Agioi Apostoloi** church, a replica of the Nea Moni. Thirteenth-century frescoes and paintings by a Cretan iconography school cover almost every inch of the interior. (Open M-F 9am-3pm. 100dr/€0.29.) The caretaker can unlock the front gate for you; ask across from the OTE.

SOUTHERN CHIOS

Only 6km south of Chios Town lies popular, sandy **Karfas**, victim of Chios's latest burst of development. Many tourists take up temporary residence here, as it is convenient to both the beach and the amenities of Chios Town. Blue **buses** run from Pl. Vournakio in Chios. Hatzelenis Tours in Chios Town can set you up with a double with bath and kitchen by the beach at **Villa Anatoli.** (☎20 002 or 32 235. Doubles 12,000dr/€35.22.) Farther south lies pristine **Emborio**, where beige volcanic cliffs contrast with black stones and deep-blue water below. The green **bus** from Chios Town drops off at the harbor. One beach is up the only road to the right (facing the water); a smaller, less crowded shore is up the stairs to the right.

NORTHERN CHIOS

Nine kilometers north of Chios Town, you'll find the pleasant, pebbly shores of **Vrondados** and **Daskalopetra.** Blue buses from Pl. Vournakio in Chios Town serve both. A 2min. walk from Daskolopetra beach takes you to the **Sanctuary of Cybele.** Here, sitting on the **Stone of Homer,** the bard is rumored to have taught to students gathered around. After Daskalopetra, the main roads wind northwest along the coast past Marmaron to **Nagos,** with its gray stone beach—perhaps a popular spot to cut Homer's classes. High in the hills toward the center of the island, the village of **Volissos,** Homer's legendary birthplace, is crowned by a Byzantine fort with a handful of modern-day habitations scattered around it. **Buses** run here from Chios.

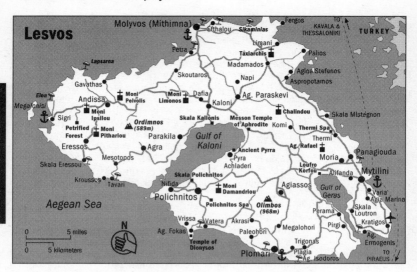

LESVOS Λεσβος

Unlike the tiny islands of the southern Aegean, Lesvos feels like its own country. Far closer to Turkey than to Athens, it's a strong Greek influence in the politically and culturally complex north Aegean. Lesvos's cosmopolitan, off-beat culture incorporates horse breeding, ouzo, and leftist politics with equal zeal. Huge, geographically diverse, and far from the mainland, the island attracts visitors who spend weeks exploring its therapeutic hot springs, monasteries, petrified forest, sandy beaches, mountain villages, seaside cliffs, and art colonies. Daytrippers may be overwhelmed; you'll need four or five days to get far beyond the main harbor.

Lesvos has one of the richest cultural and artistic legacies in the Aegean. Seventh century BC poet Sappho, fablist Aesop, philosopher Aristotle, the original epicure, Epicurus, Nobel Prize-winning poet Odysseas Elytis, neoprimitive artist Theophilos, and art publisher and critic Tériade have all called Lesvos home. Legend also has it that Lesvos's population was once entirely female. The tale may date back to the Athenian assembly's 428 BC decision to punish the unruly residents of Mytilini by executing all adult males on Lesvos; the assembly actually repealed the sentence. Still, the idea of an Amazon isle appeals to girl-power pilgrims paying homage to Sappho and the etymological roots of the word "lesbian." Poets retrace Elytis's footsteps and Sappho's fragments. Despite all the attention, Lesvos resists tourist degradations.

MYTILINI Μυτιληνη   ☎ 0251

Each morning, the wide harbor of the capital yawns into a modern, working city more reminiscent of Piraeus than of the tiny ports of nearby islands. Most come to Mytilini on business or en route to the rest of the island; aimless wandering in town will turn up crumbling buildings and quiet backgammon games alike.

▐ TRANSPORTATION

Flights: The **airport** (☎61 590 or 61 490) is 6km south of Mytilini in the direction of Varia; take a **green bus** from the intercity bus station. **Olympic Airways,** Kavetsou 44 (☎28 659 or 28 660). Open 8am-3:30pm. To: **Athens** (4 per day, 18,000dr/€52.82); **Chios** (1 per week, 14,000dr/€41.10); **Limnos** (4 per week, 16,000dr/€46.96); **Thessaloniki** (5 per week, 25,900dr/€76).

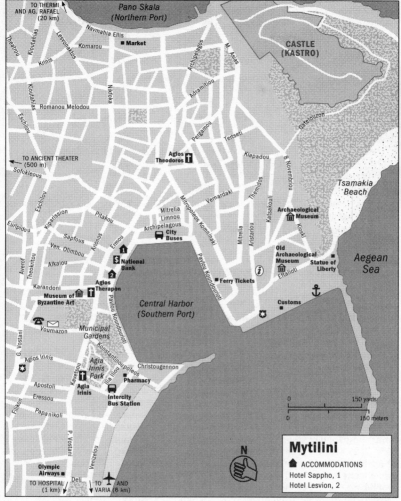

Mytilini

⬛ ACCOMMODATIONS
Hotel Sappho, 1
Hotel Lesvion, 2

Ferries: NEL Lines, Pavlou Koundourioti 67 (☎ 22 220; fax 28 601), on the east side of the waterfront, before the string of cafes. Open M-F 7am-10pm. Service to: **Chios** (3hr., 1-3 per day, 3600dr/€10.56); **Kavala** (12hr., 3 per week, 6900dr/€20.25); **Limnos** (5hr., 6 per week, 4800dr/€14.09); **Piraeus** (12hr., 1-3 per day, 7700dr/€22.60); **Thessaloniki** (12hr., 1 per week, 9000dr/€26.41); **Aivali, Turkey** (16,000dr/€46.96, includes 3000dr/€8.80 Greek port tax).

Intercity Buses: Intercity buses criss-cross the island, using Mytilini as home base. Meaning, from outlying cities, you will have to head back toward Mytilini in order to get somewhere else on the island. Other convenient transfer points are **Kaloni** and the fork for **Eressos** and **Sigri.** Schedules for the entire island are available at the bus station in Mytilini (☎ 28 873) and at most information or tourist agencies throughout Lesvos. Service to: **Aglassos** (5 per day, 650dr/€1.91); **Molyvos** (2hr., 4-5 per day, 1450dr/€4.26) via **Kaloni** and **Petra; Sigri** (2½hr., 1-2 per day, 2200dr/€6.46) via **Kaloni; Skala Eressou** (3hr., 2-3 per day, 2200dr/€6.46) via **Kaloni; Plomari** (1½hr., 3-5 per day, 950dr) via **Gera;** and **Vatera** (1½hr., 3-4 per day, 1100dr/€3.23) via **Polihnitos.** Schedules reduced Sa-Su.

Local Buses: (☎28 725), at the north end of the waterfront on Sappho run to: **Ag. Marina** (every 20-30min. 6:10am-8:40pm, 270dr/€0.79) via **Varia** (190dr/€0.56); **Ag. Rafael** (every 30min. 6am-9:30pm, 330dr/€0.97) via **Thermi** (300dr/€0.88); **Loutra** (every 1-1½hr., 6:50am-9:10pm, 270dr/€0.79) via **Koundourtias** (150dr/€0.44).

Taxis: Line up on the corner of Ermou and Vournazon.

Moped Rentals: N'Joy Rentals (☎/fax 42 242), on Tenedou, next to NEL lines ticket office, off Koundourioti. Congenial Milton offers motorbikes from 4000dr/€11.74, with discounts for longer rentals.

✦🛈 ORIENTATION AND PRACTICAL INFORMATION

Mytilini's harbor opens to the south. Cafes, bars and hotels line the waterfront street **Koundourioti** (which becomes **Sappho**) on three sides. The **old market** stretches along **Ermou,** host to pharmacies, boutiques, bakeries, and a fish market. Ermou becomes **Kavetsou** at its southern end, where it intersects **Vournazon** one block inland, on the west side of the harbor.

Banks: The inner harbor has a **National Bank** with a 24hr. **ATM** on the west side next to Hotel Sappho. Open M-Th 8am-2pm, F 8am-1:30pm.

Public Toilets: 150dr/€0.44, in the park.

Ambulance: ☎166. **Fire:** ☎199.

Tourist Police: (☎22 776), on Aristarchou near the ferry docks. Provides maps, brochures, and advice. Open 7:15am-2:15pm and 5-8pm.

Hospital: (☎43 777), southwest of town on E. Vostani. Open 24hr.

Telephone: OTE (☎24 299), on Vournazon, 2 doors up from the post office.

Internet: Get online at **Kirki Bar,** on the western edge of the waterfront next to Alpha Bank. 1400dr/€4.11 per hr. Open all day. Also at **Laser** on the eastern edge of the harbor, past the string of cafes. 600dr/€1.76 per 30min. Open all day.

Post Office: (☎28 836), on Vournazon, off Ermou on the west side of town. Offers **exchange.** Open M-F 7:30am-2pm. **Postal Code:** 81100.

🏠 ACCOMMODATIONS

Mytilini has its fair share of enterprising residents, so domatia are plentiful and well advertised. You may also be met at the ferry. Be sure to negotiate, and keep in mind that longer stays often result in lower rates. Doubles run 7000-9000dr/€20.53-26.41. Hotels along the waterfront are pricey. **Hotel Sappho,** in the center of the western waterfront, has comfortable rooms with A/C, TV, phones, and sparkling white private baths. (☎22 888 or 28 415; fax 24 522. Singles 10,000dr/€29.35; doubles 13,000-15,000dr/€38.15-45.78; triples 15,600-18,000dr/€45.78-52.82.) **Hotel Lesvion,** on the waterfront south of Hotel Sappho, has bright rooms with A/C, TV, phones, and private baths. (☎28 177; fax 42 493; lesvion@otenet.gr. Breakfast 1800dr/€5.28. Checkout noon. Singles 13,000dr/€38.15; doubles 18,000dr/€52.82.)

🍴🍷 FOOD AND NIGHTLIFE

When dining in Greece it's often best to order from the waiter's list of specials. To get close to the taverna experience, head to the alley Thasou off Ermou, north of the port, to **To Kalterimi** (☎46 571). Fresh seafood and slow-cooked grilled foods (1300-2400dr/€3.82-7.04) are the perfect complement to their wide variety of local ouzo (600-1800dr/€1.76-5.28). Walk seaward on the southwestern quay to find fresh fish, hearty food, and an amusing split view of the harbor and a busy children's amusement park at **Taverna O Stratos.** (☎21 739. Entrees 700-2200dr/€2.05. Open daily 11am-late.) **Zacharoplasteio Valentino,** El. Venizelou 6, has delicious almond confections. (☎23 989. Open daily at 9am.)

Mytilini's nightlife centers on its gyrating waterfront. Head to the hypnotic colored lights of **☒Flame,** on the northeast side of the waterfront, for pulsing beats and fashionable drinks. To take full advantage of the experience, down a few shots (800dr/€2.35) and head upstairs to Flame's trippy **neon bowling alley,** where streaking lights and glow-in-the-dark bowling balls and pins make bowling cool. (☎46 885; fax 46 886. Cocktails 2000dr/€5.87. Bowling 1200dr/€3.52 per person per game. Open daily until 2am.) On the north edge of the harbor behind the local buses, **Navagio** (☎21 310) is the refuge of the moped generation and intellectual hipsters alike. Cocktails (1800dr/€5.28) or big, gooey ice cream sundaes (1500dr/€4.40) accompany deep or frivolous conversations nicely.

For a more sedate evening, head to **Cine Arion** on Smyrnis across from the intercity bus station. American movies play nightly on the theatre's two screens. (☎44 456. Weekly schedules at the ticket window. 9 and 11:30pm, 2000dr/€5.87.)

👁 SIGHTS

ARCHAEOLOGICAL MUSEUMS. Mytilini's extensive collection of archaeological relics is divided between two museums, and tickets are good for both on the same day. The amazing **☒new Archaeological Museum,** on 8 Novembriou, is a delight to explore. Exhibits are extremely well organized and informative signs in English provide historical and cultural context. Of special interest is the museum's collection of mosaic floors from the houses of ancient Mytilini. Laid out in their original floor plan, the mosaics of the **House of Menander** (3rd century AD) include a magnificent depiction of **Orpheus,** son of the King of Thrace and the muse Calliope, which suggests the house's significance as an artisan guild. Also spectacular are the **Telaphus** and **Euripus house** mosaics. Be sure to see the collection of stylized death friezes, including an extremely rare example of a heroine figure. (☎40 223. Open daily 8am-7pm. 500dr/€1.47, students and under 18 free.) The **old Archaeological Museum,** on Eftalioti behind the ferry dock, has a collection of Lesvian artifacts organized to give a linear history of the island. The collection includes Mycenaean, Protogeometric, and Archaic pottery, Classical and Hellenistic vases and sculpture, and remnants from the excavations at Thermi, as well as masks, oil lamps, life-like figurines, and a gold-leafed crown, found and donated by fishermen. Don't miss the smaller building hiding behind the main museum, which contains rare Aeolian tablets. (Argiri Eftalioti 7. ☎28 032. Open Tu-Su 8:30am-3pm. 500dr/€1.47.)

CASTLES AND THEATERS. Nearby is the large **Gattelusi Castle.** Tucked away in a pine forest above town, the fortress stands resolute guard over photographers snapping scenic harbor shots. Originally constructed by Emperor Justinian on the site of a Byzantine castle, it bears the name of Francesco Gattelusi, who received Lesvos as dowry in 1355 after he married Justinian's daughter. Genoese, Ottomans, and Greeks have spent successive centuries maintaining the castle walls and underground tunnels. Wear good shoes for wandering the vast interior. (☎27 970. Open Tu-Su 8:30am-3pm. 500dr/€1.47, EU students and children under 18 free.) The highest point on the north side of Mytilini is the 3rd-century BC **ancient theater,** built during the Hellenistic period, where 15,000 spectators attended performances and enjoyed near-perfect acoustics. The effect was so impressive that it inspired Pompeii to build Rome's first stone theater. (Open Tu-Su 8:30am-3pm.)

> **META** Most of the large trucks causing traffic jams at the ferry docks have ΜΕΤΑΦΟΡΕΣ written on the sides. This is the Greek word for "shipping," but it transliterates directly to another English word: "metaphors." Voila: the etymological origin of the English rhetorical device which connects two different sets of ideas with one clever figurative leap, much like a large noisy truck connecting two destinations.

OTHER MYTILINI SITES. Visit the enormous late 19th-century **Church of Ag. Therapon,** on the west side of the harbor, and one block inland on Ermou *(open 9am-7pm),* and the neighboring **Byzantine Museum.** *(☎ 28 916. Open M-Sa 9am-1pm. 500dr/€1.47.)* The church towers over a fish market full of sardines, octopi, and small sharks. Inland and north of the harbor (one block off Ermou) is the impressive **Church of Ag. Theodoros,** housing the bones and skull of its patron saint.

VARIA. Only 4km south of Mytilini along El. Venizelou, the tiny, unassuming village of Varia (Βαρια) surprises wayfarers with the ◙**Theophilos Museum,** featuring the work of the famous neo-primitivist Greek painter Theophilos Hadzimichali. *(☎ 41 644. Open May-Sept. Tu-Su 9am-2:30pm and 6-8pm. 500dr/€1.47, students and children under 18 free.)* Next door, the ◙**Musée Tériade** displays an excellent collection of Picasso, Miró, Léger, Chagall, and Matisse lithographs; captions are in Greek, English, and French. Tériade, a native of Lesvos (born Stratis Eleftheriadis), was a leading 20th-century publisher of graphic art in Paris. *(☎ 23 372. Open Tu-Su 9am-2pm and 5-8pm. 500dr/€1.47, students and children free.)* Intercity **buses** to Varia leave Mytilini every hour (20min., 190dr/€0.56). Tell the driver you are going to the museum.

AGIOS RAFAEL. 20km into the hills above the capital is the monastery of Ag. Rafael in Thermi. The saint was particularly active in working modern-day miracles, making his chapel and grave a major place of pilgrimage. The door on the bottom level of the church, marked ΑΓΙΑΣΜΑ, leads to a source of holy water. Visitors can stay free for up to two nights, and nearby **Kafe-Estiatoriou O Fotis** offers "home cooking at fair prices." *(☎ 71 259. Bus from Mytilini runs every hr. for 330dr/€0.97.)*

MOLYVOS Μολυβος   ☎ 0253

Hilly and cobbled, the artists' colony of Molyvos spills from the towering castle to the sea like a gingerbread village from a children's storybook. Its quaint charm and long stretches of sand make it one of the most visited spots on the island, yet the atmosphere remains serene and the prices reasonable.

█▊ ORIENTATION AND PRACTICAL INFORMATION. Molyvos has three main tiered roads: the lowest (left as you enter town from the bus station) runs along the beach past hotels and restaurants. The middle tier is the **main road,** which traces the cliff top and runs all the way to the port on the far side of town. The upper tier, veering right and uphill as you enter town, runs through the vine-covered *agora* past shops and restaurants with fantastic views.

The **bus** stops at the base of town on the main road. **Buses** run from Molyvos to **Mytilini** (2hr., 4-5 per day, 1450dr/€4.26) via **Kaloni;** in summer, local buses run between Molyvos, **Petra,** and **Eftalou.** Check the tourist office for schedules and fares. Near the National Bank, **Kosmos Rentals** rents **mopeds** (3000-5000dr/€8.80-14.67 per day) and **cars** (10,000-21,000dr/€29.35-61.63 per day), including full insurance, tax, and unlimited mileage. (☎ 71 710; fax 71 720. Open daily 8am-1pm and 4:30-9pm.) **Taxis** (☎ 71 480) stop at the intersection on the main road heading into town from the bus stop. Just into town on the left side of the main road is the **tourist information office,** where you'll find maps, schedules, and help finding rooms. (☎ 71 347; fax 72 277; mithimna@aigaio.gr. Open daily Apr.-Oct. 7:30am-4pm.) Next door, the **National Bank** offers **currency exchange** and a 24hr. **ATM.** (Open M-Th 8am-2pm and F 8am-1:30pm.) The road forks just beyond the bank; head uphill and right at the fork at the top of the hill to the **post office** (open M-F 8am-2pm). If you head left, you'll find the local **laundry,** where 2600dr/€7.63 will get you clean clothes, or pay per individual article of clothing. (☎ 71 692. Open 9am-2:30pm and 5:30-9:30pm.) Also on the left fork is a **pharmacy** (☎ 71 427. Open 9:30am-2pm and 6:30-11pm.) Signs will direct you to the **police station** (☎ 71 222). **Internet access** is available at **Cinema Arion** (1500dr/€4.40 per hr.; open daily 8am-midnight, summer only) just up from the bus stop; **Cafe Pengola** (☎ 71 236; pergola1@otenet.gr; 1600dr/€4.70 per hr., 800dr/€2.35 minimum); and at **Molyvos Internet Center** near Conga Beach Club. (☎ 71 709. 800dr/€2.35 per 30min. Open M-Sa 10am-2pm and 6-11pm.) **Postal code:** 81108.

ꞮꞮ ACCOMMODATIONS AND FOOD. Signs for domatia dot the town and the helpful tourist office will be glad to find you a bed. Expect to pay 5000-8000dr/€14.67-23.48 for a double in the low season and 8000-10,000dr/€23.48-29.35 in the high season. ◤**Nassos Guest House,** on the hill just into town, offers cheerful rooms in an old house with high wood ceilings, private balconies, common baths and kitchen. Proprietors Marcia and Betty will make you feel at home. Veer left uphill, and then take the first switchback on the right. (☎71 432 and 71 421; nassosguesthouse@hotmail.com. Singles 7000-10,000dr/€20.53-29.35; doubles 7000-10,000dr/€20.53-29.35; triples 9000-12,000dr/€26.41-35.22. Discounts for longer stays. Reservations recommended in Aug.) **Hotel Poseidon,** on the road to the public beach, has spacious rooms with phones, TVs and fridges. Tiled private baths and little balconies complete the package. (☎71 981. ☎/fax 71 570. Breakfast 1800dr/€5.28. Singles 7500-10,000dr/€22-29.35; doubles 10,000-13,000dr/€29.35-38.15; triples 13,000-17,000dr/€38.15-49.89.) **Camping Mithimna** is 1.5km out of town on the road to Eftalou. (☎71 079. 950dr/€2.79 per person; 650dr/€1.91 per tent.)

Tavernas clustered in the harbor, at the far end of the main road, tend to be pricier than the tavernas hidden on the steep inland roads. **Taverna O Gatos,** midway up the hill before the post office, has served fresh traditional fare for over 20 years. Ask the friendly staff if you can have a rooftop seat; the view is amazing. (☎71 661. Starters 400-1600dr/€1.17-4.70, entrees 1550-1950dr/€4.55-5.72. Open 11am-late.) Herbivores rejoice, your prayers have been answered in the form of the **Friends** gyros stand, on the main road. The affable owner has created a vegetarian gyro stuffed with cucumbers, french fries, and green peppers instead of meat. (☎71 567. 500dr/€1.47.) There are several mini-markets on the main road as well.

◧◪ SIGHTS AND ENTERTAINMENT. The dominant feature of the Molyvos skyline is the **Kastro,** the medieval castle. The view alone is worth a climb up, and the castle itself is superbly preserved and occasionally plays host to theatrical events; call the town hall for information (☎71 313 or 71 323), or keep an eye out for signs. (Castle open Tu-Su 8am-7pm. 500dr/€1.47, students and children free.) **Exhibitions** by local artists and a small **archaeological museum** are in the town hall. While you're there, ask about the **Museum of Popular Art.**

On summer nights, head to **Conga's Beach Club,** accessible from both the beach-side and main roads, where pulsing music and tropical decor (complete with hammocks) entertain a tourist crowd. (Cover 1000dr/€2.93, includes a beer. Beer 1000-1500dr/€2.93-4.40, cocktails 2000dr/€5.87.) **Gatelousi Bar,** on the beach-side road, is a popular place for live, traditional Greek music. (Both open late.)

◪ BEACHES. The town's biggest draw is the long, pebbly **public beach** that stretches southward toward Petra and is accessible from the first road to the left as you enter Molyvos. Beach umbrellas abound, and showers and changing rooms are available. Watersports rev up near the Olive Press Hotel from 10am to 6pm. Rental is by the hour. (Paddleboats 2000dr/€5.87; kayaks 1500dr/€4.40; windsurfing 5000dr/€14.67; parasailing 8000dr/€23.48.) The beautiful black sand and pebble beaches of **Eftalou** (a 2001 EU Blue beach) make a pleasant daytrip from Molyvos. The bus from Molyvos drops off in the middle of the main beach. Keep walking to the end of road and around the rocks to find the **thermal baths** of Eftalou, whose 46-degree Celsius waters are good for rheumatism, arthritis, and skin diseases. (☎71 245. 800dr/€2.35 for private baths or pool. Open daily 7am-1pm and 3-9pm.) The beach continues well beyond the baths, providing ample opportunity to find a private stretch of sand.

PETRA Πετρα ☎0253

Named for the monolithic rock in the center of the town, this tiny artists' beach town suns itself on a fertile plain 5km south of Molyvos. Petra's traditional village ambience and long sandy beach make it a popular daytrip from Molyvos, as well as a worthy destination in itself.

Local buses run from **Molyvos** in the summer; the **bus** stops in the central plateia on the waterfront and picks up on the main road to Molyvos (500m from the central plateia toward Molyvos). Facing inland, the road straight ahead, **Theodokou,** hosts the **post office** (☎41 230; open M-F 7:30am-2pm). The road parallel to the water one block inland, **Ermou,** is lined with bakeries and shops. To the right on the water is **Nirvana Travel,** providing one-stop shopping for all of your tourist needs. Friendly owner Rebecca Michealides provides info, **currency exchange,** a book exchange, excursion bookings, and help with accommodations and car rentals. (☎41 991; fax 41 992; nirvanatravel@otenet.gr. Open daily in summer 9:30am-1:30pm and 6:30-10pm; available by fax, phone, and email in winter.) Next to Nirvana Travel is a **pharmacy.** (☎41 319. Open 8:30am-2pm and 5:30-9:30pm.) The **OTE,** to the left of the plateia on the road to Molyvos, provides telegram services. (☎41 399 or 41 199. Open M-F 7:30am-1:30pm.) **Taxis** are just a phone call away (☎42 022). **Internet access** is available at **Etedra** just beyond the plateia on the waterfront (☎41 170; 1600dr/€4.70 per hr.; open until midnight) and at **Reef Cafe** on the road to Molyvos, where a large selection of draft beers accompanies your surfing (☎41 488; 1000dr/€2.93 per hr.). **Postal code:** 81109.

The **Women's Cooperative of Petra,** upstairs in the central plateia (enter on Ermou), can help you find a room and serves up home-cooked meals in the summer. (☎41 238; fax 41 309. Open daily 1-4pm and 6-11pm. Rooms start at 6000dr/€17.61.) The typical beachfront taverna strip, on the road to Molyvos, is an alternative for a meal. At night, head to **Machine** bar and disco on the waterfront. (Open 10:30pm-late.) If you can peel yourself off the sand, you can watch ouzo bottling at **Ouzo Petras,** Ermou 31, an ouzo store with its own old bottling equipment. (☎41 231. Open daily 10:30am-1:30pm and 6:30-10:30pm.) Before getting happy with your brand-new bottle of liquid licorice joy, climb up the rock in the center of town (up Theodokou past the post office) to the pretty **Church of the Holy Mary with the Sweet Smile.** (Open daily 8:30am-9pm; modest dress required.) Also in town is the **Vareltzidaina House museum,** the opulent mansion of a former resident, with a collection of paintings and frescoes. (Open Tu-Su 8:30am-7pm.)

SKALA ERESSOU Σκαλα Ερεσου   ☎0253

Skala Eressou's seemingly endless beach stretches across the opposite end of Lesvos from Mytilini, completely breaking from the concrete noise of the capital. Laid-back and welcoming, Sappho's birthplace attracts an eclectic group of visitors—archaeologists, lesbian poets, and freckled families share the sand. Its western half remains one of the few legal nude beaches on the island. Perfect sunsets burn slowly down into clear nights over the mountains to the west, where the ridge forms Sappho's profile.

■▮ ORIENTATION AND PRACTICAL INFORMATION. The **main road** to Eressos and points North intersects with the long waterfront at **Pl. Anthis and Evristhenous.** To the right along the beach from the plateia are similar restaurants and cafes, while to the left (cross the bridge one block inland on **Kanari**) are more unique and interesting establishments. The streets parallel to the beach on both sides of the main road have **craft shops. Buses** run between Skala Eressou and **Mytilini,** via the fork for **Sigri** and **Kaloni** (3hr., 2-3 per day, 2200dr/€6.46). The bus stops in a large parking lot on the main road two blocks from the waterfront. Joanna and the team at **Sappho Travel,** one block from the bus stop before the waterfront, can help with accommodations, **currency exchange,** and give ▧free relationship advice. (☎52 140 or 53 327; fax 52 000; sappho@otenet.gr; www.lesvos.co.uk. Open daily 9am-11pm May-Oct.; Nov.-Apr. 9am-2pm and 5-9pm.) There are **health clinics** in Eressou (☎52 132; open Tu-Th) and Skala Eressou (☎53 221; open M, W, F 9am-1pm), behind the Hotel Sappho. The nearest **police** are in Eressou (☎53 222). In case of **emergency** call 52 122 or the **Health Center** in Antissa (☎54 440, 54 442, or 54 444). There is **no bank,** so bring either cash or traveler's checks. A few **card phones** are creatively hidden around town; one is alongside Hotel Sappho. **Postal code:** 81105.

ℍ ACCOMMODATIONS. Skala Eressou generally draws visitors for weeks of stunning sunsets; many come for vacation and end up staying for good. Consequently, studios and longer term accommodations are plentiful, although rooms for brief stays are also reasonably priced. **Sappho Travel** can help with accommodations (singles 6000dr/€17.61; doubles 12,000dr/€35.22). **Hotel Sappho,** on the waterfront to the right (facing the water), is a women's-only hotel with spacious rooms, original wall art, and a massage room. (☎53 495 or 53 233; fax 53 174. Singles 7000dr/€20.53; doubles 12,000-14,000dr/€35.22-41.10.) Farther down the beach to the right, **Villa Manilena** has well-equipped rooms with fridges, coffee makers, and beautifully tiled private baths right on the beach. (☎53 153 or 53 094. Doubles 10,000dr/€29.35; triples 12,000dr/€35.22; 5-person apartment 23,000dr/€67.50; discounts for longer stays.) There is **unofficial camping** at the far end of the beach, by the nude section farthest from town, with primitive women's facilities. This camping may be tolerated but is **illegal,** so camp at your own risk.

◪◪ FOOD AND ENTERTAINMENT. Outdoor cafes and the serene Aegean Sea surround the stone-layered **Square of Anthis and Evristhenous.** Along the beach to the left (as you face the water; cross the bridge one block inland), eclectic **▨Yamas** (☎53 693) serves home-made wheat pancakes (850dr/€2.50) and a variety of other delectable treats (500-1000dr/€1.47-2.93) all day. The longest-running bar (8 years and counting) in Skala Eressou, it also has big comfy chairs perfect for viewing the breathtaking sunset over the mountains. **Jay's Restaurant,** farther down the beach, offers a diverse menu of Eastern, Western, and **vegetarian** dishes. (Entrees 1300-2000dr/€3.82-5.87. Open daily 6pm-late.) Feel the love at **Aphrodite** (☎53 124), to the left off Kanari across the bridge, in the form of delicious, home-cooked traditional Greek dishes (1400-2500dr/€4.10-7.34). Try the specialty, stuffed grape leaves (*dolmades* 1800dr/€5.28). **The Tenth Muse,** in the main plateia, is a popular lesbian bar. (☎53 287. Cocktails 1600-2000dr/€4.70-5.87.) Revelers hang at the beachfront bars and cafes that spill onto the sand. On hot summer evenings, join the crowd for a late-night plunge in the Aegean to clear your head.

◪ SIGHTS. The 5th-century mosaics once housed in the early Christian basilica of **Ag. Andreas,** three blocks north of the beach, are now in Mytilini's Archaeological Museum. Near the church is the **Tomb of St. Andrew.** (Open 9am-1pm.) Behind the church is a small, unimpressive **archaeological museum** featuring funerary *steles* and similar items. (Open Tu-Su 8:30am-3pm. Free.) Of greater interest is the large excavation of still-vivid **floor mosaics** that began in the summer of 2000. The river, just west of Skala's center, is home to many rare and exotic birds. Peak **bird watching** season is from April to May. About 11km above Sigri on the main road is the spectacular **Ipsilou Monastery.** Situated on the peak of the Ordymnos volcanic dome, the picturesque Byzantine monastery commands an amazing view of northwestern Lesvos, and includes an ornate church and tiny museum.

▨ DAYTRIP FROM SKALA ERESSOU. A ▨**petrified forest** near **Sigri** is one of only two such forests in the world (the other is in the southwestern United States). The site is sprawled on a parched, rugged hillside about 10km above Sigri, and is connected by 2½km of walking trails. The amazing collection of fragments and unearthed trunks of 700,000-year-old trees takes at least an hour and a half to appreciate fully, and includes the largest fossilized tree in the world. In **Sigri,** the **Natural History Museum of Lesvos's Petrified Forest** has interesting, informative exhibits on a variety of plant fossils, both from the Lesvos site and from around the world, stretching back to the Paleozoic Era. The site and museum are best accessed by private vehicle, but a network of **trails** connects Eressos, the petrified forest, and Sigri (Eressos to forest, 7½km; forest to Sigri 14km; Sigri to Eressos 16km). (☎54 434; lesvospf@otenet.gr; www.aegean.gr/petrified_forest. Site open daily 8am-4pm. 500dr/€1.47, children free. Museum open daily 8am-8pm. 500dr/€1.47, children free.)

VATERA ςατερα   ☎ 0252

Near to the bubbling thermal baths of Polichnitos and backed by green hills, the long, plush beach of Vatera provides the perfect vacation escape. Fresh seafood at its beach tavernas caps off a long day in the sun and surf.

▐▌▐ ORIENTATION AND PRACTICAL INFORMATION. The **main road** from **Polichnitos,** 7km away, forms a T with Vatera's long beachside road. **Buses** enter via the main road and run the length of the beachside road between its two main resort hotels, **Aphrodite** and **Vatera Beach.** The bus can drop off and pick up anywhere along the beach. Buses run to **Mytilini** (1½hr.; M-F 4 per day; Sa-Su 2 per day; 1350dr/€3.96) via **Polichnitos.** At the T-shaped intersection, **Alfa Rent-a-Car** has cars and maps. There are no regular hours, so call a day ahead. (☎61 132; alfacar@aias.gr.) The **bank** and **post office** are both located in Polichnitos. In emergencies call the **police** (☎41 222) or **clinic** (☎41 511), both open 24hr. in Polichnitos. **Internet access** is available at **Myramida Cafe** in Polichnitos, across from the bus stop (1500dr/€4.40 per hr.). The **Aphrodite Hotel** (☎61 588, 61 788 or 61 288), 800m down the road from the main intersection, rents **bicycles** (2000dr/€5.87 per day, 500dr/€1.47 per hr.) and has **international press** and **exchange. Taxis** (☎ 42 550) are available upon request; the ride to Polichnitos runs about 2000dr/€5.87.

▐ ▐ ACCOMMODATIONS AND FOOD. Room prices shoot up during Vatera's flash-in-the-pan high season (the last week of July through August); reservations are necessary during that time. On the bright side, before or after the season you have 7km of beach practically to yourself. Family-run **Arion,** behind Taverna O Zouros, 300m down the road to the left of the intersection, has sparkling wood-accented rooms with fridges, private baths, and balconies. (☎61 331 or 61332; mobile 0932 699 219. Singles 7000-8000dr/€20.53-23.48; doubles 7000-9000dr/€20.53-26.41; triples 10,000-12,000dr/€29.35-35.22.) **Johnnie Rooms,** also to the left of the intersection, has large, immaculate rooms with A/C, fridges, private baths, and a common kitchen. (☎61 710 or 61 075. Singles and doubles 8000-10,500dr/€23.48-30.81; triples 10,000-20,000dr/€29.35-58.69.) Lavish **Camping Dionysos,** 350m from the intersection and 100m from the beach (also accessible from the main road out of town), has a pantheon of amenities: hot water showers, bathrooms, market, swimming pool, and bar. (☎61 710 or 61 151; fax 61 155. Reception 8am-midnight. Seaside gate open 9am-9pm, main road gate open 24hr. 2000dr/€5.87 per person, 1000dr/€2.93 per child; 2000dr/€5.87 per tent; 2000dr/€5.87 per car.) Two supermarkets are about 50m to the left of the intersection; tavernas are interspersed along the beachside road. Family owned and operated **Taverna O Zouros** is one of the best restaurants on the beach, with fresh seafood from 1300dr/€3.82. (☎61 353. Starters 500-1600dr/€1.47-4.70; entrees 1200-1800dr/€3.52-5.28. Open all day.) Candlelit **Mylos Cafe,** 100m to the left of the intersection on the beach, hosts a mixed crowd in search of a chill atmosphere. Beer (700dr/€2.05) and cocktails (1500dr/€4.40) accompany the mood music. (☎61 161. Open late.)

▐ DAYTRIP FROM VATERA: POLYCHNITOS SPA. The 60-92°C spring waters of Polichnitos are some of the hottest and most therapeutic in Europe. The bath houses were originally built during Byzantine times; several have been renovated for modern use. The old bath houses are still open for exploration in the field behind the renovated building, which features gender-divided showers, changing rooms, and baths. (☎41 229. Open daily 6am-noon and 3-6pm. 500dr/€1.47, towels 100dr/€0.29.). From Vatera, take the bus to Polichnitos (2-4 per day, 20min.). The spa is approximately 1½km from the bus stop. From the stop, head back down the road 200m toward Vatera and turn left at the sign for qermopiyeo (thermal springs). Follow this road through farmland and past the military installation.)

PLOMARI Πλομαρι   ☎ 0252

After arson destroyed Megalohori village in 1841, people resettled in the Turkish-inhabited region 12km south, now modern Plomari. From its earliest days, this southern coastal town has had a split personality—it's a vacation town brimming with tavernas and trinket shops, and a crumbling fishing village full of octopi nailed to telephone poles to dry in the sun. The overall effect is aided and abetted by Plomari's large ouzo industry.

◪ PRACTICAL INFORMATION. Plomari is 40km by bus from Mytilini (1½hr., 1000dr/€2.93). The **bus** stops in the main plateia, where you'll spot a **National Bank** that has a 24hr. **ATM** and offers **currency exchange.** (Open M-Th 8am-2pm, F 8am-1:30pm.) In the top left corner of the plateia a road leads to **Platanos,** a charming cobbled plateia basking in the shade of an enormous tree and ringed with tavernas and food markets. About 50m up the first street to the right from Platanos (running uphill behind the national bank) are a **pharmacy** (☎32 381; open 9am-1:30pm and 5:30-9:30pm) and a **bakery.** The street immediately to the right of the bus stop (facing inland) runs past a long gauntlet of waterfront tavernas. On the right of town on the beachside road, facing inland, are the **OTE** and the **post office,** which exchanges currency. (Open M-F 7:30am-1pm.) Services include: **police** (☎32 222); the **24hr. Health Center of Plomari,** just outside of town (☎32 151); and a **medical emergency line** ☎ 166. **Saloon Cafe,** to the right from the bus stop at the end of the line of tavernas, provides **Internet access.** (1500dr/€4.40 per hr., 1000dr/€2.93 minimum. Open 9am-evening.) **Paper Land,** in Platanos, sells **international newspapers** and books. **Taxis** (☎33 331) wait in the main plateia, next to the bus stop. On the other side of the plateia, **Oceanis Rent-a Bike** (☎32 469 or 32 498) rents mopeds (3500-7000dr/€10.27-20.53), cars (8000-14,000dr/€23.48-41.10), and a few bicycles (1500dr/€4.40). **Postal code:** 81200.

◪ ACCOMMODATIONS. While Plomari makes a wonderful daytrip, there are places to stay should you want to relax a bit longer. **⬛Pension Lida** (☎/fax 32 507), is housed in two adjacent buildings on the hill above Platanos: the old mansion of a Plomari manufacturer and the family home of its owner. Beautiful and diverse rooms are accented by Byzantine treasures tucked into walls and hardwood floors. Each opens onto stone terraces, balconies, or arched stone windows with amazing views of the village. Friendly owner **Jannis Stergellis** manufactures his own ouzo and olive oil on the premises. (☎/fax 32 507. Singles 5600-7000dr/€16.43-20.53; doubles 8000-10,000dr/€23.48-29.35; triples 10,400-13,300dr/€30.52-39.03.) **Maki's Guest House** is up the stairs to the right of Saloon Cafe; knock on the third wooden door on the left. Three pristine rooms on the waterfront have private baths, fridges, and a common balcony. (☎32 536. Singles 4000-6000dr/€11.74-17.61; doubles 7000-10,000dr/€20.53-29.35.)

◪◪ SIGHTS AND BEACHES. The local ouzo is far better than the bottled industrial variety. Try a sample at the **Barbayanni Ouzo Factory,** roughly 2km east toward Agios Isodoros on the way to Plomari, which has its very own **Ouzo Museum,** featuring the Barbayanni family's original wooden boilers. (☎32 741. Open M-F 8am-4pm.) An annual, week-long **Ouzo Festival** is held in late August and features song, dance, and, of course, free ouzo. Plomari also hosts several summertime religious celebrations and cultural events. The one-week **Festival of Benjamin,** in late June, commemorates the War of Independence leader with dancing and theatrical presentations. On August 15, the town celebrates **Panegyri** in time-honored style. Just 15km north of Plomari on the slopes of Lesvos's Mt. Olympus, you'll find the ceramic crafts center of **Agiassos.** In town, an Orthodox church treasures an icon of the Virgin Mary made by St. Lucas, originally destined for Constantinople in AD 330. When the priest transporting it heard rumors of war, he hid the icon in Agiassos's church. On August 15, Agiassos hosts **Panagia,** a grand annual celebration in honor of the Virgin Mary. The village also boasts an **Ecclesiastical Museum** with Byzantine religious works (ask church officials and priests in town) and a **Folk Museum** featuring traditional costumes.

NORTHEAST AEGEAN

Beaches appear intermittently around Plomari. To reach small, rocky **Ammoudeli Beach,** follow the waterfront road out of town to the right from the bus stop, facing the water. Continuing straight past the beach brings you to **Agios Nikolaos,** a church sparkling with icons spanning 400 years. About 3km east of town, the sandy, golden expanse of **Ag. Isodoros** beach draws a large, bronze-colored following.

LIMNOS Λημνος

According to a saying, everyone who visits Limnos cries twice: once when they arrive and once when they leave. Tiny, remote, laced with dirt roads and spotted with sheep, the island's solitude sinks in slowly. Stubborn Limnos meets travelers on its own terms, somewhere between the two-storied capital, the flamingoes of the eastern salt lakes, and the silent military presence.

MYRINA Μυρινα ☎ 0254

The island's capital and primary port is a well-proportioned fishing village. At night, the hilly skyline is dominated by an impressive, illuminated Venetian Castle. Each morning, Myrina is roused to the orange dawn by the harborside fishermen.

☰ TRANSPORTATION. Ferries: Nel Lines runs to **Alexandropoulis** (6hr., 2 per week, 3800dr/€11.15); **Chios** (10hr., 3 per week, 5400dr/€15.85); **Kavala** (6hr., 3 per week, 3900dr/€11.45); **Kos** (1 per week, 7600dr/€22.30); **Lesvos** (6hr., 6 per week, 4600dr/€13.50); **Piraeus** (22hr., 2 per week, 7500dr/€22); **Rafina** (3 per week, 5900dr/€17.31); **Rhodes** (1 per week, 9900dr/€29.05); **Samos** (1 per week, 6900dr/€20.25); and **Thessaloniki** (8hr., 2 per week, 5700dr/€16.73). Buy tickets at **Nicos Vayakos Tours** in Pl. 8 Octovriou. (☎22 460 or 22 900; fax 23 560. Open M-F 8am-3pm and 6:30-9:30pm, Sa 8am-3:30pm and 7:30-9:30pm, Su 7:30am-4pm and 7:30-9:30pm.) **Ferry Boat SAOS II** runs to: **Kavala** (6hr., 4 per week, 4000dr/€11.74); **Samothraki** (2½hr., 2 per week, 2700dr/€7.92); and **Thessaloniki** (8hr., 1 per week, 5700dr/€16.73). Buy tickets at **Pravlis Travel,** directly across the plateia from Vayakos Tours. (☎29 577 or 24 617; fax 22 471. Open daily 9am-2pm and 5-9:30pm.) Pravlis also sells tickets for **Olympic Airways** flights to: **Athens** (2 per day, 18,900dr/€55.47); **Lesvos** (4 per week, 16,400dr/€48.13); and **Thessaloniki** (6 per week, 19,100dr/€56.05). The **bus station** (☎22 464) is in Pl. El. Venizelou, the second plateia along Kyda in the far left corner between a tourist agency and a coffee shop. Although buses serve all of the island's villages, you may get somewhere and find yourself unable to return. You'll be much better off renting a **bicycle** (1500-3000dr/€4.40-8.80), **moped** (3500-9000dr/€10.27-26.41), or **car** (9000-12,000dr/€26.41-35.22); inquire on the harborfront at one of the many agencies. **Taxis** (☎23 820) are at your service in the main plateia.

◼◪ ORIENTATION AND PRACTICAL INFORMATION. The city has two main waterfronts on opposite sides of the **Kastro. Romeikos,** on the Greece-facing side, is longer, pebblier, and more popular. Once-regal Neoclassical mansions, cafes, and pricey tavernas, ideal for viewing spectacular sunsets behind Mt. Athos, line its sides. **Turkikos,** facing Turkey, is the active port, where ferries and hydrofoils dock. Its beach is sandier, shallower, and bordered by the best fresh fish restaurants in town. To get to Romeikos from Turkikos, head inland up **Kyda** (the main artery) past most of the town, and take a left at the bridge to reach the waterfront.

TALKIN' THE TALK For instant status as an honorary islander, turn your sputtering tourist Greek into a convincing local dialect. You can earn points for effort by mastering some local slang. A commonly-heard expression throughout Greece is "BRA-vo", with the accent on the first syllable for extra sass. It's used as an expression of approval ("You got a cell phone that rings to the tune of 'Blue'? Bravo!") as well as assent ("You want to go to the nude beach today? Bravo, bravo."). If you're feeling saucy, just bust out whenever you feel like it and see what happens. Ready? BRA-vo!

Kyda leads inland from Pl. 8 Octovriou, past a variety of shops and into the town's central plateia where you'll find **taxis, card phones,** and the **National Bank** with 24hr. **ATM.** (☎22 414. Open M-Th 8am-2pm, F 8am-1:30pm.) One block farther on Kyda, **Garofalidi** runs to the right. Here you will find the **post office** (☎22 462; open M-F 7:30am-2pm) and a self-serve **laundromat** in the Hotel Astron (☎24 392; priced by weight: 2000dr/€5.87 for 1-2kg, 2500dr/€7.34 for 5-6kg; open M-F 9am-2pm and 5:30-10pm, Sa 8:30am-11:30pm, Su 11am-11:30pm). Two doors down from the post office, **Joy Games** offers **Internet access.** (1200dr/€3.52 per hour, 600dr/€1.76 minimum. Open M-F 10:30am-2pm and 4-10:30pm, Sa-Su 10:30am-10:30pm.) There are several **pharmacies** on Kyda. Walk down Garofalidi past the post office until you come to a large intersection. The **police station** (☎22 200; open 24hr.) is on the corner. Turn left and take the first right, following the signs to reach the **hospital.** (☎22 222 or 22 345. Open 24hr.) In case of **fire,** call 22 199. **Postal Code:** 84100.

▗▖ ACCOMMODATIONS AND FOOD. There are many hotels in town, but they are generally quite expensive. The domatia advertised all over town are the best bet for inexpensive lodgings. **Hotel Aktaion,** on the waterfront in the first plateia on the left from the ferry dock, has clean but simple rooms with fridges and tiny private baths. (☎22 258. Singles 5000dr/€14.67; doubles 7000dr/€20.53.) **Hotel Limnos,** at the ferry dock, offers spacious rooms with balconies and harbor views, as well as A/C, TVs, and phones. The owners, Harry and Bill, can give you the low-down on Limnos. (☎22 153 or 24 023; fax 23 329. Singles 9000-13,000dr/€26.41-38.15; doubles 12,000-16,000dr/€46.96.)

The hands-down best fish in Myrina is at **To Limanaki,** on the marina around the waterfront beyond Pl. 8 Octovriou. Order from the glass tank near the kitchen, but remember that quality doesn't come cheap. (☎23 744. Entrees and fresh fish 1350-8500dr/€3.96-24.94. Open daily 7am-late.) Souvlaki and gyros sell for 400-600dr/€1.17-1.76 along Kyda; **Demis Handmade Souvlaki** (☎22 438), in the central plateia serves up a delicious, slow-grilled gyro (450dr/€1.32). The restaurants along Romeikos have menus posted along the waterfront. Be sure to get a seaside table for the view of Mt. Athos. At night, cruise the cafe/bar strip at Romeikos.

▗▖ SIGHTS AND ENTERTAINMENT. The **Kastro** that pierces the skyline and divides the waterfronts also houses several dozen deer. If you don't catch sight of them, you can at least enjoy the stunning view and the ruins of the 7th-century BC fortress, reworked by Venetians in the 13th century. Many buildings are at least partially intact within the vast ruins. Wear good shoes and allow an hour to clamber through them all. Follow signs from Myrina harbor for the easiest ascent. The network of dungeons and tunnels underlying the kastro is only for daring explorers with flashlights. In the middle of Romeikos, right next to Hotel Castro, the **Archaeological Museum** has well-staged exhibits accompanied by dramatic music. Informative banners throughout the building provide a comprehensive history of Limnos and explain the various artifacts, which include finds from Hephaestus, the Kabeiron, and Poliochni. Don't miss the interesting collection of ceramic siren sculptures or the skeleton of a sacrificed bull calf (ca. 6th century BC). (☎22 990. Open daily 8am-7pm. 500dr/€1.47, seniors 300dr/€0.88, children under 18 free.)

Limnos is home to a number of notable **archaeological sites,** which are best accessed via some form of private transportation. **Poliochni,** on the island's east coast opposite Myrina, was a prehistoric settlement in the 4th and 5th millennia BC. It underwent many building periods during its existence and is considered to be one of the most complex fortified cities of its time. Current speculation pairs the cataclysmic destruction of Poliochni in the 2nd millenium BC with that of the city of Troy, on the nearby coast of Asia Minor. Ancient **Hephaestia,** on the island's north coast, was the location of a sanctuary to the smith-god Hephaestus. Farther up the coast is the site of the 8th-century BC **Kabeiron,** or **Sanctuary of the Kabeiroi.** The Kabeiroi were a cult that practiced the mysteries for the birth of man and the rebirth of nature. Legend holds that Hephaestus moved his forge from Olympus to Limnos, indicated by the island's volcanic soil and its metal-working industry. The

Kaberoi were the sons of the Olympian smith and the nymph Kaberos, who acted as deities of seafaring, fertility, the vine, and metallurgy. One ceremony of the Kabeiroi involved the transportation of a sacred flame from Delos in the Cyclades to Limnos, where it was used to light forge fires and bless smithing activities.

Excitement on Limnos is largely seasonal. In the winter, the western salt plains of **Aliki** and **Hortaro Limni** host thousands of migrating flamingoes. On April 23, Ag. George's Day, the town of **Calliope** near Keros Beach holds a horse-racing festival. The hot springs of **Therma,** 4km outside of Myrina, can revive you after a night at Limnos's seaside discos. They usually open in midsummer and advertise their locations by postering on Myrina's harborfront.

SAMOTHRAKI Σαμοθρακη

Early on, Samothraki (also called **Samothrace**) was a place of pilgrimage for Thracian settlers who worshipped the Anatolian Great Gods that preceded the Olympian pantheon. Philip II of Macedon and bride-to-be Olympia may have met here as candidates to join the religion; Sparta's Lysander and Julius Caesar's father-in-law, Piso, were initiates, too. Unlike other mystery cults, women, slaves, and all comers could gain membership. The religious center shut down after centuries of operation, when the Roman Empire banned all non-Christian practices in the 4th century AD. When those first Thracian colonists arrived in the 10th century BC, they saw the same thing you'll see today when your ferry pulls into port: dry grassy fields spread outward from the base of the Aegean's tallest peak, the pine-blanketed 1670m Fengari "moon." Remote, scarcely developed, and full of beautiful wilderness, Samothraki attracts Greeks who would willfully choose swatting mosquitoes in a tent over clubbing until dawn. Though all kinds of people visit, there are, on the whole, more hiking boots than high heels, and guitars outnumber cell phones as hand-held accessories. This laid-back crowd lends the place a grungy *joie de vivre*—a change from the run-of-the-mill summer glitz of other islands.

KAMARIOTISSA Καμαριοτισσα ☎ 0551

Even with tourist agencies along the waterfront road and the busy comings and goings of buses and ferries, simple Kamariotissa retains the sleepy, untouched charm of the island.

✦ 🛈 ORIENTATION AND PRACTICAL INFORMATION

Everything in Kamariotissa is within a stone's throw of the waterfront. Ferries dock on the south edge of town. The north-south waterfront road runs out of town to the north and the road to Hora runs east out of town just past the bus stop (at the stop sign). **Ferries** connect Samothraki to: **Alexandroupolis** (2½hr., 1-3 per day, 2400dr/€7.04); **Kavala** (3hr., 4 per week, 3100dr/€9.10); and **Limnos** (3hr., 1 per week, 2700dr/€7.92). **Flying Dolphins** run to Alexandroupolis (1hr., 1-2 per day, 4800dr/€14.09). For tickets and schedules, ask the port police, **Saos Tours** (☎41 505 or 41 411; open 7:30am-2pm and 6-10:30pm), or **Nikis Tours** (☎41 465; fax 41 304; open 9am-2pm and 6-10:30pm). **Buses** stop on the waterfront across from Saos Tours. **Green KTEL buses** run round-trip to: Hora (6 per day 7:45am-5:30pm, 260dr/€0.76); Paleopolis (260dr/€0.76); Therma (550dr/€1.61); Fonias (5 per day 8:30am-6:20pm, 700dr/€2.05); and Profitis Ilias (4 per day 6:30am-4:15pm, 550dr/€1.61). **White local buses** run to **Kypos Beach** (3 per day, returns at 6pm, 1000dr/€2.93) via Paleopolis (250dr/€0.73), Therma (500dr/€1.47), the campsites (650dr/€1.91) and Fonias (650dr/€1.91); and to **Pahia Ammo beach** (3 per day, returns at 7pm; 1000dr/€2.93) via Hora (250dr/€0.73), Alonia (250dr/€0.73), Lakoma (350dr/€1.03), and Profitis Ilias (500dr/€1.47). **Taxis** wait on the waterfront (8am-1am). Rent **mopeds** at **Niki Rent Motor Bikes** in the flag-adorned lot on the road to Hora. (☎41 305. Mopeds start at 4000dr/€11.74 per day. Regular bikes 2000dr/€5.87 per day.)

Facing inland, past the waterfront docks on the left, a Greek flag marks the **port police.** (☎41 305. Open 24hr.) Nearby on the waterfront is the **National Bank,** which has a **24hr. ATM** and **exchanges currency.** (Open M-Th 8am-2pm, F 8am-1:30pm.) There's a **pharmacy** on the road to Hora. (☎41 217 or 41 376. Open M-F 9am-2pm and 6-10pm; hours reduced Sa-Su.) **Internet access** is available at **Para Pente Cafe,** farther down the same block on the left. (1000dr/€2.93 per hr. Open 9am-2am.) The **post office, OTE, medical clinic** (☎41 217; open 24hr.), and **police station** (☎41 203; open 24hr.) are in Hora. **Postal code:** 68002.

▐ ACCOMMODATIONS AND CAMPING

Samothraki's primary draw is its pristine wilderness; consequently many travelers breeze through Kamariotissa on their way to **Therma** and the **campsites.** Kamariotissa is the island's transportation hub and the only place to stay before early ferries; the campsites host acoustic guitar solos and late-night beach bonfires.

Brisko Rooms (☎41 328), set back off the road across from the ferry dock, has bright, spacious rooms with TVs, fridges, private baths, and balconies. Singles 6000-8000dr/ €17.61-23.48; doubles 10,000dr/€29.35; triples 12,000dr/€35.22.

Giannelou Despina (☎41 308) lets 5 rooms in the center of town, on the street next to O Stinantisi. Small and simple rooms have common balconies. Doubles 8000-10,000dr/€23.48-29.35; 10,000-12,000dr/€29.35-35.22 with bath.

Hotel Kyma (☎41 263), on the waterfront at the north edge of town, is 10m from the stone beach and has spacious rooms with balconies overlooking the sea. A/C, private baths, and fridges. Doubles 8000-14,000dr/€23.48-38.15; triples 10,000-16,000dr/ €29.35-46.96.

Camping Platia (☎98 244), 2km beyond Therma on the coast, has cold showers, bathrooms, a mini-market, and card phones. Check-out one day in advance of departure. 1000dr/€2.93 per person, 600dr/€1.76 per child; 800dr/€2.35 per tent; 650dr/ €1.91 per car; 500dr/€1.47 per motorbike.

Camping Varades (☎98 291), 1km beyond Camping Platia on the coastal road, has the same amenities, but with hot showers and a cafe. 1000dr/€2.93 per person, 600dr/ €1.76 per child; 800dr/€2.35 per tent; 650dr/€1.91 per car.

▐▊ FOOD AND NIGHTLIFE

The waterfront teems with tavernas specializing in fresh seafood. Most have no need for a menu—just go inside and point at your fish of choice. **I Sinatisi,** a few doors down from Nikis Tours, is the best in a row of fish tavernas. Excellent seafood appetizers pave the way for perfectly grilled fresh fish, with the setting sun as a natural, gorgeous backdrop. (Entrees 900-3200dr/€2.64-9.39. ☎41 308. Open until 2am.) Another excellent spot is **I Klimataria,** on the left-hand side of the waterfront, which features old standbys and some more innovative dishes, such as *yiannotiko*, pork with vegetables and cheeses. (Entrees 1000-2500dr/€2.93-7.34.) Head back to the kitchen to pick your cut of meat or prepared dish. **Cafe Moka** (☎41 039), on the waterfront, has a variety of pastries including *tyropita*, and a melt-in-your-mouth cream pie dusted with powdered sugar and cinnamon (500dr/€1.47). Wake yourself up with a shot of Bailey's in that morning *frappé* (800dr/€2.35).

Nightlife in Kamariotissa is so laid-back that it's almost non-existent. Beyond a few *barakia* (little bars), the town mostly has a drink after dinner and dozes off. **Diva** on the waterfront plays an eclectic variety of music. **Cafe Aktaion** is a popular nightspot for people of all ages. Drinks at the waterfront bars are similarly priced: beer 700-1400dr/€2.05-4.11, cocktails 1500-2000dr/€4.40-5.87.

▐▍ BEACHES AND THE OUTDOORS

The verdant gem that is Samothraki holds a wealth of hiking trails leading to cascading waterfalls, mountain vistas, and the summit of Fengari itself. Trails are generally unmarked and unexpected; the best way to explore is to rent a motorbike in Kamariotissa and then head out to the coast or the interior. The island's only **sand**

beach is the soft arc of **Pahia Ammo** on the south coast. Stony beaches ring the rest of the coast. Ask a bus driver to drop you off anywhere, then hunt out your own isolated stretch of shoreline. At the end of the line on the north coastal road is popular **Kypos beach.** White buses to: Pahia Ammo (3 per day noon-6pm, returns at 7pm; 100dr/€2.93) and Kypos (3 per day 10am-4pm, returns at 6pm; 100dr/€2.93).

The most convenient hub for outdoor activities is the town of **Therma,** which brims with dread-locked and tie-dyed alterna-types. A multitude of mini-markets and equipment stores can outfit your camping trip. Tavernas and domatia dominate the village, making it an attractive alternative to Kamariotissa, especially for stays of multiple days. **Buses** from Kamariotissa stop at the base of town, next to the refreshing **thermal springs** that give the town its name. The trail to the **summit of Fengari** is accessible from Therma. Ask around at the base of town for the best way up. Be sure to fill up your water bottles at the **fountain** at the base of town and don't hike alone. The mountain peak is usually shrouded in mist; the hike up takes 5-6hr. A lovely **waterfall** is also accessible from Therma. From the bus stop, head into town and take the left fork through town. Take the first right after a mini-market and follow this road past tavernas and a bakery. When the road dead-ends, turn left and follow the road; when it meets with an asphalt paved road, turn right. The road dead-ends again at Taverna Filarakia; turn right and head up the shaded road. The dirt trail to the falls follows the stream on the right side of the road; head right 20m before the Marina Hotel.

Enchanting ▧**Fonias** is like a cold draught of water in the scorching Aegean sun. The easy 2km hike meanders alongside a gurgling stream and beneath gnarled trees, where dragonflies hover languidly in shafts of light. The trail ends in a sheer cliff face, at a cascading **waterfall.** Shed your clothes and jump into the deep green pool at the waterfall's base. Alternatively, climb up the steep rockface to the right of the stream for a magnificent view of the falls and the mountains. The **bus** drops off at the parking lot at the trailhead. (Green buses: 5 per day 8:30am-6:20pm, 700dr/€2.05. White buses: 3 per day 10am-4pm, returns at 6pm; 650dr/€1.91.)

▧ DAYTRIP FROM KAMARIOTISSA: PALEOPOLIS

Paleopolis and the **Sanctuary of the Great Gods,** Samothraki's premier attractions, lie 6km east of Kamariotissa. (Open daily 8:30am-8:30pm. 500dr/€1.47, students free; free on Sunday.) Before the island's 8th-century BC Aeolian colonization, the chief goddess worshipped here was **Axieros,** or the Great Mother. Three other gods completed the **Kabeiroi** group: Axiokersa, Axiokerson, and Kasmilos. These gods were assimilated into the Olympian Pantheon; Axieros was recast as the fertility goddess Demeter, while two of her consorts, believed to protect sailors, were associated with the twins Castor and Pollux.

Disclosing initiation secrets was punishable by death, so the rituals remain shrouded in mystery. It seems likely that there were two levels of membership: first, the *myesis,* then the higher *epopteia.* The first purification took place in the **Anaktoron,** at the lowest part of the temple complex. The second rite took place in the **Hieron,** a courtyard whose five reconstructed columns now form the site's central attraction. In the **palace** at the southern end, aspiring initiates donned special vestments and were given a lamp. The palace adjoins the Anaktoron, with its circular wooden platform, upon which the newly inducted were presented.

The enormous cylindrical **Arsinoëin,** given to Samothraki by Queen Arsinoë of Egypt, demonstrates the importance of circles to the site. The walls (now preserved in the museum) are decorated with rosettes and heads of oxen. They once stood at the sacrificial site. The nearby **Sacred Rock** was the original center of the cult's practices. In the center, the Doric Hieron—containing pits for sacrifices, an altar for libations, and seats for the audience—saw the final stage of initiation. Confessing their worst deeds, the candidates were purified. A scrubby hillside is all that remains of an ancient **theater.** On top is the spot where the **Winged Victory** (or **Nike**) **of Samothrace** once stood upon a marble base shaped like a ship's prow. Removed to Edirne, Turkey, it was then looted by a French consul in 1683. It now sits as one of the greatest treasures in the Louvre in Paris. Above the sanctuary are the remains of the **ancient town** of Samothraki, where the apostle Paul lived for a year on his way to Kavala in AD 49-50.

Beside the ruins, the **Paleopolis Museum** is somewhat underwhelming. It houses gargantuan entablatures from the **Arsinoein** and the **Hieron,** a weathered bust of the melancholy prophet **Tiresias,** and a galling cast of the Nike of Samothrace—a "gift" to Greece courtesy of the French. The relief of dancing girls symbolizes the marriage of Cadmus and Harmonia. The dance represented the onset of winter, a time of mourning to be followed by spring's renewal of life and bursting of seed. (☎41 474. Open Tu-Su 8:30am-3pm. 500dr/€1.47, students free.)

THASOS Θασος

Just off the coast of Kavala (p. 251) lies Thasos, the green jewel of the North Aegean. According to legend, Thasos was founded when the devoted brother of Europa gave up pursuing his abducted sister and settled on this remote island. As an ancient exporter of gold, silver, and its famous wine, Thasos attracted the unwelcome attention of Phoenician, Athenian, and Roman conquerors. The Thassians who were not killed or sold into slavery were forced to hide, fleeing to mountain villages or caves. Along with most of northern Greece, Thasos returned to Greek rule in 1912 at the conclusion of the First Balkan War. Since then, massive forest fires have threatened the island's greenery, but the forests are slowly reviving; a sign states proudly upon your arrival, *"Welcome to Thassos, Forest is the Source of Life."* Today, Thasos thrives on a few trades like beekeeping, shepherding, farming, and jam-making, but tourism is making inroads. "The Green Island" fully deserves its nickname, with its cool, forested mountains, thriving agriculture, and an isolated south coast that is a hiker's paradise.

LIMENAS Λιμενας   ☎0593

The island's capital and tourist center is built atop the foundations of the ancient city, and ruins crop up sporadically in the streets. Also known as Thasos Town, Limenas sees the highest concentration of tourists, yet maintains some of the best-priced accommodations on the island. The German tourists who pack the town in the summer find it a convenient place to rent a moped and explore the island's hundreds of secluded beaches. An important note: the arrival and departure point for ferries from Kavala is not in Limenas, but in Skala Prinos (18km west). As soon as your ferry lands from Kavala, walk left to find buses for **Limenas** and **Limenaria.**

▐ TRANSPORTATION

The village of **Skala Prinos** (18km west) is the point of arrival and departure for ferries. Buses between Thasos's main villages of Limenas and Limenaria stop at Skala Prinos, in sync with the arrival of the ferries from Kavala.

Ferries: In Limenas, the gray port police building and ticket booth post schedules. Ferries go to **Keramoti** (35min., 17 per day 5am-10pm, 440dr/€1.29). From **Skala Prinos,** ferries go to **Kavala** (1½hr., 8 per day 5:45am-9:30pm, 900dr/€2.64) and **N. Peramus** (1½hr., 3 per day 6:30am-3:15pm, 900dr/€2.64). Bus schedules between Prinos and Limenas are synchronized with the ferries. You must return to Kavala for ferry connections to other islands.

Flying Dolphins: Hydrofoils zip to **Kavala** from Limenas (45min., 5 per day 8am-4:15pm, 2400dr/€7.04), and from Limenaria, on Thasos's south coast (45min.; 8:20am, 3pm; 3500dr/€10.27). Schedules are posted at the port police and ticket booth, and docked boats indicate upcoming departure times with signs on board. Tickets can be bought on board.

Buses: The station (☎22 162) is across from the ferry landing, on the waterfront. Open daily 7:30am-8:15pm. To: **Aliki Beach** (1hr., 4 per day 8:15am-4:15pm, 800dr/€2.35); **Limenaria** (1½hr., 10 per day 6:35am-7:45pm, 950dr/€2.79) via **Skala Prinos** (30min., 400dr/€1.17); **Panayia** (15min., 12 per day 6:45am-9:15pm, 260dr/€0.76); **Skala Potamia** (30min., 12 per day 6:45am-7:15pm, 340dr/€1); **Theologos**

(1½hr., 6 per day 8:15am-4:15pm, 1250dr/€3.67); and all the way around the island and back to **Limenas** (2½hr., 8 per day 6:35am-4:15pm, 2250dr/€6.60). Ask at the tourist police or bus office for schedules.

Rentals: Cars and mopeds are rented all over Limenas. **Budget** (☎23 150), on a street perpendicular to the waterfront. Cars 15,000dr/€44.02 including 100km and damage waiver. Open daily 8am-1:30pm and 5-9pm. **Billy's Bikes** (☎23 253 or 22 490) is next door. Motorbikes 4000dr/€11.74 per day and up. Open 9am-2pm and 5-9pm.

Taxi: (☎23 841), near the ports.

Water taxi: Daily from Limenas to **Golden Beach** (leaves 10:30am, returns 5pm; 1000dr/€2.93 one-way) and **Makryamos** (leaves 10:30am, returns 10:50am and 5:40pm; 500dr/€1.47 one-way).

✦🔢 ORIENTATION AND PRACTICAL INFORMATION

A small crossroads near the bus station and National Bank connects the waterfront road and **28 Octovriou**, a jungle of souvenir shops and souvlaki joints running parallel to the water one block inland. With your back to the water, to the left are the **Old Port**, the ancient **Agora**, and the nearest beach. The small central plateia lies about two blocks farther inland.

Tourist Agencies: Thassos Tours (☎22 546), under the yellow sign, is on the waterfront. Rents motorbikes (3500dr/€10.27), helps with accommodations, and has advice on tours of the island. Open daily 9am-9pm. **Thassos Tourist Services** (☎22 343), on 28 Octovriou behind the row of tavernas, has maps of the ancient agora, and **exchanges currency.** Open M-W and F-Su 9am-1:30pm and 6-9pm.

Bank: There's a **National Bank** where 28 Octovriou meets the waterfront, with an automated 24hr. **currency exchange** and **ATM.**

Police: (☎22 500), on the waterfront by the port police. Open 24hr.

Tourist Police: (☎23 111 or 23 580), with the police. Open daily 8am-10pm.

Port Police (☎22 355), in the gray building with Greek flags at the waterfront's center. Open daily 6am-11pm.

Health Center: (☎71 100), in Prinos. Open 24hr. There is no hospital on Thasos; the nearest is in Kavala.

Telephones: The **OTE** is on 28 Octovriou, a block down from Thassos Tourist Services. Open M-F 7:30am-3pm.

Internet Access: Niko's Games (☎23 150), on the corner a few doors down from Thassos Tourist Services, has 3 fast terminals. 1000dr/€2.93 per hr. Open 10am-3am.

Post Office: Head inland from Thassos Tours and turn right at the fourth corner. Open M-F 7:30am-2pm. **Postal code:** 64004.

🏠 ACCOMMODATIONS

There's no need to stay in a hotel on Thasos—the plentiful domatia are a much better deal. The streets behind 28 Octovriou are crammed with rooms to let signs; most cost 6000dr/€17.61 per single; hunt around for a good price. ▨**Hotel Athanassia** is closer to a domatia than an actual hotel, the rooms here are carefully maintained by a kind woman who will be sure to have you sign her guest book. Walk down the waterfront with your back to the Old Port and make a left after the Hotel Xenia. On the right, at the end of a narrow lane, the hotel is nearly swallowed up by grapevines and plane trees. Spacious rooms, some with baths, set in an unhurried countryside calm. Screened windows keep out the bugs: a rare amenity in Greece. (☎22 545. Singles 6000dr/€17.61; doubles 8000dr/€23.48; triples 9000dr/€26.41.) **Hotel Lido** (☎22 929), past the post office toward the plateia. Basic rooms in the middle of town. Private baths. Singles 7000dr/€20.53; doubles 8000dr/€23.48.

FOOD AND NIGHTLIFE

The waterfront is packed with cheap tavernas specializing in seafood. Most serve a similar menu of fresh fish, squid appetizers, and a few plates of schnitzel to appease the hordes of Germans.

Simi Restaurant (☎22 517), in the old port on the waterfront. One of the best-located and most popular spots in Limenas, with a laid-back atmosphere and lots of tasty fish and shellfish. Carefully prepared salads (1000dr/€2.93) are all original creations.

Selinos Taverna, 800m in from the port. Take the road past the post office, near the overgrown Temple of Hercules. Secluded and romantic, with Greek music playing softly in the background. Meat, seafood, and rabbit-food options, like *kolikomezedes* (zucchini burgers 800dr/€2.35). Entrees 1000-2300dr/€2.93-6.75. Open daily 6pm-1am.

Restaurant Syrtaki (☎23 353), past Simi and the old port at the end of the waterfront road. An ocean-oriented view and menu under a leafy canopy. Try the sun-dried grilled mackerel (1600dr/€4.70) Live Greek folk music Sa and W nights. Entrees 1200-3500dr/€3.52-10.27.

Central Bar, under a blue neon light on 28 Octovriou, has popular tables on the second floor balcony of a jewelry store. The music is loud enough to conceal your comments on the tourists strolling unaware below you.

Island Cafe, on the beach on Limenas's eastern edge just beyond the old port, is popular early in the night, when MTV blares loudly and dancing moves to the sand. Beer 800dr/€2.35, cocktails 1500dr/€4.40.

SIGHTS

Just past the Old Port are the ruins of the ancient **agora** and **acropolis,** built in the 5th and 6th centuries BC. The crumbled streets and toppled pillars invite you to scramble over them, and maps of the Old City are available at Thasos Tourist Services. Farther up the hill are the remains of a 4th-century BC Greek **theater.** Currently under restoration, little is visible beyond a tangle of stone, dirt, and uprooted trees. To find the theater, turn right behind the old port and continue to a fork in the road, just beyond the ruins of the **Temple of Dionysus.** The middle of the three paths leads to the theater. Ringing the hills around Limenas are the well-preserved marble **city walls,** inscribed with Archaic reliefs. The **Archaeological Museum** near the old port displays mosaic floors and sculptures found on the site, including a colossal 6th-century BC statue of Apollo with a ram draped over his shoulders. The **Vagis Museum,** just outside of Potamia, displays sculptures by Thassian artist Polygnotos Vagis (1894-1965). Born in Potamia, Vagis emigrated to New York at age 14, where he studied art and began mixing Archaic forms and postures with modern movement and expression. (☎61 182. Open Tu-Sa 10am-12pm and 6-7:30pm, Su 10am-1pm. Free.)

Beachgoers may have a hard time choosing among Thasos's beautiful sands. Between Panagia and Potamia, the popular golden **Chrisi Ammoudia** stretches endlessly. To the south, **Aliki**'s twin coves, formed as sand shifted over a Roman marble quarry, shelter slabs of bleached white rock and crevices ideal for snorkeling. More isolated spots can be found along the water in both directions from Limenaria—just rent a bike or head out on foot, and pick a cove. Ask at the bus station which bus heads past which beach and when to tell the driver to let you off. For a guide to the superb **hiking** in the relatively untouched interior, pick up *Walking in Thasos* at any of the tourist agencies.

LIMENARIA Λιμεναρια   ☎ 0593

Limenaria, Thasos's thriving second town, is across the island from Limenas on a glorious curve of stony beach on the island's southern tip. Much smaller and more relaxed than its bustling counterpart, Limenaria is a haven of unhurried calm, breeze-blown waves, and long, lazy sunsets. While you won't be inundated with souvenir shops, hotels here are popular and high in quality and price.

⚄🔋 ORIENTATION AND PRACTICAL INFORMATION. Limenaria's two main streets run parallel to the waterfront. One main crossroad, **Eth. Anistasis,** has **Speedy Rent-a-Car** (☎52 700; cars 12,000dr/€35.22), and beyond that, the town's **OTE.** (☎513 599. Open M-F 7:30am-2pm.) The **post office** (☎51 296; open M-F 7:30am-2pm) and **National Bank,** with a 24hr. **ATM,** are both on the far right edge of the waterfront, facing inland. The **bus stop** is on the waterfront, a few blocks left of the post office. Schedules and tickets are available at the *periptero* across from the bus stop. The **police** (☎51 111) are on the first street inland in the center of town. **Internet access** available at Rock Cave Bar (see below). **Postal code:** 64002.

🎇🍴 ACCOMMODATIONS AND FOOD. Hotels and rented rooms abound throughout Limenaria, but budget options are truly scarce. While perfect for families of vacationing Germans, the rooms will put a sizeable dent in a cost-conscious traveler's budget; search out domatia away from the waterfront. **Hotel Molos** has bright, pleasant rooms, many with balconies overlooking the water. All have baths and shared fridges. Walk down Anistassis and turn right at the waterfront. (☎51 389. Singles 8000dr/€2.35; doubles 10,000dr/€29.35; triples 15,000dr/€44.02)

The entire waterfront in Limenaria fuses into one mega-restaurant, comprised of the town's numberless tavernas and snack bars. **Il Mare,** just opposite Eth. Anistassis, serves all kinds of seafood delicacies at the romantic tables along the water. (Entrees 1500-3000dr/€4.40-8.80.) Near the edge of the waterfront to the left facing inland, you'll spot popular **O Vasilis,** draped with fishing nets; pick your still-swimming meal from the tank. (Entrees 1700-3200dr/€5-9.39.) At the other end of the waterfront is **Restaurant Maranos,** with a large wine cask lingering precariously over the entrance. It offers a shady environment, classic *rembetika*, and many fish choices. (Entrees 1000-2800dr/€2.93-8.22.)

🎇 NIGHTLIFE. Presto-change-o! Come nightfall, the wall of waterfront restaurants becomes a single long bar. **Istos Cafe-Bar, Nile Bar,** and **Larry's Bar** are all in a row, blaring a jumbled audio mess of Greek and American favorites. (Beer 1000dr/€2.93; cocktails 1500-2000dr/€4.40-5.87.) Follow the signs two streets inland to the **Rock Cave Bar,** where the DJ spins underground rock and electronica beneath a bamboo-thatched canopy. It's quiet enough to appreciate the music while holding a conversation. Three Internet-ready computers are available. (Beer 500dr/€1.47; cocktails 1000-1500dr/€2.93-4.40. Internet 1000dr/€2.93 per hr.) Popular, massive disco **Bolero,** 1.5km east of town on the road to Pefkari, booms with a different liquor promotion every night. (☎52 180. Cover 1000dr/€2.93.)

CYCLADES
Κυκλαδες

Happy is the man, I thought, who, before dying, has the good fortune to sail the Aegean Sea.
—Nikos Kazantzakis

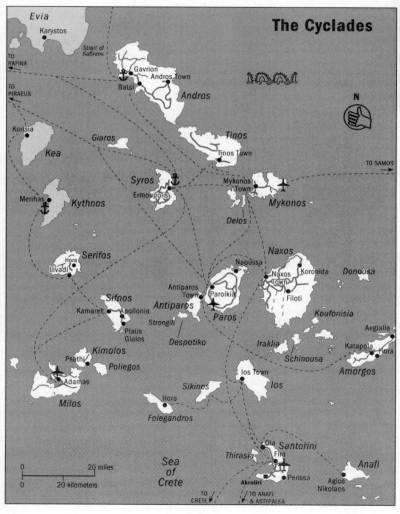

The Cyclades

Evia
Karystos
Strait of Kafireos
TO RAFINA
TO PIRAEUS
Gavrion
Batsi
Andros Town
Andros
Korisia
Giaros
Kea
Tinos
Tinos Town
Syros
Ermoupolis
Mykonos Town
Mykonos
Merihas
Kythnos
Delos
TO SAMOS
N
Serifos
Hora
Livadi
Naxos
Naoussa
Naxos Town
Koronida
Donousa
Antiparos Town
Paroikia
Filoti
Sifnos
Kamares
Apollonia
Antiparos
Paros
Koufonisia
Platis Gialos
Strongili
Aegialia
Katapola
Hora
Despotiko
Iraklia
Schinousa
Amorgos
Kimolos
Psathi
Poliegos
Ios Town
Ios
Adamas
Sikinos
Milos
Hora
Folegandros
Sea of Crete
Thirasia
Oia
Santorini
Fira
Anafi
Akrotiri
Perissa
Agios Nikolaos
TO CRETE
TO ANAFI & ASTYPALEA
0   20 miles
0   20 kilometers

When people speak longingly of the Greek islands, they are probably talking about the Cyclades. Whatever your idea of the Aegean—peaceful cobblestone streets and whitewashed houses, breathtaking sunsets, sunny hikes, Bacchanalia—you can find it here. The archipelago's name derives from their spiral shape: the *kyklos* (cyclical) pattern around sacred Delos. Today, the islands fall into a few broad groups. Although quiet villages and untouched spots still hide in their corners, the Cyclades are known as a tourist's mecca. Santorini is the most chic and expensive, with spectacular views along its black sand beaches. Mykonos ranks a close second in sophistication (and price); it uncorks some of the wildest nightlife on earth. Beer-goggled Ios can be summed up in one word: frat party. All right, that was two words, but after a night on Ios you won't be able to count either. Paros, Naxos, and Amorgos also get their share of visitors, but they're less frantic, more pristine, and attract more families and hikers. Few non-Greek vacationers sprawl in the sand on Andros, Tinos, Syros, Folegandros, Sikinos, Milos, Kimolos, Serifos, Sifnos and Kythnos (deep breath). The pint-sized Little Cyclades—Koufonissia, Donousa, Iraklia, and Schinoussa—are isolated oases blissfully untouched by tourism.

HIGHLIGHTS OF THE CYCLADES

LOSE YOUR MIND. Lose your pants. Party naked on Ios (p. 400).

SPLISH, SPLASH, take a bath in hot sulfur springs while the sun sets over lava-made cliffs and smoke-colored sand on Santorini's western coast (p. 406).

***KOSMOPOLITIKOS* MEET BACCHUS** on the streets of Mykonos (p. 368), the Aegean's premier party destination.

LEND AN EAR to the clatter of electromagnetic art in Andros Town (p. 362).

TRAIPSE through pearly sands and stunning rock formations—products of centuries of volcanic eruptions—on Milos (p. 413).

ANDROS Ανδρος

The magnificent hour-long drive from the ferry landing at Gavrio to Andros Town winds above Andros's famous, beloved beaches. This island is *the* weekend destination for Greece's wealthy ship captains, who, in their zeal to keep their hideaway unspoiled, restrict ferry access to the island. Stone walls outline green and purple tiered fields, and the island's 300 sandy beaches glow in solitude beneath the sun, each more breathtaking than the last. Andros has the distinction of being the only island in the Cyclades with a source of natural spring water. The flowing streams in the island's interior are bottled and exported for use throughout Greece. Athenians crowd in on the weekends, but Andros remains a quiet escape for those who delight in untrammeled ground and nights gazing out to sea.

BATSI Μπατσι   ☎ 0282

Humming along a stretch of golden sand, Batsi is the tourist capital of Andros, with varied food and accommodations options and the liveliest nightlife. Visitors stroll the waterfront by night, pausing for a drink at a *kafeneion*, and dance the night away in bars and clubs swelled with Athenian visitors.

■⁊ **ORIENTATION AND PRACTICAL INFORMATION.** The main **bus stop** and the **taxi stand** are at the end of the beach in a small plateia. A single **bus** motors 4-6 times per day between **Andros Town** (650dr/€1.91); **Gavrio** (300dr/€0.88), Andros's port; and **Batsi** (300dr/€0.88). From Gavrio, **ferries** sail to: **Rafina,** Athens's minor port (2hr., 3 per day 9:45am-7pm, 2500dr/€7.35); **Tinos** (2hr., 3 per day 9:45am-7pm, 1800dr/€5.28); **Mykonos** (2½hr., 3 per day 9:45am-7pm, 2000dr/€5.87). **Catamarans** shuttle between the above islands and Paros every Wednesday in half the time and

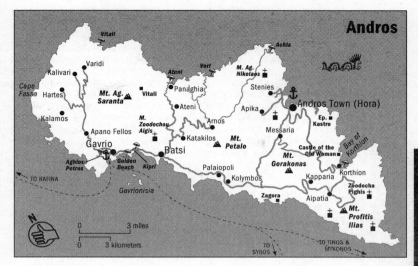

for twice the price. Check schedules and prices in Batsi at Greek Sun Travel. (☎41 198 or 41 771; fax 41 239; greeksun@travelling.gr. English spoken.) It's on the right of the wharf, above an ice cream parlor. Alternatively, try **Andros Travel** (☎41 252 or 41 751; fax 41 608; androstr@otenet.gr), located past the left end of the beach; or in Gavrio at Hellas Ferries (☎71 742 or 71 542). Beach-bound **taxi boats** dock right at the end of Batsi's wharf. (Open daily 9:30am-1:30pm and 6-9pm. Round-trip 1500dr/€4.40.) Renting a **moped** costs about 3500dr/€10.27; try **Dino's Rent a Bike,** behind the post office. (☎41 003. Open daily 8:30am-1pm and 5:30-9pm.)

In the square at the right side of the wharf, there's a branch of the **Alpha Bank** with a 24hr. **ATM.** Farther to the right and up the hill there's a **National Bank.** (Offers **currency exchange.** Open Tu-W and F 8:30am-1pm.) Along the waterfront, a **kiosk** sells **international papers** and magazines. A **pharmacy** is all the way up the hill. (Open daily 9am-1:30pm and 6:30-9pm.) At the right end of the beach you'll see the ▨Gallery Coffee & Cocktail Bar, which offers **internet access,** travel info, and a terrific breakfast for 1000dr/€2.93. (☎41 064; fax 41 620. English spoken.) Just beyond the post office, behind a playground, is a **medical office.** (☎41 326. Doctor available 9am-1pm.) In case of an **emergency** call 22 222 or 23 333. To the left of the beach, attached to Dino's, is the **post office.** (Open M-F 7:30am-2:30pm.)

🖍 🏠 **ACCOMMODATIONS AND FOOD.** It's easier but generally pricier to find accommodations in Batsi than in either Gavrio or Andros Town. Domatia in Batsi tend to be nicer than the hotels for comparable or lesser cost. Expect to pay 4000-7000dr/€11.74-20.53 per person per night (lower if you bargain). **Villa Aegeo** is worth the trek up four sets of stairs. The large doubles have a private bath, fridge, and a breezy balcony for 10,000dr/€29.35. Negotiate if you want a single. (☎41 327 or 41 714. Walk up the stairs to the right of Batsi Gold and look for the sign.) The owner of **shop #224,** with the Kodak sign at the right end of the wharf, lets nice singles for 5000-8000dr/€14.67-23.48 and doubles for 6000-10,000dr/€17.61-29.35. (☎41 322.) For rooms to the left of the beach, see Mike Marinakis at **Glari Rooms for Rent.** (☎41 350. Doubles 10,000-12,000dr/€29.35-33.22.) You can camp 300m from Gavrion if you're willing to skip the nightlife of Batsi. (☎71 444; fax 71 044.)

You'll find ▨**Restaurant Sirocco** at the top of the first set of steps on your left as you leave the beach with the water on your right; head for the string of lights and the strains of jazz. Years ago, the owner Louie was born under the bar (literally). Now he serves fabulous international food like homemade garlic bread (300dr/

€0.88), Shrimp Sirocco grilled in a spicy red sauce (3500dr/€10.27), and a curry-lover's chicken *biryani* with yogurt for 1800dr/€5.28. (Open daily 6:30pm-midnight.) Savor tzatziki (800dr/€2.35) at **The Dolphins Restaurant,** located upstairs at the right end of the wharf, as you watch waves lap the shore. (☎41 635.) There's a **fruit market** where the beach ends, on the right side of the waterfront.

◪◪ **SIGHTS AND BEACHES.** For daytime partying, there's heaps of fun to be had around the bar at **Golden Beach** (drinks 600-1200dr/€1.76-3.52), accessible by water taxi (1500dr/€4.40), taxi (1200dr/€3.52), or foot (25min.). Play beach volleyball, recline under a straw umbrella, swim in calm, shallow water—all to the tune of top 40 pop music. If you're looking for something a little more chill, walk back along the road 400m toward Batsi and descend to **Kipri.** Following the road toward Gavrion, you'll find **Agios Petros,** another secluded stretch of sand. Take a taxi to the ruins of the ancient capitol of **Paleoopolis,** where you can explore the remains of a theater and a stadium, or to the **Bay of Korthion** and Andros's finest swimming. Remnants of the **Castle of the Old Woman** are north of **Korthion,** 33km from Batsi, and are accessible by taxi, car, or moped.

◪ **NIGHTLIFE.** Begin your evening at ◪**Select,** a funky bar all the way up the hill to the right of the wharf (past the pharmacy). There's a Happy Hour (or 4) every night from 6-10pm when fun, psychedelic cocktails with plenty of toys and shiny decorations are only 1000dr/€2.93. (☎42 039.) About 75m to the right and up some stairs, you can sip a Heineken (1000dr/€2.93) or do one of Andros's local shots on the patio (free if you're lucky) at **Capriccio Music Bar.** The party moves to the indoor dance floor around midnight. (☎41 770.) **On the Rocks,** a patio bar set between the beachfront and the wharf, is a good place to find constellations, cocktails (1500dr/€4.40) and rock and dance music. (☎41 219.) Follow the Greeks to ◪**Nameless** after midnight to experience how they really party. Do tequila shots with orange slices with the town's plumber, travel agent, and off-duty police officers. Look for the artificial flames in the back right corner of the wharf's plateia. (☎41 698.) Turn right to dance underwater at **Slammer.** A black light shines on the blue-green walls; A/C works to keep you from getting really wet.

ANDROS TOWN Ανδρος ☎0282

Andros Town (commonly known as Hora) is built on an Aegean peninsula ending in a medieval castle. The quiet, cobbled streets lead past hotels, shops, and homes to the water, where blue waves pound the black rocks. Most tourists make Hora a daytrip from Batsi, but those who stay can relax with the town's 1500 residents in one of the many candle-lit open-air cafe bars.

◪◪ **ORIENTATION AND PRACTICAL INFORMATION.** The **bus** that runs between **Andros Town** (650dr/€1.91); **Gavrio** (300dr/€0.88), Andros's port; and **Batsi** (300dr/€0.88) drops you at a depot near a plateia where **taxis** wait (☎22 171). The **bus station** is coupled with a friendly restaurant. A full schedule is posted in the outdoor waiting area. Facing the white buildings with your back to the hills, walk down any lane to find the main street. The **police station** is located on the inland end. (☎22 300. Open 24hr.) Walking seaward, you will find the **OTE** (open M-F 7:30am-3pm), the **post office** (☎22 260; open M-F 7:30am-2pm), the **pharmacy** (☎22 210; open 8am-2pm), and an **Alpha Bank** that provides **currency exchange.** (☎23 900. Open M-Tu 8am-2pm, F 8am-1:30pm.) The **National Bank** (☎22 232) is in Kairis square, the town's social center. An **Internet cafe** is scheduled to open on the main street in early 2002. For **medical emergencies** dial 22 222. **Postal code:** 84500

◪◪ **ACCOMMODATIONS AND FOOD.** Rooms can be hard to find unless you're lucky and/or laden with cash. If you visit during the mid-July through August high season be prepared to spend, spend, spend. There are, however, over 50 registered domatia, which range in price from 8000-10,000dr/€23.48-

29.35 in low season and 10-15,000dr/€29.35-44.02 in high season. Keep an eye out for signs along Nimborio beach. ◪**Hotel Egli** is up the lane way from Alpha Bank. Rooms have TVs, sinks and phones. There's a sofa lounge on each floor. Reception is next door at the hotel bar. (☎22 308 or 22 159; fax 22 159; stageira.p.otenet.gr. Private bath and breakfast extra. Traveler's cheques accepted. Singles 7000dr/€20.53, doubles 9000dr/€26.41 in low season; singles 10,000dr/€29.35, doubles 15,000dr/€44.02 in high season.) **Karaoulanis Rooms,** on the left most corner (facing inland), are top of the line (kitchen, microwave, bathroom, A/C, TV) and moderately priced. Management speaks English, can direct you to most domatia in the area, take reservations, and rent you a moped. (☎24 412; riva@otenet.gr. Rooms for 2-5 people.) *Mezedes*, milkshakes, and pizza are among the tasty options served by friendly locals in Kairis Square; family-owned cafes, restaurants, and markets line the main street and Nimborio beach. Relax under the stars at the **Heaven Rock Cafe** in Kairis, or head to the Nimborio beachfront for a somewhat livelier atmosphere.

◪ SIGHTS. The **Archaeological Museum,** a large white building with a brown tile patio across from the Heaven Rock Cafe, has an excellent display on the Geometric village of Zagora and other artifacts marking Andros's ancient history, including a marvelous 2-meter marble statue of Hermes. The museum patio offers a lovely view of Andros Town. (☎23 664. Open Tu-Su 8am-3pm. 500dr/€1.47, students and seniors 300dr/€0.88, EU students free.) Turn down the lane to the left upon exiting, and travel down four sets of stairs (following the blue arrows on the left wall) to find the **Museum of Modern Art.** The building displays works by 20th-century Greek sculptor Michael Tombros. The weird noises from downstairs are not a mechanical failure—they're the clatter of electromagnetic art by Takis. Two sets of steps farther down on the right is the large space set aside for the traveling exhibitions that visit the museum every summer. (☎22 444. Open W-M 10am-2pm. June 23-Sept. 22 also open M and W-Sa 6-8pm.) At the end of the main road, just above the water, the **Maritime Museum of Andros** trots out intricate ship models. The guard next door will give you the key. (Open M and W-Sa 10am-1pm and 6-8pm, Su 10am-1pm. Free.) Continue on the main road for a view of the offshore Venetian turret.

◪◪ BEACHES AND HIKES. Gazing at peninsular Hora from the sea, **Paraporti** beach is to the left; **Nimborio** beach is to the right. Down the rocky face at the end of the peninsula is an excellent swimming hole beneath old Venetian arch ruins. Be sure to watch out for sea urchins and a surprisingly strong undertow. North of town (and virtually inaccessible) lies Achla, considered to be one of Europe's most beautiful beaches. It can be reached only by moped or fishing boat. Those yearning to see the island's more secluded spots—the many rivers, **waterfalls,** and monasteries of the island's interior—should search out **Cosmas,** who leads **hikes** on weekends or by request. (☎0977 073 088; or ask for him around Andros Town.)

TINOS Τηνος

Tinos spreads below from the summit of hulking Mt. Exobourgo. In one direction, Hora's buildings, ferries, and mystic beaches cluster together; away from the port, wildflowers, medieval dovecotes, and villages untouched by time contrast with the green mountains. The island's allure is perhaps most apparent to the thousands of pilgrims who have flocked to the Panagia Evangelistra Church in Tinos Town every year since the 1812 War of Independence. Its miracle-working Icon of the Annunciation—the *Megalochari* (Great Joy) or *Panagia Evangelistra*—was found by a nun in an underground church. Each year on the Feasts of the Annunciation (March 25) and Assumption (August 15), close to 30,000 pilgrims crawl on their knees up a red carpet from the port to the church; they then follow the icon in a 10km procession to the Kechrovouni convent.

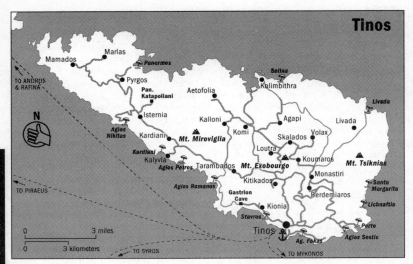

Tinos

TINOS TOWN Τηνος ☎ 0283

A stroll past the barrage of waterfront tourist shops reveals Tinos Town's dual role as tourist and religious mecca: peddlers sell both standard tourist wares and the jugs pilgrims use to carry Panagia's sacred waters home. The town is politically significant as well. On August 15, 1940, an Italian submarine torpedoed the Greek cruiser *Elli* as it docked in the harbor for the observance of a religious holiday. Mussolini declared war two months later. The Ancient Greeks believed Tinos to be the home of the wind god Aeolus; today the cool sea breeze whispers his legacy.

▐ TRANSPORTATION

Ferries: Schedules vary, check with the port police (☎22 348), in the central port, or **Blue Star Travel** (☎24 241). Ferries run to: **Mykonos** (30min., 4-5 per day, 1200dr/ €3.52); **Andros** (2hr., 2 per day, 1800dr/€5.28); **Syros** (40min., 1-4 per day 10:15am-3:15pm, 1100dr/€3.23); **Piraeus** (5½hr., 1-3 per day, 4900dr/€14.38); and **Rafina** (4hr., 2-3 per day, 3800dr/€11.15). **Catamarans** are twice as fast and twice as expensive as ferries.

Buses: Leave across the street from the National Bank 3-5 times daily to: **Pyrgos** (800dr/€2.35); **Panormos** (850dr/€2.50); **Kalloni** (630dr/€1.85); **Steni** (370dr/ €1.10); **Skalados** (450dr/€1.32); **Kionia** (250dr/€0.73); and **Porto** (260dr/€0.76). A **schedule** is posted in the KTEL ticket agency (☎22 440) across from the central port, next to Blue Star Travel. Open 8am-5pm.

Taxis: (☎22 470), next to Commercial Bank. Available 6am-1:30am.

Cars and Mopeds: It's worth getting your own wheels from a waterfront rental place. Try **Vidalis**, Zanaki Alavanou 16 (☎23 400; vidalis@thn.forthnet.gr), on the road running inland from the right of the waterfront, facing inland. Another branch is at 6 Kionion, across from the central port. Mopeds 3000dr/€8.80 and up; cars start at 8000dr/€23.48. Ask the English and French-speaking staff for **free maps**. Open 8:30am-9pm.

✈ 🛈 ORIENTATION AND PRACTICAL INFORMATION

Most ferries land at the central port across from the bus depot; catamarans and hydrofoils dock at the port to the left near a large playground. In the directions below, right and left assume you face inland. Activity centers on two main streets: sprawling **Megalochares**, and parallel pedestrian street **Evangelistras** (known as "Bazaar") to the right. Both streets lead uphill to the Neoclassical facade of the **Panagia Evangelistria Church.** Many domatia are off Evangelistras and **Alabanou,** on the right of the waterfront. Hotels, tavernas, ticket agencies, and banks face the main dock. A labeled map of Tinos is posted to the left of the central port.

Tourist Agencies: At ▧ **Windmills Travel** (☎/fax 23 398; sharon@thn.forthnet.gr), opposite the children's park by the outside port, Sharon will handle all your travel needs. Open 9am-3pm and 6-9pm.

Banks: Banks with 24hr. **ATMs** on the waterfront across from the bus depot include the **National Bank** (☎22 328) and the **Commercial Bank of Greece,** which offers **currency exchange.** Open M-Th 8am-2pm, F 8am-1:30pm.

Bookstore: International News and Magazines (☎22 581), on the left side of the waterfront, has a large selection. Open 8am-11pm.

Public Toilets: In the plateia with the dolphin statue, to the left of Hotel Lito.

Police: (☎22 100), in the same building as the **tourist police,** 5min. out of town on the road to Kionia (leave from the far left side of the waterfront).

Pharmacy: 7 Alvanou (☎23 888 or 22 438), across from the central port at the left of the harbor. Open 8am-2pm and 6-9pm.

Doctor: ☎23 341 or 22 435. Look for the red cross on Alvanou. Usually closes at noon.

Telephones: OTE (☎22 499), up Megalochares on the right. Open M-F 7:30am-3:10pm.

Post Office: (☎22 247), on the far right end of the waterfront, behind the small plateia. Sells phone cards. Open M-F 8am-2pm. **Postal Code:** 84200.

⌂ ACCOMMODATIONS AND CAMPING

Tinos has plenty of accommodations, except during the Easter festival (beginning May 5 in 2002) and during July and August weekends when vacationing Athenians descend upon the island. Most waterfront hotels are expensive, so try your bargaining skills with the crowd holding **Rooms to Let** signs when you disembark.

▧ **Dimitris-Maria Thodosis Rooms,** Evangelistrias 33 (☎24 809 or 0937 655 337), midway up the road to the left, on the 2nd floor. The traditional home with flower-laced balconies has a central kitchen and common bathrooms. Groups or families of 5-8 should ask about their more upscale apartments on G. Plati. Doubles/triples 10,000dr/€29.35; apartments 20,000dr/€58.70 for two people, 4000dr/€11.75 extra for each additional person. Cash or credit card only. Open Mar.1-Oct. 31.

Yannis (☎25 089), at the far right end of the waterfront, to the right of the Oceanis Hotel. Offers simple, hospital-style rooms (that are almost as clean) in a 75-year-old blue-shuttered home. Common baths and refrigerators, kitchen and laundry facilities available. Singles 5000dr/€14.67; doubles 8000dr/€23.48; triples with private bath and kitchen 12,000-16,000dr/€35.22-46.96.

Vincenzo Rooms to Let, 25 Martiou 8-10 (☎/fax 23 612; vincenzo@pigeon.gr); go up Alavanou, turn right onto 25 Martiou (across the street from the little boy fountain), and follow the signs. Simple rooms with common baths or **camping.** Breakfast 1700dr/€5. Laundry facilities, travel info, maps and **free internet access.** Bike rental (1000dr/€2.93; mountain bikes 3000dr/€11.75) and hiking tours offered. Call ahead for a shuttle from the port. Open Apr.-June and Oct.-Nov. Doubles 11,600dr/€34.05; campsite 1000dr/€2.93. 30% discount on weekdays.

Tinos Camping (☎ 22 344 or 22 548; fax 24 551), a 10min. walk from the waterfront to the right—signs point the way. Well kept, with kitchen and laundry, showers, and restaurant and bar. July-Aug. 1500dr/€4.40 per person; May-June and Sept.-Oct. 1200dr/€3.52 per person. 1300dr/€3.81 per tent. **Bungalows** for 1-5 people with private baths, TVs and kitchenettes 4000-7000dr/€11.75-20.53 and up.

FOOD

Tons of tavernas wait to usher you in for a bite. There's a **supermarket** two doors to the left of the post office. Small ▊**Cafe Italia,** Akti Nazou 10, behind the children's park near Windmill Travel, is a secret of gourmets, serving a range of authentic pastas (2000-2500dr/€5.87-7.35) made to the exacting standards of its expatriate Italian chef Dora. (☎25 756. Open 9am-12:30am.) **Mesklies,** on the left side of the waterfront above a green awning, is both a fine pastry shop, featuring ornately designed cakes (around 2000dr/€5.87), and a pizza restaurant. Wrap up your meal with *tyropitakia*, the dense, cheesecakey local specialty. (☎22 151. Open 7am-3am.) **Crepes,** in the back right corner of the square to the left of the hydrofoil port, are perfect for a quick meal or snack (1000-1500dr/€2.93-4.40).

◉ SIGHTS

PANAGIA EVANGELISTRA. In 1822, the Tiniote nun Sister Pelagia had a vision of the Virgin Mary telling her about an icon buried in an uncultivated field (once a church destroyed by 10th-century pirates). A year later, amid great rejoicing, the prophesied icon was unearthed and Panagia Evangelistria was built to house it. The church continues to draw daily visits from believers who consider it evidence of the Virgin's power and presence. The relic is said to have healing powers, and is credited with ridding Tinos of cholera, saving a sinking ship, and giving a blind man sight. Gifts of gold, diamonds, and jewels, and countless *tamata*—plaques praising Mary's healing powers—cover the chapel, the "Lourdes of the Aegean."

The **Well of Sanctification** is a natural spring that appeared when the icon was unearthed. Today it flows (from one of many faucets) in the church between two sets of marble entrance stairs to the chapel; visitors scoop up a bottle of it to drink or to carry as a talisman. To the right is the mausoleum of the Greek warship *Elli*, sunk by an Italian torpedo in 1940. (*Open 7am-8pm. Free. Modest dress required.*)

ARCHAEOLOGICAL MUSEUM. Tinos's small Archaeological Museum, halfway up Megalochares on the left, uphill from the OTE, exhibits sculptures from the coastal sanctuary of Poseidon and Amphitrite at Kionia, a 5th-century BC relief from a cemetary at Xombourgo, and wonderful 7th-century BC *pitnoi* (relief pottery) showing Athena bursting from Zeus's head. (*Open Tu-Su 8:30am-3pm. 500dr/€1.47, students 300dr/€0.88, EU students free.*)

PYRGOS. Take a bus 33km northwest of Tinos Town (1hr., 3-5 times per day, 750dr/€2.20) to the artsy, picturesque town of Pyrgos, home to a School for Fine Arts and inhabited by Tinos's renowned marble sculptors. Several museums and exhibitions are dedicated to past residents, such as Giannouli Chalepas, whose *Sleeping Daughter* graces Athens's central graveyard. For classy souvenirs, head to The Blue Trunk (☎31 870), where marble and (cheaper) terra-cotta statues are for sale; it's on Sardela street, near three tavernas frequented by the locals.

◩ NIGHTLIFE

Late night partyers buzz around the square to the left of the hydrofoil port. Most bars are open all day and late into the evening; clubs are open from 9pm-3am. Pop music encourages bar-top dancing under the star lights at **Koursaros Music Bar** (also known as **Corsaire**), near the water, 10m seaward from Meskelies restaurant. (☎23 963. Drinks 1200-1500dr/€3.52-4.40. Open 8am-3am.) At **Plori Cafe Yacht Club**

(☎24 824), a 7min. walk to the left along the beach road, dance on the rooftop patio or take your pick of either indoor or outdoor lounges. (Plori expects to open by 2002.) **The Kaktos Club,** inside a windmill behind the Panagia Evangelistria Church, opens its incredible hilltop view to lovers of American music; it also hosts special live music nights. For those just raring up when the bars shut down, head for the bright orange doors of **Paradise,** a 15min. walk toward Stavros beach.

BEACHES

The calm, turquoise waters of **Kardiani** and **Agios Petros,** situated at the base of the mountains, are among the islands' most spectacular beaches. Rocky **Agios Romanos** and two secluded neighboring coves are bordered by shallow waters and lined with pine and palms. **Stavros** beach, a 2km walk left out of Tinos Town, hosts a multitude of tourists on its 70m stretch of sand; **Agios Fokas** (to the right out of town) is equally touristy. For the best of the best, head east to **Agios Sostis** and **Porto.** Take the KTEL **bus** or drive all the way to the end of the road that starts at the water's edge in Porto. From there, either climb left to the nudity-strewn rock beaches or head right toward the sand. The medieval-era **dovecotes,** 2000 in total, are built of intricate white lattices and are full of nesting birds; they've become the island's symbol. To the north, lies windswept **Kolimbithra Beach** and the small shore of lovely **Panormos Bay** (2km northeast of Pyrgos). If you rent a moped or car, the landscapes along the road from Tinos Town to Panormos Bay form inspiring views. Take the KTEL **bus** from Tinos Town (3-5 per day, 200dr/€0.59) or drive left along the waterfront road to explore the ruins of the 4th-century BC **temple** of Poseidon and Amphitrite and enjoy the clear-watered, fine sand beach.

HIKING MOUNT EXOBOURGO

If you have a car or moped, the villages that ring Mt. Exobourgo (Εξοβουργο Ορος; 14km north of Tinos Town) and the site of the Venetian Fortress **Xombourgo** are great places to explore. After withstanding 11 assaults, the 13th-century island capital fell to the Ottomans in 1715, the Ottoman Empire's last territorial gain. For a resplendent panoramic view of all Tinos, drive up to the foot of the fortress itself. If you're feeling energetic, climb the mountain from the east foothill (near the village of Xinara or Loutra) on a trail lined with wildflowers and brilliant orange moss. At the gated entrance to Xombourgo, head left into the plateia to the little gate where the rocky trail to the top starts. The road detours to a church at a fork; go straight to get to the fort. Strong winds buffet Exobourgo, and the fort is occasionally closed as a result; stay low to avoid getting blown off the mountain. The delightful hike from Tinos Town to Mt. Exobourgo takes 3-4 hrs. Alternatively, the trip from Tinos Town to Loutra and back takes 3-4 hours and takes you over much of the central island. Other direct routes up Mt. Exobourgo don't cut through all the villages; wooden signposts mark these trails. Whatever your route, bring water, provisions, comfortable shoes, and a buddy. Stick to the trail and be prepared for extremely high winds at all times. There are signs for hikes around Tinos; ask a travel agent about various difficulties and lengths.

Ascent to Kitikados. Begin by heading left behind the Panagia Evangelistria Church to unmarked **Agios Nikolau** (ask if you can't find it). Follow this road straight up and to the left, where the asphalt gives way to a broad cobblestone path that takes you past two white chapels within 45min. Along the ascent, look behind you to see the ferries coming in to port. Past the second white chapel is a small stone bridge with an arch; either go over the bridge for a 15min. visit to the unremarkable village of **Kitikados,** or continue on the main trail up to the island's main asphalt road and turn left. Continue across the road until you see a small trail marked with a wooden sign bearing a hiker and the word "Ksinara." Follow this path up to the right of the windmill. Once you pass the windmill, there is another trail marker on your right. Written in Greek, it indicates a direct ascent up to Mt. Exobourgo, looming in the distance, topped by a cross revealing the **fortress** Xombourgo. **Ksinara** is straight ahead, and **Tripotamos** is behind you. You can ascend Exobourgo from this point or continue about 1½hr. through the quiet town of Ksinara.

Loutra to Xombourgo. Follow the road through town until the church plateia and then head left to the narrow dirt-and-stone trail. This pathway begins your descent to the village of **Loutra** (2hr.), where a convent school teaches young girls to weave carpets; to get there, turn right when you hit the asphalt road. Continue on the asphalt past Loutra to Skalados; turn right to find a nice hillside taverna. From the taverna, head up and right on a street with steps to another asphalt road. Walk to the right about 15min. until you see the blue sign pointing toward **Volax.** It's worth stopping here to meander through the narrow, low-arched streets and to peek into one of the many basket-weaving workshops in town. Retrace your steps to the blue Volax sign and turn left onto the road. At **Koumaros,** look for the **Association lounge** offering hospitality and dirt-cheap drinks and snacks. Once through Koumaros, the road turns into a stone stair trail that will take you up the northeast side of Mt. Exobourgo. At the foot of **Sacred Heart,** an impressive Catholic monastery, go diagonally through the plateia to the little gate on the left side. Ascend 20min. to the fort of Xombourgo for a view of the entire island.

MYKONOS Μυκονος ☎ 0289

Mykonos has long been the object of envy and desire. In ancient times, merchants vied with each other to supply pilgrims en route to the holy island of Delos. By the Byzantine and Ottoman eras, the pilgrim trade had given way to marauding pirates eager for the rich plunder to be found in the waters around the island. In the 70s, Mykonos's gay scene and wild nightlife secured the island's place among the premiere resorts of the Mediterranean. Today, the island is the playground of the sleek and chic—sophisticates the Greeks call *kosmopolitikos.* Though Mykonos's gay scene has lost its former preeminence, it's anything but dead, and Mykonosian nightlife still commands international Bacchic awe.

MYKONOS TOWN Μυκονος

Mykonos Town owes its labyrinthine streets (closed to motor traffic in the afternoon and evening) to Mediterranean pirates. The maze-city was planned expressly to disconcert and disorient marauders; the plan has a similar effect on tourists. Despite the influx of visitors, the town has resisted large hotel complexes. The drag queens and high fashion models seem to complement, not corrupt, the fishing boats in the harbor, the basket-laden donkeys, and Petros the Pelican.

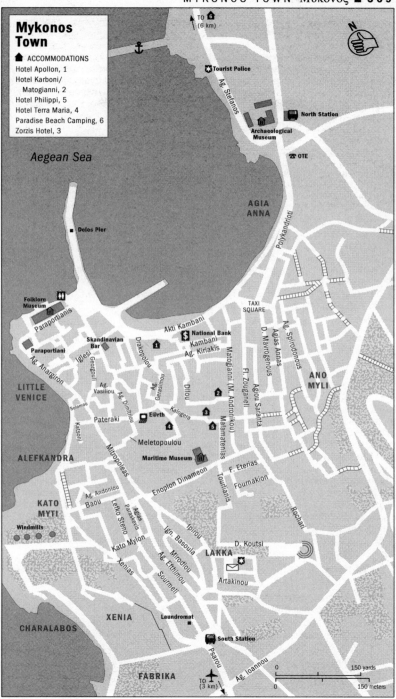

Mykonos Town

♠ ACCOMMODATIONS

Hotel Apollon, 1
Hotel Karboni/
    Matogianni, 2
Hotel Philippi, 5
Hotel Terra Maria, 4
Paradise Beach Camping, 6
Zorzis Hotel, 3

Aegean Sea

TO (6 km)

Tourist Police

Ag. Stefanos

North Station

Archaeological Museum

OTE

AGIA ANNA

Polykandrioti

Delos Pier

TAXI SQUARE

Folklore Museum

Paraportianis

Paraportiani

Ag. Anargiron

LITTLE VENICE

Akti Kambani

National Bank

Kambani

Ag. Kiriakis

Skandinavian Bar

Drakopoulou

Iglesi

Georgoui

Ag. Vasiliou

Ag. Gerasimou

Ditiou

Kalogera

Matogianni (M. Andronikou)

Fl. Zouganeli

Agiou Saranta

D. Mavrogenous

Agias Annas

Ag. Spirodonous

ANO MYLI

Solomou

Katsoni

Paterai

Ag. Dimitriou

E@rth

Meletopoulou

Maritime Museum

Mitropoleas

Matamatenias

Enoplon Dinameon

F. Eterias

Toutitianis

Fournakion

ALEFKANDRA

Ag. Andoniou

Baou

Lefko Steno

Agias Paraskevis

KATO MYTI

Windmills

Kato Mylon

Ipirou

Ign. Basoula

Mirodiou

Ag. Efthimiou

Sourmel

D. Koutsi

LAKKA

Artakinou

Rochari

XENIA

Laundromat

CHARALABOS

Psarou

South Station

Ag. Ioannou

FABRIKA

TO (3 km)

0   150 yards
0   150 meters

⌐ TRANSPORTATION

Flights: Olympic Airways (☎22 490 or 22 495; airport ☎22 327). Flights to: **Athens** (40min., 6-7 per day, 23,900dr/€70); **Rhodes** (1hr., 4 per week, 26,600dr/€77.90); **Santorini** (30min., 4 per week, 18,400dr/€53.90); **Thessaloniki** (3 per week, 31,100dr/€91.12). A taxi from Mykonos Town is the only way there (2000dr/€5.86).

Ferries: To: **Andros** (3hr., 1 per day, 2800dr/€8.20); **Ikaria** (2 per week, 3500dr/€10.20); **Naxos** (3hr., 1-2 per day, 2100dr/€6.10); **Piraeus** (6hr., 2-3 per day, 5600dr/€16.40); **Rafina** (1-2 per day, 4500dr/€13.20); **Samos** (2 per week, 5500dr/€16.10); **Santorini** (6hr., 3 per week, 3500dr/€10.27); **Syros** (2½hr., 1-3 per day, 1700dr/€4.90); **Tinos** (45min., 3 per day, 1300dr/€6.10).

Flying Dolphins: To: **Andros** (2 per day, 5500dr/€16.10); **Amorgos** (5 per week, 6400dr/€18.75); **Ios** (1 per day, 6800dr/€14.90); **Naxos** (1 per day, 3900dr/€11.47); **Paros** (1 per day, 3700dr/€10.80); **Piraeus** (1 per day, 10,800dr/€31.60); **Santorini** (1 per day, 7100dr/€20.83); **Sikinos** (1 per week, 6800dr/€19.90); **Syros** (2 per day, 3300dr/€9.60); **Tinos** (2 per day, 2500dr/€7.30).

Buses: KTEL (☎23 360) has 2 stations in town. **North Station,** uphill from the ferry dock, serves: **Agios Stefanos** beach (every 30min., 250dr/€0.73euro); **Ano Mera** and **Kalafatis** (10 per day, 250-340dr/€0.73-1); **Elia Beach** (8 per day, 350dr/€1). **South Station,** uphill from the windmills at the opposite edge of town, serves: **Agios Ioannis** (every hr., 250dr/€.73); **Paradise Beach** (every 30min., 250dr/€0.73); **Plati Yalos Beach** (every 30min., 250dr/€0.73); **Ornos Beach** (every 30min., 250dr/€0.73). Schedules are posted at the stations.

Taxis: (☎22 400 or 22 700). Available at "Taxi Square," along the waterfront.

Rentals: Agencies surround both bus stops. Get ready to bargain. **Mopeds** 5000-7000dr/€14.65-20.51 per day. **Jeeps** 12,000-16,000dr/€35.16-46.88 per day.

▣✶▮ ORIENTATION AND PRACTICAL INFORMATION

If you're facing inland, incoming boats dock at a pier on the far left of the waterfront. One road leads to the right along the water, past the beach to the center of town. Another road, parallel and north of the first, heads uphill to the **North Station** bus depot, then wraps around Mykonos Town to the **South Station.** A turnoff on the road to South Station leads to the **airport.** Everything you could need or want is near the **waterfront**—banks, travel agencies, shops, cafes, tavernas, bars, and discos—but much of the real shopping, fine dining, and partying goes on in the narrow, winding **back streets** (especially Matogianni, Kalogera, Mitropoleas, and Enoplon Dinameon). On the right side of the waterfront is a pier for excursion boats headed primarily to nearby Delos. Past the pier is a series of churches, a lovely part of town called **Little Venice** (home to the islands' classiest bars and cafes), and a small hill lined with windmills. The town's necessities—post office, police, markets, and so forth—mostly lie in the **inland** vicinity of Lakka and South Station and can be reached by following **Mitropoleas.**

Tourist Police: (☎22 482), in an office at the ferry landing. Very helpful English-speaking staff. Open daily 8am-11pm.

Banks: National Bank of Greece (☎22 932), in the center of the waterfront, offers **currency exchange** and **ATM.** Open M-Th 8am-1:30pm, F 8am-1pm.

American Express: (☎22 322), left of the bank (facing inland) inside **Delia Travel Ltd.** Limited travel services for cardholders. Commission-free check exchange. Open M-F 9am-9pm, Sa-Su 9am-3pm and 6-9pm.

International Bookstore: International Press (☎23 316), in a small plateia opposite Pierro's; follow signs from the waterfront. Eclectic books, magazines, and newspapers in English. Open daily 8am-midnight.

Laundry: (☎27 600), on Psarou, heading toward the windmills from the bus terminal. Full load 3000dr/€8.79. Open daily 8:30am-10pm.

Medical Center: (☎23 994, 995, 996, or 997; fax 27 407), on the higher road leading from the port to South Station, just beyond the turn-off for the hospital. Doctors include a general practitioner, microbiologist, cardiologist, X-ray guru, and gynecologist. Open May-Oct. 8:30am-midnight; Nov.-Mar. 8:30am-9pm. For 24 hr. **emergency** care, call an ambulance at 166, or the medical center at (094) 433 8292 or (097) 765 4737.

Police: (☎22 716 or 22 215), in Lakka past the South Station. Open 24hr.

Telephones: OTE (☎22 699), at the left end of waterfront in a big white building, uphill and to the right of the dock. Open M-F 8am-3pm.

Internet Access: E@rth Internet Club, Zani Pitaraki (☎22 791), gets connected close to little Venice. Open daily 9am-11pm. **Angelo's Internet Cafe** (☎24 106), on the street between South Station and the windmills. Both charge 1000dr/€2.93 for 20min.

Post Office: (☎22 238), around the corner from the police in Laka, behind South Station. **Exchanges currency.** Open M-F 7:30am-2pm. **Postal code:** 84600.

▌ ACCOMMODATIONS AND CAMPING

While Mykonos is certainly the most expensive of the Greek islands, affordable accommodations aren't just a pipe dream especially if you're willing to stay outside the immediate town. Most budget travelers find their niche in Mykonos's festive campsites, which offer a myriad of sleeping options beyond the standard plot of grass. The information offices on the dock are numbered according to accommodation type: 1 for **hotels** (☎24 540; open 9am-midnight), 2 for **rooms to let** (☎24 860; open 9am-11pm), and 3 for **camping** (☎23 567; open 9am-midnight).

Hotel Apollon (☎22 223), on the waterfront. The oldest hotel in town is an antique-laden house with rooms overlooking the harbor. The owner's motto is "Smile and the world's your friend." Common baths. Singles 9,000-15,000dr/€26.37-43.95; doubles 11,500-18,000dr/€33.70-52.70; triples 15,000-21,000dr/€43.95-61.53.

Zorzis Hotel, N. Kalogera 30 (☎22 167 or 24 168; fax 24 169). In its restored 16th-century building, Zorzis is by far the most elegant hotel on Kalogera. Perks include feather pillows, handmade quilts, real showers, and a roof-top deck for sunbathers. Doubles and triples 17,000-34,000dr/€50-100.

Hotel Philippi, N. Kalogera 25 (☎22 294; fax 24 680; chriko@otenet.gr), next to Zoris Hotel. Cheerful rooms around a bountiful garden provide an escape from the narrow, busy town streets. Internet 30dr/€0.09 per min. Open Apr.-Oct. Singles 8000-11,000dr/€23.44-32.33; doubles 11,000-18,000dr/€32.23-52.74.

Hotel Terra Maria, Kalogera 33 (☎24 212; tertaxma@otenet.gr). Don't confuse it with Chez Maria or the nearby Marios Hotel. A/C, private baths, fridges, TVs, minibars, and balconies. Central location, but on a quiet side street with trees out back. Breakfast 2000dr/€5.86. Singles 10,000-15,000dr/€29.30-43.95; doubles 16,000-27,000dr/€46.88-79.10; triples 21,000-34,000dr/€61.53-100.

Hotel Karboni/Matogianni (☎22 217; fax 23 264), on Matogianni, inland from the waterfront. This hotel complex has many rooms; ask about the cheaper ones in the rear. Doubles 12,000-25,000dr/€35.16-73.25; triples 18,000-27,000dr/€52.74-79.

Paradise Beach Camping (☎22 852 or 22 129; for reservations email paradise@paradise.myk.forthnet.gr), 6km from the port on the beach; the round-trip bus costs 250dr/€0.73. The liveliest place in town, this enormous complex includes every imaginable type of accommodation, eatery, and entertainment. Located directly on crowded Paradise Beach. Luggage storage 350dr/€1. Internet access 1000dr/€2.93 per 15min. 1600-2400dr/€4.69-7 per person; 900-1200dr/€2.64-3.52 per small tent, 1300-1600dr/€3.81-4.69 per large tent; 2-person beach cabin 6000-14,000dr/€17.58-41, 4-person beach cabin 12,000-28,000dr/€35.16-82.04.

Mykonos Camping (☎25 915 or 25 916; fax 24 578; mycamp@hotmail.com), on Paraga Beach. On the bus route to Paradise Beach. Free pick-up and drop-off at the port and airport. Smaller and quieter than Paradise Beach. Very clean. 1600-2400dr/ €4.69-7 per person; 900-1200dr/€2.64-3.52 per tent; 1800-2500dr/€5.46-8.47 per tent rental; 2-person bungalow 6000-12,000dr/€17.58-35.16.

⬛ FOOD

Most choose to eat out on Mykonos, but budget travelers would do well to put together a picnic from the fruit stands that surround South Station. **Mykonos Mini-Market,** a short distance from the post office, offers carbs and more. (☎24 897. Open 7am-late.) Cheap creperies and souvlaki joints are on nearly all of Mykonos's streets. Otherwise, it's possible to lounge the day away (off the beach) at the cafes that line the waterfront, all of which serve the usual Greek food suspects.

⬛ **Dynasty Thai Chinese Restaurant** (☎24 194), in Pl. Lymni, by the cinema on Meleto-poulou. It ain't Greek, but if you endure the wait for an outside table, the spicy, authen-tic Asian cooking satisfies. Thai salads 2100dr/€6.15. The owner recommends Peking duck (5000dr/€14.65). Open daily 6:30pm-12:45am.

Nikos Taverna (☎24 320), in Porto, in a cluster of restaurants inland from the excursion boat docks. Personable pelicans frequent the spot. Baked calamari and cheese 2800dr/€8.20, lamb *kleftiko* 2500dr/€7.30. Open daily noon-2am.

La Mexicana, at the end of Kalogeri. Chicken enchiladas 2550dr/€7.47, chicken or shrimp fajitas 3400-3850dr/€9.90-11.28, vegetarian dishes around 2300dr/€6.70. Happy Hour 6:30-8pm, with discounts on sangria (500dr/€1.47), frozen margaritas (1300dr/€3.81), and tequila shots. Open daily 6:30pm-12:30am.

Alexi's, in the back of Taxi Square. The oldest greasy spoon in Mykonos. Alexi puts on a show as he cooks up your gyro (400dr/€1.17) or hearty souvlaki plate (2000dr/ €5.86). Breakfast (including a fried tomato) 1350dr/€3.96. Open daily 10am-7am.

Euthymios Euthymiou, off Taxi Square. *Amigdalota* (almond dessert) 2000dr/€5.86 per box, *kalathakia* (walnut-tarts) 1800dr/€5.46 per box, and more commonplace goodies (croissants 500dr/€1.47, sandwiches 200dr/€0.59). Open daily 8am-11pm.

⬛ SIGHTS

The prime daytime activities on Mykonos are shopping and tanning, but you don't need to blow all your money. Losing yourself in the colorful alleyways of Mykonos Town at dawn or dusk is one of the easiest, cheapest, and most exhilarating expe-riences the island has to offer. A stroll to the **Castro** area—behind the Delos ferry pier, at the far left of the port if you're facing the sea—will take you to the **Parapor-tiani.** You'll recognize this cluster of white churches from picture postcards. From there, walk through **Little Venice,** where the turquoise waters of the eager Aegean lap at the legs of cafe tables and chairs. The line of stalwart **windmills** farther south along the waterfront also offers prime sunset seating.

Although cultural enrichment may not be Mykonos's primary draw, several museums fill the void. The **Archaeological Museum,** on the paved road between the ferry dock and the center of town, lacks Cycladic art but has an impressive 7th-century BC *pithos* (large terra-cotta storage jar) with relief scenes from the Tro-jan War. (☎22 325. Open Tu-Su 8:30am-2:30pm. 500dr/€1.47, students and seniors 300dr/€0.88, EU students free.) The **Aegean Maritime Museum,** around the corner from the inland end of Matogiannis, thrills with a beautifully manicured garden that houses immense nautical instruments, including ancient grave *steles* and a lighthouse. (☎22 700. Open Apr.-Oct. 10:30am-1pm and 6:30-9pm. 500dr/€1.47, stu-dents 200dr/€0.59.) **Lena's House,** part of the town's **Folklore Museum,** is a 300-year-old home with 19th-century furniture. It remains exactly as its owner left it. (☎22 591. Both open daily Apr.-Oct. 4:30-8:30pm. Free.)

PETROS THE PELICAN When it comes to glamour and beauty, even the most gawk-worthy visitors to Mykonos must compete with the island's prize pink pelicans. The first arrived in 1955, plucked out of the air by one of Mykonos' fishermen. Exhausted and mourning the death of its mate (found nearby), it had become separated from its migrating flock. The pelican was given to another fisherman, who named it Petros, for a soldier friend executed by Nazis during the World War II. Nursing Petros back to health, the fisherman created a celebrity. It wasn't long before Mykonian functions began to depend on the presence of their most famous fowl. Upon taking a trip to Tinos, the beloved bird sparked a **Pelican War**—it took an official task force comprised of the mayor, police chief, and important priests to retrieve him from the recalcitrant Tinians. Numerous official efforts were made to set Petros up with a "nice Greek girl," and distinguished people, including Jackie Onassis, have had cute girl pelicans flown to Mykonos to catch his eye. Unlike most visitors to Mykonos, however, pink pelicans practice strict monogamy, mating once and for life, and principled Petros refused to be corrupted by the charms of stardom. Meeting his end in 1985, unseen beneath a farmer's vehicle, Petros has been preserved in song (hits like "Dirge for a Pelican" and "Whitewash and Pink Feathers") and in the folklore museum, where his earthly portion is stuffed. The pelicans you see preening themselves in the streets of Mykonos today are merely trying to live up to Petros' distinguished legacy.

🌃 NIGHTLIFE

There's a good time to be had on Mykonos—perhaps the best in Greece. Come nightfall, the young and beautiful mix with mere mortals to bask in the warm embrace of chic cafes, buzzing nightclubs, and a handful of pubs. After 11pm, the bars get packed. The most popular watering holes are around Little Venice and Taxi Square. If you tire of dancing, head to **Cine Mant,** in Pl. Lymni off Meletopoulou, which shows English-language films. (☎27 109. 2 per day 1800dr/€5.28.)

🍸 **Caprice Bar,** on the water in Little Venice. Popular but unpackaged post-beach hangout with breathtaking sunsets, feel-good music, and good-time company. Cocktails 1500-2000dr/€4.40-5.86. Open Su-Th 6:30pm-3:30am, F-Sa until 4:30am.

🍸 **Montparnasse Piano Bar,** Ag. Anargyron 24. Savor the good life with a cocktail by the bay, while being serenaded by cabaret tunes from a live piano. Groovy and mostly gay. Open daily 7pm-3am.

Pierro's, on Matogianni. Pierro's gained its fame as the first gay bar in Greece and it maintains its reputation with irresistible hedonism and lively dancing. The crowd spills out into the plateia. Beer 1500dr/€4.40, cocktails 2500dr/€7.34.

Icaros, next-door and upstairs from Pierro's. Shares clientele, atmosphere, and a nightly drag show with its downstairs neighbor. Beer 1000dr/€2.93, cocktails 1500dr/€4.40. Open daily 11:30pm-4am.

Skandinavian Bar, near Niko's Taverna and the waterfront. There's something for everyone in this 2-building party complex, and though the evening starts slow, after midnight *everyone* passes through. Beer and shots around 1000dr/€2.93, cocktails upwards of 1500dr/€4.40. Open Su-F 8:30pm-3am, Sa until 4am.

Mykonos Bar, in Little Venice, next to inland side of the Caprice Bar. Watch Greek dancers perform the *zorba,* then join them until sunrise. Beer 1200dr/€3.52, cocktails around 2000dr/€5.86. Cover 1000dr/€2.93 and up. Open daily 10pm-4am.

Mad Club, on the waterfront beside Taxi Square. Serves up pounding techno in a bar-meets-jungle-gym setting. Take a break on the balcony overlooking the sea. Cocktails around 2000dr/€5.86. Cover 2000-3000dr/€5.86-8.79. Opens daily at midnight.

◪ BEACHES

Although all the beaches on Mykonos are **nude,** the degree of nudity depends on where you go. To avoid the unspectacular Mykonos Town beach, get on the bus and head out of the city. Small **Ag. Stefanos Beach** is an easy bus ride (10min., every hr., 230dr/€0.67) from the North Station, but it's close to the busy roadway leading to the airport, and its sands are often littered. The clear, shallow water of little **Ornos Beach** is a short hop away from South Station (10min., every 30min., 250dr/€0.73), as is crowded **Psarou Beach** (15min., every 30min. 8:15am-2am, 250dr/€0.73). Buses run from South Station to **Plati Yialos** (every 30min., 250dr/€0.73), where you can catch a **caïque** (around 400dr/€1.17) to Paradise Beach, Super Paradise Beach, and Elia. You can take the bus directly to **Elia** from North Station (30min., 8 per day, 350dr/€1.03) or to **Paradise** from South Station (every 30min., 250dr/€0.73). While **Super Paradise Beach** has the craziest reputation among Mykonos's bare-butt beaches, contemplative naked people while away the daylight hours at the far reaches of Elia's quiet shores, where broad sand beaches are divided by sections of craggy rock. Majestic and remote **Kalo Livadi Beach** is about a 5km walk back along the road to Mykonos from Elia. The bus to Elia stops at the turn-off, so ask the driver to let you off at Kalo Livadi to shorten your trek.

DELOS Δηλος

Apollo wher'er thou strayest, far or near,
Delos is still of all thy haunts most dear
        —Homeric Hymn to Apollo

An excursion to Delos—the sacred navel around which the Cyclades whirl—is a must-see, even for those who take little interest in mythology or history. Delos claims *the* Temple of Apollo, built to commemorate the birthplace of the god and his twin sister, Artemis. A site of religious pilgrimage in the ancient world, Delos is today something of a giant, island-wide museum.

A DRIFTING ISLAND GROWS ROOTS. After getting **Leto** pregnant with Artemis and Apollo, sleazy **Zeus** kicked her out, afraid of his wife Hera's wrath. Desperately searching for a place to give birth, Leto wandered the Aegean, only to find no room at the inn, island after island. At last she came upon a rocky, floating island shrouded in mist. Frightened, the little island bobbed about furtively until Leto swore by the river Styx that it would come to no harm, and that her unborn child would live there forever, casting light upon its birthplace. The reassured island stopped drifting, but Leto's trials were far from over: Hera conned the goddess of childbirth, Eilythia, into prolonging Leto's labor for nine days, at which point the other gods bribed Eilythia into having mercy. Leto collapsed and gave birth beside the island's Sacred Lake. Upon the children's birth, the mist disappeared and the island was bathed in radiance; because it could now be clearly seen, its name was changed from Adelos ("invisible") to Delos ("visible"). Grateful Leto promised to make the island the seat of her son's worship, and the ensuing sanctuary transformed little Delos into a major religious and commercial center.

HISTORY OF DELOS. With a central position among the Aegean islands, Delos's role as a a maritime and political powerhouse is hardly surprising. The 5km-long island is paired with larger **Rheneia,** whose inhabitants are also called Delians. Although first settled in the 3rd millennium BC, it was during the Mycenaean Period (1580-1200 BC) that Delos began to flourish. Mycenaean rule ended around 1100 BC, and a century later the Ionians dedicated the island to worshipping Leto. By the 7th century BC, Delos had become the political and mercantile center of the Aegean League of Islands, starting off three centuries of struggle for power between the Delians and the Athenians. The Delians put up a good fight, but slowly bled power to the mainlanders. During these years, the Athenians ordered at least two "purifications" of the island, in honor of Apollo. The second, in 426 BC, decreed that no one should give birth or die on its sacred grounds, meaning that all graves had to be exhumed, and the bodies within moved to a "purification pit" on nearby Rheneia. The Athenians later instituted the quadrennial **Delian Games,** where they coincidentally always came home with all the medals.

After Sparta defeated Athens in the **Peloponnesian War** (403 BC; see p. 11), Delos enjoyed independence and wealth. Sweet prosperity soured during the Roman occupation in the 2nd century BC, when prestigious Delos was reduced to the slave-trading center of Greece. By the end of the second century AD, after successive sackings, the island was left virtually deserted. Today, its only residents are legions of leaping lizards and members of the French School of Archaeology, who have been excavating here since 1873.

DELOS ARCHAEOLOGICAL SITE

*Most accessible as a daytrip from Mykonos Town. **Excursion boats** leave from the dock near Mykonos Town (35min.; Tu-Su every 30-45min. 9:30-11:30am, returns 12:20-3pm; round-trip 1900dr/€5.57). Most trips only let you explore the site for 3hr., but each boat line has several return trips in the afternoon, so you have some flexibility. Expensive **guided tours** in several languages by each excursion boat company (8000dr/€23.44, including admission to the ruins). A more affordable option is to buy the **guidebook** by Photini Zaphiropoulou (in town or at the entrance to the site), which includes info, color pictures, and a map of the site (1700dr/€5). Tinos, Naxos, Paros, and other islands offer joint trips to Mykonos and Delos but allow less time to explore. **Open** Tu-Su 8:30am-3pm. 1200dr/€3.52, students and EU seniors 600dr/€1.76, EU students free.*

Occupying almost an entire plateia mile of the small island, the archaeological site includes, in the center of the ancient city, the Temple of Apollo and the *agora*, the outlying parts of the city, Mt. Kythnos, and the theater quarter. While it takes several days to explore the ruins completely, you can see the highlights in approximately three hours. Most of your fellow ferry passengers will follow a similar route when they disembark; reverse the route if you want some privacy. As always, bring a hat, good shoes, sunblock, and a water bottle. There is an exorbitantly priced cafeteria beside the museum, so it's wiser to pack snacks.

SACRED ROAD. The path beyond the admission booth points you toward the **Agora of the Competaliasts,** where Roman guilds built their shop-shrines. Continue on in the same direction and turn left onto the wide Sacred Road. Decorating your walk are two parallel **stoas,** the more impressive of which (on the left) was built by Phillip of Macedon in 210 BC and dedicated to Apollo. Follow this road to the **Sanctuary of Apollo,** a collection of temples built in the god's honor that date from Mycenaean times to the 4th century BC. The biggest and most important of the temples is on the right. The famous **Great Temple of Apollo,** or **Temple of the Delians,** was completed at the end of the 4th century BC. Its immense, partially hollow hexagonal pedestal once supported an 8m-high marble statue of the god of light.

Following the direction of the Sacred Road north, 50m past its end, leads to the **Terrace of the Lions.** In the 7th century BC, at least nine marble lions looked onto the sacred lake from the terrace. Only five remain on Delos, and the body of a sixth, pirated by the Venetians, guards the entrance to the arsenal in Venice.

SACRED LAKE AND ENVIRONS. Proceed up the small crest left of the terrace to the **House of the Hill.** Because the building was planted deep into the earth, this archetypal Roman house is still firmly intact. Downhill lies the **House of the Lake,** with a well-preserved mosaic decorating its atrium, and the desecrated **Sacred Lake,** drained in 1925 to protect against malaria. The most mythologically potent of the island's sites, the round form of the former lake today appears as a leafy oasis with a lone palm tree at its center (honoring Apollo's birth). On the lake's south side is the expansive Roman **agora.**

AROUND MOUNT KYTHNOS. From the museum you can hike up the path to the summit of **Mt. Kythnos** (112m). Its peak offers such a sprawling view of the ruins that Zeus chose it to spy on the birth of Apollo and Artemis. Although the climb is not difficult, wear sturdy, comfortable shoes—some of the rocks dislodge easily. Ascending the mountain coming from the direction of Temple of Apollo, you will pass temples dedicated to Egyptian gods. Arguably the most spectacular antiquity on the island, the elegant bust in the **Temple of Isis** depicts the sun. The immense building blocks of the nearby **Grotto of Herakles** scream Mycenaean, but some experts suggest that it's a Hellenic knock-off of Mycenaean architecture.

At the base of Mt. Kythnos, head west along the edge of the ruins to reach the **House of the Dolphins** and **House of the Masks,** which contain their intricate, well-preserved, eye-popping mosaics of dolphins and *Dionysus Riding a Panther.* Continue up to the **ancient theater,** which has a sophisticated cistern (as cisterns go) called **Dexamene,** with nine arched compartments. Also, try to explore the maze of rooms toward the port from the theater: the **House of the Trident,** graced by mosaic of a dolphin twisted around a trident; the **House of Dionysus,** containing another mosaic of Dionysus and a panther; and the **House of Cleopatra.** The famous statue of Cleopatra and Dioscourides is sheltered in the museum.

SYROS Συρος

Syros is the capital of the Cycladic islands and, despite its small size, is also home to almost half of the Cyclades's permanent residents. Syros first rose to commercial power as a Phoenician seaport; the 13th-century Venetians turned it into the trading capital of the Cyclades until team-powered ships and the rise of Piraeus as the national port finally ended Syros's glory days. In the last 20 years, the island has regained its footing, largely due to the shipbuilding that now keeps it afloat. Internationals ship in and out of town, and windsurfing has become a favorite pastime. Escape the madness of the port town Ermoupolis by following legions of Greek families to a seaside village or beach, or by heading to the medieval settlement of Ano Syros, high above Ermoupolis on one of Syros's two peaks. Bold hikers will find uncharted terrain; everyone else can rely on the public bus system.

Syros

ERMOUPOLIS
Ερμουπολισ ☎ 0281

Bustling Ermoupolis is not only the Cyclades's largest city and capital, but (as the waterfront statue announces) it belongs to the winged messenger Hermes, god of commerce. Elegant Neoclassical buildings of Greek, Italian, and Bavarian design in Pl. Miaouli and Dellagrazia give the island an international appearance and offer a peek at the city's opulent past. They also explain its former nicknames—the "Manchester of Greece" and "little Milan." Though the city's roles in government and shipping make tourism a secondary concern, its vitality makes Syros an exciting, lively island. Athenian vacationers jam Ermoupolis's hotels from mid-July to September; you'll probably want to head for the island's countryside.

▐▀ TRANSPORTATION

Flights: There are 2-3 flights per day to Athens (15,000dr/€44). You must take a bus or a taxi to the airport, southeast of Ermoupolis (☎87 025 or 81 900).

Ferries: To: **Piraeus** (4½hr., 3-5 per day, 4750dr/€13.95); **Rafina** (4hr., 1 per day, 3500dr/€10.27); **Tinos** (45min., 2-3 per day, 1100dr/€3.22); **Mykonos** (2hr., 2-3 per day, 1750dr/€5.58); **Paros** (1hr., 3 per week, 1750dr/€5.58); **Naxos** (2½hr., 3 per week, 2300dr/€6.75); **Ios** (4hr., 3 per week, 3750dr/€11); **Santorini** (5hr., 3 per week, 4150dr/€12.18); **Crete** (10hr., 1 per week, 6700dr/€19.66); and a few smaller Cyclades. Most boats depart from the right side of the harbor. **Catamarans** or **Flying Dolphins** depart daily for Pireaus and Rafina and once per week to Tinos and Mykonos in half the time for twice the price. Schedules vary; check with a travel agency.

Buses: (☎22 575). Green **KTEL** buses leave from the depot near the ferry dock. One beach loop runs 13-18 times per day, passing through **Azolimnos** (45min., 310dr/€0.90); **Galissas** (15min., 310dr/€0.90); **Finikas, Komito,** and **Megas Gialos** (380dr/€1.12 each). Another leaves 5 times per day for the interior towns of **Episkopio** (260dr/€0.77); **Parakopi** (310dr/€1.12); **Posidonia** (310dr/€1.12); and **Manna** (380dr/€1.12). 3 to 5 shuttle buses per day go to: **Ano Syros** (260dr/€0.77); **Dili** (250dr/€0.74); **Vrontado** (250dr/€0.74).

Taxis: (☎86 222). Meet them by the winged statue of Hermes to the right of the port.

Rental Cars and Bikes: On the waterfront. Try **Enjoy Your Holidays Rent a Car,** Akti Paeidou 6 (☎87 070 or 81 336; fax 82 739), on the waterfront by the central port. Cars, motorcycles and scooters. Prices depend on season, model and duration of rental; expect a range of 4000dr/€11.74 (scooters) to 14,000dr/€41.10 and up (jeeps). You can also buy ferry tickets here. Open daily 8am-9pm.

▚▐ ORIENTATION AND PRACTICAL INFORMATION

Facing inland when you get off the ferry, head right and walk down the waterfront for 3min. to **El. Venizelou,** the town's main street, beginning at the winged **statue of Hermes.** Venizelou runs inland to **Pl. Miaouli,** a large marble plaza marked by the Neoclassical town hall. Social life centers on this plaza, and along the right side of the harborfront. Hotels and domatia can be found all along the waterfront and the surrounding streets. A labeled map of Ermoupolis and a listing of domatia are posted on two large signs at the bus depot.

Tourist Information: Look for the "i" as you head right off the ferry—the booth is behind a statue wearing the helmet of Hermes. Free, helpful info on accommodations, good maps (400dr/€1.17), and books on the island. Open daily 10am-1:30pm and 3-6pm, high season only. The **Greek Tourist Board's** Office of the Cyclades, Dodecanisou 10, offers free information and maps.

Tourist Agencies: Hellenic Star, 30 Eth. Antistasis (☎87 66; fax 87 665), at the left end of the waterfront. **Gaviotis Tours,** 12 Akti Papagou (☎86 606; fax 83 445), across from the bus depot. Open daily 8:30am-11pm. Both agencies provide schedules and prices and sell ferry, hydrofoil, and flight tickets.

Banks: National Bank, at the end of the first main street on the right off El. Venizelou (going away from the waterfront), **exchanges currency. Pireaus Bank** at the left of the waterfront, has a 24hr. **ATM.** Both open M-Th 8am-2pm, F 8am-1:30pm.

Police: (☎96 127), behind the theater off the upper right corner of Pl. Miaouli. Take the right inland street from the far right corner of Pl. Miaouli, go right at the fork and continue to the station. Very helpful. **Emergency:** ☎100; **fire** ☎199.

Port Authority: (☎88 888 or 82 690). The office is at the end of the dock all the way to the right of the waterfront, with a Greek flag in front.

Public Toilet: On the right side of the first alley off the street with the National Bank and the post office on it. Look for the "WC" sign.

Hospital: (☎86 666), at the left end of the waterfront (facing inland) at Pl. Iroön past the roundabout, a 20min. walk from Pl. Miaouli.

Pharmacy: A total of 18 are scattered throughout the city. Open M-F 8am-2pm and Tu, Th-Su 5:30-9pm.

Telephones: outside of the **OTE** (☎82 799), at the right of Pl. Miaouli. Open M, W, Sa 7am-1:30pm and T, Th-F 7:30am-1:30pm and 5:30-8:30pm.

Internet Access: Net Cafe, (☎85 330), in Pl. Miaouli, to the left of the town hall's staircase. Coffee, drinks, ice cream and erotic cartoon monitor wallpaper. 1500dr/€4.40 per hour; 500dr/€1.47 minimum. Open daily 9am-12:30am.

Post Office: (☎82 590), down the street from the National Bank. Offers **currency exchange.** Open M-F 7:30am-2pm. **Postal Code:** 84100.

ACCOMMODATIONS

Cheap domatia rooms abound (look around for "Rooms to Let" signs), and off-season prices are generally 20-40% cheaper. There's a large map with names and phone numbers of hotels at the ferry dock.

Hotel Aktaion (☎88 200 or 88201; fax 82 675; romana@otenet.gr). Look for the rooftop sign at the right end of the waterfront. Location is only the 1st of Aktaion's attractive qualities: study-like wood-and-brick rooms have TVs, A/C, telephones, as well as complimentary goodies including candy and soap. Free **internet station** for guests in reception area. Singles start at 8000dr/€23.48; doubles at 12,000dr/€35.22.

Villa Votsalo, Parou 21 (☎87 334 or mobile 093 830 05 57; fax 86 760). Walk inland on Hiou (to the left of Venizelou); parou is the first left off Hiou. Have a drink above this cozy traditional-house-turned-hotel, on the sunny roof garden bar, which has a full view of the harbor. Fridges. Singles 10,000dr/€29.35; doubles 12,000dr/€35.22.

Hotel Almi (☎82 812), on the left side of the alleyway across from the bus depot and port. Look for the dark wooden doors. A charming owner and nice rooms with TVs. Singles 6000-10,000dr/€17.61-29.35; doubles 8000-16,000dr/€23.48-46.96.

Ariadni Rooms to Let, Nikolaou Filini 9 (☎81 307 or 80 245), near the ferry dock (look for signs). A dose of luxury, the hotel prides itself on its well-deserved class "A" rating. Private baths, TVs, telephones and A/C. Doubles 10,000dr/€29.35.

FOOD

For your grocery needs, there's a **mini-market** halfway up from Hiou's plateia. (☎81 008. Open 8am-9pm.) **Hiou** hosts fruit and seafood stalls and aromatic bakeries.

Mavros (☎82 244), in the center of the ocean end of Pl. Miaouli. Serenading accordion or guitar and the big outdoor TV will entertain as you traverse the incredibly broad menu. Open daily 6am-2am.

Restaurant Bakhos (Βακχος). Walking along Hiou, turn left on Peloponnisou; the restaurant is at the end under a leafy awning. Built in 1843, the building was a functioning pottery factory until 1922. Today, it spins out seafood, pasta and Greek specialties. Open daily 10am-2am.

Kechayia Sweet Shop, on the waterfront corner of El. Venizelou. Fabulous renditions of traditional local specialties such as *chalvathopita*, a sweet concoction of almond paste, nuts, and chocolate (350dr/€1.03) and *loukoumi* (450dr/€1.32).

SIGHTS

At the **Church of the Assumption** (*Kimisis Theotokou*), on Ag. Proiou to the right of the plateia facing the town hall, you can contemplate a 1562 painting by a 20-year-old Domenikos Theotokopoulos before he was known as **El Greco** (see **It's El Greco to Me,** p. 432). Ascend the steps at the far left of Pl. Miaouli to **Ano Syros,** a medieval Venetian settlement which Syros's Catholics still call home (20min.) or take the bus from the waterfront. Continue past the summit church through labyrinthine streets to the lofty Church of Ag. George above, and look over Ermoupolis and the coast below. The town hall's **Archaeological Museum** has a small collection of Cycladic art. (☎28 487. Open Tu-Su 8:30am-3pm. Free. No cameras permitted.)

NIGHTLIFE

At night, the waterfront and Pl. Miaouli buzz with cafes, restaurants, dance clubs, and bars. If you can score a table, drink up at **Liquid** or **Cocoon.** On the right-hand strip of the waterfront, the **Cotton Club** is a hopping cafe/bar; just next to it, **Kimbara** is packed with wall-to-wall bodies and Madonna tunes. For dancing, bounce on over to **Arxaion**—it opens at 9am as a cafe and closes at 4am as a dance club. If you want some high rollin', try your luck at **Kazino Eyeou**—Aegean Casino—the only sin palace around. Men must wear pants and foreign visitors must leave their passport and 5000dr/€14.67 at the door. (☎84 400. Gambling starts 12:30pm.)

BEACHES

The closest beach is sedate **Agios Nikolau.** To get there, walk up El. Venizelou through Pl. Miaouli to the right of the Archaeological Museum. Head right and pass through Pl. Vardakas up to the right of the church of Agios Nikolau. Continue on the street until you see an archway and a stone stairway leading down to the beach. The main beach at **Galissas,** a village to the west of Ermoupolis, is beyond crowded; as *the* place to be, every inch of sand is full of sun-lovin' life. Climb past the chapel of Agia Pakou on the left side (facing the water) to discover nudist paradise: tiny, beautiful ■ **Armeos Beach.**

From Ermoupolis, **buses** travel to Galissas (13-18 per day, 310dr/€1.12), alternating between a direct 15min. route and a 45min. route that stops in other villages first (take the longer bus for a glimpse of the island). Taking the scenic route to Galissas allows you to see the rest of Syros's southern beaches. **Finikas** and **Komito** are ideal for watersports like windsurfing. **Mega Gialos** and **Azolimnos** (featuring a large metal waterslide) are more peaceful. The beach resort of **Vari** is popular with families and package tour groups because of its shallow waters and relaxed atmosphere. North of Galissas is the tiny, quiet fishing village of **Kini,** ideal for the quintessential romantic sunset. If you happen to be in this picturesque hamlet on June 29th, the **Church of Ag. Peter** invites you and every other living thing within earshot to an all-night festival. *Bouzouki* accompanies the plentiful *kakavia* (fish soup).

NAXOS Ναξος

"To Naxos steer," quoth Bacchus, "for it is indeed
My home, and there the mariner finds good cheer."
    —Ovid, *Metamorphoses*

Naxos Town's gleaming marble Portara, the lone remaining arch of the grandest Greek temple to Apollo, serves as the portal into diverse and splendid Naxos. The island is the largest of the Cyclades; olive groves, wineries, small villages, and chalky white ruins fill its interior, and sandy beaches line its shores. The ancients believed it to be the island home of Dionysus, but even without mythology Naxos has had a colorful history. Prosperous since ancient times, the island's marble rivals that of neighboring Paros. When the Venetians under Marco Sanudi conquered the Cyclades in 1207, they made Naxos the capital of their Aegean empire.

To properly experience Naxos, it's essential to escape the clutter of Naxos Town and get to the interior. Mopeds can be invaluable for combining trips to the beaches south of town and the inland sights and villages. Be careful, as even mostly paved roads have stretches of dirt with loose rocks. The villages and hikes of the **Tragea** highland valley (a vastly green olive grove) make up Naxos's most exhilarating features. Would-be hikers should pick up maps (1500dr/€4.40), or a copy of *Walking Tours on Naxos* by Christian Ucke, available from the tourist office in both English and German (4500dr/€13.21).

NAXOS TOWN Ναξος ☎ 0285

Naxos' capital reaches out to you before you've stepped off the ferry: as you drift into the harbor, the Portara juts out into the sea on a peninsula, and the Chapel of Myrditiotissa floats on an island. Once inside Naxos Town, both the twisting historic quarter and the hard-nosed modern half step forward. Tightly-packed on the hill leading up to the Venetian castle, Old Naxos snoozes behind the waterfront shops. Low stone archways and trellises of flowers drape the homes that crowd the labyrinthine streets descending from the castle; nearby. Hip bars and clubs near Ag. Georgios beach call you to shimmy after a day exploring the island.

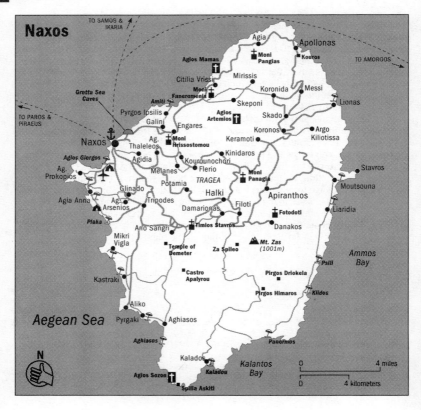

Naxos

◨ TRANSPORTATION

All **ferries** to Naxos dock in Naxos Town. There are two docks at the left end of town; the larger for large ferries, the other for smaller ferries and daily cruises. Mopeds are the easiest (and most hazardous) way to get around the island.

Flights: An **Olympic Airways** desk is housed in **Naxos Tours** (☎ 22 095 or 24 000), at the right end of the waterfront. Two flights per day to **Athens** (20,100dr/€59).

Buses: (☎ 22 291; fax 22 999), in front of the ferry dock. Check the **schedules** at the tourist office and the bus station across the street and to the left (facing inland). Buses to **Apollonas** (2hr., 4 per day, 1100dr/€3.23) and **Filoti** (30min., 5 per day, 400dr/€1.17) are often packed. Buses also run to: **Agia Anna beach** (15min., every 30min. 8am-midnight, 300dr/€0.88), via **Agios Prokopios beach**; **Apiranthos** (1hr., 4 per day 10am-3pm, 550dr/€1.61); **Engari** (1 per day, 220dr/€0.65); **Halki** (30min., 6 per day, 320dr/€0.94); **Pyrgaki Beach** (1hr., 3 per day 11am-2pm, 400dr/€1.17); **Tripodes** (3 per day 11am-2pm, 220dr/€0.65).

Ferries: To: **Amorgos** (2½-5½hr., 1 per day, 2450dr/€7.20); **Crete** (7hr., 1 per week, 5350dr/€15.70); **Donousa** (4hr., 1 per day, 1650dr/€4.85) via **Iraklia** (1hr.), **Schinousa** (2hr.) and **Koufonisia** (3hr.); **Ios** (1½hr., 1 per day, 2350dr/€6.90); **Kos** (7hr., 2 per week, 4650dr/€13.65); **Mykonos** (1½hr., 2 per week, 2050dr/€6.02); **Piraeus** (6½hr., 1 per day, 5350dr/€15.70); **Paros** (1hr., 1 per day, 1550dr/€4.55); **Rhodes** (13hr., 2 per week, 6150dr/€18.05); **Santorini** (3hr., 1 per day, 3150dr/€9.25); **Syros** (2½hr., 2 per week, 2225dr/€6.53); **Thessaloniki** (14hr., 1 per week, 9450dr/€27.73).

Taxis: (☎ 22 444), on the waterfront, next to the bus depot.

Rentals: Fun Cars (☎ 26 084) is inland and right from the roundabout. Also see **Rental Center** under **Internet Access.**

✦ ⦚ ORIENTATION AND PRACTICAL INFORMATION

Avoid the dock hawks and make your way to the waterfront ◼tourist information office (look for the "i") to find a suitable rooming situation. The waterfront to the right of the harbor, along main road **Protopapadaki**, is lined with cafes, tavernas, and clubs. After 500m the road forks inland; follow it up 70m and turn right to find the roundabout of the central square. The Old Town lies behind this main road, accessible via any of the alleyways running inland.

◼**Tourist Office:** (☎ 24 358 or 25 201; fax 25 200; chateau-zeugoli@forthnet.gr), 300m from the dock, by the bus depot. Accommodation assistance, bus and ferry schedules; car rental, **currency exchange**, international telephone, **luggage storage** 500dr/€1.47, safety deposit 500dr/€1.47, **laundry service** 2500dr/€7.34. English speakers Despina and Stavros are marvelous. Open daily 8am-11pm.

Tourist Agency: Zas Travel (☎ 23 043; fax 23 743; naxostours@naxos-island.com), along the waterfront. **Car rental** and ferry and plane tickets. Open daily 8am-11pm.

Bank: The **National Bank** (☎ 23 053) is one of many on the waterfront offering **currency exchange** and an **ATM.** Open M-Th 8am-2pm, F 8am-1:30pm.

English Bookstore: Vrakas (☎ 23 039 or 22 226), behind a jewelry shop. Look for signs reading "gold-silver used books." Vrakas buys at half the original price, sells for 200-2500dr/€0.59-7.34. Open 9:30am-11:30pm. **Zoom** (☎ 23 675), to the right of the National Bank, offers dozens of international magazines. Open daily 7:30am-midnight.

Public Toilets and Showers: Behind Toast Time on the street parallel to the waterfront. Turn left by the dock after Zas Travel and turn left again. Separate facilities for men and women. Toilets 100dr/€0.29; showers 800dr/€2.35. Open daily 6am-midnight.

Police: (☎ 23 100). On the main road heading toward Agios Georgios Beach from Pl. Protodikiou, 1km out of town. Open 24hr.

Port Police: (☎ 22 300), on Protopapadakis, across from the small port dock.

Health Center: Turn inland at the fork in the road past the OTE, at the right end of the waterfront. Follow that road for about 500m; the center will be on your left. Helicopter to Athens available for emergencies. Open 24hr.

Telephones: OTE: left of the fork in the road to the right of the waterfront, inland from Cream nightclub. Open M-F 7:30am-3pm.

Internet Access: At almost every corner. Try **Rental Center** (☎ 23 395 or 25 584) in Pl. Protodikiou. 2500dr/€7.34 per hr., 1000dr/€2.93 minimum. Friendly staff, good **car rental** rates, and lots of info on Naxos. Open 8:30am-11pm. **Veporia Play Room** (☎ 22 003), one block toward Ag. George Beach from Pl. Protodikou. Satellite TV, video games. 2000dr/€5.87 per hr., 1000dr/€2.93 minimum. Open daily 10am-late.

Post Office: Walk down the waterfront (water on your right), and continue just beyond the main street that turns left. Pass a long playground on the right, and the post office will be on your left, up one floor. Open M-F 7:30am-2pm. **Postal code:** 84300.

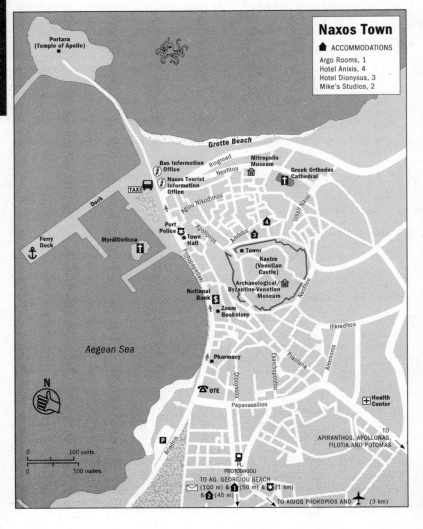

Naxos Town

▲ ACCOMMODATIONS

Argo Rooms, 1
Hotel Anixis, 4
Hotel Dionysus, 3
Mike's Studios, 2

ACCOMMODATIONS AND CAMPING

Most hotels on Naxos fill to capacity in late summer. Accommodations of all types can be arranged through the tourist office. Prices vary according to season. Naxos has three roughly equivalent **beach camping** options, and their representatives wait eagerly at the dock. **Naxos Camping,** 1500m to the right along Ag. Georgios beach, has a swimming pool. (☎23 500; fax 23 501. 1000dr/€2.93 per person; 500dr/€1.47 tent rental.) **Maragas Camping,** on Ag. Anna (a 15min. drive from Naxos Town) has studios and apartments as well as a campsite. (☎42 552 or 42 599.; fax 24 552; maragas@naxos-island.com.) **Plaka Camping,** by Plaka beach, has studio/apartment options, and a bevy of amenities including currency exchange, laundry, and supermarkets. (☎42 700. doubles 6000dr/€17.61 high season; apartments 12,000dr/€35.22. Camping 1600dr/€4.70, high season 2000dr/€5.87; tents 500dr/€1.47.)

■ **Hotel Anixis** (☎22 112 or 22 932), in Old Naxos. Rooms with baths, TVs, and balconies. Laundry and safety deposit boxes. Breakfast (1200dr/€3.52) served in the rooftop garden, overlooking the Temple of Apollo. Singles 8,000-13,000dr/€23.48-38.15; doubles 10,000-15,000dr/€29.35-44; triples 13,000-18,000dr/€38.15-52.82.

Dionysus (☎25 331), in Old Naxos near Hotel Anixis. Spartan, but very cheap. Open July-Aug. Dorms 2000dr/€5.87; singles 4000-5000dr/€11.74-14.67; doubles and triples 6000dr/€17.61.

Mike's Studios (☎23 111 or mobile (09459) 77 649), 50m from Ag. Georgios and 70m from the main square; call for a port shuttle. Brand-new rooms with bath, TV, A/C, kitchenette and laundry service. Doubles 7000-10,000dr/€20.53-29.35; up to 5 people 15,000-30,000dr/€44-88.

Argo (☎25 330 or 23 059; fax 24 910), 150m from Ag. Georgios and 400m from the square; call for a port shuttle. Multilingual owners offer rooms with private baths, phone and A/C. Rooms for 1-5 people 8000-18,000dr/€23.48-52.82.

FOOD

Wade through the sea of waterfront tables or park at one of the many new cafes. In Old Naxos, you'll stumble upon tucked-away *moussaka* havens. **Supermarkets** and fruit and grocery stands are everywhere.

■ **Taverna Vassilis** (☎23 763), on Old Market street. This charcoal grill has been cooking up delicious Greek food since 1951. Feast on calamari and wine in a romantic, narrow passageway. Entrees 1700-2500dr/€5-7.34. Open 6pm-late.

Dolfini (☎24 320), up the steps from Ergo Bank. A slice of India (via Britain), in a lush garden washed by romantic tunes. The self-proclaimed Mystic Fire Priest of Naxos challenges patrons to down their spicy dishes (curries and Thai dishes 1800-2400dr/€5.28-7.05)—soothe your fiery belly with a cocktail. Open 9am-2am.

Cafe Picasso Mexican Bistro (☎25 408). One block toward Ag. Georgios Beach from the main square. Some of the only Mexican food you'll find in Greece, from quesadillas (1300-1600dr/€3.82-4.70) to burritos (2500-2900dr/€7.34-8.50). Ease the salsa with a glass of sangria (600dr/€1.76) or a frozen margarita (1200dr/€3.52). Open 7pm-2am; kitchen closes at midnight.

Rendez-Vous (☎23 858). This bright pink waterfront palace concocts pastries: especially delicious *loukamades* (honey doughnuts; 750dr/€2.20); ice cream and fruit bowls are served with sparklers. Breakfast served. Open 6am-2am.

SIGHTS

Naxos Town is crowned by the ■**Castro,** an old Venetian castle. Of the 12 original houses within its walls, only one remains entirely intact. The Domus Della Rocca-Barozzi, vacated by its owners in 2001, is now a **Byzantine-Venetian museum.** Once per month a "Venetian Evening" is held; candles light the castle as guests revel in

singing, dancing and traditional drinks. A series of "Sunset Concerts" feature traditional Greek shadow theater *(karaghiozis)*, and traditional or contemporary
music and dancing. Run by local Naxians, the Castro is a refreshing dose of culture
and history. (☎22 387; fax 24 879; venetian@hellasnet.gr. Open daily 10am-3pm
and 7-10pm. Multilingual 30min. tours throughout the day; 2¼hr. tour Tu-Su at
11am.) Also inside the Castro sits the **Archaeological Museum,** in the former Collège
Français where Nikos Kazantzakis (see p. 33), author of *The Last Temptation of
Christ* and *Zorba the Greek*, studied. There's a significant collection of Cycladic
figurines and Mycenean vessels; tucked away in one of the rooms is the island's
historical archive. (Open Tu-Su 8:30am-2pm. 500dr/€1.47, students 300dr/€0.88;
free on Sundays and holidays.) The ◪**Mitropolis Museum,** on the left side of town, is
an architectural achievement in itself. Elevated walkways lead you through the
reconstructed buildings of a 13th century BC settlement; clear floors give the feeling of being inside them. (☎24 151. Open Tu-Su 8:30am-3pm. Free.)

From the waterfront, you can see the white chapel of **Myrditiotissa** floating in the
harbor on a man-made islet and the marble **Portara** archway, on its own peninsula.
Climb up to it and view the unfinished beginnings of an ambitious temple dedicated to Apollo, begun on the orders of the tyrant Lydamis in the 6th century BC.
This is one of the few archaeological sites in Greece where you can actually climb
all over the ruins—with no admission, and no guards, open 24 hours, it's ideal for
romantic sunsets or midnight star-gazing.

▣ NIGHTLIFE

After-hours Naxos serenades evening wanderers with music from cafes and clubs.
Take advantage of half-price happy hour, then relax all night, or get ready to join
the masses at the waterfront clubs. Mobilize around 11pm. Alternatively, spend a
low-key evening under the stars at ◪**Cine Astra** (☎25 381), on the road to Agia Anna
from Pl. Protodikliou; a 15min. walk from the waterfront. (Movies in English.
Shows 9 and 11pm. Open daily May-Oct. 2000dr/€5.87.)

Caesar's Club (☎25 203), take the inland street to the right of Naxos Tours. Climb
    upstairs, and then stumble back down after a night of boozin' and groovin' under palm
    trees overlooking the sea. Open late.

Super Island Bar and Club (☎(0946) 37 462), on the water along the paved road next
    to the bus depot. All of Naxos goes to see and be seen here. Adrenaline-pumping Euro
    beats. Open 11pm-late.

Ocean Dance (☎30 285 or 26 766), facing the water at the right end of the harborfront
    Ocean churns enough to make its namesake proud. Do your best Ricky Martin impres-
    sion atop the go-go box; you're sure to hear something you like. Open late.

Flamingo (☎23 940 or 26 285) offers a taste of the authentic with Greek music on
    select nights (10pm-2am) on a rooftop patio. Open until 2am.

Lakridi Jazz Bar, in Old Naxos on Old Market, close to the Captain's Cafe. Chill to the
    sounds of Billie Holliday in the hot Naxian night. Open 8pm-3:30am.

◤ BEACHES

North of Naxos Town, you can snorkel among caves in search of rocks and sea
urchins. You'll have to head south, however, for Naxos's busiest beach life, with
hotels, rooms to let, bars, tavernas, discos, and creperies. The most remote,
uncrowded beaches with the clearest waters are the farthest from town. There,
younger, beautiful, and scantily clad bathers frolic among visiting windsurfers
who come to Naxos from everywhere. Near town, **Agios Georgios, Agios Prokopios,
Agia Anna,** and long and sandy **Plaka** border crystal-blue water. Beware, you may
have to vie for your share of sand with the multitude of other sunbathers out to
catch some rays. On Plaka, stunning nude sunbathers stud the shore. At Ag. Georgios beach, **Flisvos Sportclub** runs windsurfing and catamaran rentals and lessons,
and organizes weekly mountain bike excursions. The complex is complete with a

WorldPhone. Worldwide.

MCI℠ gives you the freedom of worldwide communications whenever you're away from home. It's easy to call to and from over 70 countries with your MCI Calling Card:

1. Dial the WorldPhone® access number of the country you're calling from.
2. Dial or give the operator your MCI Calling Card number.
3. Dial or give the number you're calling.

         • Greece   00-800-1211

Sign up today!

Ask your local operator to place a collect call
(reverse charge) to MCI in the U.S. at:

1-712-943-6839

For additional access codes or to sign up, visit us at www.mci.com/worldphone.

www.mci.com/worldphone

It's Your World...

www.mci.com/worldphone

bar and restaurant. (☎24 308. Open 10am-7pm.) A **bus** goes from the port to the beaches every half-hour (300dr/€0.88). The more secluded beaches at **Mikri Vigla, Kastraki, Aliko,** and **Pyrgaki** are accessible by **bus** from Naxos Town. Here desert meets sea; scrub pines, prickly pear, and century plants grow on the dunes. There is a small nudist beach on the southern protuberance of **Kastraki Beach.**

DAYTRIPS FROM NAXOS TOWN

APOLLONAS AND NORTHERN NAXOS

*From Naxos Town, catch the **bus** to Apollonas for an exhilarating ride on a beautiful coastal road (2hr., 1100dr/€3.23). This bus service can be used easily to make a round trip (in either direction) of the central Naxian villages and the islands' northern coast; the bus travels on an interior and an alternate coastal route. The coast is lined with secluded, sandy beaches; those on moped can pick their spot and hike down along the goat trails.*

On the road to Apollonas you'll pass the secluded beach at **Amiti** on your left, down the road from Galini, and, further on, the monastery of **Faneromenis** (the Virgin Revealer). The main attraction of Apollonas, one of the more famous *kouroi* of Naxos, is just a short walk from the harbor. While this **kouros** is nearly 11m tall, it's not as completely sculpted than the one in Flerio (see below). From the Apollonas bus stop, walk back along the main road uphill to the fork in the road. Take a sharp right and walk up until you see the stairs at the Pros Kouro (Προς Κουρο) sign.

CENTRAL NAXOS AND THE TRAGEA

*Buses run from Naxos Town to Halki (17km, 15-20min.) Look for the turn-off to **Ano Sangri,** an isolated town of winding flagstone streets 1km west of the road. You can get off the bus at the turn-off and walk the entire way (roughly 1½hr.).*

If you're up for the 30 min. amble south of Ano Sangri, you can see the 6th-century BC **Temple of Demeter** being reconstructed with original fragments and new Naxian marble. If you have a motorbike or car, an alternate route takes you from Naxos Town through Melanes to **Flerio,** where another magnificent Naxian **kouros** sleeps in a garden. This one was probably abandoned in its marble quarry because it broke before completion. Its owner runs a small *kafeneion* in the garden. From Flerio, backtrack and follow a road through three charming villages in a river valley—**Kato Potamia, Mesi Potamia,** and, upstream, **Ano Potamia**—before reaching Halki. Maps available at the tourist office in Naxos Town (1500dr/€4.40).

Halki, a placid village surrounded by Venetian towers, marks the beginning of the magnificent **Tragea,** an enormous, peaceful Arcadian olive grove. Restoration work in the **Panagia Protothonis,** across from the bus stop, has uncovered frescoes from the 11th through 13th centuries. The priest can let you in if it is closed.

Soon after leaving Halki you'll reach Filoti (20min. walk), a village at the far end of the Tragea valley. Footpaths off the main road will lead you into the dense **olive grove.** It is easy to get delightfully lost wandering among the scattered churches and tranquil scenery of the Tragea. If you do, take note of the sun and head west to return to the main road. Naxos's largest celebration, the **Feast of the Assumption of Panagia** (the Virgin Mary) is held in Filoti from August 14 to 16.

The slopes of **Mt. Zas** near Filoti offer superb views extending to Poros and the sea beyond. Serious hikers may want to check out the **Cave of Zeus,** the spot where an eagle gave the king of the gods the power to hurl thunderbolts. This 150m-deep cave is a good 1½hr. trek uphill from Filoti. Determined mythologists, or those simply looking for a good hike with excellent views, should bring a flashlight to fully appreciate the cave. Head up the road to Apiranthos for 20-30min. until a sign points to the right for Mt. Zas. Follow this road to its end, passing through a gate, just before a clearing with a potable **spring water fountain.** From there, keep going, staying on the left (uphill) whenever possible. Look for red arrows on stones, and be prepared to share the path with goats; don't expect any signs. After 45min. you'll reach cave's mouth, marked with a simple sign that reads "cave." The grotto itself is large, cool, rather slimy, and fun to explore.

CYCLADES

APIRANTHOS

Buses run from Filoti (15min.).

The small town of Apiranthos, which houses an **Archaeological Museum** with many Cycladic artifacts, in a white building on the right side of the main street. Also in Apiranthos are a modest **folk art museum,** a **natural history museum** (near the bus stop), and a **geological museum** (beside a large church). All four are "officially" open from 10am to 1:30pm, but it all depends on tourist traffic; many of the owners moonlight as goat herders. (Single ticket to all four.) Many Apiranthos homes are 300 to 400 years old, and lie in the shadow of the two Venetian castles that preside over the town. The Zergolis family, who live in the castle by the square, may allow you to look around. The mountain views from the edges of the town are stunning, and locals are cordial to the few tourists who come this way. More information is available at the unofficial **info center** inside the pricey Yasou Snack Bar, on the right past the Geological Museum. From Apiranthos through **Koronos** and **Koronida,** a 1hr. drive away, the road snakes through interior mountain ranges. The terraced landscape, laden with fruit and olive trees, plunges into the valleys below.

LITTLE CYCLADES

Goats outnumber human inhabitants in this tiny island group. Jumping off the beaten island-hopping track into the Little Cyclades lets you pursue perfect isolation and meditation. Peaceful walks, refreshing solitude, and a breathtaking nighttime sky await the adventurous traveler.

KOUFONISIA Κουφονησια　　　　☎0285

The smallest of the inhabited Little Cyclades (and the most popular), Koufonisia surrounds itself with a sparkling selection of beaches on the southeast side of Koufonisia, **Ano Koufonisia.** The name means "hollow," earned for the caves perforating its surface; the small town of **Hora** serves as its capital. Tales of serene beaches and Cycladic relics lure visitors off of Ano Koufonisia to neighboring **Kato Koufonisia** and rocky **Keros.** There may be few alternatives to the well-worn path from beach to taverna, but Koufonisia's total simplicity makes it totally relaxing.

◼◪ **ORIENTATION AND PRACTICAL INFORMATION.** Koufonisia's commercial center consists of two main streets. One runs inland from just beyond the port to the left of the minimarket; the other springs from its left side, about 100m inland and parallel to the beach. The **ferry ticket office,** up the main road in Hora a few buildings past the blue-domed church, posts a ferry schedule on its door. (☎71 438. Open 9am-2pm and 6-10pm.) There are two **ferry** lines; one runs M, W-Th and Sa at 9:30am to **Naxos** (2½hr., 1700dr/€5) via **Schinousa** (30min., 1100dr/€3.23) and **Iraklia** (1hr., 1100dr/€3.23), and continues to **Paros** (2½hr., 1700dr/€5) and Mykonos (4½hr., 2700dr/€7.92). The other line runs daily to **Aegiali** (2hr., 1700dr/€5), and **Katapola** (3hr., 1700dr/€5) via **Donousa** (1½hr., 1400dr/€4.11). Head straight off the ferry dock toward the tiny white village and the winding lanes of Hora. The heart of Hora can be reached by turning left at the second road, just past the card phone. Be sure to bring enough money, as there is **no bank** on the island. **Currency exchange** is available at the **post office,** one block left at the first road away from the port. (Open 8:30-10am and 6:30-9:30pm.) The **OTE** is on a parallel road across from Pension Melissa. (☎22 392. Open 8am-2pm and 5-10pm.) The **medical center** (☎71 370) is on the inland road to Hora near the **police.** A few **minimarkets** are on the main road. **Postal code:** 84300.

ℹ️ ACCOMMODATIONS AND CAMPING. The small pensions around town fill up fast, so it's best to call ahead for accommodations. Many homes with rooms to let are along the main road; prices for doubles run about 8000-10,000dr/€23.48-29.35 in low season and start at 12,000dr/€35.22 in high season. **Pension Melissa** is attached to the taverna 70m along the parallel street from the inland road to Hora, just up to the left from Katerina in the center of town. (☎71 454. Doubles 9000dr/€26.41; triples 12,000dr/€35.22.) **Marousa Rooms** is attached to the mini-market across from the beach. (☎71 367. Doubles 10,000-12,000dr/€29.35-35.22.) **Harako-rou Camping** is a new site affiliated with the taverna of the same name on Finikas beach. (☎71 683. 2500dr/€7.34 for 2 people and tent rental.)

🍴📺 FOOD AND ENTERTAINMENT. Throughout town you'll find good tavernas: seafood and standard Greek fare are the unanimous favorites (entrees 1400-2700dr/€4.11-7.92). Their quality is uniform, and they're cheap. **Kohili** is the perfect spot for a croissant sandwich and a view of the harbor. (☎74 279. Open 8:30am-late.) **Kalamia Music Cafe**, 150m along the inland road by the public phone, provides drinks, sweets and internet access. (☎71 741. Open 8am-late. Cocktails 1600dr/€4.70. Internet 3000dr/€8.80 per hr., 500dr/€1.47 minimum.) The artistically inclined can wander up to **Elkazein,** a new art gallery featuring the paintings and photographs of its owners. For late-night dancing drift over to **Emplo,** a word signifying the beginning of a sea voyage. Walk up the hill path to the left of the port; listen for the Greek music.

🏖️ BEACHES. Koufonisia's beaches spool out in a continuous ribbon along the southern coast. **Amos Beach** is closest to Hora, just to the right of the ferry dock (facing inland); here you can spot nearby fishing boats and watch spirited kids' soccer games. Continuing 10min. down the road behind the sand leads you to family-packed **Finikas,** with a convenient taverna beside it. Just on the other side of the ridge from Finikas waits much quieter **Fanos.** The farther you walk the fewer people (and clothes) you'll see. A 45min. walk from Hora, 🏖️**Pori beach** is the best on the island, with water and sand magnificent even by Greek Island standards. If the sand gets too busy or begins to broil, head for the shaded rocks behind the beach to a bay that is perfect for snorkeling. Regular boats also make trips to Pori from the dock at Hora (500dr/€1.47); check the posted schedule. If these get too hectic, peace costs just 500dr/€1.47—the price of the daily ferry to Kato Koufonisia.

DONOUSA Δονουσα ☎0285

A trip to Donousa takes you back in time to the closest look at traditional life in the rural Cyclades that you may ever get. Lacking modern conveniences (banks, public transportation, a reliable tourist office), Donousa beckons those eager to abandon English.

The **tourist office** is across from the ferry dock; it sells ferry tickets and exchanges currency during its erratic opening hours. If it's closed during your visit, you can buy your ticket on the boat. **Ferries** travel to Amorgos, Koufonissia, Naxos and Schinoussa four times per week at 8am. Travel to other islands is more sporadic. Continue and bear to the right to find the **mini-market** (☎51 582). There are several tavernas, all visible from the dock, all serving similar Greek food (entrees 1000-1800dr/€2.93-5.28). **To Kima,** the island's main hangout, also sells phone cards and some groceries; it's right beside the dock. (☎51 566. Open 6am-4pm and 5pm-midnight.) Up the hill behind it is the island's sole **public phone.** You can call the **doctor** at 51 506. Vacationers most often stay in the limited domatia across the bay from the main port. Rooms run about 8000-15,000dr/€23.48-44 for a double. Try **Christos Sigalas** (☎515 70) at the Rooms to Let sign or **Venetsanou Eleutherie** (☎51 609) in the first complex at the right of the beach. Camping is permitted only on **Kedros beach,** over the hill to the right of the domatia. Some of the island's tastiest food comes from the **bakery** just above the tourist office (☎51 567).

The town **beach** allows children to splash under the watchful eyes of parents sipping Mythos. **Kedros beach,** a much nicer piece of shore, stretches out just over the ridge. Follow the road to the right of the white sign on the town beach to get to the tent-lined sand. Farther down the same road lies even more pristine **Livadi beach.**

IRAKLIA Ιρακλια   ☎ 0285

Travelers who have stumbled upon Iraklia go to great lengths to conceal their whereabouts, lest their hideaway be discovered. The island's solitude is precious, as are the close ties between the local community and its rare visitors. Whether exploring its caves, basking on its beaches, or sipping coffee under the starlight in a cafe, Iraklia's tangible and intangible charms will envelop you.

⚡🔢 ORIENTATION AND PRACTICAL INFORMATION. Ferries run almost daily to: **Donoussa** (1600dr/€4.69); **Koufonissia** (1200dr/€3.51); **Naxos** (1400dr/€4.10); **Paros** (1400dr/€4.10); and **Schinoussa** (1200dr/€3.51). Less frequent trips go to: **Amorgos** (2300dr/€6.74); **Pireaus** (5000dr/€14.67); and **Syros** (1400dr/€4.10 or 2300dr/€6.74). Schedules are posted around the harbor, or consult a travel agent. **Agiazi Travel office** (☎74 236), at the left of the beach, sells **ferry tickets.** Rent **mopeds** from **Iraklia Rent a Scooter** (☎71 564; 5000dr/€14.67 per day). From the **port,** head right past the town beach of Agios Giorgios to get to Hora. This main road splits at **Perigali,** a good place to score an island map (350dr/€1.03), marking the bottom of the ravine that runs through town. Two roads run alongside the ravine and merge at the top. The **medical center** (☎/fax 71 388) is at the top of Hora. Along the right-hand road is all-purpose ▨**Melissa,** a general store, ferry ticketer, telephone operator, post office, and domatia. (☎71 539; fax 71 561. Doubles with bath and fridge 6000dr/€17.61.) The island's only card phone is just outside. **Postal code:** 84300.

▟🔳 ACCOMMODATIONS AND FOOD. In July and August, call ahead to reserve accommodations—in most cases, your hosts will pick you up at the port. **Alexandra,** at the top of Hora on the way to Livadi Beach, has four breezy rooms with baths and fridges, a shared kitchen, and veranda. (☎71 482. Doubles 8000dr/€23.48.) **Maria's** (☎71 485), across the road, has similar rates and amenities.

Ten minutes down the road to Livadi, you'll find a delicious variety of grilled fish and Greek specialties at ▨**Giorgios Gavalas' Place.** Dance late into the night with his sons, or ask Giorgios if you can participate in the next all-male Miss Iraklia contest. Rave about your exploits to the folks back home at their **internet** station (2000dr/€5.87 per hour, 500dr/€1.47 minimum) or **international telephone.** (☎29 034 or 71 226. Traveler's checks accepted.) **Maistrali,** up the hill just before Alexandra, sells postcards, foreign papers, and books, and offers **internet access** (1000dr/€2.93 per hour); an attached restaurant serves good Greek food. (☎71 807; nickmaistrali@in.gr. Opens at 7am for breakfast.) Across the road **O Pevkos** (☎71 568) sells fresh fish. For a more energized hangout try **Bar Aki Music-Dance** (☎71 487) in Hora, a new club that has the whole island grooving to its beat.

🔳◪ SIGHTS AND BEACHES. The shallow, clear waters of **Livadi Beach** echo the serenity of everything else on the island. Wade out and look at the ruins of the **Venetian Castle** overhead. The water taxi "Anemos" will take you to **Karvounlakos** or **Alimia** beaches (3 per week, departing 11am and returning 4pm, 2000dr/€5.87); buy tickets at Perigali. To step into the Greece of 40 years ago, continue along the main road past Livadi to the town of **Panagia** (45min. from Hora), where you'll find a small taverna, a church, some cows, and not much else. The taverna, **To Steki** (☎71 579) also serves as a general store, bakery, and the only "gas station" on the island—fill up from a canister.

THE OUTDOORS. The stalactite and stalagmite-scattered **Agios Ioannis Cave,** with its tiny waterways you can crawl around in, will fascinate the adventurous. There is a rough but helpful map of the path on the back of the Iraklia map available in Perigali. Bring a flashlight, candles, and matches, and get ready to get filthy. The steep, 1½hr. **hike** begins in Panagia, where a red arrow and the word "cave" are scrawled on a barn (go through the stone doorway on the left at the beginning of town)—if you don't see it, ask in To Steki. After 20 minutes along the stone wall-lined dirt path, you'll reach a wooden fence and another painted arrow pointing you through it. Follow the stone wall on your right until it meets another stone wall. The beaten path of the ascent becomes difficult to follow; just stay near this wall. After your climb, another wooden door stands at the intersection of two fences. Through this door, you'll begin a steep but more clearly defined 30min. descent along the back side of **Mt. Pappas** toward the two cave entrances. Crawling through the small entrance (marked by a hanging bell) brings you into the caves. You'll need the flashlight right away; leaving lighted candles along the way will help mark your path. To the left as you enter is an icon of St. John, who is celebrated in an August **festival** at the cave. There are said to be 15 rooms inside the cave. Be careful: the rocks are slippery, and daylight vanishes fast.

SCHINOUSA Σχινουσα ☎ 0285

A multitude of isolated yet accessible beaches line the coast of the undiscovered island of Schinousa, all but guaranteeing an isolated communion with nature. The island is best enjoyed on foot exploring its hide-away beaches and donkey-patrolled interior, and getting to know the affable population—100 at last count.

ORIENTATION AND PRACTICAL INFORMATION. All boats dock at the tiny port of **Mersini,** with **Hora** a 10-15min. walk uphill. Call ahead for accommodations and you'll be picked up from the ferry, or grab a ride with a pension owner at the dock. **Ferries** go daily to: **Amorgos** (3hr., 2200dr/€6.46); **Iraklia** (15min., 1200dr/€3.52); **Koufonisia** (30min., 1200dr/€3.52); and **Naxos** (1½hr., 1500dr/€4.40); continuing to **Donousa** 5 times per week (1½hr., 1600dr/€4.70); **Mykonos** 2 times per week (5hr., 2500dr/€7.34); **Paros** 4 times per week (1-3hr., 1500dr/€4.40) and **Pireaus** 3 times per week. Check the posted schedules for daily routes. Nearly everything you'll need in Hora can be found on the main road, a 5min. walk from end to end. The **post office** is 100m down, on the left side. If you keep walking, you'll see a road that heads left, marked by signs for a **bakery.** The **doctor** (☎71 385) is on the same road, in a clearly marked white building. Halfway along the main road you'll see a sign pointing to Tsigouri Beach. Following this road leads to **Giorgios Grispos,** the town's travel guru, who offers one-stop tourist shopping at his **travel agency,** taverna, and domatia. (☎71 930. Open M-F 2:30-4pm and 6:30-9pm, Sa-Su 10am-2:30pm and 6-10:30pm.) Buy **ferry tickets** here or at the port and **exchange money** at poor rates. Note that there is **no bank** in town. Maps and phone cards are available at the mini-markets lining the main road. Two public **card phones** are down at the port and in the main plateia of Hora. **Postal code:** 84300.

ACCOMMODATIONS AND FOOD. Nearly every restaurant or general store in town offers several rooms to rent in addition to *moussaka* and Fanta. Centrally located **Anesis** has large, clean rooms with fridges, private baths, and panoramic balcony views. (☎71 180. Doubles 10,000-13,000dr/€29.35-38.15. Be sure to bargain.) **Agnantema** is in a new building with a prime location right next to the bakery. The rooms above their cafe overlook a rocky terrace with tables and a gazebo. (☎71 987; fax 74 077. Doubles 10,000-18,000dr/€29.35-52.82; studios for 4 people 15,000-25,000dr/€44-73.37. Cafe open 8am-11:30pm.) Enjoy traditional music and good food with a crowd of locals at **Loza Pizzeria,** off the main plateia. (☎74 004 or 71 864. Open 9am-2am.) Alternatively, gaze off the balcony as you wait for your *moussaka* at **Panorama,** a few meters past the beach turn-off on the main road. (☎71 160 or 71 957. Open 9am-midnight.)

CYCLADES

⊠⊄ NIGHTLIFE AND BEACHES. A 10min. walk down a rocky path at the beginning of Hora, off the main road, leads to **Ostria Cafe,** an outdoor beach bar and restaurant, where you can spin music with the five brothers (Manolis, Agilos, Dimitris, Christos, and Antonis) who own the joint.

Schinousa's dirt roads love pedestrians as much as they hate cars. Grab some water, glance at a map, and walk until a particularly alluring cove catches your eye. **Tsigouri Beach,** 450m down a dusty road, invites you to splash in its waves, play a round of beach volleyball, and rent kayaks or waterskis. **Livadi** is farther along the main road through Hora to the dirt tracks leading to the water; **Psili Ammos** on the other side of the island, about a 20min. walk past the bakery.

PAROS Πάρος

Paros was famous in the ancient world for its slabs of pure white marble, which were molded into the Venus de Milo, the Nike of Samothrace, and parts of Napoleon's mausoleum in Paris. In the 7th century BC, Paros was infamous as the home of sharp-tongued Archilochus, one of the earliest lyric poets, whose biting satire actually drove one scandalous Parian woman and her shamed father to suicide. Nowadays, the quarries have closed and the locals have warmed up, as Paros has become a tourist favorite among the Greek islands.

PAROIKIA Παροικια   ☎ 0284

Behind Paroikia's (PAR-ah-kia) commercial facade, flower-filled streets wind through archways past whitewashed houses and one of the most treasured basilicas of the Orthodox faith. Wander through the *agora* (marketplace) to find trendy clothing, snappy jewelry, local art, homemade goods, and the outdoor terraces of coffeehouses. While the beaches aren't much to write home about, this transportation hub is a convenient base for reaching almost any spot on the island.

▐ TRANSPORTATION

Flights: Olympic Airways (local ☎ 21 900, general information ☎ 0801 44 444), in the plateia by National Bank. Open M-F 8am-3pm. To Athens (around 2 per day, 20,400dr/ €59.77). Taxi to airport 2200dr/€6.44; bus to Aliki 300dr/€0.88.

Ferries: To: **Amorgos** (3hr., 1-2 per day, 3050dr/€8.94); **Crete** (8hr., 5 per week, 5350dr/€15.67); **Ikaria** (4hr., 5 per week, 3850dr/€11.28); **Ios** (2½hr., 7-9 per day, 2650dr/€7.76); **Kos** (1 per week, 4750dr/€13.92); **Piraeus** (5-6hr., 5-8 per day, 5000dr/€14.65); **Naxos** (1hr., 5-10 per day, 1550dr/€4.54); **Rafina** (3-5 per day, 9050dr/€26.52); **Rhodes** (16hr., 1 per week, 7550dr/€22.12); **Samos** (6hr., 6 per week, 4050dr/€11.89); **Santorini** (3½hr., 7-9 per day, 3350dr/€9.81); **Sikinos** (7 per week, 2050dr/€6); **Syros** (1hr., 3-6 per day, 1850dr/€5.42).

Flying Dolphins: To: **Amorgos** (1-2 per day, 5700dr/€16.70); **Anafi** (7100dr/€20.80); **Andros** (2 per week, 5700dr/€16.70); **Crete** (10,000dr/€29.30); **Folegandros** (3 per week, 4000dr/€11.72); **Koufonisia** (2 per week, 5600dr/€16.40); **Ios** (2-3 per day, 5000dr/€14.65); **Milos** (5900dr/€17.28); **Mykonos** (1hr., 2-4 per day, 3400dr/ €9.96); **Naxos** (4-7 per day, 2800dr/€8.20); **Rafina** (9 per week, 8300dr/€24.31); **Santorini** (3-4 per day, 6300dr/€18.46); **Sifnos** (2 per week, 2000dr/€5.86); **Sikinos** (3600dr/ €10.54); **Syros** (3-4 per day, 3200dr/€9.37); and **Tinos** (4-5 per day, 3600dr/€10.54). **Minoan Lines** go to **Piraeus** (3hr., 10,000dr/€29.30).

Buses: (☎ 21 395 or 21 133). Schedule posted a few blocks to the left of the windmill (facing inland). Prices run from 250-600dr/€0.73-1.76. Buses run to: **Aliki** and the **airport** (30min., 10 per day, 300dr/€0.88) via the **Valley of the Butterflies; Chrisi Akti** (50min., 2 per day); **Marpissa** (35min., 15 per day); **Drios** (1hr., 12 per day); **Kamares** (20min., 2 per day); **Lefkes** (25min., 8 per day); **Naoussa** (15min., 33 per day); **Piso Livadi** (40min., 15 per day); **Pounda** (15min., 15 per day).

Taxis: (☎ 22 620), inland and to the right of the windmill.

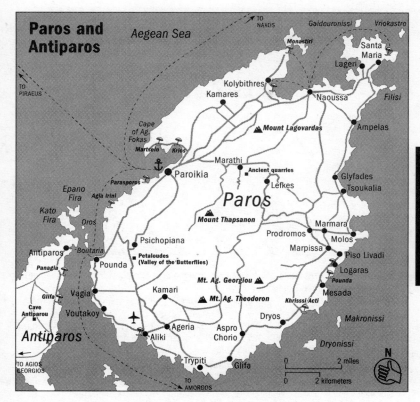

Paros and Antiparos

Aegean Sea

TO PIRAEUS

TO NAXOS

Gaidouronissi   *Vriokastro*

Monastiri

Santa Maria

Lageri

Filisi

Kolybithres

Kamares

Naoussa

Ampelas

Cape of Ag. Fokas

Mount Lagovardas

Martselo   Krios

Marathi

Paroikia

Ancient quarries

Lefkes

Glyfades

Tsoukalia

Epano Fira

Parasporos

Agia Irini

Paros

Kato Fira

Oros

Mount Thapsanon

Marmara

Psichopiana

Prodromos

Molos

Antiparos

Boutaria

Petaloudes (Valley of the Butterflies)

Marpissa

Piso Livadi

Panagia

Pounda

Mt. Ag. Georgiou

Logaras

Pounda

Glifa

Vagia

Kamari

Mt. Ag. Theodoron

Khrissi Acti

Mesada

Cave Antiparou

Voutakoy

Makronissi

Antiparos

Ageria

Aspro Chorio

Dryos

Aliki

Dryonissi

TO AGIOS GEORGIOS

Trypiti

Glifa

0   2 miles

0   2 kilometers

N

TO AMORGOS

✈ 🛈 ORIENTATION AND PRACTICAL INFORMATION

Stepping off the ferry, cheap hotels, tourist-related offices, and the town beach lie to the left. The plateia is straight ahead, past the windmill and the tourist offices. To the right, a whitewashed labyrinth brims with shops, restaurants, and cafes. To the far right around the bend, the island's party district awaits.

Tourist Agency: Polos Tours (☎22 092 or 22 093; fax 21 983), next to the OTE. Has up-to-the-minute transportation schedules and rental services. Open daily 8am-1am.

Banks: National Bank (☎21 298). From the windmill, head inland to the plateia and to the right. It's in the fortress-like building at the far corner, past the playground. 24hr. **ATM** and **currency exchange** machine. Open M-Th 8am-2pm, F 8am-1:30pm.

Luggage Storage: Agencies around the port charge 1000dr/€2.93 per piece per day.

Laundromat: Top (☎23 424). Pass the bus station and turn right just after ancient ruins. Wash, dry, and folding 2200dr/€6.46. Open daily 9am-2pm and 5:30-9pm.

Public Toilets: Beside the small blue and white church to the left of the windmill. More toilets are to the right of the windmill beside the signs for the Frankish Castle.

Police: (☎23 333), across the plateia behind the OTE, on the 2nd floor above the photo shops. Open 24hr. **Tourist police** (☎21 673), in the same building. Open daily 9am-3:30pm. **Port Police** (☎21 240), off the waterfront, past the bus station. Open 24hr.

Medical Clinic: (☎22 500). Across the street from the toilets and the small blue and white church to the left of the windmill. Open M-F 7am-2:30pm. **Emergency** care 24hr.

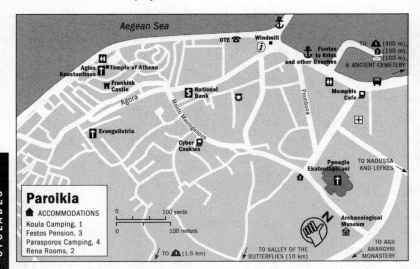

Paroikia

ACCOMMODATIONS

Koula Camping, 1
Festos Pension, 3
Parasporos Camping, 4
Rena Rooms, 2

Telephones: The **OTE** (☎ 21 399) is one block to the right of the windmill (facing inland). Open M-F 7:30am-2:30pm.

Internet Access: Internet cafes are multiplying like rabbits in Paroikia. **Cybercookies** (☎/fax 21 610), on Market street, charges 1200dr/€3.52 per hr. Special offers include 20min. free with 1 order of food, 45min. with 2 orders. Open daily 9am-2am. **Memphis Cafe** (mobile ☎ (0030) 2842 3768) is left of the windmills on the waterfront. 500dr/€1.47 for 20min. Open daily 9am-1am.

Post Office: (☎ 21 236), on the left side of the waterfront, 2 blocks past the bus stop. Open M-F 7:30am-2pm. **Postal code:** 84400.

■ ACCOMMODATIONS AND CAMPING

There are many hotels and rooms to let along the waterfront and in the Old Town; a slew of new, inexpensive pensions have opened behind the town beach to the left of the plateia. Dock hawks are known to offer good deals in Naoussa, Piso Livadi, and Antiparos, among other places; remember to insist on seeing rooms before forking over any cash. The **Room Association** (☎ 24 528) can help you hunt.

Rena Rooms (☎/fax 22 220 or 21 427). Turn left from the dock and take a right after the cemetery ruins, or call ahead for pick-up from the port. George, the owner, and his wife are both friendly and ready to help. Bright, spic-'n'-span rooms with fridges, ceiling fans, baths, and balconies. Open Mar.-Nov. Doubles 6000-13,000dr/€17.58-38.09; triples 9000-15,000dr/€26.37-43.95. 20% *Let's Go* discount.

Pelagos Studios (☎ 22 725 or 22 726; fax 22 708). Find Vassilis, the owner, in the port or call and get picked up. Fully furnished rooms with kitchen, bath, TV, and even radio. Convenient to Pariokia's nightlife, despite its peaceful setting. Doubles 10,000-18,000dr/€29.3-52.74; triples 12,000-21,000dr/€35.16-61.53.

Festos Pension (☎ 21 635; fax 24 193). From the dock, walk to the left of the windmill, and take a right to head toward the Church of 100 Gates; take another right at the end of the road. Modest, clean rooms with private baths in a central location. Laundry 1000-1700dr/€2.93-4.98. Luggage storage 300-500dr/€0.88-1.47. Check-out 10:30am. 4-bed dorm 3000-5000dr/€8.79-14.65. Singles 4500-5500dr/€13.18-16.12; doubles 6500-7500dr/€19.04-21.97.

Parasporos Camping (☎ 22 268 or 21 100), 1.5km south of the port; shuttle service available. Away from the bustle, beside Delphini Beach. Showers, laundry, and kitchen. 1300dr/€3.81 per person; 700dr/€2 per tent, 1000dr/€2.93 tent rental.

Koula Camping (☎ 22 081 or 22 082; fax 22 740), 400m north of the dock across the street from the pebbly town beach. Market, laundry, and kitchen. 1500dr/€4.40 per person; 600dr/€1.76 per tent, 1000dr/€2.93 tent rental; 1000dr/€2.93 per car.

▐ FOOD

▓ **Happy Green Cow** (☎ 24 691), a block inland off the plateia in the narrow walkway behind the National Bank. Relish vegetarian food in a psychedelic setting. Mushrooms with cheese and bechamel sauce 1900dr/€5.57. Open daily 7pm-midnight.

Apollon Garden Restaurant (☎ 21 875). Go down the winding side street off Market street, turn left 100m past the Church of 100 Gates; keep an eye out for the signs. It's not cheap, but the enthralling garden and food are worth it. Catch-of-the-day 1900dr/€5.57 for 1, 3500dr/€10.25 for 2. Open daily 5pm-1am.

Nik's Hamburgers (☎ 21 434). Walk right from the port; it's tucked away in one of the plateias. Paros's first hamburger joint, established in 1977. Nikfeast (2 burgers, chips, and salad) 890dr/€2.90, fish and chips 950dr/€2.78. Open daily 5-10pm.

Bountaraki (☎ 22 297). A 5min. walk from the center of town to the left, facing the water. The menu includes traditional dishes and vegetarian and seafood specialties (most entrees 1500-2400dr/€4.40-7.03). Open daily 1pm-midnight.

◉ 🏛 SIGHTS AND MUSEUMS

PANAGIA EKATONTAPILIANI. The **Church of Our Lady of 100 Gates** looms over Paroikia's plateia in the shape of an imperfect Greek cross. Tradition holds that only 99 of the church's 100 doors can be counted—when the 100th appears, Constantinople will once again belong to the Greeks. The Ekatontapiliani was supposedly conceived in the 4th century AD when **St. Helen,** the mother of Constantine, stopped here on her way to the Holy Land. While praying, Helen saw the True Cross and vowed to build a church befitting the site of her vision. She died before she could fulfill her promise, but in the 6th century, the Emperor Justinian commissioned young Ignatius, student of Isidorus of Miletus, to build her church. According to legend, the church's beauty drove Isidorus to a fit of jealousy, and both men died in the scuffle that ensued. The repentant architects can be seen bemoaning their fate on the sculpted bases of the columns across the courtyard. The main structure of the complex is the mammoth **Church of the Assumption.** The **Church of Agios Nikolaos** (the oldest of the three) and the **baptistry** flank this centerpiece to the north and south, respectively. Dress modestly: long pants for men, long skirts for women, and no bare shoulders. *(Open daily 8am-8:30pm.)*

OTHER SIGHTS. The collection at the **Paroika Archaeological Museum** contains more prized pieces than your average antiquities museum, including a 5th-century BC statue of wingless Nike, a large gryphon sculpture, and a piece of the marble **Parian Chronicle,** a history of Greece up to 264 BC. *(Behind the church next to the schoolyard. ☎ 21 231. Open Tu-Su 8:30am-3pm. 500dr/€1.47, students 300dr/€0.88, EU students free.)* A ramble through the Old Town will inevitably lead you past the lone remaining wall of the Venetian **Frankish Castle,** where you can see sections of marble and columns removed from the ancient Temple of Athena.

▐ ♫ NIGHTLIFE AND ENTERTAINMENT

The waterfront is the home of pulsing Parian nightlife. Throngs assemble on the sidewalk or the beach, sharing booze and singing songs. Toward midnight, the tourist traffic forms a stream flowing toward the thicket of clubs that sit at the edge of town. ▓**Pirate Blues and Jazz,** tucked away in the Old Town, anchors several mellow cafes where you'll find eclectic music offerings. (Beer around 800dr/€2.53, cocktails 2000dr/

€5.86, wine 800dr/€2.53. Open daily 7pm-3am.) The cafes are away from the dock, along the street that starts with the National Bank. **Saloon D'Or**, a popular cafe playing the greatest hits of the 70s and 80s, fills nightly with travelers. **The Slammer Bar** specializes in tequila slammers (500dr/€1.47); friendly bartenders train the uninitiated. The **Parian Experience** consists of a mind-boggling party complex that rounds out any night on Paros. Follow the spotlight and crowds to the far end of the harbor to **The Dubliner, Down Under, Cactus Shots Bar,** and the **Paros Rock Cafe,** all under one roof. Sit around or dance to any of the four simultaneously playing tunes. (Beer 700-800dr/€2-2.64, cocktails 1400dr/€4.10. 1000dr/€2.93 cover goes toward a drink.) If a night of boozing doesn't thrill you, outdoor **Cine Rex,** to the left of the dock along the waterfront, shows American movies; check signs in the plateia (2 showings per day, 1700dr/€4.98).

⛴ DAYTRIPS FROM PAROIKIA

MARATHI

Boats run from Paroikia to the beaches of Krios, Martselo, and Kaminia (15min., 4 per hr. 9:30am-7pm, 400dr/€1.17), north along the coast. The calm, secluded beaches to the south, Parasporos and Agia Irini, are an hour away by bus.

5km from Paroikia in center of the island, Marathi is home to Paros's idle marble quarries. Still considered to be among the finest in the world, Parian marble is translucent up to 3mm-thick, with one-third the opacity of most other marble. A visit to the quarries is a serious undertaking: bring a flashlight, strong shoes, and don't go alone. Nearby Lefkes, 5km from Marathi, was the largest village on the island through the 19th century, when Parians moved inland to escape plundering coastal pirates. Today, it's a quiet village of 400 inhabitants with classic Cycladic architecture, the most attractive and unspoiled town in Paros's interior.

🦋 VALLEY OF THE BUTTERFLIES

Take the bus from Paroikia to Aliki (10min., 8 per day, 300dr/€0.88) and ask to be let off at Petaloudes. Then, follow the signs up the steep winding road 2km to the entrance. Open M-Sa 9am-8pm. 400dr/€1.17.

Just 10km south of town is the cool, spring-fed Valley of the Butterflies, or **Petaloudes,** where the rare (and tongue-twisting) Panaxiaquadripunctaria moth congregates in massive numbers during its mating season, from June to late September. Every summer the moths return to mate, sleeping on the bushes during the day and getting busy at night. Because the sleeping patterns of the butterflies are vital to mating patterns, it is important to cause as little distraction as possible: don't clap or talk loudly, and don't shake the bushes.

NAOUSSA Ναουσσα   ☎ 0284

Naoussa is Paros's second port, a natural harbor cradled by long, sandy beaches in the shape of crab claws. Persian, Greek, Roman, Venetian, Ottoman, and Russian fleets have anchored here and the tradition continues today as visitors from all over the world converge on Naoussa's beaches.

📍🛈 ORIENTATION AND PRACTICAL INFORMATION. Naoussa is easy to navigate. From the bus stop facing the water, the road heading left past the little bridge leads to the beaches of **Kolibithres** and **Monastiri.** Buses go to the nude beach at **Laggeri.** To the right is a busy commercial street with Old Town just beyond it.

Buses run continuously between **Paroikia** and Naoussa (15min., every 30min., 250dr/€0.73). There are also buses from Naoussa to: **Ampelas** (4 per day, 250dr/€0.73); **Drios** (15 per day, 500dr/€1.47); and **Santa Maria** (4 per day, 250dr/€0.73). Check the schedule at the bus stop booth. **Taxi boats** leave Naoussa for nearby beaches. The blue booth across from the cafes on the waterfront sells round-trip tickets to: **Kolimbithies** (12min., every 30min. 10am-8pm, 700dr/€2); **Laggeri** (20min., every 40min., 1000dr/€2.93); **Monastiri** (15min., every 30min., 800dr/€2.53); and **Santa Maria** (40min., 1 per day, 2000dr/€5.86).

Naoussa's **tourist office,** across from the bus stop by the bridge, offers general information on the town and its accommodations. (☎52 158. Open May-Sept. 15 10:30am-6:30pm.) For more specific advice about where to stay and how to move around in Naoussa and Paros, pop into **Free Spirit Travel Agency** (☎52 251 or 53 391; fax 52294; frspirit@hellasnet.gr). To find the 24hr. **police** station (☎51 202), walk left (facing the water) up the hill and turn left on the curving road before Mike's Moto Rent; at the top of the hill, turn left again. A **medical center** is near the bus stop on the main road (☎52 304); the doctor is available 9am-10pm. For 24hr. **emergencies,** call mobile (0944) 340 0940. Farther down on the right is the **General Bookstore,** selling international magazines and some books in English. (☎51 532. Open daily 9:30am-midnight.) The **post office** is 400m down the same road, just past the Santa Maria turn-off. (☎21 236. Open M-F 7:30am-2pm.) The multilingual **pharmacy** is on the main street inland (☎51 550; **emergencies** 51 004. Open daily 8:30am-2:30pm and 5:30-11pm.) The **National Bank** is along the marina. (☎51 438. Open M-Th 8:30am-1:30pm, F 8:30am-1pm.) **Postal code:** 84401.

⌂ ACCOMMODATIONS. For a small town, Naoussa has lot of places to sleep, but package-tour groups book most hotels months in advance. Rooms to let cost roughly 7000-13,000dr/€20.51-38.09 for doubles and 8000-15,000dr/€23.44-43.95 for triples; ask at the tourist office for help. **Villa Galini** is inland past the bus stop and 700m to the right. Signs mark the way. Airy rooms with private baths, phones, and fridges, and a gregarious owner make for a pleasant stay. Call several days in advance for free pick-up from the port at Paroikia. (☎53 335; fax 53 336. Open Apr.-Sept. Doubles 6000-13,000dr/€17.58-38.09.) To the right of the waterfront with you back to the water lie a number of upscale pensions with spectacular views of the harbor. To reach **Pension Hara,** walk along the waterfront 300m past the port and climb the stairs that lead to the police station. You'll find impeccably clean rooms with balconies, TVs, and refrigerators. (☎51 011. Doubles 8000-17,000dr/€23.44-49.81.) Around the corner and up the hill a short distance is **Sakis Rooms,** with luxurious lodgings with bath, balcony, and fridge. (☎52 171; fax 24 365; www.paros-online.com. Doubles 8000-20,000dr/€23.44-58.60.) **Camping Naoussa** is on the road to Kolimbithies. Call for the port shuttle. (☎51 595. 1500dr/€4.40 per person; 1000dr/€2.93 per tent.) **Camping Surfing Beach,** 4km toward Santa Maria, offers watersports. (☎51 013 or 51 491; fax 51 937. 1500dr/€4.40 per person; 700dr/€2 per tent, 1000dr/€2.93 tent rental; 900dr/€2.64 per car, 400dr/€1.17 per bike.)

◨◪ FOOD AND ENTERTAINMENT. Naoussan kitchens cook up famously delicious seafood; their local specialty is the fish plate called *gouna.* **Diamantis,** behind the church, is an excellent choice for Greek fare. Feast on the restaurant's specialty, *lamb Diamantis,* stuffed with feta cheese, tomatoes, peppers, and onions (1900dr/€5.57). **Pervolaria** is a garden restaurant offering peaceful seduction just inland off the main road. (☎52 490. Stuffed squid 1800dr/€5.46, yogurt with fruit 1200dr/€3.52. Open daily 7pm until late.) For unbeatable *loukamades* (600dr/€1.76), turn left off the commercial street at the Naoussa pastry shop and continue past the white church to **To Paradosiako** (open 5:30pm-1am).

There are several low-key cafes and bars mixed in with the tavernas—look for dimmed lights and listen for the beat. **Varelathiko** is a huge wooden disco that draws crowds to its outdoor deck. Reminiscent of an old-fashioned barn, the place is decorated with wine barrels and lanterns hanging from the ceiling. If the main road through the plateia doesn't take you there, the current of revelers surely will. (Cocktails 1500dr/€4.40. Cover 100dr/€0.29.) If you can't stay up that late, try your luck swatting mosquitoes at the **outdoor movie theater** next to Diamantis. (Shows nightly at 10pm.) Free Spirit Travel can set you up with beachside **horseback riding.** (7000dr/€20.51 for 1hr., 10,000dr/€29.30 for 2hr.) On the first or second Sunday in July, eat, drink, and be merry as you cruise around Naoussa's harbor and watch traditional dancing at the **Wine and Fish Festival;** call the tourist office for details.

CYCLADES

EASTERN COAST OF PAROS

Road meets sea at **Piso Livadi,** 11km from Lefkes. If Paroikia's nightlife is not your bag, Piso Livadi is close to Paros's nicest beaches (from **Logara** to **Khrissi Acti**), which will warm your heart and roast your skin. Culture vultures will cringe to find that tourism spawned the town's development. **Perantinos Travel & Tourism,** across from the bus stop, provides information on accommodations as well as an international phone. (☎/fax 41 135. Open daily 9am-10pm.) In general, doubles run from 12,000-16,000dr/€35.16-46.88, depending on the season and quality. The resort-style locale will cost you a pretty penny. Up the street from the bus stop toward Paroikia are two simple hotels. **Hotel Piso Livadi** offers doubles with bath (☎41 387; 11,000-15,000dr/€32.23-43.95) and triples with bath (15,000-18,000dr/€43.95-52.74). The **Londos Hotel** has doubles (☎41 218; 9000-12,000dr/€26.37-35.16) and triples (10,000-13,000dr/€29.30-38.09).

ANTIPAROS Αντιπαρος

Literally "opposite Paros," Antiparos is so close to its neighbor that, according to local lore, travelers once signaled the ferryman on Paros by opening the door of a chapel on Antiparos. The small island is mostly undeveloped, with a modest population to match Antiparos's size. Most travelers encounter Antiparos as a daytrip to see the caves, but it's easy to find a place to stay in the quiet capital or near the beaches of this tiny island, which makes even peaceful Paros look frenetic.

ANTIPAROS TOWN Αντιπαρος   ☎ 0284

Virtually all of the island's 900 inhabitants live in town, where the ferry docks and most accommodations are.

■ ⚡ **ORIENTATION AND PRACTICAL INFORMATION.** You'll arrive in Antiparos Town by ferry; a few waterfront restaurants and several hotels and pensions are at the harbor. Tourist shops, tavernas, and bakeries line the street leading from the dock to the tree-shaded central plateia, where a cluster of bars and cafes have opened. Go through the stone archway to the right of the plateia to reach the **Castle of Antiparos,** a village built in the 1440s. Take a direct **ferry** from **Paroikia** (30min., 15 per day, 640dr/€1.88) or a bus to **Pounta** (15min., 15 per day, 250dr/€0.73), followed by a boat to Antiparos (10min., 30 per day, 250dr/€0.73). The only **bus** service on the island goes to the stalactite caves.

Waterfront **Oliaros Tours** assists with finding rooms, and has boat and bus schedules, an **international telephone,** and **currency exchange.** (☎61 231, in winter 61 189. Open 8:30am-10:30pm. Doubles with bath and fridge 5000-15,000dr/€14.65-43.95.) The **National Bank** is open only in high season (M-F 9am-1pm). The **post office** is on the left side of the street leading from the waterfront to the plateia. (Open M-F 7:30am-12:30pm.) The road bends left past the post office and passes the diminutive **OTE,** on the right just before the road opens into the main plateia. (Open M-F 9am-noon and 6-10pm.) The self-service **laundry** is closer to the water on the same street as the post office. (Open 10am-2pm and 5-8pm. Wash, dry, and soap 2000dr/€5.86.) Call the **police** at 61 202 or a **doctor** at 61 219. **Postal code** 84007.

▐ **ACCOMMODATIONS AND CAMPING.** The **Mantalena Hotel,** to the right of the dock when facing inland, has recently renovated rooms with private baths, fridges, and balconies, some of which afford a fantastic sea view. A family-owned establishment for 37 years, the hotel welcomes guests with *kourabiethes* (almond cookies). (☎61 206; fax 61 550. Doubles 8000-20,000dr/€23.44-59.60; 20% extra for another bed.) The welcoming family at the **Antiparos Hotel** rents rooms with good views of the sea. (☎61 358; fax 61 340. Doubles 10,000dr/€29.30; triples 12,000dr/€35.16.) To the right of the harbor facing inland, around the bend on the road to

Camping Antiparos, **Theologos Rooms to Let** offers sunny rooms with gleaming bathrooms and balconies. (☎61 244; fax 61 045. Breakfast 400-900dr/€1.17-2.64. Doubles 7000-12,000dr/€20.51-35.16; studios with kitchen 10,000-15,000dr/€29.30-43.95.) **Camping Antiparos** is 800m northwest of town, on the well-marked way to Ag. Yiannis Theologos Beach. The beachside site, adjacent to the nightclub, has its own mini-market and restaurant. (☎61 221. Open May-Sept. 1100-1200dr/€3.22-3.52 per person; 300-400dr/€0.88-1.17 per tent.)

⚄⚄ FOOD AND ENTERTAINMENT. The restaurants of Antiparos Town serve fresh fish pulled from the same sea that you'll gaze at while eating. Inside town, **Taverna Klimataria** trades in the view for an idyllic garden setting roofed with blazing pink azaleas. Head down the main street and turn left down the alley next to the bookstore. (Calamari 1200dr/€3.52, Greek salad 1000dr/€2.93. Open June-Sept.) Open for all-day service on the waterfront, **O Spyros** and **Zorbas** turn the catch of the day into traditional dishes. (Entrees around 1500dr/€4.40.) Following the lead of neighboring islands, Antiparos's plateia is packed with rock-and-roll watering holes. Late night, choose your favorite from among **Time Pub, Clown Pub, The Doors,** and many more (beer 500-700dr/€1.47-2). **Cafe Yam** is a trendy spot to sip a cocktail. (Beer 700dr/€2, cocktails 1500dr/€4.40. Open daily 10am-2am.)

⚄⚄ SIGHTS AND BEACHES. The cool, wet stalactite **caves** at the south end of the island are Antiparos's main attraction. (Open daily 10am-3:30pm. 1000dr/€2.93.) Names of famous visitors are written on the walls with their years of entry. Some of the stalactites were broken off by Russian naval officers in the 18th century and "donated" to a St. Petersburg museum, while still more were destroyed by Italians during World War II. Despite all this silly defilement, the caves, which plunge 100m into the earth, are simply beautiful. The site doesn't offer any postings about its peculiar history; ask if the ticket-seller is in the mood to tell stories. Excursion **buses** (20min., round-trip 1000dr/€2.93) run from Antiparos Town's port every hour from morning through early afternoon. **Psaraliki Beach,** just to the south of town, is a pleasant place to take a dip, as is **Glifa,** a few miles to the east.

AMORGOS Αμοργος

Much of Amorgos resembles its most enduring symbol, the Hozoviatissas Monastery, which burrows into the cliffs near Hora. The steep cliffs and clear waters were captured 20 years ago in the film *The Big Blue (Le Grand Bleu);* they remain just as startlingly big and blue now. King Minos of Crete was said to rule a second kingdom on Amorgos in ancient times; a 1985 discovery of Minoan artifacts atop Mt. Moudoulia affirmed the legend. Despite the recent growth of tourism, Amorgos's relative inaccessability and a local community unwilling to commercialize have preserved the pervasive peace. Infrequent ferry connections generally stop at Amorgos's two ports in succession—**Aegiali** in the northeast and the larger **Katapola** in the southwest. Be sure to disembark at the right port.

KATAPOLA Καταπολα   ☎0285

The island's central port waves to visitors with its windmill arms. Whitewashed houses, narrow streets, and the overhanging Venetian castle make up little Katapola. It's free of the bustle of many other Cycladic port towns, and retains its serene, communal atmosphere: the whole town might spend the night huddled in front of a football game.

⚄⚄ ORIENTATION AND PRACTICAL INFORMATION. Ferries from both ports of Amorgos go to: **Astypalea** (3hr., 2 per week, 2900dr/€8.50); **Donoussa** (1hr., 5 per week, 1500dr/€4.40); **Koufonissia** (5 per week, 1700dr/€5); **Mykonos** (2 per week, 3200dr/€9.39); **Naxos** (3-6hr., 1 per day, 2400dr/€7.05); **Paros** (4hr., 2900dr/€8.50);

Piraeus (10hr., 1 per day, 5300dr/€15.55); Schinoussa (5 per week, 2100dr/€6.16); Syros (4½hr., 4 per week, 3600dr/€10.56); and Tinos (3½hr., 2 per week, 3200dr/ €9.40). Once a week, there are ferries to Kalymnos and Kos, and to Santorini. Hydro-foils zoom to: Andros (4½hr., 1 per week, 8800dr/€25.83); Ios (1hr., 2 per week, 4400dr/€12.91); and Rafina (5½hr., 1 per week, 9900dr/€29.05). Frequent buses connect villages in summer, running from Katapola to: Aegiali (45min., 6 per day, 450dr/€1.32); Agia Anna (25min., 250dr/€0.73); Hora (15min., 1 per hr., 250dr/ €0.72); and Hozoviatissas Monastery (20min., 250dr/€0.73).

The town surrounds the ferry dock in a horseshoe shape, with restaurants, bars, and accommodations on either side. The large port rests at the center; most tourist services are between the ferry dock and the road to Hora. Across from the ferry dock is Synodinos Tours, which exchanges currency, has an inter-national telephone, sells tickets to ferries and hydrofoils, and rents cars and mopeds. (☎71 201 or 71 747; fax 71 278. Open daily 9am-2pm and 6-10pm.) Since there is a limited post office (open M, W, F 10am-1pm) and no OTE in Katapola, Synodinos Tours sells stamps and phone cards, and handles regis-tered mail. Agricultural Bank, across from the ferries, has a 24hr. ATM. The police (☎71 210) and port police (☎71 259; open 24hr.) are on the right on a side street heading inland from the main plateia. The nearest pharmacy is in Hora. The medical center is at the far left end of the waterfront, in the white building behind the two statues. For medical emergencies dial 71 805. There is a laundro-mat inland at the left of the waterfront. (☎71 723. Open M-Sa 8:30am-2:30pm and 6-10pm.) Public toilets are at the start of the town beach across from Amor-gos Motor Center. (☎71 007 or 71 777.) Internet access in a cafe in the central plateia. For taxis call 71 255. Postal code: 84008.

ACCOMMODATIONS AND FOOD. Katapola is a small town with a few hotels and many pensions. Pension Amorgos, at the left of the plateia above the cafes, is close to the water and has a rooftop veranda with a view, stacked above its blue-trimmed rooms. (☎71 013 or 71 350. Doubles 8000-17,000dr/ €23.48-49.89.) To reach Big Blue Pension from the ferry dock, walk toward town, turn right after the plateia and follow signs. The pension, one of many establishments cashing in on the popularity of the French film *The Big Blue*, is indeed big, with blue windows and doors. Private bath, fridges and port shuttle available. (☎/fax 71 094. Doubles 10,000dr/€29.35 in high season; 5000-7000dr/€14.67-20.53.) Titika Rooms sits under grape and flower trellises at the far right end of the beach. (Bath and port shuttle; breakfast included. Singles 6000-13,000dr/€17.61-38.15; doubles 8000-13,000dr/€23.48-38.15; triples 9000-15,000dr/€26.41-44.)

Like the island itself, Katapola's nightlife is calm and soothing. Cafes and bars are open all day, dispensing ouzo and beer amidst cool sea breezes—drink to relax, not to pass out. Dining options tend toward simple, high-quality tavernas that are easy on the wallet. Mourayio, across from the bus stop, crowds early and empties late. The restaurant stuffs smiling diners with local specialties like octo-pus (1800dr/€5.28) and *fava* (1000dr/€2.93). (Live Greek folk music. Open daily 10am-2am.) Aigaion Cafe, in the center of the main plateia, serves fruit juices, crepes, omelettes, and homemade sweets during the day, and stays on to serve coffee and drinks at night. (☎71 549. Open daily 8am-late in summer; off-season 9am-midnight.) As always, the farther from the dock, the less touristy the meal.

SIGHTS AND BEACHES. In front of Katapola's main church, a sign points to a 40min. hike to the ancient town of Minoa, inhabited between the 10th and 4th centuries BC. Look for the base of the temple among the ruins and the bust of a statue rising from within—the barely distinguishable acropolis once stood on the plateau above the temple. Various beaches provide sand and nudity outside of town, opposite the dock. Smooth-stoned, bare-skinned Plakes and Agios Pantelei-monas are quiet, yet easily accessible.

🔁 DAYTRIP FROM KATAPOLA. A trip to Amorgos is incomplete without a visit to otherworldly 🏛**Hozoviotissas Monastery**—one of the most exhilarating spectacles in all of Greece, and an inspiration to Le Corbusier among others. Built into the sheer face of the cliff, the whitewashed, 11th-century Byzantine edifice looks like a living creature growing from the rock. Legend has it that attempts to build the monastery on the shore were thwarted; when the workers discovered their tools inexplicably hanging from the cliff, they figured it was an omen and recommenced construction there. If you complete the hike (up 350 stairs), the monks may treat you to cold water, raki, and loukoumi (Greek sweets). To see more of the building, come in November when the entire island celebrates the **feast** of Panagia Hozoviotissa at the monastery. If you miss the bus back, take the stone stairway 10m uphill from the fork in the road leading away from the monastery. A 15min. climb up the stairs will lead you back to Hora. The road from the monastery also takes you to the crystal waters of **Agia Anna** and its two beaches; from the bus stop, one is at the end of the path through the clearing, the other at the bottom of the central steps. The Big Blue was filmed along these rocky shores. Catch a bus from Katapola to the monastery. (☎71 274. Open daily 8am-1pm and 5-7pm. Dress modestly: skirts for women, long pants for men, no bare shoulders.)

HORA Χωρα ☎0285

Katapola means "below the town"—the town is Hora. Also known as Amorgos Town, the island's capital lies 6km from the harbor along the island's only significant paved road. A fine example of Byzantine village planning, Hora's winding streets were constructed to deter and confuse raiding pirates, and now allow visitors to meander along the cafe-lined walk to **Pl. Loza**, at the far end of town. Sights include a 14th-century Venetian **fortress,** a row of retired windmills perched on the mountain ledge above town, 45 Byzantine churches, and the first high school in Greece, built in 1829 (on your left as you head up to OTE).

Hora is home to Amorgos's main **post office,** tucked in a corner up from Pl. Loza (☎71 250; open M-F 7:30am-2pm), and its main **OTE,** on the right at the top of town (☎71 339 or 71 699; open M-F 7:30am-3pm). The **police** are in the main plateia with the big church, next to Cafe Loza. (☎71 210. Open 8am-midnight.) The **medical center** is on the main road into Hora from Katapola. (☎71 207. Open 24hr.) If you decide to spend the night, you can contract with the domatia owners that meet your boat, or look for "Rooms to Let" signs in town. **Maria Economidou** has beautifully furnished rooms with balconies. (☎71 111; kstp@otenet.gr. Private baths and kitchenettes. Doubles 7000-13,000dr/€20.53-38.15)

Liotrivi (☎71 700), below the bus station, prepares delicious twists on Greek standards—*kalogiros* (eggplant with veal, cheese, and tomato) and *exohiko* (lamb and vegetables in pastry shell; 1500dr/€4.40) are the house specialities. **Vegara** is an eclectic cafe-bar accented by *kargiosi* (shadow theater figures) on the walls and world music on the speakers. (☎74 017. Open daily 9am-3am.) **Zygos** (☎71 350) serves peerless apple pie (600dr/€1.76) and often has live music and dancing till 5am. For a bit of history, drop by the **archaeological museum,** downhill from the large church. Peer into a giant vase encasing human skeletal fragments, or check out the remnants of Amorgos's Minoan civilization. (☎71 831. Free.)

🥾 HIKE FROM HORA. Rugged mountains and a placid coast run alongside the road from Hora to Aegiali. The 4hr. hike begins behind Hora and stretches up the mountains to the village of Potamos. Forty minutes into the hike, you'll find the crumbling Byzantine church of Christososmas (The Body of Christ), hewn out of a small cave that was once a hermit dwelling. The trail ascends past a series of monasteries before descending to views of miniature Nikouria Island, which swimmers can reach from the beach by the main road. Lonely and deserted Agios Mammas Church is the last significant marker before Potamos appears.

AEGIALI Αιγιαλη

☎ 0285

Aegiali, the island's other port, is as close as Amorgos comes to feeling touristy. As a result, the locals seem a little wearier of travelers than on other parts of the island. With a town beach and numerous rooming and camping opportunities, leisurely Aegiali serves as a base for exploring the island's northern parts.

■ **ORIENTATION AND PRACTICAL INFORMATION.** Aegiali is built up the slope of the mountain foothills. Most tourist facilities are along the waterfront. Facing inland, clubs are to the left along the beach, cafes are to the right. **Nautilus Travel** handles all ferries, **currency exchange,** and other travel services. Across the street, **Aegialis Tours** (☎73 394; fax 73 395) handles accommodations, car rental, bus and boat excursions, and stores luggage. Both agencies are just inland from the waterfront. For **ferry** and **Flying Dolphin** schedules, see the listings for Katapola (p. 397). **Buses** run between: **Aegiali-Hora-Katapola** (3 per day, 500dr/€1.47); **Meria-Hora-Katapola** (2 per day); and **Ormos-Lagada** (6 per day). Note that there is **no bank** in Aegiali. The **police** (☎73 320) are located in Langada; the **port police** are in Aegiali up the steps from the waterfront. (☎73 620. Open 9:30am-2pm and 6-9:30pm.) A **first aid station** is above the town, near the road to Potamos. (☎73 222. Open 9am-1:30pm; available 24hr. for emergencies.) A **pharmacy** (☎73 173) is up the road by the Island Market, on the right; **phones** are next door. **Taxis** (☎73 003 or 73 570) stand at the end of the beach. The **post office** also has **currency exchange;** follow signs from the waterfront. (☎73 037. Open M-F 7:30am-2pm.)

■ **ACCOMMODATIONS AND CAMPING.** Look for "Rooms for Rent" signs going up the paths in the middle of town. **Pension Christina** is up the main pathway and to the right. (☎73 236; fax 73 109. Clean rooms with balcony and private bath. Doubles 6000dr/€17.61 and up.) **Lakki Village,** at the left side of the beach, has rooms and apartments with private baths, balconies, and phones. (☎73 253; fax 73 244; medotels@otenet.gr. Breakfast included; laundry service and port shuttle available. Doubles 17,000dr/€49.89 and up.) **Amorgos Camping,** just outside town, near the road to Tholaria, is a 10min. walk from the port and beach but provides free port pickup and drop-off. The site boasts laundry and cooking facilities, safety deposit boxes, showers, a restaurant, and a bar. (☎73 500; fax 73 378. 1000dr/€2.93 per person; tent rental 500dr/€1.47.)

■ **FOOD AND NIGHTLIFE. To Steki,** at the edge of the beach, serves Greek dinners for 1500-3000dr/€4.40-8.80. (☎73 003. Open daily 6am-2am.) Follow the signs (and your nose) uphill from the waterfront to the aromatic **bakery** (☎73 225) serving yummy pastries. **Skari,** a cafe-bar at the left end of the beach, is named for both an attractive female figure and the skeleton of a ship. The funk-and-reggae fun revolves around an outside patio and inside pool tables. (☎73 016. Open daily 10am-late.) Cut loose under the stars at **Delear** (☎73 205), a club next to Skari.

IOS Ιος

☎ 0286

If you're not **drunk** when you arrive, you will be when you leave. On Ios, beers go down and clothes come off faster than you can say "Opa!" There is everything your mother warned you about—people swimming less than 30 minutes after they've eaten, wine being swilled from the bottle at 3pm, drinking games all day along the beach, men and women dancing madly in the streets, and so much more. Beer flows cheap and plentiful; Ios imports 1½ mega-truckloads of alcohol a day, and exports the same number of empty bottles each morning. The island has settled down a bit in the past few years, making a sincere and successful effort to bring families and the older set to enjoy its more peaceful side. Of its 35 beaches, only three have been fully developed for tourism, so there's plenty of unexplored territory. Those in search of quieter pleasures stay in Yialos Port, while the party animals cavort in Hora. Pilgrims to this mecca should prepare for loud music, hangovers, and the lustful stares of the inebriated.

☐ TRANSPORTATION

Ferries: To: **Anafi** (3hr., 5 per week, 2250dr/€6.59); **Folegandros** (1hr., 5 per week, 1750dr/€5.13); **Mykonos** (4hr., 1 per week, 3375dr/€9.90); **Naxos** (1¾hr., at least 3 per day, 2350dr/€6.89); **Paros** (3hr., 3 per day, 2650dr/€7.76); **Pireaus** (8hr., at least 3 per day, 5750dr/€16.85); **Santorini** (1¼hr., 3 per day, 1850dr/€5.42); **Sikinos** (30min., 5 per week, 1250dr/€3.67); **Syros** (4hr., 5 per week, 3550dr/€10.40). Once a week, ferries go to **Crete**, Skiathos, Skyros, **Thessaloniki** and Tinos.

Flying Dolphins: Catamarans are twice the speed and twice the price of ferries. To: **Amorgos** (1hr., 1 per week); **Mykonos** (2hr., 1 per week); **Naxos** (45min., 3 per week, 4700dr/€13.79); **Paros** (1½hr., 3 per week, 5300dr/€15.55); **Rafina** (4hr., 3 per week, 8950dr/€26.27); **Santorini** (45min., 4 per week, 3700dr/€10.86); **Schinousa** (45min., 1 per week); **Syros** (2hr., 3 per week, 7100dr/€20.84); **Tinos** (1 per week).

Rentals: Jacob's Moto Rent (☎/fax 91 047), by the bus stop at the port. Bikes 4000dr/€11.74; small cars 12,000dr/€35.22. Other agencies are scattered about.

⚡☑ ORIENTATION AND PRACTICAL INFORMATION

The action goes down around three locations, each 20min. apart along the island's paved road. The **port,** or **Yialos** (Γιαλοσ) is at one end; the **village,** or **Hora** (Χορα), sits above it on a hill; frenzied **Mylopotas Beach** is 3km further. During the day, the winding streets behind the church are filled with charming wares and postcard pushers; as the sun sets, they become the focus of nocturnal activity. Buses shuttle between port, village and beach (every 10-20min. 7am-midnight, 260dr/€0.76).

Tourist Information: Acteon Travel (☎91 343 or 91 002; fax 91 088). The main office is adjacent to the bus stop, but booths are set up all over the island. Sells **ferry tickets,** offers info on accommodations, and has **currency exchange,** vehicle rental, luggage storage and safety deposit boxes.

Banks: In the village, **National Bank** (☎91 565), next to the main church, has an **ATM** and handles all your MasterCard needs. Open M-Th 7:45am-2pm, F 7:45am-1:30pm. The **Commercial Bank** (☎91 474), by the main plateia next to the Lemon Club, has 24hr. **ATM.** There is an **ATM** at the port, to your left as you disembark from the ferry.

Laundry: Wash and Go Laundry (☎92 278), next to the basketball courts. Self-service wash (1800dr/€5.28) and dry (700dr/€2.05); full service 3300dr/€9.68 wash & dry.

Police: (☎91 222), on the road to Kolitsani Beach, just past the OTE. Open 24hr.

Port Authority: (☎91 264), at the far end of the harbor by Camping Ios. Open 24hr.

Medical Center: (☎91 227), in new facilities at the port, 100m from the dock. Specializes in drunken mishaps. Open daily 10am-1pm and 6-7pm. In Hora, reach 3 different **doctors** at ☎92 505, 91 137 or 92 227. All 3 are in a row next to the **pharmacy** (☎91 562 or 92 112; open daily 9am-2:30pm and 5pm-midnight).

Internet Access: At the port, **Acteon Travel** charges 2000dr/€5.87 per hr., with a 1000dr/€2.93 minimum. Open daily 7:30am-midnight. **Francesco's** hostel has internet access in its reception (2000dr/€5.87 per hr., 500dr/€1.47 minimum). **Hotel Sunrise** offers the same for 40dr/€0.12 per minute.

Ios Gym: to the right of Wash and Go Laundry. 1880dr/€5.28 per day or 8000dr/ €23.48 per week to work your little keg back into a six-pack. **Postal code:** 84001.

☐ ACCOMMODATIONS AND CAMPING

Affordable accommodations can be found in the frenetic village or in the quiet port. Each area has its own personality, so weigh your interests before climbing into bed with anything. A tent, bungalow, or room on Mylopotas Beach lets you roll hazily from your mattress to the beach, foregoing coffee for a tequila sunrise.

CYCLADES

HOTELS AND HOSTELS

Francesco's (☎91 706 or 91 713; fax 91 223; fragesco@otenet.gr), in the village. With your back to the bank, take the steps up from the left corner of the plateia, then take the first left. The Godfather of accommodations in Ios, Francesco oversees a family of hotels. Standard rooms (some with private baths and fridges) sit atop a terrace bar, where you can **get drunk** with the throngs of young internationals who frequent it. Dorms 2500dr/€7.34 and up; rooms for 2-4 people 3000-8000dr/€8.80-23.48.

Hotel Sunrise (☎91 074 or 91 527; fax 91 664; mobile 0938 10 678) at the end of the village, uphill and to the right from the bus stop. In a great location and decked out with extras including a swimming pool and restaurant/bar to help you **get drunk** (open 9am-midnight). Safety deposit boxes, laundry facilities and internet access available. Doubles 10,000dr/€29.35; 24,000dr/€70.43 in high season.

George & Irene (☎91 927 or 91 128; fax 91 512) uphill from Hotel Sunrise in the village. Dorm-style rooms with shared fridges and balconies off an open balcony where you can **get drunk** under the stars. Safety deposit boxes and laundry services available. Dorms 3000dr/€8.80; 5000dr /€14.67 in high season. Apartment for up to 7 people 4000dr/€11.74 per person.

The Corali (☎91 272; fax 91 552; coraliht@otenet.gr), on the peaceful port beach where umbrellas and beach volleyball spill onto the sand. Chill figuratively in the flowered garden and literally in A/C-equipped rooms. Safety deposit boxes. Internet access 2000dr/€5.87 per hr., 500dr/€1.47 minimum. Doubles 6000dr/€17.61; 20,000dr/€58.69 in high season.

CAMPING

Far Out Camping (☎92 301 or 92 302; fax 92 303; camping@faroutclub.com), at the center of Mylopotas beach. A luxurious, Club-Med-like campsite at rock-bottom prices, with a restaurant, a bar where you can **get drunk,** a minimarket, basketball, volleyball, a swimming pool, bungee jumping, movies, scuba-diving lessons, showers, laundry, internet access, live music, and nightly Happy Hours to **get** you **drunk.** Open Apr.-Sept. 1500dr/€4.40 per person, 2500dr/€7.34 in high season; 500dr/€1.47 tent rental; small cabins from 1800dr/€5.28; bungalows from 2000dr/€5.87.

Camping Ios (☎92 035 or 92 036; fax 92 101). For those who want affordability and similar amenities, but without the nonstop action of Far Out Camping. Open June-Sept. 1500dr/€4.40 per person; 500dr/€1.47 per tent.

◪ FOOD

Most eating on Ios coincides with boozing, peaking in the middle of the night at cheap gyro joints. More discerning palates will find several inexpensive restaurants interspersed among the ubiquitous bars and discos in Ios village, at the port, and on the beach. There's also **Ios Market** (☎91 035), across from the bus stop in Hora, and the **supermarket** in the main plateia.

Ali Baba's is located at the right end of the bar strip; ask around—it's tough to find but worth the trip. Cookie and Helen entertain with movies and occasional live bands, and generous portions of Asian and ethnic food with fill you to the brim and leave you craving more. (☎91 558. Entrees 1300-3000dr/€3.82-8.80.) **Waves Indian Restaurant and International Cuisine,** to the left of the waterfront road as you disembark from the ferries, is run by a Welsh windsurfer couple who serve hearty curries. (☎92 145. Veggie curry 2000dr/€5.87. Takeout available. Opens daily at 10am for breakfast.) **Polydoros,** 2km north (left, facing inland) of the port on Koubara Beach, is the hideout of many of Ios's residents, who delight in dishes prepared with fresh ingredients by the laid-back owner. (Shrimp with tomato sauce and feta 2800dr/€8.22. ☎91 132.)

LOOKING OUT FOR NUMBER ONE If you're travel-
ing alone in Greece, be prepared for the inevitable question: *"mono sou?"* ("just yourself?"). Answer yes and you may be asked to clarify that you really did, for some
incomprehensible reason, choose this kind of life. The solitary lifestyle is not exactly
taboo in Greece, but it's certainly not customary nor desirable. There is no Greek word
for "privacy"—the closest word translates as "loneliness" or "solitude"—and there is no
English word for *parea*, which means something like "company" (without the financial
associations) or "gang" (without the criminal implications). Your *parea* can be the
bunch of buddies with whom you do everything, or whoever you happen to be with at a
given time ("I saw Nikos and his *parea* at the club..."). So don't be offended if Greeks
commend you on your bravery, or console you for your apparent friendlessness. They
are simply concerned: they come from a country of people-persons.

SIGHTS AND BEACHES

Pay a visit to the new Ios **Archaeological Museum,** in the town hall across from the
bus stop, and bring a smile to the lonely faces of those at the door. (Open Tu-Su
8am-2pm. Free.) Centuries of storytelling have woven the myth that the great
poet, Homer, died and was buried on Ios, his mother's birthplace. Time has since
worn **Homer's tomb** to rubble, but the site still draws a few dedicated tourists. To
repent the previous night's excess at the solitary monastery, walk toward the
windmills above the village to the path near the top of the hill. There's an **Open
Theatre Festival Program** every summer, held above the windmills on the island—
inquire at a travel agency for more information.

Beyond that, **beaches** are the place to be. Most spend their days at **Mylopotas
Beach,** a 20min. walk downhill from Ios town. The beach of Mylopotas, like the
town, has music blasting everywhere. The farther you go, the fewer clothes you
will see (or wear). Alternatively, buses (25min., 2 per day, 2000dr/€5.87) make the
winding journey to the more secluded ▓**Marganaki,** the island's most beautiful
stretch of sand. **Yialos** (the port beach), **Mylopotas,** and **Manganari** all offer watersports (2000-6000dr/€5.87-17.61 per hr.). Continuing uphill from the OTE, look for
the path leading to the secluded beach and crystal pool of water at the little bay of
Kolitsani (a 15min. walk from Hora). Secluded, nudist **Psathi** on the eastern coast,
is a 7km walk along donkey trails.

NIGHTLIFE

Most of Ios's extraordinary number of bars are packed into the old village area.
Larger and louder discos line the main road, which is, in turn, lined with revelers.
Bacchantes warm up at daytime beachside bars, swill liquor from the bottle in the
main plateia at sunset, hit the village before 1am, then migrate to the discos and to
other, more private, liaisons before sunrise.

The Jungle (☎92 070), near the basketball courts, is a good place to start the night.
This Aussie-Kiwi bar serves big drinks at pub prices—or get your money's worth by entering the nightly drinking challenge-cum-kamikaze mission. On Thursday nights 8000dr/
€23.48 buys you pizza, cover immunity, a drink, and the right to **get wasted** at games
held at the 5 bars comprising the ultimate pub crawl. Open daily 2pm-late.

Disco 69 (☎91 064; disco69@otenet.gr), on the main bar street, is always jumpin' with
mainstream dance music conducive to bumpin' and grindin'...on the dance floor. **Get
smashed** or dance on the bar—both are equally likely on any given night.

The Slammer Bar, in the left inland corner of the main plateia in the village. Have the
bartender whack your helmeted head with a hammer before you **get hammered** downing the tequila slammer (tequila, Tia Maria, and Sprite; 1000dr/€2.93).

Red Bull (☎91 019), in the main plateia in the village. Fire up your mojo (shots 900dr/€2.64) to the tune of 90s rock before heading out to tackle the rest of the scene. **Get plastered** on the Red Bull and Vodka energy special (1500dr/€4.40).

Scorpion Disco, on the edge of town, en route to the beach. This crazy techno emporium, and the island's largest club, is strategically located for those heading back to Mylopotas after they **get sloshed.** Cover after 1am.

Sweet Irish Dream, in a large building near the "donkey steps." Come here after you **get pissed** (or after 2am) to dance on tables—most save it as the night's last stop. No cover before 1am. Beer 700-800dr/€2.05-2.35, cocktails 1200dr/€3.52.

Q Club, on the edge of town. Showcase your breakdancing skills to the hip hop and house spun by visiting international DJs—then go ahead and **get soused.**

FOLEGANDROS Φολεγανδρος

Named after the son of King Minos, who made the first footprints on the island's shores, Folegandros was secluded from outside influence for many centuries due to its high, rocky cliffs and inaccessible port. The dry, steep hills are terraced with low, snaking stone walls worn by centuries of fierce wind—the only tumultuous presence on the island.

HORA Χωρα   ☎ 0286

■❼ ORIENTATION AND PRACTICAL INFORMATION. After disembarking from the ferry, you can board the **bus** that runs from the port **Kararostassi** to the main town of Folegandros, Hora. Buses head to the port 45 minutes before each ferry, before returning with new arrivals (260dr/€0.76). The **post office** will be on your left as you enter town (open M-F 8:30am-2pm). From the post office, follow the heliport sign toward town to **Sottovento Travel Center** for maps (700dr/€2.05), ferry and bus schedules, **currency exchange,** and general information. (☎41 444; fax 41 430; sottovento94@hotmail.com.) At the other end of town **Maraki Travel** offers similar services as well as **Internet access** for 2000dr/€5.87 per hour, with a 1000dr/€2.93 minimum charge. (☎41 158; fax 41 159. Open daily 9:30am-1pm and 5-10pm.) Irregular **ferries** run at least 4 times per week to: **Anafi** (2600dr/€7.62); **Ios** (1½hr., 1600dr/€4.69); **Kimolos** (1½hr.); **Milos** (2½hr., 1800dr/€5.28); **Naxos** (3hr., 2500dr/€7.34); **Paros** (4hr., 2000dr/€5.87); **Pireaus** (10hr., 5300dr/€15.53); **Santorini** (1½hr., 1800dr/€5.28); **Serifos** (5hr., 1800dr/€5.28); **Sifnos** (4hr., 1800dr/€5.28); **Sikinos** (1hr., 1300dr/€3.81). Call a **taxi** at ☎(0944) 693 957. **Moped rental** is cheaper at the port (try Jimmy's, ☎41 448) than in town. Past Maraki Travel, head straight past the next two tree-filled plateias, cut across to the right, then head left. A sharp right before the **market** leads to the **police** (☎41 249). Call the **Medical Center** at 41 222. There are six **card phones** in Hora, but **no bank** or pharmacy. **Postal code:** 84011.

❰ ACCOMMODATIONS AND CAMPING. Folegandros's increasing popularity has outpaced the visibly in-progress construction of lodgings. Most housing is consequently pricey; locals tell tales of legions of travelers arriving on the morning ferry only to leave in the afternoon when they can't find a room. Fear not: welcome relief is at **Pavlo's Rooms.** About 200m from the post office, Pavlo's has simple rooms (some private baths) in a charming converted stable. (☎/fax 41 232. Laundry services, breakfast and port shuttle available. Doubles 3000-10,000dr/€8.80-29.35, with bath 5000-14,000dr/€14.67-41.10. Prices vary according to season.) **Hotel Polikandia,** near Marakis Travel, harbors rooms with breezy balconies surrounded by a pretty flagstone garden. (☎41 322; fax 41 323. Singles 13,000-19,000dr/€38.15-55.76; doubles 15,000-21,000dr/€44-61.63; triples 17,000-23,000dr/€49.89-67.50. Prices vary by season—bargain down.) **Livadi Camping** is another option; call for a port shuttle. (☎41 204 or 41 478. 2500dr/€7.34 per person.)

◧▨ **FOOD AND NIGHTLIFE.** Several fresh fruit and bread **markets** line the road from Kararostassi through Hora. At **Folegandros Snack Bar,** across from Maraki Travel, owner Michailidia makes what could be the best cappuccino outside of Italy. He also provides vegetarian foods, games, books, maps, and info about the island. (☎41 226. Open Apr.-Oct.) **To Sik** puts a twist on traditional Greek dishes; try their vegetarian vittles. (☎41 515.) Pause to appreciate the prime location of **Piatsa** (☎41 274), in the center of Kontarini square, as you wait for a delicious traditional Greek meal.

In summer, when the island's permanent population of 650 triples, Hora starts to rock. **El Greco,** on the path past Sottovento, is a bohemian cafe/bar adorned with artistic lighting and paintings. (☎41 456. Open daily Apr.-Oct. 10am-3pm and 6pm-4am. Cocktails 2000dr/€5.87.) **Avli,** the only dance club in town, plays a mixture of top 40 and Greek tracks to keep things moving at the outdoor bar. (☎41 100. Open daily 10pm-late. Cocktails 2000dr/€5.87.) **Carajo** lives up to its name with a saucy atmosphere accented by a mix of funk and latin music. (☎41 463. Open daily 10pm-late. Cocktails 2000dr/€5.87.) ▨**Kellari Wine Bar,** in Pl. Pounta next to the medical center, boasts an amazing selection of Greek wines in a small stone-walled room reminiscent of a castle wine cellar. Try dry and fruity Limnos white (800dr/€2.35 per glass) or rely on hostess Isabel's expertise. (Open daily 7:30am-late.)

◨ **SIGHTS.** The **Church of Panagia,** above the town on Paleocastro hill, is an excellent place to watch the sunset or photograph whitewashed domes against the mountains and sea. (Open daily 6-8pm in summer; in winter only for religious festivals.) A demanding hike across Paleocastro Hill leads to **Chryssopilia** (Golden Cave), once a refuge for islanders during pirate invasions. Local lore insists that there is a secret tunnel connecting the cave to Panagia, though it's uncharted.

◨ **HIKES.** The hike from Hora to **Agali** and **Agios Nikolaos** takes about an hour to Agali and another 30min. to Ag. Nikolaos beach. Start from Hora and take the road toward Ano Meria. There's about 20-30min. of asphalt until you hit one of two dirt paths leading left off the road and down to the beaches and terraced countryside. Across from one of several small white churches, you'll see the trail snaking down toward Agali. From here, you'll traverse rocky terraces and pass olive trees down the main dirt track (hang left) that heads straight to Agali. In Agali, you'll find a few tavernas, domatia, and a bunch of tents (if you climb up past the first tavernas on the right to the rocky trail that leads to Ag. Nikolaos beach). Between the two beaches are small rocky coves and beaches perfect for a cool, quiet swim. Bypass the hike on the bus from Angali and a 10-15min. walk to sun, sea, and sand

ANO MERIA

Ano Meria has many footpaths leading to secluded **beaches,** including **Livadaki,** the island's best. The steep, winding trails—the only access to these beaches—take at least an hour each; there is no taverna at the end. The Sottovento tourist office heads day-long boat tours around the island that stop at several beaches; inquire upon arrival. For a superb glance into Ottoman life, check out the **Folklore Museum** in Ano Meria. On an island whose history is empty of epoch-defining events, the olive presses, looms, and fishing nets detail the perpetual struggle against infertile soil and stormy harbors. Take the bus to Ano Meria and ask the driver to let you off there. (Open June-Aug. daily 5-8pm. Guidebook 2000dr/€5.87.)

Those planning an extended stay in Folegandros or who want a more intimate acquaintance with island culture should look into **The Cycladic School** (☎41 137; fax 41 472), run by Anne and Fotis Papadopoulous. The school leads six- to twelve-day courses that focus on drawing and painting, as well as theater, music, sailing, diving, history, and philosophy. A day at the school includes a lecture, practice time, and excursions around the island. For more information, contact Anne and Fotis Papadopoulous, GR-840-11, Folegandros, Cyclades, Greece.

SANTORINI
Σαντορινη

Whitewashed towns balanced on plunging cliffs, burning black-sand beaches, and deeply scarred hills make Santorini's landscape nearly as dramatic as the volcanic cataclysm that created it. This eruptive past— and startling beauty—have led some to believe that Santorini is Plato's lost continent of Atlantis. According to Greek mythology, Santorini arose from a clod of earth given by the sea god Triton to the Argonauts. First inhabited by the Phoenicians, the island, then called Thira, was an outpost of Minoan society by 2000 BC. Around the turn of the 17th century BC, an earthquake destroyed the wealthy maritime settlement of Akrotiri, and all hope of recovery vanished when a massive volcanic eruption spread lava and pumice across the island around 1625 BC. The destruction of Santorini heralded the fall of Minoan prominence; it is believed that the volcanic eruption lead to a series of tidal waves that wreaked havoc on Crete as well.

Natural disaster continues to threaten the safety of Santorini's residents: as recently as 1956, an earthquake caused serious damage to much of the island. The volcanoes have enriched the soil, making Santorini a green oasis among the mostly barren Cyclades. Modern Santorini is the eastern crescent of what was once a circular island, originally called Strongili (round). The ancient eruption left a crust of volcanic ash over the hollow center of the island, which later caved in to create the *caldera* (basin) that now forms Santorini's harbors and western rim.

Santorini is an easily accessible mob-scene. The coastline, neighboring islands, and volcano make it a popular site for weddings and honeymoons. It's tempting to explore via moped, but inexperienced riders and poor bikes are a dangerous combination; traveling by foot or the excellent bus service may be a better option. The island is on the expensive side, mostly due to the cost of importing water.

FIRA Φηρα   ☎ 0286

The island's activity centers in the capital, Fira (FEE-rah). Atop a hill and far from the black sand beaches, the congested assemblage of glitzy shops, whizzing mopeds, and scads of hyperactive tourists can be overwhelming to newcomers. Tourist traffic has made it almost too easy to find a hamburger or wiener schnitzel, but Fira's pristine beauty and old-school Greek food still prevail. The city is perched on a cliff, and the short walk to the *caldera*, at the town's western edge, reveals a stunning view of the harbor. All the kitsch and overcrowding still can't negate the pleasure of wandering among the narrow cobbled streets and arriving at the western edge of town in time to watch the sunset.

▐ TRANSPORTATION

Boats dock at one of three ports: Athinios, Fira, and Oia. Athinios is the most trafficked and has frequent buses to Fira and Perissa Beach (30min., at least 20 per day, 400dr/ €1.17). The **port** of Fira is down a 587-step footpath from the town; you can take a **cable car** (every 20min. 6:40am-10pm; 1000dr/€2.93, children 500dr/€1.47, luggage 500dr/ €1.47) or hire a **mule** (1000dr/€2.93). Santorini's **buses** run frequently and can take you anywhere you want to go, but be warned that their convenience leads to overcrowding. Arrive at the station 10 minutes early to make your bus. The estimated journey lengths below are based on ideal circumstances; busy buses often move much slower.

Flights: Olympic Airways (☎22 493) flies daily to: **Athens** (23,400dr/€68.56); **Iraklion** (16,200dr/€47.47); **Mykonos** (16,200dr/€47.47); **Rhodes** (23,600dr/€69.15); **Thessaloniki** (31,600dr/€92.50). From the bus depot, go across the main road, make the 1st right and then the 1st left. Open M-Sa 8am-4pm, M-Tu and Th-F 4-9pm.

Ferries: To: **Anafi** (2hr., 2 per week, 2000dr/€5.86); **Folegandros** (1½hr., 3 per week, 1200dr/€3.52); **Ios** (1½hr., 3-5 per day, 1900dr/€5.50); **Iraklion** (4hr., 1 per day, 3800dr/€11.32); **Mykonos** (7hr., 2 per week, 3700dr/€10.79); **Naxos** (4hr., 4-8 per day, 3100dr/€9.08); **Paros** (4½hr., 3-5 per day, 3300dr/€9.67); **Piraeus** (9hr., 4-8 per day, 6300dr/€18.46); **Sikinos** (2 per week, 1800dr/€5.46); **Syros** (8hr., 3 per week, 4200dr/€12.31); **Thessaloniki** (15hr., 5 per week, 10,300dr/€30.18); and **Skiathos** (12hr., 1 per week, 8200dr/€24.03). **Flying Dolphins** go to similar destinations in half the time and at twice the price.

Buses: To: **Akrotiri** (30min., 16 per day 9am-10pm, 400dr/€1.17); **Athinios** (25min., 11 per day, 380dr/€1.11); **Kamari** (20min., 35 per day, 260dr/€0.77); **Oia** (30min., 30 per day, 300dr/€0.88); **Perissa** (15min., 30 per day, 400dr/€1.17); and **Monolithos** via the **airport** (30min., 25 per day, 260dr/€0.77).

Taxis: (☎22 555) in Pl. Theotokopoulou beside the bus station.

Moped Rental: Marcos Rental (☎23 877), 50m north of the plateia. 4000dr/€11.74 per day, discounts for extended rentals. Helmets included. Open daily 8am-7pm.

⊹🔢 ORIENTATION AND PRACTICAL INFORMATION

Facing the street with the bus station behind you, walk right and uphill (north) to **Pl. Theotokopoulou,** which is full of travel agencies, banks, and cafes. At the fork in the road, the street on the right is **25 Martiou,** the main paved road. It leads from the plateia north toward Oia, and hosts accommodations, including the youth hostel. Head onto the left branch of the fork and turn onto any westbound street to find back streets with many of the best bars, stores, and discos. Farther west is the *caldera,* bordered by **Ypapantis** street, where expensive restaurants and art galleries are overshadowed by the spectacular view.

Banks: National Bank (☎22 906), on the road branching off 25 Martiou south of the plateia. Currency exchange. **24hr. ATM.** Open M-Th 8am-2pm, F 8am-1:30pm.

American Express: In the office of **X-Ray Kilo Travel and Shipping Agency** (☎22 624), on the *caldera.* All AmEx services. Open daily 8am-10pm.

International Bookstore: International Press (☎25 301), in the plateia. Many magazines, with a small selection of popular reading books. Open daily 8:30am-midnight.

Library: The Greek Cultural/Conference Center and Library (☎24 960), off 25 Martiou, on the side street before the post office. The island's only library, with info about island events. Open daily 9am-2pm and 6-9pm; off-season 9am-2pm and 5-8pm.

Public Toilets: On 25 Martiou, beside the bus depot.

Medical Center: (☎22 237). Go downhill (south) from the bus station, take the first left, then another left. Routine problems daily 9am-2:30pm. **Emergency** care 24hr.

Telephone: OTE (☎22 135), north of the plateia on 25 Martiou. Open daily 8am-2pm.

Internet Access: PC Work (☎25 551), in the upper right-hand corner of the platiea, coming from the bus stop, on the 2nd story. 700dr/€2 per 30min., 1000dr/€2.93 per hr. Open daily 9am-1am.

Post Office: (☎22 238), 50m downhill (south) from the bus stop. Open daily M-F 8am-2pm. **Postal code:** 84700.

▌ ACCOMMODATIONS

In summer, the pensions and hotels fill up quickly and prices skyrocket out of budget range. The cheapest options are the quality **youth hostels** in Fira, Perissa Beach, and Oia. Call ahead. You can find substantially cheaper places in **Karterados,** 2km south of Fira, or in the small inland towns along the main bus routes (try Messaria, Pyrgos, or Emborio). Hostels and many pensions will pick you up at the port.

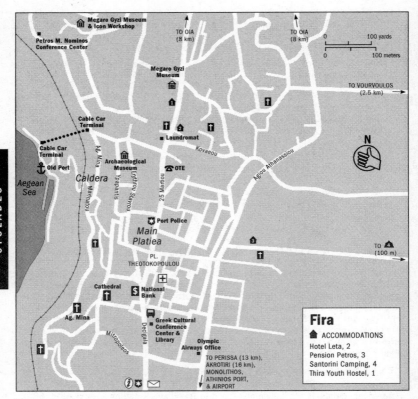

Fira

⌂ ACCOMMODATIONS

Hotel Leta, 2
Pension Petros, 3
Santorini Camping, 4
Thira Youth Hostel, 1

▓ **Pension Petros** (☎ 22 573; fax 22 615). From the bus station, go 1 block up 25 Martiou and make a right. Make a left at the bottom of the hill, then your first right. One in a line of new, and nearly identical, pensions. The owner Petros shares stories and bottles of homemade wine with travelers. All rooms have baths, TV, and fridges. Free port shuttle. Doubles 7000-17,000dr/€20.51-49.81; triples 9000-20,000/€26.37-58.60.

▓ **Thira Youth Hostel** (☎ 22 387 or 23 864), on the left roughly 300m north of the plateia, set back 25m from the road to Oia. Lonely travelers join the happy throng in the courtyard of this old aristocratic mansion neighboring Fira's *caldera.* Quiet dorm rooms and pension-quality private rooms with baths. Quiet after 11pm. No smoking in dorms. Open Apr.-Oct. 5-to-6 bed dorms 2000-3000dr/€5.86-8.79; 3-to-4 bed dorms 2000-4000dr/€5.86-11.72; doubles 5000-10,000dr/€14.65-29.30.

Hotel Leta (☎ 22 540; fax 23 903). Just 100m from the plateia: walking up the main road, follow signs to the right after the laundromat. Downstairs rooms with bath 4000dr/€11.72 per person. Upstairs rooms with A/C, TVs, baths, and fridges. Doubles 6000-16,000dr/€17.58-46.88; triples 8000-19,000dr/€23.44-55.67.

Santorini Camping (☎ 22 944 or 25 062; fax 25 065). Follow the blue signs leading east of the plateia. This shady campsite is the most festive spot in town, with a swimming pool and poolside bar, cafe, and mini-market on the premises. 24hr. hot showers. Washing machine 1300dr/€3.81 (soap included). Internet access 700dr/€2 for 30min., 1200dr/€3.52 for 21-60min. Quiet hours midnight-8am. 500dr/€1.76 per motorbike. Open Apr.-Oct. 1600dr/€4.69 per person; 900dr/€2.64 per tent; 1200dr/€3.52 per tent rental; 800dr/€2.53 per car.

◘ FOOD

Inexpensive restaurants are hard to find in Fira, but the few that are to be found are crammed between shops on the tiny streets sandwiched between the plateia and the *caldera*. The *caldera* is lined with fine dining options that impose a hefty fee for their priceless views. Generic but convenient snack shops dot the plateia.

Mama's Cyclades Cafe (☎ 24 211). Head north on the road to Oia; it's on the right side. Advertised as the best American breakfast in Greece, and they're not kidding. Mama is chatty, loud, and wants to feed all her "babies" well. Her breakfast special speaks volumes as well: pancakes, 2 eggs, bacon, hash browns, and OJ all for 2000dr/€5.86. Greek specialties complement the menu. Open daily 7am-midnight.

Restaurant Poseidon, in a garden down the stairs next to the plateia taxi stand. Excellent *tzatziki* (700dr/€2.05) and enormous entrees with 2 side dishes each. Try *tomatoklefdes*—tomatoes breaded with cinnamon-flavored fried dough (1200dr/€3.52) or their specialty *potmapauia*—beef with lemon sauce. Open daily 7am-1am.

Poldo, up the street from the National Bank. Take-out includes vegetarian entrees like falafel (900dr/€2.64), tabouli (700dr/€2), and hummus (800dr/€2.35). The long line is for the gyros: large (1000dr/€2.93) and small (500dr/€1.47). Open 24hr.

Popou, overlooking the *caldera* across the path from the Tropical Club. This candy store is full of sugary concoctions, so grab a plastic bag and start scooping (420dr/€1.22 per 100g). 14 varieties of licorice. Open daily 11am-midnight.

Kastro's Cafeteria & Bar. While you wait for the cable car next door, visit this bargain basement sister of the Kastro Restaurant. Have an omelette (1500dr/€4.40), a sandwich (800dr/€2.53), or simply a cocktail (1900dr/€5.57 and up). The pricier version is upstairs, so make sure you're in the right place. Open daily noon-3pm and 6pm-1am.

◉◘ SIGHTS AND BEACHES

The **Petros M. Nomikos Conference Center,** above the cable car station, houses an exhibition center that currently displays life-size, 3-D reproductions of the magnificent **wall paintings of Ancient Thira;** the originals are some of the most prized pieces at the National Archaeological Museum in Athens. Brightly colored and intricately detailed murals hint at the quotidian existence and imaginative life of Santorini's wealthy ancient Minoan culture. (☎23 016. Open daily May-Oct. 10am-9pm. 1000dr/€2.93, seniors and students 500dr/€1.47, children under 18 free; audio tour 1000dr/€2.93.) Just steps away from the cable cars you'll find Fira's **Archaeological Museum,** which holds an impressive array of vases, figurines, and statues from the site of Ancient Thira. (☎22 217. Open T-Su 8:30am-3pm. 800dr/€2.53, students and EU seniors 400dr/€1.17, EU students free.) The private **Megaro Gyzi Museum,** just northwest of Thira Youth Hostel, has an engrossing collection of old maps, engravings, and Greek island photographs spanning the 15th-19th centuries. A few steps away is the **icon workshop,** where Catherine and George Ioannidou recreate the religious imagery of Byzantine Greece on wood-backed canvases. The museum hosts several classical music concerts and temporary art exhibitions in July and August. (☎23 077. Open May-Sept. M-Sa 10:30am-1:30pm and 5-8pm, Su 10:30am-4:30pm. 500dr/€1.47, students 200dr/€0.59.)

Reigning over the island from its lofty height, Fira is a convenient base for exploring beaches. The black sand is hot, hot, hot—a straw mat and sandals are welcome accessories. Use your own two feet to reach one of Santorini's most secluded (though pebbly) black sand beaches: **Vourvoulou.** To get there, head north of town and follow the signs; it's a one-hour walk past fields and enclaves.

◘ THE OUTDOORS

When the hum of mopeds becomes a grating roar, hop on a boat and flee to the little islands along Santorini's *caldera* rim. The most popular boat excursion goes to the still active volcano, with a 30min. hike up the black lava rocks to see the crater. Most boats make a swim-stop afterward in nearby waters that are warmed in patches by hot sulphur springs. You'll have to swim through cold, cold water to get there, so be prepared. A longer excursion goes to the inhabited island of Thirasia; on the standard daytrip, you'll only have two hours to wander the island. Built along Thirasia's upper ridge, the villages of **Manolas** and **Potamos** have spine-tingling views of Santorini's western coast. Tour groups dock at **Korfos** or **Reeva.** From Korfos, you'll have to pant up 300 steep steps or catch a donkey ride (1000dr/€2.93) to get to the villages; Reeva provides a paved road. **Boat tours** can be arranged through agencies all over Santorini. (Volcano and springs 2500dr/€7.32, with Thirisia 4500-5500dr/€13.19-16.12.)

◤ NIGHTLIFE

Fira is host to one of the hippest disco scenes in Greece. The clubs, on the north end, gear up around 2am. Unfortunately, exorbitant covers make a club-crawl a pricey venture. Clubs generally share drink prices and covers, which vary according to the season: beer is around 800-1000dr/€2.53-2.93, cocktails around 1000-2000dr/€2.93-5.86, and covers start at 1000dr/€2.93 (soaring to upwards of 3000dr/€8.79 in the high season). A night begins at **The Blue Note,** a club/bar with techno music next to the Youth Hostel. Then onto the dance clubs: the hippest are **Koo Club** and **Enigma** (facing each other on 25 Martiou), both of which crank into the wee hours. Chill on the outdoor decks and watch the steam rise on the dance floors inside. **Trip into the Music,** next door to Kira Thira Jazz Club, keeps its dance floor crowded with a variety of tunes, including new British rock. At **Murphy's,** next to Enigma, there's energetic techno-dancing and lots of chatter all night long. **Town Club,** next to Murphy's, pumps techno through a small room with a castle motif. Try one of the following bars for some pre-booty-shaking booze:

⧯ Tropical Club. High up on the *caldera,* a native Californian mixes signature cocktails as tasty as they are creative (around 1500dr/€4.40). "Sunset coffees" like the Bob Marley *frappé* (dark rum, Kahlua, iced coffee, and cream) go well with sunset views over the *caldera.* Arrive by 8pm for prime balcony seating. Open daily noon-4am.

Kira Thira Jazz Club, across from Nikolas Taverna, on a side street parallel to the main road out of town. Mellow out to jazz (or, when there's no band, pop music) while sipping a gin fizz or piña colada (2000dr/€5.86). The brass hangs from the ceiling and the regulars kiss the DJ good night. Live jazz nightly in August. Open daily 9pm-late.

Two Brothers Bar, next to Poldo up the street from the banks. Hidden behind a medieval prison, a relaxed crowd of locals congregates to listen to Greek music. Try a watermelon shot with your complimentary one-free-shot card. 500dr/€1.47 cover goes toward the cost of a drink. Beer 700dr/€2.05. Open daily 9pm-late.

◤ DAYTRIPS FROM FIRA

AKROTIRI. The volcanic eruption that rocked Santorini in the 17th century BC blanketed Akrotiri with lava that, despite destroying the island, preserved the maritime city of Akrotiri more completely than almost any other Minoan site. In 1967, Professor Marinatos uncovered the paved streets of Akrotiri, lined with houses connected by a sophisticated central drainage system. Each house had at least one room decorated with wall paintings, some of which are the most advanced in Greece. The originals are at the National Archaeological Museum in Athens. Since no skeletons were found in the city, the theory goes that everyone escaped before the 1625 BC eruption devastated the area. (*Take the bus (16 per day, 400dr/€1.17) from Fira.* ☎81 366. *Open Tu-Su 8am-7pm. 1200dr/€3.52, students 600dr/€1.76.*)

Near ancient Akrotiri is the small modern village of Akrotiri. For fresh fishy sustenance and a fabulous sea view, head down the road to the right of the archaeological site to reach the ⧯**Dolphin Fish Restaurant,** open for lunch and until latenight for dinner; don't worry, the name is based on the popular icon in Minoan wall paintings, while the food consists of the day's catch. For a swim, continue heading away from the ancient site and past the Dolphin Fish Restaurant to the **Red Beach,** a 20min. walk from the Akrotiri bus stop. Though Santorini is famed for its black beaches, this ruddy beach is prized for its remote location and smooth sand.

PYRGOS AND ANCIENT THIRA. Once a Venetian fortress, the lofty town of Pyrgos is surrounded by medieval walls. Ottoman occupation through 1828 left a legacy of 25 blue- and green-domed churches highlighting the horizon, one of which (near the top) houses the **Museum of Icons and Liturgical Objects.** (Open Tu-Su 10am-2pm. Free.) The fortress and museum are near one another. To find them through the maze of alleyways leading up the hill, follow the signs for adjacent Kafe Kasteli. A 40min. hike from Pyrgos takes you to the **Profitis Ilias Monastery.** Built in 1711, it graciously shares its site with a radar station installed by military personnel who thought the monastery's proximity would make the station impervious to attack. (Open daily 5-9am and 5-6pm.) On July 20, the monastery hosts the **Festival of Profitis Ilias.** (*To reach Pyrgos, take the bus from Fira to Perissa (15min., 30 per day, 400dr/€1.17), and ask the driver to let you off at Pyrgos. Ancient Thira can be reached as a hike from Pyrgos. Alternatively, take a bus from Fira to Kamari (20min., 2-3 per hr., 260dr/€0.77) and climb the mountain beside the waterfront to reach the ruins.*)

From Profitis Ilias, it's approximately a 1½hr. hike to the ruins of **Ancient Thira** (open Tu-Su 8am-2pm). This trek leads along the mountain that separates Kamari and Perissa and leads to fantastic views of all Santorini. Be warned that the way is poorly marked, with narrow gravel paths on the mountainside, so shoes with good traction are a must. The ancient theater, church, and forum of the island's old capital are still visible, though less spectacular than the Akrotiri excavations.

More popular with locals than with tourists, small **Monolithos** beach is easily accessible due to its proximity to the airport (15 buses per day, 250dr/€0.73). If you want a bite to eat, the fish taverna **Skaramagas** is the least expensive on the strip. The owners catch the fresh seafood, keep what they need for the restaurant, and sell the rest to other takers. Many locals come here for lunch several times a week to enjoy calamari (1500dr/€4.40), Greek salads (800dr/€2.53), and the famed *kakavia*, or fish soup for 2000dr/€5.86. (Open May-Oct. daily 11am-midnight.)

PERISSA Περισσα

Perissa is charismatically demure—nothing is overly flashy, but the town's smooth beaches, youth hostel, nearby camping, and a casual nightlife scene make it popular with student travelers. To get there, take the bus from Fira (15min., 30 per day, 400dr/€1.17). If black sand seems passé, take the ferry to **Red Beach** at Akrotiri (☎82 093; leaves 11am, 12:30pm, returns 4pm; 1500dr/€4.40).

⚐ ACCOMMODATIONS AND CAMPING. Youthful and energetic **Stelio's Place** is a 7min. walk from the plateia: from the road leading out of town, turn left before two adjacent travel agencies; it's 50m down on your left. Stelio's has 21 spic-and-span rooms with private baths, fridges, a pool, and an adjacent bar (beer 500dr/€1.47), as well as free transportation to and from the airport or port. (☎81 860. Reservations recommended. Breakfast 1000-1500dr/€2.93-4.40. 3000-6000dr/€8.79-17.58 per person.) **Youth Hostel Perissa-Anna** is between the first and second bus stops heading into Perissa town. Alternatively, from the final stop at the main plateia by the beach, walk inland along the main street for 500m. This popular spot provides women's and coed dorms, private rooms, cooking facilities, discounts on services around Perissa, use of a nearby pool, and free safety deposit boxes. (☎82 182. 20% discount at the restaurant across the street. Hot showers 5-7pm. Luggage storage 500dr/€1.47. Linen 300dr/€0.88. Internet access 400dr/€1.17 per 15min., 900dr/€2.64 per 30min., 1500dr/€4.40 per hr. 36-bed dorm 1000-2500dr/€2.93-7.32; 10-14 bed dorm 1900-2900dr/€5.57-8.50; rooms for 3-4 people 3400dr/€9.96.) **Perissa Camping** is adjacent to the beach in one of the few tree-covered spots on the island. Enjoy their beach bar, mini-market, kitchen facilities, super-clean restrooms, discounts on nearby scuba package deals, and restaurant. (☎81 343 or 81 686. Internet access 400dr/€1.17 per 15min. 1500dr/€4.40 per person, children 750dr/€2.15; 700dr/€2.05 per tent rental.) **Domatia** in private homes offer more privacy. Proprietors hang around the dock at Athinios, but you shouldn't agree to anything before seeing the room. (Doubles 6000-10,000dr/€17.58-29.30.)

☐ FOOD. Where the main road meets the plateia, **Santo Food** crams french fries, *tzatziki*, and onions into its souvlaki. Breakfast and vegetarian sandwiches are also served. (Open 24hr.) Across the street, delicious calzones, 10 varieties of pizza, and pasta await at **Bella Aurora.** (Calzones 1500-1700dr/ €4.40-4.98. Open daily 11am-1am.) Head back across the street to the **Full Moon Bar,** where the Canadian owner lovingly taps Guinness (1500dr/€4.40) and other great drafts. DJs mastermind the music nightly, honing their craft for frequent theme nights. Listen to the Stones and the Doors while absorbing MTV, Eurosport, or CNN. (Cocktails 1500dr/€4.40, mixed drinks 1000dr/€2.93, beer 500dr/€1.47. Open daily 8am-4am.)

KAMARI Καμαρι

Although renowned for its black sand, Kamari Beach is actually covered in black pebbles, and the slippery seaweed-covered rock bottom makes wading especially difficult. But none of that really matters for most Kamari enthusiasts, who come to gawk and be gawked at from their beach chairs. The long, narrow beach area is covered in umbrellas, and pressed against the ocean by pricey hotels, upscale shops, cafes, and nightclubs. Buses come from **Fira** (20min., 2-3 per hr., 260dr/€0.77), and a rocky shuttle boat scoots between Kamari and **Perissa** (every 30min. 9am-5pm or whenever a boatload has gathered, 1000dr/€2.93). The boat leaves from in front of the Hook Bar at the right end of the waterfront, facing the sea.

▌ ACCOMMODATIONS. Throughout town, doubles range from 10,000-24,000dr/ €29.35-70.43. **Hotel Preka Maria** (☎31 266) rents rooms (12,000-15,000dr/€35.16-43.95) and furnished 3-person apartments (12,000-18,000dr/€35.16-52.74), with refrigerator, bath, and access to a swimming pool. It's on the northern end of town: heading away from the mountain, take a left before the Kali Bar and the hotel is 70m farther. **Kamari Camping** is 1km inland along the main road out of town. (☎31 453. Open June-Sept. 1200dr/€3.52 per person; 1000dr/€ 2.93 per tent.)

☐▣ FOOD AND ENTERTAINMENT. For an inexpensive snack along the waterfront, head to **Ariston,** a bakery and small grocery selling fresh bread at the northern end of the waterfront. (Open daily 6:30am-11pm.) At the northern end of the waterfront, **Mango** and **Dom** serve up a sexy combination: Mango is an upscale outdoor cafe, Dom is a futuristic indoor club. (2000dr/€5.86 cover buys 1 drink; cocktails 1700-2000dr/€4.98-5.86. Open Su-Th morning-3:30am, much later on weekends.) For quieter entertainment, see a flick at the **Open Air Cinema Kamari** (☎31 974), on the way out of town. The **Canava Roussos** winery, 1km from Kamari Camping, will wine and dine you with its red, white, and rose *bouganvilla.* The house favorite, *mavrathiko* (1000dr/€2.93 per glass), is a sweet wine made with red grapes instead of the traditional white. (Open daily 10am-8pm.)

OIA Οια   ☎0286

Dazzling sunsets made the posh cliffside town of Oia (EE-ah) famous; the little stucco buildings on said cliffside make it breathtaking. In the aftermath of the 1956 earthquake that leveled the town (and much of the northwest tip of the island), inhabitants carved new dwellings into the cliffside among the crumbled debris of the old. Peaceful window-shopping pedestrians rule on the narrow cobblestone streets at the town's many upscale boutiques. Although the budget traveler will not thrive long in Oia, it's possible to survive a pleasant day or two without too much fiscal damage. If browsing isn't your bag, hightail it over to the cliffs and secure a prime sunset view. Buses run from **Fira** to Oia (25min., 30 per day, 280dr/ €0.82), and ferries dock at Oia before continuing to Fira or Athinios.

⌐ ACCOMMODATIONS. The Karvounis family can help meet all your tourist needs. **Karvounis Tours** (☎71 290, 71 291, or 71 292; fax 71 291; mkarvounis@ote.net.gr), on the main street beside the biggest church in town, answers questions about Oia and Santorini, in addition to selling ferry and airline tickets and arranging marriages—be careful not to sign your life away. The Karvounis family's ■**Youth Hotel Oia** has impeccable rooms with baths and large mirrors for narcissism, a courtyard, and a bar open for breakfast and evening drinks. The affordable, luxurious hostel makes painfully expensive Oia bearable. Get bang for your buck during happy hour (7:30-8:30pm), with cheap drinks and a free sunset on the roof patio. (☎71 465; fax 71 291. Rooms singlesex or coed. Free safety deposit boxes. Wheelchair accessible. Breakfast included. Open May-Oct. Dorms 3700dr/€11.) Short-term domatia are rare; most proprietors expect a 5-day stay.

◻ FOOD. Dining will cost you a bit more than in Fira, but some restaurants serve exceptional food. **Petros,** Oia's oldest restaurant, at the end of the town's main road (when you're heading toward Fira from the main church), overlooks the *caldera.* Try the fresh fish soup, or any of the seafood dishes (fried calimari 2000dr/€5.86). Old Greek recipes provide a pleasant alternative to the common *moussaka,* and Petros Jr. continues the family tradition of making homemade wines. (Entrees 1000-2000dr/€2.93-5.86. Open daily 6pm-late.) Petros's family extends up the street to **Thalami Taverna,** where they cook up less exotic fare, but offer a better view of the *caldera,* all enhanced by live music on Tuesdays. (☎71 009. Chicken with blue cheese and mushrooms 2500dr/€7.33, fried tomato balls 1000dr/€1.93, Santorini salad 1700dr/€4.98.) **Restaurant Lotza** serves well-seasoned dishes like curried chicken (2500dr/€7.33), *gioourtlou* (minced meat, pita bread, and yogurt; 2400dr/€7.04), and spaghetti with seafood (2500dr/€7.33), in a bohemian atmosphere. (Open daily 9am-late.) There is a small **grocery/bakery,** near the plateia where the buses stop. Follow the signs to fresh loaves, croissants, and pies. (200-400dr/€0.59-1.17. Open M-Sa 7am-9pm, Su 7am-2pm.)

◪ BEACHES. A 20min. trip down the 252 stone stairs at the end of the main road leads to rocky **Ammoudi Beach,** where a few boats are moored in a startlingly deep swimming lagoon. It's worth climbing down and up the cliff to relax on the rocks and swim in the stunning blue water. Re-energize with a meal of fresh fish at one of the three **tavernas** at the bottom of the stairs, where meals are hauled straight from the net to the table. If you're not up for the trek back up, hire a **donkey** (1000dr/€2.93 per person) to do it for you.

MILOS Μηλος

Though the ghost of past achievements continues to loom large (plastic replicas of the Venus de Milo pop up everywhere from the archaeological museum to taverna bathrooms) there's much to enjoy in Milos that France hasn't stolen. Mineral deposits and volcanoes collaborate to create a wealth of breathtaking beaches. Feed the hunger for history stirred up by Thucydides' *Melian Dialogue* in the winding streets of Tripiti, which conceal an ancient theater and eerie catacombs.

ADAMAS Αδαμας ☎ 0287

This port town stuffs most of Milos's accommodations, food, and nightlife into the space of several blocks, causing congestion that is both vibrant and stifling. Though most sights are elsewhere, the centralized bus system makes it a base for exploring the rest of the island; a rented moped or car helps, too. Follow the waterfront to the right from the ferries to reach the center of Adamas.

TRANSPORTATION

Flights: Olympic Airways (☎22 380, at the airport ☎22 381), on 25 Martiou. Planes go once daily to **Athens** (14,700dr/€43.14). Open M-F 8am-3pm.

Ferries: From Milos, ferries follow a complex but well-posted schedule to: **Folegandros** (2hr., 3 per week, 1700dr/€5); **Kythnos** (2½hr., 1-2 per day, 2700dr/€7.92); **Paros** (4½hr., 2 per week, 300dr/€8.80); **Pireaus** (7hr., 3 per day, 5400dr/€15.85); **Santorini** (4hr., 2 per week, 3700dr/€10.86); **Serifos** (2hr., 3 per day, 1800dr/€5.28); **Sifnos** (1½hr., 3 per day, 1600dr/€4.70); **Syros** (6hr., 2 per week). The small Karamitsos ferry also goes to **Kimolos** (30min., 5 per day, 600dr/€1.76) from Pollonia.

Flying Dolphins: 6 per week go to **Pireaus, Serifos** and **Sifnos** in half the time for twice the price of a ferry.

Buses: (☎22 219). Buses stop by the Agricultural Bank on the waterfront and travel almost hourly to **Plaka, Pollonia, Tripiti,** and other destinations for around 300dr/ €0.88 each way. Check the schedule posted in the bus station or in travel offices.

Taxis: (☎22 219), stand along the waterfront. Available 24hr. Fixed fares are posted.

Moped Rental: Milos Rent a Car (☎21 994; fax 24 002), across from the port. Bikes 5000dr/€14.67 per day; cars 14,000dr/€41.10 per day.

ORIENTATION AND PRACTICAL INFORMATION

Tourist Office: (☎22 445), across from the dock. Multilingual staff. Ask for brochures, maps, ferry and bus timetables, and a complete list of the island's rooms and hotels. Open daily 10am-2pm and 7pm-1am. Pick up a **free ▓ Welcome to Milos** guide.

Tourist Agencies: RIVA Travel (☎24 024; fax 28 005; rivatr@otenet.gr), on the waterfront. English-speakers sell ferry tickets and help with bus schedules.

Banks: National Bank (☎22 077), near the post office along the waterfront with 24hr. **ATM.** There's an **Agricultural Bank** (☎22 330) in the central plateia in the harbor. Both open M-Th 8am-2pm, F 8am-1:30pm.

Police: (☎21 204), by the bus stop in Plaka.

Port Authority: (☎22 100). Open 24hr.

Medical Center: (☎22 700, 22 701, or 22 702), in Plaka.

Internet Access: Internet C@fe (☎28 011), uphill from the street to the left of the Agricultural Bank. 2000dr/€5.87 per hr.; 500dr/€1.47 minimum.

Post Office: (☎22 288). Take the waterfront road past the bus station and turn right before Agricultural Bank; it's up 100m. Open M-F 7:30am-2pm. **Postal code:** 84801.

ACCOMMODATIONS AND CAMPING

High season prices may wound your wallet, but fear not—persistence will turn up affordable private rooms in domatia hiding in Adamas's and Plaka's side streets. Book far in advance to stay in Adamas.

▓ **Semiramis Hotel** (☎23 722; fax 22 118). Follow the main road past the bus station, and bear left after the supermarket; it's straight ahead. Nikos and Petros tend excellent rooms with a shaded garden outside. Breakfast 1200dr/€3.52. If it's full, ask about its brother hotel, nearby **Dionysus,** 50m farther along the main road. Doubles 7000-16,000dr/€20.53-46.96; triples 9000-18,000dr/€26.41-52.82; cheaper downstairs rooms with common bath 5000-12,000dr/€14.67-35.22. Prices vary by season.

Kanaris Rooms to Let (☎22 184), 200m from the town center—look for the "Anezina" minibus. Private baths, fridges, balconies and ceiling fans. Doubles 5000-10,000dr/ €14.67-29.35. Prices vary by season.

Hotel Corali (☎22 216 or 22 204; fax 22 144), around the corner from Kanaris Rooms. Private baths and ceiling fans. Port shuttle. Doubles 8000-20,000dr/€23.48-58.69.

Camping Milos (☎31 410; fax 31 412; doriki1@otenet.gr; www.miloscamping.com), at Achivadolimni Beach, 7km from port; buses pick up at the dock before 6:30pm. New and sharp, with kitchen, laundry, car/bike rental, minimarket and restaurant. Bungalows with fridge and bath 12,000-17,000dr/€35.16-49.89. Camping 1500dr/€4.40 per person; tent rental 1000dr/€2.93.

FOOD AND NIGHTLIFE

Large waterfront restaurants draw tourists with their beautiful views every night. There are also several cafes peppering the waterfront, where you can watch the flood of tourists drown the island every few hours. The multitude of bakeries, creperies, and sandwich shops in the main square serve quick, cheap meals. **Psitopolio** (☎21 739), 10m inland on the street to the left of the Agricultural bank and **Aleuromulas** (☎23 117), 2km out of town on the road to Pollonia, both serve traditional, home-cooked meals. Though there isn't much of a bar or disco scene in Adamas, there are a few places to shake it to Greek tracks. Sip a drink at **Puerto,** next door to Milos Rent a Car across from the port, until the dancing gets started late into the evening. If a dark bar strikes your fancy, look no further than **Vipera Lebetina,** where DJs spin into the wee hours of the night.

BEACHES

Milos has emerged from centuries of volcanic eruptions with stunning **beaches** covered with exceptional rock formations and unique sand. Twenty-four distinctive beaches line the island's northern and southern coasts. In the north, the pools of ▮**Papafragas** are embraced by a stone arch and arms of white rock reaching into the sea, creating the impression of swimming next to snow-covered mountains. Take the bus to **Pollonia** and ask the driver to let you off at the beach. Seven buses per day journey to densely populated **Hivadolimni** beach (15min.). On the south side of the island, lively **Provatas** and **Paleohori** beaches sport bars, music, comfy beach chairs, and bus access (from Adamas; 25min., 6 buses per day). The real gem sits between them at ▮**Tsigrados beach,** where natural stores of pearlite make for deep, soft sand that glimmers magnificently in the afternoon sun. Get there by moped, or trek from Provatas (1½hr.). Ask at the a travel agencies about boat the excursions that stop at several beaches on a tour around the island. (Most run 9am-6pm and cost around 6000dr/€17.61.)

DAYTRIPS FROM ADAMAS

PLAKA Πλακα AND TRYPITI Τρυπητη

Buses from Adamas run to Plaka and Trypiti (15min., every 30min., 260dr/€0.76).

Six winding kilometers from Adamas, Plaka rests on mountaintops. Opposite the police station, follow the signs downhill through several twisty streets to the terrace of the **Church of Panagia Korfiatissa,** which leans into a view of lush countryside and blue sea only an arm's length away. Next door, the town's **Folk Museum** displays creepy mannequins in household settings. (☎21 292. Open Tu-Sa 10am-2pm and 6-9pm, Su 10am-2pm. 500dr/€1.47, students and children 250dr/€0.73.) From the bus stop, head along the paved street, down the steps, and bear right to find the large yellow **Archaeological Museum,** which houses artifacts unearthed at Fylakopi, including the mesmerizing *Lady of Fylakopi.* (☎21 620. Open Tu-Su 8:30am-3pm. 500dr/€1.47, students and seniors 300dr/€0.88, EU students free.) For a truly spectacular view, climb upward for 15min. from the bus station to the **Panagia Thalassitra Monastery** at the top of the old castle.

A 3min. walk from the Archaeological Museum leads to the tiny town of Trypiti. From there a paved road winds down past several sights. A sign marks the spot where the **Venus de Milo** was buried around 320 BC; she was moved to the Louvre in Paris in the 19th century after being discovered by a farmer tilling his fields. Farther off the path a well-preserved **theater** dating from the Roman occupation provides a riveting ocean view; ask at the tourist office about performances there. Last along the road and down a set of stairs lie signs for **catacombs** hewn into the cliff face, which are the oldest site of Christian worship in Greece. The open-air ruins are small and without on-site plaques, but peering into the unlit corridors of the cool catacombs sparks the imagination. Of the five chambers, only one is open to the public. (☎21 625. Open Tu-Su 8am-7pm. Free.) You can also still see part of a Dorian stone wall built between 1100 and 800 BC. Archaeology buffs will want to scramble among the ruins of **Filakopi,** 3km from the fishing village of **Pollonia** (Πολλο νια) toward Adamas, where British excavations unearthed 3500-year-old **frescoes** now displayed in the National Museum in Athens (see p. 104).

KIMOLOS Κιμωλοσ

Ferries run from Pollonia on Milos to Kimolos (5 per day, 600dr/€1.76).

Pedestrian-friendly Kimolos is lovely at sunset, when the colors are most vivid over the sea and islands, and the ribbon of white rock around Kimolos's edges shines. Disembark at the small port of Psathi, and head left for Aliki Beach or continue up to Hora. The **Castro ruins,** in the center of town, are just that—ruined. Wander through the alleyways and peer into the empty shells of houses, but be careful not to step on a Coke can. From the Castro, an hour's hike (or a short bus ride from the port—check posted schedules) will take you through mountains to the beautiful **beaches** of the eastern shore. To get there, walk through the minimalist town, keeping the Castro on your left. Continue past the Byzantine church and a well, and keep walking to a chapel. From there, bear right and take the bright-red downhill path toward the valley, then over a stone bridge.

SIFNOS Σιφνος

Sifniots are a festive bunch, dropping everything a whopping 13 times a year to celebrate religious festivals with food, drinking, dancing, and merriment that lasts for days. Even when they sober up and return to work, their zest persists in their happening nightlife, their distinctive cuisine, and their beaches, where people are as likely to be snorkeling or leaping from cliffs as bathing in the sun.

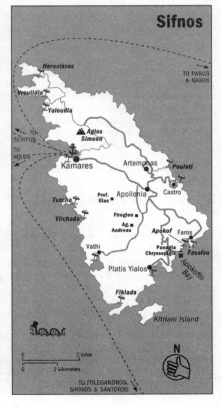

Sifnos

KAMARES Καμαρες   ☎ 0284

Kamares is a magnificent harbor filled with sailboats and yachts and surrounded by formidable brown cliffs in fierce contrast to the emerald sea. The town beach sweeps the harbor rim, and a few tavernas line its shallow perimeter. Kamares is a gentle town pleasing to the senses, where days drift easily away. Here you can secure a room, swim, dine, and peruse shops full of ornate local pottery; look for *keramiko* (ceramic) signs throughout the village.

⫶ TRANSPORTATION. From Sifnos, **ferries** head to: **Folegandros** (1hr., 3 per week, 1800dr/€5.28); **Kimolos** (1hr., 1 per day M-Sa, 1500dr/€4.40); **Milos** (1½hr., 3 per day, 1600dr/€4.70); **Paros** (2½hr., 2 per week, 1100dr/€3.23); **Piraeus** (5½hr., 3 per day, 4600dr/€13.50); **Santorini** (5hr., 1 per week, 3200dr/€9.39); **Serifos** (45min., 3 per day, 1500dr/€4.40); **Sikinos** (4½hr., 3 per week, 2000dr/€5.87); **Syros** (3½hr., 2 per week, 2200dr/€6.46). **Hydrofoils** speed daily to: **Milos** (45min., 3200dr/€9.39); **Pireaus** (3hr., 9200dr/€27); **Santorini** (2½hr., 6400dr/€18.78); **Serifos** (20min., 3000dr/€8.80). Four **buses** travel daily between a number of destinations including **Apollonia;** consult posted schedules for routes and stops. The main stop in Kamares is in front of the information office, near the port. A number of **taxis** are available on the island (☎33 719, 31 626 or 31 347). Some of the best car rental rates are at **Niki Rent a Car.** Look for the huge sign beyond the strip of cafes of tavernas. (☎33 993. Bikes 2500-5000dr/€7.34-14.67; cars 12,000-20,000dr/€35.22-58.69.)

⫶⫶ ORIENTATION AND PRACTICAL INFORMATION. Just opposite the ferry dock, the **Information Office** helps visitors find rooms, deciphers boat and bus schedules, exchanges currency, and stores luggage. (☎/fax 31 977. Open daily 9am-midnight.) The **port authority** is next door (☎33 617. Open 24hr.). The English-speaking staff at **Aegean Thesaurus Travel Agency,** along the waterfront as you walk from the dock to town, **exchanges currency,** finds accommodations, stores luggage, and sells tickets for ferries and Flying Dolphins. (☎33 151; fax 32 190; thesauras@travelling.gr. Open daily 9:30am-10pm.) **Public toilets** are next to the information office. There's an **International Press** on the main strip. (☎33 521. Open daily 9am-midnight.) In an **emergency,** call the **police** (☎31 210) in Apollonia. A **doctor** can be reached at the clinic at 31 315; call the **pharmacy** at 33 541. **Postal code:** 84003.

⫶ ACCOMMODATIONS AND CAMPING. During high season, you're unlikely to find a budget hotel room; inquire at **Room to Let** signs or ask at one of the many waterfront tavernas. **Hotel Kiki,** 10m uphill from the main road beyond the strip of cafes and tavernas, offers spotless rooms with baths, TVs, fridges, and balconies overlooking the harbor. (☎32 329; fax 31 453. Doubles and triples 13,000-16,000dr/€38.09-46.88.) **Meltemi Rooms,** behind Hotel Kiki, haolms clean rooms with A/C and private baths. (☎31 653 or 33 066. Doubles 7000-12,000dr/€20.53-35.22.) **Maki's Camping,** across the road behind the beach in Kamares, sports a taverna, laundry, and common baths and showers. (☎32 366. 1450dr/€4.26 per person; 500dr/€1.47 tent rental.) Another, more secluded campsite is calm, clean **Platis Yialos Camping,** amid trees and stone walls 10min. inland from the bus stop; it's 30min. by bus from Kamares. (☎71 286. 1200dr/€3.52 per person; 750dr/€2.20 tent rental.)

⫶ FOOD. The local Sifniot specialty of chickpea soup, called *revithada* (700dr/€2.05) is served only on Sunday. It gets polished off early, so try it for lunch. There are also several **groceries** and **bakeries.** Most of the tavernas serve food of roughly the same quality and price, but some have seaside seating. **⬛Ristorante Italiano de Claudio,** on the waterfront up the main street toward Apollonia, serves up incredible pizza (2000-3000dr/€5.87-8.80) and *rigatoni delicati* (pasta with chicken, asparagus, and cream sauce). (☎431 671. Open 1pm-late.) Across the street, **⬛O Kapetan Andreas** specializes in seafood—try the *astakomakaronada* (lobster with spaghetti). White lights adorn the tree-filled terrace like dripping stars. (☎32 356. Open noon-midnight. Lobster 1800dr/€5.28 per kg.)

■ **NIGHTLIFE.** A choice sunset-watching spot is **Cafe Folie,** at the far end of the beach. It's a bit pricey (cocktails 2500dr/€7.34), but the colorful, funky decor, Caribbean flavor, and proximity to the water justify the hefty price tag. The **Old Captain Bar,** midway along the waterfront strip, serves coffee and fruity drinks. Tap your toes in the sand to the beat of calypso and string music. (☎31 990. Open daily 11am-3am.) Farther along the road, **Mobilize** attracts a later crowd; the strobe lights pulse and the DJ takes requests until sunrise. (Open daily 10pm-6am.)

APOLLONIA Απολλωνια   ☎0284

The streets of Apollonia, the island's capital, meander haphazardly about the hill. Pick a landmark to get your bearings by the main road, where all of Sifnos's roads converge. A few steps from the main road will submerge you in narrow lanes, a maze of shops, bars, and charming houses.

■ **ORIENTATION AND PRACTICAL INFORMATION.** Everything you need to conduct business is on the main plateia, where the **bus** from Kamares makes its first stop. Buses to Kamares (10min., 270dr/€0.79) stop in the plateia in front of the post office, while those to villages and beaches such as Kastro (270dr/€0.79) and Plati Yialos (500dr/€1.47) stop around the corner near the Hotel Anthousa. Buses run to all three at least once every hour. An **International Press** is located off the plateia next to the meat market. **Aegean Thesaurus,** near the post office, is your source for **currency exchange,** accommodation assistance, bus and ferry schedules, and their 600dr/€1.76 island information packs. (☎33 151. Open daily 10am-10pm.) The **National Bank,** up the road on the left before Hotel Anthousa, has a 24hr. **ATM.** (☎31 317. Open M-Th 8am-2pm, F 8am-1:30pm.) There's an **OTE** on the road back to Kamares. (☎31 699 or 33 499. Open daily 7:30am-2:30pm.) From the other bus stop near Hotel Anthousa, head left on the road to Artemonas to find the **medical center** (☎31 315) on your left and the **police station** (☎31 210) in a small white building on your right. The **Billiard Cafe,** on the road out of Apollonia to the right, plugs you into the **Internet.** (1800dr/€5.27 per hr. Open daily 2pm-1am.) Beside the main plateia is the **post office.** (☎31 329. Open M-F 7:30am-2pm.) **Postal code:** 84003.

■ **ACCOMMODATIONS.** Summer vacancies are rare in Apollonia; call a month in advance for reservations. **Hotel Anthoussa,** above the pastry shop around the corner from the main plateia, is luxurious with A/C, TVs, phones, and daily cleaning service. (☎31 431; fax 32 220. Self-service laundry 4000dr/€11.74. Singles 7500-12,000dr/€22-35.22; doubles and triples 9000-18,000dr/€26.41-52.82.) **Hotel Sofia** is just off the plateia; head up the wide paved road from the main plateia until you see it on your left above the supermarket. (☎31 238. Doubles 16,000-20,000dr/€46.96-58.69. Prices vary by season.)

■ **FOOD AND NIGHTLIFE.** Restaurants are excellent and not as expensive as their beautiful exteriors suggest. The better tavernas are along the path across from the police. The restaurant at the **Sifnos Hotel** (☎31 624) serves the island specialty on Sundays—chick-peas with olive oil and lemon, cooked overnight in special ovens. Apostolos ladles it up along with years of wisdom about the island. The fricassee is a classic—goat and rice covered with greens and baked in a ceramic pot (1800dr/€5.27). ■**Vegera,** on the road to Artemonas, just before the National Bank, brews yummy coffees and makes crepes (1000-1800dr/€2.93-5.27) on an open-air veranda in view of the island's spellbinding sunsets. Try the caramel cake—it's sinfully delicious. (☎33 385. Open daily 9am-3am.) Stroll along the street behind Hotel Anthousa to tap into the Sifniot nightlife. **Bodgi,** a bar and coffee house, is likely to catch your eye and ear: candles light up both levels and the outside terrace, and trip-hop tickles your tympanum (open nightly until 4am). Live Greek music blares every night until sunrise at **Aloni,** where the Greeks are. Take the road toward Artemonas to get there.

⚡ **DAYTRIPS.** Travel in Sifnos is easy with the assistance of the map available at kiosks (400dr/€1.17). Pack a picnic to nibble as you explore Apollonia's adjacent hillside villages. The quiet but expansive village of **Artemonas,** a 10min. walk from Apollonia, has a magnificent view and several fine mansions built by refugees from Alexandria. Enchanting **Castro** village is 3km east of Apollonia and can be reached by bus (15min., 270dr/€0.79) or on foot (take a short cut via the stone pathway a few hundred meters along the paved road). This cluster of whitewashed houses and narrow streets rests on an ocean-facing mountaintop. You may find the tiny **Archaeological Museum** while walking through the former capital's streets. (Open Tu-Su 8:30am-3pm. Free.) There are no hotels, but ask around for domatia. Behind the Castro and below tiny **Epta Martires** church is the island's best spot for **cliff diving.** Rocks form natural platforms for jumping into the deep water below. Watch the weather; foolish courage and rough seas make a dangerous duo. From Castro, the footpath leads to the sparkling cove at **Poulati,** popular for snorkeling.

Buses run hourly to **Platis Yialos,** 12km from Apollonia, where you can rent watersports equipment. To the south, **Faros** has several popular beaches which are connected by footpath. Busy **Fasolou** and **Apokof** beaches have tavernas. Farther along the path is striking **Panagia Chrysopigi Monastery,** also accessible by the Platis Yialos bus and a 10min. walk. A bridge connects the 17th-century monastery's rocky islet to the mainland. The monastery has been known to let rooms; make reservations 2 months in advance. (☎31 482. Doubles 5000dr/€14.67.) Forty days after Easter, the two-day **festival of Analipsos** is celebrated at Chrysopigi. Other renowned Sifniot festivals fall during the summer, with one in July and four in September. Inquire at the tourist office to find out when you can join in the fun.

SERIFOS Σεριφος

Sitting atop the crumbling Castro, you can take in the full panorama of Serifos's charms, from the fertile arc of the port to the mining-ravaged hills and the untouched beaches. Poor roads restrict the plague of Athenian vacationers to the port, leaving the rest of the island blissfully undiscovered. Stony Serifos got its name from Medusa. Perseus hunted her down and turned her shocking ugliness against her with a mirror; taking her head back to Polydictes, king of Serifos, he found Polydictes putting the moves on his mom, Danae. Pissed-off Perseus flashed Medusa's head at Polydictes, turning his royal court (and the island) to stone.

LIVADI Λιβαδι   ☎0281

Livadi, Serifos's port, keeps visitors rested and full for daytime trips throughout the island. The white tower that is Hora, the island's other main town, hangs above the port, and is reachable by a hike (40min.) or the frequent bus (270dr/€0.79).

⚡ 🔋 ORIENTATION AND PRACTICAL INFORMATION

A walk along the waterfront will take you past the services. An island map that lists useful phone numbers is available at kiosks (400dr/€1.17). Regular **ferries** from Piraeus and other Western Cyclades arrive in Serifos. From Serifos, ferries travel to: **Folegandros** (5½hr.; 2 per day Tu, Th, Sa; 1800dr/€5.27); **Kimolos** (2½hr., 6 per week, 2000dr/€5.86); **Milos** (2¼hr., 2 per day, 1800dr/€5.27); **Piraeus** (4½hr., 1-3 per day, 4100dr/€12); **Sifnos** (45min., 3 per day, 1500dr/€4.40); **Sikinos** (6½hr., 3 per week, 2900dr/€8.50). **Catamarans** go once per day to Sifnos, Milos, and Piraeus, and once per week to Kythnos in half the time and for twice the money. **Buses** travel from Livadi to Hora (14 per day 7:30am-11pm, 270dr/€0.79); a return bus follows the same schedule, but with a 15min. delay. Another bus travels daily to the beach towns of **Megalo Livadi** and **Koutalas** at 10:30am, returning from Megalo

CYCLADES

Livadi at 3:45pm and Koutalas at 4pm. Buses also go to the **monastery** (30min., W and Sa 11am); they wait there for 30min. before rumbling back to Livadi. Krinas rents **cars** (12,000-16,500dr/€35.22-48.42 per day) and **mopeds** (4000-5000dr/€11.74-14.67) at the most competitive prices on the island. For **taxis,** call 51 245 or 51 435.

Krinas Travel, upstairs from Captain Hook at the inland end of the dock (☎51 488 or 51500; fax 51073; open daily 9am-midnight), and **Apiliotis Travel,** on the waterfront to the left of a supermarket (☎51 155; open daily 9am-2pm and 6-8:30pm), sell hydrofoil and ferry tickets and have English schedules. The **Alpha Bank,** with 24hr. **ATM,** is along the waterfront. (☎51 780 or 51 739. Open M-Th 8am-2pm, F 8am-1:30pm.) The **port police** (☎51 470) are up the narrow steps, marked with a large Greek flag. For **police,** dial 51 300. The **pharmacy** is two doors to the left of Apiliotis. (☎51 205. Open daily 9am-2pm and 6:30-9:30pm.) **Postal code:** 84005.

ACCOMMODATIONS AND FOOD

The small port town of Livadi is big on rooming options. **Hotel Serifos Beach** is a block back from the beach, with a large blue sign on the main waterfront road. Away from the main strip, rooms are comfortable and quiet. (☎51 209 or 51 468. Breakfast 1500dr/€4.40. Port shuttle available. Singles 9000-13,000dr/€26.41-38.15; doubles 11,000-15,500dr/€32.28-45.49.) **Hotel Areti,** up the hill on the first left as you exit the ferry, bears blue shutters and a coat of whitewash. The hotel has a harbor view, a backyard terrace, and private balconies. (☎51 479 or 51 107; fax 51 547. Breakfast 1500dr/€4.40. Open Apr.-Oct. Doubles 10,000-15,000dr/€29.35-44.) **Alexandros-Basileia,** located on Livadakia Beach, has clean rooms hidden among beautiful flowers. To find it, follow the same directions given for the Coralli Camping or call for a shuttle. (☎/fax 51903. Doubles start at 10,000dr/€29.35.) The ⬛**Coralli Campgrounds,** popular with backpackers, lie 20m from Livadakia Beach and 700m left of the port. Call for a minibus, or follow the first inland street right of the port uphill, turn left one street beyond the school, and continue toward the Coralli flags. Bungalows have TV, A/C, fridge, and private baths. A mini-market, laundry facilities, swimming pool, common kitchen, and a small restaurant are also available. (☎51 500; fax 51 073; info@corali.gr; www.coralli.gr. 1200dr/€3.50 per person, 1500dr/€4.40 in high season; 600dr/€1.76 per tent, 700dr/€2.05 in high season. Bungalows: singles 8000-15,000dr/€23.48-44; doubles 10,000-18,000/€29.35-52.82; triples 12,000-20,000dr/€35.22-58.69; quads 14,500-24,000dr/€42.55-70.43.)

Restaurants and cafes spring out from hotels and line the waterfront. Visit **Vitamine C,** near the Hotel Serifos Beach, for a breakfast sandwich (1800dr/€5.28). For an inexpensive, stick-to-your-ribs meal, head to **Stamadis,** at the right end of the waterfront on the beach. The stuffed vine leaves (1200dr/€3.52) and rabbit casserole with onions (1700dr/€5) are delightful. (☎51 309 or 51 729. Open daily 8am-late.) The restaurant at the **Hotel Anna** serves a Greek and Italian menu (☎51 666 or 51 484; fax 51 277. Open daily 6:30am-2am). The **Marinos** market, far along the waterfront, sells fresh fruit. (Open daily 7:30am-2pm and 4:30pm-midnight.)

NIGHTLIFE AND BEACHES

The **Roman** cafe, in a small shop complex by Vitamine C, has a pool table, games, and a mellow scene (☎52 242; open late). **Hook** is a rooftop dance club that plays a mix of American top 40 and Greek hits. Look for its big red sign and large globular patio lights. (☎(0932) 41 16 57. Open nightly 11pm-late). **Alter Ego Music Club** bumps and grinds next door. (Cover 1500dr/€4.40. Open nightly after 11pm.)

Serifos has many secluded sandy **beaches** awaiting your lone footprints. Follow the signs at the right side of the waterfront for a 30min. walk to **Psili Amos.** In a calm bay at the base of a mountain, this quiet beach is populated by a single taverna. Follow a map along the paved and dirt roads of Northern Serifos to the unnamed beaches hiding here. For those without a vehicle or swift-footed mule, a bus travels once daily to **Mega Livadi** and **Koutalas.**

🏃 DAYTRIPS FROM LIVADI

HORA Χωρα   ☎0281

The dense white roofs of Hora look postcard-perfect, with whitewashed houses tumbling down the hill like a handful of white dice. (*The 40min. walk there from Livadi begins at a stone staircase next to the Marinos market. The footsore can catch the hourly bus from Livadi.*) The first stop on this route deposits you at Hora's **post office** (☎51 239; open M-F 7:30am-noon) and **OTE** (☎51 399), while the second drops you in front of a well-stocked **supermarket** and a few tavernas. From here you can climb up a series of steps to the small **chapel** that crowns the town. The crumbling remains of the old **Castro** invite you to poke around them; follow the signs painted along the numerous steps up. Getting lost in Hora's maze of stony, twisty streets is even better than knowing your way around. You'll discover quiet tavernas and markets along the circuitous alleyways. The **Archaeological Museum** houses artifacts from Hora's Roman years (open Tu-Sa 9am-2pm). Domatia are available for around 12,000dr/€35.22 per double.

NORTHERN SERIFOS

Serifos's interior isn't very accessible without a car or moped, a map, and excellent driving skills. See Orientation and Practical Information (p. 419) for car rental information.

Traditional villages, scattered churches and monasteries, and traces of ruins mark the northern part of the island. With transportation, you can visit the **Monastery of the Taxiarchs,** 10km beyond Hora toward the village of Galani. Built in 1400 on a site where a Cypriot icon mysteriously appeared (and to which it returns whenever removed), the monastery also houses an Egyptian lantern and several Russian relics. Upon entering the church, notice the frescoes that have been preserved in the doorway above; there is also a 17th-century stone plate in the middle of the floor depicting the Byzantine Double Eagle. If you arrive by bus you may meet the lone monk who has lived there for 20 years. Arrange a visit by calling ahead (☎51 027). By foot, the trip takes 2hr. The monastery and town around the port have no facilities, so bring all you need if you choose to hike.

CYCLADES

DODECANESE
Δωδεκανησα

The Dodecanese are lean wolves and hunt in packs; waterless, eroded by the sun. They branch off every side as you coast along the shores of Anatolia. Then toward afternoon the shaggy green of Cos comes up; and then slithering out of the wintry blue the moist green flanks of Rhodes.

—Lawrence Durrell

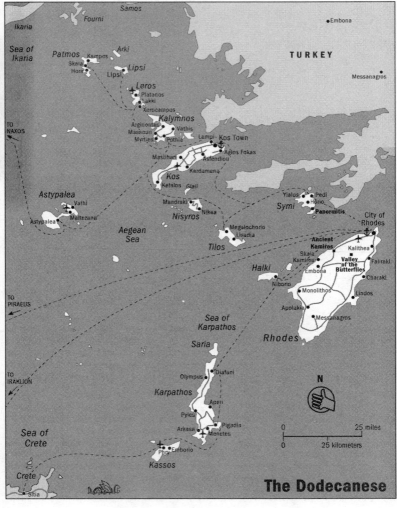

The Dodecanese

HIGHLIGHTS OF THE DODECANESE

THINK REVELATION when visiting Patmos (p. 446), former home of visionary gospel writer St. John.

SNIFF THE SULFUR of the smoking, inactive Mandraki volcano on Nisyros (p. 461).

REGENERATE with a bathtime scrubdown on sponge capital Kalymnos (p. 442).

STRAIN YOUR EARS for the sublime whisper of millions of bright beating wings in Rhodes's Valley of Butterflies (p. 436).

SQUEEZE into your tightest pants, then try to get into somebody else's on Kos (p. 436).

Scattered against the coast of Turkey, the Dodecanese, or Twelve Islands, are the farthest Greek island group from the mainland. Closer to Asia Minor than to Athens, these islands have experienced more invasions than the more central parts of Greece. In ancient times, the Dodecanese flourished before falling to Alexander the Great. A favorite target of evangelizing biblical luminaries including St. Paul and St. John, the inhabitants of the islands were some of the first Greeks to convert to Christianity. The islands prospered in the early Byzantine years, before suffering from raids that later hurt the entire empire. Crusaders stormed through during the 14th century, building heavily fortified castles as bases for their religious wars. The Ottomans ousted them in 1522, and the lucky Dodecanese received special concessions for their proximity to Turkey. The Dodecanese ultimately joined the Greek nation in 1948 after fighting fiercely in WWII.

Eclectic architecture is the most visible legacy of all these comings and goings: Classical ruins, castles built by Crusaders, and Ottoman mosques all coexist. Travelers who venture here will find landscapes ranging from Rhodes's fertile hills to the volcanic terrain of Nisyros. Kos's hopping nightlife, Rhodes's medieval city, the apocalyptic beauty of Patmos, the secluded beaches of Karpathos, and the hidden glory of Kalymnos are sure to entice even the most discriminating traveler.

RHODES Ροδος

RHODES CODES.
0241 for the northern half of the island;
0244 for all locations south of Kolymbia in the east;
0246 for all locations south of Kalavarda in the west.

The undisputed tourist capital of the Dodecanese, Rhodes has room for all, sheltering the centuries-old customs, natural resources, and serene escapes of the interior and smaller coastal towns. Sandy beaches stretch along the east coast, jagged cliffs skirt the west, and green mountains freckled with villages fill the interior; resort towns dominate the north. Kamiros, Ialyssos, and Lindos show the clearest evidence of the island's Classical past, while medieval fortresses slumber in the City of Rhodes and in Monolithos.

CITY OF RHODES   ☎ 0241

Rhodes is a city with two distinct souls. In the Old Town Greeks still inhabit their ancestors' homes, perpetuating the area's hometown feel. The New Town, on the other hand, is thoroughly modern, and is the political and economic capital of the Dodecanese. Tourism also splits along the lines of old and new: the Old Town contains virtually all of the ancient and medieval sites, while the New Town has become a magnet for party-goers, who pack its beaches with bikinis and thongs.

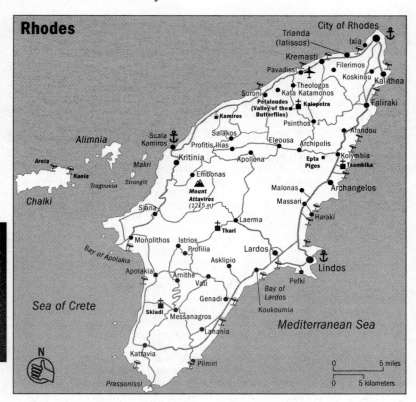

Rhodes

City of Rhodes
Trianda (Ialissos)
Ixia
Kremasti
Pavadissi
Filerimos
Koskinou
Kalithea
Theologos
Kata Katamonos
Soroni
Petaloudes (Valley of the Butterflies)
Kalopetra
Faliraki
Kamiros
Psinthos
Salakos
Scala Kamiros
Profitis Ilias
Eleousa
Archipolis
Afandou
Alimnia
Kritinia
Apollona
Epta Piges
Kolymbia
Areta
Makri
Embonas
Tsambika
Kania
Tragoussa
Strongili
Mount Attaviros (1215 m)
Malonas
Archangelos
Chalki
Massari
Siana
Laerma
Haraki
Thari
Monolithos
Istrios
Profilia
Lardos
Bay of Apolakia
Asklipio
Lindos
Apolakia
Arnithe
Vati
Pefki
Genadi
Bay of Lardos
Koukoumia
Sea of Crete
Skiadi
Messanagros
Mediterranean Sea
Lahania
Kattavia
Plimiri
N
Prassonissi

0   5 miles
0   5 kilometers

▉ TRANSPORTATION

Schedules for ferries, Flying Dolphins, and buses are at the EOT. Summer moped rental agencies are common throughout town. The bumpy, narrow cobblestone roads of the Old Town roads are dangerous on a moped: be careful.

Flights: Olympic Airways, Ierou Lohou 9 (☎24 571, reservations 24 555), near the central OTE. Open M-F 7:30am-9pm. The **airport** (☎ 83 400 or 83 403) is on the west coast, 16km from town, near Paradisi, and is accessible by public bus (5am-11pm from the west side bus station, 500dr/€1.47). Flights to: **Athens** (5 per day, 20,000dr/€58.36); **Iraklion,** Crete (2 per week, 27,000dr/€79.23); **Karpathos** (2 per day, 15,000dr/€44.01); **Kassos** (5 per week 15,000dr/€44.01); **Kastellorizo** (1 per day, 12,500dr/€36.68); **Mykonos** (2 per week, 26,500dr/€77.76); **Santorini** (6 per day, 26,500dr/€77.76); **Thessaloniki** (3 per week, 36,000dr/€105.65).

Ferries: To: **Agios Nikolaos,** Crete (3 per week, 8000dr/€23.47); **Astypalea** (2 per week, 6000dr/€17.61); **Haifa,** Israel (36hr., 2 per week, 36,500dr/€107.10); **Halki** (3 per week, 2300dr/€6.75); **Kalymnos** (3-5 per day, 4300dr/€12.62); **Karpathos** (3 per week, 4400dr/€12.91); **Kassos** (3 per week, 5300dr/€15.55); **Kos** (1-2 per day, 4000dr/€11.74); **Leros** (1 per day, 5000dr/€14.67); **Limassol,** Cyprus (17hr., 2 per week, 22,500dr/€66.02); **Milos** (3 per week, 8450dr/€24.79); **Patmos** (1-2 per day, 5400dr/€15.85); **Piraeus** (1-4 per day, 11,300dr/€33.16); **Samos** (1 per week, 6500dr/€19.07); **Sitia,** Crete (3 per week, 6400dr/€18.78); **Symi** (2500dr/€7.34); **Thessaloniki** (1 per week, 14,600dr/€42.84); and **Tilos** (3 per week, 2800dr/€8.22). Most ferries have student discounts. Daily excursions from Mandraki Port to: **Kos**

DODECANESE

(round-trip 14,000dr/€41.08); **Lindos** (2hr., 1 per day, round-trip 5000dr/€14.67); **Symi** and **Panormitis Monastery** (round-trip 5500dr/€16.14).

Flying Dolphins: Hydrofoils head to Turkey and the rest of the Dodecanese. To: **Halki** (1 per day, 4300dr/€12.62); **Kalymnos** (Th, Sa, Su, 8530dr/€25.04); **Kos** (2 per day, 6500dr/€19.07); **Leros** (M and F, 9823dr/€28.82); **Marmaris** (1 per day, 19,000dr/€55.75 including port taxes); **Nisyros** (5400dr/€15.85); **Symi** (Su-F 1 per day, Sa 2 per day, 2900dr/€8.51); **Tilos** (1-2 per day, 5300dr/€15.55). Call **Nearhos** agency for more hydrofoil information (☎ 78 052 or 78 053; fax 20 272). The **Katamaran Dodekanissos Express** (☎ 70 590) travels from Kolona Harbor between **Kalymnos, Leros, Kos, Halki, Nisyros, Tilos,** and **Symi** twice daily during the summer.

Buses: Stations lie on opposite sides of Papagou at Pl. Rimini.

East station is served by **KTEL** (☎ 27 706 or 75 134; fax 24 268). Service east to: **Afandou** (14 per day 6:45am-11pm, 500dr/€1.47); **Archangelos** (14 per day 6:45am-11pm, 650dr/€1.91); **Faliraki** (18 per day 9am-11pm, 500dr/€1.47); **Pefki** and **Gennadi** (9 per day 6:45am-7:30pm, 1350dr/€3.69); **Haraki** (10am, 800dr/€2.35); **Kolymbia Beach** (7 per day 9am-9:15pm, 700dr/€2.05); **Laerma** (M-F 1pm, 1350dr/€3.96); **Lindos** (14 per day 8:30am-7:30pm, 1050dr/€3.08); **Malona** and **Massari** (4 per day 9am-2:30pm, 800dr/€22.35); **Tsambika Beach** (9am, 750dr/€2.20).

West station is served by **RODA** (☎ 26 300). Service west to: **Embana** (3 per day, 1150dr); **Kala-varda** (8 per day 5am-9:35pm, 550dr/€1.61); **Kalithea, Calypso, Kastri** (31 per day 6:30am-10:30pm, 500dr/€1.47); **Kamiros** (2 per day 10am and 1:30pm, 1150dr/€3.37); **Koskinou** (10 per day 5:50am-9:10pm, 500dr/€1.47); **Kritinia** (1 per day, 1150dr/€3.37); **Monolithos** (M-F 1:30pm, 1500dr/€4.40); **Paradisi Airport** (24 per day 5am-11pm, 500dr/€1.47); **Peta-loudes** (9:30 and 11am, 1000dr/€2.93); **Salakos** (5 per day 6:45am-9:30pm, 900dr/€2.64); **Soroni** and **Fanes** (10 per day 5am-9:30pm, 550dr/€1.61); **Pastida** and **Maritsa** (10 per day 5:40am-9:35pm, 500dr/€1.47); **Damatria** (6 per day 6am-9:35pm, 550dr/€1.61); **Embona** (1:45pm, 1300dr/€3.82); **Kremasti** (10:20am, 8:20, 10pm; 500dr/€1.35); and **Theologos** (12 per day 5am-9:30pm, 550dr/€1.61).

Taxis: (☎ 27 666), in Pl. Rimini. Radio taxis also available (☎ 64 712, 64 734, 64 756, 64 778 or 64 790). Open 24hr.

Rentals: Mandar Moto, Zephiros 3 (☎ 34 576 or 30 665), in the Old Town. Take Sokratous to Pl. Hippokratous and continue on Aristotelous to Pl. Evraion Martiron. Mopeds 4000-7000dr/€11.74-20.54 per day. Open M-Su 8:30am-8pm. **Margartis Motors,** Ioanou Kazouli 23 (☎ 37 420 or 39 485), in the New Town near Agia Maria church. Scooters 3000-6000dr/€8.80-17.61 per day. Mountain bikes start at 1000dr/€2.93. Motor bikes 5000-12,000dr/€14.67-35.21. Open daily 8am-8pm.

■■ ◪ ORIENTATION AND PRACTICAL INFORMATION

The city is divided into two districts. **New Town** spans the north and west and **Old Town** centers around **Sokratous,** a bustling, crowded street packed with tourists ooh-ing and aah-ing at gift shops. Not the place to be, but it's a handy landmark amidst the multitude of tiny streets and pathways branching off in all directions. In the New Town, all international and most domestic ferries use the **Commercial Harbor** outside the Old Town. **Mandraki,** the New Town's more traditional Greek island waterfront, docks private yachts, hydrofoils, and excursion boats. Town beaches are to the north, beyond Mandraki, and along the city's west coast. The tourist office, both bus stations, and a taxi stand are in or around **Pl. Rimini,** beneath the fortress's turrets at the junction of the Old and New Towns. To get there from Mandraki, head a block inland with the park to your left. The New Town is a mecca for young nightlife; most tourists head to **Orfanidou,** popularly dubbed **Bar Street,** while the Greek scene huddles around **Militadou** in the Old Town.

Greek National Tourist Office (EOT): (☎ 23 255, 23 655 or 35 226; fax 26 955), up Papagou a few blocks from Pl. Rimini at the intersection of Makariou. Incredibly helpful advice on the essentials for your visit. Free maps, brochures, and accommodation advice. English spoken. Open M-F 8:30am-2:30pm.

DODECANESE

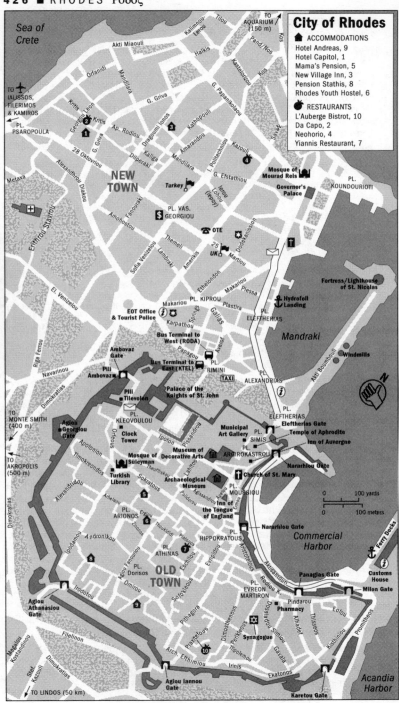

Sea of
Crete

Akti Miaouli

TO
AQUARIUM
(150 m)

City of Rhodes

🏠 **ACCOMMODATIONS**

Hotel Andreas, 9
Hotel Capitol, 1
Mama's Pension, 5
New Village Inn, 3
Pension Stathis, 8
Rhodes Youth Hostel, 6

🍎 **RESTAURANTS**

L'Auberge Bistrot, 10
Da Capo, 2
Neohorio, 4
Yiannis Restaurant, 7

TO
IALISSOS,
FILERIMOS
& KAMIROS

PL.
PSAROPOULA

Orfanidi

Mandilara

G. Griva

Kalimnou
Lerou

Tilou

Pand/Nos

Halkis

Kastellorizou

Kos

**NEW
TOWN**

28 Oktovriou

Kritis

Ap. Rodiou

Dragoumi Ionos

Kathopouli

Amarandou

Mandilara

Kazouli

Mosque of
Mourad Reis

Governor's
Palace

PL.
KOUNDOURIOTI

Turkey

I. Politechniou

G. Efstathiou

Ierou
Lofou
(lepou)

Themeli

PL. VAS.
GEORGIOU

OTE

Dodekanisou

Amohostou

Sofia Venizelou

Lambraki

Ameriks

25

UK

Mariou

Etheliondon

Makariou

Piessa

Fortress/Lighthouse
of St. Nicolas

Hydrofoil
Landing

El. Venizelou

Makariou

Karpathou

Springs

PL. KIPROU

Plastira

Gallas

PL.
ELEFTHERIAS

Mandraki

EOT Office
& Tourist Police

Bus Terminal to
West (RODA)

Papagou

Averof

PL.
RIMINI

Windmills

Ambovaz
Gate

Pili
Ambovaz

Bus Terminal to
East (KTEL)

TAXI

PL.
ALEXANDRIAS

Akti Bouriboul

Pili
Tilevolen

PL.
KLEEVOULOU

Palace of
the Knights of St. John

Ipoton

PL.
ELEFTHERIAS

TO
MONTE SMITH
(400 m)

Agiou
Georgiou
Gate

Clock
Tower

Museum of
Decorative Arts

Municipal
Art Gallery

PL.
SIMIS

Eleftherias Gate

Temple of Aphrodite

Inn of Auvergne

TO
AKROPOLIS
(500 m)

Mosque of
Suleyman

Turkish
Library

Archaeological
Museum

PL.
ARGIROKASTROU

Narahlou Gate

Church of St. Mary

PL.
MOUSSIOU

Inn of
the Tongue
of England

Narahlou Gate

**Commercial
Harbor**

PL.
ATHINAS

PL.
HIPPOKRATOUS

**OLD
TOWN**

PL.
Dorisos

Omirou

Panagias Gate

Customs
House

Milon Gate

Agiou
Athanasiou
Gate

Irodotou

PL.
EVREON
MARTIRON

Pindarou

Pharmacy

Synagogue

Arch. Efthimiou

TO LINDOS (50 km)

Agiou Iannou
Gate

Irinis

Ekatonos

Karetou Gate

**Acandia
Harbor**

DODECANESE

0   100 yards
0   100 meters

N

Tourist Office: (☎ 35 945), in the yellow building in Pl. Rimini. Bus, ferry, and excursion schedules, some accommodations advice, and **currency exchange**. Less helpful than the EOT, but has longer hours. Open June-Oct. M-Sa 8am-9pm, Su 8am-3pm.

Budget Travel: Castellania Travel Service (☎ 75 860 or 75 862; fax 75 861), in Pl. Hippokratous at the intersection of Sokratous and Aristotelous in the Old Town. Issues low-priced **ISIC** and **GO25 cards**. Free **luggage storage**. Open M-Sa 9am-9:30pm.

Consulates A **British Vice-Consul** is available M-F 9am-2pm through **Lloyd's Travel Bureau,** 25 Martiou 23 (☎ 27 306 or 27 247).

Banks: Many banks are in the New Town, few in the Old Town; **ATMs** are widespread throughout both. The **National Bank** has an office in the Old Town at Pl. Moussiou with an ATM. Open M-Th 9am-2pm, F 9am-1:30pm. In the New Town, the **National Bank** (☎ 27 031) in Pl. Kyprou has currency exchange.

American Express: Rhodos Tours Ltd., Ammohostou 23, P.O. Box 252 (☎ 38 217). Open M-F 9am-1:30pm and 5-8:30pm, Sa 7:30am-3pm.

Laundry: Happy Wash Express Service Laundry, in the New Town at 38 Alex. Diakou (☎ 35 693). 1300dr/€3.81 for wash and dry. Open daily 9am-11pm. **Express Laundry,** 5 Kosti Palama (☎ 22 514), directly across from the Pl. Rimini bus station, offers full wash and dry for 1000dr/ €293. Open daily 8am-11:30pm. The only **Old Town laundromat** is on Platonos 33, near Yiannis taverna (☎ 76 047). Open daily 8am-10pm. Wash and dry 1500dr/ €4.40.

Police: (☎ 23 294), on Eth. Dodekanisson, 1 block behind the post office. Open 24hr. **Lost and found** open M-F 8am-2pm.

Tourist Police: (☎ 27 423 or 23 329), in the GNTO building. English spoken.

Port Authority: or Central Harbor Master (☎ 22 220 or 28 888), is on Mandraki just left of the post office. Complete boat schedules. Open 24hr.

Hospital: (☎ 80 000; for a **medical emergency** dial 166), on Erithrou Stavrou, off El. Venizelou. Open for emergencies 24hr. **Visitor's clinic** open daily 1-3pm and 6-8pm.

Telephones: OTE, Amerikis 91 (☎ 24 599), at the corner of 25 Martiou in the New Town. Open daily 6am-11pm.

Internet Access: Minoan Palace, Ir. Polytechniou 13 (☎ 20 210), at corner of G. Efstathiou in the New Town. 1200dr/€3.52 per hr., 600dr/€1.76 minimum charge. Open daily 9am-2:30am. In the Old Town, **Mango Bar,** Pl. Dorisos 3 (☎ 24 877, 28 324 or 32 824). 1200dr/€3.52 per hr. Open M-Sa 10am-1am, Su 10am-midnight.

Post Office: Main branch (☎ 30 290 or 34 873), on Mandraki, along the waterfront and next to the Bank of Greece. Open M-F 7:30am-2pm. **Parcel service** 7:30am-2pm. Also a **mobile branch** (☎ 35 565) in the Old Town on Orfeos, near the Palace of the Grand Masters. From Pl. Museum, head down Ipoton and take a left onto Orfeos. Open M-F 7:30am-2pm. **Postal code:** 85100.

ACCOMMODATIONS

OLD TOWN

Most pensions are scattered about the narrow pebbled paths around Omirou; the Youth Hostel and Mama's Pension are a few steps away near Ergiou. Both are in the quiet, charming Old Town, the preferred resting place for most travelers.

■ **Rhodes Youth Hostel,** Ergiou 12 (☎ 30 491). Turn off Sokratous onto the tiny side street, next to a dilapidated building that looks like a mosque. Keep walking to a sign reading "youth hostel," where you'll take a right; the hostel will be on the left. The owners are extremely helpful. Rooms are large, clean, comfy, and simple: mainly dorm rooms, although doubles and triples are also available. For a truly economical stay ask about the bed on the roof. Services include free luggage storage, laundry (1400dr/€4.11), full kitchen. No curfew, bring your own toilet paper, and be sure to ask for sheets. Mostly shared bath. Dorms 2000-2500dr/€5.87-7.34; doubles 2500-3000dr/€7.34-8.80; triples with bath 4000-5000dr/€11.74-14.67.

Mama's Pension, Menekleous 28 (☎25 359), off Sokratous, directly above Mike's Taverna. Mike himself will treat you to a cheap room and Greek hospitality. If you're lucky, he'll serenade you with classic tunes late into the night. Singles 3000dr/€8.80; doubles 7000dr/€20.54; triples 9000dr/€26.41.

Pension Stathis, Omirou 60 (☎24 357), take Ag. Fanouriou off Sokratous and walk down to Omirou. Animated Stathis welcomes all to quiet, clean (if a bit cramped) rooms surrounding a vine-covered courtyard. English spoken. Nightly folk music from the nearby theater. Check-out noon. Singles 6000dr/€17.61; doubles 8000dr/€23.47.

Hotel Andreas, Omirou 28D (☎34 156; fax 74 285). Rooms with bunk beds are ideal for families or groups. Roof terrace offers a terrific panoramic view. Laundry, international telephone, Internet access in rooms. Singles 9000-11,000dr/€26.41-32.28; doubles 12,000-15,000dr/€35.21-44.01; triples 17,000dr/€49.88.

NEW TOWN

The New Town is somewhat charmless. Expensive hotels line the coast, but affordable pensions can be found along the narrow streets of Rodiou, Dilberaki, Kathopouli, and Amarandou.

New Village Inn, Konstantopedos 10 (☎34 937; www.rodosisland.gr), on a tiny side-street off Kathopouli. Owned and run by a helpful, hospitable couple. Open-air corridors lead to modern, sparkling-clean rooms by a tile-covered courtyard. Breakfast 700dr/€2.05. Singles 6000dr/€17.61; doubles 10,000-12,000dr/€29.34-35.21.

Hotel Capitol, Dilberaki 65-67 (☎/fax 28 645), perpendicular to Dragoumi Ionos. Quiet, spacious rooms with private baths in an old home with distinct character. Once inhabited by the mayor of Rhodes. Singles 5000-7000dr/€14.67-20.54; doubles 8000-12,000dr/€23.47-35.21; triples 100,00-15,000dr/€29.34-44.01.

◨ FOOD

In the Old Town, food tends to be mediocre, the waiters aggressive, and the prices high. The New Town cafes are similarly overpriced, but a burgeoning expat community has brought with it a sophisticated international palate.

▨ Chalki, Kathopouli 30 (☎33 196), in the New Town off Papanikolaou. The sensuous aromas of traditional Hellenic dishes draw locals and foreigners alike. Ask to enter the kitchen to pick out your meal from all the pots and pans bubbling on the stove. Entrees 1800dr/€5.28; salad 900dr/€2.64. Open daily noon-3pm and 6pm-midnight.

L'Auberge Bistrot, Praxitelous 21 (☎34 292). From the synagogue, walk south on Perikleous; take the 1st right, then the 2nd left. The covert location makes this gastronomic gem even more worthwhile. A friendly French couple has created an unforgettable bistro where jazz vibrates around artsy decor. Starters 600-1200dr/€1.76-3.52; entrees 1800-2500dr/€5.28-7.34. Open Tu-Su 7:30pm-midnight.

Neohorio, I. Kazouli 29 (☎35 116), in the New Town off Amerikis. Local grill serving the basics (gyros 250dr/€0.73; souvlaki plate 1500dr/€4.40). Carnivores welcome (sausages 600dr/€1.76; meatballs 600dr/€1.76). Open daily noon-midnight.

Yiannis, Sokratous-Platonos 41 (☎36 535), just off Sokratous away from the New Town. Good Greek food served by the cook's smiling grandmother. Try the *stifado, keftedes,* or special *moussaka* for 1100-1800dr/€3.23-5.28. Elliniko plate (a mixture of Greek *mezedes*) feeds 3 (3000dr/€8.80). Open daily 10am-midnight.

Da Capo, G. Leontos 12 (☎76 790 or 37 806), in the New Town off 28 Oktovriou. Traditional Greek food (1800-5000dr/€5.28–14.67) and an extensive list of pizzas (1600-2200dr/€4.69-6.46) on its inviting patio and balcony. Efficient service. Stands out among the New Town's restaurant options. Open daily 2pm-midnight.

⊙ SIGHTS

Few islands are known for a sight that you have to imagine; Rhodes is one of them. One of the Seven Wonders of the Ancient World, the **Colossus of Rhodes,** a 35m bronze statue of Helios at the harbor entrance of Mandraki, leaves no earthly trace today. Legend has it that the Colossus toppled in a 237 BC earthquake. Two bronze deer are now frozen right where a colossal foot would have crushed them. A new Colossus is in the works, in an effort to make Rhodes a worldwide wonder again.

OLD TOWN

Scattered throughout the pebbled inclines of the medieval Old Town (constructed by the **Knights of St. John**) are small bronze plaques that label historical sites and museums. Upon conquering the island, the Knights redecorated the capital city, giving it a homier feel and replacing Hellenistic ruins with medieval forts and castles. Material tourism abounds on **Sokratous** street, the main shopping strip, formerly an Ottoman bazaar. The street is now lined with a poor imitation of the bazaar, with rip-off jewelry stores, restaurants, and junkshops.

PALACE OF THE GRAND MASTER. At the top of the hill, the tall square tower, said to be the work of Grand Master Pierre d'Aubusson, marks the entrance to the Palace of the Grand Master. With 300 rooms, moats, drawbridges, huge watchtowers, and colossal battlements, the palace survived the long Ottoman siege of 1522 only to be devastated in 1856 by the explosion of 300-year-old ammunition in a depot across the street. At the beginning of this century, after years of use as a prison by the Turks and Italians, the citadel was restored and embellished by Italians determined to outdo even the industrious Knights. Many of the floors now bear **mosaics** taken from Kos. The interior decoration was completed only a few months before the start of the Second World War; the Italians had little chance to savor the fruits of their labor. The two outstanding exhibits on the north and southwest sides of the ground floor use archaeological findings and visual aids to tell a detailed version of Rhodes's extensive history. (☎25 500. Open M 2:30-9pm, Tu-Su 8:30am-9pm. 1200dr/€3.52, students 600dr/€1.76.) For an unparalleled bird's-eye view of the entire fortified city, wait for a Tuesday or Saturday and take a **walk** along the **city walls,** but make sure to hustle—there's only a half-hour window for admittance. (Open Tu and Sa 2:30-3pm. 1200dr/€3.52, students 600dr/€1.76.)

PLATEIA ARGYKASTROU. Dominating one side of the plateia with its beautiful halls and courtyards, the former **Hospital of the Knights** has been reborn as an **Archaeological Museum.** Its treasures include the small but exquisite first-century BC *Aphrodite Bathing* and the 4th-century *Apollo*. (☎25 500. Open Tu-F 8am-7pm, Sa-Su 8am-3:30pm. 800dr/€2.35, students and seniors 400dr/€1.17.) The cobbled **Avenue of the Knights,** or Ipoton, sloping uphill near the museum, was the main boulevard of the city 500 years ago. **Plateia Moussio** is after the low archway; to its left is the **Church of St. Mary,** an 11th-century Byzantine building that was a Gothic cathedral by the time the Knights of St. John were through with it. Most of its interior frescoes were obliterated when the Ottomans transformed the building into the Enderoum Mosque. The Italians then re-converted the mosque to a church, which has since become an **icon museum.** (Open Tu-Su 8:30am-3pm. 500dr/€1.47, students 300dr/€0.88.) The **Inn of the Tongue of England** is a 1919 copy of its 1483 predecessor, destroyed in one of many defensive battles. The Order of the Knights of St. John of Jerusalem consisted of seven different religious orders, called "tongues" because each spoke a different language. Their inns, now government offices lining both sides of Ipoton, are closed to tourists. Because each tongue guarded one segment of the city wall, parts of the wall are labeled "England" or "France" on the map.

PLATEIA SYMI. To the right inside Eleftherias Gate, at the base of the Mandraki, are the **Municipal Art Gallery**'s contemporary paintings by local and national artists. *(Open M-Sa 8am-2pm. 500dr/€1.47.)* Behind the ruined 3rd-century BC **Temple of Aphrodite** in the middle of the plateia stands the 16th-century **Inn of the Tongue of Auvergne,** with an Aegean-style staircase on the facade. (You may not realize there's anything there—the temple is literally a heap of stone and debris.)

PLANE TREE WALK. Evidence of the city's Ottoman era is most clear in Pl. Kleovoulou. A walk down **Orfeos,** better known as the Plane Tree Walk, will take you past a large **clock tower,** which once marked the edges of the wall separating the knights' quarters from the rest of the city. The walk opens onto the highest viewpoint in the Old Town. Climbing the tower leads you to a small cafe. *(Open daily 9am-11pm. 1000dr/€2.93 includes a drink at the bar.)* The **Mosque of Süleyman,** below the clock tower, dates from the early 19th century. It's distinguished by its red plaster walls, garden, and stone minaret. The original mosque was built after Sultan Süleyman the Magnificent captured Rhodes in 1522.

TURKISH HORA. The **Turkish library,** built in 1793 opposite the mosque, houses 15th- and 16th-century Persian and Arabic manuscripts. *(Open daily 10am-1pm and 4-7pm. Donation expected.)* Other Old Town Ottoman-era buildings and monuments are in various states of decay, but the 250-year-old baths and the **hamam** (Turkish bath) in Pl. Arionos are worth a peek. Note the way sunlight streams through small carved stars of one dome.

JEWISH QUARTER. Pl. Martyron Evreon (Square of the Jewish Martyrs) lies in the heart of the old Jewish Quarter. The Jewish community was an integral part of Rhodes's history from its inception. Sephardic Jews fleeing the Spanish Inquisition, added a Spanish flair to some Old Town medieval architecture. In 1943, 2000 Jews were taken from this square to Nazi concentration camps. Today, nothing remains of the Jewish heritage in Pl. Evreon: it has been overrun by tourist cafes and shops. A few streets in, however, the Jewish quarter's residential area is one of the loveliest and most peaceful parts of the Old Town. In this neighborhood, down Dossiadou, is the **Shalom Synagogue,** restored by the 50 Jewish men and women who survived the war. Services are Friday at 5pm; dress modestly. Oriental rugs cover the stone mosaic floor and "eternal lamps" hang overhead.

NEW TOWN AND MANDRAKI

If you're not blinded by the flashing display of consumer culture, you'll find stately Italian architecture throughout the modern business district. The bank, town hall, post office, and National Theater are among the Mussolini-inspired stone buildings presiding over wide Eleftherias. Opposite them is the majestic Governor's Palace and a cathedral built by the Italians in 1925. The cathedral replicates St. John's Church, leveled in an 1856 explosion. Three defunct windmills stand halfway along the harbor's pier. The **Fortress of St. Nicholas,** at the end of the pier, guarded the harbor from 1464 to the end of World War II. Opposite the cemetery is Villa Kleovoulos, which housed author Lawrence Durrell during his appointment with the Foreign Office from 1945-47. A number of Durrell's books are set in Greece, including his most celebrated *Reflections on a Marine Venus,* which takes place on Rhodes. Named after Süleyman's admiral, who died trying to capture Rhodes from the Knights of St. John in 1522, the Mosque of Mourad Reis is an important remnant of the Ottoman presence. The domed building inside is his mausoleum. Turbans indicate male graves, flowers female ones. Rhodes Town's aquarium, also a marine research center for the Dodecanese, exhibits creatures of the Aegean. (☎27 308 or 78 320. Open daily 9am-9pm. 600dr/€1.76, students 400dr/€1.17).

OUTSIDE THE CITY

Excursion boats trace the beach-filled coast from Rhodes to Lindos, leaving the city in the morning and returning in the afternoon; it's a great way to escape the crowded beaches of the western coast. The boats make several stops, including Faliraki. Schedules and prices are posted at the dock along the lower end of the Mandraki (starting at 3500dr/€10.27). **Waterhoppers** (☎38 146) and **Dive Med Centres** (☎61 115) offer **scuba diving** lessons and trips to Kalithea (lessons 15,000dr/€44.01; non-diving passengers 8000dr/€23.47), as well as trips for certified divers. **Rodini Park** is a forested area with streams, trails, a restaurant, and some small, harmless animals left over from the park's days as a zoo. Although abandoned for the last 20 years, it still makes for a serene natural escape.

◨ ♫ NIGHTLIFE AND ENTERTAINMENT

OLD TOWN

Nightlife focuses around Militado street, off Apellou. Bar after bar lines the narrow street and music pours out from everywhere. The street becomes so crowded that walking is nearly impossible; trying to get into the bars is no easier. If you do manage to get in, you'll be greeted by vocal locals.

Cafe Havana/Theater Bar, 9 Militadou (☎(0944) 314 724 or (0932) 278 587). House and pop rock the night as the charismatic bartender reels off the cocktail specialties. Try the *Scorpio* to really tickle your insides (1500dr/€4.40).

Empire Club, on Militadou next to Cafe Havana. Try the bartender's favorite shot (tequila with a squirt of orange and dash of cinnamon) to get your legs burning before hitting the dance floor. Cover 2000dr/€5.87 after 1am.

Mango Bar, Pl. Dorieos 3 (☎24 877), up Ag. Fanouriou from Sokratous. A pre-game bar, with some draft beer (400dr/€1.17). Open M-Sa 10am-1am, Su 10am-midnight.

The **sound and light show,** in the Rhodes Municipal Gardens with entrance from Pl. Rimi, is one of the Old Town's numerous attempts at a cultural offering. (☎21 922; www.greekfestival.gr. Shows in English M, Th-F, Su 8:15pm; Tu, Sa 9:15pm; W 10:15pm. 1500dr/€4.40, students 1000dr/€2.93.) **St. Francis Church** (☎23 605), at Dimokratias and Filellinon, echoes with sublime organ recitals Wednesday nights at 9pm; check at the EOT to verify schedule and time. In winter the **National Theater** (☎29 678), off Mandraki next to the town hall, stages occasional productions, and nearby **Rodon** shows new flicks and subtitled classics (1200dr/€3.52). **Folk Dance Theater,** Andronikou street, stages Greek dances and songs. (☎29 085 or 20 157. M, W, F 9:20pm. 3000dr/€8.80, students 1500dr/€4.40.)

NEW TOWN

Nightlife here is neither shy nor tame. Although popular bars and clubs are scattered throughout the New Town, crowds flock to Orfanidou, widely known as Bar Street. Popular places have expensive drinks; empty bars will cut deals. The 5min. observational walk from end to end will give you a feel for each bar's atmosphere.

Down Under, Orfanidou 37 (☎32 982). Join loud rock table-top dancers at one of the most popular bars on the strip. 90s pop music blasts until you can't hear yourself think. Drinks from 1500dr/€4.40, but keep an eye out for reps outside who can give you 2-for-1 drink coupons.

Colorado Pub, Orfanidou 57 (☎75 120). 3 rooms attract crowds by covering all necessary bases and moods. Live bands 'til 1am, a smashing club atmosphere, and an a mellow pub on the roof. Cover 1500dr/€4.40.

La Scala, a sprawling complex southwest of town by the beachside Rodos Palace Hotel in Ixia, is the king of Rhodes's nightclubs, accompanied by covers fit for royalty. Strap on your heels and shorten your skirts if you hope to fit in. Watch for special party nights.

DODECANESE

Paradiso, (☎ 32 003) next to Scala—almost as posh and a bit wilder on the dance floor. Eclectic music beats include house, reggae, rave, and down-home Greek. Have a few drinks, shed some clothing and start groovin'. Cover 3000dr/€8.80 starting at 1am.

FALIRAKI Φαλιρακη ☎ 0241

Faliraki isn't for those looking to brush up on their Greek—English is the predominant language spoken here. Here, beach bunnies hop among the sand, bars, and sandbars all day long. The bars, named for alcohol-induced impotence (e.g. The Brewer's Droop) and advertising foam parties, attract a wild crowd.

◼◼ ORIENTATION AND PRACTICAL INFORMATION. Faliraki is located 15km south of Rhodes City. There are two main bus stops in Faliraki, one on the Rhodes-Lindos road and one on the waterfront. **Buses** run to **Rhodes City** (17 per day, 500dr/€1.47) and from the waterfront bus stop to **Lindos** (14 per day, 1050dr/€3.08). Faliraki is also a base for boat trips to **Kos** (12,000dr/€35.21), **Lindos** (4000dr/€11.74), and **Symi** (6500dr/€19.07). Grab a **taxi** at the stand next to the waterfront bus stop, or call 85 444 (3000dr/€8.80 to Rhodes). Ermou is the main thoroughfare connecting the beach to the Rhodes-Lindos highway. The **Lydia Travel Agency,** right next to the Hotel Faliro on Ermou, offers currency exchange, international phone and fax services, and car rental. (☎ 85 483 or 86 135; fax 86 250. Open daily 9am-2pm and 5:30-10pm.) Directly opposite the waterfront bus stop, to the right of Ermou, is the **first-aid station** (☎ 80 000; open 8am-6pm). Dr. Zanettullis (mobile ☎ (094) 582 747) is available 24 hours a day. Another option for **emergencies** is the Faliraki 24hr. Emergency Medical Service (☎ 602 602). For an **ambulance,** call 22 222. The **pharmacy** is on the main road up to the highway; look for the green cross. (☎ 87 076. Open daily 9am-11pm.) The **Agricultural Bank,** on Ermou (open M-Th 8am-2pm, F 8am-1pm), has a 24-hour **ATM.** For internet services, **Antique Net Bar/Cafe** is the place to go. Try the Socrates (1300dr/€4.49) to set your head spinning—or thinking. (☎ 86 756. Open daily noon-3am. Internet 1500dr/€4.40 per hr.)

◼◼ ACCOMMODATIONS AND FOOD. Lodgings in Faliraki are hard to find, as most places rent their rooms to British package tour companies. A few are still holding out: **Hotel Faliro** is inland on Ermou, right before Ermou joins the Rhodes-Lindos road. Rooms are clean and a bit spartan, but offer the basics (full bath) and the superfluous (balconies). The free pool and the snack bar are perks. (☎ 85 483 or 399. Doubles 7000-9000dr/€20.54-26.41.) **Dimitra Hotel** is a fairly priced, pleasant option directly across the street from Hotel Faliro. Sparkling blue- and white-tiled hallways lead to simple, airy rooms, all with phones, baths, and balconies. (☎ 85 309; fax 85 254. Full bar and restaurant downstairs. Doubles 9,500-11,500dr/ €27.88-33.74.) The **Hotel Ideal,** again on Ermou but closer to the sea, attracts the young and wild to its drab but clean rooms. The hotel deals with tour groups but also sets aside rooms for independent travelers. (☎ 85 518; fax 86 530. Pool use and breakfast. Singles 9500-12,500dr/€27.88-36.68; doubles 9500-15,000dr/€27.88-44.01.) A great budget option is Rhodes's only **campsite** (☎ 85 516 or 85 358), off the main road 1500m north of Faliraki; ask the bus driver to let you off. It has a market, hot showers, restaurant, full kitchen facilities, laundry, and an impressive pool. (1600dr/€4.69 per person; 800dr/€2.35 for tent rental.)

Dining in Faliraki often means inhaling a burger, greasy fries, and a soda at a fast food joint. Ermou hosts most of these establishments; the Rhodos-Lindos road has other similar options. A meal will run 2000-3000dr/€5.87-8.80. For a reprieve from the typical fast-food, the Greek bakery, **Artopeio,** serves up fresh fluffy loaves of bread (200dr/€0.59) and pies of all kinds (*tiropita, spanakopita,* and sausage-pie 350dr/€1.03) at dirt-cheap prices. **Sarantis,** on the Rhodes-Lindos where Ermou ends, is a family-run restaurant focusing on seafood. (☎ 87 489. Dover sole 1950dr/ €5.72, cod 1750dr/€5.14. Open daily 5-11:30pm.)

🔊📷 **ENTERTAINMENT AND NIGHTLIFE.** With each sunset, the sun-baked masses migrate inland from the beach toward uniformly priced beer (600-700dr/€1.76-2.05) at jubilant bars on Ermou; later there is a second exodus to a handful of popular dance clubs. **Chaplin's,** on Ermou by the beach, is one of the most popular 24hr. party spots: they host a handful of dawn-to-dawn beach parties during the summer—keep a lookout for their posters. (☎85 662. Shots 500dr/€1.47.) **Jimmy's Pub** (☎85 643) inland on Ermou, is a British bar with Guinness on tap. Additional stimuli include soul music and TVs, making Jimmy's a popular spot to watch soccer. Head up to the free-of-cover **club** above the pub. The most convenient option for Ermou indulgers is **Sinners,** a popular stop-over for house and techno music. (Cover 2000dr/€5.87 includes one drink.) Friendly, new, and posh **Millennium** is set in a shopping center on Rhodes-Faliraki, and draws Faliraki's dance club junkies. (☎86 603. Cover 1800dr/€5.28 includes first drink.)

LINDOS Λινδος   ☎0244

With whitewashed houses clustered beneath a castle-capped acropolis, Lindos is perhaps the most picturesque town on Rhodes. World-famous writers, poets, painters, and professors congregate here. Vines and flowers line narrow streets, and pebble mosaics carpet courtyards. The town's appeal hasn't remained a secret, however, and in summer, the streets of Lindos make the City of Rhodes look like a desert island. The crowds, astronomical prices, room shortage, and notorious heat make lovely Lindos a better destination outside of July and August.

📷📷 **ORIENTATION AND PRACTICAL INFORMATION.** Lindos is a pedestrian-only city: all traffic stops at **Pl. Eleftherias,** where you'll find the **bus** and **taxi** stations. Buses to and from Lindos fill quickly, so it's best to arrive early. Buses connect Lindos to: **Calypso** (3 per day, 800dr/€2.35); **Esperides** (3 per day, 850dr/€2.50); **Faliraki** (13 per day 7am-6pm, 1050dr/€3.08); **Kolymbia Beach** (3 per day, 500dr/€1.47); **Pefkos** (8 per day, 500dr/€1.47); and **Rhodes Town** (13 per day, 1050dr/€3.08). Check with the tourist office about recent changes and updates to the bus schedules. **Excursion boats** from Rhodes depart at 9am and return at 5pm, hitting **Rhodes Town** and **Turkey,** among other pit stops, as they travel along the coast.

There is a tourist information booth with a very helpful and friendly staff in the plateia where buses enter town. They provide bus and excursion schedules, general info on Lindos and on the Acropolis, and help with accommodations. They also sell stamps, postcards, and newspapers. (☎31 900; fax 31 288. Open daily 7:30am-9pm.) Next to the tourist info is a 24hr. **Telebank ATM,** and past that **Acropolis** Street leads through the eastern part of town and up to the acropolis. **Apostolou Pavlou,** another main street, runs perpendicular to Acropolis just past the **Church of the Assumption of Madonna,** whose stone belfry rises above the middle of town. Note that most locals don't often use street names; it's best to orient yourself around shops and cafes, and to ask for directions accordingly. **Pallas Travel,** on Acropolis, **exchanges currency,** helps with accommodations, and arranges excursions. (☎31 494; fax 31 595. Open daily 8am-11pm. Closed in winter.)

Services huddle at the intersection of Apostolou Pavlou and Acropolis. The **pharmacy** is just past Yianni's Bar. (☎31 294. Open daily 9am-11pm.) Sheila Markiou, an American expat with oodles of humor and character, runs the superb 📷**Lindos Lending Library** with more than 7000 English, Italian, German, French, and Greek books. You can buy a book second-hand or bring an old book and trade it in. To get there, walk to Pallas Travel and bear right where the road forks; the library is up to the left. (☎31 443. Open M-Sa 9am-8pm, Su 9am-1pm.) Sheila also runs a **laundry** service out of the store (2500dr/€7.34 wash, dry, and soap). The **medical clinic** is to the left before the church. (☎31 224. Open M-Th 8am-2pm, F noon-2pm.) **Lindianet Cafe** provides cheap year-round **Internet** services. (☎/fax 32 142. 1500dr/€4.40 per hr. Open daily 10am-11pm.) **Public toilets** are across from the information office near the taxi/bus station (100dr/€0.29). The **police** are at Ap. Pavlou 521. (☎31 223. Open M-F 8am-2pm; open 24hr. for emergencies.) The **post office** is uphill from the donkey stand. (☎31 314. Open M-F 7:30am-noon.) **Postal code:** 85107.

⌐ ACCOMMODATIONS. Package tours elbow into even the tiniest pensions, making Lindos a difficult place to spend the night. One option is to arrive in the morning before the tour buses rumble in and ask the tour companies' offices if they have any empty rooms. To reach **Pension Electra,** 85107 Lindos, from the main plateia, take the first left downhill after the donkey stand and follow signs for the acropolis. Electra has clean, bright, spacious rooms with A/C, fridge and bath. Common facilities include two full kitchens, a terrace for meals, and a central garden. (☎31 266. Reservations accepted. Doubles 14,000dr/€41.08, A/C 2000dr/€5.87 per night.) **Pension Katholiki,** around the corner from Electra, has clean rooms equipped with baths, kitchens, and access to a rooftop view; inquire about the few rooms with traditional Dodecanese loft beds. (☎31 445. Doubles 12,000-15,000dr/ €35.21-44.01. A/C 2000dr/€5.87 per night.) Nikos Kritikis, the owner of the travel agency **Village Holidays** next to Yiannis Bar, owns a handful of harbor-view rooms scattered in and around Lindos. (☎31 486; fax 31 344; vi-ho@otenet.gr. Doubles 12,000dr/€35.21; quads 20,000dr/€58.69.)

◖▨ FOOD AND NIGHTLIFE. Eating poses yet another challenge to the budget traveler in Lindos. Restaurant prices range from expensive to exorbitant, leaving souvlaki-pita bars, creperies (crepes start at 800dr/€2.35), and grocery stores on the two main streets as the only cheap alternatives. "Snack bar" shops serve the healthiest option in Lindos (yogurt with honey and fresh fruit 700dr/€2.05). With the harbor below and the Acropolis above, ▨**Agostino's** restaurant provides stunning scenery and old-school *moussaka* (2000dr/€5.87) served in an earthenware pot. (☎31 218. Entrees 1500-3500dr/€4.43-10.27. Open daily 6pm-midnight.) To prepare for the climb to the acropolis, or to refuel upon your descent, have some *foccaccia* (600-900dr/€1.76-2.64) or *panzerotti* (800dr/€2.35) at **Forno Bakery,** around the corner from the bookstore. All ingredients are imported from Italy and handmade by the owner. (Open daily 8am-3pm and 6-8pm.)

Lindos' nightlife is relatively tame; municipal law requires music to stop at midnight. If you are not ready to call it a night, head to **Amphitheatre,** an open-air nightclub not far from town. Free cabs shuttle you from the Lindos plateia to the dance floor, where you can kick up your heels as you overlook the acropolis and the sea. (1500dr/€4.40 cover includes first drink. Open daily midnight-4am.) The biggest and rowdiest bar in Lindos is **Yiannis Bar.** The joint starts jumpin' around 11pm and, despite municipal rules, rocks on until the morning's wee hours. It has the largest selection of cocktails in town—get off on an orgasm cocktail (1500dr/ €4.40) as the night turns into day. (☎31 245. Open daily 8am-3am.)

◘ SIGHTS. Lindos's ancient **acropolis** stands on sheer cliffs 125m above town, caged by scaffolding and the walls of a Crusader fortress. From the highest point on the acropolis, the lowest point in the city is visible. Excavations by the Danish Archaeological School between 1902 and 1912 yielded everything from 5000-year-old Neolithic tools to a plaque inscribed by a priest of Athena in 99 BC that lists the dignitaries who visited Athena's Temple—Hercules, Helen of Troy, Menelaus, Alexander the Great, and the King of Persia. The winding path up to the acropolis is veiled in lace tablecloths sold by local women, making for a frilly ascent. Right before the final incline, don't miss the ancient Greek *trireme* (a rectangular relief etched into rock), which the artist Pythokreitos carved into the cliffside as a symbol of Lindos's inextricable ties with the sea. Lined with staircases, the daunting 13th-century **Crusader castle** towers over the entrance to the site. The arcade, built around 200 BC at the height of Rhodes's glory, originally consisted of 42 columns laid out in the shape of the Greek letter "Π." The large stone blocks arranged against the back wall served as bases for bronze statues that have been long since melted down. The remains of the **Temple of the Lindian Athena,** built by the tyrant Kleoboulos in the 6th century BC, come into view at the top of the steps. Legend has it that this area, once a tremendously important religious site, held a temple as early as 1510 BC. Kleoboulos's tomb, inscribed with Aristotle's timeless maxim, "Nothing in excess," is across the way. At the southwest foot of the acropolis rest the remains of the **ancient theater.**

Heading out of the castle, make a U-turn to your left to reach the imposing **Doric Stoa** (arcade), whose 13 restored columns dominate the entire level. Donkey rides to the acropolis aren't worth the fare (1000dr/€2.93 one-way), as the 10min. walk isn't strenuous. A cave called the **Voukopion,** on the north side of the rock face (visible from the donkey path), may have been used for special sacrifices that could not be performed in the acropolis. The cave probably dates from the 9th century BC, and was later transformed into a sanctuary for Athena by the Dorians. (☎31 258. Open M 12:30pm-6:40pm, Tu-Su 8am-6:40pm. 1200dr/€3.52, students 600dr/€1.76. Ask for the pamphlet which gives a history and explanation of the layout.

■ DAYTRIPS ON RHODES

EPTA PIGES. Eleven kilometers south of Faliraki, just before Kolymbia, a road to the right leads 3km down to Epta Piges. Constructed by Italians seeking potable water for nearby Kolymbia, the aqueduct now quenches the thirst of thrill-seekers, who slide through 150m of pitch-black tunnel. Laughers and shriekers alike end up in a large, picturesque freshwater pool; if the destination sounds nicer than the journey, take the path next to the tunnel that is used to return from the pool. A decent streamside taverna (with peacocks) sits at the entrance before the tunnel. To get there, ask a Lindos/Archangelos bus driver to let you off at the tunnel. Continue inland past Epta Piges to visit the 13th- and 15th-century frescoes of the Byzantine **Church of Agios Nikolaos Fountoucli,** 3km past Eleousa. Three **buses** per day stop at Eleousa on the way to Rhodes. Villagers in **Arthipoli,** 4km away, rent rooms.

TSAMBIKAS MONASTERY. From the coast road, Tsambikas Monastery is marked by the restaurant that sits below it. A 1km road leads up to the restaurant; the Byzantine cloister and its panoramic views are 1km farther up a steep trail. The monastery takes its name from the sparks *(tsambas)* that were reportedly seen atop the hill. Upon climbing up to investigate, locals discovered a Cypriot icon of the Virgin Mary that had mysteriously appeared here, miles and miles from home. Angry Cypriots ordered that the icon be returned, and the locals obliged, but the icon kept returning. By the third time, everyone agreed that Rhodes must be the icon's proper home. To this day, some women ascend the mountain to pray to the Virgin Mary for fertility. Should the prayer work its magic, junior should be named Tsambikos if it's a boy or Tsambika if it's a girl. Maybe it's not your first choice, but a deal's a deal. One bus runs to the long, flat, and sandy **Tsambika Beach,** 1km south of the turn-off for the monastery (750dr/€2.20). Any bus that passes the turn-off should let you off here for a worthwhile day in the sun.

KAMIROS. The smallest of the three ancient cities of the Rhodian State, Kamiros nonetheless surpasses Ialyssos and Rhodes in intricacy and preservation. The history of this ancient city has been pieced together from the evidence found in its cemeteries. People have lived here since Mycenaean times, but after the devastating earthquake of 226 BC, the city was reconstructed with a typical Hellenistic layout and design. The cistern on the north side of the temple dates from the 5th or 6th century BC, and the stone stoa (shaped like the Greek letter Π) is from at least the 2nd century BC. Visit the precinct of Athena Kamiras on the acropolis to get a clear sense of the city's impressive chessboard layout. *(Take a bus from Rhodes to Kamiros (2 per day 10am and 1:30pm, 1150dr/€3.37). ☎40 037 or 75 674. Open Tu-F 8am-6:40pm. 800dr/€2.35, non-EU students 400dr/€1.17, EU students free.)*

You can hike to picturesque **Profitis Ilias,** where three old Italian hotels long for restoration beside gorgeous orchards. Follow dirt roads to Salakos, where a path leads straight to the peak. *(Buses (5 per day, 900dr/€2.64) from Rhodes run to Salakos.)*

VALLEY OF BUTTERFLIES. Seven kilometers inland from the village of **Theologos, Petaloudes,** or the **Valley of Butterflies,** is a popular visiting spot with or without the company of the little fluttering guys. During the summer, Jersey tiger moths flock to the valley's Styrax trees, attracted to their resin (also used in making incense) and the area's unique shadiness. While resting to live out their final days in the trees, the moths fast, living only on water and body fat to conserve energy for rigorous mating sessions. After the deed is done, they die of starvation. The valley and its many trees are worth a walk throughout the year, but are a particularly welcoming reprieve from summer's sun-beaten coasts. The valley is accessible from an entrance next to an old mill, or from the main entrance farther uphill. The trail winds around a blue-green stream that collects in lily-covered pools and glides under cute little bridges. Avoid clapping and stomping to incite the moths to flight, like some foolish visitors do: noise interrupts the moths' action. *(☎81 801. Open daily 8:30am-sunset. 500dr/€1.47.)* Hike up 300m from the end of the 1km trail to the **Monastery of Kalopetra,** home to a restored mosaic, where fresh yogurt and honey from the caretakers accompany a panoramic view of the island.

KOS Κως

Kos is the spoiled child of the group. You know it at once without even going ashore. It is green, luxuriant, and a little disheveled.
    —Lawrence Durrell

Medical and literary titans have lounged on these beaches. Kos is the sacred land of **Asclepius,** god of healing, the birthplace of **Hippocrates,** father of modern medicine and the Hippocratic oath, and the home of the poet **Theocritus** and his teacher **Philetas.** In ancient times, Kos was a trading power with a population of 160,000. In Byzantine, medieval, and more recent history, its story has mirrored that of the other Dodecanese in passing under Italian, German, and British rule.

Rivaling Rhodes in sheer numbers, Kos Town tends to draw a younger, louder, more intoxicated crowd, while relatively unexplored rural Kos attracts the more sedate traveler in search of stunning beaches and serene mountain villages.

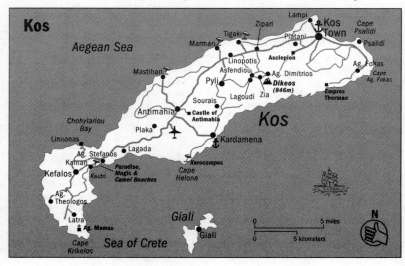

Kos Town

🏠 ACCOMMODATIONS
Hotel Afendoulis, 7
Kos Camping, 6
Pension Alexis, 4
Studios Nitsa, 1

🍎 FOOD
Ampavris Taverna, 5
Hellas, 3
Nick the Fisherman, 2

KOS TOWN ☎ 0242

In Kos Town, the minarets of Ottoman mosques spike above Italian mansions, the massive walls of a Crusader fortress, and scattered ruins from the Archaic, Classical, Hellenistic, and Roman eras. The combination of ancient, medieval, and modern makes Kos a historian's paradise by day; while its bars delight by night.

⬅ TRANSPORTATION

Flights: Olympic Airways, Vas. Pavlou 22 (☎ 28 331 or 332), has flights to Athens (4 per day, from 18,100dr/€53.23). Open M-F 8am-3pm. Sa-Su call 51 567. Olympic runs a bus (1200dr/€3.53) from their Kos Town office 2-4 times per day. Schedule posted. Taxis from Kos Town to the airport 6000dr/€17.65.

Ferries: To: **Kalymnos** (1¼hr., 1-3 per day, 1800dr/€5.28); **Leros** (2½hr., 1 per day, 2500dr/€7.34); **Patmos** (4hr., 1-2 per day, 3200dr/€9.41); **Piraeus** (11-15hr., 2-3 per day, 5200dr/€15.29); **Rhodes** (4hr., 2 per day, 4200dr/€12.35). 2 per week to: **Nisyros** (2400dr/€7.06); **Symi** (2800dr/€8.24); **Tilos** (2500/€7.35). Greek (and Turkish) boats run to **Bodrum,** Turkey every morning (10,000-13,000dr/€29.41-38.23 round-trip). Turkish boats leave in the afternoon and return the next morning (8000-13,000dr/€23.53-38.23 round-trip). Since travel is international, prices are not regulated by the Greek government.

Flying Dolphins: 2 per day to **Kalymnos** (3200dr/€9.41) and **Samos** (6700dr/
€19.71). 1 per day to: **Leros** (4300dr/€12.65) and **Patmos** (5700dr/€16.76). Two
per week to: **Agathonisi** (6200dr/€18.24) and **Tilos** (4200dr/€12.35). Also to: **Fourni**
(3 per week, 7300dr/€21.47); **Lipsi** (6 per week, 4200dr/€12.35); **Nisyros** (3 per
week, 4120dr/€12.12); **Symi** (1 per week, 5200dr/€15.29); and **Rhodes** (2 per day,
6800dr/€19.96).

Buses: (☎22 292; fax 20 263). Leave from Kleopatras street near the inland end of Pavlou behind the Olympic Airways office. M-Sa to: **Antimachia** (40min., 6 per day, 500/
€1.47dr); **Kardamena** (45min., 6 per day, 650dr/€1.91); **Kefalos** (1hr., 6 per day,
850dr/€2.50); **Marmari** (35min., 12 per day, 400dr/€1.18); **Mastihari** (35min., 5
per day, 600dr/€1.76); **Pyli** (30min., 5 per day, 400dr/€1.18); and **Tigaki** (30min.,
12 per day, 400dr/€1.18). Schedules reduced Su. Schedule posted by the stop; buy
tickets on the bus.

City Buses: Akti Koundouriotou 7 (☎26 276), on the water. To: **Asclepion** (15min., 16
per day); **Agios Fokas** (50 per day); **Messaria** (9 per day); and **Thermae** (20min., 9 per
day). Fares 150-250dr/€0.44-0.74.

Taxis: (☎22 777 or 22 333), near the inland end of the Avenue of Palms.

Rentals: Laws restricting rentals to those with proper motorbike licenses are more strictly
enforced here than on other islands. Driving behavior does not reflect this stringency,
however, and drivers should exercise caution. **Mike's** (☎21 729) is at the corner of
Amerikis and Psaron. Mopeds 3000-5000dr/€8.82-14.71 per day. Bikes 700-900dr/
€2.06-2.65 per day. **George**, P. Tsaldari 3 (☎28 480), near the port authority, rents
quality bikes. Mopeds from 4000-5000dr/€11.76-14.71 per day. Bikes 500-1000dr/
€1.47-2.94. Open daily 8:30am-8pm.

■■ ORIENTATION AND PRACTICAL INFORMATION

The dignified walls of the Castle of the Knights of St. John overwhelm the vista as
ferries pull into the harbor of Kos Town. Walk left (facing inland) from the harbor
to reach the tree-lined **Avenue of Palms,** also known as **Finikon.** Continuing along the
waterfront past the Palms leads to **Vassileos Georgios** and the rocky beach alongside it. Turn right onto the Palms, follow it to the next corner of the fortress, and
you'll come upon **Akti Koundouriotou,** another waterfront street that wraps around
the harbor. Here you'll find the city bus station, boats to Turkey, travel agencies,
restaurants, and Kos's thriving nightlife. Branching inland off Akti Koundouriotou
are the town's main arteries: **El. Venizelou** leads through a row of travel agencies
into the shopping district; **Megalou Alexandrou,** a few blocks down, heads to **Pl.
Palaiologou,** the ruins of ancient Kos Town, and eventually the inland villages. The
town's other crowded, sandy beach begins near the end of Akti Koundouriotou.

Tourist Office: Vas. Georgiou 1 (☎24 460 or 28 724; fax 21 111; dotkos@hol.gr). Free
maps and info on transportation, events, and accommodations. **Greek National Tourist
Office,** on Akti Miaouli in the same building as the tourist police, provides maps, brochures, and schedules. Open M-F 8am-8pm, Sa 8am-3pm.

Tourist Agencies: No single agency in Kos has comprehensive boat information. 2 large
ferry companies, **DANE** and **GA,** and 2 hydrofoil lines, **Ilio** and **Dodecanese Express,**
serve Kos and its neighbors. **Pulia Tours,** Vas. Pavlou 3 (☎26 388, 24 194 or 21 130;
fax 26 388), near the waterfront end of the main road, sells hydrofoil tickets, offers
rental assistance and **currency exchange.** Open daily 7am-11pm.

GA Office (☎28 545; fax 24 864), on Navarhou Ioanniou across from the National
Bank, serves the other lines and offers similar tourist services. Open 9am-10:30pm.

Banks: National Bank (☎22 167), behind the Archaeological Museum, 1 block inland
from the water on A.P. Ioannidi. 24hr. **ATM.** Open M-Th 8am-2pm, F 8am-1:30pm. After
hours, **exchange currency** at any travel agency along the waterfront.

American Express: (☎28 426). Full AmEx services at the **Credit Bank** (*Trapeza Pisteos*),
Akti Kountouriotou 5, near the bus stop. Open M-Th 7:45am-2pm, F 7:45am-1:30pm.

Emergency: (☎22 100). **Ambulance:** ☎22 300.

General Information: ☎131.

Police: (☎22 222), on Akti Miaouli in the big yellow building beside the castle. Some English spoken. Open 24hr. **Tourist police** (☎22 444) in the same building. Open daily 7:30am-2pm.

Hospital: (☎28 050). Mitropoleos 13, between El. Venizelou and Hippocrates. For **information** call ☎28 013. Open 24hr.

Telephones: OTE (☎23 399), at L. Virona and Xanthou, around the corner from the post office. Open M-F 7am-2:30pm.

Internet Access: Del Mar Internet Cafe, Megalou Alexandrou 4A (☎24 244), is small and crowded. Limited service at 1500dr/€4.41 per hr. Open daily 9am-late.

Post Office: El. Venizelou 14 (☎22 250). Follow signs from Vas. Pavlou, which lead past Pl. Eleftherias and the fruit market, and turn left onto Venizelou. Open M-F 7:30am-2pm. **Postal Code:** 85300.

🏠 ACCOMMODATIONS

Hotel vacancies are rare in summer, so start searching for rooms early. Most inexpensive places are on the right side of town if you're facing inland. It's best to seek out your own room and avoid Kos's dock hawks if your boat docks in the middle of the night, you may have no choice. Camping on public land is illegal.

🏨 **Pension Alexis,** Herodotou 9 (☎28 798 or 25 594). Take the 1st right off Megalou Alexandrou, on the back left corner of the first intersection. The aromas of fresh jasmine from the garden will delight you almost as much as Sonia and Alex's hospitality. If rooms are full, the proprietor will set you up with a mattress and sheets on the patio or cut you a deal at his elegant Hotel Afendoulis. Romantic verandas and common baths. Prices are flexible, especially if you're carrying *Let's Go*. Doubles 5500-8500dr/€16.18-25; triples 9000-10,000dr/€26.47-29.41.

Hotel Afendoulis, Evrilpilou 1 (☎/fax 25 321 or 25 797), down Vas. Georgiou. Owned by the same hospitable Alexis of Pension Alexis. All rooms have private baths and a balcony overhanging the courtyard. Doubles 7500-12,000dr/€22.06-35.29; basement rooms 6000-7500dr/€17.63-22.06.

Studios Nitsa, Averop 47 (☎25 810). Heading away from the castle, follow the main beach road around the port until it veers left; Nitsa will be on the left. Well-kept rooms come with bath, balcony, and kitchenette. Doubles 7000-14,000dr/€20.59-41.18; triples 9000-16,000dr/€26.47-47.06; quads 11,000-18,000dr-€32.35-52.94.

Kos Camping (☎23 910 or 23 275), 3km southeast from the center and accessible by public transport. Guests come back year after year to this family-operated campground to escape the frenzy of Kos Town. Mini-market, bar, laundry facilities, cooking room, post office service, pool, and security boxes. Buses run to and from the center every 30min. You can bring your own tent (1100dr/€3.24) or rent one (1300dr/€3.82).

🍴 FOOD

The fruit and vegetable **market** in Pl. Eleftherias, on Vas. Pavlou, inside a large yellow building with a picture of grapes over the doors, caters to tourists and is not as inexpensive as it looks; mini-markets have cheaper fruit (open M-F 7am-9pm, Sa 7am-6pm, Su 10am-2pm).

🍴 **Ampavris,** (☎25 696), on Ampavris. Take E. Grigoriou and then turn onto Ampavris, the road next to Casa Romana. It's about a 1km walk up the road on your left. The father and son tandem cooks and waits on tables. Stuffed flower buds 950dr/€2.79; main entrees 1500-2000dr/€3-5.50).

Hellas, (☎ 22 609) Psaron 7, at corner of Amerikis. Huge portions of tasty Greek dishes in a service-friendly, relaxing atmosphere. Lamb *kleftiko* 2300dr/€6.76, *moussaka* 1600dr/€4.71. Good vegetarian options available. Open daily 4-11pm.

Nick the Fisherman, Averof 21, at corner of Alikarnasou. Daily catches straight to your plate at the best *psarotaverna* in town, approved by all the locals. Ask for Larry's friendly service. Mussels 2000dr/€5.88, sea-urchins 1800dr/€5.29; entrees from 2000-3000dr/€5.88-8.82. Open 1pm-late.

👁 SIGHTS

ROMAN RUINS. The run-down field of ruins bounded by Nafklirou, Hippocrates, and the waterfront was once the agora; it's now dominated by a population of sunbaking youth. The remains of a **Temple of Aphrodite** and the more impressive 2nd-century AD **Temple of Hercules** lie beside two Roman roads: the **Cardo** (axis), perpendicular to Grigoriou, and the **Decumana** (broadest), parallel to Grigoriou and intersecting Cardo. Nearby is an ancient gymnasium, a swimming pool from the Roman era, and an early Christian basilica built over a Roman bath. At the end of the Decumana, the wood-sheltered 3rd-century AD **House of Europa** has a mosaic floor depicting Europa's abduction by that bully, Zeus. The **odeum,** a well-preserved Roman theater, lies across the street. The 3rd-century AD **Casa Romana,** uncovered by an Italian archaeologist in 1933, is down Grigoriou. The meager ruins of a **Temple of Dionysus** stand opposite the Casa Romana. *(Open 24hr. Free.)*

ARCHAEOLOGICAL MUSEUM. Hellenistic and late Roman sculptures dominate excavations from the island's many archaeological sights. A celebrated statue, found at the Kos Odeon and presumed to be Hippocrates, stands in the northwest room. A 2nd-century AD Roman mosaic in the central courtyard depicts Hippocrates and a colleague entertaining the god Asclepius. Statues of Dionysos, Artemis, and Aphrodite occupy the North room and Atrium. *(In Pl. Eleftherias. ☎ 28 326. Open Tu-Su 8am-2:30pm. 800dr/€2.35, students 400dr/€1.18.)*

CASTLE. Ironically, the invading Knights of St. John, who built the massive 15th-century castle, came to Kos to heal the sick. The once-removable bridge that marks the entrance to the Square of Hippocrates linked the island castle to the mainland. Destroyed by an earthquake in 1495, the fortress was rebuilt by Grand Master Pierre d'Aubusson. In the 16th century, elaborate double walls and inner moats reinforced the castle to withstand Ottoman raids; now, it's one of the best-preserved examples of medieval architecture in Greece. *(Take the bridge from Pl. Platanou across Finikis. ☎ 27 927. Ask for the helpful pamphlet available at the door. Open Tu-Su 8:30am-3pm. 1000dr/€2.94, students 500dr/€1.47, EU students free.)*

OTHER SITES. The gigantic **Plane Tree of Hippocrates,** in Pl. Platanou, allegedly planted by the great physician 2400 years ago, has grown to an enormous 12m diameter, so big that metal bars now support its branches. It's alluring to envision Hippocrates teaching and writing beneath its noble foliage; it's deflating to realize that the tree is only 500 years old. A spring beside the tree leaks toward an ancient sarcophagus used by the Ottomans as a cistern for the **Hadji Hassan Mosque.** Behind the tree stands what used to be the Italian Governor's Palace; it hasn't lost much of its big-wig aura over the years. It's now home to the police, justice, and governmental offices. The most impressive Ottoman structure is the **Defterdar Mosque** in Pl. Eleftherias. Nearby, on Diakou, is the abandoned art deco **Synagogue of Kos,** in use until World War II. The city's Byzantine **Greek Orthodox Cathedral** looms on the corner of Korai and Ag. Nikolaou. Near the Casa Romana are the ruins of an even older (5th century BC) and more striking Hellenic mansion. *(Open Tu-Su 8:30am-2:30pm. 600dr/€1.76, students and seniors 300dr/€0.88.)*

NIGHTLIFE

Prepare for masses of snugly clad youths in search of a good time. Most bars are in two districts. The first is around **Exarhia** (a.k.a. **bar street,** between Akti Koundouriotou and the ancient agora), the area around **Vas. Pavlou.** Beers go for 800-1000dr/€2.35-2.94, cocktails for 2000dr/€5.88. Most places open at 9pm, fill by 11pm, and rock on until dawn. The second district, **Porfiriou,** hops by day as sun bunnies pregame beachside for the evening's trek to the waterfront dance clubs. **Orfeas** (☎25 713), an outdoor cinema on the corner of Fenaretis and Vas. Georgiou, shows American movies (2500dr/€7.35).

- **Fashion Club,** Kanari 2 (☎22 592), by the dolphin statue rotary. Divine (peanut-vending machines) meets divine (elegant candles) at Kos's most ostentatious club, where runway models are projected on viewing screens inside. 3000dr/€8.82 cover includes first drink. No cover for the large TV-filled cafe in front. Club open daily 11pm-4am.

- **Hamam Club** (☎24 938) next to the taxi station in Pl. Diagoras. The exotic former bathhouse now refreshes and soothes you with aural massage: live outdoor acoustic sets play bluegrass and country music until midnight. After midnight, pick up the tempo inside with live international DJs spinning into the wee hours.

  Heaven (☎23 874), on Zouroudi along the waterfront. Opposite the beach—get your drink on as you soak up some sun. A loud, popular outdoor disco by night. Cover 2000dr/€5.88. Open Su-Th 10am-4am, Sa-Su 10am-dawn.

DAYTRIPS FROM KOS

ASCLEPION Ασκληπιειον. The ancient sanctuary of **Asclepion** is devoted to the healer god. In the 5th century BC, **Hippocrates** founded the world's first medical school here, forever enhancing the quality of life. Combining early priests' techniques with his own, Hippocrates made Kos the foremost medical center in ancient Greece. Present-day doctors travel here to take their Hippocratic oaths.

Most of the ruins at the Asclepion date from the 2nd and 3rd centuries BC. Carved into a hill overlooking Kos Town, the Aegean, and Asia Minor, the complex contained three levels. A sacred forest of cypress and pine trees still adjoins the site. If you ignore the swarming tourists and wander off to the wonderful world of make-believe, it's easy to envision the structures as they once stood. Inside, you'll find 2nd-century AD Roman baths, complete with *natatio* (pool), *tepidarium* (lukewarm waters), and *caldarium* (sauna). The three stacked levels, called *andirons*, remain fascinating. The lowest *andiron* holds a complex of 3rd-century AD Roman baths and a preserved cistern. Climb the 3rd-century BC steps to the remarkable second *andiron* and the elegant 2nd-century AD columns. The 60-step climb to the third *andiron* leads to the forested remnants of the **Main Temple of Asclepius** and an overview of the site, Kos Town, and the Turkish coast opposite. Although the site is remarkably preserved, much of its structure is gone: it was used for raw material by the Knights of Saint John in the building of the Kos Castle. (*3.5km northwest of Kos Town. Take the **bus** in summer (15min.), or a bike or moped. Follow the sign west off the main road, and go as straight as you can. Taxis are 500dr/€1.47.* ☎28 763. *Open daily Tu-Su 8am-6:30pm. 800dr/€2.35, students 400dr/€1.18.*)

CENTRAL KOS. Claustrophobes will be pleased at how quickly Kos Town's urban congestion gives way to pastoral landscapes north of town. The island's northern reaches stretch out flat, with bike-laned roads. Go back toward the main road, east of town, to pedal past a sandy, crowded stretch on the way to the hot springs of **Empros Thermae,** near road's end. They're marked by a cantina. **Lampi Beach** is at the northernmost tip of the island. West of Kos town and heading South, you'll find the tourist strip mall of **Tigaki** (10km west of Kos), where umbrellas and beachside tavernas reign. The beach of **Marmari,** farther south, mimics Tigaki with multicolored umbrellas blanketing the sand, but between the two lies a secluded nude beach. If cycling or motorbiking doesn't rev you up, buses run to **Empros Thermae** (9 per day), **Lampi** (34 per day), **Marmari** (10 per day), and **Mastihari** (4 per day).

The main road out of Kos Town heads 9km southwest to the modern village of **Zipari,** with the ruins of the early **Christian Basilica of St. Paul.** From there, a twisting road slowly winds through the green foothills of the Dikeos Mountains to **Asfendiou,** five small settlements that you can hike in perfect solitude. Buses from Kos go to Asfendiou (40min., 3 per day, 400dr/€1.18). Continue up this road to **Zia,** a delightful and refreshing small village set in the forests of Mt. Dikeos, host to spectacular island views and worth some wandering time. **Ag. Georgios,** in the center of town, also accommodates incredible 13th- and 14th-century frescoes. South of **Lagoudi,** the prettiest of the five villages, the road becomes narrower (a mule path) and the hills become wilder. Uphill 8km farther, you'll come to the compact ruins of old **Pyli,** which include 14th-century frescoes in a Byzantine church built within a castle. Buses run from Kos (30min., 5 per day, 400dr/€1.18).

SOUTHERN KOS   ☎ 0945

Hills, ravines, and the occasional pasture roll across Southern Kos, which is edged by the best **beaches** on the island. Get a moped to explore more freely; a private taxi will also do the trick. Heading south will land you at the most stunning beaches of the island. **Camel** is mildly busy and beautiful. **Paradise** is popular and has its own bus stop. Farther north, **Magic** has unsullied waves of pure white sand and astonishingly blue water. The bus will let you off at any of the beaches.

A few oceanside ancient columns distinguish **Kefalos,** Kos's ancient capital. Get out of this crowded, bland town to the surrounding beaches. North of Kefalos, picturesque **Limionas Beach** includes a small harbor, a smaller beach, and crashing waves. Above the beach, continue on the road past the Limionas Restaurant to the ▓**Miltos Taverna,** a true treasure for fish-lovers. (Most fish 5000-8000dr/€14.71-23.53 per kg. Open daily 9am-midnight.) Continue farther south past Limionas to **Agios Theologos,** a deserted, pebbly beach perfect for night swimming.

KALYMNOS Καλυ μνος

In Kalymnos the infant's paint-box has been at work again on the milky slopes of the mountain.
—Lawrence Durrell

Although the first inhabitants of Kalymnos have yet to be identified, the ruins at Embrio and Vathis suggest that Phoenicians successfully colonized the island around 2000 BC. Kalymnos, however, is better known for its sponge-diving industry than its ancient history. In years past, Kalymnian men would spend five or six months of the year diving in the Libyan Sea, south of Muammar Al-Quaddafi's Line of Death. Sponges still lurk in warehouses, tourist kiosks and factories, and restaurant display-cases, harkening back to the island's glory days as the sponge capital of the world. But the sponges are dying off along with Kalymnos's economy. West-coast tourism has resuscitated the economy somewhat, leaving the interior rather barren. The rugged central mountains cascade into wide beaches and blue-green water, luring the occasional intrepid mountaineer.

POTHIA Ποθια   ☎ 0243

During the turn-of-the-century Italian occupation, locals antagonized the Italians by painting their houses blue, Greece's national color. Pink and green buildings have since infiltrated Pothia's blued streets and, although slightly grayed, this relatively large town (pop. 11,500) remains more colorful than its whitewashed Aegean counterparts. Behind the bustle of the busy port, narrow back streets are lined with stellar classical leftovers. Pothia isn't made for tourists—there are few rooms, few agencies, and few attractions—but that's part of the appeal.

⊏ TRANSPORTATION

Ferries: To: **Astypalea** (7hr., 1 per week, 2700dr/€7.94); **Kos** (1hr., 2 per day, 1800dr/
€5.29); **Leros** (2hr., 2 per day, 1800dr/€5.29); **Mastihari** (3 per day, 900dr/€2.65
one-way); **Nisyros** (3hr., 2 per week, 1900dr/€5.59); **Patmos** (3hr., 2 per day,
2700dr/€7.94); **Piraeus** (12hr., 2 per day, 7200dr/€21.18); **Rhodes** (6hr., 2 per day,
4400dr/€12.94); **Symi** (4hr., 1 per week, 3400dr/€10); **Tilos** (4hr., 1 per week,
2500dr/€7.35). Daily **excursions** head to island beaches on **Pserimos** (2000dr/
€5.88 round-trip), **Vlichadi** (2500dr/€7.35).

Flying Dolphins: To: **Agathonisi** (2 per week, 4980dr/€14.65); **Astypalea** (1 per week,
5500dr/€16.18); **Fourni** (1 per week, 7100dr/€20.88); **Ikaria** (1 per week, 6180dr/
€18.18); **Kos** (3-4 per day, 3200dr/€9.41); **Leros** (3 per day, 3600dr/€10.59); **Lipsos** (2 per day, 3600dr/€10.59); **Patmos** (3 per day, 4900dr/€14.41); **Rhodes** (1 per
day, 9125dr/€26.84); **Samos** (1 per day/6145dr/€18.07); **Symi** (1 per week,
6785dr/€19.96); **Tilos** (1 per week, 4275dr/€12.57).

Buses: During the summer high season buses leave every hr. 8am-10pm (in low season
every two hrs.) to: **Kastelli** (50min., 250dr/€0.74) via **Hora** (10min.); **Myrties**
(20min.), **Massouri** (25min.), and **Panormos** (15min.). Fares 100-250dr/€0.29-0.74.
Also to: **Argos** (2 per day 7am-1:50pm, 200dr/€0.59); **Emporio** (3 per day, 300dr/
€0.88); **Plati Gialos** (3 per day 9:15am-3pm, 250dr/€0.74); and **Vilhadia** (7 per day
8am-7:30pm, 200dr/€0.88). Buses to western towns leave from the town hall in harbor center. Buses to **Vathis** (4 per day 6:30am-6pm, 300dr/€0.88) depart from the
northeast corner of the waterfront. Buy tickets before boarding at Themis mini-market,
next to the town hall, and insert them into the automated validating box on the bus, or
hand them to the driver.

Flights: Olympic Airways (☎29 265; fax 59 800). Take the first left past the National
Bank; it's 50m down on the left. Open daily 9am-1:30pm and 5-8:30pm.

Taxis: (☎50 300 or 50 303). Up Eleftherias, in Pl. Kyprou. Operate daily 7am-9pm.

Moped Rental: Magos Travel (☎28 777 or 28 652), on the waterfront near the port
police, rents scooters from 3500-5500dr/€10.29-16.18. **Scooteromania** (☎/fax 51
780) is down a little alley off the waterfront between the cafes. Mopeds 3000-5500dr/
€8.82-16.18. Open daily 8am-10pm. Both require International or EU Driver's License.

⊁▟ ORIENTATION AND PRACTICAL INFORMATION

Ferries arrive at the far left end of the port (facing inland). The road leading from
the dock bends around the waterfront until it runs into the large, cream-colored
municipal building, a church, and the town hall. Narrow, shop-lined **Eleftherias**
heads one-way inland at this point, leading to **Pl. Kyprou,** home to the **post office,
telephone, police,** and **taxis.** The waterfront road continues past town hall to a strip
of fish tavernas and one unparalleled sweet shop. The second most important avenue, **Venizelou,** intersects Eleftherias at the end of the harbor near **Agios Christos
Church.** Continue on this road to reach the western part of the island. Follow the
harbor promenade past the police station to access the road to Vathis. Most
streets in Pothia are unnamed, but following the landmarks is relatively easy.

Tourist Office: The little blue hut in the middle of the port, opposite the Neon Internet
C@fe. Very helpful advice and info on accommodation, bus and boat schedules, events
in town, and the rest of the island. (☎50 879. Open June-Oct. daily 9am-11pm.)

Tourist Agencies: It's best to consult more than one travel agency to fulfill all your tourist
needs. **Magos Travel** (☎28 777, 50 777, or 28 652; fax 22 608), on the waterfront
near the port police, sells hydrofoil tickets and **GA** ferry tickets. Open daily 9am-2pm
and 5-10pm. **DANE Sea Lines** (☎28 200; fax 29 125), next to the tourist office and
marked by a yellow flag, represents the other ferry line serving Kalymnos to Leros, Patmos, Kos, Rhodes, Piraeus, and others. They also have hydrofoil services (from 1400-
7000dr/€4.12-20.59). Open daily 9:30am-2pm and 5-9:30pm.

Banks: A few banks on the waterfront have full services, including **National Bank** (☎ 29 794), with an **ATM** and **currency exchange.** Open M-Th 8am-2pm, F 8am-1:30pm.

Police: (☎ 22 100). Go up Eleftherias and take the left inland road from the taxi plateia. English-speaking help can be found in a blue and yellow Neoclassical building on the right. Open 24hr.

Port Authority: (☎ 29 304), in the yellow building across from customs at the end of the dock. Provides ferry information. Open 24hr.

Hospital: (☎ 23 025), on the main road to Hora, 1.5km from Pothia. Open 24hr.

OTE: (☎ 28 956). From the taxi plateia up Eleftherias, take the inland road on the right across from the police. Open M-F 7:30am-3:10pm.

Internet: Neon Internet C@fe (☎ 28 343) is right on the waterfront in front of the ferry deck. Six computers and other video games. 1000dr/€2.93 per hr.

Post Office: (☎ 28 340), just past the police station on the right. Has **currency exchange.** Open M-F 7:30am-2pm. **Postal code:** 85200.

ACCOMMODATIONS

Pickings are slim in Pothia when it comes to lodgings. There are better options in Myrties or neighboring Plati Gialos, though transportation is tricky; the tourist office may help. Camping is legal on all the island's beaches, but uncommon.

Greek House (☎ 23 752). Greek House lets multiple, clean, pleasant rooms throughout Pothia. All with bath, fridge, and kitchen. The best way to find a Greek House room is to head for Ta Adelvia Flaskov, a *kafeneion* on the port a few meters away from the port authority. Singles 5000-6000dr/€14.71-17.65; doubles 8000-10,000dr/€23.53-29.41; triples 12,000-13,000dr/€35.29-38.23; rooms for a group of more than 4 also available. A/C 1000dr/€2.93 extra.

Pension Niki (☎ 48 135 or 28 528). If there are any vacancies, Niki will be waiting at the dock when you arrive. From Neon Cafe, take the small road inland to the right and walk straight; at the wedding store take a left, and ask for directions along the way. Rooms are in a quieter part of town all with baths. Doubles 5000-8000dr/€14.71-23.53.

FOOD AND ENTERTAINMENT

Nightlife in Pothia is pretty tame. Most folks enjoy a few drinks in the harbor bars and tavernas before heading to the clubs in Massouri.

Xefteris (☎ 628 642). From the town hall, head up Eleftherias and take the 1st right, then the 1st left directly into the taverna's outdoor garden. This place has been feeding the mouths and souls of Kefalonians for 85 years with fresh food cooked each morning by the 3 women who run the place. *Dolmades* (stuffed vine leaves) 1300dr/€3.82, stuffed zucchini 1200dr/€3.53. Open daily 11am-11pm.

Alachouzou (☎ 29 446) past the church and along the waterfront. This pastry-lover's paradise has been making its 5 classic honey-drenched Greek desserts for over 35 years, and it has perfected all of them. Try the house specialty, *galaktobouriko* (custard sandwiched between *phyllo* dough and drenched in sweet syrup; 500dr/€1.47. Open daily 8am-2:30pm and 6pm-midnight.

Navtikos Omilos Restaurant. Isolated at the far left end of the harbor (facing inland). Nothing fancy, but good, simple food in large portions with a relaxing view to the ocean. Spaghetti *neapolitana* 800dr/€2.35. Open daily 8am-3pm and 6:30-11pm.

Apothiki (☎ 51 890), past the town hall on the waterfront road. Pothia's trendiest nighttime haunt. Stylin' young locals sip *frappés* and cocktails as the music pounds. Open daily 10am-3pm and 5pm-2am.

Cine Oasis, at the end of a short alleyway plastered with movie posters. Nightly shows at 8:45 and 10:45pm. 1600dr/€4.71, children 1200dr/€3.53.

👁 SIGHTS

POTHIA. Learn first-hand about the island's historic industry at the sponge shop of **Nikolas Gourlas,** on the waterfront near the port police. Mr. Gourlas speaks English and will be happy to show you around the factory, where sponges are cleaned and chemically treated. (Sponges from 500dr/€1.47.) The **Nautical Museum,** on the second floor a few doors down from the town hall, houses traditional island wares and clothing in the one-room **Folk Museum,** and explores the life and work of the island's sponge divers. Read plaques about the island's famous industry, or ask the curator, a former diver, about the experience. (☎51 361. *Open M-F 8am-1:30pm, Sa-Su 10am-12:30pm. 500dr/€1.47, students 300dr/€0.88.*) Follow the blue signs from Venizelou to the **Archaeological Museum of Kalymnos,** in the former mansion of turn-of-the-century Kalymniot sponge barons Catherine and Nikolaos Vouvalis. (☎23 113. *Open Tu-Su 8:30am-2pm. Free.*)

From the port police, take the roads to the left to reach the beach at **Therma,** 2km away. Arthritic patients once came to the sanitarium to wade in its soothing **sulphur mineral baths.** A pleasant, crowded beach has replaced the baths as the main draw. A short walk around the bend leads to a quiet swimming spot. Tranquil **Vlichadia beach** (6km from Pothia), the island's only **scuba diving** site, lies west of Therma. Inconvenient buses keep it peaceful. Vlichadia also has a **Nautical Sponge Museum** at the port—ask at the tourist office in Pothia for more info.

VATHIS VALLEY. Although most of Kalymnos sprouts grass and wildflowers, thriving mandarins, limes, and grapevines cover the valley at Vathis (5½km northeast of Pothia), which begins at **Rina** village. There's no beach here, but you can swim from the pier. The exquisite scenery and quietude make sand unnecessary. Within swimming range on the north side of the inlet is **Daskaleios,** a stalagmite cave. In Rina, the **Hotel Galini** has decent rooms with baths and balconies. (☎31 241. Doubles 8500-10,000dr/€25-29.40.)

WEST COAST OF KALYMNOS

HORA

Pera Castro and Argos overlook the town of Hora, once Kalymnos's capital but now little more than another of Pothia's tentacles. One kilometer or so beyond Hora, just after the road begins to descend into Panormos, a few white steps and a sign by the side of the road lead to the **Church of Christ of Jerusalem.** Byzantine Emperor Arcadius built this church to thank God for sparing him in a storm while at sea. The half-domed stone blocks with carved inscriptions are from a 4th-century BC temple to Apollo that stood on the same site. By incorporating these pre-Christian buildings, the church served as a symbolic victory of Christianity over the Olympians. The beachside footpath leads to a quiet **cove** with strange rock formations. Bring your waterproof shoes to avoid sea urchins, if you dive in.

Hikers and **rock-climbers** have come to the right place. A guide to all the trails throughout Kalymnos (ranging from 2-7km) is available for free at the tourist office. Each walk starts and ends at different spots on the island, providing a range of landscapes from which to choose. **Rock-climbing** routes stretch along the west coast from Panormos to Armeos. You need your own equipment and there is very little organized guidance. There is, however, a free guide available at the tourist office in Pothia, detailing all the routes and their levels of difficulty.

If one of your walks leads you past the village of **Kantouni,** be sure to stop in at the 🖿**Domus Restaurant** on the waterfront. Don't miss the rooftop sunset and dance the night away at one of the most celebrated spots for quality nightlife. (☎47 959. Restaurant open daily 6:30pm-midnight, bar 11am-4am.) Encounter concealed natural platforms ideal for dives of all heights by venturing left (facing the sea) along the rocks of Kantouni beach. Another road from Panormos leads 2km to the sandy, flat and less crowded beach of **Plati Gialos,** one of the island's best. A stay at **Pension Plati Gialos** is sure to enchant guests. The pension is perched on a cliff with a memorable view of the coastline and the fresh, sun-filled rooms are a pleasure to wake up in. Follow the paved road to the top of the hill. (☎/fax 47 029; www.pension-plati-yialos.de. Doubles 7,000-10,000dr/€20.59-29.41.)

MASSOURI

The pebbly beaches and nightclubs at Massouri are always crowded. Establishments are open late, and the clientele arrives even later—always after midnight. With only one paved road running through Massouri, all the bars and clubs are within 5min. of one another on foot, and crowds in each vary from night to night. **Neon Internet C@fe** (☎48 318) has a branch here where an hour goes for 1000dr/€2.93. **Mariadis** taps Guinness (700dr/€2.05), hard cider (800dr/€2.35), and an assortment of cocktails (1800dr/€5.29). The funny barman is always up for a chat. **Nadir** bar hosts happy hour 8-9pm. (Open daily 6pm-late.) The real hot spots are the dance clubs **Club Dorian Tropical** (☎097 729 57 20) and Kalymnos's only outdoor club, **Kastro,** a little farther north on the main road.

MYRTIES

Besides its grey-sand beaches, Myrties is named for the abundance of wild blueberries that once covered its rolling hills. Short boat trips to the rocky islet of **Telendos** (15min., every 30min., 200dr/€0.59) start here. A city occupied the fault line where an AD 554 earthquake separated Telendos from Kalymnos, and traces of it have been found on the ocean floor, but the rift is invisible from the surface. The Roman ruins on Telendos are modest at best, but a few small, secluded beaches fringe the island. Turn right from the ferry dock for the best of them, including the get-naked variety. The Byzantine Monastery of **St. Constantine,** open only for liturgy, is past the beaches to the right. Its dome is visible from the Pothia-Emporios road near Myrties. Accommodations in Telendos fill up in August. Most pensions charge 5000-7000dr/€14.71-20.59 for a double.

PATMOS Πατμος

Declared the "Holy Island" by ministerial decree, Patmos makes its historical and religious significance as plain as day—portside signs warn that nudity and indecent behavior will not be tolerated here.

In ancient times, Patmians worshipped **Artemis,** the huntress said to have raised the island from the sea. **Orestes** built a grand temple to her after seeking refuge on Patmos from the Furies, who were pursuing him for murdering his mother Clytemnestra. With the arrival of **St. John,** exiled from Ephesus, Patmos became a center of fledgling Christianity. John purportedly wrote the **Book of Revelations** here, in a grotto overlooking the main town. His words "I...was on the isle that is called Patmos, for the word of God, and for the testimony of Jesus Christ" are the island's unofficial motto. In the 4th century AD, when Christianity spread with the Byzantine Empire, a basilica replaced the razed Temple of Artemis. In the 11th century, the fortified Monastery of St. John was built on a hill overlooking the entire island.

SKALA Σκαλα   ☎0247

Built along a graceful arc of coastline, the colorful port town of Skala provides a mere glimpse of the island's diverse terrain. The town didn't develop until the 19th century, when the pirate threat subsided and living by the water became safe. The main administrative buildings, home to the post office and customs house, were constructed during Italian occupation (1912-1943). Today, whitewashed churches blend in with village buildings, cafes, bars, tavernas, shops, and galleries. Skala is the most convenient place to stay on Patmos, particularly if you'll rely on the bus.

TRANSPORTATION

Ferries: Most are run by **DANE** (☎31 314; fax 31 685) or **G.A. Ferries** (☎33 133, 31 205, or 32 575; fax 32 180), both near the plateia. Ask about student discounts. 2-3 ferries per day to: **Kalymnos** (2½hr., 1900dr/€5.59); **Kos** (4hr., 3000dr/€8.82); **Leros** (1½hr., 5,200dr/€1.59). Daily to: **Agathonissi** (2hr., 1750dr/€5.15); **Lipsi** (1hr., 1400dr/€4.12); **Piraeus** (10-12hr., 6800dr/€20); **Rhodes** (9hr., 5800dr/€17.06). Also to: **Nisyros** (3 per week, 3400dr/€10); **Samos** (3 per week, 1800dr/€5.29); **Thessaloniki** (1 per week, 22hr., 12,050dr/€35.44); **Tilos** (4 per week, 3500dr/ €10.29). Private **excursion boats** go daily to **Lipsi** (1500dr/€4.40 one-way, 2500dr/ €7.35 round-trip); deals are posted on the waterfront.

Flying Dolphins: To: **Agathonissi** (40min., 2 per week, 3500dr/€10.29); **Fourni** (1hr., 4 per week, 3700dr/€10.88); **Ikaria** (50min., 4 per week, 3800dr/€11.18); **Kalymnos** (1½hr., 2-3 per day, 5200dr/€15.29); **Leros** (40min., 3-4 per day, 3400dr/€10); **Lipsi** (20min., 1 per day, 2500dr/€7.35); **Samos** (1hr., 3 per day, 3800dr/€11.18).

Buses: Bus stop right next to the Welcome Cafe at the ferry docks. To: **Hora** (10min., 11 per day); **Grikou** (15-20min., 6 per day); **Kampos** (20min., 4 per day). All fares 250dr/ €0.74, except from Skala to Hora (400dr/€1.17). Buy tickets on the bus.

Taxis: (☎31 225). Congregate in the main plateia 24hr. in summer, but are difficult to catch, especially in the post-disco flurry (3-6:30am). Taxis to Hora 1000dr/€2.93.

Car Rental: Patmos Rent-a-Car (☎32 203 or 32 923; fax 32 203). Turn left after the post office and look for it on your right, next to the Art Cafe (2nd floor). Cars 12,000dr/ €35.29 per day and up. Open daily 8:30am-1pm and 3:30-9:30pm. Discount if renting for an extended period of time.

Moped Rental: Available all over Skala. For the friendliest and most straightforward service around, **Express Moto** (☎32 088; fax 32 088) is a left after the tourist office. New models 2000-6000dr/€5.88-17.69 per day. Open daily 8am-8pm. At **Theo Girogio** (☎32 066), new models are 3000-6000dr/€8.82-17.69 per day. Open daily 8:30am-9pm. Both also rent mountain bikes (from 800-1400dr/€2.35-4.12 per day).

ORIENTATION AND PRACTICAL INFORMATION

Skala's amenities are all within a block or two of the waterfront. Excursion boats dock opposite the line of cafes and restaurants, while larger vessels park in front of the Italian building that houses the police and post office, near the main plateia. Moving straight inland from the post office, a street lined with shops and souvlaki stands leads to the OTE. Across from the Welcome Cafe, a parallel road is lined with pensions. Skala is on a narrow part of the island; you can walk from the water to the opposite coast in about 10 minutes.

Tourist Office: (☎31 666), in the big Italian building across the dock. Maps, brochures, bus and ferry schedules, and help with accommodations. Ask for the free Patmos Summertime guide, which includes maps of Skala and the island. Open daily 7am-2:30pm and 4-9pm. **City Hall** in Hora can also provide information (☎31 235 or 31 058). The **Welcome Cafe**, next to the dock, is open 24hr. and has for free baggage storage.

Port Authority: (☎31 231 or 34 131), to the left of the ferry dock, next to the snack bar. Information on ferries. Open 24hr.—just knock long and loud if it's late.

Tourist Agencies: All over the waterfront, but each offers info on only the ferry lines for which they sell tickets. Consult the tourist office or the port police for schedules, and then ask where to buy your ticket. **Apollon Tourist and Shipping Agency** (☎31 724; fax 31 819; apollon@12net.gr) sells flying dolphin tickets, can help with accommodations and rentals, and is the local agent for **Olympic Airways.** Open daily 8am-10pm.

Banks: National Bank (☎34 050), in the far end of the plateia. Cash advances on MC and Visa, **currency exchange,** and **24hr ATM.** Open M-Th 8am-2pm, F 8am-1:30pm. Exchange at **Apollon Agency** as well as most tourist agencies lining the port.

DODECANESE

Police: (☎31 303), upstairs from the tourist office. Open 24hr.

Tourist Police: (☎31 303), housed with the police above the tourist office.

Hospital: (☎31 211), on the main road to Hora, across from the monastery Apokalipsi (2km out of Skala). Open daily 8am-2pm. In an **emergency,** call the police at ☎31 303 or 31 571; they know doctors' schedules and will contact them.

Telephones: OTE (☎34 137 or 29 333); follow the signs in the main plateia. Open M-F 7:30am-3:10pm. The **Welcome Cafe** at the ferry dock also has an international phone.

Internet Access: Millennium Internet Cafe (☎29 300) past the OTE, has 4 terminals. 2000dr/€5.88 per hr., 500dr/€1.47 minimum. Open M-Sa 9am-11pm.

Post Office: (☎31 316), on the main plateia, next to the police. Open M-F 8am-2pm. **Postal code:** 85500.

ACCOMMODATIONS AND CAMPING

Even the plethora of early morning boats are greeted by a battalion of locals offering **domatia** (singles 5000-7000dr/€14.71-20.59; doubles 7000-10,000dr/€20.59-29.41). There are many rooms on Vas. Georgiou (the street leading to the OTE). Cheaper accommodations are inland, while one can expect much higher prices at the hotels that line the seafront.

■ **Flower Stefanos Camping at Meloi** (☎31 821 or 31 754), 2km northeast of Skala, 10ft. behind Meloi Beach. Follow the waterfront road past Apollon Travel as it wraps along the port and up the hill. Camping is to the left at the bottom—look for signs along the way. Mini-market, laundry facilities, spotless showers, grill facilities and shared fridges. Scooter rental (2000-5000dr/€5.88-14.71 per day). Sites 1400dr/€4.12 per person; 800dr/€2.35 per tent rental.

Pension Avgerinos (☎/fax 32 118). Follow the port-side road towards Meloi—past the electrical company a sign points uphill to your left. Clean, modern rooms all with bath, fridge, and stunning views of the whole port. Free water and family-made wine. Singles 6000-10,000dr/€17.65-29.41; doubles 7000-12,000dr/€20.59-35.29.

Pension Sydney (☎31 689; fax 32 118). Across the street from Pension Avgerinos. A 2min. walk to the sea on either side of the island. Singles 6000-10,000dr/€17.65-€29.41; doubles with balconies and private baths 7000-12,000dr/€20.54-35.22.

Jason's Rooms (☎31 832), near the OTE on the opposite side of the street. Spacious, cheery rooms run by an Italian ex-pat. Some rooms shared bath, most with balcony. Singles 6000-10,00dr/€17.65-29.41; doubles 8000-12,000dr/€23.53-35.29.

FOOD

Several seafood restaurants offering expensive fish entrees line the waterfront, and standard touristy tavernas abound. **Grocery stores** and **sweet shops** cram around the main plateia. Patmos is known more for its desserts than tavernas; try the *pouggia*, a ball of honey and nuts smothered in dough and sometimes powdered sugar (220-300dr/€0.65-0.88), or cheese pie, a pastry shell filled with local cheese, eggs, milk, and cinnamon (350-450dr/€1.03-1.32).

■ **To Kyma** (☎31 192), at Meloi beach. The 2km walk from town makes for a pleasant evening stroll. Take the waterfront road around the port and go up the hill; after you start the descent look for signs for To Kyma. This simple taverna with sweet views to the ocean serves freshly prepared fish; menu depends on what the fishermen reel in during the morning. Fish 7000-10,000dr/€20.59-29.41 per kg. Open daily noon-midnight.

Remezzo (☎31 553), along the port-side road to Meloi but before the hill. Greek dishes served right on the water with efficient service. Try the chicken speciality with orange and wine sauce (2500dr/€7.35) or the classic Greek dish, *domates yemistes* (stuffed tomatoes 1700dr/€5). Open in summer daily noon-1am, low season 6:30pm-1am.

Loukas Taverna (☎ 32 515), right next to Jason's Rooms across from the OTE. Serves up traditional Greek food in an authentic Greek taverna. Dishes include pork with mustard and wine sauce (1500dr/€4.40) and lamb cooked on the coals (1500dr/€4.40). Open summer only, daily 6pm-late.

🎵 ENTERTAINMENT

Perhaps in deference to the island's holy element, the nightlife tends to be free of the rowdy excesses found most anywhere else. The increasing number of tourists, however, ensures a standard palette of cafes and discotheques.

Art Cafe (☎ 33 092). From the plateia, take the small footpath to the right of the post office. The cafe is lined with continuously changing exhibitions of Katerina's sculpture-collages. Pleasant roof garden fit for a midday drink, and trendy atmosphere downstairs at the bar for late-night cocktails. *Frappés* 600dr/€1.76, fresh fruit juices 800dr/€2.35, cocktails 1500dr/€4.40. Open daily 9am-3am.

Koncolato (☎ 32 323), a bright club and bar popular with both regulars and tourists. Packed to the gills in summer. Participate in the *sfinakia* (shot) tradition—line up at the bar and go bottoms up in unison. Open daily 11pm-late.

Cafe Aman (☎ 32 323), a chic cafe resting below the lit church of Agia Paraskevi. Draws a pre-bar crowd early in the evening, but many stay all night. Open daily 10am-3am.

Lampsi Club (☎ 32 405), by the Eco gas station, 15min. walk from the main plateia down the road to Meloi. It has the liveliest of the few dance floors on Patmos, getting much livelier as the night wears on. Cover 2000dr/€5.88. Open daily midnight-4am.

HORA Χωρα

The white houses of Hora and the majestic walls of the Monastery of St. John the Theologian above form a landmark visible from all of Patmos. Walking barefoot along the sun-warmed cobbled lanes of the village after the tourists have left for the day is a soothing, peaceful experience—getting lost is a pleasure. Hora's streets are a maze, hiding sprawling gardens behind grand doors in the shelter of the monastery, and making it impossible to give precise directions. The map of Patmos at kiosks and tourist shops comes with a questionable illustration of the town; you'll need to pick **landmarks** to find your way back to where you started.

Take care of business before arriving, as a few cardphones and a mailbox at the bottom of the hill are the only links between Hora and the outside world. From the bus and taxi station, both the monastery and main plateia can be reached by walking left and following signs. Hora is 4km from Skala, a trip that you can tackle by **bus** (10min., 11 per day, 400dr/€1.18), by **taxi** (1000dr/€2.94), or by **foot,** although it's a steep hike. The bus stops at the top of the hill outside the town, which is also the point of departure for buses from Hora to Grikou. Hora's restaurants and cafes share the spectacular view over the surrounding countryside and the whitewashed town. Post-sightseeing hunger can be sated at **Vangelis's restaurant.** To reach it, head toward the monastery and follow signs to the central plateia. Peek into the pots and pans to pick your portion, and grab a seat on the rooftop garden to enjoy the cool evening breezes and soft Greek music. (☎ 31 967. *Moussaka* 1300dr/€3.82, entrees 1200-1900dr/€3.53-5.59. Open daily 11am-2pm and 6pm-midnight.) **Cafe Stoa,** in the main plateia across from Vangelis, is the only bar in Hora. (☎ 32 226. Cocktails 2000dr/€5.88, beer 800-1000dr/€2.35-2.94. Open daily 5pm-2am.)

▶ DAYTRIPS AROUND HORA

MONASTERY OF ST. JOHN THE THEOLOGIAN. The turreted walls and imposing gateway of the Monastery of St. John the Theologian make it look more like a fortress than a place of worship. At the time of its founding by St. Christodoulos in 1088, the monastery was a constant target of pirate raids. A memorial to St. John, who visited the island in the first century AD, was transformed into a citadel with battlements and watchtowers. As you enter the courtyard, centered around the well of Holy Water, notice the 17th-century **frescoes** on the left that portray stories from *The Miracles and Travels of St. John the Evangelist*, written by John's disciple Prochoros. To the upper right, a fresco portrays St. John's duel of faith with a local priest of Apollo named Kynops; the Saint threw the heathen into the water at Skala, where he froze into stone. The rock is still in the harbor—ask any local to point it out. The monastery holds ten chapels within its walls, which allow maximum prayer while respecting the Orthodox dictum limiting masses to one per day per altar. The **Chapel of the Virgin Mary** is covered with 12th-century frescoes, hidden behind the wall faces until 1956 tremors shook things up and exposed them. The **treasury** guards icons, a copy of St. Mark's Gospel, and an 8th-century Book of Job. Look for Helkomenos, an icon painted by **El Greco**, near the end of the exhibit. (☎ *31 398. Monastery and treasure museum open daily 8am-1pm and 4-6pm T, Th, Su. Treasury 1200dr/€3.53; monastery free. Off-season visitors may be offered an informal private tour by one of the monastery's 20 monks (down from 1700). Visitors to the monastery should dress modestly—no shorts, long skirts for women, and no bare shoulders.)*

APOCALYPSIS MONASTERY. Between Skala and the Monastery of St. John in Hora, the Apocalypsis monastery is built on the site where St. John stayed while on Patmos. Two kilometers from both Skala and Hora, on the winding road that connects them, you'll find the large white complex of interconnected buildings. Most people come here to see the **Sacred Grotto of the Revelation,** adjacent to the Church of St. Anne. In this natural cave, St. John dictated the *Book of Revelation*, the last book of the New Testament, after hearing the voice of God proclaim "Now write what you see, what is to take place hereafter" (Rev. 1:19). When God spoke to St. John, he cleft the ceiling of the cave with a three-pronged crack representing the Holy Trinity. Silver plating marks the spot upon which St. John is presumed to have slept. (☎ *31 234. Open daily 8am-1pm and 4-6pm T, Th, Su. Same dress code as St. John's: pants and long skirts for men and women respectively, no bare shoulders.*

RURAL PATMOS

Arriving in Skala, visitors are welcomed by a sign that reads *Patmos: Beautiful Beaches Nestled in Tradition.* As the sign attests, the island has no shortage of inviting beaches. For an undisputedly amazing view of Hora and Skala, visit **Aspris Bay** at sunset. To get there, take the port side road to Meloi Beach and go uphill. Look for signs on the right towards Aspris Bay. The closest shore to Skala is **Meloi,** a quick 2km walk north. Large trees flank the back of the sandy beach, so grilling in the sun is optional. A bit farther north, **Agriolivado** has yet another sandy beach, an alternative to more-crowded **Kambos,** which is a pleasant, yet discovered option for beachgoers, with frequent bus service. Its numerous hotels help pump in the tourists; the town itself has an inviting plateia and a few waterfront restaurants.

Just over the hill from Kambos, **Vagia Beach** is a world apart—rocky, secluded, and serene. Go east along the road to Livadia, and follow the path down to an appealing, unmarked beach set against a small cliff. A bit farther east, cliff-lined **Livadia beach** and **Livadia Restaurant** share spectacular views of the string of islets just offshore. While bus service extends only as far as Kambos, the hikes or bikes to farther beaches provide you with solitude and peace. North of Kambos, the beach at **Lambi** is famed for its multicolored pebbles, which are rare and growing rarer, as tourists pocket them for souvenirs. The strong winds that attack this part of the island make swimming difficult.

ASTYPALEA Αστυπαλια

Few travelers venture to butterfly-shaped Astypalea, the westernmost of the Dodecanese islands. Jagged hills and secluded orange and lemon groves make it a soothing place to unwind, but infrequent ferries and total lack of catamaran service repulses intruders almost as effectively as its mountaintop fort once did. For those in dire need of tranquility, it might be worth the effort, planning, and patience required to reach the undiscovered coves of Astypalea.

ASTYPALEA TOWN ☎ 0243

Surrounded by tawny hills, Astypalea Town is composed of Skala (or Pera Yialos) by the port, and Hora, at the top of the hill. It's the only major city on the island, and all of the services and amenities you'll need can be found here.

■✿ ORIENTATION AND PRACTICAL INFORMATION. Ferries run to: **Donoussa** (1 per week, summer only); **Kalymnos** (3hr., 1 per week, 2800dr/€8.22); **Kos** (3½hr., 1 per week, 3200dr/€9.39); **Naxos** (5½hr., 2 per week, 4800dr/€14.10); **Paros** (7hr., 2 per week, 4000dr/€11.74); **Piraeus** (10-13hr., 1-3 per week, 7000dr/€29.35); and **Rhodes** (5hr., 1 per week, 5000dr/€14.67). Check with a travel agency (see below) for more information. Daily excursions go to the neighboring islands of **Ag. Kyriakis, Kounoupi,** and **Syrna** (1800dr/€5.28). The ever-changing **bus schedule** is chalked up where the waterfront meets the main road to Hora. **Buses** run as far as **Livadia** and **Analipsi** (450dr/€1.32); frequency varies by season. Renting a **moped** is one of the best ways to see the island from Astypalea Town; try **Moto Center Astypalea** (☎61 263 or 61 541), on the waterfront near the ferry dock, or **Moto Rent Vergouli** on the main road to Hora. (☎61 351. Open 8am-2pm and 4:30-9pm.) There is only one paved road on the island; it surrounds the island from Livadi to Analipsi. Expect high prices for rentals and insurance as much of the island has only treacherous dirt roads. Just before the town's small beach, the **police** are in a small building (☎61 207; open 8am-7pm). The **port police** are in a white building with a Greek flag, on the waterfront between the town and the port (☎61 208; open 8am-10pm). In case of **emergency**, call 61 544; a **doctor** is available at 61 222.

The **National Bank** is under the Aegean hotel (☎61 224; open M-Th 8am-2pm, F 8am-1:30pm); the waterfront has a 24hr. **ATM**. A **tourist information** center (☎61 412, 61 114, or 61 206) operates in the Town Hall in **Hora**, directly across from the gift shop. **Astypalea Tours** (☎61 571 or 61 572; fax 61 328), on the main road to Hora, can handle transportation, accommodation and information questions; they're also the local **Olympic Airways** agent. Flights from Analypsis **airport** (☎61 410; open 10am-1pm and 6-10pm; flights to Athens 40min., 20,000dr/€58.69). The **OTE** is above the Maistrali Restaurant. (☎61 212. Open M-F 7:30am-2pm.) The **post office,** offering **currency exchange** (☎61 223; open 7:30am-2pm), and several **supermarkets** (open 9am-1pm and 5-9pm) are all in this section of town. **Postal code:** 85900.

✦ ACCOMMODATIONS AND CAMPING. Rooms on the island fill with an annual influx of summering Athenians in July and August, but vacancy is the norm the rest of the year. Bargain in the off season. **Mariakis Apartments,** located in the center of Hora, has rooms with telephones, fridges and some TVs. (☎61 413. Doubles 12,000dr/€35.22.) Rooms are similar to those at **Camping Astypalea,** 2.5km east of town, near Marmari; a hip bar, self-service restaurant, mini-market, post, and exchange services are bonuses. Follow signs or take a bus toward Maltezana. (☎61 338. 1100dr/€3.23 per person, 800dr/€2.35 per tent.)

◖▣ FOOD AND ENTERTAINMENT. Restaurants cluster near the waterfront in Astypalea Town and on the square in Hora. At waterside **Albatross,** tapestries and a straw roof create a cozy atmosphere to try a tasty but random assortment of Chinese, German, and Italian foods. (☎61 546. Excellent *souzoukakia* 1300dr/€3.82,

Armenkio souvlaki 1000dr/€2.93, barbecued chicken 1400dr/€4.10.) With tables stunningly set on the beach below Albatross, **To Akrogiali** serves a local Astypalean concoction, *astakomakaronada* (12,500dr/€36.68 per kg) and other daily catches from 6000dr/€17.61 per kg. (☎61 863. Open daily 8am-3am.) Finish your meal with a slice of pie (800-1300dr/€2.35-3.82) at **To Magazi,** overlooking the Castro. Follow the road across from the fifth windmill. (☎61 889. Open 10am-2pm and 8pm-2am.)

◪ **SIGHTS.** The **Archaeological Museum** in Astypalea Town houses a small, well-presented collection of artifacts unearthed from around the island, including stone inscriptions, early Christian sculptures, and Mycenaean grave finds. Before heading up to the castle, stop to see some of the better-preserved objects once held within the fortification. The museum is on the main road to Hora, just inland from the waterfront. (Open M-F 8am-2:30pm and 6pm-12:30am. Free.) In **Hora,** a striking row of windmills leads to a path up to the 1413 **Castro,** originally a line of defense built by the Knights of St. John; later, the Turks moved in, leaving the most significant architectural presence. Much of the structure remains intact. Exploring the chamber lets you gaze out across the island and nearby islets with a clear view. Occasional concerts are held there; ask at the tourist office for details. **Portaitissa Monastery** is to the right of the entrance and is the island's most sacred church.

NEAR ASTYPALEA

Head out from Hora to find good beaches. A 20-minute hike southwest along the coast takes you to **Tzanaki Beach,** an uncrowded refuge for nude bathers that's much better than **Livadia,** a beach closer to town. Four kilometers farther along a dirt path, the sand and palm trees at **Agios Konstantinos** make it the western island's best beach. Great beaches like **Ormos Kaminakia** and **Ormos Vatses** surround the southwest part of the island past Tzamaki. From there, the hidden cave of **Spilia Negrou** is accessible by boat, and worth the venture if you can convince a local fisherman to take you. A right turn after the sixth windmill in Hora begins a perilous 1hr. drive along a circuitous route leading past a military base to the monastery of **Agios Ioannis.** The monastery looks out over a small waterfall—perhaps the most charming sight on the island.

Northeast of Astypalea Town, the main road leads toward the other "wing" of the butterfly-shaped island, passing the campsite and several sandy beaches. Signs prohibiting nudity are the red flag for a good beach below. The road is a bus route, and in addition to designated stops, sympathetic drivers make informal stops.

Lackluster buildings and ominous construction mar the colorful gardens and gentle landscapes of the fishing village of **Maltezana** (officially known as **Analipsi**), 10km northeast of Astypalea Town. Home to miraculously intact **Roman mosaics and baths** next to the small port, Maltezana is accessible by **bus** (4 per day, 250dr/€0.73). **Psili Amo** beach near the airport is one of the island's best, with sands that invite everyone, but rarely see visitors. Vathi's natural harbor divides into **Exo Vathi** and **Mesa Vathi** 2km farther; there's a decent beach nearby at **Agios Andreas.** Inland dirt roads discourage moped travel, but beaches are also accessible by boat.

KARPATHOS Καρπαθος

Midway between Rhodes and Crete, windy Karpathos often receives little more than a passing glance from the deck of an overnight ferry. Those who disembark, however, bask in a warm Karpathian hospitality that exemplifies Greece's famed welcoming spirit. Karpathos wasn't always so inviting to foreigners—it fought first alongside the Spartans in the Peloponnesian War, and later fell to Rhodes in 400 BC. In 42 BC, the Romans began a series of occupations and were followed by all the usual suspects: the Arabs, the Venetians, and the Ottomans. Ottoman rule ended when Italians conquered the island during the World War I; it later passed into German hands for a few years following the end of World War II. Despite its

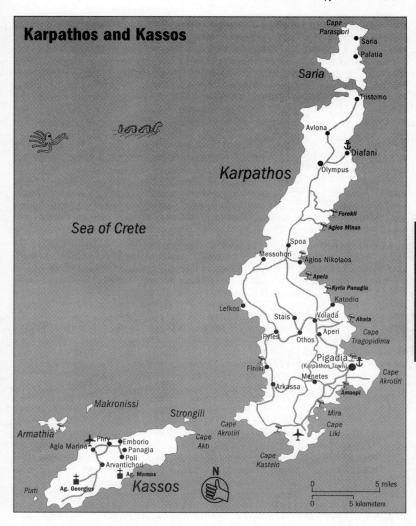

Karpathos and Kassos

Cape
Paraspori
Saria
Palatia
Saria
Tristomo
Avlona
Diafani
Karpathos
Olympus
Forokli
Agios Minas
Spoa
Messohori
Agios Nikolaos
Apela
Kyria Panagia
Katodio
Sea of Crete
Lefkos
Stais
Voladá
Ahata
Pyles
Othos
Aperi
Cape
Tragopidima
Finiki
Pigadia
(Karpathos Town)
Menetes
Cape
Akrotiri
Arkassa
Amoopi
Makronissi
Mira
Cape
Liki
Strongili
Cape
Akrotiri
Cape
Akti
Armathia
Agia Marina
Phry
Emborio
Panagia
Poli
Arvantichori
Ag. Mamas
Cape
Kastelo
Piati
Ag. Georgios
Kassos
N

0   5 miles
0   5 kilometers

DODECANESE

rowdy past, Karpathos has changed markedly in the last fifty years. Since a war-ravaged economy sent many Karpathians to the US, their prodigal Greek-American sons and daughters have returned to the island and invested heavily in it. As a result, Pigadia and the south have suddenly modernized. The mountainous north remains a world unto itself, steadfastly preserving its traditions, while gorgeous beaches stretch along the southeast part of the island.

PIGADIA Πηγαδια   ☎ 0245

Pigadia, literally "the wells," was formerly called Possi, for "Poseidon Polis," a name which drew objections because it also meant "drinking about." While this port town (also known as **Karpathos Town**) lacks the traditionalism that pervades much of the island, its turquoise waters and sea breeze ease the heat of day.

⌐ TRANSPORTATION

Schedules for ferries are available at Possi Holidays. Bus tickets are sold on board; no buses run on Sundays or local holidays.

Ferries: To: **Kassos** (1½hr., 3 per week, 1900dr/€5.58); **Piraeus** (21hr., 4 per week, 8300dr/€24.35); **Rhodes** (5hr., 3 per week, 4600dr/€13.50); **Santorini** (12hr., 1 per week, 8000dr/€23.47). For other Dodecanese islands, Rhodes is the connection hub. **Chrisovalandu Lines** and **Karpathos 1** run daily excursions to **Olympus** (leaves 8:30am, returns 6pm; 3500-5000dr/€10.27-14.67). Find them near the ferry docks or book reservations at **Possi Travel.**

Buses: 1 block up Dimokratias from the town center. Serving most southern villages (300-1000dr/€0.88-2.93); buses don't run on a regular schedule until the end of June. Check the schedule at the bus stop, at Karpathos Travel, or with Manolis (☎ 22 192). Buses to: **Aperi, Volada, Othos** and **Piles** (3 per day); **Menetes, Arkasa,** and **Finiki** (2 per day); **Amoopi** (2 per day); **Spoa Village** (1 per day).

Taxis: (☎ 22 705). Taxis run 24hr. (2000dr/€5.87 to nearby villages). Government regulated taxi prices are posted at the station on Dimokratias.

Rentals: Facing inland from the bus station, walk right 2 blocks to find **Moto Carpathos** (☎ 22 382). Fair and friendly service. Mopeds from 4500-6500dr/€13.20-19.07 per day. Insurance extra. Open daily 8am-1pm and 5-9:30pm. **Circle Rent A Car** (☎ 22 690), 1 block past Moto Carpathos. Cars 15,000-20,000dr/€44.01-58.69 per day. Open daily 8am-12:30pm and 5-8:30 pm.

☀️🔀 ORIENTATION AND PRACTICAL INFORMATION

Karpathos Town has three main roads running parallel to one another. The first runs along the water and is lined with tavernas. The second extends one block up and inland from the dock. The police and guest houses are on the third. The bus station is on Dimokratias, running perpendicular to the other main streets.

Tourist Agencies: Possi Travel (☎ 22 235, 22 627, 23 341 or 22 148; fax 22 252), nearby on Karpathion, sells ferry and plane tickets, books daily **excursions** (from 4000dr/€11.74), exchanges currency, offers bus and ferry schedules, and gives advice on accommodations and other tourist information. Open M-Sa 8:30am-1pm and 5:30-8:30pm, Su 10am-noon and 6-8pm.

Banks: National Bank (☎ 22 409), opposite Possi Travel, has **currency exchange** and an **ATM** that accepts Visa and MC. Open M-Th 8am-2pm, F 8am-1:30pm.

Police: (☎ 22 222). At the corner of Eth. Antistassis, next to the post office. Open 24hr.

Port Police: (☎ 22 227), next to the ferry dock. Open 24hr.

Hospital: (☎ 22 228), take Emboriko—the 2nd road parallel to the waterfront—straight ahead for 500m. The hospital will be on your left. English spoken. Open 24hr.

Telephones: OTE (☎ 22 609), uphill past the post office. Open M-F 7:30am-2:30pm.

Internet Access: Internet Cafe Potpourri (☎ 23 709). Take the 2nd road up from the seafront and walk straight ahead; the cafe is opposite Olympic Airways. Laid-back atmosphere and great music. Coffee 600dr/€1.76; Internet 2000dr/€5.88 per hr., half-price in winter. Open daily 8am-2am.

Post Office: (☎ 22 219). Go uphill right of the bus station and follow the signs across from the police station. Open M-F 7:30am-2pm, Sa 7:30am-1pm. **Postal code:** 85700.

▟ ACCOMMODATIONS

Illegal freelance camping is usually tolerated on the town beach to the north.

📧 **Elias Rooms for Rent** (☎22 446; www.eliasrooms.tripod.com). From the bus station, walk up the stairs past the supermarket. Rooms are quiet but centrally located, with a beautiful, breezy terrace overlooking the gulf beyond. Warm-hearted, English-speaking Elias knows a lot about the island, especially about ways to save money. Ask about the traditional rooms with lofted bed. Singles 5000-6000dr/€14.67-17.65; doubles 6000-8000dr/€17.65-23.53; triples 9000dr/€26.47.

Hotel Avra (☎22 388; fax 23 486). Facing inland at the bus station, turn right: Avra is a few doors down on the right. Rooms are bright and clean, with balcony and bath. Kitchen and card phone available. Singles 4,000-8,000dr/€11.76-23.53; doubles 6000-10,000dr/€17.65-29.41.

Harry's Rooms to Rent (☎22 188). Facing inland at the bus station, turn right and take the first left. Very clean, economical rooms with balcony and shared bath. Kind, motherly owner will try to feed you at every opportunity. Singles 4000dr/€11.76; doubles 4000-6000dr/€11.76-17.65.

🔲 🎵 FOOD AND ENTERTAINMENT

While you can always snack on savory pies (300-500dr/€0.88-1.47) and pastries (400-600dr/€1.17-1.76) from the bakeries and sweet shops, the best dinner options lie inland along the paved **waterfront** road toward the beach. More club-like nightlife is farther away, but free shuttles facilitate transportation.

📧 **Kali Karthia,** across from the Miramare Hotel on the only road heading out of town. Among the cheapest seafood options in town is the *sipia*, served like souvlaki and cooked on the coals (1500dr/€4.41). Open daily 8am-11pm.

Ideal, between the National Bank and the church on the waterfront. One of the few waterfront tavernas with cheap, tasty options serves up all the Greek basics. Pita gyros 500dr/€1.47. Open daily 6-10:30pm.

Edem Music Cafe-Bar (☎23 681), uphill from the post office. Completely packed by 10:30pm, this hotspot spins rock, reggae, and the latest Greek hits as the background for matchmaking potential. 1300dr/€3.82 optional cover includes a drink. Free shuttle to Paradiso Club (see below) leaves at 2am every night.

Paradiso Club (☎23 342), 2km out of town on the road heading for the airport. *The* place to be for late night grooving. Hops around the clock during the summer. Live music by Greek pop stars is an occasional treat. No cover.

OLYMPUS   ☎0245

Words cannot convey the isolation and insularity of Olympus, where living, centuries-old customs keep ethnographers and linguists in a tizzy. Eighty families seeking to escape attacking pirates founded the village in the 11th century, atop Mt. Profitis Ilias, 1750m above sea level. Each family built one windmill, one house, and one church. Olympus supported itself by shipping its men off to do migrant work; because women took control of the household while their husbands were away, property is inherited matrilineally. Plaster-sculpted nymphs, angels, eagles, and Venetian lions adorn house exteriors; the interiors are filled with hand-embroidered linens and ceramic plates. Tourist interest has led Olympians to preserve and, in some cases, rekindle craft traditions. Cobbler Nikolaos Kanakis still hand-crafts the leather boots that were once Olympus's standard footwear, but at 65,000dr/€190.76 per pair, these boots aren't made for walking.

📧 🇫 **ORIENTATION AND PRACTICAL INFORMATION.** Between Olympus and **Diafani**, take a **taxi** or the small **bus** that leaves Diafani (when the boat from Karpathos Town arrives; bus fare is included in the excursion ticket) and Olympus daily. A dusty **hike** along the valley floor is another alternative if you have the time, energy, and drinking water—it's a long, hot, uphill trip. **Minas,** at the village

Mayor's office, is a great resource on what the area has to offer. His perfect English and fascination with the Internet and his hometown yield a lot of information for those interested in Olympus or Karpathos.

▐▐ ACCOMMODATIONS AND FOOD. The best accommodations in Olympus are near the at **Hotel Aphrodite,** where big rooms, all outfitted with their own bath and balcony, offer breathtaking views of the ocean below. If no one's around, go to the **Parthenonos Taverna** and ask for Nikos—he owns both establishments. (☎51 307 or 51 454. Call ahead for reservations. Doubles 10,000dr/€29.41; triples 13,000dr/€38.23.) **Pension Olymbos,** around to the left of the bus stop near the start of the village, rents rooms with beautiful hand-carved beds, private baths, and peaceful balconies with mountain views. (☎ 51 009. Singles 3000dr/€8.82; doubles 6000dr/€17.65.) Farther uphill, **Hotel Astro** has simple rooms with shared bath, shared balcony, and fridge. If you can't find the owner, try asking neighbors where to look. (☎51 378. Doubles 9,000dr/€26.47; triples 12,000dr/€35.29.) The best food in town is served at the **Milos Tavern** (☎ 51 333), in the windmill above the museum. The pasta-like *makarounes*, a village specialty, are served with cheese and oil and sprinkled with onion and garlic (1200dr/€3.53). Open daily 7am-10pm.

◪ SIGHTS. Olympus itself constitutes the main sight of the region. If you want more, check out the two working **windmills** overlooking the western cliffs where Olympian women grind the flour that they later bake in huge stone ovens. While you're there, brave the tiny ladder inside the windmill and watch it whirl from behind the scenes. If you're willing to bound over stone walls, visit the three oldest chapels on Karpathos, **Agia Triada,** easily visible from the town above. Look down to the right of the bus stop for earthy red-arched roofs. Inside, 13th- or 14th-century **frescoes** represent birds and fish. Just past Parthenos Taverna, near the windmill, is the lavishly decorated **Kimisi tis Theotokou,** the largest church in the village. Gold foil blankets its altar, and breathtaking, hand-painted biblical scenes adorn the walls. If the priest isn't around, ask at the restaurant for a key.

SOUTHERN KARPATHOS

West of Pigadia, winding roads climb toward charming villages and cloud-covered mountains before descending to the beach-laden west coast.

APERI

The southern city of Aperi was the island's capital in medieval times, when Arab raids forced Karpathians to abandon their coastal homes in 1892. Although it has surrendered this official status, it remains at the heart of Karpathos. The church here holds a **Panagia** (Virgin Mary) icon revered throughout Karpathos. Legend has it that the icon was discovered when a monk was chopping wood; blood began spurting from one of the logs, tipping the monk off to the fact that this was no ordinary tree. Each time the icon was moved, it would disappear—only to reappear in an old church in Aperi. Building a bishop's church on the spot in 1886, the monk gave it a permanent home. (Open daily 8-11am.) West of Aperi, a walk through the last of Kato Horia's villages in **Pyles,** with its enchanting narrow alleyways, leads to olive groves and charming tavernas that serve the town's famous honey.

Two kilometers west of Pyles, the road hits Karpathos's stunning west coast. From Pigadia, a number of coastal towns are accessible by bus. The windswept remains of five parallel Cyclopean walls mark the town of **Arkasa,** whose acropolis is perched on the hill of Paleokastro. The notable mosaic floors of **Agia Sophia** are good reason to visit this part of the island. **Alpha Hotel,** at the north end, is one of the few hotels to accommodate independent travelers. (☎61 352. Singles 7,000dr/€20.59; doubles 10-11,000dr/€29.41-32.35.) South of Arkasa, campers find shelter in a small beach cove near the sandy shore of **Agios Nikolaos.**

North of Arkasa, the miniature fishing port of **Finiki** today consists mostly of tourist amusements. **Dimitrios Fisherman's Taverna** has earned local renown for its careful preparation of Dimitrios' daily catch. (☎61 294 or 61 365. Open M-Sa 7:30am-2:30pm and 5-10pm.) The taverna also offers some of the town's very few rooms. (Doubles 8000-12,000dr/€23.53-35.29.) Continuing north along the coast, you'll come to the small beach town of **Lefkos**, where those willing to trade sandy beaches for a rocky cove will have a gorgeous stretch of coast to call their own. Inland, forested hiking terrain is shared only with the goats.

For the island's best beaches, take the unmarked dirt roads off the Pigadia-Airport mainway (use good walking shoes or private transportation). Those seeking a full-fledged tan will adore the little stretch of sand called the **River of Birds**. Take the first dirt road headed to beautiful but sometimes crowded **Amoopi** beach and take a left as the road begins to hug the coast. Deep green-blue waves reaching for the shores across from Mira Isle can be reached by taking the first left before the built-up area preceding the airport. Long coves of sandy shores line the bay between Cape Kastelo and **Cape Akrotiri**. Follow the dirt road from the airport toward Arkasa. Stops along the way will not disappoint.

KASSOS Κασσος

The spare, rocky landscape of Kassos is billed as "tranquil," but outside the small August influx, "comatose" may be a better word. Kassos is a world apart from its crazier Dodecanese siblings. Peace and quiet are its main attractions, along with a few remote beaches, intriguing caves, and modest archaeological sites. Clusters of homes dot the arid hillside above Phry and Emporio 1km to the east: moving clockwise, these are Poli, Panagia, Arvantichori, and Agia Marina. On the other side of the hill (not visible from the ferry), the villages of Kathistres and Chroussoulas lead the way to the island's caves. You can walk the entire loop in an hour.

PHRY Φρυ ☎0245

Although the small port town of Phry isn't much to look at, it's the biggest and best that Karpathos has to offer.

▐ TRANSPORTATION. Transportation on and off the island is difficult; if you aren't flexible now, you'll learn the hard way. **Ferries** run to: **Agios Nikolaos** on Crete (5hr., 4 per week, 3500dr/€10.29); **Karpathos** (1½hr., 4 per week, 1900dr/€5.59); **Piraeus** (17hr., 4 per week, 8200dr/€24.12); **Rhodes** (6½hr., 3 per week, 5600dr/€16.47); and **Sitia** on Crete (3½hr., 4 per week, 2500dr/€7.35). **Flights** run to and from **Karpathos** (8 per week, 8089dr/€23.79) and **Rhodes** (5 per week, 15,089dr/€44.38). With island bus service cancelled, **taxis** are the most common way to get around. (☎0977 904 632 or 0945 427 308. 1500dr/€4.41 between villages.) **Moto Kasso**, on the main street in Phry, rents motorbikes. (☎41 746. Mopeds 3500dr/€10.29 per day. Open daily 9am-1pm and 3-8pm.)

⬛▐ ORIENTATION AND PRACTICAL INFORMATION. All of Kassos's tourist services are in Phry. **Kassos Maritime and Tourist Agency,** behind the church in Pl. Iroön Kasou, provides maps, friendly advice, and timetables. The **Olympic Airways** office is next door. (☎41 555. Open M-F 8am-3 pm.) The **police station** is on the airport road. (☎22 222. Open 24hr.) The **port police** are on the road to Emporio. (☎41 288. Open 24hr.) A **National Bank** representative offers **currency exchange** in the supermarket next to the Anesis Hotel. (☎41 234. Open M-F 8am-noon.) The **hospital** is on Kriti, past the bus stop (☎41 333. Open M-F 8am-3pm.) The **OTE** is a few blocks inland (open M-F 7:30am-2:30pm). **Internet access** is available at the OTE for those who really need it. (☎41 323 or 41 495; fax 41 306. Open M-Sa 7:30am-2:30pm and 5-10pm.) The **post office** is off Pl. Iroön Kasou (☎41 225. Open M-F 7:30am-2:30pm). **Postal code:** 85800.

🏠🗝 ACCOMMODATIONS AND FOOD. Kassos' hotels generally have plenty of rooms, except in August, when you should call ahead. **Anagenesis,** in Pl. Iroön Kasou next to the travel agency, has baths, sea-view balconies and kind management; inquire at the travel agency. (☎41 495 or 41 323; fax 41 730; kassos@kassos-island.gr. Singles 6500-9500dr/€19.12-27.94; doubles 9500-12,500dr/€27.94-36.76.) **Anesis,** on the main street, offers simple rooms with balconies and a taciturn owner; inquire at the supermarket below. (☎41 201; fax 41 730. Doubles 8000dr/€23.53.) **Rooms to let,** advertised by signs along the main road toward Emporio and the villages, charge 3500-6000dr/€10.27-17.61 for basic rooms. Small *kafeneia* fill the paths inside town. Restaurants set up front-row seats for the island's big daily event: the arrival of boats at the port.

🖼🐟 SIGHTS AND THE OUTDOORS. Leisurely excursions to the residential villages above Phry give insight into island agricultural life. Maneuver through roadside sheep herds to reach **Panagia** and the showy homes left behind by Kassiot sea-captains. Athenians and former Kassiots who summer here are gradually refurbishing these once-proud edifices. Panagia's annual August 15 **festival** is celebrated here. Ten minutes beyond the village of Kathistres, the entrance to the small cave of **Ellinokamara** is partially sealed by a Hellenic wall. Inside, spelunkers can clamber over slimy stones. Trek down the 1.5km footpath beyond Ellinokamara, where the cave of **Selai** bristles with stalactites and stalagmites.

From **Poli,** the 40min. **hike** to **Agios Mamas Monastery** (6km from Phry) brings you to scenic overlooks of the southeast coast. The boulders you see from the monastery are reputed to be the hulls of three ships, turned to stone by vengeful monks. The one-time monastery of **Agios Georgos at Hadies** also merits a visit, not only for the magnificent views, but also for the gorgeous **Helatros beach** below.

SYMI Συμη

Rumor has it, at least according to Symians, that visitors who daytrip here from Rhodes often end up staying for months. Indeed, both residents and foreigners alike cherish and preserve this pristine island—a refreshing mindset change after the consumer ethic of heavily touristed islands. The island's **Panormitis Monastery** (p. 460) rests in a remote spot at Symi's southern end, separated from the northern port of Yialos by an uninhabited, hiker-friendly mountain range. Indeed, until the 19th century, monasteries were the only dwellings on the island's steep, barren shores. Shipbuilding, sponge-diving, and fishing moved in later, as Symi received special treatment from the Ottoman sultans, eventually becoming the capital of the Dodecanese. Spice-growing and tourism have taken precedence in recent years, giving the island a measure of financial stability. A growing population of foreign residents gives the island a slightly cosmopolitan flair to match the colorful mosaic of houses that brighten its port.

SYMI TOWN ☎ 0246

Symi Town, the only settled town on the island, is divided into two sections. Constructed in the middle ages as a fortification against pirate raids, the village's winding pathways overlook Symi and its colorful assembly of houses. The port, **Yialos,** has most of the island's visitor services. A string of islets leads boats into the harbor, where a rainbow of houses welcomes visitors. Though many of its 19th-century houses were abandoned when the sponging industry collapsed, the Greek government declared the port a historic site in 1971.

✳🛈 ORIENTATION AND PRACTICAL INFORMATION

Ferries: Daily to **Rhodes** (3000dr/€8.82). 1 per week to: **Kalymnos** (3700dr/€10.88); **Nisyros** (2600dr/€7.65); **Tilos** (1900dr/€5.59). 2 per week to: **Kos** (2700dr/€7.94); **Piraeus** (9400dr/€27.65). There are ferry ticket offices at the dock, and another just after the footbridge, and 1 on the next block.

DODECANESE

Flying Dolphins: 4 per week to **Rhodes** (3420dr/€10.06). 3 per week to: **Kalymnos** (7200dr/€21.18); **Kos** (5200dr/€15.29). 2 per week to: **Leros** (9200dr/€27.06); **Lipsi** (8900dr/€26.18); **Patmos** (10,400dr/€30.59).

Bus: A green van stops on the east waterfront past Pl. Ikonomou. Every hr. to: **Horio** (5min., 200dr/€0.59) and **Pedhi** (10min., 200dr/€0.59).

Taxis: Most congregate near the bus stop on the east waterfront, but the island's 4 taxis can be reached at their mobile phones (get the numbers from the travel agency).

Travel Agency: Symi Tours (☎ 71 307 or 689), a block inland from the gold shop on the waterfront. Sells ferry, hydrofoil, and plane tickets, handles **currency exchange,** and helps find accommodations with friendly, efficient service. Open summer 8:30am-1:30pm and 5-10pm; winter 9am-12:30pm and 5:30-9pm.

Banks: Alpha Bank on the waterfront straight ahead as you get off the ferries. **24hr. ATM.** Open M-Th 8am-2pm, F 8am-1:30pm.

Police: (☎ 71 111), next to the Yialos clock tower, in a big white building on the waterfront. English spoken. Open 24hr.

Medical Center: (☎ 71 290), next to the church, directly opposite Hotel Kokona. Open M-F 8am-2:30pm; after hours, call the police.

Telephones: OTE (☎ 71 399), inland along the left side of the park in the middle of the harbor; follow signs from Neraida restaurant. Open M-F 7:30am-3:10pm.

Internet: Roloi, over the footbridge, set back about 50m from the 90° turn on the east side of the harbor. Open daily 9am-late. 2000dr/€5.87 per hr.

Post Office: (☎ 71 315), in the same building as the police, up the flight of stairs on the left. Open M-F 7:20am-1:30pm. **Postal Code:** 85600.

▐ ACCOMMODATIONS

Most travelers don't spend the night, but that doesn't phase the small flock of dock hawks at the port. Luckily, expensive list prices drop fast with persistent haggling. Prices listed are high-season; expect a 2000dr/€5.87 decrease in the low season.

Hotel Kokona (☎ 71 549; fax 72 620), over the footbridge to the left of the church tower. Light breezes blow the scent of lemons through the curtains. All rooms have baths and balconies. Breakfast 1500dr/€4.41. Doubles 10,000-13,000dr/€29.35-38.23; triples 12,000-15,000dr/€35.22-44.12; quads 14,000-17,000dr/€41.18-50.

Dallaras Snack Bar (☎ 72 030), in the Horio; ask around as Horio orientation is complicated. Peaceful rooms in a nearby house. Doubles 6500-9000dr/€19.12-26.47.

Hotel Maria (☎ 71 311), next to Hotel Kokona. Large rooms with kitchen facilities and baths. Wood furniture and paintings lend an intimate feel to the rooms. Doubles 7000-9000dr/€20.54-26.41.

◐▐ FOOD AND NIGHTLIFE

Waterfront tavernas pale in comparison with the eclectic menus and often more reasonable prices in **Horio.** Prices tend to creep up at midday to greet tourist boats.

Georgios' Restaurant (☎ 71 984), at the top of the 200 stairs to the Horio. Authentic, family-owned restaurant goes beyond the basic Greek menu. Try the peppers *florini* (red peppers stuffed with feta 1500dr/€4.44), and lamb *exohiko* (lamb baked in aluminum foil with potatoes, cheese, and oregano; 2000dr/€5.88). Open daily 7pm-2am.

Manos Fish Restaurant (☎ 72 429), on the port to the right of the ferries. Variable menu depends on the early morning's catch. Mix and match to your personal taste, but be sure to try the house wine (3000dr/€8.82). Open daily 11am-3pm and 6pm-midnight.

▓ **Jean and Tonic Pub** (☎ 71 819), in Horio, up the hill from George's. Happy hour 8-9pm, friendly conversation all night with expat owner, Jean, and the locals. Open 8pm-late.

To Vapori (☎ 72 540) Surrounded by a little square of bars, classy Vapori smiles with happy hour (6:30-8:30pm) and a youthful crowd. Open daily 5pm-late.

◉ SIGHTS

At the top of the road to Horio, signs point toward the small **Archaeological Museum,** which displays well-labeled Classical and Byzantine pieces, island costumes, and utensils. (☎ 71 114. Open Tu-Su 8:30am-2:30pm. 500dr/€1.47, seniors 300dr/€0.88, under 18 free.) The Archaeological Museum is housed in the **Chatzia-gapitos Mansion** (one ticket covers admission to both), which displays everyday objects owned by Symiots of yesteryear, in the village home of an old naval family. The curators of both museums are happy to explain it all to you.

In Yialos, in a yellow neoclassical building beyond the waterfront strip, floats the **Naval Museum.** It recounts the history of sponge-diving on the island with equipment and photographs. (☎ 72 363. Open daily 10:30am-3:30pm. 400dr/€1.18. Signs also lead through a maze of streets to the ruins of the old **castle,** where little remains within the Cyclopean walls aside from the **Church of Megali Panagia.**

◉ BEACHES

Symi's tiny coves shelter a few excellent beaches at **Agios Marina, Nanou,** and **Marathounda** on the east side of the island. They are the most impressive, and are accessible only by boat. Boats also go to tranquil, sandy **Sesklia Island,** south of Symi (3000dr/€8.82 round-trip). **Excursion boats** line up in the morning with destinations and prices posted (round-trip 1700-2200dr/€5-6.47). Twenty minutes below Horio is **Pedhi,** the island's only other town easily accessible by bus from Yialos. The small fishing port lacks Yialos' stateliness and Horio's architecture, but provides an unblemished beach ideal for an afternoon dip.

Find a similarly serene beach, enclosed by cliffs on each side, at **Agios Nikolaos,** an easy 30min. **hike** east. Tiny **Nos Beach** is only a 10min. walk north along the waterfront from Yialos, past the shipyard.

▶ DAYTRIPS AROUND SYMI: PANORMITIS MONASTERY

*4 weekly **tour buses** and one **tour boat** run from **Yialos;** daily tour boats from **Rhodes** stop here as well. Mopeds aren't fit for the uneven terrain around the site. By foot it's a rigorous full-day **hike.** Open daily 10am-1pm. Dress modestly; no bare shoulders or shorts. Free toilets are to the left of the complex. Museums 400dr/€1.18, under 12 free.*

In the southern part of the island, the grand Monastery of the Archangel Michael, the friend of travelers, chimes out a welcome to visitors from its elegant belltower. The monastery was built in the 15th century on the spot where a local woman happened upon an icon of Michael. As is often the way with icons, it was brought to Yialos but kept returning to Panormitis. The palatial buildings of the monastery, dominated by an elegant central belltower, contain two small **museums,** one with ecclesiastical relics and worshipers' gifts, and one with folkloric exhibits. Tokens in the museum represent supplicants' requests. Wait for the crowds to leave to really enjoy the museum. The small church focuses on an exceptional wooden altar screen, famous for its power to grant wishes.

If you want to **hike** but think the day-long trek to Panormitis is too ambitious for you, take the red paths that mark hiking trails off the main road. They lead through a forest dedicated to **James Brown** (not so fast, Americans—this James Brown was a British soldier who aided the Symian Island during World War II) to a remote **monastery** and isolated **beaches.**

NISYROS Νισυρος

Greece's *other* volcanic island, Nisyros isn't as dramatic or as crowded as Santorini, but retains its virgin landscape, hospitality, and islander community. This hidden treasure of the Aegean is a geological wonder that caters to both scientists in search of volcanic history and vacationers looking to relax on serene beaches.

MANDRAKI Μανδρακι   ☎ 0242

Nisyros's small, whitewashed port town, Mandraki welcomes guests with its modest harbor. Beyond the harbor, the winding stone-paved streets and handsome views make the city a pleasant stopover.

■✴🔧 ORIENTATION AND PRACTICAL INFORMATION

Virtually all of Mandraki lies to the right of the port. Walking along the waterfront, small alleys lead inland to residential areas and the orchards above them. Most travelers' hunger can be satiated on the waterfront and the parallel inland road.

Ferries: Daily ferries to: **Kalymnos** (2100dr/€6.18); **Kos** (1800dr/€5.29); **Rhodes** (3200dr/€9.41); **Tilos** (1500dr/€4.40). Also to: **Halki** (1 per week, 3100dr/€9.12); **Kastellorizo** (2 per week, 2900dr/€8.53); **Leros** (2 per week, 2100dr/€6.18); **Patmos** (2 per week, 2200dr/€6.47); **Piraeus** (2 per week, 7500dr/€22.06); **Symi** (3 per week, 2500dr/€7.35).

Flying Dolphins: To: **Halki** (1 per week, 6300dr/€18.53); **Kos** (6 per week/ 3400dr/ €10); **Leros** (1 per week, 4700dr/€13.82); **Patmos** (1 per week, 4800dr/€14.12.); **Rhodes** (1-2 per day, 5800dr/€17.06); **Tilos** (1-2 per day, 3200dr/€9.41).

Buses: To: **Emporio** (20min., 5 per day); **Loutra** (5min., 6 per day); **Nikea** (30min., 5 per day); **Pali** (10min., 6 per day); **Volcano** (30min., 2 per day, 350dr/€1.03); **White Beach** (5min., 6 per day). Daily excursion buses to the **volcano** run when the boats from Kos arrive. 1 per day 2000dr/€5.88 round-trip, includes entrance.

Taxis: From Mandraki, **Babis's** (☎31 460) and from Nikea, **Irini's** (☎31 474).

Moped Rentals: Nisyrian Travel (☎31 411; fax 31 610), to the left of the ferry dock, rents scooters at 5000dr/€14.71 per day. Open daily 9am-9pm.

Tourist Office: Polyvotis Tours (☎/fax 31 204), right next to the ferry dock. Provides maps and advice on transportation and accommodations. Ask to speak to Anthoula for island information. Open in summer daily 9am-3pm, off-season 10am-2pm and 6-8pm.

Travel Agency: Dimitris at **Nisyrian Travel** (☎31 411, fax 31 610), to the left of the ferry dock, is very knowledgeable. They arrange excursions, walks, accommodations, Greek Evenings, and special boat trips. Open daily 9am-9pm. **Enetikon Travel** (☎31 180; fax 31 168), on the right side of the road leading into town, on the rocks. Boat and bus schedules, excursions, accommodation advice, and **currency exchange.** Multilingual staff. Open daily 9:30am-1pm and 6-9pm.

Banks: The **Co-op Bank of the Dodecanese** (☎48 900; fax 48 902) is located on the waterfront road—from the ferry dock just walk straight. **Currency Exchange** available M-F 9am-2pm.

Port Authority: (☎31 222), in a white building near the dock. Open 24hr.

Police: (☎31 201), in the same white building as the Port Authority.

Post Office: (☎31 249), in the *same* white building. Open M-F 7:30am-2pm. **Postal code:** 85303.

🏠🍴 ACCOMMODATIONS AND FOOD

Doubles cost around 6000-7000dr/€17.65-20.59. Reserve ahead, especially during the August festival for the Virgin Mary. On the road leading left from the dock, **Three Brothers Hotel** offers well-maintained seaside rooms overlooking the ocean, with baths, balcony, fridges, and friendly service from the brothers three. (☎31 344; fax 31 640. Singles 6000dr/€17.65; doubles 8000dr/€23.53. Breakfast 1000dr/€2.94.) Across the street, **Hotel Romantzo** has rooms with baths, fridges, and a charming roof garden with an ocean vista. (☎/fax 31 340. Doubles 7000dr/€20.59; triples 9000dr/€26.47.)

Mandraki has some great dining options, most along the lines of traditional Greek island cuisine. At **Taverna Nisyros,** lady of the house Polyxenia cooks up a storm of Nisyrian specialties that will satisfy, all for under 2000dr/€5.88. Wandering away from the waterfront, a small sign points to **Y Fabrika,** on one of the side streets leading from the town hall plateia to the water. Go down the steps for books, music, and superb Greek *mezedes* at this cozy and friendly *ouzeri* (octopus 1000dr/€2.93, *raki* 350dr/€1.03, beer 400-500dr/€1.18-1.47).

▶ DAYTRIPS AROUND NISYROS

■ **MANDRAKI VOLCANO.** The volcano, dormant since 1888, is the island's main attraction. Inside the crater, the sulphur smell is overpowering and scalding steam jets up the island's pumice landscape. There are audible rumblings in parts of the crater. A 20min. walk uphill from its famous and popular neighbor, the **Alexhandros Crater** leads a quieter life. Virtually unvisited but no less spectacular, the crater is accessible via a small trail that begins behind the toilets and leads over the mountain. *(20min. bus from Mandraki, 2 per day, 350dr/€1.03) gives you 45min. to wander around in the crater. Renting a moped lets you spend more time exploring; drive carefully, as the roads are narrow. 400dr/€1.18, children under 12 200dr/€0.59.)*

MONASTERY OF OUR LADY SPILLANI. This tiny monastery nests within a deceptively inflated outer shell on the cliff at the end of the Mandraki. The monastery's sacred icon used to reside in a small cave just above Mandraki's port, but it had a habit (like most icons) of mysteriously disappearing from the sanctuary and turning up on the site of today's monastery. Monks took the hint and built a new home for the icon, making a large replica of it in 1798 to display in the new church. Recently, on the rear face of the icon of the Virgin Mary, an altar boy discovered the iconographer's hidden portrait of **Ag. Nikolaos,** which had been covered with an old cloth for over two centuries. To get up to the monastery, follow signs and climb the narrow uphill steps across from the church with the bell tower. *(Open daily 10:30am-3:30pm. Donations welcome.)*

BEACHES. The soothing sand and green waters of the area's beaches pamper swimmers enough to make up for the toe-tormenting hot black sands. Past the hot springs of Loutra, on the road to Pali, is White Beach; get there from Mandraki (6 buses per day, 250dr/€0.76). The island's best beach is larger, cleaner, and 4km east of Pali (past the Oasis taverna; ask the bus driver to let you off). Depending on demand, Enetikon and Nisyrian Travel organize trips to the nearby island of Giali for its better beaches (2000dr/€5.87 round-trip). To experience the gorgeous sands of Giali and the island's source of *kakavia* (Greek bouillabaisse), you can leave with the worker boat, which departs daily at 7:30am and returns at 3:30pm.

LEROS Λερος

From mental hospitals to military prisons to the gracefully faded Italian mansions of its harbor, Leros is both paradoxical and paradisical. The goddess Artemis, a fleet-footed hunter and generally independent woman, was the island's first occupant; she chose Leros, as did the Persians, the Knights of St. John, and the influential Italians, who saw the potential for an ideal naval base in Lakki's natural harbor during World War II. After the war, the Greek government chose Leros as a site for mental hospitals. Because these institutions garnered negative responses for their poor treatment of patients, the island was prevented from leaping onto the tourist bandwagon. In many respects, this has proved its saving grace, allowing for a degree of tourism that hasn't yet threatened the island's serenity.

LAKKI Λακκι   ☎0247

Lakki, an uninviting port town and the ferry-goer's introduction to Leros, has borne the brunt of the island's problematic recent past. The waterfront hails from the Italian occupation, and resembles an abandoned movie set populated with a cast and crew on an eternal coffee break. A grand rotary-dotted boulevard fronts quietly deteriorating art deco buildings. Public sentiment seems to be shifting in favor of preserving these edifices as a historical reminder, rather than letting them crumble as a political symbol. Unlike neighboring towns, Lakki has done little to cultivate tourism, but the town contains the island's largest stores and banks.

⬛🔽 ORIENTATION AND PRACTICAL INFORMATION. Ferries go 5 times per week to: **Kalymnos** (2000dr/€5.88); **Kos** (2100dr/€6.18); and **Rhodes** (5000dr/€14.71). There are also 6 per week to **Patmos** (1700dr/€5) and **Piraeus** (6800dr/€19.96). Kos and Patmos connect with more comprehensive ferry service. **Flying Dolphins** leave from Ag. Marina. **Taxis** (☎22 550 or 23 070; 900dr/€2.65 from Lakki to Agia Marina) are next to the police station. **Kastis Travel and Shipping**, King George 9, along the waterfront, across from the taxi stand, offers ferry tickets (including tickets for superfast ferries from Patras in the Peloponnese to Italy), airline tickets, and general tourist info. (☎22 500 or 22 872; fax 23 500. Open daily 8:30am-2pm and 5-9pm.) If Mr. Kastis is there, he'll share his grand knowledge of the island.

Virtually all tourist services are on or just inland from the waterfront. The road to the rest of the island runs perpendicular from the rotary. The closest beach is 1km west in **Koulouki**, which makes for a scenic walk along the coast. 1.5km farther beyond Koulouki, the beach of **Merikia** is even lovelier with calm water, sand, and shady trees. A **National Bank** (☎22 166) is along the waterfront, and an **Agricultural Bank** (☎24 355) sits inland from the police station, to the left where the road separates (both open M-Th 8am-2pm, F 8am-1:30pm; 24hr. **ATMs**). The **police** are at the far end of the waterfront from where ferries dock (☎22 222; nominally open 24hr.). To find the **port police**, head inland by the waterfront school near the ferry dock and take the first left into a seemingly abandoned building. (☎22 224. Open 24hr.; you may have to ring the doorbell.) A **hospital** (☎23 251 or 23 554) is two blocks inland of the waterfront school and open 24hr. For a **pharmacy,** head inland at the cinema and take the 2nd right. (☎23 367. Open daily 8am-1pm and 5-9pm.) The **post office** is a block inland from the outdoor cinema on the park. (☎22 929. Open M-F 7:30am-2pm.) **Postal code:** 85400.

🔽🔽 ACCOMMODATIONS AND FOOD. Most wisely avoid using Lakki as a base to explore the island, but ferry schedules may necessitate overnight stays here. Rooms can be pricey, but the town's unpopularity gives bargaining travelers the upper hand. **Hotel Katerina** is by far the best bet in town with clean, modern rooms all with bath, TV, and balcony. Their van may be waiting at the ferry for pickup, but if not, walk along the main street from the port, head inland at the cinema, and take the second right. (☎22 460; fax 23 038. A/C 1500dr/€4.40 per night. Breakfast 1000dr/€2.94. Singles 8000-10,000dr/€23.53-29.41; doubles 10,000-12,000dr/€29.41-35.29.) **Hotel Artemis,** a few blocks inland before the outdoor cinema, is the next best option with clean rooms all with bath, kitchen, A/C, and bar downstairs. (☎/fax 22 416. Breakfast 1500dr/€4.40. Singles 8000-10,000dr/€23.53-29.41; doubles 10,000-14,000dr/€29.41-41.18.) The large, well-maintained **campground,** 3km southeast between the mental hospital and Xero Kampos, has baths and a bar shaded by a grove of olive trees. (☎23 372 or 094 423 84 90. 1500-2000dr/€4.40-5.87 per person; 800-1000dr/€2.35-2.94 per tent; 1200dr/3.53€ tent rental.) The owner also runs **Leros Diving Center.** (Excursions from 15,000dr/€44 with proper qualification.)

There are a few exceptions to the repetitive string of restaurants along and just inland of the waterfront. The island's largest and cheapest **Spanos supermarket** lies two blocks inland from the police station. Next to the post office, inland from the outdoor cinema, **▨To Petrino** (☎24 807) serves up delectable entrees prepared from scratch right after you order. It specializes in meats with cream and mushroom sauce (*souvlaki* in cream sauce 1500dr/€4.40). Beachside **Koulouki,** 1km west of town on the coast road and an island favorite, serves lamb with pasta (1800dr/€5.29), prawns (1600dr/€4.71), and other goodies under a canopy of trees. Stay late and enjoy the seaside breezes. (☎ 24 935. Open daily 9am-midnight.) For nightlife most head to Agia Marina, but Lakki does have the **Cafe Morano,** which packs a crowd of young locals on most evenings. (☎ 25 805. Open daily 8am-3am. Beer 500dr/€1.47, cocktails 1500dr/€4.40.) Another entertainment option is Lakki's outdoor waterfront **cinema.** (☎ 25 666. Films daily 9:15pm, most in English with Greek subtitles. 1800dr/€5.29, children 1500dr/€4.40. Open mid-June-Sept.)

AGIA MARINA Αγια Μαρινα   ☎ 0247

Agia Marina is perhaps the most charming town on Leros. The small fishing boats rock back and forth in the harbor, tossed by constant wind. The small town actually supplies most island administrative and commercial services, including the island's only Flying Dolphin service. Rooms are a bit hard to find in Agia Marina; other options are to stay in **Alinda,** the beachside town across the bay, or to head up a long to road to Lakki to the town of **Platano.** As there's no beach in town, Agia Marina lends itself to eating, drinking, and promenading.

   Flying Dolphins depart from Leros to: **Patmos, Lipsi, Agathonissi, Samos, Ikaria,** and **Fourni.** Waterfront **Kastis Antonis Travel,** right near the dock, is extremely useful for exchange, excursions, and all other travel arrangements. (☎ 22 140; fax 23 500; www.dodecanesetravel.com. Open daily 8am-3pm and 5:30pm-9pm.) An **Agricultural Bank** (open M-Th 8am-2pm, F 8am-1:30pm, **no ATM**) stands by the cafes in the port; an **Emboriki Trade Bank** 24hr. **ATM** is on the Flying Dolphin pier. A 24hr. **police station** (☎ 22 221) and a number of moped rentals sit along the waterfront, alongside a burgeoning collection of boutiques and tourist shops. The **post office** (☎ 22 929) and **OTE** (☎ 23 199; fax 25 549) are in the same building along the road to Platanos' plateia. Ag. Marina's self-serve **laundry** (☎ (093) 462 349) is located on the parallel street from the main Platanos road. To reach **Agia Marina Rooms,** take a left at Kastis Travel and then another left onto the right past Marcello's Pizza. The large, comfortable rooms include bath, kitchen, fan, and balcony. The superfriendly owner can tell you all he knows about Leros, and perhaps treat you to a game of backgammon. (☎ 25 091. Doubles 8000dr/€23.53; triples 11,000dr/€32.35.)

   Agia Marina has a few excellent dining options. An absolute must is ▨**Da Giusi R Marcello's,** next to Agia Marina Rooms. The Italian couple who own the place order all their ingredients from Italy and make everything on the spot. Try their homemade pasta with mussels (3000dr/€8.85) and one of their desserts like cheesecake with raspberry. (1000dr/€2.94. ☎ 24 888. Open daily 6pm-late.) Next to Kastis Travel, **Ta Koupia** (☎ 24 204) makes some of the best chicken souvlaki around for a mere 350dr/€1.03. When the moon rises, Agia Marina becomes naughtier and livelier than its daytime calm hints. In summer at trendy **Apothiki** it's so packed that there's barely room to sway to the Greek and international dance hits. (☎ 25 785. Open daily 11pm-dawn.) **Apocalyps Club,** two doors down from To Meltemi, plays funk, soul, and jazz. (Open daily 10pm-3am.) **Enallatiko** plays the latest English hits all day and night and is a popular early-evening hangout; **Internet** service is also available. (1500dr/€4.40 per hr. ☎ 25 746. Open daily 8am-1:30am.)

CRETE Κρητη

In middle of the sable sea there lies
An isle called Crete, a ravisher of eyes,
Fruitful, and manned with many an infinite store;
Where ninety cities crown the famous shore,
Mixed with all-languaged men.
    —Homer, *Odyssey*

HIGHLIGHTS OF CRETE

DIZZY YOUR MIND clambering through the labyrinthine leftovers at Minoan palaces at Knossos (p. 474), Phaistos (p. 479).

OGLE endangered gryphon vultures and golden eagles as they soar above steep Samaria Gorge (p. 494); just don't take your eyes off the ground for too long.

MOSEY on through the rickety Venetian lighthouse to discover Hania's spectacular inner harbor shimmering on the other side (p. 489).

DANGLE YOUR TOES over the Libyan Sea from cave-riddled cliffs at Matala (p. 478).

DARE to amble through dark Dante's Gate to explore the ghost town of Spinalonga (p. 503), the last leper colony to fall in Europe.

According to a Greek saying, a Cretan's first loyalty is to his island, his second to his country. The insular Cretan mindset—shaped by centuries of bitter resistance to relentless invasion—causes them to view even their fellow Greeks as foreigners. Cretans are nonetheless friendly to the outsiders that continue to vacation on their beloved home, and visitors will enjoy a healthy dose of that old Greek hospitality. Like the long-mustached men in black who sit by the harbor polishing their high boots, the island welcomes you, but prefers to keep its distance.

Records of Cretan life reach back to 6000 BC, when neolithic inhabitants dwelled in open settlements and placed terra-cotta statuettes on mountaintops to honor their deities. When settlers arrived from Asia Minor around 3000 BC, Cretans forged a civilization that would distinguish Greece, the Mediterranean, and all of Europe. Through the next two millennia, Crete's Minoans developed unprecedented technological and artistic abilities, constructing enormous palaces which still astound archaeologists and casual observers alike. Modern excavations have turned up shards of decorated pottery, colorful frescoes, intricate jewelry, ceremonial horns, stone libation vessels, and small sculptures.

Three catastrophes—an earthquake, a tidal wave from an eruption on ancient Santorini, and a Mycenaean invasion—leveled Minoan society; three times, the Minoans rebuilt from the ground up. Distinct artistic styles accompanied each rebuilding period. The Early Period's iconography makes it famous: women on thrones appear repeatedly, leading to speculation that early Minoan society may have been the first matriarchal society. The Middle Period brought a political and artistic high point, as the Palace at Knossos (see p. 474) dominated a prosperous Aegean marine empire. Later Greeks dated their own origins to the Middle Period, when Zeus was born on Mt. Ida, the mythical Minotaur munched men in the Knossos labyrinth, and the Athenian king Theseus wrested power from Crete's Minoans and handed it to the Achaeans of mainland Greece.

In the 8th century BC, the Dorians occupied the island, carpetbagging with their own ideas about jewelry-making, sculpture, pottery, and language. Conquering Romans set up camp, only to find the island an unstable aristocratic hangout rife with intercity fighting. Next, Crete fell under rickety Byzantine rule, resulting in the construction of countless Byzantine churches, until the Arabs conquered Crete in 827. The Byzantines eventually regained the island, but lost it again to Frankish crusaders in 1204. After being sold to Venice, Crete became a commercial hub, with fortified ports ringing the island. Crete's populace split into haves and have-nots under the Venetian nobles and local merchants.

Despite Byzantine control, Cretans look back on this period far more fondly than on the Ottoman occupation that followed. From the late 17th century until Prince George's liberation of the island in 1898, Crete was Ottoman turf. After the Balkan Wars of 1913, Crete joined the Greek state. During World War II, the island combatted German occupation with passionate guerrilla resistance; the period is now regarded with great pride in Crete. From the end of the war on, Crete escaped conquerors and attacks as a part of the Greek nation.

Today, Crete is divided into four main prefectures: **Hania, Rethymno, Iraklion,** and **Lasithi.** The island's inhabitants have this division firmly etched in their minds, and transportation networks are based on the prefectures. It's easy to get around within a prefecture, but bus transportation between prefectures can be slightly more complicated, so make your plans with the divisions in mind.

> ✈ **GETTING THERE. Olympic Airways** and **Air Greece** run cheap, fast, domestic flights from Athens to **Sitia** in the east, **Iraklion** in the center, and **Hania** in the west. You might also try **Cronus Airlines** (☎ (821) 51 100) and **Aegean Airlines** (☎ (821) 63 336). Consult the **Practical Information** section of your destination for more information on flights. Most travelers take the **ferry** from Athens (**P. 81**) to Crete, landing in Iraklion, Hania, Sitia, or occasionally Rethymno or Agios Nikolaos. Boats run frequently during the summer, but often irregularly. Larger boats run more frequently and dependably. All prices listed are for deck-class accommodations; bring a sleeping bag to snooze on the deck.

IRAKLION PREFECTURE

Iraklion Prefecture revolves around its eponymous cosmopolitan capital. As with most of Crete, the touristed areas are pressed along the beaches in the north, while the southern half of the province and the mountains that sandwich each side host fewer visitors and stick more closely to traditional life.

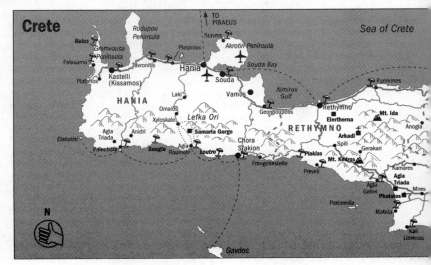

IRAKLION Ηρακλειο   ☎081

The fifth-largest city in Greece, Iraklion is Crete's capital and primary port. The chic native population lives life in the fast lane, which translates into an urban brusqueness unique among the cities of Crete, and into the most diverse nightlife on the island. While architectural aesthetes find Iraklion's unplanned jumble—Venetian monuments sandwiched between Turkish houses and two-story concrete flats—utterly offensive, others find a valuable reminder of the city's impressive history in the varied buildings. The biggest bus station and port on the island are here, making this central, capital city a convenient base to explore the island.

INTERCITY TRANSPORTATION

BY PLANE

Inexpensive flights on **Olympic Airways, Air Greece,** and **Aegean Airlines** zip between Iraklion and the other large cities of Greece. Planes fly to: **Athens** (45min., 13-15 per day, 19,300-21,300dr/€54.55-62.41); **Rhodes** (45min., 6-7 per week, 21,800-22,300dr/€63.87-65.34); **Santorini** (40min., 2 per week, 15,300dr/€44.83); and Thessaloniki (2hr., 1-2 per day, 29,800-30,300dr/€87.31-88.78). Discounts available for those under 25 or over 60. To get to and from the Iraklion airport, take **bus #1** to the **airport** from **Pl. Eleftherias** (every 10min. 200dr/€0.59). Cabs to the airport cost 2000-2500dr/€5.86-7.33. Inquire about flights at **Travel Hall Travel Agency,** Hatzimihali Yiannari 13, one block southwest of Pl. Eleftherias. (☎341 862 or 282 112; fax 283 309. Open M-Tu and Th-F 9am-4pm and 5:30-9pm, W 9am-5pm, Sa 9am-2pm.)

BY BOAT

Both **ferries** and **hydrofoils** dock at Iraklion. Boat offices line 25 Augustou, most are open 9am-9pm. Boats run to: **Athens** (14hr., 3 per day, 7000dr/€20.51); **Mykonos** (8½hr., 5 per week, 6000dr/€17.58); **Naxos** (7hr., 3 per day, 5200dr/€15.24); **Paros** (9hr., 7 per week, 5200dr/€15.24); and **Santorini** (4hr., 2 per day, 3700dr/€10.79). **Hydrofoils** serve these destinations in about half the time, for twice the price.

CRETE

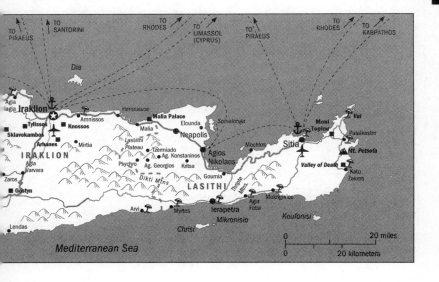

BY BUS

If you want to head out from the city, some planning is necessary, since there are several **KTEL** bus terminals. Be sure to match the station to your destination.

Terminal A (☎ 245 017 or 245 020), between the old city walls and the harbor near the waterfront, serves: **Agios Nikolaos** (1½hr., 20 per day, 1550dr/€4.55); **Arhanes** (30min., 15 per day, 400dr/€1.17); **Hersonissos** (45min., every 30min., 700dr/€2.05); **Ierapetra** (2½hr., 7 per day, 2300dr/€6.75); **Lasithi** (2hr., 2 per day, 1550dr/€4.55); **Malia** (1hr., every 30min., 850dr/€2.49); **Sitia** (3¼hr., 4 per day, 3200dr/€9.39).

Hania/Rethymno Terminal (☎ 221 765) is opposite Terminal A, beside the ferry landing. Buy tickets in the cafe building. Service to **Hania** (17 per day, 3400dr/€9.98) and **Rethymno** (1½hr., 18 per day, 1800dr/€5.28). From Hania and Rethymno, connections may be made to Plakias, Samaria, Hora Sfakion, and Akrotiri.

Terminal B (☎ 255 965). To reach Terminal B, which is outside the Hania Gate of the old city walls, take local bus #135 from Terminal A (340dr/€1). Buses run from Terminal B to: **Agia Galini** (2¼hr., 7 per day, 1800dr/€5.46); **Matala** (2hr., 5 per day, 1650dr/€4.81); **Phaistos** (1½hr., 8 per day, 1500dr/€4.40) via **Gortys** (950dr/€2.79).

⌐ LOCAL TRANSPORTATION

Taxis: Tariff Taxi of Iraklion (☎ 210 102 or 210 168). Open 24hr. When taking a taxi from the airport or port, beware of drivers who claim that a hotel you name is closed or full; they may be drawing commission from a rival hotel.

Iraklion

🔺 ACCOMMODATIONS

Hotel Paladion, 4
Hotel Rea, 2
Rent A Room Hellas, 3
Youth Hostel, 1

Car Rental: Rental car companies are scattered along 25 Augustou. Make the owners compete for your business by quoting prices from their neighbors. **Cosmos,** 25 Augostou 15 (☎241 357 or 346 173; fax 220 379), charges 10,000dr/€29.30 for a one-day rental. Renting for more days reduces the price up to 30%. Open Apr.-Oct. daily 7:30am-9pm; Nov.-Mar. 8am-1pm and 5-9pm.

Moped Rental: Inexpensive rental agencies line Handakos, El Greco Park, and 25 Augustou. Check if the quoted price includes the 20% tax and insurance (50cc bikes cost around 5000dr/€14.65 per day when you rent for several days, tax and liability insurance included).

■ ♣ ⑦ ORIENTATION AND PRACTICAL INFORMATION

The area bordered by the waterfront and **Dikeosinis, Doukos Bofor,** and **Handakos** streets contains most necessities. The city has two centers. **Pl. Venizelou** (also known to tourists as **Lion Fountain** or **Four Lion Square**), home to Morosini Fountain, is where Handakos meets Dikeosinis and 25 Augustou in the center of town. **Pl. Eleftherias** is at the intersection of Doukos Bofor and Dikeosinis on the east side of the old city. Be warned that many of the street names are given as **numbers,** so that 1866 and 25 Augostou are street names; this guide lists the address number *after* the street name.

Tourist Office: Xanthoudidou 1 (☎228 203 or 244 462), opposite the Archaeological Museum in Pl. Eleftherias. **Free city maps,** lists of hotels, message board for travelers, bus schedules, and some boat schedules. Staff is friendly and helpful but busy. Info on cultural events and museums. Open M-F 8am-2:30pm.

Travel Agencies: Several agencies line 25 Augustou. **Arabatzoglou Bros. Shipping Agents Travel Bureau,** 25 Augustou 54 (☎226 697 or 226 698; fax 222 184), has a knowledgeable staff when it comes to ferry schedules. Open 8am-9pm.

Banks: The banks on 25 Augustou have 24hr. **ATMs** and **currency exchange. National Bank,** 25 Augustou 35 (☎304 850). Open M-Th 8am-2pm, F 8am-1:30pm.

Luggage Storage: Washsalon, Handakos 18 (☎280 858). 500dr/€1.47 per day. Open 8:30am-9pm.

Bookstores: ▓ Planet International Bookstore, Kidonias 23 (☎281 558; fax 287 142), on the corner of Hortatson and Kidonias. The 4-floor megastore sells books in a number of languages, with a broad selection of classics and travel literature. Open M-F 8:30am-2pm and 5:30-8:30pm, Sa 8:30am-noon.

Library: Vikelaia Municipal Library (☎399 237 or 399 249), across from Morosini Fountain. Limited selection in English, French, Italian, Russian, and Chinese. Most international books are philosophy, literature, classics, and history—peruse them in the luxurious reading room (full A/C!) on the second floor. Open M-F 8am-3pm, also M and W 5-8pm. **Internet access** 500dr/€1.47 per 30min.

Laundromat: Washsalon, Handakos 18 (☎280 858). 2000dr/€5.86 for wash and dry, soap included. Open 8:30am-9pm.

Public Toilets: In El Greco Park, look for the underground, cage-like entrance by the swings. Also in the public gardens near Pl. Eleftherias. 150dr/€0.44. Open 6am-9pm.

Emergency: ☎ 166.

Tourist Police: Dikeosinis 10 (☎283 190 or 289 614), one block from the intersection of 25 Augustou and Dikeosinis. Open 7am-11pm.

Police: Pl. Venizelou 29, in a blue building among the cafes. Open 24hr. One station for the east side of town (☎284 589 or 282 677); another station in the same building serves the west (☎ 282 243). **Port Police** (☎244 956 or 244 912), in the harbor.

Hospital: Venizelou Hospital (☎237 502 or 237 524), on Knossou; take bus #2 from Pl. Venizelou (20min.). **Panepistimiako Hospital** (☎392 111); take a bus from Astoria Hotel in Pl. Eleftherias. The **medical center,** Iatrikos Kritis (☎342 500), is on the southern side of Pl. Eleftherias. Open 7:30am-9pm.

CRETE

Telephone: OTE, Minotavrou 10 (☎395 276 or 395 275), on the left side of El Greco Park as you enter from 25 Augustou. Open 7:30am-1pm.

Internet Access: Gallery Games Net, Korai 14 (☎282 804), is on the next street past Dedalou in the direction heading away from Pl. Eleftherias. 500dr/€1.47 per 30min. Open 10am-midnight. **Netc@fe,** on 1878, logs you in for the same fee. To reach it, walk toward the waterfront on Handakos, turn left on Vistaki, and then right onto 1878.

Post Office: Main office (☎289 995), in Pl. Daskalogianni off Giannari. Open M-F 7:30am-8pm. **Branch** in El Greco Park. Open M-F 8:30am-3pm. **Postal code:** 71001.

ACCOMMODATIONS

TOOTING THEIR OWN HORN. When taking a **taxi** from the airport or port, beware of drivers who claim that the hotel you name is closed or full. It's a common scam for taxi drivers to get payoffs from hotels for bringing customers there. Insist on your own destination, and if the cabbie won't comply, threaten to get out of the taxi.

Iraklion has a many cheap hotels and hostels, most near **Handakos** at the center of town. Others are on **Evans** and **1866** near the market.

Rent a Room Hellas, Handakos 24 (☎288 851), 2 blocks from El Greco Park. Formerly the HI Youth Hostel. Large dorm rooms, with a garden bar and casual restaurant on the 5th floor. Although not technically a hostel, Hellas retains a communal feel. Breakfast 700-1300dr/€2-3.81. Dorms 2200dr/€6.45; doubles 5000-7500dr/€14.65-21.47; triples 6000-10,000dr/€17.58-29.30. Extra bed 1000-1100dr/€2.93-3.22.

Hotel Rea (☎223 638; fax 242 189), on Kalimeraki. From Pl. Venizelou, walk down Handakos and turn right after Rent a Room Hellas. The hospitable owners provide cool, airy rooms, hot showers, and free luggage storage. Breakfast 950dr/€2.79. Rents cars (10,000dr/€29.30 per day). Singles 5000-7000dr/€14.65-20.51; doubles 7500-8500dr/€17.58-23.44; triples 9000-1050dr/€26.37-30.77.

Youth Hostel, Vyronos 5 (☎286 281; fax 222 947). From the bus station, with the water on your right, take a left onto 25 Augustou and a right on Vyronos. Midnight curfew. 24hr. hot water. Sheets 200dr/€0.59. Luggage storage 500dr/€1.47. Check-out 10am. Breakfast 700dr/€2.05; beer 400dr/€1.17. Dorms 2500dr/€7.33; singles 3000-4000dr/€8.79-11.72; doubles 5500-6000dr/€14.65-17.58; triples 7000-8000dr/€20.51-23.44.

Hotel Paladion, Handakos 16 (☎282 563). Functional, surprisingly quiet rooms conveniently close to the bustling center of town. Singles 4000-8000dr/€11.74-23.48; doubles 4500-9000dr/€13.21-26.48; triples 5000-10,000dr/€14.67-29.35.

FOOD

The ritzy cafes around the **Morosini Fountain,** near El Greco Park and in Pl. Venizelou, are perfect for lounging. Budgeteers should take a left off 1866, one block from the plateia, to reach tiny **Theodosaki** street, where 10 colorful tavernas serving big, cheap dishes (around 1000dr/€2.93) are jammed side by side. Souvlaki joints abound on **25 Augustou.**

The best show in town is the **open-air market** on 1866, starting near Pl. Venizelou. Stalls piled high with sweets, spices, produce, cheeses, meat, and Cretan muscle shirts line both sides of the narrow street. (Open M-Sa 8am-2pm, Tu and Th-F 5-9pm.) **Amalthia,** named after the goat that nursed Zeus, has cauldrons of yogurt that far eclipse the filtered, pasteurized brands found elsewhere. The store serves traditional sheep's milk yogurt (800dr/€2.53 per kg), as well as local cheeses like the special Cretan gruyère.

■ **Thraka,** Platokallergon 14. Facing the Morosini Fountain, with your back to the street, walk about 20m to the right. Barrels of fun, thanks to a 30-year tradition of serving only grilled ham gyros and souvlaki cooked over charcoal. Try the souvlaki with *thraka* bread crust (600dr/€1.76). Open M-Sa 10am-5am.

■ **Tou Terzaki,** Loch. Marineli 17 (☎221 444), behind Agios Dimitrios chapel, off Vyronos, one block from 25 Augustou. Cosmopolitan Iraklion types grab an outdoor table and order the finest of Cretan cuisine. The quiet patio seems far away from the busy city center just around the corner. Fried squid 1400dr/€4.10; stuffed tomatoes 1300dr/€3.81. Open M-Sa for lunch and dinner.

Lychnostatis, Ioannou Chronaki 8 (☎242 117), 30m past El Greco Park on the same street as the OTE. Pace your meal because pastries, fresh fruit, and ice cold ouzo are complimentary desserts. Goat with tomatoes 1100dr/€3.23. Open noon-1am.

Antonios Nerantzoulis, Agios Titou 16 (☎346 236), behind the Agios Titus Church. Family-operated since 1900, this bakery is famous for *oktasporo* (2000dr/€5.86 per kg), and baked goods. Open Sa-M and W 7am-3pm, Tu and Th-F 7am-3pm and 5-8pm.

👁 SIGHTS

IRAKLION ARCHAEOLOGICAL MUSEUM

Off Pl. Eleftherias. ☎226 092. Open M 12:30-7pm, Tu-Su 8am-7pm. 1500dr/€4.40; students and EU seniors 800dr/€2.53; classicists, fine arts students, under 18, and EU students free. Illustrated guide 1500dr/€4.40.

Iraklion's main attraction, after Knossos (p. 474), is the superb ■Archaeological Museum. While most Cretan museums offer a hodgepodge of local finds strung across millennia, the Iraklion Museum presents a comprehensive and chronologically organized record of the Neolithic and Minoan stages of the island's history. A visit to Knossos, and most any of the other Minoan palaces around the island, is incomplete without seeing the museum's inventory of the royal and everyday artifacts that once decorated the throne room and the woodshop. Of particular interest are the original **wall paintings of Knossos** on display here.

ROOM 3. In room 3 you'll find the most celebrated discovery from the palace of Phaistos (p. 479), the cryptic **Phaistos disc.** Scholars have been unable to decipher the 214 pictographs etched into the solid clay disc. The intricate impressions suggest that they were made by means of metal stamps, an ancient form of printing. The disk might convey a religious hymn or astrological chart. The plot thickens further: some archaeologists speculate that the disc didn't originate on Crete, but still can't quite place it.

ROOM 4. Three displays vie for top billing in room 4. Especially eye-catching are two topless **snake goddesses** clad in layered skirts, balancing cats on their heads and supporting flailing serpents on each outstretched arm. It's not known whether they're supposed to be goddesses or priestesses. The clothes are revealing in more ways than one: from the figure, you can see the cut and fashion of Minoan costume, the use of snakes symbols for eternity, the high status of women in the Minoan religious hierarchy, and the way the female form was idealized in Minoan society. Nearby, the **bull head libation vase** dazzles with white mustache, tight curls of hair, and red eyes made of painted rock crystal. The vase is pierced by two holes, one for filling and one for spilling. The sacred liquid used may have been blood from a sacrificial bull. While the original wood horns have not survived, one of the eyes is still preserved in its socket. Adjacent is another stately drinking vessel, an alabaster libation vase shaped like a lioness's head. Room 4's grand finale is an **ivory acrobat,** probably leaping a bull in a Minoan ritual (p. 479).

BLUEPRINTS All of Crete's palaces share a basic layout, with a vast network of rooms—sometimes rising to three stories—grouped asymmetrically around a central court. Devastating natural disasters have reduced most to ruins: first erected around 1900 BC, the palaces were destroyed by earthquakes around 1700 BC, rebuilt a century later, and promptly re-destroyed around 1650 BC. Each palace held royal apartments, artisans' workshops, extensive storehouses for oil, wine, and grain, and offices for scribes, who frantically tried to keep tabs on all the hoopla. The **west wing** was always devoted to a mother goddess, but sacred elements could be found everywhere. Near Eastern architecture from trading partners in ancient Egypt and Mesopotamia influenced their design; carefully chiseled stone in large square slabs, decorative stucco, massive pillars and ceremonial stairways, and sophisticated drainage systems made the palaces snappy-looking and functional. Shunning exterior windows, Minoan architecture disseminated light from the inside by means of light wells and wooden colonnades. Cool and airy, the interiors of Minoan palaces were bedecked with bright **frescoes** depicting bull-leaping ceremonies, magical gardens, and wild goats.

OTHER ROOMS. Look for the intricate **bee pendant** from Chryssolakkos at Malia. The pendant is composed of two bees joined delicately at their stingers, forming a cage with their antennae that encloses a golden ball and a honeycomb lying at the center—a cherished image on Crete. Room 6 stores the **Palaikastro vase**, covered with a complex pattern of spiraling tentacles that toys with your eyes. The jumble of tentacles, suction cups, seaweed, shells, and ink complement the shape of the two-headed amphora perfectly—a mix of chaos and order. In rooms 10 and 11, the **Goddess of the Poppies** stands with raised arms and opium flowers sprouting from her head. The austere power of this and other **household goddesses** shows a significant change in the Minoan concept of women the statues in room 4.

MINOAN HALL OF FRESCOES. Upstairs is the **Minoan Hall of Frescoes**, the museum's most controversial exhibit. These are the original wall paintings found at Knossos—replicas adorn the reconstructed palace. Sir Arthur Evans didn't spare these priceless finds his revisionist hand; in restoring the frescoes, he added his own ideas about the original compositions. Depicting ancient Minoan life, these frescoes capture ladies offering libations, trippy blue monkeys frolicking in palatial gardens, and Minoans in procession. They're breathtaking. But before you get too excited, check out the restoration work up close: the frescoes were reconstructed from very small original pieces, leaving room for modern day imagination. In fact, subsequent study of the **Prince of Lilies** revealed that the fragments depicted three figures: a priestess in a lily crown, and two boxers flanking her.

OTHER SITES

KAZANTZAKIS REMEMBERED. With views of Iraklion, the sea, and Mt. Ida to the west, the austere **Tomb of Kazantzakis** offers a peaceful break from crowded Iraklion. Because of his unorthodox beliefs, Nikos Kazantzakis, the author of *The Last Temptation of Christ*, was denied a place in a Christian cemetery and was buried alone in this tomb. The tomb is a wonderful place to watch the sun set, or to contemplate the city. To reach the tomb from the city center, head down Evans until you reach the Venetian walls and the Martinengo Bastion, then turn left and walk about 100m further; the tomb is atop the city walls beside the football stadium. Alternatively, you can follow the crumbling outline of the city walls to the tomb. The village of **Varvari** outside of Iraklion is home to the **Kazantzakis Museum,** where true devotees can see many of the author's original manuscripts, as well as photos of his theatrical productions. A slide show (in English) provides historical background. *(Take a bus from Terminal A to Mirtia (600dr/€1.76) and follow the signs; make sure to check return schedules. ☎741 689. Open Mar. 1-Oct. 31 M, W, and Sa-Su 9am-1pm and 4-8pm, Tu and F 9am-1pm. 1000dr/€2.93, students and children 300dr/€0.88.)*

CHURCHES. Several majestic, ancient churches hide in the modern maze of Iraklion's streets. Magnificent **Ag. Titus Church,** on 25 Augustou, is a converted mosque. Its architecture combines Muslim geometric designs and Christian regalia. The stained glass windows are all shapes rather than figures. It is lit up every night; note the *tamata* (charm-like votives) that represent the churchgoers' prayers. In Pl. Venizelou, **San Marco Church,** built in 1239, houses a changing exhibition space that features monastery frescoes from the 14th-17th centuries. (☎ *399 399, ext. 228. Open 9am-10pm. 1500dr/€4.40.)* Built in 1735, the **Cathedral of Agios Minas** graces Pl. Agia Ekaternis. (☎*282 402. Open 7am-11pm.)* **Ag. Catherine's Church of Sinai,** also in the plateia, served as the first Greek university after the fall of Constantinople in 1453. The church has six icons by the Cretan master Damaskinos as well as other icons from around Crete. (☎*288 825. Open M-Sa 9am-1:30pm, Tu and Th-F 5-7pm. 600dr/€1.76.)* San Marco and Agios Minas churches share their plaza with a small church building that contains the **Icons Museum,** a collection of Byzantine altarpieces and other ceremonial objects. (☎*288 825. Open M-Sa 8am-1:30pm, Tu and Th-F 5-7pm. 500dr/€1.47.)* A priest gives tours of the **Armenian Church.** Head away from the town center on Kalokerianou and take a right on Lasthenous after Yianni's store—the church is left of the bend. (☎*244 337.)*

HISTORICAL MUSEUM. The collection at the undervisited Historical Museum includes a scale model of the city with historical background, Byzantine and medieval works, a folk collection, photos from the World War II Nazi invasion, displays on Kazantzantkis, and perhaps the only **El Greco** painting on Crete—the 1578 work "View of Mt. Sinai and the Monastery of St. Catherine." *(On the corner of Grevenon and Kalokerianou, across from the Xenia Hotel. ☎ 283 219. Open M-Th 9am-5pm, F 9am-2pm, Sa 9am-2pm. 1000dr/€2.93, students 750dr/€2.15, under 12 free.)*

VENETIAN IRAKLION. As you rove the city, take in the various Venetian monuments: **Morosini Fountain,** centerpiece of Pl. Venizelou, and the nearby reconstructed **Venetian Loggia,** now a town hall. The 17th-century **Venetian Arsenal,** off Pl. Koundouriotou near the waterfront, and the **Koules Fortress** guard the old harbor. (☎ *246 211. Open M-F 8am-6pm, Sa-Su 10am-5pm. 500dr/€1.47, students 300dr/€0.88.)* For an unexpected dose of peace and beauty, walk along the olive tree-lined southeast section of the **Venetian walls.** Also accessible from Iraklion is **El Greco**'s home village of **Fodele,** full of orange trees and history (see **It's El Greco to Me,** p. 432).

🎬🎵 NIGHTLIFE AND ENTERTAINMENT

Trading tourist kitsch for genuine urban energy, Iraklion outdoes the resort towns with its pulsing nightlife. Day or night, the huge atrium-like **Aktarika Cafe,** across from Pl. Venizelou, brims with hip, black-clad twenty- and thirtysomething Iraklionites and the people who watch them. (*Frappés* 700dr/€2, cocktails 1700dr/€4.98. Open 9am-2:30am; DJ on duty 11am-4pm and 8pm-2:30am.) Around 11pm, the young and the restless of all nationalities overflow the small streets off **Pl. Venizelou.** To cross Androgeou street you must ford a river of chic young Cretans drinking, smoking, and chatting. As the night proceeds, these activities merge with the rhythms of techno, pop, and Greek music along the waterfront. A walk down D. Beaufort takes you to **Privilege Club** and **Yacht** next door. Continuing along the water, **Limenico** has a dance floor for bumping and a terrace for talking. The doors of Iraklion's clubs generally demand a sharp and tidy appearance (no sneakers or sloppy jeans), and ask for a 2000dr/€5.86 cover, which includes one drink.

Schedules for Iraklion's **movie theaters** are posted in front of the tourist police office. Join Greeks and tourists at sites throughout the city for Iraklion's annual **summer festival** (July-Aug.), a cultural combination of plays, concerts, theater, ballet, and folk dancing. (Shows begin at 9:30pm. Schedules at the tourist information office. Tickets around 2000dr/€5.86; reduced student prices.)

C R E T E

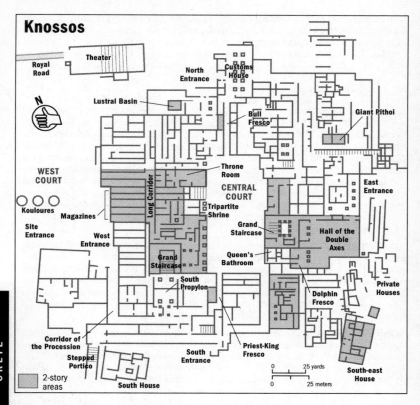

Knossos

Royal Road

Theater

North Entrance

Customs House

Lustral Basin

Bull Fresco

Giant Pithoi

Throne Room

WEST COURT

Long Corridor

CENTRAL COURT

East Entrance

Kouloures

Magazines

Tripartite Shrine

Site Entrance

West Entrance

Grand Staircase

Hall of the Double Axes

Grand Staircase

Queen's Bathroom

South Propylon

Private Houses

Dolphin Fresco

Corridor of the Procession

Priest-King Fresco

Stepped Portico

South Entrance

South-east House

2-story areas

South House

0   25 yards
0   25 meters

DAYTRIPS FROM IRAKLION

KNOSSOS Κνωσσος

From Iraklion, take bus #2 (every 20min., 300dr/€0.88), which stops along 25 Augustou and in Pl. Eleftherias. Buy your bus tickets at a nearby kiosk in advance. ☎ 231 940. Open 8am-7pm, off-season 8am-5pm. Admission 1500dr/€4.40; students and seniors 800dr/ €2.53; classicists, fine arts students, and EU students free; in winter, free on Su. Guides 1500-2200dr/€4.40-6.45. Helpful and enlightening tour in English (1hr.; 3000dr/€8.79, students 2000dr/€5.86). Make sure your guide is official and has the required papers.

Legend and fact are close cousins at the palace of Knossos, famous throughout the world and history as the site of King Minos's machinations, the labyrinth and its Minotaur, and the imprisonment (and winged escape) of Daedalus and Icarus. Cretans were once ridiculed for claiming Minoan roots, but Sir Arthur Evans won them the last laugh when his excavations confirmed their legacy.

At about 150m^2, Knossos is the largest and has the most intricate architecture of Crete's **Minoan palaces.** (The others are at Phaistos (p. 479), Malia (p. 482), and Zakros (p. 511)). Arthur Evans, one of Heinrich Schliemann's British cronies, purchased the hill that concealed Knossos in 1900. Evans spent 43 years and a fortune excavating it. Armed with the evidence he had unearthed, he set out to restore the palace with creativity and woeful inaccuracy. Walls, window casements, stairways, and columns were reconstructed in reinforced concrete, and copies of the magnificent frescoes replaced the originals, which are now a must-see in **Iraklion's Archaeological Museum** (p. 471). Indeed, a visit to Knossos is not really complete without seeing the Archaeological Museum's collection of decorations and everyday objects that cluttered the palace. Visiting throngs and the brightly painted walls make the complex look something like a Disney-esque "Minoanland." Knossos, however, is visitor-friendly and provides satisfying historical explanations, a factor which distinguishes it from other Minoan palaces.

THE SITE

CENTER STAGE. The gaping space in the middle of the site, the **Central Court,** was the heart of the palace and the arena for **bull-leaping** (see p. 479). To its left is the **Throne Room,** where the original, preserved limestone throne still sits in splendor, surrounded by paintings of gryphons. A priestess—not King Minos—probably occupied this seat. A wooden replica of the throne sits outside, erected where a pile of charred remains were found.

ROYAL QUARTERS. Leading down to the royal quarters is the grand staircase, an elegant structure that is the sturdiest part of the palace, as it was built into living rock. Because of its solid foundation, two stories below the main court survived through otherwise destructive earthquakes. Don't miss the **Queen's Bathroom,** where over 3000 years ago, she flushed her own toilet and took milk baths while gazing up at marvelous dolphin frescoes. The king had his quarters in the **Hall of the Double Axes.** The double axe, a sacred Minoan symbol, is carved all over the palace and in the Iraklion Museum. The word for double axe, *labrys*, and the tangled maze of the palace's layout (like Daedalus' maze to imprison the Minotaur) combined to form the present-day word "labyrinth."

OTHER SIGHTS. Take a break to catch the cool breeze at the **Queen's Megaron;** planners intentionally placed the queen's sitting room at this naturally air-conditioned spot. Climb above the throne room to see replicas of frescoes and the grand **pothoi**—jars so big that Minos' son was said to have drowned in one filled with honey. The areas painted red around each window and door were originally made of wood; they cushioned the walls from frequent seismic shock, but ultimately facilitated the palace's destruction by fires after the earthquake and tidal wave of Thira (modern Santorini, p. 404) in 1450 BC.

ARHANES Αρχανες

Buses run from Iraklion's Terminal A (30min., 15 per day, 380dr/€1.02).

A scenic suburb of Iraklion, Arhanes clings to its past as an ancient and medieval village in its interior old quarter, and in its museum collection and Minoan cemetery. Once used as a burial ground by Minoans and Mycenaeans, modern Arhanes is characterized by neat pastel houses with clay tile roofs and a thriving grape export industry. Arhanes's **wine factory,** behind the clock tower, is open seasonally for visiting. Only a daytrip for most visitors, Arhanes remains startlingly bereft of tourist menu billboards and harassing hosteliers.

Pleasant street-ramblings aside, Arhanes's official attractions are its **Archaeology Museum** and the sites where the collection originated. To reach the museum, head from the bus stop toward the center of town, keeping an eye out for the signs. Though the collection is small, the museum provides a good understanding of the area's sites. Its one room holds relics from Phourni, Anemospilia, and the Minoan Palace at Arhanes, as well as photos of finds now in Iraklion's Archaeological Museum (see p. 471). The most sensational of the Arhanes Museum's objects is the **bronze dagger** used for human sacrifice, found at the **Shrine of Anemospillia,** a 17th-century BC shrine on Mt. Iouktas outside of town. The sacrifices were most likely an attempt to appease the gods, perhaps to prevent the kind of earthquake that eventually destroyed the shrine. (Open M and W-Su 8am-2:30pm. Free.)

The museum's artifacts come primarily from the *tholos* graves at the nearby **Minoan Cemetery,** used throughout the Palace Period (2400-1200 BC). *Tholos* A in the burial ground was the first unlooted royal burial site found on Crete. Most of its objects have been moved to Iraklion, but some remain in the Arhanes Museum: terra-cotta *pithoi*, child and adult sarcophagi, baby burial jars, and skeletons from Phourni included. Phourni Building 4 housed a wine press and a vat for treading grapes, and an *amphora* for the wine itself. To see the cemetery after checking out its contents, follow Kapetanaki street out of town and look for signs to the site; it's northwest of Arhanes. (Open Tu-Su 8am-2:30pm. Free.)

GORTYS Γορτυνα

From Iraklion, take the bus to either Matala or Phaistos, and ask the driver to stop at Gortyna (950dr/€2.74). You can also take the bus from Mires (270dr/€0.74). ☎(0892) 31 144. Open daily 8am-6pm; off-season 8am-5pm. 800dr/€2.35; students and EU seniors 400dr/€1.17; under 18, classicists, fine arts students, and EU students free.

Gortyna, site of the Greco-Roman city Gortys, is a stimulating stop for the historically minded, 45km south of Iraklion. In 67 BC, when Crete fell to the Romans, Minoan Gortys was made its capital. From Iraklion on the paved road toward Matala, the first stop is the 7th-century **Basilica of Saint Titus,** Crete's first Christian church. Built where 10 saints were executed in AD 250, the Basilica's *berma* (half dome with windows) encompasses a courtyard of fallen columns. Behind the church is the **Roman odeon,** where the famous **Law Code of Gortys** is lodged in the walls. Called the "Queen of Inscriptions," it is the most important extant source of pre-Hellenistic Greek law. Across a small wooden bridge from the odeon is the **Platanos tree,** under which distinguished brothers Minos (an early Cretan ruler), Sarpidon (a Trojan warrior), and Rodaman (the family under-achiever) were born.

After you exit this part of the site, re-enter on the other side of the entrance booth to find a small, fenced-off **museum** with 13 sculpted figures. Left of the museum is a larger-than-life **statue** of Roman emperor Antoninus Pius. If he appears somewhat nondescript, you're on to something—resourceful Romans changed the statue's head every time a new emperor came to power.

Outside the site, you have two options. The first is an expanse of ruined structures: head 50m toward Iraklion and turn right at the sign. The **Sanctuary and Sacrificial Altar of Pythian Apollo** is the first among these ruins. Nearby is the **Nymphaion,** which was the end of an aqueduct that brought spring water from Zaros. A few steps farther is arguably the most impressive ruin at Gortys: the **Praetorium,** which was the seat of the Roman administrator. Built in the 4th century BC, the Praetorium was ahead of its time: it had a water-heating system. The 7th-century BC **acropolis** is along the other path, on the hill west of the odeon. To get there, continue 50m down the main road toward Matala, take a right after the river, and walk 200m; when you reach the corner of the fence, hike up the road for 30 minutes. Temple ruins and pottery dedicated to Athena Poliouchos are at the road's end.

ZAROS Ζαρος   ☎0894

Zaros's name has spread far and wide for its water, and little else, but this wee mountain town is a fully stocked base for a day spent hiking in the mountains of Iraklion prefecture. Zaros is the capital and political center of a union of villages that includes neighboring Vorisia, Kamares, and Moroni. Upon arrival, you may be alarmed to discover that the ultra-pure "Zaros" spring water originates in this gritty mountain town, but the surrounding landscape and warm Cretan hospitality are as refreshing as its bottled export. Zaros is busiest during the spring and fall hiking seasons; in the summer you'll have the hospitable locals all to yourself.

CRETE

⚠🏠 ORIENTATION AND PRACTICAL INFORMATION. Zaros' one main road has everything but a **bank,** which you'll find in nearby Mires. The bus stops at the downhill end of the road, near the **police station** (☎31 210). You can also call the **Mires police** (☎22 222). Two **buses** run daily from Zaros to Mires (40min., 400dr/ €1.17) and Iraklion (70min., 1050dr/€3.08). Walk uphill to reach Zaros's downtown center, which includes the **pharmacy** (☎31 386; open M-F 8:30am-2pm and 5-8pm) and the **post office** (open M-F 8:30am-1:30pm). From the bus stop, walking to the right, away from the main road leads to the **medical center** (☎31 206) and the flag-marked town hall (open M-F 9am-1:30pm); for **emergencies** at any hour call the hospital in Mires (☎(0892) 23 312). **Postal code:** 70002.

🍴🛏 ACCOMMODATIONS AND FOOD. Keramos Rent Studios is the cushier of two housing options. Walking uphill, turn left before the post office; it's 20m down the road on the left. The proprietor, George, makes all the traditional wood furniture by hand in this family-run operation; his wife, Katerina, and her two daughters tend to guests with breakfasts of fresh goat cheese from their farm and homemade Cretan delights such as *pitaraki* (Christmas pastry). Most studios have kitchenettes; all have baths and central heating in winter. (☎31 352. Singles 7000dr/ €20.51; doubles 9000dr/€26.37; triples 12,000dr/€35.16; breakfast included.) In **Charikleia Rent Rooms,** a cottage across from the police station, Georgios has clean rooms with shared baths; make friends and he'll bring you *frappés* to drink at the shady table beneath his grape arbor. (☎31 787. Singles 4000dr/€11.72; doubles 6000dr/€17.58; breakfast 1000dr/€2.93.)

Beyond the village, the main street becomes **Votomos Lane,** where a number of tavernas take shelter in the greenery. On your right, about 200m beyond the Idi Hotel (a 10min. walk from town), a restaurant run by **Petrogiannakis and Ieronimakis** is renowned for outstanding fish raised from eggs on the premises. After touring the fish farm, savor trout (1700dr/€4.98 per portion) and salmon (8000dr/ €23.44 per kg) cooked by the owner's mother. (☎31 071 or 31 454. Open 9am-midnight.) **Papadaki Rena,** 20m past Keramos Studios, sells sweets and gifts; try the *tulta* cream cake or *baklava*, for around 250dr/€0.74. (☎31 055. Open 8am-10pm.)

🔲🏔 SIGHTS AND HIKES. Zaros has been Crete's source of life-giving **water** since the days of ancient Gortys. At the water-bottling plant just above town, you can see the fleet of trucks loading bottles to carry to the far reaches of the island. There are fountains along the main street in which to wash off and quench your thirst. Every July and August, the village celebrates its aquatic bounty in a **water festival.** Zaros also holds an annual **summer festival** every August (2000dr/€5.86).

Hikes and walks through gorges and up to surrounding monasteries are breathtaking; check the map in front of the police station for route suggestions. At the end of the road beyond the Idi Hotel and Votomos tavernas is the **lake** of Votomos, which draws visiting Greeks who come to cast their fishing lines into the waters. Take the path on the left behind the lake to reach a hike through the gorge up beyond Agios Nikolaos Church. The climb makes a satisfying daytrip through the fast-changing scenery of the mountainside, but be warned that the way is often poorly marked and the path slippery with loose gravel. Another path up the mountains, starting at the nearby town of Kamares, leads to the **Monastery of Vrondisi,** where you'll find impressive frescoes said to be the work of El Greco. Every May, the annual **Paniel festival and bazaar** takes place here to commemorate the ascent of St. Thomas. Trails and streams up through the hills around the monastery lead to a cliffside sanctuary dedicated to Cretan saint **Agios Euthymios.** Shepherds keep large bottles of olive oil in the sanctuary and bring hikers into the shrines' three cave chambers to meditate before frescoes of the saint. Yet another mountain road leads to the **Kamares Cave,** where Rhea hid her infant son Zeus from his father's voracious appetite. Archaeologists have made some important finds here, including ceramics and skeletons now in the Iraklion museum.

CRETE

MATALA Ματαλα   ☎ 0892

Anyone who visited Matala 20 years ago probably has only blurry memories of a hallucinogenic trip—the caves along Matala's seaside cliffs were supposedly once full of LSD-dosed psychedelia-lovers listening to groovy music. Today's Matala is a far cry from that old hippy city. There's an admission fee and fence barring access to the caves that counter-cultural hedonists once called home. But the party isn't entirely over as a short hike beyond the main drag, magnificent nude beaches are gorgeous reminders of those bygone days.

█▚█ ORIENTATION AND PRACTICAL INFORMATION. Matala's single main street holds most necessities; when it hits the waterfront, the road bends to become a covered market with steps leading down to a taverna-lined waterfront. Before the covered market, a pension-filled road branches off, eventually heading up and over the hill to Red Beach. **Buses** go to: **Agia Galini** (45min., 3-6 per day, 700dr/€2.05); **Iraklion** (1¾hr., 3-6 per day, 1600dr/€4.69) and **Phaistos** (20min., 3-5 per day, 300dr/€0.88). **Monza Travel,** in the plateia, rents **mopeds** (4000-10,000dr/€11.72-29.30) and cars (10,000dr/€29.30) and helps with accommodations. (☎ 45 732 or 45 359; fax 45 763. Open daily 9am-10:30pm.) Several motorbike rental shops **exchange currency.** The **laundromat,** on the left side of town, charges 2500-3000dr/€7.33-8.79 per wash and dry. (Open M-Sa 9am-5pm.) The **post office** across the street opens sporadically, usually weekday mornings. The **police, hospital,** and **pharmacy** are in Mires, 17km northeast. In an **emergency,** call 22 222 for police; dial 22 225 or 23 312 for a doctor. **Public toilets** are east of the post office, on the way to the beach. **Internet access** is available at the **Kafaneio Coffee Shop,** on the right side of the road about 100m past the bus stop (750dr/€2.15 per 30min., 1200dr/€3.52 per hr.). **Postal code:** 70200.

▛ ACCOMMODATIONS AND CAMPING. Though hotels in the center of town tend to be pricey, don't try sleeping on the main beach or in the caves—it's illegal, and police raid them. Instead, look outside of town for reasonable prices in a quieter setting. **Pension Matala View,** on the road to Red Beach, offers cool rooms with private baths, balconies, and fridges, and a common kitchen facility. (☎ 45 114. Singles 4000dr/€11.72; doubles 5000-7000dr/€14.65-20.51; triples 8000dr/€23.44.) Walk 400m toward Phaistos and follow the blue signs to **Dimitri's Villa.** His gleaming rooms have baths, balconies, fridges, safes, and phones. (☎/fax 45 002 or 45 003; fax 45 740; mobile (093) 248 3939; www.c-v.net/crete/hotels/matala/dimitris-villa. Singles 5000dr/€14.65; doubles 6000-8000dr/€17.58-23.44.) If Dimitri's rooms are full, continue on to the neighboring **Georgia Hotel** (☎ 45 761), on your right, which offers rooms comparable in price and quality. If you're set on staying in town, **Matala Camping,** just off the main road east of the post office, lets you snooze in a slightly wooded grove beside the beach. (☎ 42 720. Showers available. 1100dr/€3.22 per person; 650dr/€1.91 per child; 750dr/€2.2 per small tent; 750dr/€2.20 per car; 1350dr/€3.96 per camper.)

█▜ FOOD AND ENTERTAINMENT. Only a few restaurants in town cater to the budget palate. On the west end of the beach, **Nikos at Plaka** specializes in fresh fish (breaded sole 1900dr/€5.57); they also serve traditional Greek foods for around 900dr/€2.64. (☎ 45 335. Open daily Apr.-Oct. 11am-midnight.) For good souvlaki and gyros, head to **Notos,** between the waterfront and the covered market (open daily 9am-1am). **Kantari,** on the main plateia, is a popular place to catch Latin and other world music. (☎ 45 404. Opens at 9am. Beer 500dr/€1.47; cocktails 1000-1300dr/€2.93-3.81.) Tiny **Kahlua** (☎ 45 253), near the end of the main road, has indoor and outdoor seating with a view of the beach and a laid-back bar atmosphere. **Yorgos** is owned and bartended by energetic Yorgos himself, who will win you over with his spunky dancing, chit-chat, and ice-cold beer. (☎ 45 722. Opens daily at 6pm; the partying lasts until around 6am.)

BULL LEAPING, PART I Jump. Jump. Jump. You see them everywhere in museums, the mysteriously smiling youths jumping over bull horns. Minoans made a game of frolicking with bulls in an arena, though in a very different way than today's Spanish bullfighters. Minoan bull games took place in the large central court in palaces like Knossos and Phaistos, as the main event after a boxing match. The court's ground-level exits were blocked, and fans crowded the upper windows and balconies. Scantily clad boys and girls then danced around the court, inviting the bulls to chase them. Eventually, a kid would lead a running bull up a platform, then leap over the pursuing animal. More treacherous stunts went down at mid-court, where an athlete would grab the bull's horns and launch a flip off its rearing head.

◙ ▨ SIGHTS AND BEACHES. Matala attracts visitors with its three tiers of spectacular **caves** beside the beach. As you sit in the damp interior, reflect on the caves' previous occupants—Nazis searching for British submarines, songwriter Joni Mitchell, and even Roman corpses. (Open daily 8am-7pm. 500dr/€1.47.)

Matala is blessed with some of Crete's best ▨**beaches,** many of which are spawning grounds for endangered **sea turtles.** Environmentalists run a kiosk providing info on the turtles and their habitat; if you want to support the cause, pick up a purple ▨**Save the Turtles t-shirt** (3500dr/€9.38). The main beach, a beautiful rounded cove with yellow sand and aquamarine water, captures the "here and now" spirit of Matala with a saying that is painted in block letters on the eastern side of the beach: "Today is life, tomorrow never comes." A 20min. hike past the pension-lined street and over the steep, roughly-marked hill will bring you to a magnificent strip of sand known as **Red Beach.** Bring hiking shoes, since the path is tough. Once you reach a fence, follow it to the right, and go through the goat herd gate to the shore. Cliffs surround this taverna-free nudist beach. Bring drinking water and an umbrella, as the beach has no shade, leading to speculation that it may take its name from the lobster skin-tone of unprepared visitors and not from its clay-colored sand. Five kilometers from Matala, the long, pebbly **Kommos Beach** stretches out, with one taverna and an enclave of nude bathers. Archaeologists are currently excavating a Minoan site that overlooks the beach. To get there, take the **bus** to Matala-Iraklion (260dr/€0.77) and walk a dusty 500m down to the beach.

PHAISTOS Φαιστος ☎ 0892

Buses from Phaistos go to: Agia Galini (25min., 6 per day, 450dr/€1.76); Iraklion (1½hr., 8 per day, 1300dr/€3.81); and Matala (20min., 4 per day, 300dr/€0.88). ☎42 315. Open year-round. 1200dr/€3.52; students and all EU seniors 600dr/€1.76; classics students, under 18, and EU students free.

Seated royally on a plateau with magnificent views of the mountains, the Minoan palace complex of Phaistos (also spelled **Festos**) is second in importance only to Knossos (p. 474). Phaistos attracts fewer tourists and has undergone less interpretive renovation. Four palaces have been discovered on the site: the first, built around 1900 BC, was destroyed by the earthquake that decimated Crete around 1700 BC. The second structure was leveled by a Mysterious Cataclysm in 1450 BC; traces of two even older palaces were detected by an excavation in 1952. Since the excavations, minor reconstruction work has been done on the walls, chambers, and cisterns. Built according to the standard Minoan blueprint, the complex included a great central court surrounded by private royal quarters, servants' quarters, storerooms, and chambers for state occasions.

Today visitors enter Phaistos and immediately see the **West Courtyard** and **theater area** on their right. On the left, you'll see the intact grand staircase. At its top is the **propylaea,** consisting of a landing, portico, central column, and light well. Cut through the **main hall** to reach the **central court,** which has a magnificent view of the Messara Plain. The main hall encloses a central fenced-off **storeroom,** where you can view goodies like *pithoi,* similar to those at Knossos.

CRETE

Outside of the main court, columns and boxes mark the place where sentries used to stand guard. Beyond this area, plastic-roof-covered **royal apartments** with a queen's **magaron** are similar to the famous queen's bathroom at Knossos, and a lustral basin (covered purifying pool) recalls that of the Knossos throne room. In the nearby **peristyle hall,** the remains of columns can be seen lining the walls. Northeast of the central court are the narrow halls of the palace **workshops** as well as the seven-compartmented room where the renowned **Phaistos disc,** now in the Archaeological Museum in Iraklion (see p. 471), was discovered.

AGIA GALINI   ☎1231

Agia Galini is a standard riff on the typical Cretan beach melody, though its popular beach and hilly secrets can be hard to pinpoint through the fog of package tourists that fill them. The town's main street runs down a hill from the bus station to the harbor, and contains all of the practical necessities. Off the main drag, more winding streets run so steeply that they are often composed of steps rather than pavement; most are stocked with restaurants and some accommodations. Turn left from the harbor to reach the long beach, where more tavernas await your thirst. The **bus station** has service to **Iraklion** (1½hr., 6-7 per day, 1600dr/€4.69); **Matala** (1hr., 2-5 per day, 650dr/€1.91); **Phaistos** (30min., 5-6 per day, 650dr/€1.91); and **Rethymno** (1hr., 3-4 per day, 1300dr/€3.81). **Ferries** run to **Paveli** and back once a day. They leave at 10am and return at 5pm (round-trip 5000dr/€14.65). Next to the bus station is a **taxi service** (☎91 486). Across the street, **Monza Travel** provides info and rents mopeds and cars. (☎91 278. Open daily 9am-10pm. Mopeds 4000-12,000dr/€11.72-35.16; cars 12,000-25,000dr/€35.16-73.25.) The street is full of **exchange** places. Heading downhill from the bus stop you'll pass a **doctor** (☎91 056; emergency ☎932 688) and a **pharmacy** (☎91 168. Open M-Sa 9am-2pm and 5-9pm, Su 10am-2pm). Across the street is a **police station.** (☎91 210. Open 24hr.) The **post office** is just up the street from the doctor. **Internet access** is available at Cafe Alexander, on the eastern side of the harbor (500dr/€1.47 per 20min., 1400dr/€4.10 for 1hr.) **Postal code:** 74056.

Some pensions are affordable and close to the beach. On the main road **Phaistos** offers rooms with private baths. (☎94 352. Doubles 8000dr/€23.48.) Next door, **Manos** has rooms with shared and private baths, as well as the option of a kitchen. (☎91 394. Singles 4000-5000dr/€11.74-14.67; doubles 7000-8000dr/€20.54-23.48.) The small **bakery,** on your right just next to Manos, has sweet treats for under 500dr/€1.47. **Camping Agia Galini No Problem** has a pool, mini-market, and **taverna** serving food fresh from the family farm, cooked on the embers of a traditional wood-stove (salad and 2 entrees 3500dr/€10.27). Call for the free minibus service; alternatively, walk along the beach until the path begins to climb a small hill and make a left. Continue for 20m down the path until it becomes paved; stay straight on the road, walk another 100m—the entrance to the camping site will be on your left. (☎91 386 or 91 141; fax 91 239. Laundry 1000-1200dr/€2.93-3.52. 10% discount for *Let's Go* users. 1500dr/€4.40 per person; 700dr/€2.05 children 6-12; tents 800dr/€2.53; cars 700dr/€2.05.) At night you can chill at a mellow waterfront bar or, if you're feeling saucy, trot your booty over to the **Juxebox,** where the bartender is known to toss napkins in the air to keep the party hoppin'. (☎91 154.Beer 500-1200dr/€1.47-3.52; cocktails 1500-2000dr/€4.40-5.86. Open daily 10pm-7am, happy hour until about midnight.)

HERSONISSOS Χερσονησος   ☎0897

Hersonissos's (kher-SON-i-suss) 150 bars, discos, and nightclubs, as well as mountain villages to the south, make it a playground for English and German youngsters. Bungee-jumping, bumper cars, and waterslides clutter the beachfront, and Cretan culture is preserved only in a well-polished open-air museum. You don't need to know the Greek word for vodka here—your bartender won't know it either.

✦🔢 ORIENTATION AND PRACTICAL INFORMATION

Hersonissos is just 26km east of Iraklion. The lone main road, **Eleftheriou Venizelou,** has offices, markets, and discos. Perpendicular streets lead either to the beach or to the hills. Turning right beyond the Hard Rock Cafe on your way to Iraklion puts you on **Dimokratias,** a less congested stretch of supermarkets and travel agents.

Buses: There is no bus station, just a kiosk near the Hard Rock Cafe. Bus service to: **Agios Nikolaos** (1hr., 17-20 per day, 850dr/€2.49); **lerapetra** (2hr., 1650dr/€4.84); **Iraklion** (45min., 4 per hr., 700dr/€2.05); **Malia** (20min., 4 per hr., 250dr/€0.73); **Sitia** (2½hr., 2400dr/€7.04).

Taxi: 24hr. station (☎23 723 or 22 098) on El. Venizelou beside the medical center.

Car and Motorbike Rental: Several agencies on El. Venizelou. **Eurorent,** El. Venizelou 31 (☎24 958; fax 24 371), rents cars (8000dr/€23.44 per day with full insurance and tax included) and motorbikes (5000dr/€14.65 per day).

Tourist Agencies: Mareland Travel has 5 branches; the main one is at Dimokratias 4. (☎24 424; fax 24 150. Open 8:30am-midnight.) **Zakros Tours,** Dimokratias 12 (☎22 626; fax 22 137). Open 8am-10pm. Both rent cars, sell boat and plane tickets, exchange currency, find rooms, and have maps.

Banks: Several on El. Venizelou **exchange currency** and have 24hr. **ATMs. National Bank,** El. Venizelou 106 (☎22 377). Open M-Th 8am-2pm, F 8am-1:30pm.

Public Toilets: Across from the Zakros Tours office on El. Venizelou. Free.

Tourist Police: Minos 8 (☎21 000). Turn toward the beach before Club 99 as you walk into town from Iraklion. Offers **currency exchange.** Open 8am-11pm.

Police: Minos 8 (☎22 100 or 22 222).

Medical Services: Medical Emergency of Kriti (☎22 063, 22 600, or 22 111; fax 21 987; mobile (0944) 517 170), at the corner of El. Venizelou and Kassaveti, near the Hard Rock Cafe. Open 24hr. **Cretan Medicare,** El. Venizelou 19 (☎25 141, 25 142, or 25 143; fax 24 064), in the western outskirts of town. Open 24hr.

OTE: Eleftherias 11 (☎22 299). Heading into town from Iraklion, turn right after Pelekis Jewelry. Open 7:30am-9:30pm.

Internet Access: Mouse Internet Cafe, El Venizelou 59 (☎25 292) is on your left before the public toilets (coming from the Hard Rock Cafe). 700dr/€2.05 per 30min.; 1300dr/€3.82 per hr.

Post Office: (☎22 022). Open M-Sa 7:30am-2pm. **Postal Code:** 70014.

🔥 ACCOMMODATIONS

Tour companies book up most of the rooms in town for the height of the tourist season, so consider making a reservation if you visit in late July or August.

Selena Pension, Em. Maragaki 13 (☎25 180). Walking from the bus kiosk on the main road away from Iraklion, take a left just past Enjoy Bar. Small rooms have private bath and balcony in a convenient, relatively quiet location. Singles 4000-8000dr/€11.72-23.44; doubles 8000-15,000dr/€23.44-43.95.

Camping Caravan (☎22 025; fax 24 718), in Limenas; walk or bus 2km east toward Agios Nikolaos to Lychnostatis Museum. English spoken. Restaurant and bar. 24hr. free hot water. 1300-1500dr/€3.81-4.40 per person, children ages 6-10 700-800dr/€2-2.53euro; 1000dr/€2.93 per tent; 800dr/€2.53 per car.

◐🎶 FOOD AND ENTERTAINMENT

The Hersonissos waterfront sports the usual assortment of restaurants serving "traditional Greek food"—often code for inferior pre-packaged facsimiles. A number of sandwich and fast food places line the main road. The outskirts of town contain the most peaceful and authentic eateries.

Elli Taverna, Sanoudaki 2 (☎24 758). Heading toward Iraklion, take a right after Cretan Medicare, and this modest taverna will be on your left. There's no menu, so lift the pot lids to choose from dishes such as steamed beets with oil and vinegar (800dr/€2.53), fresh, fried sardines (1500dr/€4.40), or beans (600dr/€1.76), all cooked early in the morning by the owner, in olive oil that she produces herself. Open 11:30am-1am.

Taverna Kavouri, Archeou Theatrou 9 (☎21 161). Walk toward Iraklion, turn right before the Hard Rock Cafe onto Peace and Friendship St., and then walk left around the bend. Kavouri's 15 outdoor tables under grapevines are an enjoyable, authentically Greek escape from the waterfront. Lamb 2800dr/€8.39; *moussaka* 1100dr/€3.22; chicken with lemon 1300dr/€3.81. For dessert, try fried *tiganites* with ice cream (1100dr/€3.22). Open 5pm-midnight.

Restaurant with a Roof Garden, on the lower of the 2 main streets in the small town of Koutouloufari, just uphill from Hersonissos. From the center of Hersonissos, walk about 1km uphill on one of the streets perpendicular to El Venizelou to a very small street. From Ag. Vasilioy, the restaurant is on your left. Roof garden with wide views of the coastline and bustling street. Traditional Greek food at reasonable prices. Vegetarian platter (1800dr/€5.46); lamb gyro platter (2000dr/€5.86). Open 11am-midnight.

▇ NIGHTLIFE

Hersonissos's mediocre beach confirms it: you've come for the **nightlife.** Most clubs open at dusk and close at dawn. You can't stray a block without encountering another bar or disco; they generally charge no cover, and sell beers for 800dr/€2.53 and 1300dr/€3.81, with cocktails around 1500dr/€4.40.

Black Cactus, El. Venizelou 72, is where locals and tourists alike kick off the night. Happy Hour keeps the crowd smiling from 8:30-11:30pm as the disco ball spins.

Camelot Dancing Club, on the western end of the beach, bumps until the wee hours. A diverse crowd crams the dance floor and shakes to the beat of international rave and house music.

Disco 99, back on the main street, El. Venizelou, is not as cool as its waterfront counterparts but heats up late at night. Aggressive bumping and grinding is the rule.

MALIA Μαλια ☎0897

Mediterranean climate and nearby Minoan palace aside, Malia, with its pubs and Guinness taps, comes closer to evoking the pages of *Hello!* magazine than those of Homer or Kazantzakis. Young British tourists, booked months in advance on pre-packaged holidays, leap to Malia's beach and club-crammed streets like salmon in a mating frenzy. Locals refer to these hordes as *barbares* (what the ancient Romans used to call the Greeks) and insist that there is more to Malia than simply partying like a rock star. Many visitors only come for a daytrip to see the palace. If you're ready for the mayhem of an overnight stay, however, bring a jersey from your favorite football (soccer) team, and plenty of drachmas.

▇▇ **ORIENTATION AND PRACTICAL INFORMATION. Buses,** which drop off on the main road, leave from a number of stops throughout the city for: **Agios Nikolaos** (1½hr., 2 per hr., 800dr/€2.53); **Iraklion** (1hr., 2-4 per hr., 800dr/€2.53) via **Hersonissos** (20min., 250dr/€0.74); and **Lassithi** (1½hr.; leaves 8:30am, returns 2pm; 1300dr/€3.81). **Taxis** (☎31 777 or 33 900) idle at the intersection of El. Venizelou and the National Bank road. **Altino Travel Service** (☎33 658; fax 29 620), across from the old church on the way to the beach, has maps, travel advice, exchange, Internet, and rents **cars** (13,000-15,000dr/€38.09-43.95) and **motorbikes** (5000-6000dr/€14.65-17.58 per day).

The main road from Iraklion, **Eleftheriou Venizelou,** should satisfy your practical needs with its ATMs, supermarkets, and pharmacies, while the two converging paths to the beach, full of discos and watering holes, pander to the primal. The old village (between the main road and the inland hills) has many bars and cheaper, quieter rooms; to reach its center, turn away from the beach onto 25 Martiou at the Hertz car rental agency. A number of banks on El. Venizelou have 24hr. **ATMs.** The **National Bank** is across from the taxi station. (☎31 833 or 31 152. Open M-Th 8am-2pm, F 8am-1:30pm.) There are **no police** in Malia; in **emergencies,** dial 22 222. There are two **24hr. medical centers: Medical Emergency of Kriti** (☎32 227 or 33 100), across from the old church, and **Cretan Medicare** (☎31 661, 662, or 663). The **Internet Cafe,** Dimokratias 78, is on the right-hand side, about a 10min. walk past Altino Travel Service on the way to the beach. (☎29 563. 850dr/€2.49 per 30min.) The **OTE** is in the old village; follow signs from 25 Martiou at the Bimbo Cafe. (☎31 299. Open M-F 7:30am-2:30pm.) The **post office** is off El. Venizelou behind the old church. (☎31 688. Open M-F 7:30am-2pm.) **Postal code:** 70007.

⌐⌐ ACCOMMODATIONS AND FOOD. Finding reasonably priced rooms in Malia can be a challenge, where beachside spots are either booked or pricey. The affordable housing is in the old village; wander around the side streets of **25 Martiou** and look for a place that suits you. Walking away from the bus drop-off toward Agios Nikolaos, make a right onto 25 Martiou and then a left on Konstantinou to reach **Pension Aspasia,** home to large rooms with balconies, common baths, and a roof for sunbathing. Keep an eye out for the small sign and potted plants in front. (☎31 290. Singles 5000dr/€14.65; doubles and triples 7000dr/€20.51.) **Pension Menios,** one door down from Aspasia, has more spartan rooms. (☎31 361. Singles 5000dr/€14.65; doubles 6000dr/€17.58; triples 8000-9000dr/€23.44-26.37.)

The most popular dishes in Malia are the "English" breakfast (600dr/€1.76), the "steak" dinner (1900dr/€5.57), and pizza (1500dr/€4.40). Ironically (and perhaps appropriately), the most faithful Greek food in Malia—Greek salad (1200dr/€3.52) and *stifado* (2400dr/€7.03)—is prepared by a Dutch chef, at **Petros** in the old village. (Open 5pm-1am.) On the main road, omnipresent **banana vendors** sell bunches straight from the nearby fields for 400-500dr/€1.17-1.47.

◧ SIGHTS. Though few natives take much interest in the place these days, Malia was one of three great cities of Minoan Crete. Malia's Minoan Palace lacks the labyrinthine plan of Knossos and Phaistos, but it's complex enough to rank third among Minoan architectural puzzles. First built around 1900 BC, the palace was destroyed in 1650 BC, rebuilt on a larger scale, and then destroyed again (by that Mysterious Cataclysm) around 1450 BC. Notice the Hall of Columns on the north side of the large central courtyard, with its six columns supporting the roof. The loggia, a raised chamber on the west side, was used for state ceremonies; west of it are the palace's living quarters and archives. Northwest of the loggia and main site is the Hypostyle Crypt, possibly a social center for Malia's learned. The plot is marked well enough to find these structures, and the admission fee includes entrance to a small gallery with a three-dimensional reconstruction of the site and extensive photographs of its excavation. Follow the road to Agios Nikolaos 3km to the east and turn left toward the sea, or walk along the length of the beach and then 1km through the rocky fields. (☎31 597. Open Tu-Su 8am-3pm. 800dr/€2.53, students and seniors 400dr/€1.17, EU students free.)

◧ ENTERTAINMENT. The beach road is home to many of Malia's more popular dance clubs, blaring with pop, house, international, rave, and dance music. Clubs open around 9pm, get really packed by 1am, and stay that way until 4am (weekdays) or 6am (weekends). Locals would not be caught dead partying here. Instead, all venues are filled by northern European tourists, many of whom have decided to stay in Malia for the summer and promote the club of their choice. With two halves on either side of the road, the crowd at **Malibu** blocks traffic, so you'll likely find yourself joining the party. (Cover 400dr/€1.17, redeemable at the bar after 1am. Beer and drinks 1000-1500dr/€2.93-4.40.) **Zoo** has no cover, but it does have sturdy cages for those craving a little cage-dancing. The smoke screens and strobe lights of **Apollo** enhance the hardest beats. (Cover 500dr/€1.47, redeemable at the bar. Beer and drinks 1000-1500dr/€2.93-4.40.)

At the bars toward the end of the beach road, there's less dance and more chatter, with recent Hollywood movies and old British comedies playing all day and almost all night for free; the **Charlie Chaplin** and **Oscars** have large screen TVs behind the counter (both open 11am-1am). For a quieter night of Dionysian delight, head for Old Town, where a hybrid Greek-British libation is poured down willing throats every night in open-air pubs, replete with darts and grapevines.

RETHYMNO PREFECTURE

Eastern Crete is filled with towns that survive an onslaught of Northern European tourists every summer. The western end of the island is far less built up, and each town has an individual personality. Modest seaside towns fill only short sections of the shore with tavernas, leaving long stretches to the birds, waves, and satisfied hikers. The meld of Ottoman, Venetian, and Greek architecture complements the blue waters of the southwest coast and the sheer cliffs of the Samaria Gorge.

RETHYMNO Ρεθυμνο   ☎ 0831

The capital of the Rethymno prefecture, the city of Rethymno (or Rethymnon) is steeped in ancient folklore and spiced with urban panache. According to Greek myth, Zeus was born of Rhea to the god Cronus in the cave of Idaion Andron outside of Rethymno. Cronus was on the verge of eating the baby to prevent Zeus's predicted future one-up-manship, but Cretan *kourites* (spirits) danced up a storm to distract the jealous king. Once safely away from Cronus, baby Zeus nursed from the goat Amaltheia and ate honey from golden bees.

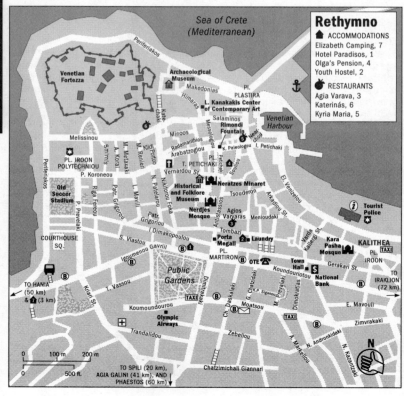

Crete's many conquerors—Venetians, Ottomans, and even Nazis—have had a profound effect in Rethymno's old city. Arabic inscriptions on the walls, a skyline full of minarets, and the Venetian fortress guarding the harbor unite into a small, distinctive cultural atmosphere that overflows the city like the Greek folk music spilling out of its cafes and garden restaurants. Even the most restless travelers may find their wanderlust inexplicably satiated as they lounge alongside contented locals, sipping *raki* into the wee hours of the morning.

■◢ 🛈 ORIENTATION AND PRACTICAL INFORMATION

Pl. Martiron, between Rethymno's **Old City** to the north and **New City** to the south, is about a 15min. walk from anywhere you'd want to go. To get to the plateia from the bus station, climb the stairs at the back of the station's parking lot onto **Igoumenou Gavriil** and go left; Pl. Martiron is to your left just after the **public gardens.** The **waterfront** lies at the northern edge of the old city, with a maze of ancient streets filling the space between the main thoroughfare of Igoumenou Gavriil and the water. The Venetian **Fortezza** sits at the western edge of the waterfront; the western end turns into a fine beach at the city's edge.

Flights: Olympic Airways, Koumoundorou 5 (☎24 333 or 22 257), opposite the Public Gardens. Open M-F 8am-8pm, Sa 8am-4pm.

Buses: Rethymno-Hania station (☎22 212), south of the fortress on Igoumenou Gavriil. Service to: **Iraklion** (1½hr., 18 per day, 1550dr/€4.40); **Hania** (1hr., 17 per day, 1600dr/€4.69); **Agia Galini** (1½hr., 3-4 per day, 1300dr/€3.81); **Plakias** (1hr., 4 per day, 1000dr/€2.93); **Arkadi Monastery** (45min., 3-4 per day, 600dr/€1.76).

Ferries: Buy tickets to Athens (7:30am, 7000dr/€20.51) at any travel office.

Taxis: (☎25 000, 22 316, 24 316, or 28 316). Available 24hr. at Pl. Matiron 4.

Tourist Office: (☎29 148), by the waterfront on El. Venizelou. **Free maps** of town; bus and ferry schedules; info on rooms and restaurants. Open M-F 8am-5pm.

Banks: The several blocks of Koundouriotou west of the public gardens sprout more than 5 banks, several with 24hr. **ATM.** The **National Bank** (on Koundouriotou) usually has the best exchange rate. Open daily 8am-1:30pm. The **International Bank** is at the intersection of Koundouriotou and Dimokratias.

Bookstore: International Press, I. Petichaki 15 (☎24 111). Sells books, newspapers, and magazines. Open 9am-11pm. **Spontidaki Toula,** Souliou 43 (☎54 307), buys and sells new and used books. Open daily 9am-11pm.

Laundromat: Tombazi 45 (☎56 196), next to the hostel. Wash and dry 2500dr/€7.33. Open M-F 8am-2pm and 5-8pm.

Tourist Police: Venizelou 5 (☎28 156; fax 53 450). Open M-F 7am-2:30pm.

Police: (☎25 247) in Pl. Iroon. Open 24hr. In an **emergency,** dial 100.

Port Police: (☎25 276), at the Venetian Port.

Hospital: Trandalidou 18 (☎27 814), in the southwest corner of town. From Igoumenou Gavriil at the bus station, take Kriari and turn left onto G. Trandalidou. Open 24hr.

OTE: Koundouriotou 23 (☎22 699). Open M-F 7:30am-8pm.

Internet Access: Cafe Galero (☎25 750), at Rimondi Fountain. 600dr/€1.76 per 30min., 1200dr/€3.52 per hr. Open daily 7am-3am.

Post Office: Main branch, Moatsou 19 (☎22 303), west of the public gardens in the New City. Open M-F 7:30am-8pm. **Caravan office,** on the beach by the 2nd dock. Open in the summer 7:30am-2pm. **Postal code:** 74100.

▛ ACCOMMODATIONS AND CAMPING

The adorable streets near the fortress and the Venetian port are lined with ideally located but expensive hotels and rooms to let.

Youth Hostel, Tombazi 41-45 (☎22 848; www.yhrethymno.com). From the bus station, walk down Igoumenou Gavriil, take a left at the park traffic light and walk through the Guora Megali gate; Tombazi is the first right. Outdoor gardens and bar bustle with friendly backpackers (beer and wine 500dr/€1.47). Outdoor beds available. Manolis and Nick make recommendations and good conversation. Hot showers 8-10am and 5-8pm in winter, more often in summer. Breakfast (400-500dr/€1.17-1.47) available until 11:30am. **Internet access** 350dr/€0.88 per 15min., 1400dr/€4.10 per hr. Reception open 8am-noon and 5-9pm. Beds 1800dr/€5.46 per person.

Olga's Pension, Souliou 57 (☎53 206; fax 29 851), off Antistassios. You'll feel like part of the family with owners George, Stella, and Iannis. Each room is carefully decorated by George with a marvelous collection of kitsch. Enjoy delicious cooking from **Stella's Kitchen** downstairs (open "early til late") or in the rooftop garden, with a view of all Rethymno and beyond. All rooms with ceiling fans, some with private bath. Singles 6000-7000dr/€17.58-20.51; doubles 7000-10,000dr/€20.51-29.30; triples 10,000-11,000dr/€29.30-32.23. Studios are available for extended visits.

Hotel Paradisos, Igoumenou Gavriil 37 (☎22 419). From the bus station, walk down Igoumenou Gavriil; the hotel is on the left, across from the entrance to the public gardens. Clean, quiet rooms make you feel like you're staying at grandma's. Doubles 7000-8000dr/€20.51-23.44.

Elizabeth Camping (☎28 694), 3km east of town on the old road to Iraklion. Take the hotel bus from Rethymno station (every 15 min. until 9pm, 170dr/€0.50). Pitch your tent on shaded grass. Free parking next to reception; otherwise, pay 600dr/€1.76 to park next to your tent. The staff lends supplies, guitars, and books to occupy you at the nearby beach. Self-service **taverna** open 8:30am-1am. Seafood grilled Tu, Th, Sa (1200-1700dr/€3.52-4.98). Laundry 1200dr/€3.52. Open from mid-Apr. to Oct. 1650dr/€4.69 per person; 1100-1500dr/€3.22-4.40 per tent, depending on size. Single person and tent 2200dr/€6.45, 10% discount with a Minoan Lines ticket.

🗺️🎵 FOOD AND ENTERTAINMENT

An **open-air market** next to the park, between Moatsou and Koundouriotou, opens Thursdays at 6 or 7am and closes around 1pm; selection diminishes by 10am. For affordable nighttime eats, tourists and locals head to **Pl. Petichaki.**

■ **Taverna Kyria Maria,** Moskovitou 20 (☎29 078), to the right down the small alley behind the Rimondi fountain. Kyria Maria serves up generous breakfasts (1200-2300dr/€3.52-6.74), rabbit with onion (1800-2000dr/€5.46-5.86), and octopus in wine sauce (2000dr/€5.86) under a leafy trellis. Exquisite, free cheese pies accompany the after-dinner shot of *raki*. Open from mid-Mar. to Oct. daily 9am-1am.

■ **Agia Varvara,** Ag. Varvaras 35 (☎28 933). Michaelis cooks traditional Greek food in his authentic taverna, a favorite among locals. The octopus (1000dr/€2.93), and Greek salad (600dr/€1.76) will satisfy you. Order the owner's home brewed *raki* (200dr/€0.59); you'll get a plate of fresh fruit. Open daily 8am-2pm and 5pm-midnight.

Katerina's, Melissinou 34 (☎57 024). Seating beneath the Fortezza, and *raki* from the lovely Katerina herself. Stuffed wine leaves are 900dr/€2.64. Lamb with Greek herbs, Greek salad, ouzo, and *tahiki* for 2 costs 4000dr/€11.72. Open daily 8am-midnight.

The bar scene in Rethymno centers around Petichaki and Nearchou streets near the west end of the harbor. The happening **Rock Cafe Club,** Petichaki 8, and the **Fortezza Disco Bar,** Nearchou 14 (☎21 493), serve pricey beers (1000dr/€2.93). They also bookend several Greek *bouzouki* bars, including **Odysseas** (☎29 233), beside the Rock Cafe. **Opera Club,** at the intersection of Salaminos and Messologiou, packs both Greek and tourist crowds onto its air-conditioned modern warehouse-esque dance floor. (☎51 593. Techno and house beats. Beer 1500dr/€4.40; cocktails 2000dr/€5.86.) For slow, steady drinks with a chatty Greek crowd, head to the bar at **Kafenio Sta Vrysakia,** Moschovitou, behind Rimnodi Fountain. (☎(09) 777 50 431. Beer 500dr/€1.47; wine 1000dr/€2.93.)

CRETAN HOMEBREW Intrigued, nervous, or delighted about what's in that **raki** Greeks are so willing to share with tourists? Here's the scoop: *raki* is a powerful form of hard liquor made from the bits of grape left over after the wine-making process (much like mainland *tsipouro*). The remnants of pulp, pits, and skin are distilled five times to make good *raki*, which should slip down your throat accompanied by a pleasant burning sensation. Beware of poorly distilled *raki*—it can be as lethal as moonshine or Irish *poitin*. (Local word has it that *raki* that's only been distilled once can blind you.) *Raki* hospitality is enshrined in the earliest Cretan laws, and there's still no tax on the substance. Ouzo is better known amongst the tourist crowd, but *raki* devotees will dismiss ouzo as a watered-down, sugary version of *raki*.

◎ SIGHTS

The **Venetian Fortezza,** a fortress built in 1580, is the highest point in the city and provides magnificent views of the coast and surrounding area. Explore ruins and pretend you're defending Rethymno from invaders for a few hours. Or just play happy tourist and bring a picnic. (☎28 101. Open Tu-Su 8am-7pm. 1000dr/€2.93, children 800dr/€2.53.) The fortress also contains the **Numismatic Museum of Athens,** which is one of the few museums in the world dedicated solely to the study of currency and coins. Rethymno's **Archaeological Museum** occupies a former Ottoman prison adjacent to the fortress. The museum has enough Minoan artifacts and information to keep archeology enthusiasts occupied for an hour or so. (☎54 668. Open Tu-Su 8:30am-3pm. 500dr/€1.47, students and seniors 300dr/€0.88.) The **L. Kanakakis Center of Contemporary Art,** Himaras 5, at the corner of Salaminus, displays 19th- and 20th-century Greek paintings, and hosts temporary exhibits. (☎52 530. Open Apr.-Oct. Tu-F 9am-1pm and 7-10pm, Sa-Su 11am-3pm; Nov.-Mar. Tu and Th-F 9am-2pm, W 9am-2pm and 5-9pm, Sa 9am-3pm. 500dr/€1.47.) The **Historical and Folklore Museum,** Vernardou 28-30, showcases artifacts of Cretan social history including farming tools, musical instruments, fabrics, and ceramics. (☎23 398. Open M-Sa 9:30am-2pm. 500dr/€1.47, students 200dr/€0.59.)

Tattooed with graffiti and untamed by museum keepers, Rethymno's Ottoman monuments are strikingly loud. Amongst these eye-poppers are the **Neratzes Minaret** on Antistassios; the former Franciscan church **Nerdjes Mosque,** a block away on Fragkiskou 1 (called St. Francis on many maps); the **Kara Pasha Mosque** on Arkadiou near Pl. Iroon; and the **Valides Minaret,** which presides over the gate called **Porta Megali** at Pl. 3 Martiou. The **public gardens,** which lie at the inland end of Igoumenou, on the corner of Pl. Mationon, provide a shady retreat from the Greek sun. Romp around the playgrounds, play chess on a big board, and be nice to the sad solitary monkey in the pen.

Rethymno's **Wine Festival** (usually in July) is a crowded all-you-can-drink celebration, with a local dance troupe performing each evening. The city's **Renaissance Festival,** featuring theater, concerts, and exhibitions, is held in the fortress in July and August. Call the tourist office for schedules and other information.

🏛 DAYTRIP FROM RETHYMNO: ARKADI MONASTERY

Take the bus the 23km from Rethymno (40min., 3-4 per day, 600dr/€1.76; return trips an hour later). ☎83 076. Site open 8am-8pm, museum 8am-1:30pm and 2:15-8pm. 500dr/€1.47. Dress modestly.

The site of one of the most famous battles in the Greek struggle for independence from the Ottomans, Arkadi Monastery (Μονη Αρκαδη) became a symbol to accompany the motto Ελευθερια η θανατος—"Freedom or Death." Modern Greeks refer to the event as the Holocaust of 1866. In November of that year, Greeks and Turks fought to a two-day standoff at the monastery. When Greek defenses finally gave way, the monks and *kleftes* holding out in the monastery set off their own ammunitions supplies, sacrificing themselves to kill hundreds of Turks. The story of Arkadi inspired support for Cretan independence in Western Europe, and the original structure has since been permanently memorialized on the 100-drachma note. Today a few monks maintain what is left of the monastery: the frame of the church and the outer complex, the roofless chamber where the ammunition was detonated, and a small museum containing a portion of the church's original decoration, including Byzantine paintings and orthodox vestments. Despite its devastation, the church is still a stunning example of 15th-century Cretan Renaissance architecture.

PLAKIAS Πλακιας ☎ 0832

Sunny and secluded, Plakias has remained wonderfully underdeveloped and inexpensive compared to most Cretan beach towns. Towering surrounding mountains and steep gorges shelter the palm trees and small olive groves. Most people stay on the main street that runs along the sandy beach; stepping inland you'll find yourself among palm fronds and the sound of chirping cicadas.

■■ **ORIENTATION AND PRACTICAL INFORMATION.** You'll be able to find anything you need either on the beach road or the paths that head inland from it. **Buses** drop off and pick up at the beach, and run to: Rethymno (4 per day, 1000dr/€2.93) and Preveli (1 per day, 400dr/€1.17). **Monza Travel** (☎31 433; fax 31 883), on the beach road, rents cars (12,000dr/€35.16) and mopeds (5000dr/€14.65). Behind Monza Travel are a **doctor** (☎31 770 or mobile 094 859 983; open M-Sa 9:30am-1:15pm and 5:15-8:30pm, Su 5:30-8:30pm) and **pharmacy** (☎31 666; open M-Sa 9:30am-1:15pm and 5:15-8:30pm, Su 5:30-8:30pm). **Police** are 20km away in Spilli (☎22 027); in an **emergency**, dial 100. The **hospital** (☎(0831) 27 814) is in Rethymno. The yellow **post office** trailer sits on the beach in summer (open M-F 8:30am-2pm); an office with permanent foundations is 1km north in Mirthios. **Internet Access** is available at Plakias Youth Hostel (250dr/€0.74 for 10min.) **Postal code:** 74060.

■ **ACCOMMODATIONS AND CAMPING.** From the bus stop, facing inland, go left and follow the signs pointing inland to reach the **Plakias Youth Hostel.** Set in an olive grove, this happening hostel goes all-out with hot showers, good music, and cheap alcohol, making it a raved-about backpacker oasis. After one day's stay you may hear the sirens singing, and never want to leave. Reception is open 9am-noon and 5-9pm, but if you arrive later, grab an open bed and settle up in the morning. Reservations recommended. (☎32 118; www.yhplakias.com. Internet access 250dr/€0.74 for 10min. Open Mar.-Nov. Beds 1800dr/€5.46; sheets 200dr/€0.59.) At **Pension Kyriakos,** a 3km walk east along the beach out of town, rooms are decked out with kitchenettes and private bathrooms. Kyriakos insists on treating all his guests to *raki.* (☎31 307. Singles 5000-6000dr/€14.65-17.58; doubles 7000-8000dr/€20.51-23.44; apartments for 3-4 11,000dr/€32.23.) To reach **Camping Apollonia,** walk westward from the bus stop and take a left at the Old Alianthos Taverna. Follow this road 100m to a complex on that includes a pool, basketball court, and snack bar—it's not a country club, it's the campsite. (☎31 318. Laundry 1000dr/€2.93. Bike rental 1500dr/€4.40 per day, motorbikes 4000dr/€11.72 per day. Open Apr.-Oct.; reception open 8:30am-9:30pm. 1300dr/€3.81 per person, 800dr/€2.53 per child ages 4-10; 750dr/€2.15 per tent; 750dr/€2.15 per car; 400dr/€1.17 per bike; 1400dr/€4.10 per caravan.)

■■ **FOOD AND ENTERTAINMENT.** To avoid the crowds, walk 40min. west along the beach to **Alyykes,** a family restaurant that only serves food fresh from its own farm. Work off your meal with a post-dinner romp on the beach 100m down the road. (☎32 116. Calamari 1200dr/€3.52; octopus 1450dr/€4.25. Open May-Oct. daily 10am-11pm.) Try the *stifado* (1300dr/€3.81) and butter beans (900dr/€2.64) at the **Old Alianthos Taverna,** at the eastern end of the beach road. (☎31 851. Open daily

11:30am-10:30pm.) Quiet Plakias starts to hum come nightfall, when its bars light up on the outskirts of town. For the best gyros/souvlaki in town, head to **Niko's,** where Beth and Niko are hospitable, and the prices are cheap. (Open daily 11am-5pm and 6pm-midnight.) Walking from the bus stop, turn west and walk for about 40m and take a right at the brown signs; Niko's will be on your right. **Meltemi,** 100m to the east past the end of town, grinds nightly from 11pm to 6am. If you want to dance with the Greeks, don't arrive until late, or rather, early. (☎31 305. Beers 1000dr./€2.93.)

⚑⚑ HIKES AND BEACHES. Life on the beach can sometimes be dull, but not in Plakias, where there are endless environments to explore. Take a walk through one of the massive gorges in the area, or trek through small villages that dot the hills around Plakias. You can take a **bus** to **Preveli Monastery,** or ask either in town or at the hostel for directions on how to complete the fantastic (but complicated) 2-hour **hike.** (Open daily 8am-1:30pm and 3:30-8pm. Modest dress required. 700dr/ €2.05, students 350dr/€1.03, under 14 free.) From there you can reach **Preveli Beach** by walking 1km along the road to a dirt parking area; make the one-hour climb down. Scramble up again to catch the Preveli-Plakias bus back, or take the ferry to **Plakias** (1000dr/€2.93) or **Agia Galini** (2500dr/€7.33).

HANIA PREFECTURE

The westernmost tip of Crete is ringed with gorgeous beaches and cloven by the wildly popular Samaria Gorge. Tourists flock to these natural wonders in droves, but Hania is also Zorba country, with small villages and beaches off the beaten track and awaiting exploration. If you want to party in a beachside club, look no further. If you want to flee pounding techno and foam-filled orgiastic scenes, seek out a moped, and escape will be yours.

HANIA Χανια ☎0821

Crete's second largest city, Hania (KHAHN-ee-ah) reacts to its yearly avalanche of summer tourism with Cretan hospitality, despite the port town's urban sophistication. Down by the Old Venetian Harbor, the revelry starts. Visitors meander through winding streets, listening to folk music from streetside cafes or waiting for the setting sun to silhouette the lighthouse and nearby Ottoman domes. A day in Hania is easily spent people-watching from cafes, window shopping, or absorbing the aura of the old town by casting maps aside and blazing a route of your own.

⚑⚑ ORIENTATION AND PRACTICAL INFORMATION

To get to the city center from the bus station, turn right onto Kydonias, walk for one block, then turn left onto **Zymvrakakidon,** which runs along one side of a large public plaza called **Pl. 1866.** At the far end of Pl. 1866, the road becomes **Halidon** and leads to the **Old Venetian Harbor,** full of outdoor restaurants and narrow alleyways. Intersecting with Zymvrakakidon and Halidon at their meeting point is another major road, **Skalidi,** to the left (facing Halidon); to the right it becomes Chatzimichali, and then Giannari. A short distance further, Giannari forks into Tzanakaki and El. Venizelou. If you're arriving by ferry, you'll dock in the nearby port of **Souda.** Take the bus from the dock, which stops at the supermarket on Zymvrakakidon by Pl. 1866 (15min., 270dr/€0.80). Hania's business district is across from the **Municipal Market** near the intersection of **Gianari** and **Tzanakaki.** Its shops and restaurants cluster around the splendid Venetian Harbor. Sunbathers should head west of the harbor along the waterfront to find a long, thin stretch of well-populated sand at **Nea Hora.**

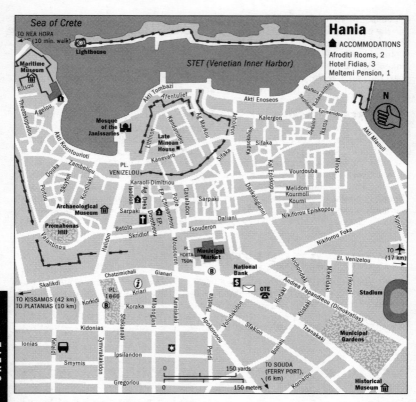

Flights: Olympic Airways, Tzanakaki 88 (☎57 701, 702 or 703), near the public gardens. Tickets sold M-F 8am-3pm. Phone reservations M-F 7am-6pm, Sa 8am-3pm. Flights to **Athens** (4 per day, 19,400dr/€46.26).

Buses: The **central bus station** (☎93 306) fills a block within Kydonias, Zymvrakakidon, Smyrnis, and Kelaidi. Service to: **Elafonissi** (1 per day, 2500dr/€6.45); **Hora Sfakion** (3 per day, 1500dr/€4.40); **Iraklion** (17 per day, 2900dr/€8.50); **Kastelli** (14 per day, 1000dr/€2.93); **Paleohora** (4 per day, 1600dr/€4.69); **Platanias** (every 30min., 350dr/€1.03); **Rethymno** (17 per day, 1600dr/€4.69); **Samaria Gorge** (4 per day, round-trip 2800dr/€8.39); and **Sougia** (1 per day, 1550dr/€4.40). Schedules and fares change depending on season, so call ahead.

Ferries: ANEK Office, Pl. Market 2 (☎27 500). *Lato* and *Lissos* go to **Piraeus** (9½hr., 8:30pm, 5900dr/€17.29). Call ahead in July-Aug. about an additional morning departure between 8 and 9am, with a 30% discount fare. Open 7:30am-8:30pm.

Moped and Car Rental: Several agencies are on Halidon. Mopeds 4000-7000dr/ €11.72-20.50 per day. Cars go for around 8000-13,000dr/€23.44-38.09 per day. Make sure to ask if unlimited kms are included in the price, and beware of scams.

Tourist Office: Kriari 40 (☎/fax 92 624), just off Pl. 1866. Free maps of Hania and Crete. Open M-F 7:30am-2:30pm. Private tourist agencies near Pl. 1866 offer travel advice in English. The **Tourist Information Center,** Kanevaro 10, on the east side of the harbor, has info on rooms to let. Open M-F 9am-2pm and 6-9pm, Sa 9:30am-2pm.

Banks: National Bank (☎28 810), on the corner of Nikiforou, Foka, and Tzanakaki streets. **ATM.** Open M-Th 8am-2pm, F 8am-1:30pm.

Luggage storage: You can leave your bags at the bus station while looking for a room. 500dr/€1.47 per bag. Open 6am–6:30pm and 7:30-9pm.

Police: Irakliou 23 (tourist ☎53 333, general ☎28 730). Open 7:30am-8pm.

Emergency: ☎100. 24hr. **ambulance:** ☎166.

Hospital: (☎27 000). Located in Mournies, 6km south of Hania. Outpatient clinic open M-Sa 12:30-2pm and 6-9pm, Su 8am-9pm.

OTE: Tzanakaki 5 (☎35 519). Open 7am-10pm. Telex and telegram M-F only.

Internet Access: Sante (☎94 737), a cafe toward the west end of the harbor on the waterfront, offers Internet access upstairs. 500dr/€1.47 per 30min., 1000dr/€2.93 per hr., 500dr/€1.47 deposit. Open 9:30am-1am. **Vranas Internet Cafe,** on the corner of Kalinikou Sarpaki and Agion Deka, beside Mitropeleos Square (☎58 618). 1000dr/€2.93 per hr. 200dr/€.59 deposit. Open 8am-late.

Post Office: Tzanakaki 3 (☎28 445). Open M-F 7:30am-8pm, Sa 7:30am-2pm. **Postal Code:** 73100.

ACCOMMODATIONS

Inexpensive pensions are hard to come by, but the best prices are found in the Old Town. Pensions in the New Town have dazzling views of the harbor and are near noisy night spots. Small hotels sprout from the beaches to the west, but expect to pay dearly for the brown sands of **Nea Kydonia** and **Agia Marina**. The **Association of Rooms to Let: Unikreta Travel Agency,** Dor. Episkopou 20, one block left of harbor center, can help you find a room. (☎43 601; fax 46 277. Open M-F 9am-2pm.) Also worth trying are the Tourist Office and Tourist Information Center (see listings above). Beware of people at the bus station trying to entice visitors to stay in their rooms: hawking at the station is illegal.

Hotel Fidias, Sarpaki 6 (☎52 494). Walking toward the harbor on Halidon, turn right onto Athinagora; half a block past the cathedral on the right, Athinagora becomes Sarpaki and the pension is on your right. Irasmos, the owner, provides bright, comfortable rooms with balconies as well as invaluable travel tips; free luggage deposit; laundry downstairs. English spoken. Reception open 7am-10pm. Dorms 2000-3000dr/€5.86-8.79; singles 4000d/€11.72; doubles 4000-6000dr/€11.72-17.58; triples/dorms 6000-9000dr/€17.58-26.37, depending on season. 15% senior discount in winter.

Meltemi Pension, Agelou 2 (☎/fax 92 802), at the west side of the harbor, next to the Naval Museum. High ceilings, private showers, and clear views of the harbor will make you feel like the king of budget travelers. The **Meltemi Cafe** downstairs serves *frappés* (600dr/€1.76), breakfast (1300-1600dr/€3.81-4.69), and cocktails (1300dr/€3.81) come nightfall. English spoken. Takes reservations, but no credit cards. Singles 7000dr/€20.51; doubles 8000-12,000dr/€23.44-35.16; triples 15,000dr/€43.50.

Aphroditi Rooms, Ag. Deka 24 (☎57 602), has affordable doubles and triples in a pleasant location near the harbor. Most rooms have private bathrooms and kitchen facilities; laundry downstairs. Doubles 5000dr/€14.65; triples 10,000dr/€29.35.

FOOD

You could construct a fantasy meal from the exotic foodstuffs and affordable snacks available at the open-air **Municipal Market** in (surprise!) Pl. Market. Wheels of cheese, fresh catch of the day, and homegrown vegetables accompany the many bakeries and small cafes. Inside, **Restaurant Bonne Petite** provides cooked seafood, if you can't fry your own. (Open Sa-M and W 8am-2pm, Tu and F 8am-2pm and 6-9pm.) For other cheap options, try the **supermarket** (☎90 558) in Pl. 1866, on the right coming from Halidon. (Open Sa-Th 8am-9pm, F 8am-6pm.)

CRETE

Anaplous (☎ 41 320), on the right from the harbor on Sifaka. This romantic open-air bistro is set in pink stone ruins. Flowering vines dangle from the restaurant's only ceiling. Nikos, the innovative chef, boasts of offering the only *pilino* (pork and lamb cooked 6-7hr. in fresh clay) in Greece. Breaking the clay (7000dr/€20.51) may also bust your wallet, but it serves 3. Other dishes average 1900dr/€5.57. Stellar vegetarian options abound, like *boureki* (seasoned zucchini, 1680dr/€4.98). Anaplous moves to a Venetian house across the street during winter. Open daily noon-3pm and 6pm-midnight.

Tamam, Zambeliou 49 (☎ 96 080). Tamam may not catch your eye among the multitude of beautiful open-air restaurants on and around Zambeliou, but the stellar food is a secret of the natives. Intimate dinners such as stuffed peppers with cheese (1300dr/€3.81), *hounkiar beyiendi* (chicken in eggplant puree, 2100dr/€6.15), and vegetarian alternatives delight locals and visitors alike. Open daily 1pm-12:30am.

Akrogiali, Akti Papanikoli 19 (☎ 73 110), on the waterfront in **Nea Hora,** a 12min. walk westward along the water past the Maritime Museum. Scarf down fresh seafood snatched straight out of the Mediterranean as you gaze across the road at Hora's white beaches. Open M-Sa 6pm-1am, Su 11am-1am.

Bougatsa Iorthanis, Apokoronou 24 (☎ 91 345). This authentic breakfast joint is famous for its *bougatsa,* (goat cheese in a tasty pastry covered with sugar), which is made by only one family in Hania. Portions cost 600dr/€1.76. Open daily 9am-1pm.

🎵 ENTERTAINMENT

Rock clubs such as **Mythos,** Akti Koundourioti 52, and **Street,** right next door, provide a club/bar scene and cheesy club-pop for a 2000dr/€5.86 cover that includes one free beer or drink (ensuing beers and drinks 1000-2000dr/€2.93-5.86). The clubs are open until 3:30am on weekdays, and until the crowds flee on weekends. **Mylos,** a must-see dance club for red-blooded beach-party devotees, is only a 2000dr/€5.86 taxi ride away in Platanias (see **Near Hania,** p. 493). **Anecdote,** Zambeliou 45, an "everybody knows your name" type bar, serves up free nuts and old American jazz to a mostly local crowd. (Beer and wine 600dr/€1.76, pitcher of raki 1000dr/€2.93.) For nightly traditional music and dancing in a relaxed setting, sit down and sip a slow drink with the older locals in the narrow confines of **Kafe Kriti,** an outpost of Cretan culture on Kalergon on the east side of the harbor.

👁 SIGHTS

VENETIAN INNER HARBOR. A long, hot walk to the **Venetian lighthouse,** an odd tower of stone, provides a superb view of Hania from the water. This tower guards the entrance to Hania's stunning architectural relic, the Venetian Inner Harbor. The inlet has retained its original breakwater and Venetian arsenal, and the Egyptians restored the lighthouse during their occupation of Crete in the late 1830s. On the west side of the main harbor, the **Maritime Museum** describes the tumultuous (often ferocious) 6000 years of Crete's naval and merchant history in maps and models. The second floor houses a large exhibition on Crete's remarkable expulsion of the Nazis in 1941. (☎ 91 875. *Open daily Apr.-Oct. 9am-4pm, Nov.-Mar. 9am-2pm. 600dr/€1.76, students 350dr/€1.03.*) In the **Venetian Shiphouse,** at the east end of the harbor where Arhdeon meets Anti Bnoseos, a temporary museum is set up with a new theme each summer—consult the tourist office. The melange of Ottoman and Venetian architecture in the **waterfront alleys** reflects the city's past. At the corner of Kandanoleu and Kanevaro, just north of Kanevaro on **Kastelli Hill,** visitors can look upon more ancient reminders of Hania's ancient Kydonian Bronze Age prosperity, including the **Late Minoan House** (c. 1450 BC) and other fenced-off and unmarked monuments.

MUNICIPAL GARDENS. On the left as you walk down Tzanakaki from the city center. Greeks of all ages flee heavily touristed streets in favor of the floral shade of the **Municipal Gardens**, *Dimotikos Kypos*, once the property of a *muezzin* (Islamic prayer caller). Multi-faceted, the garden also features an **open-air movie theater** that screens international films (☎41 427; 1800dr/€5.46), in addition to a zoo of several goats, many birds, and a flock of free-range pigeons. UNICEF sets up an annual **International Fair** in the gardens—see the tourist office for details.

SFAKIANAKI. This tree-lined 19th-century neighborhood is beyond the gardens to the east. The **Historical Museum and Archives**, Sfakianaki 20, may not cater to English speakers, but its small display of Cretan weaponry, photos of 19th-century generals, and tattered Cretan flag will surely enthrall Greek speakers and costume specialists. (☎52 606. Open M-F 9am-1pm. Free.)

ARCHAEOLOGICAL MUSEUM. The **Archaeological Museum,** on Halidon about 40m past the cathedral, features a broad collection of Cretan artifacts, ranging from early Minoan to Hellenistic times. Once a Venetian monastery, then the mosque of Yusuf Pasha, these high-ceilinged halls are lined with mosaics, grave steles, clay shards of Linear B, and even some scraps of Linear A: get your gold, glass, stone, or clay! (☎52 606. Open T-Su 8:30am-3pm. 1000dr/€2.93, students 300dr/€0.88.)

▶ DAYTRIPS FROM HANIA

PLATANIAS Πλατανιας

30min. from Hania by bus (every 30min., 350dr/€1.03).

Platanias (plat-AHN-yaas) shelters long, pretty beaches and seemingly thousands of tourists for every local. Platanias's fame sprang from a large rock island just off-shore, better known as Kracken, the petrified sea monster. Perseus turned the Kracken to stone with the aid of Medusa's severed head. (For a cinematic retelling, check out the special effects wizardry of *Clash of the Titans*.) Present-day Platanias's most famous phenomenon, swanky rock club **Mylos,** beats any MTV beach party for sheer numbers of gyrating hot bodies and hard, pumping beats. The converted, well-polished bread mill draws nightly crowds of suavely dressed young Europeans from midnight until morning. Take the last bus from Hania, get off at the bus stop at Platanias Center, and continue walking away from Hania. After about 450m, a huge sign will alert you to the right-hand turnoff that leads past an enormous parking lot to Mylos, the **beach,** and booty aplenty. (Beer 1500dr/€4.40. Cover 2000dr/€5.86, includes one drink. To get home, either take a cab for 2000dr/€5.86, or party until the 6:30am bus arrives the next morning.)

AKROTIRI PENINSULA

*Note: Akrotiri Peninsula is most easily navigated by car. Using the bus, you will need two days to visit all of the sites, due to inconvenient bus times. However, it is quite easy to visit both beaches **or** both monasteries in one day.*

Just northeast of Hania is the sparsely populated peninsula of Akrotiri, home to Zorba's hill at Stavros, several monasteries, and sheltered aquamarine coves. At the small, white sand beach of **Kalatnos,** 16km from Hania, sunbeds with umbrellas go for 1000dr/€2.93euro per day. Kalatnos lies on the route of the bus to **Stavros,** another glorious beach with a handful of demure resort hotels, all looking up at a mining hill you may recognize from the movie *Zorba the Greek.* Take the bus (1hr., 4 per day, 400dr/€1.17) and get off at the end of the line in front of **Christiana's Restaurant** (☎39 152), where you can eat breakfast, lunch, or dinner for a reasonable price; have a talk with Nikos (the bartender) over a drink, and listen to live traditional Greek music every Thursday night starting at 8pm. On the sand, you can rent an umbrella and a deck chair for 1000dr/€2.93 per day, or take a walk down to the rockier, though more private and no less lovely, end of the beach. Get your refreshments 30m inland at **Zorba's Original Tavern.** Both Stavros and Kalatnos make excellent daytrips for travelers staying in Hania and hankering for more secluded, unpolluted beaches.

About 6km from Kalatnos on the way to Stavros (16.5km from Hania) is the monastery of **Agia Triada** (☎ 63 310), which was built in 1606 near ruins of a Minoan temple (c. 1700 BC) and has produced traditional olive oil since 1632. Enjoy a peaceful walk through the grounds and small museum, with its collection of mostly 19th-century pieces and three Byzantine paintings (1635-45). You can bottle the experience in the form of Agia Triada olive oil (600dr/€1.76 for 250ml, 1200dr/€3.52 for a pretty bottle). Modest dress is requested: long skirts for women, long pants for men, and no bare shoulders. (Open 8am-2pm and 5-7pm. 300dr/€.88.) Monastery buffs who just can't get enough may want to trek the 4km up a stubby Cretan hill (complete with wild goats and narcissus flowers) to **Gouverneto,** a similar but smaller monastery. (☎ 63 319. Open 7am-2pm and 4-7:30pm.)

BALOS

The secret lagoon of Balos rests on the northwestern tip of Crete. Chartered boats reach this shore, and some travelers brave the hassle of driving, but are richly rewarded for it. To drive from Hania, take the main road (Skalidi) out of Hania going west along the northern coast and following signs for Kissamos and Kisari. Go through Kissamos approximately 2km past the town, take a right turn towards Balos and Kiliviani. Continue to follow signs for Balos and soon the road will change from pavement to a dirt road that grows increasingly treacherous as it winds on. You'll see a small white chapel on your right—keep going. Once you reach a parking lot (after 90min. of driving), take the small path to your left and hike for 30min. through goat country, to the mind-blowing **blue lagoon** with bright white sand and shallow waters. You will feel that you have found your paradise. If you get greedy for pleasure, continue to drive down the coast through Platanos towards Kefali, and pick your spot among the breathtaking stretch of beach. Or take the less travelled route southward to Elafonisi, to pass the late afternoon without the usual swarm of tourists.

SAMARIA GORGE Φαραγγι της Σαμαριας

*Open May 1 to Oct. 15 6am-4pm. For gorge information, call the **Hania Forest Service** (☎(0821) 92 287), or pick up info at the tourist offices in Hania, Rethymno, or Iraklion. **Buses** for Omalos and Xyloskalo leave Hania (3 per day, 1500dr/€4.40). Early buses (6:15-8:30am) can get you to Xyloskalo in time for a day's hike; the 1:45pm bus will get you to Omalos, ready to go the next day. If you want to spend the night in Omalos, rest up at **Gigilos Hotel** on the main road. (☎0821 67 181. Singles 4000-5000dr/€11.72-14.65; doubles 6000dr/€17.58.) From **Rethymno,** take the 6:15 or 7am buses through Hania to Omalos (2550dr/€7.33). Early risers can take the 5:30am bus from **Iraklion** through Rethymno and Hania to Omalos (3850dr/€11.32). **Admission** 1200dr/€3.52, children under 15 and organized student groups free. Hang on to your ticket; you have to give it back at the gorge's exit.*

The most popular excursion on Crete is the five- to six-hour hike down the longest gorge in Europe, the Samaria Gorge, a formidable 16km pass through the **White Mountains National Park.** Sculpted by rainwater over the course of 14 million years, the gorge retains its allure despite mobs of international visitors. Those who remember to take their eyes off their feet may be knocked off of them by the scenery: epiphytes peek out from sheer rock walls, wild flowers border the path, wild *agrimi* goats clamber around one of their last natural homes, and endangered gryphon vultures and golden eagles soar overhead. Humans have settled here for centuries, as the 1379 church of **Saint Maria of Egypt,** the source of the gorge's name, attests. While under Ottoman rule, Cretan rebels hid out in the gorge's caves.

Though it's possible to reach the gorge from any number of major tourist towns, **Hania** is the closest and allows the for the most flexibility. The 44km, 1½-hour bus ride from Hania to **Xyloskalo** places you at the start of the trail and provides passengers with views of small mountain towns and more goats! The base town boasts no more than toilets, a cafeteria, a shop, and the ticket booth—the last of their kind that you'll see for several hours. From Xyloskalo, you begin a long descent, following a noisy but nearly dry river, and passing between cliff walls as high as 600m and as narrow as 3½m. Much of the hike is shaded by clumps of pines and by the walls of the gorge itself. The hike ends in the small beach town of **Agia Roumeli** on the south coast (see below)—from there, experienced hikers can try the ten-hour hike to **Hora Sfakion** (see below) along one of the more outstanding coastlines in the country, or a path from Xyloskalo that ascends **Mt. Gingilos** to the west. If you're only interested in the dramatic tail of the gorge, you can start at Agia Roumeli; the path to the trail begins behind Hotel Livikon at the rear of the village. Known as "Samaria the Lazy Way," the two-hour climb to the north takes you to the gorge's narrow pass: the **Iron Gates**.

Whichever route you choose, bring water, trail snacks, and supportive shoes with good tread. The gorge is dry and dusty in summer, and well-worn stones on the path are very slippery. Often, the altitude makes the top of the gorge cold and rainy. If you get tired on the hike, keep an eye out for the **donkey taxis** that patrol the trail, although they can be few and far between. Be sure to bring enough **cash** to get to the gorge and home again as there are no banks on either end. Pack a bathing suit so you can rinse off after a hard day at the beach in Agia Roumeli. Please observe the Hania Forest Protection Service's rules concerning litter.

AGIA ROUMELI. This town exists solely for you, the hikers, because you are tired and hungry at the end of the gorge. Here you will find nothing but a beach, restaurants, grocery store, souvenirs, and lodging. If you need a rest, sleep right where the path meets the town, at **Hotel Livikon,** in a room with a balcony and bathroom. (☎91 363. Doubles 6000dr/€17.58; triples 7000dr/€20.51.) **Ferries** run from Agia Roumeli quite frequently from April to October to **Hora Sfakion** (2 per day, 1500dr/€4.40) and to **Sougia** and **Paleohora** (1 per day, 1000-2100dr/€2.93-6.16). From November to March, there are three ferries per week; call in advance for their times. The last **bus** from Hora Sfakion waits for the last ferry. The bus and ferry are scheduled at 7:30 and 6pm respectively, so you can make the complete round-trip from Hania, Rethymno, or Iraklion in one day if you leave on a morning bus. (One-way bus from Hora Sfakion to Hania 1600dr/€4.69, to Rethymno 1600dr/€4.69, to Iraklion 3100dr/€9.08.)

CRETE

BULL LEAPING, PART II While many Minoans enjoyed jumping over bulls (see **Bull Leaping, Part I,** p. 479), one Minoan queen jumped a bull. Poseidon, the sea god, had given **King Minos** a white bull specifically to slaughter in the god's honor, but Minos neglected to axe the bull as promised. Aphrodite then set out for twisted retribution: she filled his wife **Pasiphaë** with a burning lust for the fine bull. Pasiphaë hired master engineer **Daedalus** to build a sexy cow costume to catch the bull's eye. After a (literal) roll in the hay, Pasiphaë gave birth to the hideous **Minotaur,** a fearsome beast with a bull's head (and a bullheaded attitude to match), a man's body, and a taste for human flesh. Minos shut the bully bastard into an inescapable **labyrinth** designed by Daedalus; to feed the monster, he taxed mainland Greece seven maidens and seven youths every year. The Minotaur gobbled the young'uns year after year until dashing Athenian prince **Theseus** volunteered to be sacrificed. Theseus met, wooed, proposed to, and conspired to escape with **Ariadne,** Minos and Pasiphaë's all-human daughter. Ariadne gave Theseus a ball of string to find his way around the labyrinth; within the maze, he killed the monster, retraced his path, and escaped by ship with Ariadne. Theseus then ditched Ariadne on the beach of Naxos (p. 380), Bacchus' favorite hangout. Men. Soon, Bacchus himself quieted Ariadne's grief and married her. Back in Crete, Minos imprisoned Daedalus and his son **Icarus** for their role in the whole mess. Resourceful Daedalus manufactured wax wings for them, going for the ultimate jailbreak. With freedom in sight, Icarus ignored Dad's warning not to fly so close to the sun; his wings melted, and he plummeted to his death.

HORA SFAKION Χωρα Σφακιων   ☎ 0825

The extremely small port town of Hora Sfakion, often called simply Sfakion, lacks the intimacy of Plakias to the east or Paleohora to the west, but serves as the transportation hub of the south coast. Its quiet streets and tavernas are a necessary resting spot following the Samaria Gorge hike, and the location makes it a convenient base for daytrips to the area's smaller gorges and lovely beaches.

■▨ ORIENTATION AND PRACTICAL INFORMATION. The town consists of one main harborfront road, which opens off a plateia 50m uphill from the ferry dock. Four **buses** per day go to: **Hania** (2hr., 1600dr/€4.69; last at 7pm); **Rethymno** (1½hr., 1600dr/€4.69; change at Vrises); and **Iraklion** (3100dr/€9.08; last at 7pm; change at Vrises). Buses leave Vrises for **Rethymno** and **Iraklion** every hour on the hour. Buses also run to **Agia Galini** (2hr., 2200dr/€6.45). If your ferry is late, don't worry—the buses wait for the boats to arrive. Boats from Hora Sfakion travel to **Agia Roumeli** (1¼hr., 4 per day, 1500dr/€4.40). From April to October, most routes stop in **Loutro**. In winter, travelers go by foot or fishing boat. As always, it is a good idea to check schedules with the ticket office (☎91 221). Boats also run to **Gavdos,** a sparsely populated island that is the southernmost point in Europe (Sa-Su 9am). **Caïques** to Sweetwater Beach leave at 10:30am and return at 5:30pm every day (500dr/€1.47 each way). Uphill from the plateia on your right, you'll find the **OTE** (☎91 299; open M-F 7:30am-3:15pm) and, eventually, farther up the hill, the flag-bedecked 24hr. **police station** (☎91 205) and **port police** (☎91 292). Walking from the plateia toward the street, you'll see the **post office** on your left (☎91 244; open M-F 7:30am-2pm) and the helpful travel agency, **Sfakia Tours,** right next door (☎/fax 91 130; open 8am-9:30pm), where you can get bus tickets and rental cars (9000dr/€26.37 per day). **Postal code:** 73011.

▛▙ ACCOMMODATIONS AND FOOD. Hotel owners in Hora Sfakion are aware their town is a convenient rest stop after the Samaria Gorge, and their prices reflect this. The cool, grotto-like **Hotel Xenia,** at the far end of the street, has pleasant and spacious rooms with refrigerators and phones. Enjoy a good breakfast for 900dr/€2.64 under their flowery veranda. (☎91 490; fax 91 491. Doubles 8000dr/€23.44.) **Lefka Ori,** on the waterfront, rents rooms with views of the harbor. (☎91 209. Doubles with bath 6000dr/€17.58.) **Hotel Alkyion,** also on the waterfront, has neat and tidy rooms with private balconies and bathrooms. Sip free coffee on the upstairs balcony overlooking the harbor. Late risers beware: checking out after noon will cost you 50% more. (☎91 180; fax 91330. Open 8am-1pm. Doubles 5000-8500dr/€14.65-24.91; triples 7000-9500dr/€20.51-27.84. Laundry service 1500dr/€4.40 per load.) No-frills **Stavris** modestly awaits at the end of the back street. (☎91 220 or 91 201; fax 91 152. Singles 4500-5000dr/€11.72-14.65; doubles 5000-6000dr/€14.65-17.58; triples 6000-7000dr/€17.58-20.51.) The town's restaurants are limited to those downstairs from the hotels (entrees average 1500-2500dr/€4.40-7.33). **Hotel Alkion** has excellent stuffed eggplant and meatballs (1500dr/€4.40) with a free shot of *raki* after dinner. The **supermarket** is a good place to stock up on food. The only disco, **Underground,** rocks nightly, if you're not too exhausted from your hike. (Open nightly 10pm-morning. No cover.) In the mood for exhibitionism? Make a trip to **Sweetwater Beach,** where sunbathers strut their stuff in the buff. To walk there, take the main road westward out of town and follow the clearly marked sign from the main road down to the pebbly shore.

PALEOHORA Παλαιοχωρα   ☎ 0823

Once a refuge for the embattled rear guard of the 1960s counterculture, Paleohora (pahl-eo-KHOR-ah) has since calmed down to a state of contented middle-aged charm. The town, 77km south of Hania, is a peninsular retreat flanked by a rocky harbor on its east side and smooth beaches on its west, all set against the splendor of the Cretan mountain backdrop.

TRANSPORTATION. One to two **ferries** per day leave this modest port for: **Sougia** (45min., 1000dr/€2.93); **Agia Roumeli** (1½hr., 9:30am, 2100dr/€6.15); **Loutro** (2¼hr., 2700dr/€7.91); and **Hora Skafion** (2½hr., 2800dr/€8.20). One boat per day departs Paleohora for **Elafonisi** at 10am and returns at 4pm (1hr., 1300dr/€3.81 each way). A boat goes to **Gavdos** three times a week (3½hr.; post boat leaves M and Th 8:30am, returns 2:30pm, tourist boat goes at the same time Tu; tourists may ride either boat; 3100dr/€9.08 each way.) More tourist boats run in summer. For information about boats, tickets, and much more, visit the friendly people at **Notos Rentals** (☎42 110; fax 41 838). **Syria Travel** (☎41 198; fax 41 535) is a general tourist office that is helpful for ferry information and tickets, as well as basic information about the region. The **bus station** is on Venizelou on the northern edge of town. Buses run to **Hania** (2hr., 3 per day, 1600dr/€4.69) and **Samaria** at 6am (1400dr/€4.10). For a taxi, call **Paleohora Taxi Office** (☎41 128 or 41 061).

ORIENTATION AND PRACTICAL INFORMATION. The lodgings and restaurants of Paleohora town cluster around the main thoroughfare, **Venizelou,** which runs down the center of the peninsula from north to south. Heading north on Venizelou takes you to Hania, and south to the ruins of an **old castle.** Venizelou crosses **Kentekaki,** which leads west to the beach and east to the harbor.

Walking toward the center of town from the bus station, you'll find the **National Bank,** with a 24hr. **ATM** three blocks up on your right. (☎41 430. Open M-Th 8am-2pm, F 8am-1:30pm.) Half a block farther and also on your right is the helpful **tourist office.** (☎41 507. Open W-M 10am-1pm and 6-9pm.) A block and a half farther, on your right again, is the **OTE.** (☎41 299. Open June-Sept. M-F 7:30am-10pm; Oct.-May M-F 7:30am-3pm.) The **port police** (☎41 214) are farther down the main street. Turning left toward the harbor at the OTE leads to the **police station** (☎41 111), one block down on your left. The port lies past the police station toward the harbor. Notos Rentals (See above) also runs a **laundry, exchanges money,** and has **internet access** (500dr/€1.47 per 15min., 900dr/€2.64 per 30min., 1500dr/€4.40 per 1hr.) All facilities are open 8am-2pm and 5-11pm. There is a **doctor** on Venizelou (☎41 380), one street past the bus station heading away from town; the **public health center** (☎41 211) is behind the OTE, heading away from the beach. There is a **pharmacy** on Venizelou across from the OTE. (☎41 498. Open 8am-2:30pm and 5-11:45pm.) To find the **post office,** head to the beach from the OTE and make a right. (☎41 206. Open M-F 7:30am-2pm.) **Postal code:** 73001.

ACCOMMODATIONS AND CAMPING. Some small hotels line the road closest to the harbor. In the middle of the harbor stands a tall white building marked **Dream Rooms,** run by the cordial Nikos Bubalis and his bubbly wife. Rooms with balconies look out onto the picturesque harbor and the surrounding mountains. (☎41 112. Singles 4000-5000dr/€11.72-14.65; doubles 5000-7000dr/€14.65-20.51; triples 6000-8000dr/€17.58-23.44.) A bit farther along the waterfront going away from the ferry dock is **Christos Restaurant and Hotel,** which has comfortable doubles with private bath. (☎41 359. Doubles 7000-9000dr/€20.51-26.37.) Away from the harbor, **Savas Rooms** offers quiet, shady rooms with private bathrooms. To get there, walk from the bus station 50m north on Venizelou toward Hania; Savas is on your left at the edge of town. (☎41 075. Doubles 6000-7000dr/€17.58-20.51.) **Camping Paleohora** is a 10min., well-marked walk east of town. With its own on-site restaurant, the campsite is across the street and within earshot of Club Paleohora, the town's popular disco, and a beautiful **beach.** To reach it, walk north on Venizelou (away from town), turn right just after the bus station, take the second left on the last paved road before the beach, and walk 1km to the site. (☎41 120. Open Apr.-Oct. 1000dr/€2.93 per person, 500dr/€1.47 per child, children under 4 free.; 500dr/€1.47 per tent; 500dr/€1.47 per car; 500dr/€1.47 per child, children under 4 free.)

◨◪ FOOD AND ENTERTAINMENT. Markets and **tavernas** are fixtures along Venizelou and its surrounding streets; several restaurants serve traditional Greek food along the waterfront from standard tourist menus at mid-range prices (*tzatziki* 400-600dr/€1.17-1.76, *moussaka* 1000-1200dr/€2.93-3.52, baklava 500-700dr/€1.47-2.05). Notable among these is **Christos Restaurant.** Vegetarians and carnivores alike will appreciate the homemade Greek, Asian, and European dishes at the ◪**Third Eye Vegetarian Restaurant;** to get there, turn right after the pharmacy, walk three blocks, turn left, take an immediate right, and the Third Eye will be on the left. All things veggie are delicious and under 950dr/€2.75, while meat lovers are penalized in price but fortunately not flavor. Nourish your mind and body with scrumptious falafel and pumpkin and yogurt pastry, each 950dr/€2.75. (☎41 234. Main dishes are around 1400dr/€4.10. Open Apr.-Oct. 8am-3pm and 6pm-midnight.) **Club Paleohora,** across from Camping Paleohora, is the town's popular, music-pumping, open-air disco. Follow the directions to the campsite, or take the minibus that transports clients from **Skala** bar in front of the port to the disco every 30min. from midnight to 4am. (☎42 230. Drinks 800-1500dr/€ 2.53-4.40. Cover F-Sa 1000dr/€2.93 includes one beer. Open M-Sa 11pm-5am, Su 11pm-6am.)

◪ DAYTRIP FROM PALEOHORA: ELAFONISI (Ελαφονισι). Elafonisi is a beach across from a small uninhabited island at the southwestern corner of Crete. Tourists tumble on the soft, white sand of the mainland side of the beach 10am to 4pm, but wading 100m through crystal-clear water will wash you up on the shores of the island beach. On its mainland side are sunchairs (1000dr/€2.93), restrooms (150dr/€.39), and a taverna with prices steeper than the face of the Cretan Mountains. (Open 8am-8pm. Souvlaki 800dr/€2.53, burgers 800dr/€2.53, beer 500dr/€1.47.) If the sun hasn't drained all of your energy, a 200m walk up the road from the beach to the next taverna will get you more baklava for your buck. If you miss your boat and want to stay overnight in Elafonisi, **Elafonisi Restaurant Bar** has private bungalows or rooms for reasonable prices. (☎0822 61 274. Singles and doubles 6000-8000dr/€17.58-23.44.)

Too much sun worshipping? Then pay homage of another sort at the cliffside monastery of **Chrisso Kalitissas,** which is operated by an order of nuns. Built from and supported by the cliffs, it's blessed with a magnificent ocean view. Reach it by walking 5km up the road from Elafonisi. The monastery will be in view on your left when you come to an unmarked but well-paved road; turn left, then make another left at the end of this road. *(Take the ferry from Paleohora along the south coast (leaves 10am, returns 4pm; 1300dr/€3.81 each way), or take the bus from Hania (leaves 8am, returns 4pm; 2500dr/€7.33 each way. Monastery free. Open daily 7pm-sunset.*

ANIDRI. Escape the crowds at Paleohora's beach at nearby Anidri Beach, which may be reached by car or on foot. An adventurous **day-hike** from Paleohora takes you to the picturesque village of Anidri and then on to Anidri beach itself. To begin the hike, take the road out of town past Camping Paleohora for about five minutes until the road forks; the low road to the right takes you along the coast to the beach, the higher road to the left will take you through the mountains to the village cafe (about 1hr. walk). Walk straight past its open patio and onto a road with a sign pointing to a church. Follow this road to its end and make another right. You'll reach a stone road with a sign pointing back to the cafe; turn left and go down it to the dry riverbed. Follow the signs and stone markers through the small gorge to the beach (about 40min. from town). The beautiful path is poorly marked and fairly difficult—your only company will be roaming **goats.** Make sure to wear sturdy walking shoes, and bring water and trail snacks.

The beaches at the bottom, especially the beach farthest to your left, are smooth, unblemished strips of pale sand surrounded by sheer cliffs and crystal clear water. No need to weigh yourself down with a bathing suit—going nude is perfectly normal here. To head back, walk eastward along the dirt road that traces the waterfront, which will return you to the right branch of the fork near Camping Paleohora. This path can be a gentle alternative for reaching the beach without risking the snares of the mountain path (45min.).

LASITHI PREFECTURE

Lasithi Prefecture isn't much for first impressions—heavily touristed towns such as Malia may rub you the wrong way—but hope is not lost. The road east from Iraklion along the north coast passes through jammed, overpriced resort towns with mediocre beaches crowded against the ocean by tavernas and an imported northern ambience. As the road continues east along the coast, however, it becomes gradually quieter and more scenic; inland, it hits smaller villages sustained not by tourism but by thriving local agriculture. Heed the advice of locals who nudge you toward the island's eastern edge, where stretches of pristine coastline fill the gaps between white villages and olive plains.

AGIOS NIKOLAOS Αγος Νικολαος   ☎ 0841

Occupying a small peninsula on the northeast edge of Crete, Agios Nikolaos is a nouveau chic resort town where posh vacationers huff and puff their way up steep, boutique-lined streets, then stop in at a harborside cafe to catch their breath with a cigarette. Meander through its sparkling, hilly streets and you'll find beach-obsessed patrons, one-stop holiday-makers, and hikers on their way to more obscure destinations. There are few bargains in Agios Nikolaos or in its satellite beach towns, but the intense nightlife, diverse array of intriguingly glamorous tourists, and remnants of indigenous Cretan culture make for a lively combination.

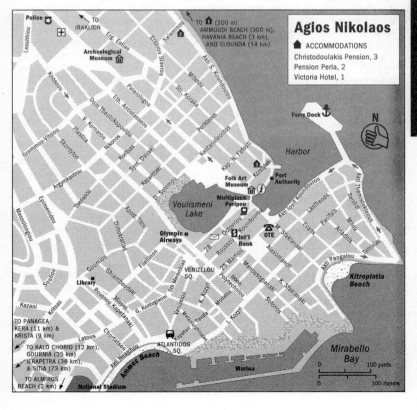

Agios Nikolaos

⌂ ACCOMMODATIONS
Christodoulakis Pension, 3
Pension Perla, 2
Victoria Hotel, 1

CRETE

⌐ TRANSPORTATION

Flights: Olympic Airways Office, Plastira 20 (☎28 929), overlooking the lake. Open M-F 8am-3:30pm. The closest **airport** is in Iraklion.

Buses: (☎22 234), in Pl. Atlantidos, across town from the harbor. To: **Ierapetra** (1hr., 7-9 per day, 750dr/€2.53); **Iraklion** (1½hr., 20 per day, 1450dr/€4.40) via **Malia** and **Hersonissos; Kritsa** (15min., 8-11 per day, 250dr/€0.88); **Lasithi** (1½hr., 2 per week, 1150dr/€3.52); **Sitia** (1½hr., 3-5 per day, 1550dr/€4.69). Buses to **Elounda** (20min., 14-20 per day, 250dr/€0.88) and **Plaka** (40min., 6-8 per day, 360dr/€1.17) leave from the tourist office.

Ferries: Nostos Tours, R. Koundourou 30 (☎22 819), sells tickets for departures all over Crete. Open 8am-1:30pm and 5-9pm. To: **Karpathos** (7hr., 3 per week, 4100dr/€12); **Kasos** (6hr., 3 per week, 3300dr/€9.68); **Piraeus** (12hr., 5 per week, 7500dr/€21.98) via **Milos** (7hr., 4 per week, 5000dr/€14.65); **Rhodes** (12hr., 3 per week, 6300dr/€18.46); **Sitia** (1hr., 5 per week, 1600dr/€4.69); **Spinalonga** (2 per day, 3000dr/€8.79). Ferries to **Cyprus** and **Israel** also available.

Taxis: 24hr. station (☎24 000 or 24 001), at the bridge beside the tourist office. Taxis abound around the monument on El. Venizelou.

Car and Moped Rental: Shop around on A. Koundourou. Car rentals average 10,000-12,000dr/€29.30-35.16 per day, motorbikes 4000-6000dr/€11.72-17.58 per day.

⚔🛈 ORIENTATION AND PRACTICAL INFORMATION

Agios Nikolaos is easy to navigate—it's set on a small peninsula, with beaches on three sides and most services, hotels, restaurants, and discos in the center. Facing the water from the bus station, turn around 180 degrees and walk straight onto **S. Venizelou.** Continue straight on this road until you reach Venizelou Sq., a rotary with a monument. If you stay on the right, you will head down to the harbor on **Roussou Koundourou.** Don't confuse the nepotistic street names: R. Koundourou, I. Koundourou, S. Koundourou…

Tourist Office: S. Koundourou 21A (☎22 357 or 24 165; fax 82 534). Cross the bridge at the harbor and take a right to reach the tourist office. Assists with accommodations, **exchanges currency,** sells phone cards and stamps, provides transportation schedules and a **map.** Open Apr.-June and Sept.-Nov. 8am-9:30pm, July-Aug. 8am-10:30pm.

Banks: Several on 28 Octovriou have 24hr. **ATMs.** The **National Bank** (☎28 735) is open for **currency exchange** M-Th 8am-2pm, F 8am-1:30pm; the bank's ATM is on R. Koundourou.

Emergencies: For **24hr. emergencies,** go to **Cretan Medicare,** Palaiologou 20 (☎27 551, 552, or 553; fax 25 423).

Police: Stavrou 25 (☎22 321); walk up Paleologon; it is just beyond the hospital. 24hr.

Tourist Police: Stavrou 25 (☎26 900), in the same building as the police. Regulates hotels, registers complaints, and gives general info. Open 8am-2pm.

Medical Care: There is a hospital (☎25 224) on Paleologou, at the north end of town. From the lake, walk up Paleologou, 1 block past the archaeological museum.

Pharmacies: Dr. Theodore Furakis (☎24 011), in Pl. Venizelou. Open M-F 8am-2pm.

OTE: (☎95 333), on the corner of 25 Martiou and K. Sfakianaki. Open M-Sa 7am-midnight, Su 7am-2:30pm.

Internet Access: ▧ **Multiplace Peripou,** 28 Octovriou 25 (☎24 876). Internet 1500dr/€4.40 per hour. Sells CDs and books. Open daily 9:30am-2am.

Post Office: 28 Octovriou 9 (☎22 062). Open M-Sa 7:30am-8pm. Branch at Metamorphosis 8 (☎22 276) for packages only. Open M-F 7:30am-2pm. **Postal code:** 72100.

ACCOMMODATIONS

Many larger hotels in Agios Nikolaos fill up months in advance. There are lots of **pensions** offering clean, cheap rooms, but their rooms are also in great demand, so make a reservation. Look for cheaper accommodations inland on the east side of the harbor, although some pensions on the western waterfront are also affordable. The **tourist office** has a bulletin board with many of Agios Nikolaos' pensions and their prices. Prices listed are reduced 20-40% in the off season.

Christodoulakis Pension, Stratigou Koraka 7 (☎22 525). With your back to the tourist office, turn right and climb the street next to the taxi station, then make the 2nd left onto Stratigou Koraka. Airy and light with a convenient location, common kitchen facilities, and large common balconies for sunbathing. Singles 4000dr/€11.72; doubles 6000dr/€17.58; triples 7500dr/€21.98.

Pension Perla, Salaminos 4 (☎23 379 or 26 523). Walk away from the harbor on S. Koundourou. Big rooms, some with balconies and harbor views. Comfortable TV lounge and fridge space. All but 2 rooms have private bath. Singles 4000dr/€11.72; doubles 5000-8000dr/€14.65-23.44; triples 6000-9000dr/€17.58-26.37.

Victoria Hotel (☎22 731; fax 22 266), about 1km from the harbor on S. Koundourou, near Amoudi Beach. A clean, white stucco hotel. Rooms with baths, phones, and balconies. Breakfast included. Singles 6000dr/€17.58; doubles 7000-9000dr/€20.51-26.37; triples 8000-11,000dr/€23.44-32.23.

FOOD

While Agios Nikolaos's waterfront suffers from a super-chic strain of the tourist-restaurant virus, there are tasty and semi-cheap eats to be found. **Spar Supermarket** is near the archaeological museum on Paleologou. (Ouzo 1150dr/€3.52 for 700ml.)

Sarri's, Kuprou 15 (☎28 059), 1 block from Pl. Venizelou. Sarri's serves freshly harvested food from the family farm. Vine-covered retreat is a rustic getaway from the nearby city center. Post-feast, enjoy the free *raki* under a quiet arbor. *Tzatziki*, chicken, potatoes, and a glass of wine 1800dr/€5.46. Open 8:30am-4pm and 6pm-midnight.

Loukakis Taverna, S. Koundourou 24 (☎28 022), a 10min. walk past the tourist office. The business from locals hasn't slowed since this family-run taverna opened in 1952, and the tourists are fairly innocuous. Veal *stifado* 1200dr/€3.52, chicken *okra* 1200dr/€3.52, and vegetarian dishes 400-900dr/€1.17-2.64. Open 9am-11pm.

Cafe-Creperie Central, R. Koundourou 6 (☎22 011). This sunny cafe folds up sweet and savory crepes (750-950dr/€2.15-2.79, additional toppings 100dr/€0.29), along with a spread of baked goods (sandwiches 450-550dr/€1.32-1.62).

SIGHTS AND BEACHES

Around hilly Agios Nikolaos you'll find a bathtub for goddesses, goat-inhabited archaeological sites, and cheap shopping.

FESTIVALS. Every two years, the last week of June or the first of July brings **Nautical Week,** when Greek seamen race in the waters around Agios Nikolaos. (The festival is coming in 2002). For landlubbers, there's nightly music and dancing around town. Call the tourist office for details. Facing the harbor are two islands. On the near one, endangered mountain goats, nicknamed Kri-Kri, have booted off human inhabitants. The Greek government has barred people from the Kri-Kri's island because of its archaeological value; the people of Agios Nikolaos have ordained it the Island of All Saints. Every year on the last weekend of June, the fisherman dock their boats in the harbor and gather passengers to ferry over to the island for the **Feast of All Saints.** The rest of the year, only the goats may set foot on Kri-Kri Island. The more distant island is also uninhabited; the municipality limits its use to the Boy Scouts.

CRETE

MARKET. You can shop for inexpensive clothes at the weekly **market,** where sundry items like paintings, knock-off Prada bags, swimming trunks (300dr/€0.88), and underwear (4 for 1000dr/€2.93) can be purchased. Goodies like watermelon (100dr/€0.29 per kg), tomatoes (50dr/€0.15 per kg), and Cretan honey (1000dr/€2.93 per 500g) are sold at the top of the hill. (On Eth. Antistassios, next to the lake. Open W 7am-1pm.)

MUSEUMS AND ARCHAEOLOGICAL SITES. Head away from the harbor and lake on Paleologou to reach the **Archaeological Museum,** which houses an extensive collection of artifacts, including Minoan sarcophagi (bones still inside), a well-documented coin collection from Greek and Roman times, and art from the underrepresented 7th-century Daedalic period. Don't miss the strange bowl of knuckle bones in the 10th room. (☎24 943. Open Tu-Su 8:30am-3pm. 500dr/€1.47; students 300dr/€0.88; EU students, classicists, fine arts students, and under 18 free.) Train your eye before you buy crafts at the weekly market by visiting the **Folk Art Museum,** next to the tourist office. Colorful tapestries, embroidered clothes, furniture, and icons are lovingly displayed in this private museum by the woman who assembled them. (☎25 093. Open Su-F 10am-4pm. 500dr/€1.47, under 12 free.)

One kilometer before Kritsa on the road from Agios Nikolaos, Crete's Byzantine treasure, the **Panagia Kera,** honors the Dormition of the Virgin in several narrative cycles. A patchwork of smoky 14th-century paintings adorns the central nave, while the wings bear 15th-century Byzantine frescoes. (Open 8:30am-3pm. 800dr/€2.35, students and seniors 400dr/€1.17.)

BEACHES. All of Agios Nikolaos's beaches are rated blue flag beaches by the EU, which means they're the cleanest of the clean. The constant sunshine and lack of rain makes these beaches perfect for sunning. Three of the more mediocre beaches are a quick walk from the main harbor, but the farther you venture, the better it gets. Lazy folks sunbathe on the concrete piers that jut out from S. Koundourou, while others head to **Ammos Beach** by the National Stadium, **Kitroplatia Beach** between Akti Panagou and the marina, or **Ammoudi Beach** farther up S. Koundourou away from town. Those with greater aspirations catch the hourly bus to Ierapetra or Sitia and get off at **Almiros Beach** (1.5km east of Agios Nikolaos), the area's best beach. Almiros is Agios Nikolaos's only natural beach, and nature abounds just up the hill, where an EU-protected **wildlife reserve** merits exploration. A river runs through the reserve and gushes cold water into the sea at Almiros; the hot springs hidden under the ocean surface mix with the cold jet for a titillating hot-cold swim. Sandy **Kalo Horio,** 10km farther, is less crowded; take either bus and tell the driver to let you off at the **Kavos Taverna.** Another beautiful, somewhat touristy spot is **Havania Beach,** at the Havania stop on the Elounda bus.

▣ ♫ NIGHTLIFE AND ENTERTAINMENT

Join the happy throng at the upscale clubs around the harbor on I. Koundourou or S. Koundourou. Alternatively, take in a movie at the **open-air theater** on Kazantzaki; from October to April, flicks are also available indoors at the **Rex** theater on M. Sfakianaki (1500dr/€4.40).

■ **Multiplace Peripou,** 28 Octovriou 25 (☎24 876). After dinner, Greek youths stream in to sip *frappés* (500dr/€1.47) and play or watch a game of backgammon. View of the lake and seashells preserved under glass tabletops. 1-stop entertainment spot with a cafe, Internet access (1500dr/€4.40 per hr.), and book and record store. From Oct.-May, the club cafe hosts live music twice a week, from Greek traditional to jazz acts. Occasional cover 2000-3000dr/€5.86-8.79. Open 9am-2am.

Rififi (☎23 140). A harborside rendezvous with a large balcony for backpackers and other tourists to view the passing traffic as they sip *frappés* (700dr/€2) and alcohol (cocktails 1500dr/€4.40, beer around 1000dr/€2.93). Open 11am-3am.

Sorrento Bar, on the harbor waterfront. A good place to begin a night of debauchery, with dancing bartenders and free shots of "fluffy" at the door. Cocktails 1500dr/€4.40, beer 900dr/€2.64. Open 9pm-3am.

Lipstick Night Club (☎22 377), on the waterfront; look for a pink neon sign. Join modern Bacchic frenzy with local kids. Free tequila at the door and shooters with drinks on F. Open 10:30pm-late. Happy Hour at the bar from 8-10:30pm.

⚑ DAYTRIPS FROM AGIOS NIKOLAOS: SPINALONGA

There are 2 ways to get to Spinalonga: Nostos, in Agios Nikolaos, offers guided boat rides and walking tours of the island for a combined price of 3000dr/€8.79. Bring your bathing suit; most boats make 20min. swim stops. If you don't want a guide, you can get there more cheaply by taking one of the frequent buses to Elounda (250dr/€0.72) and taking a ferry from Elounda to Spinalonga. Once you arrive at Spinalonga, there is a 500dr/€1.47 entrance fee for adults, 300dr/€0.88 for students. Under 18 free.

The most touted—and most disconcerting—excursion in eastern Crete is the trip to Spinalonga Island (Σπιναλογκα). A short distance across the clear sea from Plaka, the island is painted with a dichromatic scheme: robust green brush softens the harsh lines of the orange stone fortifications. This island-wide museum's simple coloring doesn't even hint at the island's long and bizarre history.

In 1204, after purchasing the entire island of Crete, the Venetians destroyed fortresses in Barba Rossa and Agios Nikolaos before investing 75 years building a third, almost impregnable fortress on Spinalonga. When Crete gained independence in 1898, the Greeks were determined to rid the island of all outsiders, including the Turks who had overtaken Spinalonga. In a kill-two-birds-with-one-island scheme, they established a leper colony there, simultaneously frightening away the Turks and sequestering the infected, who had previously inhabited mountain caves. On October 22, 1903, the first lepers arrived at their new home. In 1957, following the development of an effective treatment for leprosy, the colony was closed and the surviving residents were taken to Athens and cured. Spinalonga had been the last leper colony in Europe. The island was reopened in 1970, leaving a good 13 years to insure the absence of bacteria for visitors' safety.

When you arrive at the island, you will enter as the lepers did, through **Dante's Gate,** a grim, dark procession through an iron-barred tunnel to **Market St.,** past reconstructed Venetian and Turkish houses. For the first 9 years of the colony's existence, the lepers were not only poor, but also exploited by their corrupt governor. It was only in 1913 that inhabitants began receiving social security payments of one drachma per day—a large allowance at the time.

At the end of the street is the **Church of Agios Pandelemonis,** founded by the Venetians in 1709 and dedicated to the Roman doctor Pandelemon, the saint of the sick in the Greek Orthodox faith. Stairs lead from the church to the **laundry,** where water was collected into tubs, heated over fires, and used to rinse bandages. The **hospital,** halfway up the hill, is identifiable by its 8-window facade. It's lofty location theoretically allowed the wind to carry away the odor of rotting flesh.

Beyond the laundry are steps to the sea, to the right of these are the modern concrete **apartment buildings** that housed the lepers. At the bottom of the steps is the original arched entrance to the **fortress.** In front is the **disinfecting room,** where everything from bedsheets to clothing to coins was sterilized. Continuing on the path around the rest of the island, you will find the small orange-roofed **Church of Ag. George.** Built in 1661 by the Venetians, this is where lepers took communion. Past this church, at the top of the ramp leading back to Dante's Gate, is the cemetery and its 44 unmarked graves.

LASITHI PLATEAU ☎0844
Οροπεδιου Λασιθου

The inland route to Agios Nikolaos bypasses the jagged northern coastline and traverses the Lasithi Plateau, ringed by steep, crumbling mountains. This rural plain is home to 12 small, whitewashed villages full of exhausted donkeys and farmers tilling their fields. The residents of the region once harnessed the plains' persistent breezes with thousands of wind-powered water pumps; black-and-white pictures of their windmill-strewn fields adorn the walls of travel agencies across the northern coast. Since electric pumps have taken over in recent decades, a few of the windmills have been downsized, but otherwise modern life has taken the coastal road and bypassed Lasithi. Only a daytrip to the Dikteon Cave for most travelers, the tranquil plain boasts sufficient natural wonders and Old World hospitality to make a longer stay worthwhile.

▐ TRANSPORTATION. It's best to visit Lasithi on wheels (with a rental **car** or **moped**). Those who use the infrequent bus service may find themselves stranded for hours in one town, or limited to the few towns within walking distance.

If you're coming from **Iraklion,** take the coastal road 8km past Gournes, and then turn right on the road to **Kastelli** (not the one on the west coast). After about 6km the road forks right to Kastelli; stay left, heading toward **Potamies,** pausing to ogle the giant plane tree in the center of the town: it takes 12 men to wrap their arms around the trunk. Continuing on through Krassi, the main road winds around mountain ridges, cuts through the ruins of the stone windmills of the Seli Ambelou pass, and finally descends into the Lasithi Plateau.

If you're heading from **Malia,** you have two options. To reach the more manageable road, head west along the coastal road and turn left about 3km outside of town at the turn-off for **Mochos;** this road takes you onto the road that passes through Krasi, described in the directions from Iraklion. Your second option from Malia is to follow **25 Martiou** out of town, and follow the signs. This road is faster than the Mochnos route, but it is largely unpopulated and involves even more hairpin turns. **Buses** run between Lasithi Plateau and **Agios Nikolaos** (1½hr., 2 per week, 1150dr/€3.52), **Iraklion** (2hr., 2 per day, 1450dr/€4.40), and **Malia** (1 per day; leaves Malia 8:30am, leaves Lasithi 2pm; 1250dr/€3.81). The bus arrives first in Tzermiado, and then takes about 45 minutes to make its way around the whole plateau, so you can stop at any town that pleases you.

▐▐ ORIENTATION AND PRACTICAL INFORMATION. All the basics can be found in Tzermiado, the capital of Lasithi and the first and only large village you pass through upon entering the plain. The bus stops at the center of the town's main plateia in front of the Kronio Restaurant. The **tourist police** for Lasithi Plateau are in Agios Nikolaos, but the regular police station is a few doors down from Kronio. (☎22 208. Open 24hr.) The **OTE** is farther down the same road. (☎22 299. Open M-F 7:30am-3:10pm.) The **Agricultural Bank** across the street from the Kronio exchanges currency. (☎22 390. Open M-F 8am-1:30pm.) The **pharmacy** is 100m from the bus stop along the road to Agios Nikolaos. (☎22 310. Open 10am-1pm and 6-9pm; hours extended M-F.) A **medical center** (☎22 602) is open 24hr. for emergencies and basic primary care; walk away from the police station on the road with the Agricultural Bank, make your first left, and follow this road for 1km. The **post office** is next door to Kronio. (☎22 248. Open M-F 7:30am-2pm.) **Postal code:** 72052.

▐▐ ACCOMMODATIONS AND FOOD. In **Tzermiado,** you'll find **Hotel Kourites** by following the road with the pharmacy and the hotel beyond the Texaco. If no one is at reception, check in at the hotel's other building and taverna. The big bedrooms come with baths, balconies, and breakfast. (☎22 194. Singles 6000dr/

€17.58; doubles 8000-10,000dr/€23.44-29.30.) In **Agios Konstantinos,** your only option is **Maria Vlassi Rent Rooms,** behind Maria's embroidery shop on the road from Tzermiado. (☎31 048. Singles 3000dr/€8.79; doubles 4000dr/€11.72.) In **Agios Georgios,** there are several good choices: **Dias Hotel,** on the main road, has sunny rooms with sinks and 24hr. hot water. The rooms are decorated with the owner's handmade crafts; you may find her sewing when you arrive. (☎31 207. Singles 2500dr/€7.33; doubles 4000dr/€11.72; breakfast 600dr/€1.76. Student discount 500dr/€1.47.) **Hotel Maria,** on the opposite side of town, offers a hipper spin on traditional style; go to Rea Taverna on the main street to request a room. (Singles 5000dr/€14.65; doubles 6000-7000dr/€17.58-20.51.)

Most restaurants in Lasithi Plateau are linked to hotels. An exception to the rule is ◪**Kronio Restaurant,** the oldest taverna in Lasithi, at the center of **Tzermiado.** There's more to this place than the delectable food (*moussaka* 1200dr/ €3.52, *stifado* 1600dr/€4.69, Greek salad 800dr/€2.53): the corner at Kronio is a convention spot for the outgoing villagers to settle utilities bills, and a favorite coffee shop of the village priests. The **Kri Kri Taverna,** in the center of town, lavishes tender affection on its food. Ivy-covered walls and a homey fireplace make a strange but splendid combination (*moussaka* 1200dr/€3.52, omelette 700dr/€2). On the main road in **Agios Konstantinos,** the **Dikti Taverna** has excellent *moussaka* (1000dr/€2.93) and Greek coffee (150dr/€0.44). In **Agios Georgios,** the only restaurants are attached to hotels. In **Psychro's Taverna O Stavros,** the owner delights visitors with gifts of flowers and raki after a meal. (Tzatziki 500dr/€1.47; beer 300dr/€0.88.)

◪ **SIGHTS. Agios Georgios** is home to a **folklore museum,** which houses models of humans that are more amusing than edifying. Next door is the **El. Venizelou Museum,** a hall dedicated to honoring the former prime minister of Crete and president of Greece, who was born in Hania. (Open Apr.-Oct. 10am-5pm. Admission to both museums 800dr/€2.53, students 500dr/€1.47, under 12 free.)

The village of **Psychro** serves as a starting point for exploring ◪**Dikteon Cave,** 1km away. At the turn of the century, archaeologists found hundreds of Minoan artifacts crammed into the cave's ribbed stalactites; many are now at Iraklion's **Archaeological Museum.** Arthur Evans, who also dug up Knossos, excavated this spot and, in a blast of misguided enthusiasm, blew apart the entrance. To get there, follow signs from Ag. Georgios. Local members of the Association of Ass Drivers (insert joke here) will probably offer to taxi you (4000dr/€11.72 round-trip); the uphill walk is grueling, but it should take less than an hour. (Open 8:30am-3pm. 800dr/€2.53, students and seniors 400dr/ €1.17, EU students free.) For a nice daytrip, take the bus to Psychro, visit the Dikteon Caves, and then take the 1½hr. walk across the flat plain to Tzermiado, where you can grab a bite to eat.

The **Kronion Cave** may play second fiddle to Dikteon, but it's free from Dikteon's crowds and merits a brief side trip. Clear signs in Tzermiado will direct you to the 2km route to the grotto, the mythical home of Zeus's parents, Cronus and Rhea. The last kilometer is badly marked and manageable only by foot. Stay on the people path (there are many goat paths), and don't forget a flashlight.

IERAPETRA Ιεραπετρα   ☎0842

Although German tourists have made inroads, Ierapetra (ear-YEP-eh-tra) still welcomes more Greeks than foreigners. It's outed as Europe's southernmost city, but the title is dubious: the most urban aspect of Ierapetra is its tangled, unplanned streets, and it's otherwise quite small. After centuries of foreign rule by Arabs, Venetians, and Turks, the city's architecture reflects its worldly past, but in everyday life, the traditional rural ethic shines through in the hospitality of the locals.

🔒🔐 ORIENTATION AND PRACTICAL INFORMATION. Ierapetra can be difficult to navigate despite its small size. It has three main plateias, connected by three roads running north-south. With your back to the **bus station,** Lasthenous 41 (☎ 28 237), **Pl. Plastira** will be on your right. Walking straight for a block on **Lasthenous,** which then turns into **Koundouriotou,** brings you to **Pl. Eleftherias,** the central square. Keep walking in the same direction for about 100m to reach another plateia: **Pl. Kanoupaki.** South of it is the Old Town district. Pick up a free **map** of the city from one of the travel agencies along the waterfront. The **Ierapetra Express office,** Pl. El. Venizelou 25, is helpful. (☎ 28 673 or 22 411. Open 8am-1:30pm and 4-9pm.) The **police station,** in Pl. Eleftherias (☎ 22 560), is in the big yellow building on the waterfront. Ierapetra is under the jurisdiction of the Agios Nikolaos **tourist police** (☎ (0841) 26 900). The **National Bank,** in Pl. Eleftherias, has a 24hr **ATM.** (Open M-Th 8am-2pm, F 8am-1:30pm.) **Radio Taxi** (☎ 26 600 or 27 350) lines up cars in Pl. Kanoupaki. The **hospital** is north of the bus station, left off Lasthenous at Kalimerake 6. (☎ 22 48 8 or 22 766. Open 8:30am-1:30pm; 24hr. **emergency** care.) The **OTE** is at Koraka 25. (Open M-F 7:30am-1pm.) Chic **Polycafe Orpheas,** Koundouriotou 25, just past Pl. Eleftherias, offers **Internet access** at 1000dr/€2.93 per 30min. (☎ 80 462. Open M-Sa 9am-11pm.) The **post office** is on V. Kornarou, on the west side of the old town. (☎ 22 271. Open M-F 7:30am-2pm.) **Postal code:** 72200.

🔒 ACCOMMODATIONS. For the most part, Ierapetra makes its beds for upscale tourists, who want only the best after a day snoozing on Chrissi Island. When bargain-hunters land in town, they avoid the mainland and knock on doors in the streets surrounding the bus station. Make a sharp right out of the bus station and you'll see signs leading to many moderately priced pensions, including the sparkling **Cretan Villa,** Lakerda 16. The 205-year-old building's white stucco-walled, brick-floored, high-ceilinged rooms hide a central garden. The owner, a University of Missouri alum, speaks fluent English. All rooms have private baths with sparkling tiles. (☎ 28 522. www.cretan-villa.com. Singles 7000-9000dr/€20.51-36.37; doubles 10,000-12,000dr/€29.3-35.16; triples 12,000-15,000dr/€35.16-43.95.) Find **Hotel Coral,** Ioanidou 18, in the Old Town, by following Kyrva from Pl. Kanoupaki and taking a right after passing the port police. It has large rooms with private bathtubs, fridges, and free luggage storage. (☎ 22 846 or 28 743. Doubles 5000-7000dr/€14.65-20.51; triples 8000dr/€23.44; A/C 1500dr/€4.40 extra per night.) Outdoor enthusiasts can pitch a tent at **Koutsounari,** 7km from Ierapetra on the coastal road to Sitia near their restaurant, bar, and beach. Take the bus to **Sitia** via **Makri Gialo** (20min., 1 per hr., 220dr/€0.65) and ask to be let off at the campgrounds. (☎ 61 213. 1300dr/€3.81 per person; 900dr/€2.64 per tent.)

🔋 FOOD. Most of Ierapetra's waterfront restaurants are identically priced. Locals and tourists of all ages and sizes frequent **Veterano,** in Pl. Eleftherias, a cafe/dessert bar with an ideal view of the palm-edged main plateia. Sip your cappuccino, spy on the bustling populace, and contemplate a second piece of *kalitsounia* (200dr/€0.59), an Ierapetrian sweet cheese tart. (Open 7:30am-midnight.) Spiros, the friendly owner of **Kotaki,** on Stratigou Samovil, offers generous portions of traditional meals and fresh catch (*giovetsi* 1800dr/€5.46) straight from the Libyan Sea. (Open 9am-midnight.) **Napoleon,** Stratigou Samovil 26, on the waterfront near the old town, is the oldest restaurant in Ierapetra. Every day, the charismatic couple in charge cooks up seasonally priced fish, meats for 1500dr/€4.40, and vegetables for 800dr/€2.53. (Open M-Sa 8am-midnight.)

🔲 SIGHTS. Few of Ierapetra's historical sights are open for visiting. In the Old Town are a 19th-century **mosque** and a decaying **Ottoman fountain** (*Krini*) covered with Greek graffiti. The 13th-century restored **Venetian fortress** (*Kales*) at the south end of the old harbor is a pleasant lookout, though there's not much room to stretch your legs. (Open Tu-Su 8:30am-3pm. Free.) The **Kervea festival,** held each summer in July and August, features music, dance, and theater performances at the fortress; call the town hall for information (☎24 115). Ierapetra's **Archaeological Museum**, at Pl. Kanoupaki on the waterfront, has Minoan artifacts from the south coast and a worthwhile collection of Greco-Roman statues. One unique sarcophagus in the second room, adorned by hunting scenes, embodies the simple elegance of Minoan painting. (Open Tu-Sa 8:30am-3pm. 500dr/€1.47, EU students free.)

⚡ DAYTRIP FROM IERAPETRA: CHRISSI. Ierapetra's star attraction is Chrissi, an island eight nautical miles away from the mainland. Free from stores and crowds, Chrissi is completely flat, adorned by green pines and surrounded by transparent green sea. Most beaches on the island are spread with very fine, flour-like sand. Pack a lunch and bring water; there's nothing but a taverna near the dock, which tends to be pricey (open all day). **Ferries** depart May through October daily at 10:30am and 12:30pm, returning at 5pm and 6pm, respectively (6000dr/€17.58, including return; 1500dr/€4.40 beach chair charge).

SITIA Σητεια ☎0843

A winding drive on coastal and mountain roads from Agios Nikolaos leads to the fishing and port town of Sitia. Despite strong efforts to promote tourism, Sitia has maintained a teflon resistance to each summer's batch of holiday-makers, staying devoted to its residents. Tourists blend with locals at the harborside tavernas, and pelicans walk the streets at dawn. Sitia makes a great base for your exploration of Crete's east coast, and it's the most convenient port for departures to Rhodes.

⚜ 🛈 ORIENTATION AND PRACTICAL INFORMATION

Pl. Iroon Polytechniou sits at the center of town on the waterfront; most practical necessities can be found here. With your back to the bus station, exit to the right. Make another right, then a left, and **Venizelou** will take you there.

Flights: Airport (☎24 666) connects to Athens (3 per week, 2 per week in winter; 23,200dr/€68.09). No buses to airport. Taxis cost 1000dr/€2.93 for the 1km ride.

Ferries: Port Office (☎25 555). Three ferries per week go to: **Kassos** (4hr., 2600dr/€7.62); **Karpathos** (5hr., 3400dr/€10.26); and **Rhodes** (12hr., 6000dr/€17.58). Five per week go to: **Piraeus** (16-17hr., 7600dr/€22.27) via **Agios Nikolaos** (1½hr., 1600dr/€4.69) and **Milos** (9hr., 5200dr/€15.24).

Buses: The station (☎22 272) is outside of town off Venizelou. To: **Agios Nikolaos** (1½hr., 4-6 per day, 1550dr/€4.55); **Ierapetra** (1½hr., 3-5 per day, 1300dr/€3.81); **Iraklion** (3¼hr., 3-5 per day, 2950dr/€8.64); **Kato Zakros** (1hr., 1-2 per day, 1050dr/€3.08); **Vai** (1hr., 3-5 per day, 600dr/€1.76).

Taxis: (☎22 700) in Pl. Venizelou. Usually available 24hr. on weekends.

Rentals: Porto-Belis Travel, Karamanli 34 (☎22 370; fax 23 830) rents **cars** (8000-10,000dr/€23.44-29.30) and **mopeds** (8000dr/€23.44 and up).

Tourist Office: (☎28 300), on the waterfront. From Pl. Polytechniou, head along the water to the east; the small white building will be on your left. **Maps, currency exchange,** info on accommodations. Open 9am-9pm.

Banks: National Bank (☎22 250 or 22 218), in Pl. Venizelou. 24hr. **ATM.** Open M-Th 8am-2pm, F 8am-1:30pm.

Tourist Police: Therissou 31 (☎24 200). From the plateia, follow Kapetan Sifi 2 blocks to Mysonos; go left and continue until it becomes Therissou. Open 7:30am-9pm.

Police: (☎22 266 or 22 259), in the same building as the tourist police. Open 24hr.

Hospital: (☎24 311), off Therissou past the youth hostel, away from town. Open 24hr.

CRETE

OTE: Kapetan Sifis 22 (☎ 28 099). From the main plateia, head inland past the National Bank for 2 blocks. Open M-F 7:30am-10pm.

Internet Access: Upstairs at **Ianos Internet,** Venizelou 159, by the water for 1300dr/€3.81 per hr.

Post Office: Main branch, Dimokritou 8 (☎ 22 283; fax 25 350). From the plateia on the waterfront, walk inland on Venizelou and go left on Dimokritou; it will be on your right. Open M-F 7:30am-2pm. **Postal Code:** 72300.

ACCOMMODATIONS

Call ahead for reservations in August. The youth hostel is friendly, but for more privacy, look behind the west end of the waterfront on Kornarou and Kondilaki.

Youth Hostel, Therissou 4 (☎ 22 693). From the bus station turn left and walk inland and follow the signs for the main road to Iraklion and Agios Nikolaos. As you bear left, the street becomes Therissou; the hostel is 150m up. Reception 9am-noon and 6-9pm; if no one is around, find a bed and register later. Call ahead for a free ride from the bus station. Common kitchen. 24hr. hot water. Dorms 1700dr/€4.98; singles 2500dr/€7.33; doubles 4000dr/€11.74; triples 5000dr/€14.65. Camping on the small lawn 1200dr/€3.52 per perso, tents free.

Venus Rooms to Let, Kondilaki 60 (☎ 24 307). Walk uphill on Kapetan Sifi from the main plateia and make your first right after the OTE. All rooms have balconies and access to common kitchen facilities. The luxurious top floor offers a flowered balcony. Doubles 7000dr/€20.51, with bath 10,000dr/€29.30.

Rooms to Let Apostolis, Kazantzakis 27 (☎ 22 993 or 28 172). From the main plateia, head inland on Kapetan Sifi and turn left onto Foudalidi, then right one block farther onto Kazantzakis. Bright granite stairs lead to spacious rooms with private baths and fans. A basic common kitchen area opens onto a balconied dining area. Doubles 7500-8500dr/€21.98-24.91; triples 9500-10,500dr/€27.84-30.77.

FOOD

The waterfront offers typical tourist fare to light *bouzouki* strumming. There's less of a view of the water but more local life at the tavernas on the inland streets.

Cretan House, K. Karamanli 10 (☎ 25 133), right of the main plateia as you face the water. Most diners eat on the waterfront, but the interior is more colorful. The amicable staff serves a huge variety, including Cretan recipes like *mezethra, kouloukopsomo,* and *staka*. Entrees around 1400dr/€4.10. Open 9am-1:30am.

Taverna Michos, V. Kornarou 117 (☎ 22 416), one block up from the main plateia. Serves swordfish-prawn souvlaki with rice and delicious Cretan vegetables (1600dr/€4.69), and lamb stew in wine sauce (1600dr/€4.69). Whet your appetite with their *dolmades* (800dr/€2.53). In winter, live music on F-Sa. 15% discount for seniors.

Mike's Creperie, El. Venizelou 162 (☎ 25 207), left of the main plateia. Sweet and salty crepes spice up the waterfront. Crepes around 800dr/€2.53. Open M-Sa 10am-4pm.

SIGHTS

Away from the waterfront on the hill high above town, the **fortress** may not offer much protection but it does make for a sweet view. (Open Tu-Su 8:30am-3pm. Free.) It hosts Sitia's **Kornareia Festival,** running from June to August, with free open-air theater and concerts of traditional and popular Greek music and dancing. Contact the tourist office for details. The **Archaeological Museum,** directly behind the bus station, is the product of the rich excavation sites around Sitia, where many prominent sanctuaries and villas were located in Minoan times. Be sure to note the Late Minoan Palaikastro Kouros statuette—

a small ivory and gold masterpiece with strong Egyptian influences. (☎23 917. 500dr/€1.76, students and seniors 300dr/€0.88, EU students and under 18 free. Open Tu-Su 8:30am-3pm.) Sitia's **Folk Art Museum** houses traditional 19th-century Cretan items and has a beautiful collection of fabrics and garments from the early 20th century; walk up Kapetan Siphi from the main plateia and the museum is on the right. (☎22 861. Open M 9:30am-1:30pm and 5-8pm, Tu-F 9:30am-2:30pm and 5-9pm, Sa 9:30am-2:30pm. 500dr/€0.47.) The town's **beach** extends 3km east toward Petra. Close to town, the beach is narrow and squeezed out by a busy roadway, but the road turns inland farther down, leaving an empty expanse of beach.

🔊🎵 NIGHTLIFE AND ENTERTAINMENT

People-watching is a Sitian pastime, especially along the row of restaurants and cafes near the main plateia, where moonlight softens the rugged boats and colors the evening. A night out begins here at places like **Scala**, El. Venizelou 193, a bar with late-night DJs that draws a younger crowd. (Cocktails 1500dr/ €4.40. Open 5pm-3am.) **Iannos Internet Cafe/Bar,** El. Venizelou 159, packs in the late crowd for drinks, chatter, and music from an in-house DJ. (Cocktails 1300dr/€3.81. Open 9am-4am.) After midnight, everyone heads to **Hot Summer,** about one kilometer down the road to Palaikastro by the beach, where a swimming pool replaces the staid dance floor. The über-chic, the young, and the talkative self-segregate at three fully-stocked bars, and half the fun is figuring out which crowd is where. (Cover around 1000dr/€2.93, redeemable at the bar; cocktails 1800dr/€5.46.) Around 3am, head westward several kilometers out of town to **Planetarium Disco,** where you can unwind on the balcony or shuffle your feet at one of Crete's largest clubs. (1500dr/€4.40 cover, includes one drink. Open in summer 1am-dawn.)

🏖 DAYTRIP FROM SITIA: VAI Βαι

Buses from Sitia (1hr., 4-6 per day, 650dr/€2.35) via Palaikastro (300dr/€0.88) stop in the parking lot in front of the beach. (Parking: cars 600dr/€1.76; motorbikes 250dr/ €0.74.) A tourist information booth offers currency exchange. First aid at the back of the parking lot. For emergencies call the police (☎61 222).

Not long ago, tourists headed east to Vai to get off the beaten path. Today, several buses roll into this outpost daily, depositing tourists eager to swim at a smooth, sandy **beach** and rest under the shady fronds of Europe's only indigenous **palm tree forest.** Legend has it the forest sprouted from dropped date seeds that 2nd-century BC Egyptian soldiers littered on their way to war. In the 60s and 70s, Vai became a haven for British bands like Cream and Led Zeppelin, who would camp out, rock out, and smoke out under the palms. Nowadays camping, fires, and drugs are all prohibited to keep the forest (and the visitors) healthy.

For more secluded bathing and an umbrella-free beach, face the water and head up and over the craggy hill. Those in search of a more secluded beach experience should go left along the cliff to a perfect stretch of sand. Although camping is forbidden in the park itself, many unfurl sleeping bags in this cove to the south of the palm beach. If sandy pajamas and the possibility of arrest don't appeal to you, rent a room in quiet **Palaikastro,** 8km back toward Sitia. Although there is one **restaurant** and a **snack bar** (small sandwiches 500-600dr/ €1.47-1.76) in Vai, you're better off packing a **picnic** or eating in Palaikastro or Sitia. A **watersports center** offers jet-skis (6000dr/€17.58 for 10min.), and scuba diving (15,000dr/€14.65 per session). (Open 10am-6pm; reduced prices for larger parties.) Try a banana, grown on a local plantation, or buy a bunch from the stand in the parking lot (600dr/€1.76 per kg.).

CRETE

PALAIKASTRO Παλαικαστρο   0843

The slow pace of life in town and the excellent beaches that dot the periphery of the village of Palaikastro create an ideal balance of tranquility and diversion.

✳❓ ORIENTATION AND PRACTICAL INFORMATION

Palaikastro is a stop on two bus routes, running from Sitia to Vai and Kato Zakros. **Buses** leave from the main plateia for: **Sitia** (30min., 3-4 per day, 500dr/€1.47); **Vai** (15min., 3-4 per day, 300dr/€0.88); and **Kato Zakros** (30min., 1-2 per day, 650dr/€1.91). You may buy tickets at the kiosk in the plateia or on the bus. For **taxis** call 61 380 or 61 271. The village has the bare necessities in its main plateia. **Lion Car Rental,** in the plateia across from the church, rents **cars** for around 10,000dr/€29.30 per day. (☎61 482 or 61 511, mobile (0944) 58 1665; fax 61 482. Open 9am-1pm and 6-9pm.) The **tourist information office,** 100m down the road to Sitia on your right, has an **ATM, currency exchange,** room and restaurant info, and free **maps.** (☎61 225; fax 61 547; www.photoart.gr/itanos. Open M-Sa 9am-10pm.) Across the street is a **pharmacy.** (Open 9am-2pm and 5-11pm.) A few doors away is the **police station** (☎61 222), one flight upstairs in a building marked by Greek flags. A **doctor** (☎61 204) visits the village once per week, seeing patients in the mayor's building, down the road immediately left of the tourist office. The **OTE** (☎61 225) is in the same building as the tourist office. **Internet access** is available at **Kazamias Rent-a-Car,** just past the tourist office. (☎61 093. Open 9:30am-1:30pm and 5:30-9:30pm. 600dr/€1.76.)

🏠📱 ACCOMMODATIONS AND FOOD

You can find rooms and hospitality in the home of **Yiannis Perakis.** From the bus, take the right fork of the main road away from Sitia and continue for 200m to Pegasos Taverna on your left. Take the small gravel road to the left immediately before Pegasos, and follow it around a bend to the left. Inquire for rooms at the first door to your left. Lemon trees and bougainvillea invite you into bright rooms with shared baths and balconies. (☎61 310. Singles 3000dr/€8.79; doubles 5000dr/€14.65; triples 6500dr/€ 19.05.) On the same path as Yiannis, **Pegasos Rooms,** above Pegasos Taverna, offers balconies, fridges, and private baths. (☎61 479. Singles 6000dr/€17.58; doubles 8000dr/€23.44; triples 9000dr/€26.37; 5-person apartments 12,000dr/€35.16.)

For the basics, visit the village's **mini-market** and **bakery** opposite the church entrance, 20m down the road to Vai. **Restaurant Mythos,** in the plateia, is a local favorite with good prices. (Traditional dishes such as *moussaka* and *stifado* 1000-1400dr/€2.93-4.10, vegetables 600dr/€1.76. Open 6am-1am.) **Hotel Hellas** serves all the standards and has the best view of the plateia. (Greek salad 750dr/€2.15, stuffed eggplant 950dr/€2.79. Open 8:15am-1am.) Choose your feast at **Vasios Nasiakos,** a family restaurant 300m past Pegasos in the next village, Agathias. (Entrees with vegetables 1000-1300dr/€2.93-3.81. Open summer 7pm-1am.)

🌊 BEACHES

If you're looking for activities outside of Palaikastro, take the bus headed for Kato Zakros and ask the driver to let you off at **Chochlakes.** From this village, you can walk through the valley to the secluded beach and bay of **Karoumes.** Take the road east from Palaikastro on its way to the tiny village of **Agathias,** beyond which lie many of Crete's most scenic and least visited beaches. Past Agathias, the road forks; its right branch leads to the **Minoan Palace** at **Roussolakos;** the left branch leads to **Chiona Beach.**

⚡ DAYTRIP FROM PALAIKASTRO

VALLEY OF DEATH AND ZAKROS   ☎ 0843

Buses travel from Sitia to Kato Zakros, stopping in Palaikastro and Zakros (1hr., 2 per day, 1050dr/€3.08). Ask the bus driver to drop you at the gorge's entrance, approximately 2km down the road from Zakros's main plateia. The 11am bus from Sitia allows enough time to hike the gorge, visit the ruins, grab a bite to eat, and take a quick swim. Zakros's bus stop is in the main plateia, with taxis and the police station (☎ 93 323).

A 4-km natural gorge, named the ■Valley of Death, connects the quiet village of Zakros or Apo Zakros (upper Zakros) to the beach enclave of Kato Zakros (lower Zakros). The wildlife showcases the area's natural diversity: goats graze by the mountain road, snakes and scorpions slither in the valley, and elegant geese strut the streets of Kato Zakros.

Those seeking a physical challenge should hike (4km, about 70min.) through the **Valley of Death** (or **Death's Gorge**), leading from Zakros to Kato Zakros. Although Samaria is larger, Death's Gorge equals it in beauty and far surpasses it in tranquility. Although it's impossible to wander too far astray in a gorge, the path is poorly and sporadically marked with crude red arrows. Bring along plenty of water and trail snacks, good hiking shoes, and long pants to protect against stray brambles. Keep an eye out for **phaskomilo,** a tea plant with small, fuzzy, green leaves. Its scent is naturally refreshing, a marked change from the odor of the onion plants (identified by their small purple flowers) that also inhabit the valley.

At the end of the gorge, turn left on the dirt path—bear right when you see the sign for the palace that leads you to the coast and the **Minoan Palace** (☎ 93 105) of Kato Zakros. Destroyed in 1450 BC, the royal rubble extends up a hill and is still undergoing excavation. Minoan kings once bathed in pools near the bottom of the hill, now home to innumerable turtles. (☎ 93 105. Open 8am-3pm, last entrance 2:30pm. 500dr/€1.47, students and seniors 300dr/€0.88, EU students free.)

Continue along the path away from the palace to Kato Zakros and its wheelchair-accessible beach. The waterfront is largely free from clutter and deck chairs, and the beach is pleasant, if pebbly. Restaurant **Nikos Platanias** has exceptionally friendly, multilingual waiters who serve up fish from the Mediterranean and veggies from the owner's farm. (☎ 93 375. Entrees around 1300dr/€3.81.) To stay overnight, ask at the restaurant or follow the signs to **George's Villa** (300m up the road). George treats his guests to his own good humor in rooms that overlook the brilliant Mediterranean and unspoiled beach. Call for a ride from the bus stop. (☎ 26 883. Doubles 8000-12,000dr/€23.44-35.16; triples 9000-13,000dr/€26.37-38.09.)

CRETE

CYPRUS Κυπρος

Would that I go to Cyprus, the island of Aphrodite,
Where the Loves who soothe mortal hearts dwell.
    —Euripides

From the ancient temples and Roman mosaics scattered on its shores to the Green Line that runs through its capital city, Cyprus is an island of ancient harmonies and modern tensions. After enduring a succession of conquerors that reads like a who's who list of historical peoples (the Phoenicians, Greeks, Persians, Ptolemies, Romans, Arabs, Crusaders, Ottomans, and Britons have all passed through), the island now exists independently, although uneasily. Contrasting landscapes—sandy beaches, the cool Troodos mountain air, the developing industrial cities—mean that a change of pace is just a short bus ride away. Times are changing, too: flashy signs aimed at tourists have replaced the scrawled graffiti that once proclaimed the unification of Cyprus; a deeper search proves that Cyprus does have a memory. Conversations with elder Cypriots can yield nostalgic ruminations well worth a night at a small kafeneion. Although visiting Cyprus can be expensive, more and more tourists seem convinced that the trip is worthwhile.

HIGHLIGHTS OF CYPRUS

STAY OVERNIGHT AT A MOSQUE-TURNED-HOSTEL, sup with poets at an art cafe, and stare into the foundations of one of the world's oldest cities at Larnaka (p. 519).

FROLIC on the fabulous beaches of frenetic Agia Napa (p. 526).

CROSS THE GREEN LINE to Turkish-occupied territory in Lefkosia, the world's last divided city (p. 544).

DIP YOUR TOES in the Aphrodite's Divine Tub of Love and Beauty (p. 538).

HIKE the shady, piney Troodos Mountains, where French poet Arthur Rimbaud once hid out (p. 540).

HISTORY AND POLITICS

ANCIENT AND MEDIEVAL CYPRUS

REALLY OLD. The remains of round stone and mud dwellings date settlement on Cyprus back to roughly 7000 BC. Millennia later, Cyprus's wealth of copper and ore made it the most popular island around, leading to an increase in Cypriot trade and cultural exchange during the **Bronze Age** (2500-1050 BC). Linguists are unsure whether *Kypros*, from which the word "copper" is derived, first referred to the island or to the metal itself.

3000 BC: POPULARITY CONTEST	The discovery of copper in the foothills of the Troodos mountains makes centrally located Cyprus the place where the cool kids go. Copper is used to make shiny, pretty things.

In the midst of all the copper-working, **Mycenaean** (see p. 7) traders from the Peloponnese swung by, initiating a long-lasting Hellenic influence in Cyprus. The 12th century BC saw the rise of city-kingdoms Paphos, Salamis, Kition, and Kourion; the spread of Greek language; and the use of basic written notation. The

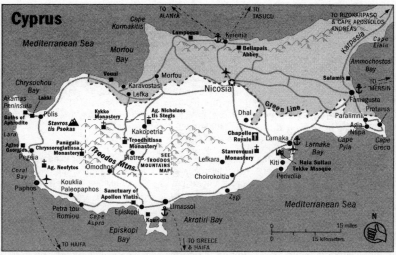

Cyprus

Mediterranean Sea

TO ALANYA
TO TASUCU
TO RIZOKARPASO & CAPE APOSTOLOS ANDREAS

Cape Kormakitis
Lampousa
Kyrenia
Bellapais Abbey
Cape Elaia

Morfou Bay
Karpasia
Ammochostos Bay

Chrysochou Bay
Vouni
Morfou
Nicosia
Salamis
TO MERSIN

Akamas Peninsula
Lakki
Karavostasi
Lefka
Famagusta

Baths of Aphrodite
Polis
Kykko Monastery
Ag. Nicholaos tis Stegis
Dhali
Green Line
Paralimni
Protaras
Agia Napa

Lara
Stavros tis Psokas
Kakopetria
Chapelle Royale
Larnaka
Cape Pyla
Cape Greco

Agios Georgios
Panagia Chryssoroglatissa Monastery
Troodhitissa Monastery
Larnaka Bay

Pegeia
Ag. Neofytos
Omodhos
Platres
Troodos Mtns
SEE TROODOS MOUNTAINS MAP
Lefkara
Stavrovouni Monastery
Kiti
Hala Sultan Tekke Mosque

Coral Bay
Kouklia
Paleopaphos
Choirokoitia
Perivolia

Paphos
Sanctuary of Apollon Ylatis
Zygi

Petra tou Romiou
Cape Aspro
Episkopi
Kourion
Limassol
Akrotiri Bay

Episkopi Bay
TO GREECE & HAIFA
Mediterranean Sea

TO HAIFA

N

0   15 miles
0   15 kilometers

arrival of **Phoenician** traders and bullies in the first millennium BC forced the Greeks to share political control until the **Assyrians** arrived in the 7th century BC; the Assyrians dominated the island for a century, until the **Egyptians** seized control for a brief spell. They were soon overthrown by the **Persian** king. Pro-Hellenic **Evagoras I** forced the Persians out of Salamis and spread the Greek language throughout his kingdom, initiating the most significant Cypriot resistance to Persian rule.

GETTING IT TOGETHER. As Persian expansion stagnated, **Alexander the Great** (see p. 12) absorbed Cyprus into his growing empire. In 295 BC, following Alexander's death, the rather strict **Ptolemies of Egypt** claimed Cyprus, abolished the city-kingdoms, and unified the island. While cultural and religious institutions remained unchanged, the Greek alphabet came to replace the local syllabic script. Two centuries later, in 58 BC, Rome annexed the island, and in AD 45 the apostle **Paul** and the Cypriot apostle **Barnabas** introduced Christianity to the island. The new faith spread, and when the Roman governor converted in 46, Cyprus won the prize for becoming the world's first Christian territory.

BYZANTINE TO OTTOMAN RULE

AD 1191: SHIPWRECKED!	Richard the Lionheart's fiancée and sister claim mistreatment at the hands of Cypriots following an emergency docking in Limassol. Rich captures island; mother warns, "You are *not* bringing that *thing* into my house!"

ISLAND FOR SALE. After Constantinople was proclaimed capital of the eastern half of the divided Roman empire (see p. 14), Roman civic thought, Greek philosophy, and Greek Orthodoxy were synthesized on Cyprus. These centuries were bad times for the Cypriots: devastating earthquakes rocked their world in AD 332 and 342, a 40-year drought left everyone thirsty, and fierce Arab raids in the 7th century made the islanders feel like fish in a barrel. In 1191, **Richard the Lionheart**, en route to the Crusades in Jerusalem, overran the island; he took provisions for the Christian armies and robbed the island of its treasures. Unable to carry the island around, he sold it to the **Knights Templar.** In turn, they passed responsibility on to **Guy de Lusignan,** a minor French noble who had been involved in the Crusades.

NOT A NICE GUY. The feudal system of the **Lusignan Dynasty** (1192-1489) oppressed the lower classes and suppressed Cypriot traditions and religion, but bestowed Gothic churches, cathedrals, and castles upon the area. The Crusaders were forced to retreat after getting beaten up in Palestine, so the Lusignans invited Crusader families to hang out in Cyprus. As a result, in the late 13th century Cyprus became the wealthiest island in the eastern Mediterranean. Profiting from the Lusignans' dynastic intrigues, the **Venetians** annexed the island in 1489. Even with strengthened Cypriot military defenses, however, the island was no match for the encroaching Ottomans. In 1570, following a two-month siege, Lefkosia surrendered to the Turks under Lala Mustafa. The fall of Famagusta one year later marked the beginning of the **Ottoman period** in Cyprus, as well as the introduction of a brand new ethnic element to the island.

1821: GREEK WAR OF LIBERATION	The sultan smells a conspiracy on Cyprus. Four hundred and eighty-six Christians are convicted of sympathizing with the mainland freedom-fighters; heads roll. See **Greek Nationalist Revolt,** p. 16.

Cypriot peasants welcomed the Ottoman abolition of feudalism, probably because they acquired lands in the process. The Orthodox Church also flourished, serving as a powerful administrative machine for the sultan. In the 19th century, Great Britain defended the Ottoman territories against Russian expansion in an effort to defend its own colonies. Landing at Larnaka in July of 1878, British forces assumed control of Cyprus as a **military base.** Although Cypriots received no political freedom under the British, as a consolation prize they gained many public works including roads, railways, schools, and hospitals.

CYPRUS IN THE 20TH CENTURY

In 1955, **General George Grivas,** in conjunction with **Archbishop Makarios,** founded the **EOKA** (National Organization of Cypriot Fighters), an underground *enosist* (pro-union) movement demanding union with Greece. When the United Nations vetoed the Greek request to grant Cyprus self-government, an enraged Grivas and the EOKA initiated guerrilla warfare aimed at the British government. In response to increased EOKA activity, the underground Volkan (Volcano), under the leadership of **Rauf Denktaş,** founded the **TMT** (Turkish Resistance Organization). The TMT was a paramilitary organization designed to fight the *enosists* and to push for **taksim,** or a partitioning of the island between Greece and Turkey. Weary of the perpetual violence, Britain, along with the foreign ministers of Greece and Turkey, agreed in 1959 to establish an **independent Cypriot republic.** On August 16, 1960, Cyprus was granted independence and became a member of the UN; in March 1961, it was admitted to the British Commonwealth.

1963: KEEP YOUR HANDS TO YOURSELF	Fighting breaks out in Cyprus when Prez and Veep disagree. The British government posts soldiers across the center of Lefkosia, telling both groups to stay on their own side, or they will turn this island around and go straight home.

LET'S BE FRIENDS. The new **constitution** stipulated that a Greek Cypriot president and a Turkish Cypriot vice president be appointed through popular election, and that the Greek-to-Turkish ratio in the House of Representatives would be 70 to 30. In 1959, **Archbishop Makarios** became the mixed republic's first president, and **Fazıl Küçük,** leader of the Turkish Cypriot community, was elected to the vice presidency unopposed. In 1963, Makarios proposed 13 amendments to the constitution intended to make bicommunal life easier, including the abolition of the president's and vice-president's veto power and the introduction of majority rule (in a country where the Greek Cypriots are the huge majority). When the unenthused Turkish government threatened to use military force if these amendments were implemented, renewed violence broke out between the EOKA and the TMT, resulting in the division of Nicosia along the **Green Line** (p. 545). In February 1964, the UN dispatched a "temporary" peacekeeping force that has been renewed indefinitely and remains in place today.

BREAKING UP IS HARD TO DO. In 1968, Makarios and Küçük were both re-elected by an overwhelming majority, although in the years following they were subject to several coup attempts. In 1971, General Grivas snuck back into Cyprus to found the militant EOKA-B and to revitalize the call for *enosis*. The violence exploded into an international affair in 1974, when the Greek Cypriot National Guard (sans General Grivas, who died in Limassol the same year), assisted by the military junta in Greece, overthrew Archbishop Makarios and replaced him with Nikos Sampson, an EOKA member who favored immediate *enosis*. This new government lasted all of five days, after which the Turkish army invaded Cyprus from the north to protect Turkish Cypriots from the National Guard. Early in 1975, the North declared itself the Turkish Federated State of Cyprus (TFSC), officially partitioning the island.

RECENT YEARS

In November 1983, Turkish-occupied Cyprus proclaimed itself independent as the **Turkish Republic of North Cyprus (TRNC).** Although only Turkey has recognized the new state, the TRNC has established trade relations in Europe and with several Arab states. In 1992, the UN significantly pared down its peacekeeping mission, leaving Cypriots to resolve their situation without much international intervention. **Glafkos Clerides,** former head of the conservative **Democratic Rally (DISY),** became head of the Republic of Cyprus in 1993. Led by Rauf Denktaş, North Cyprus still lags behind the Republic of Cyprus economically, but has retained the support of Turkish-Cypriots and, in recent years, thousands of settlers from mainland Turkey. The two men still lead their respective island halves today, and hope for cooperation is growing.

EU OR NOT EU? Greek officials are hopeful for the Republic of Cyprus's acceptance into the European Union, a prospect with uncertain implications for the political status of North Cyprus. Turkey was not a candidate for admission to the EU in either the first or second round, and has warned that it would seek to annex North Cyprus if the Republic of Cyprus were to join the EU. In early August 1997, Turkey and North Cyprus agreed to work toward partial defense and economic integration. The agreement came just five days before UN-sponsored talks between Greece and Turkey, and incensed the Greek government.

WE CAN WORK IT OUT. The peace talks' hope for cooperation faded further in late 1997, when the Republic of Cyprus placed an order for a shipment of **S-300 missiles** from Russia. Both the Turkish government and the Turkish Cypriot government threatened that the delivery of these weapons would prompt an immediate increase in the Turkish military presence on the island. The missiles were deployed to Crete instead. In the past few years, negotiations to resolve the missile situation have progressed in fits and starts with periodic US involvement, including the mediation efforts of the current US Ambassador to the UN, **Richard Holbrooke.** While missiles are still a sore subject for both sides, talks begun in 2000 about the political status of the island have been somewhat successful. Though Clerides and Denktaş don't meet face to face, they have been discussing the formation of a federation or a loose confederation of the Greek and Turkish Cypriot governments. As of July 2001, the talks remained inconclusive; tensions rose in June 2000 after a massive **fire** of mysterious origins devastated the agricultural plains of Cyprus.

CYPRIOT SPECIAL EVENTS

Cypriots observe not only Greece's holidays (see p. 34), but also hold their own regional and local festivities. Below are a few of the most significant:

Dec. 26: Boxing Day. The day after Christmas. Cypriots still celebrate this throwback to the days of British colonization.

Feb. 18-March 13: Carnival. The most notable celebrations are in Limassol (p. 528).

March 18, 2002: Green Monday, the beginning of Lent. In areas of more strict observance, this day initiates seven meatless weeks of Lenten fasting.

Apr. 1: Greek Cypriot National Day, commemorating the creation of the Republic.

June 24, 2002: Kataklismos, or Flood Festivals. Across Cyprus, **Pentecost** marks the beginning of days of feasting and celebration, remembering Noah's deliverance from the Flood and paying homage to Aphrodite.

Oct. 1: Cyprus Independence Day.

ESSENTIALS

ENTRANCE REQUIREMENTS. Tourists with valid passports from Australia, Canada, Great Britain, Ireland, New Zealand, and the US do not need a **visa** to enter Cyprus for stays of up to 90 days; South Africans can stay without visas for up to 30 days. Citizens of Turkey do need visas (£5). Tourists wishing to stay longer should probably first leave Cyprus and then reenter.

GETTING THERE

YOU CAN'T GET THERE FROM HERE. Southern Cyprus is not accessible from northern Cyprus, nor is northern Cyprus accessible from southern Cyprus. If your travels originate in North Cyprus and you have a Turkish stamp in your passport, you can *never* enter the south. The quickest way to get to the south from the north is to fly somewhere else first, then hop a plane to southern Cyprus. To get to there without flying you must take a detour: catch a ferry to **Taşucu,** Turkey, a bus to **Marmaris,** a ferry to **Rhodes,** and on to southern Cyprus (2 days). Ask the Turkish authorities not to stamp your passport: a **Taşucu** stamp reveals that you've been to North Cyprus.

Cyprus lies 64km from Turkey, 160km from Israel and Lebanon, and 480km from the nearest Greek island. **The Republic of Cyprus** (southern Cyprus) is accessible from Greece and other European and Middle Eastern countries by airplane or ferry. Both **Limassol** and **Larnaka** are accessible by ferry from a number of points, including Rhodes, Crete, and Hafia. There are two international airports, in **Larnaka** (p. 519) and **Paphos** (p. 533); see the **Transportation** section for each city for more information on fares and routes. Cyprus is accessible by plane on **Olympic Airlines** (US ☎ (800) 223-1226; Cyprus ☎ (04) 62 79 50; www.olympic-airways.gr), **Cyprus Airways** (US ☎ (212) 714-2190; Cyprus ☎ (02) 44 30 54; www.cyprusair.com.cy), and many major airlines. Roundtrip fares from Athens to Larnaka cost about US$145 (for more information on finding flights, see **Essentials,** p. 61).

CONSULATES AND EMBASSIES

CYPRIOT EMBASSIES

Australia: 30 Beale Cr., Deakin, Canberra, ACT 2600 (☎6281 0832; fax 2810 860).

Canada: 365 Bloor St. E., Suite 1010, Box #43, Toronto, ON M4W 3L4 (☎(416) 944-0998; fax 944-9149).

Greece: 16 Herodotou, Athens (☎ 723 27 27; fax 453 63 73).

UK: 93 Park St., London W1Y 4ET (☎ (0171) 499 82 72 or 4; fax 491 06 91).

US: 2211 R St. NW, Washington, D.C. 20008 (☎ (202) 462-5772; fax 483-6710).

FOREIGN EMBASSIES IN CYPRUS (LEFKOSIA)

Australia: High Commission, Annis Comninis 4 (☎ 753 001; fax 766 486), 500m east of Pl. Eleftherias off Stasinou. Open M-F 7:30am-12pm, 12:30-3:15pm.

Canada: Odos Them. Dervi 15 (☎ 451 630; fax 459 096).

Egypt: Egypt 3 (☎ 465 144; fax 462 287). Open M-F 8am-2pm.

Greece: Lordou Vyronos 8 (☎ 441 880; fax 473 990). Open M-F 9am-noon.

Israel: I. Grypari 4 (☎ 445 195). Open M-F 8am-4pm.

Lebanon: Vas. Olgas 1 (☎ 442 216; fax 467 662). Open M-F 8:30am-1:30pm.

Syria: Androkleous 1 (☎ 474 481; fax 446 963). Open M-F 8am-2pm, Sa 8am-1pm.

UK: High Commission, PO Box 1978 Alexander Pallis (☎ 861 100 or 861 342 or 3; fax 286 1150). Open M and W-F 7:30am-2pm, Tu 7:30am-1pm and 2-5:30pm.

US: PO Box 4536 Metochiou and Ploutarchou, Engomi (☎ 776 400; fax 720 944). Open M-F 8am-5pm, except for US and Cyprus holidays.

MONEY

The main unit of currency in the Republic of Cyprus is the **pound (£),** which is divided into 100 cents. Coins come in 1, 2, 5, 10, 20, and 50 cent denominations; bank notes in denominations of £1, 5, 10, and 20. Cyprus imposes no limit on the amount of foreign currency that may be imported, but amounts in excess of US$1000 should be declared on Customs form D (NR). No more than £50 in Cypriot currency may be brought into or taken out of the country. Banks are generally open M-F 8:30am-12:30pm; see the **Practical Information** section of each city for more detailed info. The prices quoted below were effective in the summer of 2001. As inflation and exchange rates fluctuate, present prices may differ by as much as 30%. (For information on traveler's checks, ATMs, credit cards, and other financial matters, see **Money** p. 42).

CYPRIOT POUND (£)		
US$1 = £0.66	£1 = US$1.53
CDN$1 = £0.43	£1 = CDN$2.37
UK£1 = £0.93	£1 = UK£1.07
IR£1 = £0.73	£1 = IR£1.37
AUS$1 = £0.33	£1 = AUS$3.01
NZ$1 = £0.27	£1 = NZ$3.71
ZAR1 = £0.08	£1 = ZAR12.62
EUR€1 = £0.57	£1 = EUR€1.75
100DR = £0.17	£1 = 597DR
TL1,000,000 = £0.49	£1 = TL2,052,001

GETTING AROUND

A reliable highway system serves much of Cyprus, but take caution on the winding mountain roads. **Cars** drive on the left side of the road; be prepared for British rotaries. Almost all Cypriot rental cars have manual transmission and standardized rates: the cheapest compact cars should cost £13 per day, small **motorbikes** £5, and larger motorcycles £7-8. Cypriot law requires that seatbelts be worn in front seats of cars, and an **international driver's license** or a **national driver's license** from your home country is required. A temporary Cypriot driver's license, good for six months, can be obtained from district police stations with a photo ID and £3.

CYPRUS

There is one island-wide **bus schedule** available at tourist offices. This schedule provides all necessary information, including prices for buses and private taxi service. Bus service is less frequent in winter and is less dependable in rural areas of Cyprus. Buses run between all major cities except **Paphos,** which requires a connection in Limassol in order to reach Larnaka or Lefkosia. **Service taxis** are the most reliable form of transportation on Cyprus and are quite affordable; each taxi seats 4-7 passengers. Alternatively, **private taxis** provide a reasonable alternative. Hitchhiking is uncommon, and neither locals nor tourists are likely to offer rides. Limited bus service is available to the **Troodos Mountains.** See the **Getting There, Getting Around,** and **Practical Information** for each town or city for more information.

PRACTICAL INFORMATION

199 for ambulance, fire, or police; **112** if calling from a cell phone. **192** for queries about domestic telephone numbers; **194** for international queries.

BY MAIL. Post offices are open Monday through Friday from 7:30am to 1:30pm. Some have afternoon hours (4-6pm) and Saturday hours (8:30-10:30am). Poste Restante (see **Keeping in Touch,** p. 57) is available in Lefkosia, Larnaka, Paphos, and Limassol. **Airmail** is available and takes 3-4 days to travel to Europe. Faster, more expensive, courier services are also available. The cost of sending a 20g letter varies by destination: to **Europe** and **Middle East,** 31¢; **US, Australia, New Zealand** and **South Africa** 71¢. Sending a **postcard** costs 26¢ to each of the above destinations.

BY PHONE. Southern Cyprus has fairly reliable telephone service (administered by **CYTA**). Direct overseas calls can be made from all public phones, but you need a **phone card** to activate them even if you plan to use your own service provider. Cards are available in $3 or $5 denominations and are sold at banks and kiosks. Private phones in hotels may have a 10% surcharge. For instructions on how to call in and out of Cyprus, see **Keeping in Touch,** p. 57.

PHONE HOME	The country code for Cyprus is **357**. The international access code for Cyprus is **080.**

ACCOMMODATIONS. In general, off-season prices (Oct.-May) are about 20% lower than the high-season rates quoted in this book. Lefkosia, Paphos, and Larnaka all have HI youth hostels; expect hostels to be clean, if a bit run down, with free showers, kitchens, and common rooms. Although Cyprus has few formal campgrounds and camping in unmarked areas is illegal, some travelers still sleep on beaches and in forests. Women should not camp alone. It is generally a good idea to make reservations in advance; the Cyprus Tourist Office (p. 519) can help travelers find rooms. For more information on Accommodations, see p. 53.

TIPS FOR TRAVELERS. Getting around in Cyprus is like traveling in Greece: most Cypriots speak English, and the country's main industry is tourism. There are a few additional things to be aware of when visiting this divided island. Picture taking is forbidden at the top of Mt. Olympus and at the Green Line in Lefkosia (p. 544). **Women** (or anyone) traveling alone should feel safe, as the police take the harassment of women very seriously in Cyprus. It was only two years ago that homosexuality was legalized in Cyprus, but **gay and lesbian travelers** shouldn't have any trouble getting around the country. A few stares and comments may be thrown your way, but as with any form of hassling, ignore it and keep moving. In general, Cypriots are known for their hospitality and truly enjoy showing travelers around their country. For more information on **Specific Concerns,** see p. 71. **Tipping** is customary in restaurants and some hotels, but *not* for taxis.

CTO OFFICES. Tourist offices in Cyprus are extremely helpful and efficient. There are offices in Limassol, Lefkosia, Larnaka, Paphos, Polis, Agia Napa, and Platres. The main office is the **Cyprus Tourism Organization (CTO)**, P.O. Box 4535, Lefkosia 1390 (☎(02) 337 715; fax 331 644; cytour@cto.org.cy). The CTO offices provide free maps and info on buses, museums, and events. A particularly helpful publication available at tourist offices is *The Cyprus Traveler's Handbook* (free). Officials generally speak English, Greek, German, and French.

Greece: 36 Voukourestiou, Athens (☎361 01 78; fax 364 47 98).

UK: 213 Regent St., London W1R 8DA (☎(0171) 569 8800; fax 287 6534; ctolon@cto-lon.demon.co.uk).

US: 13 E. 40th St., New York, NY 10016 (☎(212) 683-5280; fax 683-5282; gocyprus@aol.com; www.cyprustourism.org).

COASTAL CYPRUS

Nothing draws visitors to Cyprus like its magnetically lovely beaches. The volume of coastal tourism in the area contributes to the island's colonial feel—in the summer it seems as if Brits outnumber Cypriots. Still, merely a block's stroll inland leads to Cypriot culture, particularly in Paphos, where nearby monuments make for a quick transition between marble and sand.

LARNAKA Λαρνακα   ☎04

Larnaka gets its name from the ancient Greek word for coffin *(larnax)*, an allusion to the final resting place of **St. Lazarus** in the city's central church. Tropical Larnaka (pop. 71,000) is one of the oldest continually inhabited cities in the world. Segments of the ancient city walls and aqueducts, Bronze Age temples, and the Hala Sultan Tekke Mosque—which dates back to the first Arab invasion of Cyprus in AD 647—poke through into the present. Elsewhere, graffiti reading *"Hellas, Enosis, EOKA"* elicits memories of the violent movement for union with Greece a few decades ago. Larnaka has lately become a leisure hotspot, quieter and cleaner than Limassol, and a convenient base for travelers.

▐ TRANSPORTATION

Flights: (☎643 000). Most flights into and out of Cyprus land at the **Larnaka Airport** located (5km) west of town. **Taxis** to the center of town cost £3-5 and are the main mode of transport. **Buses #22** and **24** run from the airport to Larnaka (Su-Tu and Th-F every hr. 6:45am-4:45pm plus 1 bus at 5:45pm in summer, W and Sa 6:45am-12:45pm; £0.50) and from Larnaka to airport (every hr. 6:30am-5:30pm plus one bus at 7pm in summer, W and Sa 6:45am-12:30pm; £0.50).

Buses: Intercity buses leave from Leforos Athinon by the marina on the waterfront opposite Four Lanterns Hotel. Check the bus schedule on the sandwich board where the buses stop, and double-check with the bus driver, as schedules change frequently. **Kallenos Buses** (☎643 492 or 665 814) go to **Lefkosia** (M-F 5 per day 7am-4pm, Sa 4 per day until 1pm; £1.50) and **Limassol** (M-F 4 per day 8am-4pm, Sa 3 per day until 1pm; £1.70). **EMAN** (☎03 721 321) buses go to **Agia Napa** (M-Sa 9 per day 8:30am-5:30pm, Su 4 per day until 4:30pm; £1). **A.L.** (☎650 477) bus # 6 or 7 leaves Pl. Lazarus and stops at **Ag. Helenis, Artemidos, Meneou,** and **Kiti** (13 per day M-F 6:40am-5:45pm, Sa last bus at 2pm, extra bus in summer M-F 7pm; £0.50).

Service Taxis: Travel & Express (☎661 010), main branch in Pl. Vasileos Pavlou, directly across from the CTO. All of the service taxi agencies in Larnaka have joined to form one company, Travel & Express. You might see different names on signs for taxis, such as **Kyriakos,** or **Makris**—they're all the same. Taxis run to Lefkosia every 30min. 6am-7pm, Su every hr.; £2.50, Su £3. To Limassol same times; £3, £3.50.

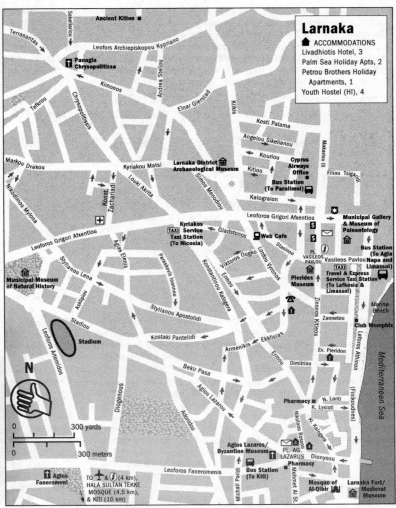

Larnaka

🏠 ACCOMMODATIONS
Livadhiotis Hotel, 3
Palm Sea Holiday Apts, 2
Petrou Brothers Holiday
   Apartments, 1
Youth Hostel (HI), 4

Private Taxis: Makris' private taxi service (☎652 929), across from the CTO, is shamelessly expensive, but it's 24hr. (£0.65 per km in the day, £0.90 per km at night). **Travel & Express** (☎652 929, 655 333 or 652 644) also operates private taxi services, but different numbers apply to order a taxi. Starting price £1.40 plus £0.25/km, after 8:30pm £2 plus 0.30/km. Rates listed also apply if you flag down a taxi on the street.

Car Rental: Phoenix Rent-A-Car, Makariou III 65 (☎623 407; fax 650 460; www.phoenix.com.cy). Prices from £15 per day. Unlimited mileage. Minimum age 25.

✦🛈 ORIENTATION AND PRACTICAL INFORMATION

Leoforos Athinon (a.k.a. the **Finikoudhes,** "Palm Tree Promenade," or simply **Athinon**) runs along the waterfront in the heart of the tourist district and hops with various eateries and night spots. On one end of Athinon there is the **Marina,** which hosts mostly foreign yachts. In front of the Marina is the **Plateia Evropi**

(Pl. Europe), and **Pl. Vasileos Pavlou** marks the city center one block in, where most practical facilities (including the post office, police station, and tourist office) can be found. On the other end of Athinon, the **Larnaka Fort** marks the juncture between Athinon and **Piyale Pasha,** and between the Greek neighborhood and the old Turkish quarter. Less commercial restaurants can be found on Piyale Pasha.

Tourist Office: CTO (☎654 322), in Pl. Vasileos Pavlou, provides information and maps for all of Cyprus. A little patience yields a plethora of information from local ladies. Open winter M-F 8:15am-2:30pm and 3-6:15pm, Sa 8:15am-1:30pm. Open summer Th-Tu 8:15am-2:15pm and 4-6:30pm, Sa 8:15am-1:30pm. Spring and fall season hours change, so be sure to check the schedule posted on its front door. The **Larnaka Airport Branch** (☎643 575) of CTO is open daily 8am-11pm.

Banks: The main branches of 3 major banks are in or near Pl. Vasileos Pavlou, across the street from the CTO. **Bank of Cyprus,** next to the AmEx office, has a 24hr. **ATM,** traveler's checks, and **currency exchange.** (☎653 183). Open M-F 8:15am-12:30pm. **Popular Bank,** also called **Laiki** (☎814 340). Open M-F 8:15am-12:30pm. The **National Bank of Greece** and the **Hellenic Bank** have 24hr. **ATM** services throughout the city.

American Express: (☎843 333; fax 622 535), in the office of **Mantovani Plotin Travel,** across from the CTO. No traveler's checks or currency exchange. Money check forms available for those drawing funds from AmEx cards, but come before noon to draw funds, because Mantovani writes out its checks to local banks, which close at noon. Open M-F 8am-1pm and 2:30-5:30pm, Sa 9am-noon.

Police: (☎804 040), on the corner of Makariou III, 1 block north of the tourist office along Vasileos Pavlou, past the post office, in a building resembling a small fort. English spoken. Open 24hr.

Hospital: There is an old hospital in Larnaka with very few facilities and a new hospital outside of town that is modern and fully equipped. The **old hospital** (☎652 007 or 630 322) is on Grigori Afxentiou Avenue; from the CTO cross the intersection and continue on Stasinou all the way. It's a long walk to the **new hospital** (☎27 999 or 28 111); take **bus #2** from Ermou (6:30am-5:30pm plus a 7pm bus in summer).

Copy/Fax Center: The **Rouvas Copy Center,** Zinonos Pierides 9 (☎658 150; fax 626 659) makes copies, and offers **fax** service. Helpful, efficient staff. Copies £0.05/£0.40 color; faxes to the USA £1.70/page, to Europe £1.20/page.

Telephones: CYTA, Z. Pierides 7-9 (☎640 257). Follow Lordou Vyronos toward the waterfront; the office is on the right, before Zinonos Kitieos. Open M-F 7:30am-5:30pm, W until 1:30pm, Sa until 1pm; off-season M-F 7:30am-1:30pm, Sa until 1pm. £3, £5, or £10 **phone cards** available at most kiosks. **Telecard phones** throughout the city.

Internet Access: Web Internet Cafe, Lordou Vyronou 54 (☎654 954; www.webcafe.com.cy), with computer use £2 per hr.; printing £0.05 per page. **Alto Cafe** (☎659 625), on the corner of Grigori Afxentiou and Ougko, serves mainly as a trendy evening hangout, but has several computers ready for web-surfers. £2 first hr., £1 each additional hr.; printing free for a few pages, £0.10 for larger bulks. Open daily 10am-2am.

Post Office: Main branch, in Pl. Vas. Pavlou right behind the CTO (☎802 406). Open Sept.-June M-Tu and Th-F 7:30am-1:30pm and 4-6pm, W morning hours only, Sa 8:30-10:30am; July-Aug. M-Tu and Th-F 7:30am-1:30pm and 3-6pm, W morning hours only, Sa 8:30-10:30am. **Postal code:** 6900. **Pl. Ag. Lazarus branch** (☎630 182) open all year M-F 7:30am-1:30pm, also Th 3-6pm. **Postal code:** 6902.

▲ ACCOMMODATIONS

While Larnaka is less expensive than neighboring Agia Napa, rooms are just as scarce in summer. Pricey resort hotels line the waterfront, but cheaper options can be found a few blocks inland. Prices tend to be £8-11 less in winter. For those staying in the area for more than 5 days, Larnaka is a good base. Flats can cost £5-10 less per person for longer stays.

■ **Youth Hostel (HI),** Nikolaou Rossou 27 (☎621 188), near Pl. Ag. Lazarus, across the street from the Livadhiotis Hotel, next to the mosque. JP, the personable owner, welcomes travelers of all ages. The hostel is a bit dim, but very clean and efficiently run. Housed in the living quarters of a former **mosque**, the hostel contains 3 large rooms (female, male, coed) with at least 10 beds each, 1 room for a family, 3 full baths, and a kitchen with fridge, stove, sinks, dish ware. No luggage storage, but there is a safe for valuables. Sheets £1. The hostel, but not the front desk, is open 24hr; guests can sign in anytime. Private space may be available in the low season, but in high season it is advisable to call in advance to reserve a bed. Dorms £4 per person.

Petrou Bros. Hotel Apartments, Armenikis Ekklisias 1 (☎650 600/601; fax 655 122; www.petrou.com.cy), 2 blocks from the waterfront. Follow Lordou Vironos toward the waterfront; the hotel is at the corner of Ekklisias and Zinonos Pierides. Bright, modern, spacious flats with baths, telephones, kitchens, balconies, A/C. Breakfast £1.50, 24hr. reception, laundry, travel services, free parking. Doubles £25; quads £35; 6-person suite £45; off-season £8-11 less. Cheaper prices arranged for stays two weeks and longer; mention *Let's Go* to the manager for a 10-15% discount.

Palm Sea Beach Holiday Apts, Evanthias Pieridou (☎659 232; fax 625 726; www.palmsea.com; phasarias@hotmail.com) 3 blocks from Pl. Vasileos Pavlou between Athinon and Zinonos Kitios. Great views of the ocean from in-room balconies, all with bath, kitchen, TV and fold-out couch. Attentive, English-speaking staff. Peak summer season rates begin at £22, 10% discount if paid in euros.

Livadhiotis Hotel Apartments, Nikolaou Rossou 50 (☎626 222; fax 626 406; livadhiotishotapts@cytanet.com.cy) directly across from the youth hostel, next to Pl. Ag. Lazarus. A bit on the expensive side, but excellent for families, with large rooms. Located only a few streets away from Athinon. All rooms include bath, TV, A/C and fridge. Doubles £20; quads £22; suites (six people and up) £36. Up to £8 cheaper in winter.

◖ FOOD

Most of Larnaka's tavernas and bars are on the waterfront. Cypriot families seek out the smaller tavernas outside of town, fast-food chains cater to local youth.

■ **Cuckoo's Nest,** 10 Piyale Pasha (☎628 133). Walk about a block away from Larnaka's Fort on Piyale Pasha; don't blink or you'll miss it. The owner, a Greek Cypriot, preserves the Greek feel with native dishes and entertaining anecdotes. Try the popular *mezedes* for 2 (£10), steak (£2.50), or the classic fish & chips (£3-5). Open daily 5pm-late.

■ **Kali Kardia,** Zehra 8. Go south on Piyale Pasha from Larnaka Fort and turn right on Barbaros, the third road off Piyale. If you want a hearty meal with no frills dirt cheap this is your place. One woman runs the whole shebang, four tables and a kitchen. Just the basics, but served to perfection: kebabs, souvlaki, or salads (£1 for take-out, £2 for dining in) with a cold beer. Open daily 6pm-midnight.

1900 Art Cafe, Stasinou 6 (☎653 027), across the street from the tourist office. Van Goghs dot the walls and international music wafts out onto the one-table balcony, where patrons sip carafes of local wine (£3-6) and coffee (£1). Serves some of the only vegetarian dishes available in the city. Most main dishes £4. Open daily 6pm-late.

Mavri Helona, (Black Turtle) Mehmet Ali 11 (☎650 661), on a small side street by the church of Ag. Lazarus. A welcoming and boisterous crowd of musicians and assorted locals carouse. Most come for the nightly live music more than the cuisine, but no one goes hungry as *mezedes* (£7) and kebabs (£2.50) delight.

Militzis Restaurant, Piyale Pasha 42 (☎655 867), 1 block south of Larnaka Fort on the seafront. Catch some cool sea breezes on even the most sweltering of days and relish the captivating view, spacious veranda, and excellent food. Three large clay ovens create *psita*, cooking up an assortment of fresh meat (£4) and lamb dishes (£4.25). Local wines £3-6. Open daily 12:30pm-midnight.

👁 SIGHTS

Within walking distance of each other, Larnaka's major historical sights draw the many tourists passing through the city. The CTO offers **free walking tours** for travelers in a hurry, including "Larnaka Old & New," (W 10am) beginning at the CTO (☎654 322) and "Skala—Its Craftsmen," (F 10am) from Larnaka Fort (☎630 576).

▨ CHURCH OF AGIOS LAZARUS. Rebuilt after a devastating fire in 1970, this beautifully adorned 9th-century church rests on the sepulcher of Lazarus, whom Jesus raised from the dead. The church is one of the most important Orthodox pilgrimage sites, especially on the Saturday of Lazarus during Lent. Legend holds that Lazarus journeyed to Cyprus and became the island's first bishop, living in Kition for 30 years before dying again. Lazarus's tomb is down the steps near the *iconostasis*. The church's belfry was added in 1857 and lends a Byzantine ambience. (*Take the first left north of the Larnaka Fort. Dress modestly: long skirts for women, pants for men, no bare shoulders. Wrap skirts provided at the door for those who are forgetful. Museum ☎652 498. Open in winter 8:30am-1pm and 3-5pm except W (no afternoon hrs.); in summer same morning hours, afternoon 4-6:30pm. Museum £0.50. Church services 6:30-8:30am.*)

▨ HALA SULTAN TEKKE MOSQUE & SALT LAKE. This must-see mosque's setting is exotic and picturesque: it hangs over the edge of the Salt Lake, which dries up completely in summer. Before it dries flamingoes combine with the palm trees to create a peculiarly tropical backdrop. Also called the **Tekke of Umm Haram,** it was constructed in AD 1550 during the Arab invasion of Cyprus and rebuilt in 1816 over the site where Umm Haram (Muhammed's maternal aunt) fell from a mule and broke her neck around AD 649. The mosque is one of the most sacred pilgrimage sights for Muslims after Mecca, Medina, and Jerusalem. It also houses the tomb of King Hussein's great-grandmother, who died in exile in Cyprus in 1929. (*Take bus #6 or 7, bound for Kiti, from Pl. Ag. Lazarus (every hr. 6:40am-7pm, Sa until 2pm; £0.50). Tell the driver "Tekke." After you're dropped off, walk along the paved road for 1km. Open daily 7:30am-7:30pm, off-season 5am-5pm. Free.*)

PIERIDES FOUNDATION MUSEUM. This private museum was the home of Demetrios Pierides (1811-1895), a collector of Cypriot artifacts; his descendants still occupy the top floor of the house. Bronze Age ceramics, Roman blown glass from 54BC, Cypriot folk wood carvings and silverware, as well as some of the earliest cartography of the island are examples of just some of Pierides' treasure, displayed in four large rooms. A fascinating display of a reconstructed Cypriot room shows the costumes, furniture, and tools of a typical household of a century ago. Modern sculptures, chiefly from the past decade, are displayed in the adjacent yard. (*Zinonos Kitieos 4, diagonal from CTO entrance.☎652 495. Open M-Sa 9am-1pm, Su 11am-1pm. £1, under 12 free.*)

LARNAKA FORT. Built by Venetians to protect Larnaka harbor in the 15th century and rebuilt by Ottomans in 1625, the small fort served as a prison during the British occupation (1878-1959). Climb the sea wall for a panoramic view of the surrounding town, and peer through the same slits that the Venetians used to gaze anxiously at the sea. In summer municipal plays are put on in the refreshingly cool courtyard. There is small museum right below the seawall. Ask the guard for information on the history of the fort. (*At the southern end of Athinon and a block east of Pl. Agiou Lazarou.☎630 576. Open M-F 8am-5pm, summer until 7pm. £0.75.*)

KITION. Now underground, the temple complex of the ancient city forms the substratum of Larnaka. It was settled in the early 13th century BC by refugees from the Peloponnese. The four main small temples at the site were damaged in 4th-century BC wars with the Phoenicians and Egyptians, and were later leveled by earthquake and fire in 280BC. Part of the ancient Cyclopean wall and the Temple of Astarte, the Phoenician God of fertility, still remain. *(The entrance to the site is hard to find; watch small street signs carefully when following directions. About a 20min. walk from Athinon in Larnaka; going on a moped may be a better option. Walk north from the archaeological museum on Kilkis with the museum on your left. Turn left on Leontious Machaira, and left again on Ioanni Paskirati; entrance is at the end of the road. Open M-F 9am-2:30pm.)*

TORNARITIS-PIERIDES MUSEUM OF PALEONTOLOGY. Five colonial-style warehouses are home to the Paleontology Museum and Municipal Gallery. The Paleontology Museum is two rooms filled with wood, fossilized fish, and the bones of pygmy elephants and hippopotami who once mysteriously migrated to Cyprus. Pieces date back over 490 million years to the Cambrian period. The enthusiastic curator has created an exhibit aimed at families —if a child can find a shell or fossil in good condition, the little tyke can place it in the exhibit! The Municipal Gallery's small but impressive set of modern abstract works and rotated featured collections inspect Cypriot politics and culture. Each month brings a different exhibit; the CTO has info on exhibit listings. The curator is eager to expound on the art and to refer aesthetes to private galleries throughout the island. *(Pl. Evropis, in the old customs warehouse at the end of Athinon opposite the Marina. Call a day in advance to arrange a tour. Gallery ☎ 628 587, Paleontology ☎ 658 848. Open Tu-F 10am-1pm and 5-7pm, Sa-Su 10am-1pm; off-season daily 4-6pm. Free.)*

OTHER SIGHTS. The **Larnaka District Archaeological Museum** has two main rooms, one dedicated to ceramic artifacts from the prehistoric period to the middle Bronze Age, and the other full of findings from ancient Kition. *(Follow the signs and head west on Leoforos Grigori Afxentiou; turn right on Klimonos. It's at the intersection of Kilkis and Klimonos. ☎ 630 169. Open M-F 9am-2:30pm. £0.75, Cypriot citizens free.)* In the center of the **Municipal Gardens,** view the stuffed aviaries, with a pelican, ducks, seagulls, turkeys, buzzards, canaries, flamingos, and peacocks. The **Municipal Museum of Natural History** contains over 5000 individually labeled Cypriot insects. Stuffed local animals—from street cats to extinct moufflons— fill six small rooms. *(On Stadiou across from the stadium, in the Municipal Gardens. Open Tu-Su 10am-1pm and 4-6pm. £0.20.)* Muslims anxious to teach travelers about their religion still use the medieval **Mosque of Al-Qibir** as a place of worship. *(Across the street from the Larnaka Fort.)*

🏛️🏖️ NIGHTLIFE AND BEACHES

The area around the **Hard Rock Cafe** shimmies with fun, teen-centered nightlife. **Stone Age Pub** (☎ 624 526), **Hard Rock Cafe** (☎ 624 292), and the **Camel** form a triangle. Walk down Athinon toward the fort and take a right onto a small footpath (officially called Watkins St.) in between the Chicago Bar and the Navy Marine Kebab House. Join the teenage locals for a cocktail at the Stone Age (£2.50-3.50), some snacks at the Hard Rock (£2-3) or a few beers at the Camel (£1-3). **Club Memphis,** on Athinon next to the Times Cafe, hosts infamous foam parties. A dubious entrance leads to an underground craze of intense dancers shakin' it to a wide range of tunes from Britney Spears to Nirvana until the wee hours of the morning. The most visited club in Larnaka, Memphis has grown even more popular with recent glitzy renovations. (Cover £5, one drink included. Open nightly 10pm-4am.)

If you prefer your fun in the sun, check out the Marina area for watersports, although you'll do better to explore beaches out of town. Pretty, less-crowded white sand **beaches** are situated to the northeast, on the way to Agia Napa (EMAN buses 8:30am-5pm, £1). You can also try a **Larnaka-Napa Sea Cruise** day trip organized by a private company; see **Mr. Karotsakis,** who oversees watersports and sea cruises. (☎ 656 949/954; larnaka.napa.sea.cruises@cytanet.com.cy.) Otherwise, you're left with the bustling beach—a dismal mixture of packed dirt and cigarette butts crammed with baking vacationers.

⚡ DAYTRIPS FROM LARNAKA

PANAGIA ANGELOKTISI

Take bus #6 or 7, bound for Kiti, from Pl. Ag. Lazarus (every hr. 6:40am-7pm, Sa until 2pm; £0.50), tell the driver "Panagia Angeloktisi." Open M-F 8am-4pm, Sa 10am-4pm, Su 9am-noon. Modest dress required: long skirts for women, pants for men, no bare shoulders. Donations welcome.

The church "built by the angels," Panagia Angeloktisti, lies in **Kiti,** a little residential village. Much of the church was built in the 11th century, atop (and incorporating) the 5th-century ruin of a prior sanctuary. A spectacular 6th-century **mosaic** in the central apse depicting the Virgin Mary with Christ is the oldest Cypriot mosaic still in its original setting. The church's narthex was built in the 14th century by the Gibelets, a Roman noble family prominent in medieval Cyprus.

STAVROVOUNI MONASTERY

Open daily 7:30am-noon and 3-5pm. No photography or video. Free. Note: women are not allowed to enter the monastery, only the church at the foot of the entrance, and only with proper attire (long skirt required).

Panoramic views of Cyprus's countryside, from Larnaka to Lefkosia and beyond, spread out below "Cross Mountain" monastery's 700m peak, which is just 40km outside Larnaka. This 4th-century monastery was founded by Constantine the Great's mom and Saint Helen—the woman responsible for his conversion. Stavrovouni was erected atop the ruins of an ancient temple dedicated to Aphrodite. On the way home from Jerusalem, Helen is said to have left a fragment of the True Cross there, following a dream's instructions. Despite adhering to a strict regimen, the devout monks find the time to be eminent icon painters and produce some of the island's best honey and cheese. At the foot of the rocky cliff is the small 18th-century monastery of Agia Varvara, also noted for its monks' icon painting.

DHERYNIA

Two kilometers north of Paralimni and a stone's throw from the Green Line is the small village of Dherynia, home to many refugees from Famagusta. The **Paralimni-Dherynia Bus Co. headquarters** (☎821 318) in Paralimni sends a bus to Larnaka, which passes through Dherynia and Frenaros on its way, reversing direction in Agia Napa (M-F 6 per day 6:10am-4:30pm, Sa 9:30am, 2pm; £1. In winter last bus at 2pm M-F with one extra bus Sa at 1:30pm; £1). **Police** can be found at Ammochostou 47, near the traffic light on the road for Paralimni. Several tourist lookouts nearby allow views of Turkish-occupied **Famagusta.** The closest viewpoint can be found following signs from the main road to the ⚑**Famagusta Beach View.** (☎823 003; £0.50). The View is owned and run by Annita, whose family was among those that fled from Famagusta in 1974. The UN has declared Famagusta a closed area, and no one is allowed in or out. Virtually a ghost town, the hotels loom desolate and trees overgrow streets frozen in time. At night the coastline is pitch black, except for 4 lights in the distance from military station points.

LEFKARA

Take the Lefkara bus from Pl. Ag. Lazarus (1 per day M-Sa 1pm, returns to Larnaka 7am. The bus goes to Pano Lefkara and Kato Lefkara; get off at Pano Lefkara.

Although a visit to Lefkara requires an overnight stay, you may never want to leave after one trek up to this lovely village. The old Greek section is home to the Church of Timo Stavrou, which dates back to the 11th century. Artisans from Lefkara produce the famous Lefkaritiko lace from which Leonardo da Vinci designed an altar cloth for the Milan Cathedral. Lefkaran silver craftsmen are also known for their exquisite work. The owners of Jackie's Studio in the Greek section will let you meander through their home, a wonderful example of an old Cypriot house restored to preserve its original architecture.

CAPE GRECO

East of Agia Napa on **Kyrou Nerou,** resort hotels give way to an empty coast preserved as a national forest. Several rough surface roads connect mainland Cyprus to the sea; the mostly unmarked hiking trail, 8km from town, leads to **Cape Greco.** For a solitary—and breathtaking—communion with Cyprus's southeast coast, trek around Cape Greco and the Red Villages on a rented moped or bicycle.

Maps of hiking trails can be obtained from the **CTO** and are quite helpful. The cape has remained undeveloped because of a military radar installation, giving aspiring secret agents the chance to swim beneath two space-age radar dishes. On Kyrou Nerou, the main road, signs point to **Agiou Anargyroi,** a small church that stands in splendid isolation over the sea. Next to the church, stairs descend to **sea caves** large enough to wander inside: a flashlight is helpful. There are no hotels, no tavernas, and no sand—just craggy coves cascading into the magnificent blue sea.

AGIA NAPA (Αγια Ναπα)   ☎03

Agia Napa thrives on the heavy tourist traffic of sunbaked visitors. Mopeds zip past beaches that once sparkled but have since been tainted by a vast array of multicolored English-language signs. This once-quiet farming and fishing village has become a haven for young tourists ready to get freaky around the clock. Thirty years ago, most tourists flocked to **Famagusta,** 16km to the north, allowing Agia Napa's ruined monastery and white sandy beaches to lie peacefully vacant. When Turkish forces occupied Famagusta in 1974, Agia Napa was transformed almost overnight into a glitzy, brassy tourist resort.

■■ ⚑ **ORIENTATION AND PRACTICAL INFORMATION. AirTour-Cyprus,** Dinoysos Solomos 18, near the post office. (☎722 133; fax 722 134; airtour@cytanet.com.cy. Books flights, organizes tours, rents cars and mopeds. Open M-F 9am-1pm and 4-7pm, Sa 9am-2pm; winter afternoon hours 2:30-5:30pm) The **bus station** is across from the Hellenic Bank. **EMAN** (☎721 321) provides service to: **Larnaka** (M-Sa 9 per day 8am-5pm, Su 4 per day 9am-4pm; in winter 5 per day 8am-4pm; £1); **Lefkosia** (M-Sa 8am, £2); and **Paralimni** via **Protaras** (M-Sa 20 per day 9am-8pm, Su 5 per day 9am-6pm; in winter M-Sa 8 per day 9am-5pm; £0.50). Expensive but effective **Agia Napa Taxi** (☎701 777), across the street from the monastery on Makarios, offers 24hr. service and negotiable rates. **Bikes and mopeds** are ideal transportation in Agia Napa. To reach **Ham-Yam's Car, Motorcycle & Bicycle Rentals,** take a right on Nissi from Makarios. Ham-Yam's is the only place to offer full insurance coverage, and is worth the slightly higher prices. Daily scooter rentals start at £7.50. (☎721 825. Open daily 8am-8pm, off-season and Su closes at 1pm.)

Trying to navigate Agia Napa by addresses and street signs is an exercise in futility. Instead, establish landmarks using a map. The town centers on the **Agia Napa Monastery** and the bar and taverna-laden streets that wind up the hill from it to the **Square. Makarios,** in front of the monastery, is the main road, with banks, shops, and most tourist services along it. Uphill, Makarios becomes **Dimocratias,** which leads north to Paralimni. Toward the sea, **Leoforos Nissi** heads west of Makarios to Larnaka and Nissi beach. A free **map** will help; get one from the **CTO,** Kyrou Nyrou 12, just off Makarios. (☎721 796. Open M-Sa 8:30am-2:15pm with afternoon hours 3-6pm every day except W.) The **Hellenic Bank,** on Makarios, has a 24hr. **ATM.** For **Internet access** head to **Virtuality,** Eleftherias 2, uphill from the monastery (☎723 290. Open M-Sa 12:30pm-2am, Su 4:30pm-2am. £2 1st hr., £1 each additional hr.) The **police** (☎721 553) are north of town on the road to Paralimni. The closest **hospital** (☎821 211) is 7 km north in Paralimni. The **post office** is at D. Liperti 1A. (☎721 550. Open M-F 7:30am-1:30pm, Th 3-6pm, Sa 8:30-10:30am.) **Postal code:** 5330.

⌐⌐ ACCOMMODATIONS AND FOOD. Inexpensive rooms are always elusive in Agia Napa, and in August they're nearly nonexistent—many tour groups book entire hotels so **call ahead** for reservations. To get to **Kyriakos Rooms,** Democratias 36 (☎701 389), go up the road to Paralimni until you have to turn. A left, a right, and a walk to the top of the hill will land you there. Each clean room features a balcony, bath, hot water, stove, and refrigerator. Price varies according to length of visit, but expect less than £7 per night. Just before Kyriakos Rooms are the **Paul Marie Hotel Apartments,** which offer currency exchange, a pool table, two bars, a rooftop pool, and 24hr. service. Rooms are clean and spacious, with fridges, A/C, and balcony. (☎722 481; fax 722 706. Studio £26; 1 bedroom £34.)

Good, cheap food is also hard to find in Agia Napa: try the supermarkets and 24hr. takeout shops, which serve the same food as restaurants, at cheaper prices. **Napa House Restaurant Taverna,** Democratias 4, on the road up to Paralimni on your right, serves decent American dishes laced with a Greek touch. (☎722 174. Main main dishes £3-6. Local wines £5-7.) **Jasmin's Inn,** D. Solomou 1, provides variety, large portions, and entertainment. The fearsome "Viagra cocktail," (£5 for 2 people; £10 for 4) stimulates table-top dancing and karaoke after 11pm. (☎721 731. Open daily 8am-2am, closed off-season. Main dishes £3-5.) The **Happy Eater,** D. Solomou, across from Jasmin's Inn, offers the cheapest and tastiest take-out in town. (☎721 436. Vegetarian dish £1.60, gyros plate £1.80.)

◙ SIGHTS. Amid the frenzied pace of the town the 16th-century Venetian **Monastery of Agia Napa** stands as a tranquil reminder of the town's Christian roots. Just outside the walls a 600 year-old sycamore tree spreads its thick branches to encompass shade-seekers. The inside is very cheery: pink flowers and a small wishing well surround a single palm tree that puts a tropical twist on this Mediterranean monastery. In the small chapel, a few icons hang and the well of the **Miracle of Panagia**—the inspiration for the monastery—rests in the corner, small and unornamented. According to Christian belief, the Virgin Mary appeared here to save a group of Christians from pirate attacks. Destitute and dehydrated, the Christians would likely have perished had not the Virgin Mary directed them to the corner spring. (Open daily 9am-10pm. Greek Orthodox Services no longer performed in the monastery. Anglican services Su 11am; Catholic services Su 5pm.)

The **Tornaritis-Pierides Municipal Museum of Marine Life,** Agias Mavris 1825, in the basement of the town hall, catalogues Cyprus's coral-reefed beaches through a collection of giant shells, fossilized fish, and stuffed migratory birds and marine animals from around the Mediterranean. There's also an explanation of local efforts to save sea turtles, common victims of beachside development. (☎723 409. Open M-Sa 9am-2pm. £1, students and soldiers free.)

◪ NIGHTLIFE. After dark, the bass thumps at Agia Napa's watering holes and discos and continues far into the wee hours of the morning. Accompanied by flashing neon lights and the grinding bodies of youthful revelers, the party never ends in Agia Napa. After sundown, people gather near **the Square** to sample drink specials at such pubs as the **Volcano Pub** (☎721 049), **Minos Pub,** and **Mariella Pub.**

The crowds dwindle after 1am as people migrate to the dance clubs. Nearly all of the club culture in Agia Napa is 20-something non-Cypriots. **Gas,** on Makariou, can cram 2000 people into its cavernous, bubble-filled, retro interior; two rooms of 70s and 80s hits and garage music blast from state-of-the-art electronic equipment. Open 1-4am. **The Castle,** Tefkrou Anthia 37, has three dance arenas, multiple DJs, 13 bars, and a "Chill-Out" area (with full bar, of course). (☎723 276. 18+. Open daily 12:30am-4am.) Smaller clubs, such **Starsky & Hutch,** and **Carwash** (70s and 80s, baby) are more retro in their music offerings. There's also the option of a bar turned club, such as **The Planet** (☎09 499 30), which is mainly for chillin', but sports a wide dance floor. Look for the big black planet hovering above the square: there's your spot. While the pubs have no cover, the clubs often charge £5 (or £3 with the flyer handed out in the Square); women may get a break on cover.

CYPRUS

LIMASSOL Λεμεσος   ☎ 05

A perpetual barrage of cultural festivities entertains foreigners and natives in this bustling industrial metropolis. Limassol is an unrepresentative but cordial introduction to Cyprus as port of entry for most passenger ferries. A maximum of 2 hours from almost anywhere on Cyprus and a transportation hub for many of the bus routes around the island, it makes an excellent base for further exploration. A walk along the seafront, separated from the main road by a row of palm trees and extensive landscaping, provides a break from the noisy city. The region's jewels—the ruins of Kourion and the gorgeous beach that dwells below—lie 10km to the west on the Akrotiri Peninsula (p. 532).

▐ TRANSPORTATION

Most intra-Limassol buses run up and down the main sea-side road and come every ten minutes; buses stop all along the road and can drop you off anywhere. **Bus #1** runs to the port from the station near the Anexartisias market, and **bus #30** runs from the **new port** to downtown Limassol (every 10 min., Sa every 30min., £0.35). After ships arrive, buses wait near the customs building; otherwise, the stop is outside the port gates. A taxi to town costs £2.50.

> **Buses:** Check times with the CTO. **Intercity Buses** (☎ 06 643 492) and **Nea Amoroza Bus Service** both go to **Lefkosia.** Both depart from the Old Port on the sea front road (M-F 6 per day 6am-6pm, Sa 4 per day 7am-2:30pm; £1.50.) **Intercity** also goes to **Larnaka** (M-F 4 per day 8am-4pm, Sa 3 per day; £1.70) and **Paphos** (M-Sa 9:15am and 1:30pm, £1.70.) To reach the **Troodos Mountains,** contact **Kyriakos,** Thessalonkis 21 (☎ 362 061), which serves **Platres** (6 per week; M-Sa 11:15am, return 7am; £2). Buses to Polis are via Paphos; buses to Agia Napa, Paralimni, and Protaras are via Larnaka. The **Episkopi Village** and **Kourion archaeological site bus** stops at the Limassol Castle (every hr. 9am-1pm; returns 11:50am, 2:50, 4:50pm June-Sept.; £0.70).
>
> **Ferries: Poseidon Lines** (☎ 575 666; fax 575 577). Open M-F 8am-1pm and 3-7pm, Sa 9am-1pm. **Salamis Tours** (☎ 860 000; fax 367 374) run to: **Haifa,** Israel (11hr., 2 per week, £70); **Rhodes** (18hr., 2 per week, £64); and **Piraeus** via **Rhodes** (45hr., 2 per week, £74). Ask for student discounts on ferry tickets. **Cruises: Salamis Tours** (☎ 860 000; fax 367 374), **Louis Tourist Agency** (☎ 363 161; fax 363 174), and **Paradise Island Tours** (☎ 357 604; fax 357 884) stop at Haifa, Israel and Port Said, Egypt.
>
> **Service Taxis:** Run 6am-6:30pm to **Lefkosia** (£3.45), **Larnaka** (£3), and **Paphos** (£2.50). Contact **Travel and Express** (☎ 362 061, 363 484 or 365 550.) Free port pickup.
>
> **Private Taxis: New Faithful Taxis** (☎ 354 444, 365 527 or 377 633).
>
> **Bike and Moped Rentals:** Agencies cluster on the shore road, near the luxury hotels. Try **MikeMar** on Ag. Georgiou A, next to Pizza Hut (☎ 327 611. Open M-F 8:30am-7pm, Sa 8:30am-1pm.) £10 for a 50cc scooter, £3 for a mountain bike. For longer rentals, you'll find lower rates in Polis.

◈ ▐ ORIENTATION AND PRACTICAL INFORMATION

Centrally located on the south coast and 50-70km from other major cities in southern Cyprus, Limassol is the island's transportation hub. Passenger boats arrive at the **New Port,** 5km southwest of the town center at the **Old Port.** The Old Port area contains the one and only significant structure in Limassol, the **medieval castle.** Tourist shops crowd the castle in the day, while candle-lit local tavernas offering fresh fish fill after 10pm. The blocks neighboring the town hall contain all the necessary tourist services. A number of dining and entertainment venues are east on **Ag. Andreou,** parallel to the waterfront two blocks inland. Approximately 6km east of the town center, a row of resort hotels and apartments lines the waterfront.

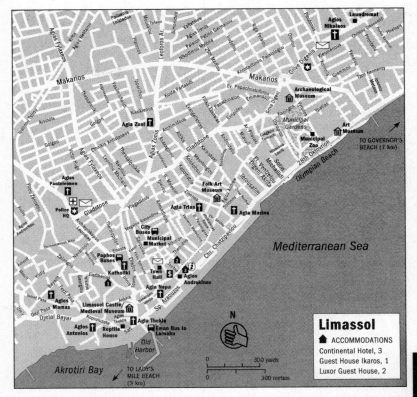

Limassol

🏠 ACCOMMODATIONS
Continental Hotel, 3
Guest House Ikaros, 1
Luxor Guest House, 2

Tourist Office: CTO, Spiro Araouzos 115a (☎362 756; fax 746 596), on the waterfront 1 block east of the old port along the main beach road. Open M-Tu and Th-F 8:15am-2:30pm and 4-6:30pm, W 8:15am-2:30pm, Sa 8:15am-1:15pm. Office at the **New Port** (☎571 868) opens immediately following arrivals. Another office in **Dassoudi Beach,** George I. Potamos Yermassoyias 35 (☎323 211), opposite the Park Beach Hotel and a few houses down (open same hours as Limassol office except closed Sa)

Tourist Agencies: Salamis (☎860 000; fax 367 374), on 28 Octovriou, offers package tours, ferry and airplane tickets, and cruises. Open M-Sa 8am-1pm and 3-6pm.

American Express: Archiepiskopou Kyprianou 1 (☎362 045; fax 378 042), is in the offices of **A. L. Mantovani and Sons.** Open M-F 8am-12:45pm and 2:30-5:30pm.

Banks: All 3 major banks are in the town center around Agia Napa church. Open M-F 8:15am-12:30pm with 24hr. **ATM** service. **Popular Bank,** one block from the Old Port CTO, has a convenient ATM for travelers waiting for the bus.

Bookstores: Kyriakos Bookshop, Panayides Building 3, Grivas Dighenis (☎747 555), at the roundabout near the Museum of Archaeology. The largest selection of paperbacks, dictionaries, educational books, and magazines in the city. Open M-Sa 8am-1pm, and 4-7:30pm except W and Sa. **Marilyn's Book Swap,** Kitou Kyprianou 51 (☎353 564). Open M-F 9am-1pm, Sa 9am-2pm. Wide selection of second-hand books; trade one in for store credit.

Laundromat: Quick Service, Grive Digenis 175a (☎587 056), past the roundabout. Self-service or leave it with them (£2). Open M-F 7am-7pm, Sa 7am-3pm.

Police: (☎805 050), on Gladstone and Leondios next to the hospital. Open 24hr.

Hospital: Government General Hospital, (☎305 777) outside of Limassol near the village Polemidia; take the #15 bus, which stops near the Municipal Market.

Telephones: CYTA on the corner of Markos Botsaris and Athinon.

Internet Access: C&P Computer Center 286C and 288A Agiou Andreou beyond the footpath (☎746 210). A bit expensive, but worth the convenience. High speed modems and the closest internet to the center of town: £3 per hr., minimum charge £2. Printing available. Open M-Sa 8am-3pm. **World Explorer Net Cafe,** Gladstonos 37 (☎347 795), 5 blocks in from the beach front road but cheaper than C&P: £2 per hr., £0.50 minimum charge. Open daily 1pm-1am.

Post Office: The main office (☎802 259) is next to the central police station on Gladstone. Open May-Sept. M-Tu and Th-F 7:30am-1:30pm and 4-6pm, W 7:30am-1:30pm, Sa 9-11am. Oct.-June daily 3-5pm except W. **Postal Code:** 3900.

ACCOMMODATIONS

Quirky yet friendly guest houses around the town center are Limassol's budget best since the town has no youth hostel. Those craving more than the absolute basics, however, may prefer the more upscale hotels on the waterfront.

Luxor Guest House, Ag. Andreou 101 (☎362 265), one block in from the CTO and to the left on the footpath, convenient to the town's attractions. Understated decor lends a simple elegance to this guest house, and the paternal manager will treat you like his own. Some private baths, most shared. Full kitchen available. 2 rooms have balconies. Singles £6; doubles £10; triples £18. Open year-round.

Guest House Ikaros, Eleftherias 61 (☎354 348), take Eirinis off the main road and take your fourth left. Tapestries, fish tanks, animal skins, lawn ornaments, and chandeliers. Cheap, big rooms with shared bath. In high season call for reservations, though dropping by randomly will land you a room on occasion. Singles £5; doubles £10.

Continental Hotel, Spiro Araouzos 137 (☎362 530; fax 373 030), right next to the CTO on the main seaside road. Well priced for a seaside hotel; affords privacy and convenience. Private baths, phones, TVs, balconies. Breakfast included. Singles £15; doubles £25; triples £35; quads for families £40; A/C £2 extra. Discounts for children, rates decrease by £5 in winter.

FOOD

There are tavernas, small kebab houses, and cafes throughout the city. The best option for the health and wealth-conscious traveler is the **Municipal Market,** in a huge warehouse on the corner of Saripolou and Kanari. A lunch of fruits, veggies, bread, and cheese costs less than £1. (Open M-F 6am-1pm.)

Sidon, Saripolou 71-73 (☎871 614). Walk along the footpath of Ag. Andreou with the Luxor guest house on the right. Lebanese restaurant in a beautiful setting—soft lights, open air rooms with twining flowering vines. Main dishes £5.50-12. Open daily 7-11pm.

Cuckoo's Nest, Ag. Andreou 228 (☎362 768), past the footpath with the Luxor glasshouse on the left. Cheap village wine (£3 per bottle) and local gossip flow freely under the fishing nets strewn across the ceiling. Main dishes £1.25-3. Open 10am-late.

Ta Kokkalakia, Ag. Andreou 239 (☎340 015), past the footpath and before the Folk Art Museum. The zebra hides aren't likely to win points with animal rights activists, but the exotic garden and bar will please even the toughest critic. Eclectic African menu including ostrich steak and South African sausage, and an impressive South African wine selection. Try the Kokkalakia mixed grill, touted by the owner as a dish for the truly gutsy (and those not afraid of heart attack risk). Main dishes £5-11. Open M-Sa 7pm-2am.

Mikri Maria, Ankara 3 (☎357 676). Endearingly unpretentious, serving exquisite food cooked over hot coals. Try the delicious grilled *lountza* and *halloumi* or the refreshing *tzatziki*. Live guitar music in winter. Main dishes £3-5.50. Open M-Sa until 10:30pm.

👁 SIGHTS

CASTLES. The **Limassol Castle,** where Richard King of England married Queen Berengaria in 1191 (crowned the Queen of England), is the lone building of historical significance in Limassol. Richard gained possession of Cyprus after defeating Cypriot Isaac Comnenus, who had reportedly mistreated some survivors of a shipwrecked fleet on the way to the Third Crusade (see p. 15). The original Byzantine fort was largely destroyed—only its western wall remains. In the early 14th century, the Knights Templar fortified the castle's walls and covered the Gothic windows. Later, the Knights of St. John converted the great Western Hall into a Gothic church and turned the chapel into a series of prison cells. The Ottomans claimed the castle in 1570, and the spacious West Hall was used as a prison under the British regime until 1940. Today, it is the **Cyprus Medieval Museum,** home to a scattered collection of medieval armor and religious objects. *(☎305 419. Open M-F 9am-5pm, Sa-Su 10am-1pm. £1.)* The **Kolossi Castle** played a crucial role during the Crusades, when both the Knights Templar and the Knights of the Order of St. John briefly made it their headquarters. *(9km west of Limassol; take bus #16 (every 20min., £0.40). ☎234 907. Open daily 9am-7:30pm. £0.75.)*

SITES. The **Archaeological Museum,** on the corner of Kaningos and Vyronos, offers a collection of funerary *steles,* jewelry, statues, and terra-cotta figurines from the Greek bronze age—an impressive and informative collection worth the visit. *(☎305 157. Open M-F 9am-5pm and Sa 10am-1pm. £0.75.)* Kids and snake lovers may enjoy the **Reptile House,** at the Old Port, showcasing scaly critters from around the world, with eight species local to Cyprus, plus crocodiles, iguanas, tortoises and poisonous spiders. *(☎372 779. Open daily 9am-6pm. Adults £1.50, children £1).* The attractive **Municipal Gardens,** on the waterfront between Olympion and Vyronos, are home to Cyprus's largest zoo and the **Municipal Open Air Theatre,** which hosts concerts and local theatrical performances. *(Check with the CTO for upcoming performances, and keep your eyes open around the city for posters advertising about events.)*

BEACHES. The city's long stone beach might be a little too rocky and too near the busy port for the discerning beach-goer, but a new breakwater past the town center has made the area more pleasant for swimming. **Dassoudi Beach,** 3km east of Limassol, is slightly better. *(Take bus #6 from the Kanaris market. Every 15min., £0.50.)* Further east about 7km beyond Dassoudi beach, surprisingly uncrowded **Governor's Beach** is perhaps the best bet near Limassol: sand, clean waters, and quiet. A bus leaves the Old Port at 9:50am each morning *(£2 roundtrip; children under 10 free).* **Ladies Mile Beach**—so named because the wife of the British Governor of Limassol used to ride her horse along the mile long beach—just west of the new port, is popular with locals and tourists alike. Clear blue seas preside over light grainy sand. *(Take bus #1.)* On your way to Kourion, be sure to spend some time at luckily undiscovered **Kourion beach.** It's almost always windy and the waves break heavily, but the beauty of the beach makes bearing the elements worthwhile.

FESTIVALS. Limassol hosts a plethora of special events throughout the year; pamphlets with details are available at the CTO. At summer's end, Limassol's gardens are transformed into a tribute to Dionysus for the Limassol **wine festival,** where participants fill bottles with as much of the local wine as they can guzzle. The general intoxication is enlivened by music, dance, and theater. (Admission £1.50.) From May to August, Limassol's cultural selection of activities is centered at **Kourion.** People flock from around the world for **Shakespeare Nights** at the theater of ancient Kourion. Hand-picked performers from all of Cyprus and abroad work year-round to produce weekend shows. **Carnival,** 50 days before Orthodox Easter (usually in February), is celebrated with more vim and vigor in Limassol than anywhere else in Cyprus.

♠ NIGHTLIFE

Local bars and cafes are sparse near the center of Limassol, but a few can be found on Ag. Andreou and near the castle. **Paradozo,** Irinis 140, is an open-air bar with plenty of nooks for conversation, after you battle your way through the wave of cologne and perfume. (Open 8pm-2am, weekends until 3-4am.) The 200-year-old building of **The Green Movement,** past the Cuckoo's Nest, is a testament to Limassol's fine architectural past with white columns protruding from a marble patio. It serves as a bar, a stage for spontaneous jam sessions, and a meeting room for political and environmental discussions among local students and intellectuals. (☎ 369 595 Open M-Sa 6pm-2am.)

Dance clubs, discos, and bars are at the edge of town in the tourist district. Taxis are probably the safest bet—just tell the taxi driver "tourist area" (£3-5). For disco dance clubs, **The Hippodrome,** on Georgiou, is the place to get down as the neighboring bars die down after 1am. Music includes popular dance hits and house, punk, R&B—you'll know it's time to break it down when the glowsticks start flashing. **The Basement Club,** a few bars down from the Hippodrome on Georgiou, hosts a diverse crew of merrymakers and is one of the last clubs to close down. Ladies can march in free of charge with a flyer.

♠ DAYTRIP FROM LIMASSOL: KOURION

12km west of Limassol. Buses leave Limassol Castle bound for ancient Kourion every hr. on the hr. (10am-1pm), returning at 11:50am, 2:50, and 4:50pm (£0.80). Drivers to Kourion usually go via Episkopi village. There are no signs for Kourion until you're within about 2km of the site, so a map is essential. Open year-round 8am-7:15pm. £1. Guidebook (£3) available at reception area. Handicap accessible.

Recall vivid images of mythology and ancient life through the remarkably well-preserved ruins of Kourion. First settled during the Neolithic period, Kourion was colonized during the 14th and 13th centuries BC by Achaeans from Argos; it would become famous for its **Sanctuary of Apollo Hylates,** fittingly meaning "of the forest" (8th century BC, 3km west from main road), and its **Stadium** (2nd century AD, 1km west of the main settlement and the basilica). In the 4th century AD, an earthquake destroyed several Cypriot coastal cities, leveling Kourion. The city was rebuilt in the 5th century, only to burn in a 7th-century Arab raid. As a result, the **Temple of Apollo** and other parts of the Sanctuary of Apollo are largely reconstructed. A photo of the pre-reconstruction sanctuary hangs in the front office.

The majestic 2nd century Roman **amphitheater** opens to a splendid view of the sea. It is used for **Shakespeare Nights** in June (see **Festivals,** p. 531), occasional summer concerts and theatrical productions, and weekend theater in September. The oldest structure on the site, the theater was used for dramas during Greek and Roman times, but by 300 AD, civilization-on-display had degenerated into a playland replete with animal fights and professional wrestling.

PLANET OF THE GRAPES The Ancient Greek god of wine, Dionysus, was always described as a joyful character: no wonder! Visit Omodos, a village renowned for its wine production, and you'll feel the same. The grapes that drape the hills of Omodos are squeezed into a wide variety of wines. The most distinctive of these is a sweet red wine called *Komandaria* drunk as an after-dinner treat. In addition to the mainstream reds and whites, hardy souls can try Greece's answer to Guinness—a thick, black wine called *Limnio* that may just leave you on knees begging old Dionysus for mercy. All of these wines can be tasted free of charge at the wine cellar, ■ **To Katoi,** where the smiling owner will gladly raise his glass with you.

CYPRUS

Adjacent to the amphitheater lie the **Baths and Annex of Eustoios,** built in 360 AD with exquisite mosaic floors dating to the 5th century. Look for the finely detailed round mosaics of a pheasant and a fish, the best preserved of all the floors. Across the road from the basilica lie a group of ruins under excavation. In the northwest corner are the remains of the **House of Gladiators** and its mosaic gladiator pin-ups. The **House of Achilles,** next to the ancient theatre, has mosaic floors depicting the Rape of Ganymede and Achilles's revelation to Odysseus of his identity.

PAPHOS Πάφος   ☎ 06

Paphos—the favorite city of Aphrodite—was made the capital city of Cyprus under the Ptolemies of Egypt. The city grew fabulously wealthy, developing into a cosmopolitan commercial center and remaining so under later Roman conquerors. When a 4th century BC earthquake ended its supremacy, the capital—and the political and social prestige—moved to Salamis (near modern Famagusta), and Paphos dwindled. As the upper half of the modern city goes about its business largely without regard for tourism, the lower half is overrun with tourists.

▐▀ TRANSPORTATION

Flights: CTO (☎ 932 841). Most flights arrive in Larnaka, but **Paphos International Airport** receives various European airlines and chartered flights. Get there by private taxi from the city center or Kato Paphos (£7-8). **ALEPA** (☎ 934 410) runs to the airport (5 per day 9am-5pm; £0.50, plus £0.50 per piece of luggage); call for reservations.

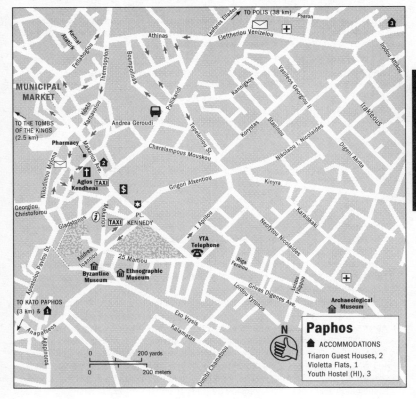

Paphos

⌂ ACCOMMODATIONS
Triaron Guest Houses, 2
Violetta Flats, 1
Youth Hostel (HI), 3

Buses: Nea Amoroza Co., Pallikaridi 79 (☎236 822 or 236 740), in Pl. Kennedy goes to **Polis** (11 per day M-F 6:20am-7pm, Sa 6 per day 9am-4pm; £1); some continue on to **Pomos Village** (2 per day M-F 11am and 4pm, 3 per day Sa; £1.10). Service to **Limassol** (M-Tu and Th-F 2:30pm, W and Sa 10:30am and 1pm; £2).

City Buses: ALEPA Bus (☎934 410 and 934 455) runs the municipal bus #11 between Ktima Paphos and Kato Paphos (every 15min., £0.50). Catch one in Ktima Paphos, up the road from the post office at the market, or in Kato Paphos at any of the yellow benches on the road to town. ALEPA bus #10 goes to **Coral Bay** (20 per day, £0.50) along the coastal road. Bus #2 starts at Geroskipou Beach with stops along the coastal road (every 15-20min. 6am-7pm). Check the schedules available in the tourist office.

Service Taxis: To: **Limassol** (every 30min. M-Sa 6am-6pm, Su 7am-5pm; £2.75). Contact **Travel & Express** on Eagorou (☎933 181).

Moped Rental: There are several shops in Kato and Ktima Paphos and along Apostolos Pavlou, the coastal road. Cheaper options lie along Ap. Pavlou. Rent early in the day; rentals often run out during peak seasons. £3-8 per day. **4U Car & Bike rentals** (☎944 085 or 09 466 026) is on Tomb of the Kings avenue. Mountain bikes £3, scooters £7 per day. **Pentaras Rentals,** Ag. Antoniou 5 (☎941 965 or (09) 603 838), in Kato Paphos, has a few cheap cars and bikes (£5-15 per day). Call ahead. Open M-F 8am-1pm and 2:30-7:30pm, Sa-Su 8-1pm.

✦ 🚺 ORIENTATION AND PRACTICAL INFORMATION

Paphos is divided into two sections. **Ktima Paphos** (the upper section, referred to simply as "Paphos") is centered on **Pl. Kennedy,** where you'll find the shops, budget hotels, and services. **Kato Paphos** (the lower section) lies roughly 3km south, hosting luxury hotels and most of the city's nightlife. **Leoforos Apostolos Pavlou** runs south from Ktima to Kato Paphos. **Vasileon** runs up the coast to Coral Bay and is lined with costly resorts. Unless noted, everything listed below is in Ktima Paphos.

Tourist Office: CTO, Gladstone 3, just outside of Pl. Kennedy (☎932 841; fax 932 841). Open in summer M-Tu and Th-F 8:15am-2:30pm and 2:45-7pm, W and Sa 8:15am-1:30pm. In winter same hours except afternoon hours change to 3-6:15pm.

Travel Agency: Iris Travel, Gladstone 10A (☎948 933 or 937 585; fax 93 960; iris.travel@cytanet.com.cy), opposite CTO. Very helpful and competent staff. Ferry tickets to Rhodes, Crete, and Israel (from £44, student discounts up to 20%). Airline tickets to London and Greece (about £40, student discounts up to 40%). Open M-Sa 8:30am-1pm and 3-6pm except no afternoons W and Sa; in summer afternoon hours 4-7pm. Helpful **VK Developers,** El. Venizelou 56, is close to the hostel next to the Alpha Bank (☎910 400; fax 910 195). Open M-F 8am-1pm and 4-7pm, Sa 9am-1pm.

Banks: Concentrated around Pl. Kennedy on Makariou. All have 24hr. **ATMs.** Open M-F 8:30am-12:30pm. ATMs can be found on any major road.

Police: (☎806 060) on Grivas Digenes, in Pl. Kennedy, opposite the Coop Bank. English spoken; provide helpful tourist information. Open 24hr.

Hospital: Paphos General (☎803 100), is a long walk away on Neophytos Nicolaides, offers free first aid. English spoken. **St. George's Private Hospital,** El. Venizelou 29 (☎947 000), on the way to the youth hostel, has casualty and ambulance services. English spoken. Open 24hr.

Telephone: CYTA (☎930 228), on Grivas Digenes. Open daily 7:30am-1:30pm.

Internet Access: Scattered throughout the city. **Maroushia Fashion Cafe,** 6 Pl. Kennedy (☎947 240; maroushia@cylink.com.cy). Check email (£2 per hr.) while young locals play pool or converse over an afternoon *frappé*. Maroushia, the lively owner, has also opened a branch in Kato Paphos on Poseidonos, the main beach road.(☎910 657).

Post Office: Main branch, (☎940 223) on El. Venizelou. Open M-F 7:30am-1pm and (except W) 3-6pm, Sa 8-10am. The post office in **Kato Paphos** (☎940 226) is on Ag. Antoniou. **Postal Code:** Ktima Paphos 8900; Kato Paphos 8903.

ACCOMMODATIONS

Finding affordable accommodations in Paphos is a chore. Solo travelers should stick to the guest house or the youth hostel if they have their own transportation; groups might try renting a flat. Prices are higher in tourist-filled Kato Paphos.

■**Triaron Hotel Guest House,** Makarios 99 (☎932 193; fax 936 227), from Pl. Kennedy Makarios is the narrow road directly to the left as you face Pallikaridi. Airy, high-ceilinged rooms, a common living room with TV, kitchen access, and an owner very glad to help out with any queries about the town make this ideally-located budget option a brilliant choice. Shared bath. Singles £5; doubles £8-12.

Violetta Flats, Dionissiou 7 (☎934 109; fax 220 734), in Kato Paphos. 7 flats with kitchen, TV, and private bath. Rooms are large, with small personal touches that warm them up. Well situated for enjoying the nightlife, poorly situated for avoiding it. Singles £8-15; doubles £10-18; larger rooms for up to 5 people £28. A/C £2 extra.

Youth Hostel (HI), El. Venizelou 45 (☎932 588). Walk 15min. from the plateia on Pallikaridi to Venizelou, then turn right. Out of the way, but clean and cheap. 2 single-sex rooms with 8 beds each, one mixed room, and one family room available. Kitchen and laundry facilities. No curfew, but lights out around 11pm. £5 per bed for the first night, £4 per night thereafter.

FOOD AND NIGHTLIFE

Restaurants in Kato Paphos are geared to money-laden foreigners, while in Ktima Paphos local tavernas are hidden among the winding streets. ■**Vasano Kebab House,** Agapinoros 25 in Kato Paphos, has only the basics, but every morsel is prepared to perfection, and the locals know it—no evening passes without a full house. On the road down from Ktima to Kato Paphos, take a left onto Pinelopis and then a right onto Agapinoros. (☎242 635. Main dishes £1-2.) **Athens,** Pallikaridi 47, is the place for anyone who remotely likes sugar. Traditional pastries, cookies, and *pites* are freshly baked every morning. (☎32 613. Pastries £0.40 and under.)

Virtually all of the area's nightlife centers on Ag. Napas and Ag. Antoniou, a couple of blocks inland from the waterfront in Kato Paphos. **Club 12,** on Ag. Andreou, draws all the crowds after 1am with heavy bass and the latest techno tunes—be prepared for wild dancing on the bars and tables. (☎(0191) 230 4848. Cover £5.) **Summer Cinema** (☎247 747 or (09) 632 229), on the waterfront, is a trendy open-air club just far enough from package hotels for the locals to call it their own. **Bubbles,** on Ag. Antoniou, hops from 10pm till late (3-4am). Every Thursday, "Carwash Night Back in Time" turns back the clock with 70s and 80s hits. A more laid-back atmosphere is found at **Different** (☎934 668), farther down on Ag. Antoniou. Panos, the owner, enthralls all, gay and straight, with stories and jokes—especially after a Strawberry Kiss, a must-try cocktail made just for you.

SIGHTS

TOMBS OF THE KINGS. Apostolou Pavlou street, connecting Ktima and Kato Paphos, is lined with monuments to the Roman, early Christian, Byzantine, and Venetian periods of Cypriot history. About 2km before Kato Paphos, a sign directs you to Paleokastra's **Tombs of the Kings.** Although those interred in the stone tombs were local aristocracy, not kings, the 2nd century remnants bear a strong resemblance to Egyptian peristyle court tombs. The larger tombs consist of an open court encircled by burial chambers, with Doric columns carved out of the underground rock, and stairways leading down to the interiors. These Hellenistic and Roman tombs were later used as hideouts by Christians fleeing persecution. The most impressive are tombs three, four, five, and eight, which have extensive underground passages to wander through. (☎940 295. Open 7:30am-7:30pm. £0.75.)

MOSAICS OF KATO PAPHOS. Over 2000m^2 of mosaic floors from the **House of Dionysus,** the **House of Theseus,** and the **House of Aion** lie under weather protection tents adjacent to the ruins of the houses they were originally kept in. Some of the city's, and the Eastern Mediterranean's, most extensive ancient relics were discovered accidentally by a farmer plowing his fields. In 1962, they were excavated by a Polish expedition that found largely intact mosaics covering 14 rooms of the expansive Roman House of Dionysus. The mosaics are not unique for their time period, but are amazingly well preserved (and thus rare) examples of the norm for aristocratic decor during the Roman Period. The floors depict scenes from Greek mythology and daily life using the naturally occurring hues of the stones. The House of Theseus, toward the water, dates from the 2nd to 6th centuries AD. These ruins reveal what was once a decadent building with marble statues, columns, and mosaic floors. The most famous mosaic, now housed in the warehouse, comes from the House of Theseus and is a vibrant, circular representation of the clash between Achilles and Theseus. *(Enter through the gate at the start of the pedestrian way past the parking lot on the Paphos Fort road. Walk up the dirt path about 200m to the reception booth.* ☎940 217. *Open daily 8am-7:30pm. £1.50. Guidebook £3.)*

MUSEUMS OF KTIMA PAPHOS. The **Archaeological Museum,** on Grivas Digenes, 1km from Pl. Kennedy, has an array of Bronze Age pottery, tools, sculpture, statues, and artifacts from the houses of Dionysus and Theseus. *(☎940 215. Open M-F 9am-2:30pm and 3-5pm, Sa 10am-1pm. £0.75.)* The private collection at the **Ethnographic Museum,** displayed in the owner's home at Exo Vrysi 1, just outside Pl. Kennedy, takes you through different historical phases of Cypriot life, complete with traditional costumes and daily tools. The garden is the highlight of the museum, with a 3rd-century-BC Hellenistic tomb, Christian catacombs, and *kleftiko* ovens. *(☎932 010. Open M-Sa 9am-6pm, Su 9am-1pm. £1. Guidebooks £3.)* Across the way, the **Byzantine Museum,** Andreou Ioannou 5, has icons and religious relics from local monasteries and churches, including frescoes, vestments, and manuscripts. The main attraction is the oldest icon in Cyprus, of Agia Marina, dating to the 7th or 8th century. *(☎931 393. Open M-F 9am-4pm, Sa 9:10am-1pm. £1, guidebook £3.)*

CATACOMBS OF AGIA SOLOMONI. Descend into the dark catacombs that include a chapel with deteriorating Byzantine frescoes. Dedicated to Ag. Solomoni (Hannah), the chapel sits on the site of an old synagogue. A marked tree—said to cure the illnesses of those who tie a cloth to it—marks the entrance to the catacombs. St. Paul was whipped for preaching Christianity at nearby **St. Paul's Pillar,** on the site of the Catholic church. *(Tombs on Ap. Pavlou. Open 24hr. Free.)*

OTHER SIGHTS. The remnants of an *agora* are north of the mosaics, enclosed in Kato Paphos's archaeological park. The limestone Roman **odeon,** a small, roofed theater, is still used for dance and song performances. Pick up a schedule at the CTO. *(Open daily 8am-7:30pm. Entrance is free along with your ticket for the mosaics— the sites are side by side.)* Built in the late 7th century on a hill overlooking the harbor, the **Byzantine Castle** *(Saranda Kolones)*, named as such for its many granite columns, was intended to protect inhabitants from Arab pirates. An earthquake destroyed most of the castle in 1222, but part of its fort and some ruins remain. No one knows exactly when the **Paphos Fort,** at the end of the pier, was built, but some speculate that the Lusignans built the it after *Saranda Kolones* was destroyed. The Turks completely rebuilt it between 1589 and 1593. *(Open 10am-5:45pm. £0.75.)*

◪ BEACHES

The two most popular beaches stretch along **Geroskipou** to the east and **Coral Bay** to the north (big, sandy, and touristy—luxury hotels line the way). For Geroskipou, take bus #2 from Ktima Paphos (5 per day, 6:25am-7pm, £0.50); to reach Coral Bay, take bus #10 from the Market in Pano Paphos (every 20min., £0.50). **Cape Lara** is host to lovely, empty beaches, and is a nesting site for

Green and Loggerhead Turtles from June until September. The ◼**Lara Sea Turtle Project** was conceived in 1971 to protect the turtles by ensuring that nesting continues. After traveling the Mediterranean, the turtles return to the beach where they were born to lay their eggs. Turtle nests can be viewed in the Project's hatchery enclosure. Alas, there's no public transportation to Cape Lara; your best bet is a jeep excursion or motorbike. Follow signs for **Agios Georgios** from Coral Bay to the pebbly beach that sits below the church. **Sundy Beach,** 2km down the road to Cape Lara, parades umbrellas for rent. Farther along a nearly deserted, unnamed beach stretches for about 1km.

◪ DAYTRIPS FROM PAPHOS: KOUKLIA

Adjacent to the modern village of Kouklia are the ruins of the great **Temple of Aphrodite** and **Paleopaphos** (Old Paphos), once the capital of a kingdom encompassing nearly half of Cyprus. The temple itself was the kingdom's religious center and a destination for pilgrims from every corner of the Roman world. Built in the 12th century BC, it thrived until the 4th century AD, when the edicts of Emperor Theodosius and a series of earthquakes reduced it to rubble. The scant remains make little sense without a guide. *A Brief History and Description of Old Paphos*, published by the Department of Antiquities, is available in the adjoining **Paleopaphos Museum.** (☎432 180. Open M-F 8am-7pm, Sa-Su 9am-5pm. Admission to ruins, city, and museum £0.75. The sites are best seen from excursion buses. Renting a moped is not advisable—the road is hazardous; service taxis are a much safer bet.)

POLIS Πολις   ☎06

Polis is the quietest and the smallest of Cyprus's major seaside towns. The town is separated from the coast by cornfields; just when it seems you'll be landlocked forever, the sea appears in the distance. Polis retains its own ways and life goes on with a peaceful rhythm. Tourism has made just enough inroads to make for sufficient rooms, but the beauty of its natural treasures has remained unscathed.

▤ TRANSPORTATION. Nea Amoroza Bus Co. (☎236 740 or 236 822) passes through Polis from Paphos (10 per day M-F 6:30am-7pm, 5 per day Sa 9am-4pm; £1). **Spirides Taxi Service** (☎516 161) is in the plateia. **Pegasus** (☎321 374), also in the plateia, rents cars, mopeds ($4 per day), mountain bikes ($3 per day), and apartments. **Odysseas Car Rentals Ltd.** (☎322 236 or 09 675 610) on a side street right off the Plateia rents cars, mopeds (from £6 a day) and motorbikes (from £6 a day). The **Lemon Garden** (☎09 647 729), away from the plateia past the Hellenic Bank, rents and sells **sports equipment** such as jet skis, mountain bikes ($2.50-3 per day, discounts for longer rentals), and diving equipment ($5-15).

▨▨ ORIENTATION AND PRACTICAL INFORMATION. Polis can be difficult to navigate, though most tourist destinations are clearly marked and consolidated in the plateia. The plateia, about 1½km inland from the shore, is home all of the town's tourist services. The **CTO** office is the island's newest, offering enthusiastic advice for daytrips and accommodations. (☎322 468. Open in summer Su-Tu and Th-F 9am-1pm and 2:30-5:45pm, W and Sa 9am-1pm; in winter Su-Tu and Th-F 9am-9pm, W and Sa 9am-1:45pm.) The **police** are one block from the plateia in the direction of the beach, and speak some English. (☎321 451. Open 24hr.) Around the plateia you'll find three **banks** with 24hr. **ATMs.** (Open M-F 8:15am-noon.) Two **pharmacies** (☎321 253 or 321 167) are down the street from the post office. High speed **internet access** can be found above **The Piazetta** at Pavlou Georgiou 3. (☎321 518. $2.50 for 1hr.) The **hospital** (☎321 431) is about a short walk from the plateia toward the campground. The **post office** is also in the plateia. (☎321 539. Open M-F 7:30am-2pm, Th 3-5pm.) **Postal Code:** 8905.

ACCOMMODATIONS. The cheapest and most reasonable accommodations in Polis are the various **rooms to let** throughout the town. Women with rooms to let often wait at the bus stop in the hopes of winning over guests with a sales pitch. It's generally not good practice to commit to a room without checking it out. **Elena's Rooms to Let** are a 5min. walk from the beach, along the main road that leads uphill from the beach to the plateia. Rooms are simple but clean and have all the necessities, including refrigerators. Most have private baths and some have balconies. (☎321 244 or (09) 675 474. £10-15 per night.) The **Lemon Garden** has a unique combination of quality rooms, food, and atmosphere. All rooms come with kitchenette, private bath, A/C, a view, and swimming pool access. (☎321 443. Doubles £20; quads £36 for families in the high season. If you arrive late ring the bell; the owner and her family live right upstairs.) Other inexpensive rooms to let (£5-6 per person) on the road to Latsi and the road to the beach are clearly marked; inquire at a cafe if you get tired of looking. Campers are in luck: the **campground** (☎321 526), 1½km from the town center in a fragrant, seaside eucalyptus grove, is open from Mar.-Oct. To get there just follow the signs. It has shower facilities, a playground, a mini-supermarket, and a bar that hosts beach parties every Thursday and Sunday. (£1 per person, £1.50 per tent, tent rental £2.)

FOOD. The plateia cafes and restaurants serve pretty uniform fare (Cypriot with an Italian flare), but a few places a bit away from the center of things provide some delectable surprises. At ◼**Mario's Garden Cafe,** located down a set of stairs beyond the Akamas Hotel, a formerly dilapidated Turkish house has become a whimsical garden cafe and bar, with statues, quirky furniture, and a central bonfire. Mario doesn't cook up a full menu every day (drinks, salads, and some snacks are always available) but he saves his best for Sunday when he stirs up a *meze*-style all-you-can-eat buffet (£5). For convenient dining, visit **Lemon Garden Taverna,** right below the hotel. Try the classic *pastitsio* (£3.50), or if you happen to drop by in the morning, sample their rich and extensive breakfast menu. (Main dishes £2.50-5.50. Open 8:30am-11pm.) In town, **Arsinoe,** across from the church, serves the catch of the day, and comes recommended by locals. (Swordfish £4.50, fish *meze* £6. Open 8am-1pm and 7pm-1am.)

SIGHTS. The churches of **Agios Andronikos** and **Agia Kyriaki** in Polis were built in the 15th century. In the latter half of the 16th century, invading Ottomans converted Agios Andronikos into a mosque and plastered over its frescoes. Both of the churches are closed and no longer in use. The **Baths of Aphrodite,** carved out of limestone are the mythical site of Aphrodite's first encounter with, and later marriage to, Akamas, the son of Theseus. The goddess would come here to cleanse herself after nocturnal exploits. There's no word on modern-day naughtiness but according to legend, all who bathe in the pool stay forever young. *(Take a bus from Polis M-F 9:30, 10:30am, 2:30pm; £0.50.)*

HIKING THE AKAMAS PENINSULA. The easternmost home of European vegetation, the peninsula contains a remarkable array of about 600 plant species and over 160 bird species, some of which (especially the stationary varieties) are marked along the trails. Stretching to the Cape of Arnaouti, this area is a must for travelers. The two primary hiking trails, the **Aphrodite** and the **Adonis,** begin at the Baths. Both take 2-3hr., although with a side trip to **Fontana Amaroza** (the Fountain of Love), the Aphrodite trail can take closer to half a day. The trails take the same path for the first 2km, leaving coastal scrub behind in favor of fragrant forest. They split at the ruins of **Pyrgos tis Rigainas,** believed to be a medieval monastery, where picnic tables and a potable well sit among huge oak trees. From here, the Adonis continues left, running along a series of placid streams and returning to the main road just east of the tourist pavilion. The Aphrodite continues to the right, ascending **Mt. Sotiras** before descending toward the coast into a field cleared by a forest fire. It then hugs the coast all the way back to the Baths. Near the coast, the turnoff for Fontana Amaroza (the Fountain of Love) leads to a shipwreck and sea caves, as well as the fountain itself. While it may have worked wonders in the past, today the *fontana* is an unimpressive stagnant pool; the point of the hike is more at the scenery than the fountain itself. The CTO has free maps of the Akamas Peninsula and a helpful booklet on the vegetation and animal life.

TROODOS MOUNTAINS Τροοδος

Comprised of some of the world's most geologically distinct terrain, winding and underdeveloped roads, crisp mountain air, authentic village life, and Byzantine churches hidden amid pine-covered mountains, the Troodos are the perfect escape for hikers who want to avoid Cyprus's summer heat. A peaceful and rejuvenating natural experience in June and early July can turn frustrating and costly in August, when the urban crowds descend, especially on weekends. In winter, **Mt. Olympus,** the highest point in Cyprus (1951m), plays host to hundreds of skiers.

Public transportation between villages and around the area is infrequent; scheduled stops are unreliable at best, nonexistent at worst. In the mountains, those over 17 can easily rent mopeds. Cars are available in Limassol, Paphos, or Lefkosia for those over 23. Be careful: mountain roads are steep, winding, and bumpy.

PLATRES Πλατρες   ☎05

Fresh mountain air and the sound of rushing streams combine to make Platres a glorious natural escape. Devoted to eateries and accommodations, relatively cheap and accessible by public transportation, the town offers no sites of its own, but evokes a relaxing communion with your surroundings. It's a great base for exploring Troodos and visiting the surrounding mountain villages, and it will offer a soothing welcome after a long, full day of hiking.

⌷ TRANSPORTATION. From Limassol, a **Kyriakos service taxi** leaves for Platres at 11:30am, returning to Limassol at 7am. (☎05 362 061. M-Sa, £2.) Kyriakos has an office in Platres (☎364 114) for transit in the area. **Pantelis private taxis** run within the mountain villages (☎423 333 or 09 429 453; £5 to Troodos Sq., £7 to Omodos). **Top Hill Souvenirs,** on the main street, down the hill from the post office, rents **mountain bikes.** There are some great bike routes in the Troodos—ask the staff for guidance. (☎421 729. 21-gear bikes £4 per day, helmets included. Open 10am-6pm.)

◼▟ ORIENTATION AND PRACTICAL INFORMATION. Platres is divided into the **pano** (upper) and **kato** (lower) sections. Pano Platres contains most tourist facilities, while Kato Platres is largely residential. Hiking trails are the area's main form of entertainment. The **tourist office** is left of the parking lot in the plateia. (☎421 316. Open M-F 9am-3:30pm, Sa 9am-3pm.) The **Bank of Cyprus** is opposite the tourist office, and **Popular Bank** is just up the hill. Both have a 24hr. **ATM.** The **hospital** is between Pano and Kato Platres and is no longer open 24hr., but keeps a doctor's number posted on the door for emergencies. (☎421 324. Open 7am-7pm.) The nearest **pharmacy** is in Kakopetria. (☎924 492. Open M-Sa 8:30am-1:30pm and 3:30-7:30pm.) The **police** are opposite the tourist office in a converted military chapel. (☎421 351. Open 24hr. English spoken.) The **CYTA,** next to the post office, sells phone cards. (Open M-F 7:30am-2:30pm.) The **post office** is to the left of the tourist office. (☎422 624. Open M-F 3-5pm; in winter M-F 7:30am-noon and 3-5pm.) **Postal Code:** Kato 4815, Pano 4820.

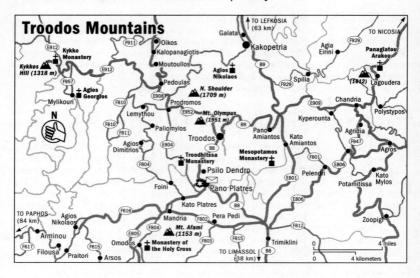

Troodos Mountains

TO LEFKOSIA (63 km)
Galata
TO NICOSIA
Oikos
Kakopetria
Agia Eirini
Panagiotou Arakou
E912 Kykko Monastery
F911
Kalopanagiotis
F929
Moutoullos
Agios Nikolaos
B9
Kykkos Hill (1318 m)
E912
Spilia
(1612) Lagoudera
F957
Pedoulas
F929
Aglos Georgios
N. Shoulder (1709 m)
Chandria
E909
Mylikouri
F810
E908
Prodromos
Polystypos
Lemythou
E952 Mt. Olympus (1951 m)
Kyperounta
Agridia
F810
Paliomylos
B9
F947
F811
Pano Amiantos
Troodos
Agios Dimitrios
E804
B8
Kato Amiantos
Agros
Troodhitssa Monastery
Mesopotamos Monastery
F801
E806
F804
Psilo Dendro
E801 Pelendri
Kato Mylos
Foini
Pano Platres
Potamitissa
B8
E806
Kato Platres
Zoopigi
TO PAPHOS (84 km)
Agios Nikolaos
F616
Mandria
Pera Pedi
F802
F812
Arminou
F804
Mt. Afami (1153 m)
F815
Trimiklini
0   4 miles
F617 Filousa
E805
Omodos
Monastery of the Holy Cross
F803
TO LIMASSOL (38 km)
B8
0   4 kilometers
Praitori
Arsos

ⅢⅢ ACCOMMODATIONS AND FOOD. From the post office, go down the hill and bear left to find **Kallithea Hotel**, where the kind owner offers simple rooms, some with a balcony or patio. (☎421 746; fax 05 422 241. Singles £15 high season, £11 low season; breakfast included.) Ask about the rooms across the street, which offer large serene balconies (£12 per person high season; breakfast included.) **To Psilo Dendro**, a fish farm 2km north of Platres on the road to Troodos, serves sumptuous trout under a canopy of tall trees. (Whole trout £4.20. ☎05 422 050. Open 8am-5pm.) Directly below the hill from the post office is the **Petit Palais Hotel Restaurant**, with a large selection of main dishes (£3-5) and crepes (£1-2). Try house favorites moussaka (£4.50) or lamb (£5). Cafes serving standard snack foods line the plateia. For picnics, two large **grocery stores** are downhill from the post office; bear right one block past Lanterns. **Sofoula Supermarket** (open 8am-8pm) and **Cherryland** (open 8am-8:30pm) stock all the necessities, plus ice cream bars.

ⓝ HIKING. Psilo Dentro restaurant marks the starting point for three main hiking trails. A helpful map of Platres area hikes and bicycle routes is available at the Platres tourist office. Most hikes lead toward various views of ▧**Kaledonia Falls,** the Troodos region's most celebrated and picturesque spot. Although the falls are not impressively high, the sparkling cold water is striking. Left of the restaurant, a path accessible by car and mountain bike quickly reaches the falls, affording postcard views before continuing through a forested path for 3km (about 1-2hr. uphill). The trail ends by the Troodos's presidential palace, built by the famous French poet **Arthur Rimbaud.** The house is not open to the public; intense security surrounds the place, especially when the president is in residence. At the end of the trail, veer left to reach the Platres-Troodos road. To the right of the restaurant, the path joins with an easterly trail before reaching a junction. From here, yellow signs lead to both the top of Kaledonia falls or the southern shoulders of Mt. Olympus. Also to the right of the restaurant, the least impressive but most ambitious trail leads to the unremarkable **Mesopotamos Monastery;** the 9km (a generous 4hr.) dirt track is accessible to mountain bikes.

OMODOS ☎05

A small village 10km southwest of Platres, Omodos is home to lush green hills that surround the town on all sides and harbor the grapes that produce the region's famous wine. The town will endear itself to you with its cobbled plateia and quiet afternoon siesta hours. Occasional tourist buses bring sporadic bursts of people in search the handmade cordial lace crafted by women on the doorsteps of the town.

7 PRACTICAL INFORMATION. No buses run to Omodos; grab a **taxi** (£6-7) from Platres. There is **no CTO**, but this small residential village is very easy to navigate; if you get lost a bit of wandering will quickly lead you back to a familiar street or to the plateia. The **hospital** (☎421 254) is directly outside of the plateia and holds unreliable hours, but the **doctor** is always on call (☎(097) 26 965). The closest **police** station is in Pano Platres. The **post office** is on the street to your left when facing the monastery's entrance. (Open officially M-F 3-8pm, but since the post office doubles as a *kafeneion*, the postmaster can usually be found sitting outside, ready to help). **Postal Code:** 4820.

⌂▢ ACCOMMODATIONS AND FOOD. There are basically two options for shacking up in Omodos. Ask for a room at the cafes that line the plateia— almost all of them have rooms at around £15 for a double. The other option is to head over to the **Linos Souvenir Shop,** the last shop on the plateia on the right as you face the monastery. The lady who runs the shop distributes contact information for **Village Houses,** a small company that owns multiple rooms throughout the town. The recently renovated rooms are pleasant and airy. All include balcony, fridge, and full bath. (☎731 076 or 422 361; fax 733 190. £15 per person.) For your dining pleasure, **Taverna Makrinar** is planted in the heart of Omodos (follow signs from the plateia). *Bouzoukia* strum into the night in this traditionally decorated taverna: locals swear by the authentic food. Try the *moussaka* (£3) with a glass of local wine. On the outskirts of town **Omodos Taverna** and its pleasant veranda stare down upon the green hills of the town. The house specialty is the *stifado* (£4.50), beef cooked with tomato, onion and vinegar. (☎421 493. Open 12:30-4pm.)

▣ SIGHTS. For immersion into old school Greek life, visit the simply named **House Museum.** The curator and former resident of the home has collected traditional objects from her home and others to create dynamic antique displays including beautiful hand-made lace coverings, a traditional bridal dress from 1900, jugs for storing wine, a traditional dome-like stove, and an old loom the owner still uses to weave rag-rugs (which are for sale upstairs). (Open M-Su 9am-9pm.) The upper level of the famous 14th-century **Monastery of the Holy Cross** is closed to visitors due to the reconstruction following a 1996 earthquake, but the church and a number of other structures remain. Alive with biblical history and gory splendor, the church contains the bloodstained piece of rope used to tie Christ that St. Helen brought with her; it lies hidden from the public. The skull of Apostle Philipos, the bones of 26 saints, and a unique icon of Christ whose glazed eyes seem to follow your each and every move are some of the amazing relics contained within the monastery. (Open M-Sa 8am-6pm, Su noon-6pm.)

TROODOS Τροοδος ☎05

Penetrating Cyprus's clear skies in the mountains that bear its name, the Troodos district hoards magnificent views of the entire island. However, Troodos village is merely an aggregate of tourist and camping facilities providing another launch point for exploration. Just 10km north of Platres, the area can be reached by **Clarios Bus Co.** in Lefkosia if you make reservations. (☎02 753 234. Leaves from Lefkosia M-F 11:30am, returns 6:30am; £1.10.) A **private taxi** costs £25 from Lefkosia and £5 from Platres. You can also **hike** uphill (at least

2hr.) from Platres. The **Troodos campground,** 2km north of the plateia in a pine forest, provides laundry facilities, a mini-market, a bar/restaurant, and a first aid station, plus a relaxed, upbeat atmosphere for young travellers and families alike. The exceptionally accommodating owner will be happy to answer your questions and offer assistance. (☎422 249. £1.50 per person.) Troodos also has a **Youth Hostel:** walk past town, down the mountain and follow the signs. Flaying to the minimalists, the hostel provides bare necessities: beds, bathroom, sometimes running water. In the winter, a stove is available for heating. Plenty of space but a gender divide: 2 female rooms, 2 male rooms, and 4 family rooms. (☎420 200, £5 first night, £4 each additional night.)

◪ TROODOS TRAILS. Four spectacular hikes originate in the Troodos area. Detailed maps are available at all Cyprus tourist offices. From Troodos, **Artemis** begins 200m up the road to Prodromos. The circular trail wraps around **Mt. Olympus** for 7km, or roughly 3½hr. Although relatively flat and mostly covered in black pines, the hike provides majestic views of Cyprus in its entirety. From the Troodos post office, the **Atalante** trail mimics the Artemis trail at a lower altitude. The trail runs 12km (about 5hr.), ending at the Prodromos-Troodos road, near the chromium mine camp. A fresh mountain water spring 3km into the hike will sustain hikers, allowing ceaseless photography of the striking views from Limassol to the Northern occupied territory, and everything in between. The 3km **Persephone** trail leaves from the coffee shop in Pl. Troodos and gradually descends to a breathtaking lookout point among huge slabs of limestone rock. The **Kaledonia** trail, the shortest, begins 2km from Troodos on the road to Platres, passes the Kaledonia Falls, and ends at Psilo Dentro restaurant near Platres.

KAKOPETRIA Κακοπετρια ☎02

Kakopetria is popular with urban Cypriots and foreign tourists alike. Traditional wood and stone village houses perch beside the mountain stream that flows through the center of town. According to local legend, the large rock perched on the hillside once rolled over and crushed a couple as they walked past the church, initiating a tradition in which newlyweds sit on the rock to ensure marital stability. Lately, Kakopetria has become a model of the nation's trend toward "agrotourism," ideally a seamless blend of tourism and tradition. While a bit contrived, the result is an aesthetic success, incorporating tasteful tourism into its lively plateia.

◪⃞ ORIENTATION AND PRACTICAL INFORMATION. Clarios (☎753 234) runs buses to **Lefkosia** from **Kakopetria** (M-F 9 per day, 4:30am-2:30pm; Su 6am, 4:30pm; £1.10). Some buses continue to **Troodos** by reservation. **Private taxis** to Lefkosia cost £15. Kakopetria consists of the main street, **Makarios,** which leads into the old section of the village, passes through the plateia, and continues to the adjoining village of Galata. The "Old Road" lies across the stream and can be accessed off Makarios at the Village Pub. **Hellenic Bank** (☎926 636), **Popular Bank** (open M-F 8:15am-12:30pm), and **Bank of Cyprus** (☎450 530; open Tu, Th-F 9am-1pm and M, W 8:30am-5:30pm) are in the plateia and have 24hr. **ATMs.** The **police station** is right up the hill from the Bank of Cyprus. (☎922 420 or 922 255. Open 24hr.) There is a **pharmacy** on Makarios. (☎ 924 492. Open M-Sa 8:30am-1:30pm and 3:30-7:30pm.) The **post office** is up the hill from the Bank of Cyprus. (☎922 422. Open M-F 7:30am-1:30pm.) **Postal Code:** 2810.

◪⃞ ACCOMMODATIONS AND FOOD. Kakopetria has a number of budget domatia above or behind restaurants, many along the stream with clearly visible signs. For a longer, considerably more expensive getaway, try staying in one of the agrotourism inns, gorgeous restored homes rented out for several days or weeks. When you arrive in Kakopetria head over to the **◪Serenity Cof-**

TUTTI FRUITY Citrus fruits, apples, and watermelons are succulent treats hard to find in most of the world. Cyprus' booming **agrotourism** industry brings people to traditional holiday homes, allowing them to assimilate the nature and tradition of country life. These old dwellings have been beautifully restored and allow city-folk to catch a glimpse of old village farming life and work—for a fee. Saturday morning *laiki agora* brings together farmers from nearby villages, promoting the trade of their produce to visitors shacking up in nearby hotels and inns, combining tourism and the agricultural industry. Bargain with the wrinkled men selling fresh fruit, and become part of a tradition older than most of the *archaia* you visit.

feeshop and Inn, in the old village, a few meters past the Linos Taverna. Try to squeeze your way into one of their 3 exquisite rooms. Outfitted with huge, traditional canopied beds, these cheery rooms get even brighter with gorgeous balconies that overlook the mountain stream. All rooms have refrigerators. (☎922 602. Singles ₤15; doubles ₤20.) Also very pleasant is the **Hekali Hotel,** Gr. Digenis 2. From the plateia turn right at the police station, continue up the road, turn left when you see the Minaides Hotel, and left again onto Gr. Digenis. The hotel features very comfortable, bright modern rooms with full amenities: TV, radio, phone, balcony, and A/C (₤2 per night). The downstairs includes a full bar, dining hall, and couches with TV. (☎992 501; fax 922 503. Handicapped accessible. Singles ₤15; doubles ₤22.)

Kakopetria has more dining options than neighboring towns. Restaurants on the plateia cater to tourists and serve mostly mainstream dishes, while those in the old village serve more authentic Cypriot cuisine. Only a few meters away from the Serenity Coffeeshop, the ◪**Linos Taverna** serves up some sumptuous dishes. Chomp on their specialty—a mixed dish combining five main dishes of your choice (₤8)—while you listen to soft Cypriot music in a quiet old wood house. For slightly upscale eating, follow the signs over a log bridge to arrive at **Maryland at the Mill,** looking out over a neighboring former mill along the stream. This restaurant has become internationally reknown for its fresh trout specialty (₤6.15) among other succulent dishes. (☎ 922 536. Open daily noon-11pm. Reservation highly recommended weekends and June-Sept. Call at least 2 days in advance.)

◪🗺 **SIGHTS AND ENTERTAINMENT.** Well-preserved village houses line the cobbled streets. Kakopetria and its smaller neighbor, **Galata,** have five Byzantine churches between them. The most notable, 11th-century **Agios Nikolaos tis Stegis,** shines 3km southwest of Kakopetria on the road to Troodos. Local buses fetch the elderly from surrounding villages for Sunday morning services. Frescoes dating back to 1320 ornament the walls. Ask the obliging caretaker for a tour detailing the history of the church and its frescoes. (Open Tu-Sa 9am-4pm, Su 11am-4pm.)

For ambitious hikers looking for a long daytrip, an 8km uphill hike on a well-maintained trail from Ag. Nikolaos tis Stegis to Troodos Sq. will test your mettle. Buses departing from Troodos for Kakopetria and Lefkosia at 6:30am are by reservation only; call **Clarios Bus Co.** (☎753 234). The monastery of **Panagiatou Arakou,** 16km southeast of Kakopetria in the village of Lagoudhera, displays elaborate 12th-century frescoes, including a dome depiction of Christ Pantokrator restored in 1968. (Open 8am-7pm daily.)

Nightlife in Kakopetria centers on its cafes in the plateia and its single nightclub. Teenagers mull around the plateia before kicking up their heels at **Clarion Brand Disco,** Makarios 21, across the stream from the plateia; there's a pub upstairs and dancing to Greek dance hits downstairs. (Cover ₤3-5. Open F-Sa 7pm-2am.) For a less raucous night, stroll the byways of Old Kakopetria and savor mountain views.

CYPRUS

⚡ DAYTRIP FROM KAKOPETRIA. Kykko Monastery, (Μονη Κυκκο) 20km from Pedhoulas in the northwest part of the mountains, prides itself on being the wealthiest and most prestigious monastery on Cyprus. Standing strong and solitary in the depths of the Troodos mountains, this architecturally intricate building is the result of centuries of renovation after each of four accidental fires in AD 1365, 1541, 1751, and 1813. The most recent renovations have been underway since 1987; the building as it stands now remains true to Byzantine architecture but the actual structure is virtually modern. The monastery was founded in the early 11th century by the hermit Isaiah. Isaiah is said to have had a dream where the Virgin Mary came to him and declared that the famed **Icon of the Virgin Mary**, painted by the Apostle Luke, should be moved from Constantinople to the island of Cyprus. The Byzantine Emperor ceded the icon only after his daughter fell ill; it is said that after the icon arrived in Cyprus his daughter became well again. The celebrated icon has survived intact, but is too holy to be viewed directly and is consequently stored in a gold casing in the monastery's church, directly to the left of the iconostasis. During the Cypriot struggle for independence (p. 514), Kykko was a communication and supply center and the home of **Archbishop Makarios III.** Only 1.5km away was the secret headquarters of the first military leader of the struggle, General George Grivas. Today, the monks are very aware of their monastery's historical importance and are willing to give extensive explanations upon request. The sanctity of the space prohibits photography in the church and museum, but a video is on sale in the giftshop.

From the Leonidou station in Lefkosia, Kambos (☎09 623 604 or 94 253) sends buses to Kykko Monastery (departs at noon, returns to Lefkosia 6am the next day; ₤1.50 each way, ₤2.50 with luggage). Most tourists reach Kykko by car. Rentals are available in Lefkosia (p. 544) or Limassol practical information (p. 528). Rooms are available, but are meant for those who've come for religious purposes. Call (942 319) a day in advance to reserve a room. (Monastery ☎942 736. Open Nov.-May daily 10am-4pm, June-Oct. 10am-6pm.)

NICOSIA Λευκωσια ☎ 02

Landlocked Lefkosia, sliced in two by the barbed-wire Green Line, has the dubious distinction of being the last divided city in the world. The more modern New City is separated from the Old by Venetian walls, built on top of the ancient Roman town of Ledra in a failed attempt to fend off Ottoman cannons. In 1570, the Ottomans took only 7 weeks to conquer Lefkosia, proving the uselessness of the walls. They ruled the city for several hundred years before British imperialists arrived in 1878. The British governed Cyprus until it gained independence in 1960, when Lefkosia became the capital of the island nation; British colonial rule paved the way for present day tourism. In the aftermath of 1974, Lefkosia was split into Turkish and Greek sections, and remains under the watchful eye of the UN. Passage across the Green Line is permitted from the Ledra checkpoint on the southern side.

LEFKOSIA (SOUTH NICOSIA)

The Old City of Lefkosia, the name officially given to their half of Nicosia by the Greek Cypriots, caters to history buffs and politically inclined tourists. Outside the Venetian walls that embrace the Old City, the New City sprawls, an expanding metropolis. At the moment, the city is restoring the old Laiki Yitonia (the pedestrian area of the Old City) and constructing new museums and monuments, catering to tourists as it preserves its history. The New City is geared toward bureaucrats rather than backpackers; most museums, tourist districts, restaurants, and hotels are found in the Old City. The city offers the chance to discover the island without the frills of coastal tourism, giving a poignant, intimate view of the political strife that has shaped modern Cyprus.

CROSSING THE GREEN LINE The infamous Green Line is Nicosia's main attraction. The only spot on the border where photography is permitted is Ledra, where the military has erected a makeshift shrine to the north. Crossing the Green Line from the south is fairly easy—just follow the strict regulations, and don't bother trying to get information about North Nicosia on the southern side: Greek Cypriots have not crossed the line for over 20 years. You will not be permitted to cross if you are a Greek citizen or if you are of Greek descent. Head for the **Ledra Palace Checkpoint** between the Greek Cypriot and Turkish walls. This former hotel, its interior gutted and its exterior marred by bullet holes, stands on neutral territory in the buffer zone; it currently houses the UN headquarters in Cyprus. You must show your passport on the Greek Cypriot side and again on the Turkish side, where you fill out a general information form in order to receive a special visitor's visa (the Turkish side once charged a border fee but no longer does; you may be asked to pay £1 at most). **Do not let them stamp your passport.** If they stamp your passport, you will not be readmitted to Greek Cyprus. They will, however, give you a form to be stamped by someone at another window. Hold on to this form—you will need it to cross back after your visit.

1. You may enter North Cyprus 8am-1pm, but must return by 5pm. No exceptions. You cannot start a trip through North Cyprus and Turkey by crossing the Green Line; guards will not allow you to cross with a large backpack or bag. If you remain in North Cyprus later than 5pm the only way for you to re-enter Southern Cyprus will be to cross over to Turkey and then take a boat or plane back to the country.

2. Cars are not allowed—you must cross by foot.

3. As in other areas of Lefkosia and Cyprus, do *not* take pictures of anything that has to do with the military or police.

4. You are prohibited from buying anything on the Turkish side. Any items purchased in the north will be confiscated upon your return to the south. If you wish to buy food, you must exchange your much desired Cypriot pounds for Turkish lira after you have crossed the border to Northern Cyprus.

5. If you have a problem, ask the UN soldiers (in blue berets) for help.

▣ TRANSPORTATION

Buses: Intercity Buses (☎665 814), in Pl. Solomos, run to **Larnaka** (7 per day M-F 9am-6:30pm, Sa 11am, 1pm; £1.50). **Intercity Buses** and **Alepa** (☎09 625 027) both leave from Pl. Solomos and run to **Limassol** (9 per day M-F 6am-5:45pm, Sa 10am, 12:45, 2pm; £1.50). **Nea Amorza** (☎236 822) and **ALEPA** (☎664 636), near Pl. Solomos, run to **Paphos** M-F via **Limassol** (2 per day 6:30am and 3:45pm, plus W and Sa 12:45pm; £3). **Paralimni-Dherynia**, Stasinou 27 (☎444 141), runs to **Agia Napa, Parlimni,** and **Protaras** (M-F 1:30pm, £2.50). **Pedoulas-Platres Bus** (☎09 618 865) runs to **Pedoulas, Platres,** and **Prodromos** (M-Sa 12:15pm, £2). **Clarios** (☎753 234), 200m east of Pl. Eleftherias on Costanze Bastioon, runs to **Kakopetria** (13 per day M-Sa 6:15am-7pm, £1.10; Su 8am, 6pm, £1.90) and **Troodos** (M-F 11:30am, £1.10). **Kambos,** on Leonidou, runs to **Kykko Monastery** (M-Sa leaves at noon and returns 6am the next day, £2). A free route map of all the urban **Lefkosia buses** is available at the CTO (☎674 264).

Service Taxis: Travel & Express (☎07 774 74 or 757 616) runs taxis (M-Sa every 30min. 6am-6pm, Su 7am-5pm) to: **Limassol** (£3.45), **Larnaka** (£2.40), and **Paphos** (£6). Call ahead. **Solis** (☎666 388), on Tripolis Bastion, runs taxis (M and W-Sa noon, £5) and a minibus (M-Tu and Th-Sa noon, £4) to **Polis** via **Limassol** and **Paphos.**

Private Taxis: Are easily summoned from sidewalks and corners. Taxi stations are in Pl. Eleftherias, or call **Travel & Express** (☎757 616) for private service as well. Open 24hr. Private taxis are expensive, running about £0.65 initial charge and £0.22 per km daytime, or £0.88 initial charge at night and same amount per km.

✦ 7 ORIENTATION AND PRACTICAL INFORMATION

The easiest way to orient yourself in Lefkosia is to use the Venetian walls. The Green Line, running east to west at the north end of the city, divides the **Old City** into Greek and Turkish sectors. Within the walls, travelers can find most budget lodgings, museums, tavernas, and sights. From **Pl. Eleftherias,** Evagoras heads southwest into the New City, while **Lidras** street, the primary pedestrian and tourist core, runs to the north, where it intersects the Green Line. Intersecting Evagoras are Makarios Ave., Diagoras, and Th. Dervis, which leads to the youth hostel. **Laiki Yitonia,** southeast of Lidras street, is the prominent pedestrian and tourist district. The New City is more spread out, making transportation on foot difficult. Sheet metal barriers or white and blue dividers confront you when you walk down the streets of the Old City. **Do not ignore the signs forbidding photography.**

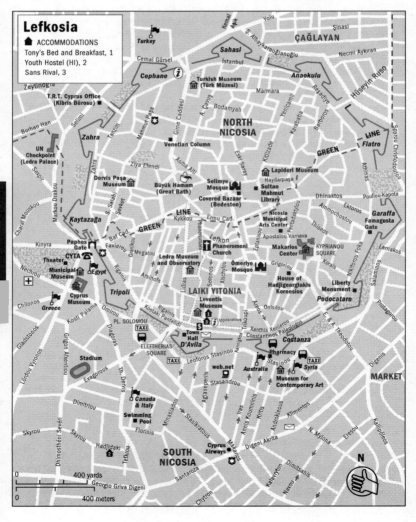

Lefkosia

🏠 ACCOMMODATIONS
Tony's Bed and Breakfast, 1
Youth Hostel (HI), 2
Sans Rival, 3

Tourist Office: CTO, Aristokypros 11 (☎674 264; fax 660 778), in the Laiki Yitonia. Entering Pl. Eleftherias from the New City, turn right and follow signs from the post office. Free maps, a list of buses, and a guide to events in the city. Open M-F 8:30am-4pm, Sa 8:30am-2pm. Free English-language walking tour through the old village of Kaimakli offered M, more general walking tour of Lefkosia Th; both leave from the CTO at 10am and last 2hr.

Embassies and Consulates: See p. 516.

Banks: Bank of Cyprus: main branch, Phaneromeni 86 (☎674 064), offers **ATM** and **currency exchange.** Open M-F 8:15am-12:30pm. A convenient branch (☎436 161) in Laiki Yitonia on Drakos with 24hr. **ATM.** Open M-F 8:30am-12:30pm. Additional ATMs throughout the city, most 24hr.

American Express: A.L. Mantovani and Sons, Agapinoras 2D (☎ 763 777), 1km south of Pl. Solomos down Makarios. Open M-F 8am-12:45pm and 2:30-5:30pm, Sa 9am-noon. Currency exchange, and traveler's check exchange.

Public Toilets: In the parking lots along the Venetian walls (follow the W/C signs). Surprisingly sanitary and toilet paper is blessedly abundant.

Police and Fire Station: (☎802 200). The two buildings are next door to one another, 150m east of Paphos Gate on Digenis, inside the wall. Additional police station in the New City at the corner of Santaroza and Makarious (☎304 967). Both open 24hr.

Hospital: (☎ 801 400), at Omirou and Nechrou streets. Open 24hr.

Telephone: CYTA, Egypt 14 (☎702 276). Customer service open M-F 7:15am-1:30pm; cashier open M-F 7:15am-6pm, Sa 7:15am-1pm. 24hr. telecard machine outside.

Internet Access: Web.net cafe at Stasandrou 10C (☎753 345; fax 753 184), at the border of the New City. New computers, efficient service £2.20 per hour, discount for students. Drinks £0.60-1.30. Open M-Sa 10:30am-midnight, Su 5:30pm-midnight.

Post Office: Main office (☎303 219 and 303 123) on Constantinos Paleologos, east of Pl. Eleftherias. Open M-F 7:30am-2pm and 3-6pm except W no afternoon hours, Sa 8:30-10:30am. Branch offices on Digenis, Palace, and Loukis Akitas (☎302 531). **Postal Code:** 1903.

▐ ACCOMMODATIONS

▧ **Tony's Bed and Breakfast,** on the corner of Solon and Hippokratous (☎666 752 or 667 794; fax 662 225), in the Laiki Yitonia. Traditional decorations and a Victorian staircase lead to rooms of various sizes, all with radio, phone, hot water pots, fridge, A/C and TVs. Guests can enjoy their breakfast on a spacious rooftop patio. Sparklingly clean. Singles £20; doubles £25-28; triples £30; quads £35. 20% discount with student ID.

Youth Hostel (HI), Hadjidaki 1 (☎674 808 or 09 438 360), in the New City off Diagoras Dervis. An old home with a sprawling, enclosed garden, this hostel will feel like grandma's house. The 11pm noise curfew keeps the peace and tends to attract slightly older travelers. 2 rooms for women, 2 rooms for men, 2 for families/couples, and 1 attic room as a single. Full kitchen, 1 bath. Sheets £1. Dorms £4; attic room £6.

Sans Rival, Solon 7 (☎669 383), in the Laiki Yitonia. Generally booked. Elevators take you to spacious, albeit spartan, rooms. A/C in summer, full central heating in winter. Singles £15; doubles £20.

▐ FOOD

Dining in Lefkosia includes tavernas with live music, pubs, pizzerias, and full restaurants. Touristy joints around Laiki Yitonia serve Cypriot *mezedes;* smaller restaurants cater to locals in the backroads in the Old City smaller restaurants. For a cheap option, head to the **municipal market** on the corner of Digenis Akritas and Kallipolis, a huge warehouse filled with food stands. Hanging pigs will either stir your hunger or make you a vegetarian. (Open 6am-1pm and 4-6pm.) A colorful streetside **produce market** near Pl. Eleftherias along Constantinos Paleologos beckons veggie lovers. (Open W 9am-1pm and 4-6pm.)

▨**Zanettos Taverna,** Trikoupi 65 (☎765 501), near Omeriyeh Mosque in the Old City. Open since 1938, this oasis in the central of Cyprus's capitol manages to provide its guests with a taste of *kypriatiko paradosiako faghito* (traditional Cypriot cuisine). The *Halloumi* specials (£2) make for splendid starters and the meat *meze* for 2 (£14) will satisfy all your carnivorous cravings. Open daily 12:30-4pm and 7:30pm-midnight.

Savvas, Solon 65 (☎668 444), in the Laiki Yitonia, serves up exactly what a Cypriot mother would put on the table for her children. Join the locals on lunch break for traditional homemade dishes; for a true native experience try the *bambies* (baked okra stewed in a tomato, onion, and garlic sauce). All main dishes £1-2, with a glass of local wine (£0.50). Open 10am-5:30pm.

Berlin #2 Cafe (☎474 935), on the corner of Lefkon and Phaneromni. This popular takeout joint serves up *kebab*, salad, and pita (£2) in the shadow of a UN guard station. Open M-Sa 7am-midnight.

👁 SIGHTS

▨**THE STATE GALLERY.** Formerly known as The Lefkosia Municipal Gallery of Contemporary Art, this gallery is housed in a graceful converted hotel building constructed in 1925. Small rooms off spacious hallways showcase the paintings and sculpture of renowned contemporary Greek artists, such as Andreas Charalambides and Georghios P. Georghiou. Be sure to check out the installations on the third floor as well. *(Crete 1. On the edge of the New City across from the Bayraktar Mosque. ☎304 992. Open M-F 10am-5pm and Sa 10am-1pm. Free.)*

FAMAGUSTA GATE. Along the Venetian Walls at the end of Theseus street is the recently restored Famagusta Gate, the largest, best preserved, and most famous of all the gates that surround old Nicosia. The main entrance to old Lefkosia, built in 1567, it now hosts plays, concerts, exhibitions, and lectures; check the schedule at the CTO or pick one up at the Town Hall. *(Open M-F 10am-1pm, 4-7pm in winter and 5-8pm in summer. Free.)* Not far down Korais street, walking away from Famagusta gate toward the Laiki Yitonia, is a marble monument, the **Freedom Statue** or *Agalma Eleftherias*, depicting 14 Cypriots, each representing a period of the island's history, being released from the iron bars that have restrained them.

LEVENTIS MUNICIPAL MUSEUM. This museum, which won the European Museum of the Year award in 1991, chronicles the history and social development of Lefkosia from 3000 BC to recent years. Peer through the glass at your feet as you walk over an excavated portion of a Medieval House from the Nicosia area. The 2nd floor consists mainly of traditional costumes, household items, and weaponry. Don't overlook the photographic chronology or the courtyard garden with its authentic Turkish baths. *(Hippocratis 17 in the Laiki Yitonia, off Solon. ☎671 997 or 661 475. Open Tu-Su 10am-4:30pm. Free. Handicapped accessible.)*

PHANEROMENI CHURCH. A point of nationalist pride to Greek Cypriots, the Phaneromeni Church survived a Turkish attempt to transform it into a mosque. Dating to the 14th century, the ornate *iconostasis* is engraved with Old Testament images. *(In the center of the Old City off Ledgras street. Open daily 6:15am-1pm and 3:45-7pm. Free, but donations are welcome.)*

PLATEIA ARCHBISHOPRIC KYPRIANOS. The Plateia consists of four main buildings of historical and touristic interest: the first is the **Makarios Cultural Center,** the largest of the buildings, in the middle of the plateia. The Center contains four galleries, the most impressive of which is the **Byzantine Museum** on the first floor. The museum contains over 150 icons from the 8th to 18th centuries, most of which were collected by the first Bishop of Cyprus, Makarios III. On the second floor is an **Art Gallery** containing an impressive collection of European oil paintings mostly from the 17th century. The **1821 War of Independence Gallery,** on the third floor, hosts a varied selection of war-related paintings from the 17th century to the modern day (see War for Independence p. 16). On the second and third floors the **Cypriot Contemporary Painting Gallery** displays a collection of constantly shifting exhibits by contemporary Cypriot painters. (☎ 430 008. *Byzantine Museum open 9am-4:30pm and Sa 9am-1pm. All other galleries share the same hours, but close from 1-2pm. £1.)* The second building of interest is **Saint John's Cathedral,** in the courtyard of the Makarios Center, built in 1662 by Archbishop Nikiforos with a single nave and five pointed arches. The tablets adorning the entrance were transferred from Venetian and Frankish buildings. *(Open M-F 9am–noon and 2-4pm, Sa 9am-noon. Free.)* The third building is the **Ethnographic Museum of Cyprus,** previously called the Folk Art Museum, to the left of the Makarios Center. The Museum is housed in a magnificent 15th century monastery, and contains Cypriot woodcarving, embroidery, pottery, basketry, and metalwork from the 18th to 20th centuries. *(☎ 432 578. Open M-F 9am-4pm, Sa 10am-1pm. £1.*

HOUSE OF HADJIGEORGIAKIS KORNESIOS. Near Pl. Kyprianos is the luxurious, 18th-century home of the famous *dragoman,* or Ottoman tax-collector and interpreter. Kornesios was actually a Greek Cypriot who, through clever strategy and knowledge of many languages, rose to the prestigious and lucrative position of tax-collector in Cyprus for the Ottoman Emperor. In 1804 the Cypriots raided his house, but the *dragoman* and his family escaped through a hidden passage. With an enchanting courtyard and a floor plan in the shape of the letter π, the monument is a significant example of the urban architecture of the last century of Ottoman rule. *(Patriach Gregory 18. ☎ 305 316. Open M-F 8am-2pm, Sa 9am-1pm. £0.75.)*

CYPRUS MUSEUM. Here you'll find the most extensive collection of ancient art and artifacts on the island, from pre-Hellenic periods through the Byzantine era. Amateur archaeologists can compare local jewelry across eras, while everyone will feel dwarfed by ancient, larger-than-life terra-cotta figures. *(Mouseiou 1, near the Paphos Gate. ☎ 303 112. Open M-Sa 9am-5pm, Su 10am-1pm. £1.50.)*

OTHER SIGHTS. Ledra Museum and Observatory. From this vantage point atop the Woolworth building tourists can take in the Northern part of the city. The free binoculars and informational plaques help locate astonishing sights, such as the **Cathedral of Saint Sophia,** a structure greatly resembling a palace that was finished in 1319. *(☎ 679 369. Corner of Arsinois and Ledra. Open daily 10am-6:30pm, £0.50.)*

🎦 🎵 NIGHTLIFE AND ENTERTAINMENT

For late night entertainment, scattered coffeeshops, pubs, and dance clubs keep Lefkosia jumping. Most of Lefkosia's **bars** and **pubs** can be found in the Old City near or around Pl. Eleftherias. A word of caution: many cabaret clubs surround Pl. Eleftherias. Women should not walk alone through the neighborhood around Pl. Eleftherias past 2am when the bars have closed and the younger crowd at surrounding cafes has abated. **Dance clubs** appear mostly in the outskirts of the New City, while Makariou is filled with cafes for the younger crowds. For popular tunes, the neighborhood known as Engomi, around Leoforou Goudia, is home to some of the most popular clubs, among them **Martini.** (☎ 781 059. Open Su-Th 8pm-2am, F-Sa 8pm-4am.) Expect **Sfinakia,** Santaroza 2, to be packed every night of the week. (☎ 766 661. Open daily 9pm-3am.)

CYPRUS

Mike & Alexander's Pub and Restaurant, Pl. Eleftherias, Pantelidi St., Laiki Yitonia (☎451 174). Catering to a varied clientele, the pub offers both a cafe for relaxation and a pub for revelry. Crowded and bustling until 2am every night of the week. Beer £1.50-2.60. Open daily 8am-2am.

Ta Kala Kathoumena, Nikokleous 21 (☎664 654), tucked into an alley behind Phaneromni Church. Lefkosia's young collegiate intellectuals gather at night for debate, backgammon, and drinks (£0.40-£1.20). Open M-Sa 11am-midnight, Su 6pm-midnight.

The Zoo, Stasinou 15 (☎758 262). Draws a slightly older crowd. Upscale joint has a fancy restaurant upstairs and club downstairs. Open daily 8:30am-1am, F-Su until 4am.

NORTH NICOSIA

North Nicosia is overrun with green-clad troops, who have been instructed to be kind to tourists. Unlike the conservationism affecting its southern counterpart, modernization has seized the Old City of North Nicosia. The glitzy highrises of Girne Caddeşi contrast with the barbed wire and oil barrels of the Green Line and the crumbling walls of the Old City.

⚡🔢 ORIENTATION AND PRACTICAL INFORMATION

From the south at the **Ledra Palace** crossing, a roundabout with a Turkish victory monolith in the middle is 500m up the street. Follow the city walls to **Girne Gate** (Kyrenia Gate). From there, **Girne Caddeşi,** the main street, runs to the main square, **Atatürk Meydanı,** and continues to the Green Line.

Because of the fluctuating value of the Turkish lira, prices for goods and services in North Nicosia are listed in US dollars. For **police,** dial 155; **emergency ambulance,** dial 112; **fire,** dial 199. The helpful **tourist office,** at the extreme northwest of the city on Bedrettin Demirel Cad., 2km from Girne Gate, is a good place to begin your tour of the city. (☎228 96 29. Open M 9am-6pm, Tu-F 9am-5pm; in winter M-F 8am-5pm.) Only **Turkey** has a full embassy in North Cyprus, at Bedrettin Demirel Cad. (☎227 23 14. Open M-F 9am-noon.) The following countries have "representative offices," offering some consular services: **Australia,** 20 Güner Türkmen Sok. (☎227 73 32; open Tu, Th 8:30am-12:30pm); **Germany,** #15 28 Kasım Sok. (☎227 51 61); **UK,** 29 Mehmet Aleif Cad. (☎228 70 51 or 228 38 61; open M, W, F 9am-1:30pm; Tu, Th 9am-1:30pm and 2:30-5pm); and **US,** 6 Saran Sok. (☎225 24 40; open M-F 8am-1pm and 2-3:30pm). Several offices along Girne Cad. offer **currency exchange** (open M-F 8am-1pm and 2-4pm). **ATMs** are near Atatürk Meydanı; the one outside **Türkiye İş Bankası** takes foreign cards. The **police** (☎228 33 11) are on Girne Cad. close to Atatürk Meydanı. A **hospital** (☎228 54 41 or 223 24 41) is 3km from the town center on the road to Girne, roughly 700m from the Victory Monument. Look for the *Hastane* sign. **Pembe Telefon,** 30m right of the post office, has metered booths and sells phone cards. (Open M-F 7:30am-2pm and 3:30-5:30pm.) **Restaurants** crowd the area near Girne Gate; typical Turkish fare goes for around $3.50.

👁 SIGHTS

The **Selimiye Camii** mosque, formerly **Agia Sophia Cathedral,** is a bizarre sight: a seemingly ancient cathedral looming in the shadow of its two soaring minarets. Despite the *seccade* (prayer rugs) and Islamic calligraphy, the saints carved in the arches above the door and the flying buttresses testify to the edifice's original purpose. Refurbished by the Ottomans in 1570, the Roman Catholic cathedral was originally built in the Gothic style in 1326 by French architects at the behest of Queen Alix of Champagne. From Atatürk Meydanı, with Girne Gate at your back, continue down Girne Cad., looking left for the twin minarets. Beside it is the **Bedesten,** the 14th-century Orthodox **Cathedral of St. Nicholas.**

With your back to the mosque, head straight for a block and take a left to get to the 700-year-old **Büyük Hamamı,** once part of a 14th-century church. Since the time of the building's construction, the city has risen about 2m, leaving the *hamam* slightly subterranean. (Open daily 8am-10pm. Bath, exfoliation, and massage by professional male masseur $15.) Just a dice throw away is the **Kumarcılar Hanı** (Gamblers' Inn). Formerly for 17th-century traveling merchants, it now houses Northern Cyprus's Antiquities Department (open M-F 8am-2pm). A block or two to the east and beyond the Selimiye Mosque is the Gothic-era **Haydarpaşa Camii,** once a Lusignan church, and today a gallery. Face the Green Line and follow it to the right to the **Derviş Paşa Museum.** The former mansion of a notable 20th-century Cypriot newspaper owner, it has been converted into an unimpressive ethnographic museum displaying clothing and household goods. (Open M 9am-2pm and 3:30-7pm, Tu-Su 8am-7pm. $1.80, students $0.40.)

CYPRUS

DAYTRIPS TO TURKEY

The Turkish Aegean coast is full of ancient Greek ruins, funky beach towns, beautiful mosques, and moving war memorials. Daytrips to Turkey are cheap and easy from several Greek islands, including Samos (p. 332), Kos (p. 437), and Chios (p. 336). To go for the day, just catch a ferry to the Aegean coast. Not every Turkish daytrip is accessible by direct ferry. If your destination is Çanakkale, Eceabat, İzmir, Efes, or Selçuk, you'll need to head to Bodrum or Kuşadası and catch a bus to your destination. Bus connections are listed below, with prices in US$ (as the Turkish lire is unstable). For more info, check out *Let's Go: Turkey 2002*.

GETTING TO TURKEY As of August 2001, citizens of Australia, Canada, Ireland, the UK, and the US require a visa to enter Turkey. A visa costs US$45. Citizens of New Zealand and South Africa do not need visas to enter Turkey. New Zealanders may stay for up to three months with a valid passport, South Africans for up to one month. Ferry schedules are variable, so check with a tourist office when making plans. For info on purchasing tickets, see the Practical Information section for each town. Ferries run from the following Greek islands to towns on the Aegean coast (3000dr/€8.80 Greek **port tax** not included here):
Samos: From Samos Town 5 per week to: **Kuşadası** (1¼hr.; 10,000dr/€29.35 one-way, 14,000dr/€41.09 for an open-return ticket). **Chios:** From Chios Town to **Çeşme** (45min., 1 per day, 17,000dr/€49.89). **Kos:** From Kos Town for **Bodrum** (1 per day 10,000-13,000dr/€29.35-38.15 round-trip). Some boats leave in the afternoon and return the next morning (8000-13,000dr/€23.48-38.15 round-trip).

BODRUM ☎252

The "Bedroom of the Mediterranean," Bodrum comes to life at night. While Bodrum's nightlife is notorious, the surrounding Acadian Peninsula is famous for its silica beaches, lush forests, secluded coves, and ancient ruins. As a multitude of visitors agree, it's easy to get sucked into Bodrum's rhythm of sun, shopping, sight-seeing, and watersports—an innocent prelude to nightfall's bacchanalian delights.

◆⚡ ORIENTATION AND PRACTICAL INFORMATION

Small blue signs label the streets of Bodrum; main streets radiate from the **Castle of St. Peter.** The main commercial drag, **Cumhuriyet Cad.,** runs along the beach. **Kale Cad.** runs from the left of the castle to a mosque. **Belediye Meyd Cad.,** the street to the left of the mosque, becomes **Neyzen Tevfik Cad.** along the west harbor coast.

See **Getting to Turkey** (above) for Kos-Bodrum **ferries.** Travel agents sell tickets back to Greece. **Bodrum Express Lines** (☎316 40 67 or 316 10 87; fax 313 00 77) has offices in the *otogar* (station) and near the castle. Walk past the castle toward the sea; the office is on the left. **Bodrum Express** also runs **hydrofoils** to **Kos** (20min.; daily 9am, return 4:30pm; $18, round-trip $28) and **Rhodes** (2¼hr.; M-Sa 8:30am, return 5pm; $46, round-trip $57). Contact **Pamukkale Lines** (☎316 66 32) for **buses** to: **İzmir** (4hr., 4am-7pm, $7) and **Selçuk** (3hr., 2am-6pm, $8). The **tourist office,** 48 Barış Meydanı, gives away free brochures and **maps** at the foot of the castle. (☎316 10 91; fax 316 76 94. Open daily Apr.-Oct. 8:30am-5:30pm; Nov.-Mar. M-F 8am-noon and 1-5pm.) **ATMs** pepper shopping areas. In an **emergency,** dial 316 12 15. The **police,** 50 Barış Meydanı, are at the foot of the castle, next to the tourist office. (☎316 10 04. Open 24hr.) If you need a place to sleep it off, try ■**Emiko Pansiyon**, Atatürk Cad., 11 Uslu Sok.; from the *otogar*, follow Cevat Şakir Cad. toward the water, turning left onto Atatürk Cad. After 50m, turn right down the alley marked with the pension's sign, it offers eight simple rooms with hardwood floors and bath. (☎/fax 316 55 60; emiko@turk.net. Guest kitchen. Breakfast $2. Laundry $3. Singles $7, doubles $12; Aug. singles $10, doubles $16.) Another option is the **Otel Kilavus**, No. 25 Atatürk Cad., near the mosque on the way to the castle. A modern hotel with a garden, pool, and bar, Kilavus has 12 rooms with large baths and phones. (☎316 38 92. Singles $10, doubles $16; June-Aug. singles $13, doubles $20.)

🅝 🅙 NIGHTLIFE AND ENTERTAINMENT

All of the following except for Halikarnas Disco are on Cumhuriyet Cad. For a wild taste of England in Turkey, hop over the western ridge of Bodrum to Gümbet, where more discos and bars glitter in the night (30min. walk or 10min. *dolmuş* ride; *dolmuş* leave the *otogar* every 10min.; $0.40).

■ **Halikarnas Disco**, Z. Müren Cad. At the end of Cumhuriyet Cad., 1km from the center of town. The second-largest open-air disco in the world, Halkarnas juts into the ocean, where its strobe lights reflect off the sails of nearby yachts. There's a **foam party** on Saturdays in July and August. $12 cover charge includes one local drink. Beer $3; cocktails $6.

■ **Temple** (☎316 17 21). A popular club where edgy dancing coincides with sly socializing, as the spasmodic dance floor lights dart above the flicker of candlelight from the dark wooden bar. Beer $2; *rakı* (a potent Turkish liquor) $2. Open daily 7pm-5am.

■ **Hadi Gari** (☎313 80 97). Next to the luminous castle, the oldest disco in Bodrum fuses elegance and funkiness. Stylish customers groove on the outdoor dance floor. Others recline on cushions in the softly lit interior. Beer $3; *rakı* $3.60; cocktails $4-8. Restaurant by "day" (6pm-midnight), dance club by night (midnight-4am).

Greenhouse (☎313 09 11). A much-favored dance bar that extends onto the beach, with a laid-back atmosphere. Enthusiastic international and Turkish DJs. Everyone ends up here. Beer $1.80; *rakı* $3; cocktails $5. Open daily midnight-5am.

Sensi (☎316 68 45). For a riotous ride in bar craziness, join the mostly British crowd at Sensi, where table dancing, karaoke, and wig-wearing 70s nights keep this joint quaking. Beer $1.80; *rakı* $2; cocktails $3.60-5. Open daily 5pm-5am.

ÇANAKKALE ☎286

Çanakkale, though not terribly scenic, is an easy base for exploring Gallipoli and Troy. The easiest way to get to Çanakkale is by bus from İzmir (5hr., $8). **Dolmuş** ($0.50-1) run from under the small bridge over the Sarı Çay inlet to **Troy** (25min., leaving throughout day when the *dolmuş* fills ($0.75). **Ferries** to Eceabat (30min., every hr.) require a token ($0.50) from the window next to the small PTT booth. Practically everything relating to the mechanics of budget travel (food, accommodations, and travel agencies) lies within the one-block area around the **ferry dock** and the clock tower. The English-speaking staff at the **tourist office**, 67 İskele Meydanı, distributes maps. (☎/fax 217 11 87.) The **police** (☎212 14 66) are on İnönü Cad., next to the PTT. **Tours** of the Gallipoli battlefields and the city of Troy are available and include lunch, an English-speaking guide, transportation, and admission to the sights. ■**TJ's Tours** (☎814 29 40; fax 814 29 41; TJs_TOURS@excite.com), provides daily tours to Gallipoli (12:30pm, $19) and to Troy (8:45am, $14) when there's sufficient demand. Call ahead to reserve a space. **The Hassle Free Travel Agency**, 61 Cumhuriyet Meydanı (☎213 59 69; hasslefree@anzacamp.com), provides daily Gallipoli tours (Apr.-Nov. 11:45am, Dec.-Mar. 10:45am; $19), and almost-daily Troy tours that depart from Anzac House (Apr.-Nov. 8:45am, Dec.-Mar. 7:45am; $14).

TROY

Take a dolmuş from Çanakkale; they run from under the small bridge on Atatürk Cad. (25min., every hr. $0.75). Open daily June-Sept. 8am-7pm, Oct.-May 8am-5pm. $3, students $1.50.

For the casual visitor with no particular attachment to **Homer,** Troy's jumbled, partially excavated ruins don't immediately strike the romantic imagination. For lovers of Greek myth, archaeology, or Homer's poems, however, it's a magical gold mine among ancient sites. A tour (see p. 553) is a good idea, since a guide's explanations of Troy's history and the excavation process liven it up.

Troy's lifetime spans a huge continuum of civilization, from the early Bronze Age to the late Roman Empire. During 110 years of sporadic excavation, archaeologists have split these into numbered periods. Troy began as a fishing settlement in 3000-2500 BC, evolved into an affluent city-state from 2500-2200 BC, and eventually became the city of Homer's **King Priam** from 1275 to 1240 BC (though the date is disputed), before its fall to ruin for four centuries. Reborn as a fishing village around the 3rd century BC, Troy rose to importance as VIPs from Alexander the Great to Julius Caesar took an interest, hoping to associate themselves with the legendary city. The fall of Rome wrecked Troy again; after being inhabited for 35 centuries, the city lay buried for 13 more until **Heinrich Schliemann** (p. 119) arrived to dig it all up. Schliemann helped himself to some ancient treasure; his keepsakes can be seen today in the Pushkin Museum of Fine Art in Moscow.

SELÇUK   ☎ 232

Selçuk serves as a base for exploring nearby Ephesus, and offers a few notable archaeological sites of its own. The Selçuk castle dominates the city's skyline, along with the Basilica of Saint John, where the apostle John is buried, the İsa Bay Camii, and the ruins of the Temple of Artemis. The House of the Virgin Mary *(Meryemana)* can also be reached from Selçuk.

ORIENTATION AND PRACTICAL INFORMATION. The İzmir-Aydın road, **Atatürk Cad.,** is one of Selçuk's main thoroughfares. **Dr. Sabri Yayla Bul.,** also called **Kuşadası Cad.,** meets Atatürk Cad. from the west, and **Şahabettin Dede Cad.** meets Atatürk Cad. from the east to form the town's main crossroads. Selçuk is reachable by **bus** from **Bodrum** (3hr., 2am-6pm, $8) or **İzmir** (take a Bodrum- or Kuşadası-bound bus and ask to be let off at Selçuk; 1hr.; $2). Buses head to: **Bodrum** (3hr., every hr. 8:15am-1:15am, $4.50); **İstanbul** (10hr., 5 per day 9:45am-12:30pm, $10); and **İzmir** (1hr., every 30min. 6:20am-8:30pm, $1.25). **Minibuses** run to **Kuşadası** (20min.; every 15min. May-Sept. 6:30am-11:30pm, Oct.-Apr. 6:30am-8:30pm; $0.80). The **tourist office,** 35 Agora Çarşısı, Atatürk Mah., at the intersection of Kuşadası Cad. and Atatürk Cad., has free **city maps.** (English spoken. ☎ 892 63 28; fax 892 69 45. Open M-F 8:30am-noon and 1-5pm; Apr.-Dec. also Sa-Su 9am-5pm.) A **bank,** 17 Namık Kemal Cad., **exchanges currency** and **traveler's checks** and has an **ATM.** (☎892 61 09 or 892 65 14. Open M-F 8:30am-5:30pm.) The **police** (☎892 60 16) have an office beside the bank, and a booth at the corner of the *otogar* on Atatürk Cad.

SIGHTS. The stunning Selçuk mosque **İsa Bey Camii** was built in 1375 on the order of Aydınoğlu İsa Bey. It features columns taken from Ephesus, which the Ephesians, in turn, had pilfered from Aswan, Egypt. Restored in 1975, the mosque has regained much of the simple elegance that was eroded by 600 years of wear and tear. Inside the courtyard is a collection of Ottoman and Selçuk tombstones and inscriptions. The mosque's facade features Persian-influenced geometric black and white stone inlay. (Open 10min. before and 10min. after times of prayer.) A few hundred meters down Dr. Sabri Yayla Bul., walking away from town with the tourist office on your right, are the sad remains of the **Temple of Artemis.** Once the largest temple in existence and among the Seven Wonders of the Ancient World, it now consists of a lone reconstructed column twisting upwards from a bog that approximates the area of the temple's foundation. (Open daily 8:30am-5:30pm. Free.)

▥ EFES MÜZESI (EPHESUS MUSEUM). Directly across from the town's tourist office, Selçuk's Efes Müzesi houses a world-class collection of Hellenistic and Roman finds from Ephesus; most earlier pieces are in Vienna. The collection includes an infamously erect Priapus statue, **Beş,** that graces postcards throughout Turkey. While this particular piece was found in the vicinity of Ephesian brothels, the image of the generously endowed demi-god wasn't a smutty novelty, but a fairly common image in the ancient world. The museum houses an excellent collection of statuary, including a multi-breasted statue of **Artemis,** exquisite busts of Eros, Athena, Socrates, and emperors Tiberius, Marcus Aurelius, and Hadrian. (Open daily 8:30am-noon and 1-7pm; in winter 8:30am-noon and 1-5:30pm. $3.)

EPHESUS   ☎ 232

> *From Kuşadası or Selçuk, take a free **shuttle service** from any hotel. Otherwise, from the Kuşadası otogar, take a **dolmuş** to Selçuk and tell the driver to stop at Efes (30min., $0.80). From the Selçuk otogar, take a Pamukkale-bound dolmuş to Kuşadası (5min.; every 15min., Nov.-Apr. every 30min.; $0.60). **Taxis** run from Selçuk to Ephesus ($4) and to the House of the Virgin Mary (9km, $15 round-trip including 45min. to visit the site). Ephesus is an easy **walk** (3km, 25min.) from Selçuk along a fig tree-shaded path, beside Dr. Sabri Yayla Bul. Bring water and sunscreen. A good guidebook to Ephesus costs about $2.50 in Kuşadası's souvenir shops or at the entrance to the site; it provides the history of the ruins and a more lengthy explanation of the many sights. ☎892 64 02. Open daily 8am-7pm. $5.60, students $2.50. The best time to visit is early in the morning.*

From early archaic times to the 6th century AD, Ephesus has enjoyed perpetual glory and prosperity. The ruins here rank first among Turkey's ancient sites in sheer size and state of preservation; extensive marble roadways and columned avenues give an authentic impression of this ancient gateway to the eastern world.

Once you reach the site, you'll see the **Vedius Gymnasium** on the left, down the road from Dr. Sabri Yayla Bul. toward the lower entrance. It was built in AD 150 to honor then-emperor Antonius Pius and **Artemis,** the city's patron goddess. Beyond the roadside vegetation, the remains of the **stadium** open up in a horseshoe. The original Greek semi-circular theater followed the land's contours to add natural emphasis to the staged dramas. Romans plunked their own stadium right on top of the Greek theater, interpreting "drama" in another way: bloody gladiator games, wild beast hunts, and public executions. Just inside the lower entrance, a dirt path leads off to the right. On the right side of the fork, you'll find the ruins of the **Church of the Seven Councils,** where the Third Ecumenical Council met in AD 431. Beside it lies the ruined **Archbishop's Place,** destroyed by Arabs in the 6th century AD.

At the main entrance gate, a tree-lined path points to the **Arcadiane,** Ephesus's main thoroughfare. Buried under a dense swarm of tourists, the 30m by 145m **Grand Theater** is a stunning, heavily restored beast; its *cavea* (seating area), carved into the side of Mt. Pion, seats 25,000. The **Street of Curetes** begins at a slight incline. Ruts in the road are evidence of the heavy traffic between the temple and the city, and gaps between the slabs reveal glimpses of the city's **sewer system.** At the very bottom of the Street of Curetes is the **Library of Celsus,** restored by Austrian archaeologists. The large building behind the library was probably the **Temple of Serapis,** an Egyptian god of grain. Farther up the Street of Curetes, the imposing ruins of the AD 118 **Temple of Hadrian** are on your left, marked by a double-layered column construction. A little farther up the hill on the left are the ruins of the exquisite **Fountain of Trajan.**

Two pillars in the middle of the road mark the **Gate of Hercules;** farther uphill and to the left is the **Prytaneion.** Dedicated to the worship of **Vesta** (Hestia to the Greeks, and goddess of hearth and home), the Prytaneion contained an eternal flame tended by Vesta's priestesses, the **Vestal Virgins.** Vesta was vital to the Romans, and the Vestal Virgins thus gained a social standing *almost* as high as men. (Thanks, guys.) Immediately adjacent, the **odeon,** or *bouleterion,* remains in fine repair. The **state agora** on the right was the heart of political activity from the 1st century BC until the city's final demise. On the left lie the upper **baths.**

APPENDIX

CLIMATE

The climate is fairly uniform throughout Greece; the islands are a bit milder, and higher altitude areas (especially in the north) are cooler—expect it to be much colder on mountainous hikes. **Summer** is sunny, hot, and dry. **Winter** temperatures hover around 50°F. October to March is the rainy season.

Avg. Temp. (lo/hi),	JANUARY		APRIL		JULY		OCTOBER	
Precipitation	°F	in.	°F	in.	°F	in	°F	in.
Athens	55/43	2.5	68/52	0.9	91/73	0.2	75/59	2.0
Thessaloniki	48/36	1.8	68/50	1.6	90/70	.9	72/55	2.3
Trikkala	48/32	3.4	70/46	3.2	95/66	0.8	77/54	3.2
Naxos	59/50	3.6	68/55	0.8	81/72	0.1	75/64	1.8

To convert from degrees Fahrenheit to degrees Celsius, subtract 32 and multiply by 5/9. To convert from Celsius to Fahrenheit, multiply by 9/5 and add 32.

°CELSIUS	-5	0	5	10	15	20	25	30	35	40
°FARENHEIT	23	32	41	50	59	68	77	86	95	104

METRIC CONVERSIONS

1 inch (in.) = 25.4 millimeters (mm)	1 millimeter (mm) = 0.039 in.
1 foot (ft.) = 0.30 m	1 meter (m) = 3.28 ft.
1 mile = 1.61km	1 kilometer (km) = 0.62 mi.
1 ounce (oz.) = 28.35g	1 gram (g) = 0.035 oz.
1 pound (lb.) = 0.454kg	1 kilogram (kg) = 2.202 lb.
1 fluid ounce (fl. oz.) = 29.57ml	1 milliliter (ml) = 0.034 fl. oz.
1 gallon (gal.) = 3.785L	1 liter (L) = 0.264 gal.
1 square mile (sq. mi.) = 2.59km²	1 square kilometer (km²) = 0.386 sq. mi.

TELEPHONE CODES

See **Keeping in Touch** (p. 57) for full information and advice about telephone calls in Greece and Cyprus, including international access.

		COUNTRY	CODES		
Australia	61	Greece	30	South Africa	27
Canada	1	Ireland	353	Spain	34
Cyprus	357	Italy	39	Turkey	90
France	33	Japan	81	UK	44
Germany	49	New Zealand	64	US	1
		GREECE	**30**		
Aegina	0297	Iraklion	081	Parga	0684
Agios Konstantinos	0235	Kalamata	0721	Paros	0284
Agia Galini	1231	Kalambaka	0432	Patmos	0247
Alexandropoulis	0551	Kalavrita	0692	Patras	061
Amorgos	0285	Kalymnos	0243	Piraeus	01
Andros	0282	Kardamyli	0721	Poros	0298
Arahova	0267	Karpathos	0245	Rafina	0294
Astypalea	0243	Karpenisi	0237	Rethymnon	0831
Athens	01	Karystos	0224	Rhodes (City of)	0241
Kephalonia	0671	Kassos	0245	Samos	0273

GREECE	30				
Chios	0271	Kavala	051	Samothraki	0551
Corfu	0661	Kos	0242	Santorini	0286
Corinth	0741	Kyllini	0623	Serifos	0281
Delphi	0265	Kythera	0736	Sifnos	0284
Dimitsana	0795	Lefkada	0645	Sithonia	0375
Edessa	0381	Limnos	0254	Sitia	0843
Epidavros	0753	Matala	0892	Skiathos	0427
Folegandros	0286	Methoni	0723	Skopelos	0424
Halkida	0221	Metsovo	0656	Skyros	0222
Hania	0821	Milos	0287	Sparta	0731
Hersonissos	0897	Monemvasia	0732	Symi	0246
Hora Sfakion	0825	Mt. Athos	0377	Syros	0281
Hydra	0298	Mytilini	0251	Thasos	0593
Ierapetra	0842	Nafpaktos	0634	Thessaloniki	031
Igoumenitsa	0665	Nafplion	0752	Tinos	0283
Ikaria	0275	Naxos	0285	Volos	0421
Ioannnina	0651	Olympia	0624	Zagorohoria	0653
Ios	0286	Paleohora	0823	Zakynthos	0695
CYPRUS	357				
Agia Napa	03	Limassol	05	Paphos	06
Larnaka	04	Nicosia	02	Platres	05

GLOSSARY OF GREEK TERMS

acropolis a fortified, sacred high place atop a city
adelfos brother
adelfi sister
afto this
aftokinito car
agape love (see *erotas*)
agora the ancient city square and marketplace
alithea truth
ammos sand
amphora a two-handled vase for oil or wine storage
angouri cucumber
apse nook beyond the altar of a church
architrave lintel resting on columns and supporting the entablature, below a frieze
arni lamb
astinomeio police
astra stars
Archaic Period 700-480 BC**arnaki** lamb
Asia Minor Turkey, particularly its once-Greek Aegean coast
aspro white
astakos lobster
atrium house's open interior courtyard; typically Roman
avga eggs
avgolemono egg-lemon soup
avrio tomorrow
basilica church with a saint's relic; especially holy

bouleterion meeting place of an ancient city's legislative council
bouzouki stringed instrument
Byzantine Period AD 324-1453
caïque fishing or passenger boat, usually wooden
capital decorated top of a column
castro castle or fortifications
cella inner sanctum of a classical temple
chora (hora) village
chrono year (or time, in a grandiose sense)
chryso gold
cigara, or **tsigara** cigarettes
Classical Period 480-323BC
Corinthian column ornate, leaf- or flower-engraved top (or capital) of a column
cornice top of the entablature of a temple
Cyclopian walls massive irregular-cut Minoan and Mycenaean stone walls, so called because only a Cyclops could lift such stones
demos people, citizens
dimarchio town hall
dolmades warm stuffed grape leaves with sauce of egg and lemon
dolmadakia cold stuffed grape leaves

domatia rooms to rent in private homes; rooms to let
Dorian referring to invaders of 1100 BC
Doric column cigar-shaped columns with wide fluted shafts, cushion tops (or capitals), and no bases
efimerevon 24hr. pharmacy
eleftheria freedom
eleftheri/os single, free
entablature upper parts of a temple facade, atop columns
epicremeni/os upset, sad, disappointed
erotas erotic love or sex; "let's do it"="na kanome erotas" (see *agape*)
erotevmeni/os madly in love
etos year
exoteriko international
exedra curved recess in classical/Byzantine architecture
exonarthex outer vestibule in a Byzantine church
Faneromeni Virgin Revealer
feta soft, white, omnipresent goat-milk cheese
filaki (accent on Ia) kiss
filaki (accent on ki) jail
forum Roman marketplace
frappé Greek iced coffee
frieze illustrated middle part of a temple exterior (in particular, the entablature); see *metopes* and *triglyph*

frappé whipped, frothy frozen coffee drink
frourio medieval fortress or castle; often called a Castro
gaiduri donkey (masculine)
gaidara donkey (feminine)
galaktopoleio dairy shop
galaktobouriko cream pastry
Geometric Period 1100-700 BC
ghala milk
glika sweets
gyro greasy, pita-wrapped lamb sandwich (mmm)
haroumeni/os happy
Hellenistic Period 323-46 BC
heroon shrine to a demigod
hora (chora) island capital or main town in an area
iconostasis screen that displays Byzantine icons
Ionic column slender column topped with twin scrolling spirals and with a fluted base
iperastiko long distance (phone calls, transportation)
kafeneion cafe
kaimaiki specialty ice-cream with *mastika* (gum)
kalamarakia baby squid
kasseri hard yellow cheese
kastro castle or fortifications
Katharevoussa uppity "pure" Greek literary language, taken from ancient Greek
kathemera every day
kathemerino daily
katholikon monastery's main church or chapel
kato hora the lower part of a village
kefalos head
kefi The Mood for fun
KKE Greek communist party
koine "common" Greek used before the Byzantine era
kore female statue
kotopoulo chicken
kouros male nude statue
ktapodhi octopus
KTEL inter-city bus service
ladhi oil
leoforos avenue
leoforeo bus
libation gift of food or liquor to a god
limani port
logariasmo check
magiritsa tripe soup with rice
malaka common obscenity that connotes masturbation
mastika chewing-gum or gum
mavro black
megalo big (opposite of *mikro*)
megaron large hall in a house or palace
melizanes eggplants

meltemi an unusually strong north wind in the Cyclades and Dodecanese
metopes painted or sculpted square block in a Doric frieze that contains scenes with figures; *metopes* are separated by *triglyphs*
meze, mezedes, mezedakia appetizers to go with ouzo
mikro small (opposite of *megalo*)
Minoan Period 3000-1250 BC
mitera mother
moni monastery or convent
moro/moraki baby
moschari veal
moussaka a lasagna-like dish made with layered eggplants, meat and potatoes
moustarda mustard
Mycenean Period 1600-1100 BC
naos holy innermost part of a temple or church
narthex vestibule on the west side of a Byzantine church
nave church aisle
ne yes
Neolithic Period 3000-2000 BC
nomos Greek province
nosokomeio hospital
ohi no
odeion semi-circular theater
odos road
ohi no
oikos house
omphalos belly-button
opa! much-used expression; hey!; oops!; look out!
ouzeri *ouzo* tavern serving *mezedes* and other yummy treats
ouzo national brew of Greece
omorfia beauty
ora time (hour)
OTE the Greek national telephone company
paleohora old town
palaestra classical gymnasium
Panagia the Virgin Mary
pano high or upper
panigiri local festival, often religious
Pantokrator a mosaic or fresco of Christ in a Byzantine church dome
papaki duckling (slang for moped)
parea a group of friends
patera father
pedi child; "ela, pedia" means "come on, kids"; used to call the *pareia* at any age
pediment triangualar, sculpture decorated space in an ancient temple's facade

peplos mantle worn by ancient Greek women; Athena's nightgown
periptero street kiosk
peristyle colonnade around a building
philos buddy, friend
pima poem
piesi high blood pressure, nerves
piperi pepper
pithos ceramic storage jar
plateia town square
pleio ferry
polis city-state
portico colonnade or *stoa*
pronaos outer column-lined temple porch
propylaion sanctuary entrance flanked by columns
prytaneion administrative building
psaras fisherman
psaria fish
psomi bread
raki Cretan local liquor
retsina sharp white wine
rhyton cup shaped like an animal's head
Roman period 46 BC-AD 324
satyr lusty follower of Dionysus
simera today
skala port for an inland town
souvlaki oh-so-tender meat on a skewer (usually lamb)
spili, spilia cave, caves
stele a stone slab that marks a tomb
stoa in ancient market-places, an open portico lined with rows of columns
taverna restaurant or tavern
techni art
tholos Mycenean earth-covered, beehive-shaped tomb
tiri cheese
triglyph part of a Doric frieze comprised of 3 vertical grooves that alternate with *metopes*
trireme ancient ship with 3 sets of oars
tsipouro mainland bathtub liquor
tsoutsoukakia meat balls in tomato sauce
varka boat
volta evening walk
vouno mountain
voutiro butter
xechasmeni/os forgotten
xeri dry
xeri carpi nuts, dry snacks
yiayia grandmother
yialos waterside (port, beach)
zaccharoplasteio sweetshop
zakhari sugar

GREEK ALPHABET

The Greek alphabet has 24 letters; the chart below can help decipher signs. The left column gives the name of each letters in Greek, the middle column shows lower case andcapital letters, and the right column shows the pronunciation.

LETTER	SYMBOL	PRONOUNCIATION	LETTER	SYMBOL	PRONOUNCIATION
alpha	α A	*a* as in father	nu	ν N	*n* as in net
beta	β B	*v* as in velvet	ksi	ξ Ξ	*x* as in mix
gamma	γ Γ	*y* as in yo or *g* as in go	omicron	o O	*o* as in row
delta	δ Δ	*th* as in there	pi	π Π	*p* as in peace
epsilon	ε E	*e* as in jet	rho	ρ P	*r* as in roll
zeta	ζ Z	*z* as in zebra	sigma	σ (ς) Σ	*s* as in sense
eta	η H	*ee* as in queen	tau	τ T	*t* as in tent
theta	θ Θ	*th* as in health	upsilon	υ Y	*ee* as in green
iota	ι I	*ee* as in tree	phi	φ (φ) Φ	*f* as in fog
kappa	κ K	*k* as in cat	xi	χ X	*ch (h)* as in horse
lambda	λ Λ	*l* as in land	psi	ψ Ψ	*ps* as in oops
mu	μ M	*m* as in moose	omega	ω Ω	*o* as in glow

COMMON WORDS AND PHRASES

USEFUL PHRASES

yes	ναι	NEH
no	οχι	OH-hee
ok	ενδαξι	en-DAX-ee
please/you're welcome	παρακαλω	pah-rah-kah-LO
thank you (very much)	ευχαριστω πολυ	ef-khah-ree-STO (po-LEE)
sorry/pardon me	συγνομη	sig-NO-mee
Do you speak English?	μιλας αγγλικα;	mee-LAHS ahn-glee-KAH?
I don't speak Greek	δεν μιλαω ελληνικα	dhen mee-LAHO el-leen-ee-KAH
I don't understand	δεν καταλαβαινω	dhen kah-tah-lah-VEh-no
How much?	πσπο κανει;	PO-so KAH-nee?
Can I help you? (Literally: Tell me)		oh-REES-teh
Leave me alone!	ασεμε	AH-se-me
Help!	Βοηθεια!	vo-EE-thee-ah!
shit	σκατα	ska-TA
darling	λατρεια	lah-TREE-ah
maybe; I'm thinking about it	το σκεπτομε	toh SKEP-to-meh
it does (not) matter	(θεν) πειραζι	(then) peer-ADZ-ee
I love you	Σ'αγαπαω	SAH-gap-AH-o
I miss you	Μου λιπις	mou LEE-pis
I want you	Σε θελο	seh THEL-oh

GREETINGS

good morning	καλημερα	kah-lee-MEH-rah
good evening	καλησπερα	kah-lee-SPE-rah
good night	καληνυχτα	kah-lee-NEE-khtah
hello/goodbye (polite, plural)	γεια σας	YAH-sas
hello/goodbye (familiar)	γεια σου	YAH-soo
Mr./Sir	κυριος	kee-REE-os
Ms./Madam	κυρια	kee-REE-ah
What is your name?	Πως σε λενε;	pos-se-LEH-neh?

APPENDIX

My name is ...	Με λενε	me-LEH-neh ...

why?	Για τι;	yah-TEE?
where? who? when?	που; πιος; ποτε;	POO? pYOS? POH-teh?
Where is...?	Που ειναι;	pou-EE-neh...?
Where are you going?	Που πασ	POU-pahs?
I'm going to...	Πηγαινω για	pee-YEH-no yah...
When do we leave?	Τι ωρα φευγουμε;	tee O-rah FEV-goo-meh?
stop	στασι	STA-si
I need a ticket	Χπειαζομαι ισιτεριο	chree-AH-soh-meh eeseeTERio
Can I see a room?	Μπορω να δω ενα δωματιο;	bo-RO nah-DHO E-nah dho-MAH-tee-o?
here, there	εδω, εκει	eh-DHO, eh-KEE
left	αριστερα	ah-rees-teh-RAH
right	δεξια	dhek-see-AH
I am lost	χαθηκα	HA-thee-ka
I am ill	Ειμαι αρροστος	EE-meh AH-ross-toss
airplane	αεροπλανο	ah-e-ro-PLAH-no
airport	αεροδρομειο	ah-e-ro-DHRO-mee-o
bus	λεωφορειο	leh-o-fo-REE-o
ferry	πλοιο	PLEE-o
port	λιμανι	lee-MA-nee
suitcase	βαλιστα	vah-LEE-tsah
ticket	εισιτηιριο	ee-see-TEE-ree0o
train	τραινο	TREH-no

What time is it?	Τι ωρα ειναι;	tee-O-rah EE-neh?
Monday	Δευτεπα	def-TEH-ra
Tuesday	Τριτι	TREE-tee
Wednesday	Τεταπτη	teh-TAR-ti
Thursday	Πεμπτη	PEHmp-tee
Friday	Παρασκευι	pah-rah-skeh-VEE
Saturday	Σαββατο	SAH-vah-to
Sunday	Κυριακη	kee-ree-ah-KEE
yesterday	χθες	KTHES
today	σημερα	SEE-mer-a
tomorrow	αυριο	AV-ree-o
morning	πρωι	pro-EE
evening	βραδι	VRAH-dhee
later tonight	αποψε	ah-PO-pseh
first	πρωτο	PRO-to
last	τελευταιο	teh-lef-TEH-o

bank	τραπεζα	TRAH-peh-zah
church	εκκλησια	eh-klee-SEE-ah
doctor	γιατρος	yah-TROS
hospital	νοσοκομειο	no-so-ko-MEE-o
hotel	ξενοδοχειο	kse-no-dho-HEE-o
market	αγορα	ah-go-RAH
museum	μουσειο	mou-SEE-o

pharmacy	φαρμακειο	fahr-mah-KEE-o
police	αστυνομεια	as-tee-no-MEE-a
post office	ταχυδρομειο	ta-khee-dhro-MEE-o
restaurant	εστιατοριο	es-tee-ah-TO-ree-o
room	δοματιο	dho-MAH-teeo
toilet	τουλετα	twa-LE-ta
open, closed	ανοιχτο, κλειστο	ah-nee-KTO, klee-STO

COMMERCE

I need	Χρειαζομα	khree-AH-zo-meh
I want	Θελω	THEH-lo
I would like ...	Θα ηθελα	thah EE-the-lah ...
I will buy this one	Θα Αγορασω αυτο	thah ah-go-RAH-so ahf-TO
Do you have?	Εχετε;	Eh-khe-teh?
bill	λογαριασμο	lo-gahr-yah-SMO
water	νερο	ne-RO
good	καλο	kah-LO
cheap	φτηνο	ftee-NO
expensive	ακριβο	ah-kree-VO

NUMBERS

zero	μηδεν	mee-DHEN
one	ενα	Eh-nah
two	δυο	DHEE-o
three	τρια	TREE-ah
four	τεσσερα	TES-ser-ah
five	πεντε	PEN-dheh
six	εξι	E-ksee
seven	επτα	ep-TAH
eight	οκτω	okh-TO
nine	εννια	en-YAH
ten	δεκα	DHEH-kah
eleven	ενδεκα	EN-dheh-kah
twelve	δωδεκα	DHO-dheh-kah
thirteen	δεκατρια	DHEH-kah TREE-ah
fourteen	δεκατεσσερα	DHEH-kah TES-ser-ah
fifteen	δεκαπεντε	DHEH-kah PEN-dheh
sixteen	δεκαεξι	DHEH-kah E-ksee
seventeen	δεκαεπτα	DHEH-kah ep-TAH
eighteen	δεκαοκτω	DHEH-kah okh-TO
nineteen	δεκαεννια	DHEH-kah en-YAH
twenty	εικοσι	EE-ko-see
thirty	τριαντα	tree-AN-dah
forty	σαραντα	sa-RAN-dah
fifty	πενηντα	pen-EEN-dah
sixty	εξηντα	ex-EEN-dah
seventy	εβδομηντα	ev-dho-MEEN-dah
eighty	ογδοντα	og-DHON-dah
ninety	ενενηντα	en-EEN-dah
hundred	εκατο	ek-ah-TO
thousands	χιλιαδες	hil-ee-AH(dhes)
million	εκατομμυριο	eka-to-MEE-rio

Money From Home In Minutes.

If you're stuck for cash on your travels, don't panic. Millions of people trust Western Union to transfer money in minutes to over 185 countries and over 95,000 locations worldwide. Our record of safety and reliability is second to none. You can even send money by phone without leaving home by using a credit card. For more information, call Western Union: USA 1-800-325-6000, Canada 1-800-235-0000.

www.westernunion.com

The fastest way to send money worldwide.

INDEX

A

ABOUT LET'S GO

FORTY-TWO YEARS OF WISDOM

For over four decades, travelers crisscrossing the continents have relied on *Let's Go* for inside information on the hippest backstreet cafes, the most pristine secluded beaches, and the best routes from border to border. *Let's Go: Europe*, now in its 42nd edition and translated into seven languages, reigns as the world's bestselling international travel guide. In the last 20 years, our rugged researchers have stretched the frontiers of backpacking and expanded our coverage into the Americas, Australia, Asia, and Africa (including the new *Let's Go: Egypt* and the more comprehensive, multi-country jaunt through *Let's Go: South Africa & Southern Africa*). Our new-and-improved City Guide series continues to grow with new guides to perennial European favorites Amsterdam and Barcelona. This year we are also unveiling *Let's Go: Southwest USA*, the flagship of our new outdoor Adventure Guide series, which is complete with special roadtripping tips and itineraries, more coverage of adventure activities like hiking and mountain biking, and first-person accounts of life on the road.

It all started in 1960 when a handful of well-traveled students at Harvard University handed out a 20-page mimeographed pamphlet offering a collection of their tips on budget travel to passengers on student charter flights to Europe. The following year, in response to the instant popularity of the first volume, students traveling to Europe researched the first full-fledged edition of *Let's Go: Europe*. Throughout the 60s and 70s, our guides reflected the times—in 1969, for example, we taught you how to get from Paris to Prague on "no dollars a day" by singing in the street. In the 90s we focused in on the world's most exciting urban areas to produce in-depth, fold-out map guides, now with 20 titles (from Hong Kong to Chicago) and counting. Our new guides bring the total number of titles to 57, each infused with the spirit of adventure and voice of opinion that travelers around the world have come to count on. But some things never change: our guides are still researched, written, and produced entirely by students who know first-hand how to see the world on the cheap.

HOW WE DO IT

Each guide is completely revised and thoroughly updated every year by a well-traveled set of nearly 300 students. Every spring, we recruit over 200 researchers and 90 editors to overhaul every book. After several months of training, researcher-writers hit the road for seven weeks of exploration, from Anchorage to Adelaide, Estonia to El Salvador, Iceland to Indonesia. Hired for their rare combination of budget travel sense, writing ability, stamina, and courage, these adventurous travelers know that train strikes, stolen luggage, food poisoning, and marriage proposals are all part of a day's work. Back at our offices, editors work from spring to fall, massaging copy written on Himalayan bus rides into witty, informative prose. A student staff of typesetters, cartographers, publicists, and managers keeps our lively team together. In September, the collected efforts of the summer are delivered to our printer, who turns them into books in record time, so that you have the most up-to-date information available for your vacation. Even as you read this, work on next year's editions is well underway.

WHY WE DO IT

We don't think of budget travel as the last recourse of the destitute; we believe that it's the only way to travel. Our books will ease your anxieties and answer your questions about the basics—so you can get off the beaten track and explore. Once you learn the ropes, we encourage you to put *Let's Go* down and strike out on your own. You know as well as we that the best discoveries are often those you make yourself. When you find something worth sharing, please drop us a line. We're Let's Go Publications, 67 Mount Auburn St., Cambridge, MA 02138, USA (feedback@letsgo.com). For more info, visit our website, www.letsgo.com.

Will you have enough stories to tell your grandchildren?

Yahoo! Travel

DO YOU YAHOO!?

CHOOSE YOUR DESTINATION SWEEPSTAKES

No Purchase Necessary.

Explore the world with Let's Go® and StudentUniverse!
Enter for a chance to win a trip for two to a Let's Go destination!

Separate Drawings! May & October 2002.

GRAND PRIZES:
Roundtrip StudentUniverse Tickets

✓ **Select one destination and mail your entry to:**

☐ Costa Rica
☐ London
☐ Hong Kong
☐ San Francisco
☐ New York
☐ Amsterdam
☐ Prague
☐ Sydney

* Plus Additional Prizes!!

Choose Your Destination Sweepstakes
St. Martin's Press
Suite 1600, Department MF
175 Fifth Avenue
New York, NY 10010-7848

Restrictions apply; see offical rules for
details by visiting Let'sGo.com or sending SASE
(VT residents may omit return postage) to the address above.

Name: _____

Address: _____

City/State/Zip: _____

Phone: _____

Email: _____

Grand prizes provided by:

 StudentUniverse.com   Real Travel Deals